Thomas Moran

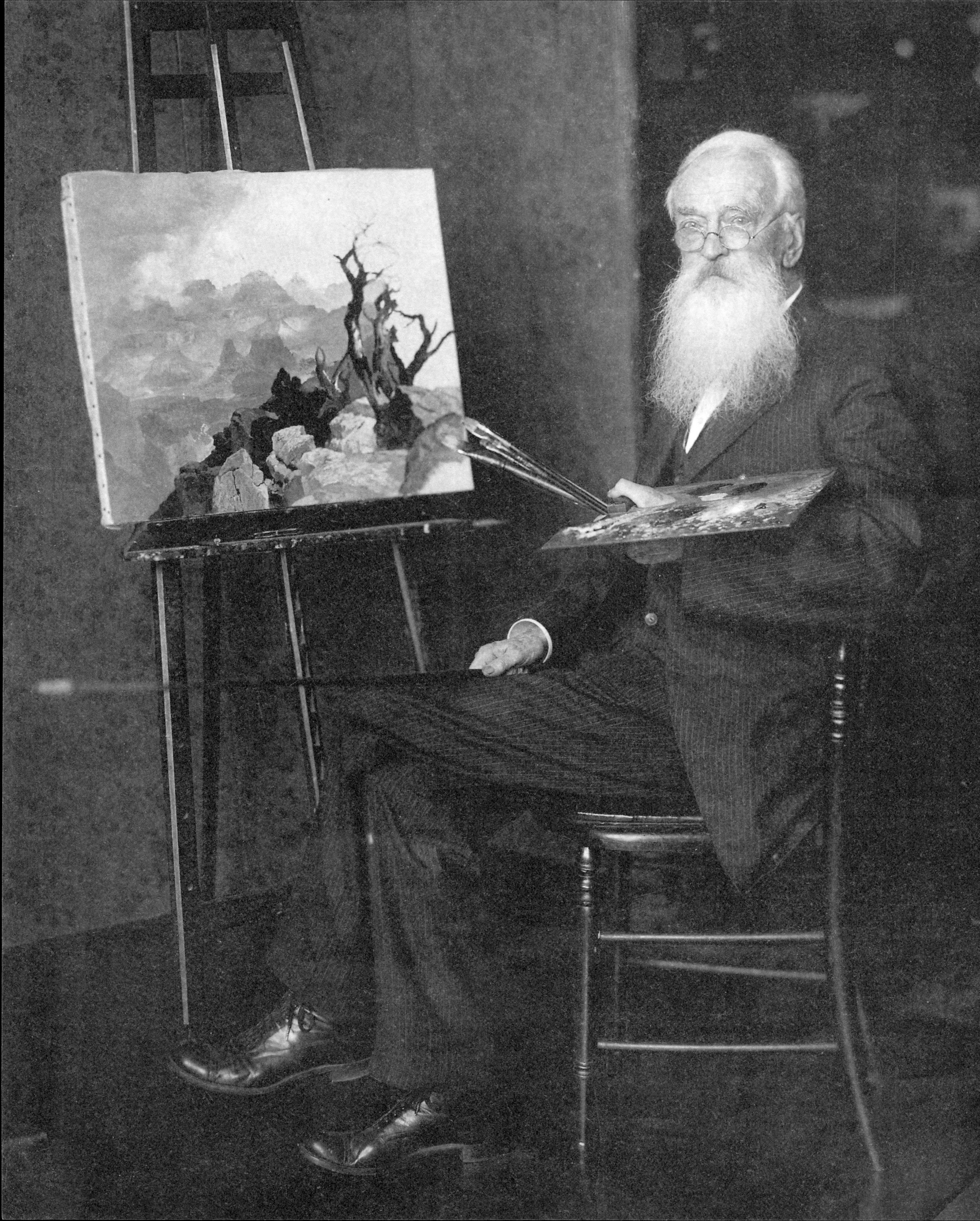

Thomas Moran

Nancy K. Anderson

with contributions by

Thomas P. Bruhn, Joni L. Kinsey, and Anne Morand

National Gallery of Art, *Washington*

Yale University Press, *New Haven and London*

THE EXHIBITION IS MADE POSSIBLE BY GENEROUS SUPPORT FROM THE BOEING COMPANY

The exhibition has been organized by the National Gallery of Art, Washington, in association with the Gilcrease Museum, Tulsa

Exhibition Dates

National Gallery of Art, Washington
28 September 1997–11 January 1998

Gilcrease Museum, Tulsa
8 February–10 May 1998

Seattle Art Museum
11 June–30 August 1998

Frances P. Smyth, *Editor-in-chief*
Tam Curry Bryfogle, *Editor*
Margaret Bauer, *Designer*

Type was set in Adobe Caslon, Myriad, and Snell Roundhand. Printed on Gardapat 135gsm by Arnoldo Mondadori Editore, Verona, Italy.

Clothbound books distributed by Yale University Press, New Haven and London

Library of Congress Cataloging-in-Publication Data

Anderson, Nancy K.
Thomas Moran / Nancy K. Anderson; with contributions by Thomas P. Bruhn, Joni L. Kinsey, and Anne Morand.

p. cm.

Catalog of an exhibition held at the National Gallery of Art, Washington, Sept. 28, 1997–Jan. 11, 1998, the Gilcrease Museum, Tulsa, Feb. 8–May 10, 1998, and the Seattle Art Museum, June 11–Aug. 30, 1998. Includes bibliographical references and index.

ISBN 0-300-07325-9 (cloth)
ISBN 0-89468-225-3 (paper)

1. Moran, Thomas, 1837–1926—Exhibitions.

I. Moran, Thomas, 1837–1926. II. National Gallery of Art (U.S.) III. Thomas Gilcrease Institute of American History and Art. IV. Seattle Art Museum. V. Title.

N6797.M576A4 1997
760'.092—dc21 96-23435

Illustrations

COVER: Thomas Moran, *Hopi Village, Arizona* (detail), 1916, Heckscher Museum of Art, Huntington, New York, August Heckscher Collection [cat. 97]

BACK COVER / PAGE 2: Thomas Moran, c. 1915, photograph by Henry Havelock Pierce, Boston, courtesy East Hampton Library

PAGES 6–7: Thomas Moran, *Portneuf Cañon, Idaho,* 1879, Gilcrease Museum, Tulsa, Oklahoma [cat. 55]

PAGES 12–13: Thomas Moran, *Grand Canyon of the Yellowstone* (detail), 1872, Department of the Interior Museum [cat. 41]

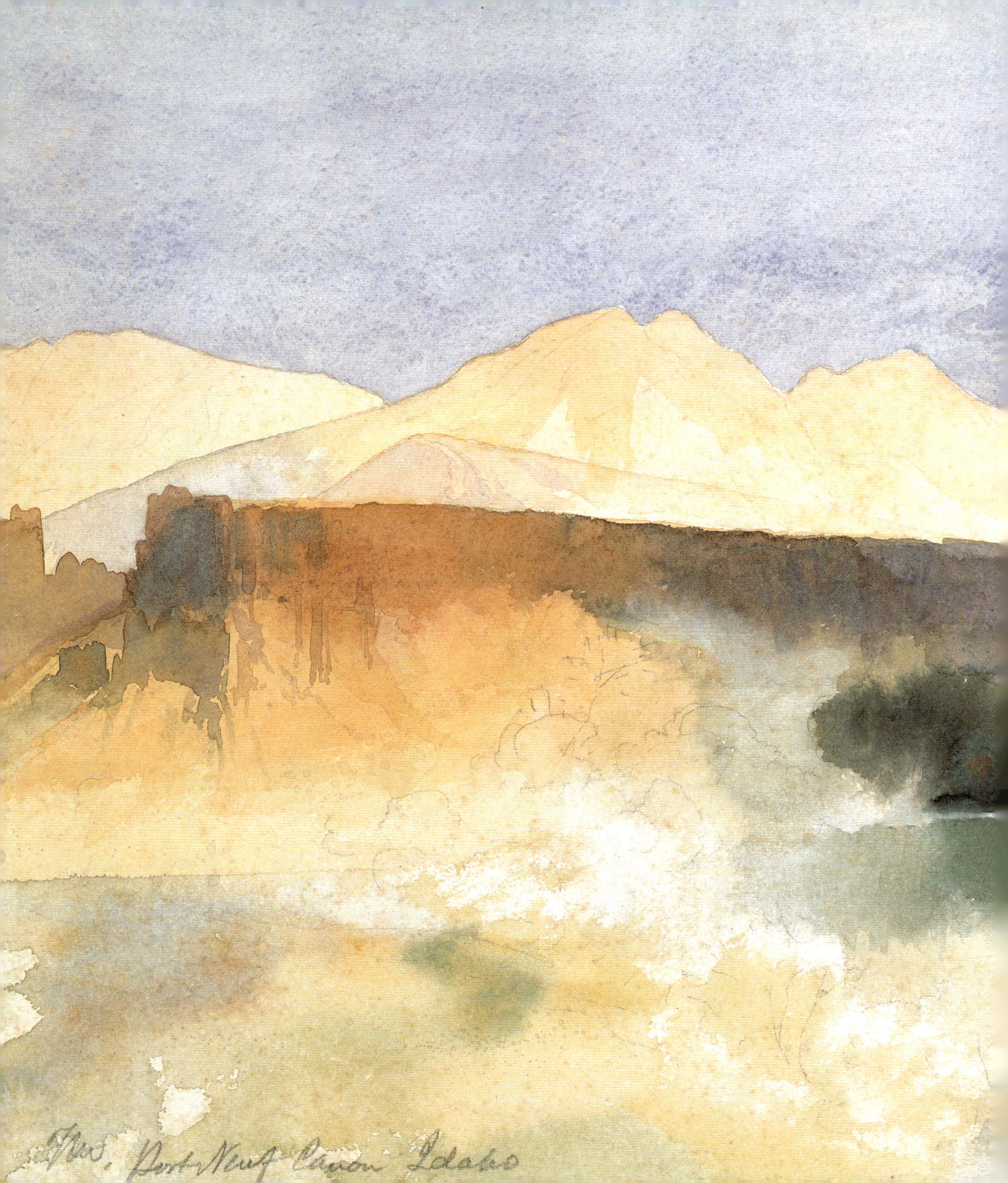
Port Neuf Canon Idaho

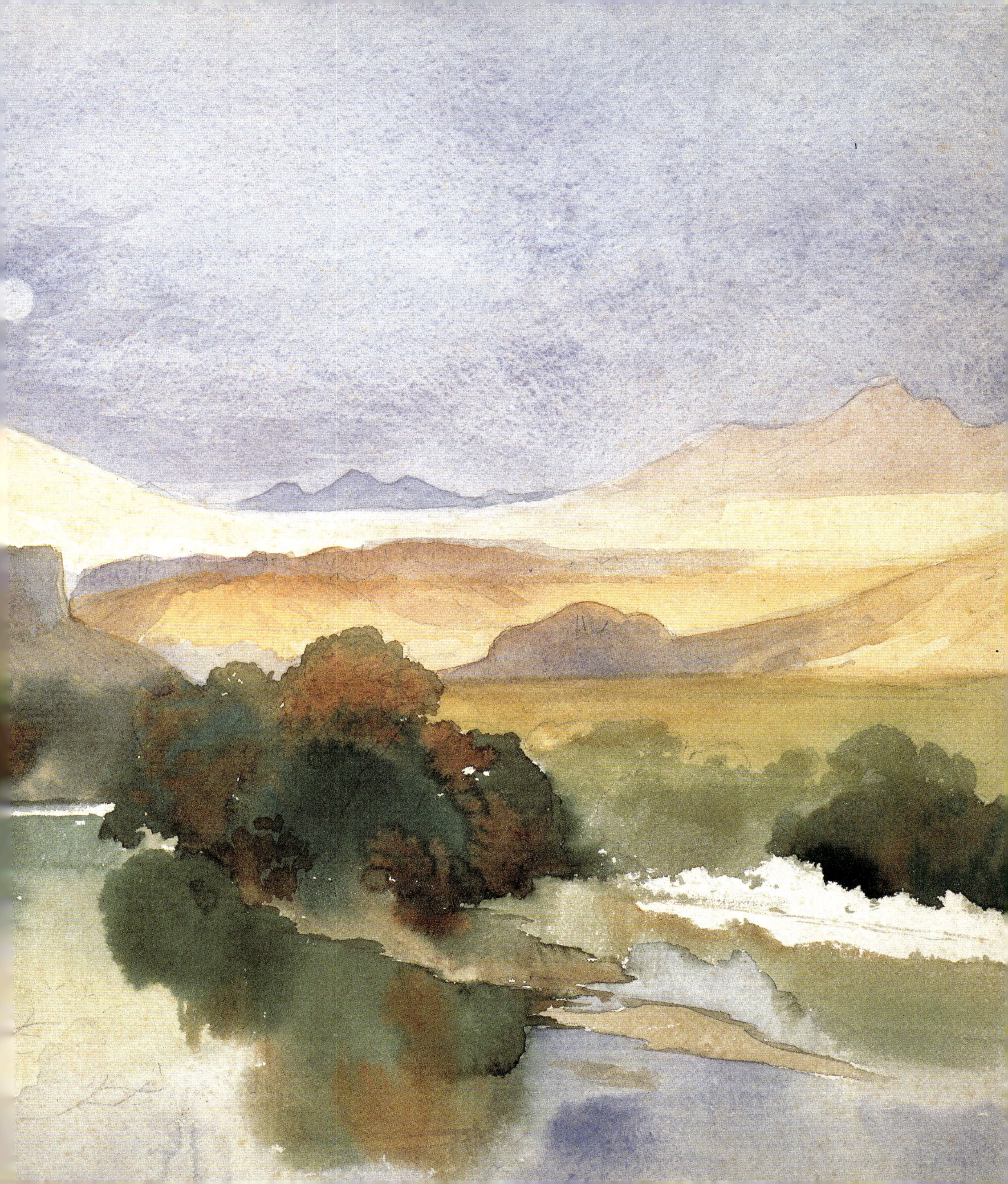

LENDERS TO THE EXHIBITION

The Anschutz Collection
The Art Institute of Chicago
Autry Museum of Western Heritage, Los Angeles
Berea College Museum, Berea, Kentucky
G. Andrew Bjurman
Joan and Jerry Blank
Buffalo Bill Historical Center, Cody, Wyoming
The Chrysler Museum, Norfolk
The Cleveland Museum of Art
Cooper-Hewitt National Design Museum, Smithsonian Institution, New York
The Corcoran Gallery of Art, Washington, DC
Dr. Donald and Kathryn O'Connor Counts
The Cummer Museum of Art & Gardens, Jacksonville, Florida
Denver Art Museum
Department of the Interior, Yellowstone National Park
Department of the Interior Museum
The Detroit Institute of Arts
Gilcrease Museum, Tulsa
Heckscher Museum, Huntington, New York
Paul Hertzmann and Susan Herzig, Paul M. Hertzmann, Inc.
Hevrdejs Collection
Jefferson National Expansion Memorial, National Park Service, St. Louis
David H. Koch
Mr. and Mrs. Robert A. Levinson
Manoogian Collection
Anthony R. Mayer
The Metropolitan Museum of Art, New York
Montgomery Museum of Fine Arts
Merl M. Moore Jr.
Museum of Fine Arts, Boston
Museum of Western Art, Denver
National Archives, Washington, DC
National Gallery of Art, Washington
National Museum of American Art, Smithsonian Institution, Washington, DC
The Nelson-Atkins Museum of Art, Kansas City
New Britain Museum of American Art
North Carolina Museum of Art, Raleigh
The Philbrook Museum of Art, Tulsa
Private Collections
Private Collection, courtesy Jordan-Volpe Gallery
Private Collection, courtesy Lagakos-Turak Gallery
Union Pacific Historical Museum, Omaha
Robbie and Sam Vickers
Leonard Walle
Washington County Museum of Fine Arts, Hagerstown, Maryland
The White House
Yale Collection of Western Americana, Beinecke Rare Book and Manuscript Library, New Haven

ALTHOUGH THOMAS MORAN has long been recognized as one of the premier landscape painters of the nineteenth century, this exhibition is the first retrospective of his work ever held. Moran's finest oil and watercolor paintings have been brought together through the extraordinary generosity of the Gilcrease Museum, holder of the largest collection of works by Moran; the Department of the Interior Museum, lender of two important paintings purchased by Congress for the Capitol; the Cooper-Hewitt National Design Museum, recipient of a major gift of works from the artist; as well as numerous other museums and private collectors.

The opening of the Moran exhibition and the publication of the catalogue coincide with the 125th anniversary of the founding of Yellowstone National Park. In honor of this occasion the Department of the Interior has agreed to lend Moran's original Yellowstone watercolors, completed during his first trip west in 1871. According to Ferdinand Hayden, leader of the Yellowstone expedition Moran accompanied, these watercolors played a decisive role in the passage of the bill that created the first national park. For an artist who later signed his name, Thomas "Yellowstone" Moran, this anniversary year is an especially appropriate time to celebrate his remarkable achievement.

Moran's paintings of the American West, particularly those of Yellowstone and the Grand Canyon, brought him immediate and enduring fame. It is one of the highlights of this exhibition that his three most famous western landscapes—*Grand Canyon of the Yellowstone* (1872), *Chasm of the Colorado* (1873–1874), and *Mountain of the Holy Cross* (1875)—will be shown together for the first time. Moran had hoped to exhibit the three works as a western "triptych" at the Centennial Exposition in 1876, but his plans were foiled when Congress refused to lend the first two pictures.

In addition, the exhibition includes several of Moran's finest marine paintings, a number of European and Mexican views, a selection of Long Island scenes, and a group of stunning but little-known Pre-Raphaelite landscapes from the first decade of his career.

The exhibition and catalogue have been organized by Nancy K. Anderson, associate curator of American and British paintings at the National Gallery of Art. Anne Morand, curator of art at the Gilcrease Museum, has generously assisted at all stages of development, as have a host of scholars, collectors, and dealers.

The National Gallery of Art wishes to thank The Boeing Company, in particular chief executive officer Philip M. Condit, for its generous sponsorship of the exhibition and the catalogue. Boeing's support has immeasurably enhanced the Moran project.

The Seattle Art Museum also wishes to acknowledge Mr. Condit and The Boeing Company for the generous grant that will allow the Moran exhibition to be seen in the Pacific Northwest.

At the Gilcrease Museum a group of individuals and foundations provided the support that will enable the exhibition to travel to Tulsa. They include The Williams Companies, Inc., Grace and Franklin Bernsen Foundation, The Mervin Bovaird Foundation, The Helmerich Foundation, The John Steele Zink Foundation, Lorene Cooper Hasbrouck Charitable Trust, and the Maxine and Jack Zarrow Foundation.

Many of the works in this exhibition are privately owned, and several have not been seen publicly since the nineteenth century. The National Gallery, the Gilcrease Museum, and the Seattle Art Museum express their gratitude to all the lenders, private and public, who have graciously agreed to lend their paintings and make possible the presentation of this important exhibition.

Earl A. Powell III
Director, National Gallery of Art

IN A LETTER WRITTEN late in 1916 to William Henry Holmes, curator at the National Museum in Washington, Thomas Moran noted that he would be eighty years old on 12 January 1917, and then went on to remark, "we have lived in a wonderful age." Moran's letter has become emblematic of this exhibition and catalogue project, for the artist was both right and wrong in his statement. He and Holmes had indeed lived through a remarkable period, and both had made substantial contributions to the cultural history of the nation. Surprisingly, however, Moran was incorrect about his date of birth, for the legal certificate on file in Bolton, England, indicates that he was born 12 February 1837. The difference is slight, but one date is accurate and the other is not, even though Moran repeated the erroneous date for years when asked to supply biographical information.

During the five years that the Moran project has been under way, we have sought to explore the "wonderful age" in which Moran lived—all eighty-nine years—as not just the backdrop for, but the actual milieu in which he created the works of art that are the focus of the exhibition. In writing the catalogue, we have sought to correct "errors" of statement and others of omission, recognizing that our publication comes very early in what we anticipate will one day be a substantial Moran bibliography.

In preparing for the exhibition and accompanying publication, we have made extensive use of two major collections of Moran archival material. The first, located at the East Hampton Library, in East Hampton, New York, was the gift of Ruth Moran, the artist's daughter. Supplementary materials were added by Fritiof Fryxell, longtime friend of Ruth Moran and an early Moran biographer. The second and larger collection is one of the treasures of the Gilcrease Museum in Tulsa, Oklahoma. Purchased by Thomas Gilcrease from the estate of Ruth Moran, the collection encompasses a large number of valuable primary documents, including the artist's early "Opus List," which is reproduced in this volume as Appendix 2. The collection also preserves the notes for two unfinished manuscripts about Thomas Moran by individuals who knew him: Nina Spalding Stevens and Esther Singleton. Additional biographical notes by Ruth and Mary Moran, the artist's daughters, are housed in the Gilcrease Archive.

In addition to the East Hampton and Gilcrease archives, we reviewed contemporary newspaper and periodical articles related to the artist and his work. In the hope that others who carry on Moran studies will not have to repeat the task of searching for the same references, but rather can add to them, we have included a chronological listing of bibliographic sources at the end of this volume, giving the major newspaper and periodical articles, dissertations, and books on Moran in publication order. Far from definitive, the list is offered as a starting point for those who wish to follow the rise of the artist's reputation and gauge the tenor of subsequent commentary in the order in which it appeared.

Among the secondary sources cited in the bibliographies, several deserve special notice. Thurman Wilkins' biography (1966) was the first comprehensive account of Moran's career and thus an invaluable guide for all who have studied the artist since. Carol Clark's examination of Moran's western watercolors, both in an exhibition format (1980) and as a dissertation study (1981), is also a critical tool. In 1986 Anne Morand and Nancy Friese published a catalogue of the Moran print collection at the Gilcrease Museum that remains a key resource for the artist's work on paper. In 1989 Joni L. Kinsey completed her dissertation on Moran's work with the western surveys, later published as *Thomas Moran and the Surveying of the American West* (1992), an insightful analysis of one of the most important periods of Moran's career. Anne Morand's recent *Thomas Moran: The Field Sketches, 1856–1923* (1996), lavishly illustrated and thoughtfully organized, will serve as a standard reference work for generations of Moran scholars.

In our own contribution to the growing Moran bibliography, we have attempted to add both documentary information and interpretative commentary. The catalogue includes four biographical essays exploring the major periods of Moran's professional career, each of which introduces a section of color reproductions of works in the exhibition. The color plates are accompanied by excerpts from contemporary sources, including newspaper and periodical reviews, when such commentary was available. Following these essays is an extensive chronology of Moran's life and work, illustrated with numerous archival photographs. Two additional essays amplify our consideration of Moran's oeuvre. In the first, Thomas P. Bruhn discusses Moran's substantial contributions to the fields of American etching, engraving, and lithography. In the second, Joni L. Kinsey examines the enormous body of work Moran created for commercial purposes, including a large number of illustrations for books and magazines.

Three appendices follow. The first reproduces both the text and images from Louis Prang's 1876 portfolio *The Yellowstone National Park, and the Mountain Regions of Portions of Idaho, Nevada, Colorado, and Utah.* The fifteen chromolithographs included in the set were based on watercolors by Moran. In recent years it has become common practice to sell individual plates from the series without the accompanying text. In the interest of scholarship and connoisseurship we have reproduced the text and images as they appeared in the original publication, one of the most important illustrated works of the nineteenth century. The images reproduced here are from one of two sets in the collection of the Gilcrease Museum.

The second appendix is a transcription of what has come to be called Moran's "Opus List." Between 1863–1868, while still a developing artist, Moran kept a list of works to which he assigned "Opus" numbers. Corresponding numbers appear near Moran's signature on the surface of many early paintings. Matching the opus numbers on the paintings with those on Moran's list yields significant information, including original titles, dates, and commentary regarding painting materials, patrons, and prices. Known opus works are illustrated.

The third appendix consists of four letters dating from 1873. Three were written by Justin E. Colburn, correspondent for the *New York Times;* the fourth by Thomas Moran. All four document the journey that the two men made when they accompanied John Wesley Powell to the Grand Canyon in the summer of 1873. The immediacy of the commentary and the informed nature of the observations lend a perspective to that important trip unavailable through any other source.

During his long life Thomas Moran produced an enormous body of work that included highly accomplished engravings, etchings, lithographs, sketches, drawings, and illustrations, as well as the oil and watercolor paintings for which he has long been celebrated. Although much research has been done on Moran, much more remains to be undertaken. It is our hope that this catalogue will serve not only as a visual record of the exhibition, but also as a reference tool for future scholars of Moran's life and art. NKA

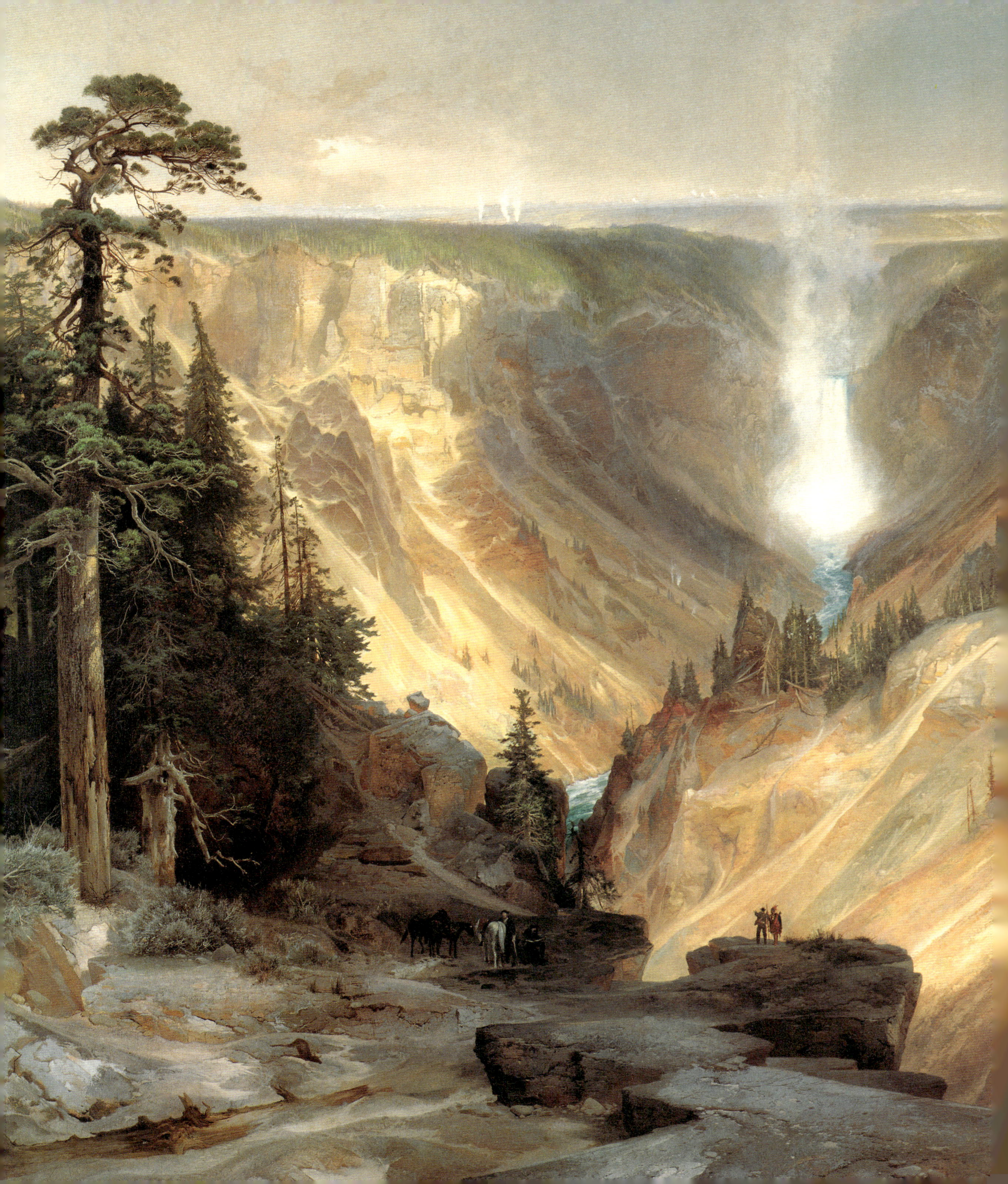

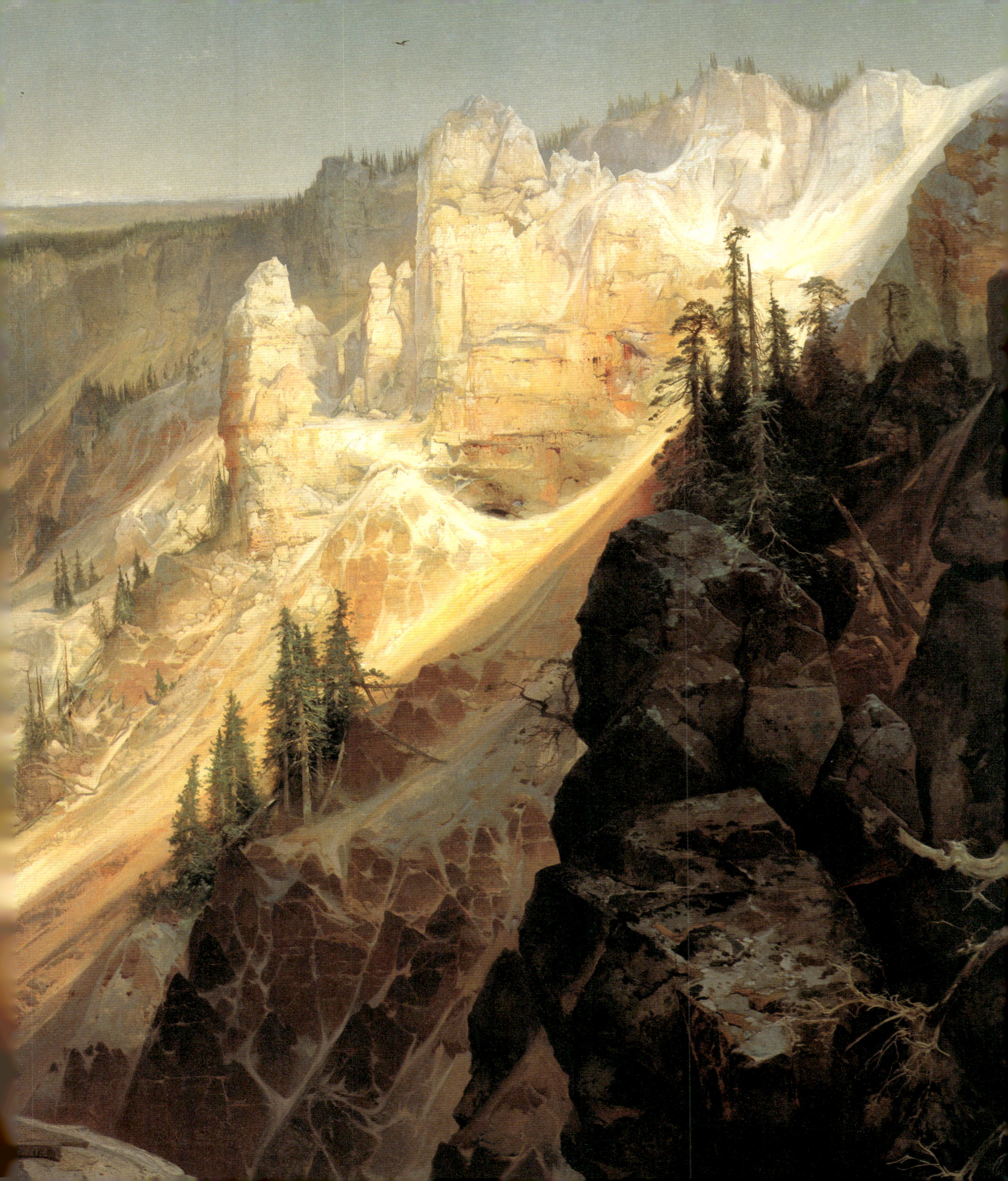

ACKNOWLEDGMENTS

FROM THE EARLIEST stages of development the Thomas Moran exhibition and catalogue have been collaborative efforts. Both have benefited from the enthusiastic support and full cooperation of numerous Moran scholars, including the late Thurman Wilkins, whose groundbreaking biography appeared in 1966 and whose revised edition of that work will be issued in 1998. Carol Clark, whose fine work on Moran was critical to our study, provided information and support throughout. Steve Good and Phyllis Braff of the Moran Catalogue Raisonné Project also made substantial contributions. Without the daily assistance, however, of Anne Morand of the Gilcrease Museum, this project would not have come to fruition. Anne's mastery of the enormous Moran archive at the Gilcrease, and her familiarity with the Moran bibliography were a constant source of wonder. For her unfailing cheer and skilled guidance, I remain profoundly grateful.

An exhibition and publication of this scope draw upon the expertise, energy, and good will of many people. I gratefully acknowledge the assistance of friends and colleagues at the three sponsoring institutions.

At the National Gallery of Art director Earl A. Powell III and deputy director Alan Shestack have been very supportive from the outset. Elizabeth Driscoll Pochter, administrator for policy and programs, provided assistance at critical stages of development. In the department of American and British paintings Nicolai Cikovsky Jr. and Franklin Kelly provided encouragement and guidance; Deborah Chotner searched tirelessly for photographs of the "Opus" works listed in Appendix 2 and assisted with catalogue illustrations; Stephenie Schwartz supplied invaluable help with correspondence, computers, and catalogue research. I would also like to thank curatorial colleagues in other departments who have been especially supportive, in particular Ruth Fine in modern prints and drawings, Sarah Greenough in photography, Virginia Clayton and Gregory Jecman in old master prints, and Nancy Yeide and Anne Halpern in curatorial records and files. In the exhibitions office D. Dodge Thompson, Ann Bigley Robertson, and Jonathan Walz skillfully guided the project from beginning to end. In the secretary-general counsel's office Marilyn Tebor Shaw administered all contracts. In the treasurer's office Nancy Hoffmann was responsible for insurance arrangements. Stephanie Belt and Lisa Mariam assisted in coordinating loans from the Gallery's collection. In conservation Ross Merrill, Michael Skalka, Sarah Fisher, Michael Swicklik, Judith Walsh, and Stuart Wolffe provided numerous insights gleaned from their study of Moran's painting technique and materials. Special thanks are due many members of the library staff who responded to every request, however obscure, and delivered their findings with unfailing good cheer: Lamia Doumato, Ted Dalziel, Thomas F.J. McGill Jr., Frances Lederer, Roberta Geier, Anna Rachwald, Ruth Philbrick, Gregory P.J. Most, Nicholas Martin, and Thomas O'Callaghan. Susan Farr provided much-needed computer assistance at critical junctures throughout the project. In the editors office Frances P. Smyth, Tam Curry Bryfogle, and Margaret Bauer oversaw production of the catalogue, with assistance from Mariah Seagle and freelance copyeditor Nancy Eickel. Susan Arensberg and Isabelle Dervaux coordinated production of brochures and wall texts, and Elyse Kunz assisted in developing video programs. Thomas Valentine and John Conway oversaw numerous audiovisual programs. In imaging and visual services Ira Bartfield, Lorene Emerson, Bob Grove, Dean Beasom, James Locke, Alexi Bryant, Christina Moore, and Sara Sanders-Buell went to great lengths to secure high-quality tranparencies and photographs for the exhibition and catalogue. In corporate relations, Sandy Masur secured generous funding for the National Gallery. During the early stages of the project fundraising efforts were initiated by Elizabeth Perry, Laura Smith Fisher, and Joseph Krakora. Chief registrar Sally Freitag and art handler Daniel Shay and his crew managed the task of gathering the works for the exhibition with remarkable efficiency. Plans for the design and installation of the exhibition were initiated by the late Gaillard Ravenel and guided to completion by Mark Leithauser, Donna Kwederis, Gordon Anson, William Bowser, Jane Rogers, Barbara Keyes, Steve Wilcox, Richard Ford, Hugh Phibbs, and Jenny Ritchie. In the education division Lynn Russell, Faya Causey, Anne Henderson, Julie Springer, and Elisa Patterson planned and executed tours and lectures as well as teacher and school programs, while Donna Mann prepared the feature on Moran for the Gallery's Web site. Deborah Ziska and Nancy Starr oversaw publicity for the exhibition with skill and good humor.

I would also like to acknowledge the many contributions of the Gilcrease Museum, our partner in the Moran project. Special thanks go to former director Joan Carpenter Troccoli who championed the exhibition from the beginning, and current director J. Brooks Joyner who has supported the project with equal enthusiasm since he arrived at the museum in 1996. In addition to curator Anne Morand, we have been assisted by Gary Moore, Michael Sudbury, Ken Busby, Dan Swan, Deborah Burke, Kevin Smith, Sarah Erwin, Lisa Kahn, Shane Culpepper, Joe Chalakee, Nancy Apgar, Sharyn Barhoover, Vail Wilcox, Beverly Wilcox, Carol

Diebolt, Pat Peters, Jo Ann Mckinney, Hubert Noble, Kathryn Jarboe, and Norma Ewing. Among trustees and association members William C. Kellough, David James, Hans Helmrich, Milann Siegfried, Debbie Branch, and Jack Short deserve special thanks.

At the Seattle Art Museum, third venue of the exhibition, director Mimi Gardner Gates has been an energetic supporter of the project from the start. Trevor Fairbrother and Zora Hutlova Foy have overseen the many details associated with the installation. Special thanks are due Tom and Anne Barwick and the American Art Council of the Seattle Art Museum for their longstanding support of the exhibition and its Seattle venue.

During the course of our research the contributors have benefited from the persistent efforts of librarians and individual researchers in two cities central to Thomas Moran's life and career: Bolton, England, the artist's birthplace, and East Hampton, New York, site of his summer residence. In Bolton, A.C. Bell, librarian for the *Bolton Evening News* and *Bolton Journal*, kindly searched nineteenth-century newspapers to help locate undated references included in a Moran family scrapbook; Mrs. Eileen Voce, intrepid genealogist, helped with family history; Lucy Whetstone, assistant keeper of art at the Bolton Museum and Art Gallery, and Shaun Greenhalgh provided help with references and photographs. In East Hampton we owe special thanks to Dorothy King, librarian for the Moran Archive at the East Hampton Library, and Mrs. Condie Lamb, current owner of Thomas Moran's house.

For several years the catalogue authors have benefited enormously from the energy and diligence of numerous volunteers who read microfilm, tracked down references, searched for photographs, and generally assisted in every possible way: Anne Clark, Jennifer Harper, Kim Latta, and Jenny Parker deserve special thanks. Helena Wright, National Museum of American History, assisted in countless ways, as did Sarah Kelly, who volunteered a year of her time to help with the Moran project. Working closely with Sarah and all other Moran enthusiasts was Merl M. Moore Jr., who made his way through many reels of microfilm searching for critical references and who cheerfully volunteered to be "our man" at the National Archives. For his help with this project and many others we are especially grateful.

At a critical point in this project Sally Mansfield assumed the role of exhibition and research assistant. With unflappable good humor and dogged determination, she pursued every lead, answered every call, and examined every detail during the preparation of the catalogue. I am especially grateful for her dedication to this project.

During the several years of travel and research that preceded the exhibition and publication, the contributors have incurred many debts to fellow curators, scholars, dealers, collectors, and friends who assisted in innumerable ways. Inevitably, some of these individuals have accepted new positions at different institutions, but we remember them in the context of the Moran project and take pleasure in acknowledging the invaluable assistance of: Gail A. Anderson; Cheryl A. Brutvan, Albright-Knox Art Gallery, Buffalo; Jane Myers, John Rohrbach, Rick Stewart, Milan Hughston, and Paula Stewart, Amon Carter Museum, Fort Worth; Darlene Dueck, The Anschutz Collection, Denver; Judith E. Throm, Archives of American Art, Smithsonian Institution, Washington, DC; Suzanne Folds McCullagh, Kimberly S. Rhodes, and Stephanie Skestos, The Art Institute of Chicago; Joanne D. Hale and James H. Nottage, Autry Museum of Western Heritage, Los Angeles; Thomas and Anne Barwick; George Miles, Beinecke Library, Yale University, New Haven; Frederick D. Hill, James Berry Hill, and Bruce Weber, Berry-Hill Galleries, Inc., New York; Candace Krauss, Briarhurst Manor, Manitou, Colorado; Linda S. Ferber, Barbara H. Millstein, and Teresa Carbone, Brooklyn Museum of Art; Sarah E. Boehme and Peter Hassrick, Buffalo Bill Historical Center, Cody, Wyoming; Ellen Halteman, California State Railroad Museum, Sacramento; Joseph Cleary and Betty Dickert, Cleary-Dickert House, Jacksonville, Florida; Marilyn Symmes and Liz Marcus, Cooper-Hewitt National Design Museum, Smithsonian Institution, New York; Marisa Keller, Linda Simmons, and Dare Hartwell, Corcoran Gallery of Art, Washington, DC; Anne Wheeler and Byron Price, Cowboy Hall of Fame, Oklahoma City; Diane De Grazia, Cleveland Museum of Art; Eric Paddock, Colorado Historical Society, Denver; Kahren J. Arbitman and Sally A. Metzler, Cummer Gallery of Art & Gardens, Jacksonville, Florida; Carl David; Joan Troccoli and Lewis I. Sharp, Denver Art Museum; Nancy Rivard Shaw and Jim Tottis, Detroit Institute of Arts; Diane Dillon; Ivy F. Strickler, Drexel University Collection, Philadelphia; Bill Eloe; Lois Fink; Jane Montgomery and Ann Powell, Fogg Art Museum, Harvard University Art Museums, Cambridge; Mike Foster; Don Fowler, University of Nevada, Reno; Michael Godfrey; William Goetzmann; Amy Eller, Guild Hall Museum, East Hampton; Charles Hillburn, Gulf States Paper Corporation, Tuscaloosa, Alabama; Sharman Robertson, Hallmark Historical Collection, Kansas City, Missouri; Sandy Falkenhagen, Harbert Corporation, Birmingham, Alabama; Anne Cohen DePietro and William H. Titus,

Heckscher Museum of Art, Huntington, New York; Paul Hertzmann; Judy L. Larson, High Museum of Art, Atlanta; Caroline Hinkley; Stuart Feld and M. P. Naud, Hirschl and Adler Galleries, New York; Perry Houston; Amy Myers, Huntington Library, Art Collections and Botanical Gardens, San Marino, California; Jody Hawley Ochoa, Idaho State Historical Museum, Boise; Peter G. Boag, Idaho State University, Pocatello; Elizabeth Ann Wilcox and Sarah Sullivan, Independence Seaport Museum, Philadelphia; Christine Hennessey, Inventory of American Paintings, Smithsonian Institution, Washington, DC; Nan and Roy Farrington Jones; Vance Jordan, Jordan-Volpe Gallery, New York; Alan, Mary, and Colleen Kollar; Francis O. Krupka; Helen Lane; Sarah Weatherwax, Susan Oyama, and Kenneth Finkel, Library Company of Philadelphia; David Kresh, Katherine Blood, and Walter Zvonchenko, Library of Congress, Washington, DC; Olivia Lincoln and Margaret Donlan; Eileen Fort, Los Angeles County Museum of Art; Mary Lublin; James Maroney; Joan Barnes and Jonathan Boos, Masco Corporation, Taylor, Michigan; Robert Mayo, Gallery Mayo, Richmond; Martha Sandweiss and Linda Delone Best, Mead Art Museum, Amherst; H. Barbara Weinberg and Kevin Avery, Metropolitan Museum of Art, New York; Katherine B. Crum, Mills College Art Gallery, Oakland, California; Margaret Lynne Ausfeld, Montgomery Museum of Fine Arts, Alabama; Pat Moore; Sophia Hewryk, Moore College of Art and Design, Philadelphia; Erica Hirschler, Shelley Langdale, Carol Troyon, Sue Walsh Reed, and Page Hamilton, Museum of Fine Arts, Boston; Ed McCarter, Jim Zeender, and Chris Kent, National Archives, Washington, DC; Claire Bunkham, National Gallery, London; Elizabeth Broun, William Truettner, Denise Dougherty, Richard Murray, Patricia M. Lynagh, Cecilia H. Chin, Melissa Kroning, and Merry Foresta, National Museum of American Art, Smithsonian Institution, Washington, DC; Julie Aronson, Nelson-Atkins Museum of Art, Kansas City, Missouri; Laurene Buckley, New Britain Museum of American Art, Connecticut; John W. Coffey, North Carolina Museum of Art, Raleigh; Thomas Nygard; Marcia Eymann, Oakland Museum, California; Alex Molitor, Old Cathedral Cemetery, Philadelphia; Susan Haskell, Peabody Museum of Archaeology and Ethnology, Cambridge, Massachusetts; Cheryl Leibold, Pennsylvania Academy of Fine Art, Philadelphia; Gerald Peters, Catherine Whitney, and Kelly Keto, Gerald Peters Gallery, Santa Fe; William Lang, Philadelphia Free Library; Darrell Sewall and Carolyn Peter, Philadelphia Museum of Art; Lori Morse, *Philadelphia Inquirer;* Marcia Y. Manhart and Richard P. Townsend, Philbrook Museum of Art, Tulsa; Stacey Roman; A.W. Potter, Royal Academy of Arts, London; Miss Ann Reilly, St. John the Evangelist Church, Philadelphia; Paul Benisek, Santa Fe Railroad, Chicago; Rona Schneider; Robert D. Schwarz, Frank Schwarz Gallery, Philadelphia; Edward Shein; Marc Simpson; Thomas Southall; Andrew Smith; Ira Spanierman, David Henry, and Amy Young, Spanierman Gallery, New York; Bruce B. Eldredge and Janis L. Ziller, Stark Museum of Art, Orange, Texas; George Turak; Charles Tyler; Joe McGregor and Carol Edwards, United States Geological Survey, Denver; Don Snoddy, Union Pacific Historical Museum, Omaha; Lori Olson, American Heritage Center, University of Wyoming, Laramie; Samuel Vickers; Leonard A. Walle; Nina Angeli Walls; Ginny White; Rex W. Scouten, Betty Monkman, and Lydia Tederick, White House, Washington, DC; Jonathon Williams; Susan Williams; Barbara A. Wolanin, United States Capitol, Washington, DC; Robin Frank and Laura Mills, Yale University Art Gallery, New Haven; Susan Kraft and Michael V. Finley, Yellowstone National Park, Wyoming; Richard York, Richard York Gallery, New York; Barbara L. Beroza, Yosemite Museum, Yosemite National Park, California. NKA

NOTES TO THE READER

Dimensions are given in centimeters, height before width, with inches following in parentheses.

Bibliographic sources are cited in short forms throughout the texts and notes, with full references provided in the Bibliography at the end of the book. Critical references to Moran's life and work are listed chronologically at the beginning of the Bibliography; additional general sources are listed alphabetically in the following section.

Some quotations from contemporary sources may contain eccentric spellings of familiar words. Very occasionally obvious misspellings have been corrected and commas added to clarify meaning often indicated by spacing in original documents. Whereas titles of periodicals may have varied slightly when originally published, we have chosen to use consistent citations throughout.

Works of art cited in the Chronology are often identified by numbers assigned in original exhibition lists or catalogues. Such catalogues bear titles that, unless otherwise specified, include the names of institutions that sponsored the exhibition. When numbers are cited simply as "no." (rather than "cat. no."), the source for the citation was not the exhibition catalogue itself but is given at the beginning or end of the entry.

LIST OF ABBREVIATIONS

AAA Archives of American Art

ABVM Church of the Assumption, Blessed Virgin Mary, Philadelphia

AFS Artists' Fund Society

AIC Art Institute of Chicago

AWCS American Water-Color Society

BAA Brooklyn Art Association

CA Century Association Records of Exhibitions 1881–1924 (microfilm)

Corcoran The Corcoran Gallery and School of Art Archives

DCAA Washington (DC) Art Association

EHL Moran Archive, East Hampton Library

EH Star *East Hampton Star*

Fryxell, UW Fritiof Fryxell papers, American Heritage Center, University of Wyoming

GA Gilcrease Archive (Thomas Moran papers at the Gilcrease)

Gilcrease Gilcrease Museum, Tulsa

GTNP Grand Teton National Park, Colter Bay, Wyoming

Hayden IC Hayden papers, incoming correspondence, United States Geological Survey, National Archives

JNEM Jefferson National Expansion Memorial

LC Library of Congress

LCP Library Company of Philadelphia

MFA Boston Museum of Fine Arts, Boston

NA National Archives, Washington, DC

NAD National Academy of Design, New York

NGA National Gallery of Art

NMAA National Museum of American Art

NYEC New York Etching Club

NYPL New York Public Library, Gilder papers

NYT *New York Times*

PAFA Pennsylvania Academy of Fine Arts, Philadelphia

Powell IC Powell papers, incoming correspondence, United States Geological Survey, National Archives

PSE Philadelphia Society of Etchers

SAA Society of American Artists (originally American Art Association)

SAE Society of American Etchers

SFRR Santa Fe Railroad Archive

SPE Society of Painter-Etchers (London)

ULC Union League Club

YJ Yellowstone Journal

YNP Yellowstone National Park

Catalogue

On 27 February 1812 George Gordon, Lord Byron, addressed his peers in the House of Lords for the first time. Not yet the famous poet he would soon become, Byron spoke passionately about the "unparalleled distress" he had witnessed among textile workers living near his estate in Newgate.[1] His remarks were offered in support of an unsuccessful attempt to defeat a bill that sanctioned the use of the death penalty for "frame-breakers"—those who damaged newly installed textile machinery. Byron delivered his speech shortly after arriving in London from Nottingham, the seat of much labor unrest, where, he noted, "not twelve hours elapsed without some fresh act of violence."

The violence Byron witnessed was born of frustration, poverty, and inexorable change. The economic and social transformation that would later be described as the Industrial Revolution had begun several decades before Byron rose to speak, but the full impact of mechanization—massive unemployment and devastating poverty—did not gain national attention until the frustration of those displaced by new "laboring-saving" machines exploded in angry riots.

It was the textile industry that first felt the hand of revolution, for the introduction of the spinning jenny and power loom quickly transformed a domestic craft into a factory industry. Thomas and Mary Moran of Bolton,

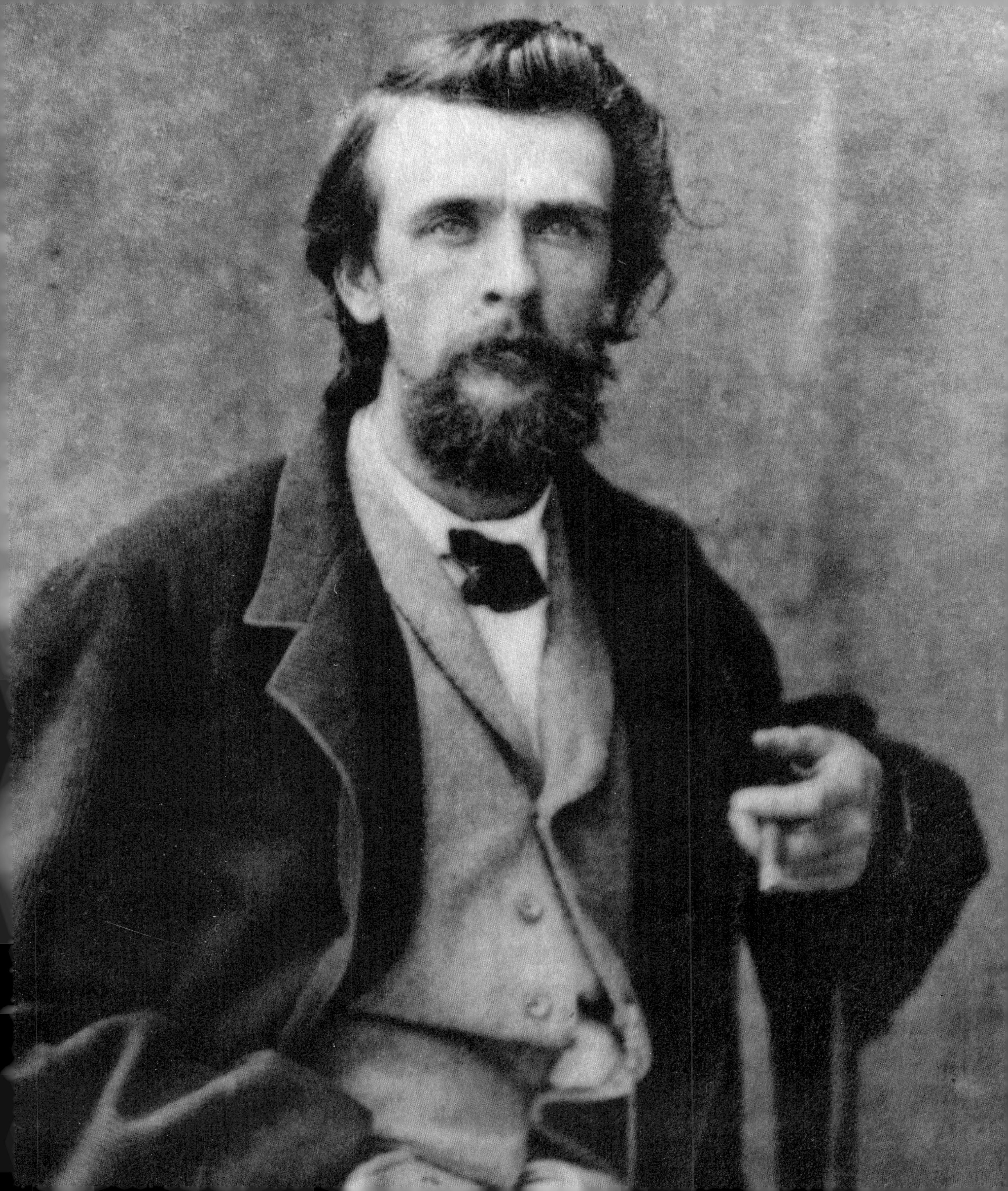

Preceding page: Thomas Moran, c. 1855, courtesy East Hampton Library.

1. *View of Bolton,* 1842, lithograph after a painting by Selim Rothwell, courtesy Bolton Museum and Art Gallery (England).

2. Paul Weber, courtesy Free Library, Philadelphia, Prints and Picture Collection.

3. James Hamilton, courtesy Free Library, Philadelphia, Prints and Picture Collection.

England, descendants of a long line of hand-loom weavers, were caught in the midst of the resulting turmoil.

Bolton, a factory town north and west of Byron's Newgate, gained a measure of unwanted notoriety when Friedrich Engels, in his classic study of the English working class, described Bolton as "among the worst" of the industrial towns surrounding Manchester, the acknowledged heart of the Industrial Revolution (fig. 1). Engels' assessment was based on personal experience:

> It has, so far as I have been able to observe in my repeated visits, but one main street, a very dirty one, Deansgate, which serves as a market, and is even in the finest weather a dark, unattractive hole in spite of the fact that, except for the factories, its sides are formed by low one- and two-storeyed houses. Here, as everywhere, the older part of the town is especially ruinous and miserable. A dark-coloured body of water, which leaves the beholder in doubt whether it is a brook or a long string of stagnant puddles, flows through the town and contributes its share to the total pollution of the air, by no means pure without it.[2]

By the time Thomas and Mary Moran's fifth child, a son they named Thomas, was born in February 1837, conditions for many in Bolton had become desperate. Peter Ainsworth, one of Bolton's two members of Parliament, reported to the House of Commons that "he had gone over the town with an honorable and gallant gentleman accustomed to witness the consequences of war, who had seen towns besieged and all the other miseries and privations which belong to such events, and who said he had never witnessed scenes in which wretchedness so deplorable was depicted."[3] Many years later Thomas Moran's youngest daughter, Ruth, noted succinctly that Bolton, the family's ancestral home, "was not pastoral England."[4]

The privations of the 1830s extended into the following decade, and coupled with near famine among the unemployed, the 1840s quickly became known as the "hungry forties." Bleak living conditions, poor prospects, and a growing family were undoubtedly the critical factors in Thomas Moran's decision to emigrate to America, but according to his wife, the immediate impetus came from a visiting American, George Catlin. Years after the fact Mary Higson Moran wrote that her husband

1

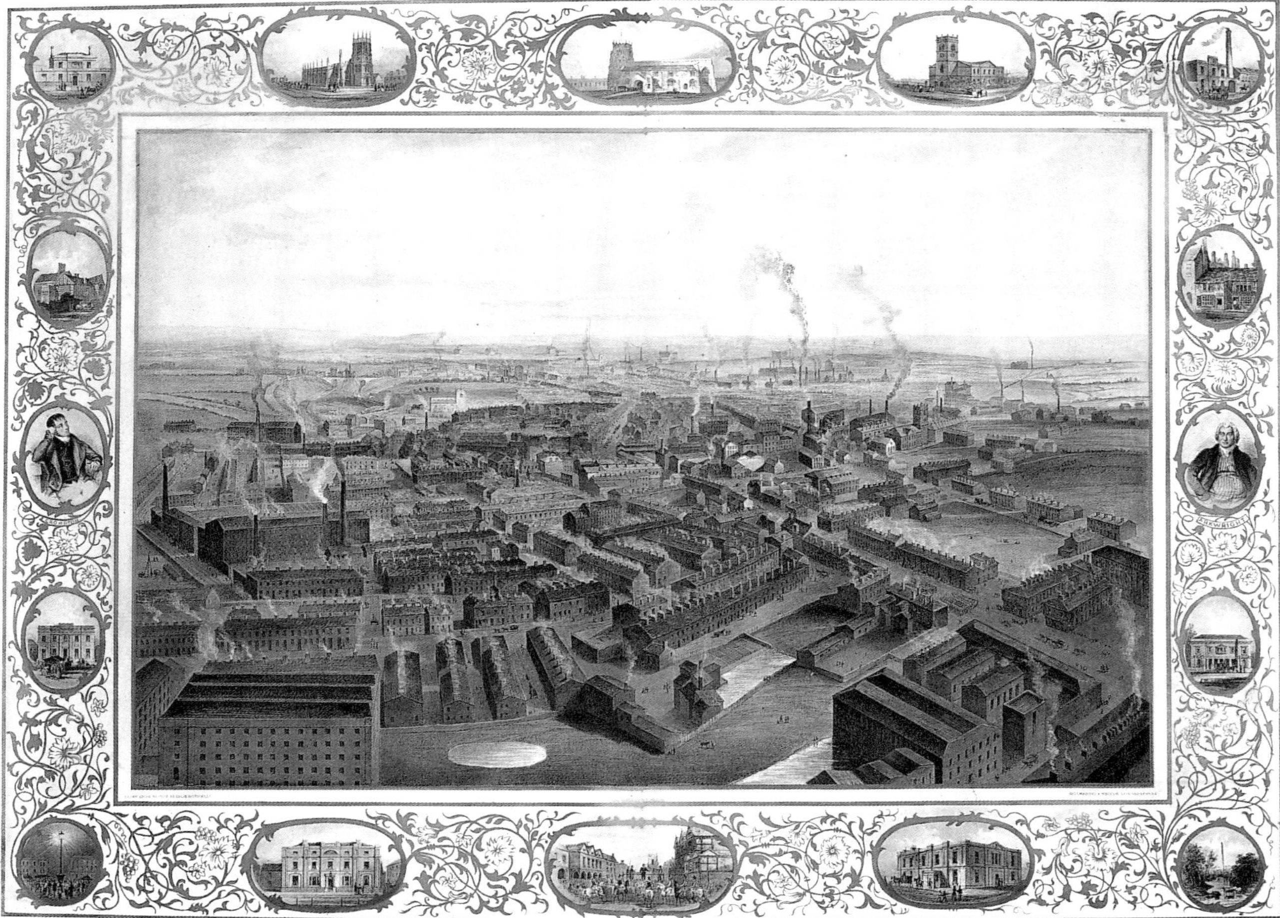

decided to try his luck in America after hearing Catlin lecture in London.[5] The famous Indian painter had arrived in England in January 1840 in a pique of anger after Congress had failed to purchase the Indian paintings and artifacts that he called his "Indian Gallery." Threatening to sell his collection abroad, Catlin installed the Indian Gallery in London's Egyptian Hall. As much a showman as an artist, he lectured regularly on North American Indian life and other topics. It is not clear what remarks by Catlin sparked Thomas Moran's interest in America, but in 1842 he set sail for the United States. Two years later, in the spring of 1844, his wife and seven children joined him.

2

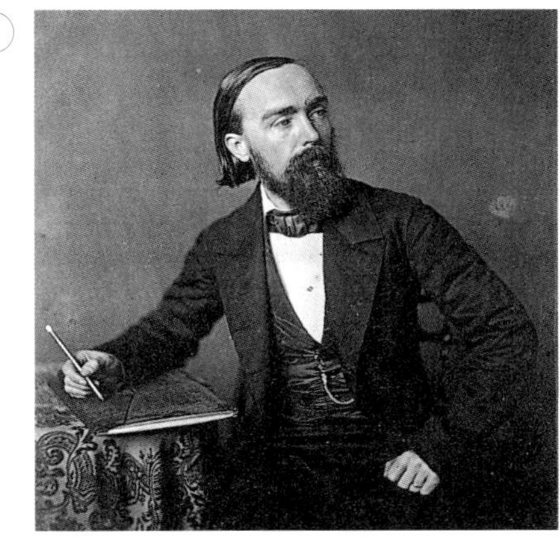

3

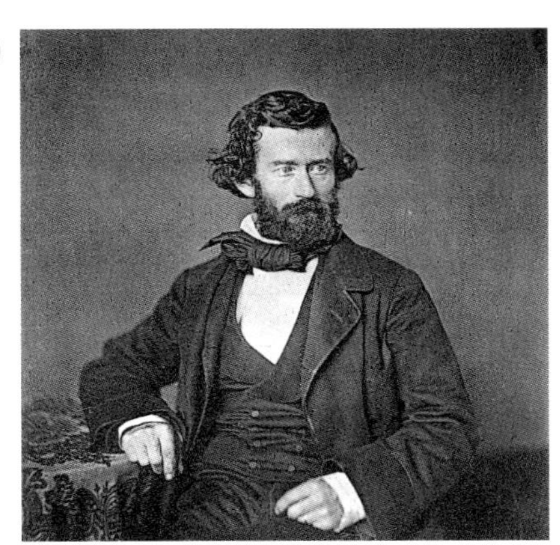

Capitalizing on his skills as a weaver, Thomas Moran settled his family in Kensington, a working district of Philadelphia. Years before the Moran family arrived, Kensington had become such a mecca for displaced textile workers that it had become known as "Little England."[6] Numerous mills on the tributaries of the Schuylkill River and burgeoning textile factories allowed older members of emigrant families to continue weaving while their children, through the public school system, acquired the skills that would allow them to break free of the textile trade.

Edward Moran, the eldest of Thomas and Mary Moran's children, was the first in the family to strike out on his own. Eight years older than young Thomas, Edward began working at his father's side at Ormrod's mill in Bolton while still a child. It was there that he had been playfully admonished for drawing pictures on newly woven cloth. By his own account, his early interest in drawing had been encouraged by a neighbor, a French housepainter with a reputation for decorating the interiors of local homes with whimsical designs.[7] By necessity such interests were put aside following the family's move to America, for Edward was obliged to assist his father in support of the growing Moran family. It was not until the early 1850s when introductions to Philadelphia artists Paul Weber and James Hamilton (figs. 2, 3) resulted in enough guidance and encouragement for the aspiring artist to risk leaving the weaving trade he had come to "detest."[8] A room over a cigar shop became his "studio" and odd jobs for a lithographer provided his first paycheck. In 1854 he made his professional debut at the Pennsylvania Academy of the Fine Arts in Philadelphia, exhibiting four paintings. Well before that date he had assumed a role that his brother Thomas would acknowledge many years later: "He taught the rest of us Morans all we know about art and grounded us in the principles we have worked on all our lives....It is scarcely probable that any of us would have been painters had it not been for Edward's encouragement and assistance. Such ability as we had was doubtless latent in us, but he gave us our bent, and such successes as we have attained, we primarily owe to him."[9]

In 1853, one year before Edward exhibited at the Pennsylvania Academy for the first time, Thomas entered an apprenticeship with Scattergood and Telfer, a Philadelphia engraving firm. Having recently completed grammar school, Moran chose, or more likely was persuaded by his father, to enter the work force rather than continue his studies in high school. Approximately two years later, for reasons not entirely clear, Moran terminated his apprenticeship prematurely.[10] Shortly thereafter he began working in Edward's studio. Resolute in his determination to become an artist despite family opposition and extremely modest means, Thomas set about acquiring the requisite skills. He turned first to his brother.

Eclectic Apprenticeship

In 1888, at the height of his success as a painter, Edward Moran published two articles in *Art Amateur* that were intended as instructional aids for those interested in marine painting.[11] In the first of these essays Edward praised the "powerful marines" of J.M.W. Turner and noted that he had drawn attention to these particular pictures "because the work of accomplished painters will necessarily, and properly, have great influence upon students and amateurs, and it is essential that they be directed to the right examples." The work of Turner was critical to the artistic development of both Thomas and Edward Moran, but for many years they knew his imagery primarily through illustrations and engravings. The "accomplished painters" who served as "the right examples" for both Thomas and Edward during their early years in Philadelphia, and from whom they received valuable professional and personal advice, were Paul Weber and James Hamilton.

Weber had arrived in Philadelphia in 1849, a refugee of political rather than industrial revolution. Born and educated in

Darmstadt with additional training in Frankfurt and Munich, Weber was a mature painter when he arrived in the United States. A landscape specialist, he traveled extensively in the Northeast and created works that celebrated the rich colors and textures of American forests, particularly those surrounding Philadelphia (fig. 4). A widely admired series of paintings of forest interiors completed by Thomas Moran in the 1860s clearly reflects Weber's influence. Although Weber returned to Europe in 1861 and remained there for the rest of his life, he continued to send paintings to Philadelphia dealers for sale and to the Pennsylvania Academy for exhibition. Thomas and Edward Moran undoubtedly studied these works carefully, but clearly the personal relationship they had enjoyed with Weber was no longer possible.

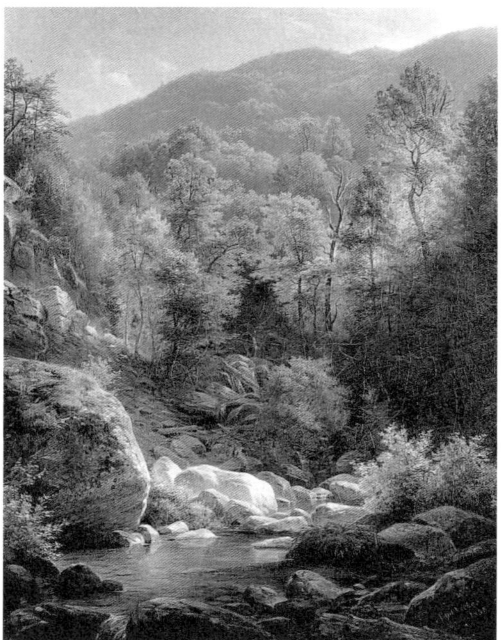

4

4. Paul Weber, *Scene in the Catskills,* 1858, oil on canvas, courtesy Corcoran Gallery of Art, Gift of William Wilson Corcoran.

5. Thomas Moran painting in a forest, c. 1864–1865, photograph by John Moran, courtesy East Hampton Library.

6. *The Hillsides of the Tohicon, Point Pleasant, Bucks County, Pa.,* c. 1865, photograph by John Moran, Collection of Leonard A. Walle.

At the time of Weber's departure Edward was well on his way to establishing a reputation as a skilled marine painter. Thomas, however, was still very much a student. Aside from his brother, the artist to whom Thomas was most indebted during this formative period was James Hamilton. In later life, Moran repeatedly described Hamilton as his "teacher," although he invariably disclaimed any formal instruction.

Like Moran, Hamilton was the son of emigrant parents. Fifteen years old when he arrived in Philadelphia in 1834, Hamilton resisted, as Moran would later, a life in trade. Instead, seeking out John Sartain, a well-known Philadelphia engraver, Hamilton showed him "a bundle of drawings" and asked for "a fair opinion."[12] According to Sartain, "there was sufficient proof of talent to justify the warmest encouragement, and earnest advice was given him not to be diverted from his purpose, but to devote himself to Art as the *one* vocation of his life." Hamilton took the advice to heart, obtained instruction in drawing, and eventually became a drawing instructor himself. It was Sartain who described Hamilton as "a most devoted admirer and student of the works of Turner," qualifying his remark by noting "as far as we are able to know them by engraved copies." In 1854, two years after Sartain made this observation, Hamilton traveled to England to study Turner's work firsthand along with that of other English landscape artists. He returned to Philadelphia steeped in English painting shortly before Thomas Moran terminated his apprenticeship and entered Edward's studio. In pictures characterized by strong color, dramatic light, and richly textured paint, Hamilton demonstrated what he had learned abroad. Quickly dubbed "the American Turner," he produced a body of work that was significantly different in conception and execution from that produced by Paul Weber.

Sartain's remark that Hamilton knew Turner as well as one could through "engraved copies" is telling, for without access to formal training, aspiring artists with meager resources, like Hamilton and the Moran brothers, by necessity took their lessons where they could. Aside from exhibitions at the academy and displays in dealers' shops, access to original works of art was limited. Available in greater numbers, however, were prints, engravings, and illustrated books. John Sartain, for example, had in his Philadelphia shop a large collection of European and American prints, and as mentor to Hamilton and later to Edward and Thomas Moran, he surely made these works available for study. Also accessible were illustrated books produced in great numbers during the nineteenth century. Family accounts of Thomas Moran's early years note that as his watercolors became more accomplished he succeeded in persuading at least one Philadelphia bookseller, C. J. Price, to accept his watercolors in exchange for books.[13] Among these were several publications with illustrations by Turner.

There is no doubt that Moran profited from the personal guidance he received from Weber, Hamilton, Sartain, and others, but it is also clear that Moran was a voracious reader from his earliest days.[14] Although of limited means, he grew to maturity in a city ornamented with libraries, a city that viewed itself as the cultural capital of the nation. For an obsessive autodidact like Moran, Philadelphia offered an ideal point of departure.

Moran's visual debt to others is evident in numerous early works. Drawings, watercolors, and oils inscribed "after Claude," "after Turner," or "after Isabey" define Moran's self-selected "academy" and confirm European influences. Less obvious perhaps are the textual sources for his imagery.

As might be expected from any artist whose youthful curriculum was hobbled together from resources at hand, Moran's early work reflects multiple enthusiasms. The most successful paintings from the 1860s, Moran's formative decade, may be the landscapes (often forest interiors) that testify to a sustained admiration (and perhaps market) for Pre-Raphaelite precision and detail. A large exhibition of British paintings (including works by the English Pre-Raphaelites) was shown at the Pennsylvania Academy of the Fine Arts in 1858. But well before that important event, lengthy excerpts from Ruskin's laudatory reviews of earlier Pre-Raphaelite exhibitions had appeared in *The Crayon* (published 1855–1861), a periodical that Moran and other members of his circle undoubtedly read.[15] Ruskin, who later remarked that his own early work found a wider and more sympathetic audience in America than in Europe, was a formidable voice during the 1850s and 1860s when Moran was assembling his syllabus of instructive reading. The English critic's enthusiasm for Turner and the Pre-Raphaelites enjoyed wide distribution in America through both the popular and specialized press.

5

Moran was well acquainted with Ruskin's views as expressed in *Modern Painters*, but perhaps of greater practical use were the instructive chapters in a lesser-known publication, *The Elements of Drawing*, subtitled *Three Letters to Beginners.*

Published in 1857, Ruskin's drawing manual was addressed to the "solitary student." With respect to "sketching from nature," Ruskin promoted direct imitation of nature's "vital facts" as the path to "truth." He advised students to begin by studying a single leaf and expand their range of vision gradually, avoiding any view that would make a "pretty" picture. He suggested that in preparation for study "in the field" the serious student select one plate from Turner's *Liber Studiorum*, hold the image up to a window, and trace the etched outline as accurately as possible. For students unable to obtain an image from the

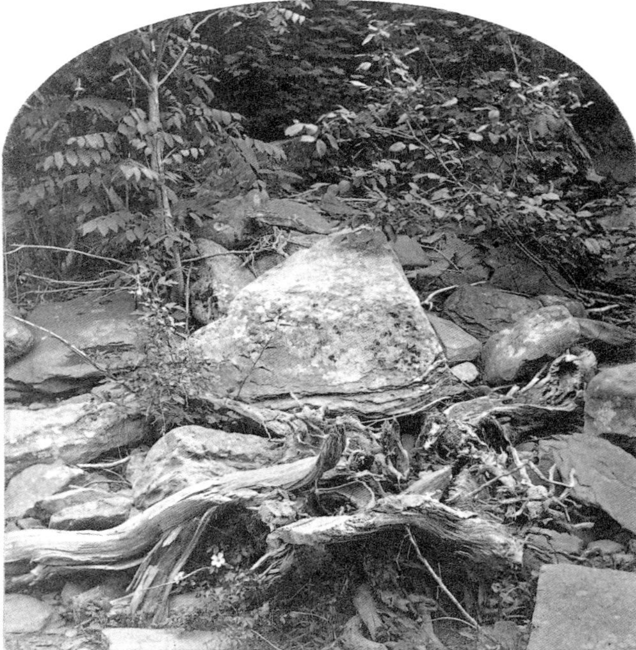

6

Liber, Ruskin recommended using a photograph to perform the same exercise. A cautionary footnote, however, accompanied Ruskin's text. Recognizing the inevitable gulf between the engravings of Turner and the field sketches of even the most dedicated student, Ruskin noted that even if strictly followed his method of instruction might lead to truth in manner but not in imagination.[16]

While aspiring to imitate Turner's imaginative feats, Thomas Moran and his brothers heeded Ruskin's advice to study the facts of nature. During the 1860s the Moran brothers spent a good deal of time sketching along the tributaries that fed the Schuylkill River and in the forests surrounding Philadelphia (see Chronology). An older brother John, who became an accomplished photographer, produced a number of stereo views that documented these forays, including several images that isolate the lichen-covered boulders Ruskin directed students to single out for study (figs. 5, 6).

Ruskin's recommendation that Turner's *Liber Studiorum* be used as the primary "text" for the study of drawing is intriguing, for there is strong evidence that Thomas and John Moran undertook a similar project with only limited success. In the list Thomas made of works completed between 1863 and 1868 (see Appendix 2), he added the notation "for 'Studies for Pictures'" to selected drawings that, when photographed by John, could have constituted a photographic "Liber."[17] John produced a similar volume for the Artists' Fund Society of Philadelphia in 1869 with twenty photographs of paintings by members of the society, including a work by Thomas Moran. Although described as an annual, the publication appears to have been a unique attempt by the society to extend its influence and increase revenue. If the Artist's Fund volume was a financial failure, as appears likely, the Moran brothers may have modified or abandoned their plan to publish a similar volume dedicated primarily or exclusively to images by Thomas.

The single painting by Thomas Moran included in the Artist's Fund Society album was "The Pictured Rocks of Lake Superior," which he had based on drawings from his first major sketching expedition.

Hiawatha's Landscape

In the summer of 1860 Moran and Isaac L. Williams, another Philadelphia artist, traveled to Lake Superior, where Moran wrote to Mary Nimmo, his future wife, that he had seen "the great sight, the Pictured Rocks," and that they had "exceeded [his] expectations though in a manner different from what I had supposed them."[18] That Moran had expectations confirms that Lake Superior was a deliberate rather than a random destination. Indeed this trip established a pattern that Moran would repeat frequently. Inspired by texts, in this case by Longfellow's enormously popular poem *The Song of Hiawatha,* Moran made a literal journey to the physical landscape that had served as the setting for the poem.[19] During the coming decades he would also make a number of imaginative journeys to the more illusory landscapes created by such literary figures as Percy Bysshe Shelley, Samuel Taylor Coleridge, Robert Browning, and, ironically, Lord Byron.

Moran's trip to Lake Superior also represents one of the earliest manifestations of his market acuity. By the time Longfellow completed *Hiawatha* in 1855, his popularity was such that four thousand copies of the poem were sold on the day of publication. Fifty thousand copies had been sold in the United States by April

7

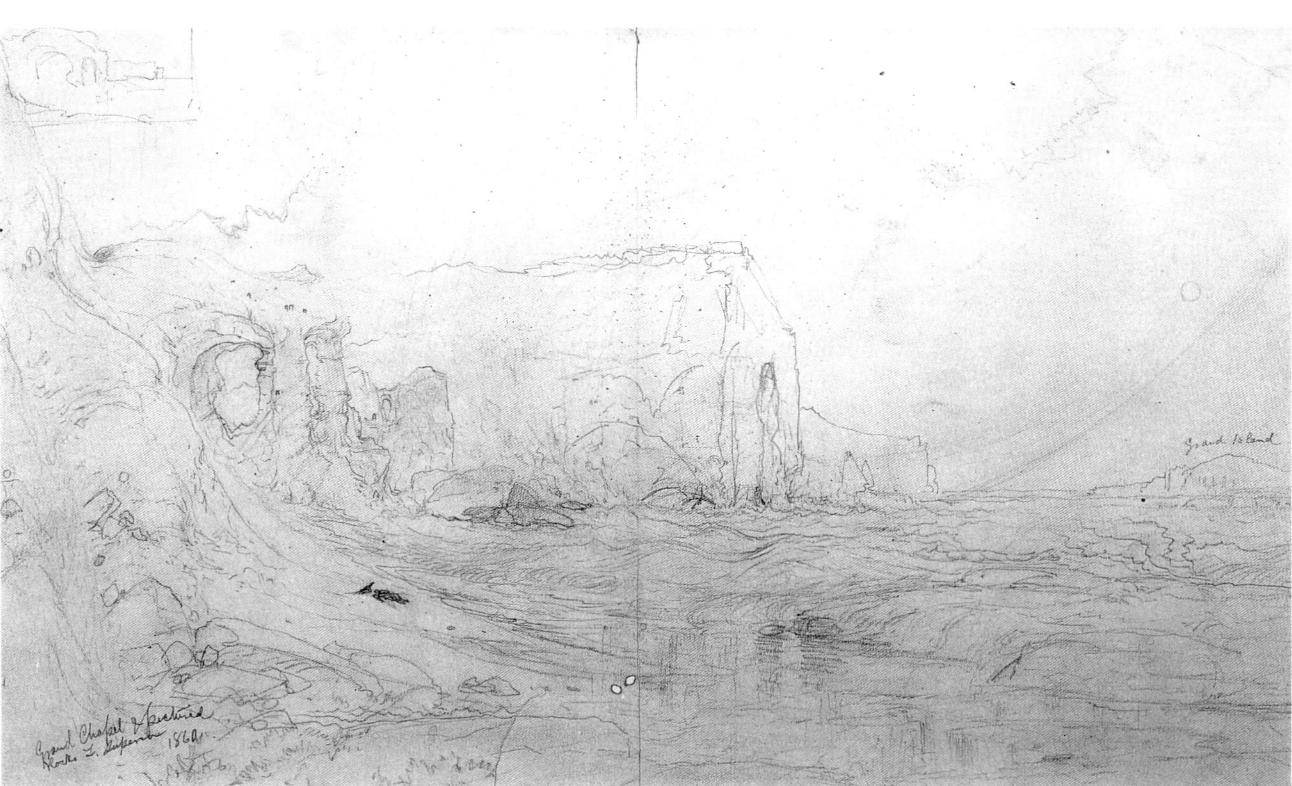

8

7. Detail from Thomas Moran, *Our Camp at the Pictured Rocks, L. S.,* 6 August 1860, graphite and crayon, courtesy Museum of Fine Arts, Boston, Gift of Maxim Karolik.

8. Thomas Moran, *The Grand Chapel and Pictured Rocks, L. Superior,* 1860, graphite, courtesy Gilcrease Museum, Tulsa, Oklahoma.

9. J. M. W. Turner, *The Golden Bough,* c. 1834, oil on canvas, courtesy Tate Gallery, London.

10. Thomas Moran after J. M. W. Turner, *The Golden Bough,* 1862, oil on canvas, present location unknown.

9

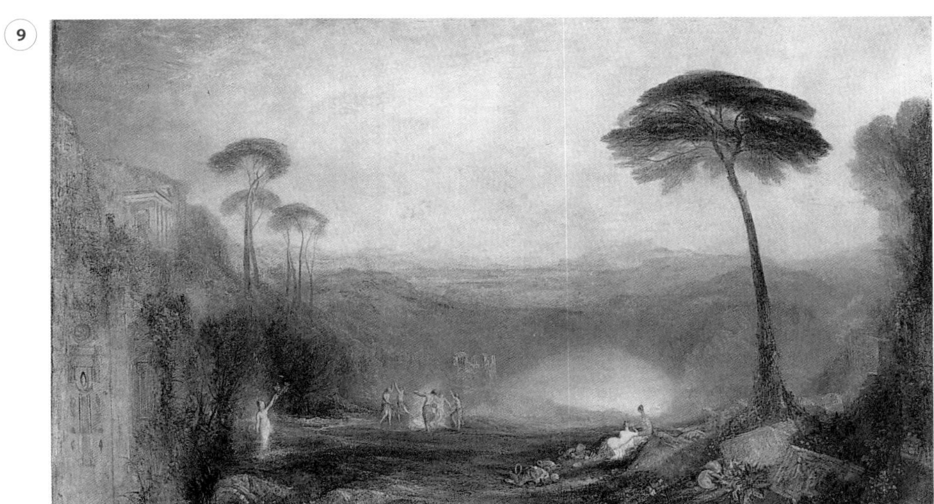

10

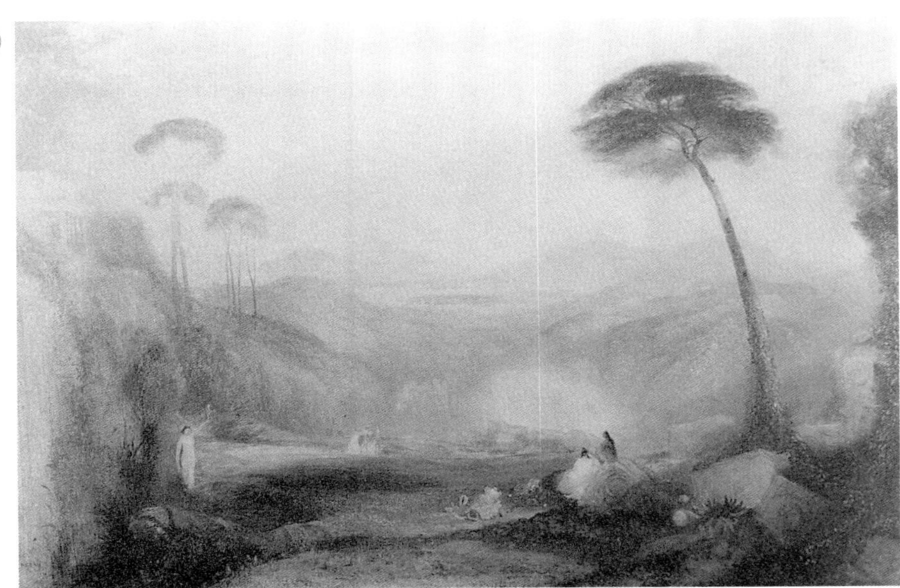

1857. It is impossible to know which edition of the poem Moran read or perhaps owned, but Ticknor and Fields, Longfellow's Boston publisher, included notes from the author in its 1856 edition that advised the reader interested in further information about the "Pictured Rocks" to consult "Foster and Whitney's Report on the Geology of Lake Superior Land District, Part II. p. 124."[20] Longfellow then offered an extended excerpt from the report. As others have noted, this report contains a tantalizing invitation: "So far as we know none of our artists have visited this region and given the world representations of scenery so striking, and so different from any which can be found elsewhere. We can hardly conceive of anything more worthy of the artist's pencil."[21]

Pencil sketches were in fact exactly what Moran brought back from his trip to Lake Superior. In one such image, inscribed "Our Camp at the Pictured Rocks, L. S." (fig. 7), Moran included an artist's easel supporting a work that appears quite similar to a pencil sketch in the collection of the Gilcrease Museum, "The Grand Chapel and Pictured Rocks, L. Superior" (fig. 8). Such sketches provided the raw material that Moran eventually used to produce paintings and illustrations for the market.[22] In 1860, however, the visual delivery system that would serve Moran so well a decade later (publications such as *The Aldine*, founded 1868, and *Scribner's Monthly*, founded 1870) was not yet firmly in place. Thus, although he had identified a subject with great popular appeal, he was not able to capitalize immediately on the market for images of a landscape that much of the public had come to know first through a work of literature.

Following Turner's Trail

In the spring of 1862 Thomas and Edward Moran traveled to England, where both had been born. Since emigrating to America, however, the brothers knew the country best as it had been painted and drawn by Turner. Perhaps encouraged by James Hamilton, who had made a similar pilgrimage eight years before, they sailed for Britain to see what they could not see in reproduction: Turner's color.[23] Already "apprenticed" to Turner by choice, they went abroad to study both the master's paintings and his subjects.

According to family lore, Thomas spent several weeks at the National Gallery in London, ferreted away with original works, teaching himself to paint by copying pictures by the artist he esteemed above all others. There may be some truth to the well-worn tale, for Moran made several paintings that are direct copies of Turner originals—*The Golden Bough* (figs. 9, 10), for example, which he inscribed "after Turner,"[24] and *Ulysses Deriding Polyphemus*, which he is known to have admired. Moran's copy of *Ulysses* is identifiable above the fireplace in a photograph of his East Hampton studio taken at least twenty years after this youthful journey (fig. 11).

There is no doubt that Turner's color—both in oil and watercolor—made a tremendous impact on Moran, for it is clear that when he saw the landscape of Yellowstone for the first time nearly a decade later it was Turner's palette that served him so well. Of equal importance, however, during Moran's study tour abroad, was the sketching trip he and Edward undertook along the southern coast of England following—quite literally—in Turner's footsteps (see Chronology).

Many years later, referring to this early trip, Edward commented on Turner's disregard for topographical accuracy:

> It is not to be supposed that Turner's sketches of particular localities are strictly correct. I once took a lot of Turner's engravings of views on the English coast, and went with them, as nearly as I could judge, to the exact spots from which they must have been taken—at Hastings, Dover and other southeastern points—going out in a boat and rowing about until I found the right place. Well, the result settled all doubts as to his accuracy. He is very inaccurate—willfully so. He would move a steeple from left to right of a given point without scruple, but his were always possible changes; his knowledge of the forms of land and sea and cloud was so thorough that he could do pretty much as he pleased with them, and yet keep within the bounds of naturalness.[25]

The revelation Edward described regarding Turner's "inaccuracy" was not lost on Thomas, who later summoned Turner's example when stating his own position regarding topographical truth:

> Turner is a great artist, but he is not understood, because both painters and the public look upon his pictures as transcriptions of Nature. He certainly did not so regard them. All that he asked of a scene was simply how good a medium it was for making a picture; he cared nothing for the scene itself. Literally speaking, his landscapes are false; but they contain his impressions of Nature, and so many natural characteristics as were necessary adequately to convey that impression to others.... The literal truth counts for nothing; it is within the grasp of any one who has had an ordinary art-education. The mere restatement of an external scene is never a work of Art, is never a picture.[26]

Although Moran would later travel with survey expeditions whose mandates dictated accurate topographical reporting, he rarely bowed to such demands when composing studio paintings. James Hamilton may have introduced him to the concept of artistic "license" before his journey abroad, but the experience of bobbing about in a boat off the English coast, with engravings by Turner in hand, noting how church steeples had been moved in accordance with artistic necessity, sanctioned the practice. Whenever attacked for "inaccuracy," Moran offered the Turner defense. He too had little interest in topographical truth.

Thomas and Edward Moran returned to Philadelphia in the fall of 1862. In February of the following year Thomas married Mary Nimmo (fig. 12). Clearly a match based on affection,

11. Interior of Moran's East Hampton studio, showing his copy after Turner's *Ulysses Deriding Polyphemus* over the fireplace, courtesy East Hampton Library.

12. Mary Nimmo Moran, 1863, courtesy East Hampton Library.

11

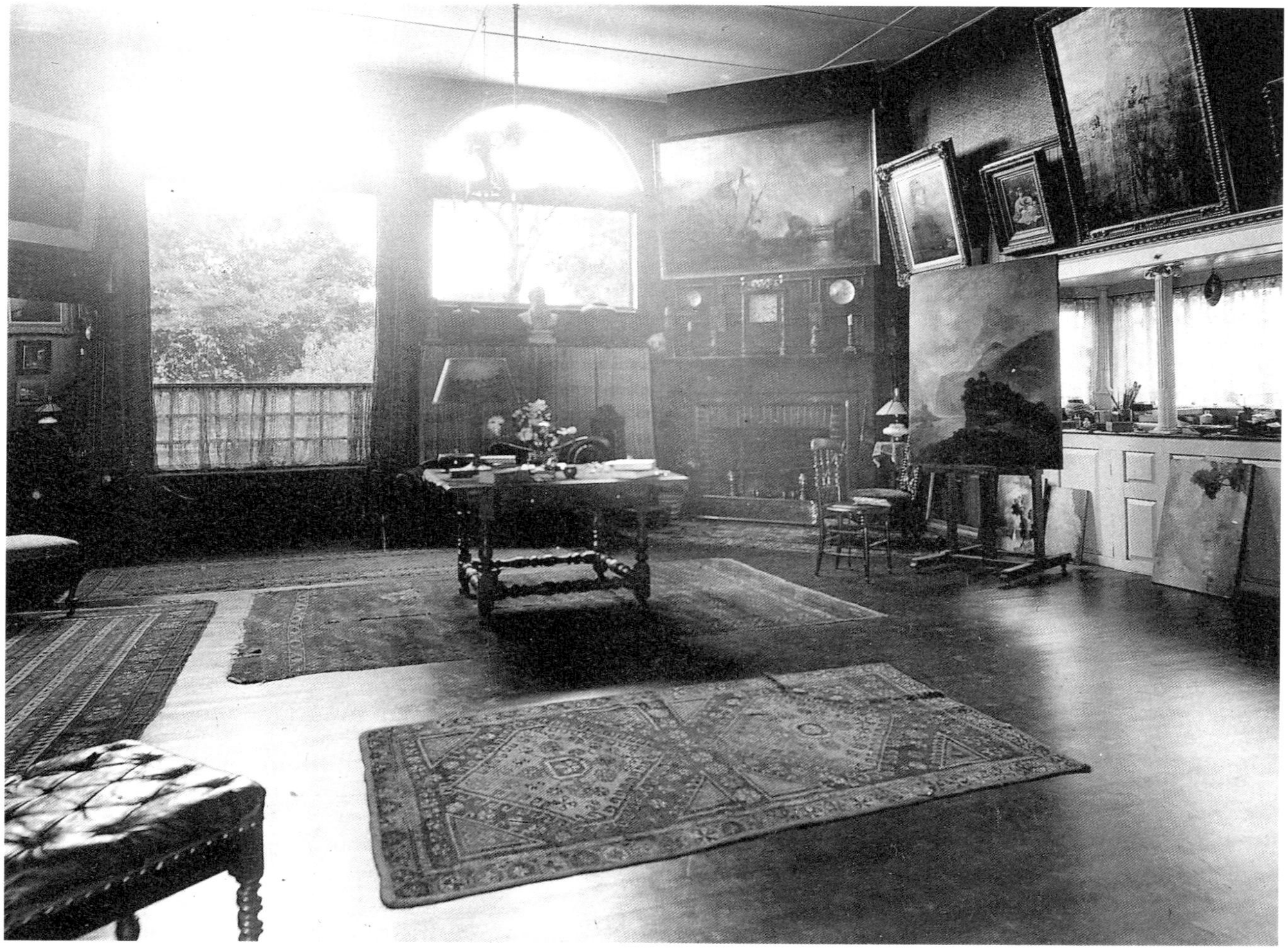

the union also became an extraordinary working partnership. During the early years of their marriage Mary contributed to the support of the family (three children were born between 1864 and 1870)[27] by teaching drawing at home. She was also her husband's business partner, largely responsible for coordinating the details related to the staggering number of commissions Moran received for illustrations. Later, with her husband's assistance, Mary became an accomplished etcher whose work was widely exhibited and highly praised. Until her death in 1899, she ran the Moran household with such efficiency that Thomas was freed of most domestic tasks and thus able to devote himself almost entirely to his work. Following Mary's death, the Morans' youngest daughter Ruth assumed the responsibility of caring for her father until his death in 1926. Thomas Moran's astonishing productivity was, in large measure, made possible by a domestic support system that continued for sixty-three years.

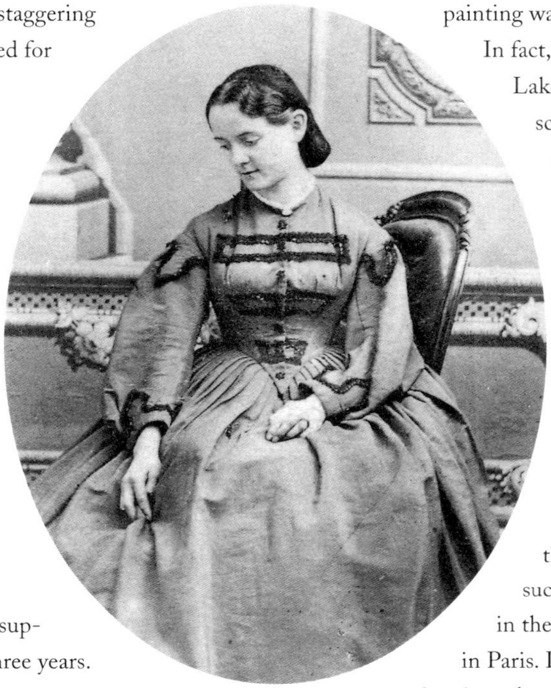

12

Return to Europe

In June of 1866 Thomas, Mary, and their young son, Paul, sailed for Europe, where they remained for much of the following year. Although Thomas had begun to exhibit regularly at the Pennsylvania Academy of the Fine Arts and had sold a number of works for respectable prices, this second trip abroad was also, in many respects, a study tour. It was during this journey that he visited the studio of Camille Corot, sketched in the Forest of Fontainebleau near the village of Barbizon, traveled through the Alps and northern Italy, and spent several weeks sketching in and about Rome. Despite his declared wish to paint American subjects in an American manner, Moran incorporated so much of what he admired in the work of European masters that throughout his career even American critics invoked the names of Salvator Rosa, Claude Lorrain, Alexandre Calame, Camille Corot, Narcisse Diaz, as well as Turner in reviewing his work.[28] It was the European sojourn of 1866/1867 that allowed Moran to study in depth original paintings by many of these artists, whose work he had known primarily in reproduction.

Headquartered in Paris during much of this period, Moran was also able to study an enormous cache of European paintings assembled in the French capital for the Exposition Universelle that opened on 1 April 1867. Moran himself was a contributor to the Exposition having brought two works from America for that purpose. One of these, *Children of the Mountain* (cat. 7), he completed abroad. In later years the painting was often described as a western scene. In fact, Moran had been no further west than Lake Superior by 1867, and the mountain scene was pure invention. The picture contains no figures; rather, the "children" of the title are "the cataract, the storm cloud, the rainbow, the mist, the eagle and the rock."[29]

Moran's decision to journey to Paris with an unfinished picture that he hoped would be accepted for inclusion in one of the largest European art exhibitions of the decade reflects a level of ambition not usually attributed to the artist. Equally impressive was his success in placing another large painting in the concurrent exhibition at the Salon in Paris. Listed in the catalogue as *Une forêt en Amerique*, the painting was most likely the picture Moran recorded in his ledger as Opus 22, *The Woods Were God's First Temples* (fig. 13). Among the largest of his early works, the picture was one of a series of forest interiors that Moran completed during the decade of the 1860s. Intricate, precise, and captivating in their detail, these paintings represent one of the earliest manifestations of a theme central to the artist's mature work. And once again their heritage is literary.

Solitude

Like the Lake Superior pictures begun in 1860, *The Woods Were God's First Temples* is the visual equivalent of a popular poem: William Cullen Bryant's "A Forest Hymn" (1824), which opens "The groves were God's first temples." By the time Moran began painting forest scenes, the sanctity of American wilderness, often represented by images of pristine eastern forests, had been the staple of more than one generation of American artists. Moran's variation on this theme reflects not only his enthusiasm for the painting techniques of the English and American Pre-Raphaelites but also his transformation of the American forest into a New World sanctuary for that most celebrated creation of the English romantics—the solitary poet-hero.

13

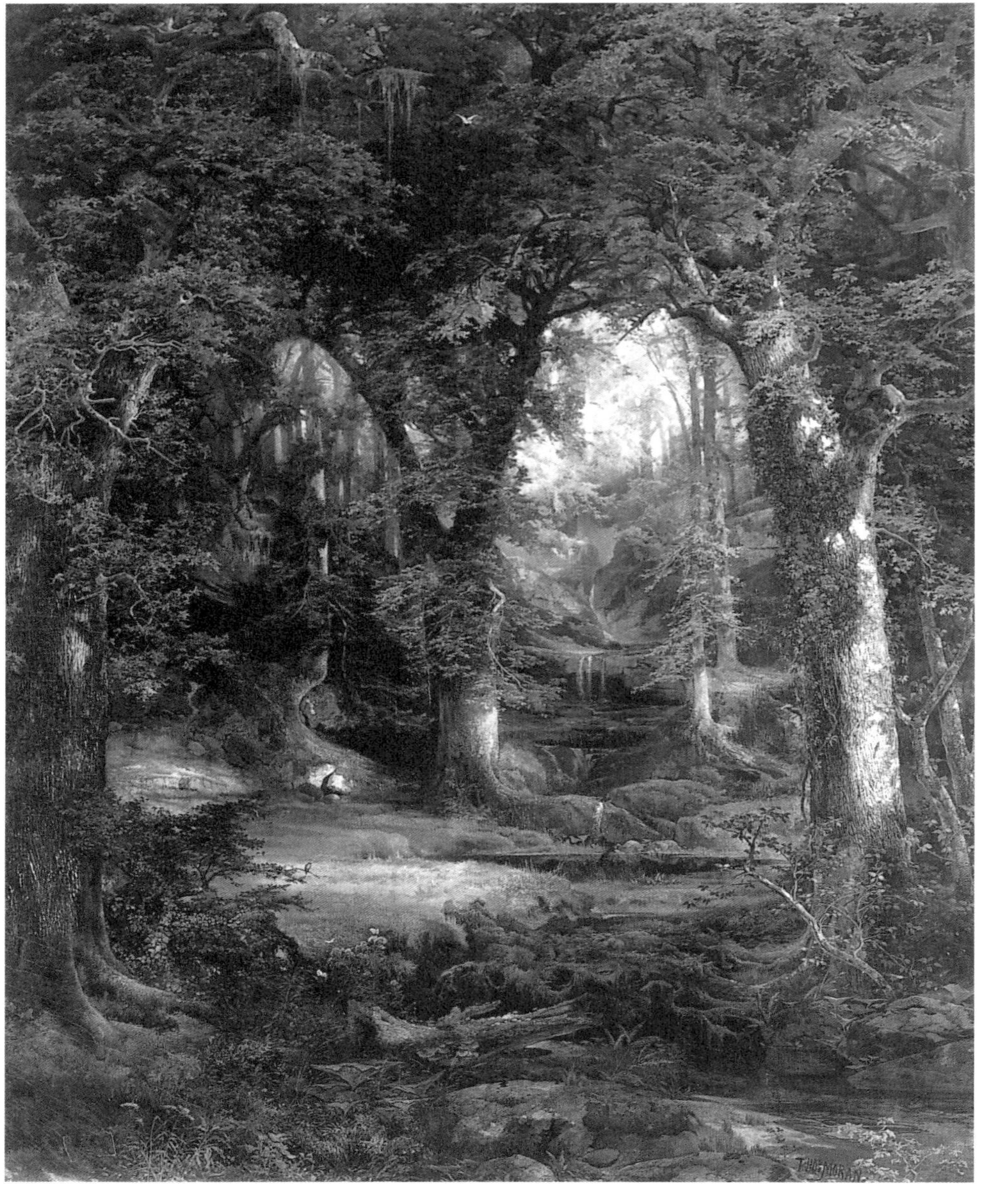

13. Thomas Moran, *The Woods Were God's First Temple*, 1867, oil on canvas, courtesy The Haggin Museum, Stockton, California.

Evidence of Moran's acquaintance with the literature that gave rise to the figure of the wandering poet appears early, for in 1857 he exhibited the painting *"Among the Ruins—there he lingered"* at the Pennsylvania Academy, its title taken from Shelley's poem *Alastor, or the Spirit of Solitude*. Published in 1816, *Alastor* was Shelley's first important work, but by no means the first of its kind. Four years earlier Lord Byron had completed the first two cantos of his youthful exposition of the theme, *Childe Harold's Pilgrimage*. In both works solitary young men of poetic temperament travel through the landscape of Europe searching for truth and beauty among the ruins of decaying civilizations.

Although the present location of Moran's painting based on *Alastor* remains unknown, a watercolor of the same subject does survive. Titled *Ruins on the Nile*, the composition includes the requisite broken columns and other debris of a fallen civilization (fig. 14). Sitting amid the ruins is the solitary poet-hero, surrogate for both author and reader.

Moran was well acquainted with the poetry of Shelley, Coleridge, Wordsworth, and Keats, but the literary figure to whom he was most indebted was Byron. The artist may have responded to Byron's poetry on his own and for personal reasons, but by the time he was mature enough to read Byron's work, the poet's chief visual interpreter was J. M. W. Turner. Early in his career and repeatedly in later years Moran stated that Turner was

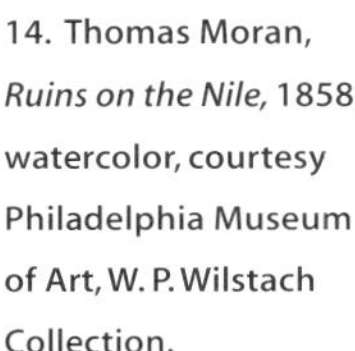

14. Thomas Moran, *Ruins on the Nile,* 1858, watercolor, courtesy Philadelphia Museum of Art, W. P. Wilstach Collection.

15. Edward Moran, *Jacques and the Forest of Arden,* oil on canvas, courtesy Museum of Fine Arts, Boston, Gift of Harold W. Dana.

16. Sir Charles Locke Eastlake, *Lord Byron's "Dream,"* 1827, oil on canvas, courtesy Tate Gallery, London.

14

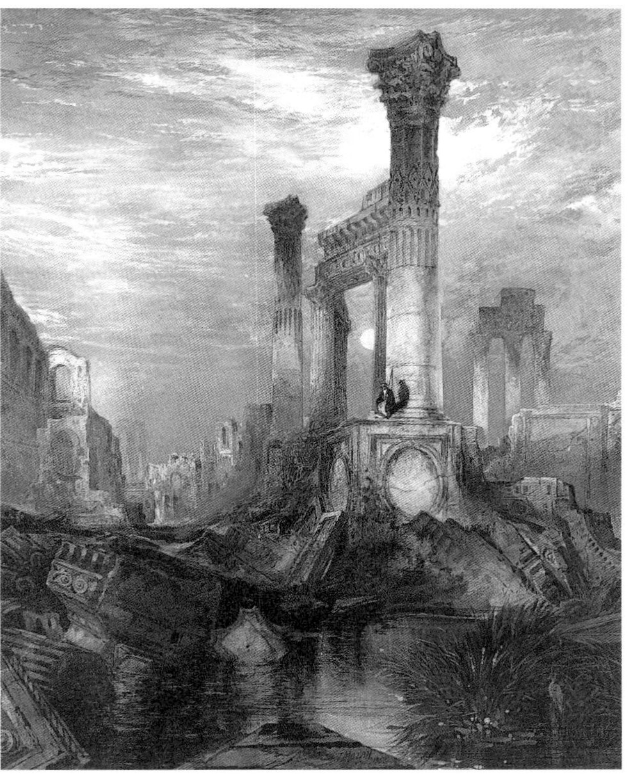

15

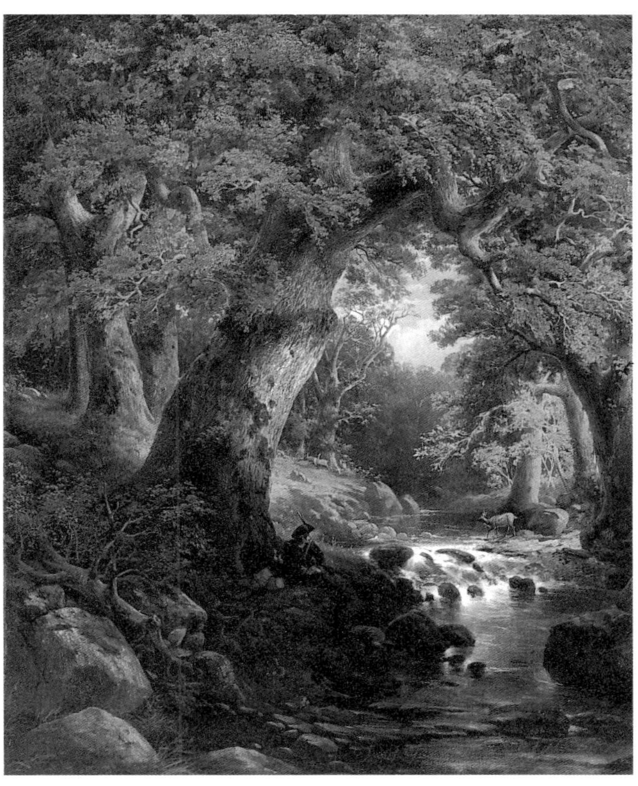

the artist he admired most. Traditionally such statements have been interpreted as references to Turner's technique, his color, and his landscape subjects. Of equal importance, however, was the avenue Turner opened to Byron, for to a degree difficult to understand today, Byron defined and then became the solitary artist, the poet-hero of his age. The persona he created was enormously attractive, and Thomas Moran was far from the only artist who fell under his spell. But for Moran the effects were significant and enduring—not because he would continue to paint "literary" pictures, although he did, but because Moran succeeded in redefining visually several of the key elements of Byron's romanticism.

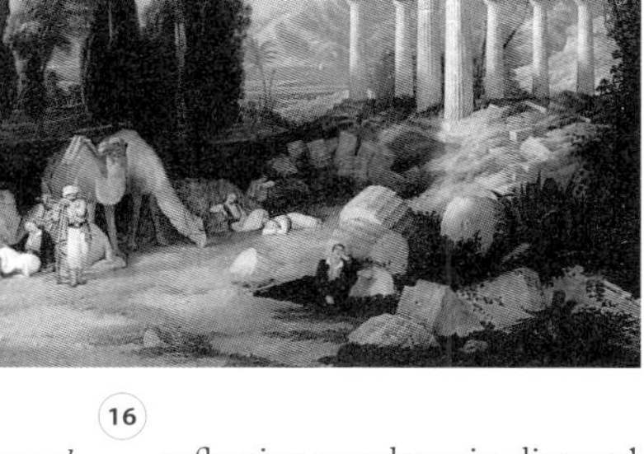

16

A hint of what was to come may be seen in *The Autumnal Woods* (cat. 6), one of Moran's most successful paintings of a forest interior.[30] Like others in the series, *The Autumnal Woods* combines a canopied forest glade, a distant lake surrounded by wooded hills, a quiet pool, and an extraordinary display of lush foreground foliage. The leaves and lichens that Ruskin advised young artists to study in detail are present in abundance. Also present is a solitary reclining figure.

Edward Moran, in another early painting based on a literary work, *Jacques and the Forest of Arden* (Shakespeare's *As You Like It*), used a similar compositional format, including canopied trees shading a reclining figure in the foreground (fig. 15).[31] More to the point, however, may be several European works. Charles Eastlake's painting *Lord Byron's "Dream"* (fig. 16), based on Byron's poem "The Dream," has been described as the "definitive image of a melancholy or reflective wanderer in distant lands."[32] Engraved in 1834 and distributed in large plate format, the image was widely known. Eastlake's interpretation of the Byronic landscape—complete with contemplative figure (Byron) amid the ruins of civilization—may have inspired Turner's *Childe Harold's Pilgrimage*—

Italy (1832) based on Byron's most famous poem.[33] Turner's painting was well known to both Moran brothers, for in March 1868 a Philadelphia newspaper noted that Edward Moran had opened a new studio in which "a copy, painted with some care, of Turner's 'Childe Harold'" hung above the piano.[34] The reclining contemplative figure appears in another landscape Thomas Moran knew well: Turner's *Solitude*, plate 53 in his *Liber Studiorum* (fig. 17). Initially published in 1814, Turner's etching is a landscape view with framing trees, a foreground pool, and lush foliage—a setting fit for solitary contemplation.

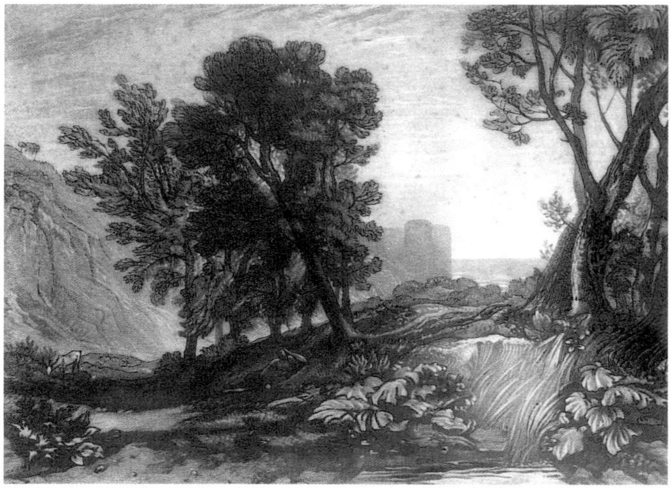

In a painting like *Ruins on the Nile* Moran invented a setting for the poet-hero he had followed through Europe via Shelley's *Alastor*. In coming years he would perform the same imaginative task countless times as he became one of the most prolific illustrators of books and periodicals in nineteenth-century America. In paintings like *The Autumnal Woods*, however, he produced pictures much less reflective of a single text and far more revealing as the work of a young artist attempting to balance the dictates of Ruskin, the model of Turner, the technique of the Pre-Raphaelites, the seductions of the Romantic poets, and the advice of his mentors. In so doing, Moran created images that testify to the skillful adaptation of European themes and models by a young man who consciously aspired to be a poet-artist himself.[35]

In *The Autumnal Woods* Moran provided an American bower for Byron's solitary poet. Deftly transforming European precedent, he placed his contemplative figure in an American forest in full autumnal glory. Clearly based on close firsthand observation, Moran's forest interior was constructed leaf by leaf following Ruskin's instruction and the Pre-Raphaelites' example. The result is a wonderfully American hybrid. Lord Byron's poet, bereft of ancient ruins, reclines in the natural sanctuary of a Pennsylvania forest.

Four years after he completed *The Autumnal Woods* Moran created the finest of his early lithographs, *Solitude* (fig. 18), later described as a "view on the south shore of Lake Superior."[36] Moran may have incorporated details from sketches executed in Michigan nearly a decade earlier, but it seems just as likely that he drew upon his European experience,—particularly his acquaintance with the work of Alexandre Calame. Whatever the source of individual compositional elements the collective whole represents the next step in Moran's redefinition of the romantic state of "solitude." Gone is the leafy bower with its soft mottled light. A mountain lake and cascading water have replaced the quiet pool and trickling stream of *The Autumnal Woods*. Thunder clouds threaten, and twisted pines betray earlier elemental battles. No velvet-clad poet reclines beneath these trees.

17

A decade after *Solitude* was completed, the lithograph was published as an illustration in an article about Moran, with a caption that identified it as "from a painting."[37] During the course of his career Moran created several paintings titled *Solitude* that are closely related to the early lithograph. One of these, a picture signed and dated 1897, recently came to light (cat. 84). Similar in terms of composition, the lithograph and the painting are nevertheless quite different. In the 1897 painting Moran modified many of the Calame-like elements. The thunderheads and the alpine firs have been replaced by blue sky, soft pink clouds, and western pines. The most significant change, however, appears in the distance, where a range of snow-capped peaks rises above the more modest mountains that defined the horizon in the earlier lithograph. This recently rediscovered painting was occasionally listed in exhibition catalogues with an amplified title that included the words "Rocky Mountain Waterfall." The juxtaposition of Moran's early lithograph with his late reworking of the theme may offer the most dramatic example of the kind of transformation that the artist effected throughout his career. Steeped in the tenets of European romanticism, particularly as manifest in the life and poetry of Byron, Moran capitalized on the eclectic nature of his artistic apprenticeship, gradually assembling a visual vocabulary that allowed him to recast romantic concepts as basic as "solitude" first in the forests of Pennsylvania and later in the Rocky Mountains.

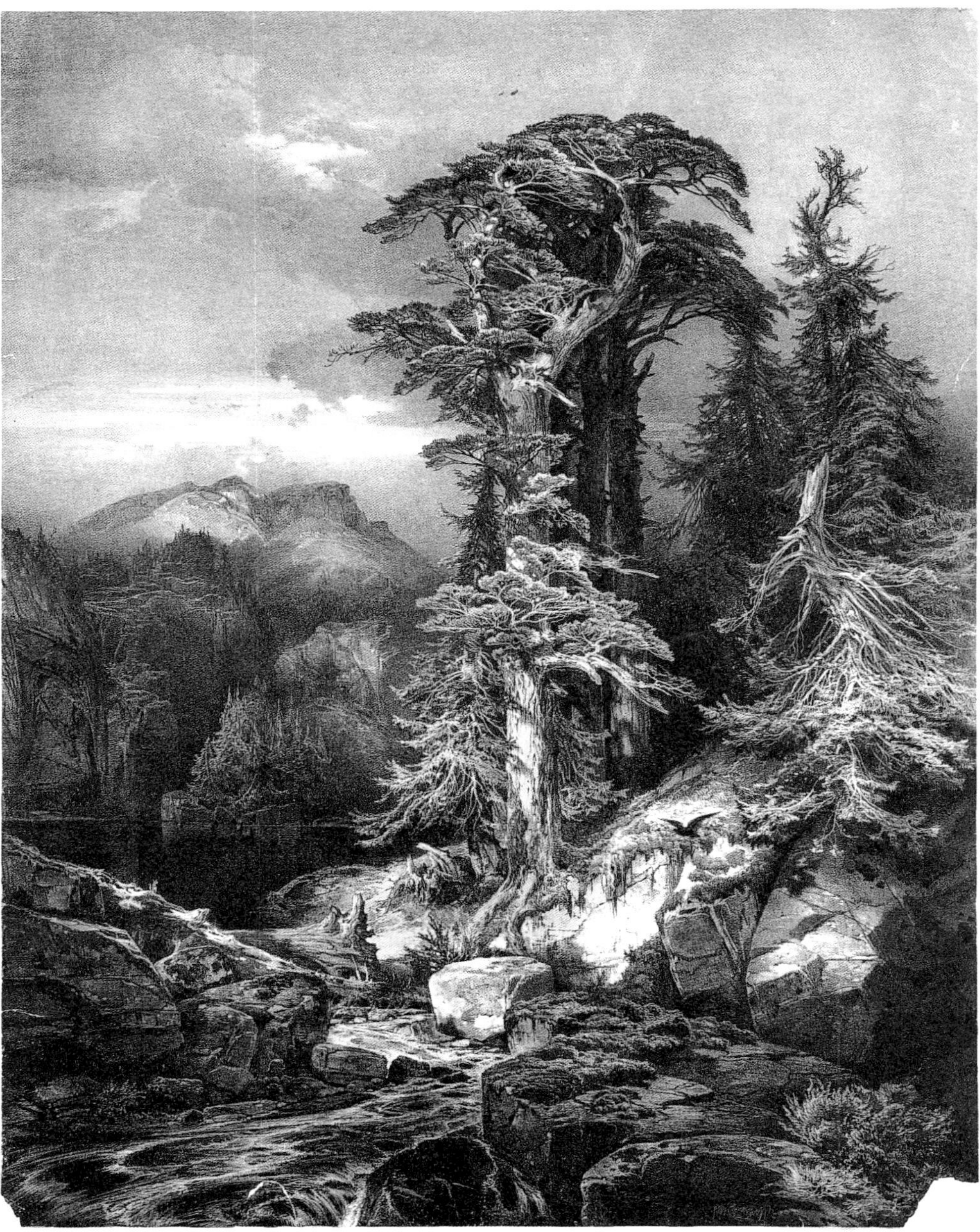

17. J.M.W. Turner, *Solitude,* 1814, etching and mezzotint, courtesy National Gallery of Art, Washington.

18. Thomas Moran, *Solitude,* 1869, lithograph, courtesy Gilcrease Museum, Tulsa, Oklahoma.

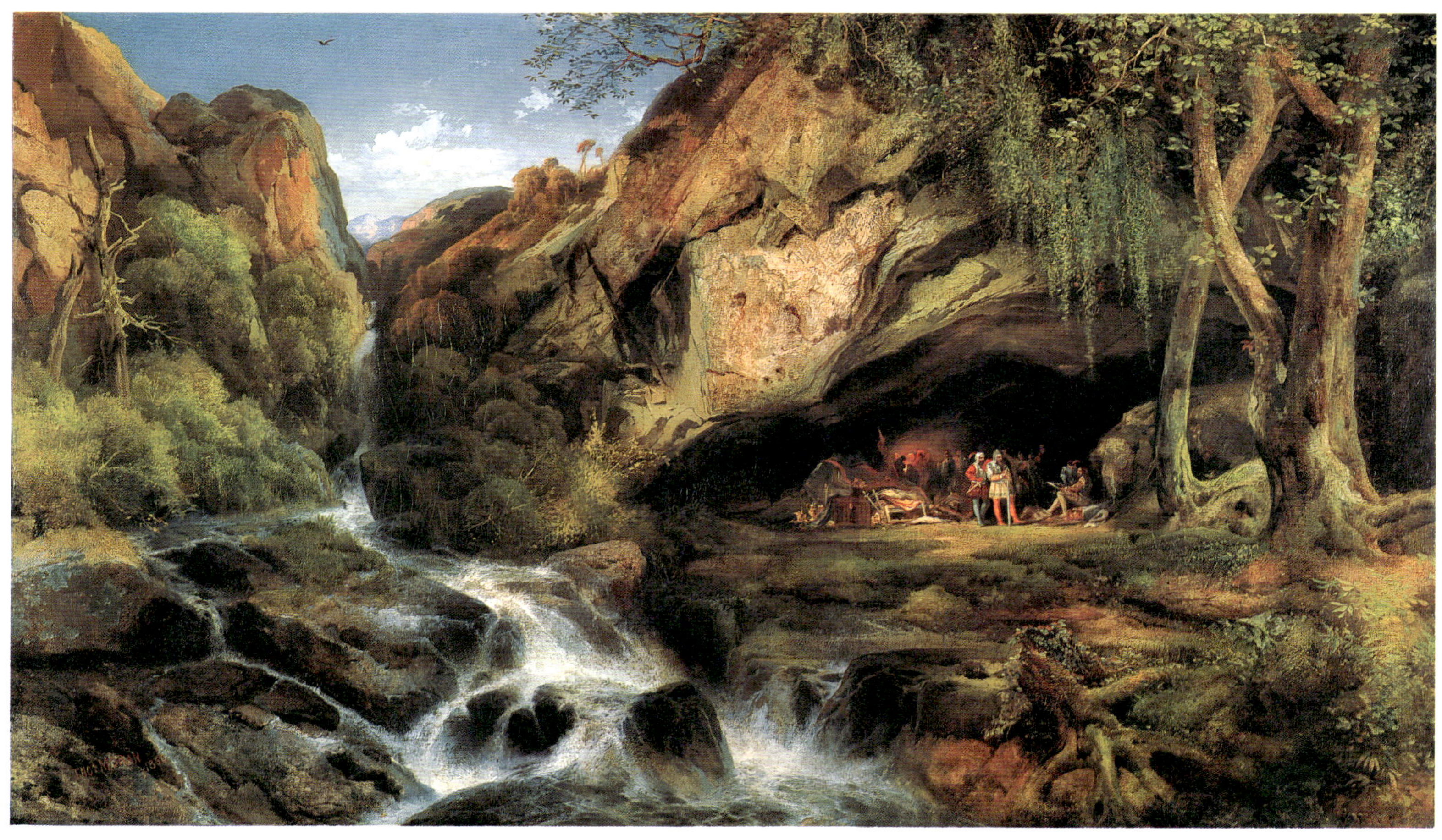

I

Salvator Rosa Sketching the Banditti

1860, oil on canvas
101 x 169.6 (39 ¾ x 66 ¾)
The Chrysler Museum, Norfolk, Gift of Walter P. Chrysler Jr.

THE EVENT WHICH most singularly marked the fearless enterprises of Salvator in the Abruzzi, was his captivity by the banditti, who alone inhabited them, and his temporary (and it is said voluntary) association with those fearful men. That he did for some time live among the picturesque outlaws, whose portraits he has multiplied without end, there is no doubt; and though few of his biographers allude to the event, and those few but vaguely, yet tradition authenticates a fact, to which some of his finest pictures afford a circumstantial evidence....

The genuine banditti...of the seventeenth century were no vulgar cut-throats. ...They were, in fact, more nearly allied to the brave, bold Condottieri, and the black and white bands of Medici and of Suffolk, in the fifteenth and sixteenth centuries; and though, when unhired, they lived at large and wild, with their hand against every man, and every man's hand against them, yet they occasionally rivalled in dignity and importance the standing armies of existing legitimates, fighting like them for hire in any cause that paid them....Like the marine letter of marque, half pirate, and half national, their troops were regularly enrolled and disciplined; and though their ranks were filled with the wild and the worthless—with men born out of the pale of civilized society, or driven beyond it by their crimes,—yet many among them were of a superior cast: they were outlawed gentlemen of Naples, escaped from the wheel and the scaffold, to which their efforts in the cause of their country had condemned them; who, seeking shelter in the savage wilds of the Abruzzi, became, by their talents and rank, chiefs and leaders of men associated and armed against society under the influence of far different causes. It is an historical fact, that the number, skill, valour, and fidelity of these bands had rendered them, at the period here alluded to, so formidable in the eyes of the Austro-Spanish government, and so respectable in the estimation of the people, that, by a strange inversion of principle, these natural enemies of society frequently became its chosen champions....The time spent by Salvator among these outlaws has never been verified; but it is probable, and indeed evident, that he remained sufficiently long to fill both his imagination and his memory with accumulated combinations of the magnificent and the terrible. It is not impossible that the adventurous artist owed the security in which he pursued the interests of his art, in such abodes of violence and danger, to the exertion of talents both musical and poetical, not less calculated to amuse his ferocious hosts by the midnight fires of their earth-embosomed dens. (Morgan 1824, 108–119)

2

Dusk Wings

1860, oil on canvas
50.8 x 76.2 (20 x 30)
Montgomery Museum of Fine Arts, The Blount Collection

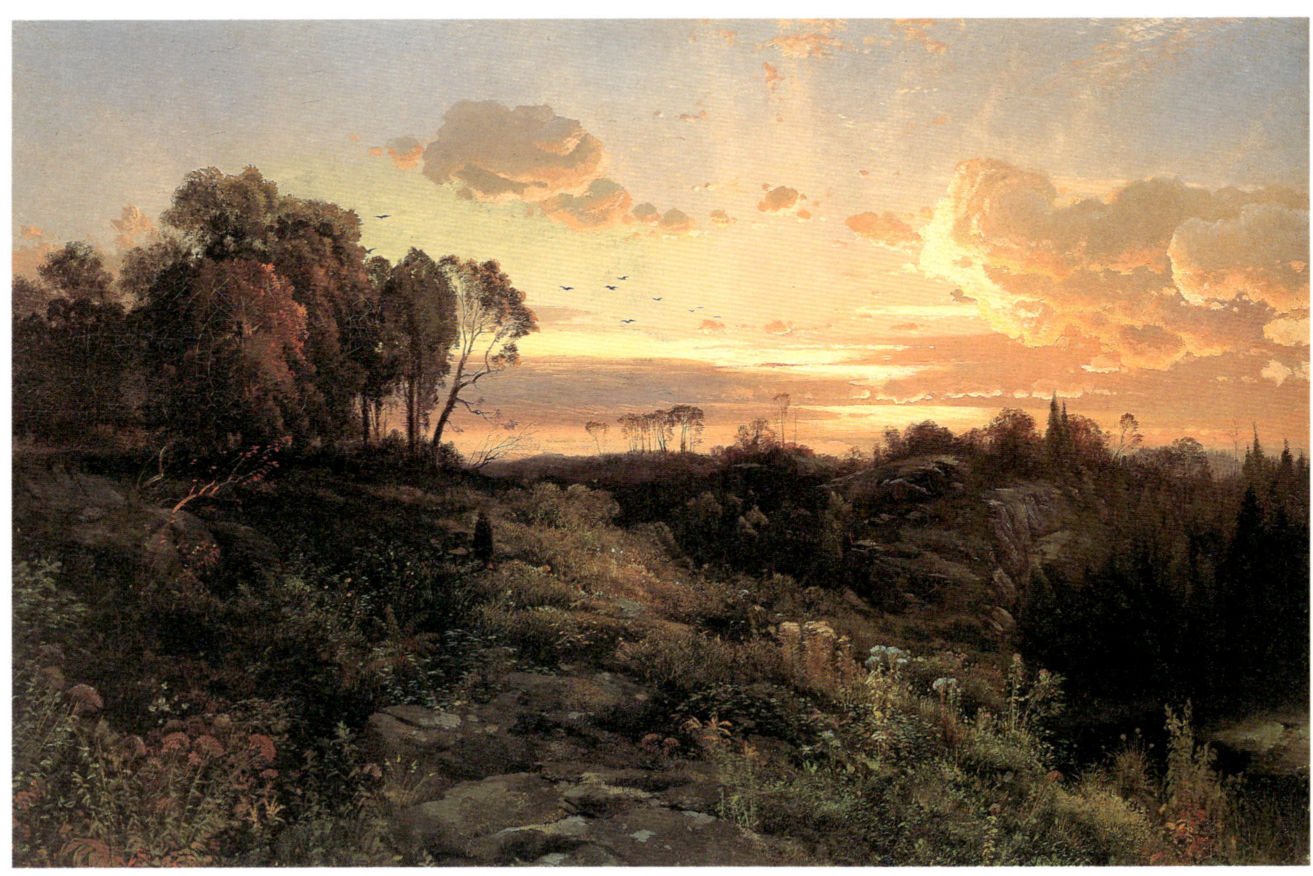

3

Slave Hunt, Dismal Swamp, Virginia

1862, oil on canvas
85.7 x 111.8 (33 ¾ x 44)
The Philbrook Museum of Art, Tulsa, Oklahoma, Gift of Laura A. Clubb

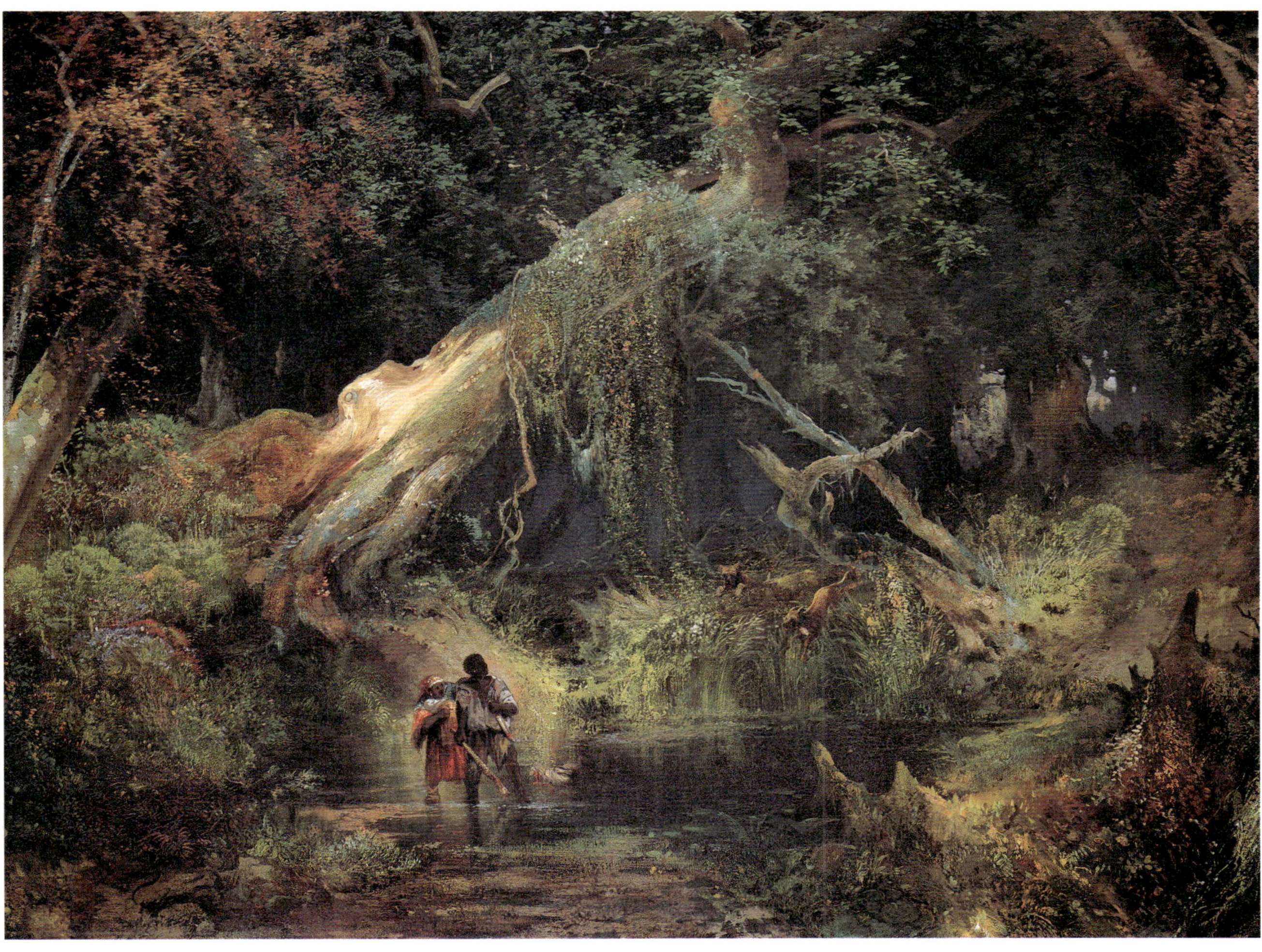

Away to the Dismal Swamp he speeds,—
His path was rugged and sore,
Through tangled juniper, beds of reeds,
Through many a fen, where the serpent feeds,
And man never trod before.

THE READER WHO consults the map will discover that the whole eastern shore of the Southern States, with slight interruptions, is belted by an immense chain of swamps, regions of hopeless disorder, where the abundant growth and vegetation of nature, sucking up its forces from the humid soil, seems to rejoice in a savage exuberance, and bid defiance to all human efforts either to penetrate or subdue. These wild regions are the homes of the alligator, the mocassin, and the rattlesnake. Evergreen trees, mingling freely with the deciduous children of the forest, form here dense jungles, verdant all the year round, and which afford shelter to numberless birds, with whose warbling the leafy desolation perpetually resounds. Climbing vines, and parasitic plants, of untold splendor and boundless exuberance of growth, twine and interlace, and hang from the heights of the highest trees pennons of gold and purple,—triumphant banners, which attest the solitary majesty of nature. A species of parasitic moss wreaths its abundant draperies from tree to tree, and hangs in pearly festoons, through which shine the scarlet berry and green leaves of the American holly.

What the mountains of Switzerland were to the persecuted Vaudois, this swampy belt has been to the American slave. The constant effort to recover from thence fugitives has led to the adoption, in these states, of a separate profession, unknown at this time in any other Christian land—hunters, who train and keep dogs for the hunting of men, women, and children. (Stowe 1856, 1:255)

4

Cresheim Glen, Wissahickon, Autumn

1864, oil on canvas
74 x 92.4 (29 ⅛ x 36 ⅜)
Hevrdejs Collection

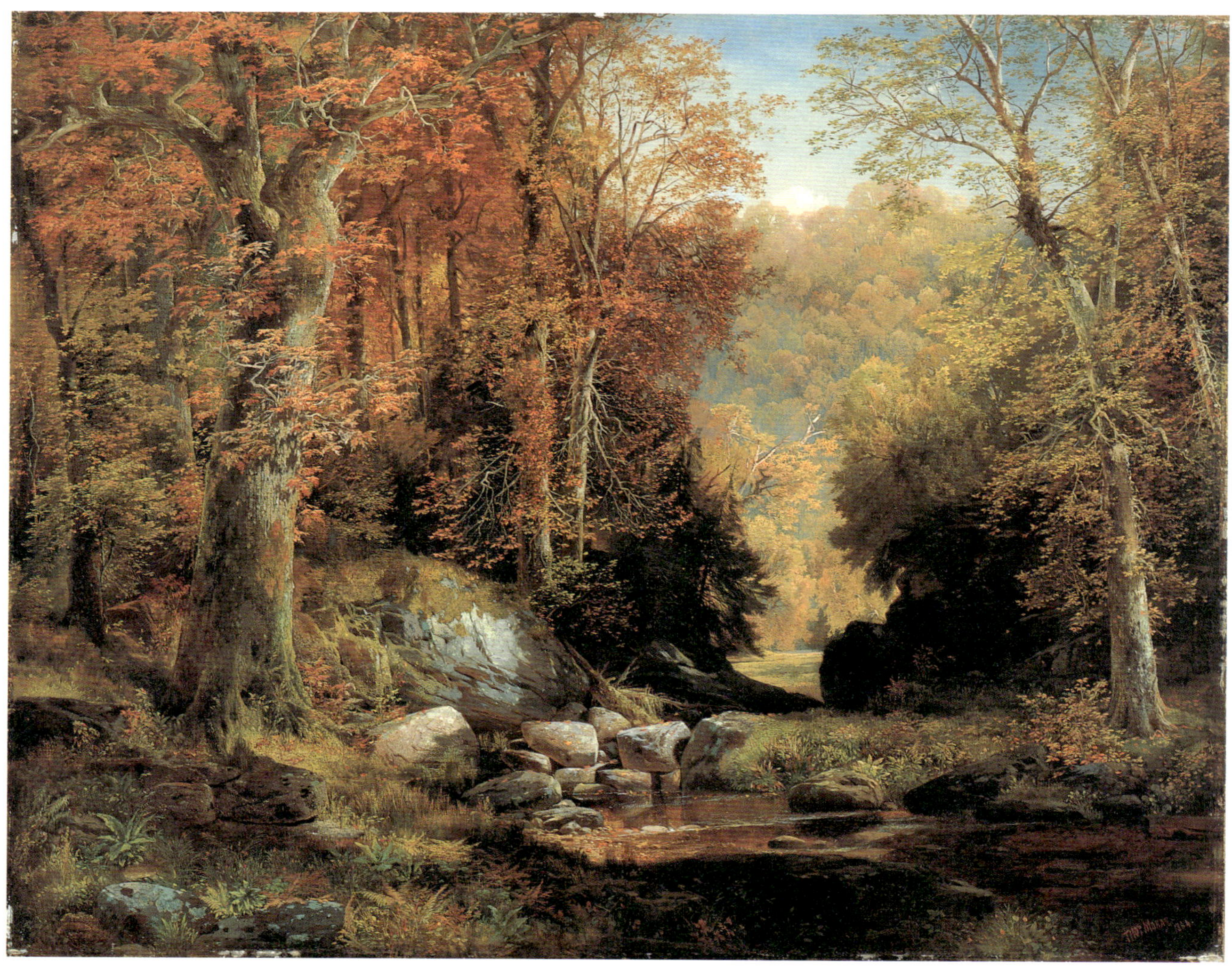

ONE OF THE most picturesque places in the valley of the Wissahickon is where Creasheim's creek runs into the larger stream. Here a pool, dark and deep, lurks under a huge overhanging rock. It is called the Devil's Pool, and the glen which surrounds it is a highly-prized resort for picnic parties, on account of its beauty and retirement. (Crane 1871, 237)

THERE IS NO other city where the varieties of wild landscape so closely surround and so boldly invade a civilization given over to material industries. Besides the broad Delaware, the exquisite Schuylkill, a stream far more beautiful than the Arno, bathes one side of the city, and into this Italian sheet of water slides the wild Wissahickon, coming down pure from its "savage gorges and cold springs" as primitive as a stream of the wilderness, yet easily accessible to the most sedentary citizen. (Strahan 1875a, 7 – 8)

See also Appendix 2, Opus no. 5.

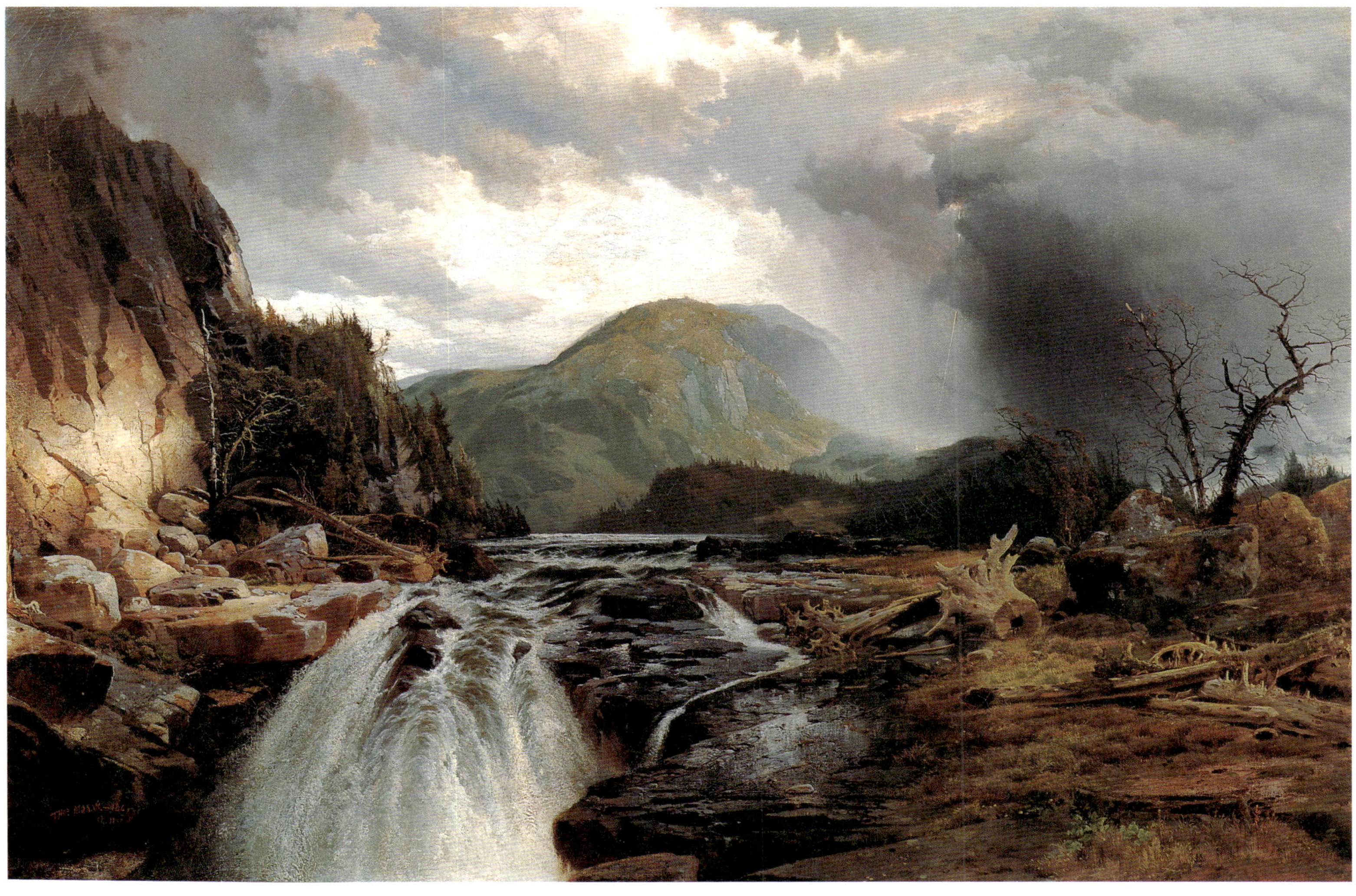

5

The Wilds of Lake Superior

1864, oil on canvas
76.2 x 114.3 (30 x 45)
New Britain Museum of American Art, Charles F. Smith Fund

THE SALE OF this fine collection of paintings commenced last evening. A very large company was present and a spirited competition for many of the pictures took place. We only mention the prices brought by the principal works: ... "Wilds of Lake Superior," Moran, $610....

The sale last evening was very well attended, and bidding was spirited, and there were many fine bargins. We have never, in our experience, met with a more select and appreciative audience, even at a Fine Art Sale, and it sat out, with unexampled patience, until 11½ o'clock, the entire sale. (*Phila. Evening Bulletin*, 24 Mar. 1865)

See also Appendix 2, Opus no. 11.

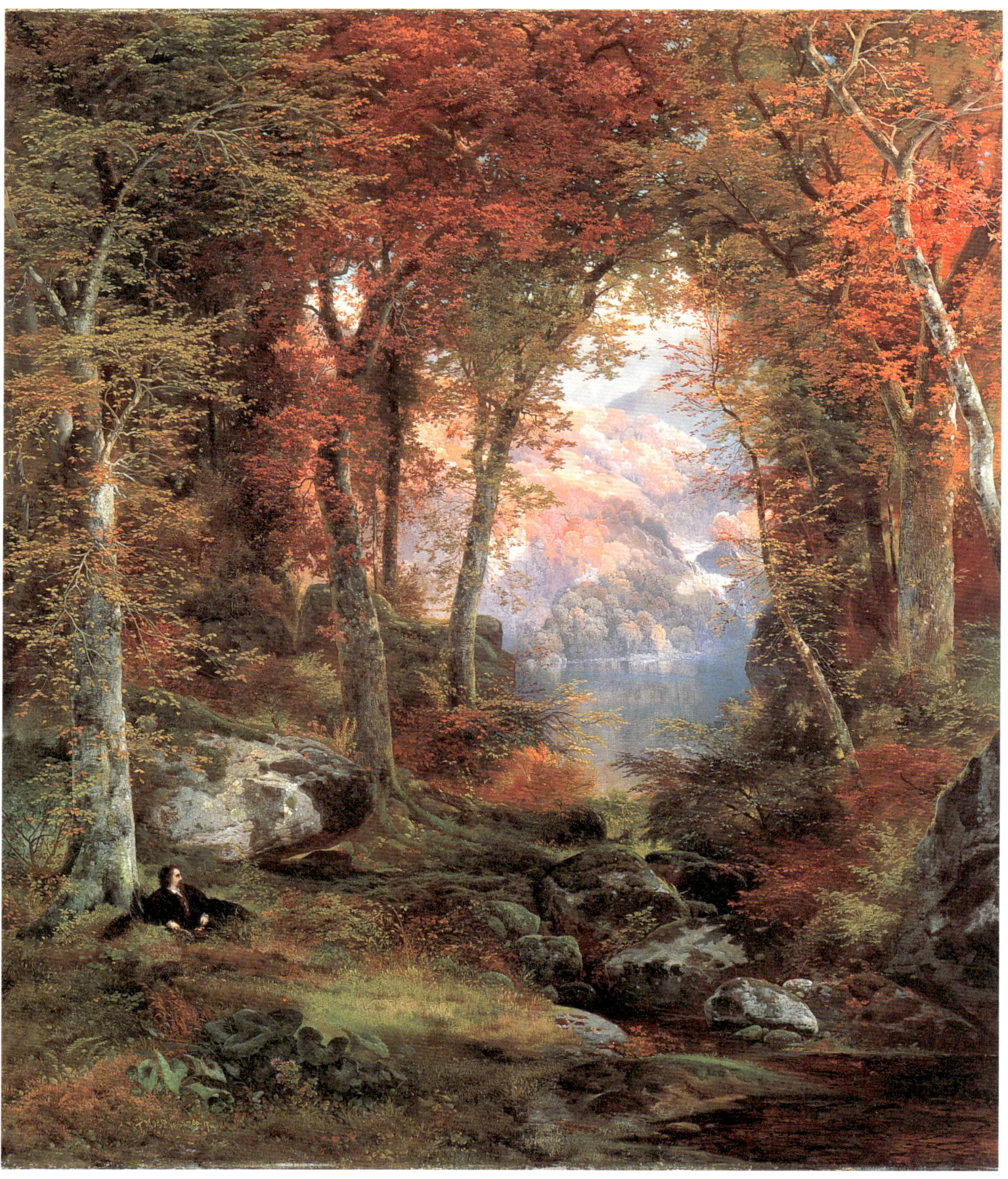

6

The Autumnal Woods (formerly titled "Under the Trees")

1865, oil on canvas
101.6 x 87 (40 x 34¼)
Manoogian Collection

FAIRMOUNT (PARK) we may remark *en passant,* is rich in ravines.... Look into and along its depths, up its sloping, hilly sides, and through its long ranks of trees—is it not a majestic and impressive scene? An aisle of God's great forest-temple, it dwarfs all the cathedrals that man has reared; it is worthy of its boundless dome—the sky. The noonlight, which is so intense here, loses its brightness as it struggles through the multitudinous foliage, and goes wandering among the trees and slopes. Here and there at the hither end a tree stands out strongly, distinguishable from its leafy companions; but as we advance we find ourselves in what is neither light nor darkness, but a tender twilight shade hovering about the greenery which surrounds us, and of which we may almost be said to be a part, so deeply has it interpenetrated our thoughts and feelings. We stand among these gigantic forest fathers like one of themselves. That magnificent tulip poplar on the other side of the brook, and this grand old fellow here—they have strengthened and enlarged us, lesser and weaker children of nature. We should like to embrace them, but our arms are too short. We should like to shake hands with them, but we cannot reach high enough. The lowest branch is full sixty feet above our heads. This is not tall talking by any means, but short talking,—it is so far below the magnitude of these old forest kings. They wait their poets, who to largeness of imagination will add a greater knowledge of nature than most poets possess. The only American singer who could make us see them in his song is Mr. Bryant, who is at once a naturalist and a painter, and whose word-pictures are perfect, accurate in all their details, and everywhere comprehensive and harmonious. His genius would be at home among these poplars, pines, chestnuts, beeches, and birches, and would look lovingly upon the smallest wild flower at his feet. We city folk, who escape into nature less frequently, are not so familiar with forest scenery, and not so happy in describing it. (Strahan 1875a, 128–129)

See also Appendix 2, Opus no. 17.

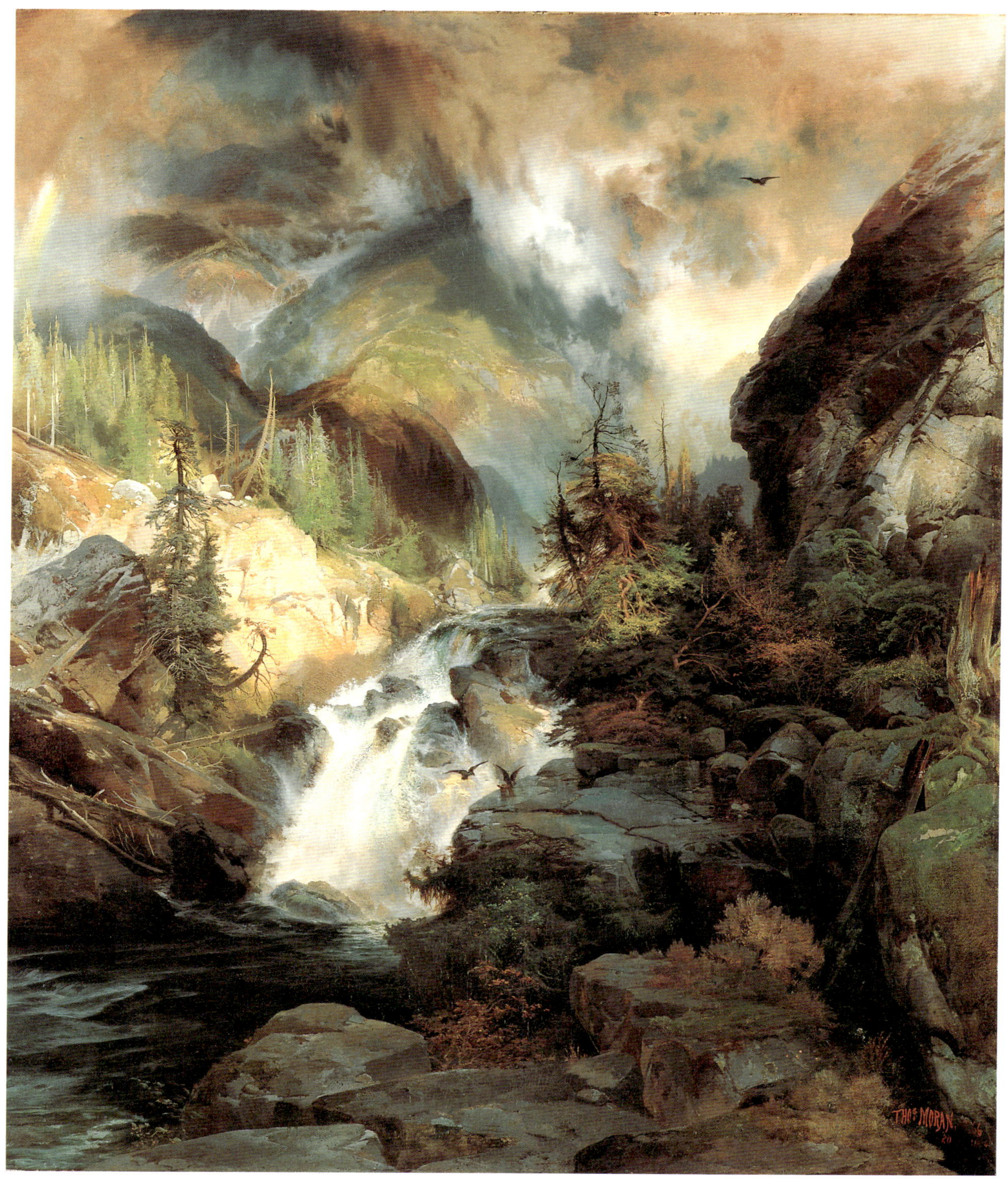
THOs MORAN

7

Children of the Mountain

1867, oil on canvas
157.8 x 132.4 (62 1/8 x 52 1/8)
The Anschutz Collection

THOMAS MORAN has his studio in Wood street. This young artist when abroad paid particular attention to the pictures of Turner, and has since his return to this country been assiduous in his study of nature in all her manifestations. The sketch of his last and best work, "The Children of the Mountain," is on exhibition at the Artists' Fund rooms. The "children" are not of human birth, but the cataract, the storm-cloud, the rainbow, the mist, the eagle and the rocks. (*NY Post*, 27 Nov. 1865)

MR. THOMAS MORAN is finishing a large picture called "The Children of the Mountain," with a daring effect of clouds and wilderness. Mr. T. Moran is undoubtedly a poet, though he occassionally leaves it a little uncertain whether he controls, or is controlled by, the frenzy. This grand picture is partially an amplification of one of those rich charcoal drawings recently published in photography. (*Phila. Evening Bulletin*, 6 Dec. 1865)

IN 1866 MR. AND MRS. Moran and their little son, Paul, sailed for England *en route* for Paris where they took a studio 50 rue de l'Ouest. Moran was fortunate in seeing his canvas *Children of the Mountain* hung in the Paris Exposition, the chief object of the trip. (Ruth B. Moran, biographical notes, EHL)

MR. THOMAS MORAN contributes... his "Children of the Mountain," which attracted the notice of all American visitors at the Paris Exposition. (*Phila. Evening Bulletin*, 6 Apr. 1868)

SEVERAL OF OUR home artists have made known their intention to furnish an art department in the coming Industrial Exhibition. Mr. Thomas Moran has consented to exhibit some of his largest and most important pictures, including, probably his great painting, "The Children of the Mountain." (*Newark Daily Advertiser*, 12 July 1872)

THE ART GALLERY has been much improved. Last night for the first time, a change in the arrangement of the light partially brought out the beauty of Moran's fine picture, "The Children of the Mountain." The conception of the artist is a grand one. There is the mist born of the mountain air rising from a deep gorge in thick fantastic wreaths and veiling the setting sun; rays of pale golden light fall upon a mass of rocks and the pine trees that grow above them. Opposite is a dark, slippery precipice that casts a shadow of blackish green upon a deep and angry pool into which pours a foaming torrent. Above all the eagle soars, one wing dipping in the cloud. Mr. Moran's forte is in rock painting, and in this he seems to excell. (*Newark Daily Advertiser*, 23 Aug. 1872)

THIS PICTURE exhibits some of the finest rock painting in the world, the conception is very fine and the whole scene in entire harmony. (*Newark Daily Advertiser*, 28 Sept. 1872)

See also Appendix 2, Opus no 21.

8

Forest Scene

1870, oil on canvas
50.8 x 40.6 (20 x 16)
Private Collection

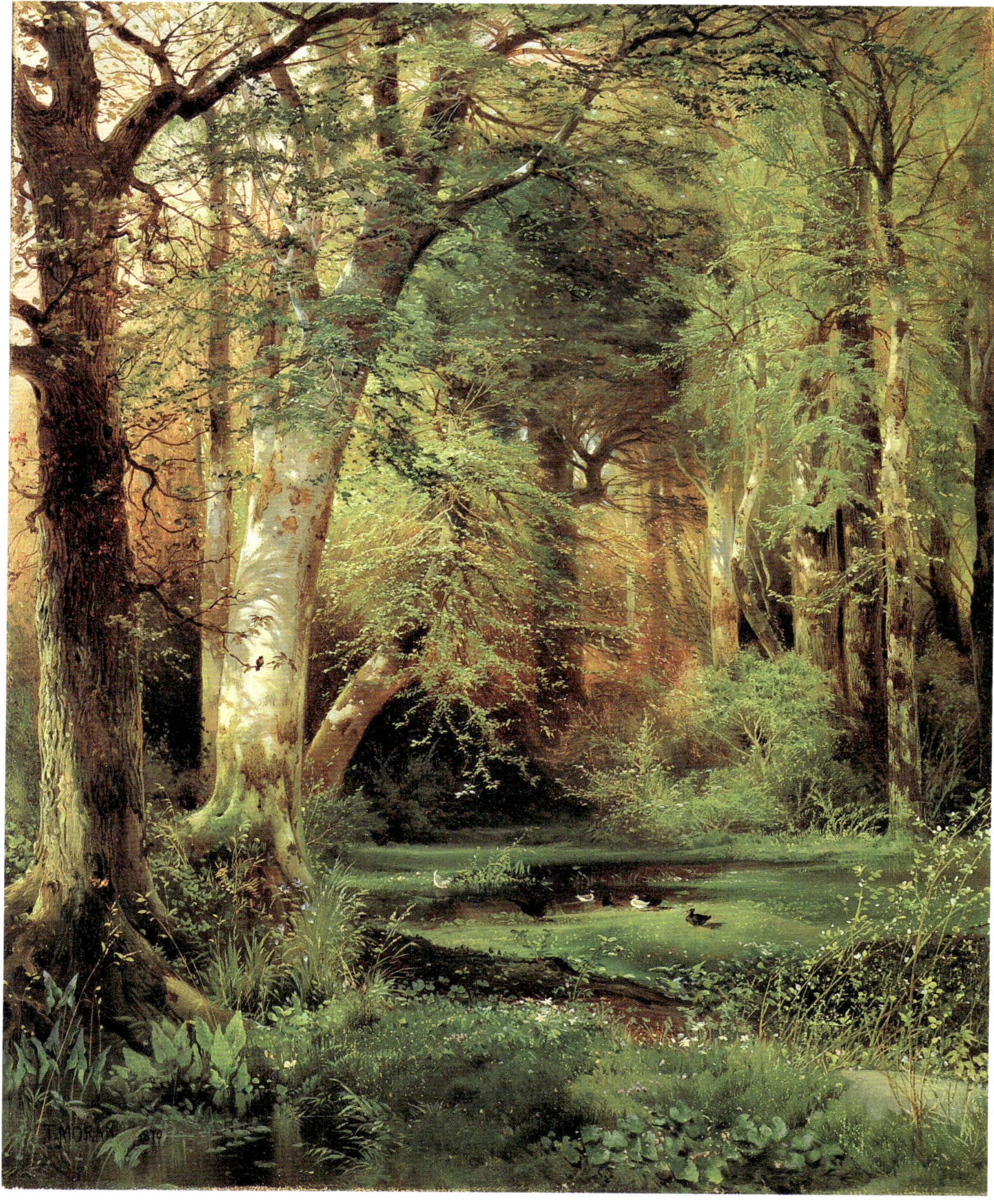

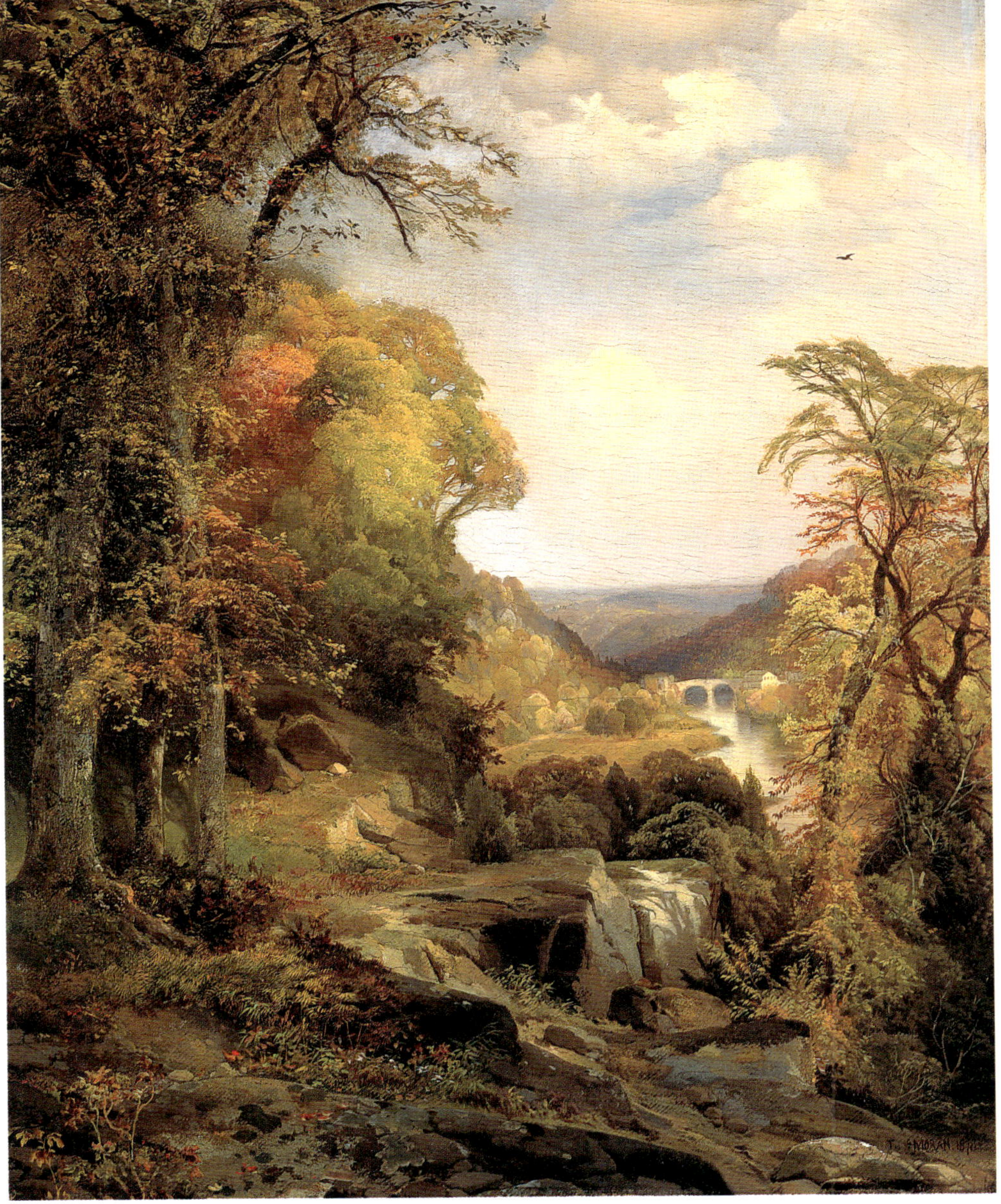

9

On the Wissahickon near Chestnut Hill

1870, oil on canvas
50.8 x 41.3 (20 x 16 ¼)
Private Collection, courtesy Lagakos-Turak Gallery

FAIRMOUNT PARK, in addition to the extensive lands on the east and west banks of the river, embraces...the Wissahickon Creek for six miles from its mouth, and sufficient territory on both sides to make a grand drive. A road at present runs through the valley, and has been in use for many years by residents at Chestnut Hill, a collection of handsome country places near the source of the Wissahickon. Although merely a country road, it is the most attractive drive out of Philadelphia, on account of the magnificent scenery which it presents. There are not many such streams as the Wissahickon, none perhaps in this country, and few in the world. For several miles it picks its way daintily between two rows of high hills.... Sometimes it is only a noisy brook running over pebbly bottoms, and anon a flashing cascade leaping from rock to rock with shouting noise. Then it widens out into a sober river which flows into a peaceful lake, so quiet that down in its depths the trees that meet above it are reflected with every delicate outline of foliage.... Romancers have woven the queer legends of the Wissahickon, which date back a couple of centuries, into interesting tales that are still read with avidity. The artists of to-day, like those of the last generation, have made its haunts their out-door studios. Many of its phases have been transferred to canvas; and others, where ruins of old mills and picturesque, odd-fashioned bridges relieve the landscape, afford studies of rare beauty. (Crane 1871, 235–237)

On Christmas Day 1872 Thomas Moran sent his friend Richard Watson Gilder (fig. 1) a gift, with a note that read in part: "Accept this slight offering as an indication of the esteem and gratitude that I feel toward you, for the unselfish interest you have always evinced in my success. It is to you that I owe the great prosperity that has followed me."[1] At the time Moran wrote this note, Gilder was managing editor of *Scribner's Monthly Magazine*. Two years earlier Gilder had hired Moran to rework a number of amateurish field sketches that had been submitted as illustrations for an article by Nathaniel P. Langford about a strange land in the Far West called Yellowstone, full of hot springs and geysers.[2]

Rarely is the turning point of an artist's career as easy to identify as in the case of Thomas Moran. Commissioned by Gilder to amend illustrations of a landscape he had not yet seen, Moran was astute enough to recognize an opportunity not to be missed and resourceful enough to find a way to journey to Yellowstone himself just a few months later. As he acknowledged in his Christmas message, Moran was indeed much indebted to Gilder.

The article that changed the course of Moran's career appeared in *Scribner's* in May and June of 1871. Titled "The Wonders of the Yellowstone," the narrative had been written by a member of the Washburn-Doane expedition, a group of private citizens who had ventured into Yellowstone the

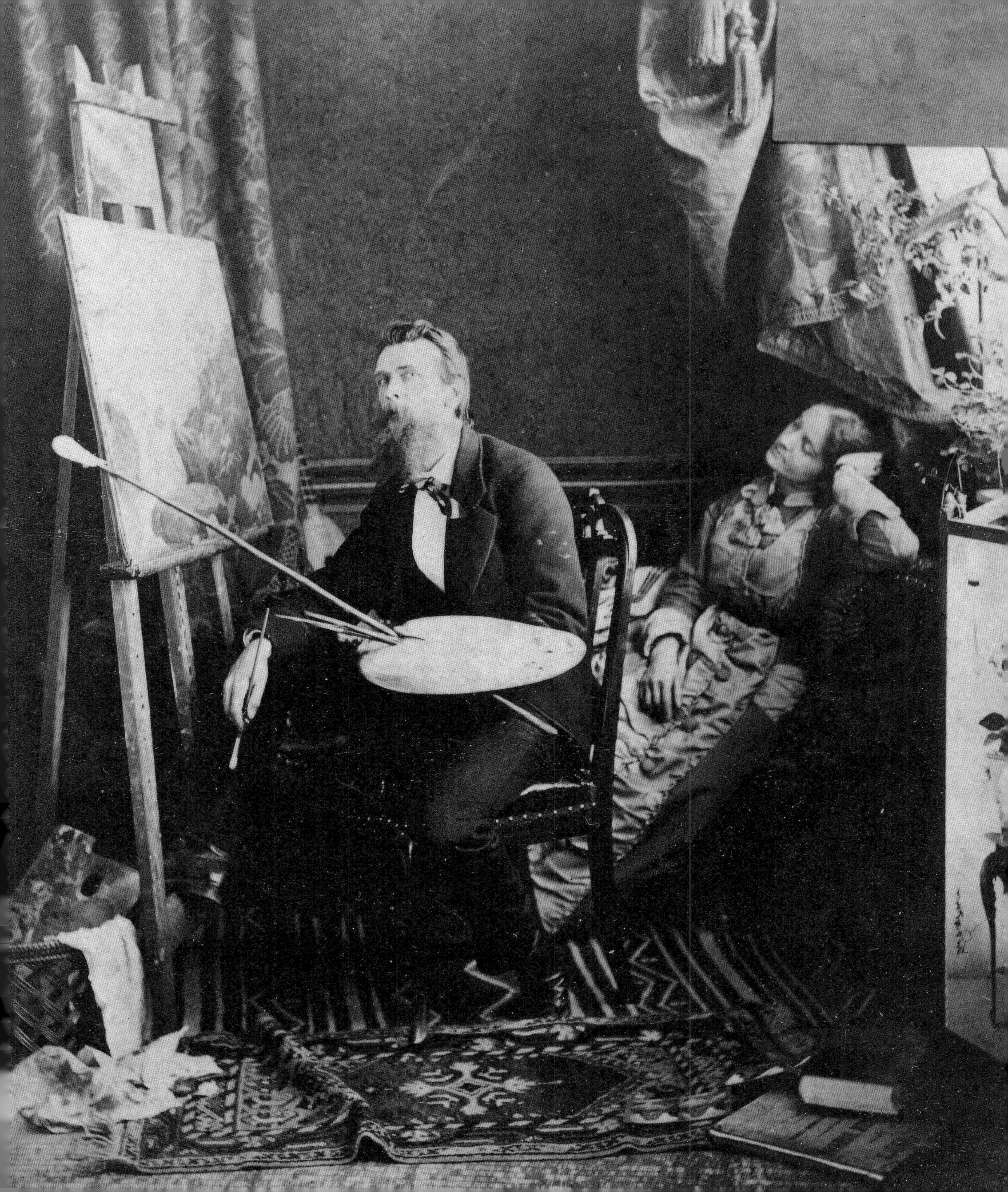

Preceding page: Thomas Moran in his studio with Mary, 1876, courtesy East Hampton Library.

1. Richard Watson Gilder, published in *Letters of Richard Watson Gilder* (Boston, 1919).

2. *Temporary and Permanent Bridges and Citadel Rock, Green River,* 1868, photograph by Andrew Joseph Russell, Yale Collection of Western Americana, Beinecke Rare Book and Manuscript Library, New Haven.

previous year to see if stories of geysers and mudpots might be true. According to the article, the stories were more than true. Langford's report piqued the interest of many, including Ferdinand Vandeveer Hayden, a geologist of wide-ranging interests, who had skirted but not penetrated Yellowstone several years earlier. It was Hayden, who, in the summer of 1871, would lead the expedition to Yellowstone that unexpectedly included Thomas Moran.[3]

Although *Scribner's* later published a number of illustrations based on sketches Moran completed in Yellowstone, the magazine did not sponsor his trip. Instead Moran obtained private funding, borrowing $500 from Roswell Smith, publisher of *Scribner's* (with his *Children of the Mountain* [cat. 7] as collateral), and an additional $500 from Jay Cooke, financier of the Northern Pacific Railroad, to whom he promised a group of Yellowstone watercolors.

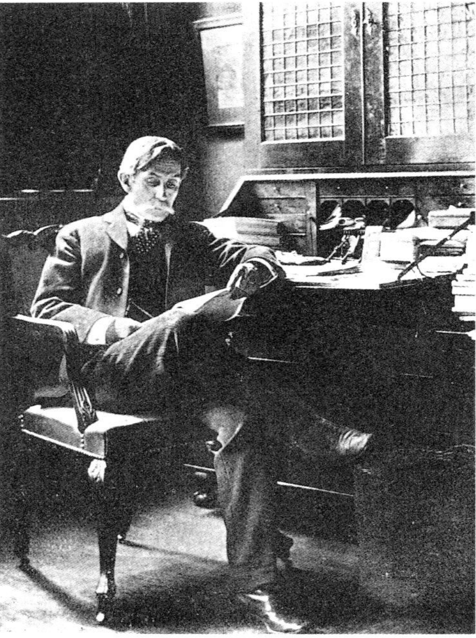

1

Early in June 1871 A.B. Nettleton, office manager of the Northern Pacific Railroad and a friend of Moran's, wrote to Hayden and asked if the young artist might join the upcoming expedition, noting, "He, of course, expects to pay for his own expenses, and simply wishes to take advantage of your cavalry escort for protection."[4] Two weeks later, in a follow-up letter to Hayden, Nettleton described Moran as an artist "of much genius" who "desires to take sketches in the upper Yellowstone region from which to paint some fine pictures on his return," adding, "That he will surpass Bierstadt's Yosemite we who know him best fully believe."[5]

By the time Thomas Moran boarded the train for his first trip west, Albert Bierstadt had been exhibiting large-scale paintings of the Rocky Mountains and Yosemite for more than a decade. As Nettleton noted, Bierstadt was indeed the competition. But Bierstadt had not been to Yellowstone. The speed with which Moran found his way to Yellowstone suggests that he was well aware of the lucrative market Bierstadt had created for spectacular views of the Far West. A large-scale painting of a relatively unknown western wonderland might garner Moran the same financial rewards that by 1871 had made Bierstadt one of the most successful artists of the nineteenth century.

In 1859, when Bierstadt journeyed west for the first time, he had at his command the technical skills and European experience that allowed him to recast traditional landscape compositions in Rocky Mountain garb. Twelve years later Thomas Moran arrived in Green River, Wyoming, with very different skills. They were, however, precisely the right skills for the landscape he would be the first artist to paint.

Green River

Yellowstone was Moran's ultimate destination in the summer of 1871, but before he reached the land of geysers and hot springs, he completed a field study that he later inscribed "First sketch made in the West" (cat. 10). Modest in size, the watercolor study was the first of many that Moran would make of the sculpted and striated cliffs near the railroad town of Green River, Wyoming. Surprised by a landscape unlike any other he had ever seen, Moran may not have immediately known that the lessons of Turner and the literature of romance had provided him with the ideal visual vocabulary to turn a hot, dusty, desert landscape into a western Xanadu.

Three years before Moran reached Green River, Union Pacific railroad crews had arrived in force (fig. 2). Engaged in a spirited race with their Central Pacific counterparts to span the continent by rail, the vanguard of the Union Pacific contingent had set up shop near the banks of the Green River, where they began construction of temporary and permanent bridges across the water. Over flat land the crews had been able to lay between one and three miles of rail a day, but constructing a bridge required considerably more time. Anticipating a profitable delay, speculators had arrived in advance of the railroad crews, and quickly a town was born. By the time Thomas Moran arrived, the founding fathers could boast a schoolhouse, church, hotel, and brewery—none of which would ever appear in a Green River painting by Moran.

In 1871 Moran did not linger in Green River. He was on his way to join Hayden's survey party in Montana, and it was the landscape of Yellowstone that was foremost in his mind. Before leaving Green River, however, he did secure a number of sketches of Citadel and Castle Rocks—the enormous buttes that dwarfed the burgeoning town below—and these he put to very good use, later, when he returned east.

Unlike Yellowstone, the landscape of Green River had not been "previewed" for eastern viewers through illustrations published in *Scribner's*. The multicolored, castellated buttes were an entirely fresh subject for paintings. Moran made the most of this opportunity, claiming the landscape as his own through a series of paintings completed over a period of forty years. Among the most successful and revealing of these is *Green River Cliffs, Wyoming* (cat. 61). Broad in its vista, the composition includes a sparsely foliated foreground through which a caravan of Indians makes its way toward a village on the horizon. In the far distance are the cliffs of Green River, cast in hues of orange, lavender, and pink. Wisps of clouds, also tinged with the pink of the setting sun, dust the sky.

Geographic distance from the landscape itself may have encouraged Moran's contemporaries to believe that the artist had actually seen such a sight, just as temporal distance might tempt twentieth-century viewers to make the same assumption. In fact, Moran never saw Indians in the vicinity of Green River, and the neon hues of the cliffs are more the figments of fantasy than the facts of geology.

Andrew Joseph Russell, a photographer who traveled with the Union Pacific construction crews to document the progress of the railroad, took a number of photographs at Green River in 1868. Russell's photographs are works of art in their own right, but when juxtaposed with Moran's paintings of the same geography, they serve as revealing touchstones.

In the photograph *Temporary and Permanent Bridges and Citadel Rock, Green River*, Russell recorded parallel lines of track and a smoking engine directed toward the viewer. In the middle distance a watertower echoes the shape of Citadel Rock looming above. Construction workers pose on the track they have laid and stand atop stone battlements they are preparing for the permanent bridge. Russell's camera clearly captured the arrival of the mechanical age in Green River, Wyoming.

In Moran's painting, however, all signs of the railroad and its attendant community have been excised. Instead, the languorous river lies undisturbed and free of bridges. Exotically clad Indians more suggestive of figures from the *Arabian Nights* replace the railroad crew photographed by Russell. Far from a report of what Moran saw in the West, *Green River Cliffs, Wyoming*, is a carefully constructed fiction that taps the same vein of romantic nostalgia that made *Hiawatha* a bestseller.

2

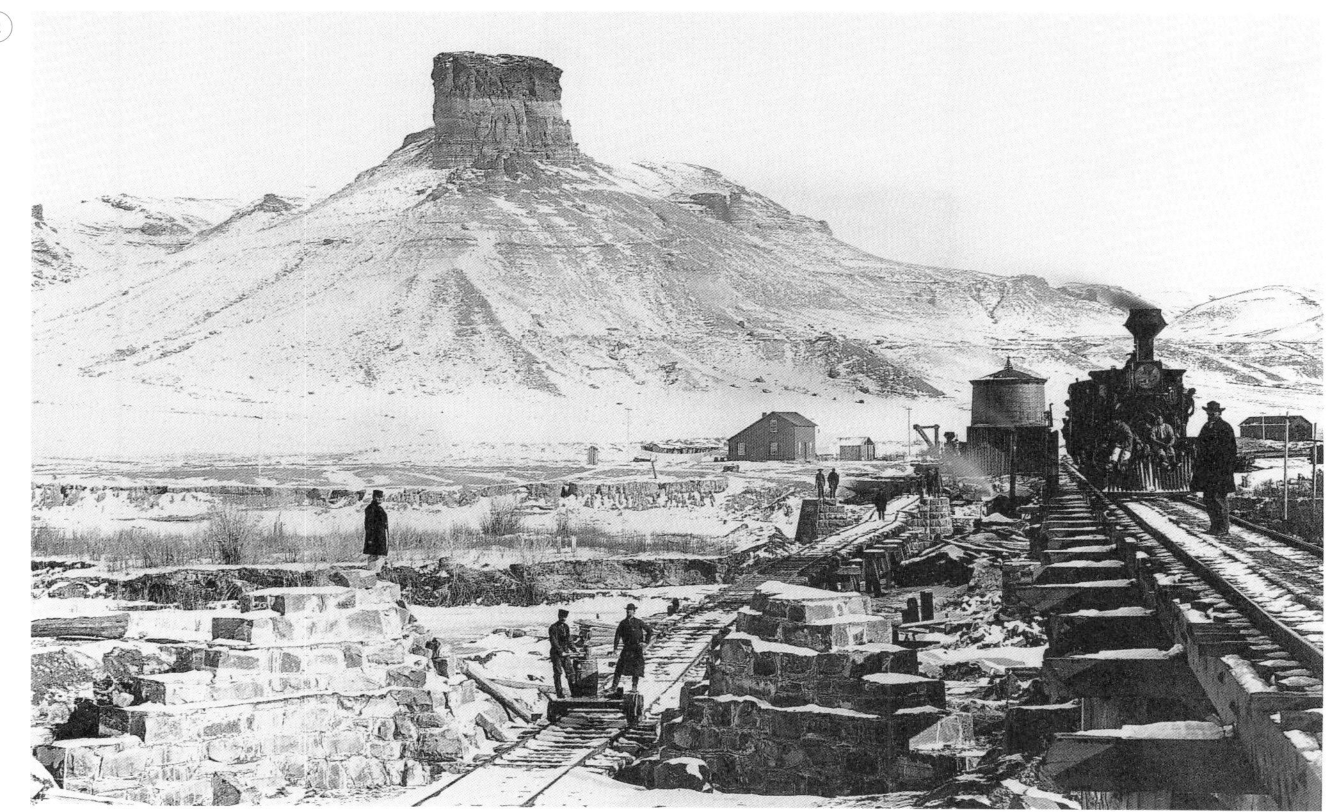

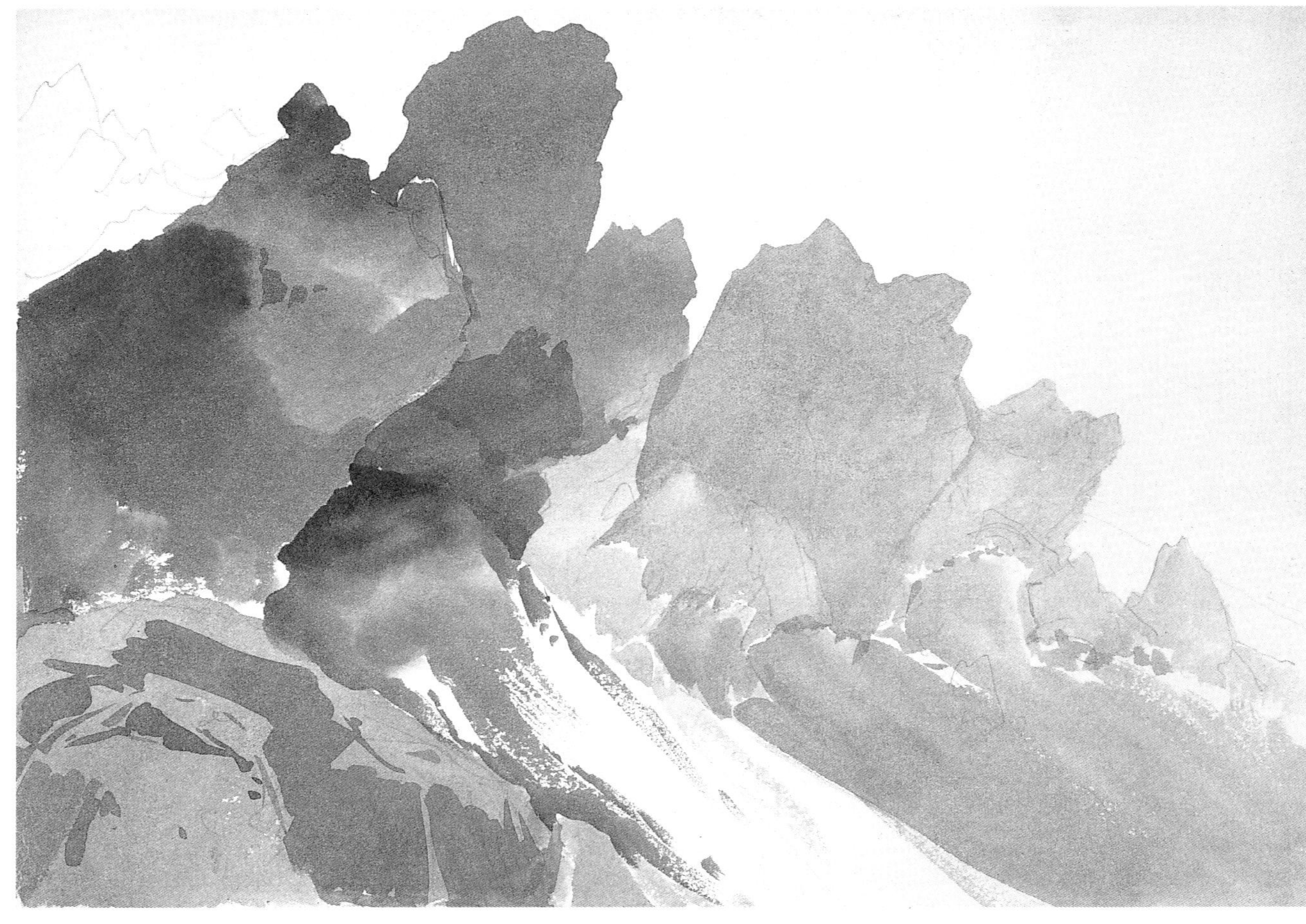

3. Thomas Moran, *Devil's Den* [?], from the Yellowstone sketchbook, 1871, graphite and watercolor, courtesy Department of the Interior, Yellowstone National Park.

4. William Henry Jackson, 1873, courtesy Colorado Historical Society.

5. *Crystal Falls, Cascade Creek,* 1871, photograph by William Henry Jackson, courtesy Department of the Interior, Yellowstone National Park.

6. Thomas Moran, *Crystal Falls,* 1871, watercolor, courtesy Department of the Interior, Yellowstone National Park. See also cat. 20.

Under no obligation to produce topographical views of Wyoming, Moran may have taken his cue yet again from Turner. The church steeple on the southern shore of England that the Moran brothers discovered Turner had "moved" for artistic purposes was a minor infraction compared to the wholesale erasure Moran exercised on the Green River landscape. Describing Turner's practice as that of an imaginative artist who took from a landscape not its literal truth but rather those elements that would allow him to make a good picture, Moran again followed his master's lead.

With evidence at hand of the extent to which Moran manipulated the Green River landscape, it is important to recall that as an artist Moran was in the business of making pictures for a market. In 1871 he went west specifically to gather the raw material (drawings, sketches, photographs) that would allow him to produce images that could be bought and sold in a commercial market. The compositional formula he devised for views of Green River fed the lingering hunger for spectacular New World landscapes, which would surpass that for views of Europe, and at the same time tapped an increasingly nostalgic view of American Indian life fanned by the relentless popularity of works like *Hiawatha.* Moran's Green River images proved so popular, spoke, in other words, so clearly to a romantic and already nostalgic impression of the West, that the artist continued to sell variations on the theme well into the twentieth century.

Yellowstone

From Green River, Wyoming, Moran traveled to Corinne, Utah, then on to Virginia City, Montana, where he joined Hayden's expedition. On 11 July the *Helena Herald* reported that the survey party was preparing to depart. In identifying the members of the group, the article noted that the expedition would serve art, science, and commerce, adding,

"We doubt not that the report of this scientific expedition will attract thousands of tourists to the country of the Yellowstone."[6] The *Herald* was correct in recognizing multiple agendas associated with the Hayden expedition, but even they could not have anticipated the full impact of the journey. Rarely had art, science, and commerce joined with politics, as they would in 1872, to legislate a new idea.

Moran's reason for making the trip was clearly defined: he was gathering the raw material he would need to compose images for a wide range of uses. The journal he kept of his Yellowstone adventure includes detailed descriptions of rock formations (fig. 3), foliage, and the extraordinary colors of Yellowstone—all elements that might be incorporated in future illustrations and paintings. At one point along the trail he observed that the outlet of a lake passed through "an immense gorge in the mountains bordered with great cliffs & peaks of limestone, some of them isolated & forming splendid foreground material for pictures."[7]

At the time of his departure Moran could not have known that William Henry Jackson (fig. 4), a young photographer, would be his companion through Yellowstone and that the images they would produce together would have an enormous impact when they returned east. Jackson had preceded Moran to the West by several years and had worked with Hayden in the field the previous summer. Moran, no stranger to photography himself (his brother John was a skilled photographer), quickly struck up a friendship with Jackson. For more than six weeks they worked together in Yellowstone, selecting the best subjects and points of view for photographs and sketches. A Jackson photograph of Crystal Falls and a watercolor of the same subject by Moran confirm that they often worked side by side, each benefiting from the expertise of the other (figs. 5,6).

On 7 August Hayden's survey party received word that their military escort had been told to return to Fort Ellis. Moran, Jackson, and several other members of the group decided to return as well. Moran noted in his journal, "as the Wonders of Yellowstone had been seen I concluded to return."[8] Arriving in Virginia City (fig. 7), he was quoted by the *Helena Herald* as declaring, "all the phenomena described by Messrs. Langford and Trumbull have been seen and the half was not told by them." The reporter went on:

> Mr. Moran pronounced the country the most wonderful region on the Continent. All the phenomena which elsewhere is found scattered and distributed over widely separated portions of the globe, is here crowded into a region which does not exceed eighty miles in length. What Humboldt traveled twenty thousand miles to see, may have been seen at a glance. Mr. M. has photographic views of the falls, cascades and canyons

5

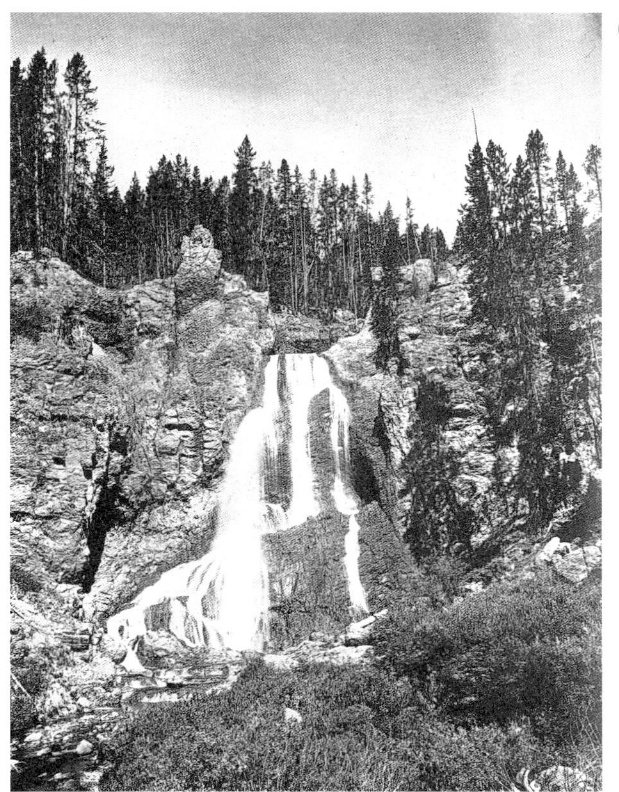

6

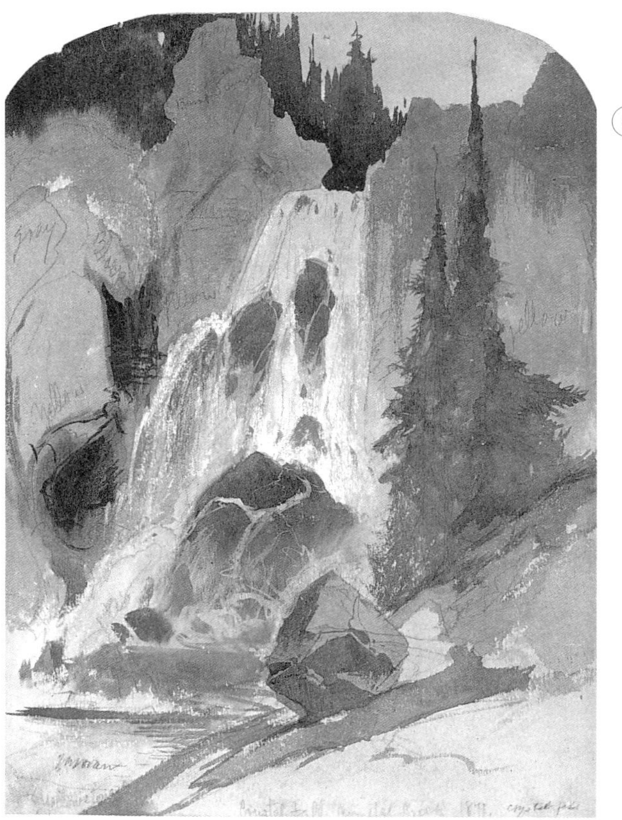

of the Yellowstone, and of many points of interest in that vicinity. He is a landscape painter of very fine powers, and we may expect some result of his visit to this country within the next year.[9]

Because Moran was not employed by the survey, he was not bound by its "scientific" mission. He was not compelled, in other words, to report literal facts of geography or geology. Rather he was free to use the drawings, sketches, and photographs he had assembled (fig. 8) to compose studio paintings for an audience eager to see more of Yellowstone following the enticements *Scribner's* had offered the previous year.

Shortly after returning to the East, Moran moved with his family to Newark, New Jersey. It has been suggested that the move was prompted by Moran's wish to be closer to Richard Watson Gilder, his link to *Scribner's Magazine*.[10] This may be true, for Moran moved just a few doors away from Gilder and nearly as close to Alexander Drake, the art director for *Scribner's*. Recognizing the financial potential in providing a successful magazine with commissioned illustrations, he positioned himself to take advantage of the new market. At the same time, he was preparing to challenge Albert Bierstadt, long the dominant figure in western landscape painting, with an enormous Yellowstone canvas.

Moran quickly became his own best publicist. Early in October 1871, the *Newark Daily Advertiser* reported that Moran was about to become a resident and that he had just returned from an expedition to Yellowstone, bringing with him "the most remarkable portfolio, perhaps, that it has ever fallen to the lot of an artist to fill." Noting that illustrations of Yellowstone had appeared in *Scribner's* and had inspired "incredulity," the reporter declared:

Mr. Moran assures me that they fall modestly short of the vast fantastic freaks of Nature which they attempt to represent.... Mr. Moran says he could only describe it as a country bespattered with rainbows. It seemed unreally strange, like a dream-land, and he could hardly believe at times that he was not in a dream instead of an exploring expedition. He fears that he will need strong affidavits to defend his pictures against the charge of exaggeration. The wonderful brilliancy of his mineral specimens, confirm, however, on a small scale, both description and picture. It is a very happy fortune that this *terra incognita* is to be introduced to the eyes of men by an artist of Mr. Moran's extraordinary genius for natural scenery. Those best acquainted with his works anticipate that the new pictures will take a rank in American Art as eminent as the subjects they illustrate hold among the characteristics of the American continent. He will immediately settle down to his work in Newark, N.J., and some time next year, I suppose, the world of art will be agog with the freshest and richest sensation it has enjoyed for some time.[11]

Moran had succeeded in setting the stage for the debut of his most ambitious painting.

While Moran began to work on his Yellowstone picture in Newark, F. V. Hayden (fig. 9) had undertaken a promotional campaign of his own in Washington. Preparing the survey report he was required to present to Congress, Hayden was also involved in the initial discussions that eventually led to the formation of Yellowstone National Park. As early as January 1872 Washington newspapers began to report that a bill providing for such a park was "under consideration" in Congress.[12] In one notice a member of the Committee on Public Lands was quoted as saying

7. Virginia City, Montana, 1871, photograph by William Henry Jackson, courtesy Department of the Interior, Yellowstone National Park.

8. *Castle Geyser and Fire Hole Basin,* 1871, photograph by William Henry Jackson, courtesy Department of the Interior, Yellowstone National Park. See also cat. 38.

9. Ferdinand Vandeveer Hayden, c. 1875, silver albumen print, courtesy National Portrait Gallery, Smithsonian Institution.

7

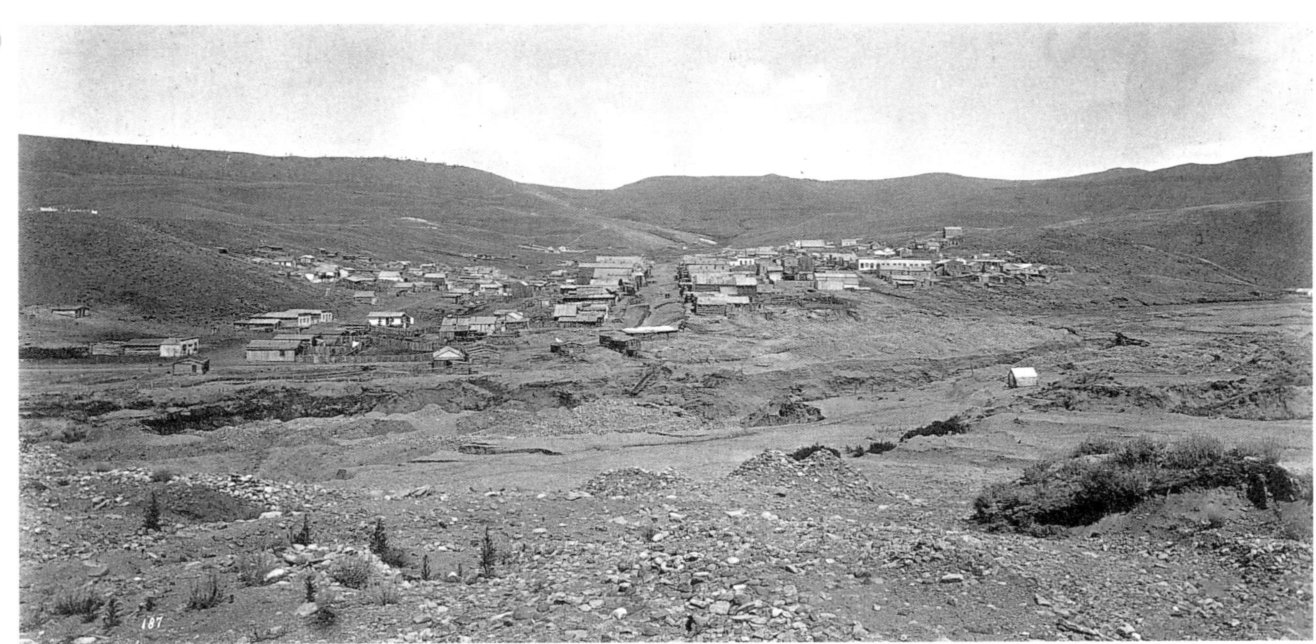

"it was thought best to pass this bill at once, before any private claimants could lay title to any portion of the land."[13] In February *Scribner's* published an article by F. V. Hayden titled "Wonders of the West: More about Yellowstone." In his update on Yellowstone Hayden pressed his cause: "Why will not Congress at once pass a law setting it apart as a great public park for all time to come, as has been done with the not more remarkable wonder, the Yosemite Valley?"[14]

8

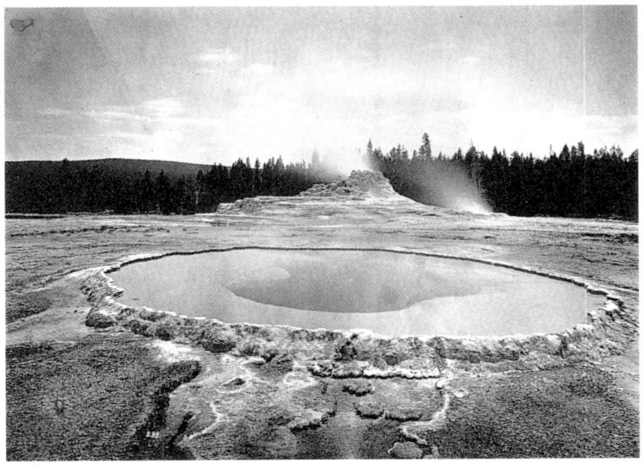

By the end of February, in an astonishing display of expeditious deliberation, both the Senate and the House had agreed to the proposal. On 1 March the bill was passed, and the following day it was signed by President Ulysses S. Grant. Years later William Henry Jackson wrote that during the Yellowstone debate "the watercolors of Thomas Moran and the photographs of the Geology Survey [Jackson's] were the most important exhibits brought before the Committee"; he quoted historian Hiram M. Chittenden's supporting opinion: "They did a work which no other agency could do and doubtless convinced every one who saw them that the regions where such wonders existed should be carefully preserved to the people forever."[15] If, as Jackson wrote, Moran's Yellowstone watercolors were instrumental in the formal establishment of the national park, they also served as an appetizer for the large oil painting Moran would place on exhibition in Washington just a few weeks later.

Ten days after the Yellowstone bill passed, Moran reported to Hayden that his large picture was "more than half finished." He apologized for not sending the painting Hayden had commissioned but insisted, "It was of the first importance to me to get the big picture out before any one else dabbled with the subject."[16] Like a miner laying claim to the mother lode, Moran was anxious to make public his artistic deed of ownership. Well before his Yellowstone painting was finished, Moran welcomed visitors to his studio: "several art-critics went over to the Newark studio of Thomas Moran, an artist of considerable local fame, to see an immense picture upon which he is at work illustrating the Grand Canyon of the Yellowstone, and they returned very enthusiastic about it.... The connoisseurs who have seen this picture declare that it is superior to Bierstadt's *Yosemite* and that Moran is certainly the coming man in art."[17] Another lengthy description of the work-in-progress concluded: "this remarkable picture [is] a great and so far successful effort to depict for us the culminating wonder of a region new and strange to us, as different in all its pictorial elements for form and color, as if it were a sudden revelation of another world, governed by other laws than those of the nation which we know."[18] Moran continued to work on his Yellowstone painting through April, all the while entertaining visitors, including several members of the board of directors of the Northern Pacific Railroad who had a vested interest in the commercial potential of Yellowstone.[19]

Moran had been so successful in engineering advance publicity for the painting that he must have been disappointed with its first showing in New York. *Grand Canyon of the Yellowstone* (cat. 41) was displayed in the exhibition room of Leavitt and Co. auctioneers on 2 May 1872. The viewing was private, brief, and unusual. Clarence Cook, art critic for the *New York Tribune*, later reported that the picture was poorly shown, flanked by "two tables filled with a forlorn collection of miscellaneous books waiting their turn to be knocked down to the lowest bidder.... There were no flowers, no birds in cages, no delicately printed programmes, no tin tubes, no drapery. A zealous friend, going to the hall in the afternoon to see how things were getting on, was troubled in spirit to find the picture in its bare frame standing up against a back-ground of nothingness."[20] In describing the less-than-favorable viewing conditions, Cook seized the opportunity to skewer subtly Bierstadt and other artists whose private viewings of important paintings were indeed often replete with flowers, birds, and tin tubes. Moran need not have worried about the details of presentation, however, for Cook went on to praise his painting in lavish terms: "In truth, there was no need of any decorations or allurements. The people who came to see this picture came from curiosity or interest, and the picture kept them there by its own intrinsic truth, sublimity, and beauty. Next to Church's 'Niagara' —for to that noble picture the first place must long be given— next to Church's masterpiece, Mr. Moran's 'Great Cañon of the

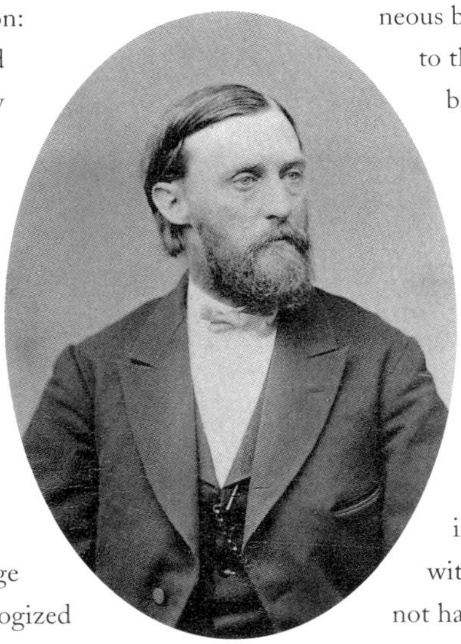

9

Yellowstone' will, we are sure, be received by the best judges in America as the finest historical landscape yet painted in this country."[21]

According to Cook, F. V. Hayden was present that evening, and "in an impromptu description of the picture given at the request of many persons present, showed, point by point, the artist's devoted adherence to facts." Echoing Hayden, Cook wrote: "color, form, space, proportion, all were true; if the picture had no other merit it had this, that a mine of scientific illustration is to be found in it."[22] Noting that scientific fact could as easily be found in photographs and maps, however, Cook declared that a work of art must offer more—it must reflect imagination. This he declared he found in Moran's painting. For young Thomas Moran, who had boldly challenged Bierstadt at his own game, Cook's review served as an important stamp of approval.

Just before Moran exhibited *Grand Canyon of the Yellowstone* in New York, a Newark newspaper reported that the picture would also be placed on view in Washington, adding that it "ought to become the property of the government."[23] It is not clear who initially proposed offering the painting to the federal government or when the campaign began, but once it was under way, Moran played an active role in the sales effort.

On 9 May 1872, approximately two months after the passage of the Yellowstone Park bill, *Grand Canyon of the Yellowstone* went on public view at the Smithsonian. Almost immediately Moran began lobbying for exhibition space in the Capitol, and less than two weeks later he had succeeded in placing the picture in the "old Hall of Representatives where every member of Congress will see it."[24] At the same time he entertained another invitation: "Major Powell of the Colorado expedition sent for me this morning and offers to take me with him this summer and pay my R.R. fare from Chicago to Salt Lake City and back and provide everything during the expedition and give me $500 for a picture of the Grand Cañon of the Colorado."[25]

At mid-century four important survey expeditions were under way. Led by John Wesley Powell, Clarence King, George Wheeler, and F. V. Hayden, the expeditionary forces were charged with mapping and measuring the Far West for commercial as well as scientific purposes. Although sponsored by the federal government, each survey was dependent on annual funding. Thus Powell, King, Wheeler, and Hayden were forced to compete with one another for congressional allocations. In 1872 Hayden took full advantage of the attention Moran's Yellowstone images had garnered to promote his own plans for future survey activities—a tactic not lost on his competitors. Within a short time Moran received invitations to travel west from Powell, King, and Wheeler, further testifying to the impact of his Yellowstone paintings. Moran had won, in effect, an open ticket for travel west with any survey party.

In June 1872 Congress purchased *Grand Canyon of the Yellowstone* for $10,000. Weeks of promotional effort by Moran, Hayden, and others had, quite literally, paid off. After a short eastern tour, the painting was installed in the Capitol, the first landscape to enter its collection. Much has been written about the composition, color, and "geology" of the painting both by Moran's contemporaries and by modern art historians (see cat. 41). Equally important is the manner in which Moran sought to balance the often opposing mandates of art and science. As already noted, Moran had declared himself unfettered by any slavish adherence to facts. His was an art inspired as much by the imaginative nature of poetry as by the literal lay of the land. Yet contemporary reviews of the painting, often quoting Hayden, praise the "accuracy" of the picture:

> The perfect success which Mr. Moran has achieved in this wonderful painting is due to a happy and, we believe, unique combination of gifts and acquirements. It is evident that the painter of this picture possesses in a high degree the poetic instinct, as well as entire familiarity with nature. He not only understands the methods of art but the processes and work of nature, so far as the faithful interpreter of natural scenery must know them. In all the rush of enthusiasm and glow of artistic power, he seems never to forget the faithful manipulation by which absolute truth is caught and fixed in the splendor of picturesque art. It is noble to paint a glorious and inspiring poem; it is satisfying to render nature with firm mastery of technical detail. In "The Grand Cañon of the Yellowstone" Mr. Moran has done both.[26]

Moran's early success lay in his ability to manipulate truth and art. In large measure he did so by employing a cultural vocabulary that was born as much of literature as of painting, a vocabulary widely understood by his contemporaries.

Universally praised for their contributions to science, the western survey expeditions also carried the romantic overlay of the sacred pilgrimage, the poetic quest. Thus it is not surprising to find Nathaniel Langford, in the first important article on Yellowstone, reporting that during a particularly difficult trek through fallen trees and underbrush a member of his party was reminded of lines from Byron's *Childe Harold*: "There is a pleasure in the pathless woods,/There is a rapture on the lonely shore."[27] For all his inventive gifts, however, even Byron could not have imagined a landscape as bizarre and wondrous as Yellowstone. As locus for an American version of the heroic quest, Yellowstone challenged even the phantasm of Coleridge.

Like costume dramas, the survey expeditions were often clothed, descriptively, in the language of romantic poetry. Even

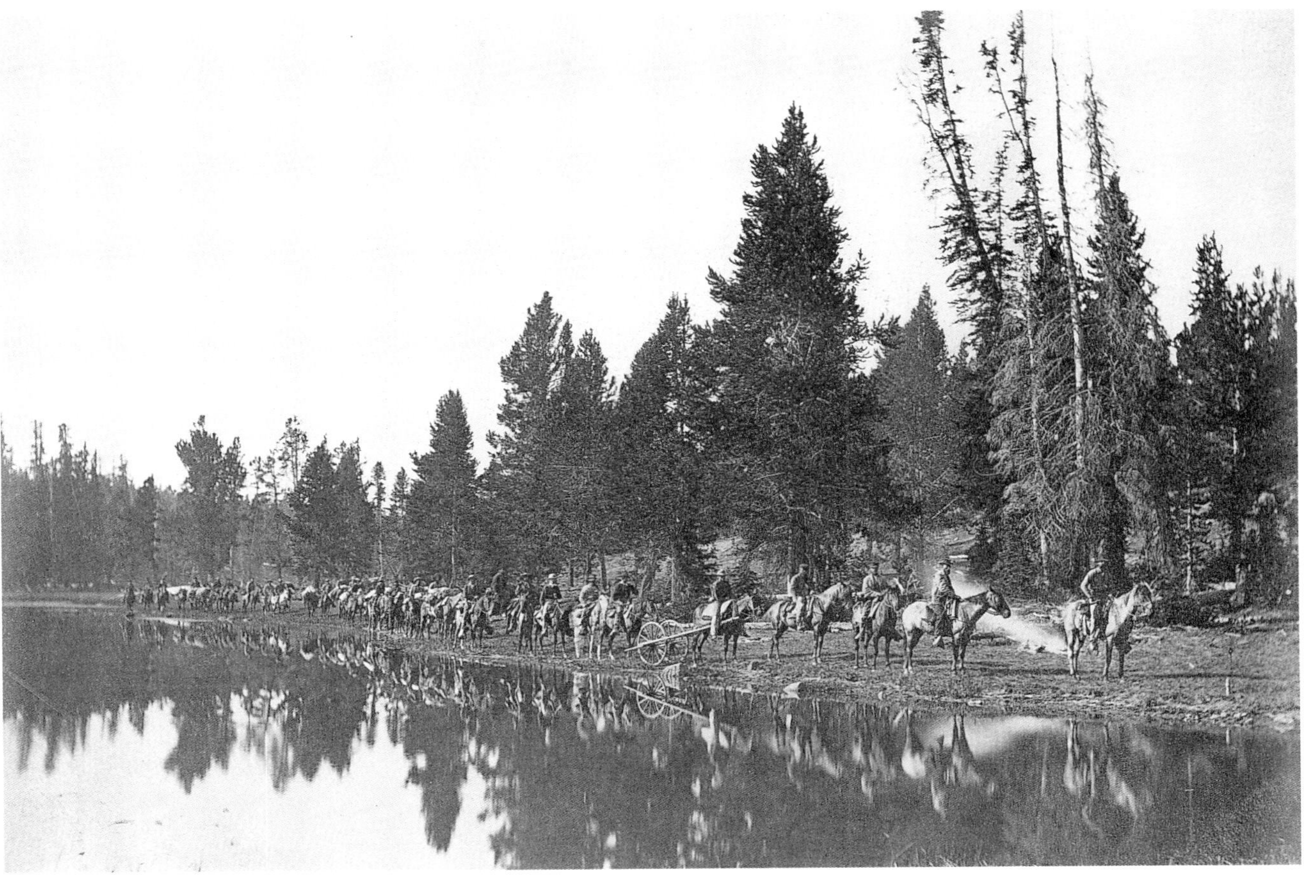

10. *Pack Train of the U. S. Geological Survey,* 1871, photograph by William Henry Jackson, courtesy Department of the Interior, Yellowstone National Park.

the expedition leaders, scientists to the core, were steeped in the language of Shelley and Byron, Longfellow and Scott.[28] The great western surveys, enterprises as commercial and political as they were scientific, became secular pilgrimages—a uniquely American variant on a European model. Thus Jackson's photograph of the expedition party en route to Yellowstone (fig. 10) resembles nothing so much as a buckskin version of Chaucer's pilgrims setting out for Canterbury.

Like others of his age, Moran was both a self-proclaimed romantic and a shrewd businessman. Keenly attuned to the market, he skillfully cast what Langford described as the "profound and solemn solitude" of Yellowstone's grand canyon into an image that simultaneously celebrated the American landscape and the heroics of the ultimate secular pilgrim—the expedition scientist. In *Grand Canyon of the Yellowstone*, his large painting of solitude redefined, Moran placed Hayden, pilgrim/poet/scientist, on a rocky precipice above a geologic timetable. Unlike Shelley's Alastor or Byron's Childe Harold, who struck melancholy poses among the ruins of civilization, Hayden contemplates both an ancient past and a promising future. It was Hayden, after all, who championed the National Park bill by skillfully demonstrating the mutually beneficial interests of science and commerce. And it was Moran who knew how to construct a picture—how to marshall what he had learned from teachers as varied as Turner and Byron—to create an image described by his contemporaries as both a document and a poem.

Colorado Chasm

On 28 June 1873 Moran wrote to F. V. Hayden to advise him that despite earlier plans he would not be joining Hayden's survey party that summer. Concerned that Hayden might not reach the Grand Canyon as initially proposed, Moran explained that he had already "made a number of contracts to furnish pictures of the region, amounting in all to about 100," and thus could not risk failing to see the site before fall, when he would need to begin work on the commissions; Moran would be traveling to the Grand Canyon with John Wesley Powell instead.[29] By this time he had seen photographs of the Grand Canyon taken on George Wheeler's recent expedition, and he clearly recognized that the landscape offered rich "material for pictures."[30]

11. John Wesley Powell, courtesy National Archives, Washington, DC.

Early in July Moran set out on his second major trip west, expecting to reach "the cañons" about 15 July. Inhospitable terrain made travel difficult, however, and it was not until early August that Moran stood above the Colorado River on the rim of the Grand Canyon for the first time:

> It was by far the most awfully grand and impressive scene that I have ever yet seen. . . . Above and around us rose a wall of 2000 feet and below us a vast chasm 2500 feet in perpendicular depth and ½ a mile wide. At the bottom the river, very muddy and seemingly only a hundred feet wide, seemed slowly moving along but in reality is a rushing torrent filled with rapids. A suppressed sort of roar comes up constantly from the chasm, but with that exception every thing impresses you with an awful stillness. The color of the Great Cañon itself is red, a light Indian Red, and the material sandstone and red marble and is in terraces all the way down. All above the cañon is variously colored sandstone, mainly a light flesh or cream color and worn into very fine forms. I made an outline and did a little color work but had not time nor was it worth while to make a detailed study in color. We made several photos which will give me all the details I want if I conclude to paint the view.[31]

For several days Moran, Powell, and their companions pursued different "views" of the canyon from various points along the rim. By mid-September Moran had gathered the sketches, color studies, and photographs he needed for the staggering amount of work he had outlined in a letter home: "70 drawings for Powell, 40 for Appleton, 4 for Aldine, 20 for Scribners all from this region, beside the water colors and oil pictures."[32]

Once back in Newark, and though pressed to complete the many illustrations for which he had accepted commissions, Moran wasted little time in setting to work on the large painting he would soon describe as a "companion" to his Yellowstone picture. By 25 November he had "finished the design for it in charcoal."[33] On Thanksgiving Day John Wesley Powell visited the artist and was "delighted" with the work, which Moran had begun to call "Chasm of the Colorado."[34]

In his ledger Moran wrote that he began to paint *Chasm of the Colorado* (cat. 47) in January 1874. On a canvas the same size as his Yellowstone picture, Moran created a second western landscape that he clearly intended to market as a pendant to the Yellowstone painting purchased by Congress. Again well before the painting was finished, he launched his promotional campaign. By late January he had left a photograph of the picture (probably the finished charcoal) with a Washington friend, who promised to forward it to the Honorable Marcus L. Ward, representative to Congress from Newark.[35]

When he had completed *Chasm of the Colorado*, Moran followed the same exhibition pattern he had established with his Yellowstone painting. On 30 April he welcomed friends and neighbors to a private viewing in Newark. The following day the picture was placed on public view for the first time. In what may be the first review, the art critic for the *Newark Daily Advertiser* recalled that when Moran first exhibited his earlier Yellowstone painting the work had been described as a "brave picture." According to the *Advertiser's* critic, "brave" was the appropriate adjective because "in its very truth of coloring it seemed to be an absurdity."[36] Conceding that Moran had not exaggerated the color of Yellowstone, the reviewer applied the same adjective to *Chasm of the Colorado*. In this instance the "bravery" was defined as Moran's attempt to capture the enormous expanse and depth of the canyon—a canyon unlike any other Moran's contemporaries had ever seen.

Early in May Moran placed the picture on exhibition in New York.[37] Lengthy reviews quickly followed. More than one critic described the landscape as a view of hell and the literary precedent as Dante's *Inferno*:[38] "The scene is a tumultuous and even appalling chaos of cliffs and chasms, a wildly-broken plain of cyclopean rocks without a tree or shrub to vary its savage grandeur. Midway in the picture, through a deep rift in the rocks, one traces far below the narrow thread of the Colorado; while in the near foreground are frightful chasms reaching to unknown depths. These dark abysms seem fairly infernal; it is as if hell itself were gaping. . . . Altogether, it is the wildest, and, we may say, fairly diabolical scene man ever looked upon."[39]

Following its New York debut, Moran shipped *Chasm of the Colorado* to Washington, where it was displayed at the Corcoran Gallery of Art. As early as 13 June the *Washington Evening Star* declared that "this picture ought to be owned by the government as a companion to the Yellowstone landscape."[40] In nearly record time the deal was done, and on 14 July the *Star* reported that Congress, "on the unanimous recommendation of the Joint Committee on the Library," had purchased *Chasm of the Colorado* for $10,000.[41] As a lobbyist, Moran had proven himself extraordinarily able.

As noted above, *Chasm of the Colorado* had been described, shortly after its public debut, as a "brave" picture. The word is apt and perhaps more resonant than initially intended. *Chasm of the Colorado* is not a "pretty" picture; nor is it comforting. Indeed one critic declared that "standing before the painting, the first impression is of chaos. . . . There is no sign of life anywhere—no human interest; not even a bird flecks the sky, nor so much as a lizard crawls on the pitiless rocks. Here and there a few stunted clumps of olive-green sagebrush or rugged mesquit bushes appear to enhance the forlornness of this utter solitude. It is awful."[42]

The "solitude" perceived here is much removed from the solitude earlier commentators had praised in Moran's Pre-

Raphaelite paintings of forest interiors. In the Grand Canyon Moran had found a landscape capable of inspiring that "frisson" of terror that stalwart romantics had pursued for decades—both in literature and life—often in the mountain passes of the Swiss Alps. In a striking twist on European precedent, however, Moran's flirtation with terror comes from looking into the depths of the earth rather than scaling its heights.

Thus Dante's journey into the depths of hell provided the metaphor most frequently used by those attempting to describe Moran's newest painting. Writing for the *Atlantic Monthly*, Clarence Cook invoked the Italian poet:

> The subject of this important work is the chasm or pit worked by the Colorado River in the sandstone rock over which it flows at this point.... The landscape of Mr. Moran's first picture was equally awful and desolate with that shown us in the present work, but its terror was lessened by the beauty and variety of the color with which nature veiled her work of change and destruction. Here, we have no such charm. We are led into a region where the eye has hardly a resting-place, no resting-place, in fact, unless it be turned upward to the sky. For this serene heaven—serene except where in one portion it darkens with the wrath of thunder clouds and the stream of deluging rain—looks down upon the very pit of hell. Only Dante's words seem fit to describe this scene.[43]

Dante's descent through the circles of hell was but the first part of a longer journey through purgatory to paradise. It was a poetic pilgrimage well known to Moran's contemporaries and thus a useful metaphoric touchstone for those attempting to describe the unusual character of the Grand Canyon. In his review Cook posed a rhetorical question: "Did Dante in his wanderings ever see such a country? Perhaps Vesuvius or Etna might show something as full of fear if one climbed down into their craters. But even there, the limited area of the desolation would not allow the mind to forget utterly the supreme loveliness of the nature that lies so near. Here there is no loveliness for hundreds of miles, nor anything on which the healthy human eye can bear to look (the scientific eye excepted)."[44] Touching on the enterprise of American science, the reviewer placed the expedition scientist, the secular pilgrim, within a European literary tradition that was centuries old. Never mind that the grail was as commercial as it was scientific; the visual and verbal vocabulary were born of poetry.

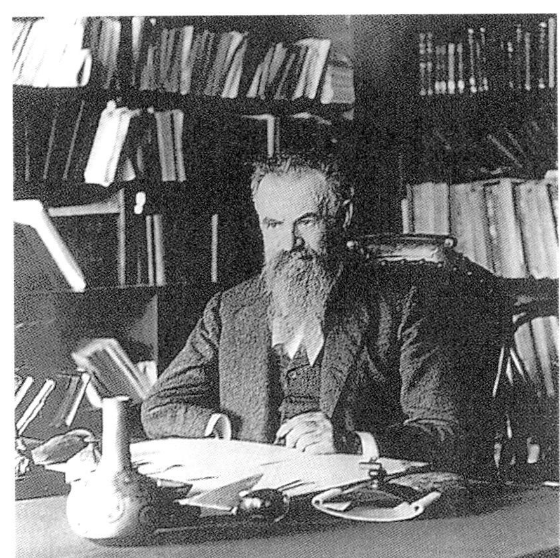
11

"The Great Fact"

In the summer of 1873, determined to reach the Grand Canyon, Moran had selected as his guide, John Wesley Powell (fig. 11), the survey leader whose account of his harrowing journey down the Colorado River in 1869 had already made him famous. Five years after he led Moran to the rim of the Grand Canyon, Powell published one of the most farsighted and sobering documents ever issued by the U.S. Government Printing Office: *Report on the Lands of the Arid Regions of the United States*. In his study Powell wrote candidly about the scarcity of water in the West and the ramifications this unavoidable fact would have for future development. Powell's message was not the one railroad promoters and other western boosters wanted heard. Developers of all types, eager to encourage settlement, had long trumpeted the Far West as Nature's garden. Yet Powell, though attacked for the candor of his report, was not alone in his assessment. Five years earlier Justin E. Colburn, a correspondent for the *New York Times* and Moran's traveling companion on his way to join Powell at the Grand Canyon, had raised similar alarms. From several points along his journey west Colburn had sent letters to the *Times* (see Appendix 3), describing in particular the desolate landscape of the Plains and Southwest. Although he had not intended to "write one word" about the landscape between Omaha and Ogden, because the route of the Union Pacific Railroad had been so frequently described, he found that his "impressions and expectations, formed from reading," were "so at variance with the truth, and the facts so different from the notions that extensively prevail that something new to many readers seems quite possible to be written."

Colburn had unexpectedly stumbled upon the rhetorical gap between the western "garden" described in promotional literature and the bleak landscape he saw out the window of the train on which he traveled west: "When one goes to sleep at night of the first day from Omaha, the last arable land on the whole journey has been seen. The supper-station, Grand Island, is on the verge of 'The Great American Desert' of the maps of fifteen to twenty years ago. The train has entered the rainless realm where drouth and aridity hold indisputable sway. This is the great fact, the fact gigantic in proportions when considered in its economical aspects and its importance to the American nation."

For Colburn, Powell, and a handful of others water was the critical economic, political, and social issue of the West. Water, as one reviewer noted, also played a central role in Moran's *Grand*

12. ***Mountain of the Holy Cross,*** **1873, stereograph by William Henry Jackson, Collection of Leonard A. Walle.**

13. **Thomas Moran, *Holy Cross Trip—Camp Vexation,* 12 August 1874, graphite, courtesy Jefferson National Expansion Memorial, National Park Service.**

Canyon of the Yellowstone and *Chasm of the Colorado*: "Although the places depicted in the two paintings are several hundred miles apart, and though the geological structures of the two are widely different, there is yet a superficial resemblance between the two subjects, owing chiefly, no doubt, to the fact that in both we are shown the tremendous action of water, first, in denuding a vast tract of country, and then in boring and cutting its way down to a lower level through immensely thick layers of stratified rock."[45] Many of Moran's contemporaries saw Dante's hell in *Chasm of the Colorado*, but others saw a geologic textbook in which the chief protagonist was water: the mighty Colorado River, a silver thread at the center of the picture, the roiling thunderstorm at the left, and the hot, steamy mist rising from the canyon walls.

Following his initial visit in 1873, Moran returned to the Grand Canyon many times. Over a period of five decades he created hundreds of Grand Canyon images, but perhaps none as richly complex as *Chasm of the Colorado*, for woven together in this single image are threads of epic and romantic literature, of ancient pilgrimages and modern expeditions, of art and science. Fortunate in his companions, Moran reaped the rewards of Powell's experience and Colburn's candor. Dante's Virgil could not have served him better.

Mountain of the Holy Cross

On 14 March 1874, before he had finished *Chasm of the Colorado*, Moran deposited a photograph at the copyright office in Washington, D.C., that allowed him in effect to stake visual claim to the subject of his next major painting, *Mountain of the Holy Cross* (cat. 53).[46] At the time he had not yet seen the mountain with the cross of snow. As had been the case with the Yellowstone and Grand Canyon subjects, Moran saw images created by others—field sketches and photographs—and quickly recognized the aesthetic and economic viability of a new subject.

During the summer of 1873, on the Hayden expedition that Moran had declined to join, William Henry Jackson had taken his first photographs of Colorado's Mountain of the Holy Cross (fig. 12). Located approximately 100 miles west of Denver, in rugged terrain, the mountain had long been a staple of local lore. In August 1873, however, when Hayden and Jackson settled on their itinerary, few had actually seen the peak. The journey was difficult and the weather unsettled, thus Jackson secured only a few glass plate negatives.[47] Yet the resulting photographs were enough to send Moran to Colorado the following summer.

Traveling first to Denver, Moran and his companions set out on a mountain trek that proved as arduous as that reported by Jackson the previous year (fig. 13). By 24 August Moran was able to write to Mary that he had seen the mountain and, en route, "one of the most picturesque waterfalls" he had ever observed. Already composing his Holy Cross painting, at least in his mind, Moran declared that he would "use" the waterfall "in the foreground of the picture."[48]

Pleased that Colorado's legendary mountain might soon become the subject of a painting by Moran, Denver's *Rocky Mountain News* reported: "Mr. Moran made a portfolio of sketches, including the Holy Cross, from which he intends to make paintings, the principal one to be of the Cross. Mr. Moran pronounces the view which is obtained from that locality one of the grandest he has ever seen, and says that no better subject could be presented for the pencil and brush of the artist."[49]

By early September Moran had returned to Newark. Though clearly eager to stake claim to another spectacular western landscape, Moran may have had difficulty balancing his commercial commitments with his wish to undertake a major new painting, for *Mountain of the Holy Cross* was not completed until April of the following year. Once again the artist invited friends and neighbors to a private viewing. Shortly thereafter the *Newark Daily Advertiser* described the finished painting as "grandly successful."[50]

By 1875 Moran was far more experienced in the subtleties of marketing a major painting than he had been in 1872 when

Grand Canyon of the Yellowstone was first shown in the company of used books. Following the private viewing in Newark, Moran placed *Mountain of the Holy Cross* on exhibition at Schaus Gallery in New York. A privately printed exhibition announcement stated that Moran had "penetrated this wilderness and made the studies for the picture" the previous summer. On 10 April the *New York Times* declared the painting "decidedly superior to either of the two former pictures of western scenery painted by Mr. Moran.... In its general treatment, 'The Mountain of the Holy Cross' reminds us strongly of the studies of Calame, that almost unrivaled painter of wild mountain scenery, though at the same time we fully recognized the fact that Mr. Moran's work bears the unmistakable stamp of originality and we think that it will unquestionably take rank as one of the finest examples of American landscape art that has yet been produced."[51] The comments were perceptive, for Moran's western paintings were very much rooted in European tradition. Alexandre Calame was the recognized master of European mountain landscapes at mid-century, thus the link with Moran was offered as a compliment.[52]

It is not clear if Moran intended to undertake a third lobbying campaign to sell his latest picture to Congress. It is certain, however, that by early June he had arranged for the painting to be placed on exhibition in Washington at the Corcoran Gallery. Corcoran records indicate that Moran offered the picture to the gallery shortly after it arrived, but the Corcoran declined to purchase it.[53] If Moran also attempted to promote the painting to members of Congress, the effort came to naught, for by early November the work was on view in Boston, where it remained through December.[54]

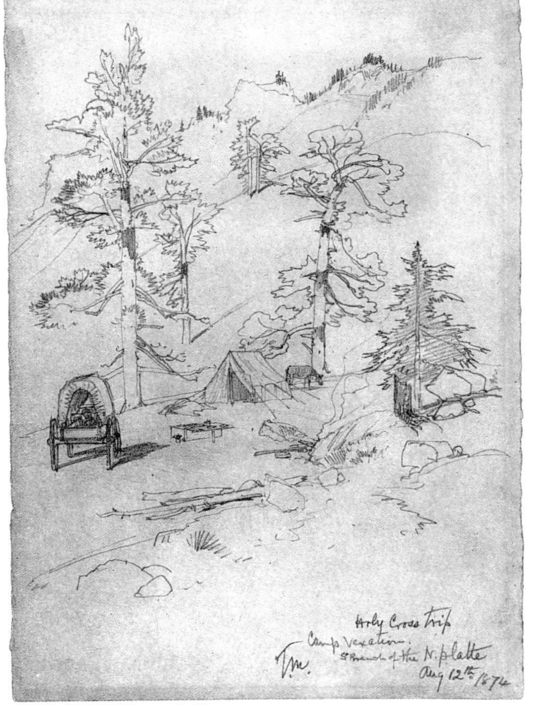

13

In 1876, during the celebration of the nation's centennial, Moran attempted to bring together his three great western landscapes: *Grand Canyon of the Yellowstone*, *Chasm of the Colorado*, and *Mountain of the Holy Cross*. Hoping to exhibit the three works in the art gallery of the Centennial Exposition in Philadelphia, Moran tried to borrow back the two paintings he had sold to Congress. Congress refused. Moran was thus thwarted in his effort to exhibit what had become, in essence, a western triptych.

In addition to other works by Moran, *Mountain of the Holy Cross* was shown at the exposition, where it received an award but did not sell. In 1879, when Moran sent the painting to London for exhibition, it remained unsold. Early in 1880, however, the picture was purchased by Dr. William Bell, an English physician and railroad entrepreneur. Eventually the painting was installed in the home that Bell maintained in Manitou, Colorado, and therein lies the tale of the ultimate redefinition of the religious pilgrimage and the quest for the grail.

William Bell was a founding member of the consortium that built the Denver and Rio Grande Railroad, a line that ran between Denver and Mexico City. Like Jay Cooke, chief financier of the Northern Pacific Railroad, Bell saw prosperity ahead if potential passengers could be lured to stops along the railroad line. Just as Cooke stood to profit from the public's fascination with Yellowstone, Bell saw profit in promoting the therapeutic properties of the mineral water located at Colorado Springs and Manitou, two newly established communities on the rail line south of Denver. Soon dubbed the "Saratoga of the West," the area became an attractive destination for well-to-do invalids and their families.

By the time Bell installed *Mountain of the Holy Cross* in Manitou, the painting was nearly as famous as the fabled waters. Ironically, the overt religious symbolism of the picture—symbolism that may have rendered a sale to Congress difficult, if not impossible—was precisely the message Bell wished to convey. When Moran decided to reconfigure the topography of the landscape near the Mountain of the Holy Cross and "use" the waterfall he had sketched on his journey in the foreground of his painting, he created an image in which "holy" water seemed to be streaming from the mountain with the cross of snow. Wise in the ways of the market, Moran undoubtedly recognized in the Mountain of the Holy Cross a geographic anomaly that would be widely interpreted as a natural sign of divine favor—one of the central tenets of nineteenth century American social, political, and religious thought. Bell took the symbolism further, squeezing from the image railroad tickets and water treatments. Twice a week he opened his home to pilgrims who wished to look upon Moran's painting before making their way to the water cure. Throughout his career Moran's best patrons were often those who had something to sell along the iron tracks of a railroad line.

14. Albert Bierstadt, photograph by Napoleon Sarony, New York.

15. Chamber of the House of Representatives, U.S. Congress, before 1901, with Bierstadt's *Settlement of California—Bay of Monterrey* and *Discovery of the Hudson River* installed at the left and right of the Speaker's podium, courtesy Architect of the Capitol, Washington, DC.

Head to Head

From the time A. B. Nettleton of the Northern Pacific Railroad first suggested that Moran would "surpass" Bierstadt (fig. 14) if he had the opportunity to visit Yellowstone, the names of the two artists were often linked. Although only seven years older than Moran, Bierstadt had succeeded in establishing himself at such a young age that the two seemed to be of different generations. It was Bierstadt who had dazzled American and European audiences with enormous paintings of the Rocky Mountains and the Sierra Nevada during the 1860s. And it was Bierstadt who, in 1865, had sold *The Rocky Mountains, Lander's Peak*, for an astonishing $25,000. In aspiration and temperament the two artists were very different men. Yet in 1878 they very nearly came to blows. Not surprisingly, the issues were money and government patronage.

In 1872, when Congress purchased Moran's *Grand Canyon of the Yellowstone*, the $10,000 price was widely reported. In 1874 the purchase of *Chasm of the Colorado* for the same sum also became a news event. Undoubtedly many artists took note of such congressional largess. But Bierstadt may have paid particular attention to such reports, for he had been attempting to reap similar rewards from Congress for several years.

As early as 1866 Bierstadt had begun a campaign to win the commission for two paintings to be placed on either side of the Speaker's platform in the House of Representatives. Originally he had proposed filling the coveted spots with western landscapes: a Rocky Mountain scene and a Yosemite view. As an alternative he suggested paintings illustrating important events in American history—the discovery of the

14

15

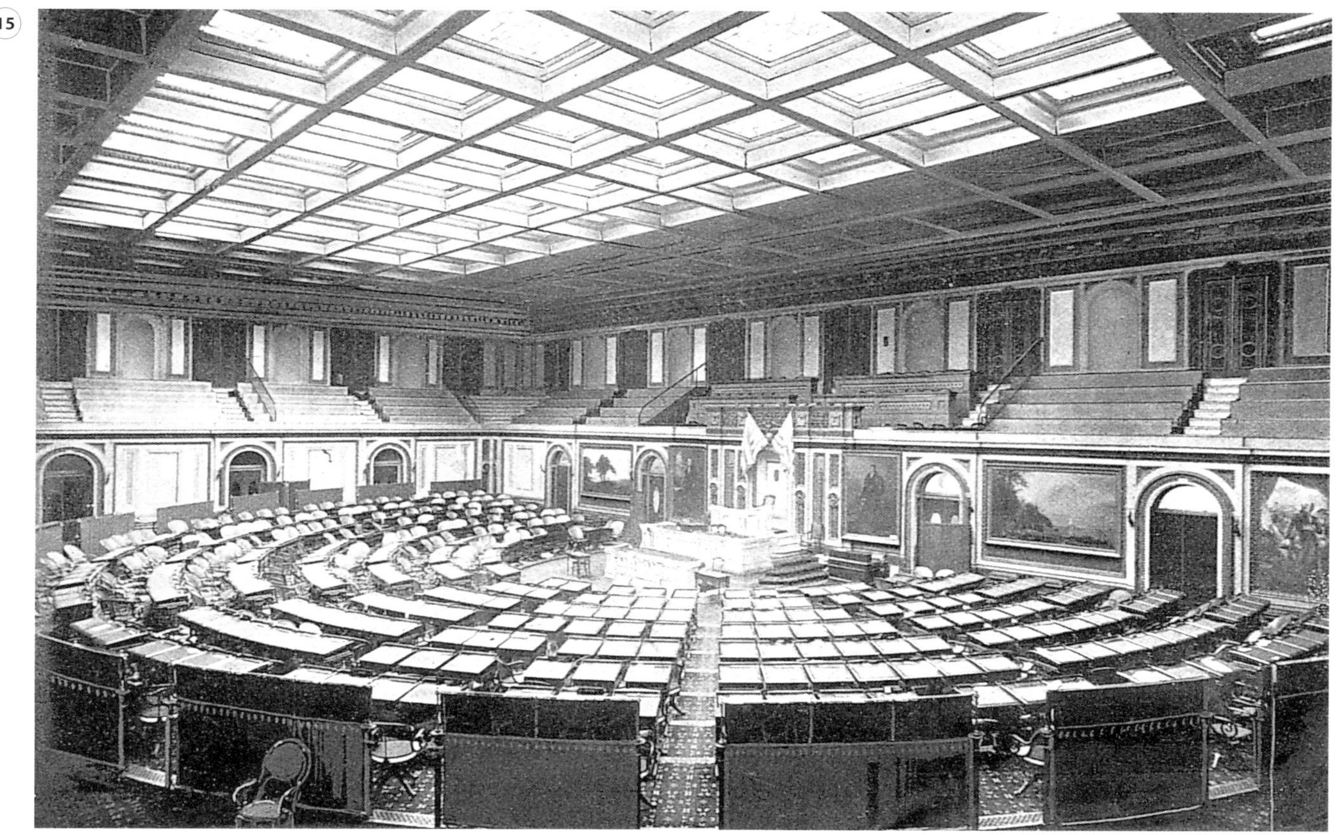

Hudson River, for example. Bierstadt may have doomed his own proposal, however, by asking for the enormous sum of $40,000 per painting. Subsequently, declaring the "honor" worth something, he indicated he would reduce the price to $30,000 for each picture. The Library Committee viewed both proposals as outrageous and decided to shelve the issue for an indefinite period.[55]

The purchase of the Moran paintings several years later revived Bierstadt's interest in the commission for the House chamber, and by late fall 1874 he had succeeded in installing two of his paintings, *Discovery of the Hudson River* and *Autumn in the Sierras*, in the House of Representatives (fig. 15). Covering all bets, he chose to offer a traditional history painting and a western landscape. The sketches for *Autumn in the Sierras* had been completed on an expedition to California with Clarence King, a circumstance that may reflect Bierstadt's awareness of the role Hayden and Powell had played in the successful sale of Moran's paintings. In March 1875 the Library Committee voted to purchase Bierstadt's *Discovery of the Hudson* for $10,000. No appropriation was made for the Sierra picture. Bierstadt may have been advised that current opinion favored a second history subject rather than a landscape, for shortly thereafter he began *Settlement of California—Bay of Monterey, 1770.*

News of the purchase of one Bierstadt painting and the rejection of another undoubtedly reached Moran without delay. Both artists knew that one panel in the House chamber remained to be filled, and both determined to win the prize. In February 1878 a disagreement had broken out over the continued exhibition in the Capitol of a privately owned painting. Favoritism was implied when a petition from a second artist who wished to hang a picture in the Capitol was rejected.[56] The principals were Bierstadt, whose *Discovery of California* had hung unpurchased in the House chamber for more than two years, and Moran, who wanted to offer a newly completed painting, *Ponce de Leon in Florida* (cat. 54), as a candidate for the remaining space in the House chamber. Unsuccessful in his attempt to dislodge Bierstadt's painting, Moran arranged for his picture to be shown at the Corcoran. The rancor continued, and late in June supporters of both artists were lobbying Congress.[57] Bierstadt won the battle, less on merit than on the compromise premise that Congress had already purchased two paintings by Moran and only one by Bierstadt.

Neither artist emerged from the competition unscathed, but the most unfortunate result may have been that in seeking government patronage both felt compelled to abandon the panoramic western landscapes that had brought them great success and to turn instead to history paintings—a genre for which neither had demonstrated any special gifts.

West Again

Setting aside the disappointment he must have felt at the outcome of his skirmish with Bierstadt, Moran quickly made plans to return west. Accompanied by his brother Peter, Moran was clearly on a mission to collect new material for pictures. Surviving sketches indicate that Thomas and Peter traveled to Donner Pass in the Sierra Nevada range and sketched near Lake Tahoe and Salt Lake City before turning north toward Fort Hall and the Snake River country of Idaho. It was during this trip that Thomas Moran sketched the Teton Mountains for the first time. Several years earlier F. V. Hayden had named one of the Teton peaks "Mount Moran" in his honor. At the end of the journey Moran returned to Green River and the same railroad station where his western odyssey had begun eight years earlier. During that short period of time he had achieved a measure of success most of his contemporaries would never know. He had staked visual claim to two of the most phenomenal landscapes on the American continent: Yellowstone and the Grand Canyon. Inevitably, every other painting of those geologic wonders would be judged against his standard.

Extraordinarily productive, both as an illustrator and as a painter, Moran had captured the attention of the public and the press with his large western landscapes. Carefully composed and skillfully executed, *Grand Canyon of the Yellowstone*, *Chasm of the Colorado*, and *Mountain of the Holy Cross* had become iconic images by the end of the decade. Inextricably linked to political, commercial, scientific, and social issues, the paintings came to reflect much more than aesthetic concerns. Moran's western triptych may in fact be seen as one of the most powerful statements ever made regarding land use. Simultaneously embraced by those who won legislative approval for the concept of "national parks" and by those who actively promoted settlement of the West, Moran's images were compelling enough to validate the proposition that both conservation and commerce were well served when landscapes as spectacular as Yellowstone and the Grand Canyon were left relatively untouched.

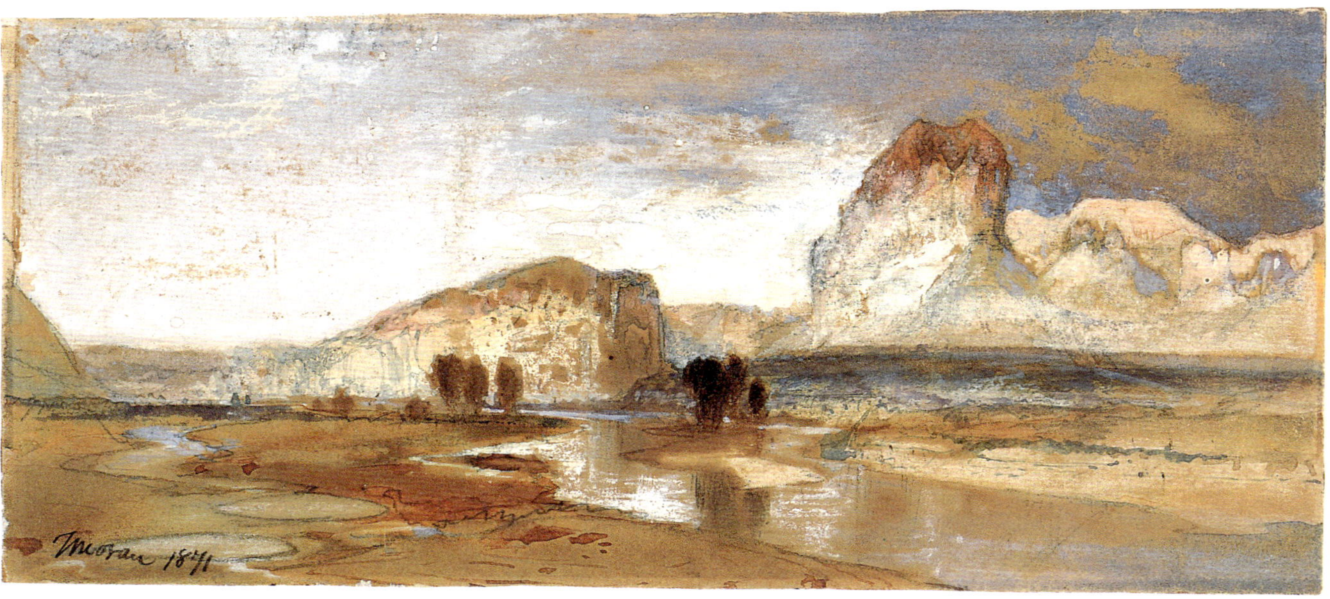

10

"First Sketch Made in the West at Green River, Wyoming"

1871, watercolor
8.9 x 19.7 (3½ x 7¾)
Gilcrease Museum,
Tulsa, Oklahoma

YELLOWSTONE NATIONAL PARK WATERCOLORS CATALOGUE NOS. 11–22

WE LATELY TOOK great pleasure in looking over a number of sketches made by Mr. Thomas Moran in the Yellow Stone region. They were, of course, extremely interesting on account of their entirely unique and picturesque subject matter. The Geysers, both spouting and in repose, the singularly-shaped beds of mineral matter deposited by the springs, the lovely and lofty terraces built by the slow and silent action of the waters, the unfamiliar vegetation and the wild and broken surface of the land—all these are features of which any at all adequate rendering must be interesting. Mr. Moran's sketches certainly were so. But their greatest interest does not lie in their subject matter so much as in the artist's own qualities which they display. The prevailing characteristic of the sketches is not, as might have been expected, boldness or brilliancy, but extreme delicacy. The drawing is necessarily slight, and not specially remarkable in any regard. But the color is very beautiful. The effects are extremely varied and subtle, and most of the color pure and strong. Mr. Moran has seized it with facility and fixed it with precision. There are some water-views, and some combinations of the strange rock color, of which we have seldom seen the equal in refined and firm rendering. These sketches of Mr. Moran bespeak the trained perceptions of a gifted and conscientious artist. He has just finished a considerable series of drawings from them for Mr. Jay Cooke. (*NYT,* 14 May 1873)

BACK IN WASHINGTON, that winter of 1871–1872, in the proceedings before Congress for the creation of the Yellowstone National Park, the water colors of Moran and the photographs of the Geological Survey were the most important exhibits brought before the Committee. "They did a work which no other agency could do and doubtless convinced every one who saw them that the regions where such wonders existed should be carefully preserved to the people forever." (Jackson 1936, 157)

11

Great Springs of the Firehole River

c. 1871, watercolor
20.6 x 28.3 (8⅛ x 11⅛)
Department of the Interior, Yellowstone National Park

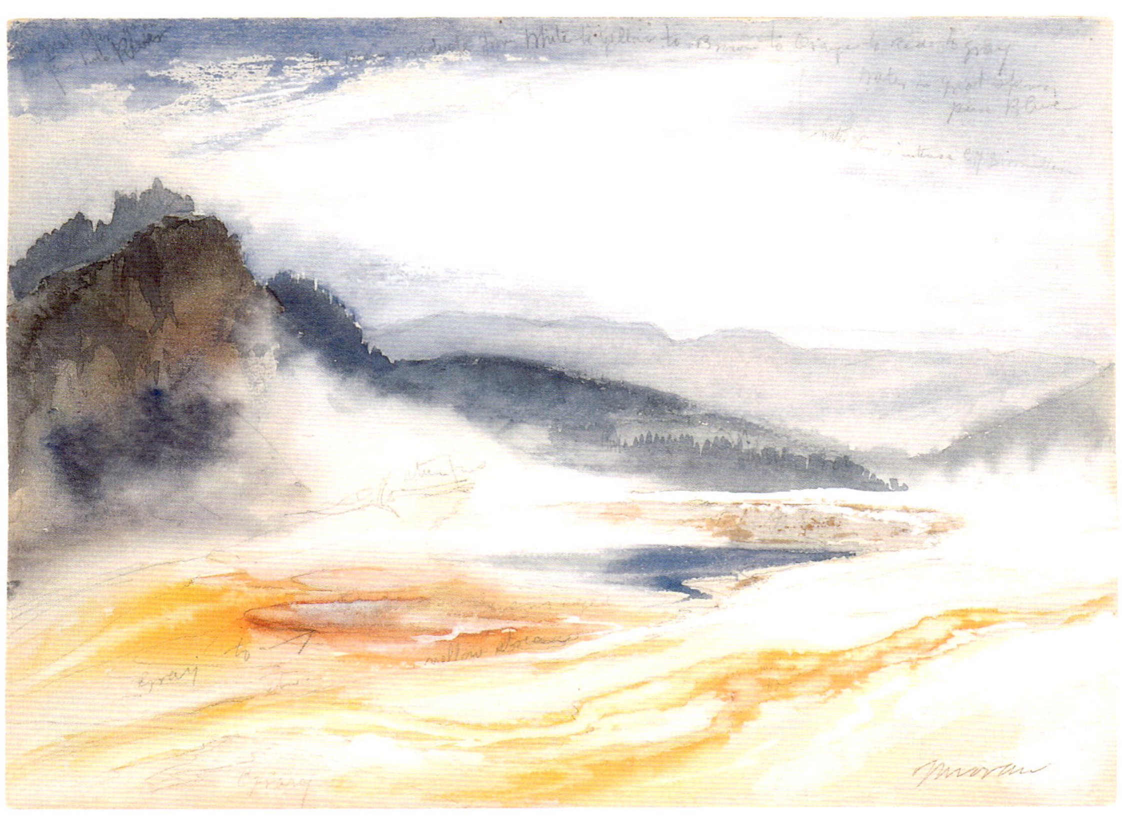

AFTER ENCOUNTERING many obstructions, we arrived at the Fire-Hole Basin, and spent five days in exploring its wonders, making charts, sketches, photographs, and taking the temperatures of the springs. The boiling-point of water at this elevation is about 192° to 196°. We ascertained the temperatures of more than six hundred hot springs in this valley, and there were as many more that were dying out, to which we did not think it worth while to give our attention. Many also must have been overlooked by us; so that within an area of about five miles square we may estimate the existence of about 1,200 to 1,500 springs, with basins of all sizes, from a few inches in diameter to three hundred feet. The springs in this valley are of three kinds, but varying much in their active power: 1st, those in which the ebullition occurs only at intervals, and which may therefore be called intermittent springs; 2d, such as are constantly boiling and bubbling up, therefore permanent springs; 3d, those whose surface is always undisturbed, and in which there is no bubbling or boiling up. The first class reach the boiling-point only when in operation—when in a state of repose the temperature of the water is as low as 150°. The second class have a temperature equal to boiling water, or not far below it—in this region, varying from 180° to 196°. Some of the largest of the springs are in a constant state of agitation.... The basin is about two hundred feet in diameter, and the sides of the crater, which have been much broken down, are about thirty feet deep. The crater is so filled with dense steam that it is only at periodical times that it is cleared away so that one can catch a glimpse of the seething caldron below. From one side of it five streams of water are ever flowing, which in the aggregate form a river ten feet wide and two feet deep. The delicate shades of coloring from the iron and sulphur are most finely displayed upon the surface over which this water flows. (Hayden 1872a, 395)

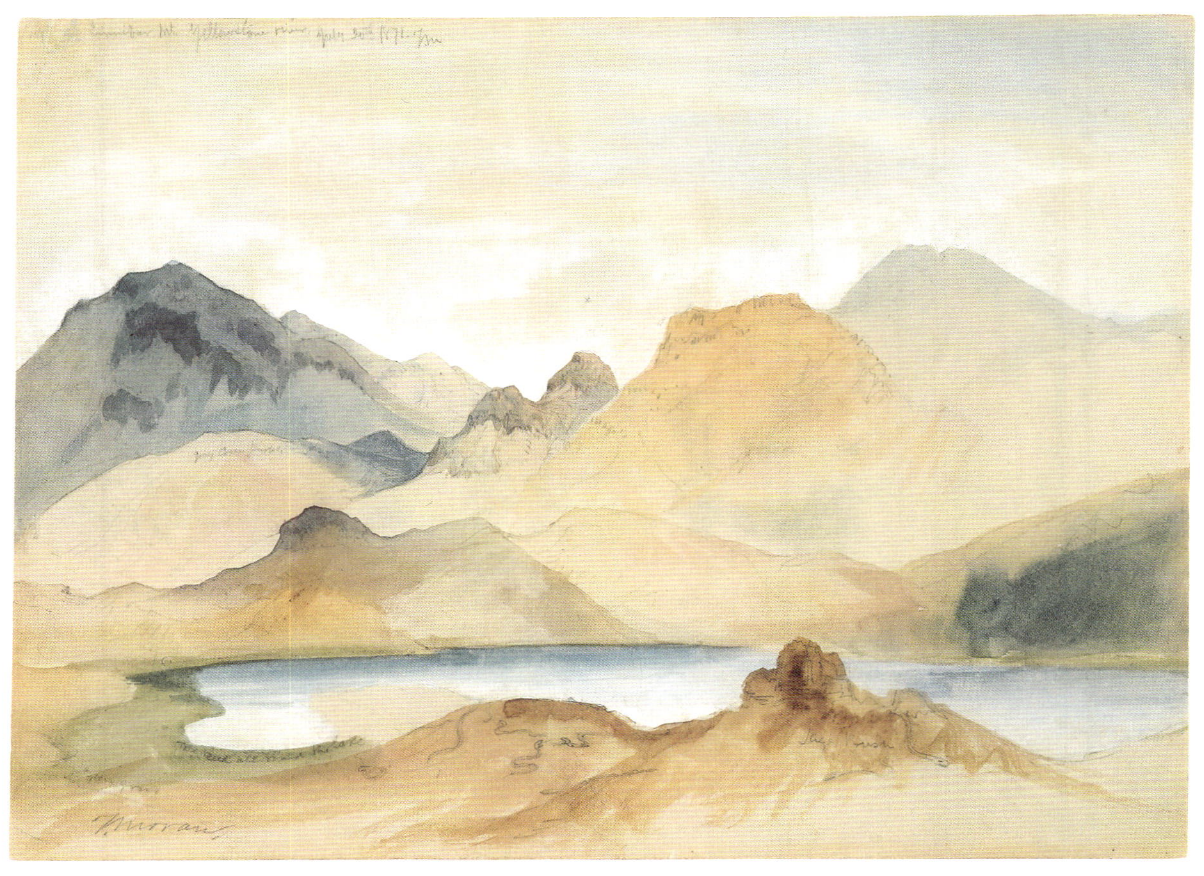

12

Cinnabar Mountain, Yellowstone River

20 July 1871, watercolor
26.2 x 35.9 (10 5/16 x 14 1/8)
Department of the Interior, Yellowstone National Park

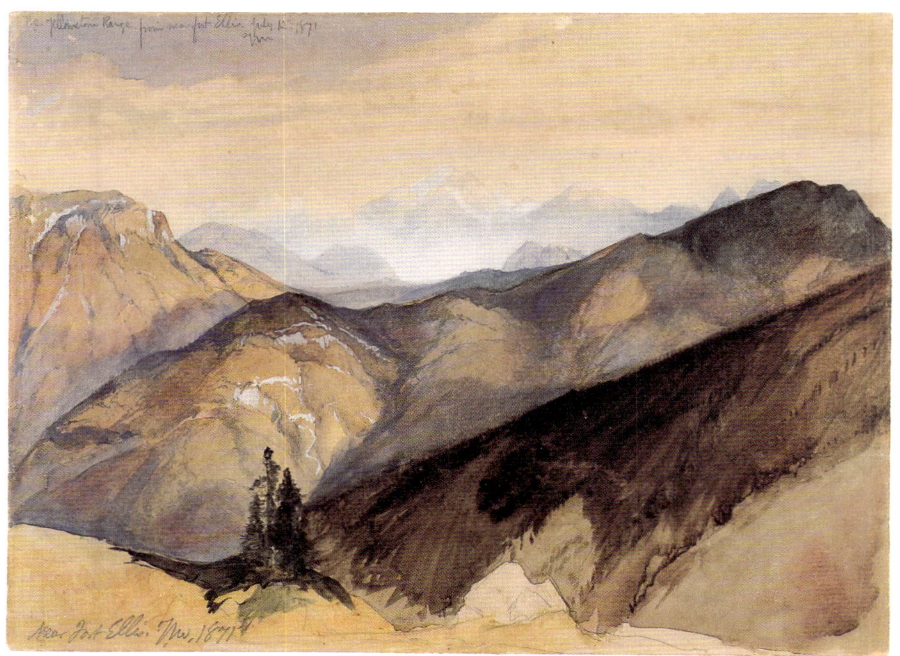

13

The Yellowstone Range from near Fort Ellis

12 July 1871, watercolor
25.7 x 34.9 (10 1/8 x 13 3/4)
Department of the Interior, Yellowstone National Park

14

The Devil's Slide, Yellowstone

1871, watercolor
26 x 17.8 (10 ¼ x 7)
Department of the Interior, Yellowstone National Park

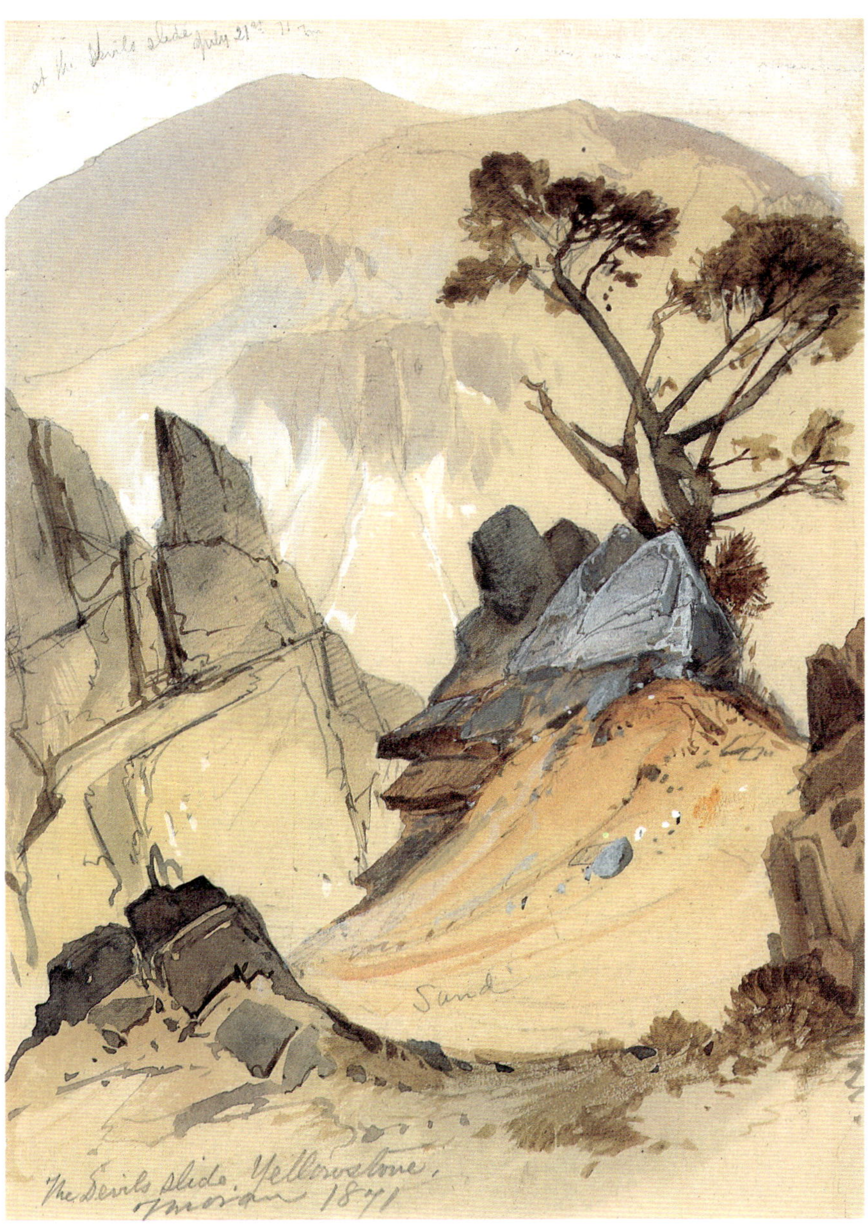

AFTER TRAVELING six miles over the mountains above the cañon, we again descended into a broad and open valley, skirted by a level upland for several miles. Here an object met our attention which deserves more than a casual notice. It was two parallel vertical walls of rock, projecting from the side of a mountain to the height of 125 feet, traversing the mountain from base to summit, a distance of 1,500 feet. These walls were not to exceed thirty feet in width, and their tops for the whole length were crowned with a growth of pines. The sides were as even as if they had been worked by line and plumb—the whole space between, and on either side of them, having been completely eroded and washed away. We had seen many of the capricious works wrought by erosion upon the friable rocks of Montana, but never before upon so majestic a scale. Here an entire mountainside, by wind and water, had been removed, leaving as the evidences of their protracted toil these vertical projections, which, but for their immensity, might as readily be mistaken for works of art as of nature. Their smooth sides, uniform width and height, and great length, considered in connection with the causes which had wrought their insulation, excited our wonder and admiration. They were all the more curious because of their dissimilarity to any other striking objects in natural scenery that we had ever seen or heard of. In future years, when the wonders of the Yellowstone are incorporated into the family of fashionable resorts, there will be few of its attractions surpassing in interest this marvelous freak of the elements. For some reason, best understood by himself, one of our companions gave to these rocks the name of the "Devil's Slide." (Langford 1871, 6–7)

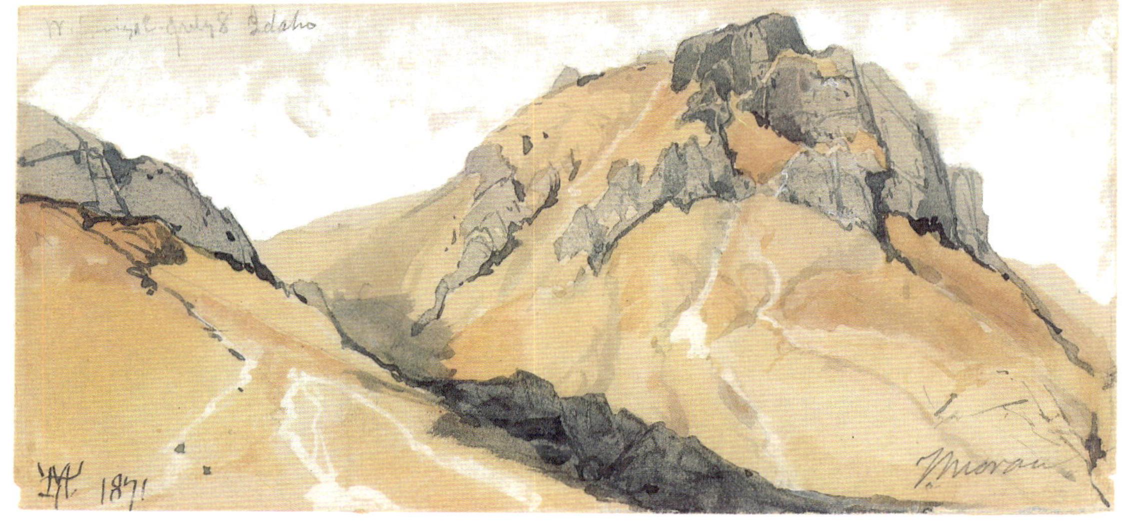

15

Warm Springs Creek, Idaho

1871, watercolor
8.6 x 18.1 (3 3/8 x 7 1/8)
Department of the Interior, Yellowstone National Park

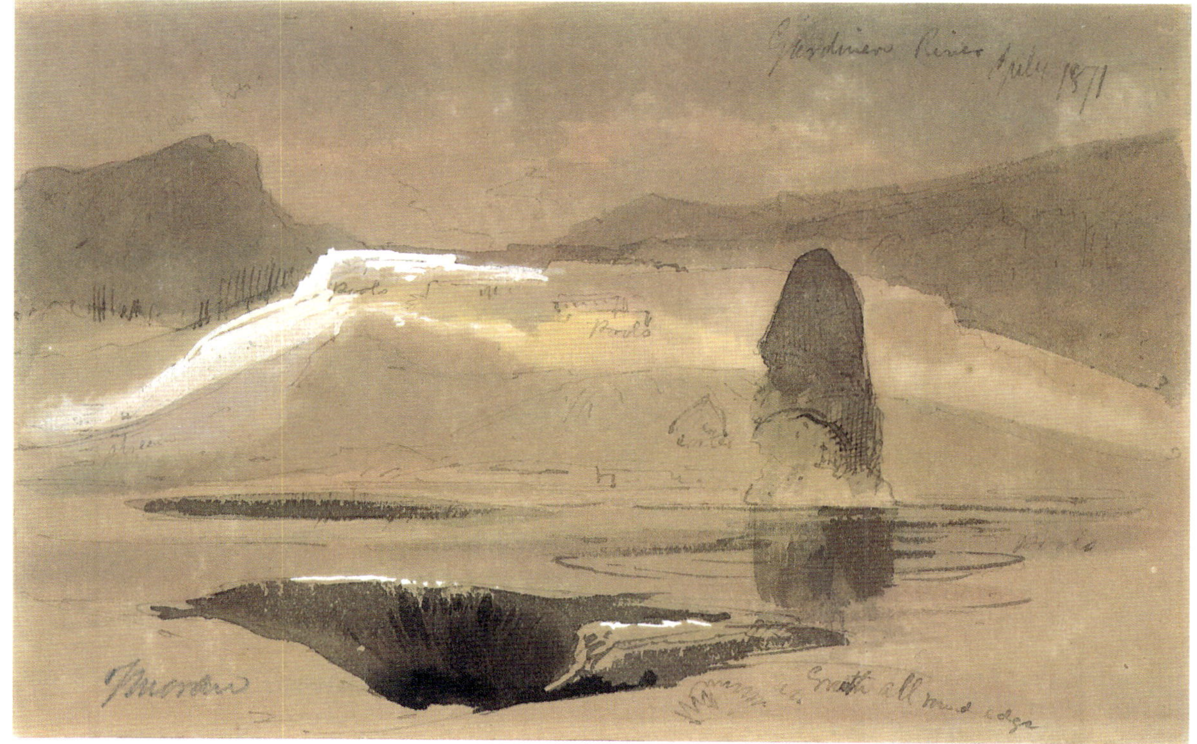

16

Gardiner River

July 1871, watercolor
12.7 x 19.7 (5 x 7 3/4)
Department of the Interior, Yellowstone National Park

17

Liberty Cap and Clematis Gulch

1871, watercolor
17.5 x 25.4 (6 7/8 x 10)
Department of the Interior, Yellowstone National Park

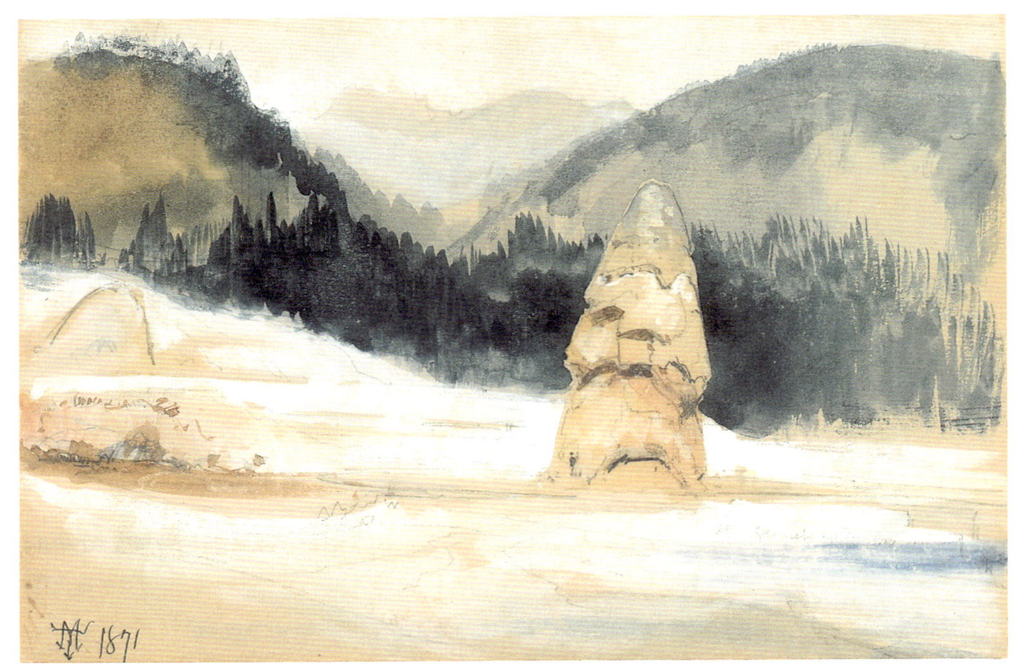

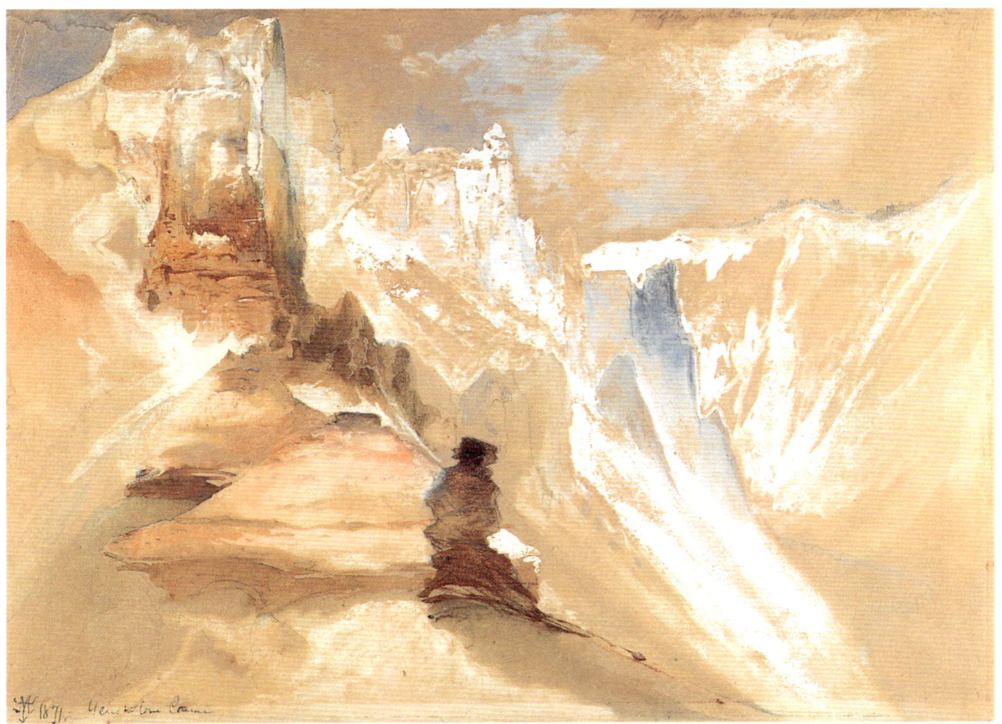

18

Yellowstone Canyon

1871, watercolor
26.4 x 35.9 (10 3/8 x 14 1/8)
Department of the Interior, Yellowstone National Park

19

Sand in the Canyon

1871, watercolor
14.6 x 25.2 (5 ¾ x 9 15/16)
Department of the
Interior, Yellowstone
National Park

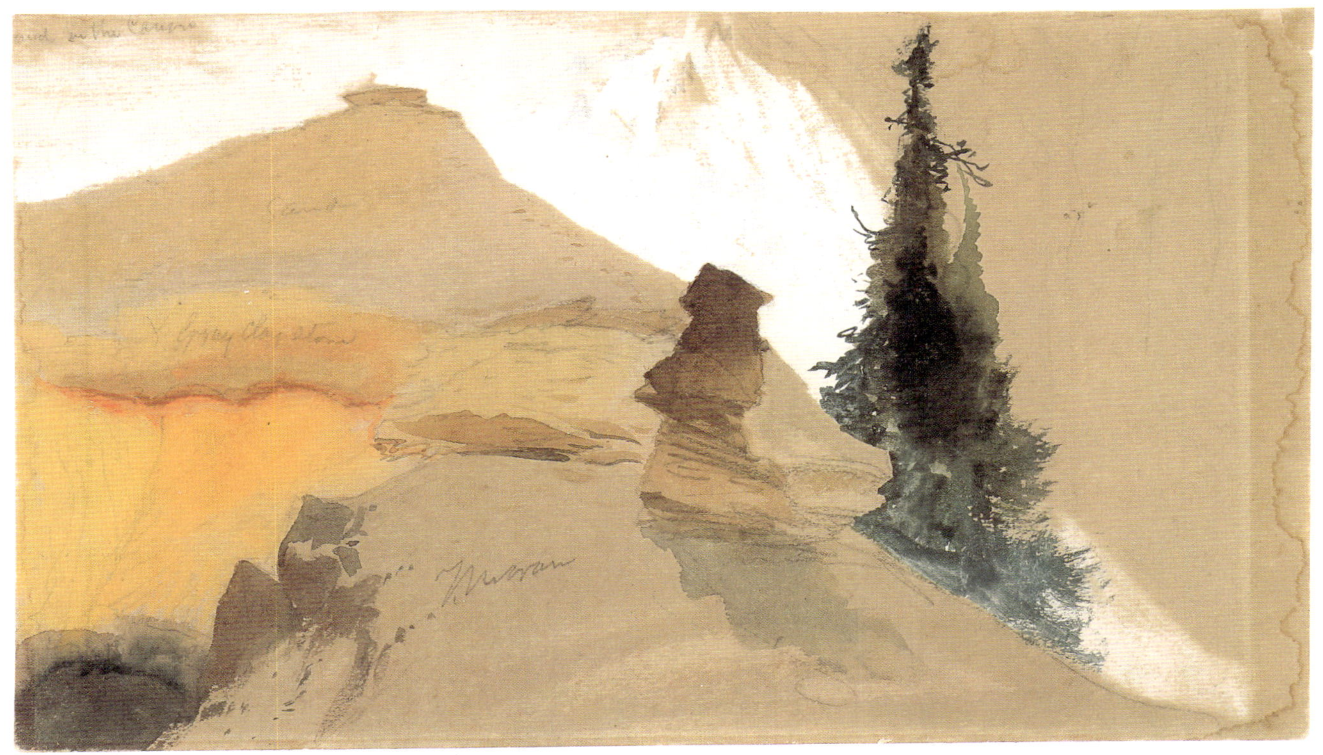

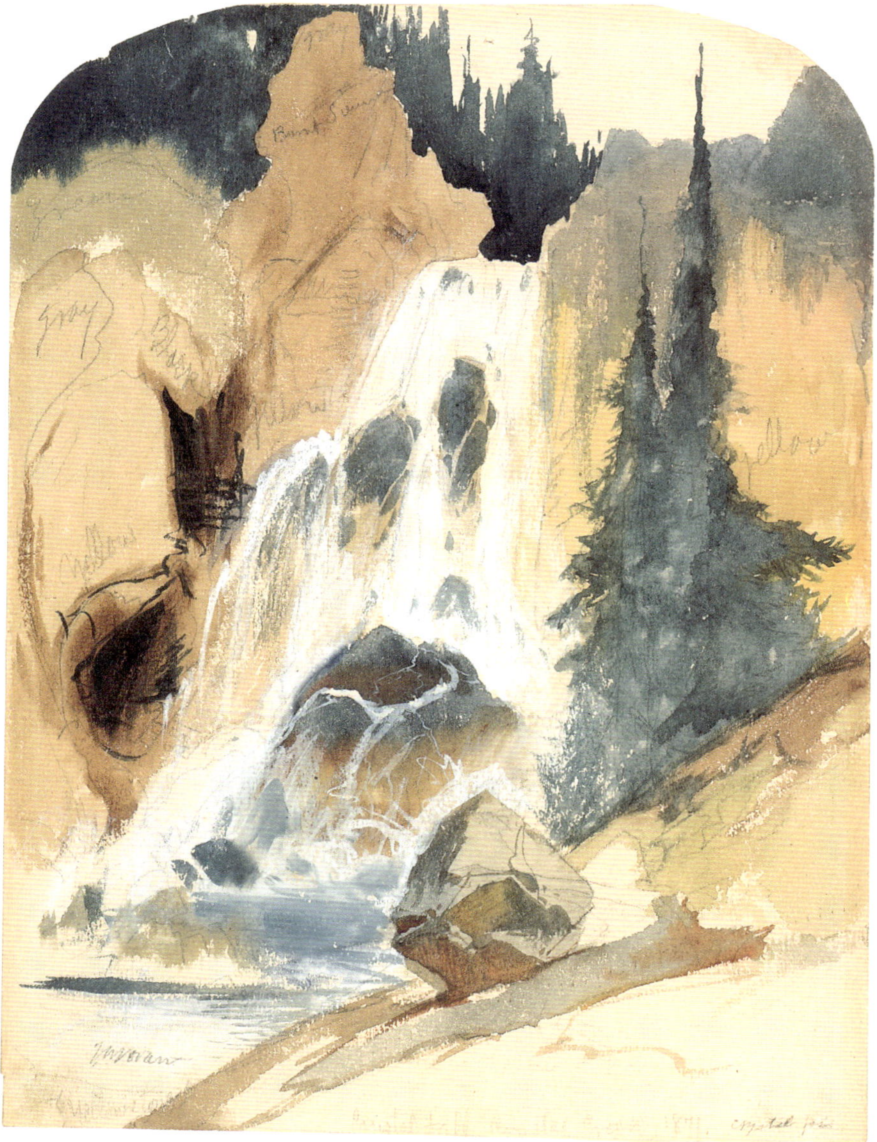

20

Crystal Falls

1871, watercolor
27.9 x 20.6 (11 x 8 ⅛)
Department of the Interior, Yellowstone National Park

NEAR THE FOOT of the gorge the creek breaks from fearful rapids into a cascade of great beauty. The first fall of five feet is immediately succeeded by another of fifteen, into a pool as clear as amber, nestled beneath overarching rocks. Here it lingers as if half reluctant to continue its course, and then gracefully emerges from the grotto, and, veiling the rocks down an abrupt descent of eighty-four feet, passes rapidly on to the Yellowstone. It received the name of "Crystal." (Langford 1871, 11 – 12)

21

Tower Creek

1871, watercolor
19.7 x 26.8 (7¾ x 10 9/16)
Department of the Interior, Yellowstone National Park

TOWER CREEK IS a mountain torrent flowing through a gorge about forty yards wide. Just below our camp it falls perpendicularly over an even ledge 112 feet, forming one of the most beautiful cataracts in the world. For some distance above the fall the stream is broken into a great number of channels, each of which has worked a tortuous course through a compact body of shale to the verge of the precipice, where they re-unite and form the fall. The countless shapes into which the shale has been wrought by the action of the angry waters, add a feature of great interest to the scene. Spires of solid shale, capped with slate, beautifully rounded and polished, faultless in symmetry, raise their tapering forms to the height of from 80 to 150 feet, all over the plateau above the cataract. Some resemble towers, others the spires of churches, and others still shoot up as lithe and slender as the minarets of a mosque. Some of the loftiest of these formations, standing like sentinels upon the very brink of the fall, are accessible to an expert and adventurous climber. The position attained on one of their narrow summits, amid the uproar of waters, and at a height of 250 feet above the boiling chasm, as the writer can affirm, requires a steady head and strong nerves; yet the view which rewards the temerity of the exploit is full of compensations. Below the fall the stream descends in numerous rapids, with frightful velocity, through a gloomy gorge, to its union with the Yellowstone. Its bed is filled with enormous boulders against which the rushing waters break with great fury. (Langford 1871, 8–9)

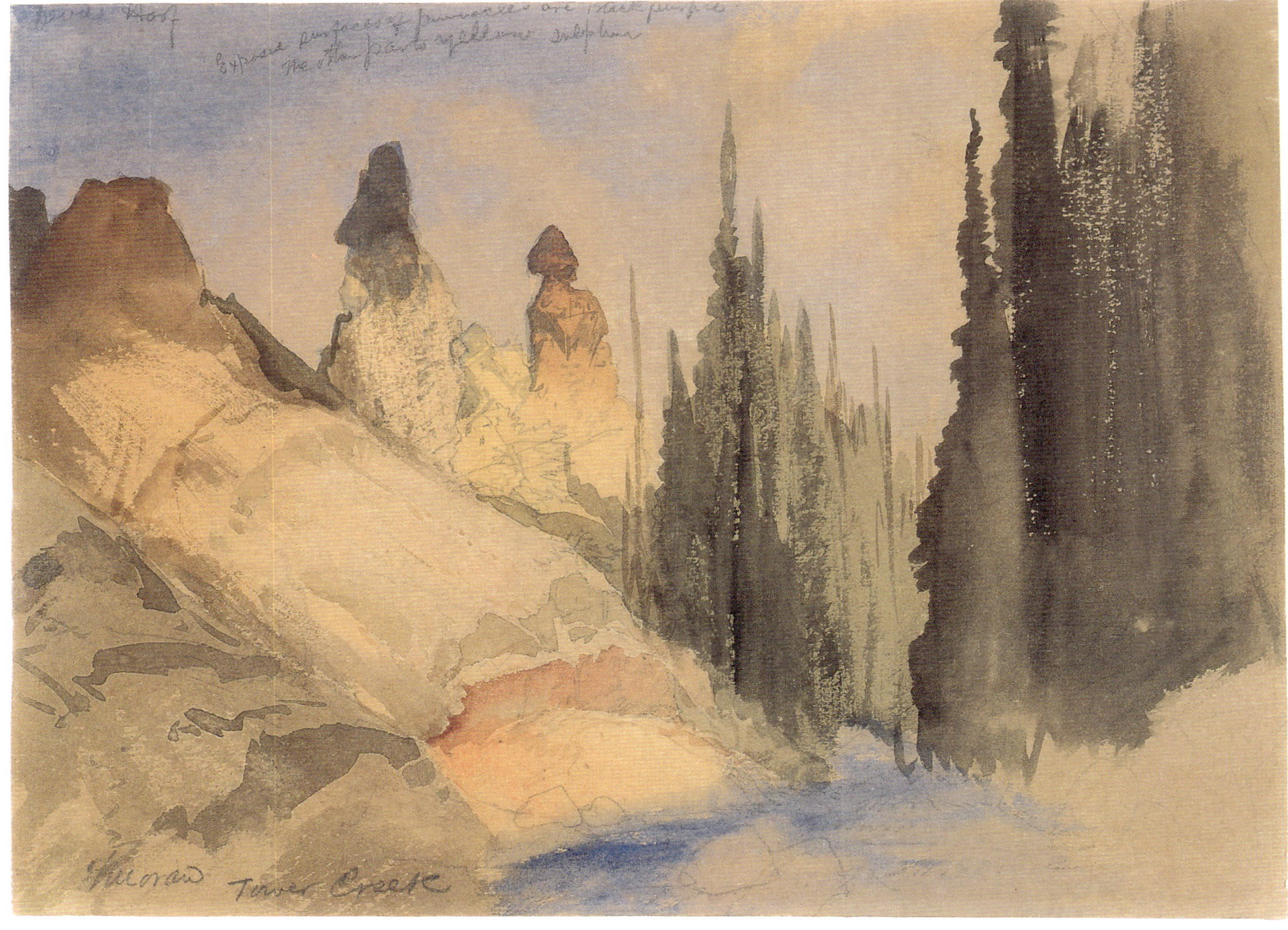

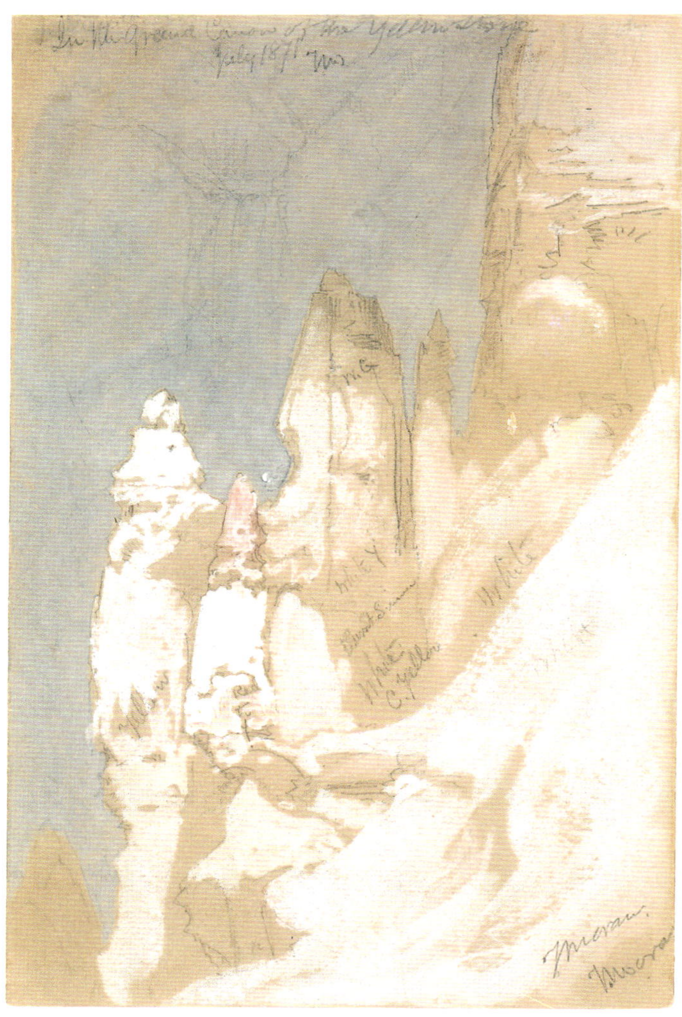

22

In the Grand Canyon of the Yellowstone

July 1871, watercolor
19.5 x 12.7 (7 11/16 x 5)
Department of the Interior, Yellowstone National Park

FROM A FIRST view of the cañon we followed the river to the falls. A grander scene than the lower cataract of the Yellowstone was never witnessed by mortal eyes. The volume seemed to be adapted to all the harmonies of the surrounding scenery. Had it been greater or smaller it would have been less impressive. The river, from a width of two hundred feet above the fall, is compressed by converging rocks to one hundred and fifty feet, where it takes the plunge. The shelf over which it falls is as level and even as a work of art. The height, by actual line measurement, is a few inches more than 350 feet. It is a sheer, compact, solid, perpendicular sheet, faultless in all the elements of grandeur and picturesque beauties. The cañon which commences at the upper fall, half a mile above this cataract, is here a thousand feet in depth. Its vertical sides rise gray and dark above the fall to shelving summits, from which one can look down into the boiling, spray-filled chasm, enlivened with rainbows, and glittering like a shower of diamonds. From a shelf protruding over the stream, 500 feet below the top of the cañon, and 180 above the verge of the cataract, a member of our company, lying prone upon the rock, let down a cord with a stone attached into the gulf, and measured its profoundest depths. The life and sound of the cataract, with its sparkling spray and fleecy foam, contrasts strangely with the sombre stillness of the cañon a mile below. There all was darkness, gloom, and shadow: here all was vivacity, gayety, and delight. One was the most unsocial, the other the most social scene in nature. We could talk, and sing, and whoop, waking the echoes with our mirth and laughter in presence of the falls, but we could not thus profane the silence of the cañon. Seen through the cañon below the falls, the river for a mile or more is broken by rapids and cascades of great variety and beauty.
(Langford 1871, 13)

23

Cliffs, Green River, Wyoming

1872, watercolor
15.7 x 29.7 (6 3/16 x 11 11/16)
Museum of Fine Arts, Boston, M. and M. Karolik Collection

Washington only

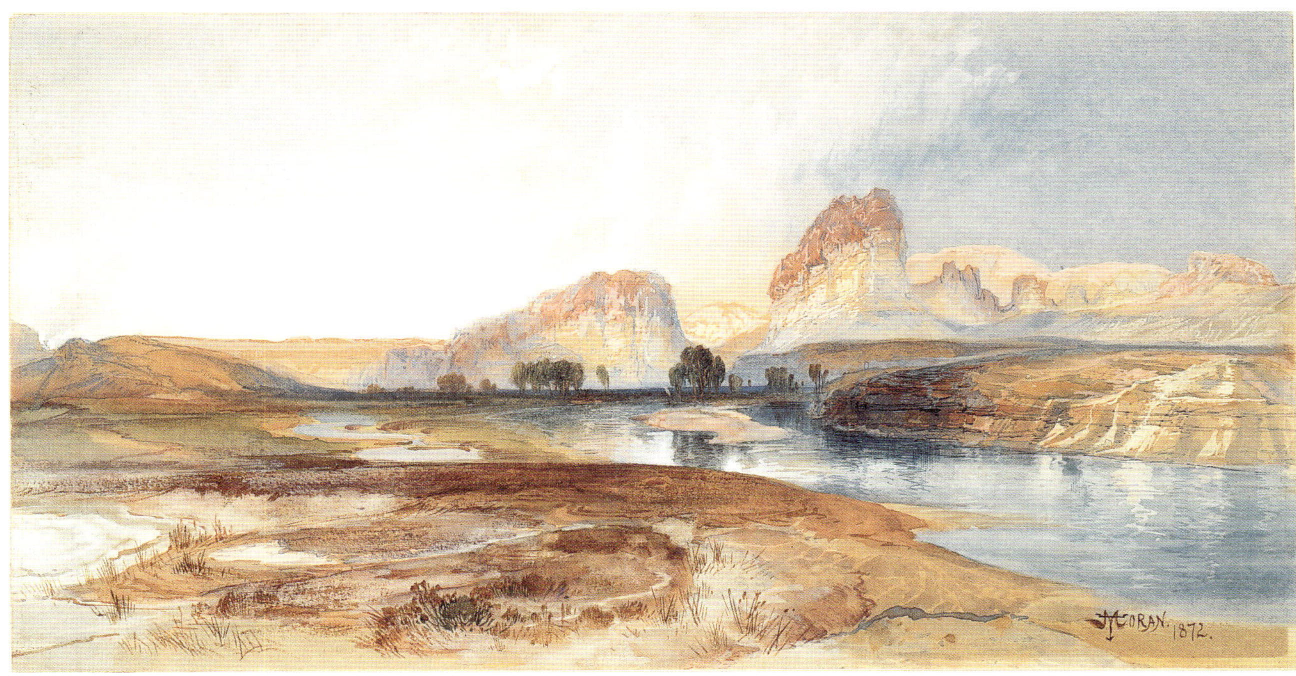

ONE PICTURE GIVES a view on Green River, the head waters of the Colorado, which is fully as wonderful in its illustration of the local color of the cliff and rock formation of the region as [Moran's] "Chasm of the Colorado." In the present work, which is in reality a study from nature, there is a castellated cliff, 1,000 feet high, formed of a yellow-toned sandstone and capped with red or blood-covered lava, which as it has become disintegrated by the action of the atmosphere runs down its perpendicular sides, one color mingling with another in rich confusion, until at the base it assumes a gray-green tone of surpassing brilliancy.
(*NY Post*, 18 Nov. 1874)

BLACKMORE WATERCOLORS
CATALOGUE NOS. 24–39

PUT ON YOUR best strokes this summer so as to be ready for a big campaign next summer—I think you ought to try hard to complete Blackmore's pictures—It was a sad event, the death of his wife. Now he wishes to have them as a sort of monument to her memory. (Hayden to Moran, 29 Aug. 1872, GA)

WE WISH TO show our really high estimate of Mr. Moran in specifying a series of water-color drawings from the Yellowstone region which we have seen, and which include in parcels the principal features of the Capitol landscape, with many other studies. They will amount, we learn, when complete to nearly twoscore, and have been obtained by an English purchaser for ultimate presentation to the Queen. They are abundantly finer works than the painting we have been admiring. They are rapid, racy, powerful, romantic specimens of water-color sketching, showing in each example faculties that any artist ought to glory in. (*The Nation* [5 Sept. 1872], 158)

TO SAY THAT these drawings are the most brilliant and poetic pictures that have been done in America thus far, is unfortunately not to say much; because our work in landscape to the present time has been plain prose, or weak idyl, or outheroding of Herod; anything, in short, but poetry. This, with a few sweet exceptions, is the main outcome of our landscape painting. But Mr. Moran's water-colors show a strong man rejoicing to run a race; and with all his senses alive for rich and strange and tender shimmering color, rainbow and mist, with fleeting cloud, and more hues than Iris with her purfled scarf can show. His love of form is as strong as his love of color, and his lines betray the same innate grace of spirit, the same delicately moving mind. In these drawings, as in the large picture bought by the Government and now hanging in the Capitol, the artist is on such strange, unaccustomed ground, that one suspects some trick, some stage-play, and fears to be caught with unrealities. Tame conventional people, who make a fetish of the Frenchman, and look upon Theodore Rousseau as the speaker of the last word in landscape art, blame Moran for not leaving the strangeness out of his pictures, and for not making the Yellowstone synonymous with the Seine. But those who can love Rousseau, and Turner, and Corot, and Raphael, with one and the same heart—nor hear any division in the concord of sweet sounds they make—will ask only how this new painter has solved his problem, and whether the Yellowstone is as weirdly poetic on his canvas as it is in nature. But who will look at Mr. Moran's pictures and ask themselves how he has delivered the message given him for us—whether he has belittled it, or clouded it, or slipped it, or given it in all the fullness of which he is capable, and with all simplicity—will, we think, agree with us that the messenger was well chosen, and that the wild western desert has found in him a most faithful because most poetic voice. (*Scribner's* [Jan. 1873], 394)

IN 1871 AN opportunity was offered [Moran] of accompanying the United States' exploring expedition conducted by Professor Hayden to the Yellowstone River in Wyoming territory. This river courses through a most extraordinary region. It is of sulphureous formation. Hot springs and geysers abound, and the sulphur rocks and cliffs assume the most fantastic shapes, and are tinted with vivid blue, red, and especially yellow colours. Sometimes one can, without any stretch of fancy, imagine himself in some deserted city of the orient, whose highly-coloured walls, battlements, palaces, minarets, and towers yet remain, while all the inhabitants are gone except the vulture and the kite and the lizard. Through a narrow tortuous seam in the singular country winds the Yellowstone River; the gorge is often 1,000 feet deep. Mr. Moran took many careful sketches, chiefly in water-colours, of these impressive scenes, some of which, I believe, are now owned at Salisbury, England. (Benjamin 1882, 91)

IT IS TRUE that Englishmen here have shown a greater appreciation of my work than Americans.... In the Museum at Salisbury are 16 watercolor drawings of the fine scenery of the Yellowstone Park, made by me for another English gentleman, Mr. Wm. Blackmore, who presented them to the Museum. He had travelled much in the Western territories, and his wife died almost within sight of the Park, after enduring great hardships of travel to see the marvellous scenery of that wonderland. (Thomas Moran, in "Bolton Artists in the New World: The Moran Family," *Bolton Journal* [England], 22 Apr. 1882)

HIS SERIES OF exquisite water-colors, relating to Yellowstone Park, were purchased by the late William Blackmore of London, who, at his death, bequeathed them to his brother, Dr. George Blackmore, founder of the Salisbury Museum, which was presented to that city by Dr. Blackmore, and is entirely devoted to the relics of the native races of North America, and where these famous water-colors may now be seen. (Teetor 1889, 6)

24

The Yellowstone Range, near the Crow "Mission"

1872, watercolor
17.8 x 34.9 (7 x 13 ¾)
Gilcrease Museum, Tulsa, Oklahoma
Blackmore Set, no. 1

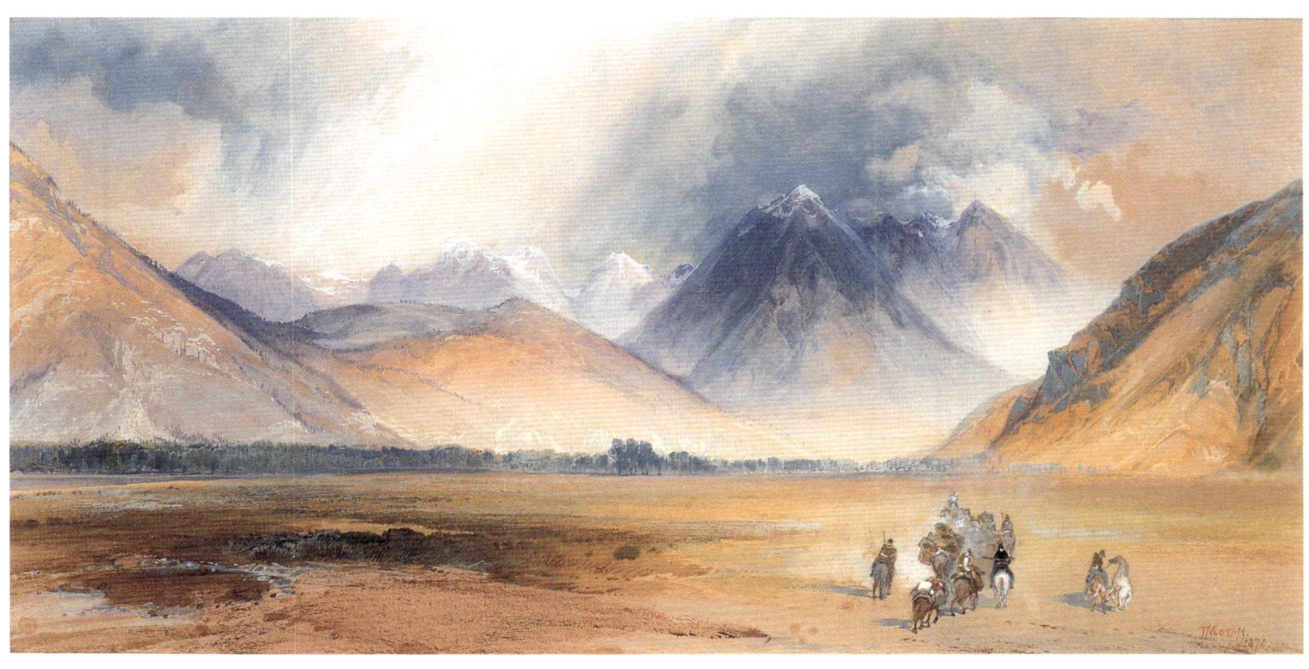

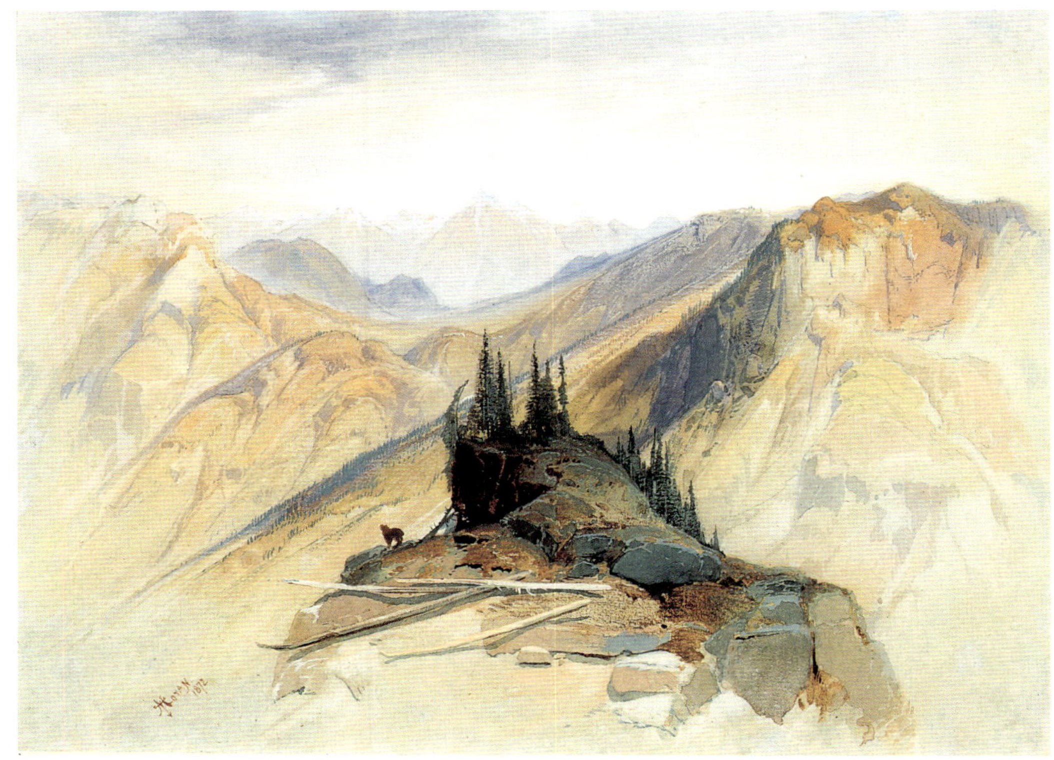

25

The Yellowstone Range, near Fort Ellis

1872,watercolor
20.3 x 27. 9 (8 x 11)
Gilcrease Museum, Tulsa, Oklahoma
Blackmore Set, no. 2

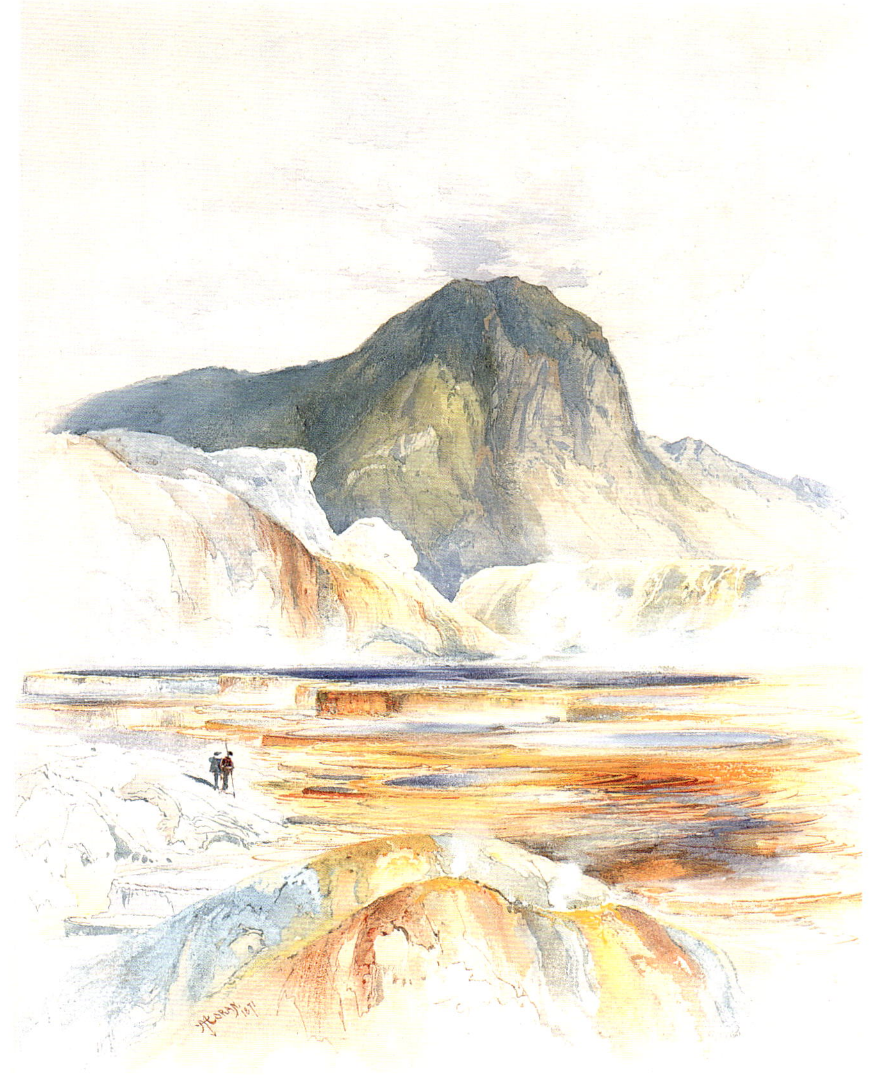

26

The Hot Springs of Gardiner's River, Upper Pools

1872, watercolor
28.6 x 21.6 (11 ¼ x 8 ½)
Gilcrease Museum, Tulsa, Oklahoma
Blackmore Set, no. 3

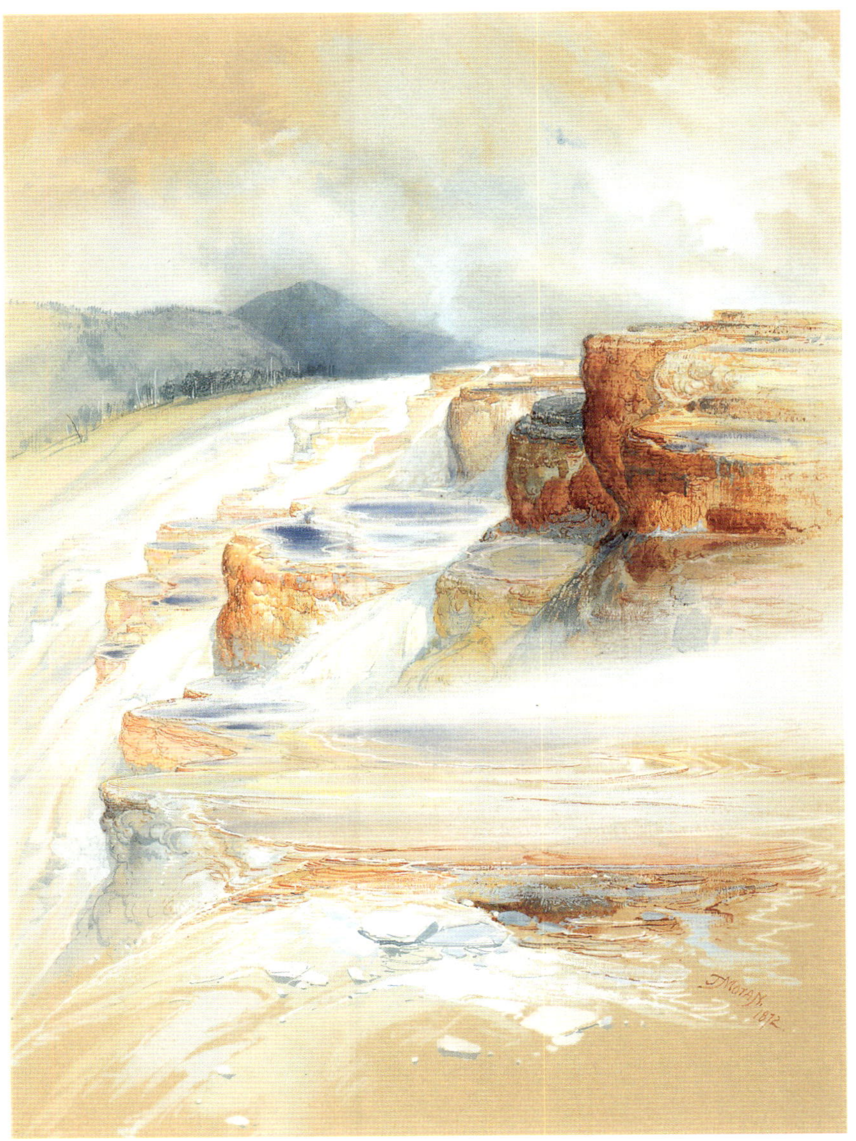

27

The Hot Springs of Gardiner's River, "Diana's Baths"

1872, watercolor
34 x 24.8 (13 3/8 x 9 3/4)
Gilcrease Museum, Tulsa, Oklahoma
Blackmore Set, no. 4

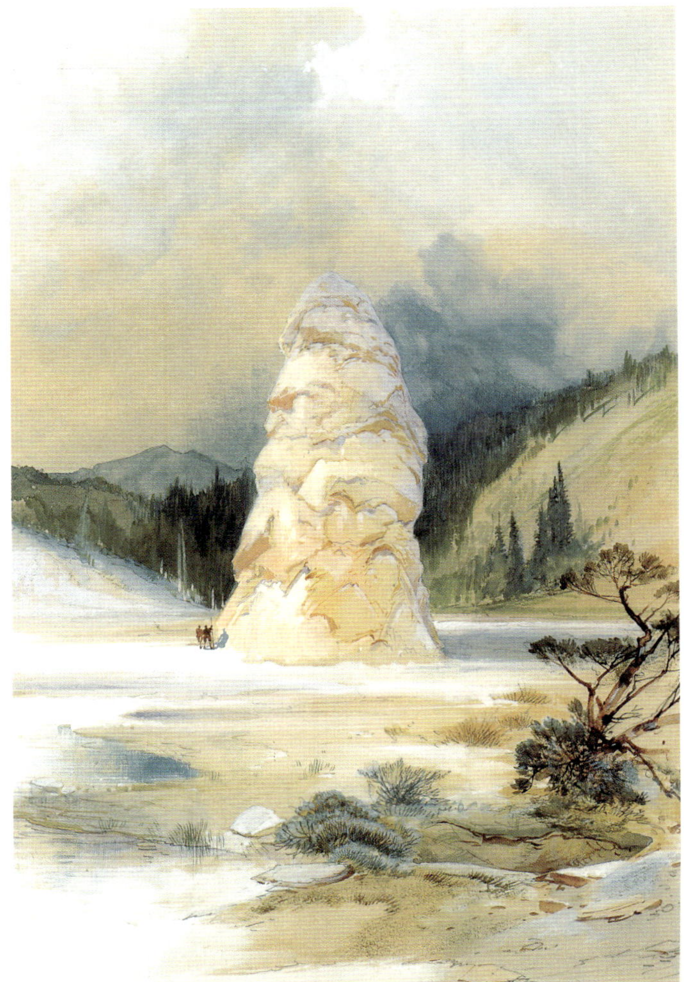

28

The Hot Springs of Gardiner's River, Extinct Geyser Crater

1872, watercolor
26 x 17.2 (10 1/4 x 6 3/4)
Gilcrease Museum, Tulsa, Oklahoma
Blackmore Set, no. 5

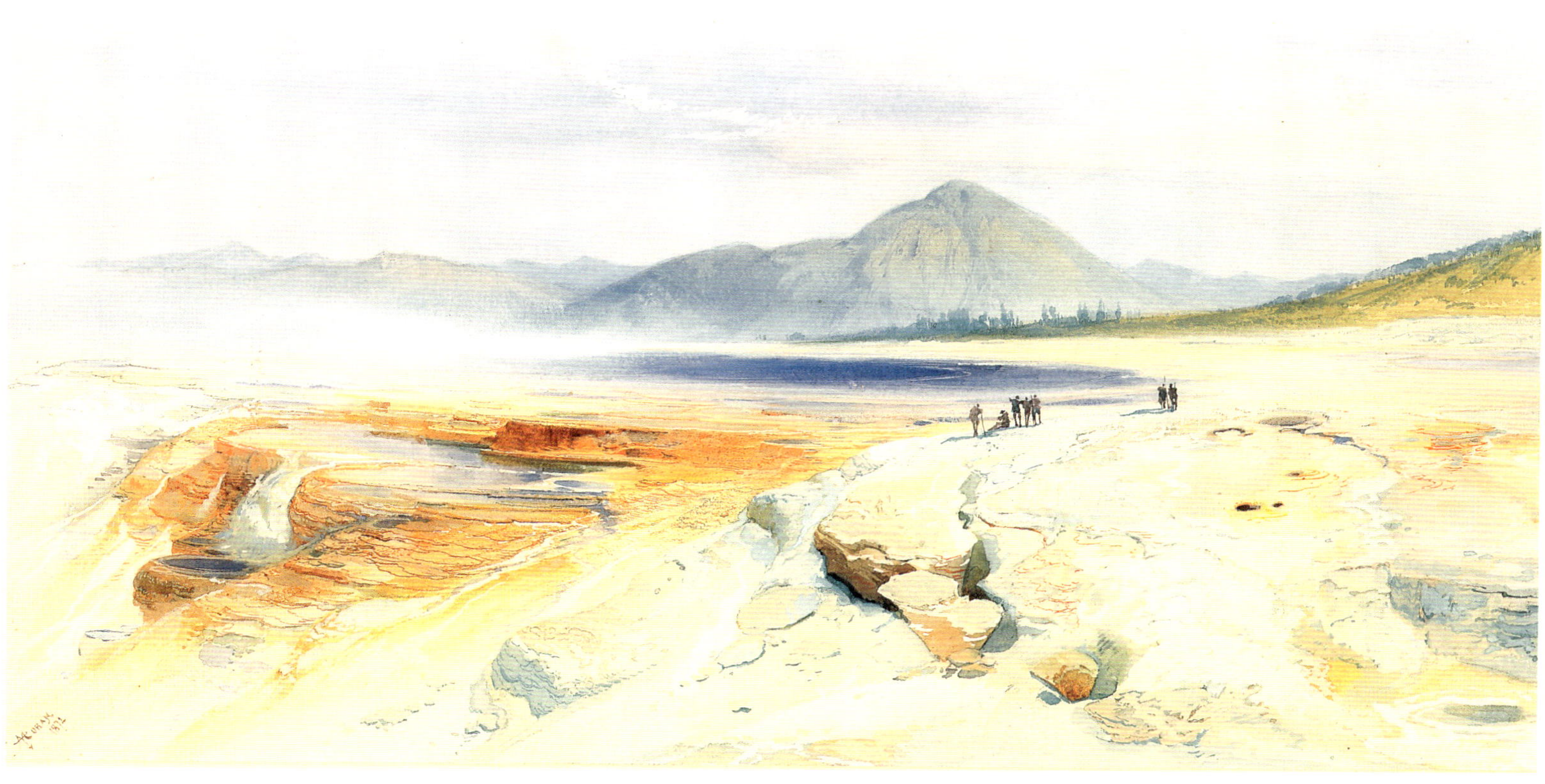

29

The Great Hot Spring, Gardiner's River

1872, watercolor
21.9 x 43.3 (8 5/8 x 17 1/16)
Gilcrease Museum,
Tulsa, Oklahoma
Blackmore Set, no. 6

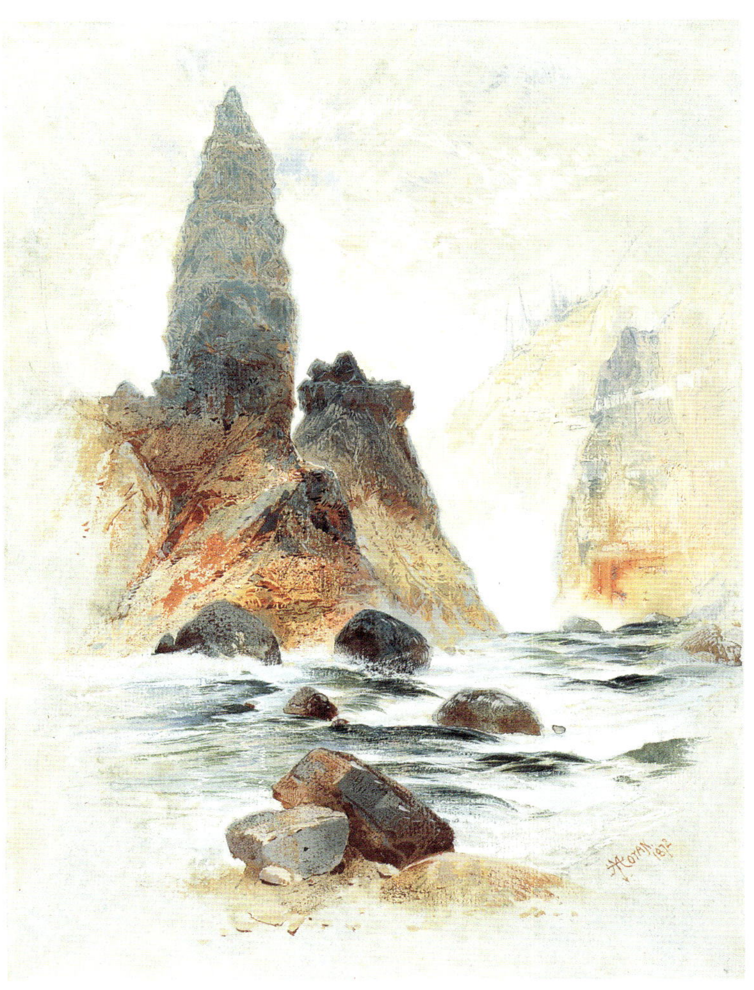

30

The Towers of Tower Falls

1872, watercolor
27 x 20 (10 ⅝ x 7 ⅞)
Gilcrease Museum,
Tulsa, Oklahoma
Blackmore Set, no. 7

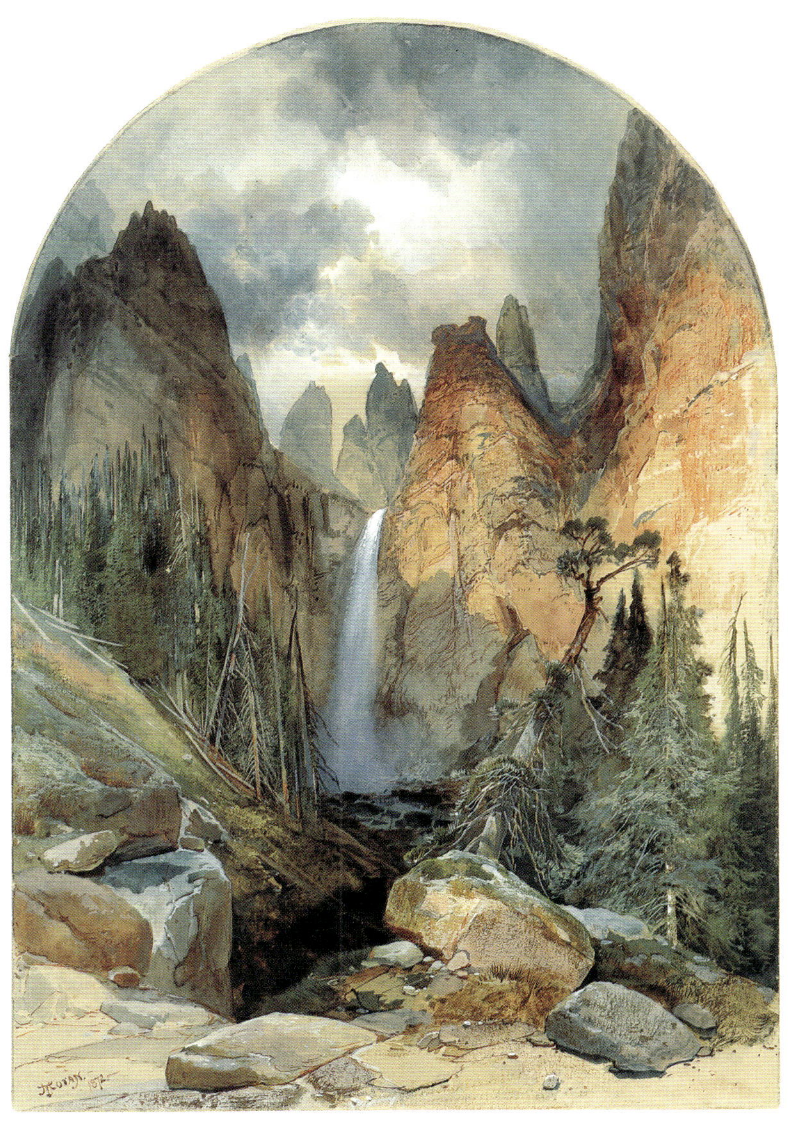

31

Tower Falls

1872, watercolor
28.6 x 19.7 (11 ¼ x 7 ¾)
Gilcrease Museum,
Tulsa, Oklahoma
Blackmore Set, no. 8

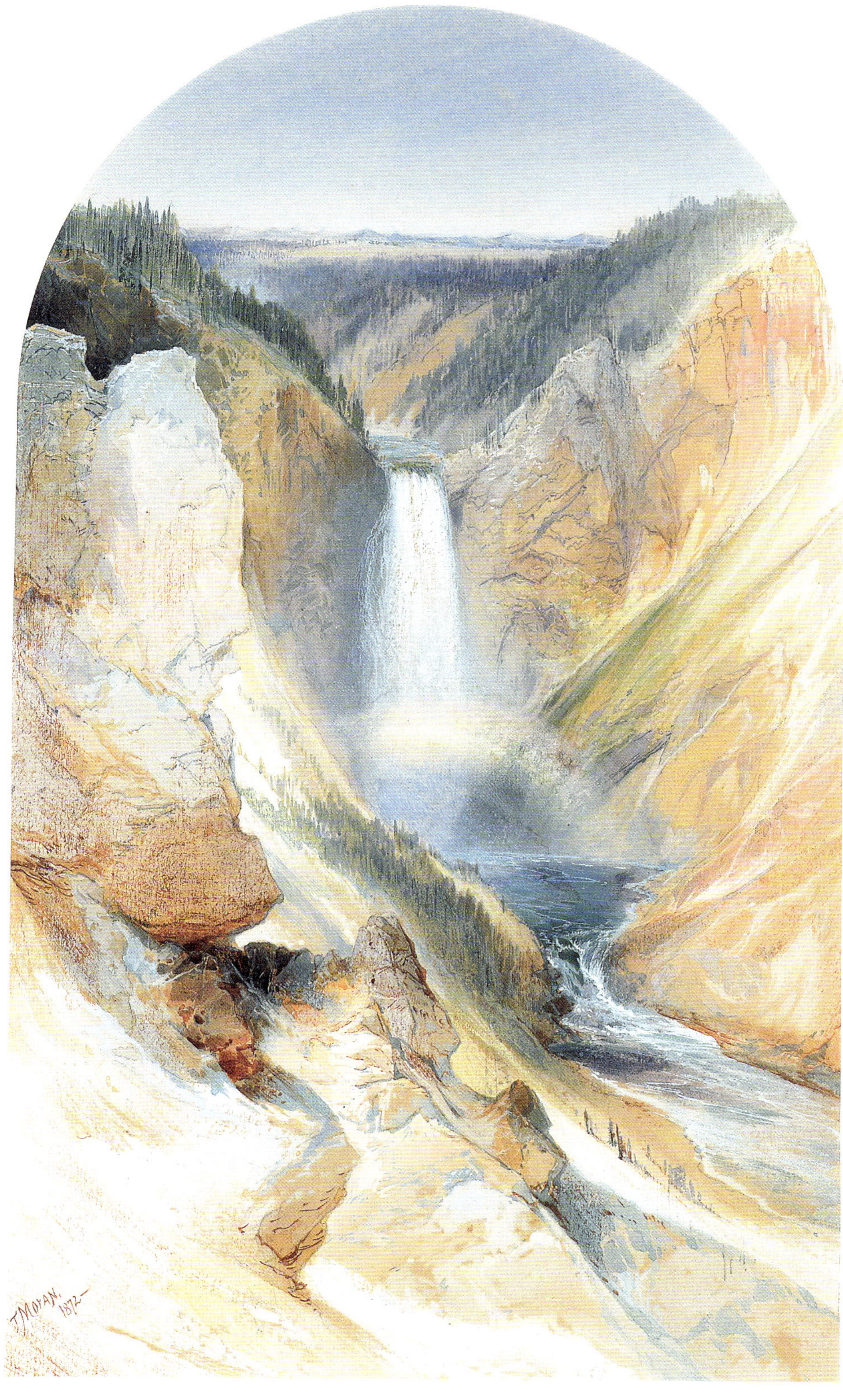

32

Wyoming Fall, Yellowstone River

1872, watercolor
33 x 19.1 (13 x 7½)
Gilcrease Museum,
Tulsa, Oklahoma
Blackmore Set, no. 9

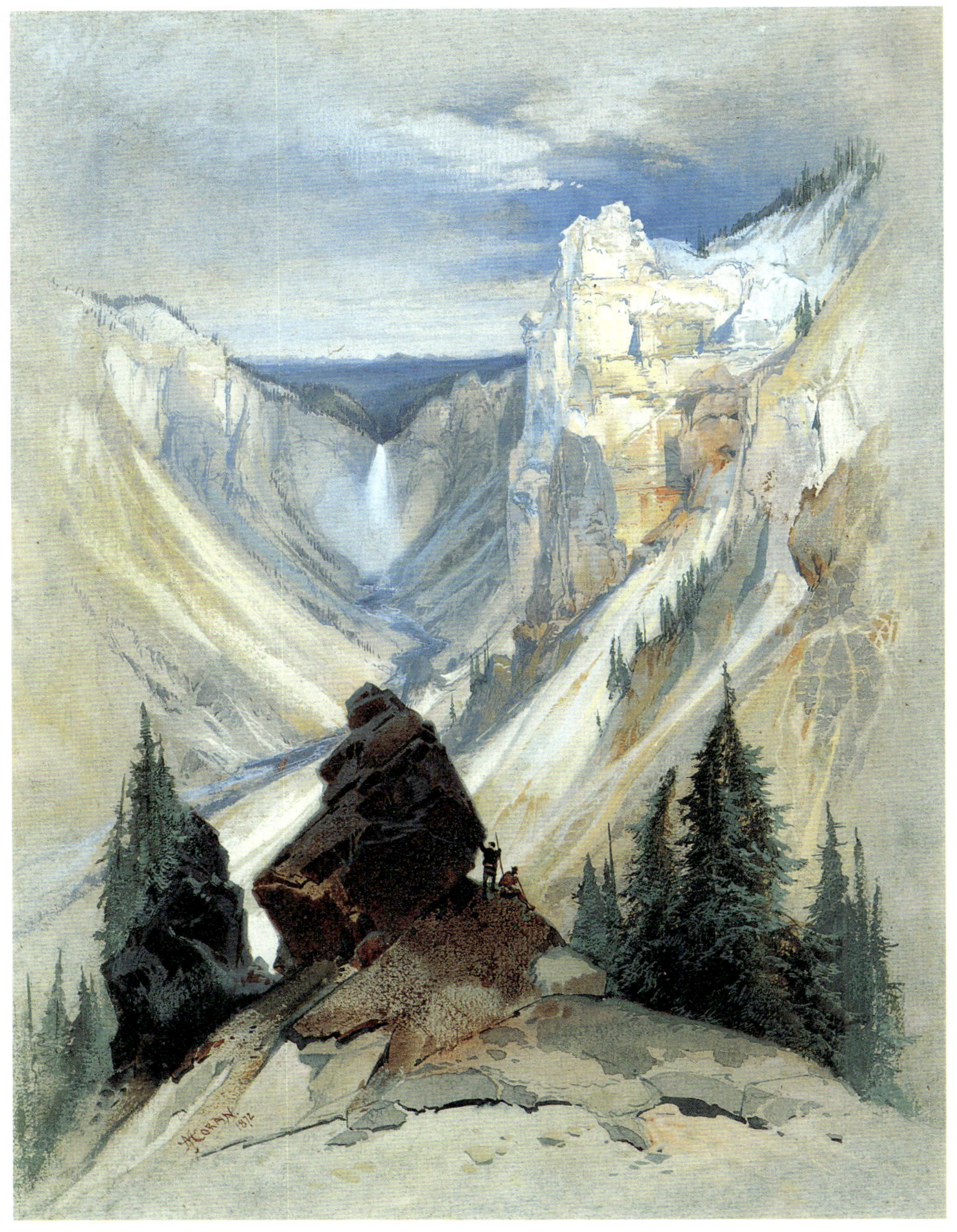

33

The Grand Cañon of the Yellowstone

1872, watercolor
28.6 x 20.3 (11¼ x 8)
Gilcrease Museum,
Tulsa, Oklahoma
Blackmore Set, no. 10

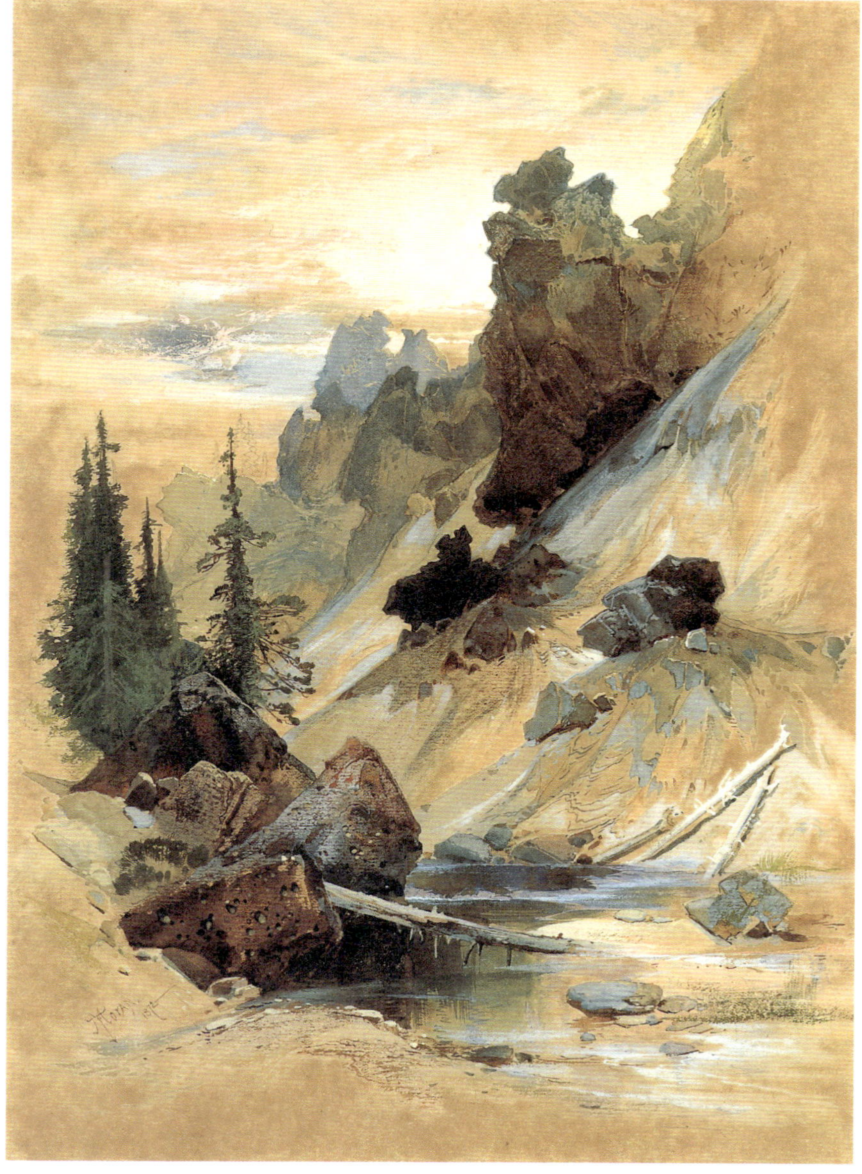

34

The Devil's Den on Cascade Creek

1872, watercolor
33.3 x 24.5 (13 1/8 x 9 5/8)
Gilcrease Museum,
Tulsa, Oklahoma
Blackmore Set, no. 11

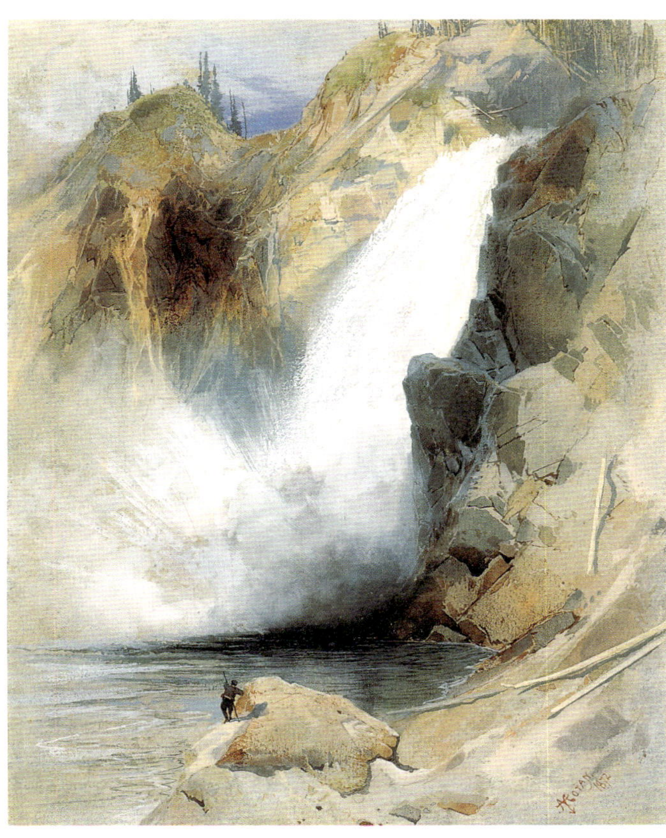

35

The Upper Falls of the Yellowstone

1872, watercolor
26 x 20.6 (10 ¼ x 8 ⅛)
Gilcrease Museum,
Tulsa, Oklahoma
Blackmore Set, no. 12

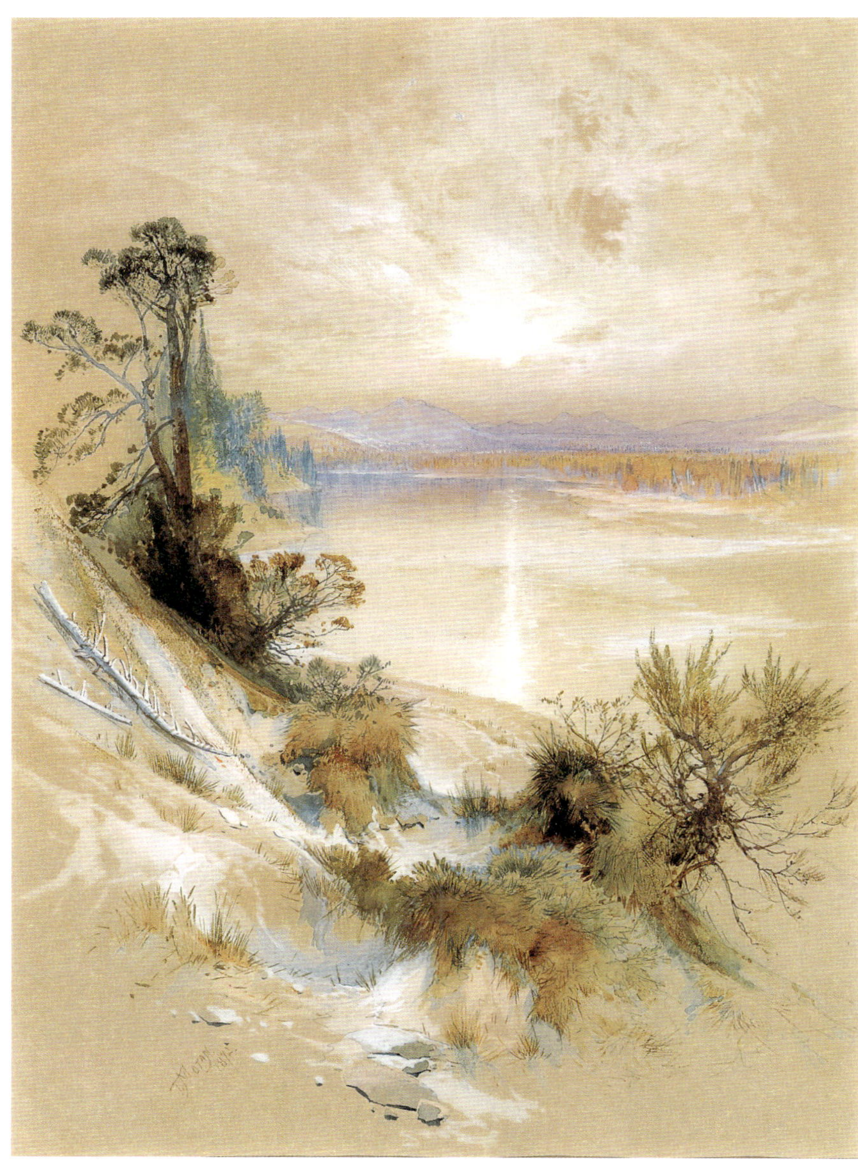

36

The Yellowstone River, at Its Exit from the Yellowstone Lake

1872, watercolor
33 x 24.1 (13 x 9 ½)
Gilcrease Museum,
Tulsa, Oklahoma
Blackmore Set, no. 13

37

The Yellowstone Lake with Hot Springs

1872, watercolor
16.8 x 34.3 (6⅝ x 13½)
Gilcrease Museum,
Tulsa, Oklahoma
Blackmore Set, no. 14

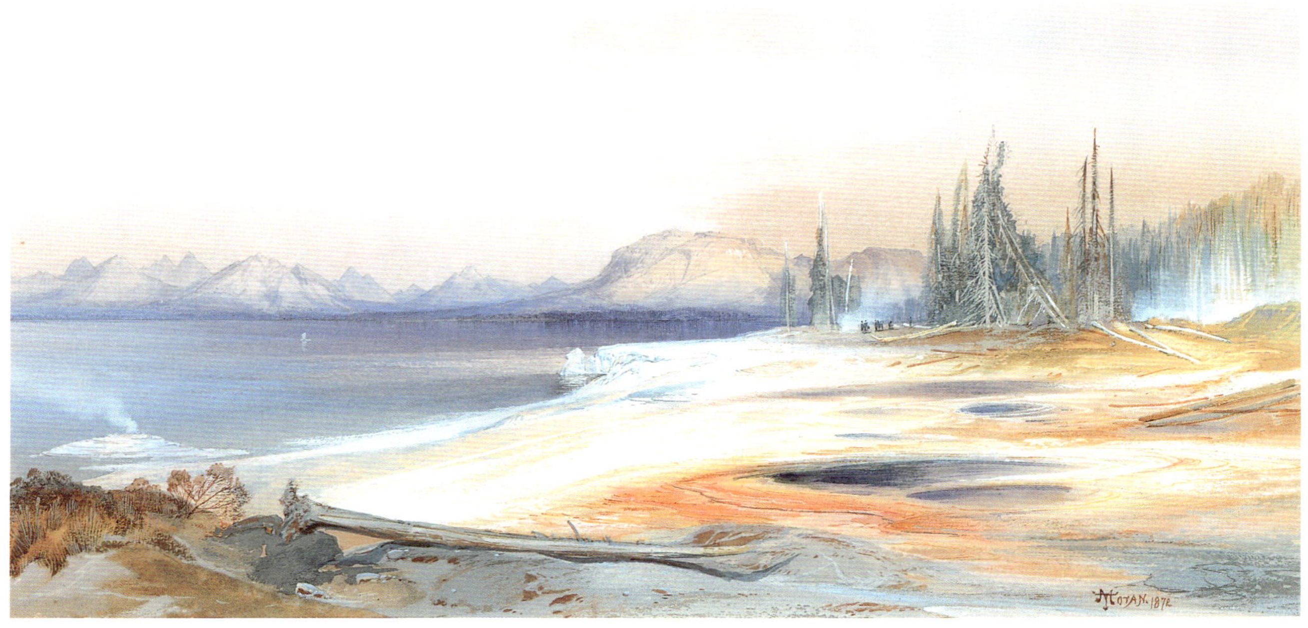

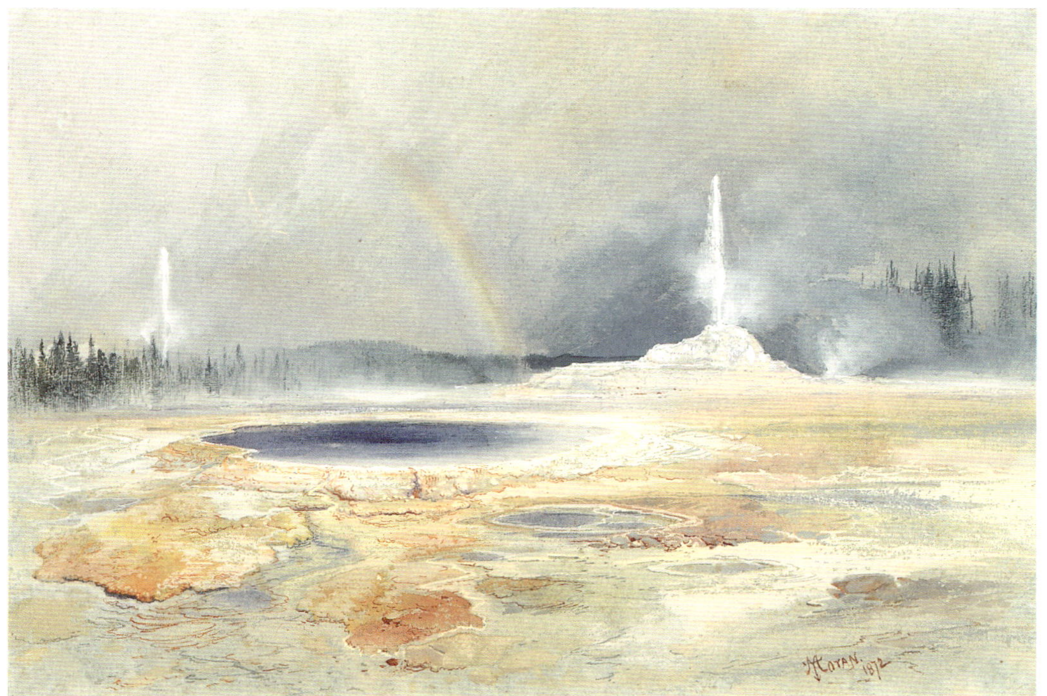

38

The Castle Geyser, Fire Hole Basin

1872, watercolor
19.1 x 27.9 (7½ x 11)
Gilcrease Museum,
Tulsa, Oklahoma
Blackmore Set, no. 15

39

The Grotto Geyser, Fire Hole Basin

1872, watercolor
22.9 x 33.7 (9 x 13 ¼)
Gilcrease Museum,
Tulsa, Oklahoma
Blackmore Set, no. 16

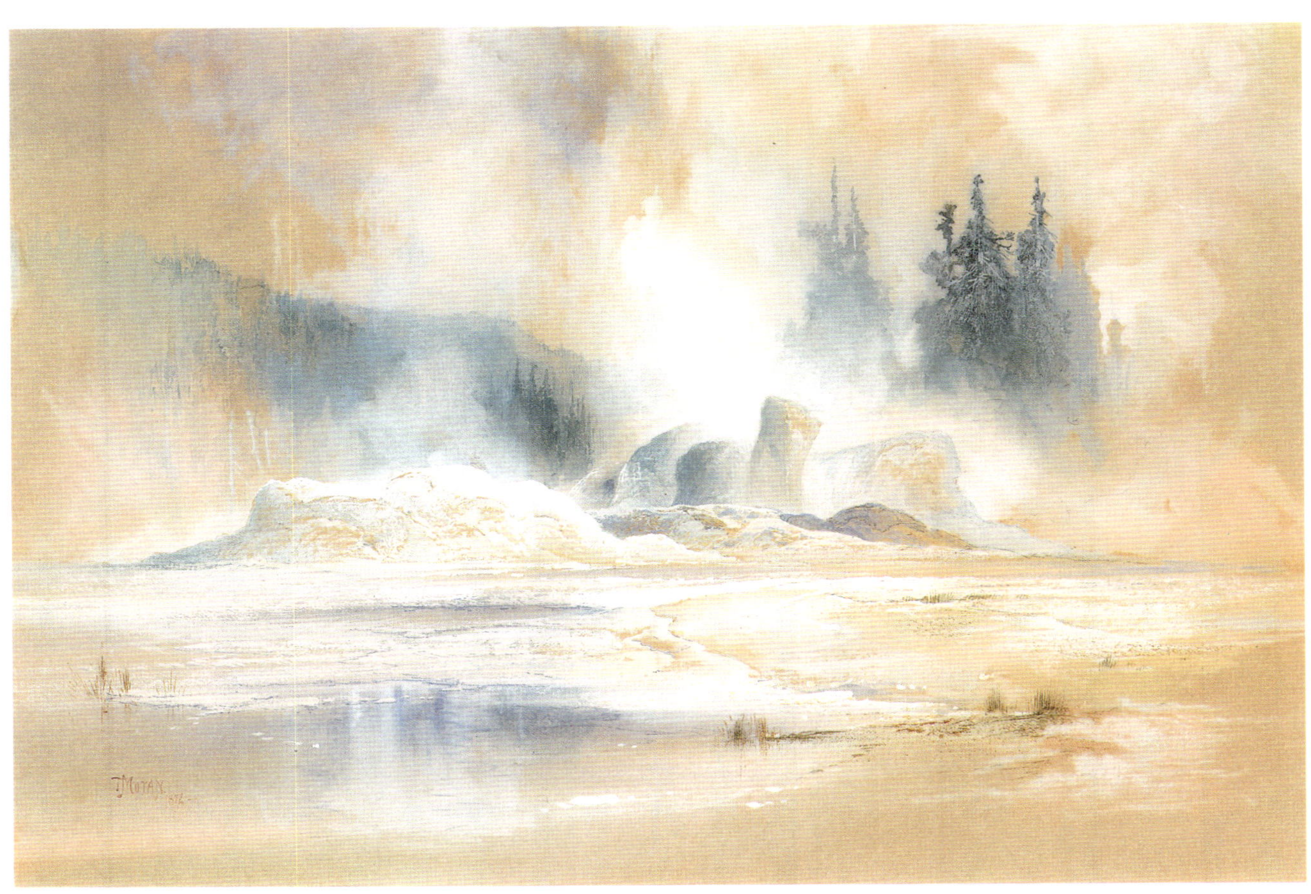

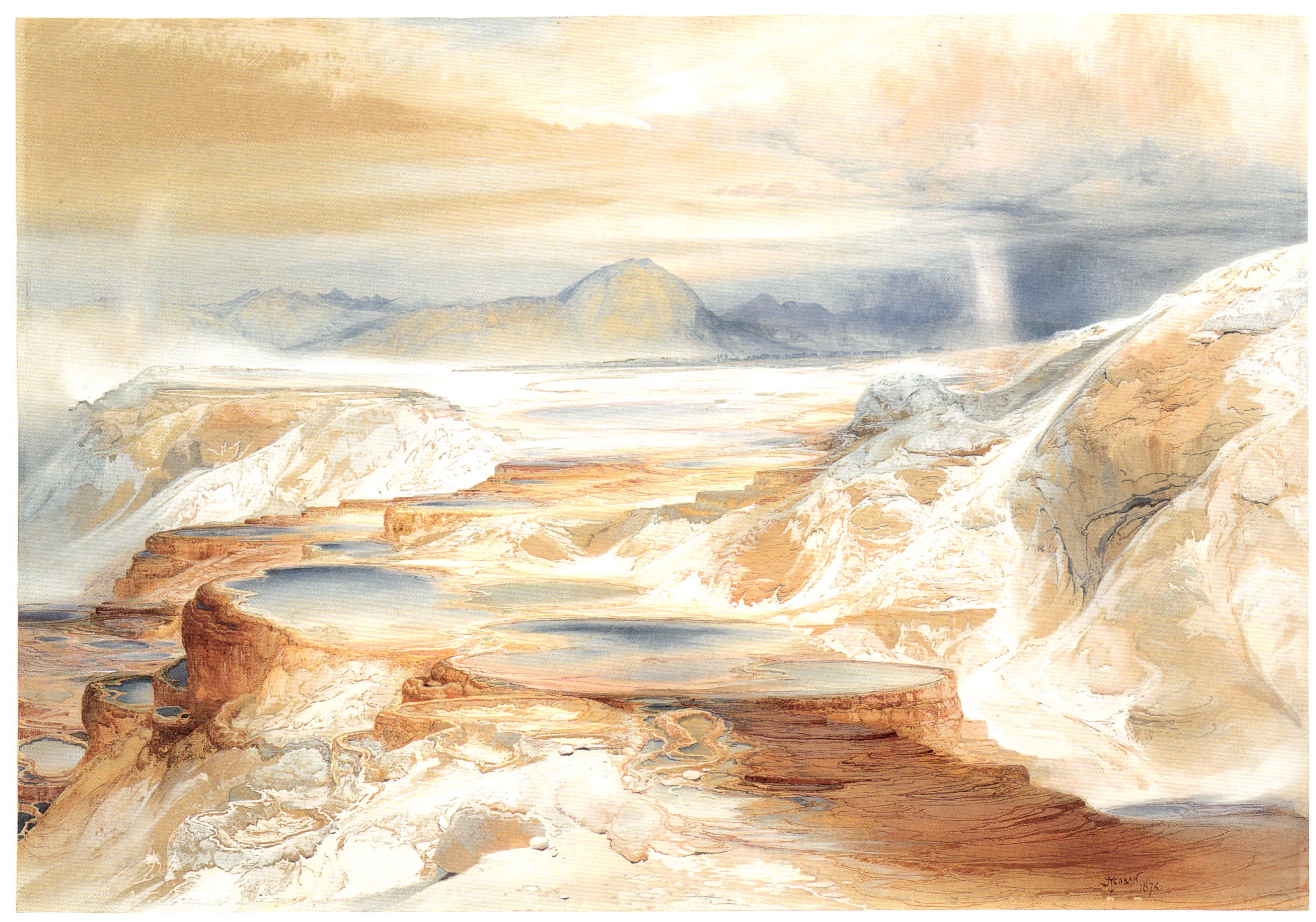

40

Hot Springs of Gardiner's River

1872, watercolor
51.4 x 72.7 (20 ¼ x 28 ⅝)
Private Collection, Washington, DC

Washington only

FROM THE RIVER our path led up the steep sides of the hill for about one mile, when we came suddenly and unexpectedly in full view of the springs. This wonder alone, our whole company agreed, surpassed all the descriptions which had been given by former travelers. Indeed, the Langford party saw nothing of this. Before us arose a high white mountain, looking precisely like a frozen cascade. It is formed by the calcareous sediment of the hot springs precipitated from the water as it flows down the steep declivities of the mountain side. The upper portion is about one thousand feet above the waters of Gardiner's River. The surface covered with the deposit comprises from three to four square miles. The springs now in active operation cover an area of about one square mile, while the rest of the territory is occupied by the remains of springs which have long ceased to flow. We pitched our camp upon a grassy terrace at the base of the principal group of active springs. Just in the rear of us were a series of reservoirs or bathing-pools, rising one above the other, semi-circular in form, with most elegantly scalloped margins composed of calcareous matter, the sediment precipitated from the water of the spring. The hill, which is about two hundred feet high, presents the appearance of water congealed by frost as it quickly flows down a rocky declivity. The deposit is as white as snow, except when tinged here and there with iron or sulphur. Small streams flow down the sides of the snowy mountain, in channels lined with oxide of iron colored with the most delicate tints of red. Others present the most exquisite shades of yellow, from a deep bright sulphur to a dainty cream-color. In the springs and in the little channels is a material like the finest Cashmere wool, with its slender fibers floating in the water, vibrating with the movement of the current, and tinged with various shades of red and yellow, as bright as those of our aniline dyes. These delicate wool-like masses are undoubltedly plants, which seem to be abundant in all the hot springs of the West, and are familiar to the microscopist as diatoms. Upon a kind of terrace covering an area of two hundred yards in length and fifteen in width are several large springs in a constant state of agitation, but with a somewhat lower temperature than the boiling-point. The hottest spring is 162°; others are 142°, 155°, and 156°, respectively. Some of them give off the odor of sulphuretted hydrogen, lime, soda, alumina, and a small amount of magnesia. It is beautifully clear, and slightly alkaline to the taste.

The water after rising from the spring basins flows down the sides of the declivity, step by step, from one reservoir to the other, at each one of them losing a portion of its heat, until it becomes as cool as spring-water. Within five hundred feet of its source our large party camped for two days by the side of the little stream formed by the aggregated waters of these hot springs, and we found the water most excellent for drinking as well as cooking purposes. It was perfectly clear and tasteless, and harmless in its effects. During our stay here all the members of our party, as well as the soldiers comprising our escort, enjoyed the luxury of bathing in these most elegantly carved natural bathingpools, and it was easy to select, from the hundreds of reservoirs, water of every variety of temperature. These natural basins vary somewhat in size, but many of them are about four by six feet in diameter, and one to four feet in depth. With a foresight worthy of commendation, two men have already preempted 320 acres of land covering most of the surface occupied by the active springs, with the expectation that upon the completion of the Northern Pacific Railroad this will become a famous place of resort for invalids and pleasure-seekers. Indeed, no future tourist in traveling over the Far West will think of neglecting this most wonderful of the physical phenomena of that most interesting region. (Hayden 1872a, 389–391)

I AM OVERRUN with work on the Yellowstone & the interest in them seems to increase. I lately finished a very large drawing of Hot Springs (20 x 30 inches) which will be exhibited in New York in a couple of weeks. (Moran to Hayden, 24 Nov. 1872, Hayden IC, NA)

I SHALL SEND down the large water color drawings of the Springs next week to Barlow on Penna Av. [Washington, D.C.] for exhibition for a week or two. It will attract attention I think. (Moran to Hayden, 28 Jan. 1873, Hayden IC, NA)

SINCE HIS LATE sale, the walls of Barlow's gallery look comparatively bare.... The most notable things to be seen there just now are Moran's striking water color drawing of the hot springs on Gardner's river,—a characteristic type of Yellowstone scenery...so surprising and peculiar in its effect as to attract constant attention without the aid of newspaper notice. (*Evening Star* [DC], 15 Mar. 1873)

THE HOT SPRINGS of Gardner River in the Yellowstone Park repeats the startling color effects of Mr. Moran's famous Yellowstone picture with an admirable mastery of technique and perfection of detail. (*Boston Transcript*, 7 Dec. 1875)

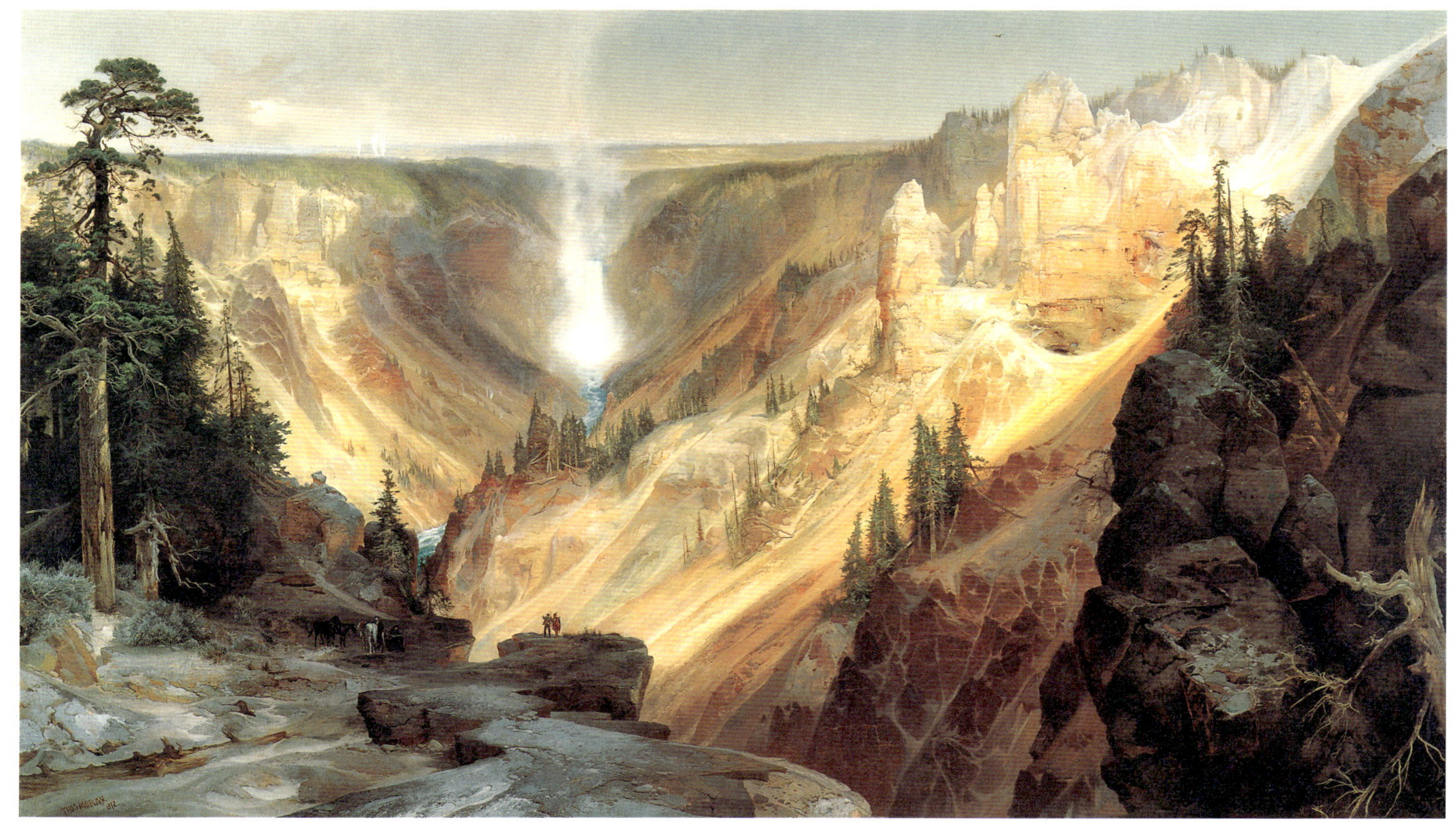

41

Grand Canyon of the Yellowstone

1872, oil on canvas
213.4 x 365.8 (84 x 144)
Department of the Interior Museum

I HAVE BEEN intending to write to you for some months past but I have been so very busy with Yellowstone drawings, & so absorbed in designing & painting my picture of the Great Cañon that I could not find the time to write to anybody. The picture is now more than half finished & I feel confident that it will produce a most decided sensation in art circles. By all artists, it has heretofore been deemed next to impossible to make good pictures of strange & wonderful scenes in nature; & that the most that could be done with such material was to give topographical or geological characteristics. But I have always held that the grandest, most beautiful, or wonderful in nature would, in capable hands, make the grandest and most beautiful or wonderful pictures; & that the business of a great painter, should be the representation of great scenes in nature. All the above characteristics attach to the Yellowstone region, & if I fail to prove this, I fail to prove myself worthy of the name of painter. I cast all my claims to being an artist, into this one picture of the Great Cañon & am willing to abide by the judgment upon it. All my friends in this region declare that it is already a great success, but I cannot feel confident about it, until you have seen it. In fact I cannot finish it until you have seen it, as your deep knowledge of nature & her workings would make your judgment on the truths of the picture of far greater value to me, than that of any other man in the country. Your knowledge of cause & effect in nature, would point out to me many facts connected with the place that I may have overlooked, & if your duties or time would allow you to come & see the picture, you would add another to the many great obligations I am under to you. I was delighted to see Jackson the other day & I believe he was favorably impressed with the picture. I have made two large drawings of the Yellowstone for *Harper's Weekly*, one in the Great Cañon & the other the valley from the lower Cañon [published 5 Apr. 1873]. I am also engaged to the "Aldine" to make five or six large drawings for that paper, but I find but little time for drawings since I commenced the picture.

I now want to make another request of you. I am desirous of placing you on horseback as one of the figures in the foreground. To do this will make it necessary for me to have a photograph of you, the head to be just the right size. A head alone would do, say this size. [sketch] If you have such a photo I would thank you very much for it. I have done nothing on your picture or that for Jim [Stevenson, Hayden's assistant], but you will appreciate the reason. It was of the first importance to me to get the big picture out before any one else dabbled with the subject & when I have done this, you shall not wait long for yours. (Moran to Hayden, 11 Mar. 1872, Hayden IC, NA)

I KNEW THE ARTIST was going to paint a big picture, but I didn't know how big it would be. It was not begun till he had been back from his summer rambles many months. When I think of his carrying that immense canvas across his brain so long, I wonder that he didn't go through doors sidewise, and call to people to look out when they came near.

Watching the picture grow was like keeping one's eye open during the successive ages of world creation—from darkness to the word Good. The outline was thrown upon the bare canvas in a single day. Afterward great streaks of, to me, meaningless color flashed hither and thither. I saw only hopeless chaos. Then blue sky appeared; by and by, delicate indications of cloud, mist, mountain, rock, and tree crept down the canvas, slowly gathering body and tone; till at last the artist's full, glorious Idea shone perfect in every part.

I believe I have had almost as much worry and pleasure over it as the painter himself, although I put brush to it but once. My figure had a vast deal of action, he said, yet, on the whole, he thought it would look better the other side of a pine tree. I take satisfaction in knowing it's there, even if nobody can see it.

I dropped in last evening just about dusk. A shadowy glow from the western window half illumined the big canvas.

"Well, how comes on the Baby?" I said.

"Oh, She's behaved like a lady today. I guess we'll carry her out tomorrow." And so we talked on about the picture in a low tone of voice, as if it were a child lying asleep there in the twilight.

Tomorrow the critics and the public will come rustling and gossiping about it.

I know what some of the critics will do. Because it is a "new departure" in art; because it is something altogether fresh and daring—they will do as the American Jacks tars at Port Mahon did when they saw the French sailors going about with short tails to their jackets—they won't stand that sort of thing. They will "pitch in!"

They will prove that the noble fellow's great-great-uncle, on his mother's side, was hung for horse-stealing; some time in the latter part of the last century. (Gilder 1872, 242)

THE PAINTING OF the "Grand Canyon" measures some fourteen feet by seven, and if ever a subject justified the use of a gigantic canvas surely this one does. The point of sight chosen by the artist is on an elevation several miles below the great fall, towards which we look as the central point of interest in the picture. This fall is of three hundred and fifty feet and ninety feet in width, yet at the distance which we view it and dwarfed by its colossal surroundings of cliff and peak, it is more an object of grandeur than of beauty. But the story of its great volume is suggested by the cloud of spray forever rising from the depths carried upward far above the highest peak, and, as in the picture here the frail background upon which the sun paints rainbows as he nears the West. As the artist places his spectator standing on great rocks in the foreground higher than the summit of the distant fall, he not only overlooks all the intervening gorge, but away beyond the canyon toward the region of the lake itself, and the great volcanic cones ten thousand feet above the level of the sea.

But it is in contemplating this great rent in the earth's surface below the fall, and between that and the point on which he stands, that the spectator's wonder culminates. And he needs to be fortified by the perusal of the statement of the prosaic geologists, to accept this painter's story of forms and color-forms before which those of the Yosemite are tame, and colors which surpass in beauty and variety the Autumn glories of our forests. To right and left the great rocks rise in the most fantastic shapes, more like the forms that clouds take, than anything more subject to gravitation. Shapes suggesting cathedral domes and turrets, peaks and pinnacles, Norman keeps, with battlements and bridges, a thousand forms which play with the imagination whichever way it turns. And yet not alone by these fantastic shapes is the imagination stirred, for color in most unexpected fashion comes into add its completing glory to the wonderland. But who can describe color as it is shown here, where the rocks and the earth from which they rise the great river and the river's bed exhibit hues as many and as brilliant as a stormy sunset: Looking from the heights above, said a spectator, it is as if a million rainbows had made their home among the rocks. The source of all this color is, as the reader doubtless knows, the minerals of the region. Says Lieut. Doane: "The combinations of metallic lustres in the coloring of the walls is truly wonderful, surpassing, doubtless, anything of the kind on the face of the globe.... Promontories stand out in all manner of fantastic forms, affording vistas of wonder utterly beyond the power of description...."

Mr. Moran has chosen, as the hour of the day at which we are presumed to look upon the scene depicted by him, the early afternoon, when only the deeper cavities are in shadow and a broad belt of light traverses the middle distance, bringing out the marvelous coloring of rocks and stones; of the great sloping beds of sulphur, of volcanic ashes and of the various tinted salts which are the soil of this strange land. The rocks of the foreground are in gray shadow. Pines innumerable stud the declivities and top the summits, these dark objects lending brilliance by contrast to the already prismatic tinted rock forms to which they are opposed.

But, however earnest our effort, we must fail to do more than awaken curiosity to see a work so indescribable as this remarkable picture—remarkable as being a great and so far successful effort to depict for us the culminating wonder of a region new and strange to us, as different in all its pictorial elements of form and color, all if it were a sudden revelation of another world, governed by other laws than those of the nature which we know." ([D.O.C. Townley], *NY Mail,* 25 Mar. 1872)

THE CANVAS MEASURES fourteen by seven feet. The artist has chosen a mass of great rocks some distance below the fall as the point of sight, so as to display the fantastic rock-formation, all sorts of shapes...and the brilliant colors...of the vast gorge. Beyond, in the distance, is the huge fall, three hundred and fifty feet high, and ninety feet in width, dwarfed by the colossal surroundings of cliff and peak, its greatness shown only by the volume of spray carried upward beyond the highest cliff; and the point of observation,—the rocks in the foreground,—being higher than the summit of the fall, further beyond a glimpse is given of the region of the lake itself, and the great volcanic cones, ten thousand feet above the level of the sea. (*Boston Advertiser,* 1 Apr. 1872)

WHEN, SOME WEEKS ago, we heard, by the way, that a young and almost unknown American artist was hard at work painting a large picture of the Great Cañon of the Yellowstone River, we heaved a natural sigh, and tried to be resigned. We took it for granted, in our haste, that it was simply a new chapter in the old story. Another acre of canvas was to be spoiled in an attempt to prove that Nature, in constructing the American continent, had gone clean daft, and forgotten her own laws; somebody else was groaning and laboring over mountains that after all would turn out a ridiculous muss; some other mighty landskip [*sic*] was to be boiled down to academic glue in a Dusseldorf saucepan. We had meekly hoped there had been a turn in the tide. We were fresh from contemplating with a not unjustifiable pleasure the ignominious downfall of certain pretenders who had too long abused the patience of good men, and whose tricks and manners were enough to make the Muses turn in their coffins; and it was not a welcome thought that there were others standing ready to take their places, and made the old nuisance eternal.

Thursday evening we found the auction-room of Mr. Leavitt, in Clinton Hall, well filled with people, invited to look at the new picture for an hour or two before it should be sent away to Washington. The artist, a modest and withdrawing man, who had painted his picture in earnest solitude, desired, now that, like spoken words, it was no longer his, it should be placed in the fullest light of publicity, but it was impossible to find a room in which it could be shown for any length of time. At length, after much searching, one hospitable door turned on its hinges, and for a few hours it was given shelter in the dusty auction-room, flanked with two tables filled with a forlorn collection of miscellaneous books waiting their turn to be knocked down to the lowest bidder. There was none of that professional festivity that has come to be the expected thing at all picture exhibitions in New York. There were no flowers, no birds in cages, no delicately printed programmes, no tin tubes, no drapery. A zealous friend, going to the hall in the afternoon to see how things were getting on, was troubled in spirit to find the picture in its bare frame standing up against a back-ground of nothingness. Generous efforts were made to cover this nakedness with a few fig-leaves of upholstery, but it was too late, and a quaint bit of stuff, like a blanket in the alarm of fear caught up, made a satire of the usual paraphernalia of such occasions.

In truth, there was no need of any decorations or allurements. The people who came to see this picture came from curiosity or interest, and the picture kept them there by its own intrinsic truth, sublimity, and beauty. Next to Church's "Niagara"—for to that noble picture the first place must long be given—next to Church's masterpiece, Mr. Moran's "Great Cañon of the Yellowstone" will, we are sure, be received by the best judges in America as the finest historical landscape yet painted in this country. In its origin, no less than by its actual achievement, it deserves to be placed so near to the most famous picture that has as yet come out of an American studio. Mr. Church's picture was the slow result of the most abundant studies; there never was a picture painter anywhere to which went more earnest, more devoted, more joyous labor. And the same earnestness, the same simple-hearted, sincere devotion, the same delight in labor for its own sake, have created Mr. Moran's "Cañon." It is true that it was painted many hundred miles away from the scene it represents, but that was not to be helped. All the multitude of sketches and studies out of which it has been composed were made on the spot, and study and observation have so filled the artist's mind with the scene itself that it does not need the testimony of learned geologists like Mr. Waterhouse Hawkins and Professor Hayden to convince us of the truthfulness of the result; we feel that truthfulness appealing to our own consciousness for confirmation. An eminent geologist said last night: "I have never been to this place, but I will vouch for the scientific accuracy of this picture. I have never seen any place like it, but I know from this picture that it exists. I have seen famous pictures of the Rocky Mountains that I knew must be false, for no such mountains exist, or can exist. This scene is stranger, grander, more abnormal than even the valley of the Yo Semite, but Mr. Moran's picture makes doubts of its possibility impossible." Professor Hayden, in an impromptu description of the picture given at the request of many persons present, showed, point by point, the artist's devoted adherence to facts. Color, form, space, proportion, all were true; if the picture had no other merit it had this, that a mine of scientific illustration is to be found in it.

But the artist seeks for other satisfactions in a picture; scientific accuracy he can find in photographs and surveyor's maps; here in a work of art he asks the added charm of beauty, the light of life. And no one will be disappointed who seeks these on Mr. Moran's canvas, for before he was a scientific observer he was an artist, and it is with the eye of imagination, the desire for beauty, that he has lingered over this majestic scene. The composition is arranged with great skill, and there is a simple reliance upon the intrinsic value of the lines, and forms, and colors, that lay about him, without resort to sensational tricks that we feel most grateful for. The tree drawing is most satisfactory, and the variety, the richness, the delicacy of the color must surprise those who have learned from other artists that Nature in those parts is dressed mostly in hodden gray. There is an exquisite passage of color in the stream as it appears in the center of the picture below the great fall, and again a rich chord in the rocks at the right, stained with the crushed wine of the hidden ores, and veiled with the cream and gold of the sulphur deposit. It is, indeed, a most extraordinary spectacle to which the artist introduces us, but while we stand lost in the wonder of it, we feel that there is a weird beauty about it more impressive and more abiding." (Clarence Cook, *NY Tribune,* 4 May 1872)

TO THOSE WHO have considered Mr. Moran's paintings deficient in warm and truthful coloring, this work of his will be an unexpected pleasure. Nothing can exceed the brilliancy of his coloring in this picture, unless it is the manner in which he has graduated and subdued it in his treatment of aerial perspective. This is most evident where the green mossy banks are seen through their thick curtain of spray in the distance, and in the intense contrast of his cold gray rocks in the shady foreground with the brilliant sunlit walls of the chasm on the other side of the torrent. If it be urged that the almost prismatic tints of the basaltic rocks are too brilliant, not only have we the testimony of Dr. Hayden (a travelling companion of the artist, who was present at the meeting, and volunteered some useful explanations), that in gazing on the scene Mr. Moran was puzzled what colors to select to represent the actual richness of its yellows and red; but any one who has travelled among the porphyry-colored defiles of the Tyrolese Alps, or witnessed an Italian marble quarry gleaming in the sunshine, will bear testimony that there is nothing in Mr. Moran's representation of the rich oxides and sulphurets of rock scenery to surpass the bounds of nature. Upon the whole this great painting will go far to enhance the value of American art, and if Mr. Moran had not already claimed that position this last work of his would unquestionably place him in the very foremost rank of American landscape painters. (*Newark Daily Advertiser,* 4 May 1872)

THOMAS MORAN, one of Philadelphia's artists, has been gradually but surely twining for himself a wreath of laurel, and now, at one bound, by his last, greatest work, the "Grand Cañon of the Yellowstone," he has won the day, and will stand henceforth in the front rank of American painters. This picture, which he has but lately completed, is now on exhibition at the Smithsonian Institution, and will well repay a visit to those who adore the beautiful and the grand.

Every inch of the canvas, which is a large one, glows with beauty in the elaborate finish of the picture, while the lofty and grand ideal of the whole scene is the handiwork of sublimity itself.... To the left, in the foreground, towers a huge tree, beneath whose shade are picketed some horses. Standing upon a huge rock, directly in the front center of the picture, are two human figures, contemplating the awful sublimity of the scene. We could willingly spare this feature of human life. This picture is so awing in its beauty, so solemn in it magnificent grasp of nature, that we would like to think of it, as hedged around by solitude, with no sound save the thunder of the river leaping into the cañon, and no spectator save the solitary eagle, resting on wide spread pinions far above the scene.

Mr. Moran may well feel proud of this last best achievement of his brush. The picture is worthy to rank in the same class with Church's "Andes," and Bierstadt's "Yosemite," and as a faithful portrayal of one of the wildest and most beautiful phases of American scenery, is as much a valuable contribution to science as it is a superb painting. (Unidentified newspaper clipping, c. 11 May 1872, EHL scrapbook)

MR. THOMAS MORAN'S picture of the Yellowstone Cañon is the most remarkable work of art which has been exhibited in this country for a long time.... In the great size of his picture (about twelve feet by seven), the startling character of the geologic forms, the brilliant colors he has had to deal with, and in the manifold planes of distance presented by the view, all needing clear definition yet gradation, and all threatening to claim special and undue attention while requiring to be subordinated and harmonized to the whole—the artist has had a task of no common magnitude. A patent obstacle to the unity of the work, also, is the independent and, so to speak, rival significance and importance of the splendid mass of rockwork at the right, and the cañon proper with its waterfall. It is a favorite theory with some art critics that too great grandeur of subject in landscape painting may be as fatal to success as tameness or insignificance of theme, crushing and bewildering the artist by its splendor or variety, and calling unwelcome attention from its own wealth and immensity to his poverty and littleness of description. In the present work the artist has had not merely one but two such subjects to deal with—the superb cliffs with their exceptional coloring, and the equally superb waterfall, one of the most striking cataracts on this our continent of magnificent objects and colossal proportions. By his masterly arrangement, his ingenious combination and subordination of details, and his boldness yet harmony in coloring, he has blended the two to an impressive and artistic whole, and gone far to demonstrate his own theory, that any, the most imposing of Nature's works is legitimate matter judicious delineation.

The perfect success which Mr. Moran has achieved in this wonderful painting is due to a happy and, we believe, unique combination of gifts and acquirements. It is evident that the painter of this picture possesses in a high degree the poetic instinct, as well as entire familiarity with nature. He not only understands the methods of art but the processes and work of nature, so far as the faithful interpreter of natural scenery must know them. In all the rush of enthusiasm and glow of artistic power, he seems never to forget the faithful manipulation by which absolute truth is caught and fixed in the splendor of picturesque art. It is noble to paint a glorious and inspiring poem; it is satisfying to render nature with firm mastery of technical detail. In "The Grand Cañon of the Yellowstone" Mr. Moran has done both. He has produced a painting which has, we suppose, but a single rival in American landscape art; in certain elements of greatness will be acknowledged to excel even this, and it is not likely soon to be surpassed by the work of any hand save, perhaps, that of Thomas Moran himself. (*Scribner's* [June 1872], 251–252)

THIS GRAND PAINTING, now in Statue Hall, at the Capitol, is the most wonderful picture by far that we have ever beheld—more wonderful even than Bierstadt's "Yo Semite," or "Rocky Mountains"—the scene is so unique, so entirely different from anything ever seen or painted before, and none who listened to Captain Hayden's description of it could imagine for a moment that the wonderful coloring is exaggerated in the slightest degree. Indeed, we sincerely believe the artist when he tells us that quite a large amount of coloring had to be taken out of the cliffs for the sake of giving the true effect in shadow and distance. (Mary E. Nealy, *Sunday Morning Chronicle* [DC], 9 June 1872)

IT IS BUT a few years since the wonders of the Yosemite Valley, now of world-wide fame, have been known to any save Indians; and a shorter time still it is since any one has dreamed of there being scenes, still farther removed from the centres of civilization, that are of even more striking character, although some might claim they were more of the sensational characteristics of nature than its grandeur. But little indeed is known of the wonderful region of the Yellowstone, in Wyoming Territory, and other wild regions in that and Colorado Territory. Occasionally a correspondent has penetrated the region, and sent home glowing words of description, that were often laughed at by the practical New Englander, as high-colored and too sensational. And this is what the prosy and practical will say of Thomas Moran's "Grand Canyon of the Yellowstone," which will be shown to the people of Boston for a short time, by Elliot, Blakeslee & Noyes, 127 Tremont street, previous to its delivery to the Government at Washington, it having been purchased by Congress, at the price of ten thousand dollars, for the adornment of the Capitol.

The coloring of the gigantic walls and domes and pillars, seemingly carved by man's own hands instead of the action of water and convulsions, aided by chemicals and oxides inherent in the earth here, is often gorgeous, frequently giving an antique appearance as of some pile of ancient ruins, covered with fragments of stained glass, or isinglass with a bright fire burning behind it. One might almost doubt the correctness of the coloring of Mr. Moran, and think his eyes were playing him some Aladdin or Cinderella trick of fancy, if it was not for the assertion of Professor Hayden, who says that "the painting is in this regard, as also in its definition of geologic forms, strictly true to nature." Lieutenant Doane, in his report published by the War Department, says, "The walls of the canyon are gypsum, in some places having an incrustation of lime as white as snow, upon which the rays of the sun produce a dazzling effect, rendering it almost painful to look into the gulf below. In others the rock is crystalline, and almost wholly sulphur, of a dark yellow color, with streaks of red, green, and black, caused by the percolations of hot mineral waters, of which thousands of springs are seen, in many instances flowing from spouts high upon the walls on either side. The combinations of metallic lustres in the coloring of the walls is truly wonderful, surpassing, doubtless, anything of the kind on the face of the globe."

As a work of art, of course, the painting is full of sensations; but they are those of nature, and are not objectionable. The distance off beyond the mountains, in its immensity, will take the eye from the colors and the spouting geysers nearer to the spectator; which is the best evidence, after all, of the artistic merits of the work. Every one should see this painting, as it is the revelation of a new world of wonders on our northwestern borders, and one which will please while it will instruct. (*Boston Transcript,* 22 June 1872)

MR. THOMAS MORAN, an artist hitherto better known to the public interested in art by his lithographic drawings, and his drawings-on-the-block for wood-engravers than for his painted pictures, has just finished a work in oils, which, whatever may finally come to be thought of it in its relation to the landscape art of our own time or of other times, cannot but be admitted, by whoever will study it, a work of real artistic and scientific importance. The subject is the Grand Cañon of the Yellowstone River with the Lower Falls, and it is a lively presentment of one of the most wonderful wonders in a land made by Nature, when, to use the language of her child, the artless Pike, "she had her high-heeled shoes on." So faithful to the facts of the place is the picture, that those who have seen both assure us we might as well be on the spot as looking at this canvas.... One does not need to be instructed in art to enjoy it; its appeal is to the general love of nature, to the love of color, and of grandeur in forms and lines. Perhaps, also, it appeals a little to the pleasure we all may have, and not be ashamed of it, in the fact that this wonderful place is not merely a bit of the continent, but is, indeed, the private property of every man, woman, and child of us, being in the very middle of that generous tract of 3,578 square miles which by the energy and persistence of Professor F. V. Hayden, backed by good men and true in both Houses, Hon. S. C. Pomeroy in the Senate, and Hon. W. S. Claggett in the House, has been set apart forever as a public park for the people of the whole United States to walk abroad and recreate themselves. (Cook 1872b, 246–247)

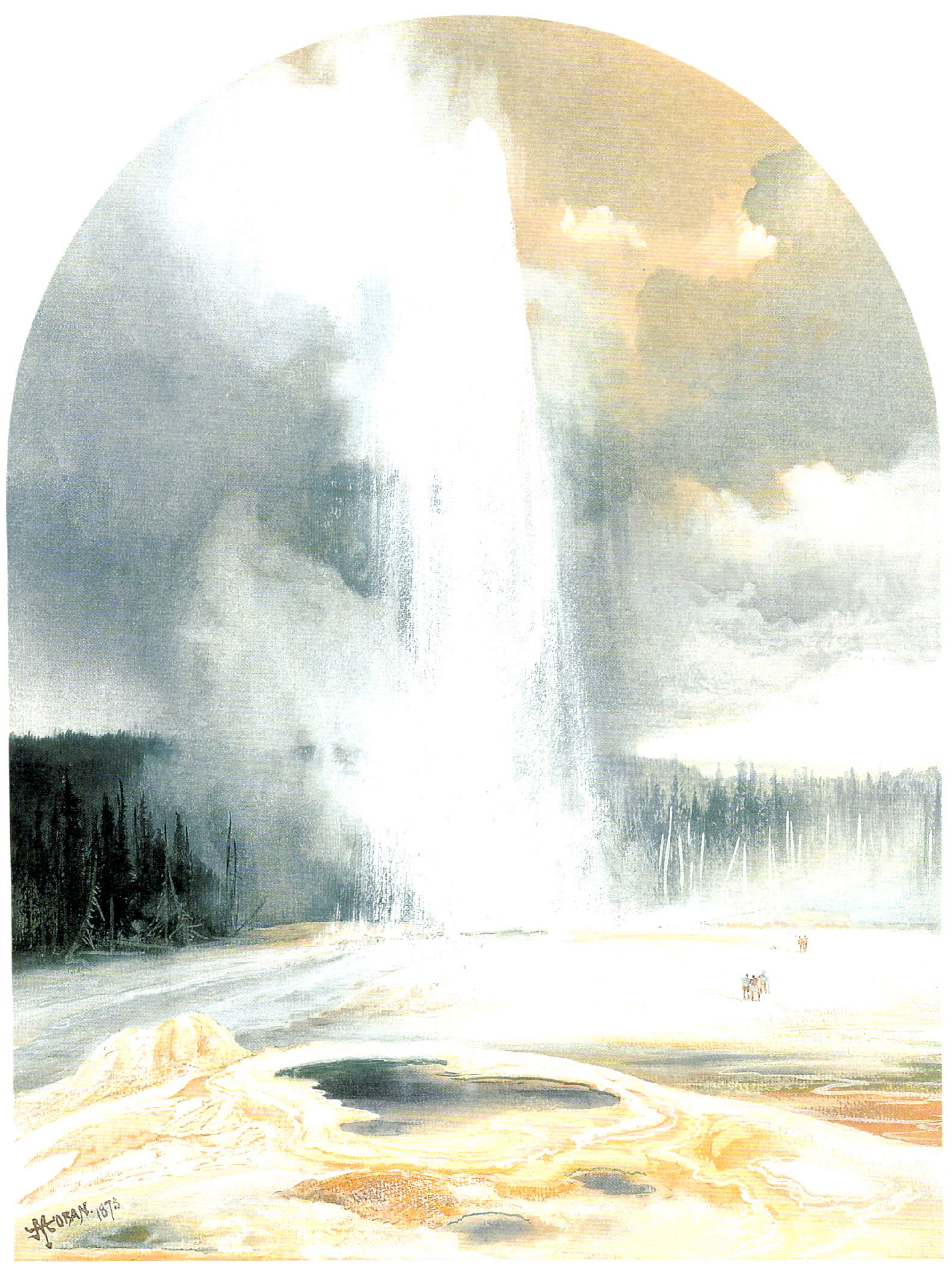

42

Old Faithful

1873, watercolor
45.7 x 34.3 (18 x 13½)
Museum of Western Art, Denver

Washington only

HURRYING DOWN the Firehole, thinking the wonders of the Yellowstone country had been left behind, and anxious only to reach the settlements of the Madison Valley, the expedition of 1871 was startled and astonished to see at no great distance an immense volume of clear, sparkling water projected into the air to the height of one hundred and twenty-five feet. "Geysers! Geysers!" exclaimed one of the company, and, spurring their jaded horses, they were soon gathered around an unexpected phenomenon—a perfect geyser. The aperture through which the column of water was projected was an irregular oval, three feet by seven in diameter. The margin of sinter was curiously piled up, the exterior crust filled with little hollows full of water, in which were globules of sediment, gathered around bits of wood and other nuclei. This geyser stands on a mound, thirty feet above the level of the surrounding plain, its crater rising five or six feet higher. It spouted at regular intervals nine times during the explorers' stay, the columns of boiling water being thrown from ninety to one hundred and twenty-five feet at each discharge, which lasted from fifteen to twenty minutes. They gave it the name of "Old Faithful."
(Richardson 1873, 135–136)

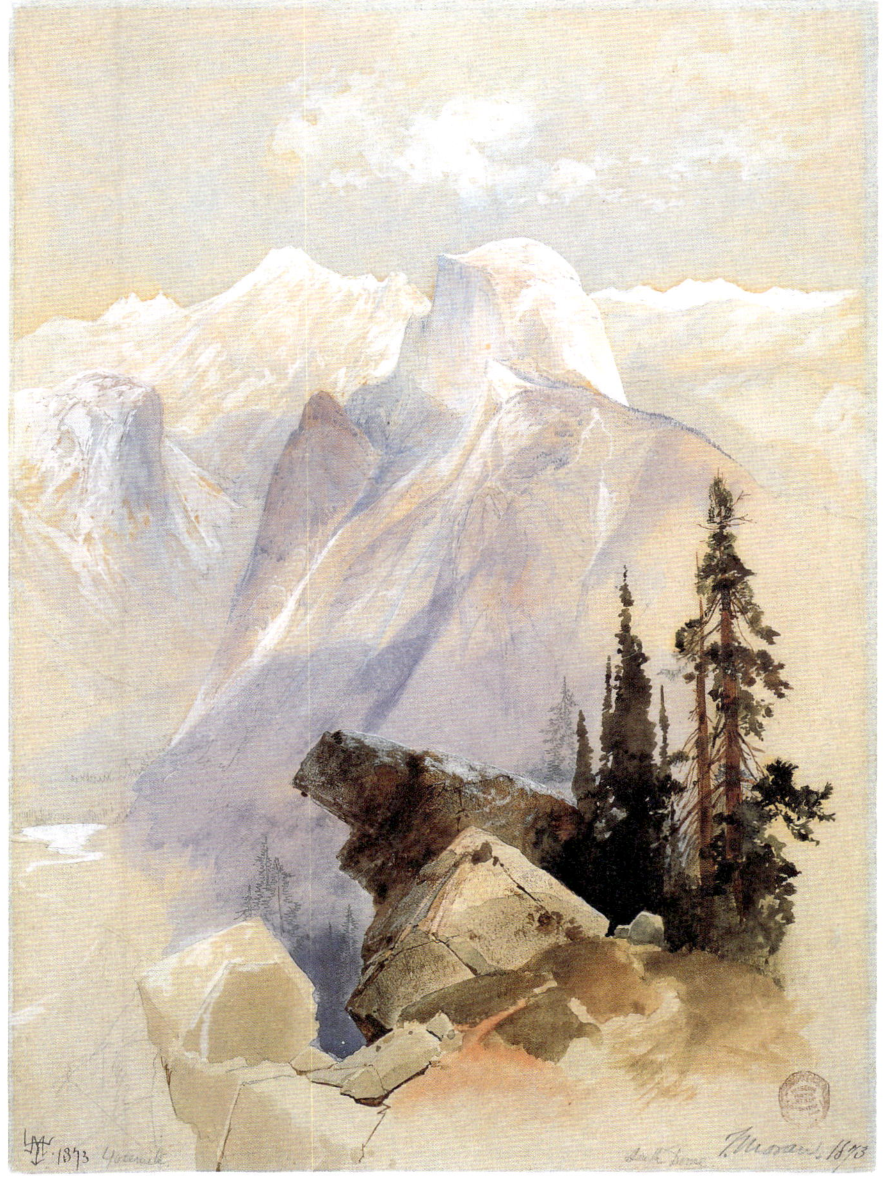

43

Half Dome, Yosemite

1873, watercolor
36.8 x 26.4 (14½ x 10⅜)
Cooper-Hewitt National Design Museum, Smithsonian Institution, Gift of Thomas Moran

Washington only

THE REGION OF the Yellowstone River has come to be regarded as an enchanted land. We have heard so much about its lofty peaks, its upspouting geysers, and the wondrous effects of color which adorn the mountain sides that we are tempted to think that the halo of romance has been cast around the locality, and disbelieve the truth of such pictures as "Cliffs in the Grand Canon of the Yellowstone"...and "The Great Blue Spring, Yellowstone Park." Nor do we wonder at those who declare those tints a palpable intensification of nature, for no one who was not familiar with similar natural phenomena would believe that the hues are, if anything, over somber in color. We have never been up the Yellowstone, but a few months have elapsed since we stood in Geyser Canyon, in California, and reasoning from the information we obtained there we can thoroughly endorse Mr. Moran in the rendering of the play and brilliancy of color he has put upon his paper. But he must change his key of color when he comes to deal with the domes of the Yosemite Valley, for his sketch from "Glacier Point"...is anything but true to nature. (*NY Mail,* 18 Feb. 1873)

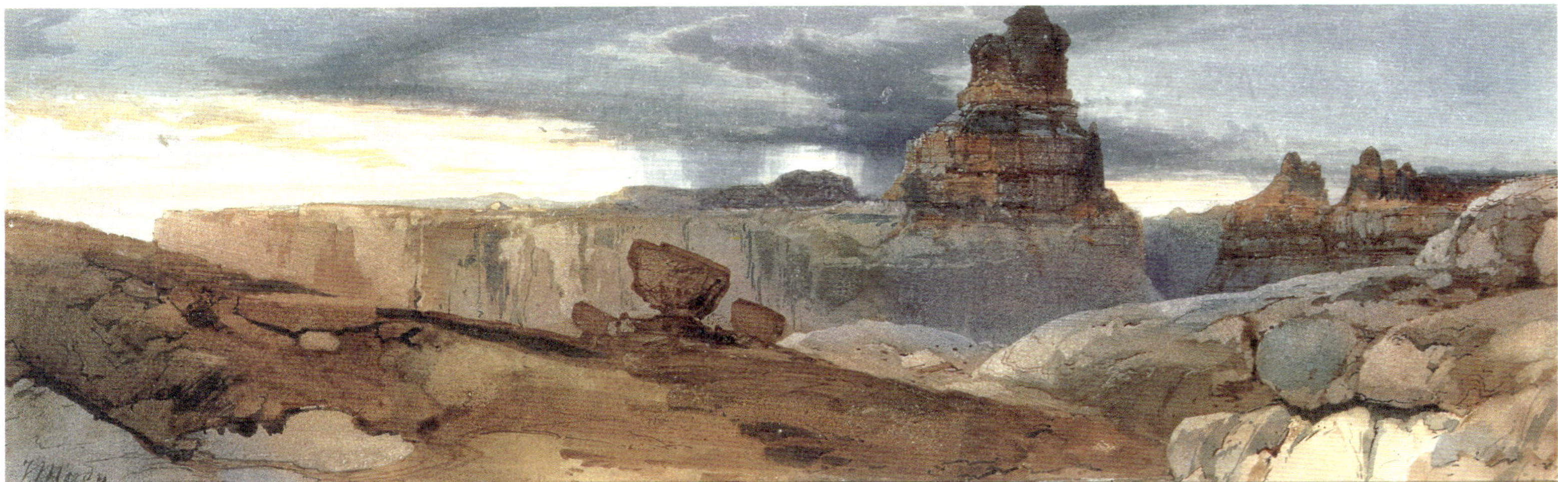

44

Shin-Au-Av-Tu-Weap (God Land), Canyon of the Colorado, Utah

1873, watercolor and pencil on paper
12.2 x 37 (4 3/16 x 14 9/16)
National Museum of American Art, Smithsonian Institution, Gift of Dr. William Henry Holmes

Washington only

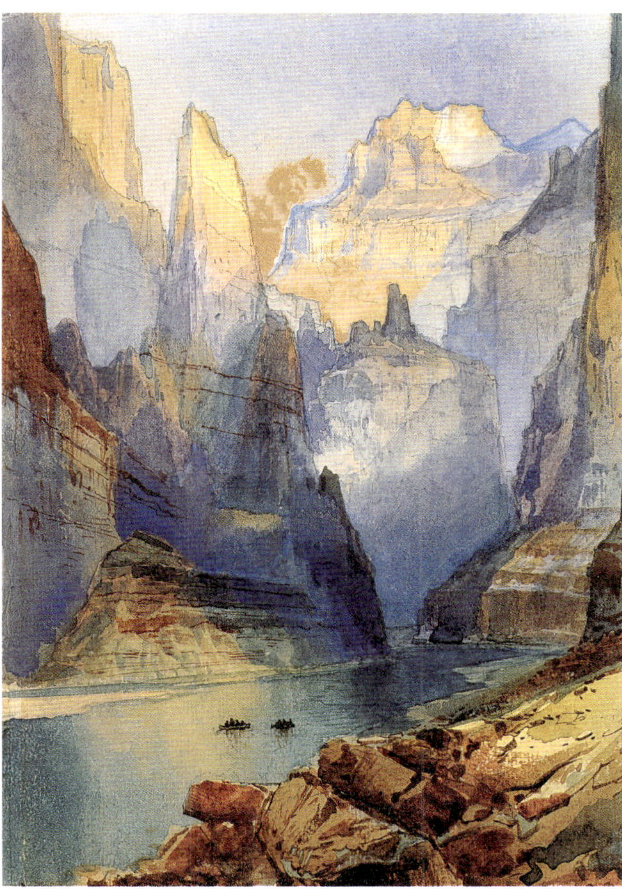

46

Zion Valley

1873, watercolor
21.6 x 15.2 (8 ½ x 6)
Gilcrease Museum,
Tulsa, Oklahoma

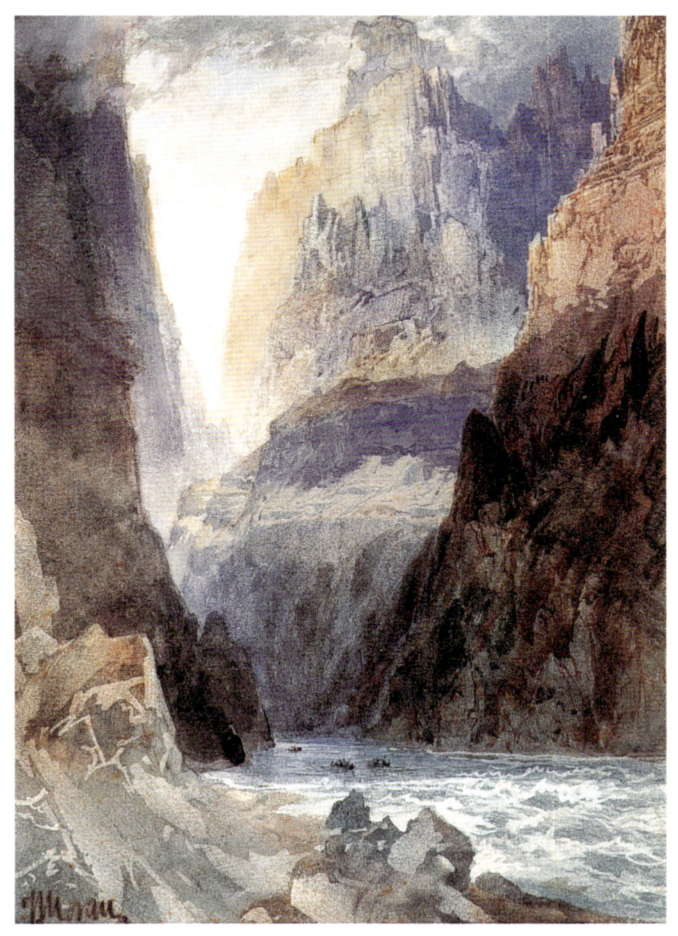

45

Zion Canyon

1873, watercolor
21.6 x 15.2 (8 ½ x 6)
Joan and Jerry Blank,
Miami

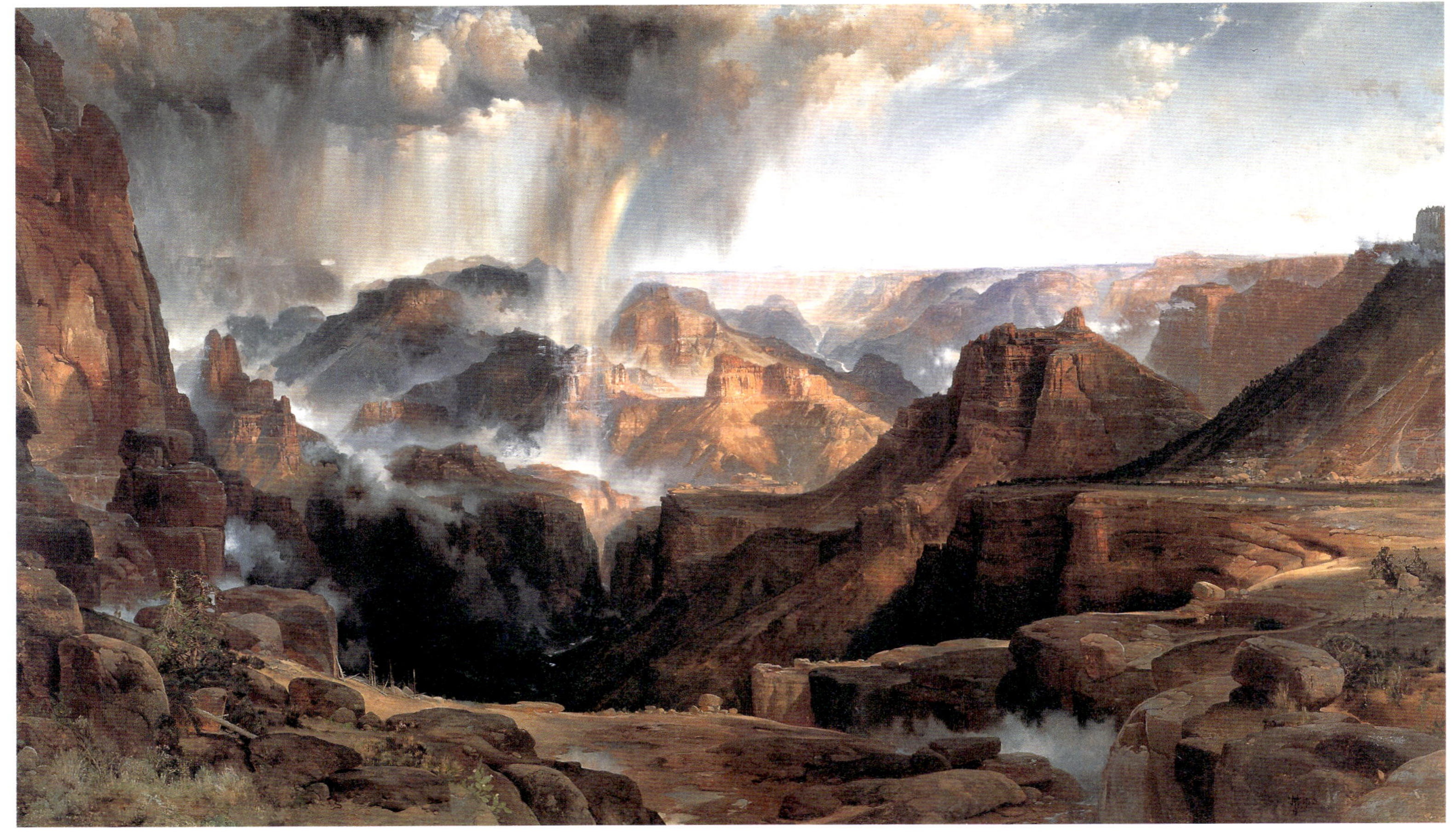

47

Chasm of the Colorado

1873–1874, oil on canvas
213.4 x 365.8 (84 x 144)
Department of the Interior Museum

MR. THOMAS MORAN acted like a good neighbor and townsman in giving the first view of his new and grandest picture, the *Chasm of Colorado* to our Newark people....The verdict was unanimous and four or five hundred people passed an evening to be remembered, in studying, criticizing and finally applauding this remarkable picture. When Mr. Moran painted the *Yellowstone* now in the Capitol at Washington and the property of the Government, the remark was made that it was a 'brave picture,' brave because in its very truth of coloring it seemed to be an absurdity. So novel was it in all its effects that it needed some sort of an affidavit to certify its genuineness. That it found within itself, because such true perspective and faithful handling of natural tints of cloud and sky as we are familiar with could not have been worked out by a dishonest hand, and so those who looked believed in its astounding colors.

There is something of the same bravery in the *Chasm*. A picture, the back ground of which is more than a hundred miles from its foreground, in which the field is so large that no standard of comparison, like a human figure, can be introduced, yet which shall be so grandly filled in as to compel belief, is a bold task. Yet the eye rests happily on all its thunderous beauties, the cool foreground, the middle ground crowded with cities and stately castles wrought by the hand of God, where no man ever dwelt, and the flat sky-line crowned with clouds beyond. If in any of these effects we are cheated, it is a charming deception. (*Newark Daily Advertiser*, 1 May 1874)

THE GRAPHIC SAYS of Mr. Moran's *Chasm of the Colorado:* This, his latest work, is equal in vigor to any yet produced by him. Sensational, indeed, it is, and there may be some who will carp at it for being that; but it may be well to remember that in art the "sensational" is a legitimate element, else to what intent and purpose had Milton delineated Satan and Dante Hell?...This *Chasm of the Colorado* ...is volcanic, basaltic, and—begging Nature's pardon for being so familiar—more suggestive of a grand transformation scene gone wild than of anything else that we can hit upon at short notice for a comparison. The forms everywhere are of the most fantastic and wizard mould. Some of the peaks look like those old feudal castles that from their dizzy heights frown upon the reaches of the Rhine. In true relation with the tremendous spasm of rocks is the phase of sky which the artist has introduced. It is somewhat phenomenal and bears evidence of having been a witnessed fact. Not exactly a water-spout, but something like one, a column of water comes sheer down upon the chasm from a rolling bank of clouds. It is evidently a very strange region, this Chasm of Colorado, and Mr. Moran has rendered its features with appreciative force...It has become customary to speak of this Colorado region as the "Switzerland of America," but really we do not see what the comparison has to rest upon. For native savageness these volcanic tracts of the great West are as different from the Alps of Europe as are the wild Comanches or Sioux from the "merry Swiss boy" who blows his Alpine horn among the reverberating rocks of his mountain home. Mr. Moran has done well to select these strange and startling phases of American nature for his canvasses. The time cannot be far distant when to visit those scenes will be as much "the proper thing" as it now is to whittle one's name upon the Pyramids of Egypt. (*Newark Daily Advertiser*, 13 May 1874)

THE HEIGHT and depth of many of the peaks and chasms of this region, as we are told by the explorers, are measured by hundreds of feet, in some cases by thousands, yet it is difficult for the most enthusiastic admirer of Mr. Moran's works, even if gifted with the most ardent imagination, to realize this fact by an inspection of his picture. In fact, the painting does not impress us in the remotest degree with the idea that we are looking on some of nature's grandest and noblest works, nor even that we have before us hundreds of square miles of country. It rather gives us the belief that we are looking through a rocky pass of limited dimensions. It is true that we have been told in explanation of this apparent shortcoming on the part of the artist, that the atmosphere of these regions is so pellucid and rarified that heights of 500 feet look to be but seventy or eighty, and that a mountain, distant fifty miles, appears as if it could be reached in a morning's walk. Further, that amid these arid regions grow no trees or shrubs, by which the heights of the surrounding peaks can be compared. All this, though true enough, must be taken for what it is worth. It is for the artist to discover some means by which the comparative height of his peaks and the depth of his chasms will become so apparent as to impress the beholder with the natural grandeur of the scene depicted. This Mr. Moran has failed to do, and consequently he has failed in producing a true work of art. The technical merits of the composition are sufficiently good, though it may be doubted where the Chasm of the Colorado ever displays such brilliant tints as are to be found on the artist's canvas. (*NYT*, 18 May 1874)

MOST PERSONS unfamiliar with the scenery in that part of the country imagine that it must be exaggerated, both in forms and color; but this is not so. From what we have ourselves seen of nature in the interior, as well as from the artist's assurance, we are satisfied that the picture is underwrought rather than exaggerated in either respect. To be sure, in general effect not less than in detail, the canvass looks like a gorgeous memory of dreamland, but it is in reality a faithful transcript of nature, and as such is not only well worth seeing, but deserving of careful study. This picture ought to be owned by government as a companion to the Yellowstone landscape in the old House hall, by the same artist. (*Evening Star* [DC], 13 June 1874)

THE SUBJECT OF Mr. Thomas Moran's latest large picture is Titanic. It represents a broken and deeply furrowed mass of rock, leading by devious angles from the main cañon of the Colorado River, near the line which separates Arizona from Utah. Standing before the painting, the first impression is of chaos, confusion....

In spite of the sunlight here and there, and the blue sky beyond the tumult of the showers, the sensitive spectator will be dismayed. This seems to be a glimpse of another planet; the weary and troubled eye longs to find repose in some sweet pastoral landscape, which, besides this enormous grandeur, would dwindle into absurd pettiness.... All is terrible, fantastic and weird. And though the marvelous faithfulness of detail attests the photographic accuracy of the picture, one must be smitten with a sudden incredulity as to the actual existence of the scene; it may have been the grotesque glimpse of a dream!

The manipulation of the work is absolutely perfect. The texture of the rocks is a miracle of art. It is not paint that one sees; it is a description so accurate that a geologist need not go to Arizona to study the formation. This is geology and topography. That it is also bold to audacity, is apparent from what has been already said. Few men have ever undertaken a work which might have so easily been a monumental failure. Few men could have achieved so signal a success; let this be said to the artist's honor. (*Scribner's* [July 1874], 373–374)

MR. THOMAS MORAN, who two years ago painted a remarkable picture of the Cañon of the Yellowstone,—now the property of the nation,—has just completed another large work representing the *Chasm of the Colorado*....

The subject of this important work is the chasm or pit worked by the Colorado River in the sandstone rock over which it flows at this point, as the subject of the other picture was the chasm worked in the limestone rock by the Yellowstone River. The landscape of Mr. Moran's first picture was equally awful and desolate with that shown us in the present work, but its terror was lessened by the beauty and variety of the color with which nature veiled her work of change and destruction. Here, we have no such charm. We are led into a region where the eye has hardly a resting-place, no resting-place, in fact, unless it be turned upward to the sky. For this serene heaven—serene except where in one portion it darkens with the wrath of thunder clouds and the stream of deluging rain—looks down upon the very pit of hell....

Did Dante in his wanderings ever see such a country? Perhaps Vesuvius or Etna might show something as full of fear if one climbed down into their craters. But even there, the limited area of the desolation would not allow the mind to forget utterly the supreme loveliness of the nature that lies so near. Here, there is no loveliness for hundreds of miles, nor anything on which the healthy human eye can bear to look (the scientific eye excepted), and this scene is only the concentrated ghastliness of a ghastly region....

As there is no claptrap about Mr. Moran, so there is none about his pictures, and the faults we discover in this latest work are the result of trying to do too much—at least, this is our way of explaining the difficulty. The picture not only crowds too much incident into its comparatively narrow frame, but the subject it deals with is one that never should have been attempted—partly because it is impossible to do justice to it, and again because art is not concerned with it, if it were possible. Mr. Moran showed wiser in his first picture. He chose a simpler subject, or at any rate one with more unity. Perhaps we may go so far as to say that the first picture had a subject, and this one has none. It was said by one who looked at it, "There is no use in trying to paint all out-of doors."...

Though the composition is muddled and confused, and the color monotonous, and the sense of height absent, yet there is distance wonderfully expressed, most exquisite painting of sky and cloud over the plateau at the right, and lovely lightness and motion in the mist that forms in the clefts of the rocks, and rises to be dispersed in the palpitating heat of the upper air. All that is most difficult to be expressed by paint is expressed here with a skill that approaches perfection, and if, as we think, Mr. Moran has failed to cope with the difficulties of his subject, he has yet in this picture given new evidence, if any were needed, of his ability to deal with the beauty and the serenity of the nature we all know and love. (Cook 1874, 375–377)

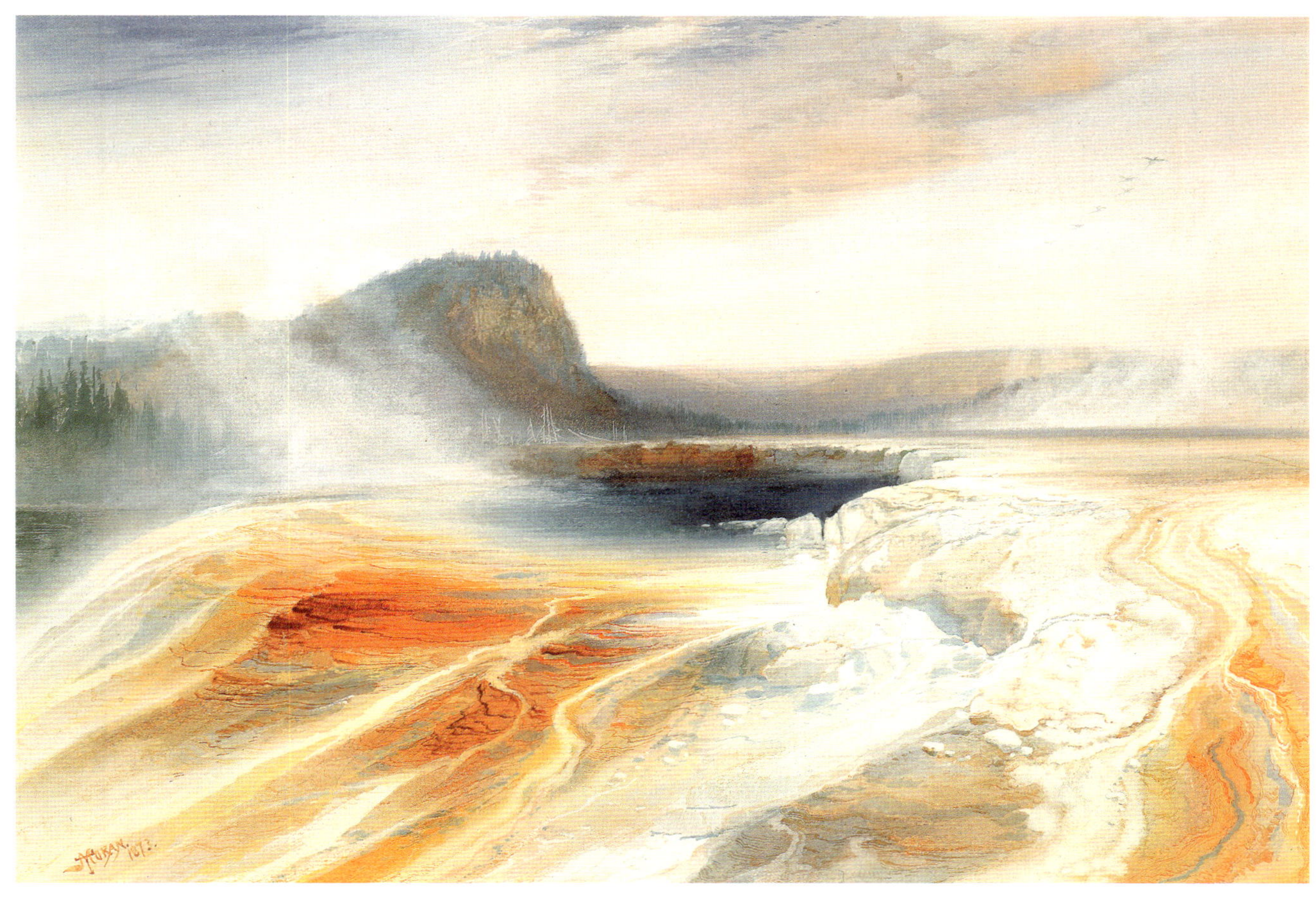

48

Lower Geyser Basin

1873, watercolor
24.1 x 34.9 (9 ½ x 13 ¾)
Gilcrease Museum,
Tulsa, Oklahoma

49

Shoshone Falls, Idaho

c. 1874/1875, watercolor
25.4 x 35.6 (10 x 14)
The Chrysler Museum,
Norfolk, Gift of Mr.
Hugh Gordon Miller

Washington only

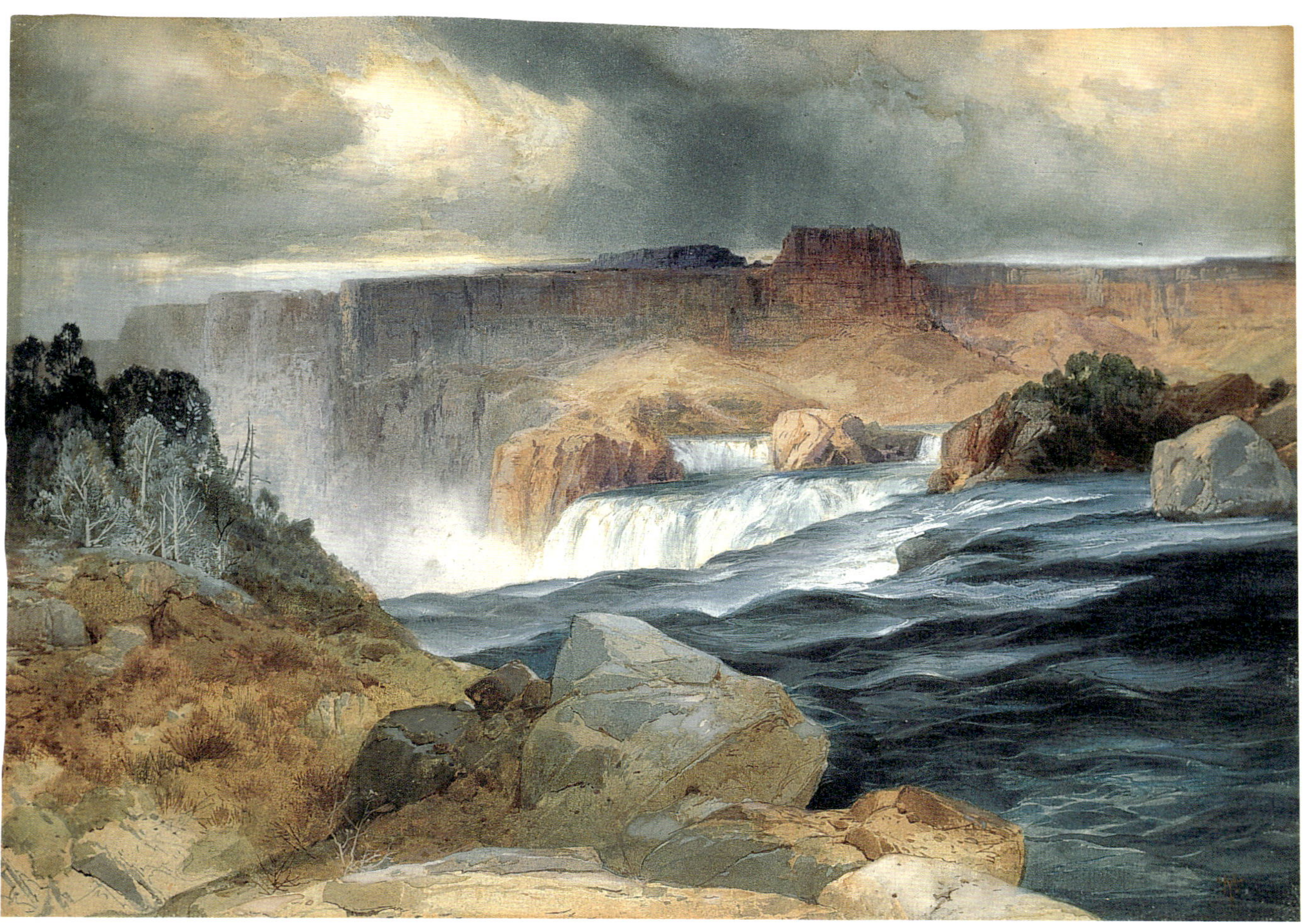

See Appendix 1.

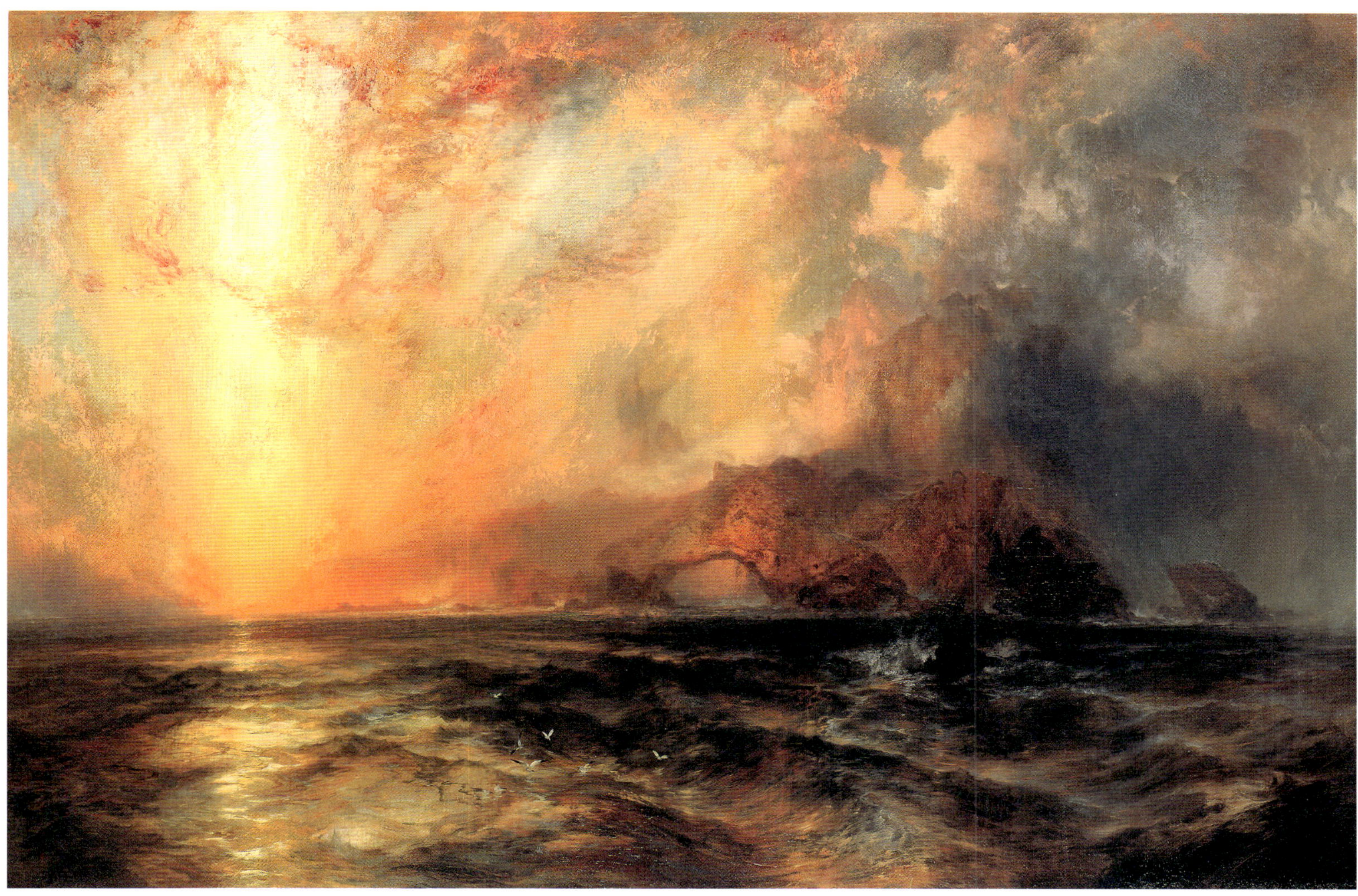

50

"Fiercely the red sun descending / Burned his way across the heavens"

c. 1875, oil on canvas
84.8 x 127.2 (33 3/8 x 50 1/16)
North Carolina Museum of Art, Raleigh, Purchased with funds from the North Carolina Art Society (Robert F. Phifer Bequest)

The Song of Hiawatha, Canto IX

On the shores of Gitche Gumee,
Of the shining Big-Sea-Water,
Stood Nokomis, the old woman,
Pointing with her finger westward,
O'er the water pointing westward,
To the purple clouds of sunset.
  Fiercely the red sun descending
Burned his way along the heavens,
Set the sky on fire behind him,
As war-parties, when retreating,
Burn the prairies on their war-trail;
And the moon, the Night-sun, eastward,
Suddenly starting from his ambush,
Followed fast those bloody footprints,
Followed in that fiery war-trail,
With its glare upon his features.

(Longfellow 1856)

PROFESSOR LONGFELLOW hit on the richest of all veins of gold when he wrote the "Song of Hiawatha." The rarity of the measure, the novelty of the subject, the beauties of the poetry, the fearful difficulties of the Indian names, and the remarkable facility of imitation, set the whole nation talking about it.... It is stated that over thirty thousand copies of the "Song of Hiawatha" have been sold already, and this is quite up to the sale of Uncle Tom's Cabin during a like period of time. ... Hiawatha is the rage just now and bids fair to continue so for sometime to come. (*Phila. Evening Bulletin,* 26 Mar. 1856)

MR. MORAN HAS attempted to illustrate these lines from Hiawatha: "Fiercely the red sun descending,/Burned his way along the heavens." There is no denying the fact that Mr. Moran is an artist;...but no artist has as yet succeeded in depicting a great sunset. Red paint won't do it, even when thrown on the canvas *à la Turner.* So here the translation of that glory that seemingly lifts up the earth to the gate of heaven is a failure. There is power, there is a something akin to grandeur, yet the sunset is a failure. The water is in Moran's happiest vein, it is the fathomless sea, solemn in its power, subdued in the light that falls upon it. Moran is fast taking place as the best marine painter in the Union. (*Newark Daily Advertiser,* 3 Dec. 1881)

51

Mosquito Trail, Rocky Mountains of Colorado

1875, watercolor
24.8 x 36.2 (9 ¾ x 14 ¼)
Private Collection

Washington only

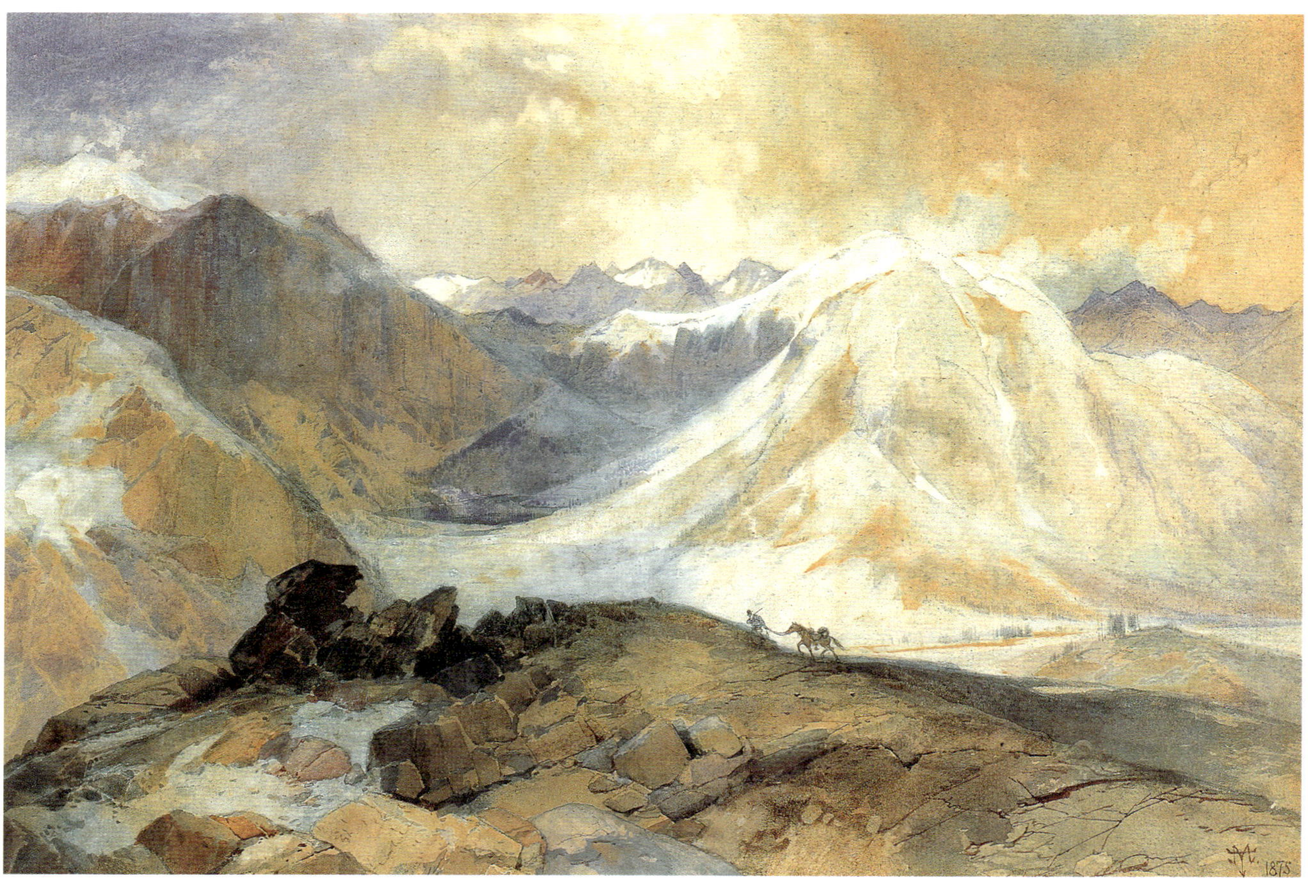

See Appendix 1.

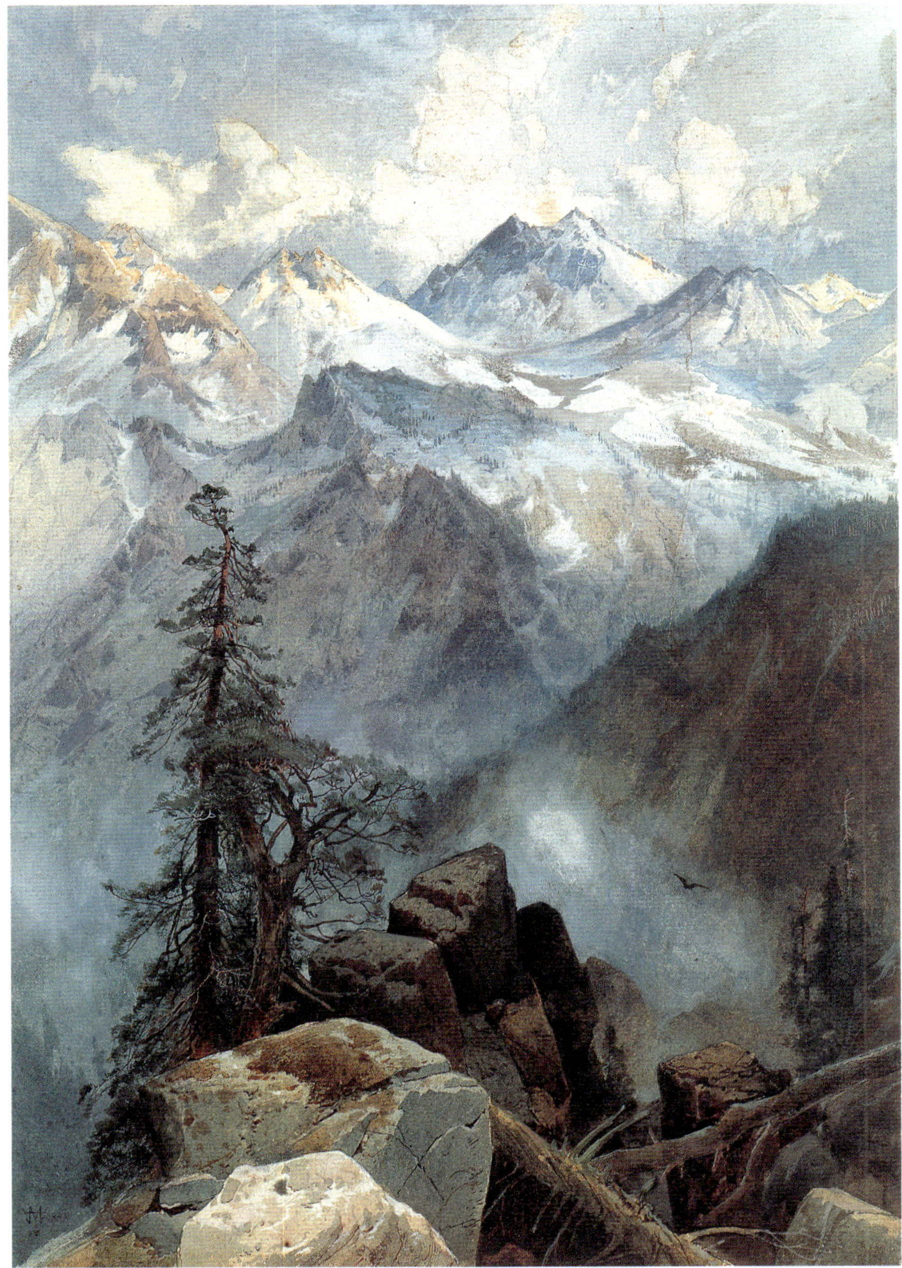

52

Summit of the Sierras

1872/1875,
gouache on paper
36 x 25 (14 1/8 x 9 7/8)
The Art Institute
of Chicago, Gift of
Mrs. Byron Harvey

Washington only

See Appendix 1.

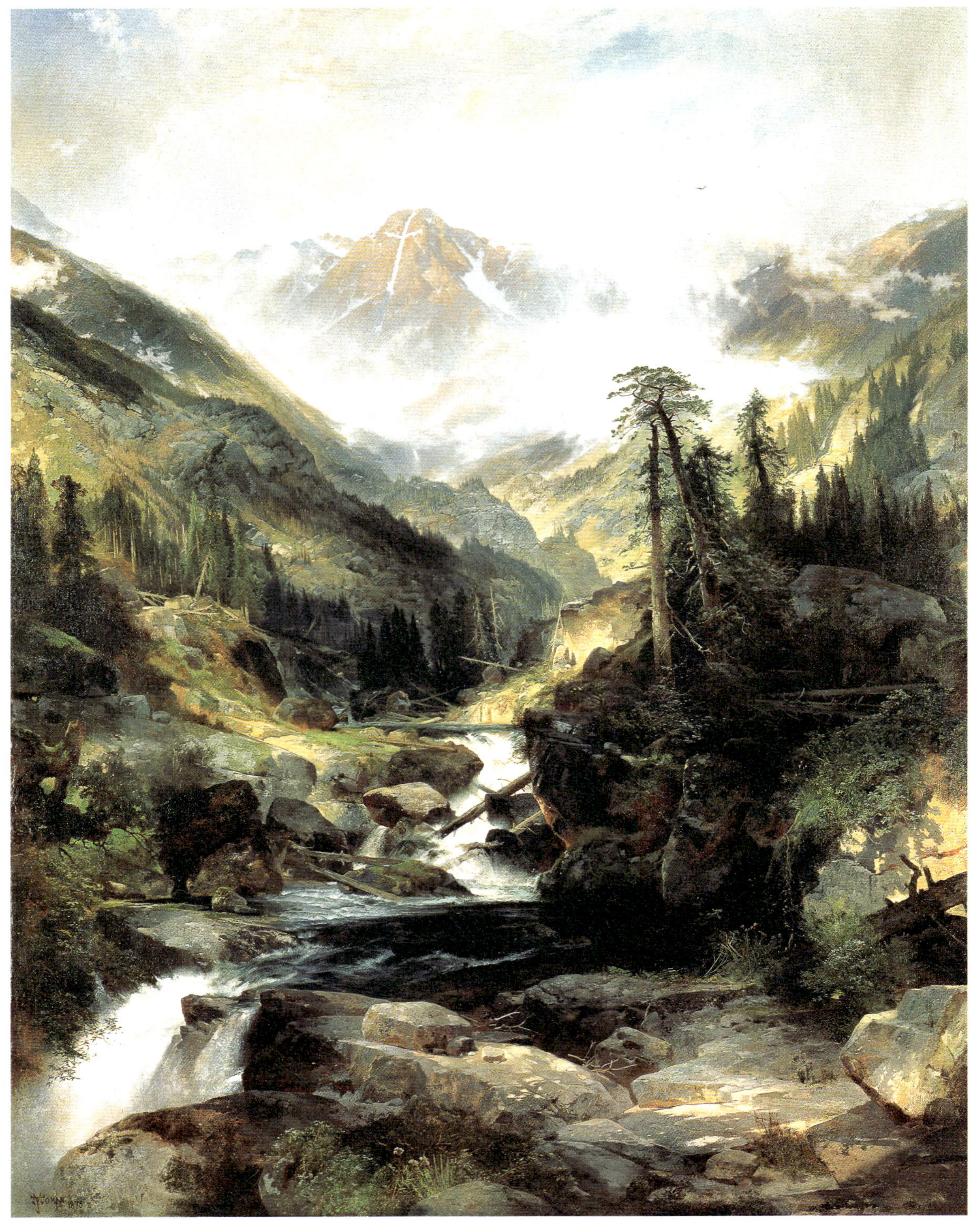

53

Mountain of the Holy Cross

1875, oil on canvas
208.6 x 163.2
(82 ⅛ x 64 ¼)
Autry Museum of Western Heritage, Los Angeles, Gift of Mr. and Mrs. Gene Autry

MR. MORAN made a portfolio of sketches, including the Holy Cross, from which he intends to make paintings, the principal one to be of the Cross. Mr. Moran pronounces the view which is obtained from that locality one of the grandest he has ever seen, and says that no better subject could be presented for the pencil and brush of the artist. We feel confident his painting of the Mount of the Holy Cross will add brilliancy to his already world-wide reputation. (*Denver Rocky Mt. News*, 1 Sept. 1874)

MR. THOMAS MORAN respectfully announces that his New Picture, "The Mountain of the Holy Cross," is now on Exhibition at the Gallery of W. Schaus, 749 Broadway. New York, April 6th, 1875.

The Mountain of the Holy Cross is situated in the heart of the Rocky Mountains of Colorado, about 150 miles west of Denver, on the Pacific slope of the range. The name was given by the old Spanish missionaries, who penetrated these regions to christianize the Indians, long before the settlement of the Western States, and was suggested by the very perfect Cross, formed by two great crevices high on the face of the mountain, running nearly at right angles to each other, and filled with perpetual snow.

Although placed on the face of a great peak, 13,000 feet above the level of the sea, yet it is visible from but few points in the region.

The Holy Cross Creek which flows from the base of the mountain into Eagle river, is supplied entirely by the melting snows, and is the very ideal of a picturesque stream, bordered by pines and firs, and in its rapid descent, is broken into a hundred cascades by accumulated rocks. In many places the valley exhibits glacial action of a former period in the furrowed and polished surfaces of the outcropping "Roches Mouttons." In the Summer of 1874, Mr. Moran, accompanied by a few friends, penetrated this almost unknown wilderness and made the studies from which the picture was painted. (Printed announcement, Apr. 1875, director's records, Corcoran)

NOW THAT Mr. Thomas Moran's new picture, the "Mountain of the Holy Cross," which has been on strictly private view at his house in this city for a few days, is on exhibition at Schaus' in New York, we may be permitted to say a word of praise for what we regard as a grandly successful picture. The distances are not so immense as in the "Chasm of the Colorado" or "The Yellowstone," and the eye can measure somewhat accurately the magnificent ten mile perspective at the back of which is the "Holy Cross," a snow crevasse, filled the year round in the form of a cross, which lies upon the almost perpendicular face of a bald mountain of reddish rock. A little imagination will transmute a snow drift on the right into a prone figure with hands outstretched and imploring to the symbol of salvation. Not only the popular eye, that which almost unconsciously loves true perspective, honest color and just drawing, will admire this. It will satisfy the love of the artistic sense and live in the memory. (*Newark Daily Advertiser*, 5 Apr. 1875)

OF THE WORK itself we may say that it is decidedly superior to either of the two former pictures of Western scenery painted by Mr. Moran. Though unexceptionable, so far as mere mechanical execution goes, both the two works referred to fell far short of giving the true sentiment of mountain scenery. The spectator did not feel, as he should have done when standing before Mr. Moran's canvas, impressed either by the vastness of the space covered, the height of the mountain peaks in the distance, or by the profound depth of the rocky valleys or cañons in the foreground. As mechanical reproductions of the grander Western mountain scenery the pictures referred to deserved commendation, but they could scarcely be considered as taking rank among works of high art. In "The Mountain of the Holy Cross," now on exhibition at the Schaus Gallery, Mr. Moran has been strikingly successful in his translation of our Western mountain scenery. In the foreground we have the Holy Cross Creek, a wild and tortuous stream, lashing itself into foam against the numerous dark and jagged rocks that impede its course, its banks bordered by pines and firs and the bright-colored but scanty herbage usually found beside a mountain water-course. Up this brawling stream the eye is led to the mysterious white cross near the summit of the vast and distant mountain, a work of Titans we should be disposed to pronounce it were we not assured that the cross was carved by the hand of Nature herself. Above the rocky peaks rolls a fine mass of gray clouds, and in the middle distance—"The mists that round the mountain curl Melt into light."

To the technical merits of Mr. Moran's work the highest praise may be awarded. The foreground is charmingly painted, the color is unusually pure and truthful, the rocks have all the solidity of nature, the foliage is crisp and well defined, and there is motion in the water. At the same time the aerial perspective has been managed with so much skill that the spectator really feels as if the grand mountain on which shines the glittering cross were many miles away. In its general treatment, "The Mountain of the Holy Cross" reminds us strongly of the studies of Calame, that almost unrivaled painter of wild mountain scenery, though at the same time we fully recognized the fact that Mr. Moran's work bears the unmistakable stamp of originality and we think that it will unquestionably take rank as one of the finest examples of American landscape art that has yet been produced. Mr. Moran may well be proud of a work exhibiting so much technical skill, combined with such noble simplicity and even severity of treatment, and all who take an interest in the progress of American art must gratefully recognize the fact that at last we have among us an artist of native birth eminently capable of interpreting the sentiment of our wilder mountain scenery in a style commensurate with its grandeur and beauty. (*NYT,* 10 Apr. 1875)

MR. THOMAS MORAN... exhibits at Schaus's his recently-painted view of "The Mountain of the Holy Cross," in Colorado. The scene of the painting is a most picturesque one, with the high, snowy mountain at the head of a deep ravine, through whose rocky bottom the stream from the mountain wildly plunges. Far up the mountain-side, and above all vegetation, two snow-filled crevices unite in forming a gigantic cross, which is visible at a great distance. The scene is one of the most excessive loneliness and remoteness; not the slightest trace of man appears in the wild glen, whose vegetation is torn and gnarled by winter storms. The mountain is about one hundred and fifty miles west of Denver, and is in the very heart of the Rocky Mountain range. The name was given to it by the old Spanish missionaries, who penetrated to this region two or three centuries ago, and were naturally greatly impressed by this marvellous apparition of the chief symbol of their religion. The accessories of the landscape are very fine, and the tangled undergrowth and twisted pine-trees are a fit setting for the silent peak at the top of the ravine. The studies from which the picture was painted were made last summer, when Mr. Moran, with a few friends, penetrated the wilderness. (*Appleton's* [24 Apr. 1875], 535)

MR. THOMAS MORAN is already known to our readers as...the painter of two large and remarkable pictures, "The Grand Cañon of the Yellowstone River," and "The Chasm of the Colorado." A third work by this industrious artist now claims our attention, having recently been on exhibition at the gallery of Schaus & Co. It is a view of "The Mountain of the Holy Cross," so called because of a peculiarity of the bare rocky wall which springs to the summit from the body of the mountain. In this wall are two comparatively narrow transverse fissures, filled with ice and snow, which mark a very distinct cross on the face of the great height. This, at first sight, might seem too bizarre a matter for successful pictorial treatment; but Mr. Moran, by virtue of his careful study of rock structure, and his apparently instinctive sympathy with mountain-nature, has avoided all appearance of sensationalism in his use of it. The astonishing novelty of his subject in the Yellowstone picture laid that work open, perhaps, to some slight reproach of making an appeal to our interest that bordered on the factitious, but it cannot be even suspected in the present case. "The Mountain of the Holy Cross," too, is much in advance of the "Yellowstone" in another particular—that of general composition. There was a massive realism and sturdy directness in the latter which was very attractive; it seemed as if the artist had seized a great block out of the mountains and flung it before us with something of a giant's strength; but it wanted rounding, nevertheless, and was too abrupt in its presentation. The present effort is more comprehensive. The painter has got farther away from his subject, and so thrown it into a better focus. "The Mountain of the Holy Cross" is an impressive and pleasing picture; and the eye, resting upon the solemn rocks of the foreground, touched here and there with sunlight, the swirling rush of the indigo-tinged river, and following the flood back in its windings through the glen, finds an abundant variety of interest before it reaches the snowy cross on the lofty mountain, walling in the scene. We might, it is true, make some complaint of a certain effect of confusion that struck us as resulting from the crowded presence of the clouds high up in the middle and right of the picture, and of some deficiencies of strong and accurate definition in the heights sloping upward in the left background; but we have no intention of dwelling on these points, for Mr. Moran is, in the main, successful; and, good as were the qualities of his two larger works previously exhibited, he has here gone beyond his own earlier success, in combining those qualities to a more completely satisfying end." (*Scribner's* [June 1875], 252–253)

BEYOND A QUESTION, in the painting of this picture, Mr. Thomas Moran has made one of those exceptional professional leaps which bridge the chasm between reputation and immortality. Church did not more certainly do so, in his "Niagara" and "Heart of the Andes," two pictures closely following each other and combining to form the ladder (if so humble an image may be used) up which he rose from an ordinary appreciation to that of a magnate of the first rank in the art-world; Bierstadt did not more certainly do so, in his "Rocky Mountains," at once supplying the strongest proof of the power with which he could depict composite nature, and of the fact that, this excellence reached at a single bound, he could never go beyond. (*The Aldine,* July 1875, 379)

MORAN'S MOUNTAIN of the Holy Cross, which is on exhibition of the gallery of L. A. Eliot & Co., adjoining the Globe Theatre, deserves to rank among the finest works that have hither to come from the easel of a native artist. It is a strikingly beautiful picture in every essential. The drawing throughout is wonderfully clear and decisive. The masses of rock in the foreground for texture, truthfulness of form, color, and general treatment, are equal to anything we have seen from a modern hand. Not the slightest detail has been neglected, and yet the effect of them is superbly broad and natural.... The whole is vividly impressive. The spectator stands before it absorbed in thought, and presently becomes fascinated with the poetry that pervades it. In subject, treatment, color, atmosphere, drawing and handling, the work is worthy of the highest praise. It is a masterpiece, and we do not know which of our artists could have painted it as well as Mr. Moran has done it. The public should not neglect to pay it a visit. (*Boston Transcript,* 9 Nov. 1875)

MORAN'S LARGE and masterly painting, "The Mountain of the Holy Cross," now on exhibition at the gallery of L. Eliot & Co., adjoining the Globe Theatre, is attracting a great deal of attention from connoisseurs and the public in general. It is a superb piece of work, technically considered, and is in advance of even the very best the artist has previously given us. The coloring is exceedingly rich and harmonious, the drawing is wonderfully clear and true, and the textures throughout are reproduced with a skill and a conscientiousness but seldom seen in paintings of this size. Perhaps the finest bit of art in the work is the mass of rocks in the foreground. These are almost perfect, not only in their finely varied forms, their color, and their solidity, but in their admirable relief. The shrubbery and the foliage are painted with a free but at the same time a careful hand, and, even though occupying a subordinate place in the picture, are finished to a high degree. Mr. Moran's touch has greatly improved in firmness, crispness and certainty, and in this canvas he shows a thorough command over the techniques of his art. The only point in which he really seems to have failed is in giving distance. The picture seems to lack atmosphere. The objects in the middle and extreme distance are quite as strongly defined as are those in the foreground, and even the far-away mountain, with its cross of snow embedded in the fissure of the rocks, shows every marking on its surface. It has been said, in excuse of this apparent fault, that the atmosphere in this region is so clear and pure, that distant objects are seen in all their minuteness of detail. It may be so, but the lack of space is felt nevertheless. Beyond this, we have only praise to bestow upon the painting, which is an honor to American art, and is well worth the seeing by every person of taste and culture. (*Boston Evening Gazette,* 14 Nov. 1875)

THE PICTURE IS in moderate and grateful tone, very different from the extraordinary color in Mr. Moran's previous works upon this region. The composition is pleasing and regular, even to the point of conventionality, and there is much faithful and skilful painting of details. The perspective along the reaches of the river is managed in a masterly manner.... [there is] one failing of the picture, —which for chaste and harmonious tone and composition and artistic handling is entitled to rank very high among the best landscapes—and that fault is the weakness of aerial perspective. The mountain cross is not far enough away. (*Boston Transcript,* 16 Nov. 1875)

THERE IS NOW on exhibition at the art gallery of Messrs. Pettes & Leathe, Nos. 606 and 608 Washington avenue, a magnificent painting by Thomas Moran, entitled "The Mountain of the Holy Cross." It is a most successful effort to portray a remarkable view in the Rocky mountains.... Thousands of people in St. Louis, if they have not seen the precise scene depicted by Mr. Moran, are yet familiar with Rocky mountain scenery in general, and all such will realize the truthfulness of this delineation in its general characteristics. The cross is but an incident in the picture, and whilst it is a prominent feature, it is not by any means a predominant one. Strike it entirely out, and the painting would simply lose the significance of its title; it would still remain a beautiful and artistic representation of mountain scenery. All the details are wrought out with marvelous fidelity. The sky is such as belongs to a mountainous country; the rocks have all the solidity of nature, the foliage is crisp and well defined, and there is motion in the water. At the same time the aerial perspective has been managed with such skill that the spectator almost feels as if the grand mountain on which shines the glittering cross were miles away. The painting will remain on exhibition a short time. (*St. Louis Republican,* 18 Feb. 1876)

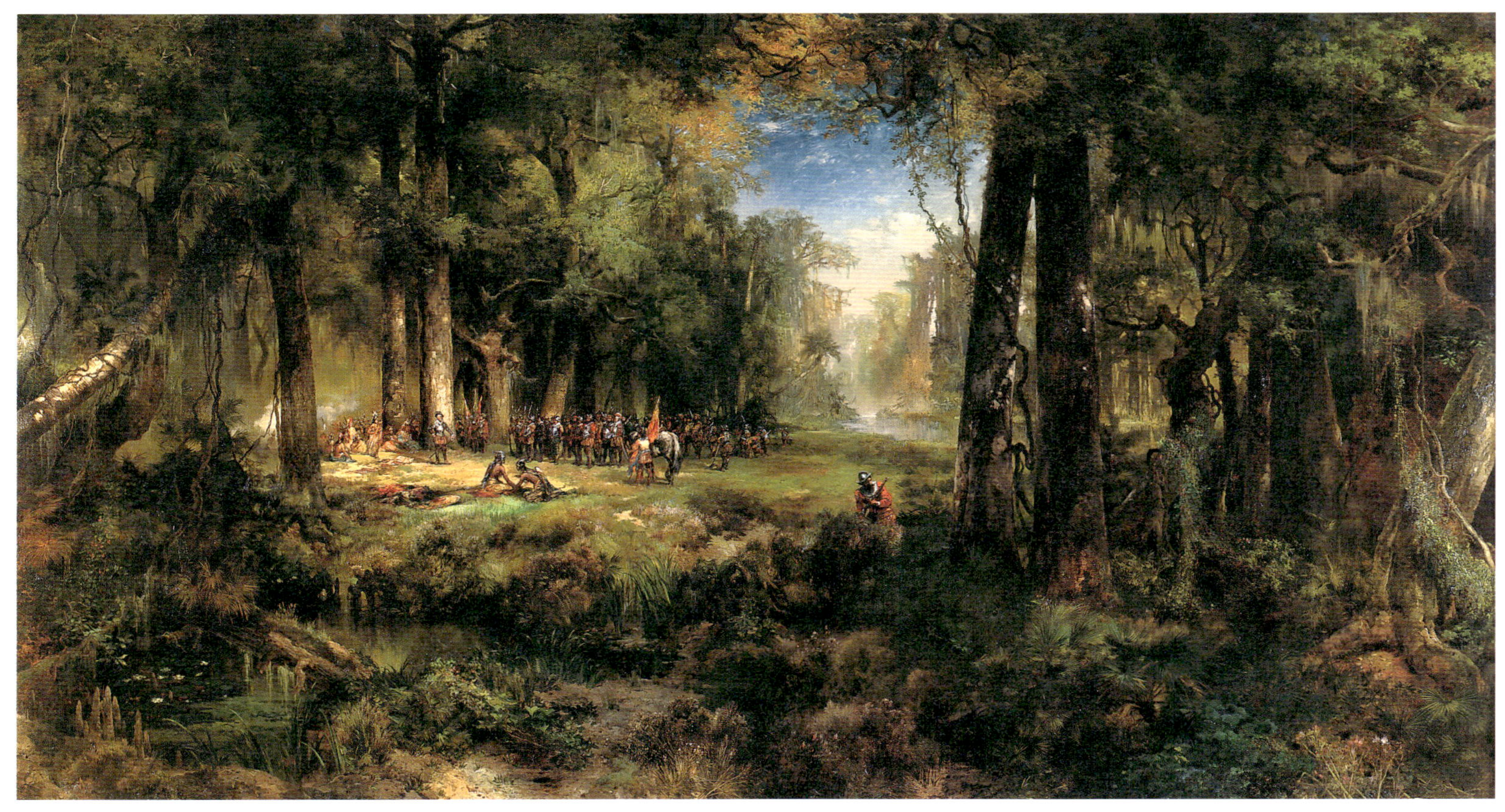

54

Ponce de Leon in Florida

1878, oil on canvas
160 x 292.1 (63 x 115)
The Cummer Museum of Art & Gardens, Acquired for the people of Florida by The Frederick H. Schultz Family and Barnett Banks, Inc. Additional funds provided by the Cummer Council

MR. THOMAS MORAN'S lately completed large painting of the Discovery of Florida by Ponce de Leon will soon be placed on exhibition at the Corcoran Gallery, where the public is invited by the artist to call and inspect it after it shall have been put in position. This work has been on private view for some time past in the Wright Building, on G street, where, in spite of limited space and inadequate and unsuitable light, it created a decidedly favorable impression upon artists and connoisseurs who had the opportunity to see it. Many of these regard it as Mr. Moran's best effort; but upon this point there is likely to be a difference of opinion, even among the artist's friends.... it is a pleasing and impressive canvas, and contains much painting of a very high order of merit. As commemorating a historical event of great importance in the ante-revolutionary period of our history, it would make a fitting companion to Bierstadt's "Discovery of the Hudson River," hanging on the south wall of the House, —that is, to fill the panel now occupied by that artist's other picture, the "Discovery of California," which, we understand, the library committee of Congress have decided not to purchase. (*Evening Star* [DC], 20 Apr. 1878)

MR WORTHINGTON of Georgetown called. He surprised me by his criticism upon Moran's Ponce de Leon, the trees of which he insists as an old resident of Florida, are utterly unlike the timber of that state. He says that the live oak is black in bark, grows up straight, has enormous boughs, & that none of the trees represent the bark of Florida timber. & that the fallen *birch* is utterly absurd, as that tree is not known there. If this be so, the prospect of selling the picture is a poor one. (William MacLeod, 29 Apr. 1878, curator's journal, Corcoran)

UNDER THE RECENT re-enactment of the joint resolution requiring the removal from the Capitol of all works of art not belonging to government, Bierstadt's large picture representing the discovery of California will have to be taken from the Hall of the House, where it has hung so long in spite of the Congressional rule above referred to, and which, other artists say, was rigidly enforced against everything else.... An earnest movement has also been made by the friends of Mr. Moran for the purchase of his "Ponce de Leon in Florida," now on exhibition in the Corcoran Gallery. The main objection urged against the purchase of the latter is the fact that the nation has already bought two of Mr. Moran's paintings—the Canon of the Yellowstone and the Canon of the Colorado, which hang in the room opening out of the east gallery of the Senate. The friends of other artists insist they ought to have a chance, and that the walls of the capitol should not be covered by the works of a few men to the exclusion of others. (*Evening Star* [DC], 22 June 1878)

IN 1878 I PAINTED the large picture of Ponce De Leon in Florida 4 x 7 feet & tried to sell it to Congress to fill a panel in the House of Reps but failed & Bierstadt picture of the Discovery of California was bought for the place, most of the Com being... indifferent & the chief excuse being that they had already bought two pictures from me. But professing at the same time that they preferred mine. It is now in the Corcoran Gallery but as yet unsold. 1878. (Old Book of Lists, GA: "Sold at my sale in 1882 [*sic*—1886] for 2000 to Knoedlers—they sold it to Ponce de Leon Hotel Florida" [added in pencil])

THOMAS MORAN'S new picture of the "Exploration of Florida by Ponce de Leon"... is also in the Gallery. We look out from a shadowy, marshy foreground, under the colonnade of forest-trees, upon a clearing bounded by gigantic trees of cypress and live-oak, with a vista of tall palmettos and a dreamy bit of river beyond. On the sunlit open-ing, under the trees drooping with moss, stand De Leon and his soldiers in the picturesque military garb of the time, confronting a tribe of Indians, as though he was about to resume his exploring march. Altogether there is a charming blending of knightly romance and primeval sylvan solitude in this picture, which is executed with elaborate finish. It was painted with a view of disposing of it to Congress, as a pendant to the "Discovery of the Hudson," by Bierstadt, filling a panel in the House of Representatives. (*Art Journal* 4 [July 1878], 223)

FIFTY-FOURTH Annual Exhibition of the Academy of Design—Important Pictures—First Notice. Over the best landscape by William Hart which we have seen for a long time hangs, on the east wall, "Ponce de Leon in Florida"... by Thomas Moran. It is a strong picture, though, as in the case of the Inness, we can hardly see the reason for its great size. It is, however, a grandiose subject, treated with a thorough and masterly grasp. The eye is led through an opening between the magnificent tree forms to the skilfully introduced mass of figures in the glade. (*NY Herald,* 28 Mar. 1879)

NO; SIZE WILL not help a picture. On the contrary, it becomes at once an element of weakness, unless the subject and the style are on an equal scale. One end of the South Room is half filled with a gigantic composition by Thomas Moran, representing Ponce de Leon and his Spanish hunters for gold and the fountain of immortal youth. It is Florida.... The Everglades are there—very much there, one may say: and the bright groups of horsemen and Indians at a distance represent well enough the imaginary scene. There is a black lizard in the left foreground, and Spanish moss hangs from moldering trees. But it is waste energy. Since Leutze's time, no one except the wild Western Congressman cares for such spectacular affairs.... But in this picture there is no strong interest. The filibuster and his party are doing nothing. We are therefore cast back on the technical merits of the painting. One it has. Mr. Moran is almost always strong in perspective, and his craft in that respect does not desert him.... Moran is therefore best when he adheres to some homely, everyday scene which does not demand warmth of color or a draft upon the imagination.

The good perspective of Thomas Moran might be profitably imitated by a host of painters here. (*NYT*, 7 Apr. 1879)

A LARGE PAINTING by Thomas Moran, "Ponce de Leon in Florida,"... is the most ambitious landscape in the [NAD] exhibition. There is shown a vast deal of earnest work and high purpose, and, if the result is not wholly satisfactory, much must be conceded to the difficulties of the plan. (*Art Journal* 5 [May 1879], 159)

THOMAS MORAN, honored by an appreciative nation with various commissions for the Capitol, and with successive summer excursions of a romantic and to him inexpensive nature, shows the result of some of his travels in a Florida scene, "Ponce de Leon."...Moran's "Florida," with Ponce de Leon's explorers, is a rich and imposing drop curtain.... Both of the landscapist's contributions aforesaid have an almost terrifying ease and mastery of style, and this not in the way of slickness or emptiness, but with downright fecundity of varied effects; but the artist's determination is to teach Nature how to look, not to learn how Nature looks. (*Boston Transcript*, 20 May 1879)

NOR HAS Mr. Moran's genius confined itself to the delineation of the sublime scenery of the great west. He has also visited the south, and revelled in its gorgeous colours and its affluence of tropic vegetation. The music of the palm has touched his soul, and the tender azure of the skies which overarch Mexico's Gulf has kindled his fancy. Among the number of admirable paintings suggested by such scenes may be mentioned his "Ponce de Leon in Florida." This is a large canvas, and represents a clearing, or rather an opening, in a dense, luxuriant grove of palms and oaks, draped with the long festoons of Spanish moss. A little on one side of this clearing De Leon and his companions are seen coming to a halt. The grouping of the figures is excellent and attractive; but the chief merit of the painting is the poetic faithfulness with which the character of a southern forest is suggested. The pendulous masses of graceful foliage are most effectively rendered, and make this one of Mr. Moran's finest works. (Benjamin 1882, 92)

MORAN'S "Ponce de Leon" hangs midway of the galeria in the Biltmore hotel, a picture of the school of another day, rich with his eternal genius and power.

The patina of age gives glory to the winey browns and greens, the luscious shadows of the big painting. The virgin forest spreads its pageant before the feet of the adventurer. Century old trees gather together in a mighty regiment, towering higher and higher so that they shut out the light from lush undergrowth that is never touched by the sun. In their midst is a clearing above which stretches the blue mantle of the sky that is like a royal canopy fastened to the tree tops. In the shadows the white men and the red men stand together, trying to bridge the gulf that separates one world from another. (*LA Herald*, 1 Jan. 1927)

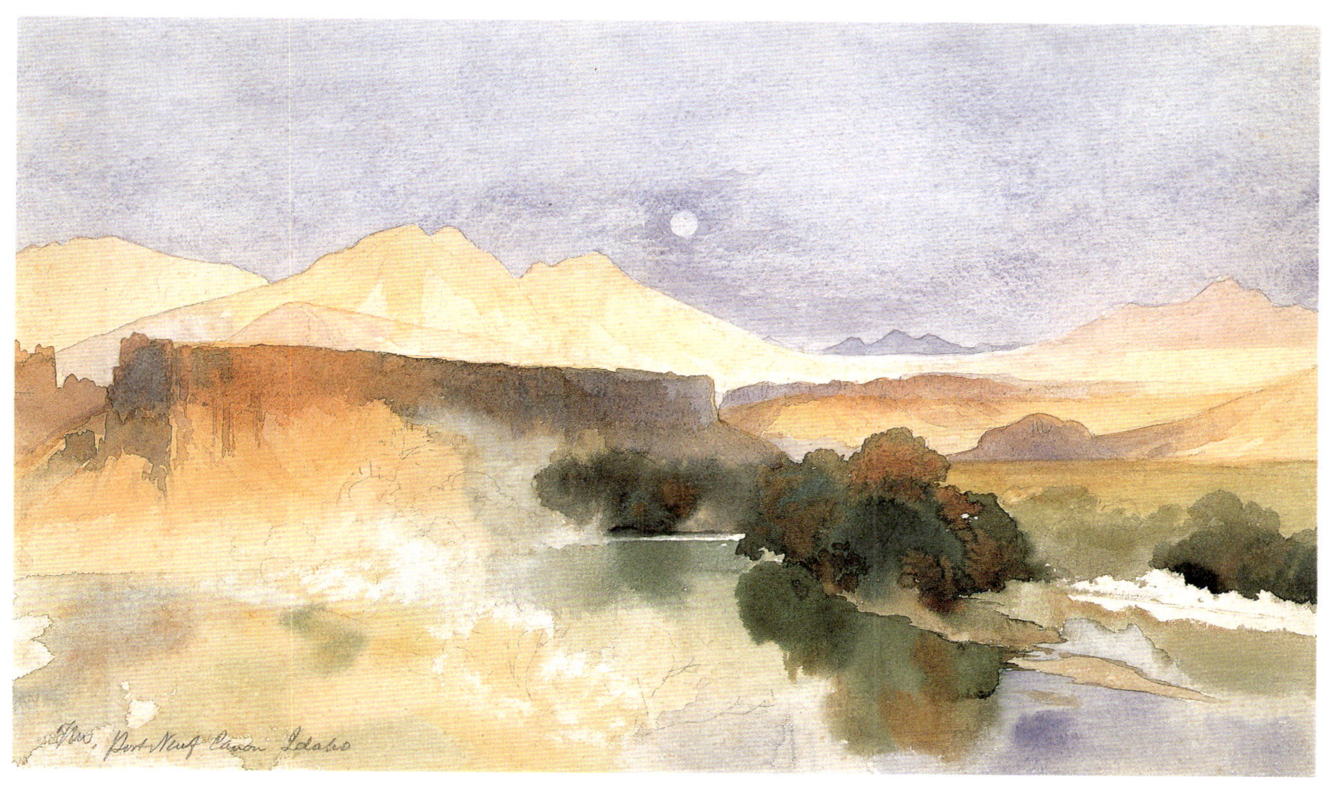

55

Portneuf Cañon, Idaho

1879, watercolor
30.5 x 50.2 (12 x 19 ¾)
Gilcrease Museum,
Tulsa, Oklahoma

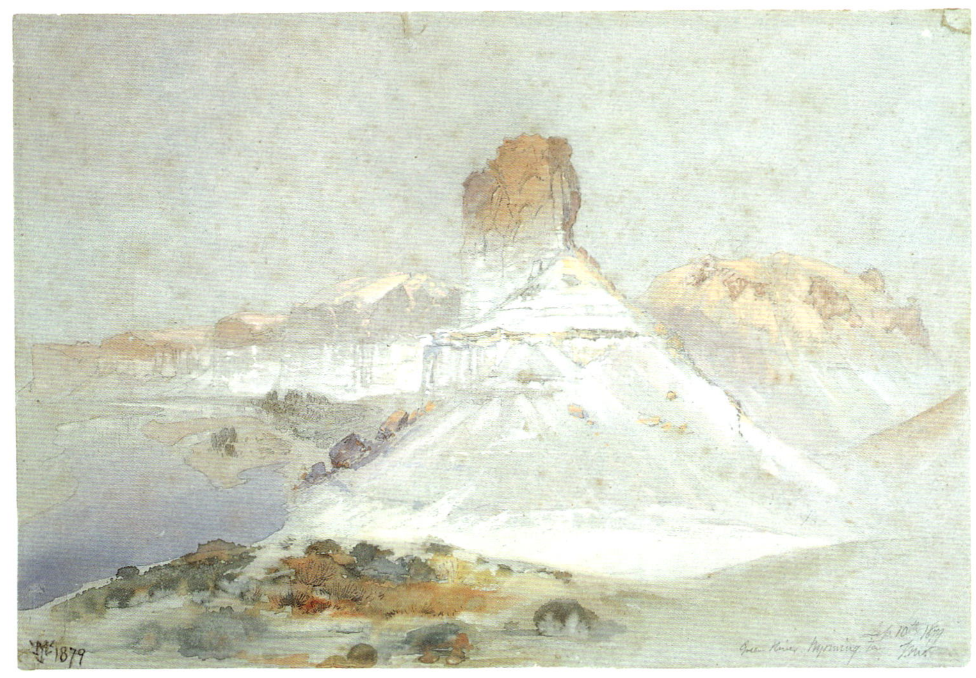

56

Green River, Wyoming

1879, watercolor, pencil, and opaque white on paper
26.4 x 37.2 (10 ⅜ x 14 ⅝); Jefferson National Expansion Memorial, National Park Service

57

Green River Buttes, Wyoming

1879, watercolor
26 x 35.2 (10 ¼ x 13 ⅞)
Gilcrease Museum, Tulsa, Oklahoma

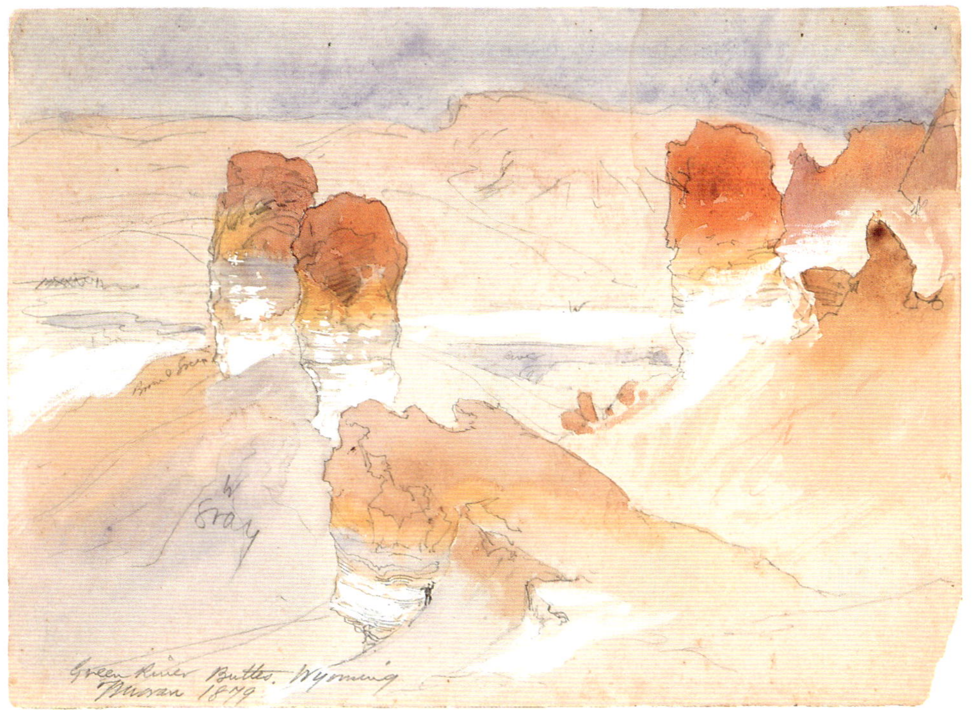

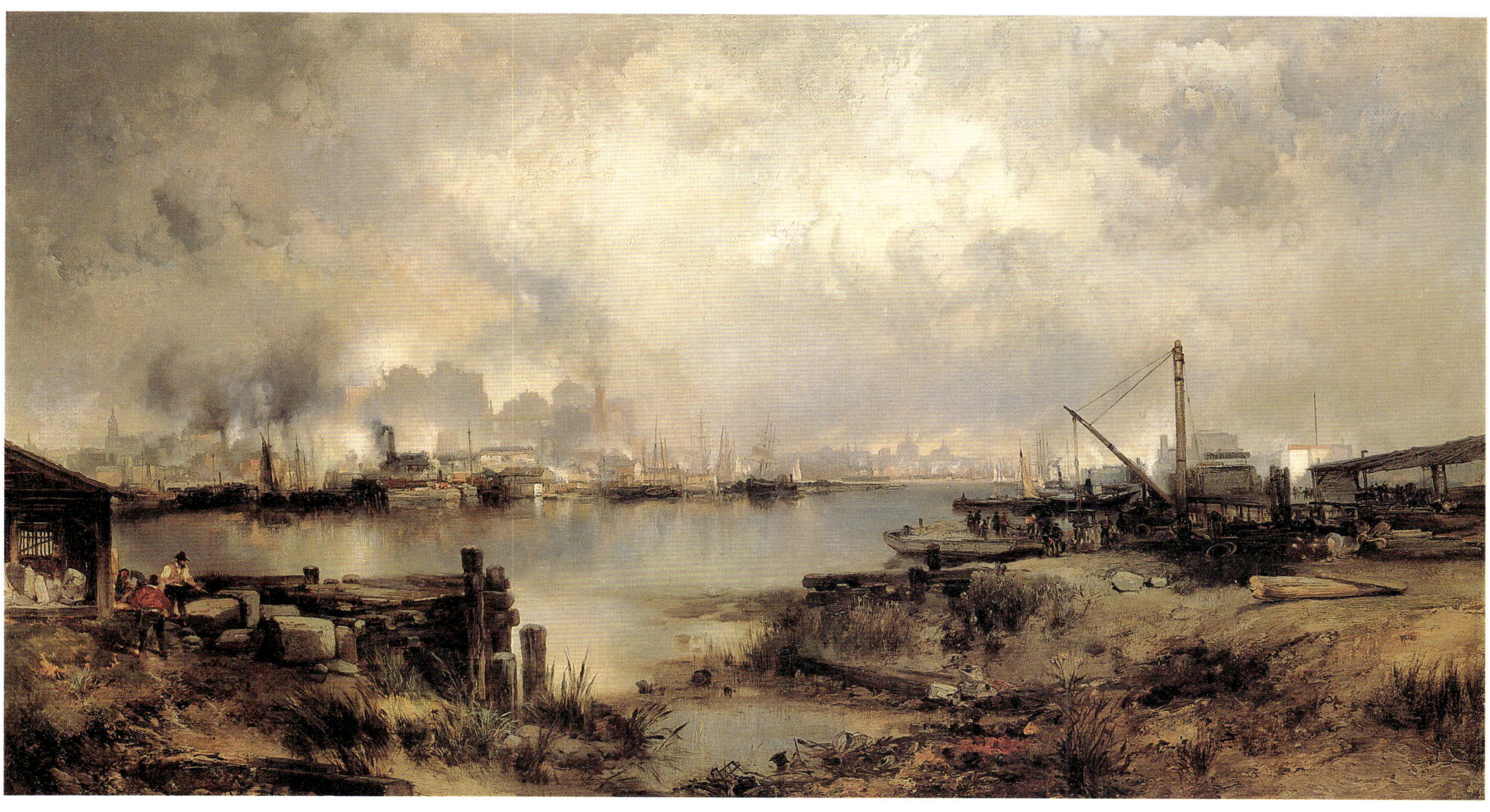

58

Lower Manhattan from Communipaw, New Jersey

1880, oil on canvas
64 x 114.9 (25 3/16 x 45 1/4)
Washington County Museum of Fine Arts, Hagerstown, Maryland

THOMAS MORAN...shows...a view of sugar bakeries at Communipaw. Let us not deny the finished ability of this prolific artist in expressive brush-work; the remarkable length of his catalogue of the conventional formulae which may be taken for the conventional textures and growths of nature, is most imposing. His touch for grass, his touch for pine trees, his touch for rocks, his touch for mud and gravel, his touch for cloud, is ready at a moment's notice, whereupon the thing is in a moment defined. A turn of the wrist, a play of the astonished bristles, and the thing is painted. It is like seeing a juggler's exhibition to inspect his facility. The temptation that goes with this least reassuring of the gifts of the gods is to rest content with superficial impressions. Mr. Thomas Moran's..."Communipaw" is a silver dazzle of sugar-baking palaces rising among the mists and exhalations of a universal thaw, which expresses itself in front by "realistic" mud and "practicable" slush, that assault the senses like the smell of washing-soda in the stage presentment of "L'Assommoir." (Strahan 1879, 4)

OF PICTURESQUE elements existing on every hand without limit, those embraced in a view of Jersey City across Morris Canal appear in a picture characterized by some of Thomas Moran's best qualities. It is a gray day, showing but dimly the New York Post-Office and other great buildings of the quarter across the North River. But the poetry of the air makes itself felt along that artificial water-course about the depots beyond, and among those common scenes of commercial industry in a manner which the artist has perhaps never so forcibly realized before. The picture will probably be seen in the spring exhibition. (*Art Amateur*, Feb. 1880, 52)

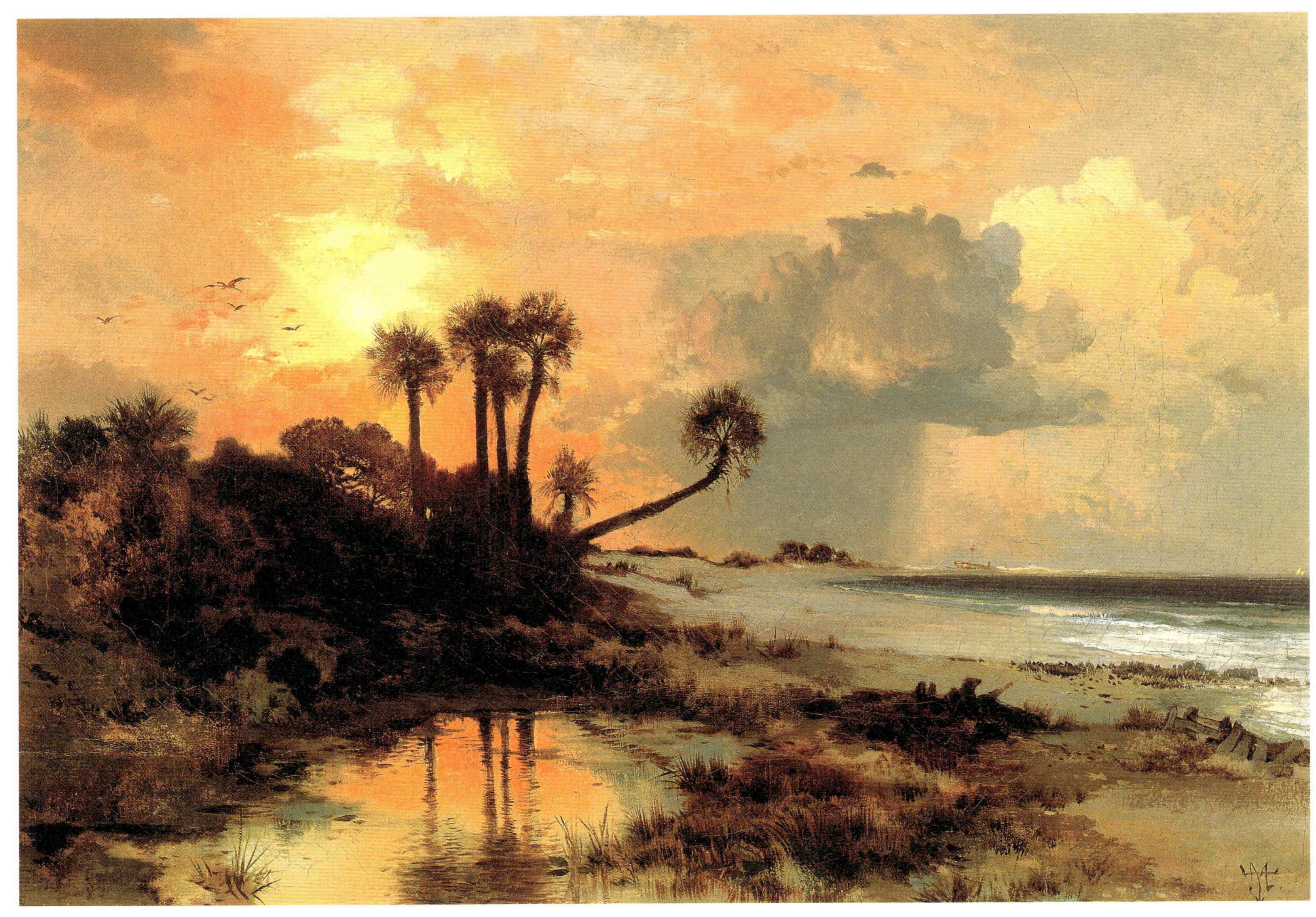

59

Fort George Island

1880, oil on canvas
27.9 x 40.6 (11 x 16)
Robbie and Sam Vickers

AT THE MOUTH of the St. Johns River, which, taking its rise in the wonderful springs and impassable swamps of southern Florida, rolls its waters four hundred miles due north to the Atlantic, lies the Island of Fort George. It is one of that chain of Sea Islands—so famous for their long-fiber cotton in the old times before the war—which stretch along the coast from Savannah to St. Augustine.

Of the throngs of tourists who every winter pass this island in their search for health or pleasure in the land of Ponce de Leon, comparatively few even know of its existence. Yet it would be hard to find a spot combining more advantages and delights than this....

The island of Fort George received its name from a fortification of some kind, probably not very considerable, which stood in colonial times upon a point of land on the northern shore, built to withstand attacks from the Spanish.... Some slight remains of earth-works alone show where it stood....

The island has an area of some twelve hundred acres of low wooded plateau, surrounded mostly by a band of salt meadow of varying width, beyond which, on the eastern and southern sides, three or four miles of fine beach stretch along the sea. Toward the northern end the land rises somewhat irregularly, culminating in Mount Cornelia, the highest point on the coast south of Cape Hatteras.... A pleasant, home-like hotel affords accommodation for visitors to the island; boats are at hand for sailing or fishing, or excursions to the neighborhood; miles of avenues have been cut with fine taste and discrimination in all directions throughout the woods, and connected with the drive upon the beach....

And to Fort George nature has been very bountiful. About forty kinds of trees grow upon its surface, our northern pines and cedars—their foliage becoming softer and finer in this southern latitude—mingling with the huge live oak, the luxuriant magnolia and the stately palm.... The air and sea teem with life in inexhaustible variety....

Over wood and plain and sea and sky the sunset throws a glory of its own. The scene is one of perfect repose and peace. Standing here, we cannot wonder that a universal sentiment has inspired the poets of all times to find their ideal of peace and felicity in far-off islands of the sea; that Pindar sang in sweetest numbers of the "Islands of the Blest," of our own Whittier: "I know not where His islands lift / Their fronded palms in air, / I only know I cannot drift / Beyond His love and care." (Dodge 1877, 652–661)

By 6 June 1881 Thomas and Mary Moran were comfortably settled in their new home in New York City.[1] After a decade in Newark, and several years after Richard Watson Gilder had made the same decision, Moran moved his family and his studio to Manhattan. By the end of the year Gilder would be named editor-in-chief of *Century Magazine*, successor to *Scribner's*, and Moran would be elected an Associate of the National Academy of Design. Still close friends, Moran and Gilder had chosen to settle their families in the city that had emerged as the art and publishing capital of the nation. For more than three decades New York (and soon East Hampton) would serve as Moran's professional home base. During that period he also continued to travel to distant ports—always with sketchbook in hand.

Just a few weeks after moving to New York, Moran joined his old friend William Henry Jackson on a trip to the Southwest. Several years earlier, while traveling with F. V. Hayden's survey party, Jackson and several of his companions had, in their own words, "discovered" the extraordinary cliff dwellings at Mesa Verde in southwestern Colorado.[2] Although others had clearly preceded them to the site, Jackson was the first to photograph the dwellings.[3] Traveling with him at the time was Ernest Ingersoll, correspondent for the *New York Tribune*, who wrote an account of their adventure

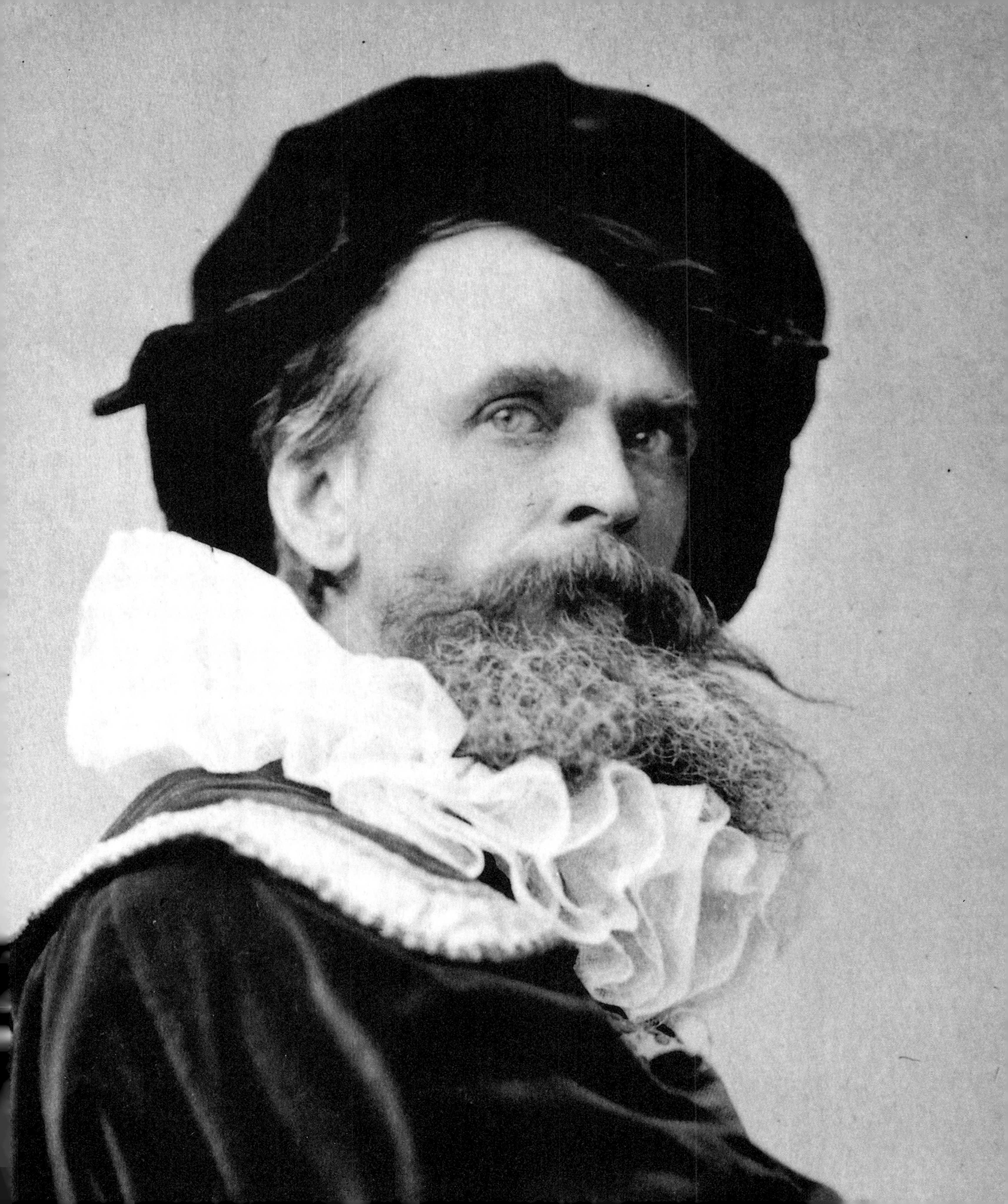

that attracted considerable attention when published 3 November 1874.[4] Ever alert to intriguing and marketable subjects for pictures, Moran undoubtedly saw Jackson's photographs and may have read Ingersoll's report as well, but it was not until 1881 that he journeyed to the land of pueblos and cliff dwellings himself.

1

Moran traveled first to Denver, where he was joined by Jackson, who had recently established a business in the city, and by Ernest Ingersoll, who was then employed by *Harper's Magazine*.[5] Aboard the Denver & Rio Grande Railroad, Moran and his party journeyed south into New Mexico, the southern terminus of the rail line. In so doing, they traveled through territory relatively unexplored by artists. Moran spent several weeks sketching, not only in New Mexico but also in Colorado, Utah, and Wyoming. Not surprisingly, however, when he returned east, it was the land of the pueblos that commanded attention. The *New York Independent*, for example, reported that the artist had "visited many of the Indian pueblos and made a large number of studies."[6] Once again Moran had identified a fresh subject for paintings that had already received attention in the popular press. Ingersoll's prose served as an effective drumroll for the paintings Moran quickly began to produce.[7] Ironically, some of the first fruits of his sketching trip to the Southwest were seen abroad before they were seen in the East, for early in 1882 Thomas and Mary Moran, accompanied by their three children, returned to Bolton, England.

Home Again

In many ways Moran's trip to Bolton was a triumphant return. Celebrated in local newspapers as a native son who had achieved success in America, Moran was the subject of sustained applause. Ever the businessman, he had not traveled empty handed. At Bromley's Art Gallery in Bolton, Moran mounted a sizable exhibition. The *Manchester Guardian* recorded the numbers: "22 oil paintings, 100 water colour drawings, and a series of 25 illustrations from Longfellow's 'Hiawatha.'" The *Guardian* went on to note that Moran also brought with him a series of etchings (as had Mary), a number of proof engravings of illustrations he had published in *Scribner's* and other magazines, and a complete set of his Yellowstone chromolithographs published by Prang.[8] Sales were apparently brisk, for a Boston newspaper later reported: "His paintings and etchings have been warmly commended by critics, and he has sold nearly all of them to eager purchasers."[9] The true highlight of the European trip came later, when Thomas and Mary visited London and met John Ruskin (fig. 1).

As noted earlier, Moran had become acquainted with the writings of Ruskin while still an aspiring apprentice in Philadel-

2

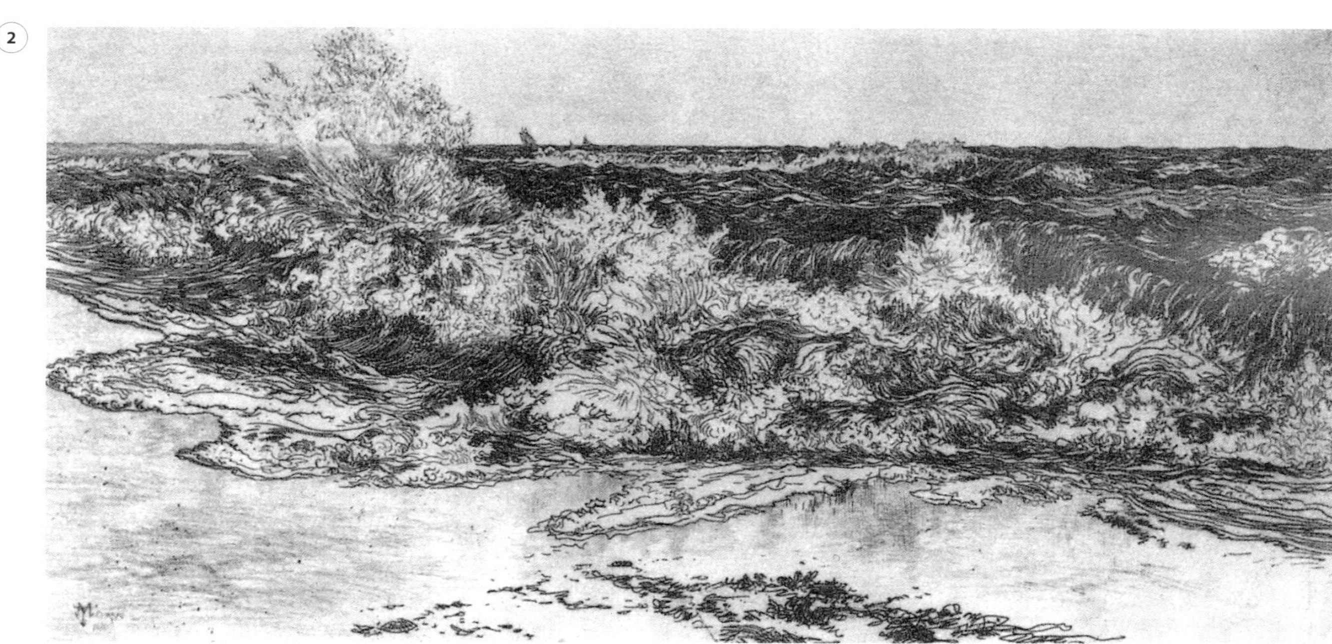

3

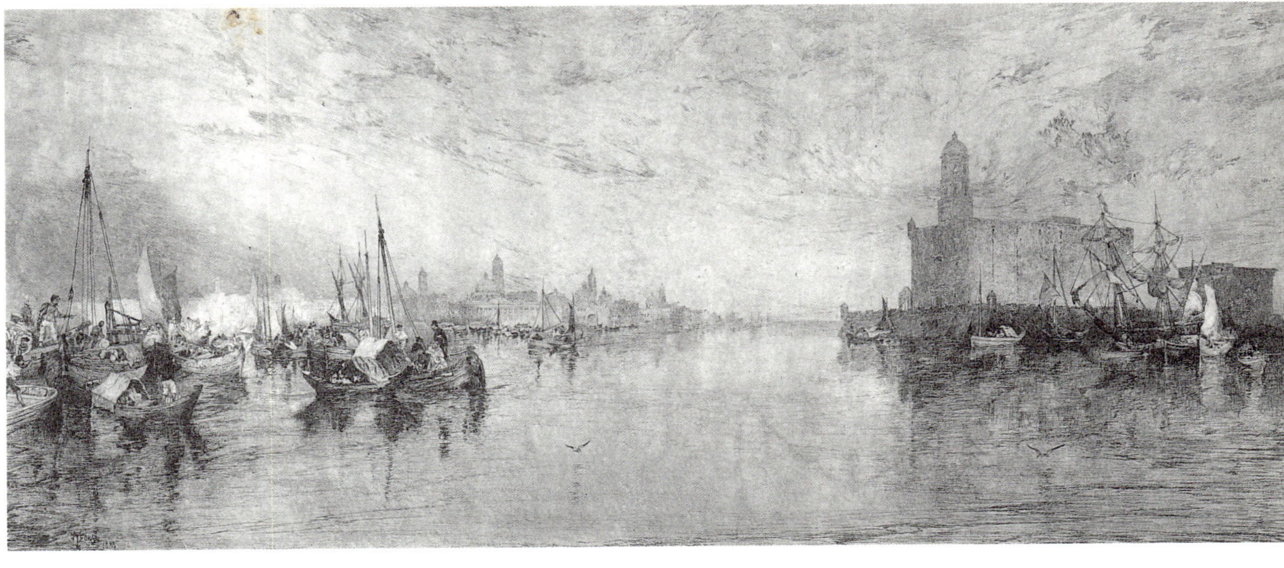

Page 119: Thomas Moran, c. 1884, photograph by Napoleon Sarony, New York, courtesy East Hampton Library.

1. John Ruskin, courtesy East Hampton Library.

2. Thomas Moran, *The Resounding Sea*, 1880, etching, courtesy Gilcrease Museum, Tulsa, Oklahoma. See also cat. 66.

3. Thomas Moran, *The Harbor of Vera Cruz, Mexico*, 1885, etching, courtesy Gilcrease Museum, Tulsa, Oklahoma.

phia during the 1850s. Thirty years later his admiration for Turner's champion had not diminished. Well before his return to America the *New York Herald* reported that Ruskin had not only expressed admiration for Moran's work, he had also purchased "two pictures and six etchings (including three by Mrs. Moran)." In addition, the *Herald* noted: "Of one of Mr. Moran's etchings, 'The wave breaking on the shore,' Mr. Ruskin was especially complimentary, saying it was 'the finest piece of water drawing he had ever seen by any man'" (fig. 2). Reporting that Ruskin had ordered a set of Moran's Yellowstone chromolithographs, the *Herald* concluded: "Mr. Ruskin's pleasure in examining the work of and meeting so ardent and talented a disciple of Turner as Mr. Moran, must have naturally been great, and he called several times upon the artist."[10]

Hearing words of approval from Ruskin regarding his own paintings and etchings, as well as those of Mary, must have been one of the high points of Moran's professional life. As a young man Moran had made literal copies of works by Turner. While abroad in 1862 he had studied works from the Turner bequest—works ordered and arranged by Ruskin. Most important, however, Ruskin must have recognized, especially in the Yellowstone images, that Moran had put the lessons of Turner to good use, for while the landscape was American, the aesthetic and technical provenance of Moran's imagery was clearly British.

The Moran/Ruskin meeting was recorded in several American newspapers—often with a hint of pride that works by two American artists had been purchased by the eminent English critic. Although well along in years, Ruskin remained an art celebrity in 1882, and his stamp of approval was a marketing tool that Moran put to good use.

Mexico

Just a few weeks after returning from Europe, Moran sailed again. Accompanied by Arthur G. Renshaw of the Mexican National Railroad and a mining engineer identified only as Mr. Hahn, Moran began a journey that would take him first to Cuba, then on to Mexico. Although the circumstances that prompted the trip are not clear, Moran took full advantage of the opportunity to sketch yet another distant landscape about which much had already been written.[11] Tireless in his pursuit of new subject matter, Moran completed a large number of sketches including several extraordinary views of the Trojes Mine in central Mexico (cat. 64).

Ironically, it was during the Mexican trip that Moran made written reference to an even more distant port—one that eventually became, perhaps, his most popular subject. Shortly after arriving in Vera Cruz, Moran wrote to Mary sharing news of his trip (fig. 3). In describing the Mexican coastal city, he called Vera Cruz "another pictorial place like Venice. A quiet smooth sea reflecting the castle and buildings. Very green water."[12] At the time he made the comment, Moran had not been to Venice. He had, however, seen many images of Venice—a substantial number by Turner.

Venice: "A Boast, a Marvel, and a Show"

In February 1886, at Ortgies Gallery in New York, Moran placed more than sixty works on exhibition prior to auction.[13] In accounting for such a large display of works by a single artist, the *New York Herald* reported, "Mr. Moran and his wife, Mary Nimmo Moran, leave for a European trip in June, and therefore the former decided to dispose of his unsold works by auction."[14] In fact,

Thomas Moran made the European trip alone, departing in April rather than June.[15] By 1 May he had arrived in Venice. Two days later he wrote to Mary: "Venice is all, and more, than travellers have reported of it. It is wonderful. I shall make no attempt at description but will tell you all when I get back."[16]

Only one letter survives from Moran's Venetian sojourn, thus we cannot know with certainty who the artist saw while abroad. It seems likely, however, that he visited the salon of a much-beloved hostess with American ties, Mrs. Arthur Bronson. Mrs. Bronson, born Katharine de Kay, was a sister of Helena de Kay, wife of Moran's close friend, Richard Watson Gilder. Described as one of the founders of the Anglo-American colony in Venice, Mrs. Bronson had arrived in the city in 1876. She maintained her home and salon in the Casa Alvisi, a small palace, located at the mouth of the Grand Canal directly opposite Santa Maria della Salute. James McNeill Whistler and John Singer Sargent were frequent visitors, as were Henry James and Robert Browning. It was Browning who described Mrs. Bronson as the "best Cicerone in the world; she knows everything and teaches me all she knows. There never was such a guide."[17] Considering the close relationship Moran enjoyed with Gilder, Mrs. Bronson's brother-in-law, it seems unlikely that Moran would forgo meeting and benefiting from Mrs. Bronson's guidance as well.

4. J.M.W. Turner, *Bridge of Sighs, Ducal Palace, and Custom-House, Venice,* c. 1833, oil on canvas, courtesy Tate Gallery, London.

5. Thomas Moran's Venetian gondola on Hook Pond, East Hampton, courtesy East Hampton Library.

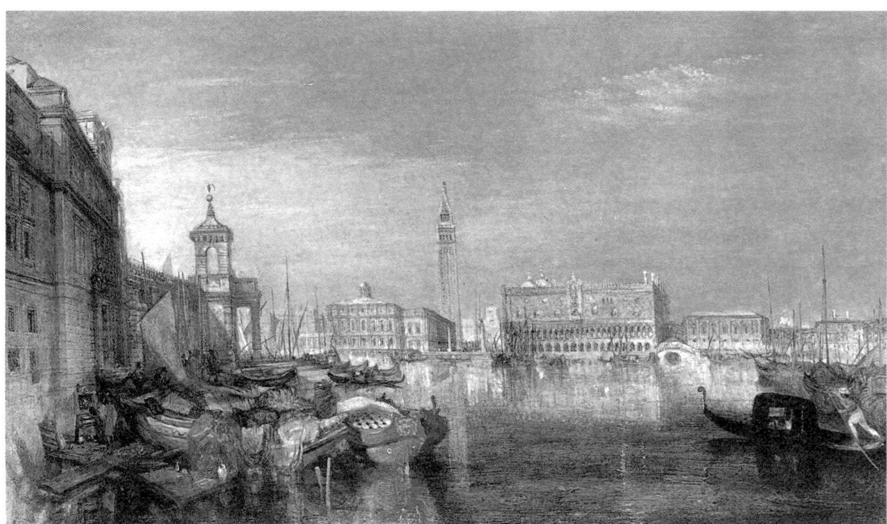

4

While Gilder probably provided Moran with an introduction to the city's most gracious hostess, Venice was clearly a city Moran already knew well—at least visually—before he arrived. Once again, his tutors were Byron, Turner, and Ruskin.

Ruskin visited Venice for the first time in 1835; many additional trips would follow, the last in 1888. Enchanted by the city and passionate about the preservation of its architectural treasures, Ruskin wrote extensively about the "jewel on the Adriatic." In March 1851 the first volume of *The Stones of Venice* was published simultaneously in England and America. The second and third volumes appeared two years later. Several excerpts were published in *The Crayon* in 1855, giving the book wide currency in American art circles.[18]

Like Moran, Ruskin "knew" Venice visually before he actually visited the city, because he had seen Venice through Turner's eyes before he departed England. Turner had traveled to Venice as early as 1819, following in the footsteps of the figure who seemed to be at once Childe Harold and Lord Byron. It was Byron who wrote of Venice in the fourth canto of *Childe Harold's Pilgrimage*:

> I loved her from my boyhood; she to me
> Was as a fairy city of the heart,
> Rising like water columns from the sea,
> Of joy the sojourn, and of wealth the mart;
> And Otway, Radcliffe, Schiller, Shakespeare's art,
> Had stamp'd her image in me, and even so,
> Although I found her thus, we did not part;
> Perchance even dearer in her day of woe,
> Than when she was a boast, a marvel, and a show.

It is interesting to note that the first oil painting Turner completed of a Venetian subject was titled *Bridge of Sighs, Ducal Palace, and Custom-House, Venice: Canaletti Painting* (fig. 4). The picture was exhibited at the Royal Academy in 1833 accompanied by lines from Byron's *Childe Harold*: "I stood upon a bridge, a palace and/A prison on each hand."[19] Turner's painting was given to the National Gallery, London, in 1847 and thus would have been part of the collection Thomas and Edward Moran traveled abroad to see in 1862. In 1890, shortly after returning from his second trip to Venice, Moran exhibited his own version of the "Bridge of Sighs" at the National Academy of Design in New York.

In November 1882, four years before Moran made his first trip to Venice, *Century Magazine* published an article on the city by Henry James. James began his essay by noting: "Venice has been painted and described many thousands of times, and of all the cities of the world it is the easiest to visit without going there. Open the first book and you will find a rhapsody about it; step into the first picture dealer's and you will find three or four high colored 'views' of it."[20] According to James, so much had been written about Venice, so many photographs had been taken, so many pictures had been painted that nothing new remained to be said. Characteristically, James went on to write a lengthy article.

5

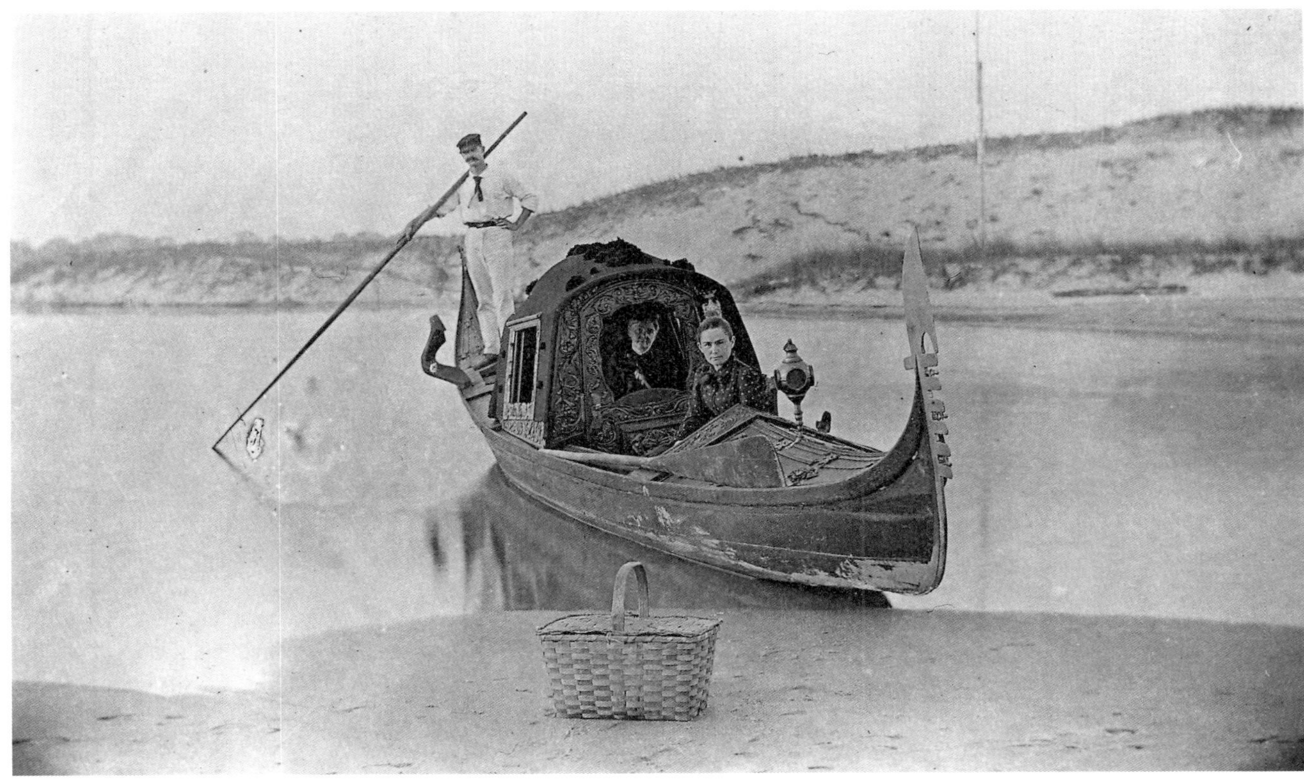

When Moran returned from Venice in 1886, he was in a similar position. A decade earlier he had returned from distant lands bringing back the first watercolors ever seen of marvelous geological formations and wondrous new landscapes. With a temporary corner on the market, he had managed to define (even copyright) some of the most remarkable of these—Yellowstone, the Grand Canyon, and Mountain of the Holy Cross, in particular. When he returned from Venice, the situation was reversed. Other artists had preceded him by many years, and as James noted, the city and subject were so well known that nothing remained to be said. Nevertheless, Moran set to work immediately, using his sketches to produce studio oils. At the National Academy annual exhibition the following spring, Moran submitted two works, both Venetian subjects: *The Church of Santa Maria della Salute, Venice*, and *The Gate of Venice*. From that moment forward Moran contributed a Venetian painting to the academy exhibition nearly every year he participated. The subject became his "best seller."

As others have noted, works of art with Venetian subjects enjoyed extraordinary popularity during the second half of the nineteenth century.[21] Nostalgia for a non-industrial past certainly played a role, as did the dreamlike, otherworldly quality of a city floating on water. Travel literature, eagerly read, and often of high quality, also contributed to widespread interest in the city.

For Moran, known to be an admirer of Ruskin, Turner, and Byron, the three figures primarily responsible for the resurgence of interest in Venice in the nineteenth century, the city had enormous appeal. Moran's debt to Turner's Venetian pictures was immediately recognized by his contemporaries and surely contributed to the popularity and marketability of his pictures.

Like Turner, Moran made full use of the reflective interplay that occurred when architecture and exotic vessels were mirrored by the surface of the sea. The resulting mix of bright color and shimmering light produced the poetic or "dreamlike" quality that Moran's contemporaries frequently noted in his Venetian paintings. Using a compositional technique quite like that he had employed with his Green River pictures, Moran often "anchored" his Venetian paintings with recognizable architecture and then freely invented foreground elements. Thus as Citadel Rock and Castle Rock immediately defined a Green River landscape, Santa Maria della Salute, the Campanile, and the Doge's Palace set the scene in Venice. In place of the Indian caravans that frequently made their way across the foregrounds of Moran's Green River pictures, gondolas and fishing vessels filled with brightly costumed figures often float in the foreground of Venetian paintings.

6. Thomas Moran, *The Grand Canyon of the Colorado,* 1892–1908, oil on canvas, courtesy Philadelphia Museum of Art, Gift of Graeme Lorimer.

7. *Hance's Trail Down,* 1892, photograph by William Henry Jackson, courtesy East Hampton Library.

In *The Fisherman's Wedding Party, Venice* (cat. 76), for example, Moran placed decorated vessels with their colorfully attired revelers in the left foreground.

Like his Green River paintings, Moran's views of Venice were nostalgic fictions. As noted earlier, the railroad had replaced the Indian in Green River by the time Moran visited the site. Although gondolas and fishing boats still plied Venetian waters in the 1880s, the point of comparison was with an industrialized America pushing full speed into a new age. In Moran's paintings Venice served as a dreamy, poetic refuge from rapid change.

Poetic associations may have gotten the best of Moran during his second visit to the city in 1890, for he returned home with a gondola, which he subsequently launched on a pond near his summer residence in East Hampton (fig. 5). Reporting on what was surely one of the most unusual events of the season, the *East Hampton Star* noted:

> Artist Moran has placed his Venetian gondola upon Hook Pond, and on Tuesday a party consisting of himself, Dr. Herrick, Dr. Monroe, and their ladies, enjoyed a sail around the pond on that novel craft. The gondola is 38 feet long, and about four or five feet wide at the centre, and is propelled by a gondolier who stands upon the stern and works the oar upon a curiously shaped arm, by which he is enabled to guide the boat as well as propel it without taking the oar from the water.... This is probably the only Venetian gondola in America, and it has a peculiar mark of distinction, having been at one time owned by the poet Browning.[22]

Several years later, a visitor to Moran's studio inquired about the gondola and recorded the artist's response:

> "That is Robert Browning's gondola that we bought in Venice. It is the gondola which the poet used all the time he was in the city of the Adriatic. In it he wrote 'In a Gondola.' There are the chairs that were always in the boat, and were used by Mr. Browning." Mr. Moran pointed to two antique, heavily carven ebony chairs beside the old fireplace. "Robert Browning bought them in one of the old palaces, as I learned from the poet's gondolier, who was in our employ the entire time we were in Venice."[23]

Robert Browning's gondola did not fare well in East Hampton's Hook Pond and before long was relegated to the status of yard ornament. There it became a particularly apt totem for the artist who may have painted more views of Venice than any other American of the nineteenth century.

Return West

In March 1892 the *East Hampton Star* quoted a biographical sketch of summer resident Thomas Moran that identified him with an earlier generation of painters: "Among our older American painters who have achieved great eminence in the past, there is no one who has a greater enthusiasm for his art than has Thomas Moran. He is the youngest old man—with possibly two exceptions—both in person and in the character of art

6

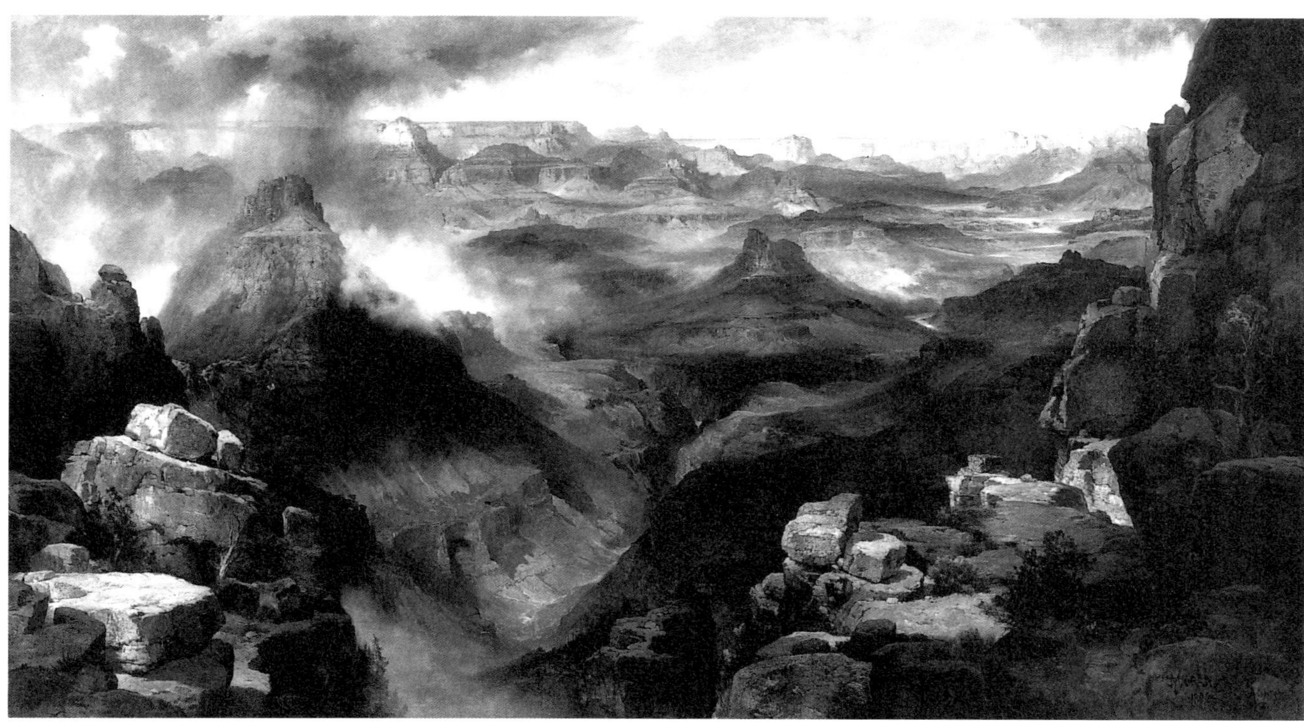

who can be found at the present moment with a palette on his thumb."[24] Moran was fifty-five years old at the time the East Hampton article appeared and, ironically, just about to depart on a rigorous trip to the Grand Canyon and Yellowstone—the landscapes that had made him famous two decades before. Accompanied by his twenty-eight-year-old son, Paul, Moran journeyed first to Chicago, where he entered into a business relationship with the Atchison, Topeka, and Santa Fe Railroad. Anxious to promote themselves as the rail route to the Grand Canyon, the Santa Fe Railroad subsidized Moran's 1892 trip in exchange for the copyright of a painting that could be used for promotional purposes (fig. 6).[25] Over time the Santa Fe Railroad became one of Moran's best patrons, sponsoring numerous trips to the canyon and extended stays at the El Tovar Hotel.

In 1892 the company's advertising agent, C. A. Higgins, traveled with Moran to the Grand Canyon. On 21 May they reached Flagstaff, Arizona, where they were joined by William Henry Jackson. Although both Moran and Jackson had visited the canyon earlier, they had not done so together, nor had they visited the south rim. Thus the collaboration between artist and photographer that had proven so rewarding in Yellowstone in 1871 took place at the Grand Canyon for the first time in 1892.

Early in June 1892 Moran, Jackson, and their companions reached the rim of the canyon. There they were met by legendary guide and raconteur, John Hance (fig. 7). Hance had arrived at the canyon a decade earlier in search of mining opportunities but had quickly perceived that tourism would prove more profitable. His "ranch" near Grandview Point was, in effect, the canyon's first hotel, and it was there that Moran and his party stayed early in their journey as they made their way down the canyon to the river. All the while Moran sketched and Jackson took photographs. Several days later Moran described the descent in a letter to Mary, noting that as they neared the river the route became so treacherous they had to let themselves down with ropes. He continued, "We were all very tired having descended more than 5000 feet from the brink to the river, but it was a glorious trip."[26] Jackson took a number of photographs from the floor of the canyon before they began their ascent. As Moran noted, "We had to mount all the falls again by the ropes we came down on, which we accomplished all right and just at dark camped under some rocks about 2 miles from Hance's cabin in the canon. After a good supper we wrapped ourselves in our blankets and laid on the open ground and slept the sleep of the tired."[27] It was likely at this camp that Moran completed one of the most remarkable of his Grand Canyon watercolors, *In the Lava Beds* (cat. 71). The image is small and elegantly spare. All around are the lava cliffs that proved such an impediment to their canyon descent. In the middle distance smoke from the evening campfire drifts upward. At the right, beneath massive boulders, are the tiny figures of Moran's fellow travelers. In the foreground, fragile and isolated, is Jackson's camera. Mounted on spindly legs that look to have been painted with single strokes of a tiny brush, the camera seems aptly emblematic of the fragility of the human enterprise in a landscape as overpowering as that of the Grand Canyon. Less than 10 x 12 inches in size, Moran's *plein-air* watercolor stands in marked contrast to the enormous paintings that brought him great acclaim. *In the Lava Beds* serves as a fitting reminder that Moran's remarkable *plein-air* studies frequently exhibit an intimacy that did not transfer to his studio oils. Much less iconic than the monumental canvases, they record the artist's personal response rather than a market mandate.

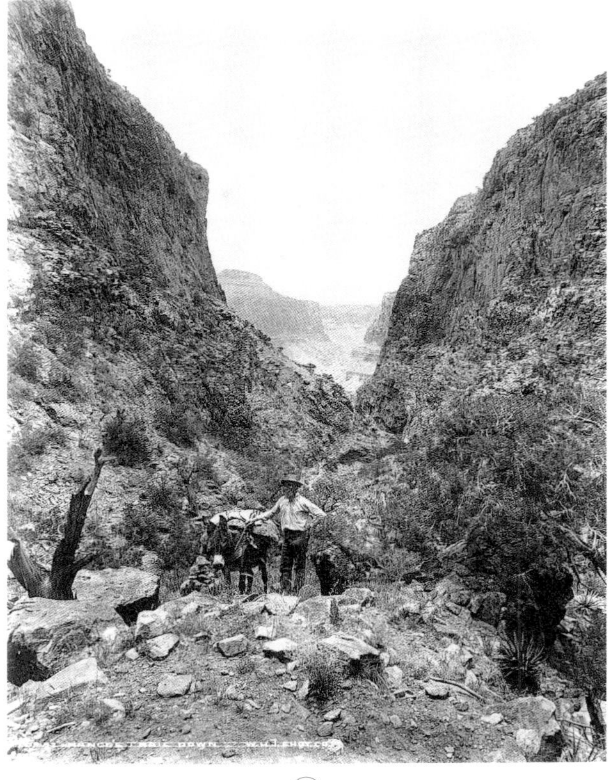
7

After a week at the Grand Canyon, Moran and his party returned to Flagstaff. From there Mr. Higgins returned to Chicago, and Paul to East Hampton. Moran and Jackson, however, journeyed on—first to Denver, then to Yellowstone.

The purpose of the journey was reported by Denver's *Rocky Mountain News*: "Mr. Moran is on his way to Yellowstone National Park. He will be accompanied on his trip by W. H. Jackson of this city and the world's fair commissioners of Wyoming, the object of the trip being to secure materials for a large picture to be exhibited at the world's fair."[28]

When Moran returned to Yellowstone in 1892, he found himself a celebrity. In a letter to Mary he wrote: "I have been made much of at all the places in the park as the great and only 'Moran' the painter of Yellowstone and I am looked at curiously by all the people at the Hotels."[29] Jackson and Moran spent many days in the park visiting sites they had been the first to photograph and paint nearly twenty years earlier. Keenly aware of changes in the landscape, Moran noted, "The Great Blue Spring that I drew for Prang's work is about ten times as large as when I saw it last and has become the greatest geyser in the basin" (Appendix 1).[30]

Although he visited many sites within the park, Moran chose to meet his obligation to the exposition committee by returning to the subject of the painting that Congress had purchased twenty years earlier. On a canvas even larger than the first (8 x 14 feet) Moran revisited, visually, the Grand Canyon of the Yellowstone (fig. 8). Although the view down the canyon is the same, the two paintings are significantly different. In the later work Moran's brushwork is far looser and geologic concerns more relaxed. In the foreground at the left, where the figures of Hayden, Jackson, and Moran had provided scale and historical presence in the earlier painting, all signs of human presence have been erased. Even the towering trees that framed the first picture have been reduced in size. Instead Moran concentrated on Yellowstone's spectacular color. No longer fearful of disbelief, Moran was free to celebrate the luminous colors of the canyon with paint that is remarkably thin and transparent.

Ironically, just prior to his return to the Grand Canyon and Yellowstone in 1892, the *East Hampton Star* published a biographical sketch of Moran that included the comments:

> Two decades ago, when Mr. Moran made a journey through the Yellowstone region and spent many enchanted months in the wildest portions of the Rockies he was convinced that no greater mine of pictorial wealth could be found than in the country upon whose inspiring grandeur he then feasted his eyes. He did not dare to paint nature as she was in these parts. Untraveled folk would call him mad and say the burning colors of his mountains and ravines did not exist, or, if they did, they were not as he showed them. As it was, when our painter returned from the West laden with a store of marvelous canvases, he was forewarned by his brother painters that it would be little better than professional suicide to exhibit such startling views in a public gallery as those he privately displayed. It did not take many years of persistent painting and exhibiting of his Yellowstone and various Rocky Mountain pictures to convince the long-eared public that what he presented was the modified truth of nature and not eccentric nightmares of color and design.[31]

8

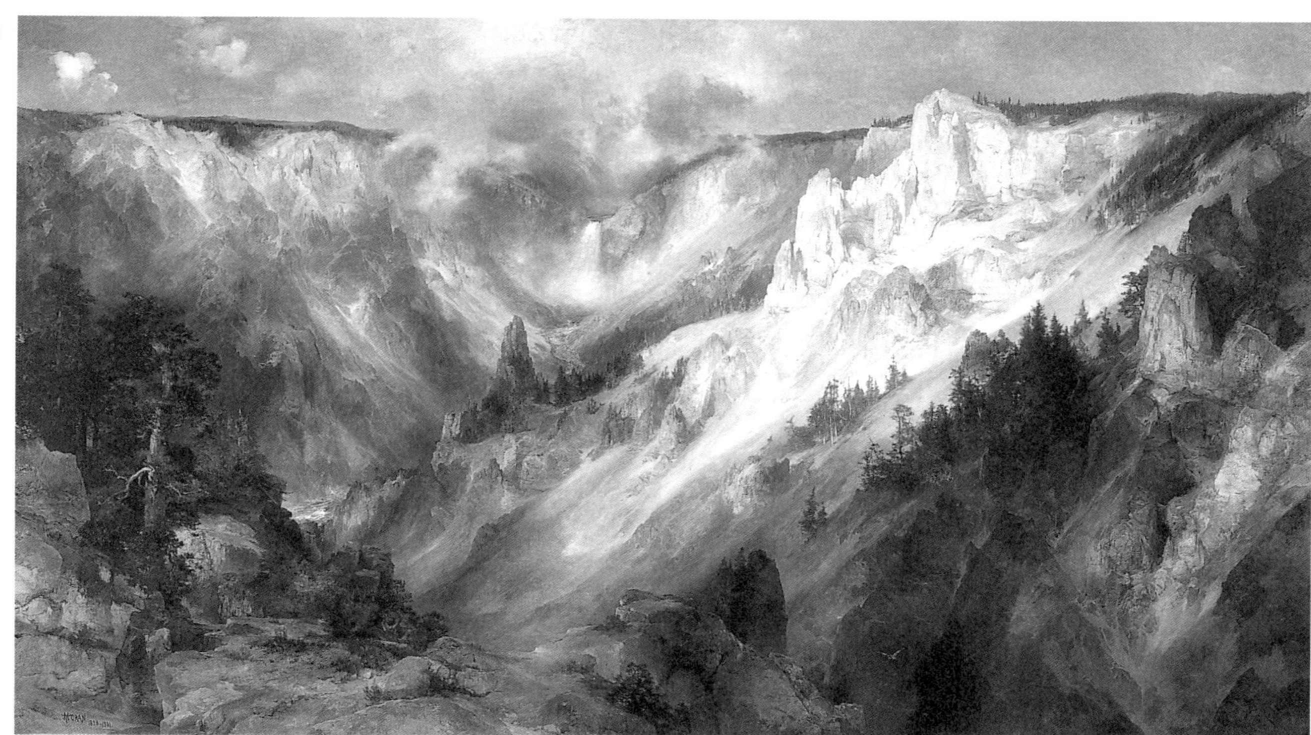

8. Thomas Moran, *The Grand Canyon of the Yellowstone,* 1893–1901, oil on canvas, courtesy National Museum of American Art, Smithsonian Institution, Gift of George D. Pratt.

9. Thomas Moran's house at East Hampton, 1995.

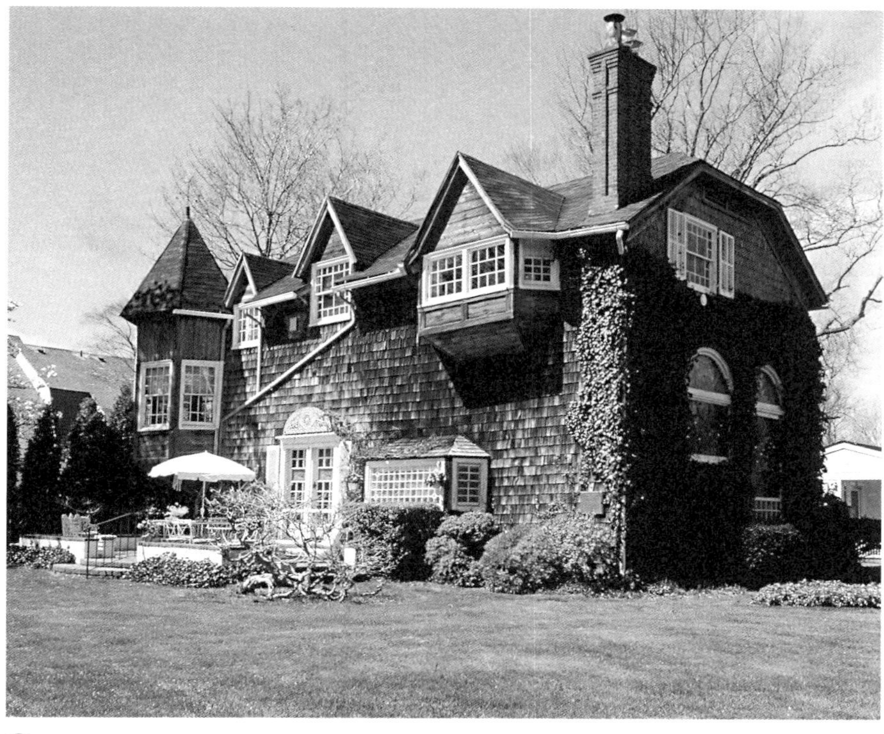

9

By 1892 Yellowstone had been visited by enough "long-eared" tourists that Moran no longer had to fear being labeled "dishonest" for his depiction of the canyon's startling color.

In 1893 Moran's late version of *Grand Canyon of the Yellowstone*, along with an earlier painting of North Atlantic icebergs, *Spectres from the North* (cat. 70), was exhibited at the World's Columbian Exposition in Chicago. Neither picture drew special attention and both remained unsold at the time of the artist's death. Well aware of changes in the market, Moran told a Denver reporter in June 1892, "I prefer to paint western scenes, but the Eastern people don't appreciate the grand scenery of the Rockies. They are not familiar with mountain effects and it is much easier to sell a picture of a Long Island swamp than the grandest picture of Colorado."[32] Times and the picture market had changed.

Loss

When Moran returned home in August 1892, it was to the house and studio that he and Mary had built eight years earlier in the village of East Hampton on Long Island. Both had first visited the area in 1878 when they were invited to accompany members of the Tile Club on a sketching trip. Enchanted by the village and the surrounding countryside, they later purchased property on Main Street near Town Pond. In 1884 they built the home that initially served as a summer residence but quickly became the center of Moran family life (fig. 9).

In June 1898, shortly after the outbreak of the Spanish American War, a military camp was hastily built near Montauk, on the eastern tip of Long Island. Later in the year, when Theodore Roosevelt's Rough Riders and other soldiers began to return from Cuba ill with fever, a tent hospital was added to the Montauk camp. By late September two additional hospitals in East Hampton were also treating fever-ridden soldiers.[33]

For months residents of East Hampton and other Long Island communities helped care for the soldiers. Mary Moran and her daughter Ruth were among many volunteers acknowledged in the *East Hampton Star* as having contributed to the effort. In September 1898 the *Brooklyn Eagle* reported on the kindness of East Hampton residents, noting: "Many of the cottagers at East Hampton now send their carriages daily to the soldiers hospitals to give the men a drive on pleasant days, and the sight of a group of troopers in blue or in the faded buff uniform of the Rough Riders, carefully wrapped in blankets, driven by a liveried coachman, is frequently met on the village drives or along the picturesque lanes."[34]

Such kind ministrations had tragic consequences for the Moran family the following year, when first Ruth and then her mother became ill. After a long convalescence Ruth recovered, but on 25 September 1899 Mary Moran died. She was buried the following day in the cemetery across the street from the East Hampton home she and Thomas had built fifteen years earlier.[35]

Following her mother's death, Ruth became her father's constant companion and business partner for the remainder of his life. Despite Ruth's dedication to his well-being, Moran never fully recovered from the loss of Mary.

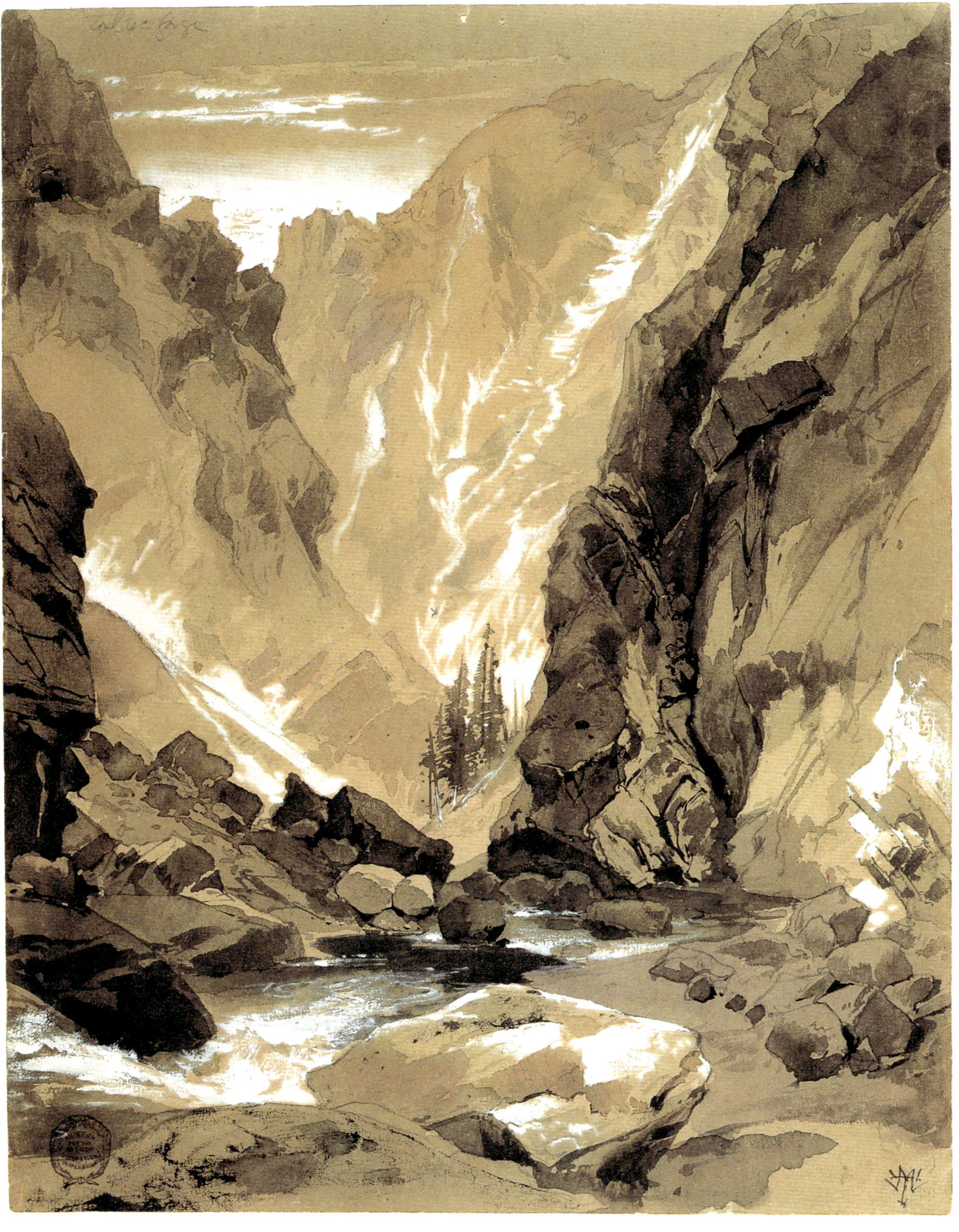

60

Toltec Gorge, Colorado

c. 1881, watercolor
31.9 x 24.1 (12 $^{9}/_{16}$ x 9 ½)
Cooper-Hewitt National Design Museum, Smithsonian Institution, Gift of Thomas Moran

Washington only

SIX MILES ahead lay the cañon of which we had heard so much,—the Toltec Gorge, whose praises could not be overdrawn. Evidently his majesty had entrenched himself in glories beside which any ordinary monarch would lose his magnificence. Was this king of cañons really so great he could afford to risk all rivalry? Here, on the left, what noble martello-tower of native lava is that which stands undizzied on the very brink of the precipice? I should like to roll it off, and watch it cut a swath through that puny forest down there, and dam up the whole stream with its huge breadth....

In the most secluded nook of the mountains we come upon Phantom Curve, with its company of isolated rocks, made of stuff so hard as to have stood upright, tall, grotesque, and sunburned. ...Miles away you can trace these black pinnacles, like sentinels, mid-way up the slopes; but here at hand they fill the eye....

Winding along the slender track, among these solemn forms, we approach the gorge, the vastly seamed and wrinkled face of whose opposite wall confronts us under the frown of an intense shade,—unused to the light from all eternity; but on this, the sunny side, a rosy pile, lifts its massive head proudly far above us, its square, fearless forehead,—

Fronting heaven's splendor,
Strong and full and clear.

How should we pass it? On the right stood the solid palisade of the sierra, rising unbroken to the ultimate heights; on the left the gulf, its sides more and more nearly vertical, more and more terrible in their armature of splintered ledges and pike-pointed tree-tops,—more often breaking away into perpendicular cliffs, whence we could hurl a pebble, or ourselves, into the mad torrent easily seen but too far below to be heard; and as we draw nearer, the rosy crags rise higher and more distinct across our path. We turn a curve in the track the cars leaning toward the inside, as if they, too, retreated from the look down into that "vasty deep," and lo! a gateway tunneled through,—the barrier is conquered!

The blank of the tunnel gives one time to think. Pictures of the beetling, ebony-pillared cliffs linger in the retina suddenly deprived of the reality, and reproduce the seamed and jagged rocks in fiery similitude upon the darkness. In a twinkling the impression fades, and at the same instant you catch a gleam of advancing light, and dash out into the sunshine,—into the sunshine only? Oh, no, out into the air,—an awful leap abroad into invisible bounded space; and you catch your breath, startled beyond self-control!

Then it is all over, and you are still on your feet, listening to the familiar ring of the brown walls as they fly past.

What was it you saw that made your breathing cease, and the blood chill in your heart with swift terror? It is hard to remember; but there remains a feeling of an instant's suspension over an irregular chasm that seemed cut to the very center of the earth, and, to your dilated eye, gleamed brightly at the bottom, as though it penetrated even the realms of Pluto. You knew it opened outwardly into the gorge, for there in front stood the mighty wall, bracing the mountain far overhead, and below flashed the foaming river. This is the sum of your recollection, photographed upon your brain by a mental process more instantaneous than any application of art....

Our train having halted, the Artist sought a favorable position for obtaining the sketch of Toltec Gorge which adorns these pages, the Photographer became similarly absorbed, and the remaining members of the expedition zealously examined a spot whose counterpart in rugged and inspiring sublimity probably does not exist elsewhere in America. A few rods up the cañon a thin and ragged pinnacle rises abruptly from the very bottom to a level with the railway track. This point has been christened Eva Cliff, and when we had gained its crest by dint of much laborious and hazardous climbing over a narrow gangway of rocks, by which it is barely connected with the neighboring bank, our exertions were well repaid by the splendid view of the gorge it afforded. (Ingersoll 1885, 116–118)

AN HOUR'S RIDE from Antonita brings the traveler to the brow of a precipitous hill, from whence he looks down on the picturesque valley of the Los Pinos. As the advance is made around the mountain spurs and deep ravines, glimpses are caught of profound depths and towering heights, and then the train, making a detour of four miles around a side cañon, plunges into the blackness of Toltec tunnel, which is remarkable in that it pierces the summit of the mountain instead of its base. Twelve hundred feet of perpendicular descent would take one to the bottom of the gorge, while the seared and wrinkled expanse of the opposite wall confronts us, lifting its massive bulwarks high above us....

When the train emerges from the tunnel it is upon the brink of a precipice. A solid bridge of trestle-work, set in the rock after the manner of a balcony, supports the track, and from this coigne of vantage the traveler beholds a most thrilling spectacle. The tremendous gorge, whose sides are splintered rocks and monumental crags and whose depths are filled with the snow-white waters of a foaming torrent, lies beneath him, the blue sky is above him and all around the majesty and mystery of the mountains. (*Rhymes of the Rockies; Or, What the Poets Have Found to Say of the Beautiful Scenery on the Denver and Rio Grande Railroad* [Chicago, 1891], 27)

Toltec Gorge

Against the snows of cloud hills high,
    Majestic mountains, centuries old,
Reach rugged heights far up the sky,
    Like Babel's tower in story old.

The winds of night in furious rage
    Beat 'gainst the wall 'twixt earth and Heaven;
Each element tireless war did wage;
    Backward, defeated each was driven.

The warm Chinook o'er the prairie sighed;
    The north wind fled to frozen seas;
The chill east wind in coast fogs died;
    The avalanche crashed amid the trees.

Furrowed and tortured, in silent woe,
    One mountain bore the storms of ages,
And sun of summer or winter's snow
    Left no trace on its mystic pages.

But a drift of snow that lay long hidden
    In creviced niche on a lean peak's crest,
Wept bitter tears that crept unchidden
    Far down the mountain's unyielding breast.

The river down in the valley knew,
    For the stream whispered when they met—
The brook and river—and, laughing, too,
    The hills had never a thought as yet.

In years the mountain's heart of rock
    Yields to the subtle brook, and fast,
With thunder peal and earthquake shock,
    Crashed chasm open—defeat at last.

Centuries pass. The deep drifted snows
    Fade 'neath summer suns, and the stream
Widens the gorge, and misty breath throws
    High up black walls that silvery gleam.

But a web is cast of iron strong,
    Like a spider's home of thread-like coil.
The brook is tamed, and its echoing song
    Praises the power of human toil.

(Patience Stapleton, in *Rhymes of the Rockies*, 1891, 28)

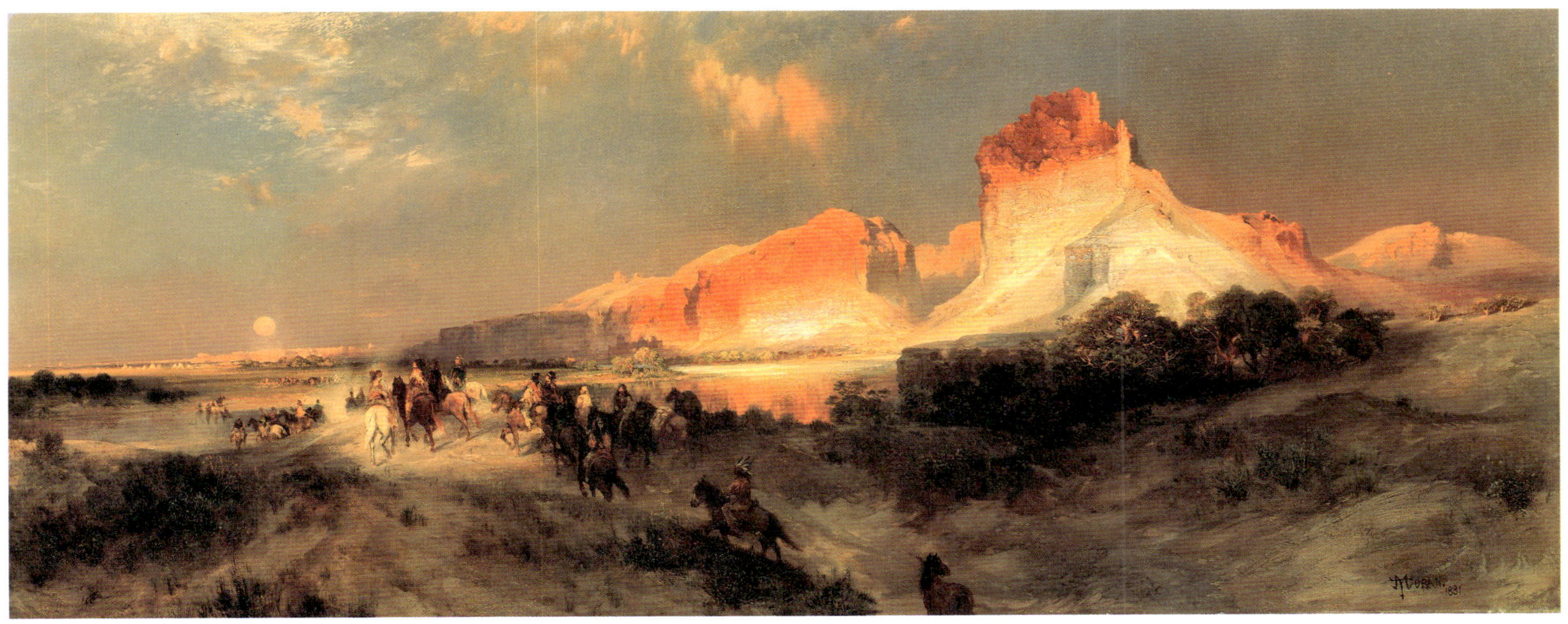

61

Green River Cliffs, Wyoming

1881, oil on canvas
63.5 x 157.5 (25 x 62)
Private Collection, Colorado

MR. MORAN employs colour with great mastery; there is no thinness or weakness evident in his paintings. The texture of rocks and foliage is carefully and truthfully reproduced. He is partial to the brighter aspects of nature, and succeeds in representing them without conveying the impression of garishness. A painting he has recently completed shows a sublime, isolated peak, cloven in the centre, that soars like a Titanic feudal tower above the banks of the Green River, a tributary of the Colorado. The colours of this natural fortress are vivid copper, streaked with vermilion, and merging into leaden grey. It is painted sun-smitten against the foreboding gloom of a coming storm. The broad river flows grandly at its base through an endless plain that fades off like the ocean into the infinite. In the foreground a troop of Indian warriors, in the gay accoutrements of battle, are guiding their spirited ponies through long sere herbage to the river's brink. The colours in this painting, with the contrasted greys and reds, are very striking, and yet are so admirably harmonised that one is convinced without hesitation that the scene must be strictly true to nature. (Benjamin 1882, 92)

62

Cliffs of the Upper Colorado River, Wyoming Territory

1882, oil on canvas
40.6 x 61 (16 x 24)
National Museum of American Art, Smithsonian Institution, Bequest of Henry Ward Ranger through the National Academy of Design

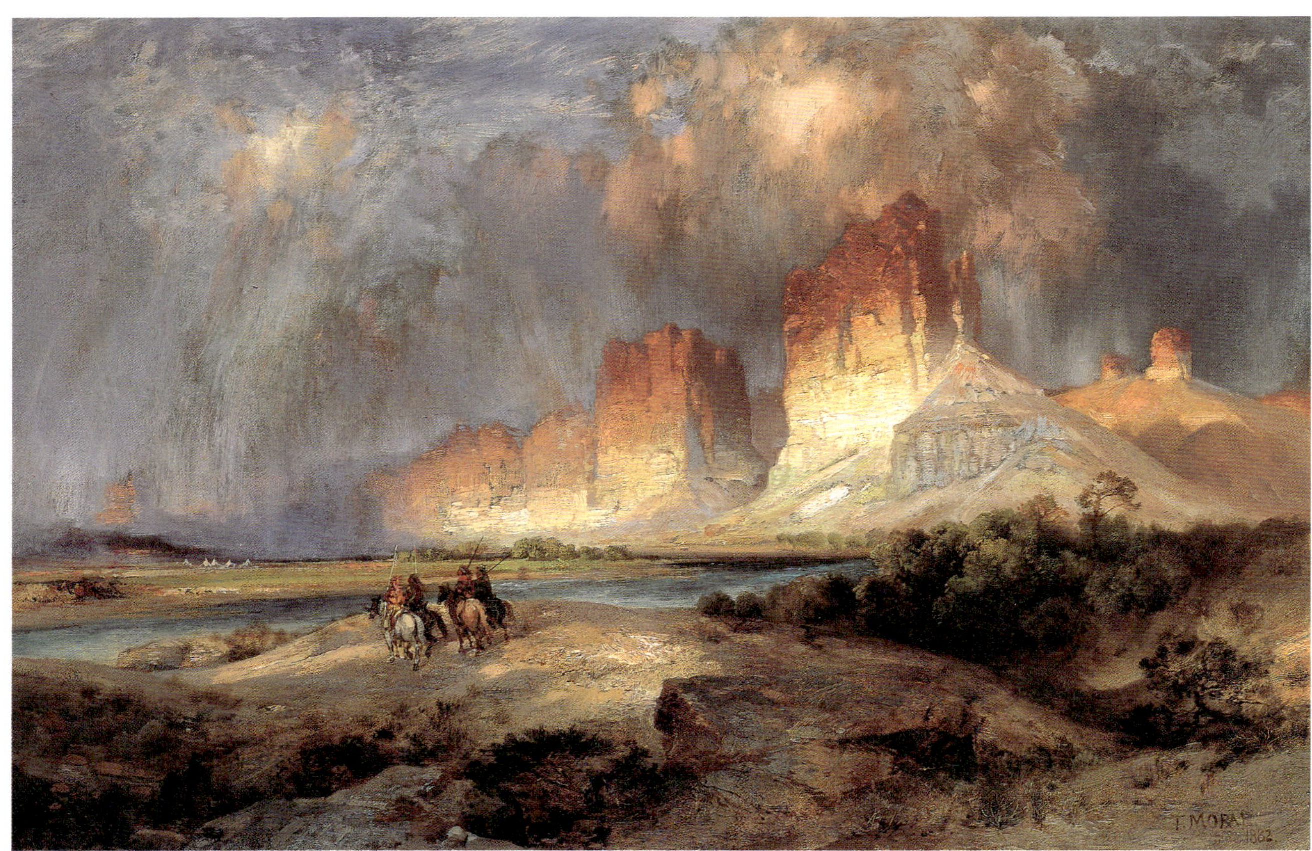

63

Pass at Glencoe, Scotland

1882, watercolor
50.8 x 76.2 (20 x 30)
Gilcrease Museum, Tulsa, Oklahoma

HOISTED ONCE more upon the roof of a Highland coach, in the best of spirits, pipes and cigars, flasks of the real mountain tonic within easy range, there was not a merrier party within the rocky shores of Scotland. There is something very invigorating about a Highland coach. the four spirited horses, the smoothness of the roads, the humor of the driver, who is generally a character, the delightful feeling of utter abandon....

The American tourist who has never visited the Yosemite Valley or the Cañons of Colorado, can form but little idea of the Wildness and grandeur of Glen Coe. Our ride that day of 20 miles led us through wilds where cultivation is unknown, and where the lonely shepherd's is the only human foot that treads the heath. Rocks on every hand—mountains on every side.

"Crags, knolls and stones confusedly hurled, the fragments of an earlier world." ([Viator],"Scotland: Coaching," *NY Mail,* 20 May 1872)

THE "Bridge of Three Waters, Pass of Glencoe, Scotland," where the massacre of the MacDonalds took place, is painted with the love and the spirit of a Highlander, and one might fancy that the artist had worked to the sound of the bagpipes. Mr. Moran possesses something of the feeling for color that made Turner immortal. ("Art Notes," *The Critic* [27 Feb. 1886], 108)

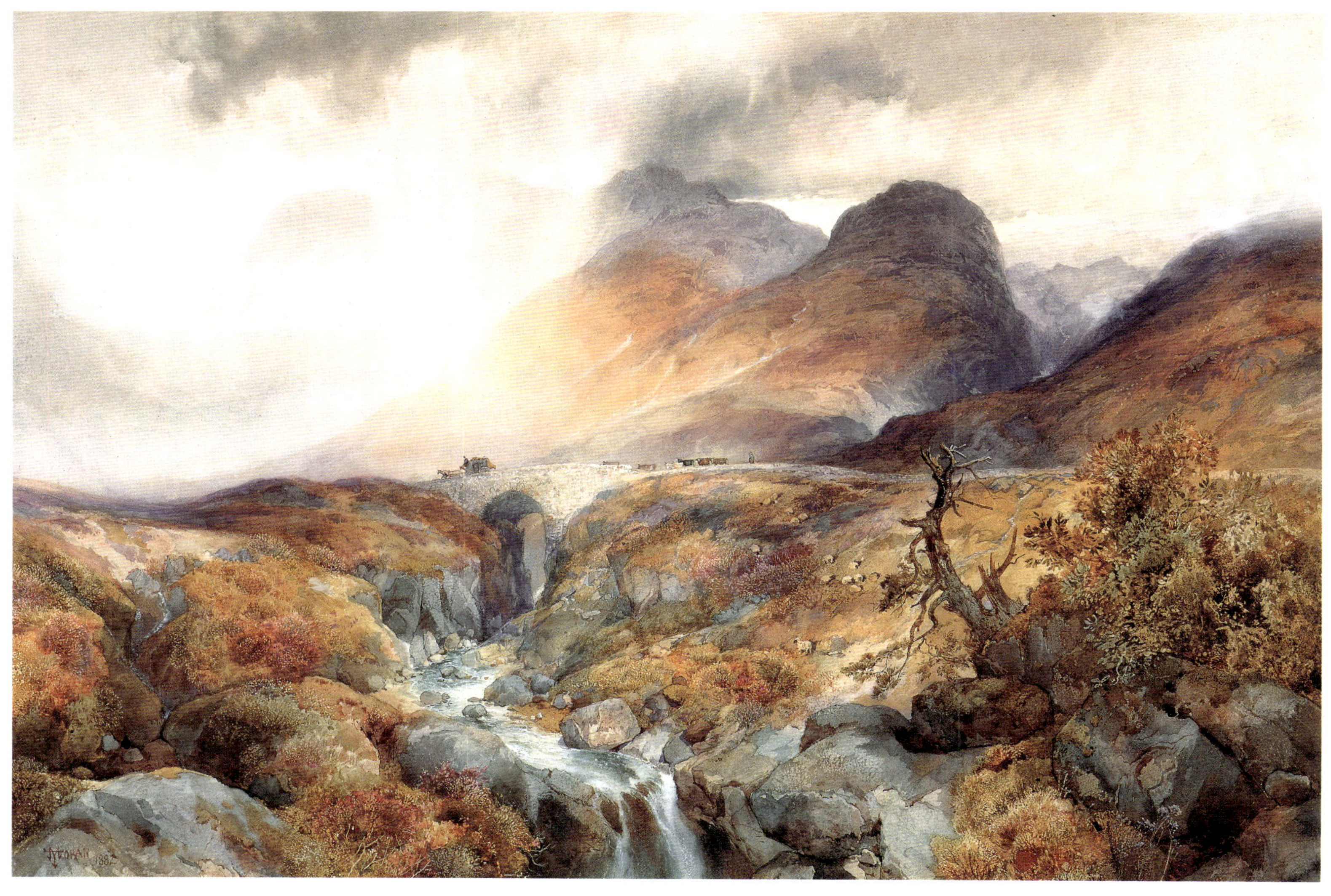

64

Trojes Mine

1883, watercolor
25.4 x 36.8 (10 x 14½)
Private Collection

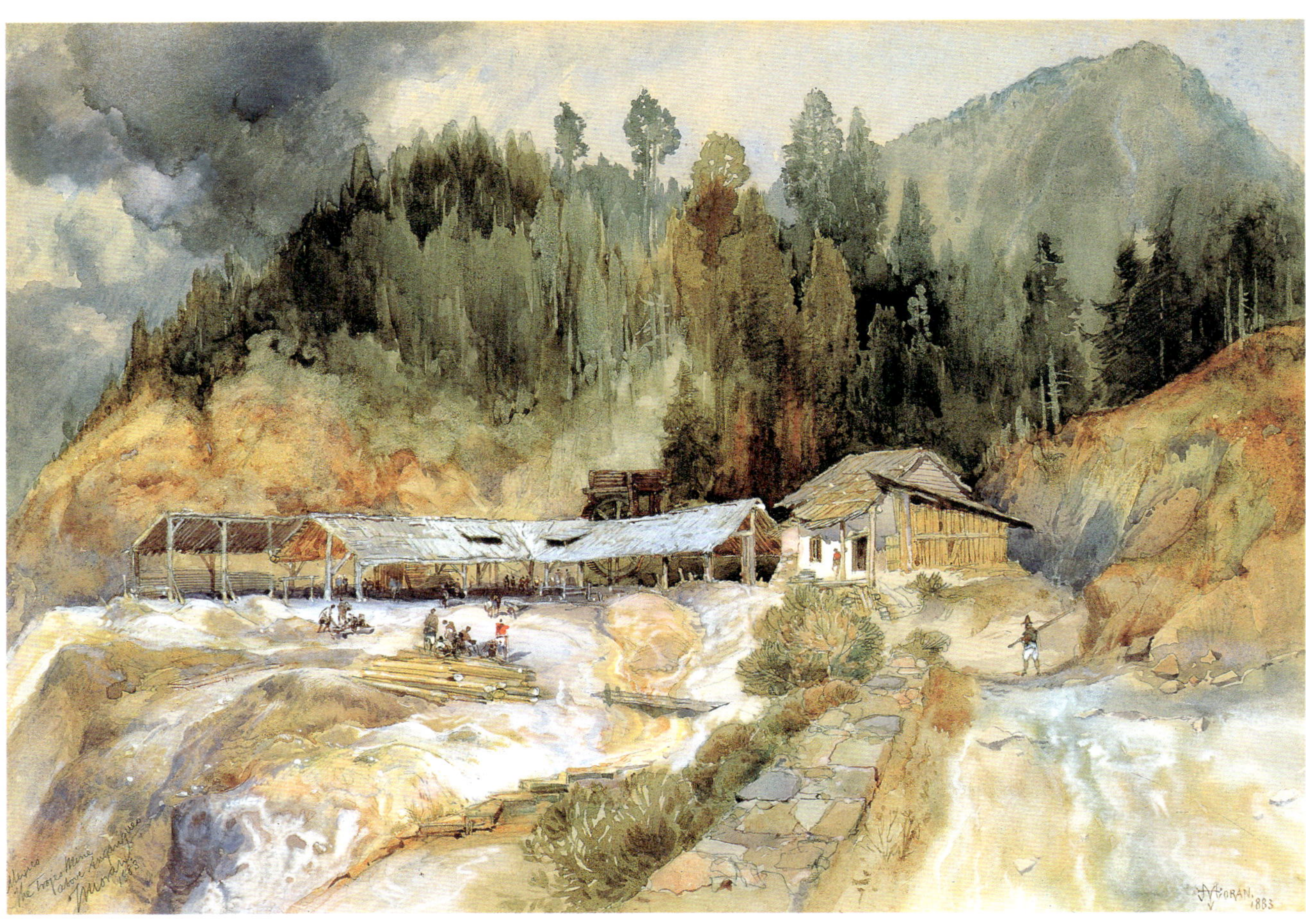

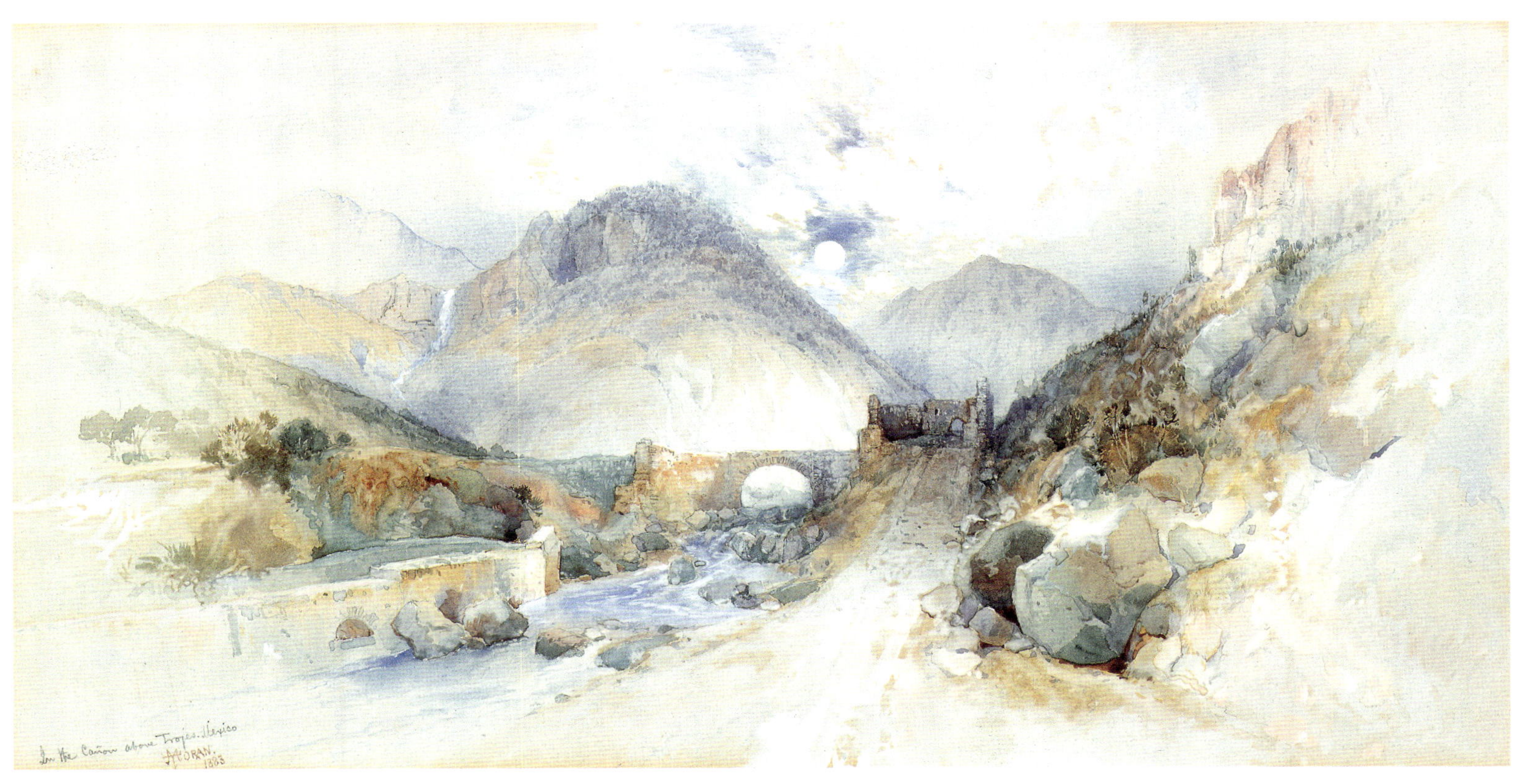

65

In the Cañon above Trojes, Mexico

1883, watercolor
27.9 x 54 (11 x 21 ¼)
Private Collection

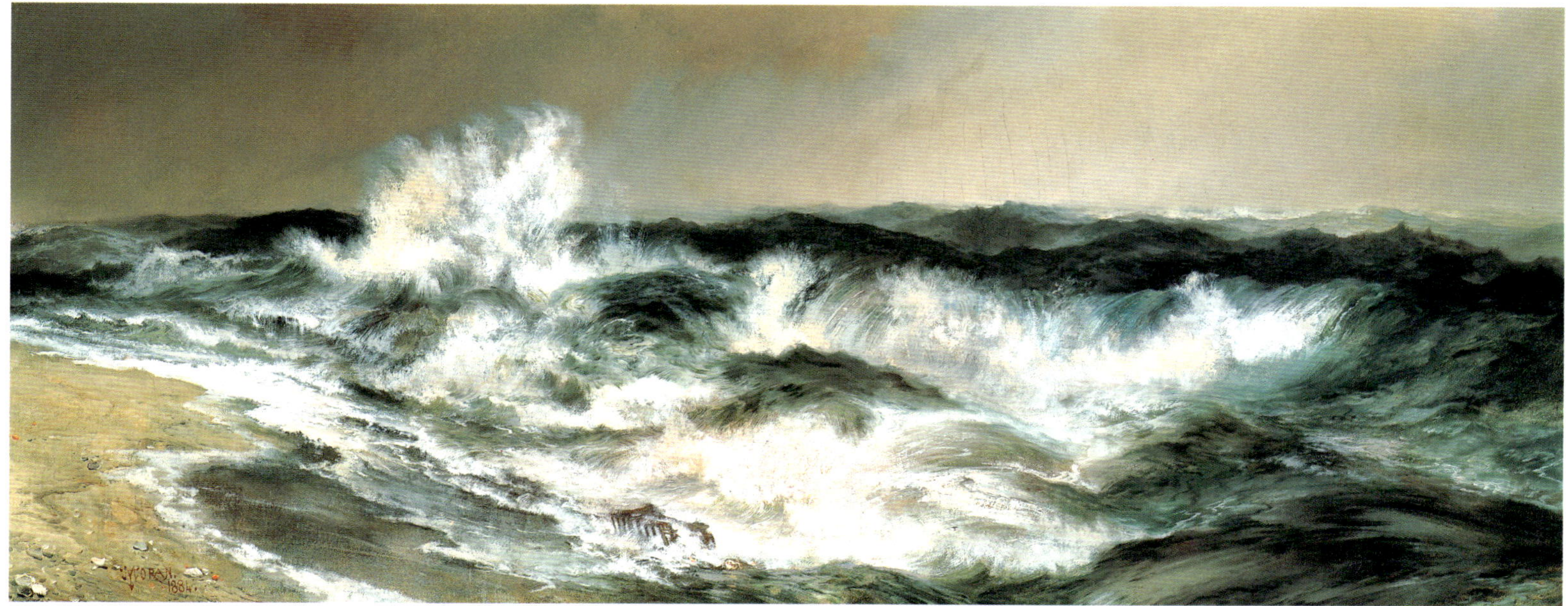

66

The Much Resounding Sea

1884, oil on canvas
63.9 x 158.2 (25 3/16 x 62 5/16)
National Gallery of Art, Washington, Gift of the Avalon Foundation

LIKE UNTO the blast of boisterous winds, which rushes down to the plain, urged by the thunder of Father Jove, and with a dreadful tumult is mingled with the ocean; and in it [rise] many boiling billows of the much resounding sea, swollen, whitened with foam. (*The Iliad of Homer,* trans. Theodore Alois Buckley [New York, 1857])

67

Cloudy Day at Amagansett

1884, oil on canvas
40.6 x 50.8 (16 x 20)
Private Collection, Seattle

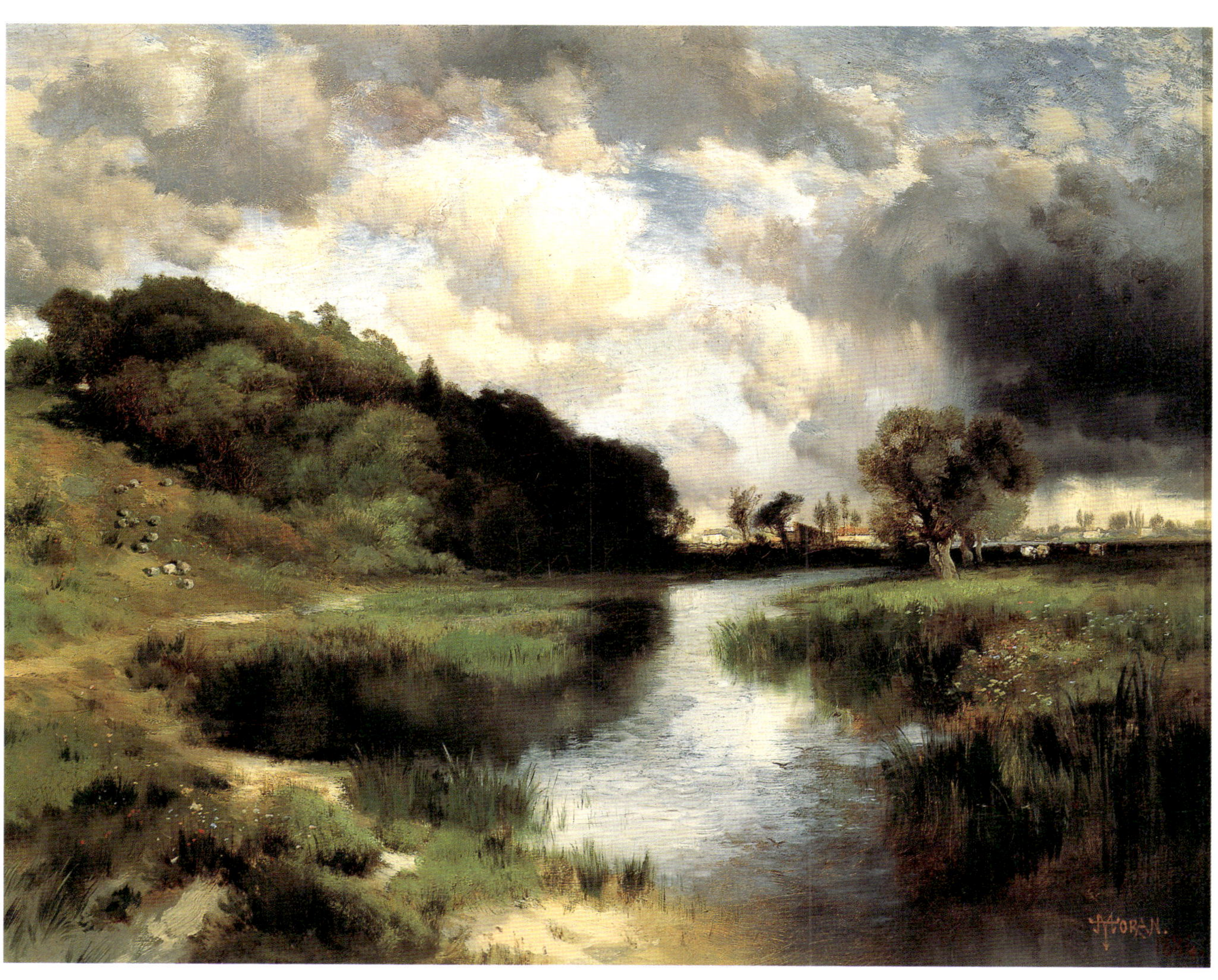

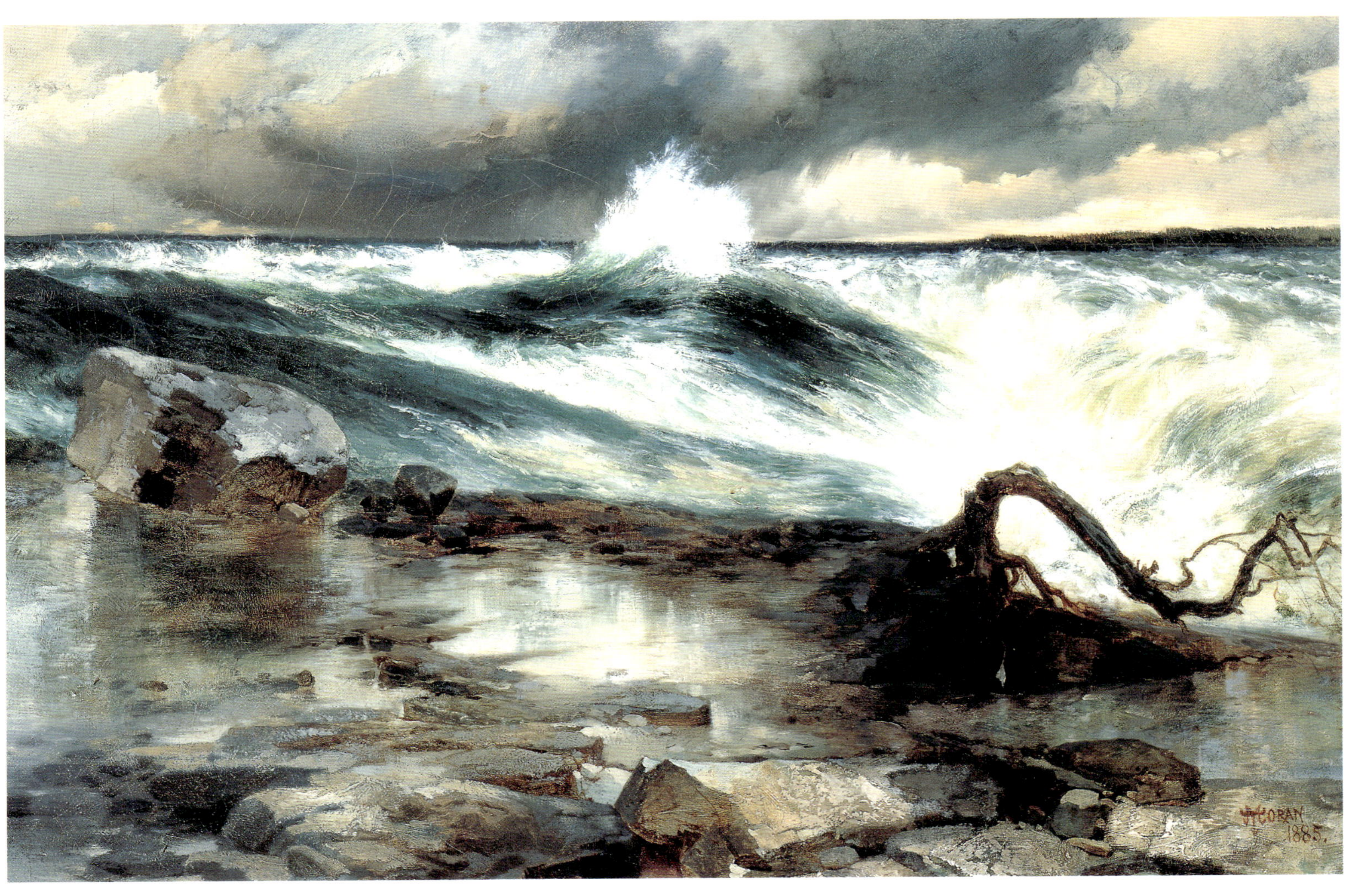

68

Rapids above Niagara

1885, oil on canvas
51.4 x 76.8 (20 ¼ x 30 ¼)
Dr. Donald and Kathryn
O'Connor Counts

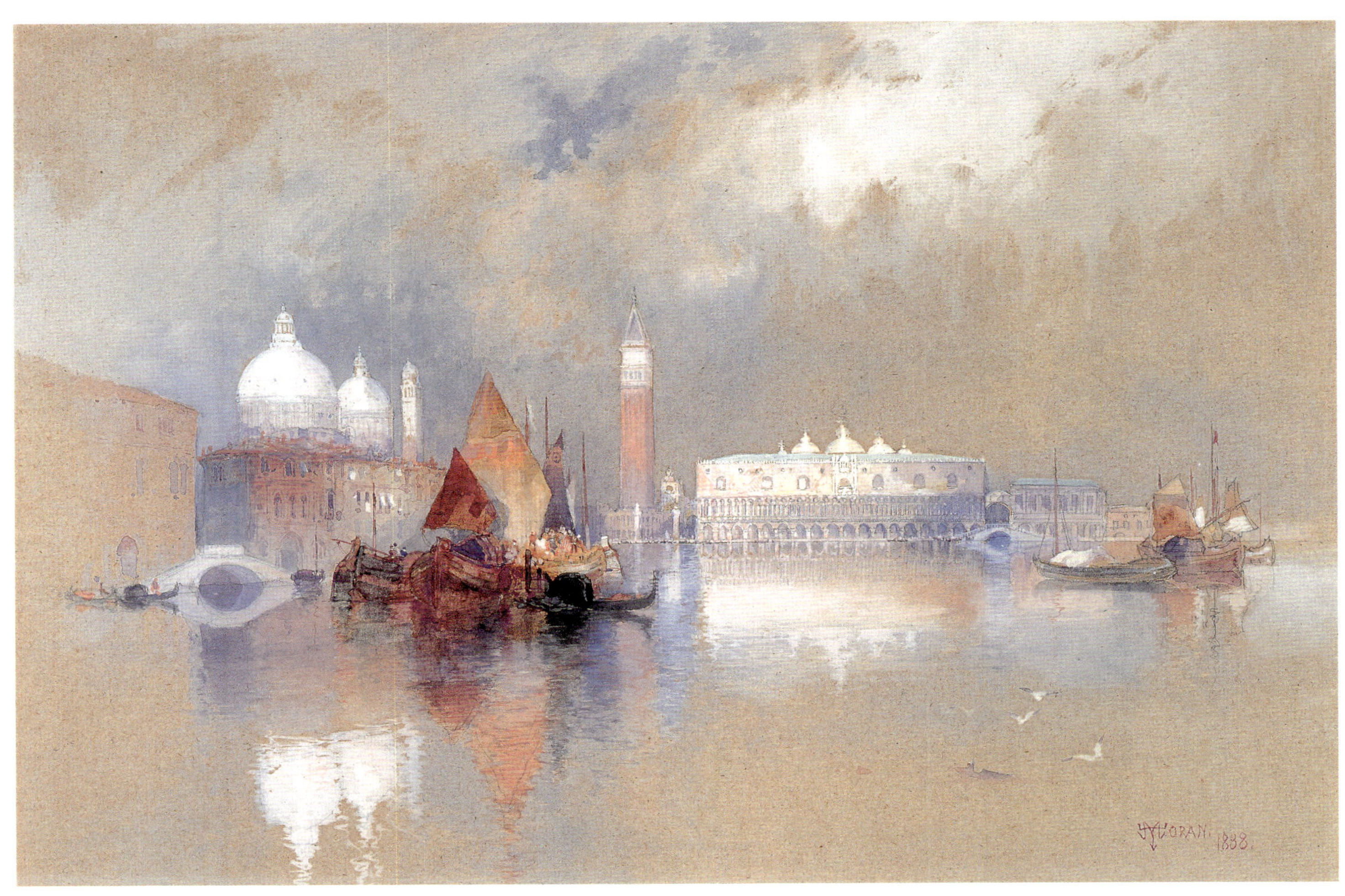

69

View of Venice

1888, watercolor
28.6 x 41.6 (11¼ x 16⅜)
Corcoran Gallery
of Art, Washington, DC,
Gift of James Parmelee

Washington and
Seattle only

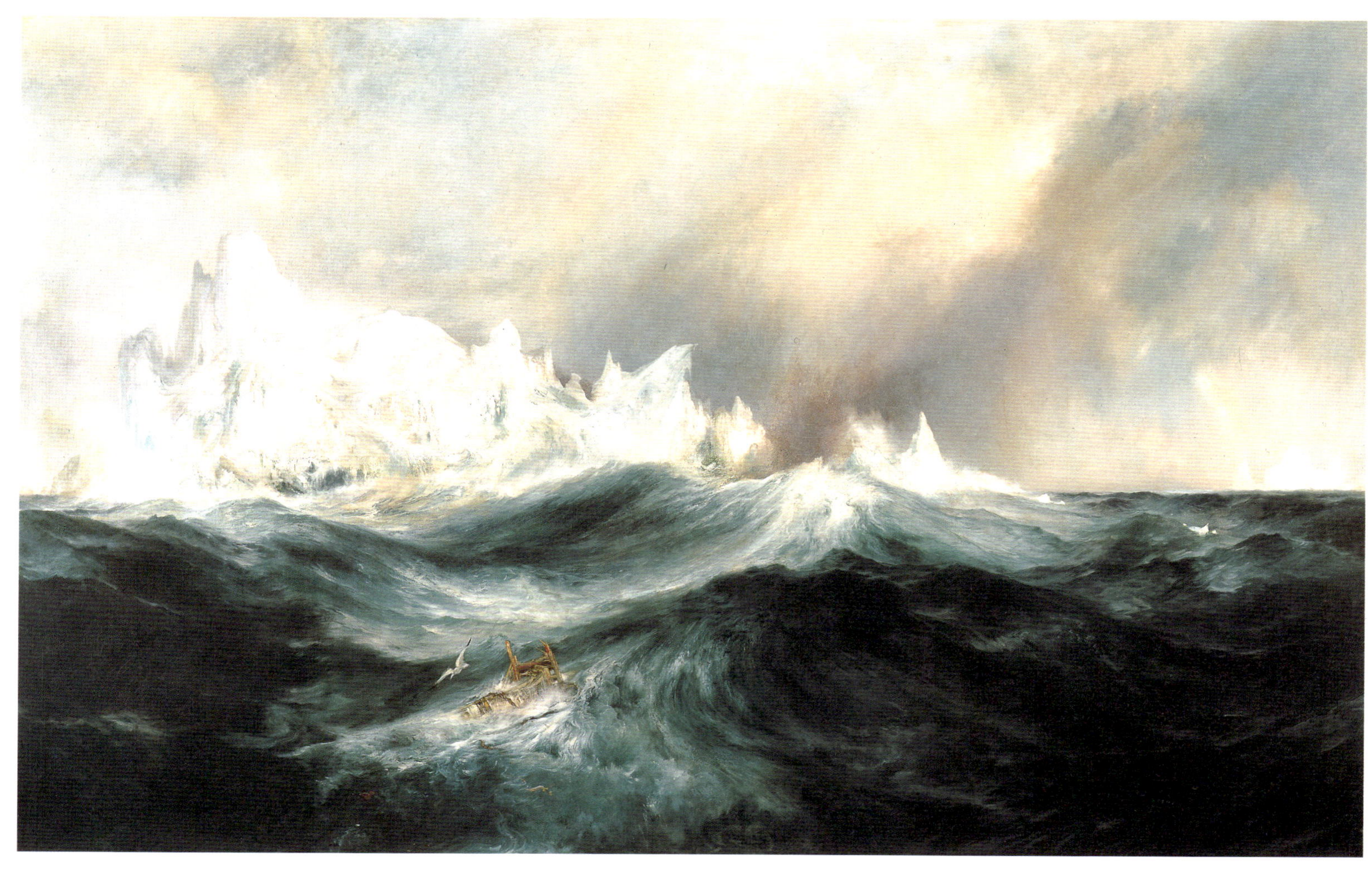

70

Spectres from the North

1891, oil on canvas
188 x 299.7 (74 x 118)
Gilcrease Museum,
Tulsa, Oklahoma

ICEBERGS, PAINTED from sketches made…in the spring of 1890 on the trip to Antwerp. It was painted immediately after my return, in Easthampton, & first exhibited there in the old Clinton Academy. I think it one of my best works. It was part of my exhibit at the Great World's Fair in Chicago in 1893. (GA ledger)

THOMAS MORAN'S large painting "Ice-bergs in Mid Ocean" was put on exhibition in Clinton Hall Friday afternoon, for the purpose of raising money to build a suitable walk from the bathing houses to the beach. The admission was 50c and enough cash was taken to do away with further inconveniences in regard to walks upon the beach. (*EH Star,* 30 Aug. 1890)

SPECTRES FROM THE NORTH is the title of the large painting from the brush of artist Thomas Moran, which was exhibited in Clinton Hall on the afternoon of Aug. 29. The picture, which measured six by eight feet, was stationed in the proscenium, and had been tastily draped by the ladies of the committee in charge. Mr. Moran took his subject for the picture from a view he obtained of three large ice bergs in the middle of the Atlantic during his recent return trip from Europe, and has succeeded in making a realistic picture, embracing beautiful sky, the dark rolling ocean, and three majestic and stately ice bergs. The longer one looked at the picture the more true to nature it appeared, and one could easily imagine he was being rocked by the boundless waves as he sat and gazed at the wonderful portrayal of oceanic grandeur. The artist has informed us that there are some details about the work which are yet unfinished.…Mr. Moran will exhibit his picture at the different clubs in New York this winter, and in the spring it will be put on exhibition at the national academy. (Unidentified newspaper clipping, EHL scrapbook)

A PLACE OF honor is given to a large painting by Mr. Thomas Moran, *Spectres from the North.* It is a scene from mid-ocean. An iceberg the size of an island occupies the middle distance and is seen through the spray of great billows that charge against its front with as much fury as if it were solid rock. A comrade 'spectre' is seen in the right distance and the foreground is full of tumbling waves. No sail disturbs the savage grandeur of the scene. The iceberg rises into pinnacles, and in places is brilliant with the rainbow colors that sunlight produces when penetrating great masses of ice. One thinks of the paintings of Bradford, who has long held a monopoly of such subjects, but only to the credit of Mr. Moran. He has kept the marvelous play of colors in the berg, but softened them by distance and by interposing atmosphere in which the moisture of the ocean is understood, while the clouds of spray from the surf reduce the brilliancy of the iridescence still more. The waves of the foreground are painted with surprising power, magnificently drawn and magnificently colored. It is a living scene without human life, and marks a point in the artist's career which calls for congratulations. (*NYT,* 17 Jan. 1891; repr. *EH Star,* 23 Jan.)

71

In the Lava Beds

1892, watercolor
24.1 x 31.1 (9 ½ x 12 ¼)
G. Andrew Bjurman

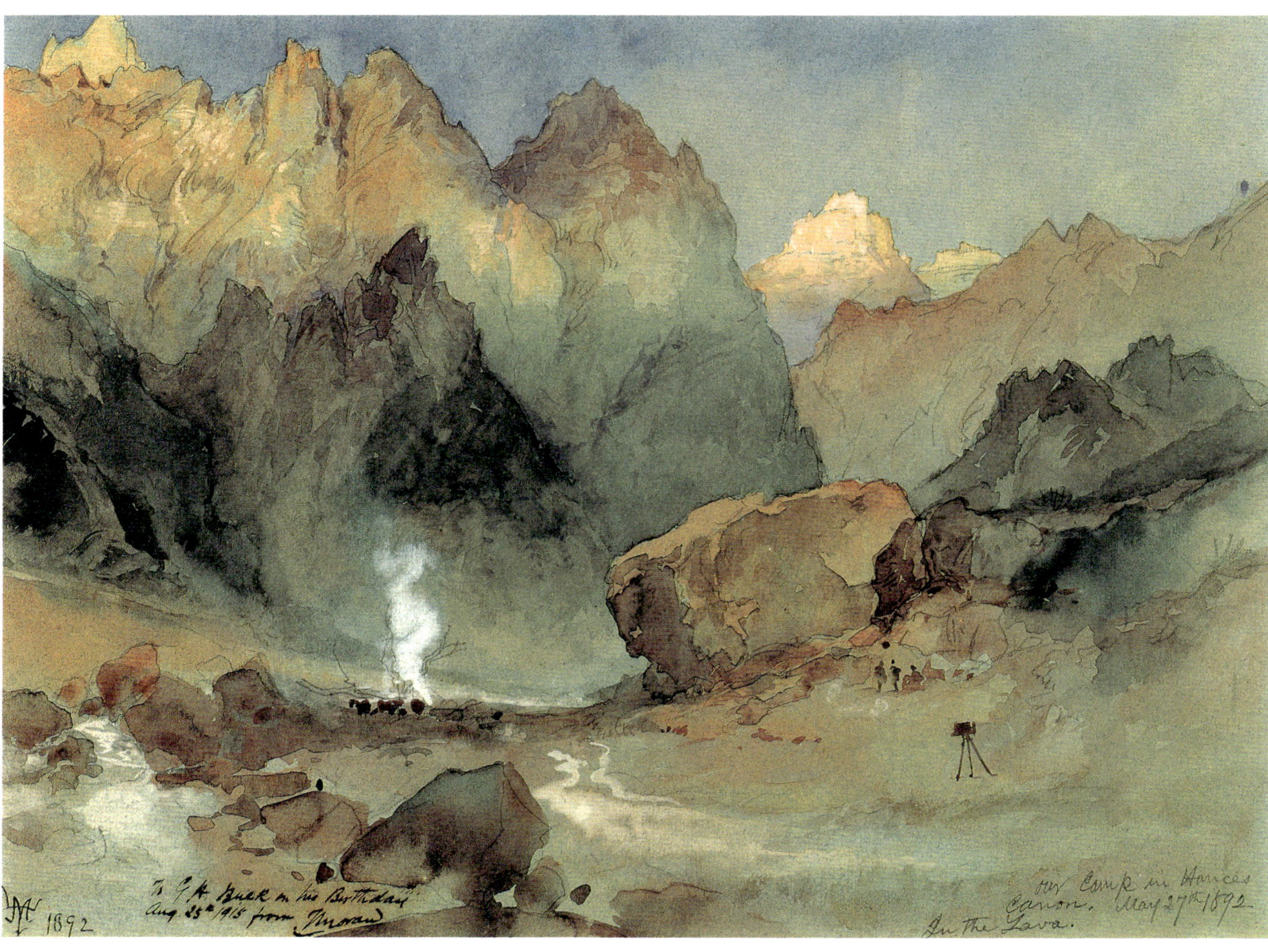

AFTER DINNER we started for the river. The trail was easy enough until we struck the first waterfall in the lava. Here we let ourselves down with ropes and in the same way of six waterfalls. Jackson's photos will show you how we did it. We reached the river about 4 in the afternoon. It was very full and muddy and it seemed to me that the rapids were equal to the Whirlpool rapids at Niagara. Black lava 2000 feet in height was all around us except an occasional glimpse of the higher sandstone peaks in the openings. We were all very tired having descended more than 5000 feet from the brink to the river, but it was a glorious trip. After photographing for an hour, we began the return to where we were to camp for the night about 2 miles up. We had to mount all the falls again by the ropes we came down on, which we accomplished all right and just at dark camped under some rocks about 2 miles from Hance's cabin in the Cañon. After a good supper we wrapped ourselves in our blankets and laid on the open ground and slept the sleep of the tired. (Moran to Mary Nimmo Moran, from Denver, 5 June 1892, in Bassford and Fryxell 1967, 90–91)

72

Smelting Works at Denver

1892, watercolor
24 x 31.8 (9 3/8 x 12 1/2)
The Cleveland Museum of Art, Bequest of Mrs. Henry A. Everett for the Dorothy Burnham Everett Memorial Collection

Washington only

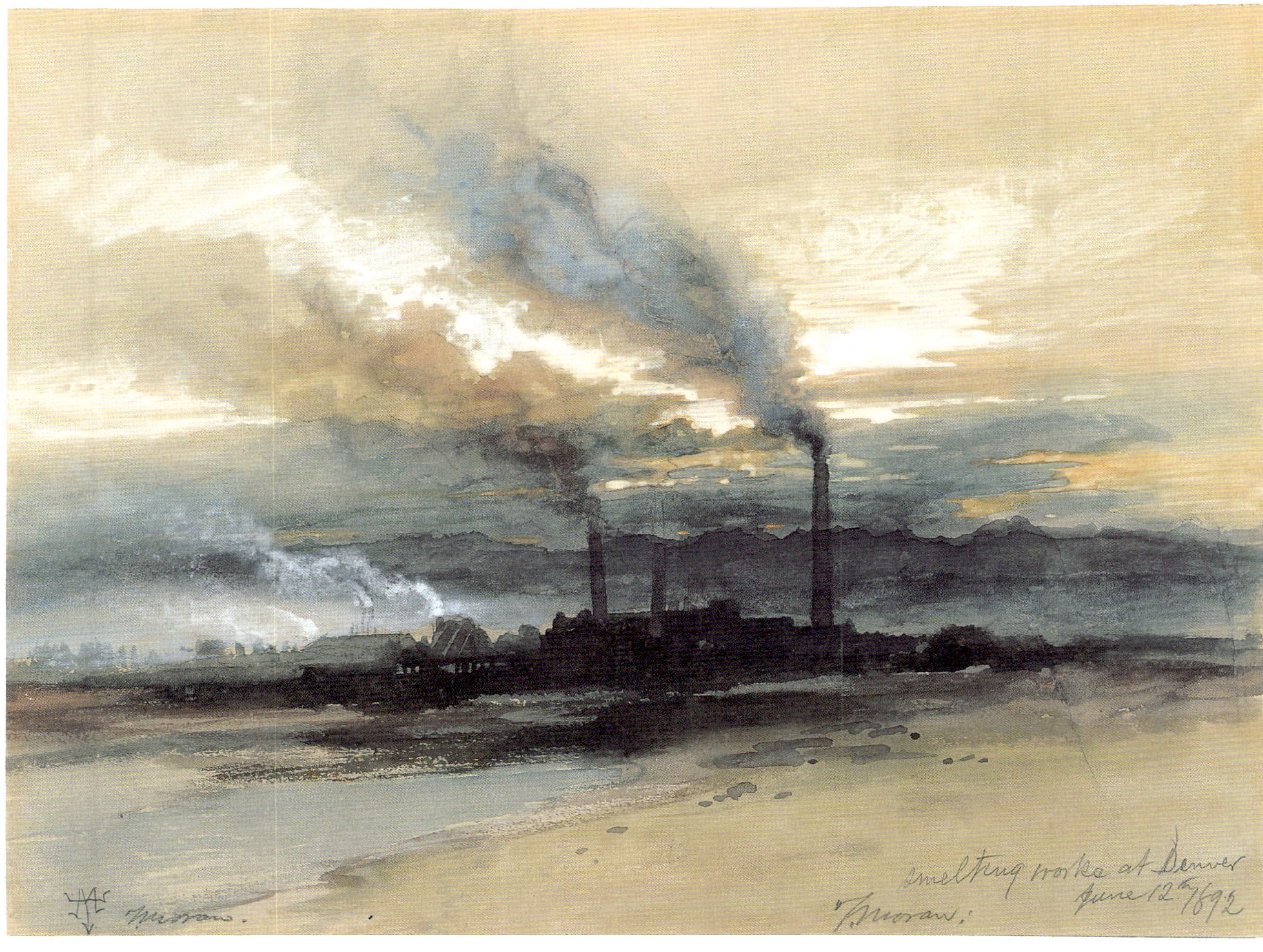

NOTABLE AMONG the latter is a little classic, *Smelting Works in Denver.* Not a thrilling theme, you'll admit. But behold what the artist-soul of him has done with it. Black masses against a yellow and orange sky make it a thing to carry away for a low hour, if you have such. (*Santa Barbara Morning News*, 16 June 1925)

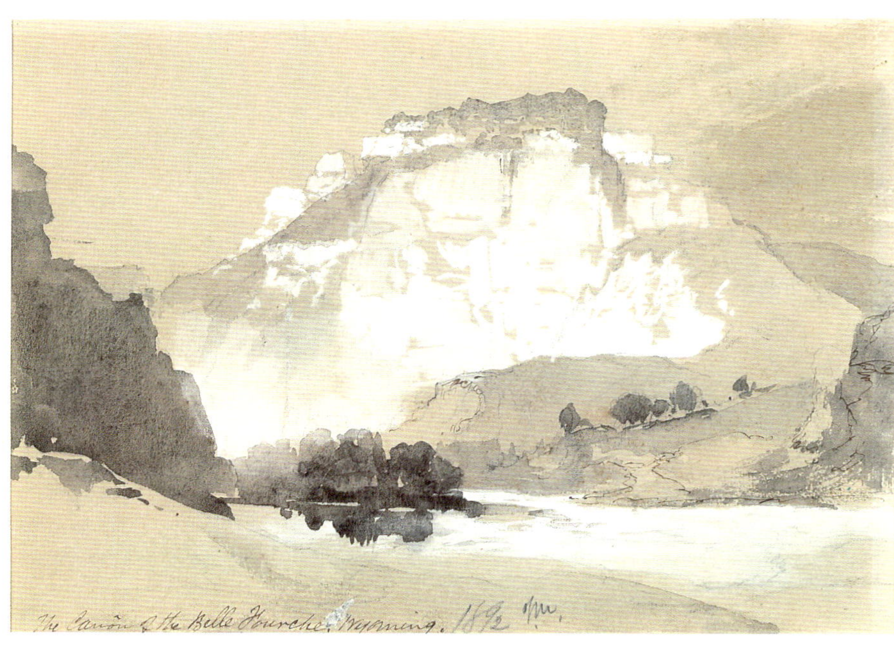

73

Cañon of the Belle Fourche, Wyoming

1892, pen and ink,
pencil and ink wash,
heightened with white
17.8 x 24.6 (7 x 9 11/16)
National Museum of
American Art,
Smithsonian Institution,
Gift of Dr. William
Henry Holmes

Washington only

74

Chama below the Summit

1892, watercolor
21.9 x 30.2 (8 5/8 x 11 7/8)
Cooper-Hewitt
National Design
Museum, Smithsonian
Institution, Gift of
Thomas Moran

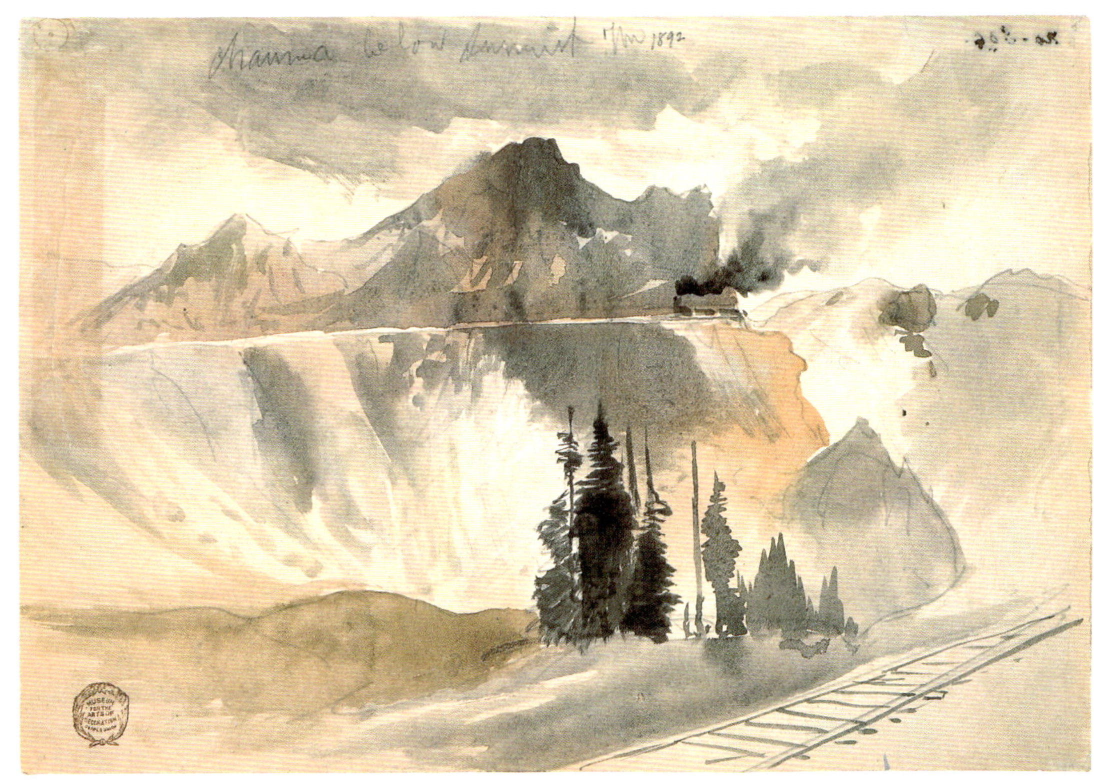

75

Hot Springs, Yellowstone

21 July 1892, watercolor
25.4 x 30.5 (10 x 12)
Cooper-Hewitt National Design Museum, Smithsonian Institution, Gift of Thomas Moran

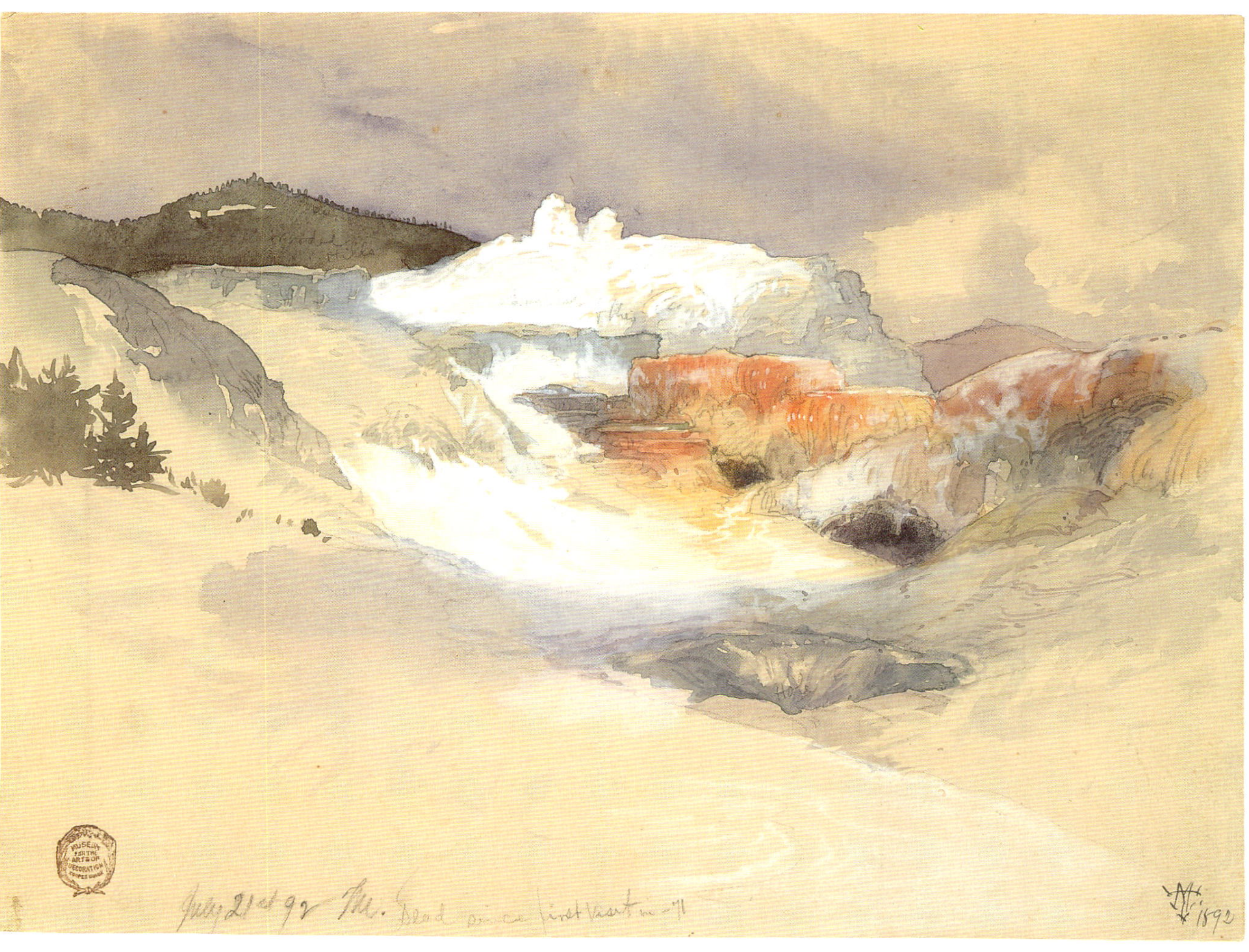

76

The Fisherman's Wedding Party

1892, oil on canvas
61 x 83.8 (24 x 33)
The Detroit Institute of Arts, Bequest of Alfred J. Fisher

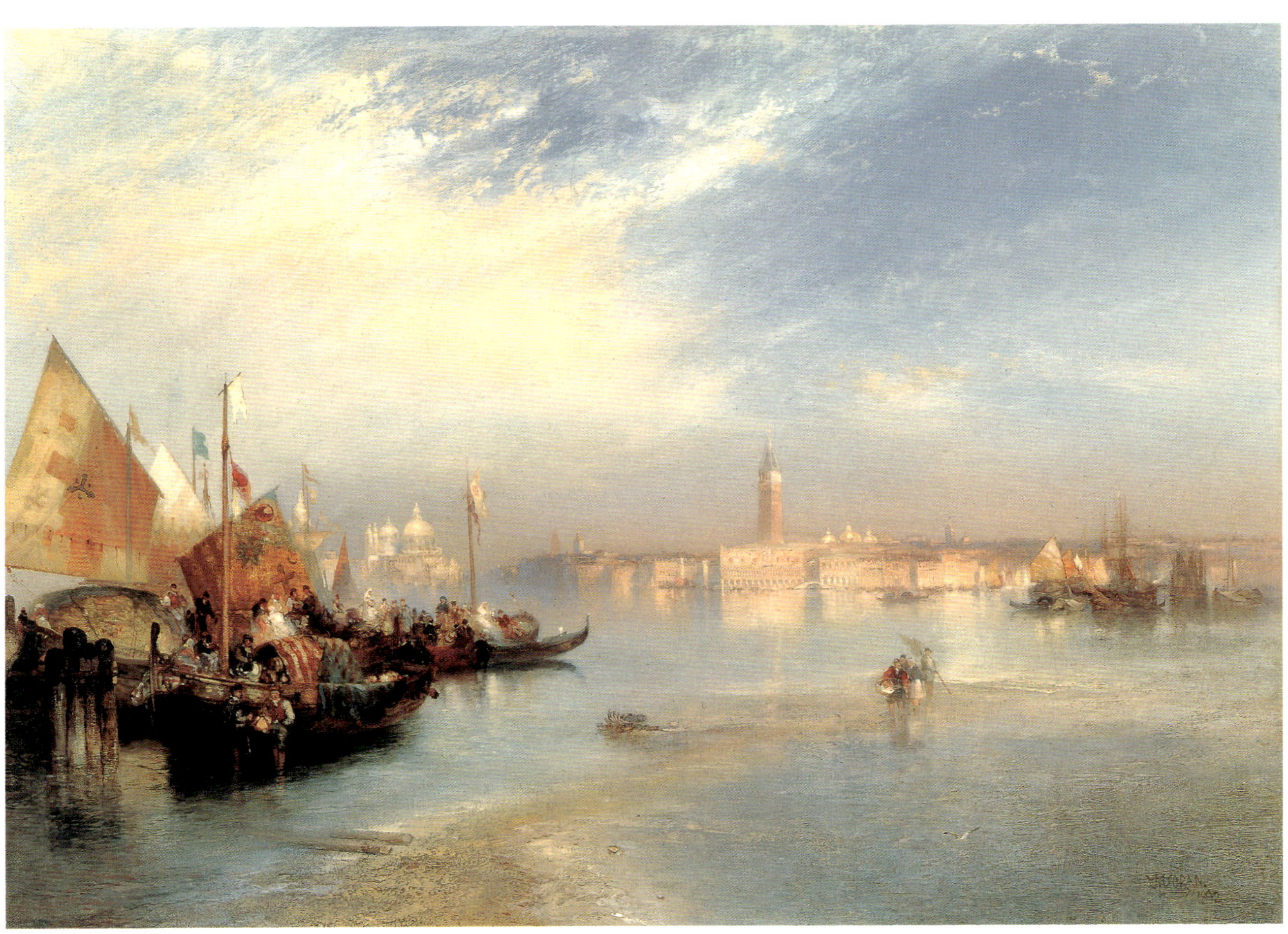

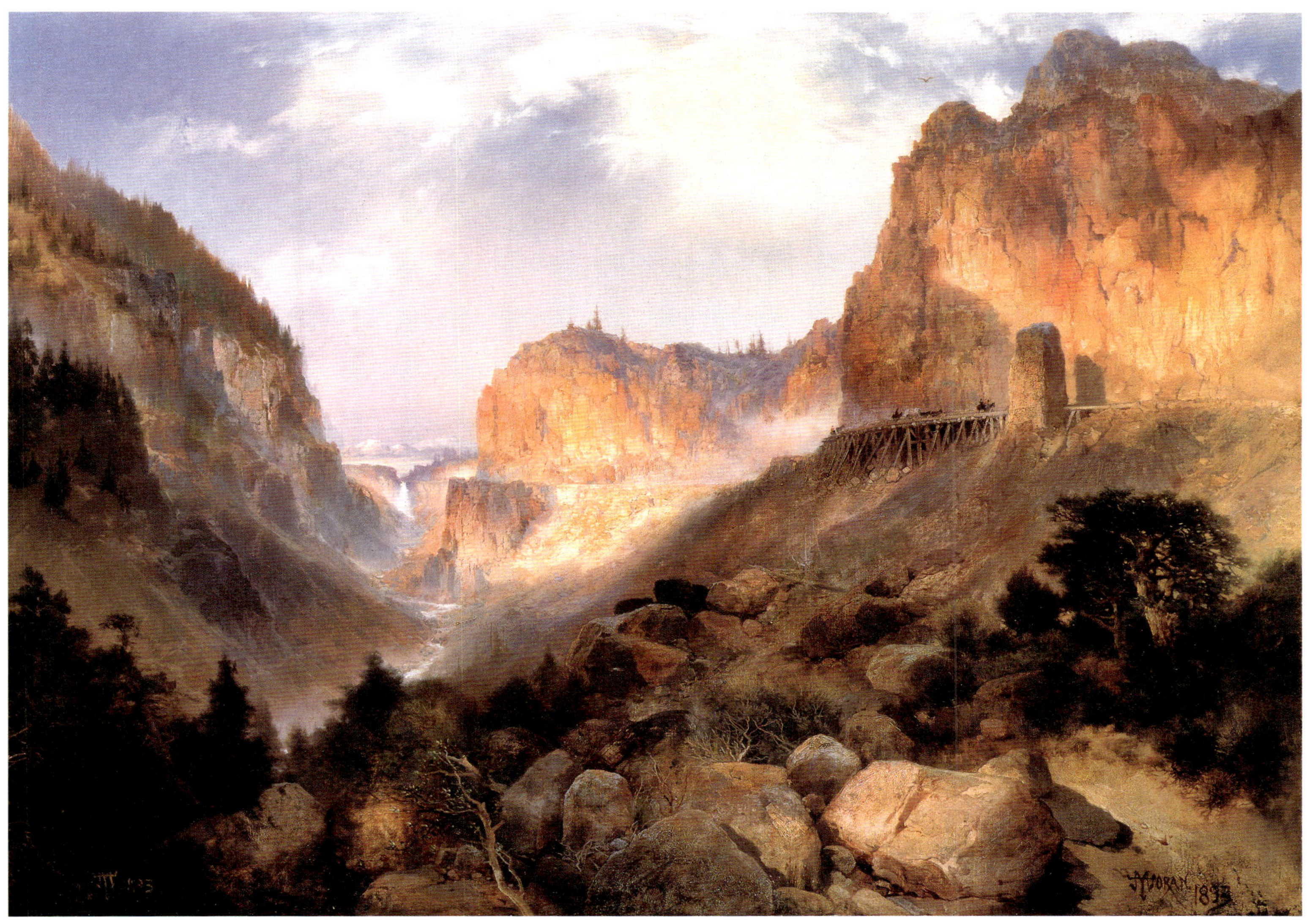

77

Golden Gateway to the Yellowstone

1893, oil on canvas
92.1 x 127.6 (36 ¼ x 50 ¼)
Buffalo Bill Historical Center, Cody, Wyoming

POSED ON THE trestled road, I looked back at the Golden Gate Pass. It is one of those marvellous vistas of mountain scenery utterly beyond the pen or brush of any man. Paint cannot touch it, and words are wasted. War, storms at sea, and mountain scenery are bigger than any expression little man has ever developed. Mr. Thomas Moran made a famous stagger at this pass in his painting; and great as is the painting, when I contemplated the pass itself I marvelled at the courage of the man who dared the deed. But as the stages of the Park Company run over this road, every tourist sees its grandeur, and bangs away with his kodak. (Frederic Remington, "Policing the Yellowstone," *Harper's Weekly* 39 [12 Jan. 1895], 35)

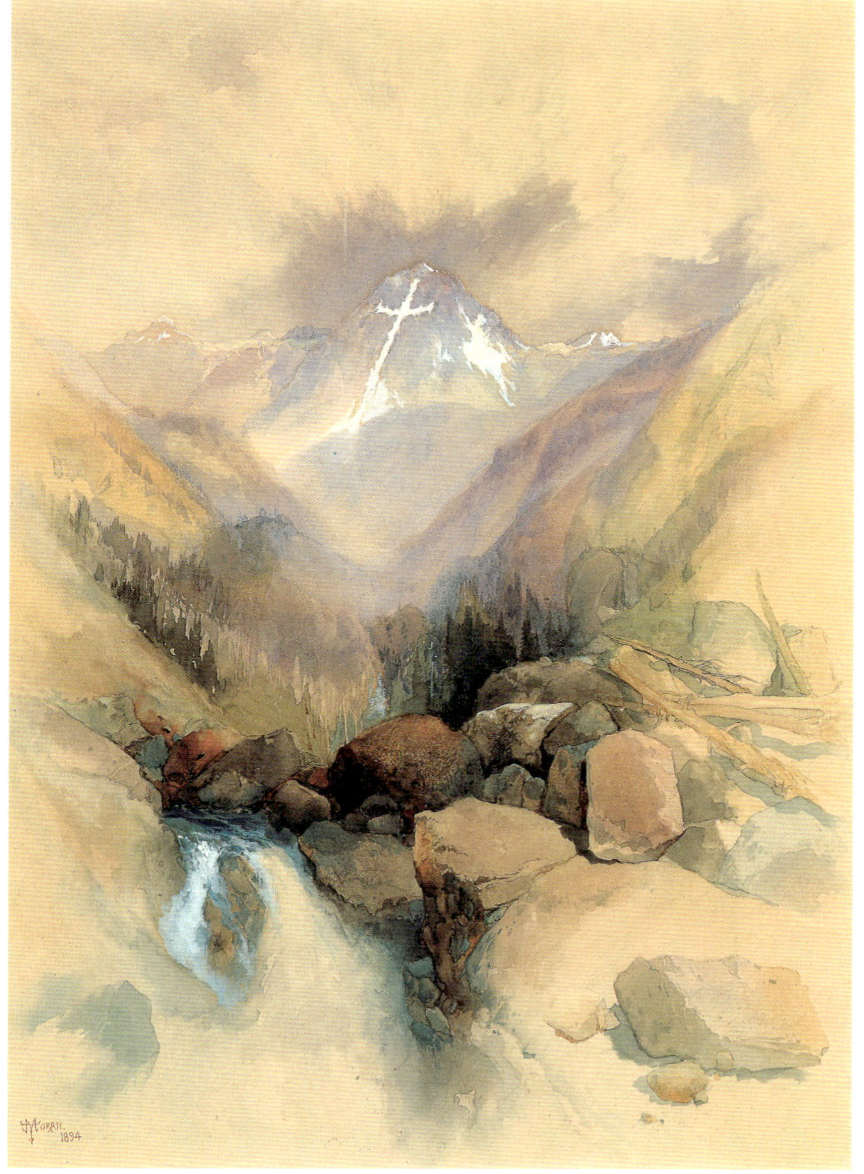

78

Mountain of the Holy Cross

1894, watercolor
48.9 x 35.6 (19 ¼ x 14)
Denver Art Museum,
Anonymous Gift

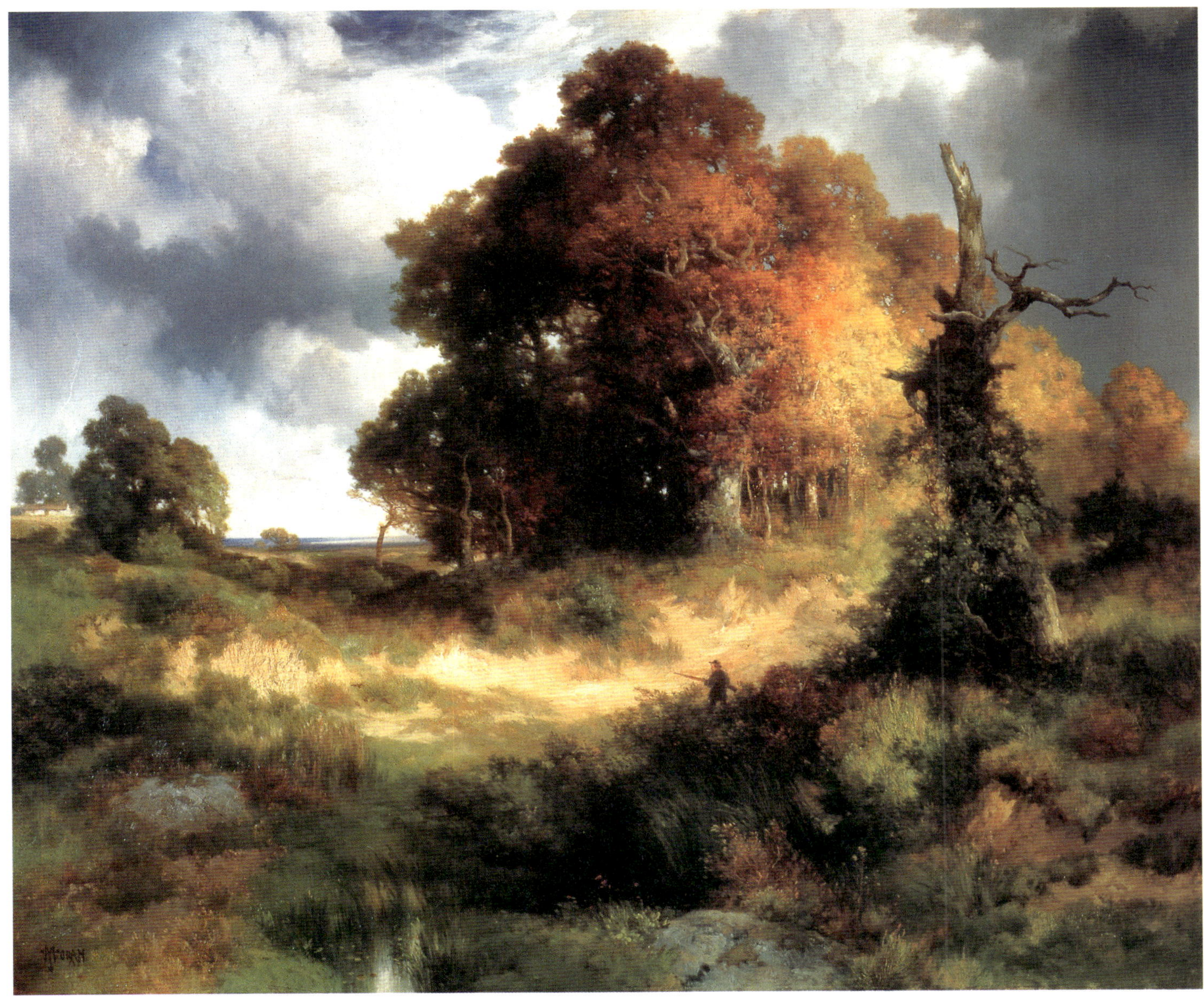

79

Autumn

c. 1893–1897, oil on canvas
76.2 x 91.4 (30 x 36)
The Philbrook Museum
of Art, Tulsa, Oklahoma,
Gift of Laura A. Clubb

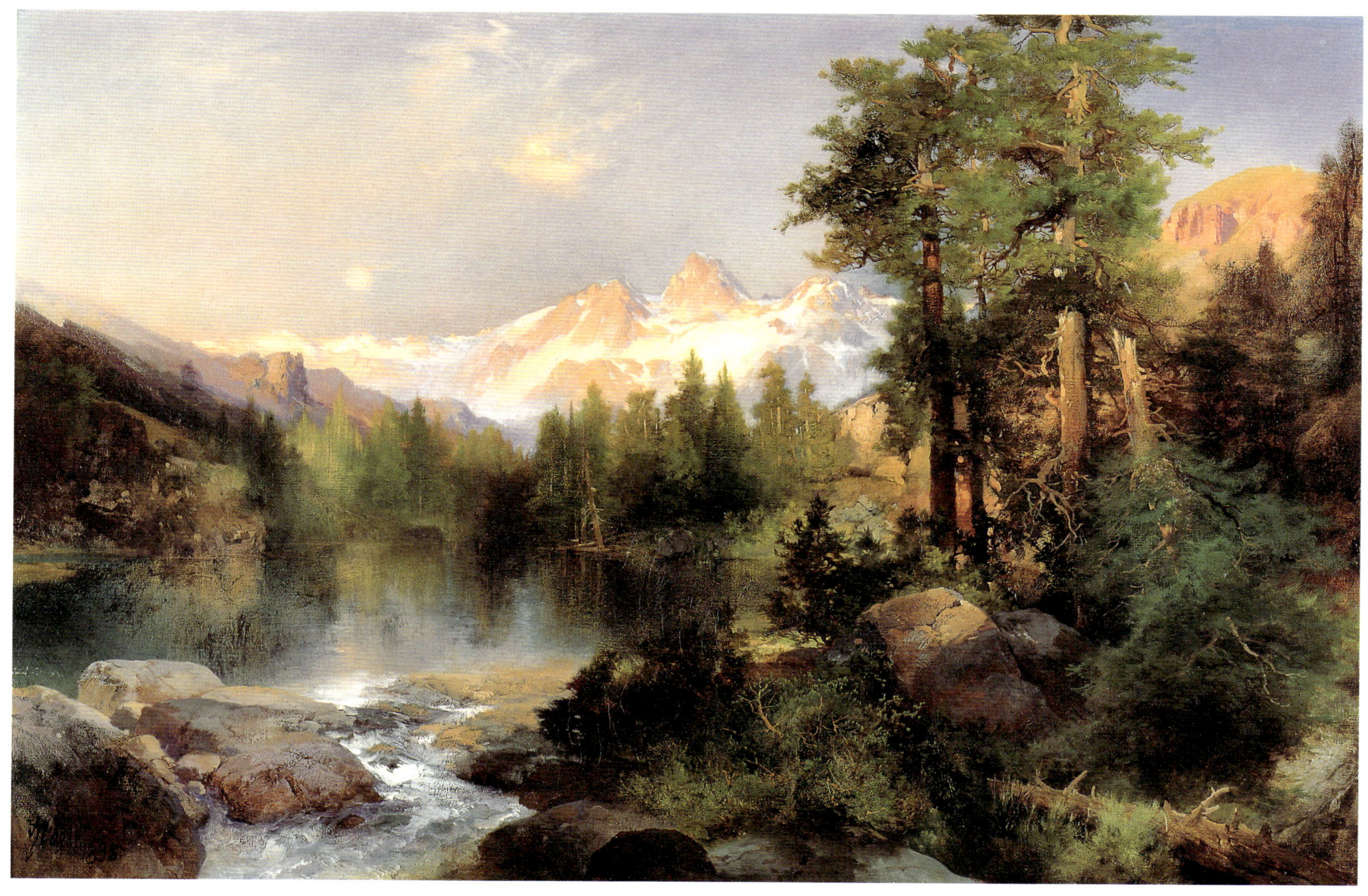

80

The Three Tetons

1895, oil on canvas
52.4 x 77.5 (20 5/8 x 30 1/2)
The White House

Washington only

THIRTY-SEVEN mounted men and twenty-five pack animals could hardly fail to disturb the unbroken slumber of a region which, from every rock and tree and mountain, answers to the faintest sound with reduplicated murmurs. But as we looked before us and beheld, rising through the morning vapors, the glinting sides and summits of the Tetons, we felt that even this country, desolate and virgin as it was, had a thrilling history. Those grand old mountains covered with eternal snow had, by their very isolation, pointed the way to the Pacific to all the early explorers, from the days of Lewis and Clark, through the mountain passes and river mazes of this the most intricate part of the continent. Guided by them, Hunt in 1811 led his little half-starved band out of the almost inextricable wilderness of the Bighorn Mountains, and pursued his long and tortuous journey to the Columbia. Often did they serve during his years wandering to guide Bonneville to the friendly wigwams of the Bannacks or Shoshones. And in the recent history of the country, the first sight of them has often assured the perplexed gold-hunter that he was on the right path to the Northern Eldorado. Rough, jagged, and pointed, they stood out before us nearer than I had ever before seen them, shining like gigantic crystals in the morning sunbeams....

After a ride of ten miles, we arrived at mid-day at the Middle Fork of the Snake, or the Mad river of Mr. Hunt. It is not as large as the North Fork, but much more rapid. All day the Tetons reared their heads in full view. From the summit, midway to the base, they seemed to be covered with perpetual snow. In the buttressed sides, as the eye scanned them critically, many places were seen where the rocks were nearly vertical, and which it would be impossible to scale. They were apparently intrenched in a wilderness of rocks, as inaccessible as their summits....

Eight miles of difficult travel took us fairly into the Teton basin. This basin, hid away among the mountains, is like an oasis in the desert. It embraces an area of about eight hundred square miles, and is carpeted with the heaviest and largest bunch-grass I have ever seen. It is bounded on three sides by a range of snow-capped mountains, and forms a complete *cul-de-sac.* Camas and yamph grow all over it in great abundance, and in the lowlands and along the streams are found large patches of strawberries of the finest flavor. Our entrance into this valley was effected by traveling over high tablelands and rolling foot-hills, which for a distance of twelve or fifteen miles were covered with vegetation. Innumerable crystal streams flow from the surrounding mountains into the Teton river, which traverses the valley longitudinally....

There is no greater wonder in mountain scenery on this continent, than the tendency it has to shorten distance to the eye and lengthen it to the feet. A range of mountains apparently ten miles distant may be fifty miles away. A plain, to all appearances as smooth as a floor, is often broken into deep ravines, yawning chasms, and formidable foot-hills. Everything in distance and surfact is deceptive.

(Langford 1873, 129–157)

HAD OUR first sight of the great Teton some 70 miles away.

The Tetons are now plainly visible but not well defined owing to the mistiness of the atmosphere. They loom grandly above all the other mountains An intervening ridge dividing us from the Teton Basin stretches for miles to the north of a beautiful pinkish yellow with delicate shades of pale cobalt while the distant range is of an exquisite blue with but little definition of forms on their surfaces....

Following a trail leading up the edge of the Canon we found that it led down into the Canon which has a beautiful stream flowing through it fringed with Water Elms, Pine Cottonwoods &c....

The Tetons here loomed up grandly against the sky & from this point is perhaps the finest pictorial range in the United States or even in N. America....

It is very hot this afternoon & so very smoky that the Teton peaks can scarcely be seen & at times are entirely obscured so that sketching is out of the question & we spend our time working up some of our sketches made previously....

The peaks of the Tetons are from this point entirely hidden from view but a number of other fine peaks present themselves in view. The view is very magnificent. The opposite mountain rises 5000 feet about the river with a granite base surmounted by sandstone & capped with tremendous precipices of limestone. The slopes are covered in place with a growth of large pines but the summit is nearly bare of vegetation.

(Moran's diary, 22–27 Aug. 1879, GTNP)

81

June, East Hampton

1895, oil on canvas
50.8 x 76.2 (20 x 30)
Private Collection

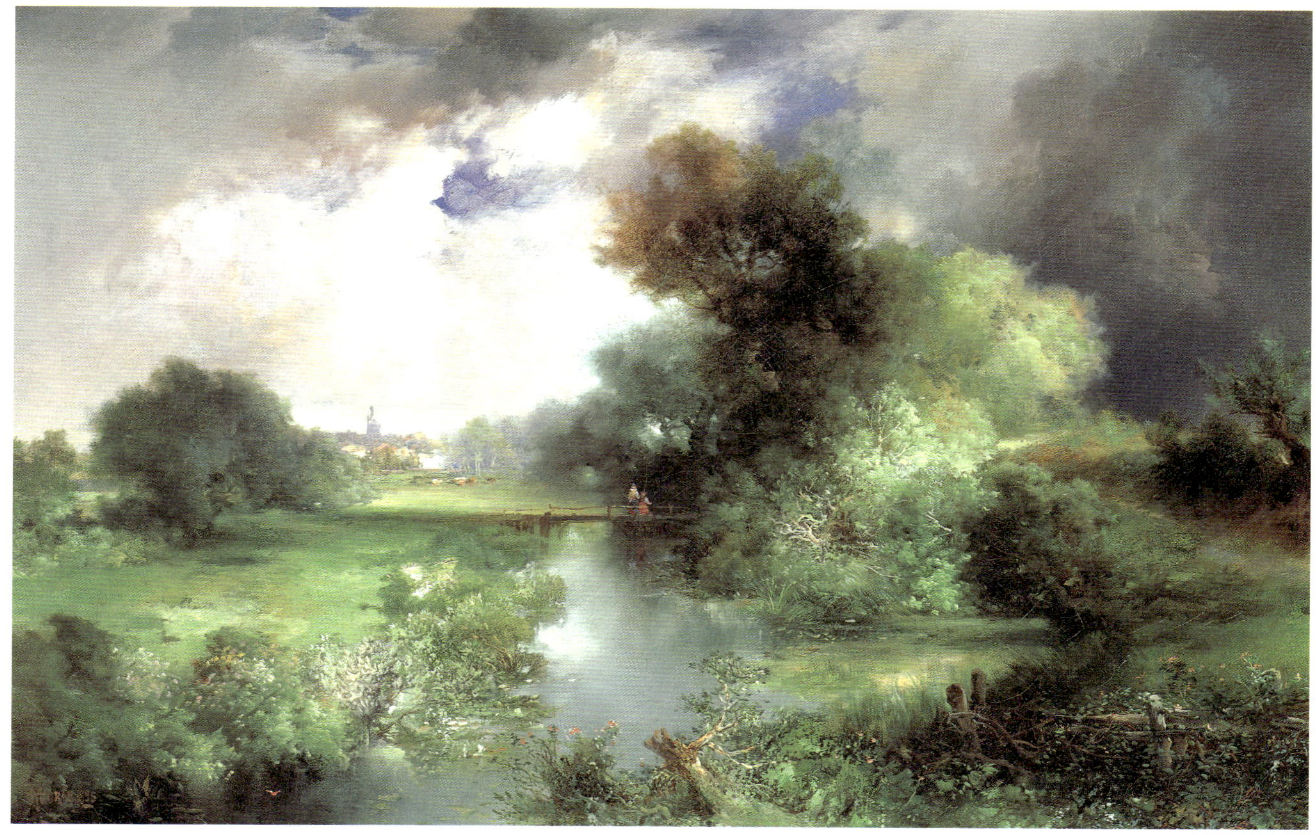

JUNE, EAST HAMPTON... presents a smiling picture of a neighborhood landscape, almost like England in its general aspect, but quite true enough in observation to be American. (*NY Sun*, Feb. 1897)

82

Green River, Wyoming

1896, oil on canvas
51.1 x 76.8 (20 ⅛ x 30 ¼)
Private Collection,
courtesy Jordan-Volpe
Gallery

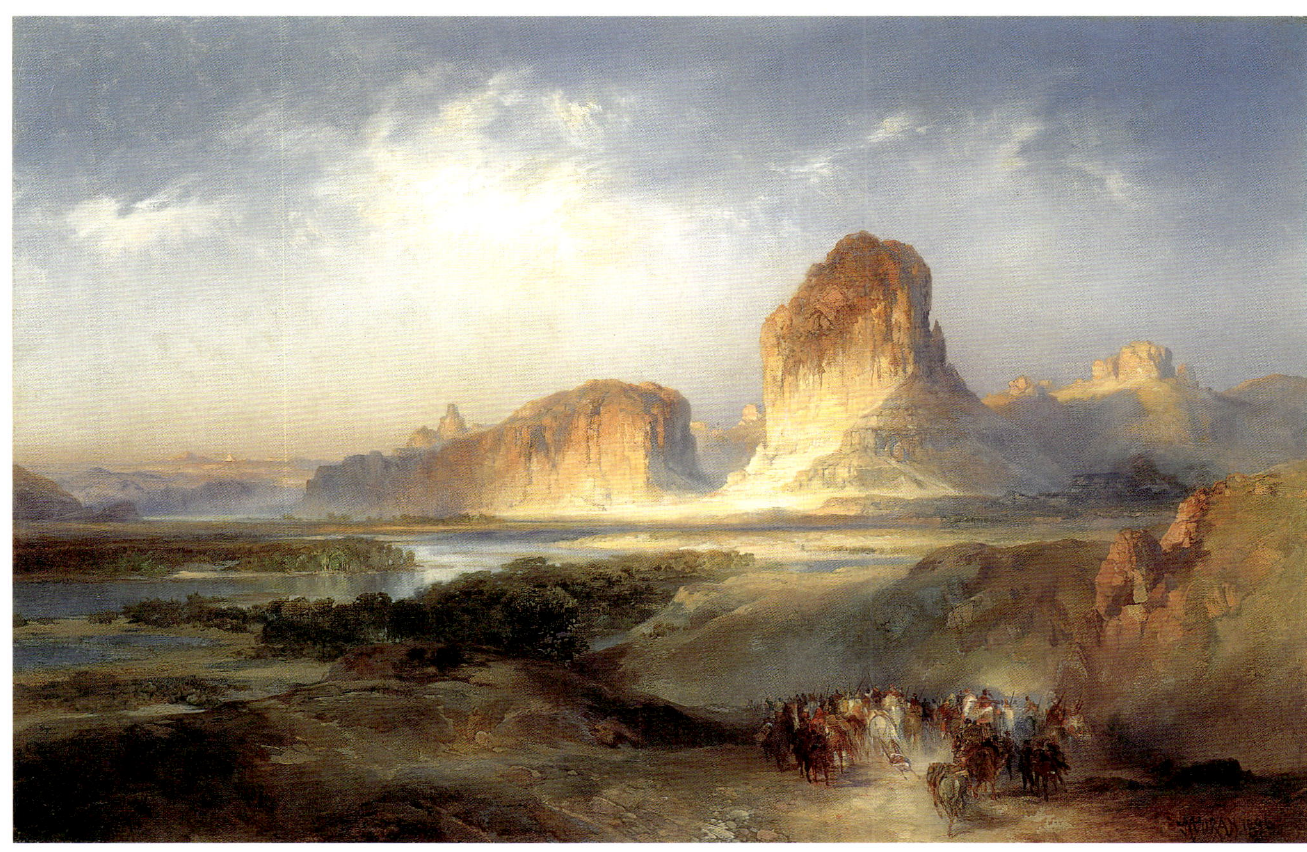

THOMAS MORAN...with his..."The Cliffs of Green River, Wyoming."...I think me there is no better exponent of God's own architecture. From the base to the pinnacle the volcanic upheaval and descendant stand in sullenness and pride, dignified and morose, yielding nothing but a diversified quality and quantity, unintelligible, unconquered, but brought nearer home by Mr. Moran than by any other artist throughout the length and breadth of the land. (Lockington 1901, 68)

83

The Teton Range

1897, oil on canvas
76.2 x 114.3 (30 x 45)
The Metropolitan Museum of Art, Bequest of Moses Tananbaum, 1937

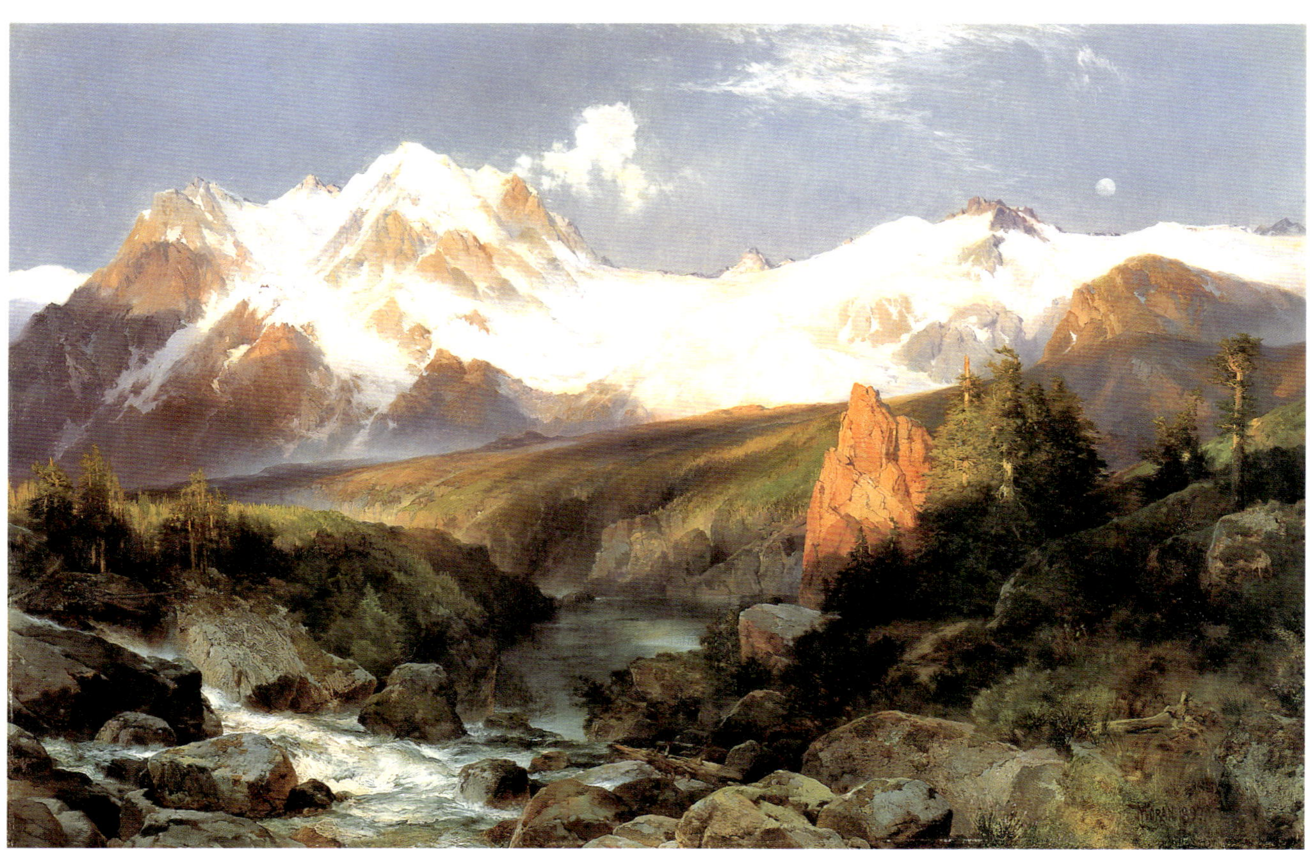

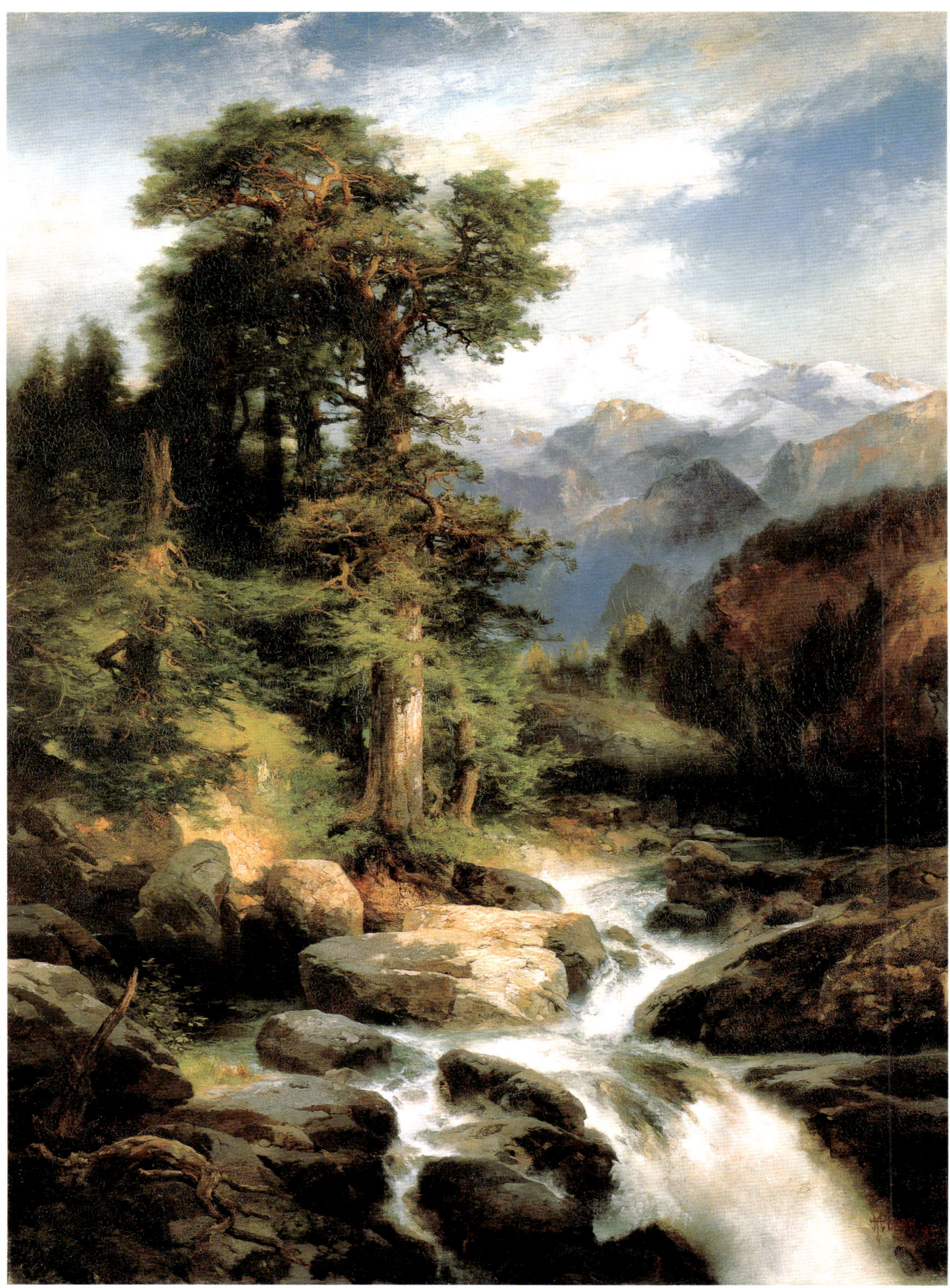

84

Solitude

1897, oil on canvas
119.4 x 86.4 (47 x 34)
Private Collection

85

Landscape

1898, oil on canvas
51.4 x 76.5 (20 ¼ x 30 ⅛)
David H. Koch

Washington and Tulsa only

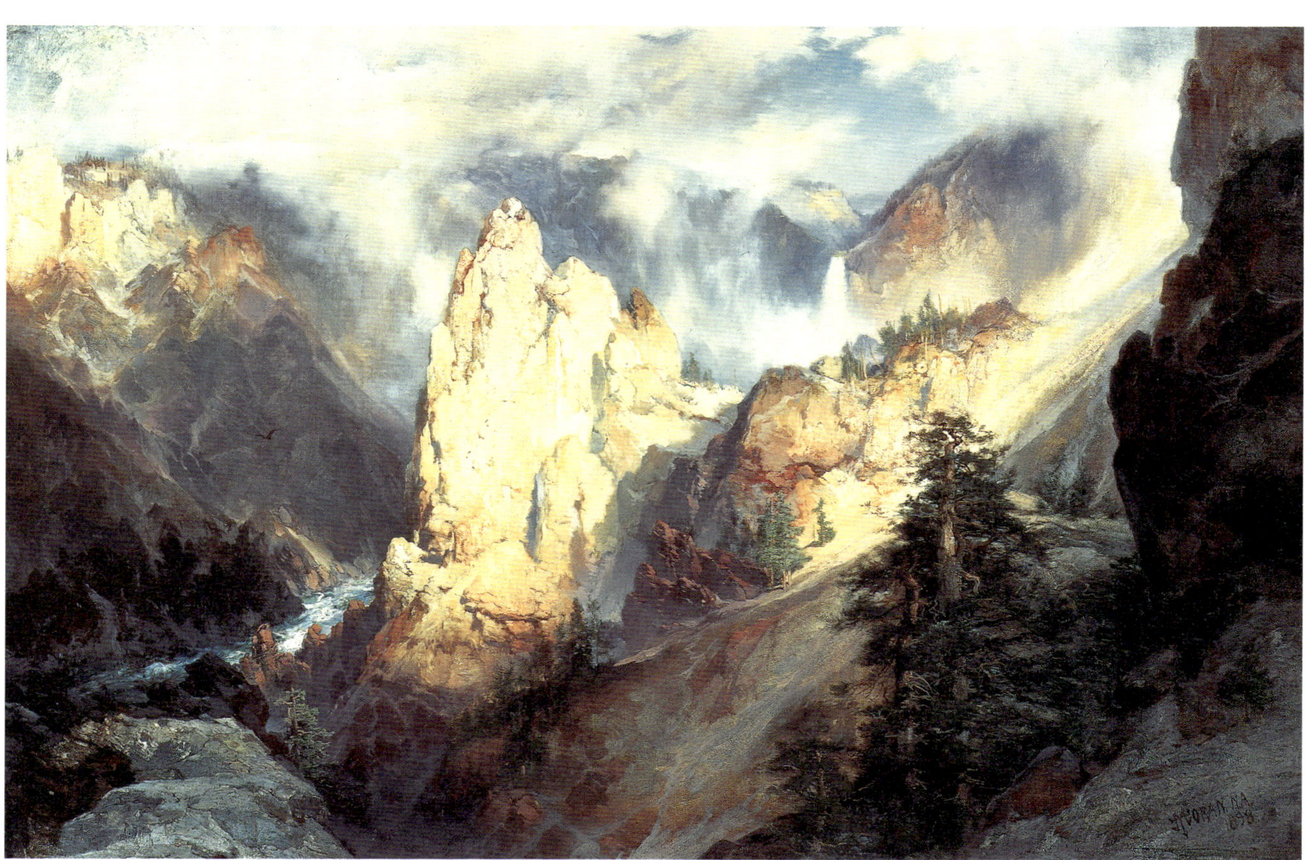

86

In the Teton Range

1899, oil on canvas
106.7 x 76.2 (42 x 30)
Museum of Western
Art, Denver

Washington only

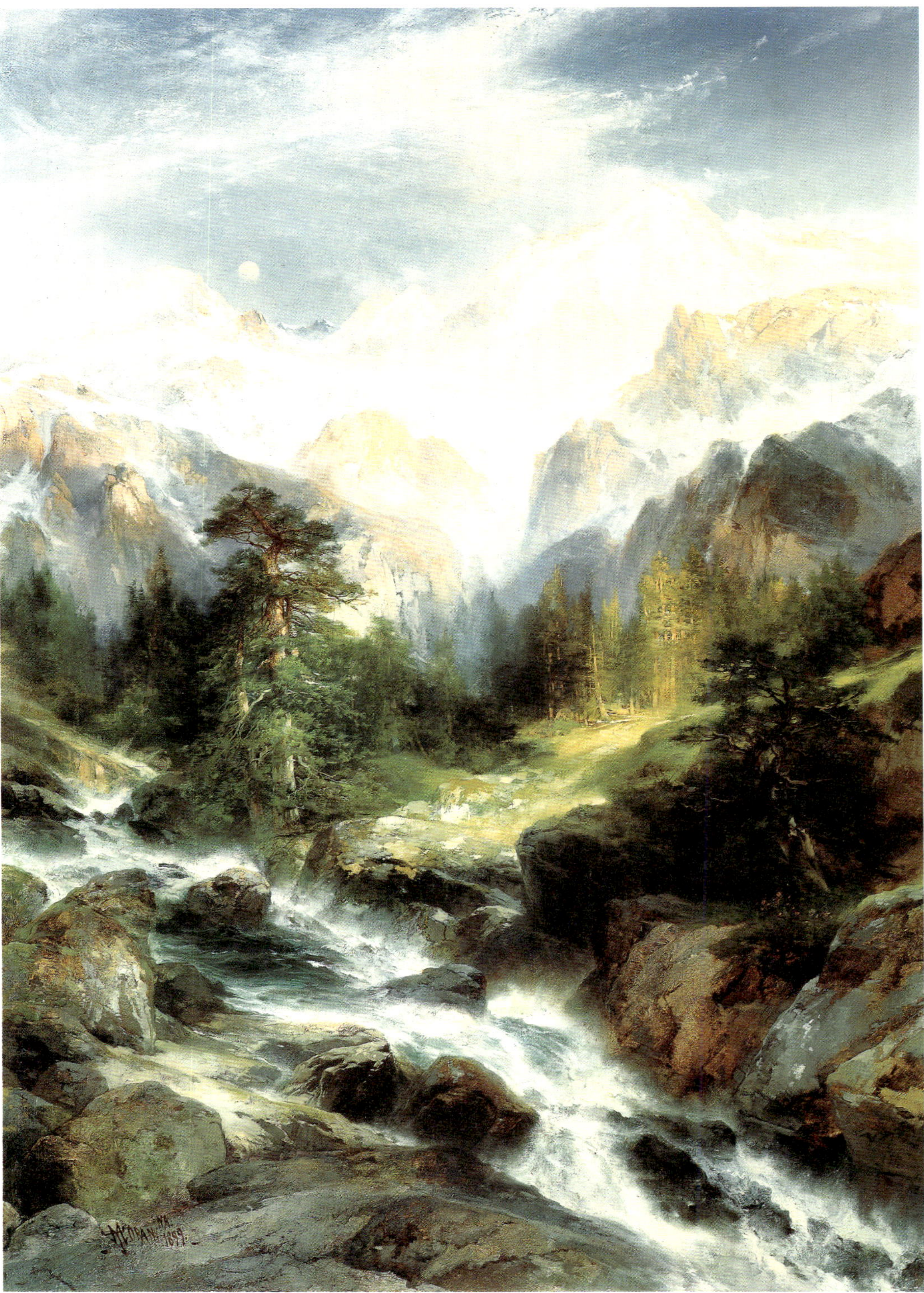

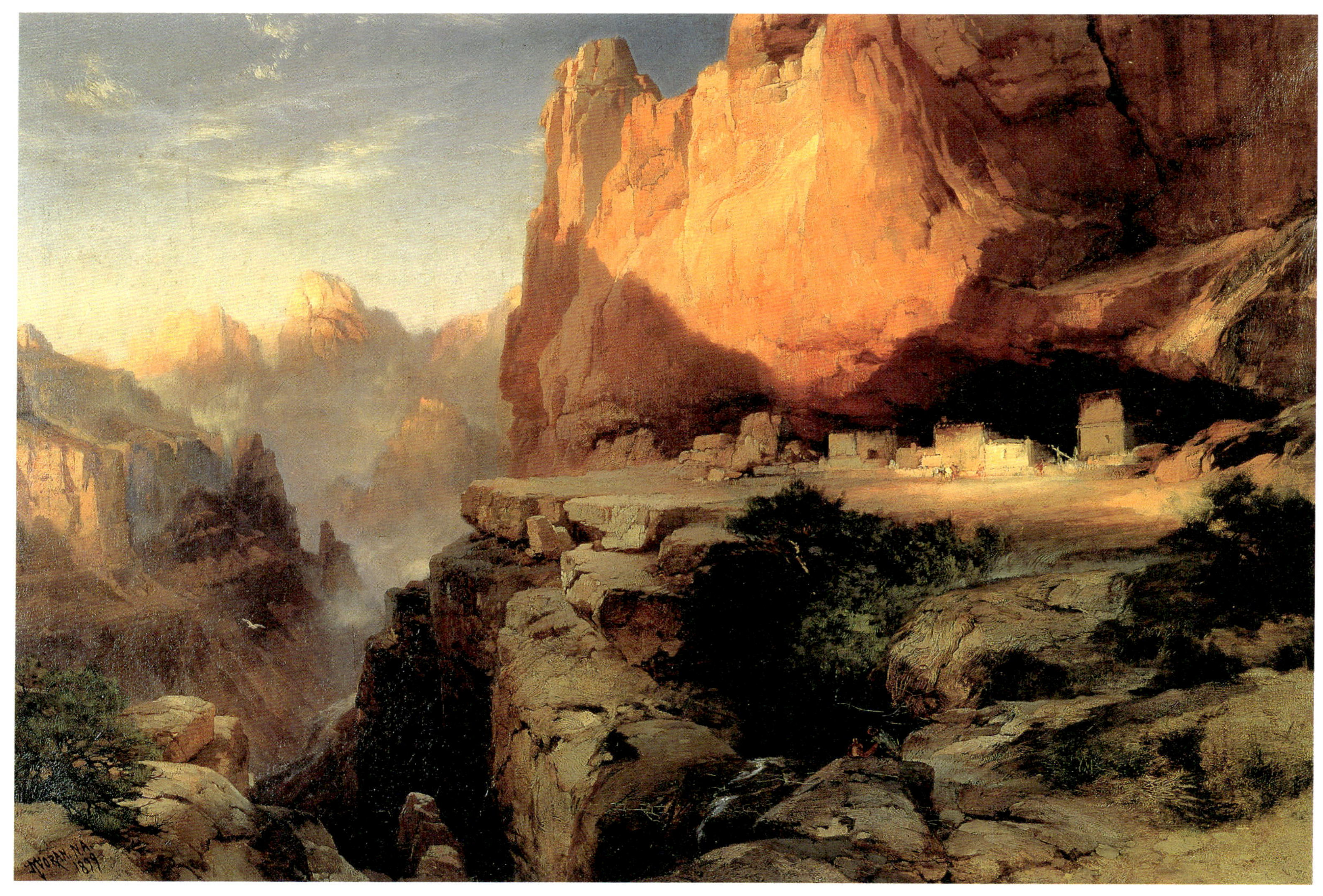

87

Cliff Dwellers

1899, oil on canvas
51.1 x 76.5 (20 1/8 x 30 1/8)
Berea College,
Berea, Kentucky

DISCOVERED LATELY...by the Hayden Geological Survey....On the terraces of the more open cañons are multitudes of picturesque ruins; in the bottom lands are the remains of towns; in the wilder cañons the houses are perched upon the face of the dizzy chasm....They are so high that the naked eye can distinguish them merely as specks. There is no access to them from above on account of the rocks that project overhead, and no present way of reaching them from below, although doubling paths and footholes in the rocks show where the way was trodden of old by human feet....

The cliffs in some part are limestone, but more frequently sandstone, with alternating strata of shales and clay. The softer layers are hollowed out, leaving caves, whose solid stone ledges serve as the floors and roofs of the cliff dwellings. A few houses have two stories, and one shows four stories, but generally they are not higher than a man's head. Division walls are built from the rear of the opening and running outward to the front of the cave, which is so neatly walled by masonry of the prevailing stone that the artificial work is scarcely noticeable by a casual observer....As to the habits of these dwellers in mid-air we know almost nothing....It is assumed that the present Pueblo Indians are the descendants of these people, from the fact that their huts to-day resemble the ancient cave houses. The absence of implements of warfare, either completed or unfinished, gives rise to the opinion that they were a peaceful race. Near some of the cities thousands of flint arrow heads were found sticking in the cliff—all pointing toward the city—showing that some strong invader had attacked them. (*NY Post*, 17 Oct. 1879)

AT SEVERAL POINTS upon the rim of the Grand Cañon, both east and west of the stage terminus, the razed walls of ancient stone dwellings may be seen....

The most famous group, and the largest aggregation, is found in Walnut Cañon, eight miles southeast from Flagstaff. This cañon is several hundred feet deep and some three miles long, with steep terraced walls of limestone. Along the shelving terraces, under beetling projections of the strata, are scores of these quaint abodes. The larger are divided into four or five compartments by cemented walls, many parts of which are still intact. It is believed that these ancient people customarily dwelt upon the plateau above, retiring to their fortifications when attacked by an enemy. (Higgins 1897, 25)

In the summer of 1900, just a few months after his wife's death, Thomas Moran, accompanied by his daughter Ruth, returned to Yellowstone. Thirty years had passed since Nathaniel Langford's article describing a western wonderland near the Yellowstone River had piqued Moran's interest and sent him west to join F. V. Hayden's survey party. That trip had changed both the course of Moran's career and the nation's legislative agenda.

By 1900 Moran had spent nearly three decades signing his paintings with a colophon that included three letters: TYM. The name he had invented for himself was Thomas "Yellowstone" Moran. During that same thirty-year period Congress had amplified the original Yellowstone legislation, setting aside additional "parks," including Yosemite in 1890. Inextricably linked through his paintings to numerous landscapes that eventually became national parks, Moran would one day be described as the "father" of the national park system.

By the time Moran and his daughter arrived in Yellowstone in the summer of 1900, much had changed. The isolated landscape Jackson had photographed and Moran had sketched in 1871 had become a tourist mecca. The railroads, stage lines, and hotels that transported and served increasing numbers of tourists were thriving. Congressional action may have curtailed commercial excess within the park, but outside the entry gates commercial enterprise was faring very well.

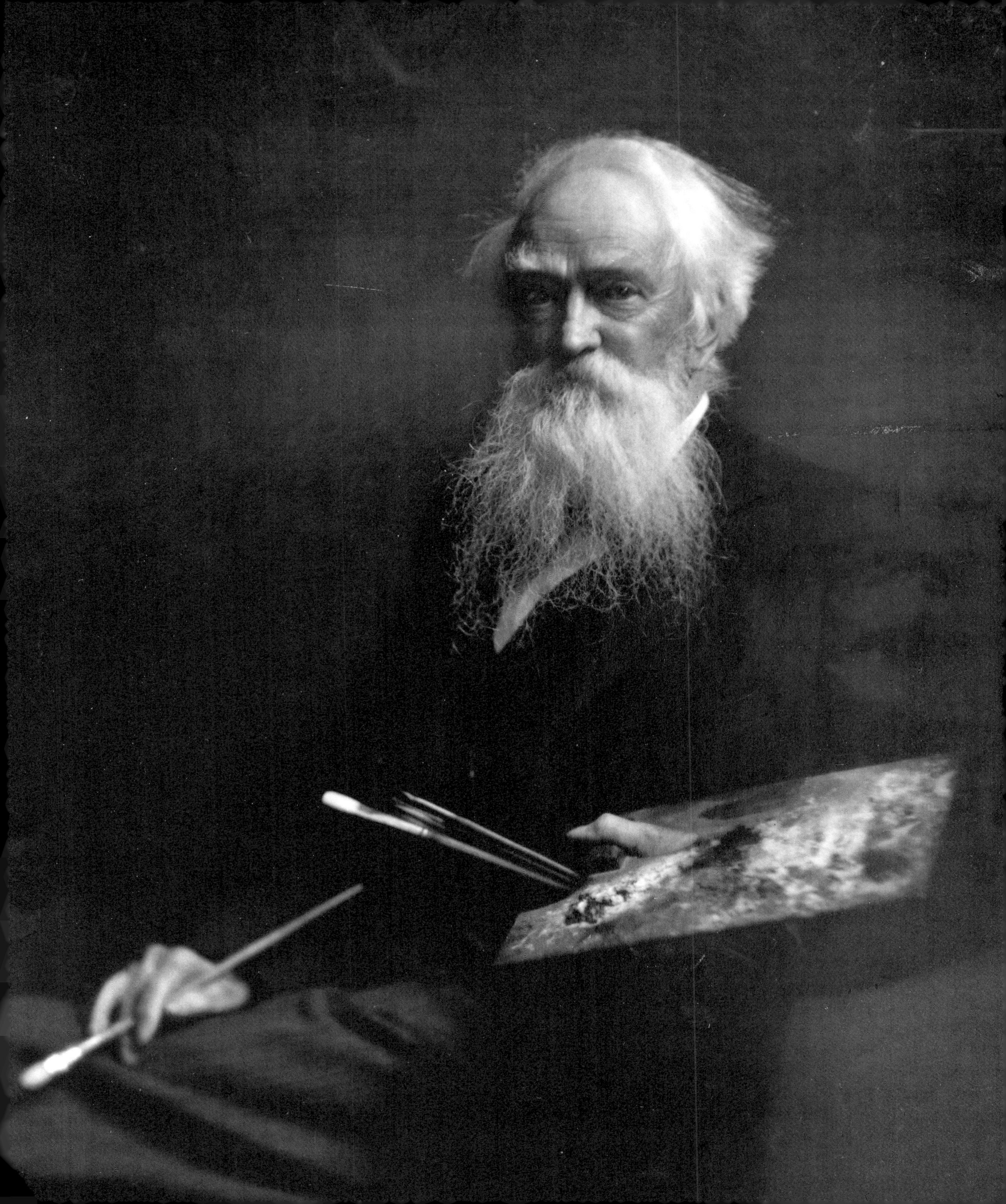

Moran's trip to Yellowstone in 1900 was part of a larger journey that included stops in Utah and Idaho. It was the Idaho leg of the trip—the rail and stage expedition to Shoshone Falls on the Snake River—that resulted in Moran's last major western landscape.

Preceding page: Thomas Moran, 1921, photograph by Glenhills, Santa Barbara, courtesy East Hampton Library.

1. Thomas Moran, *The Falls of the Snake River,* illustration from "Idaho Scenery," *The Aldine* (June 1876), 195.

Shoshone Falls

As had been the case with the pivotal paintings of the 1870s, including *Grand Canyon of the Yellowstone*, Moran had produced images of Shoshone Falls (perhaps using photographs by Timothy O'Sullivan) before he had actually visited the site. In June 1876, for example, *The Aldine* published an illustration titled "The Falls of the Snake River" by Thomas Moran (fig. 1). A similar view of the falls was included in the set of fifteen chromolithographs based on paintings by Moran published in 1876 by Louis Prang (Appendix 1). Photographs of spectacular western landscapes had sent Moran west in earlier years, and in 1900 they may have done so again.

Unlike Yellowstone, Shoshone Falls was, at the turn of the century, a "fresh" subject for pictures. The large size of Moran's finished painting (6 x 11 feet) suggests that from the outset he conceived of the work as a picture for a special exhibition. Indeed, it is likely that Moran's trip to the Snake River in 1900 was prompted by his wish to exhibit a large painting of a new western subject at the Pan-American Exposition in Buffalo, New York, the following year.

Like Yellowstone, the Grand Canyon, and Mountain of the Holy Cross, Shoshone Falls had enjoyed considerable "press" before Moran began his large canvas. As early as 1866 the *Philadelphia Evening Bulletin* reprinted an extensive article from a Salt Lake City newspaper titled "The Niagara of the West—The Great Shoshone Falls." Describing the falls as "a world wonder which for savage scenery and power sublime stands unrivaled in America," the author continued in a nationalistic vein: "As tourists tell, the cataracts of Southern Asia and the falls of the fair Rhine; the Victoria Falls, of Zambezi, Africa, as explored by Livingston, and the Fall of Staubach, Switzerland, as immortalized in Byron's *Manfred*, may each have special points, but as a whole, for wildness and for witchery, for width and volume, this 'Niagara of the West' will stand second to none of all."[1] Additional testimonials were offered by Albert D. Richardson, who wrote in 1867 that the cataract was "unequaled in the world, save by Niagara," and by an unidentified author (perhaps Timothy O'Sullivan), who wrote in the September 1869 issue of *Harper's Magazine* that Shoshone Falls was "one of nature's greatest spectacles."[2] Even Clarence King, in his classic 1872 publication *Mountaineering in the Sierra Nevada*, described the "incessant roar" of the cascading water and compared the grandeur of the falls to that of Niagara.[3] Despite the tantalizing nature of these early descriptions, Shoshone Falls had not become the subject of a major picture before Moran journeyed to the site in 1900.

In a letter written many years later, Ruth Moran recalled the visit she and her father made to Idaho, noting that Moran "was tremendously impressed by the Falls, and told me when he saw them that not since his first sight of the Yellowstone and the Grand Canyon had he been so stirred and thrilled as by Shoshone." She went on to comment that "there were no houses nor people to spoil the grandeur of the mighty torrent of water."[4] In fact, by the time Thomas and Ruth Moran arrived, Shoshone Falls had been a tourist attraction for a number of years.

Although the Shoshone Falls site was not directly served by a rail line, the potential for tourist traffic had been anticipated more than two decades before the Morans arrived. In 1876 Charles Walgamott had fenced the area around the falls in an attempt to establish squatter's rights to a site he predicted would become a tourist destination. Before long Walgamott began operating a stage line to ferry visitors to the falls from the nearby town of Shoshone. For the comfort of overnighters a "hotel" constructed entirely of tents was erected. Some years later the Union Pacific Railroad began to promote special excursions to the falls as part of an extended Yellowstone tour.[5] By 1900, the date of Moran's visit, Shoshone Falls had won a place on the tourists' map of the West.

Predictably, Moran's painting betrays not the slightest hint of tourism. Exercising the same editing privileges he had employed with his Green River pictures, Moran stripped the site of all human reference and produced a painting of a grand but forbidding landscape.

As noted above, early visitors to Shoshone Falls frequently compared the cataract to Niagara, the American standard by which all other waterfalls were judged. Western enthusiasts were quick to point out that Shoshone Falls was approximately fifty feet higher than Niagara and the rush of water over the lava cliffs every bit as magnificent as that of the eastern cataract when the Snake River was swollen with winter runoff.

By the time Moran actually saw the falls, the Niagara comparison had been made repeatedly. In fact, as Linda Hults has pointed out, Moran may have consciously tipped his hat to the most famous image of Niagara created during the nineteenth century, Frederic Church's *Niagara* (1857), when he composed his view of Shoshone Falls.[6] Despite the compositional echo of Church's *Niagara*, Moran's *Shoshone Falls* (cat. 88) is clearly a western landscape and its stark and forbidding character more closely aligned to the artist's own *Chasm of the Colorado*. Clarence King, perhaps the most gifted writer to describe the Snake River landscape and the falls, anticipated Moran's view when he wrote:

Dead barrenness is the whole sentiment of the scene.... Above the brink, the whole breadth of the river is broken by a dozen small, trachyte islands, which the water has carved into fantastic forms: rounding some into low domes, sharpening others into mere pillars, and now and then wearing out deep caves. At the very brink of the fall a few twisted evergreens cling with their roots to the rock, and lean over the abyss of foam with something of that air of fatal fascination which is apt to take possession of men. In plan the fall recurves up stream in a deep horseshoe, resembling the outline of Niagara. The total breadth is about seven hundred feet, and the greatest height of the single fall about one hundred and ninety. Among the islands above the brink are several beautiful cascades, where portions of the river pour over in lace-like forms. The whole mass of cataract is one ever-varying sheet of spray.[7]

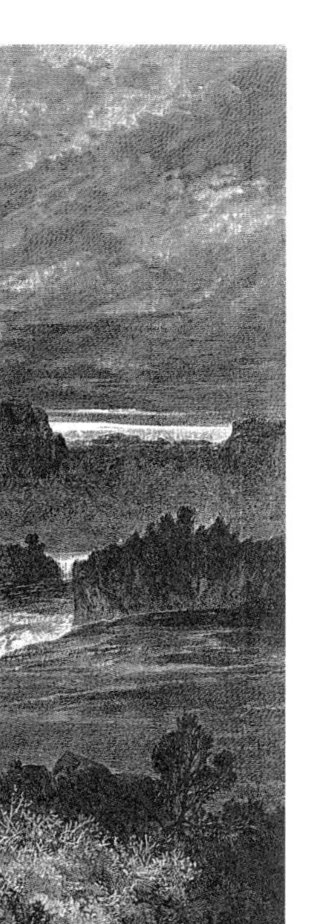

1

Like *Chasm of the Colorado*, Moran's painting of Shoshone Falls is a roiling, turbulent, statement about the power of water. Carving its way through lava rock, the Snake River is the violent protagonist of the picture. Coursing through a gorge flanked by stone battlements, the steel grey water of the river plunges more than 200 feet over a serrated edge. Thunderclouds, dark and threatening, move swiftly along the distant horizon. The "roar" Clarence King described is palpable.

Ironically, at the time Moran visited the falls, that roar was about to be significantly reduced. In October 1900, just a few months after Moran's visit, the major newspaper in the Washington/Idaho area reported that an enormous irrigation project was about to be undertaken: "News of the organization of the greatest irrigation project ever launched in this state, if not in the northwest, has leaked out tonight. Moreover, the projectors of the undertaking propose to do what has always been supposed to be impossible—they will take water from the Snake River some miles above Shoshone Falls and irrigate 200,000 acres of the wonderfully fertile land that stretches away on the plateau 1000 feet above the tumbling river."[8] The process by which Idaho would become the third most heavily irrigated state (behind California and Texas) had begun. During the coming decades a series of dams would harness the river and the "savage grandeur" of the scene, as captured in Moran's painting, would be diminished.

In January 1901 Moran exhibited *Shoshone Falls* at the National Academy of Design in New York. In a review of the exhibition Charles Caffin began by applauding "the increased recognition given to younger members of the Academy." He went on to write that despite this hopeful development it would be "churlish" to bemoan the presence of the "Old Guard." Among this group Caffin singled out Moran, focusing his attention on the artist's large western landscape:

"The Shoshone Falls of Snake River, Idaho," by Thomas Moran, N.A., represents a brave and earnest effort to portray a grand phase of nature. The canvas is very large, but the painter has not relied upon size to suggest bigness, having resolutely attacked the big elements of his subject—the rock formation, like giant ramparts and bastions, and the plunge of the mass of water. On these there is an infinity of patient labor expended, which leaves, however, no sense of niggling detail. The composition counts fairly as a whole, and possesses an impressiveness which cannot be reasonably ignored. That our preference may not be for the grand and panoramic in nature is beside the question. Wisely or unwisely the artist has attempted their portrayal, and from this point of view with remarkable success.[9]

Caffin's review of *Shoshone Falls* serves as an apt marker of the change of tone that began to characterize commentary about Moran's work during the early years of the twentieth century. Respectful rather than enthusiastic, Caffin prefaced his remarks with appreciative acknowledgment of the battles an earlier generation had fought, noting that the "Old Guard" had labored "under difficulties of which the younger generation can have little or no conception" and in so doing had done "their share in building up a national art."[10]

When shown at the Pan-American Exposition just a few months after its debut at the National Academy of Design, *Shoshone Falls* was awarded a silver medal. Nevertheless, the picture was the last of Moran's large panoramic western landscapes and remained unsold at his death.[11] Taste and the times had changed.

"Working as Hard as Ever"

In June 1901 Edward Moran, Thomas Moran's elder brother, died. It was Edward whom Thomas acknowledged as his earliest mentor—the person who offered encouragement and studio space when Thomas had nothing more than ambition.[12] Eight months after Edward's death, in February 1902, John Moran died. Five years older than Thomas and a skilled photographer, John had remained in Philadelphia when his brothers moved north. Close companions when young, the brothers had pursued similar careers each initially dependent upon the support of the others. In less than three years Thomas Moran had lost three of the most important people in his life. In 1907 he lost his only son. Paul Moran, who shared his father's interest in painting, died in Los Angeles at age forty-three.

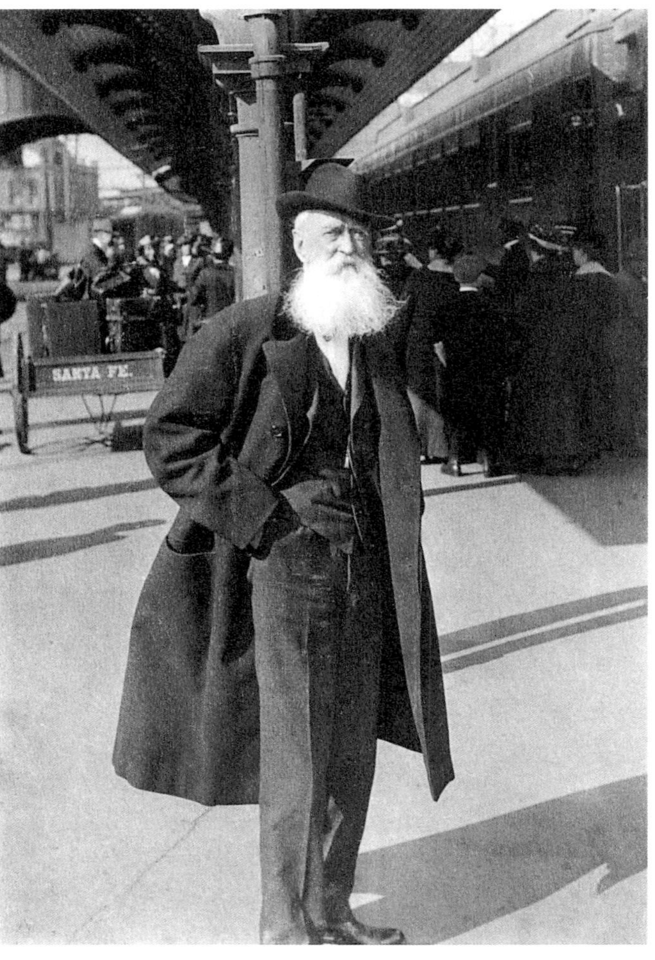

2

2. Thomas Moran on the Santa Fe Railroad, Los Angeles, courtesy East Hampton Library.

3. Advertisement for Santa Fe Railroad published in *Fine Arts Journal,* January 1909.

Despite such sadness and loss—or perhaps because of it—Thomas Moran turned his full attention to work during the first decade of the twentieth century, producing an astonishing number of paintings. These he aggressively marketed through private galleries throughout the country. His business relationship with Moulton and Rickets Gallery in Chicago, for example, was such that he painted pictures on order—often by subject. Moran's best patron, however, was neither a gallery nor a collector but rather the Santa Fe Railroad (fig. 2).

Following Mary's death, Thomas and Ruth Moran spent nearly every winter during the next two decades at the Grand Canyon. In exchange for rail passes and hotel accommodations, Moran produced paintings of the canyon that were used as promotional tools in hotels, offices, and railroad cars. Additional images were distributed on calendars, in guidebooks and brochures, even on stationery. Eventually Moran became so closely identified with the canyon that the railroad used his picture in advertisements (fig. 3).

When not wintering in the Southwest, Ruth and Thomas Moran were often traveling. Blessed with health and energy, Moran maintained a daunting travel schedule that included four trips to Europe during the last years of his life. In 1911, just back from one of his European expeditions, Moran told a reporter from the *New York World*: "I looked at the Alps, but they are nothing compared to the majestic grandeur of our wonderful Rockies. I have painted them all my life and I shall continue to paint them as long as I can hold a brush. I am working as hard as ever I did.... I go to California in the Autumn. There I will paint all winter. I have hundreds of sketches of the Rockies and the Sierra Nevadas, of course, for I have been making them for years, but I still want more."[13] The extensive and detailed ledgers Moran kept during this period testify not only to his productivity but also to his active engagement in the sale of his work. Capitalizing on subjects that had demonstrated market strength, Moran produced a large number of Venetian, Grand Canyon, Yellowstone, and Green River images. Although often repetitive, some of the late works do rival in quality the paintings that broke new ground many years earlier.

As he grew older, Moran came to be described as the "dean of American painters." He also became the subject of numerous newspaper and periodical "profiles." Surprisingly, the articles frequently echo commentary published many years earlier. In 1900, for instance, Richard Ladegast, wrote that Moran "has never been a mere copist, even of Nature. All that he does is directed by an imagination so poetical, and yet so clear, and truthful, that his work is more akin to creation than reproduction."[14] That same year Frederick W. Morton credited Moran with being a "pioneer" in the article he wrote for *Brush and Pencil*, describing the artist's "mental bent" as "poetic" and declaring that his "chief characteristic" is "a rich, almost exotic, imagination."[15] Even Moran's well-known admiration for Turner was addressed late in his career when a critic for the *New York Times* wrote: "He has been called 'an artist spoiled by too much study of Turner,' a criticism which has always seemed rather paradoxical, for it is difficult to conceive how the influence of the great English master could spoil any painter. If Thomas Moran sees Venice and even the majestic scenery of our far West as Turner might have seen them, the visions which he transcribes are none the less strong or entrancing on this account."[16]

3

Thomas Moran Sketching at

Grand Canyon

of Arizona

A large painting of the Grand Canyon of Arizona, by Thomas Moran, N. A., hangs in the National Capitol at Washington, D. C.

Mr. Moran was the first American artist of note to visit this world's wonder. He still frequently goes there to get new impressions. In his summer home at Easthampton or in his New York City studio, usually may be seen several canyon canvases under way.

Quoting from Chas. F. Lummis, in a recent issue of *Out West* magazine: "He (Moran) has come nearer to doing the Impossible than any other meddler with paint and canvas in the Southwest."

Other eminent artists also have visited the titan of chasms. They all admit it to be "the despair of the painter."

You, too, may view this scenic marvel as a side trip on the luxurious and newly-equipped

California Limited

en route to or from sunshiny California this winter.

Only **two days** from Chicago, three days from New York, and one day from Los Angeles. A $250,000 hotel, El Tovar, managed by Fred Harvey, will care for you in country-club style. Round-trip side ride from Williams, Ariz., $6.50.

Yosemite also can be reached in winter from Merced, Cal., nearly all the way by rail.

Write for our illustrated booklets: "Titan of Chasms" and "El Tovar."

W. J. Black, Passenger Traffic Manager
A. T. & S. F. Ry. System
111 Railway Exchange, Chicago

Santa Fe
All the way

Richard Ladegast was correct in stating that Moran was not a copist. More than many of his contemporaries realized, Moran was an imaginative painter. He was also a skilled promoter. Although genuinely interested in literature, music, and the related arts, Moran consciously cultivated an image that combined, in a somewhat improbable way, the most attractive traits of the romantic poet and the expedition artist. Skillfully employing the technical vocabulary of artists he admired, including Turner, with subject matter that extended the range of the romantic landscape, Moran created a number of works that redefined several tenets central to the romanticism of his day. From the ancient volcanic landscape of distant Idaho, for example, he created a solitude more profound, more threatening than any conjured by Byron or Dante.

Open and candid regarding his lack of interest in topographical views, Moran was never just a reporter. Even the field studies he gathered as raw material for studio paintings betray his self-stated interest in making pictures not documents. Despite the enormous size of his most famous works, Moran may have been at his best in the small watercolor sketches he produced in the field. Nowhere perhaps is the romanticism of the age summarized more elegantly than in the small watercolor based on field studies Moran created in 1873 of the tiny boats carrying the Powell expedition down the Rio Virgin between the walls of Zion Canyon (cat. 46). Rarely has the human enterprise appeared so fragile or so heroic.

Self-cast as the artist/pilgrim in wondrous but difficult landscapes, Moran created and then marketed images that were born as much of imagination as of experience. A master at mixing fact and fiction, Moran used the technique to great advantage, producing some of the most remarkable landscapes of the nineteenth century.

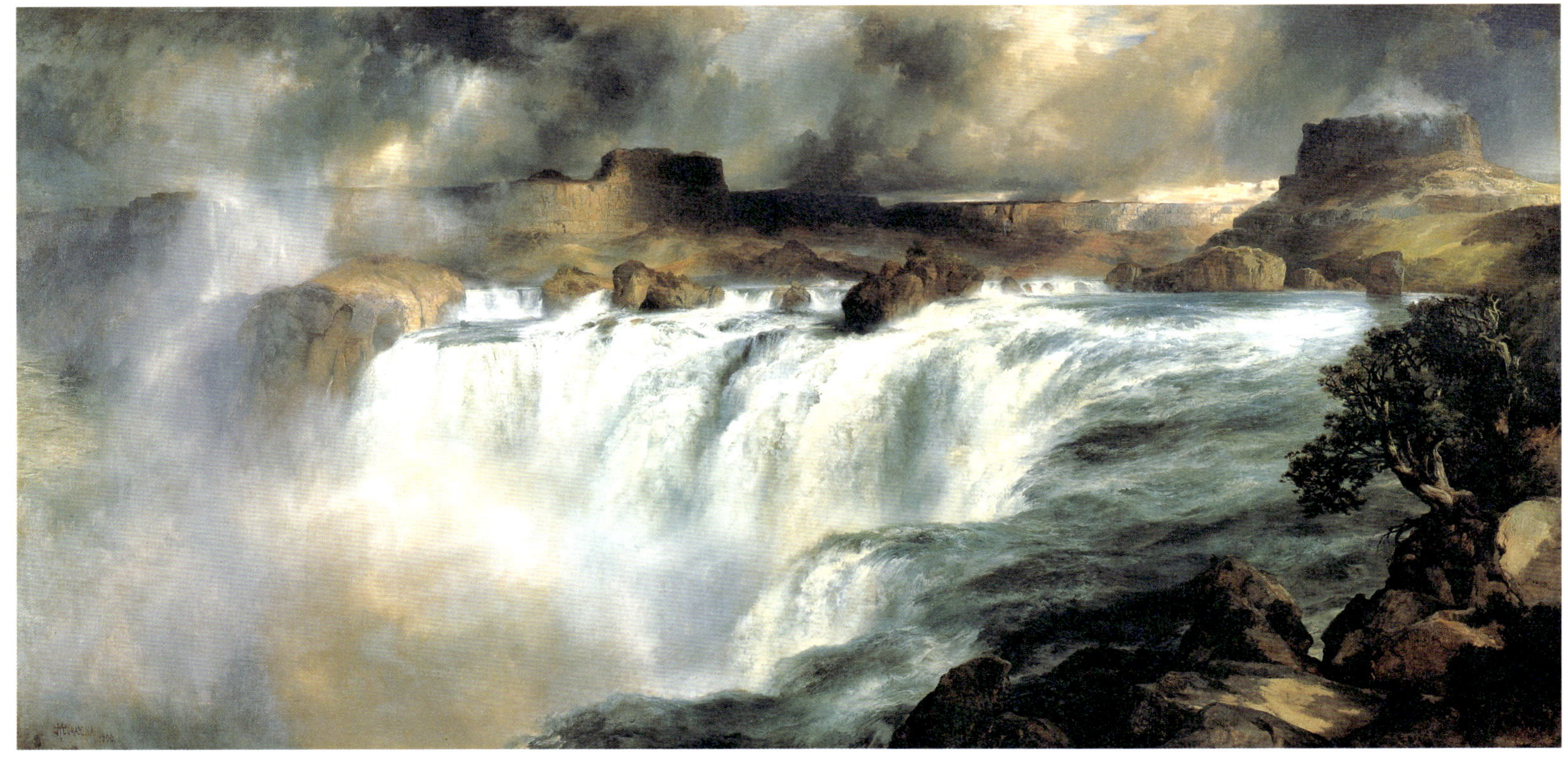

88

Shoshone Falls on the Snake River

1900, oil on canvas
182.9 x 365.8 (72 x 144)
Gilcrease Museum,
Tulsa, Oklahoma

AWAY IN THE wilds of Idaho, midway between Salt Lake and Oregon, the air is thundering and the earth is rent by a cataract as imposing as Niagara. Situated on the sage-brush plains, which calmly sleep between the Rocky Mountains and the Cascade Range, and are alike untenanted by Ceres or the god of gold, the Great Shoshone is a world wonder. (*Phila. Evening Bulletin*, 17 July 1866; from the *Salt Lake (Union) Vidette*, May 31)

STILL THE RIVER was invisible in its winding chasm, one thousand feet below the surface of the plain; but now at three miles we heard more clearly its thrilling roar, and saw the mist with its violet tinge of rainbow, which arises forever and ever, as if old Shoshonee were taking a vapor-bath or smoking his pipe.

At last we alighted on a broken floor of brown lava, descended the precipice for three hundred feet by a natural rock stairway, walked a few hundred yards across a terrace of grass, lava and cedars; and stood upon a second precipice.

Peering over the edge, five hundred feet beneath us we saw the river, after its terrific leap, peaceful as a mirror. Half a mile above, in full view, was the cataract. It is unequaled in the world, save by Niagara, of which it vividly reminded us. It is not all height like Yosemite, nor all breadth and power like the Great Falls of the Missouri, nor all strength and volume like Niagara; but combines the three elements....

Down the stream I could find no place where I dared attempt to descend the almost unbroken wall to the water's edge. But just below the brink I crept out to the edge of the projecting rock. Clinging to a hardy cedar, I saw the peaceful waters two hundred and fifty feet below me. Above, the surface of the water is broken into five channels by little islands. Thence I saw the river come gliding swift, clear and smooth to the dizzy edge; the long plunge; and the caldron, which boils beneath, under wafting clouds of spray. The fall itself is of purest white, interspersed with myriads of glassy drops —a cataract of snow with an avalanche of jewels. Mocking and belittling all human splendor, Nature is here in her lace and pearls, her robe of diamonds and tiara of rainbow. (Richardson 1867, 497, 499)

THEN LEAVING this they moved northward toward the falls of the Snake River, designated, in the vicinity of Salt Lake, as the Great Shoshone Falls.... Standing upon the craggy rocks that jut out from and form the walls of the table-land below the falls, one may obtain a bird's eye view of one of the most sublime of Rocky Mountain scenes. Even in this location, which is many feet above the falls, the air is heavy with moisture, which is attributable to the mist into which the river's great leap slivers the water. From the position on the crags you have also a grand sight of the different falls, of which the main one seems but the culmination. Each small fall is in itself a perfect gem with a setting of grandeur in the glorious masses of rock.... There is in the entire region of the falls such wildness of beauty that a feeling pervades the mind almost unconsciously that you are, if not the first white man who has ever trod that trail, certainly one of the very few who have ventured so far. From the island above the falls you may not see the great leap that the water takes, but you will certainly feel sensible of the fact that you are in the presence of one of one of Nature's greatest spectacles as you listen to the roar of the falling water and gaze down the stream over the fall at the wild scene beyond. (John Samson [Timothy O'Sullivan?], "Photographs from the High Rockies," *Harper's New Monthly Magazine* 39 [Sept. 1869], 475)

WE WERE breakfasting when the sun rose, and shortly afterward, mounting into the saddle, headed toward the cañon of the Shoshone.... A few miles in front the smooth surface of the plain was broken by a ragged, zigzag line of black, which marked the edge of the farther wall of the Snake cañon. A dull throbbing sound greeted us. Its pulsations were deep, and seemed to proceed from the ground beneath our feet. Leaving the cavalry to bring up the wagon, my two friends and I galloped on, and were quickly upon the edge of the cañon-wall. We looked down into a broad, circular excavation, three quarters of a mile in diameter, and nearly seven hundred feet deep. East and north over the edges of the cañon, we looked across miles and miles of the Snake plain, far on to the blue boundary mountains. The wall of the gorge opposite us, like the cliff at our feet, sank in perpendicular bluffs nearly to the level of the river, the broad excavation being covered by rough piles of black lava and rounded domes of trachyte rock. An horizon as level as the sea; a circling wall, whose sharp edges were here and there battlemented in huge, fortress-like masses; a broad river, smooth and unruffled, flowing quietly into the middle of the scene, and then plunging into a labyrinth of rocks, tumbling over a precipice two hundred feet high, and moving westward in a still, deep current to disappear behind a black promontory. It is a strange, savage scene: a monotony of pale blue sky, olive and gray stretches of desert, frowning walls of jetty lava, deep beryl-green of river-stretches, reflecting, here and there, the intense solemnity of the cliffs, and in the centre a dazzling sheet of foam. In the early morning light, the shadows of the cliff were cast over half the basin, defining themselves in sharp outline here and there on the river. Upon the foam of the cataract one point of the rock cast a cobalt-blue shadow. Where the river flowed around the western promontory, it was wholly in shadow, and of a deep sea-green. A scanty growth of coniferous trees fringed the brink of the lower cliffs, overhanging the river.... The mere suggestion of trees clinging here and there along the walls serves rather to heighten than to relieve the forbidding gloom of the place. Nor does the flashing whiteness, where the river tears itself among the rocky islands, or rolls in spray down the cliff, brighten the aspect. In contrast with its brilliancy, the rocks seem darker and more wild. The descent of four hundred feet, from our stand-point to the level of the river above the falls, has to be made by a narrow, winding path, among rough ledges of lava. We were obliged to leave our wagon at the summit, and pack down the camp equipment, and photographic apparatus upon carefully led mules. By midday we were comfortably camped on the margin of the left bank, just above the brink of the falls. My tent was pitched upon the edge of a cliff, directly overhanging the rapids. From my door I looked over the cataract, and, whenever the veil of mist was blown aside, could see for a mile down the river. The lower half of the cañon is excavated in a gray, porphyritic trachyte. It is over this material that the Snake falls....

In the early spring, when swollen by the rapidly melted snows, the river pours over with something like the grand volume of Niagara, but, at the time of my visit, it was wholly white foam.... Immense volumes of foam roll up the cataract-base, and, whirling about in the eddying winds, rise often a thousand feet in the air. When the wind blows down the cañon, a gray mist obscures the river for half a mile; and when, as is usually the case in the afternoon, the breezes blow eastward, the foam-cloud curls over the brink of the fall, and hangs like a veil over the upper river.... Incessant roar, reinforced by a thousand echoes, fills the cañon. Out of this monotone, from time to time, rise strange, wild sounds, and now and then may be heard a slow, measured beat, not unlike the recurring fall of breakers....

Night is the true time to appreciate the full force of the scene. I lay and watched it many hours. The broken rim of the basin profiled itself upon a mass of drifting clouds where torn openings revealed gleams of pale moonlight and bits of remote sky trembling with misty stars. Intervals of light and blank darkness hurriedly followed each other. For a moment the black gorge would be crowded with forms. Tall cliffs, ramparts of lava, the rugged outlines of islands huddled together on the cataract's brink, faintly luminous foam breaking over black rapids, the swift, white leap of the river, and a ghostly, formless mist through which the cañon-walls and far reach of the lower river were veiled and unveiled again and again. A moment of this strange picture, and then a rush of black shadow, when nothing could be seen but the breaks in the clouds, the basin rim, and a vague, white centre in the general darkness.

After sleeping on the nightmarish brink of the falls, it was no small satisfaction to climb out of this Dantean gulf and find myself once more upon a pleasantly prosaic foreground of sage. (Clarence King, *Mountaineering in the Sierra Nevada* [Boston, 1872]; repr. Lincoln, NB, 1970, 188–191)

I FIRST VISITED Shoshone falls in company with two traveling women whose names I have long forgotten, and a stage driver by the name of Joe Mason.... It was along about the last days of August or first of September, 1875. While more than fifty years have elapsed since that day the experience of the trip made such a deep imprint on my young mind that the picture is flashed before me often and clearly....

There was just an Indian trail down the hill, so...we hoofed it down to the river where we went from place to place finding new points of interest, each location seeming better than the one we had just left....

That day while eating our lunch at the falls we built imaginary hotels to accommodate tourists who would be attracted to this beauty spot. We could all see the possibilities of a great pleasure resort. No country in the world could produce a location where beauty, grandeur and power was so artistically and profusely intermixed. And with all this natural display no one had cared to own or claim the land adjoining to Shoshone falls.

This impressed me and I inquired as to how the land could be procured. I was informed that the land was unsurveyed...and all that was required to secure the land was to use a squatter's right and hold possession, which required the posting of a notice on the land making claim to all you pretended to fence.... Along in the early part of the summer of 1876 I...put up a pair of bars across the trails near the top of the hill and had the country fenced around Shoshone falls... both up and down the river....

We knew [after 1879] that the railroad was building but had no idea that it had gotten that far into Idaho. Shoshone was quite a little city of tents and was to be quite a prominent point. Everything was business and bustle....

We inaugurated a daily stage line from Shoshone to Shoshone Falls.... Presently the travel began to come but it came in spurts and spells.... During that season we handled several excursion parties including the Omaha Business Men's association of some forty-five people, and the Colorado Press association of about the same number.... In 1883 we sold our holdings to a syndicate of capitalist[s].... (Walgamott 1926, 57–60)

IT IS STILL rare to meet anyone who has seen the Falls of the Snake; and people look with mild surprise upon those who, having visited Shoshone, presume to compare it with Niagara. Yet no one possessed of a keen eye for the beautiful and the picturesque can visit the two places without feeling that the Idaho cataract, high up in the great table-land amid its lava beds, and those wonderful mountain skies and in that mountain atmosphere, is incomparably the more attractive, and, indeed, except in volume of water, the more wonderful, as well as more interesting, of the two....

There was never a day during our Shoshone visit that, for a moment, the region did not become a hideous reality from which I longed to escape. But all such moments were followed by hours when the very height of the walls that hemmed us in, and the wild noise of the falling river fascinated and exhilarated. You should see the river gather itself together for its leap into the lower depths of the cañon; should listen to the roar it makes; should feel the earth tremble with the shock; should watch the rising mists, ghost-like in the moonlight; should give days to the isolated place, to know the fascinations of Shoshone Falls. Telling one how high the Falls are, how deep the cañon is, gives no idea of the place itself... full of novelties and strange sights. Night-loving bats live in the caverns that honeycomb the cliffs; and on top of the high, slim pinnacle of red rock, rising amidstream, an eagle has her nest and rears her brood. There are points overlooking the Falls where, unless strong, you will feel ill and dizzy; and there are others where you will delight to sit and read....

At Niagara the river falls two hundred and twenty-five feet in twenty-five miles. At Shoshone the Snake descends five hundred feet in four miles. The Great Fall of Shoshone is crescent-shaped, and is two hundred and twenty-five feet high by nine hundred and fifty feet wide. The plunge is unbroken. Facing it one sees a quivering wall of water that stretches from one side of the cañon to the other. The roar is deafening, and its force so great that the displaced air is as fierce as a tornado. The earth trembles from the blow it receives. You yourself are drenched with spray; and the rising mist is like a fog at sea, blown hither and thither, and so catching the sun's rays as to form arch upon arch of glorious color. (Roberts 1888, xi, 155–156, 164)

THOMAS MORAN of New York who has earned the reputation as among the foremost of distinctively American painters, is a guest at The Knuirford with his daughter, Miss Moran, enroute to Shoshone Falls on the Snake river, which he will sketch and color in water, and then paint in oil during the fall or winter in his New York studio. (*Salt Lake City Daily Tribune*, June 1900, EHL scrapbook)

THE LARGEST and most attractive picture in the art gallery at the Pan-American is Thomas Moran's painting of the Shoshone Falls, Snake River, Idaho. The picture is twelve feet six inches by twelve feet and occupies a prominent position in the large exhibit. Mr. Moran has at his East Hampton studio a photograph of the painting which is thirty two inches long and is one of the finest specimens of photographic art we have ever seen. (*EH Star*, 26 July 1901)

THE PUBLIC library will have on exhibition during the next ten days a painting by Thomas Moran, an artist who has recently become a resident of Santa Barbara, after spending two winters as a visitor.

The painting is of the Shoshone Falls, Snake River, Idaho, and is considered by connoisseurs one of the artist's most important canvases. It is one of three paintings that Mr. Moran has made of the most impressive landscapes of America: one of the Grand Canyon of Arizona, one of the Yellowstone Canyon and this of Shoshone Falls. The canvas is 6 by 12 feet, and was painted in 1900 immediately after the artist's visit to the west when the work was accomplished in one month. (Unidentified newspaper clipping, 1920, EHL scrapbook)

"SHOSHONE FALLS," the magnificent oil painting by Mr. Moran that was shown at the public library for several weeks, about 18 months ago, and which was so warmly praised by thousands of people, is now in the painter's studio at his residence. Mr. Moran considers this the grandest waterfall he has ever seen, in that it has a most magnificent background of rocky lava bluffs, which rise to a height of 1000 feet above the mighty torrent, while Niagara, for instance, has a background altogether plain and uninteresting, comparatively flat. In the former picture the mad tumult of water in its wild rush has almost the effect of taking one's breath away, and the drawing and coloring are such as could only be the work of real genius. (*Santa Barbara Sunday Morning Press*, Dec. 1921 clipping, EHL scrapbook)

89

Looking up the Trail at Bright Angel, Grand Canyon of Arizona

1901, watercolor
37.8 x 26.4 (14 ⅞ x 10 ⅜)
Cooper-Hewitt National Design Museum, Smithsonian Institution, Gift of Thomas Moran

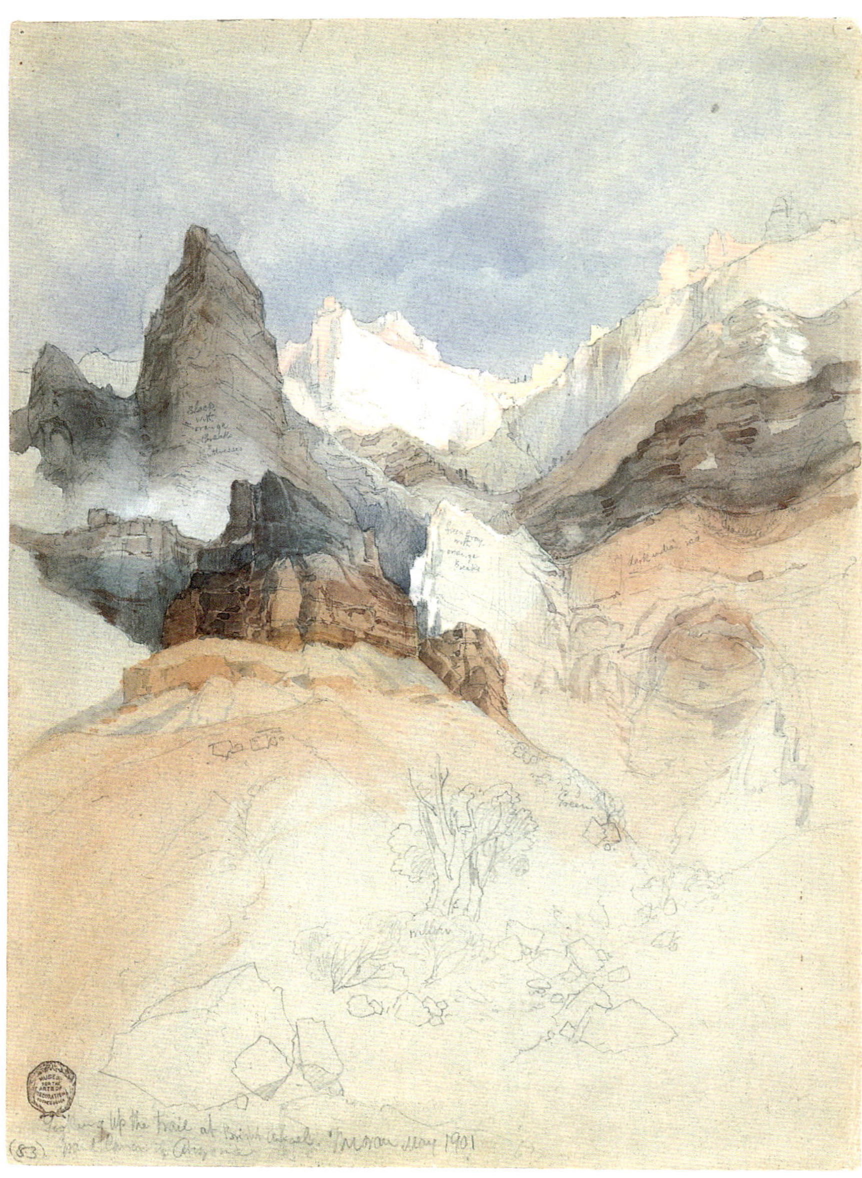

ONLY BY descending into the Cañon may one arrive at anything like comprehension of its proportions, and the descent cannot be too urgently commended to every visitor who is sufficiently robust to bear a reasonable amount of fatigue.... Not the most fervid pictures of a poet's fancy could transcend the glories then revealed in the depths of the Cañon; inky shadows, pale gildings of lofty spires, golden splendors of sun beating full on façades of red and yellow, obscurations of distant peaks by veils of transient shower, glimpses of white towers half drowned in purple haze, suffusions of rosy light blended in reflection from a hundred tinted walls. Caught up to exalted emotional heights the beholder becomes unmindful of fatigue. He mounts on wings. He drives the chariot of the sun.

Having returned to the plateau, it will be found that the descent into the Cañon has bestowed a sense of intimacy that almost amounts to a mental grasp of the scene. (Higgins 1897, 14, 18)

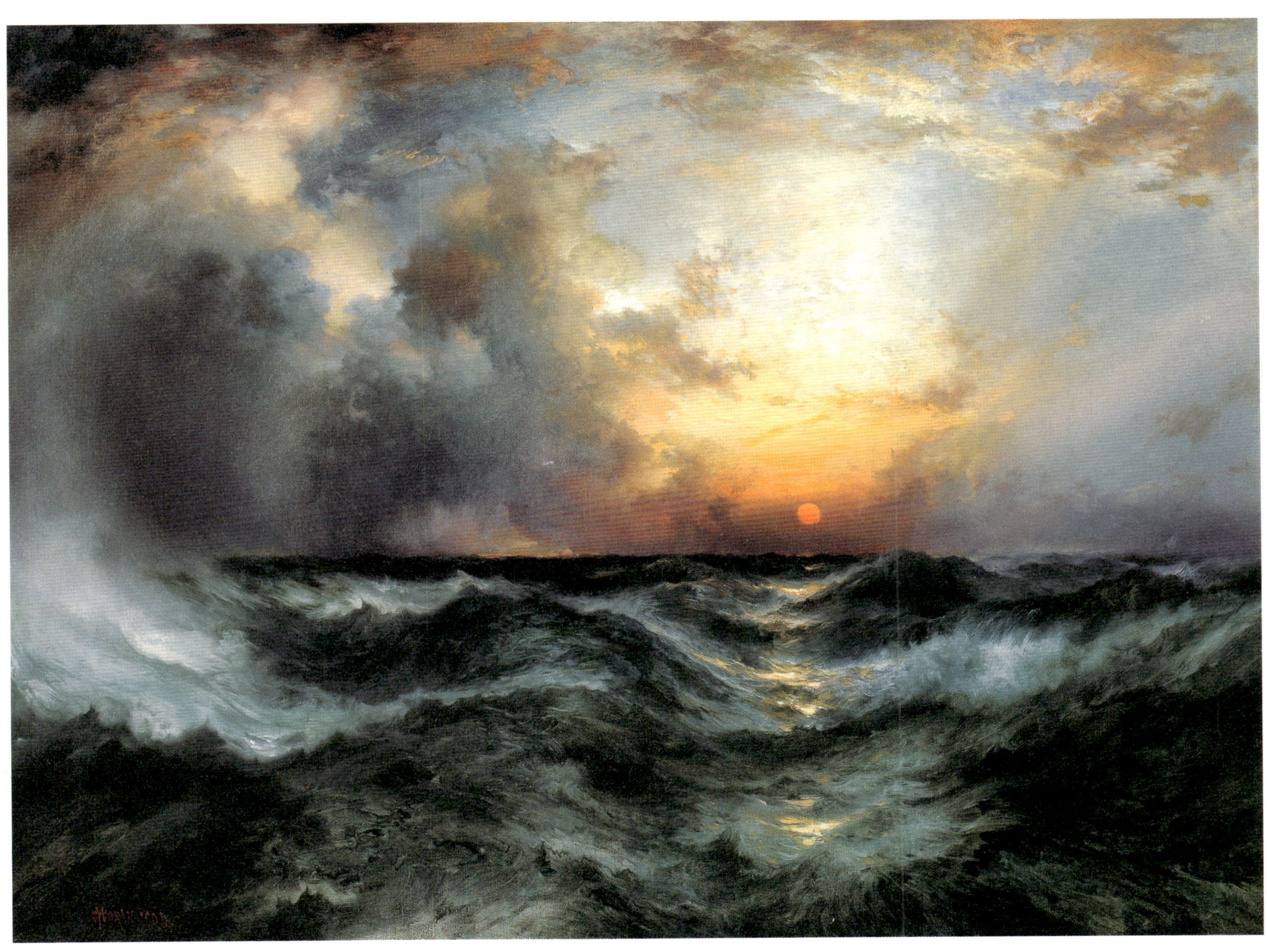

90

Sunset in Mid-Ocean

1904, oil on canvas
76.2 x 101.6 (30 x 40)
Private Collection

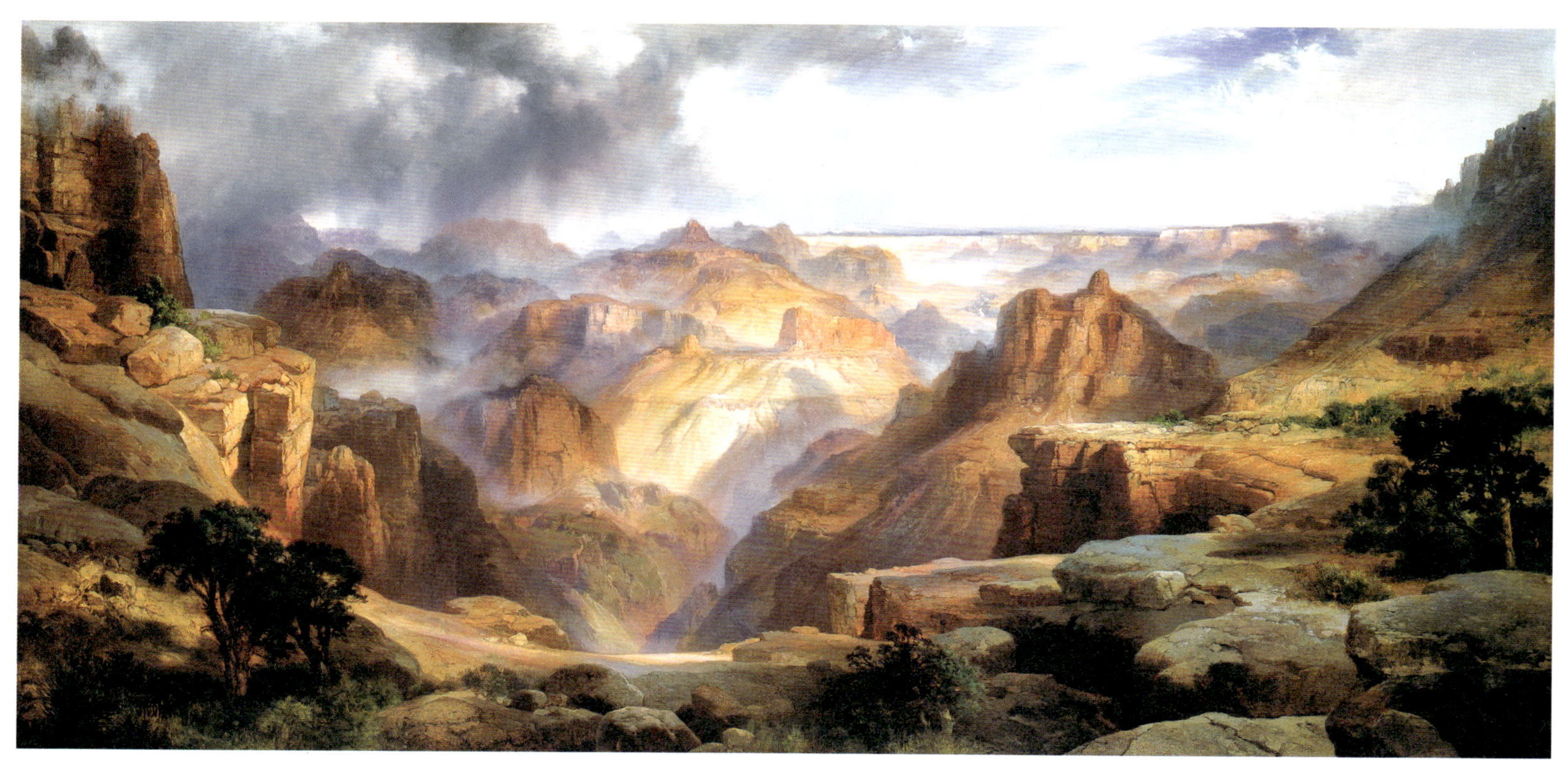

91

Grand Canyon

1904, oil on canvas
76.2 x 152.4 (30 x 60)
Private Collection

Washington only

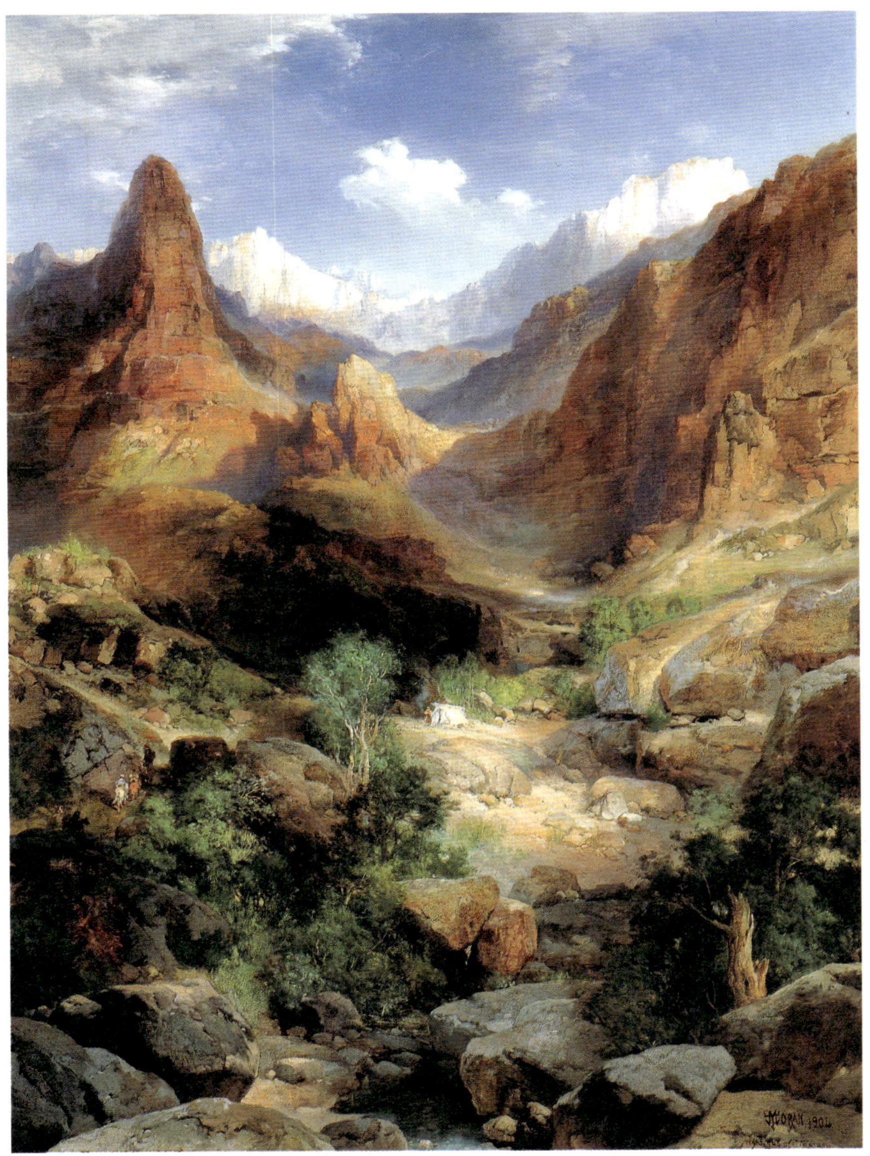

92

Bright Angel Trail

1904, oil on canvas
101.6 x 76.2 (40 x 30)
Private Collection

AFTER THE CLOUDS had lifted and the sun was shining once more, the party assembled, in riding array, to take "The Trail to Those Below." There was much amusement and snapping of cameras in the little corral beside the hotel at the mounting of the mules. Pete and Johnny, two wise little animals whose packs were larger than themselves, led the way down the Bright Angel Trail, looking back occasionally to see that the long line of riders were following properly. The descent seemed perilous or safe as one had fear or confidence, and while some of the party rode down with joy, to others the trip meant heroism. The guides were watchful, the mules sure of foot and the plateau was reached without mishap. For two hours the way lay along the side of a creamy cliff and some one cried with wonder, "Oh! how strange, the Canyon is all yellow and white." But five hundred feet below the rim, the Canyon began to be all red, in an infinite variety of shades and hues, and, looking up, the vast golden rocks became but as the foam upon the crest of the sea. The plateau was soft with sage brush and although the snow still covered the ground about the hotel, here was found a small, but fertile garden, with roses and chrysanthemums blooming luxuriantly under vivid green trees. (Stevens 1911, 113)

93

Indian Pueblo, Laguna, New Mexico

1905, oil on canvas
50.8 x 76.2 (20 x 30)
Private Collection, Colorado

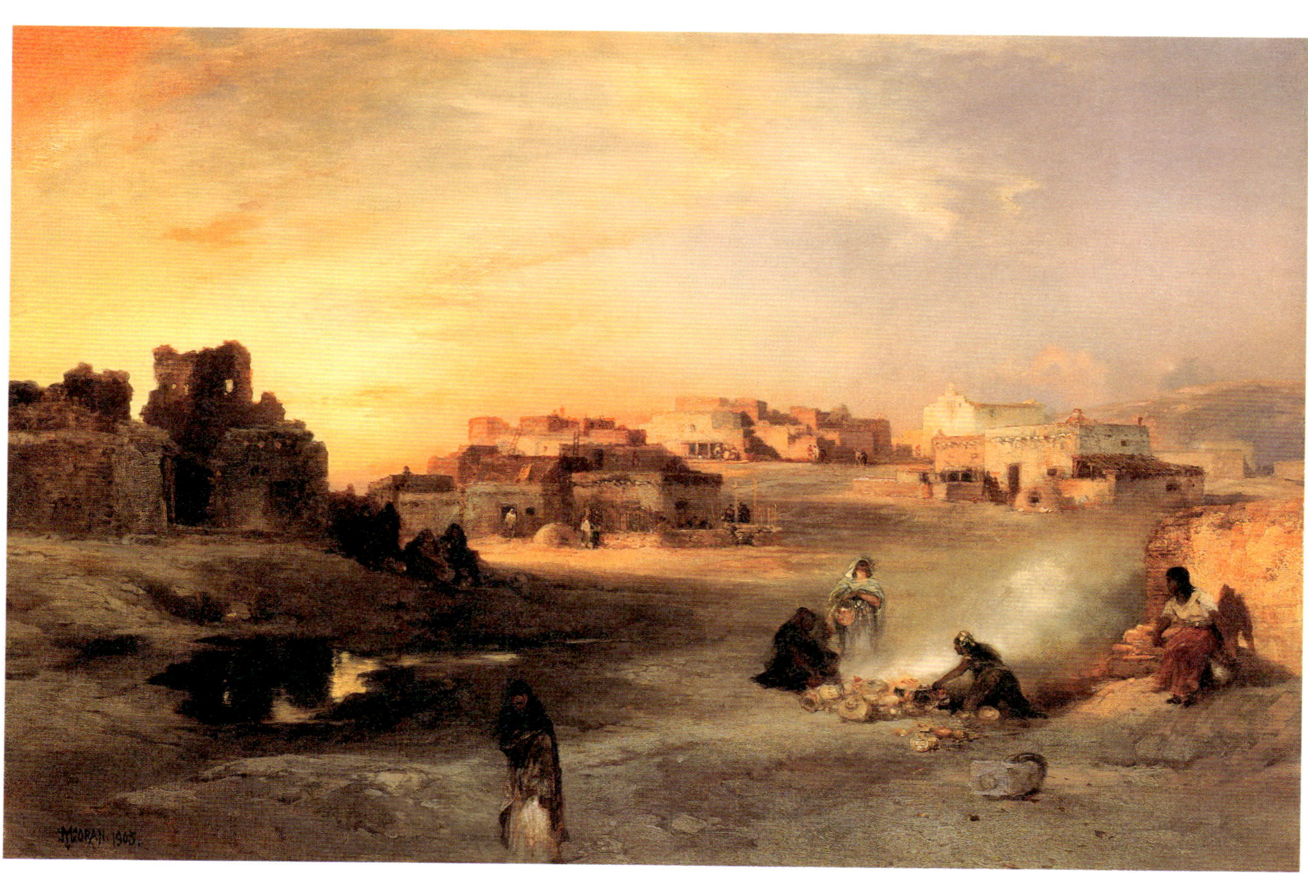

94

Tantallon Castle, North Berwick, Scotland

1910, oil on canvas
76.8 x 101.6 (30 ¼ x 40)
Private Collection

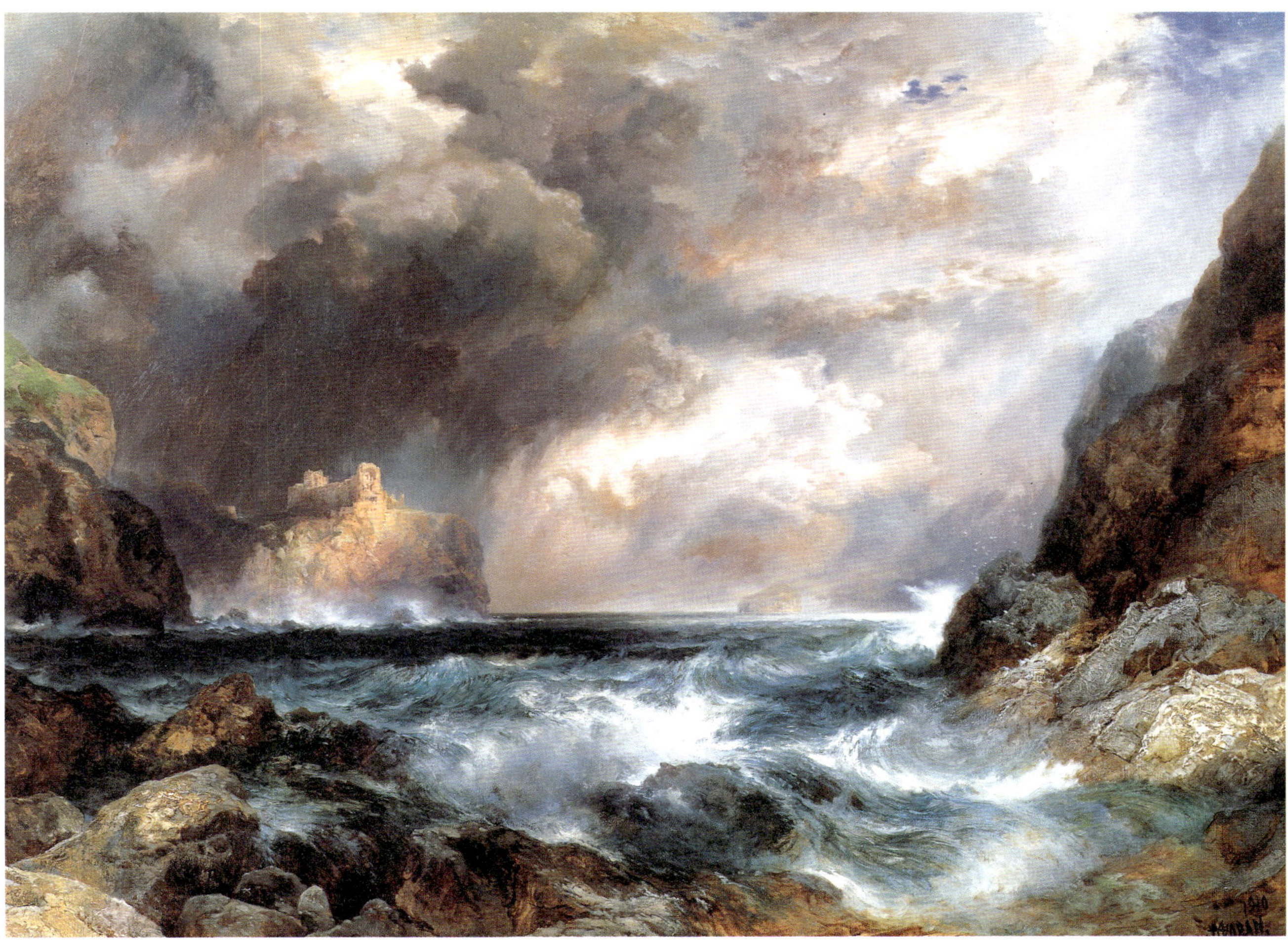

Marmion, Canto V

But scant three miles the band had rode,
When o'er a height they passed,
And, sudden, close before them showed
His towers, Tantallon vast;
Broad, massive, high, and stretching far,
And held impregnable in war,
On a projecting rock they rose,
And round three sides the ocean flows,
The fourth did battled walls enclose,
And double mound and fosse.
By narrow drawbridge, outworks strong,
Through studded gates, and entrance long,
To the main court they cross.
It was a wide and stately square:
Around were lodgings, fit and fair,
And towers of various form,
Which on the court projected far,
And broke its lines quadrangular.
Here was square keep, there turret high,
Or pinnacle that sought the sky,
Whence oft the Warder could descry
The gathering ocean-storm.

(John Dennis, ed., *The Poetical Works of Sir Walter Scott,* vol. 2 [London, 1892], 156–157)

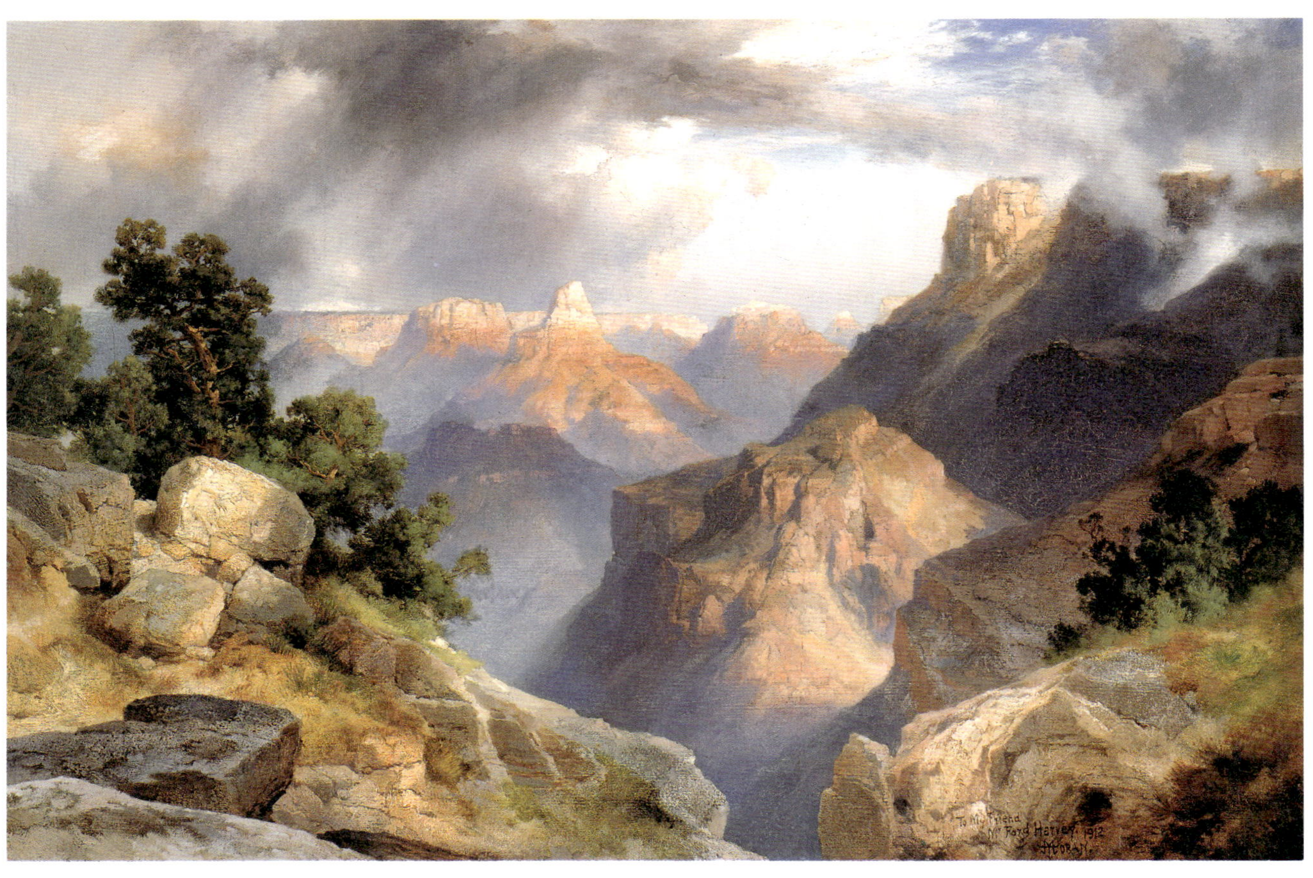

95

Grand Canyon

1912, oil on canvas
40.3 x 60.6 (15 7/8 x 23 7/8)
The Nelson-Atkins Museum of Art, Kansas City, Missouri, Bequest of Katherine Harvey

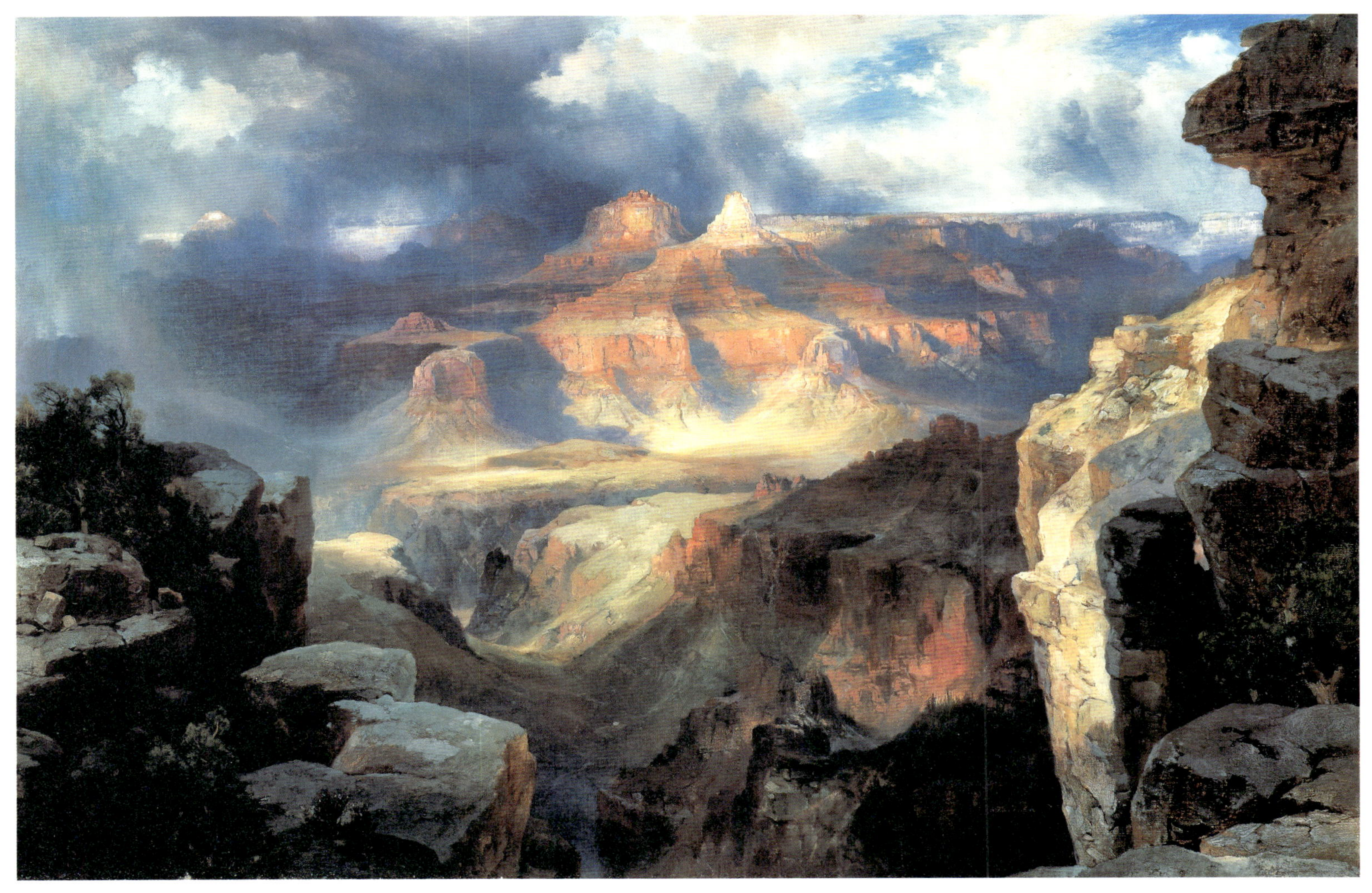

96

A Miracle of Nature

1913, oil on canvas
51.1 x 76.5 (20 1/8 x 30 1/8)
David H. Koch

Washington and Tulsa only

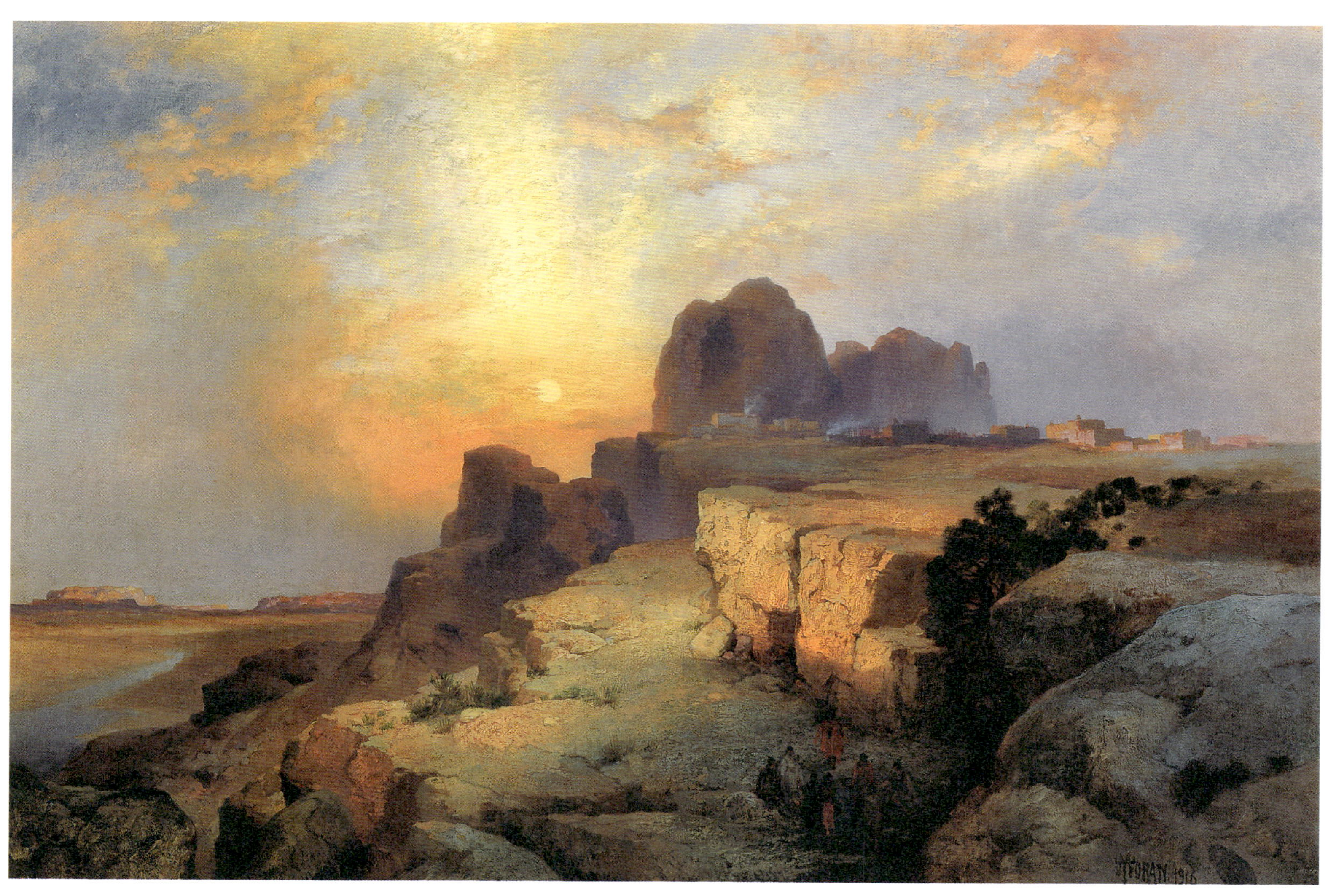

97

Hopi Village, Arizona

1916, oil on canvas
50.8 x 76.2 (20 x 30)
Heckscher Museum
of Art, Huntington,
New York, August
Heckscher Collection

Chronology 1837–1926

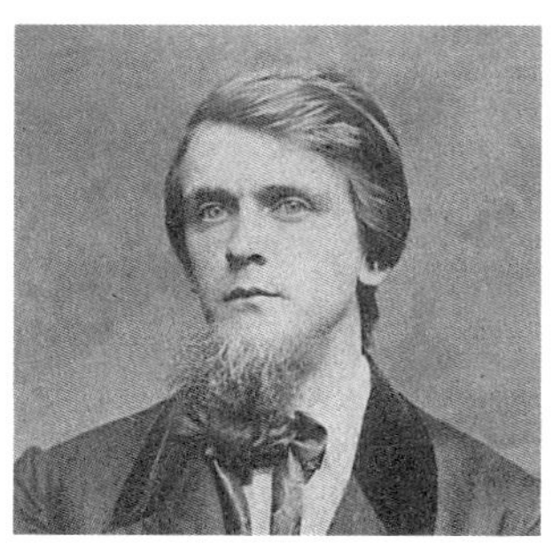
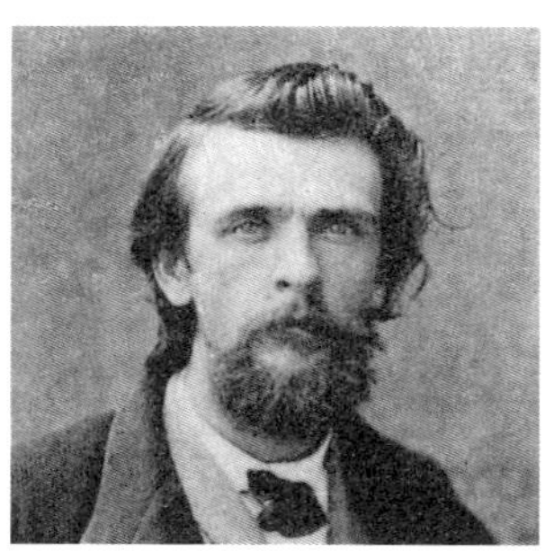
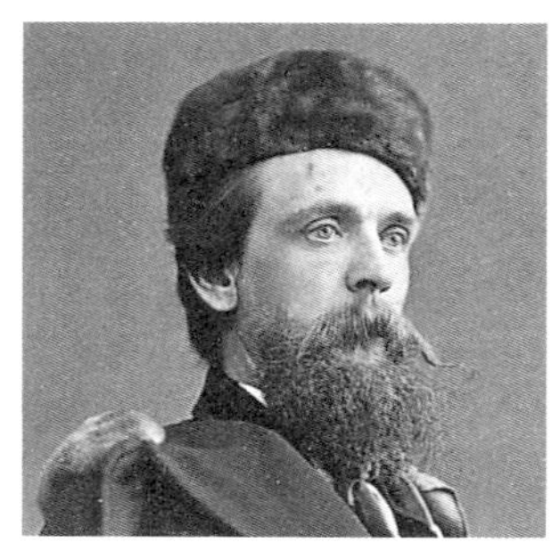
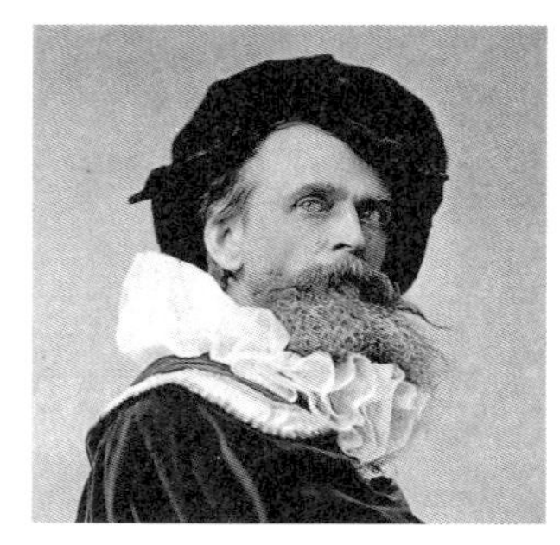

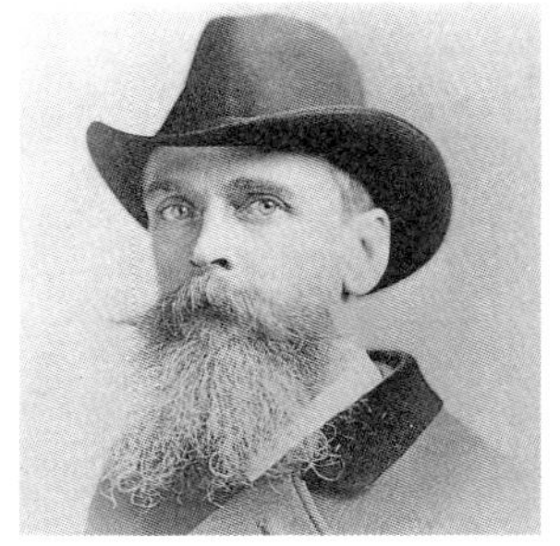
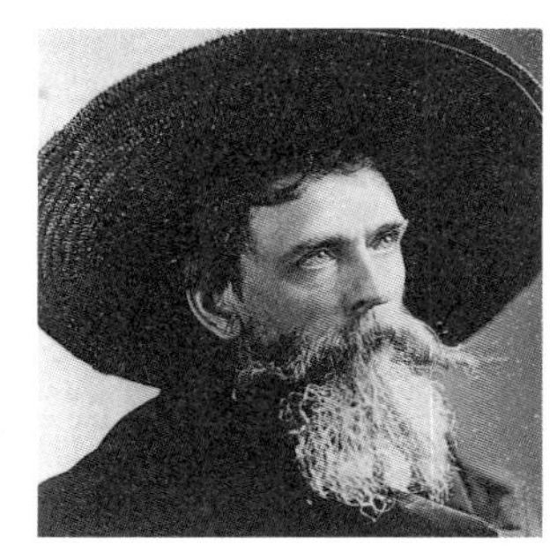
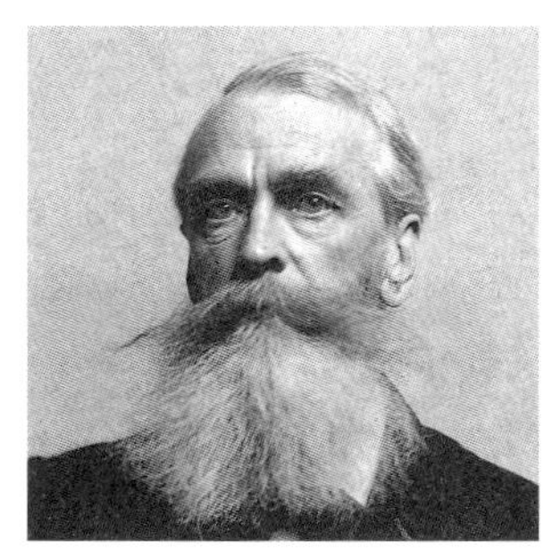
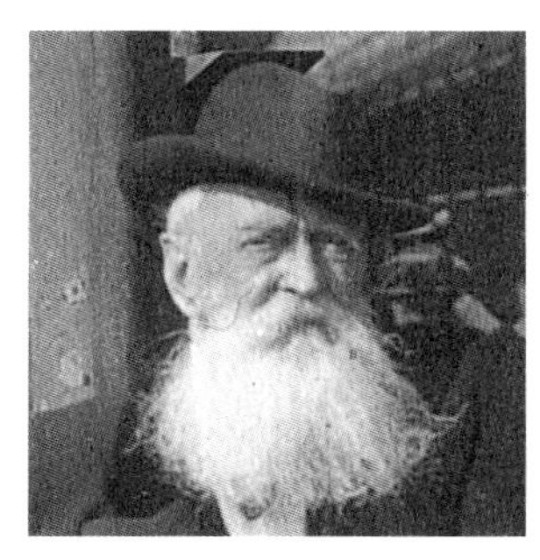
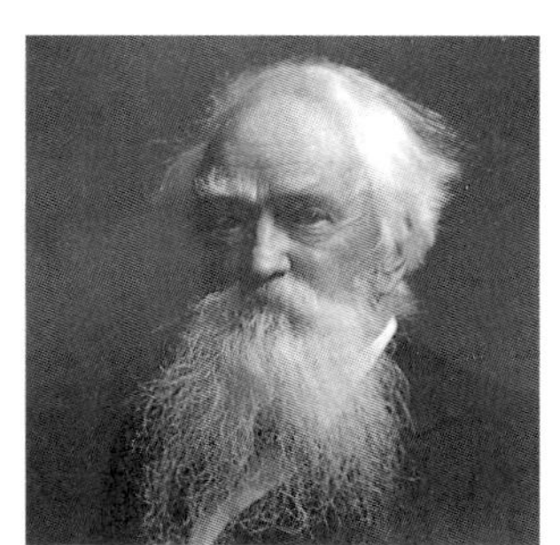

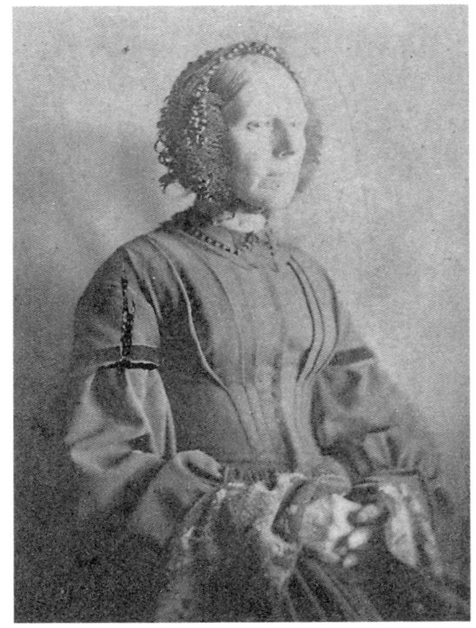

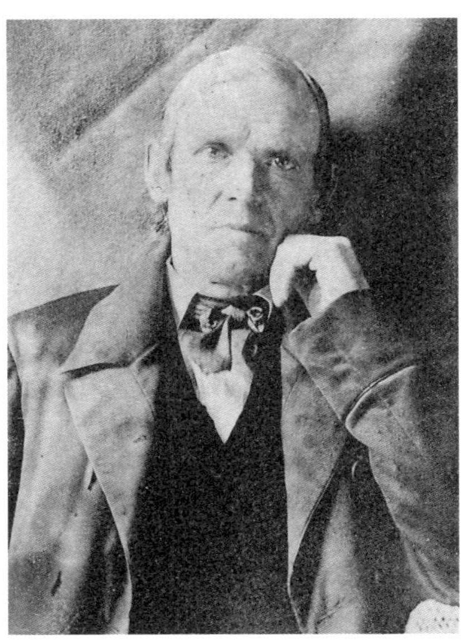

Moran's parents, Mary Higson Moran and Thomas Moran Sr., courtesy East Hampton Library.

• 1837 •

12 February. Thomas Moran born at 6 Duncan St., Bolton, Lancashire, England. Fifth child, fourth son of Thomas (1802–1862) and Mary Higson Moran (1807–1883). Older siblings: Edward (1829–1901); John (1831–1902); James (1833–before 1850); and Sarah (1835–?). Younger siblings: Elizabeth (1839–?); Peter (1841–1914); William (1846–1871); Mary (1849–1933); and James (1852–1860). (Birth certificates of Thomas, Elizabeth, and Peter Moran, Bolton district registry; 1850 and 1860 U.S. Census; EHL; interment records, Old Cathedral and West Laurel Hill Cemeteries, Phila.)

• 1842 •

Thomas Moran (Sr.) emigrates to the U.S., eventually establishing a mill at Carrocksink [currently Cohocksink], near Philadelphia. (*Bolton Journal*, 22 Apr. 1882)

• 1843 •

Mary Higson Moran takes sons Edward and Thomas to see George Catlin's traveling exhibition and Indian troop in Manchester, England. (Shaun Greenhalgh, 24 June 1987, quoting Mary Higson Moran, Gilcrease research files)

• 1844 •

13 April–31 May. Mary Moran; children Edward, John, James, Sarah, Thomas, Elizabeth, Peter; and Mary's mother, Sarah Higson, travel from Liverpool to Philadelphia aboard *Thomas P. Cope*. Sarah Higson dies en route. (Harrison 1978, 43–44; passenger lists, Phila., 1800–1882, NA)

30 July. Thomas (Jr.), John, and Peter Moran become naturalized citizens. (Naturalization records, U.S. Circuit Court, Phila.)

• 1845 •

Thomas Moran (Sr.) listed as a weaver in Kensington, an outlying district of Philadelphia, until 1857. (M'Elroy's Phila. City Directory)

• 1846 •

7 November. Thomas Moran (Sr.) applies for naturalization; granted to him and remaining unnaturalized family members, 2 Oct. 1849. (Naturalization records, U.S. Circuit Court, Phila.)

• 1850 •

10 August. U.S. Census lists Moran household as: Thomas Moran 48, weaver, born in Ireland; Elizabeth [Mary] 42; John 18, printer; Sarah 15; Thomas 13; Elizabeth 11; Peter 9, all born in England; William 7, Mary 5, born in Pennsylvania; William Thompson 28, warper, born in England, and Susan 20, born in Pennsylvania. (Schedule 1. Free Inhabitants in ... 3rd Ward ... Kensington ..., 139)

• 1852 •

Thomas Moran (Jr.) completes studies at Harrison's Grammar School on Master St., Kensington. (Moran's copy of *Flora's Lexicon*, EHL; Curtis 1897, 325)

• 1853 •

Moran enters apprenticeship with Scattergood and Telfer, a wood engraving firm in Philadelphia; he later terminates apprenticeship prematurely. (*Boston Transcript*, 1 Dec. 1875; notes by Ruth Moran and Mary Tassin Moran, 1903, and by Thomas Moran, GA; M'Elroy's)

Moran completes *Catawissa Valley*, inscribed "one of my earliest drawings on wood. T. Moran 1853" (EHL).

• 1854 •

9 May–27 June. PAFA annual exhibition. Edward Moran exhibits for first time, showing *View on the Susquehanna* (no. 356). (*Phila. N. American and Gazette*; Rutledge 1955, 144)

• 1855 •

Edward Moran moves from Kensington to Philadelphia. (M'Elroy's; Rutledge 1955, 144)

10 April. PAFA annual exhibition. Edward Moran exhibits four paintings. (*Crayon*, 7 Mar., 159; Rutledge 1955, 144)

• 1856 •

Thomas Moran (Jr.) joins brother Edward at 186 Locust St., Phila. (M'Elroy's; Rutledge 1955, 144, 145)

15 April. Moran sketches and dates *Bridge over the Schuylkill, Philadelphia* (Gilcrease).

Moran's siblings Edward, John, Sarah, and Peter Moran (left to right), courtesy East Hampton Library.

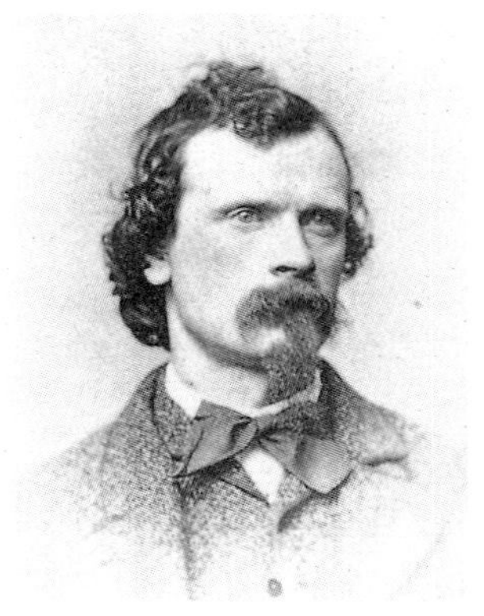

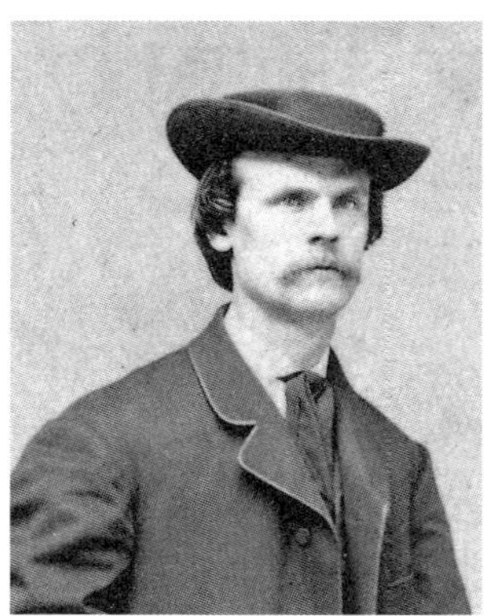

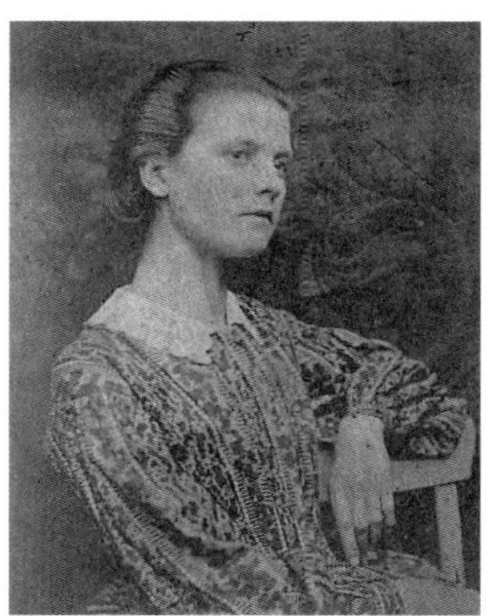

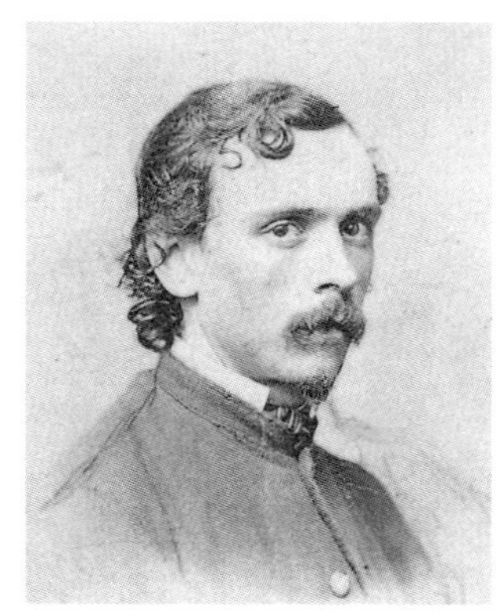

Interior of James S. Earle & Son Gallery, Philadelphia, stereograph by John Moran, courtesy Library Company of Philadelphia.

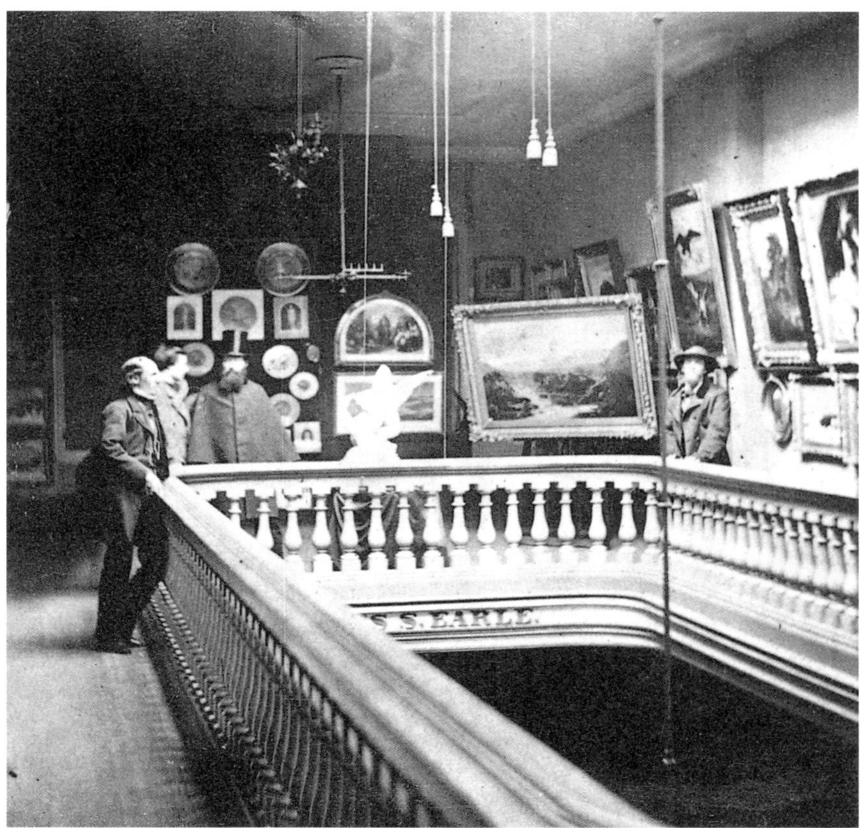

30 April. *Phila. Evening Bulletin* reports opening of PAFA annual exhibition. Moran exhibits for first time with six watercolors, *Absecom*; *Sketch on the Delaware*; *Evening on the Danube*; *Martello Tower, on the Kentish Coast*; *Landscape, Showery Weather*; *Embarkation on Lake Shalimar* (nos. 367, 368, 391, 394, 437, 439). Edward Moran exhibits six paintings. (Rutledge 1955, 144, 145)

• 1857 •

10 March–16 May. First annual exhibition of DCAA. Moran exhibits *View on Tacony Creek* (no. 24). Edward Moran exhibits two works. (Cobb 1963–1965, 122, 124; *Crayon* [June], 186; Yarnall and Gerdts 1986, 2465, 2466, 2469)

23 April. *Phila. Evening Bulletin* advertises sale at James S. Earle Gallery on 24 Apr. of a collection of oil paintings by "prominent American and European Artists," including Thomas and Edward Moran.

27 April–20 June. PAFA annual exhibition. Moran exhibits *"Among the Ruins—there he lingered"* and four watercolors, *Coast Scene*; *On Raritan Bay*; *The Narrows—Entrance to NY Bay*; *Dunure Castle* (nos. 152, 401, 404, 411, 417). Edward Moran exhibits five paintings. (*Phila. Evening Bulletin*, 27 Apr. and 17 June; Rutledge 1955, 144, 145)

18 May–20 June. NAD annual exhibition. Edward Moran exhibits for first time, with *New Castle on the Delaware* (no. 180). (Cummings 1865, 356; Cowdrey 1943, 2:30)

27 October. Thomas Moran sketches and dates *Falls of the Schuylkill* (MFA Boston).

• 1858 •

Moran listed as an artist at 515 Chestnut St., Phila., and with brother Edward at 915 Sergeant St. Thomas Moran (Sr.) listed as a paper carrier at 828 Centre St. with son Peter, a lithographer. (M'Elroy's; Rutledge 1955, 144, 145)

At Children's Hospital Benefit in Philadelphia, Moran exhibits *Sepia Drawing* and *Scene on Pine Creek, Tioga Co.* (nos. 138, 140). Edward Moran exhibits three works. (Yarnall and Gerdts 1986, 2464, 2468)

10 February. DCAA annual exhibition opens. Moran exhibits *Welsh Mountain Stream* (no. 26). Edward Moran exhibits two paintings. (Cobb 1963–1965, 124; Yarnall and Gerdts 1986, 2463, 2466, 2468)

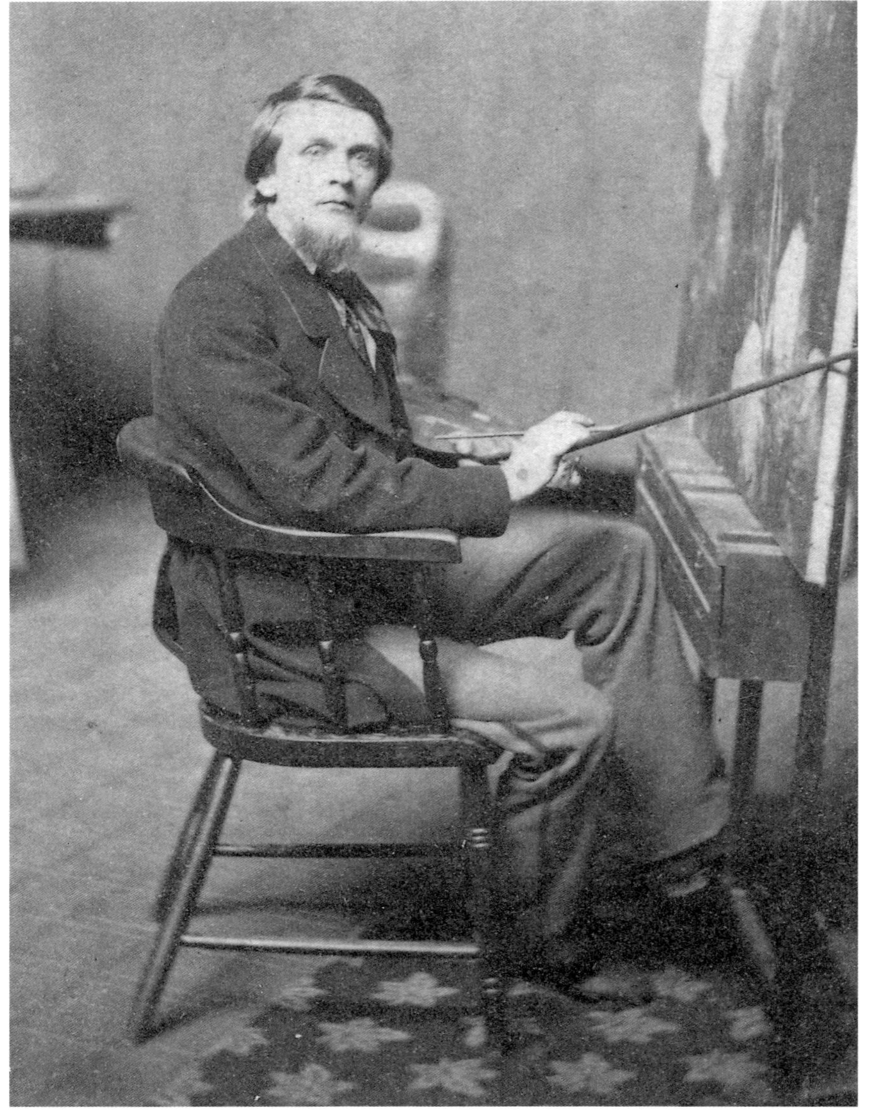

Thomas Moran, c. 1860, courtesy East Hampton Library.

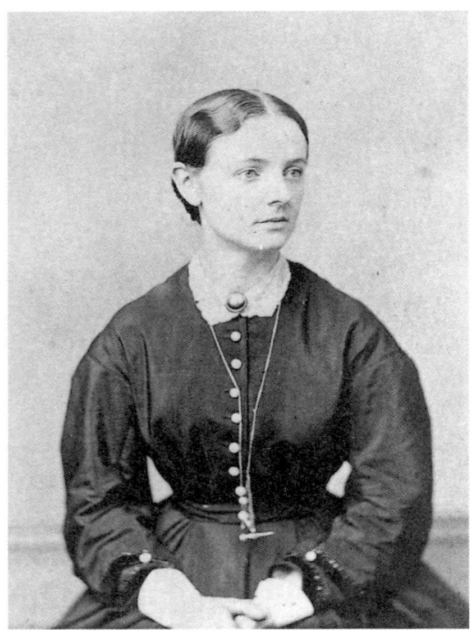

Mary Nimmo Moran, courtesy East Hampton Libary.

20 April–19 June. PAFA annual exhibition. Moran exhibits *Waiting for the Tide*; *View on Tacony Creek*; *Haunted House*; and two watercolors, *Studies*; "*There is a temple in ruin stands...*" (nos. 262, 286, 289, 368, 380). Edward Moran exhibits eight paintings. (*Phila. N. American and Gazette*, 19 Apr., 15 June; Rutledge 1955, 144, 146)

• 1859 •

Thomas, Edward, and Peter Moran all listed at 915 Sergeant St.; Thomas Moran (Sr.) at 828 Knox (formerly Centre) St. with son Peter. (M'Elroy's; Rutledge 1955, 144, 145)

3 January. *Crayon* announces opening of DCAA annual exhibition. Moran exhibits *Haunted House* (no. 44). (Yarnall and Gerdts 1986, 2465, 2467)

25 April–25 June. PAFA annual exhibition. Moran exhibits *Marine—near Cape Elizabeth, Maine*; *Deserted Fortress*; *Summer Morning on the Coast*; *Coast of Newfoundland* (nos. 132, 188, 299, 337). Edward Moran exhibits seven paintings. Peter Moran exhibits for first time, with three works. (*Phila. News*, 25 Apr. and 20 June; Rutledge 1955, 144–146)

• 1860 •

Moran listed at 828 Knox with his father and brother John, a photographer; at 915 Sergeant with brothers Edward and Peter; and at 726 Sansom St. with engraver Samuel Sartain and painter and graphic artist Stephen J. Ferris. (M'Elroy's; Cohen's City Directory; Rutledge 1955, 72, 144, 145)

John Sartain, engraver (and father of Samuel), demonstrates etching technique to Thomas Moran and Stephen J. Ferris. (Wray 1893, 53–54)

12 March. Edward Moran is elected an Academician of PAFA. (Goodyear 1973, n.p.)

23 April–30 June. PAFA annual exhibition. Moran exhibits *Sunset*; *First Ship*; *Sketch on the Coast*; and *Rocky Coast* (nos. 103, 123, 131, 290). Edward Moran exhibits four paintings; Peter, one. (*Phila. News*, 23 Apr. and 29 June; Rutledge 1955, 145, 146)

24 April. *Phila. Press* reviews PAFA exhibition: "Mr. T. Moran has two excellent marine pieces, Nos. 123 and 131."

29 June. U.S. Census lists Thomas Moran (Sr.) 58, "Ledger Currier," value of personal estate 800, born Ireland, and his household as: Mary 54; John 29, artist;

Sarah 25; Thomas 23, artist; Elizabeth 21; Peter 19, glass painter apprentice; William 14; Mary 11; James 8, all born England [*sic*]; Valentine Stause, 22, Clerk, born Russia [husband of Sarah]. (Schedule 1. Free Inhabitants in ... 20th Ward ... Phila ...., 221)

3 July. *Phila. Press* reviews PAFA exhibition: "From T. Moran there is a fine 'Sunset,' a 'Sketch on the Coast,' and 'A Rocky Coast.' This last has the water a little too white."

Mid-July. Moran and Isaac Williams, another Philadelphia artist, leave for a trip to Lake Superior. (Morand 1996, 14–16)

23–24 July. Moran sketches and dates *Old Mill Wheel at Marquette, Lake Superior* (MFA Boston).

25 July. U.S. Census lists Edward Moran 32, artist, value of personal estate 1000, born England, and his household as: Elizabeth 29, and James 10, both born Pennsylvania. (Schedule 1. Free Inhabitants ... East Ward, 10th District ... County of Phila., 191)

25 July. Youngest Moran brother, James, has died at age 8. (Interment records, Old Cathedral Cemetery, Phila.)

26 and 29 July. Moran sketches and dates *Miners Castle, Pictured Rocks, Lake Superior*, and *At Miners River, Pictured Rocks, Lake Superior* (Gilcrease).

6 and 7 August. Sketches and dates *Our Camp at the Pictured Rocks, Lake Superior*; *Looking from the South Entrance of the Great Cave, Pictured Rocks, Lake Superior*; *Great Cave, Pictured Rocks from the East*; *Side of the Entrance to the Great Cave, Pictured Rocks*; and *Entrance to the Great Cave, Pictured Rocks* (MFA Boston; Gilcrease).

9 August. Moran writes Mary Nimmo, his future wife: "Since my last letter we have seen the great sight, the Pictured Rocks. They exceeded my expectations though in a manner different from what I had supposed them. But I will tell you all about them when I come back which will not be long now as we have got sketches of the important points. We left here in a Mackinaw boat with only another man and ourselves on last Sunday morning at 9 o'clock and reached the farthest point about 2 o'clock having rowed the whole distance of 12 miles. We then landed and pitched our tent on the sand beach, lit a fire, cooked our dinner ... took a sail to the great cave and made a sketch. We slept on the beach 3 nights and got back here on Wednesday night .... I shall stay here about a week longer to finish my sketches." (Bassford and Fryxell 1967, 23–24)

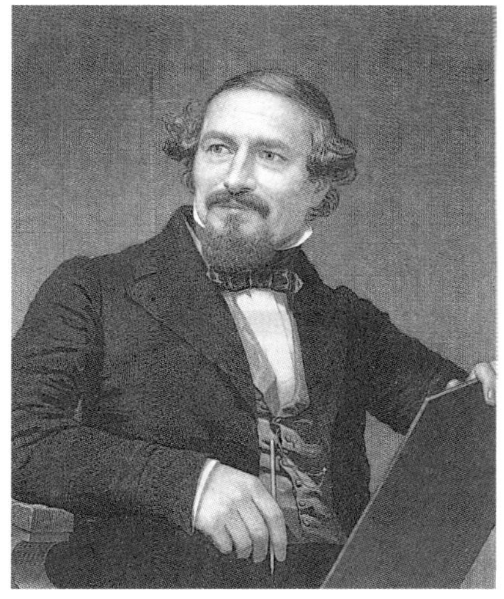

John Sartain, engraving, Collection of Merl M. Moore Jr.

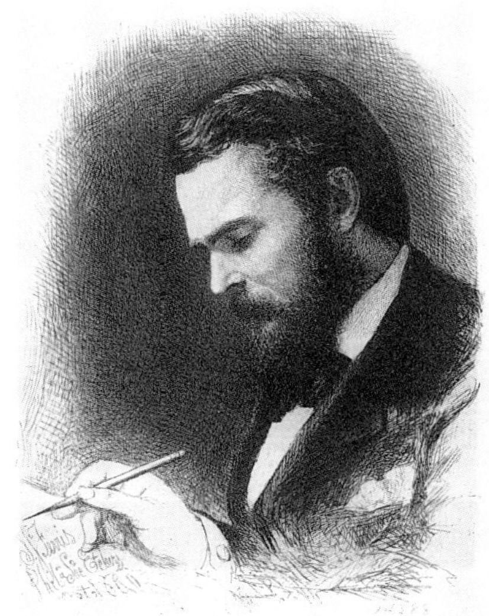

Stephen J. Ferris, *Self-Portrait*, 1880, etching, courtesy National Museum of American History, Smithsonian Institution, Graphic Arts Collection.

August. Moran sketches *In the Forest of Munising, Lake Superior*, inscribed "Aug. 1860" (Gilcrease).

22 August. On his return trip to Philadelphia, sketches and dates *St. Clair Flats, Michigan*, and *Mill at Newport River, St. Clair, Michigan* (Gilcrease; MFA Boston).

5 September. Sketches and dates *Delaware Water Gap* (Gilcrease).

1 November. Sketches, dates, and inscribes two scenes in environs of Philadelphia: *Crescentville* and *From Nature, Green Lane* (Gilcrease).

5 December. Completes and dates a *cliché-verre, Flight into Egypt* (Gilcrease).

• 1861 •

Moran listed at 927 N. 11th with his father and brothers John and Peter; and at 726 Sansom with Samuel Sartain and Stephen J. Ferris. Peter Moran listed again at 915 Sergeant with his brother Edward. (Mc'Elroy's; Rutledge 1955, 72, 144, 145)

Moran inscribes and dates sketch of *Manayunk*, an industrial town on the Schuylkill River west of Philadelphia (Gilcrease).

12 February. Thomas Moran is elected an Academician of PAFA. (Board minutes, PAFA archives)

Spring. Thomas, John, and perhaps Edward and/or Peter Moran go to Catawissa, PA, on the Susquehanna River, to sketch and photograph. Some of Thomas' sketches are used as illustrations for "Catawissa Railroad," in *Harper's Monthly*, June 1862. (Thomas J. Evans, 25 Oct. 1985, Gilcrease research files; sketches at Gilcrease, EHL, MFA Boston; photographs by John Moran, LCP)

22 April–29 June. PAFA annual exhibition. Moran exhibits *Flight into Egypt*; *Salvator Rosa Sketching Banditti*; *Grand Portal of Pictured Rocks, Lake Superior*; *Pictured Rocks from Miner's River, Lake Superior*; *Sunset in the Woods (Autumn)* (nos. 52, 159, 177, 233, 514). Edward Moran exhibits ten paintings; Peter, one. (*Phila. Evening Bulletin*, 22 Apr. and 17 June; Rutledge 1955, 145, 146)

Elizabeth Moran Ferris, 1878, portrait drawing by Stephen J. Ferris, courtesy National Museum of American History, Smithsonian Institution, Graphic Arts Collection.

Thomas Moran Sr., courtesy East Hampton Library.

Mary Nimmo Moran, 1858, tintype, courtesy East Hampton Library.

Thomas and Edward Moran (?) in *Killing the Snake,* 1863, stereograph by John Moran, Private Collection.

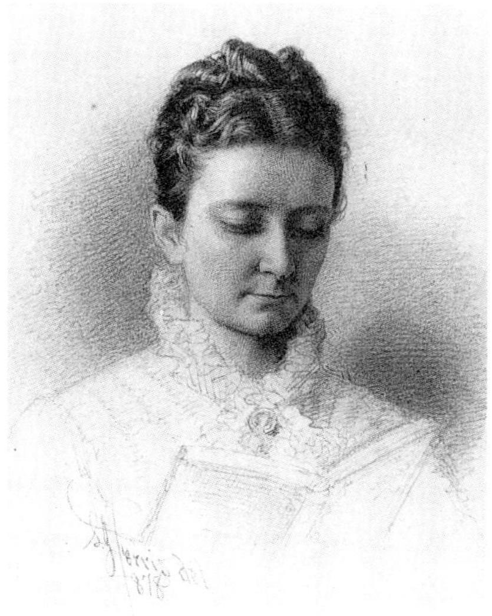

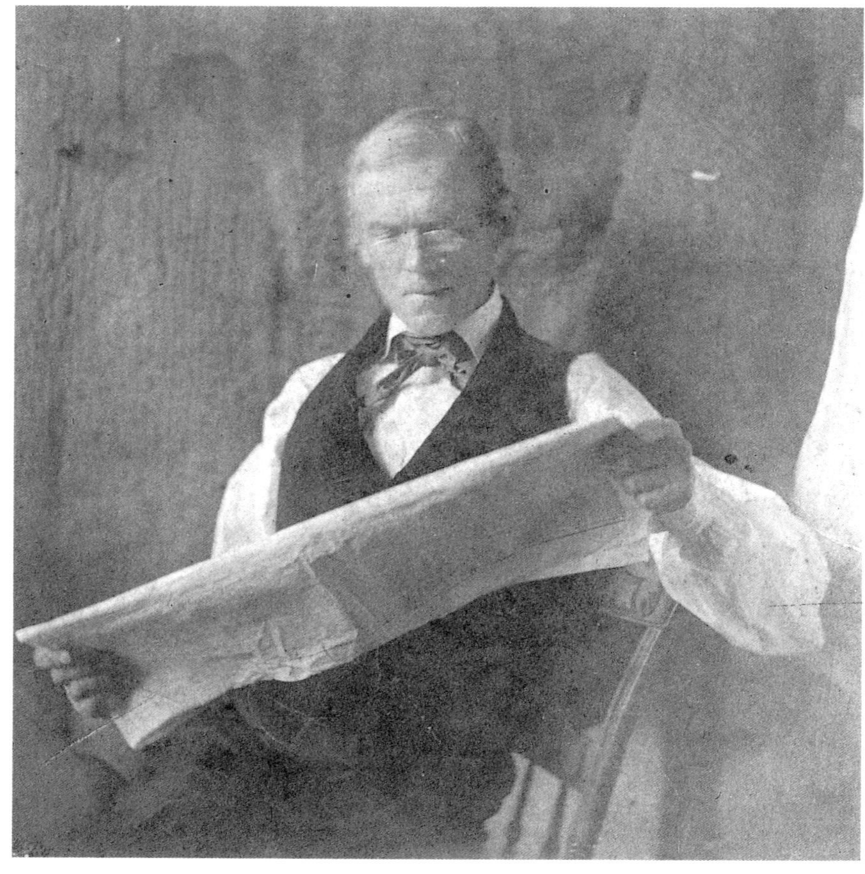

30 November. James S. Earle Gallery advertises in *Phila. Evening Bulletin* "Elegant Exhibition" of oil paintings, including works by Thomas Moran.

• 1862 •

Moran listed at 806 Coates with his father, brother John, and Stephen J. Ferris. (Mc'Elroy's; Rutledge 1955, 72, 144, 145)

Elizabeth Moran marries Stephen J. Ferris. (*Biographical Album* 1889, 327)

20 February. Thomas Moran (Sr.) dies; burial at Cathedral Cemetery. (*Phila. Inquirer*, 22 Feb.; *Phila. Public Ledger*, 21–22 Feb.)

20–21 March. At BAA, Moran exhibits *Classic Ruins* (no. 60). (Marlor 1970, 281, 403)

28 April–28 June. PAFA annual exhibition. Moran exhibits *Composition—on the Schuylkill*; *Valley of the Catawissa in Autumn*; *Evening—Scene on the Little Schuylkill*; *Summer on the Susquehanna*; *Evening on the Susquehanna near Williamsport*; *Columbia Bridge over the Schuylkill*; *View near Kellyville* (nos. 15, 90, 119, 132, 151, 214, and no. 812 of supplement). Edward Moran exhibits nineteen paintings; Peter, three. (*Phila. Evening Bulletin*, 21 Apr. and 21 June; Rutledge 1955, 145, 146)

May. Thomas and Edward Moran travel to England, probably arriving in Liverpool.

June. "Catawissa Railroad," *Harper's Monthly*, 27: "A work of great merit... produced by the artist Thomas Moran of Philadelphia [probably *Valley of the Catawissa in Autumn*]... attracted considerable attention and elicited the highest encomiums from connoisseurs at the recent artists' reception of Philadelphia."

3 June. *Phila. Evening Bulletin* reviews PAFA exhibition: "Passing by the many beautiful foreign works, the exhibition is especially valuable as evidence of the merit of the artists of Philadelphia.... Among these will be found not a few which are worthy of any Art school in Europe.... In landscape are those of Weber, Richards, Lewis, Haseltine, and the brothers Moran—who, by the way, have recently sailed for Europe."

14, 16–17 June. Moran inscribes and dates *Liverpool*; in Bolton, his birthplace, sketches and dates *Forthill Bridge at Bolton, Lancashire*, and *Tonge Fold* (Gilcrease; Bolton Museum and Art Gallery).

25, 27 June. Traveling south, sketches and dates *Windsor* and *Windsor Castle*; then back in London, *In Greenwich Park*; *Houses of Parliament from Hungerford Bridge*; and *St. Paul's from under Waterloo Bridge* (Gilcrease; Corcoran).

1 July. Still in London area, sketches and dates *From Waterloo Bridge* and *Richmond* (Gilcrease).

4–5 July. Traveling to the eastern coast, sketches and dates *Margate*; then moving south, *Ramsgate* (Gilcrease).

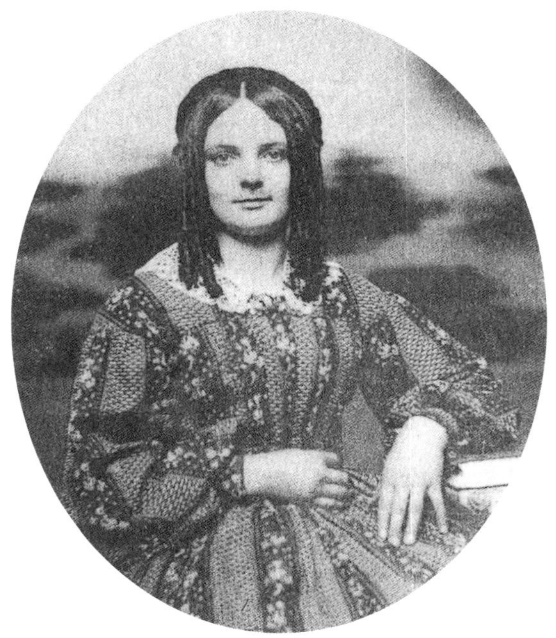

7–8, 12 July. Continuing along coast, sketches and dates *Sandown Castle*; inscribes and dates *Sandown Castle, Deal*; *Dover*; *At Dover*; *Margate*; then *Arundel Town and Castle*; and *Hastings* (Gilcrease; EHL).

13–15 July. Sketches and dates *Cliffs of Ecclesborne, Near Hastings*; *East Cliff, Hastings*; inscribes and dates *Portchester* (Corcoran; Gilcrease).

19–22 July. Sketches and dates *Bexhill*; inscribes and dates three sketches titled *Hastings* and another, *On the Beach, Hastings*; then completes two more dated and inscribed *Hastings* (Gilcrease; MFA Boston).

24, 26, 29 July. Inscribes and dates *Town and Castle of Lewes*; *Arundel Town and Castle*; *Carisbrooke Castle, Isle of Wight* (Gilcrease).

Fall. Thomas and Edward Moran return to Philadelphia.

13 November. *Boston Transcript* reviews exhibition in Boston at Messrs. Sowle & Jenks: "The two brothers Moran … have three or four wood scenes of great merit."

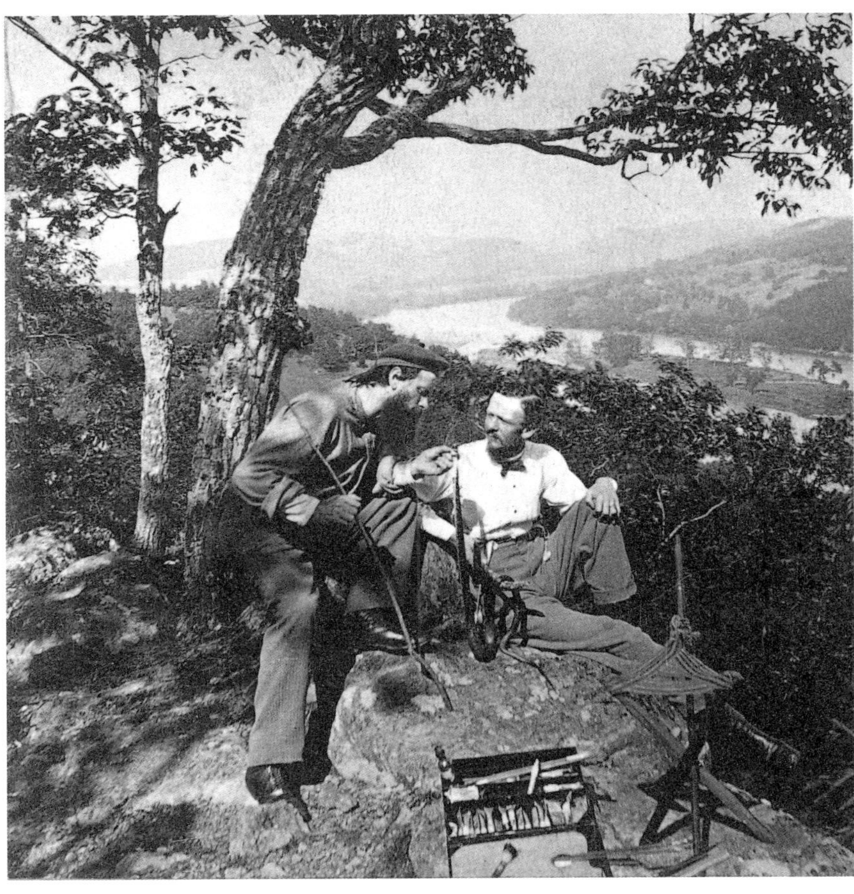

• 1863 •

Moran listed at 806 Coates with brother John and Stephen J. Ferris; and at S.W. 8th and Coates with his mother and brother Peter. Peter listed again at 915 Sergeant with brother Edward. (McElroy's; Rutledge 1955, 72, 144, 145)

Shoenberger Collection exhibited in Pittsburgh, including Moran's *Golden Bough* (no. 23). (Yarnall and Gerdts 1986, 2467)

9 February. Moran marries Mary Nimmo (1842–1899) of Crescentville, PA, at the Church of the Assumption, Blessed Virgin Mary, Phila. (Marriage records, ABVM)

7 May. PAFA annual exhibition opens. Moran exhibits *Evening on the Susquehanna*; *Landscape*; *Hastings, South Coast of England*; *Summer Moonlight*; "*On the Lone Chorasmian Coast*"; *Watercolor Drawing*; *Watercolor Drawing*; *Kilchurn Castle, Scotland*; *Autumn on the Susquehanna, near Catawissa* (nos. 33, 80, 128, 161, 406, 411, 436, 468, 476). Edward Moran exhibits seven paintings; Peter, one. (*Phila. Evening Bulletin*, 4 and 7 May; Rutledge 1955, 145, 146)

July. Moran begins to paint *Wissahickon in Summer*, first work noted on what will become his "Opus List." (See Appendix 2)

August. Moran begins to document his own work, assigning Opus numbers.

Fall. John Moran and "his artist brothers" travel to Delaware Water Gap to sketch and photograph. Sellers 1863, 435: "Mr. [John] Moran … returned from the Delaware Water Gap … [with] a rich treat in pictures … one called *Killing the Snake* … [in which] an artist's box of colors is partially shown … indicating the calling of the two venturesome ones who … made the capture [Thomas and Edward?]."

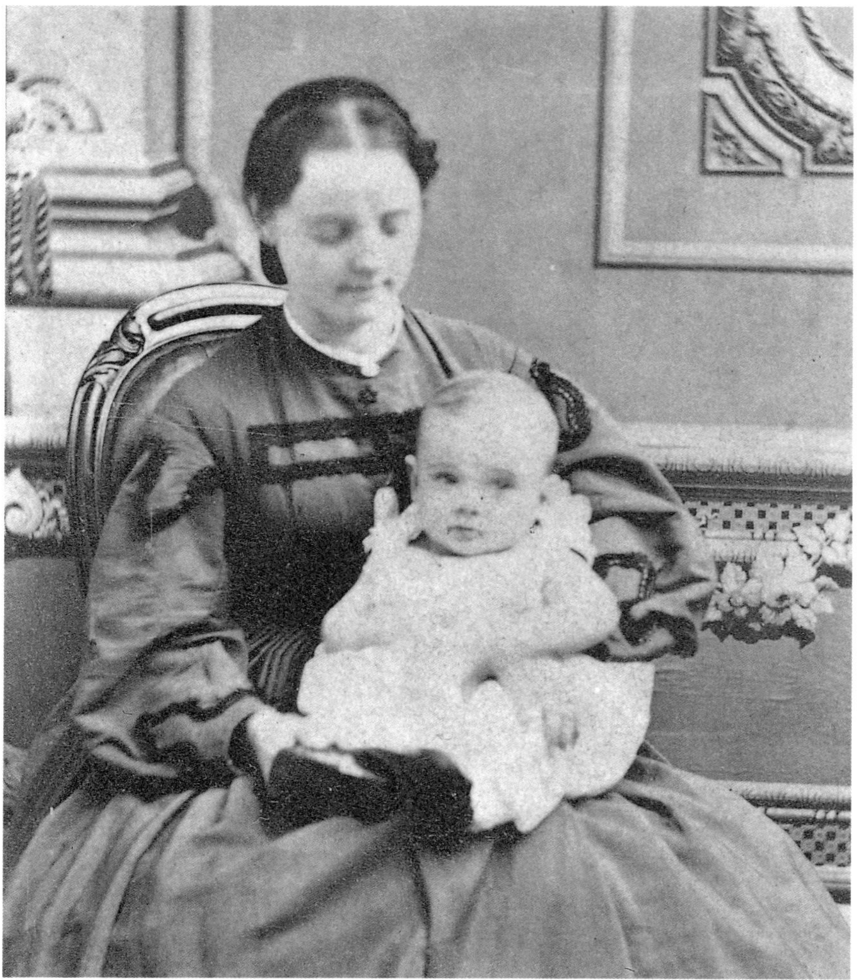

Mary Nimmo Moran with first child, Paul, courtesy East Hampton Library.

September. Moran sketches and dates *Wissahickon* (Gilcrease).

October and November. Paints Opus 2, *Autumn on the Wissahickon*, "incited by a most glorious Autumn."

December. Paints Opus 3, *Okehampton Castle*, to fulfill a commission.

27 December. Sellers 1864, 31, mentions visit to John Moran's studio: "What gives such a charm to all Mr. Moran's pictures is the thorough knowledge he has of painting and all the elements of a good picture. He showed us some studies he had made from his brother's [Thomas'] landscapes in oil, which certainly seemed to have been taken from nature."

28 December. *Phila. Evening Bulletin* advertises auction the next day by F. Gabrylewitz (Phila.) of paintings by "P. F. Rothermel, James Hamilton, E. & T. Moran . . . J. L. [Isaac] Williams . . . and other American and European artists."

• 1864 •

Moran listed at 838 Race St. (Rutledge 1955, 144, 145)

January. Paints Opus 4, *Canadian Waterfall, Sunset.*

10 February. *Phila. Evening Bulletin* mentions AFS reception at PAFA the previous day: "Mr. Moran, Mr. Schuessele [*sic*], Mr. Bonfield, Mr. F. de B. Richards and several other artists deserve to be named for the excellence of the works they presented."

April. Paints Opus 5, *Creisham Glen, Wissahickon, Autumn.*

11 April. First child, Paul Nimmo Moran, born to Thomas and Mary Nimmo Moran. (Baptismal and birth records, ABVM)

25 April. *Phila. Evening Bulletin* reports opening of PAFA annual exhibition. Moran exhibits *Windsor Castle*; *Autumn on the Wissahickon*; *Okehampton*; and *Autumn* (nos. 31, 63, 167, 199). Edward and Peter Moran each exhibit one painting. (Rutledge 1955, 145, 146)

30 April. *Phila. Evening Bulletin* reviews PAFA exhibition: "Mr. T. Moran exhibits several landscapes, the most ambitious of which (no. 31, 'Windsor Castle') we like least. The haze in the atmosphere has a smeared look, and the details are not happily executed. His two autumnal views, 199 and 63, are much more interesting pictures, and show not only fine effect but admirable painting of foliage and rocks."

May. Moran paints Opus 6, *Reminiscence of the Passaic.*

14 May. *Round Table*, 344: "T. Moran has painted this year a picture which is in many respects better than anything he has heretofore done, an 'Autumn on the Wissahickon.' The splendid brilliancy of our October landscape is portrayed with truthfulness and grace, and with a care for which we had hardly given Mr. Moran credit. There is some bad drawing in the foreground, which is, too, rather glaring in color, but the whole is real and effective, and among the most attractive landscapes of the exhibition. After looking at this work, it was with surprise that I turned to . . . 'Windsor Castle', by the same artist. Here is a large picture painted in a Turneresque manner, thin and yellow and unmeaning. The trees are the mere suggestions, or rather shadows of trees; the color of the whole is one sickly yellow green; and though it may be an excellent

likeness of Windsor Park—from the numerous prints we see of this same view there is doubtless truth in the main prints of the picture—it certainly bears no resemblance to anything that grows upon this side of the Atlantic. O Mr. Moran, we are glad to welcome your truthful hills and autumn woods, but not any more Turner and Windsor Castle, if you please."

June. Moran paints Opus 7, *Nutting, Autumn*, for presentation to the "Sanitary" [Great Central] Fair.

7–29 June. Great Central Fair for the Benefit of the Sanitary Commission, Phila. Moran serves on fine arts committee and exhibits *Autumn on the Wissahickon*; *Creisham Creek*; *Reminiscence of the Passaic*; *Fall Scenery* [*Nutting, Autumn*]; *Cost of Loyalty in East Tennessee*; *Susquehanna*; *Ascending a Greenland Glacier*; *Ruined Fortress* (nos. 19, 26, 513, 734, 782, 848, 920, 939). Edward Moran exhibits eight paintings; Peter, one. (*NY Post*, 6 June; *Phila. Evening Bulletin*, 28 June; Great Central Fair cat.)

18 June. *Round Table*, 10, describes a watercolor by Moran in Great Central Fair: "an autumn wood view, which looks like a repetition of that shown at the Academy [*Autumn on the Wissahickon*, see 14 May]."

29 June–5 July. Great Central Fair closes, but art gallery remains open. (*Phila. Evening Bulletin*, 28 June, 6 July)

5–6 July. Sale of paintings from Great Central Fair to benefit the Sanitary Commission. Moran's *Fall Scenery* [*Nutting, Autumn*] sells for a reported $74. (*Phila. Evening Bulletin*, 7 July; *Round Table*, 16 July, 74; Appendix 2)

16 July–17 November. William Moran serves in Union Army as a private, Capt. Bender's 196 Regiment, Pennsylvania Infantry, only Moran brother to serve in Civil War. (Company muster rolls, NA)

July and August. Moran takes sketching trip along Pennsylvania Central Railroad. Selected sketches result in illustrations for "River Scenery of Pennsylvania," *The Aldine* (1878). (Morand 1996, 23–25)

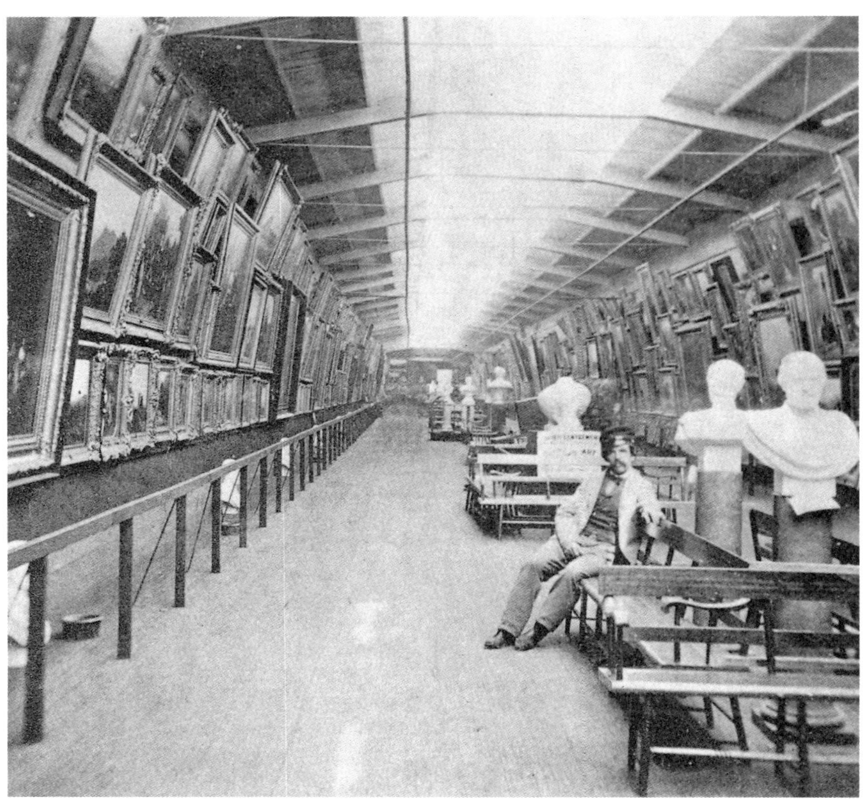

Picture gallery at Sanitary Fair, Philadelphia, 1864, stereograph by John Moran, courtesy Library Company of Philadelphia.

26 July. Inscribes and dates *Huntingdon* (Gilcrease).

3–6 and 8–9 August. Inscribes and dates *Huntingdon from Warriors Ridge*; *Huntingdon*; and *Warriors Ridge, Huntingdon, Pa.*; then *Juniata below Huntingdon* and *Johnstown*; then *Willmore*; then *On the Conemaugh below Lockport*; *Conemaugh at Lockport*; and *Conemaugh at Bolivar* (Gilcrease; MFA Boston).

11–25 August. Following the Conemaugh River, inscribes and dates *Conemaugh below Johnstown* and *Willmore* and inscribes four versions of *Gallatzin*; then inscribes and dates *Spruce Creek* and *Water Street*; then *Juniata at Spruce Creek*; *Tussey Mountain, Spruce Creek*; two versions of *Spruce Creek*; *Mill Creek*; *Near Mapleton*; *Juniata at Mill Creek*; and another *Mill Creek* (Gilcrease; EHL).

September. Paints Opus 8, *Juniata, Evening*.

November. Paints Opus 9, *Autumn Afternoon, Wissahickon*, and Opus 10, *Woods in Autumn*.

25 November–16 January 1865. James L. Claghorn Collection exhibited at PAFA to benefit U.S. Christian Commission, "contributing to the comfort of our brave soldiers." Includes Moran's watercolor *Kilchurn Castle* (U. S. Christian Commission cat., no. 240). (*Phila. Evening Bulletin*, 26 Nov., 5, 8, 12 Dec.)

December. Paints Opus 11, *Wilds of Lake Superior*.

• 1865 •

Moran listed at 1812 Wood with his brother Peter. (Mc'Elroy's; Rutledge 1955, 144, 145)

4 January. Auction of paintings from reception to benefit AFS (29 Dec.). Moran contributes *Woods in Autumn*

(which sells for $180, one of the highest prices in the sale); *Greenland Glacier*; and *Summer Shower* (cat. nos. 1, 17, 40). Edward contributes two paintings. (*Phila. Evening Bulletin*, 30 Dec. 1864; *NY Post*, 30 Jan. 1865; Appendix 2)

February. Paints Opus 12, *Farewell of Summer*.

March. Paints Opus 13, *Conemaugh, Autumn*.

15 March. *Phila. Evening Bulletin* announces auction by Earle & Sons at PAFA of "elegant collection of Paintings, comprising the latest and finest importations and also a large number of the works of our Philadelphia artists, prominent among whom are Thos. Moran."

23 March. At Earle & Sons sale Moran's *Wilds of Lake Superior* brings $610. (*Phila. Evening Bulletin*, 24 Mar.; Appendix 2)

7 April. *Phila. Press* mentions "Next Fine Arts Exhibition" at PAFA, for which James Hamilton, Moran, and others form exhibition committee.

24 April–10 June. PAFA annual exhibition. Moran exhibits *Autumn on the Wissahickon*; *Landscape*; and *Farewell of Summer* (nos. 636, 670, 775). Edward Moran exhibits eight paintings; Peter, four. (*Phila. Evening Bulletin*, 5 June; Rutledge 1955, 145, 146)

25 April. *Phila. Press* reviews PAFA exhibition: "Three Morans are exhibitors.... Mr. T. Moran gives us...'Autumn upon the Wissahickon.' The picture is very pleasant in its technical execution, but is too rawly gay in color, and wants the application of some tolerably unscrupulous glazing to produce a greater sobriety in its general tone."

29 April. *Phila. N. American and Gazette* reviews PAFA exhibition: "T. Moran, a brother of Edward Moran, has a picture, 'Autumn on the Wissahickon' (no. 636), which depicts the lovely scene when the colors of fall have touched the foliage. The gradations of the distance, it will be noticed, are finely marked by the lessening foliage, the winding road, teams, dust, and cattle. The foreground is loosely sketched in and stands out in high contrast to the remainder."

May. Moran paints Opus 14, *Wood Scene, Autumn*.

1 May. *Phila. Press*: "We...can scarcely compliment Mr. T. Moran upon his color in...'Farewell of Summer.' It is much too gay and flowery. This is a somewhat generic error in the translation of nature by the gentlemen bearing this name. It, however, makes them popular, and, because popular, successful painters."

24 May. *Phila. Evening Bulletin* advertises sale at Thomas Birch & Sons gallery that includes works by Thomas and Edward Moran.

June. Moran paints Opus 15, *Juniata, below Huntingdon*.

23 June. *Phila. Press* mentions national competition with prizes sponsored by Phila. Sketch Club (Edward Moran, v.p.) as an "excellent and honest effort to advance the cause of American art.... Contributors must be residents of the United States.... The list will be closed on the first of October."

July–August. Moran goes on sketching trip to Pike County, PA, visiting the Delaware Valley Resort Cataract Region. (Morand 1996, 27–29)

22–30 July. Sketches and dates two versions of *Milford*; sketches two versions of *Raymondskill*; inscribes and dates eleven sketches of either *Sawkill* or *Sawkill Falls*; sketches and dates two versions of *Milford*; two versions of *Vandermark*; and *Hemlock Root, Vandermark* (Gilcrease; MFA Boston; EHL).

3–5, 7–9, and 12 August. Returning to Sawkill, sketches and dates *Sawkill*; *Sawkill Fall*; and *Picnic Rock, Sawkill*; another version of *Vandermark*; then two more versions of *Sawkill*; *Sawkill Fall*; *Adams Creek*; and *Hemlock, Sawkill Fall*; then *Lower Fall of Adams Creek*; then two versions of *Sawkill*; several versions of *Adams Creek*; and *Bull Run, Milford*; then another *Sawkill* (Gilcrease; MFA Boston).

30 September. *Round Table*, 60: "Thomas Moran has spent the summer among the waterfalls of Pike county. Other artists may have been as industrious as he, but none can show a larger collection of studies, for Moran possesses a singular facility of execution, and many of these sketches are remarkable examples of his power of expressing the character of scenery in broad masses of light and dark. But this very facility, however admirable in sketching, is very dangerous in painting; and, if he be not very careful to keep it in check, will render his pictures liable to severe criticism."

September and October. Moran paints Opus 17, *Autumnal Woods*.

27 October. *Phila. Evening Bulletin*: "The Philadelphia School of Design for Women has arranged to have a course of lectures before the pupils. The lecturers are Prof. A. R. Thomas, Prof. T. C. Porter, S. J. Ferris, T. W. Braidwood (Principal at the School), and T. Moran, the landscape painter." According to his ledger, Moran "Made 24 studies for the School of Design for Women during 1865 & early 1866." (Appendix 2)

November. Moran paints Opus 16, *Clearing in the Mountains*.

14 November. *Phila. Evening Bulletin* advertises paintings by Moran for sale at James S. Earle & Sons on 16–17 Nov.

24 November–21 December. AFS exhibition. Moran exhibits *On the Conemaugh* and drawings *Children of the Mountain*; *Morning*; and *Evening*. (Henry Tuckerman, *NY Post*, 27 Nov.; *Phila. Evening Bulletin*, 9 Nov.)

5 December 1865–3 January 1866. Phila. Sketch Club first annual prize exhibition

at PAFA. Edward Moran exhibits four works. "It has begun to be felt that it is now time to uphold our own noble artists in the eyes of American patrons and try to stop the influx of cheap foreign journey work gotten up with contemptuous haste for the Western market." (Phila. Sketch Club cat.; *Phila. Evening Bulletin*, 6 Dec.)

6 December. *Phila. Evening Bulletin*: "Mr. Thomas Moran is finishing a large picture called 'The Children of the Mountain,' with a daring effect of clouds and wilderness. Mr. T. Moran is undoubtedly a poet, though he occasionally leaves it a little uncertain whether he controls, or is controlled by, the frenzy. This grand picture is partially an amplification of one of those rich charcoal drawings recently published in photography."

• 1866 •

Moran listed at 1812 Wood, Phila., and 50 rue de l'Ouest, Paris. (Mc'Elroy's; Rutledge 1955, 145; Salon cat., 150)

Moran exhibits *Autumn on the Wissahickon* (no. 8) at the Utica [NY] Art Association annual exhibition. (Yarnall and Gerdts 1986, 2467)

January and May. Moran paints Opus 18, *Evening on the Juniata*.

19 January. *Phila. Evening Bulletin*: "A great sale of Oil Paintings takes place this evening... at Scott's Art Gallery.... The collection embraces several very interesting subjects from the easels of some of our most talented artists, among which we notice S. B. Waugh, T. Moran."

February. Moran records: "The Track of the Storm. An allegory of the war for the republic. Charcoal drawing on paper." (Appendix 2)

6 March. *Phila. Evening Bulletin* publishes article on Moran's *Track of the Storm*, one of his few images related to the Civil War.

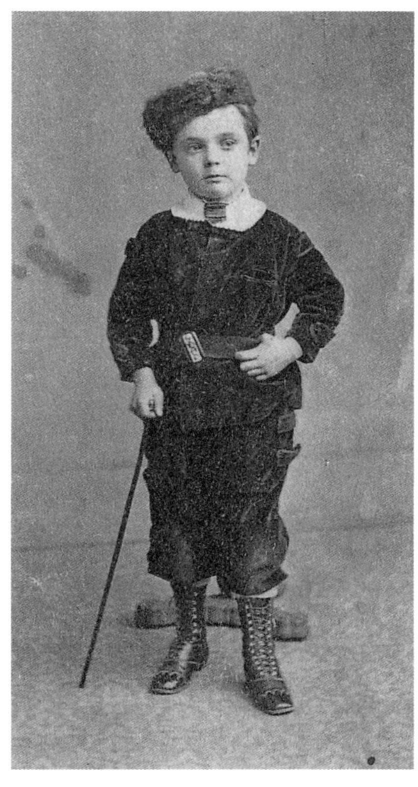

Paul Nimmo Moran, c.1868, courtesy East Hampton Library.

16 April – 4 July. NAD exhibition. Moran exhibits for the first time with *Under the Trees* (no. 474). Edward Moran exhibits two paintings; Peter, one. (*NYT*, 17 Apr.; Naylor 1973, 647, 653)

18 April. *Phila. Evening Bulletin* advertises sale at A. S. Robinson's of American and foreign oil paintings on 18 – 19 April: "134—Thomas Moran, Philadelphia, 'Coast of New Brunswick.'" Reviewer calls sale "one of the finest collections of paintings ever offered to the public in America.... there are hundreds visiting it today."

23 April. PAFA annual exhibition opens. Thomas, Edward, and Peter Moran do not exhibit. Reviewer remarks on the prejudices of the hanging committee: "Next in order of preference come the New York and foreign artists, thus rendering it necessary to place many worthy conceptions of our own painters in inferior positions. The watchword of the Academy should be 'Encouragement to Philadelphia Art.' Two prominent artists of our city, Messrs. Thomas and Edward Moran, have recently contributed to the New York Spring Exhibition some of their best works. It was thought proper by those in charge of that establishment to give these gentlemen's pictures such elevated places that it is a matter of regret to their admirers that they were ever confided to the hands of a strange committee." (*Phila. Evening Bulletin*, 20 and 22 Apr.)

5 May. *Round Table* reviews PAFA exhibition: "Of the usual contributors, some are remembered by their absence, such as the brothers Moran."

May. Moran paints Opus 19, *Shores of Lake Superior*.

23 May. *Boston Transcript*: "We invite the attention of lovers of nature and the best works in art to two paintings, to be seen in the windows of Childs & Jenks's Gallery of Art.... They are entitled 'June,' by W. T. Richards of Philadelphia, and 'October,' by Thomas Moran of the same city, and are both in the style called pre-Raphaelite.... Moran is a later disciple of the same class, and is making for himself a sure place as a delineator of autumnal effects. He has all the merits of Cropsey's coloring, with less of hardness and lack of atmosphere."

2 June. *Phila. Evening Bulletin* mentions local artists preparing to take their summer holidays, with a number going abroad: "He [Thomas Moran] has taken with him a number of unfinished works, including a splendid landscape which he intends to place in the Paris Exhibition of 1867."

5 June. Moran requests passport for himself, wife Mary, and son Paul, which is granted 8 June. (Application no. 26741, NA)

16 June. Moran and family depart for Europe on the steamship *Etna*. (*NYT*, 17 June)

October. In Paris, Moran paints Opus 20, *Morning in Autumn*.

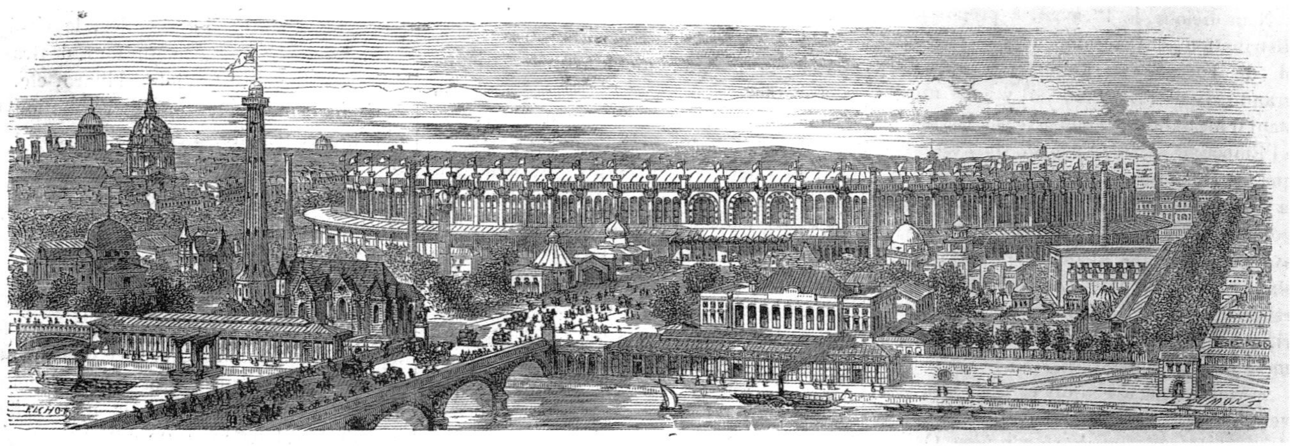

View of the Exposition Universelle, Paris, published in *L'Exposition Universelle… Illustrée,* vol. 2 (Paris, 1867).

Thomas Moran, *Rome from the Claudian Aqueduct,* 1867, graphite on paper, courtesy East Hampton Library.

December. Moran finishes Opus 21, *Children of the Mountain*, which he had begun in Philadelphia.

15 December. *Phila. Evening Bulletin*: "That excellent association of Philadelphia artists, known as 'The Artists' Fund Society,' have recently got possession of beautiful new rooms at 1334 Chestnut street… which they intend to keep open for the free exhibition of pictures by members of the Society and others. A fine collection of original works is now on exhibition and will be sold at auction on Tuesday evening next…. Among the artists contributing to this sale are… E. Moran, T. Moran, P. Moran…. The proceeds… are for the maintenance of the gallery."

17 December. At AFS Moran exhibits a painting based on Thomas Moore's poem, *Lalla Rookh*. According to the *Phila. Evening Bulletin*: "Mr. T. Moran has several masterly works, and… 'Arrival of Lalla Rookh at the Imperial Palace,' is a wonderful romance on canvas, which is worthy of Turner's best efforts."

18 December. *Phila. Evening Bulletin* announces postponement of AFS sale until January 1867 "in order that the public may have a longer opportunity to examine the fine works in the new Galleries."

• 1867 •

Moran again listed at 1812 Wood, Phila., and 50 rue de L'Ouest, Paris. (McElroy's; Rutledge 1955, 145; Salon cat., 150)

Early 1867. Moran meets Jean-Baptiste-Camille Corot at his Paris studio, which he recalls years later: "I remember him well… and had a pleasant visit with him, though we had to converse through an interpreter, as he understood no English and I no French. He was at work in his Paris studio and was full of life—a bright, wide awake, cheerful old fellow at 80. 'Papa' Corot they called him. It was not until he had become an aged man that he was appreciated, and even then the popularity of his pictures was nothing to what it is now. 'When I was painting good pictures,' said he, 'nobody would have them, but now that my eyes are poor I can't seem to paint enough.' At that time he was turning out those gray pictures that you find in every American auction at the rate of two or three a day, and when you consider the vast number of imitations that have been turned out it is easy to see that there are Corots—real and bogus—enough to fill a museum. I could at that time have bought almost anything that had Corot's name on it for $50 to $100, but I was studying and hadn't the money." (*Brooklyn Daily Eagle*, 18 Aug. 1889)

22 January. *Phila. Inquirer* notes that Moran's *View on Lake Superior* (no. 138) is included in a lottery to support the Crosby Opera House Art Association of Chicago. Catalogue entry (p. 18) reads, "A landscape, by one of the most poetic of our modern students of nature." Edward Moran's *Children of the Seashore* is also included (p. 22).

19 February. AFS reception at new galleries. Moran exhibits *Autumn* and *Autumn Morning* (cat. nos. 5, 31). Edward Moran exhibits one painting; Peter, two.

20, 23 February. *Phila. Evening Bulletin* reviews AFS reception: "The attendance was so large as to show how rapidly the public interest in the institution is increasing…. Owing to the crowds it was not possible to make special note… of the works of other artists…. But there are five pictures by the Morans"; "Mr. T. Moran's 'Autumn Morning'… is a warm, poetical, delicious landscape."

23, 26, 27 February. On a trip to Italy, Moran sketches and dates *Civitavecchia*; then *Ruins of the Palace of the Caesars, Rome*; then *Colosseum, Rome*, and two versions of *Palace of the Caesars, Rome* (Gilcrease). (Morand 1996)

March. Sketches in the Campagna, inscribing several images "March": *Aqueduct on the Campagna, Rome*; *Claudian Aqueduct, Rome*; *Campagna near Rome*; and *Rome from the Aqueduct*. At the Villa Borghese, sketches and inscribes *Alpine Pine in the Villa Borghese, Rome*; *Oaks in the Villa Borgese, Rome*; and *Pines in the Villa Borgese, Rome* (Gilcrease).

6, 12 March. Sketches and dates *Rome from the Claudian Aqueduct*; then *Lake Nemi* (EHL; Gilcrease).

Later March. Sketches and inscribes *Passage of the St. Gotthard, near Amsteag* (Gilcrease).

1 April. Sketches and dates *Argegno, Lake of Como* (Gilcrease).

1 April – 31 October. Exposition Universelle in Paris. Moran exhibits *Autumn on the Conemaugh, Pennsylvania*, and *Children of the Mountain* (nos. 62, 63), both brought to Paris for the exhibition. (*Phila. Evening Bulletin*, 2 Apr.; Leslie 1868, 39)

Spring. Moran finishes Opus 22, *The Woods Were God's First Temples*, a painting begun in the spring of 1866 and brought to Paris.

5 April. *Phila. Evening Bulletin* lists American artists contributing works to the Paris Exposition, including "T. Moran, Philadelphia—'Autumn on the Conemaugh River'—C. L. Sharpless [owner]."

15 April. Salon opens in Paris. Moran exhibits *Une forêt en Amerique* (cat. no. 1095).

16 April. AFS reception. *Phila. Evening Bulletin*, 17 Apr.: "There are excellent works by Rothermel, Hamilton, the Morans ... and many other favorites."

22 April – 1 June. PAFA annual exhibition. Moran exhibits *Autumn Landscape* (no. 118). Edward Moran exhibits one work. (*Phila. Evening Bulletin*, 22 Apr., 29 May; Rutledge 1955, 145, 146)

1 – 13 May. Moran and family travel from Liverpool to New York aboard the steamer *City of New York*. (*NYT*, 14 May)

23 May. *Phila. Evening Bulletin* reviews PAFA annual exhibition: "'An Autumn Landscape,' by T. Moran ... elicits many expressions of pleasure from those who study its beauties of color and sentiment."

June. Moran paints Opus 24, *Rome, from the Campagna, Sunset*.

16 June. Second child, Mary Scott Moran (1867 – 1955), born to Thomas and Mary Nimmo Moran. (Moran family monument, South End Cemetery, East Hampton)

21 June. Thomas Eakins writes his father about sending Moran's picture (presumably *Children of the Mountain*) via direct steamer from Paris to Philadelphia. (Foster and Leibold 1989, 146)

June and July. Moran paints Opus 25, *Last Arrow*.

July. Paints Opus 23, *Temple of Venus and Castle of Baiae*.

August. Paints Opus 27, *Lake of Como*.

September. Paints Opus 26, *Evening after Rain, Fontainebleau*, Opus 28, *Bay of Baiae, Sunrise*, and Opus 29, *Pozzuoli and Bay of Baiae*.

September and October. Paints Opus 32, *Hiawatha*.

October. Paints Opus 30, *Forest of Fontainebleau*, and Opus 31, *From the Quay at Naples*.

November. Thomas Eakins, in a letter to his family, says he has returned Moran's picture from "the Great Exhibition." (Foster and Leibold 1989, 149)

14 November – 11 March 1868. NAD's first annual winter exhibition, which incorporates works from AWCS exhibition and Exposition Universelle. Moran exhibits *Children of the Mountain* (cat. no. 671), back from Paris. (*Putnam's Magazine* [Jan. 1868], 132; *NYT*, 7 Mar.)

3 December. At AFS sale Moran's *Forest of Fontainebleau* brings $80. (*Phila. Evening Bulletin*, 30 Nov., 3 Dec.; Appendix 2)

13 December. *Phila. Evening Bulletin*: "Mr. Thomas Moran is ... very well represented on the walls of the Artists' Fund galleries at present. His manner in landscape painting has changed of late years, and is now as individual as that of any painter of the day. Several of the works now exhibiting are from studies made in Italy and elsewhere during his late European tour. They are charming in composition and splendid in color. Avoiding the extreme of realism, and yet equally avoiding technical faults, Mr. Moran's works are poems as well as pictures. The romantic is a distinct but not obtrusive element in them, and they create ever new impressions in the mind of the careful observer."

December 1867, January 1868. Moran paints Opus 33, *Scene on the Tohickon Creek*.

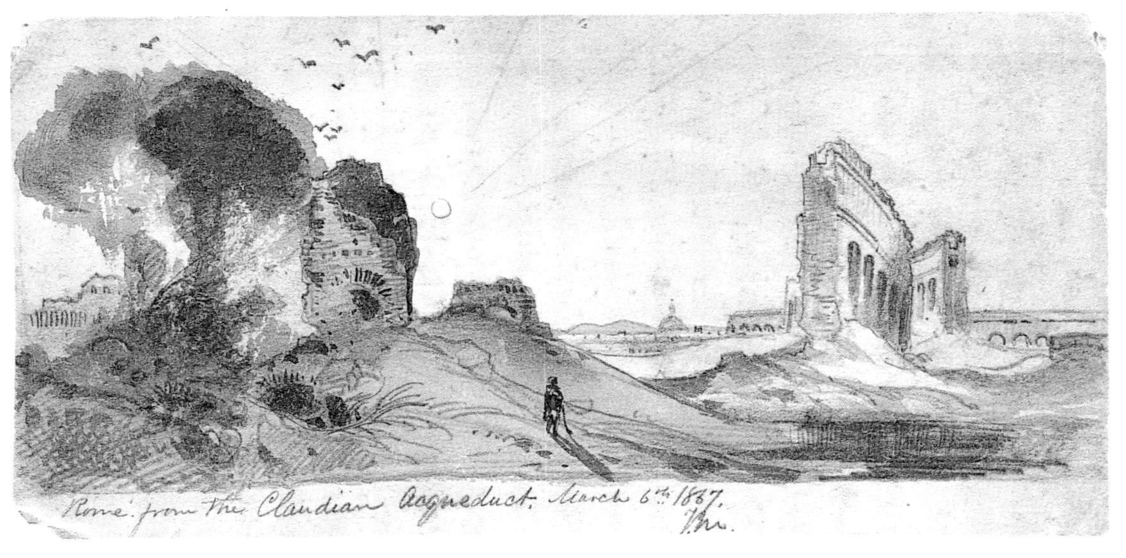

• 1868 •

Thomas and Edward Moran live in independent households in Philadelphia. Peter Moran shares a home with his mother, with brothers John and William, both photographers, and with Stephen J. Ferris. (Gopsill's Phila. City Directory; Rutledge 1955, 72, 144, 145)

February and March. Thomas Moran serves as chairman of AFS exhibition committee and contributes *Sketches*; *Grecian Ruin*; *Children of the Mountain*; *Remorse of Cain* (cat. nos. 46, 54, 137, 146). Edward Moran exhibits three paintings; Peter, two. (*Phila. Evening Bulletin*, 13 Feb.; Moran's ledger also lists *Rome, from the Campagna, Sunset*; *Last Arrow*; and *Hiawatha* [Opus nos. 24, 25, 32])

14 February. *Phila. Evening Bulletin* reviews AFS exhibition: "In the first room, on entering, the visitor will be struck with the large canvas by Thomas Moran, a copy of one of the most important works of Turner in the National Gallery of London, and catalogued as 'Ulysses deriding Polyphemus.' It is gorgeously rich in color, and perhaps will give a better idea of Turner's grand manner than can be derived from any of the few original pictures by him that have been brought to this country. Mr. T. Moran's own style is well represented in the exhibition by two landscapes in oil, and by several drawings of great strength and beauty."

March. Moran paints Opus 34, *Hiawatha and the Serpents*, and Opus 35, *Remorse of Cain*.

4 April. AFS reception. *Phila. Evening Bulletin*, 6 Apr.: "The oil paintings are creditable to the industry and enterprise of the Fund Associates. Mr. Thomas Moran contributes two large pictures, his 'Children of the Mountain,' which attracted the notice of all American visitors at the Paris Exposition, and a late work, the 'Remorse of Cain.'"

27 April. *Phila. Evening Bulletin* reports opening of PAFA annual exhibition. Moran does not exhibit but is on the managing committee. Edward Moran exhibits four paintings. (Rutledge 1955, 145)

June. Moran completes eight drawings, six of which are engraved by Samuel Sartain and appear as illustrations in Reverend Daniel March's *Night Scenes in the Bible*, published in 1868. (Appendix 2)

June. Paints Opus 36, *Sacrifice of Isaac*, and Opus 37, *Wood Scene, Autumn*.

Summer. Paints Opus 39, *Rome with St. Peter's and the Castle of St. Angelo.*

October. Paints Opus 38, *Autumn on the Wissahickon*, in exchange for money and clothing.

November. Thomas and Edward Moran elected honorary members (nonresident participants) of AWCS of NY, although Thomas does not exhibit with society until 1873. (Foster 1982, 137)

November. Moran paints Opus 40, *Alpine Peak, Evening*, Opus 41, *Lake Superior Morning*, and Opus 42, *Waterfall*, his last designated Opus. Moran later wrote, "Ceased numbering in 1868."

December. Gives Opus 42, *Waterfall*, to Thomas Eakins for Christmas.

• 1869 •

Thomas and John Moran living in independent households in Philadelphia. Edward and Peter listed separately as well as with their mother, brother William, and Stephen J. Ferris. (Gopsill's; Rutledge 1955, 72, 145)

11 March. *Phila. N. American and Gazette*: "Artists' Fund Annual.... To extend the influence of the society, as well as to increase its means, the members have published a volume containing twenty photographs by John Moran, of as many original paintings by the members of the society. The photographs are large, on large cardboard, handsomely bound.... Thomas Moran [contributes] 'The Pictured Rocks of Lake Superior in the Morning';... Peter Moran, 'A Herd Scared by a Thunderstorm,'... Edward Moran, 'Lost at Sea.'... The landscapes are all interesting and are happily relieved by the marines and interiors and studies of cattle. The work of the photographer has been achieved with signal success, so that it will be difficult to find... any ornament... that is so desirable and procurable." (One copy owned by LCP)

24 March. *Phila. N. American and Gazette* mentions works by Thomas, Edward, and Peter Moran included in M. Thomas & Sons "Sale of Oil Paintings. Comprising important parts of Two Private Collections."

15 April. Edward Moran resigns from PAFA following dispute about exhibition policies. (Letter to board, Harriet Sartain Collection, Historical Society of Pennsylvania, AAA)

26 April. PAFA annual exhibition opens. Thomas Moran exhibits *Dreamland*; *Children of the Mountain*; *Ripening of the Leaf*; *Bridge and Castle of St. Angelo*; *Remorse of Cain*; *Mountain Stream*; *From Longfellow's "Hiawatha"*; *Ruins of the Palace of the Caesars*; *River Bank*; *Charcoal Drawing*; *Hemlock Forest* (nos. 84, 106, 119, 164, 166, 175, 190, 219, 251, 255, 261). Mary Nimmo Moran exhibits at PAFA for the first time, with *Wood Scene* (no. 8). (*Phila. N. American and Gazette*, 26 Apr.; Rutledge 1955, 146)

26 April. *Phila. American and Gazette* reviews PAFA exhibition, listing Thomas as both an Academician and a member of the exhibition committee: "Of the more conspicuous productions of the Philadelphia School of Art, we notice the following:... 'Dreamland,' by Thomas Moran. This young artist has given us in Philadelphia a lovely revelation of the golden visions that dance through a painter's fancy, and although Mr. Moran has other pictures in the exhibition on which he has expended more time and care, we think his fame for this season may safely rest exclusively on this one. He has evidently

read Ruskin to some purpose, and has given us in this ideal scene one of those superb designs that only rarely make their appearance in the galleries of an academy. The rarity of such pictures shows how little of the ideal is, after all, prevalent among artists, either abroad or at home, realism having swept all before it, and brought art down to the level of humdrum details. Fortunately Mr. Thomas Moran had a predecessor in Philadelphia in this line. Mr. James Hamilton, who, after encountering an amount of ridicule sufficient to have frightened most artists, has firmly established his ideas and his style; and we see in Mr. Moran's 'Dreamland' that Hamilton's wonderful success is inducing others to adopt the ideal, and leave off painting brass kettles and mullein stalks."

25 May. *Phila. Press* reports on art in Philadelphia and PAFA exhibition: "We could point out two or three dozen first-class pictures in this very exhibition.... Thos. Moran's 'Dream Land,' (reminding one of F. Danby's poetical productions), and 'Ruins of the Palace of the Caesars;' and 'Cattle and Bridge of St. Angelo.'" Article goes on to complain that Philadelphia art is often maligned, citing H.T. Tuckerman's *Book of the Artists*, which gives Philadelphia only 25 pages out of 640, and "Edward, Thomas, and Peter Moran, with Bispham, Bonfield, J.G. Brown, G.C. Lamdin, E.D. Lewis, T.B. Read, W.T. Richards, three Smiths, H.J. Hazeltine, and several other of our really eminent local artists did not receive all together as much notice as would extend over a single page." (See Tuckerman 1867)

17 November. *Phila. Evening Bulletin* advertises Moran's lithograph: "*Swarthmore College*. A Magnificent Drawing on Stone, By Thomas Moran. Of this new and beautiful *Collegiate Institution* of the Society of Friends. Size of the Picture, 14 inches by 6 inches. Price, $1.00. For sale by Uriah Hunt's Sons."

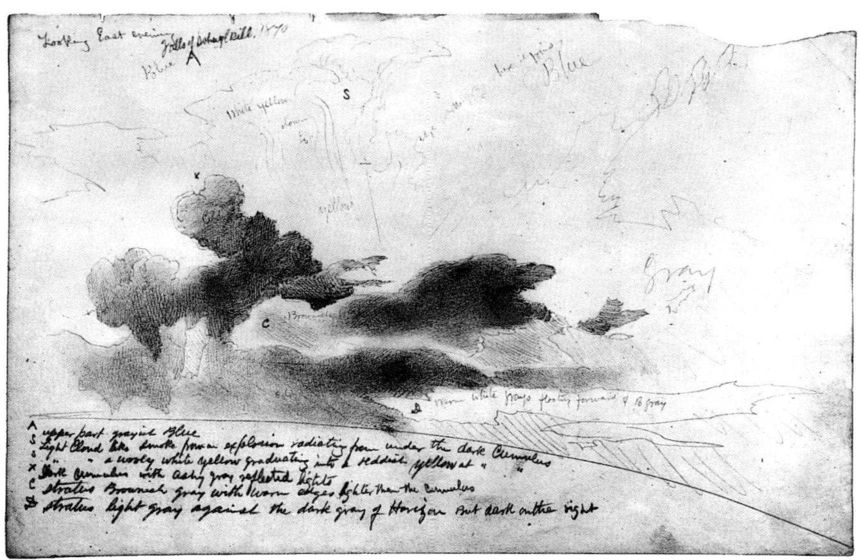

Thomas Moran, *Falls of the Schuylkill (Cloud Study)*, 1870, graphite on newsprint, courtesy Gilcrease Museum, Tulsa, Oklahoma.

21 December. Moran's *Kilchurn Castle* (no. 134) included in PAFA exhibition of the Claghorn Collection, along with Edward's *Towing a Disabled Brig*. (Yarnall and Gerdts 1986, 43, 2469, 2464)

• 1870 •

Moran's *Landscape* (no. 153) exhibited in Harrison Collection at the Gallery of Joseph Harrison Jr., Rittenhouse Square, Phila. Edward Moran is represented by one painting. (Yarnall and Gerdts 1986, 43, 2464, 2468)

Spring. Exhibition of Pittsburgh Art Gallery. Moran exhibits *Ripening of the Leaf*; *Children of the Mountain*; *Hiawatha and Pearl Feather*; *Roman Campagna* (nos. 7, 21, 53, 58). Edward Moran exhibits one painting; Peter, four. (Yarnall and Gerdts 1986, 44, 2462, 2466, 2467, 2469)

21 March. *Phila. Evening Bulletin* mentions Philadelphia School of Design for Women: "The use of oil colors is explained by Mr. Thomas Moran."

15 April. *Phila. Evening Bulletin* announces D'Huyvetter sale at B. Scott's: "Purchasers must not forget the claims of the American artists represented: Thos. Moran's 'Sunshine on Snow,' a little in the manner of Jacobsen's favorite picture, is one of the best landscapes he has lately turned out."

18 April. *Phila. Evening Bulletin*: "[Swiss painter Alexandre] Calame is well represented... in Philadelphia in the collections of Mr. J. Bohlen, Mr. J.R. Claghorn and Joseph Harrison. Upon two, at least, of our excellent landscape painters, Calame had a strong educational influence—Paul Weber and Thomas Moran."

20 April. *Phila. Evening Bulletin* comments on D'Huyvetter sale: "Nearly half the pictures in the catalogue were disposed of last night by Mr. Scott, at his Galleries... and the remainder will be sold this evening. The attendance was considerable, comprising many of our recognized leaders in taste, but the prices obtained were low. Some of them were as follows:... 'Winter' [Sunshine on Snow], by T. Moran, $97 ½."

28, 30 June, 8 August. Moran sketches and dates *Falls of the Schuylkill* and *West, Time, ½ past 6 O'Clock* (cloud study); then *Storm—Evening Looking Southwest*; then *Falls of Schuylkill* (Gilcrease).

20 August. Second daughter, Ruth Bedford Moran (1870–1948), born to Thomas and Mary Nimmo Moran. (Moran family monument, South End Cemetery, East Hampton)

September. Moran sketches and dates two versions of *Falls of the Schuylkill* and *Wissahickon* (Gilcrease; EHL).

Ruth Moran, c.1874, courtesy East Hampton Library.

Thomas Moran (with fish) on the Hayden expedition to Yellowstone, 1871, photograph by William Henry Jackson, courtesy East Hampton Library.

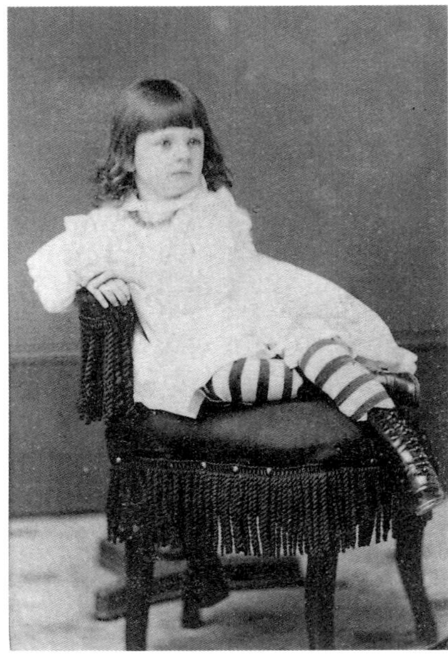

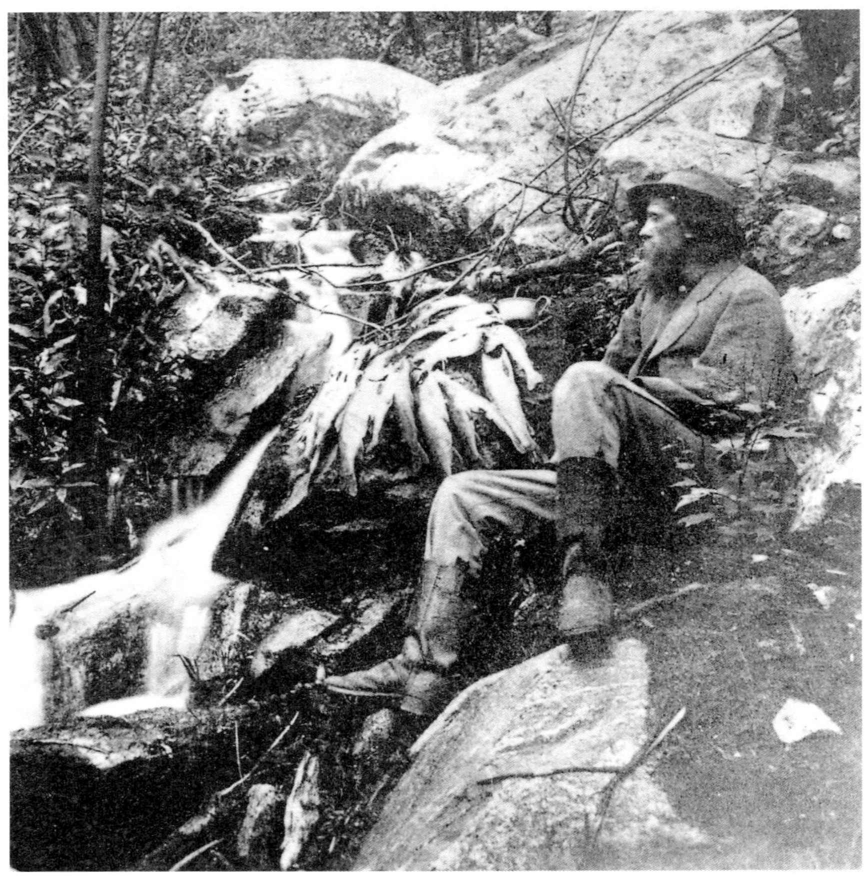

22 September. Sketches and dates *Schuylkill Falls* (EHL).

Fall. Paints two scenes from West Laurel Hill Cemetery—*View from Pencoyd Point* and *View up the Schuylkill*—for the Smiths, owners of the cemetery company, in exchange for four lots. (GA Old Book of Lists)

November. *Scribner's Monthly* begins publication. Moran contributes illustration for T. Edwards Clark's "Bottom of the Sea" in premier issue.

1 November. *NY Post*: "E. Moran, the marine painter of Philadelphia, will sell his entire collection of finished works and sketches, consisting of seventy-five or eighty examples, through Messrs. Earle & Son, of that city, about the first of December."

8–10 December. First art reception and exhibition of the ULC of Phila. Moran serves on hanging committee and contributes *Brook Scene*; *View in Laurel Hill*; *View in Laurel Hill* (nos. 43, 90, 91). Edward Moran exhibits six works; Peter, one. (Whiteman 1978, 5; Yarnall and Gerdts 1986, 43, 2462–2463, 2466–2468)

Winter. Richard Watson Gilder, managing editor of *Scribner's* art department, commissions Moran to illustrate Nathaniel P. Langford's "Wonders of the Yellowstone." (*Scribner's*, May and June 1871)

• 1871 •

Thomas and John Moran living in separate households in Philadelphia. Edward listed there with his mother and brothers Peter and William, then moves to E. 17th St., NY. (Gopsill's; NAD summer exh. cat.)

26–29 April. 3rd art reception of ULC of Phila. Moran exhibits *On the Schuylkill*. (Yarnall and Gerdts 1986, 43, 2469)

May and June. Nathaniel P. Langford's "Wonders of the Yellowstone" published in *Scribner's*. Illustrations by Moran are based on field sketches made by 1870 Washburn-Doane expedition members Charles Moore and Walter Trumbull. Fourteen ink wash drawings made for the engraver are now at Gilcrease. (Treuttner 1976, 241–242; Morand 1983, 4–8)

7 June. A. B. Nettleton, office manager of Northern Pacific R.R. (Phila.), to F. V. Hayden: "My friend Thos. Moran, an artist of Philadelphia of rare genius, has completed arrangements for spending a month or two in the Yellowstone country, taking sketches for painting. He is very desirous of joining your party at Virginia City or Helena, and accompanying you to the headwaters of the Yellowstone. I have encouraged him to believe that you would be glad to have him join your party, and that you would in all probability extend to him every possible facility. Please understand that we do not wish to burden you with more people than you can attend to, but I think that Mr. Moran will be a very desirable addition to your expedition, and that he will be almost no trouble at all, and it will be a great accommodation to us

F.V. Hayden, courtesy Smithsonian Institution Archives.

Thomas Moran in *At the Mammoth Hot Springs, Gardiner River,* 1871, photograph by William Henry Jackson, courtesy East Hampton Library.

William Henry Jackson, courtesy Colorado Historical Society.

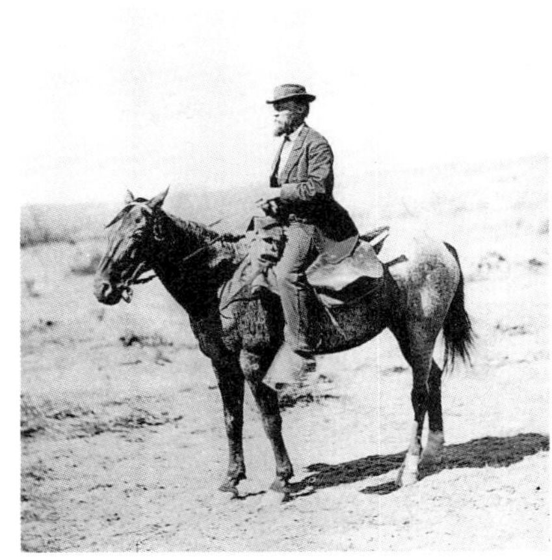

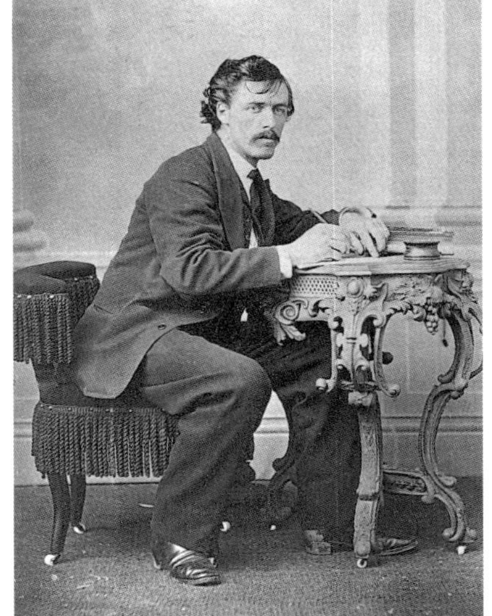

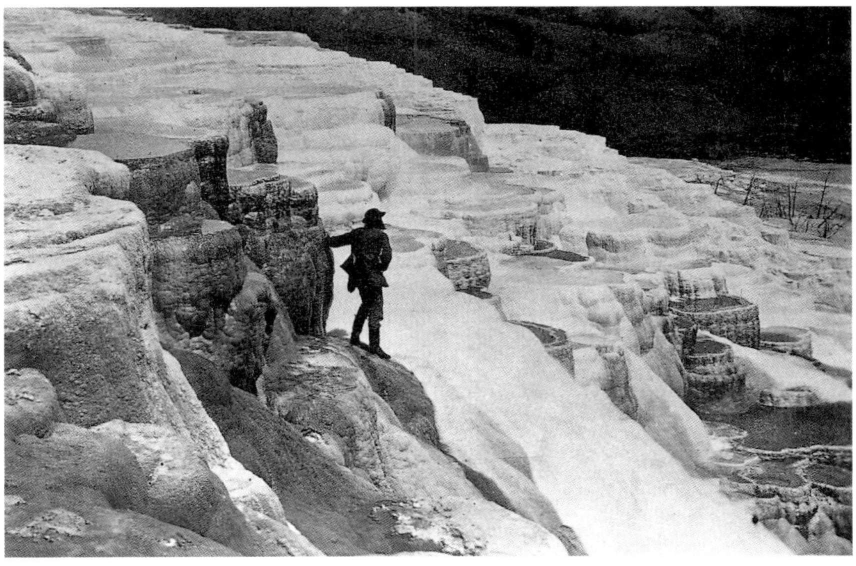

and to the road, if you will assist him in his efforts. He, of course, expects to pay for his own expenses, and simply wishes to take advantage of your cavalry escort for protection." (Hayden IC, NA)

16 June. Nettleton to Hayden in Ogden, UT: "This will introduce my friend Thomas Moran of this city, of whom I think I wrote you at Ogden. Mr. Moran is an artist (landscape painter) of much genius, who desires to take sketches in the upper Yellowstone region from which to paint some fine pictures on his return. That he will surpass Bierstadt's Yosemite we who know him best fully believe. He goes out under the patronage of Mssrs. Scribner & Co Publishers N.Y. and our Mr. Cooke on whom (as well as himself) you will confer a great favor by receiving Mr. Moran into your party when you start for the Yellowstone Country." (Hayden IC, NA)

July. Moran arrives in Green River, WY, via Union Pacific R.R. Completes and inscribes "First sketch made in the West at Green River, Wyoming, 1871" (Gilcrease).

July. Arrives in Corinne, UT, by train. Traveling by stagecoach, joins Hayden expedition at Virginia City, MT. Survey party proceeds on horseback to Fort Ellis. (Inscribed sketch at EHL; Jackson 1936, 152)

4, 7, 8 July. Moran sketches and dates *Beaver Head Canyon, Montana,* and *South West Canyon*; then *Sulphur Spring Creek near the Madison*; then *Warm Springs Creek, Idaho,* and *Ruby Range from near the Gallatin* (MFA Boston; YNP).

11 July. *Helena Herald* [MT]: "In our Virginia [City] correspondence yesterday, the names of the gentlemen composing this Expedition were given, with their respective specialties in all branches of natural sciences and in art, with the single exception, we think, of Mr. Moran, landscape painter, who is directly in the interest of the N. P. R.R. Company. The scientific corps was fitted out by direction of the Secretary of the Interior, and is complete in every detail. Yellowstone Lake will be navigated and sounded; the altitude of the mountain ranges and peaks definitely ascertained; in fact a complete and exhaustive report of the physical features and phenomena of this wonderful region, will be presented to the country. An Agricultural and Geological map, drawn upon the immense scale of four miles to the inch, will accompany the report to the Secretary of the Interior, while the geological collections will be deposited, as required, in the Smithsonian Institute.... We doubt not that the report of this scientific expedition will attract thousands of tourists to the country of the Yellowstone."

11 July. Moran's travel journal: "On Tuesday last started from camp [Ft. Ellis] in company with Hayden, Jackson (the photographer) Elliot (draughtsman) Thornborn (topographer) Dixon (Jackson's assistant) Dr Campbell, Lt. Gerome, & Lt. Norton of Fort Ellis, for a small lake in the Mountains about 15 miles distant. About one half of the distance lays through dense forests with a great deal of fallen timber, making it very difficult to travel through with horses. The path in many places very precipitous & dangerous. One part of the route lay through magnificent forest of pines & firs all growing straight as ships mast, & growing but a few

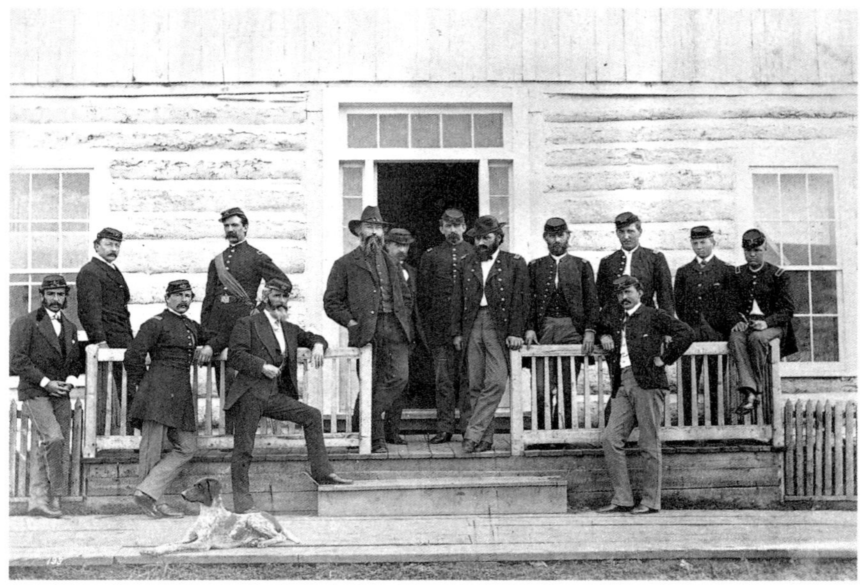

expect to see any finer general view of the Rocky Mountains. We got back to Camp [Fort Ellis] at 7½ p.m." [rest of page torn off] (YJ)

15 July. With preparations complete, Hayden's expedition departs Fort Ellis, entering the Yellowstone valley 30 miles due east. Ascending the valley ten miles farther, they pitch a permanent camp near Bottler's Ranch, close to the lower canyon. From this point they change their mode of travel to pack animals. (Hayden 1872a, 388; for spelling of "Bottler's" see Whittlesey 1988, 27; and Modelski 1984, 90)

15–20 July. "Left [Fort] Ellis for Yellowstone camp Trail Creek"; "Left camp on Trail Creek in company with Stephenson, Jackson & Dummy, for the Crow Agency. Stayed at the Agency all night. We were each presented with a buffalo robe by Major Pease"; "Left the Agency at 12 o'clock, did some photographing in the Lower Canyon & reached Boettlers [*sic*] ranch at ½ o'clock that night after a severe ride in the dark of 35 miles from the Agency"; "remained in camp at Boettlers"; "Left Boettlers in Co with Jackson, Dixon, Ellick, Jose, & Crissman. Reached the Middle Canyon in the afternoon. Camped for the night. Did some tall fishing, photographed & sketched some next morning"; "Left the Middle Canon & went as far as the devil's slide on Cinnabar Mt where we camped for the night." (YJ)

21–24 July. "Sketched & photos in the morning. The main party passed us in the forenoon. Went on in the afternoon as far as the Hot Springs on Gardners River"—sketches and dates *Yellowstone above Boettlers Ranch* (JNEM); "in camp at Hot Springs [3 days]. Left in the afternoon & went as far as day light allowed & camped in a small Ravine near the Yellowstone." (YJ)

25–31 July. "Left camp in the ravine early & touched the Yellowstone at [Baronett Bridge]. Thence to Tower Falls"—sketches and dates *Near Meadow Creek* (Cooper-Hewitt); "Remained at Tower Falls sketch-

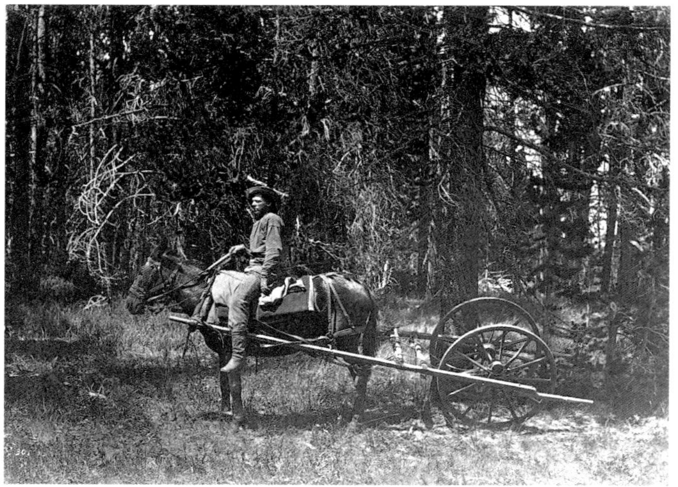

feet apart. Passed over debris of a great land slide, where the whole face of the mountain had fallen down at some time, laying bare a great cliff some 500 feet high. The view of the lake, as we approached it, was very beautiful.... The Mountains surrounding it are about 11,000 feet high... having snow still upon them.... After descending to the shore of the lake, some of the party fished in it & caught a few of the finest trout that I have yet seen. After a rest... all the party started back for camp excepting Jackson, Dixon & myself, we having concluded to remain over until the next day for the purpose of photographing & sketching in the vicinity. Made a large fire & cooked our supper of black tailed deer meat.... during the night it rained a little but not enough to wet us to any extent. Got up early enough in the morning to get our breakfast, & commence photographing as soon as the sun rose. The outlet of the lake is through an immense gorge in the Mountains bordered with great cliffs & peaks of limestone, some of them isolated & forming splendid foreground material for pictures. Sketched but little, but worked hard with the photographer selecting points to be taken &c.... Jackson got 13 negatives during the day, which considering the difficulties quite a feat I think. Started back for camp at 3½ o'clock. Clouds began to gather & a rain set in the Mts all around us but did not fall heavily on us. Jackson's pack mule & traps got pretty well shaken up in the return by having to force a passage between trees not wide enough apart to allow free passage of the pack. When about half way back Dixon's horse got his foot fast between two fallen trees & in his frantic efforts to extricate himself he struck Dixon, who had dismounted to help him, square on the top of the head with his fore foot, peeling his scalp & hurting him considerably. The view from the Mountains south east of our Camp & on the road to the lake looking toward the Yellowstone Country glorious, & I do not

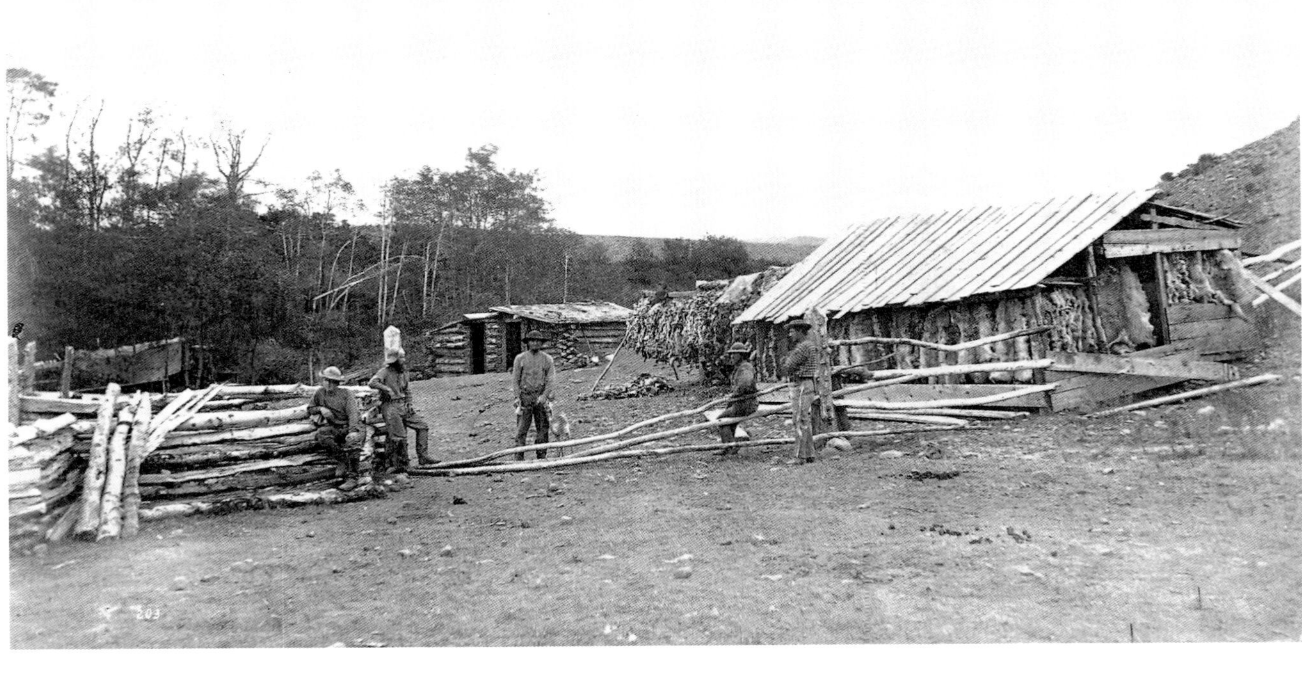

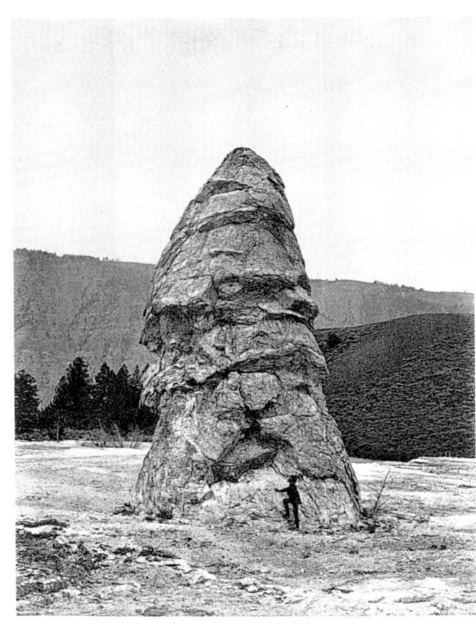

Col. Baker and Officers, Ft. Ellis, 1871, photograph by William Henry Jackson, courtesy Yellowstone National Park.

The Expedition Odometer, 1871, photograph by William Henry Jackson, courtesy Yellowstone National Park.

Bottler's Ranch, 1871, photograph by William Henry Jackson, courtesy Yellowstone National Park.

Liberty Cap, 1871, photograph by William Henry Jackson, courtesy Yellowstone National Park. See also cat. 17.

ing & photographing"; "Left Tower Falls. Halted at noon on Mt. Washburne. Arrived at Yellowstone falls in the evening"; "Sketching & photographing about the Falls"; "Photographing & sketching around the Falls & Canon"; "Still at the Falls"; "Left the falls, reached Crater Hill, large Sulphur Spring & many Mud Springs. Left at noon & camped at the Mud Volcano." (YJ)

1–5 August. "Photog. & sketching at Mud Volcano. Left Mud Volcano at noon & reached the Yellowstone Lake where the whole party & escort were encamped"; "Made photographs & sketches of the Lake & river in forenoon, followed the main camp in the afternoon to the border of the Lake. 30 miles through heavy timber & was lost for several hours at night in a dense forest on a mountain side covered with fallen trees. Got into camp at 10½ o'clock"; "Moved camp a few miles farther round the lake to the Hot Springs"; "remained all this day at the same camp. Did some sketching about the springs. Took the boat to the springs farther round the lake & had a hard pull to get back as the lake was rough & the wind against us"—sketches and dates *Yellowstone Lake* (JNEM); "Camp moved to the springs visited yesterday." (YJ)

6–10 August. "Jackson, Dixon, & myself started out to find the Madison Lake to get a photograph of it, but after travelling through heavy forests until two o'clock, gave up the search & got back to camp at evening"—sketches and dates *Yellowstone Lake* (JNEM); "In camp all day. Photo. some of the springs in the evening. Lieut. Doane arrived from Ellis with an order for the return of the escort to the fort. Grugan & Tyler invited me to return with them, & as the Wonders of the Yellowstone had been seen, I concluded to return. 4 Biscuits a day for last 5 days"—sketches and dates *Great Blue Spring of the Lower Geyser Basin of Fire Hole River, Yellowstone,* and *Fire Hole River* (YNP; Clark 1981, no. 8); "Set out with Jackson, Smith, & the escort across the country for the geysers in Fire Hole River, led by Doane. Struck the river 9 miles below the geysers & camped." Jackson records: "We were now prepared to return to our base, and we left the lake by way of Pelican Creek and crossed over to the East Fork of the Yellowstone. At Soda Butte we laid over one day, while I completed my first series of hot spring pictures"—Moran sketches and dates *Lower Entrance to Madison Canyon*; *In Lower Madison Canyon*; and *In the Madison Cañon* (JNEM; Gilcrease; YNP). Moran records: "Went to the geysers. Helped Jackson during the day & returned by myself to camp"—sketches and dates *Ravine in Madison Canyon* (JNEM); "Started down the Madison &

camped on a dull spot on the edge of the River near a bit of burnt timber, after passing through the Upper Canyon with the great cliff on it." (YJ; Jackson 1940, 202)

11–14 August. "Moved across the country & reached the 2nd Canyon of the Madison & camped in it. It is a grand canyon"; "Passed out of the Canyon into the open country & camped near the basaltic ridge"; "Reached the ranches & camped on the road to Virginia City near Hayden's old camp." According to Jackson, "the party made its way back to Botelers' Ranch by the same route we had followed on our ascent. We had spent exactly forty days in the Yellowstone." Moran continues: "Camped at Bradleys Ranch on Warm Springs Creek." (YJ; Jackson 1940, 202)

25 August. Moran sketches and dates *Left Half Beaver Head Cañon* (YNP).

29 August. *Helena Herald*: "Mr. Thomas Moran, one of the artists who accompanied Professor Hayden to Yellowstone Lake, returned last evening *en route* for the States. He says that the exploring party ... discovered many curiosities that were not seen by the party last year.... At Gardner's river, seventy-five miles beyond Bozeman, they visited the hot springs, discovered some time before by some of the citizens of Bozeman. Mr. Moran says they constitute one of the most remarkable curiosities of the world.... He had a number of photographic views and some outline drawings of his own, which gave an idea of the springs and the scenery in the vicinity.... There was every evidence, Mr. Moran says, that a fresh eruption had taken place at the Mud Volcano, as trees were broken down in all directions around it, and completely bespattered with mud. At the lake, the party had constructed a boat, visited the islands and inlets, and found many things of great interest. They had also visited the Geyser basin, and while there, witnessed the eruption of one geyser, not described by the party last year, which by actual measurement, projected water to the height of 300 feet. A new geyser region has been discovered by the denizens of the hot springs on Gardiner's river, some miles up the stream which, at the time Mr. Moran left, had been only from a distance of four or five miles. It was reported to be very lively in action, but discovered too late in the day to be visited, and admit of a return to camp. A party was to visit it a few days after Mr. Moran left."

16 September. *NY Post*: "T. Moran, the celebrated landscape artist, has just returned from the wonderful Yellowstone region, with subjects for several large paintings exhibiting the peculiar and magnificent scenery of that grand and unique region. He accompanied Professor Hayden's Government Expedition, as a guest, but returned somewhat in advance of that party. He confirms all the marvellous stories that have been told of the Yellowstone."

27 September. *Boston Transcript*: "T. Moran has just returned from the Yellowstone region with a number of sketches in pencil and water-colors, which will form the material for a series of paintings, exhibiting the peculiar scenery of that very extraordinary country."

6 October. *Newark Daily Advertiser*: "A New York correspondent, judicious and reliable, writes us about the scenery of the Yellowstone River and the picture which Mr. Moran, about to become a resident of Newark, is to paint here from his sketches made while acting as artist of the Yellowstone Expedition.... Mr. Thomas Moran, of Philadelphia, completed his sketches some time since and returned alone, bringing the most remarkable portfolio, perhaps, that it has ever fallen to the lot of an artist to fill. Some of the astonishing features of the scenery were sketched by a soldier of the expedition last year, and were brought out in Scribner's Monthly, with a narrative by Gov. Langford. They excited much wonder, not unmixed with incredulity."

13 December. Moran's younger brother William dies at age 25. (*Phila. Public Ledger*, 15 and 16 Dec.; interment records, Old Cathedral Cemetery, Phila.)

Winter. Moran and family move to Newark, NJ. (Moran to Hayden, 11 Mar. 1872; Holbrook's Newark City Directory)

• 1872 •

Moran listed at 61 Sherman Ave., then moves to 166 Brunswick St., Newark. (Moran to Hayden, 11 Mar. and 6 April; Holbrook's)

January. *Scribner's* publishes Isaac Bromley's "Wonders of the West" with illustrations by Moran.

3 January. *National Republican* [DC]: "Professor Hayden, who recently explored the Yellow Stone river, is busily engaged on his report, which is to be sent to Congress about the middle of February. It is proposed to get out an illustrated edition, which, when finished, will be one of the most valuable acquisitions to any library."

February. *Scribner's* publishes Hayden's "Wonders of the West II" with illustrations by Moran.

23 February. Moran and many "distinguished journalists" attend reception held by *The Aldine*. Mark Twain and Bayard Taylor both speak. ([D.O.C. Townley], *NY Mail*, 26 Feb.)

2 March. President Ulysses S. Grant signs bill to make Yellowstone the first national park, following passage by the Senate (30 Jan.) and House (27 Feb.). (*Congressional Globe*, 42nd Cong., 2nd sess., pp. 697, 1228, 1416; Statutes 1871/1873, 17:32; and *NY Mail*, 25 Mar.)

11 March. From his Newark studio Moran writes Hayden that his large painting of the Grand Canyon of the Yellowstone is "now more than half finished" and asks for a photograph of Hayden so he might include him as a figure in the picture. (Hayden IC, NA)

1 April. *Boston Daily Advertiser* reports the visit of "several art-critics" to Moran's Newark studio to see his unfinished *Grand Canyon of the Yellowstone*; they were "very enthusiastic about it."

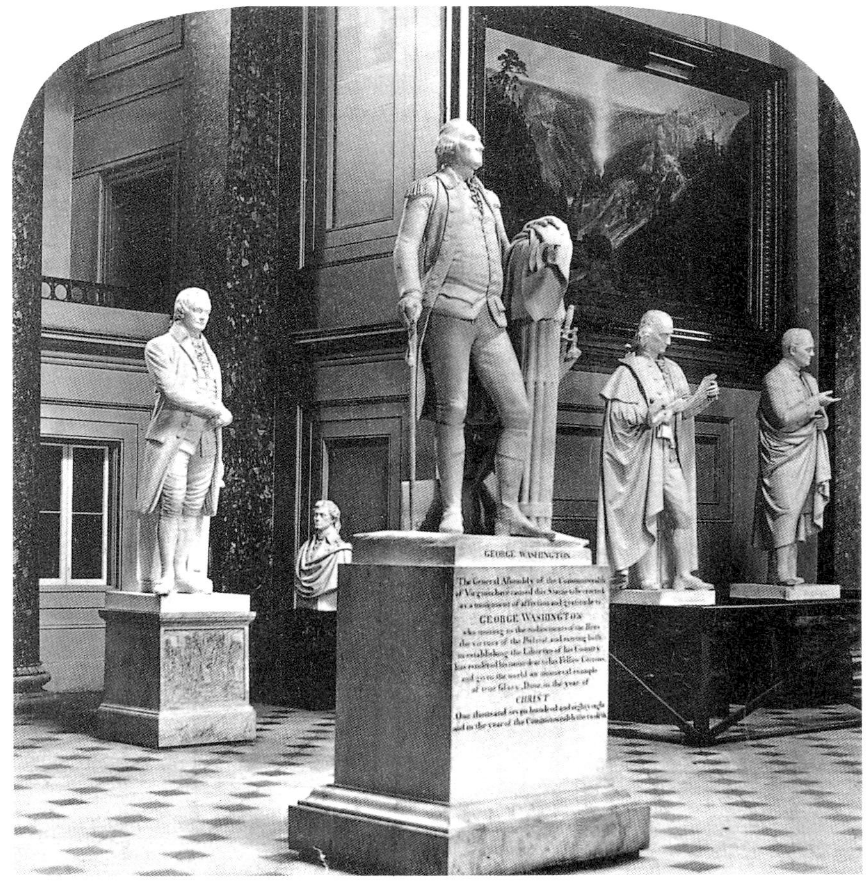

Moran's *Grand Canyon of the Yellowstone* in the U.S. Capitol, 1872, stereograph by Charles Bierstadt, Collection of Merl M. Moore Jr.

6 April. Moran acknowledges receipt of photographs from Hayden, adding "The picture is all that I ever hoped to make of it & the indications are that it will make a sensation wherever it is exhibited." Moran notes that he is eager for Hayden to see the painting and criticize its "geology." (Hayden IC, NA)

12 April – 4 July. NAD spring exhibition. Moran exhibits *Autumn on the Conemaugh* (no. 292). (*Christian Union*, 17 Apr.; *NY Tribune*, 1 July; Naylor 1973, 647)

15 April. From his Newark studio Moran writes Hayden to ask for advance payment for drawings for government publication, citing expenses associated with his Yellowstone painting and adding: "Mr. [Howard] Carroll a N.Y. critic [*NYT*] was over last Saturday, also Mr. Brooks of the *Tribune*. Both were impressed & are as Gilder says 'enthused.' They are going to write it up in the various papers & in Boston. Mr. Warner of the *Hartford Courant*, comes tomorrow to see it. I am confident of finishing this week." (Hayden IC, NA)

18 April. [D.O.C. Townley], *NY Mail*, comments on NAD exhibition: "'Autumn on the Connemh' [*sic*], by Thomas Moran ... does not fairly represent the artist.... This painting was done in 1865, seven years ago, since when Mr. Moran's progress has been as marked as that of any school-boy between seven and fourteen."

20 April. Moran writes Hayden that his "big" Yellowstone picture is "finished except the figures & the frame will be finished on Tuesday morning next. I hope, & believe, it will meet all the expectations raised of it." (Hayden IC, NA)

26 April. Moran to Hayden, acknowledging receipt of advance payment and reporting that "President Smith, Vice Pres. Rice & part of the directors of the N.P. R.R. were over to see the picture yesterday & were decidedly enthusiastic over it. So far I have been unable to obtain any gallery in N.Y. for the private view, but hope to do so tomorrow, & the 'view' will take place next Thursday afternoon & evening, when all the directors of the N.P. R.R., Jay Cooke, Gen. Nettleton & all New York will be present. I wish you could also be present, & hope your business engagement may permit it. I have the picture in the frame & it looks stunning. I should like to have taken the pic. to Washington in the early part of next week but the prestige it will give it by exhibiting it to N. York is of so much importance that I thought it best to wait a few days in order to reap this great advantage. I confidently hope to be able to accompany your expedition the coming summer & to find some new subjects for important pictures." (Hayden IC, NA)

29 April. *Newark Daily Advertiser*: "Mr. Thomas Moran will be happy to receive at his studio ... on Tuesday afternoon and evening, all of his Newark friends ... who may desire to see, before it leaves the city, his large painting of 'The Grand Cañon of the Yellowstone.' This remarkable picture covers a space of twelve by seven feet, and has been visited during its painting by connoisseurs and critics from New York ..., who have expressed their opinions in the warmest terms of admiration. It is a faithful likeness of one of the most wonderful ... scenes of the famous valley of the Yellowstone river, and will soon be removed to Washington where it will be exhibited in the hall of the Smithsonian Institution. Mr. Moran, who was the artist of the late government expedition to that country, is now a resident of our city and with the generosity of a true artist, invites all who would like to see it to do so to-morrow at his residence in Brunswick street, near the terminus of the Broad street horse-car railway. The painting is the finest work of art ever produced in our State—full of vigor, rich coloring and vivid effects, and ought to become the property of the government."

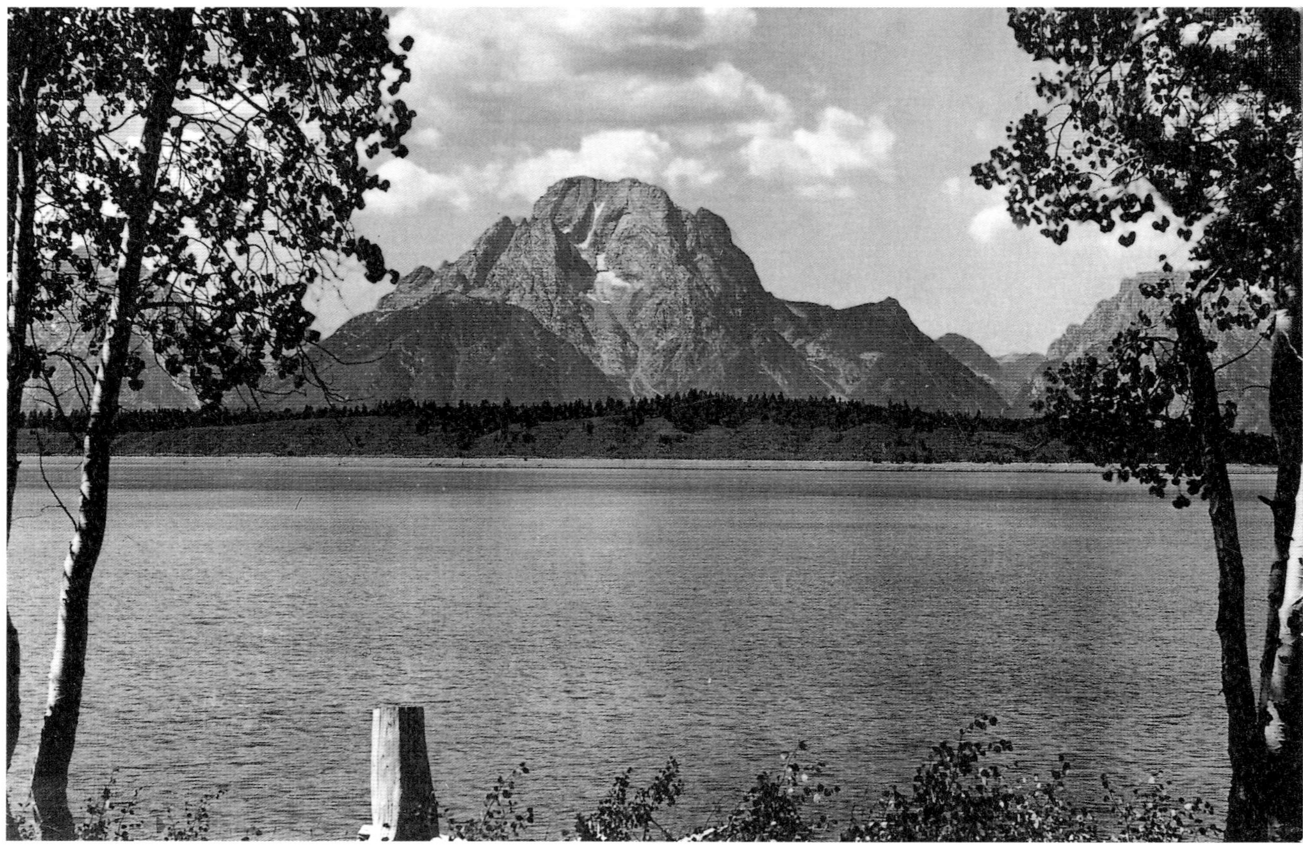

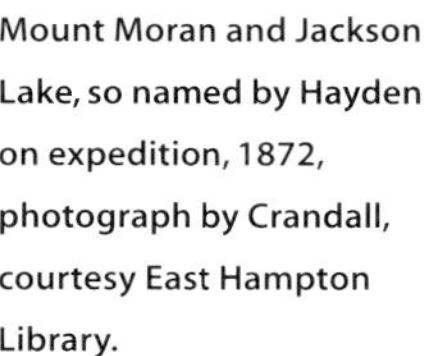

Mount Moran and Jackson Lake, so named by Hayden on expedition, 1872, photograph by Crandall, courtesy East Hampton Library.

1 May. *Grand Canyon of the Yellowstone* leaves Moran's studio for exhibition in New York. (Hayden IC, NA)

1 May. [D.O.C. Townley], *NY Mail*: "Tomorrow afternoon and evening the 'Grand Canyon of the Yellowstone' by Thomas Moran will be exhibited in the large exhibition room of Messrs. Leavitt and Co. Clinton Hall, to the friends of the artist who have been invited to a private view. After this exhibition the painting will be taken to Washington at the request of Dr. Hayden of the U.S. Exploring Expedition and there exhibited. ... We shall indeed be disappointed if it fails to prove in every respect a work of surpassing interest, and to excite more comment and admiration than any landscape yet painted in this country."

2 May. [D.O.C. Townley], *NY Mail*: "Thos. Moran's painting—'The Grand Canyon of the Yellowstone'—as announced yesterday, will be exhibited this afternoon and evening at Leavitts'.... We saw it yesterday afternoon, and do not hesitate to say that the completed work fully sustains the good opinion we expressed of it when we saw it a month ago, unfinished, at Newark. It is, to our mind, a most remarkable work of Art—remarkable in its successful treatment of a subject of extraordinary difficulty—one in which the order of nature seems set aside; and it is thoroughly admirable in its *technique*. By this work Mr. Moran has established his claim to rank among the first landscapists of America."

8 May. *NY Post*: "[Moran's Yellowstone picture is] a literal transcript of nature.... The first view of this picture causes a feeling of disappointment, owing to its extreme brilliancy of color, but after a few moments of study the composition is felt to be in harmony throughout; the gorgeous tones of the foreground blend in subtle gradations with the receding colors which lead off into the perspective, and are in effect refined and beautiful. The picture is carefully painted, and, what is remarkable in so large a work, it will bear a close examination. The structure, texture and character of the rocky formation of these remarkable cliffs are most vividly rendered, and the artist is to be congratulated upon the success of his work." (Repr. *San Francisco Daily Evening Bulletin*, 20 May; and *Helena Herald*, 30 May)

9 May. *National Republican* and *Evening Star* [DC]: "Mr. Thomas Moran's great picture of the Grand Canyon of the Yellowstone, which produced such a decided sensation in New York last week, will be open to public inspection today, the great hall of the Smithsonian Institute. This picture, which the art critics of New York place upon the same level with Church's Niagara, should be seen by all interested in art matters, or who love the beautiful and grand in nature."

13 May. *NY Post* previews June edition of *The Aldine*: "The full-page picture underneath the title, 'Kwasind, the Strong Man,' drawn by T. Moran, is a marvellous triumph in the representation of forest shade and dense foliage."

15 May. [D.O.C. Townley], *NY Mail*: "Thos. Moran's remarkable work, 'The Grand Canyon of the Yellowstone,' will, on its return from Washington, be exhibited at Goupils' for one month."

18 May. From Washington Moran writes his wife Mary regarding his efforts to have his Yellowstone painting placed in the Capitol. Appointment with Senator Charles Sumner was disappointing. (EHL)

20 May. Moran writes Mary that he has obtained permission to install his painting in the Capitol and continues: "I am sick of Washington and want to get home bad but I must see the thing through and shall do all I can to sell it. I shall ask $20,000.00. Two of the explorers of the Colorado, Wheeler and Powell, both want me to go with them this season. I have seen some of their photos and the region is quite as wonderful and as remarkable as the Yellowstone, but of course my going with them is out of the question. King's expedition people also desire me to accompany them, which when Hayden hears it, will make him all the more anxious for me to accompany him, but unless the picture is sold to Congress I shall not go on any of them. These other expedition people opened their eyes when they saw my pictures and sketches." (Fryxell, UW)

21 May. In daily letter to Mary, Moran reports that the Yellowstone picture will be installed the next day "in the old Hall of Representatives where every member of Congress will see it.... I shall have a fair show now at least and if I cannot sell to Congress it will not be for want of an opportunity of letting them see the picture, but because they will not buy a picture. Congress will adjourn on the 29th of May so I shall not have very long to wait to know the result. I have had a hard day's work but feel good on it." (EHL)

22 May. Moran reports to Mary: "I got the picture up in the place I wanted this morning. The light is good and the picture looks well." He also mentions offer from John Wesley Powell to take him to see the Grand Canyon of the Colorado and concludes: "The time occupied in the trip would be 4 months. Of course I shall not go, but I said I would consider it." Finally, he notes that he will meet with the Librarian of Congress the following day regarding the sale of his Yellowstone picture. (Fryxell, UW)

22 May. [D.O.C. Townley], *NY Mail*, previews June edition of *Scribner's*, with "a second installment of 'Traveling by Telegraph,' lavishly studded with illustrations; several of which are of Moran's best and worthy of places of honor anywhere."

24 May. Moran asks Hayden for his assistance in selling *Grand Canyon of the Yellowstone*: "Since you were here before, I have succeeded in getting the picture placed in the old Hall of Representatives, & it has created quite a sensation there. It was quite evident that it was useless to continue its exhibition at the Smithsonian, so far as getting Congressmen to see it was concerned. Many of the members have expressed the opinion that Congress should purchase it. Mr. Spofford the librarian thinks so too. Now the members have nearly all seen it, & the only thing remaining to be done is to bring the matter before the Joint Committee of Congress on Library, to find if they will introduce a resolution to that effect. I asked [Henry] Dawes what he thought of the chances, & he made a favorable reply. Your assistance towards this end would be most valuable. I want your immediate influence with Dawes & [James] Garfield in order to bring the matter before the House Committee, of which Mr. [John] Peters is chairman, the other members being [William] Wheeler & [Lewis] Campbell. The Senate Committee are [Justin] Morrill ... (chairman) & [Timothy] Howe & [John] Sherman. I am likely to find how Morrill would stand this forenoon through a friend. Could I see you at the old Hall of Reps. at 2 o'clock. I will be there at 2, 3, & 4 o'clock. Whatever movements I make to bring it before Congress must be done immediately as so little of the session remains. Kellogg desires to see you as soon as possible." (Hayden IC, NA; *Bio. Congress* 1989)

25 May. *Boston Transcript*: "A surprisingly beautiful work of art, now on exhibition in Washington, namely, Moran's painting of the Yellowstone Cañon, was on Tuesday placed in the old Hall of Representatives at the Capitol, and hourly attracted immense crowds of spectators, both general and connoisseur. Moran is a young artist, and until very recently comparatively unknown. He has undoubtedly made his reputation on his representation of the cañon, which is Bierstadt repeated, but perfectly original."

26 May. Moran and Hayden breakfast in Washington with William Blackmore, English entrepreneur who will travel to Yellowstone with Hayden shortly. (Taylor 1980, 25)

Summer. Moran: "In Summer of 1872 made sixteen water color drawings of the Scenery of Yellowstone region for Mr William Blackmore of London for $800.00." (GA Old Book of Lists)

June. D. Appleton and Company begins publication of *Picturesque America*, issued in 48 parts over two years; Moran contributes numerous illustrations. (Rainey 1994, 77)

June. *Scribner's*, 251–252, discusses Turner's *Slave Ship*, Church's *Parthenon*, and Moran's *Grand Canyon of the Yellowstone*: "Mr. Thomas Moran's picture of the Yellowstone Cañon is the most remarkable work of art which has been exhibited in this country for a long time."

June. *The Aldine* publishes Moran's *Kwasind, the Strong Man*, to illustrate "The Noble Savage," which discusses Longfellow's *Song of Hiawatha*: "Mr. Moran has caught the spirit of his original, the wild and primitive feeling in which these Indian traditions originated. His characteristic excellences—power and imagination—are represented as well as they can be without color, in which he excels. For what he is, he has no master in America."

1 June. *Appleton's*, 612: "Mr. Moran is fortunate not only in the splendor of his subject [*Grand Canyon of the Yellowstone*], but in having painted a picture that is likely to rank with the great landscapes of Church, Bierstadt, and Gifford."

3 June. *National Republican* [DC]: "Thomas Moran's painting of the Grand Canon of the Yellowstone, now on exhibition in the old Hall of Representatives, is, we learn, offered for sale to the Government. The subject itself is most fitting for a great painting to adorn the Capitol, and there are three or four places in the building waiting to be filled with works of national interest and artistic value. This painting is declared by the art critics to stand, in point of artistic merit, second only to the greatest painting by an American artist, which is claimed to be Church's Niagara, and it is stamped with most, if not all the excellencies of that work. Congress should not run the risk of its going into some private collection by waiting till next session before ordering its purchase. Without wishing to make any unjust comparisons we believe the picture is far more valuable than any now owned by the Government, and worth much more than Congress will be asked to appropriate. It may be worthy of consideration that there is not in the Capitol a picture of American landscape or American scenery of any kind, if we are not mistaken, painted by a native born American citizen. This is therefore an occasion when encouragement to American art by Government patronage will be properly and judiciously extended."

8 June. Moran copyrights *Grand Canon of the Yellowstone*. (Copyright no. 6141 C, EHL)

10 June. Congress acts "To enable the joint committee on the library to purchase Moran's large painting of the Canyon of the Yellowstone, ten thousand dollars." (Statutes 1871/1873, 17:347, 362)

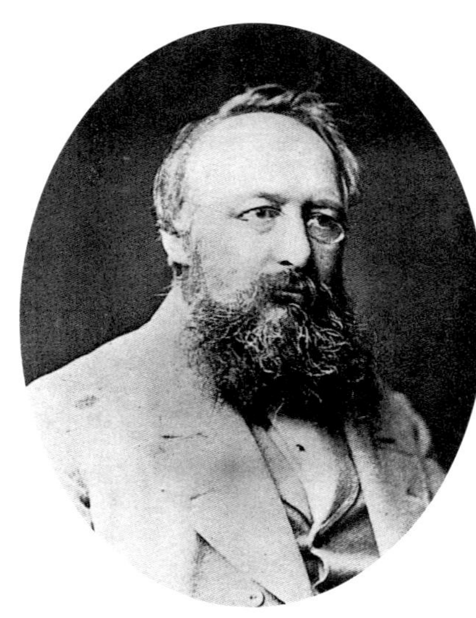

William Blackmore, photograph published in Herbert O. Brayer's *William Blackmore: The Spanish Land Grants of New Mexico and Colorado, 1863–1878* (Denver, 1949).

12 June. *Newark Daily Advertiser*: "Mr. Moran's picture of the Yellowstone Cañon, previous to its actual delivery and sale to the Government, which will be in July ... will be taken to Boston and placed on exhibition for a short time. When it is brought back it will be placed opposite the northeast grand stair case of the Capitol, a worthy place for a noble picture. The price paid by Government was $10,000. Newark feels an especial pride in this success of one of her artists, as the picture was painted here and here first exhibited." (Repr. *San Francisco Daily Evening Bulletin*, 29 June)

17 June. *Boston Transcript*: "The Canyon of the Yellowstone, as rendered by Thomas Moran, in his great picture, now on exhibition at the gallery of Elliot, Blakeslee & Noyes ... is prominent among the attractions of the season, not to be omitted by citizens or visitors."

20 June. [D.O.C. Townley], *NY Mail*, previews July magazines: "*Scribner's* opens with a comprehensive article ... on 'West Point.' ... The illustrations are lavish and of varied merit, the frontispiece is one of Moran's superb scenes—up the river from Garrison's."

24 June. From Newark, Moran writes J.W. Powell to decline his offer of travel to the Grand Canyon, citing the press of work. (Powell IC, NA)

12 July. *Newark Daily Advertiser* reports that Moran will contribute works to the upcoming Newark Industrial Exposition.

25 July. *NY Post*: "Thomas Moran's remarkable painting, 'The Grand Cañon of the Yellowstone,' is now on exhibition at the Goupil Gallery. This fine picture was noticed in the *Evening Post* on its first exhibition here, at the Clinton Hall Gallery ... previous to its removal to Washington and purchase by the government by order of Congress. Its first exhibition here was very brief, and but few had an opportunity of seeing it. The work is now to be exhibited for a period of two weeks or longer, after which it is to be removed to Washington, where it will be hung at the head of the grand staircase in the Senate wing of the Capitol. The picture is entitled to more than ordinary notice from the fact that it is the only landscape ever bought by order of Congress and the first work of art purchased solely on its merits as such."

28 July. *NYT*: "[Moran] has certainly chosen a grand subject [*Grand Canyon of the Yellowstone*] whereon to exercise his skill, and we have the assurance of those who have spent months in wandering about these regions, and are perfectly familiar with the scene Mr. Moran has spread before us, that the composition is most faithful to the original in every detail."

2 August. *NY Post*: "The exhibition of Moran's great painting, 'The Grand Cañon of the Yellowstone,' which has attracted so much attention at the Goupil Gallery during the past week will close on Saturday next; therefore lovers of art who desire to see this fine picture in its present favorable position should avail themselves of the opportunity at once. The painting is to be removed to Washington on Monday next, when it is to be delivered to the government. It has been assigned a position at the head of the grand staircase in the Senate wing of the Capitol."

3 August. *Newark Daily Advertiser*: "While speaking of the [Newark Industrial Exposition] we regret to say that efforts to

secure for the exhibition, one of Newark's brightest gems of art (Moran's 'Yellow-Stone' picture) have failed, as the painting has been purchased by Government for $10,000, and is to be delivered this day. However, Mr. Moran takes a lively interest in the exhibition, and will contribute a fine collection, among them is 'Storm in the Mountains' 6 feet by 5 feet, 'Dream-land,' 'Hemlock Forest,' &c."

After 3 August. Unidentified newspaper clipping: "It is a very dangerous thing for an artist to risk his reputation in painting a big picture of the most tremendous eccentricity in which nature is known to have indulged; but Mr. Moran has taken the risk, and, so far as we can judge, has used it to advantage." (EHL scrapbook)

9 August. *NY Post*: "Mr. Thomas Moran has deposited with the government, in the Capitol building, the painting of the Yellowstone Cañon, which was purchased by the government from him last session. It will be immediately put in position in the place allotted to it by the Library Committee."

14 August. *Newark Daily Advertiser*: "Mr. T. Moran will exhibit [at the Newark Industrial Exposition] his celebrated painting of the 'Children of the Mountain,' 'Dream Land' and one of his great Hiawatha pictures, also some elegant water-color sketches of Yellowstone scenery."

24 August. Thomas and Mary Moran depart on a trip to Yosemite: "Mrs M & I went to the Yo Semite in August 1872 & made a number of pencil & ink sketches & 4 sketches in water colors." (YJ; GA Old Book of Lists)

29 August. Hayden to Moran, from Montana Territory: "We elected you Honorary Member of the U.S. Geological Survey No. 2. Blackmore was elected No. 3 & Langford No. 4." (GA)

September. Hayden's survey party names a peak of the Teton range after Moran at suggestion of R. W. Gilder, editor of *Scribner's*. (Bassford and Fryxell 1967, 133; Hayden IC, NA)

5 September. *The Nation*: "Mr. Thomas Moran has delivered to Congress his picture of the Yellowstone Valley, the instance being the first in our history where a work of art that is neither heroic art nor historical art has been chosen for national purchase. The painting obtained from Mr. Moran is a landscape; or, to do more justice to its scope and multiplication of points of sight, a diorama; or, to rise with the occasion in qualifying a picture that explains the marvels of geological formation and natural chemistry, it is a chart of physical geography."

5 October. Thomas and Mary Moran return from Yosemite. (GA Old Book of Lists)

24 November. Moran to Hayden, from Newark: "I... have an order from Jay Cooke for 16 water color drawings & many others from other parties, so you can imagine I am pretty busy. Colorado Powell was very much disappointed that I did not go with him last summer & he offered me great inducements, but the Yellowstone is my love. I shall come to Washington this winter & shall bring with me all the Yellowstone work that I have been doing as well as some other material." (Hayden IC, NA)

Winter. Watercolors of Yellowstone Moran painted for William Blackmore exhibited at Goupil's, NY. (*Scribner's*, Jan. 1873, 394; Blackmore 1872)

• 1873 •

January. *The Aldine* publishes "Pictured Rocks of Lake Superior" with drawings by Moran: "The chief feature of the Pictured Rocks can only be represented by *color*, and must, therefore, be left to the imagination of the reader; enough remains, however, when this is subtracted, to startle the artist, and to call forth the utmost skill of the pencil. What they are, translated in black and white, Mr. Moran has shown us. His illustrations are full of power, and are strikingly suggestive of the wild and magnificent scenes in which the Pictured Rocks are set—the old forests by which they are crowned and the stormy waters from which they rise."

January. *Scribner's*, 394: "A collection of water-color drawings, by Mr. Thomas Moran, the subjects taken from the Yellowstone country, have been lately removed from Goupil's, where they were seen by many persons—although not, strictly speaking, on exhibition—and have been sent to England by their purchaser, Mr. William Blackmore."

January. *Scribner's*, 399: "[John W. Palmer, ed.] *Songs of Nature* (Scribner, Armstrong & Co.) is a beautiful volume of verse and picture, especially suited to the holiday season. This is the fourth and final volume in the re-issue of Folk Songs.... There is a noble design by T. Moran on the first page, illustrating Bryant's Forest Hymn. ...and other well-known artists have helped to make the present one of the most attractive volumes ever printed in the country."

21 January. *Newark Daily Advertiser*: "Mr. T. Moran has just completed a set of water color drawings of the Yellowstone country for Jay Cooke, of Philadelphia."

28 January. Moran writes Hayden from Newark to ask for Yellowstone "specimens." (Hayden IC, NA)

31 January. O. B. Bunce, ed., *Appleton's*, writes Hayden: "Mr. Moran is now making drawings of scenes along the Union and the Pacific roads. I am extremely grateful to you for your offer to give him the use of [Jackson's photographs] and also for your consent to prepare the article." (Hayden IC, NA.; cited in Lindquist-Cock 1967, 146 n 45)

February. Junius Henri Browne in *Scribner's* describes Moran's *Grand Canyon of the Yellowstone*: "The only really good picture that is to be found in the Capitol.... This picture was taken to Washington at the strong urging of persons who thought the government ought to buy it and put it in the Capitol. When it reached Washington it was allowed a resting-place in the Speaker's Room, and during some weeks was seen by a great many members

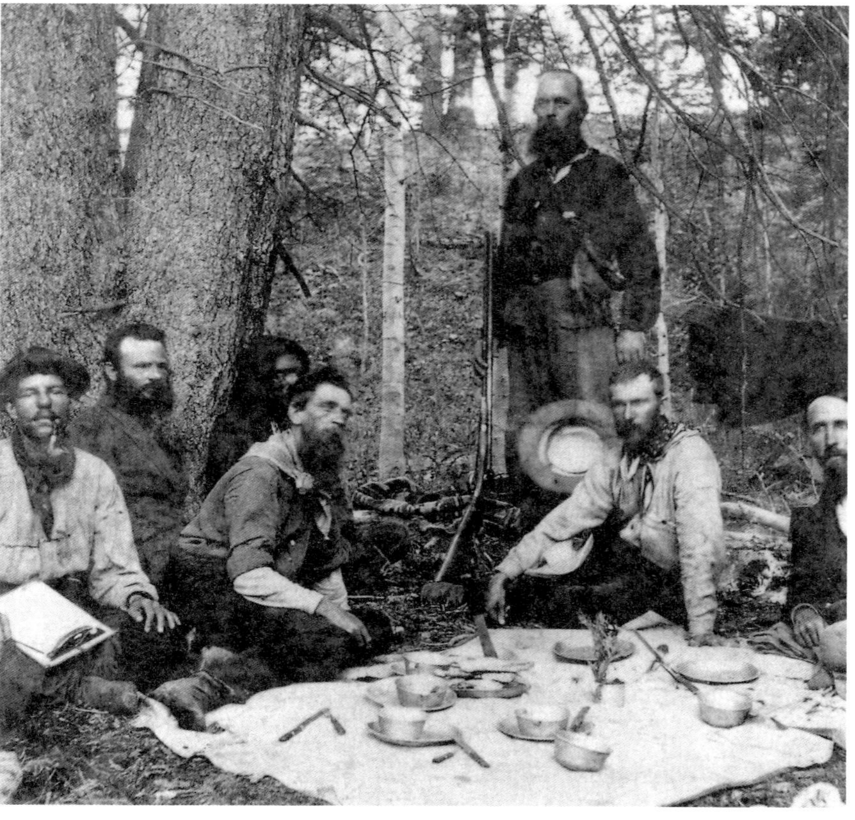

Powell expedition, 1873, showing John Wesley Powell (second from left) and Thomas Moran (fourth from left), courtesy East Hampton Library.

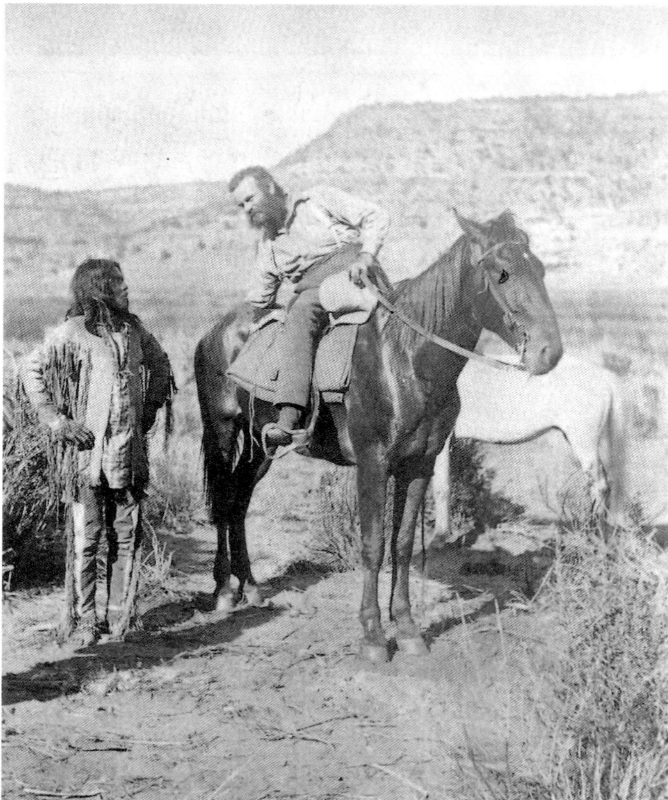

Major Powell in southern Utah, 1873, photograph by John K. Hillers, courtesy East Hampton Library.

of Congress and by visitors to the Capitol. Finally it was purchased, and it is a pleasant thing to be able to say, considering how much talk there is of speculation, and jobbery, and improper influences used, in every Congressional grant of money, that Mr. Moran's picture was bought on its own merits, and that the money paid for it came to the artist undiminished by a penny of brokerage disguised under whatever name."

6 February. *NYT* reports opening of annual AWCS exhibition at NAD. Moran exhibits *Cliffs in the Grand Canon of the Yellowstone*; *South Dome from Glacier Point*; *Great Blue Spring, Yellowstone Park*; *Hiawatha and the Serpent*; and two works called *A Suggestion* (cat. nos. 46, 175, 238, 310, 311, 327).

16 February. *NYT* reviews AWCS exhibition, with "two sketches by John Ruskin (Nos. 271 and 319) and some good drawings in black and white by Thomas Moran."

25 February. *Boston Transcript* quotes *The Nation*'s review of the AWCS exhibition: "Mr. Thomas Moran exhibits nothing but studies, but studies in great variety, from dark caprices apparently printed off from an inky sponge, and very suggestive in their way, to the caprices of Yellowstone scenery, which strike the eye as odd, and nothing more."

March. *The Aldine* publishes "Yellowstone Region" with illustrations by Moran.

10 March. Moran writes Hayden to thank him for Yellowstone specimens and adds: "I have got your drawings under way, one of which is particularly good, the great Blue Spring of the Lower Geyser Basin, which I will send to you at once if you desire it. Will have the two drawings for Mrs. Hayden done by the first of May." (Hayden IC, NA)

19 March. *NY Post* previews April's *Aldine*: "The reading matter of this handsome and unique monthly rivals the art department, and that needs no praise at this period of its success. The full-page illustrations [include]... 'Tower Creek, below the Falls' from Thomas Moran... These are all in *Aldine* style; and that term has become specific and well defined. An attractive paper, both in literary interest and art illustration, is 'The Yellowstone Region,' in which the illustrations, four in number, from Thomas Moran (whose 'Grand Cañon of the Yellowstone' was purchased by the government at Washington last fall), are very handsome."

31 March. Moran writes Hayden to express regret that the survey was not given proper credit when Moran's Yellowstone illustrations were published by *Harper's*: "If I draw any more Yellowstone for publication, I will make it a condition that proper credit is given to the Survey." (Hayden IC, NA)

April. *The Aldine* publishes another "Yellowstone Region" with illustrations by Moran.

4 April. From Newark, Moran writes to thank Hayden for naming a peak after him ("Mount Moran" in the Tetons) and to say he expects to travel with the survey that summer. (Hayden IC, NA)

5 April. *Harper's Weekly* publishes R. W. Raymond's "Heart of the Continent: The Hot Springs and Geysers of the Yellow Stone Region" with illustrations by Moran.

12 May. From Newark, Moran acknowledges payment of $150 from Hayden for drawings: "I do not think I can get off before the 15th of June, as I have to go into Maine for a week in the beginning of June. I saw Wheeler's photos from the Grand Canon of the Colorado today. They are poor & Jackson will knock spots out of them." (Hayden IC, NA)

28 May. Moran advises Hayden that he has agreed "to accompany a sort of newspaper & literary party on a fishing excursion into Maine, if it will not interfere with joining your party in the matter of time. They start on the 6th of June & I expect to return & be ready to start for the west about the 15th or 16th of June." (Hayden IC, NA)

28 June. Moran writes Hayden about a change of plans: "There were a number of reasons which made it imperative upon me to reach the Grand Canon of the Colorado this summer if it were possible to do so, & also to reach it at a time that would enable me to return east by the 1st of September. Under the impression that you would go there, I made a number of contracts to furnish pictures of the region, amounting in all to about 100, but your last letter left me in doubt as to whether you would go there at all & in any event that you would not go down until the end of your season, which would imply a very late return. This seemed to render my chances of reaching that region very remote, & although exceedingly desirous of accompanying your Survey this summer, I felt it obligatory on me to accept the offer made by Maj. Powell as the only chance of getting there within the limits of the time that I could give to it & I have agreed to accompany him. Mr. Colburn has also concluded to go. I hope that you will not feel that I do not appreciate your great kindness & the invaluable opportunity of seeing the region of your present Survey, but my business relations with others & my intense desire to see the Grand Canon force me to change my original plan of accompanying you this summer & I hasten to write that you may make no provision in reference to my joining your party in the field." (Hayden IC, NA)

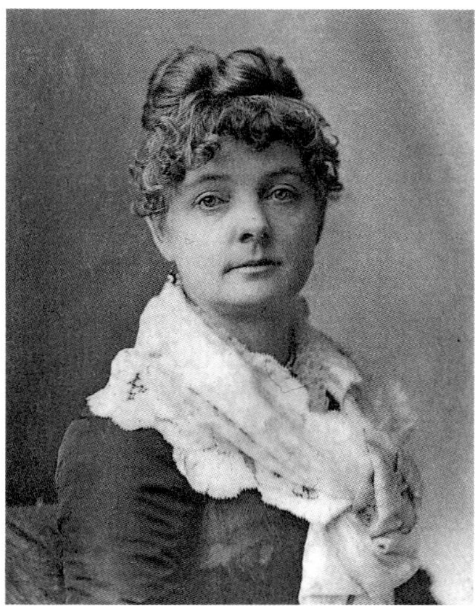

Mary Nimmo Moran, c. 1875, courtesy East Hampton Library.

5 July. Moran writes his wife Mary from Cheyenne, WY, en route to the Grand Canyon. He is traveling with J. E. Colburn of *NYT*. (Bassford and Fryxell 1967, 27; see also Appendix 3)

6 July. Moran arrives in Salt Lake City, then writes Mary on 9 July: "We go tomorrow morning certain. We leave here by R. R. to Lehi 40 miles then take the stage to Fillmore 110 miles, where we shall be met by ambulance and horses so that we can ride on horseback or in wagon as we please. Powell will leave us at Fillmore and will not join us again for 3 weeks as he goes off to make treaties with the Indians. We shall reach the Canons about the 15th of July. We had rather a dull day yesterday making a few visits and killed the afternoon at Camp Douglas. The officers there, like the officers at all military posts, are splendid fellows. Today Maj. Gordon escorted me around to the various saloons in town but saw nothing different from such places in any of the western towns. In the afternoon Powell and I went to Brigham Young's house and I was introduced to all the leading Mormons." (Itinerary, YNP sketchbook; Bassford and Fryxell 1967, 29)

10–16 July. Travels to Springville; Spanish Fork Canyon; back to Springville; on to Steward's and Mt. Nebo; ascends Mt. Nebo, descends and rides toward Fillmore, stopping at Mona or Willow Creek; then on to Cedar. (YNP sketchbook; Colburn, 23 July, see Appendix 3)

17 July. Reaches Fillmore, where he writes Mary: "We arrived at this place this morning after a very severe ride of two days. The day after I wrote you last, we rode to a ranch at the foot of Mt. Nebo and concluded to ascend to the top. Nebo is the highest mountain in Utah or Nevada being 12000 feet. Before sundown we ascended about 2000 feet and made our camp for the night, cooked supper, played a game of Euchre, wrapped our blankets round us and went to sleep. We were up and off again by 6 o'clock. It was an awful climb but we made the top by 12½ o'clock having mounted 6500 feet. We made coffee from the snow and remained up about two hours. It was the most magnificent sight of my life and no person who has not ascended to such an elevation can have the faintest conception of the glorious sight. It seems as if the whole world was laid out before you; and although I do not think I would undergo the labor of another ascent, I would not have missed this for ten times the fatigue. I stood it first rate but Powell, Colburn, and Pilling were sick and vomited when we got down.... We came to this point by private team. We are just 160 miles south of Salt Lake City. We leave here tomorrow morning and shall make a bee line for the Grand Canon, which we shall reach in 5 days. We shall travel but 30 or 40 miles a day. We go the rest of the distance on horseback, and Powell has the animals all ready. We shall return to Salt Lake on horseback and so get out of the

horrid stage ride. It is an awful country that we have been traveling over and I cannot conceive how human beings can stand to live on it." (YNP sketchbook; Bassford and Fryxell 1967, 31–32)

18–23 July. Travels from Fillmore to Dog Valley; Beaver; Parowan; Karmano; and Toquerville. (YNP sketchbook)

23–26 July. Sketches and dates *Utah, Rio Virgin*; *Approach to Toquerville*; *Near Toquerville*; *Toquerville from the Lava Road*; and *Colburn Butte Taylor Canyon*; then *Gate of Little Zion Valley*; then *Canon near Tocquerville, Lava Lower Hills* (Gilcrease; JNEM; YNP sketchbook).

27 July–1 August. Travels from Toquerville to Sheep Troughs, sketching and dating *Road to Kanab*; *Cathedral on the Road to Kanab*; *From Humian Hills North, Creek Domes, Rio Virgin*; *From Humian Hill, Rio Virgin Chasm*; *Look up the Virgin from Humian Hill*; and *Volcano Cones Humian Ledge, Rio Virgin*. In Zion Valley: *Looking up the Valley, Right Hand Side, from above the Ranch, Looking toward the Gates*; *Cathedral Mountain from Gorge, on Way to Grafton*; and *Virgin Tower from Grafton*; then *Zion*; *Capitol Dome*; *Dome Opposite Heaps from below the Ranch, the Citadel*; *Sphinx, the North Gate, Zion*; *Monument*; *Zion Canon no. 6*; *Above the Cave 2*; *Cave 2 no. 4*; *Virgin 2. no. 3*; and *Zion no. 2, Narrows*. Travels back to Sheep Troughs, sketching *Mosque near Kanab* and *Entrance to the Valley of Enchantment, Zion, Rio Virgen [sic], S. Utah*. Travels to Pike, then on to ranch (YNP sketchbook).

2 August. From Kanab, Moran writes Mary about his trip to the Canyon of the Virgin with John Hillers, expedition photographer. (Bassford and Fryxell 1967, 35–36)

7 August. *Evening Star* [DC], reporting on Powell expedition, states that Moran and Colburn intend to return to Salt Lake City by 10 Sept.

7, 10 August. Moran sketches and dates *Cliffs a Yellow Gray with Outcropping of Red at Intervals near Kanab*; *Near Kanab*; and *Kanab*; then *Side Gulch, Grand Canyon*, and *Lava Overflow at the Foot of To Ro Weap* (YNP sketchbook; EHL; YNP).

13 August. From Kanab, Moran writes Mary telling her the party had reached the rim of the Grand Canyon and was setting out to view it from another vantage point. (See Appendix 3)

25 August. Sketches and dates *Grand Canon Colorado* (YNP sketchbook).

3 September–4 October. Cincinnati Industrial Exposition. Moran exhibits *French Coast near Dieppe* (cat. no. 45). (Yarnall and Gerdts 1986, 2469)

6–10 September, 4 October. Sketches and dates *Long Valley Orange Cliff*; then *Monroe in the Sevier Valley* and *Volcanic Cones and Salt Mines at Salina Utah, Sevier Valley*; then *Drinkers Bridge over the Sevier*; then *Little Cottonwood Canyon from Sandy*; then *Hook Pond from the Volcano* (YNP sketchbook).

21 October. *Helena Herald* publishes an article on Jay Cooke's home: "One of the last of his purchases was a small album of Moran's views on the Yellowstone, for which he gave $1,000."

25 October. Moran to Hayden, from Newark: "I am at work on the design of the Chasm of the Colorado & it promises splendidly." (Hayden IC, NA)

25 November. Moran to Hayden: "I have not yet touched paint to the Colorado Chasm, but have finished the design for it in charcoal." (Hayden IC, NA)

4 December. Moran to Hayden: "Powell came to see me Thanksgiving day & brought in a set of the Indian pictures. As you say, they are stunning. I am having a picture painted from one of them. He was highly delighted with the design for the Chasm of the Colorado. He also commissioned me to paint him quite a large picture of the Grand Canon of the Colorado." (Hayden IC, NA)

26 December. Sending New Year's greetings to Hayden, Moran promises to speak with publishers of *The Aldine* about using a Mountain of the Holy Cross image. He also reports that Yellowstone images were published in latest installment of *Picturesque America*. (Hayden IC, NA)

• 1874 •

Moran listed at 166 Brunswick, then moves to 9 Thomas St., Newark. (Moran to McLeod, 15 May; Holbrook's)

January. *The Aldine* publishes "Utah Scenery" with illustrations by Moran: "Mr. Thomas Moran has visited some of the most picturesque places in Utah Territory, and his pencil has faithfully reproduced them for *The Aldine*."

5 January. From Newark, Moran writes Hayden that he is about to travel to Washington. (Hayden IC, NA)

29 January. Moran writes Hayden that he left a photograph of his Grand Canyon painting to be forwarded to Representative Marcus L. Ward of New Jersey. (Hayden IC, NA)

29 January–28 February. AWCS annual exhibition at NAD. Moran exhibits *Sulphur Spring, Yellowstone Country* (cat. no. 254), owned by Clarence Cook. (*NY Graphic*, 29 Jan.; *NYT*, 8 Feb.)

14 February. *Evening Star* [DC] reports that joint congressional committee on Library of Congress directs removal of Moran's painting of the *Grand Canyon of the Yellowstone* from the old hall of the House of Representatives to a position in the rear of the ladies' gallery of the Senate.

27 February. Moran notes: "3 Yellowstone drawings of Prang Com[mission]. for 12. viz Devils Den, Hot Springs, Towers

[of] Tower Fall 300. In all I made 24 drawings for Mr. Prang for his work in chromo of the National Yellowstone Park in which work he used 15 of them. Mr. Kirkpatrick of Newark afterward bought two of them, the Canon of the Rio Virgen & the Upper Fall of the Yellowstone." (GA Old Book of Lists)

18 April. *Appleton's* begins series of articles, "Cañons of the Colorado and the Moquis Pueblos," with illustrations by Moran. (Sequels on Apr. 25, and May 2, 9, 16, 23, and 30)

27 April. *Newark Daily Advertiser*: "Moran's picture of the Chasm of the Colorado will be privately exhibited to invited guests on next Thursday [30 Apr.] evening at Upper Library Hall, and on Friday evening will be publicly shown to all who come."

2 May. *Newark Daily Advertiser*: "Moran's picture attracted a large crowd of admirers yesterday and will remain on exhibition throughout to-day."

4 May. *Newark Daily Advertiser*: "Mr. Moran's painting is to be taken to New York this week and placed on exhibition there."

5 May. Lavish praise for Moran's *Chasm of the Colorado* is published in letter to the editor of *Newark Daily Advertiser*.

9 May. *NY Mail*: "Mr. T. Moran has completed a painting of the 'Chasm of the Colorado,' which will be exhibited on private view next Monday evening at the Leavitt Art Rooms ... and subsequently at Goupil's Gallery."

12 May. *NYT*: "Mr. Thomas Moran's new picture, 'The Chasm of the Colorado,' was exhibited last evening at the Leavitt Art Rooms .... The canvas is a very large one, and represents one of those wild rock-strewn scenes, in which enormous masses of granite have been piled one upon the other by some tremendous agency that has now receded and left them for man to wonder at its power. It would be unfair to criticize any painting seen only under an artificial light, and of this it need only be said here that it is evidently a very strong picture and very brilliant in color, and one on which the artist has labored conscientiously, introducing more detail than is usually to be found in such works. It will be on view at the Goupil Gallery during the week, when the public will have an opportunity of judging of its merits."

12 May. *NY Tribune*: "Mr. Thomas Moran, who two years ago painted a picture, 'The Cañon of the Yellowstone,' which gave him a national reputation—a reputation not diminished by the fact that the work was afterward purchased by the government and placed in the Capitol—has just completed another important picture, which was exhibited a week or so ago in Newark, where the artist lives, and again last evening at Leavitt's room on Broadway to a small party of personal friends and members of the press. It is now on exhibition at Goupil's Gallery ... where it will remain for two weeks. It will, it is hardly necessary to say, repay many visits and the most careful study. It is a strange theme, treated with real power and with a skill rare, at this time, anywhere, either at home or abroad. The work deserves a more extended notice, which it must receive at some other time."

12 May. *Newark Daily Advertiser:* "'The Chasm of the Colorado,' was privately exhibited [in NY] last evening to members of the press."

12 May. *NY Post*: "Thomas Moran's painting of 'The Chasm of the Colorado' ... is evidently a faithful study of the topographical formation of that remarkable region which it portrays, containing cañons, sandstone cliffs and other marvelous features. The foreground, representing a distance of about a mile in width, assumes the form of an amphitheater. Here we see upon the rocks which arch the sides of a minor chasm the effect of the disintegrating process which separates the chalk from the sandstone, and gives to this scenery its wonderful character.

Leading off into the distance are seen a number of cliffs which resemble ruined towers and castles. The artist says that the sandstone here is formed in upright columns, and as the chalk disappears from the interstices, the columns assume these delusive shapes, as shown in the picture. The distance given in the view is about one hundred and twenty-five miles, and through the transparent atmosphere peculiar to the region the course of the Colorado may be traced for many miles through the Grand Cañon, the sides of which are said to be six thousand feet in height.

The perspective of the picture is one of the most remarkable points in the work. The scene is drawn under a passing storm, the features of which add to the brilliancy of the picture. The work is strong in color, and every detail is worked up with the most conscientious care. The artist, to his credit be it said, has simply given us a view of the landscape as he saw it; he has copied a leaf from Nature's book."

15 May. From Newark, Moran writes William MacLeod, curator of the Corcoran, asking if he might arrange to show *Chasm of the Colorado*: "The picture is the proper companion of the Yellowstone Cañon and I hope Congress may be induced to look on it in that light, but as things look at present, its purchase by the Govt. seems extremely unlikely. It is universally conceded that it surpasses the Yellowstone picture, but of that you will soon have an opportunity of judging." (Letter 317, director's records, Corcoran)

20–25 May. Series of letters between Moran and MacLeod regarding possible exhibition of *Chasm of the Colorado* at the Corcoran. (Letters 318, 319, and letterpress volumes, director's records, Corcoran)

25 May. Letter to the editor of *NYT*: "There are some who find fault (as did your critic [see entry for cat. 47]) with Moran's painting of the 'Chasm of the Colorado,' on the ground that it does not impress the beholder with a sense of vastness commensurate with the actual size

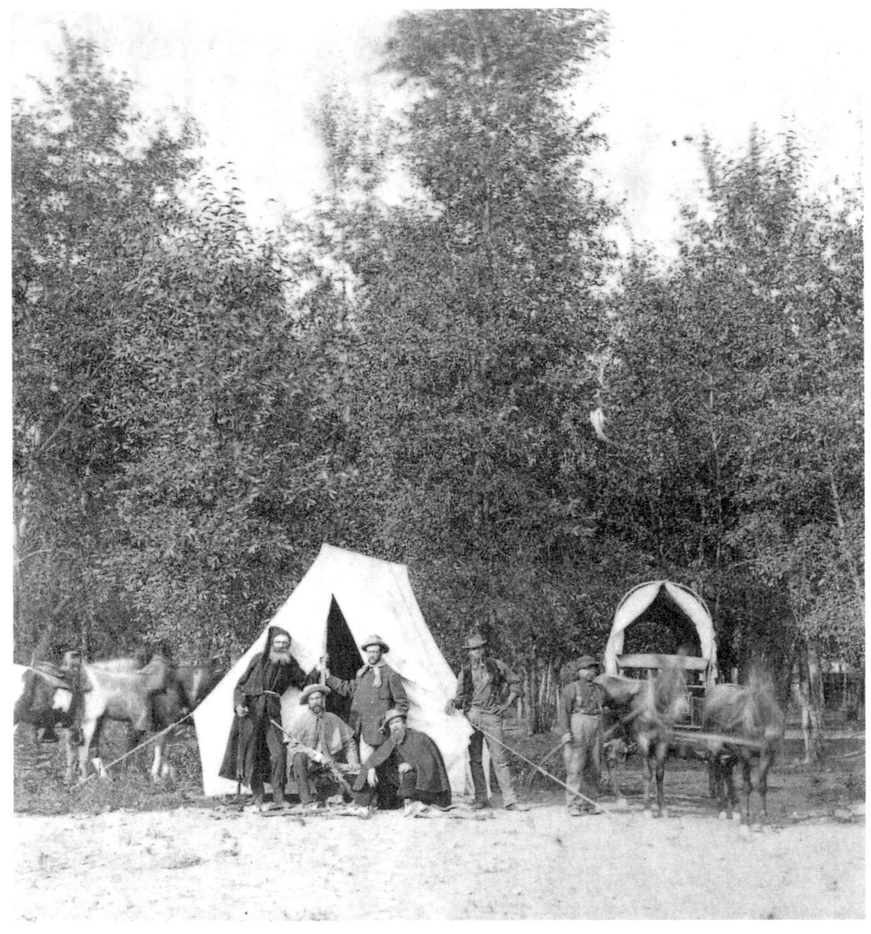

Members of expedition to Mountain of the Holy Cross, 1874, courtesy East Hampton Library.

and distances. I suppose it would have been easy for the artist to have thrown in a few pigmy human figures, in which case there would have been no difficulty (especially with the aid of a yard-stick) in judging the height of the rocks in the immense foreground from which the height of the distant peak could have been approximately estimated. But it seems to me that the absence of human figures attests the instinct of a genuine artist. The same painter has made use of a group of explorers, with their horses, in his splendid picture of 'The Yellowstone Cañon'; but in the present scene it would have been necessary to draw them much smaller. They would have presented an insignificant appearance and would, according to the opinion of many, have been out of keeping with the peculiar phase of nature exhibited.

But after all, figures or no figures, the impression of immensity should be given. That it is given by means of the shrubbery, and tree-growth in the foreground, and still more by the painter's masterly drawing and bold and skillful manipulation of light and shade, I think many hundreds will testify who have had the pleasure of seeing, at Goupil's, this most daring, able, and interesting rendering of a splendid and extraordinary scene."

4 June. Moran's *Chasm of the Colorado* is hung at the Corcoran. (Curatorial records, Corcoran)

8 June. *Evening Star* [DC]: "There is now in the Corcoran Art Gallery a new painting, by Mr. Thomas Moran. It is called the 'Chasm of the Colorado,' and is a view of a portion of the Grand Gorge of the Colorado river, which was first explored and mapped a few years since by Maj. J. W. Powell. The scene lies in northern Arizona, about four hundred miles south of Salt Lake City. The painting is of the same size as the Yellowstone picture at the Capitol, and it can be seen by all visitors to the Gallery, in the room east of the stairway, adjoining the main picture hall."

17 June. Bill passed by Congress appropriates funds "to enable the Joint Committee on the Library to purchase such works of art for ornamenting the Capitol as may be ordered and approved," enabling purchase of Moran's *Chasm of the Colorado.* (Statutes 1873/1875; U.S. House 1873/1874)

26 June. Moran's *Chasm of the Colorado* is removed from Corcoran Gallery. (Curatorial records, Corcoran)

3 July. Moran copyrights *Chasm of the Colorado.* (Copyright no. 8847 E, EHL)

14 July. *Evening Star* [DC]: "Congress, on the unanimous recommendation of the Joint Committee on the Library, purchased Moran's great painting, the 'Chasm of the Colorado.' By direction of the same committee the spacious hall on the second floor of the Capitol, and looking out upon the eastern portico of the Senate extension, has been set apart for its accommodation, together with the companion painting, the 'Grand Canon of the Yellowstone,' by the same artist, and now in the national statuary hall."

8 August. Moran joins group in Denver to travel via Fairplay, CO, to the Arkansas River, Tennessee Pass, and Eagle River to the Mountain of the Holy Cross. (*Denver Rocky Mt. News*, 1 Sept.)

9, 10 August. Sketches and dates *Camp of the Two Pines*; then *No. 2 Camp of the Evening Star, on the Platte* (recto), and *Pike's Peak from the Road to Fairplay* (verso) (JNEM).

10, 11 August. From Turkey Creek, CO, Moran writes his wife Mary about his departure from Denver. Traveling with him are J. S. Delano (son of the Secretary of the Interior), Col. W. L. Woods, James

Studio and home of Thomas Moran, Newark, New Jersey, courtesy East Hampton Library.

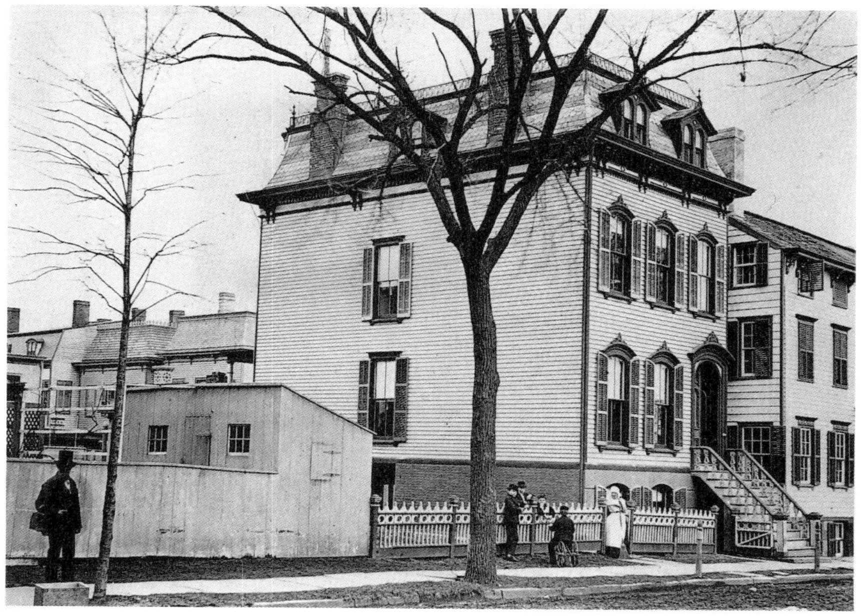

3 September. *Denver Rocky Mt. News*: "Mr. Thomas Moran ... left Denver Tuesday night for the east .... He will at once commence work on a painting of the Mount of the Holy Cross, and hopes to have it completed by January 1, 1875. Mr. Moran considers the two paintings alluded to [*Grand Canyon of the Yellowstone* and *Chasm of the Colorado*], and the one about to be begun, three of the grandest subjects on this continent, especially the latter."

8 September. *Newark Daily Advertiser*: "Mr. Thomas Moran, the artist who has produced some of the finest pictures which adorn our national capitol, has just returned from the Rocky Mountains, where he has been engaged in sketching for a new picture."

Stevenson [assistant to F. V. Hayden], a driver for the wagon, and a cook. The next day he writes Mary from the Platte River about his journey into the Colorado mountains. (Bassford and Fryxell 1967, 45–47)

12 August. Sketches and dates *Holy Cross Trip, Camp Vexation, S. Branch of the N. Platte* (JNEM).

13 August. From camp at South Park, Moran writes Mary that he is within three days of seeing the Mountain of the Holy Cross. (Bassford and Fryxell 1967, 49)

18, 20, 23, 26 August. Sketches and dates *Camp on the Upper Arkansas in Tennessee Pass*; then *Camp on Eagle River*; then *Delano Valley, Eagle River;* then *Upper Twin Lake* (JNEM; Gilcrease).

24 August. Moran to Mary, from camp on the Arkansas River: "Of all the hard climbing that I have experienced, this beat it. Almost perpendicular, covered with burnt & fallen timber, lying 3 or 4 deep. It was only by slow & persevering effort that the horses could get through & we had to walk a good part of the way. When we got to the top the view was perfectly magnificent. 2,000 feet below us lay the Moutonnee Valley with the Holy Cross Creek rushing through it & at the head of the valley the splendid peak of the Holy Cross, with the range continuing to the left of us .... In the Valley is one of the most picturesque waterfalls that I have ever seen. I shall use it in the foreground of the picture. We had a glorious campfire that night, and Jim says that in all his experience, he had never seen worse travelling .... We have had a most delightful, but hard trip & as we are now out of the woods, I consider it over. It will probably be the 5th of September before I reach home .... I have not done much sketching, but have done a good deal of looking." (Bassford and Fryxell 1967, 51–57)

30 August. Moran and party return to Denver. (*Denver Rocky Mt. News*, 1 Sept.)

September. *The Aldine* publishes "Storm in Utah" with illustration by Moran: "Both the artist and the engraver have succeeded in catching the spirit of nature in the remarkable picture representing Utah scenery. The rush of the water, the solidity of the rocks, the feeling of wind and strife of elements have been wonderfully depicted. As a specimen of fine and delicate engraving, equal to that of a steel-plate, nothing has ever been seen in *The Aldine* to surpass this."

November. Moran's *Cliffs of Green River*, in a gold frame, is listed as the most expensive "Aldine Art Union Prize, Series A" at $500. (*Aldine Art Union*, "Prospectus—1874–1875.")

18 November. *NY Post*: "Thomas Moran, the well-known painter of the 'Chasm of the Colorado' and 'The Grand Cañon of the Yellowstone,' both of which pictures were purchased by resolution of Congress and are now in the possession of the government at Washington, spent the summer on the western slope of the Rocky Mountains in sketching the impressive scenery of that wild and picturesque region. Mr. Moran returned to his studio in Newark early in October, and since that time he has been engaged upon several commissions .... Another interesting picture, which is also drawn from studies made last summer, gives a view of the famous 'Mountain of the Holy Cross.' As is known to many, this cross is formed by two ravines on the mountain-side crossing each other, both of which are filled snow. To the right of this great natural cross, and almost at its foot, there appears a great snowy chasm, which is in effect like a kneeling figure and lends a weird interest to the scene. Both pictures will be finished during the present month."

17 December. In response to request from editor of *American Cyclopedia*, Moran submits a biographical statement for publication. (Letter, LC mss div.)

19 December. Moran writes Powell from Newark to compliment him on his recent article in *Scribner's* and to say he has not yet finished the drawings Powell ordered "but will have them soon." (Powell IC, NA)

• 1875 •

25 January. *Newark Daily Advertiser*: "Moran, the artist, is engaged upon a painting of 'The Mountain of the Holy Cross,' to be chromoed."

30 January – 27 February. AWCS annual exhibition at NAD. Moran exhibits *On the Schuylkill* and *Near Hastings, England* (cat. nos. 371, 384). (*NY Post*, 1 and 26 Feb.)

5 March. Moran writes William Trost Richards advising him to ask Hayden for photographs of the Rocky Mountains and noting: "I have nearly finished my picture of the Mt. of the Holy Cross. It is 5 x 7 feet." (Fryxell, UW)

9 March. *Newark Daily Advertiser*: "Mr. Thomas Moran has nearly finished his picture of the 'Mountain of the Holy Cross,' which is said to be as well executed as his 'Falls of the Yellowstone' and the 'Grand Cañon of the Colorado.'"

5 April. *Newark Daily Advertiser* reports that Moran's new picture, *Mountain of the Holy Cross*, which had been on private view at his house, is on exhibition at Schaus' Gallery, NY.

6 April. *Boston Transcript* reports Moran's recent completion of *Mountain of the Holy Cross*: "Mr. Moran has given the marvelous effect of this strange freak of nature without making it too prominent."

8 April – 20 May. NAD annual exhibition. Moran exhibits *Overland Train, Green River, Utah*, and *Cupica Bay, Honduras* (cat. nos. 280, 459). (*Boston Transcript*, 2 Apr.)

9 April. *Boston Transcript* reviews April's *Aldine*: "The mountain scenery of Utah is represented with much force and grandeur in three large engravings on wood by Thomas Moran, that rank high as genuine works of art."

14 April. *NY Post* comments on *Mountain of the Holy Cross*: "The perspective effect is remarkably fine, and every detail of running water, crumbling rock and forest verdure is drawn and painted with the greatest care and a fidelity worthy of the highest praise. The painting is not so large as his 'Grand Chasm of the Yellow Stone' and its companion piece, which were purchased by order of Congress, but in its artistic qualities it shows a decided advance over those great works."

15 April. *The Independent* [NY]: "At Mr. Schaus's little gallery, there is an undoubted original by an American artist well worthy of special study. It is a view by Mr. Moran of one of the most remarkable objects in mountain scenery, being an accurate reproduction of the eminence among the Rocky Mountains called the Mountain of the Holy Cross. The cross at the summit of the mountain is formed by fissures in the rocks which are filled with perpetual snow, and the effect is most remarkable. The picture is a noble representation of wild mountain scenery, and the foreground is painted with great delicacy and beauty, giving the characteristic shrubs which grow in the locality with accuracy of form and color, or, at least, with an appearance of fidelity which only the visitor to the locality could question."

17 April. *NYT* reviews NAD exhibition: "'The Overland Train'... by Mr. Thomas Moran, gives a view in Utah, in which rocks and water are bright with all the prismatic colors. It is a picture that we cannot admire. If it be really an attempt to represent truthfully the local color of certain districts in Utah, then we think the attempt had better not been made. There are scenes that no artist can paint, and colors in nature that no artist can transfer to his canvas. We do not believe in Mr. Moran's Utah any more than we do in Mr. Bierstadt's California."

24 April. *NY Post* reviews NAD exhibition: "One of the best landscapes in the collection (on many accounts it seems to us the very best) is Thomas Moran's 'Green River in Utah.' This painting has more color in it than almost any one on exhibition."

24 April. *Appleton's*, 535: "[Moran's] painting of 'Green River,' in Utah, at the Academy, is in many important respects the finest landscape in that exhibition."

26 April. Moran to William MacLeod: "I expect to bring my new picture of 'The Mountain of the Holy Cross' to Washington about the middle of May." (Letter 579, director's records, Corcoran)

May. *Art Journal* reviews NAD exhibition: "Thomas Moran's 'Overland Train, Green River, Utah,' is chiefly remarkable as a study of the peculiar local colour of the region."

1 May. *Appleton's*, 568: "'The Overland Train, Green River, Utah,' by Thomas Moran, is in the front rank among the landscapes.... As a palette of color, this picture suggests the works of Samuel Coleman, but, in the Utah landscape, color and tone have a meaning and language of weather and climate, such as is seldom equaled; and the drawing, too, has a precision and force which, if the picture had no color at all, would still give it fullness and brilliancy. The variety of the cloud-forms, and their effects in the quiet river, make the spectator think of Turner, so changeful are they in kind and in theme; but it is Turner in his best days, not lurid, and with the lineaments of his landscape blurred and fantastic."

10 May. Moran writes Powell that *Mountain of the Holy Cross* "has been on exhibition for some time & has received the highest praise from the artists & the public with a fair share of newspaper laudation." (Powell IC, NA)

Exhibition announcement for *The Mountain of the Holy Cross,* courtesy Gilcrease Museum, Tulsa, Oklahoma.

Mr. Thomas Moran
respectfully announces that his New Picture,
"The Mountain of the Holy Cross,"
is now on Exhibition at the Gallery of
New York, April 8th, 1875. W. SCHAUS, 749 Broadway

12 May. Moran to MacLeod: "I will send the picture of 'The Mountain of the Holy Cross' to the Gallery so as to arrive on the 25th of this month. I had hoped to have sent the picture earlier but at the urgent request of a number of New Yorkers I have kept it on exhibition longer than I at first intended. It has been a decided great success in New York with the artists. All conceding to it the highest praise." (Letter 597, director's records, Corcoran)

22 May. *NY Tribune*: "The exhibition of Mr. Thomas Moran's picture, 'The Mountain of the Holy Cross,' which has been on view during the last three or four weeks at Schaus's Gallery ... will close on Monday next [24 May]. Owing perhaps to its striking subject this has been one of the artist's most popular pictures and everybody will regret its removal."

29 May. *Mountain of the Holy Cross* arrives in Washington for installation at the Corcoran. (Curatorial records, Corcoran)

10 June. Moran writes MacLeod with regret at not having seen him in Washington when *Mountain of the Holy Cross* was hung at the Corcoran and asking when the committee will meet to decide whether to purchase the painting. (Letter 621, director's records, Corcoran)

12 June. *NY Post* reports that Moran's *Overland Train, Green River, Utah,* sold at Schenck's Gallery for $645.

14 June. MacLeod to Moran: "After due examination of your picture of the 'Holy Cross' and deliberation upon your offer of it for sale, the Committee respectfully declined purchasing it." (Letterpress volumes, director's records, Corcoran)

July. Henry James in *The Galaxy*, 95, writes in regard to NAD exhibition, that American landscape painting is superior to figure painting and "some of the rocks were most delectable—those, for instance, of Mr. Thomas Moran, in his picture of certain geological eccentricities in Utah. The cliffs there, it appears, are orange and pink, emerald green and cerulean blue; they look at a distance as if, in emulation of the vulgar liberties taken with the exposed strata in the suburbs of New York, they had been densely covered with bill-posters of every colour of the rainbow. Mr. Moran's picture is, in the literal sense of the word, a brilliant production. We confess it gives a rather uncomfortable wrench to our prosy preconceptions of the conduct and complexion of rocks, even in their more fantastic moods; but we remember that all this is in Utah, and that Utah is terribly far away. We cannot help wishing that Mr. Moran would try his hand at something a little nearer home, so that we might have a chance to congratulate him, with a good conscience, not only upon his brilliancy, but upon his fidelity."

29 July. *Newark Daily Advertiser*: "Mr. Thomas Moran, the celebrated landscape painter, is spending the Summer with his family at Blairstown, Warren county." Later in the summer Moran visits Pikes County, PA, among other places. (Letters 637 and 651, director's records, Corcoran)

October. *Scribner's* publishes John Wesley Powell's "Overland Trip to the Grand Cañon" with illustrations by Moran.

19 October. *Boston Transcript*: "Thomas Moran's large and beautiful picture of 'The Mountain of the Holy Cross' is expected in Boston early in November, when it will be placed ... in the gallery of L. A. Elliot."

25 October. *Boston Transcript*: "Thomas Moran's large picture [*Mountain of the Holy Cross*] will shortly be placed on exhibition in the gallery of L. A. Elliot & Co. It has for several months formed one of the chief attractions of the Corcoran Art Gallery in Washington."

26 October. *Mountain of the Holy Cross* leaves Washington for Boston. (Curatorial records, Corcoran)

29 October. *NY Post*: "Thomas Moran's picture of 'The Mountain of the Holy Cross' is to be placed on exhibition in Boston early next month."

1 December. *Boston Transcript*, prompted by interest in *Mountain of the Holy Cross*, publishes perhaps the first detailed biographical sketch of Moran.

6 December. *NY Post*: "A large and valuable collection of American and European oil paintings owned by Mr. Louis Prang, of Boston, was opened for exhibition at the Leavitt Art Rooms... yesterday morning. Many of the subjects of these paintings have been published under the name of 'Prang's Chromos,' and are well known to the public, but the originals have never before been offered for sale, as they are now." Moran is one of the artists whose work is included.

7 December. *Newark Daily Advertiser*: "The Centennial Commission has issued a list... of the applications of New Jersey exhibitors for... the Centennial Exhibition.... It may be said to the credit of New Jersey that few of them are frivolous or unworthy....those from Essex county [include]:...Thomas Moran, Oil Paintings."

7 December. *Boston Transcript*: "Three more paintings by Thomas Moran have been added to the exhibition of his noble work, 'The Mountain of the Holy Cross,' at Eliot's gallery. One is a very ambitious and largely successful essay at the Turneresque, 'Azure Cliffs of Green River at Sunrise.' The composition—a wood-crowned crag jutting forth in soft but dense shadow... with an obelisk-like peak rearing itself to immense heights, beside the track of the vertical flood of yellow light striking upwards from the rolling vapors of sunrise—is very powerful, and the brave color very successful, while the atmospheric effect is less so. A wide landscape of Utah mountain ranges and intervales, called 'The Temples of the Rio Virgen,' bathed in warm and rich colors and a hot, hazy summer atmosphere, is also a very handsome picture."

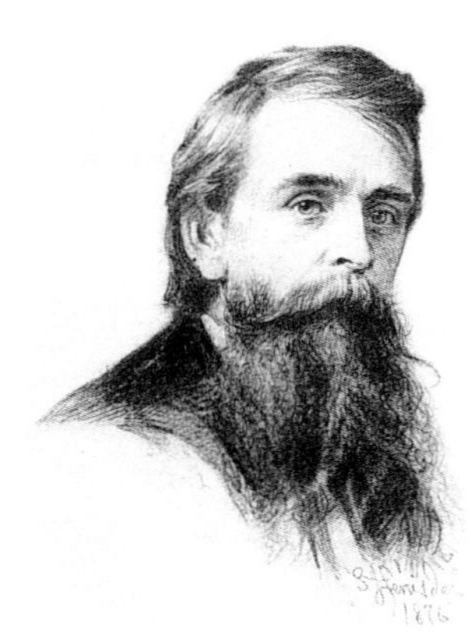

***Thomas Moran*, portrait drawing by Stephen J. Ferris, 1876, courtesy Smithsonian Institution.**

21 December. *Boston Transcript*: "The exhibition of Thomas Moran's large and beautiful picture of 'The Mountain of the Holy Cross,' at the gallery of L. A. Elliot & Co., will close on [31 Dec.]. It will then be sent to St. Louis for exhibition."

• 1876 •

L. Prang issues *Yellowstone National Park, and the Mountain Regions of Portions of Idaho, Nevada, Colorado, and Utah*, described by Ferdinand V. Hayden and illustrated with 15 chromolithographs based on watercolors by Moran. (See Appendix 1)

At Rochester Academy of Art, Moran exhibits *Dreamland* and *Valley of the Rio Virgin, S. Utah* (nos. 165, 166); at Chicago Academy of Design, he exhibits *Ride for Life: Plains of the Humboldt* (no. 158). (GA ledger)

January. *The Aldine* publishes "Glories of Southern Utah" with prints of Moran's *Azure Cliffs of Green River* and *Elfins' Water Pocket* and says of *Rock Rover's Land*: "In many regards this picture has never been excelled by any artist... it adds materially to the reputation of Mr. Moran as one of the high priests of continental scenery."

26 January. *Newark Daily Advertiser*: "Mr. Thomas Moran, the landscape painter, accompanied by his wife and three children, has left Newark for a long visit to Philadelphia."

31 January–26 February. AWCS annual exhibition at NAD. Moran exhibits *Solitude* (no. 122). (*NY Post*, 1 Feb.)

16 February. *St. Louis Republican*: "'Mountain of the Holy Cross,' now on exhibition at Pettes & Leathe's. 'It is, without question, the greatest painting produced so far by an American artist' (*New York Herald*)."

March. *The Aldine*, 91–92, reviews AWCS exhibition, noting that after only a few years American watercolor painting has become equal in quality to that of the old world and adding: "Thos. Moran conveys the feeling of his subject very forcibly as well as carefully, in 'Solitude.'"

4 April. House of Representatives debates whether or not to lend two Moran paintings in the Capitol to the Centennial Exhibition; vote is nay. (*Congressional record*, 44th Cong., 1st sess., 4:2185.)

5 April. *Newark Daily Advertiser*: "The House of Representatives yesterday defeated a joint resolution authorizing the removal of Moran's paintings of the Yellowstone and Colorado cañons to the Centennial. The argument in opposition was that the Capitol should not be denuded of its decorations. Mr. [Fernando] Wood and Mr. [Samuel Sullivan] Cox both opposed the resolution, Mr. Wood claiming that the Centennial was a private affair. The Government will send big guns, models of ships, collections of minerals, Indian blankets and implements, curiosi-

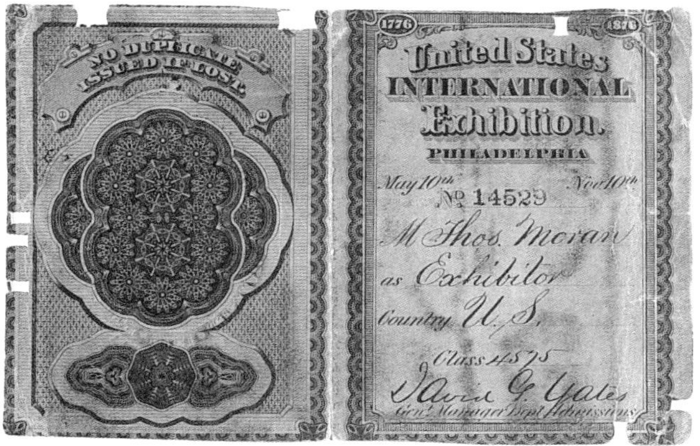

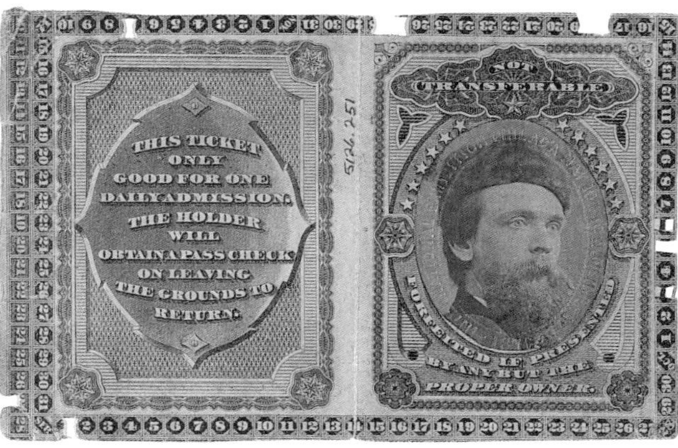

Moran's exhibitor's pass for the Centennial Exposition, Philadelphia (recto and verso), 1876, courtesy Gilcrease Archive.

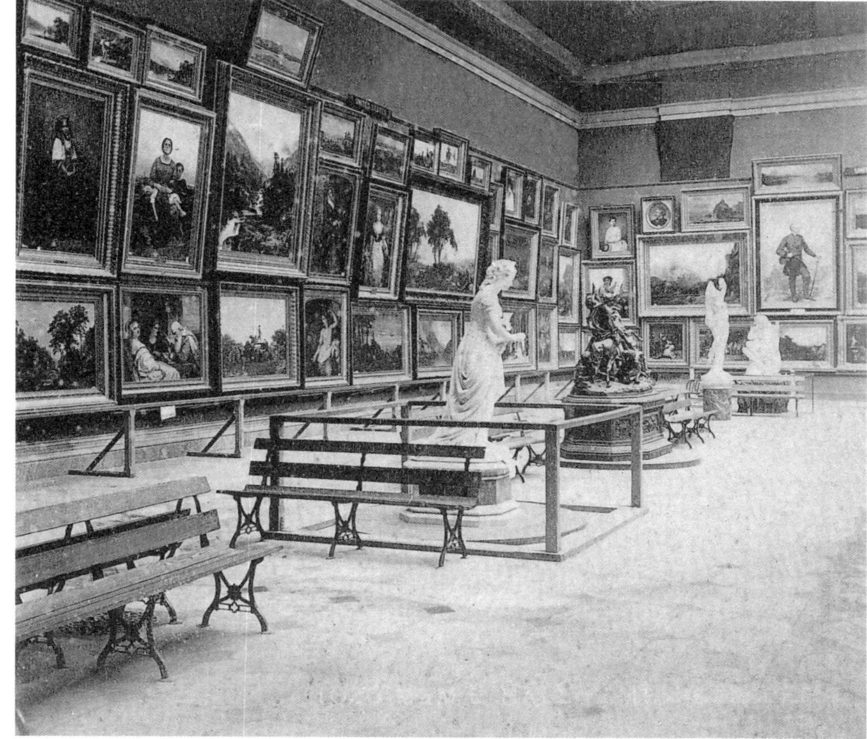

Interior of the Centennial Exposition art gallery, displaying Moran's *Mountain of the Holy Cross* (center left), stereograph, Private Collection.

ties and the like, at a cost of $2,000,000, but will not have a picture in the gallery of arts."

24 April–5 June. PAFA annual exhibition. Moran exhibits *Ride for Life* (no. 50), owned by J. Snedecor. (Falk 1989, 33, 342)

10 May–10 November. Centennial Exhibition in Philadelphia. Moran is awarded both a medal and a diploma, exhibiting *Mountain of the Holy Cross*; *"Fiercely the red sun descending..."*; *Valley of the Rio Virgin, Utah*; *Dream of the Orient* (nos. 196, 1039, 1047, 1049), six drawings based on Longfellow's *Hiawatha*, and, with AWCS of NY, *Hot Springs of the Yellowstone, Wyoming Territory* (no. 376). Edward, Peter, and John Moran also exhibit. Thomas Moran's exhibitor's pass, personalized with his photograph, shows that he visited the exhibit many times. (Ingram 1876, 73; *International Exhibition* 1876; exhibitor's pass, GA)

29 May. Moran writes Powell hoping to meet soon in Philadelphia and asking whether Powell plans to go to the Grand Canyon this summer: "If you can make me one of your corps I think I would go too.... I am just finishing a pretty large picture of a side gulch in the Grand Canon, a great amphitheatre with fall that I think will please you. The subject is based on the illustration opposite page 64 in your report." (Powell IC, NA)

5 June. Moran writes Henry Wadsworth Longfellow asking for the opportunity to show him his proposed illustrations for *Hiawatha*. (Letter, Houghton Library, Harvard University)

July. Women's Centennial Committee of Wisconsin commissions Moran to paint two pictures. Thomas and Mary Moran spend several days in Madison sketching: "Painted two views of the Lakes at Madison, Wisconsin, 30" x 45", for $1000 each. They were for a nucleus at the University of Wisconsin and Mrs. [Alexander] Mitchell paid one thousand and Ole Bull gave a concert to pay for the other." *Sunset on Lake Mendota* and *Sunrise on Lake Monona* were late additions to the Centennial Exhibition, hung in Memorial Hall to represent the state of Wisconsin. Both were destroyed in 1884 in a fire at the university. Mrs. Mitchell became an important patron for Moran. (GA ledger; Madison newspaper clipping, 7 Dec., EHL scrapbook; Taylor 1936, 90)

27 July. Moran sketches and dates *First Lake, Madison, Wisconsin*. Also dated 1876 are sketches *Madison, Wisconsin*, and *Third Lake, Madison, Wisconsin* (Gilcrease).

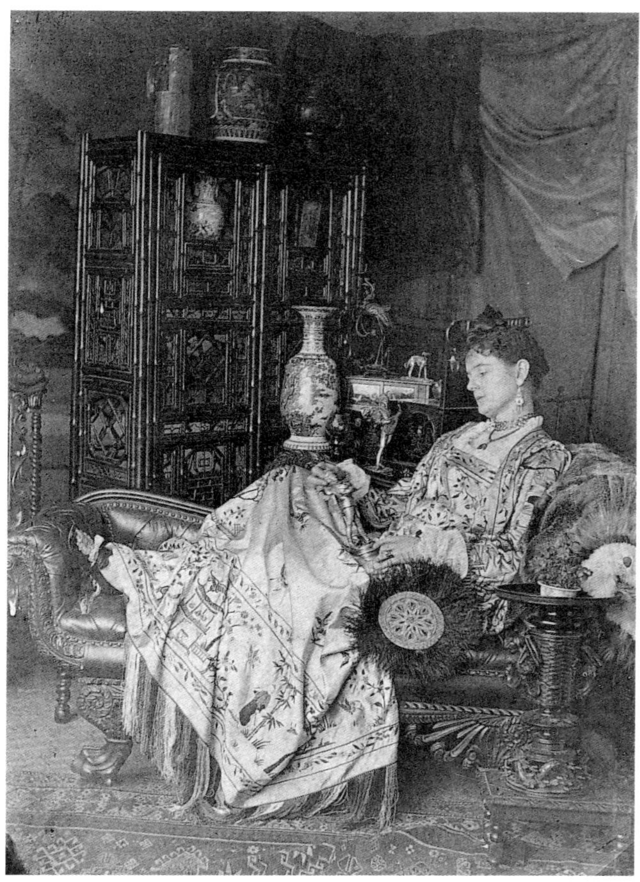

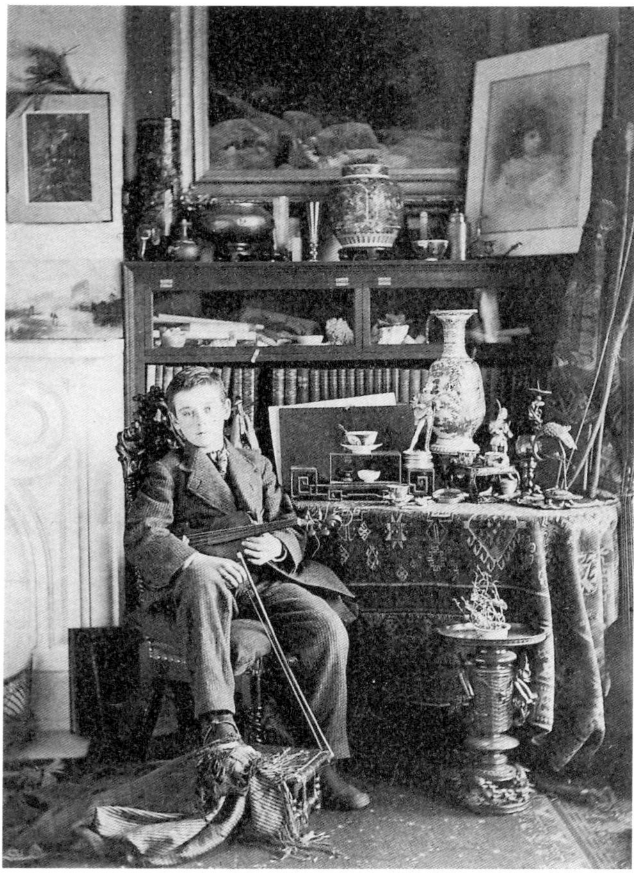

Mary Nimmo Moran in costume in Moran's Newark studio, 1876, courtesy East Hampton Library.

Paul Nimmo Moran, 1876, courtesy East Hampton Library.

3 August. From Madison, Mrs. Sarah F. Dean to her brother, Lucius Fairchild: "I had a lovely time with Thomas Moran the artist and his wife, who is something of an artist too. They were consigned to me by Mrs. Mitchell and I drove or sailed with them all the time they were here." (Kellogg 1926, 13n)

16 August. *Newark Daily Advertiser*: "Mr. T. Moran, whose fame as a landscape painter is already national, has received a munificent order from [Mrs. Mitchell], the subject to be chosen from sketches made at a recent visit to the four lakes of Wisconsin."

18 August. *NY Post*: "Thomas Moran, who went to Colorado last June to paint two large pictures of the mountain scenery, for which he had received commissions, has begun his homeward journey, and is passing a few weeks in Wisconsin."

20 September. *NY Post* reports opening of Chicago Interstate Industrial Exposition. Moran exhibits *Azure Cliffs of Green River* (no. 161). (GA ledger)

28 September. *Newark Daily Advertiser* and *Boston Transcript* announce Moran's Centennial award for excellence in landscape painting for *Mountain of the Holy Cross*. Peter and Edward Moran also receive awards. (Walker 1877, 89; *Phila. Evening Bulletin*, 10 Nov. 1914)

4 December. *Newark Daily Advertiser*: "During the present week an Art Exhibition will be opened at Upper Library Hall. . . . Among the Newark artists represented will be Thomas Moran."

6 December. *Boston Transcript*: "Mr. Thomas Moran has nearly completed his series of illustrations in India ink of Longfellow's 'Hiawatha,' which are being etched by his brother Peter, who, by the way, was the only etcher awarded a medal at the Centennial."

11 December. *Newark Daily Advertiser*: "The popular interest which has been recently exhibited in works of art in this city is altogether unprecedented. It is usually conceded that in a manufacturing town the cultivation of refined taste is neglected for the acquirement of useful knowledge and the accumulation of wealth. But ever since the advent here of Thomas Moran, the distinguished landscape painter, the people of Newark have shown great interest in the exhibition of pictures whenever really meritorious works of art have been placed on view. This fact has induced some liberal spirited citizens to collect a gallery of paintings, the like of which has never been seen outside of the largest cities in this country. The pictures are by the most distinguished American artists, and have nearly all been loaned for the occasion by the artists themselves, who all take a

deep interest in extending the love of art throughout the community. In this collection Bierstadt will be represented by two important pictures, Eastman Johnson will have three of his best works, Ed. Moran will send two grand marine views, and McEntee, Gifford, Church, DeHaas, David Johnson, Story, Inness, Miss Odenheimer, and, in fact, all the leading artists, will be represented by works upon which they rely for their reputation. T. Moran will exhibit his charming view of the Plains of the Rio Virgin, which was awarded a medal at the Centennial Exhibition. A striking feature of the collection will be a facsimilie [painted by Thomas Moran] of one of J. M.W. Turner's most famous pictures, 'Ulysses deriding Polephemus' [*sic*], which was purchased by the British Government for $60,000. To-night there will be a private view of the collection, at Upper Library Hall, and to-morrow the gallery will be open to the general public."

12 December. *Newark Daily Advertiser*: "Yesterday evening there was opened in Upper Library Hall probably the most meritorious exhibition of paintings ever held in this city.... The copy of one of Turner's pictures...was painted by Moran, and it is a relief to turn to the works in his own style, which are as beautiful as Turner is homely. 'Rock River Land' is one, and it is a noble picture, to which we shall do justice hereafter. Another is 'The Azure Cliffs of Green River,' which we must also defer."

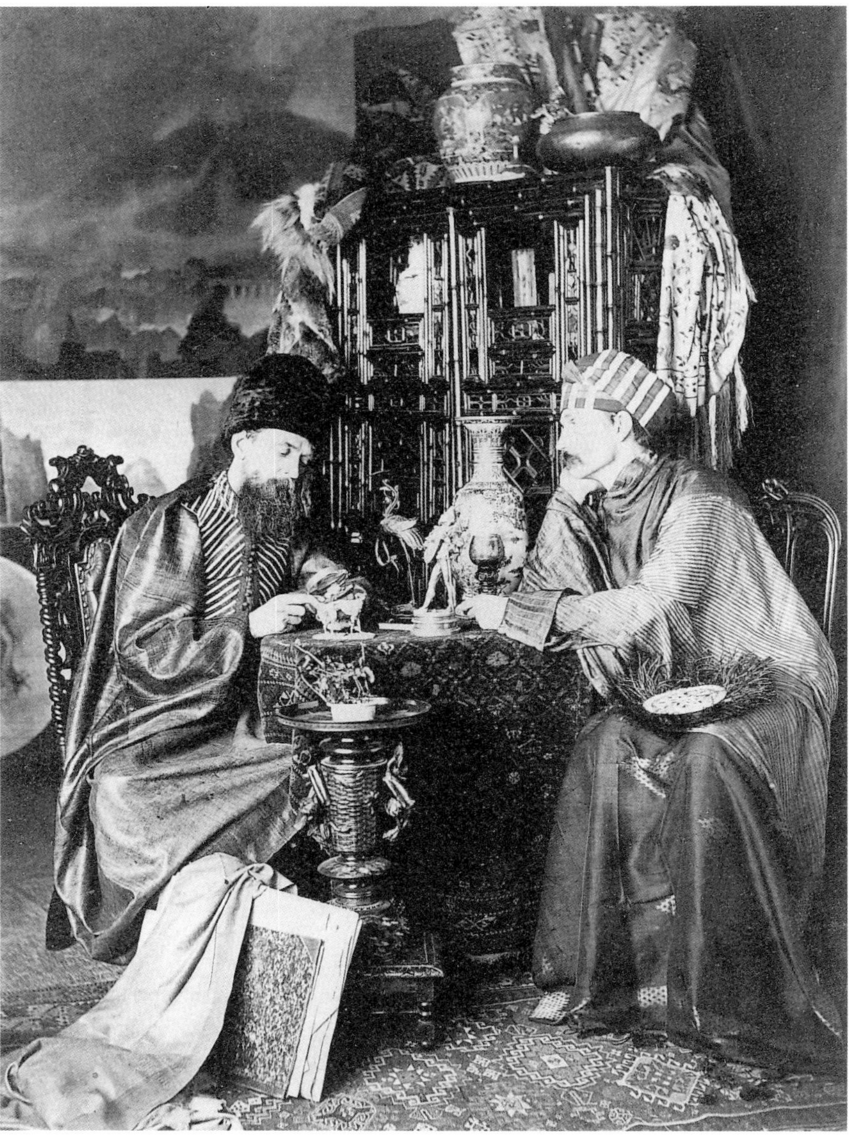

Thomas Moran and Newark artist John Bolles in costume in Moran's studio, 1876, courtesy East Hampton Library.

20 December. *Newark Daily Advertiser*: "The art reception, given by the Essex Club at their elegant mansion on Park place, was the paramount social event last evening.... The spacious apartments on the second floor were transformed into a series of picture galleries, the walls of which were covered with examples of foreign and domestic art, the owners of which had generously contributed them for the occasion.... The rooms were radiant with lights from endless rows of gas jets effectively distributed under the supervision of Mr. T. Moran."

27 December. From Newark, Moran writes Prang & Co., having received a copy of the Yellowstone portfolio: "a most sumptuous & magnificent work." (Moran archive, NGA; see Appendix 1)

28 December. *Newark Daily Advertiser*: "During yesterday and last night there was a perfect rush of visitors at Upper Library Hall to see the excellent display of pictures which has been there for the past two weeks. As the time draws near for the close of the exhibition public interest increases, and a very earnest general request has been made that it be continued for a short time longer. In response to this demand the managers have decided to allow the pictures to remain on view one night longer, but as they have to be returned to their owners on Saturday, tonight and to-morrow will be positively the last opportunity to see them.

Last evening a new picture was added to the collection, and has attracted universal admiration. It is a small but exquisitely painted view of the Golden Cliffs of Green River, in Wyoming Territory, by Thomas Moran. The artist has chosen one of the glowing sunset effects to which the peaks are indebted for their name. Those who know Moran only through his larger and more ambitious pictures are naturally surprised that the same hand that displayed on canvas the grandeur of the Canon of the Yellowstone and the Chasm of the Colorado would have the delicate touch necessary to the production of the little gem now on exhibition in the Loan collection. There are many, however, who infinitely prefer his smaller works to greater achievements, as the delicate little canvases of Meissonier may be preferred to the grander paintings of Horace Vernet."

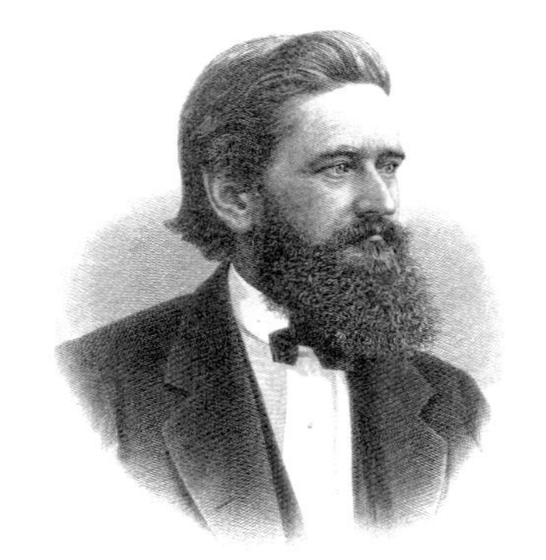

Louis Prang, courtesy National Museum of American History, Smithsonian Institution, Graphic Arts Collection.

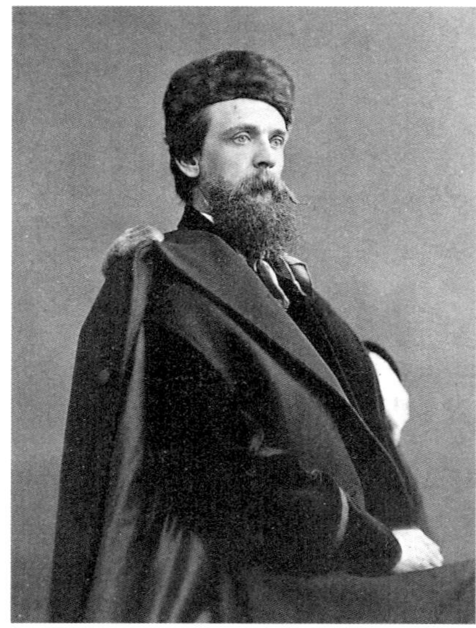

Thomas Moran, 1877, courtesy East Hampton Library.

• 1877 •

February. *Scribner's* publishes Edward Seymour's "Trout Fishing in Rangeley Lakes" with illustrations by Moran.

11 February. *NYT* lists Thomas and Mary Moran traveling on steamship *San Jacinto* from New York to Savannah, en route to Fort George Island, FL (at the mouth of the St. Johns River 25 miles from Jacksonville). Moran sketches extensively around Fort George and Lake Isabel, later producing five illustrations for September *Scribner's* article "Island of the Sea." (Morand 1996, 44–46)

15 February. *The Nation* reviews Prang's Yellowstone portfolio: "There can be no doubt that this work of Mr. Moran's was worth doing, and worth doing so well; and it is especially to be commended that Mr. Prang was willing to undertake so costly an enterprise.... Concerning Mr. Moran's artistic qualifications, we can cheerfully say that we think he is at his best when working on paper instead of on canvas. The Yellowstone studies present a series of color-effects taken from regions confessedly out of the plane of common human experience, and accordingly we do not pretend to judge them; we only wonder how scenes described in the text as ideally glorious should generally look crude and shocking in the water-colors; and again, we cannot but be a little surprised to find the bold, not to say violent, scale of color used for the topographic curiosities of the Yellowstone adopted afterwards, with not much chastisement, for subjects like the mountain of the Holy Cross and other scenes more or less out of fairyland. We humbly confess, however, that the only way to judge these views perfectly would be to get a camping outfit, go into the West, and successively put a mule at every one of the summits, passes, and natural belvederes from which the startling results we see were obtained.... The boldness and facility of the drawing are really impressive. The artist of an exploring party, it is evident, cannot dawdle over his task; when he comes home he must do one of two things; he must work up photographs—a process which inevitably produces dead, coaly-looking pictures—or he must give broad, spirited results, with his sketches for the base. The latter process is the best, and we must not complain too much of the perpetual Turner sky and Calame pine-trees in works done under such difficulty and with so much enterprise. On the whole, the untravelled world is under vast obligations for these vivid reports of regions we shall not all live to see in any other form."

22 February. Moran sketches and dates *St. Augustine* (Gilcrease).

March. *American Journal of Science and Arts*, 229–230, reviews Prang's Yellowstone portfolio: "This volume of colored sketches... is magnificent in scale and beautiful in execution. Mr. Moran is well known for his fine landscapes; and it is fortunate that such a painter has been over the wonderful Yellowstone region with his pencil. The colors of the landscapes will be thought too brilliant by those who have not visited the region, and perhaps in one or two cases the artist has allowed his feelings in that exhilarating atmosphere to influence in some degree his brush. But, in other cases, that for example of the scenery along the Cañon of the Yellowstone, as we understand from one who has visited the region, the colors even fall short of the reality."

March. In Florida, Moran sketches and dates *Ghost House*; two works inscribed *Fort George Island*; and *From Point Isabel, Fort George Island* (Gilcrease; MFA Boston).

1, 5 March. Sketches and dates *Fort George Island, Florida*; *From Shell Hummocks, Fort George Island*; and three works inscribed *Fort George Island*; then *Palmetto Trees at Lake Isabel, Fort George Island, Florida*; two inscribed *Lake Isabel, Fort George Island, Florida*; and three inscribed *Fort George Island* (Gilcrease; EHL; MFA Boston).

9 March. *Newark Daily Advertiser* reviews Prang's Yellowstone portfolio: "It is a genuine triumph of American graphic art.... The coloring is perfect and the perspective admirably maintained."

20 March. *Boston Transcript* quotes the *Boston Evening Gazette*: "Mr. Thomas Moran, the painter of Yellowstone fame, has just returned from Florida, where he and his wife have been visiting Mrs. Alexander Mitchell, a wealthy patron of art. Mr. Moran has brought back a portfolio full of sketches of Southern scenery, which is as different from the brilliant Yellowstone as possible. While South, he visited Mrs. Harriet Beecher Stowe, at her orange grove, and hung from moonlit balconies in old St. Augustine, listening to the music of guitars and castanets. If he puts all he saw on canvas, he will have some beautiful pictures."

3 April–2 June. NAD annual exhibition. Moran exhibits *On the Border of the Forest*; *Cliffs of the Upper Colorado*; *Near Waverly Park—N.J.*; *Cloudy Day*; and *Arkansas Divide, Rocky Mountains* (nos. 39, 112, 253, 294, 366). Mary Nimmo Moran exhibits for the first time, with one work. (*NY Post*, 9 Jan.; Naylor 1973, 653, 656)

17 April. *Newark Daily Advertiser* reviews NAD exhibition: "[Moran] surprises his friends by showing a wonderful versatility in his picture called 'On the Edge of the Forest,' painted in such cool grays and browns, and so entirely different from what the public has seen in his Yellowstone series that one can scarcely recognize his work. In this trying light it appears to lack warmth in the green of the foreground and the grays of the sky and the far off horizon. But for vigor, firmness, and decision of handling, as well as composition and conception, it is not excelled in the whole exhibition. Who among our artists can paint rocks like him? The delicate crisp touch of his brush shows a facility and perfection that is not excelled anywhere."

22 April–4 June. PAFA annual exhibition. Moran exhibits *Sunset: Castle Cliff, Colorado*, and *Golden Cliffs on Green River* (nos. 229, 234), both owned by D. P. Secor. (Falk 1989, 33, 342)

28 April. *NY Post* reviews NAD exhibition: "Mr. Thomas Moran's landscapes are five in number; but, if we except the bright little 'Rocky Mountains'... with its real snow and its sense of the out-doors, one of them tells the story of all, and that one is the 'Near Waverly Park.'... It is as spacious and as breezy as a Lambinet, and at the same time finely mysterious. The materials of the scene are very simple—a bare heath, a few ugly trees, a country road, common enough clouds; not much more than John Crome used to use in producing his best effects. There is no attempt at pictorial deception, nor any slurring or muddling of details. Comparing it with Mr. Miller's small landscape... the details seem to be affectionately cherished; comparing it with Mr. W. T. Richards's landscape... they seem to be cordially despised; comparing it with the artist's other landscapes... they seem to be moderately well respected. Take your position fifteen feet away from the little picture, and there is something about its openness, and atmospheric rotundity, and amplitude and clearness which makes one think of Cicery. There is not a painting in the exhibition that excels in these qualities; and it is all the more pleasant to say so because Mr. Moran this year has climbed into the company of the most growing American artists. He has excelled himself superbly."

10 and 15 May. First *NY Post* then *Boston Transcript* publish articles criticizing NAD's process of electing Academicians and Associates: "Thomas Moran, who enjoys a national reputation, is also among the rejected."

17 May. *Boston Transcript*: "Edward Moran has put on exhibition at the Kurtz Gallery, New York, preliminary to his departure for Europe, about 120 of his paintings and sketches, with a view to their public sale."

18 May. *Boston Transcript*: "Mr. Thomas Moran of New York has sent to Williams & Everett a fine work which he entitles 'A Dream of the Orient,' a gorgeous picture not unlike some of Turner's pictures of Italy. On the shore rise splendid palaces, and before these float a regal fleet decorated with painted sails and brilliant hangings. A glowing sunlight floods the whole picture. Through study of the works of the great English painter, Mr. Moran has no doubt become familiar with his methods. The present picture, though original in subject, is treated in such a way as to call to mind effects of light and color for which Turner was famous, showing that contact with his work has influenced very largely the thought and purpose of our artists."

27 August. *Newark Daily Advertiser*: "Thomas Moran and Mrs. Moran are spending a few weeks in Wisconsin, and will return early in September."

29 October. American Art Association [later SAA] founded at meeting in the home of Richard Watson Gilder and Helena de Kay Gilder, in protest of practices of NAD. Moran is among founding members. (*Art Journal* [Mar. 1878], 94; *NY Post*, 29 and 30 Oct.; Lansdale 1911, 725)

6 December. *Newark Daily Advertiser* announces opening of 2nd annual loan exhibition of American art at Upper Library Hall, Newark. Moran exhibits *Cloudy Day* (no. 70).

27 December. *Boston Transcript* quotes *NY Tribune* concerning art matters in New York: "Not the least interesting of the coming displays will be that of the American Art Association in March and April.... there is work and earnestness of purpose in the men connected with the movement, and their exhibition will be a beautiful affair and an event in the art history of the United States. At present there are less than twenty people in the association, namely, Walter Shirlaw, the president of it; Mr. St. Gaudens, the vice president; Wyatt Easton, the secretary; Louis Tiffany, treasurer; and Messrs. Dielman, Coleman, Swain Gifford, Homer Martin, Sartain, LaFarge, Thomas Moran, Lathrop, Julian Wier, and Mrs. Gilder, members, with perhaps three or four others."

• 1878 •

Moran records: "During the past seven years (1878) I have made about 400 or 500 illustrations on wood nearly all done at night." (EHL)

5 January. *Evening Star* [DC]: "Mr. Thomas Moran, with whose fine paintings and attractive book illustrations the people of Washington are familiar, is in the city for a prolonged visit. We understand he will have some of his lately finished pictures on view shortly, and it is not unlikely that he may open a studio here at no distant day."

11 January. William MacLeod notes: "Maj. Powell & Mr Moran artist called. The latter advised me to apply poppy oil to Des Goffes & the 'Weeper' & clean the 'Monk'. Maj. Powell thinks Bierstadt's Mt. Corcoran not truthful in form of the mountain—too much of a precipice. Mr Moran thinks it the best Bierstadt we could buy." (Curator's journal, director's records, Corcoran)

26 January. *Evening Star* [DC]: "The reception of the Washington Art Club on Tuesday evening was pronounced a great success, as well in the display of pictures on the walls as in the large assemblage of appreciative people gathered together to enjoy it.... with the exception of some excellent and characteristic examples contributed by Miss Searle, of Dusseldorf, and by Mr. Thomas Moran and Mr. F. Waller, of New York, the exhibition was a purely local one.... Washington seems to have been during the week quite a gathering point for artists from other places. Among those who were here—some of them being still in the city—may be named... Messrs. Bierstadt, Moran and Waller, painters."

4 February–3 March. AWCS annual exhibition at NAD. Moran exhibits woodcut and original engraved by F. S. King for Scribner & Co. (cat. no. 564). (*Evening Star* [DC], 5 Jan.)

23 February. *Evening Star* [DC]: "Not a little feeling is entertained in art circles at the manner in which the rule of Congress prohibiting the exhibition of private works of art in the Capitol building is violated or ignored by somebody assuming to have authority in the premises. In spite of this very proper provision, one large picture, the property of the artist who painted it [Albert Bierstadt], has been given a conspicuous place in the House side for more than two years past, yet when another artist of acknowledged ability and reputation several weeks ago asked for a similar opportunity to exhibit for a period of only thirty days an original painting illustrating an interesting episode in early American history, his request was quietly 'laid on the table,' and remains up to this time, so far as can be learned, without any action,—the other picture meantime still holding its position. A proceeding which smacks so much of favoritism as this is alike unfair to artists and discreditable to those guilty of such discriminations. All applicants of equal or nearly equal merit ought to be put upon the same footing in regard to facilities for exhibiting their works, or, still better, the wholesome prohibitory rule should be rigidly enforced in all cases. A body like Congress can afford to be just, between man and man, even if it doesn't know much about art."

March. John Moran in *Art Journal* discusses purpose of SAA and notes that the new organization of artists will hold its first annual exhibition in the Kurtz Gallery, NY.

6–29 March. First SAA exhibition at Kurtz Gallery. Moran exhibits *Kanab Canon, S. Utah*; *Autumn Afternoon*; *Fort George Island, Florida*; and *Twilight*. (*Boston Transcript*, 6 Mar.; *NYT*, 1 Apr.; *Phila. Telegraph*, 13 Mar.)

13 March. *Phila. Telegraph* reviews SAA exhibition: "Mr. Thomas Moran—who once was a Philadelphian, but who for many years past has had his headquarters in New York—has four pictures, one—'Kanab Cañon, in Southern Utah'—in the old Moranish manner with which all good Philadelphians are, or ought to be, familiar. The others—entitled, respectively, 'An Autumn Afternoon'; 'Fort George Island, Florida'; and 'Twilight'—are not in Mr. Moran's accustomed style, and they indicate that the artist has been giving discriminating study of late to the works of some of the best French landscapists. Be that as it may, they are good pictures, worth looking at and worth the buying of any one having a large store of the current money of the nation to draw upon."

16 March. *Evening Star* [DC]: "The Society of American Artists have decided to open their annual exhibition rooms free to the public on Sunday afternoons. This step is a wide departure from the rule of the more conservative Academy of Design, and one which will probably shock the sensibilities of not a few staid New Yorkers, but it will certainly draw the great heart of the people closer to the new organization, which aims to be the exponent in this country of liberal and progressive art."

17 March. *NYT* reviews SAA exhibition: "La Farge is here, Whistler, Homer Martin, and William Hunt, R. Swain Gifford, Wyant, and Thomas Moran... one of the best known favorites of the older exhibitions. In him the breath of progress has stirred to curious results. He seems to be striving after the methods of Diaz.... 'Fort George Island, Florida,' has external resemblances to the work of that painter, and so has... 'An Autumn Afternoon.' In his old style—what we may dub his 'Yellowstone style'—is... 'Kanab Cañon, Southern Utah,' but... 'Twilight,' is Diaz again. Evidently, Mr. Moran is anxious to hit on some popular vein."

April. *Art Journal*, 126, reviews SAA exhibition: "Thomas Moran has made some strong and effective imitations of Diaz or Rousseau."

April. "A New Departure in American Art," *Harper's Monthly*, mentions Moran as being a member, by election, of the SAA.

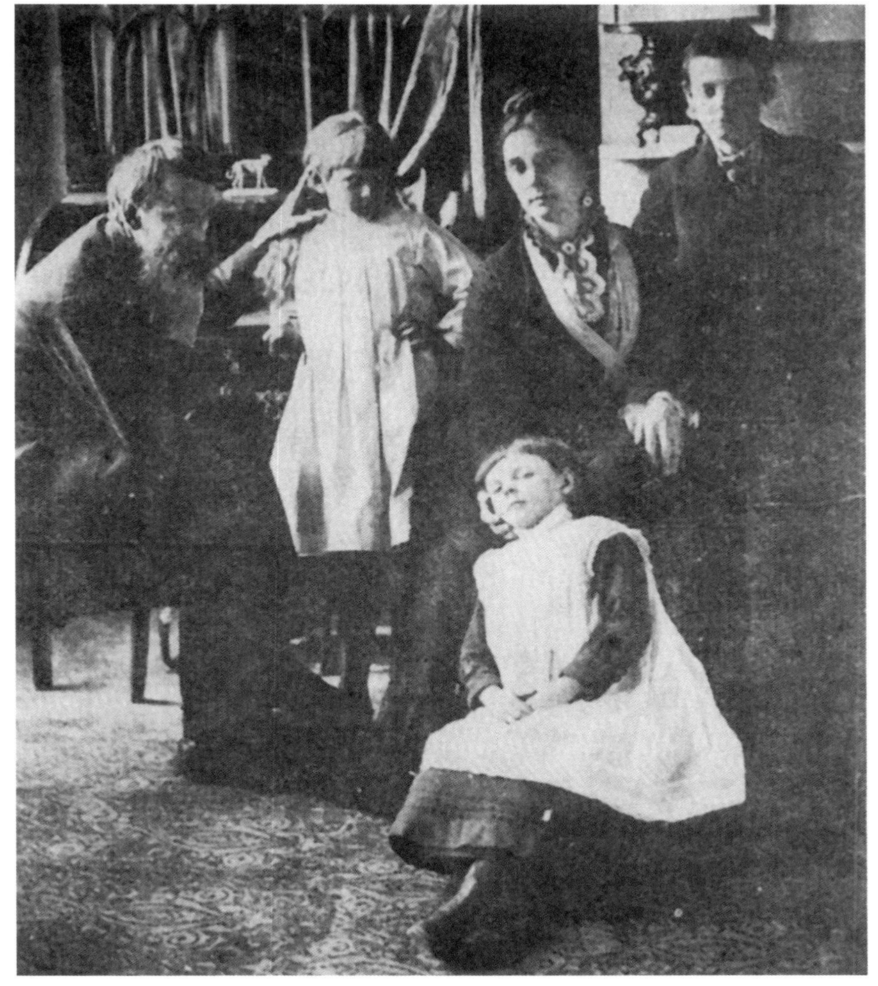

Moran family at Newark, 1878, photograph published in the *East-Hampton Star*, 7 January 1887, courtesy Miss Dorothy King and *East-Hampton Star*.

2 April–1 June. NAD annual exhibition. Moran exhibits *Summer Shower*; *Watering Place*; and *Dream of the Orient* (nos. 157, 698, 716). (*Evening Star* [DC], 30 Mar.; Naylor 1973, 653)

10 April. *NYT* reviews NAD exhibition: "Here is Mr. Thomas Moran, who is frankly Turneresque, because he admires Turner and finds that the public likes his interpretations of that eccentric genius.... 'A Dream of the Orient'... is not so bad a dream, as dreams go. This will not please those who have got to like the twang of Turner, but how few, comparatively, have seen Turner's pictures, and how few of those who have seen them learn to appreciate them?... 'A Summer Shower'... in which the styles of Diaz and Turner are by no means disagreeably blended; for, if Mr. T. Moran be somewhat lacking in imagination, his execution is marvelously facile and his knowledge of what the people like remarkably sure."

13 April. MacLeod notes: "Mr Moran called & left directions for receiving his picture when ready." (Curator's journal, director's records, Corcoran)

18 April. *Newark Daily Advertiser* reviews NAD exhibition: "There are some very interesting oil paintings [including] a lovely landscape by Thomas Moran... 'A Summer Shower.' His other contributions [are]... 'The Watering Place,' and... 'A Dream of the Orient.' This same 'Dream of the Orient' seems to affect the metropolitan critics very much, like shaking a red rag at a bull. It makes them mad at once and they say very disagreeable things about it. And yet it is really beautiful, no matter what they say, and admirably illustrates the title. It is an agreeable combination of delicate tints and indefinite forms—not a picture perhaps but simply a fantasy and as such a thing of beauty, worthy of the fertile imagination and skilful hand that produced it."

20 April. *Evening Star* [DC] notes that Moran's recently completed *Discovery of Florida by Ponce de Leon* will soon be exhibited at the Corcoran Gallery. It has been on private view in the city for some time.

22 April–18 May. BAA exhibition. Moran exhibits *Twilight* and *Fort George Island, Florida* (nos. 43, 273). (Marlor 1970, 281, 392)

23 April. MacLeod records: "Went to see Mr Moran's picture of Ponce de Leon in Florida and found it a very fine work. Have sent word to Mr Barlow to send it up to-morrow." (Curator's journal, director's records, Corcoran)

24 April. MacLeod: "Moran's picture of the Discovery of Florida by Ponce de Leon... was hung... in the S.W. Gallery." (Curator's journal, director's records, Corcoran)

24 April–5 June. PAFA annual exhibition. Moran exhibits *Mountain of the Holy Cross, Colorado*; *Cloudy Day*; *Near Waverly, N.J.*; *On the Coast of Florida*; and *Cliffs on the Upper Colorado, Wyoming* (nos. 97, 220, 236, 270, 293). Mary Nimmo Moran exhibits one work. (Falk 1989, 33, 341–342)

27 April. Moran writes MacLeod giving title of his painting as "Ponce de Leon in Florida" and asking him to "put a card on the picture with title." (Letter 1334, director's records, Corcoran)

27 April. *Evening Star* [DC]: "Mr. Moran's large new picture of 'Ponce de Leon in Florida,' to which reference was made last week, is now on exhibition in the Corcoran Gallery. It is well worthy the attention of connoisseurs and the public."

29 April. *NY Herald* reviews NAD exhibition: "Thomas Moran has produced a fine picture, full of strength, in his 'The Watering Place.'... Its chief fault... is a slight spottiness in effect. But how excellent is the sky, pure and real is its line and full of slow motion in the good cloud forms; how suggestive of action is the figure of the horseman at the rise of the moorland; and how admirably is the eye carried from the man and horse past the cattle by the pool to the blue bird flying over it in the shade. The color is rich and real, if slightly opaque, and the vista into the woods on the right is rendered with great skill."

Thomas Moran, *Near Feltville, N.J.*, 1878, graphite, wash, and gouache on paper, courtesy Gilcrease Museum, Tulsa, Oklahoma.

1 May. Exposition Universelle opens in Paris: "An engraving by F.S. King, of one of Thomas Moran's landscapes, was the only work in the Exposition representing this artist, who ranks in his own land among the foremost. The truth is, the commissioners appointed by the President to select pictures did not invite Mr. Moran to contribute, and thus one of the most eminent of American landscapists was virtually unknown at the Exposition.

It is very much to be regretted that such important works as Mr. Moran's 'Grand Cañon of the Yellowstone,' painted after his return from the Hayden exploring expedition, and 'The Chasm of the Colorado,' sketched during the Powell expedition, and both purchased by Congress to adorn the Capitol, could not have been sent to Paris in 1878, as well as his famous 'Mountain of the Holy Cross.' Such works are truly representative of American landscapes and landscape painters. At the Lotos Club exhibition of paintings, held the last of February in the present year, Mr. Moran exhibited a new and strikingly beautiful picture, called 'Castellated Colorado,' which was at once sold for $1,000, and purchased by an American who intends sending it to the next exhibition of the Royal Academy in London. This striking and curious picture showed a long range of immense castle-like rocks, which towered heavenward like a row of St. Peter's domes, only a thousand to fifteen hundred feet high instead of a few hundred. A placid stream, lined with trees, flows at their base, while far away to the left stretches a plain over which gallops a troop of horsemen. The sky is intensely clear and blue, contrasting strongly with the reddish and yellow tints of the rocks." (Gonse 1879, 2; *The Aldine* 9 [1878–1879], 265)

17, 21, 22 June. MacLeod records: "Mr T. Moran landscapist, called. He is here to sell his 'Ponce de Leon' to Congress"; "Mr Moran got permission to remove cotton screen from over the east Gallery, in order that the 'Ponce de Leon' may be seen to better advantage by the Committee from Congress who are to call & examine it. Senator Howe called while I was out, to examine it"; "Mr Moran has taken leave. His picture will remain for a season. Will sell it to the Gallery, but will name no price." (Curator's journal, director's records, Corcoran)

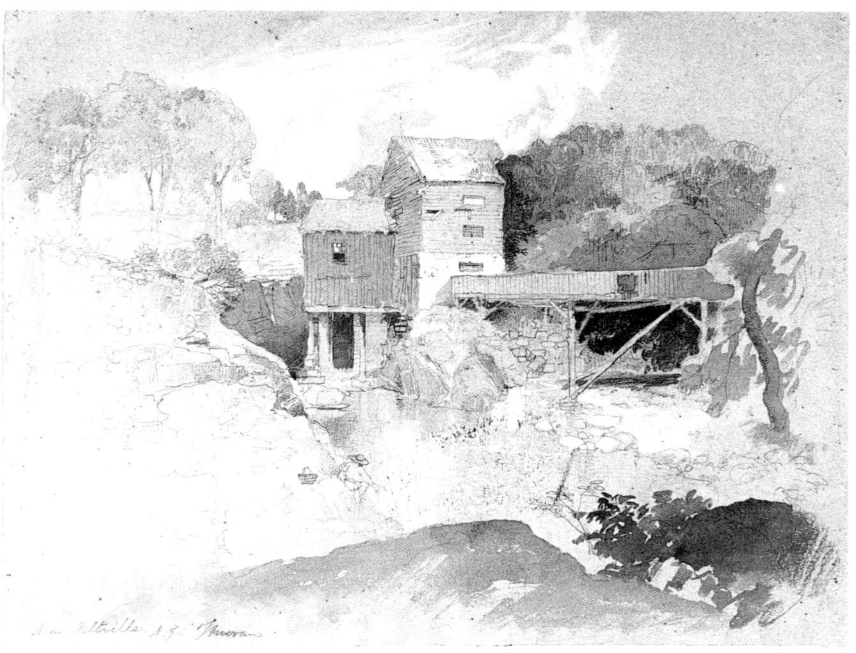

22 June. *Evening Star* [DC] reports resolution requiring "removal from the Capitol of all works of art not belonging to government." Bierstadt's *Discovery of California* must be purchased or removed. Moran and friends lobby for purchase of *Ponce de Leon*, but Congress ultimately purchases the Bierstadt.

Late July. Moran records: "Feltville, New Jersey (deserted village), family there with artist friends." (GA ledger; Morand 1996, 46, 53)

20, 30 July, and August. Sketches and dates three versions of *Feltville* (Gilcrease).

Early September. Morans visit East Hampton, Long Island, staying at Gardner's Hotel as guests of the Tile Club. Thomas Moran sketches extensively, filling small sketchbook (Gilcrease). (Rattray 1941, 49, 133)

7–9, 14 September. Sketches and dates four drawings inscribed *East Hampton*; then *Pig-Pen, East Hampton*, and *East Hampton*; then *Montauk Light*; *Montauk*; and *Looking South, Montauk* (Gilcrease).

19 September. From Newark, Moran writes Powell to say he met the artist S.R. Gifford while at Montauk Point, and "in talking over our western experiences he said that he had a great desire to read your account of the Canons of the Colorado which he had often heard spoken about & he wanted to know how he could get a copy. I told him they were now scarce but that I thought you would let him have a copy & I promised to write you on the subject. If you can let him have a copy

please send it to my care & I will deliver it to him & have him sign the receipt for it.

I have just rec'd a letter from Cap. Dutton on the subject of bringing the Canons before the British public in the *London Graphic* or *London News.* I think it can be done with much advantage to your Survey as well as to myself, as I propose to shortly exhibit my pictures in England.

I wish it was not so expensive running down to Washington, as I could then run down & talk the matter over with him.

I have now finished a large Canon picture which I wish to present to you in acknowledgement of the innumerable courtesies & favors you have done me in years past. I shall send it down to you in a few days." (Powell IC, NA)

11 November. Moran to MacLeod: "Although I have made no formal offer of 'Ponce de Leon in Florida' to the Art Committee of the Corcoran Gallery, yet I suppose they are aware that I have it for sale. Now I do not want to make a formal offer of the picture to them, unless I had some reason to believe that they would take the propriety of its purchase into serious consideration. Do you know how they look upon it, or what they think of it. My reason for asking about it at present, is that before a great while I shall want to exhibit the picture in New York & other places, & when I have brought it from Washington, there is no probability that I should have it down there again. Of course I should be very glad indeed if it should find a resting place in such fine company, & I think we could come to a satisfactory understanding in regard to the price if the Art Committee desired.... Can you not find out for me the feeling of the Committee on the subject & let me know? I could then lay my plans for the future movements of the picture & you would confer an obligation.... P.S. I have taken a studio in New York & shall go into it about the first of Dec. & when you are in New York, shall be pleased to have you call." (Letter 1469, director's records, Corcoran)

13 November. MacLeod records receipt of a letter from Moran wishing "to know if Art Committee has passed upon his Florida picture." (Curator's journal, director's records, Corcoran)

13 November. *Boston Transcript* reports that Moran is awarded bronze medal at exhibition of Massachusetts Charitable Mechanic Association.

18 November. MacLeod to Moran: "I have delayed replying... until I could inform you of definite action of the Art Committee or the Board upon your offer to sell 'Ponce de Leon.' I have to state that nothing has been done. They know of your offer, and have not even inquired the price. Indeed, they show no disposition to purchase anything at present, and perhaps will take the steps to do so before their annual meeting in January. There are several pictures before them for purchase. If however anything should occur favorable to buying, I will let you know." (Letterpress volumes, director's records, Corcoran)

9 December. *Newark Daily Advertiser*: "An original Turner picture... has just been rescued from obscurity in a West Jersey farm house at Hammonton, Atlantic county, by Mr. Thomas Moran, the artist, who now has it in his possession and is engaged in cleaning off the dust and smoke which begrimes its surface, preparatory to exhibiting it to connoisseurs at his studio in New York. The story is that twenty-five years ago a young English artist named John Butterton, came to Philadelphia with the picture in his possession. Mr. Moran, then a boy, saw it and has ever since remembered it with enthusiasm but lost trace of it.... Recently the following advertisement appeared in Scribner's Magazine:

Picture For Sale.—For sale, an important picture, by Turner, the famous English painter. For particulars and price address J. B., Post Office box 146 Hammonton, N.J.

Mr. Moran recognized the initials at once and went to Hammonton, where he found Butterton, the proprietor of a nursery, who recognized him and showed him the picture. He was anxious to place it where it would be appreciated and finally fixed the terms at so reasonable a figure that Mr. Moran immediately concluded the bargain and brought it to Newark. He does not state the cost, but says it is valued by experts at from \$25,000 to \$30,000. It is said to be the largest Turner picture ever seen in America and measures three feet eight inches by four feet eight inches, being double the size of the 'Slave Ship.'"

• 1879 •

9 January. Exhibition at ULC of NY. Moran exhibits *Plains of the Humboldt* (cat. no. 29). *NY Post*, 10 Jan.: "The meaning of Mr. Wyant's, Mr. Swain Gifford's, Mr. Thomas Moran's and Mr. George H. Boughton's landscapes lies behind the paint thereof."

15 January–8 February. Boston Art Club exhibition. Moran exhibits *Watering Place* (no. 160). (Chadbourne, Gabosh, and Vogel 1991, 277)

28 January. Moran sketches and dates *After the Thaw, near Communipaw Ferry* (Guild Hall, East Hampton).

3 February–1 March. AWCS annual exhibition at NAD. Moran exhibits *Afternoon Ride* and *Teton Range, Idaho* (cat. nos. 121, 201). (*Newark Daily Advertiser*, 29 Jan. and 6 Feb.; *The Aldine* 9 [1878–1879], 270)

4 February. Moran asks MacLeod to return *Ponce de Leon* to him since the Corcoran does not seem to want to purchase it: "Art Matters are improving in every way in New York with the revival of business. Many men who have been students abroad are returning & taking studios in New York.... I have taken a studio in... Booth's Theatre Building [23rd St. and 6th Ave.]." (Letter 1517, director's records, Corcoran)

8 February. MacLeod to Moran, confirming that he will return *Ponce de Leon*. (Letterpress volumes, director's records, Corcoran)

18 February. Moran writes Powell to request prepayment for a Green River picture and adds: "I am now settled at work in my New

York studio getting ready for the spring exhibitions." (Powell IC, NA)

March. Samuel G.W. Benjamin in *Harper's Monthly*: "The number of those who have made a specialty of black and white, whether for illustration or otherwise, is so large that as we turn to them a wide field opens upon us.... Mr. Thomas Moran ranks with Mr. Fenn as a vivid delineator of landscape, handling a vigorous and versatile pencil, and inspired by poetic fervor."

Booth's Theater Building in New York, where Moran established his studio in 1879.

6 March. Moran attends Baltimore reception at home of well-known connoisseur and collector, Mr. William T. Walters (who was also a trustee of the Corcoran and the Peabody Institute). (*NY Post*, 7 Mar.)

8 March. *Newark Daily Advertiser*: "There is trouble in the Society of American Artists of New York. The society is about to hold its regular exhibition. Yesterday it was announced in select circles that the Hanging Committee had actually rejected a picture by Thomas Moran, late of this city, one of the Vice Presidents of the society. Investigation revealed that Mr. Moran had sent in two pictures; that one was a large canvas 4½ by 3 feet, a 'Scene in Florida,' the other was about 20 by 24 inches, a wood interior, entitled 'Woodland Reflections,' with a female figure. The small one the Committee accepted and placed on the line, but the large one, the 'Scene in Florida,' the committee decided unanimously was not worthy of a place on the line, and concluded to return it to Mr. Moran rather than risk a public offence or injure its sale by hanging it high. Mr. Moran was full of righteous wrath when he learned of the decision, and ordered both pictures back to his studio. Some of his friends were equally indignant, and R.C. Minor and Wordsworth Thompson withdrew their pictures.... The Hanging Committee consists of Homer Martin, J.A. Weir and W.M. Chase, and they remain firm. It is charged that they have given preference to their own pictures."

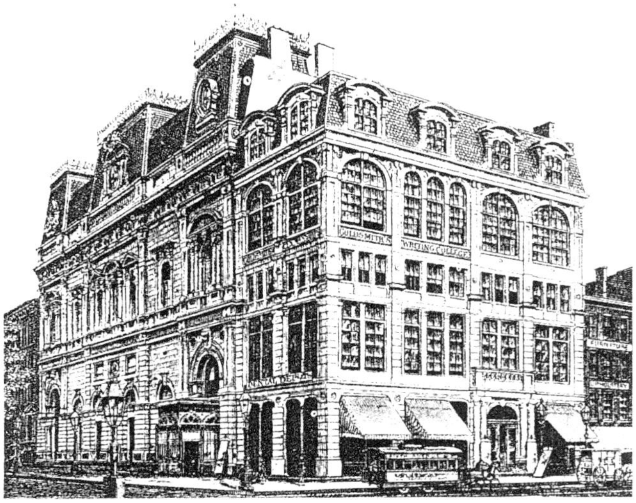

8 March. *Boston Transcript*: "Thomas Moran, a member of the Society of American Artists, sent in his resignation yesterday because of the rejection of a large landscape of his by the hanging committee."

9 March. Moran writes Powell, concerned that two previous letters remain unanswered and saying if Powell cannot send the amount of money Moran requested to please send something, as he is hard pressed with bills. (Powell IC, NA)

13 March. Reception for ULC of NY. *NY Post*, 14 Mar., comments on Moran's painting: "The Florida landscape which the Society of American artists refused to hang... is deeper in meaning and riper in pictorial effect than three-fourths of the landscapes in that society's exhibition."

17 March. Moran to Powell: "I received your letter & the postal orders for which thanks. A few days before receiving it I had a letter from Donaldson which I did not understand, as he said you had asked me to send the picture of the Rio Virgen. I wrote him that I had not heard from you to that effect. The picture of the Rio Virgen I had already sold to a Mr. Johnson in New York but on receiving your letter, I saw him & arranged to give him another subject in place of it, so I can let you have that picture. Shall I send it down to you in Washington? Let me know immediately as I want to do a little work on it before it leaves my studio. Hoping your plans for the Surveys are working out to your satisfaction." (Powell IC, NA)

29 March. *NY Post* previews NAD exhibition: "Mr. Thomas Moran's very large tropical landscape with figures represents an historical scene.... Especial attention is due to Mr. Thomas Moran's small landscape—Long Island flats in the foreground, the towers of the Brooklyn bridge beyond, and a locomotive at the left—as a study of mist and smoke."

31 March. President Rutherford B. Hayes writes letter of introduction from Washington to commanding officer at Fort Hall, Idaho Territory, for "Mr. Thomas Moran a distinguished American artist, for whom I bespeak such attention and courtesy as he would extend to myself." (Fryxell, UW)

31 March. Reception at NAD. *NY Post*, 1 Apr.: "For the first time in the history of these exhibitions not a single foreign picture was to be seen."

1 April–31 May. NAD annual exhibition. Moran exhibits *After the Thaw—Communipau Ferry*; *Ponce de Leon in Florida...*; and *Woodland Reflections* (no. 289, 317, 472). Mary Nimmo Moran exhibits three paintings. (*NY Post*, 3 Jan.; Naylor 1973, 653, 656)

2 April. *NY Post*: "The regular monthly reception of the Art Students' League was noticeable for the display of a series of pictures and studies by Mr. Thomas Moran, who recently somewhat famously resigned from the Society of American Artists. As the management of the league is supposed to be in harmony with that of the young society, the presence of Mr. Moran in such force and with such a welcome caused comment beyond the praise that works so clever were sure to elicit."

4 April. *Newark Daily Advertiser*: "The [NAD] exhibition, as a whole, is very fine, the artists having evidently done their best to make it so.... One of the largest pictures in the exhibition is by Thomas

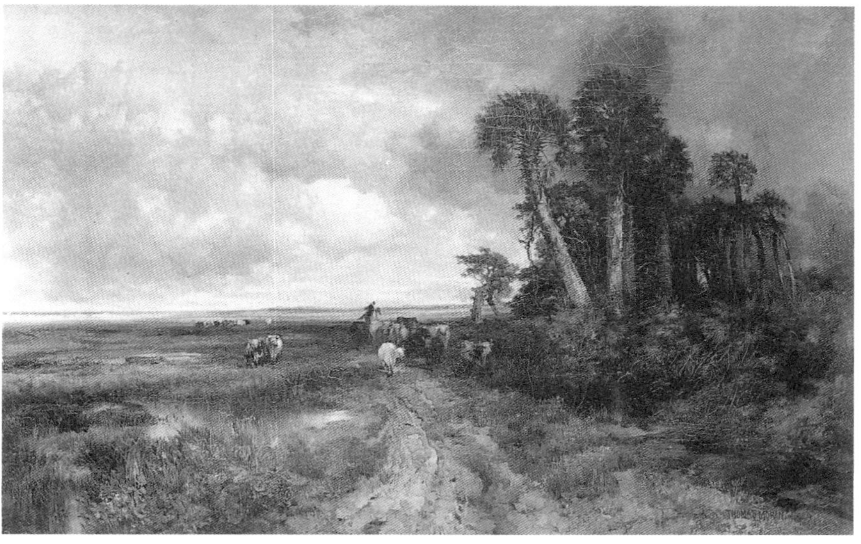

Thomas Moran, *A Road near the Sea, East Hampton,* 1880, etching, courtesy Gilcrease Museum, Tulsa, Oklahoma.

Moran ... 'Ponce de Leon in Florida .... ' It represents the depth of a tropical forest, with a group of Spaniards in the centre and some Indians regarding them."

28 April – 2 June. PAFA annual exhibition. Moran exhibits *Bringing Home the Cattle, Coast of Florida,* and *Plaza*, owned by Scribner & Co. (nos. 221, 365). (Falk 1989, 33, 342)

5 May – 4 August. 111th Exhibition of the Royal Academy of Arts, London. Moran exhibits *Mountain of the Holy Cross* (cat. no. 488). (*Art Journal* 5 [Aug. 1879], 256)

8 May. *The Independent* [NY] reviews PAFA exhibition: "Mr. Thomas Moran's 'After a thaw / in Communipaw' is an odd and affected picture, in which we fail to detect a particle of truth or of genuine artistic merit. It is an excess of an effete English-school mannerism. It is particularly unpleasant by reason of its want of values and the patchy style of its composition. If we would cut out a bit here and a bit there, we might get several agreeable sketches by themselves. As a whole, it is disjointed, and the color has a raw, unbaked look."

9 May. *Boston Transcript*: "Thomas Moran, the artist, and his brother [Peter] will make a summer trip to the Rocky Mountains, and the latter will study the Indians as a subject for pictures."

12 May. *Newark Daily Advertiser*: "Mr. Moran's picture, recently rejected in New York, was sent on to the Philadelphia Academy for exhibition. The New York Society of American Artists remonstrated relative to the hanging of Moran's and Eakin's pictures in the exhibition. A delegation was sent there to confer with the Academy people and to arrive at some definite understanding with them. Although the result of the meeting was not made public, a member of the Academy Hanging Committee states that the decision was satisfactory to both parties and the meeting was harmonious. To-day the galleries of the Academy will be entirely rehung, and Mr. Moran's picture will not be seen in the exhibition hereafter."

20 May. *Newark Daily Advertiser* reports on SAA at PAFA: "They were invited here after the close of their exhibition ... in New York. Part of their newspaper fame here has arisen from the little misunderstanding they have had with their Philadelphia hosts. As representatives of the Munich school of art they naturally object to any picture which does not conform to its rules, especially when it is brought into what they intend shall be an exposition of their peculiar theories. Their work was brought here with such an understanding, and a large gallery assigned to them for such a purpose. But much to their dismay when a deputation came down to look after the Munich school of art, they found that a picture by Mr. Thomas Moran, 'Bringing Home the Cattle,' which for reasons sufficiently clear to themselves had been emphatically rejected by these revolutionary artists in New York, had been classed here among their pictures. Irreverent Philadelphians, unable or unwilling to see the difference between a Moran and a Shirlaw, or a Chase, had put the obnoxious landscape in a post of honor .... Great dissatisfaction was the result."

June. *Art Journal*, 191 – 192: "The American Art Gallery is a new and most important departure in the interest of Art. It has long been felt that American painters were ... without an adequate means of reaching the public, the galleries of the dealers being for the most part given up to important pictures. This is now changed .... Messrs. Moore and Sutton have taken Kurtz's Gallery ... and, with an additional room, opened them as a permanent gallery and sales-room for American paintings and works of Art. The initiative took place on Monday, May 3rd, and the opening was most auspicious, many persons going so far as to say that it was the best exhibition of exclusively American pictures, for its size, that had been seen in New York for many years .... Among the artists represented are Inness, De Haas, Brown, Wyant, R. Swain Gifford, Edward Moran, Colman, Dielman, Thomas Moran."

Summer. Morans rent Conkling House in East Hampton for the season. (Rattray 1941, 49, 86)

11 July. On Long Island, Moran sketches and dates *Montauk* (EHL).

18 July. *NY Post*: "Upon the studio doors of nearly all our prominent artists are cards bearing the words 'Out of the city for the summer.' ... Mr. A. H. Baldwin returned to New York this morning from Easthampton .... 'A jolly party we had

down there. Peter and Thomas Moran are there; also Professor John F. Weir, J. H. Dolph, Jervis McEntee, Samuel Colman and A. F. Bunner. Such a picturesque place it is! We all did some sketching and found plenty of material.' The Morans will start for a trip out west in the Rocky Mountains in a few days."

August. Moran travels to the Southwest and the Donner Pass region of Sierra Nevada mountains with his brother Peter. (Morand 1996, 49–53)

5, 8, 11–14 August. Sketches and dates *Murphy's Cabin from Keseberg's Camp, Donner Party*, and *Tahoe*; then another *Tahoe*; *Chinese Wheel for Raising Water, Elko*; and *Ruby Range*; then *On the Border of Great Salt Lake, Utah*; then *Upper End of Cottonwood Canyon*; then *In Little Cottonwood Canyon*; *Upper End of Little Cottonwood Canyon*; *Upper End of Cottonwood Canyon*; and *Near the Summit of Cottonwood Canyon*; then *Alta, Utah* (Gilcrease; Cleveland Museum of Art; MFA Boston; EHL; Cooper-Hewitt).

21 August. Moran records: "Left Fort Hall with Cap. A. H. Bainbridge & 20 men, 2 wagons. On way to Taylors Bridge very hot. Mirage. Dogs exhausted. Pete sick. Reached Taylors Bridge late in afternoon. 27 miles. Desolation. Abandoned town. R. R. Bridge over the Snake.... Discharged soldier in the morning came into camp & made disturbance.... Highway robber. Dismal Camp. Furious wind all night driving sand everywhere almost Blinding. Gray dismal morning. Black Basalt. Abomination. Rushing river like Niagara Rapids." (Diary, GTNP)

22 August. "Left Camp at Taylors Bridge at 7 o'clock. Cold & windy with dust following & blinding us all the way. At noon passed Black Jacks on Willow Creek. All sage plain proposed irrigation. Arrived at 12 at Buck from Connecticut. 7 miles to South Fork of Snake.... two hours to get across on the opposite side. Had terrible time to get the Heavy wagons up the embankment & through the willows 40 feet. 12 mules soldiers yelling & beating the mules. Got up all right & went into Camp in a beautiful spot on the north bank of the river. Soldiers bathing. Watering the stock near Taylors Bridge. Had our first sight of the great Teton some 70 miles away. Indian herder[s] seldom speak & keep studiously apart from the other men.... Amusing to see the mules inquisitively surrounding the teamster who was handling rations. Fires all over the country." (Diary, GTNP)

22 August. Sketches and dates *Snake River above Taylor's Bridge* (JNEM).

23 August. "Following foothills surmounted by basalt over a plain covered with fine bunch grass.... a beautiful grazing & farming Country with means of easy irrigation from South fork of the Snake which is a splendid current & clear as crystal. We are directly opposite Crater Buttes across the Snake.... The Salmon river range close in the distance enveloped in a delicate blue haze. To the east lies the Snake river range, a low line of mountains separating us from the Teton Basin.... At 11:20 reached a fine cold stream, probably Moody Creek where we rested ½ hour to water the animals. The Tetons are now plainly visible but not well defined owing to the mistiness of the atmosphere. They loom grandly above all the other mountains. An intervening ridge dividing us from the Teton Basin stretches for miles to the north of a beautiful pinkish yellow with delicate shades of pale cobalt while the distant range is of an exquisite blue." (Diary, GTNP)

24 August. "Teton River Camp.... a wind blowing nearly as bad as at Taylors Bridge, driving the dust everywhere & covering our breakfast. Cold but bright overhead. The Tetons from this camp [were] very well defined... before the sun rose but soon disappeared when the atmosphere lighted. ... Reached Canon Creek at 11 o'clock after a 15 mile ride over rolling country covered with excellent grass.... We struck the canon at a point where it is about 800 feet in depth with very precipitous banks covered with the debris from the basaltic columns with which the upper edge is fringed.... following a trail leading up the edge of the Canon we found that it led down into the Canyon, which has a beautiful stream flowing through it fringed with Water Elms, Pine Cottonwoods &c.... About a mile above we found a depression in the side of the Canon down which we could make our way to a flat space.... here the wagons were unloaded & after packing the material on the pack Mules the Wagons... were sent back to Boqua.'... We made our camp on the flat in the Canon. Caught a few Mountain trout & ascended the Canon again to get a glimpse of the Tetons, but from this point only the top of Mt. Moran is visible." (Diary, GTNP)

25 August. "We were out of Bed this morning at 5.30. It was very cold & ice had formed on the tin cups. In another hour we were under way over what appeared to be a rolling but smooth country, but as we advanced we found our mistake. Every mile we found a gulch bordered with aspens in depth from 100 to 200 feet but we found no difficulty in crossing any of them. After passing the divide between the Teton Basin & our last camp, we found a gently rolling country descending to the Basin. The Tetons here loomed up grandly against the sky & from this point is perhaps the finest pictorial range in the United States or even in N. America. After descending the slope about 3 miles we came upon a small ice cold stream & determined to camp." (Diary, GTNP)

26 August. Sketches and dates *Three Tetons* (GTNP). "From Camp this morning our way lay over a smooth rolling country descending gently to the bottom of the Teton Basin... through which the Teton river flows.... The Teton river can be forded at almost any point.... At the mouth of the Canon we found a pretty good camping spot on the edge of the banks of the river which are here about 14 feet high. A fine growth of pine fills the river Bottom & good grazing for animals covers the space between ourselves & the hills. It is very hot this afternoon & so very smoky that the Teton peaks can scarcely be seen & at times are entirely

obscured so that sketching is out of the question & we spend our time working up some of our sketches made previously." (Diary, GTNP)

27 August. "After a good night's rest we got up on the morning of the 27th at an early hour.... the Cap., Pete, myself & two men started on a trip up the Canon. We proceeded over a not difficult way about 6 miles & ascended to the top of a granite cliff about 500 feet to get a good view of the Canon that leads up to the right of the Tetons. The peaks of the Tetons are from this point entirely hidden from view but a number of other fine peaks present themselves.... The view is very magnificent. The opposite mountain rises 5000 feet above the river with a granite base surmounted by sandstone & capped with tremendous precipices of limestone. The slopes are covered in places with a growth of large pines but the summit is nearly bare of vegetation. We remained on the cliff some 3 hours sketching & afterward amused ourselves by rolling down great granite boulders over the precipice upon which we stood & watching their descent as they went rebounding from rock to rock & crashing through the brush & dead timber at the base with a noise like the report of musketry & echoing reverberating through the Canon. Descending to the valley we found red raspberry & [black] currants plentiful with which we regaled ourselves.... We returned to Camp early in the afternoon. The fires in the surrounding mountains had become so dense as almost to obscure the peaks of the Tetons & the sun went down in fiery redness. A strong & cold wind began to blow soon after & during the night a violent thunder storm continued until nearly day break accompanied by rain in the canon & snow on the peaks. Heavy storm clouds hung over the range dropping snow or rain occasionally & a cold wind blew." (Diary, GTNP)

27 August. Sketches and dates *Entrance to the Teton Canyon* (GTNP).

28–29 August. "We broke camp & left the Canon at 6.30. After an uncomfortable breakfast prepared under difficulties of rain & a cold wind. As we left the Canon & came into the open plain the sun broke through the dense clouds that overhung the mountains for a time and showed his face fitfully all day.... we proceeded to the Teton River near its junction with Bear Creek where we intended to camp but after a rest of a couple of hours... we concluded to go on some 8 miles to our old Camp on the other side of the Teton Valley where we arrived about 4 o'clock. ... It was cold & windy during the evening & considerable snow fell on the mountain during the day.... A roaring camp fire dispelled the cold, & our camp being in a sheltered spot we slept comfortably & next morning... we followed our old trail toward Canon creek for some time when we were again joined by Beaver Dick who guided over a new route to Boqua's.... We journeyed along & reached Boqua's ranch early in the afternoon & found that the party we had left in charge of the wagons was camped on Moody Creek near its junction with the South fork of the Teton River some four miles further on.... It was very cold during the night, heavy ice forming on the water in our buckets.... The Cap ordered the start but left 3 men at the camp.... We proceeded on our way toward the S fork of the Snake River, & when about 8 miles on our way we descried the men with the Indians coming along. We halted for half an hour until they came up. They had all their worldly goods with them packed on 3 Horses consisting of beaver, otter, deer, bear, & other skins....We bought some otter skins from them, but a coveted gray bear skin the squaw would not part with.... We recrossed the Snake River without accident & arrived at Willow Creek at its junction with Sand Creek at 3 o'clock & went into Camp. Cedars, Cottonwood in the bottoms & a beautiful day. The ever present Crater Buttes on our right all day backed by Salmon River Ranges." (Diary, GTNP)

1, 10–12 September. Sketches and dates *Green River*; then *Green River, Wyoming Territory*; *Green River from the Ferry*; and *Green River* (Gilcrease; JNEM; Cooper-Hewitt; present location unknown). Of the nearly 50 extant sketches from the summer trip, 17 represent Green River. (Morand 1996, 51–53)

22 September–11 October. At Exposition in St. Louis. Moran exhibits *Passing Shower*; *On the Edge of a Wood, N.H.*; and *October in New Hampshire*. (*Art Amateur* [Sept.], 76)

23 October. *The Independent* [NY]: "Thomas Moran, in company with his brother, Peter Moran, the animal painter, spent the past summer among the Sierra mountain range of California, the Elcho and Ruby ranges in Nevada, and the Wahsatch range in Utah. They made a series of landscape studies in water colors."

9–13 December. First exhibition of the Springfield [MA] Art Association. *American Art Review* (Jan. 1880), 130: "Most of the contributors were local artists, but well-known New York and Boston names, such as... Thomas Moran... were also represented."

22 December. *NY Post*: "One of the latest, most varied and brightest collections of pictures ever seen at a club reception in this city now enlightens the walls of [the Lotos Club]. There are seventy-six examples, almost exclusively by American artists, including... the 'Bathers' by T. Moran."

27 December. *Newark Daily Advertiser*: "There are so many attractions [this season]... that there is some danger that our art loving citizens... will overlook a most meritorious exhibition of paintings in Upper Library Hall. It must not be confounded with the 'galleries' that come here to be sold at auction—gilt frames with the pictures thrown in—for every picture is by a leading artist, and... we find such names in the catalogue as DeHaas, Geo. Inness, Morston Ream (one of the best painters of fruit in the world), Cropsey, the two Morans, Bierstadt... and more than a score of others of equal merit."

• 1880 •

January. Moran in Europe. Autobiography of Francis Coates Jones says he saw Moran on train to Paris from London "starting on the seven hour trip with a bundle one foot long, a violin case under one arm and clutched under the other, a live cat." (DeWitt McClellan Lockman papers, AAA, roll 503, p. 8)

3 January. *Newark Daily Advertiser* discusses pictures at Upper Library Hall: "Of... captivating character is... 'Landscape,' by Mr. Thomas Moran. The elements are disturbed, and the picture suggests the dashing new school, which was introduced by the late Fortuney."

February. S. R. Koehler in *American Art Review*, 151, says Moran has completed 9 etching plates, including *Study of Trees* (first plate etched in 1860); *Bazaar*; *Bridge and Trees*; *Evening*; *Study of Willows*; *Passaic Meadows*; *Ku-Ra-Tu. A Pah-Ute Girl*; *Yellowstone River*; and *Empty Cradle*: "There is a marked difference in these plates, owing to the fact, undoubtedly, that the artist has been experimenting.... The touch in Mr. Thomas Moran's etchings is peculiarly attractive. There is a nervous vitality in it, which makes every line an interesting subject of study."

2 February–1 March. At NAD Moran exhibits with AWCS, *Morning* (cat. no. 169), and with NYEC, *Empty Cradle*; *In the Marshes*; *Head Waters of the Yellowstone*; *Bazaar; Study with Willows*; *Bridge and Trees*; and *Evening* (cat. nos. 169, 383, 403, 430, 472, 475, 477). (*American Art Review* [March], 214)

3 February. *Newark Daily Advertiser* reviews AWCS exhibition: "It would have paid you to have come over to secure... 'Morning,' $75, by Thomas Moran, a beautiful picture, full of feeling, with just a tinge of the impressionists' dashy features in the trees and their foliage."

19 February. *NY Post*: "The brothers Peter and Thomas Moran are the American etchers represented in the February... *American Art Review*, the former appearing in 'Noonday Rest'—some horses and mules under a shed—and the latter in 'The Passaic Meadows.' The Moran family are much interested in etching: Mrs. Thomas Moran and her son Paul, Mrs. Peter Moran, her brother-in-law Mr. S. J. Ferris, and his son G. Ferris, have all done excellent work with the needle. Mr. Thomas Moran's present example is a very delicate, almost gray-toned landscape."

28 February. *NY Post* reviews AWCS exhibition: "Mr. Thomas Moran—past finding out though his color-scheme in oils is sometimes—vindicates his reputation anew in the intellectual apprehension and the manual certainty of his delicate atmospheric study, 'Morning.'"

March. *Art Journal*, 92–93, reviews AWCS exhibition: "'Morning' by Thomas Moran, is an effective bit of work by an artist who, in the language of others, often gives us very clever thoughts of his own.... When one studies the etchings of such artists as R. Swain Gifford, Farrer, Bellows, Moran, or the Messrs. Smillie... and discovers how admirably they have labored in the field, he is more encouraged than by any other sign of progress now evident in American aesthetics; for there is no medium in pictorial Art by which the genuine artistic nature can better give expression to the more profound and emotional sentiments inspired by the harmonies of Nature."

March. *American Art Review*, 214, discusses AWCS exhibition: "A black and white room competes with the regular black and white exhibition only in the matter of etchings.... Thomas Moran [inclines] to a soft massiveness and mystery, with the woods and waters of his favorite Yellowstone."

12 March. Moran records: "Sold *Mountain of Holy Cross* to Dr. W. A. Bell of Manitou, CO, for $4500." (GA small notebook 1877/1882, 30; in Partial Memorandum Concerning Pictures 1879–1882, 1, Moran notes price as $5,000)

22 March. *NY Post* notes the Morans will be represented at the loan exhibition in the new Metropolitan Museum of Art.

26 March. *NY Post* previews NAD exhibition, mentioning that about 500 works were rejected, that the "New-School" artists are only imperfectly represented, and that "a view of New York by T. Moran" is included.

30 March–29 May. NAD annual exhibition. Moran exhibits *Sunrise on the Colorado River*; *Arkansas Diredo, Rocky Mountain*; *Bringing Home the Cattle, Coast of Florida*; and *Grey Day* (nos. 8, 363, 390, 410). Mary Nimmo Moran exhibits one work. (*NY Post*, 13 Jan.; Naylor 1973, 654, 656)

5 April–30 May. PAFA annual exhibition. Moran exhibits etchings *Bridge and Trees*; *Evening*; *Headwaters of the Yellowstone*; *Empty Cradle*; *Study of Willows*; *Newark Meadows*; and *Bazaar* (nos. 276, 320, 331, 373, 379, 380, 383). Mary Nimmo Moran exhibits four etchings and a painting. (Falk 1989, 33, 341–342)

6 April. Moran, involved in formation of a new art association in Newark, writes to R. H. Latimer for a sample charter. (NYPL mss, Ford Collection, N15, 1076)

17 April. *NY Post* reviews NAD exhibition: "Mr. Thomas Moran's view in the Newark meadows, 'A Gray Day,' is facile in composition and perspective but the distant buildings seem unnecessarily lofty."

10 May. Moran is proposed for membership in the NYEC. (Minutes, NYEC)

19–30 May. BAA exhibition. Moran exhibits *Color Study* (no. 229). (Marlor 1970, 281, 392)

June. *American Art Review*, 363: "The majority of [auction] sales of American pictures seem to have taken place in Boston.... *Study in Wales*, by Thomas Moran, brought $48."

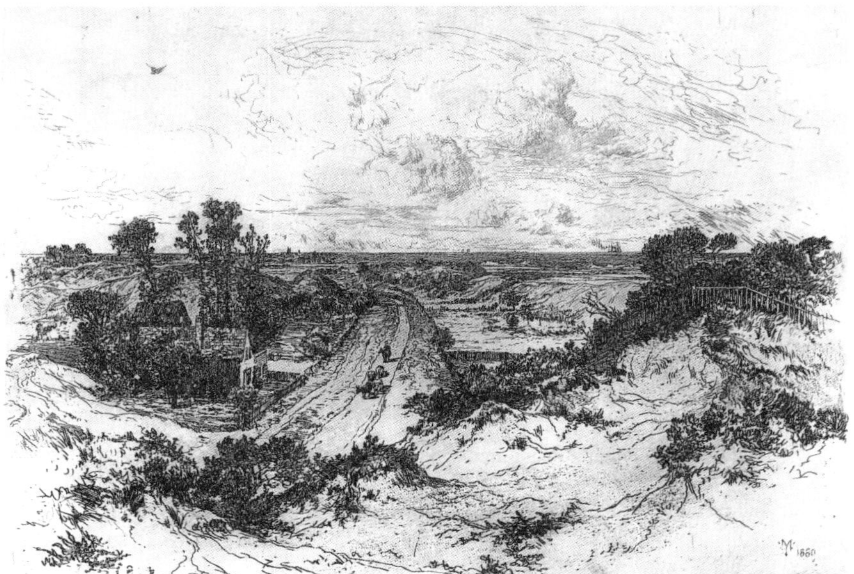

Thomas Moran, *A Road near the Sea,* 1880, etching, courtesy Gilcrease Museum, Tulsa, Oklahoma.

4 June. *Boston Transcript* comments on exhibition of original designs for Christmas cards by Louis Prang & Co. in NY: "Several well-known artists of New York and of Boston are among the competitors, and the work of Thomas Moran, F. S. Church and W. S. Macy, among others, is easily identified."

12 June. Moran sketches and dates *Baltimore from Federal Hill* (EHL).

Summer. Rents Conkling house in East Hampton for the season. (Rattray 1941, 49, 86; Morand 1996, 53–56)

23, 29 June. Sketches and dates *East Hampton Beach* and *East Hampton* (EHL).

6, 12, 23 July. Sketches and dates *East Hampton*; *Sand Hill Road to Georgica Pond, East Hampton*; and *Watermills, Long Island* (Gilcrease; EHL).

2 August. Sketches and dates *East Hampton* (EHL).

3 August. *Boston Transcript* reports upcoming Louisville Industrial Exhibition: "Among the pictures, some two hundred in number, which will be forwarded by Louis R. Menger, from New York studios, to the Louisville exhibition, are Thomas Moran's large work, 'Ponce de Leon in Florida.'"

5, 12, 15 August. Sketches and dates *East Hampton*; *Evening, East Hampton*; and *Sassafras Trees, East Hampton* (EHL; Gilcrease).

27, 28 August. Sketches and dates *East Hampton* and a view of East Hampton (EHL).

2, 5 September. Sketches and dates *Montauk* and *Napeague* (Gilcrease).

8 September–20 October. Annual art exhibition of the Inter-State Industrial Exposition in Chicago. Moran exhibits *New York from Jersey City* and etchings with NYEC, one of which—*Bazaar*—is called "a forcible piece of work." Mary Nimmo Moran also exhibits etchings with NYEC. (*American Art Review* 2 [Nov.], 19–21)

10, 12 September. Moran sketches and dates *Egypt Road*; then *Pond from Egypt Road* and two sketches inscribed *Amagansett* (EHL; Gilcrease).

22 September. *Denver Rocky Mt. News*: "Lovers of the Beautiful will be interested in learning that Moran's great painting, the 'Mountain of the Holy Cross,' has been placed at the disposal of St. Andrew's church, Manitou, and will be on exhibition for a limited period, on Wednesdays and Saturdays, from 9 to 4 p.m., at the residence of Dr. W. A. Bell, in that charming vicinage. This great masterpiece of art is alone worthy a trip to Manitou."

According to Henry Teetor in *Magazine of Western History* (1889), 4–8: "Whilst [*Mountain of the Holy Cross*] was being exhibited in the Royal Academy in London, Mrs. Bell saw it there and wrote to her husband to see it on its return to New York. Dr. Bell (who was then and had been for some years the vice-president of the Denver & Rio Grande Railway Company) was in New York attending the now historic contest in the Supreme Court of the United States, for the possession of the Grand Canon of the Arkansas between his company and the Atchison, Topeka & Santa Fe Railroad Co. Being greatly struck with the beauty and merit of the painting, and naturally associating it in his mind with the herculean efforts of his road to penetrate these Rocky Mountain fastnesses, he entered into an understanding with Mr. Moran that he would purchase the painting if his company won its suit before the Supreme Court. Within three months the painting was his, and now reposes permanently at his home in Manitou, at the gate of the mountains, and with surroundings in every respect fitting its great artistic merits."

26 October. *Newark Daily Advertiser*: "We have noted the return to town of our justly celebrated artist, Thomas Moran, who, we understand, has been spending the Summer season at East Hampton, a quaint picturesque old town on Long Island, with plenty of material for those with an artistic eye, where he has accumulated a portfolio of delightful sketches, which we hope to see carried out to a greater extent on some worthy canvas or in the effective method of the etching tool. His talented wife, known to the art world as M. Moran, has also been busy with her pencil and brush, getting material for work which we shall probably have opportunity to admire when our next exhibition is open."

7 December–1 January 1881. BAA semi-annual exhibition. Moran exhibits *New York from Jersey City* and *Bathers* (nos. 78, 171), "both as important as anything Mr. Moran has done, perhaps." (Marlor 1970, 392, 281; *Art Journal* 7 [Jan. 1881], 32)

22 December. *Newark Daily Advertiser*: "The annual exhibition of the Salamagundi Club of New York opened with a private view on Saturday evening last.... Among the contributors were Thos. Moran and M. N. Moran, of this city, who exhibited a number of etchings, the subjects of which were taken from studies made while away during the Summer. They were very well spoken of, and Mrs. Moran, who seems to have caught the spirit of that style of art, especially received many favorable criticisms from the artists present. We shall expect to see some fine examples from both Mr. and Mrs. Moran when our regular Academy exhibition is open."

• 1881 •

Maintaining studio at Booth's Theater Building, Moran moves residence in June from Newark to 51st St. and 7th Ave., NY. (Holbrook's; New York City Directory)

Ladies Art Association of NY hires Moran to teach an etching class. (Peet 1988, 14)

January. *Art Amateur*, 25, reviews art exhibition at Lotos Club, calling Moran's *Communipaw Flats* an "excellent picture" but "too old an acquaintance for present comment."

10 January. Moran is elected a member of the NYEC. (Minutes, NYEC)

15 January. First issue of *The Critic* published, with editors Jeannette L. and Joseph B. Gilder, siblings of Richard Watson Gilder. Moran contributes illustrations. (*NYT*, 21 Nov. 1909)

21 January–23 February. AWCS annual exhibition at NAD. Moran exhibits *Montauk Point*; *Neshaminy Creek, Pa.*; *Oak Grove, Amagansett*; *Feudal Stronghold*; *Sketch in Northern Arizona*; *Morning*; *Near Bordentown, N.J.* (cat. nos. 23, 116, 137, 194, 250, 261, 425) and serves on hanging committee. (*Art Journal* [Mar.], 95)

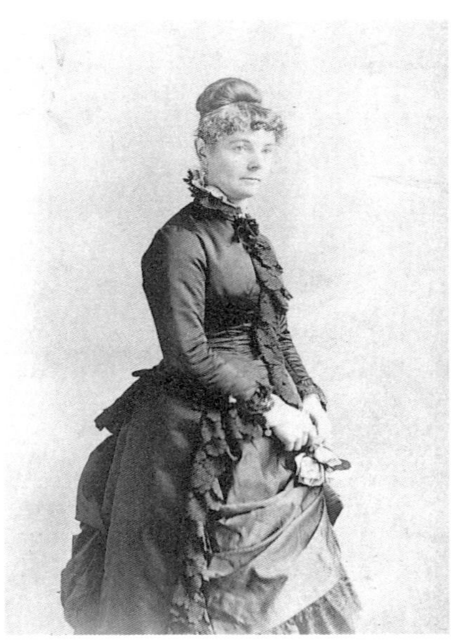

Mary Nimmo Moran, c. 1878, photograph by Napoleon Sarony, New York, courtesy East Hampton Library.

22 January. *Newark Daily Advertiser* reviews AWCS exhibition: "Notwithstanding the pitiless storm there was a large attendance of artists and critics, who were jubilant over the unanimous verdict that it is the most extensive and important collection of works ever displayed by the Society, both as the number and the merit of their exhibits. It was also a demonstration of the rapid advance that has taken place in the production of watercolor art. The hanging committee, of which T. Moran, of Newark, was one of the most efficient members, displayed unusual discrimination and impartiality in placing the bewildering mass of pictures, which fill four or five large rooms, and the catalogue, which is itself a work of art, is uncommonly well classified to facilitate the desires of spectators and buyers. All of our foremost artists are represented, and the prices established are almost if not quite up to the value of oil paintings of similar merit. Among the conspicuous examples are several from S. Coman, T. W. Wood, H. Farrer, Quarterly, the Morans, H. P. Smith, who has rapidly assumed a place in the front rank, Bellows and a host other well-known names. The exhibition will open to the public on Monday and is richly worth a visit from amateurs."

27 January. *Newark Daily Advertiser* reviews AWCS exhibition: "Thomas Moran and Edward Moran, and still further M. Nimmo Moran... are all well represented in the collection.... Thomas Moran has seven drawings in the exhibition; his... 'Montauk Point' commands attention. But I must look at Mr. Moran's work when there is more favorable opportunity to appreciate him."

29 January–19 February. At Boston Art Club Moran exhibits *New York from Jersey City* and *Bringing Home the Cattle, Coast of Florida* (nos. 57, 96). (Chadbourne, Gabosh, and Vogel 1991, 277)

February. Edward Strahan reviews AWCS exhibition for *Art Amateur*, 48–50: "The Moran family communicates the tradition of art from torch to torch, from influence to influence. No less than nine of the name are known as exhibitors.... Mr. Thomas Moran has a large, highly finished composition showing the lighthouse, the ponds, the hills, and the distant sea of Montauk Point; at the fresh-water pools a mounted Indian herdsman, sole vestige of the old red kings of Long Island, drives to water the cattle which inherited right gives him the privilege of rearing."

11 February. Mary Nimmo Moran is unanimously elected a member of NYEC. (Henry Farrer to Mary Nimmo Moran, EHL)

March. *Art Amateur*, 72, reviews Boston Art Club exhibition: "Your landscapists are on hand in force—Thos. Moran with two of his grandiose compositions."

8–19 March. At BAA Moran exhibits watercolors *Morning, Salt Ponds at East Hampton*; *On the Neshaming Creek, Penn.*; *Sunset in North Arizona*; *Feudal Stronghold*; *Near Bordentown, N.J.*; *Oak Grove, Amagansett, L.I.*; *Near the Grand Canyon, N. Arizona*; and *Morning* (nos. 185–187, 471, 491, 527, 530, 537). (Marlor 1970, 281, 392)

23 March–14 May. NAD annual exhibition. Moran exhibits *Sunset, Long Island Sound*; *Reminiscence of Florida*; *Green River, Wyoming*; *Path to the Village* (nos. 33, 305, 364, 435) and serves on hanging committee. Mary Nimmo Moran exhibits two works. (*Newark Daily Advertiser*, 25 Mar.; Naylor 1973, 654, 656; *Art Journal* 7 [June], 192)

4 April. First annual exhibition of SPE opens in London. Moran exhibits *Above Lower Falls, Yellowstone*; *Sounding Sea*; *Coast of Long Island*; *Twilight, Bridgehampton Road*; *Study in Southern Utah*; *Montauk Ponds*; *Rainbow*; *Southerly Wind*; *A Bazaar*; *Three Mile Harbor*; *Sassafras Grove*; and *Study of Willows*. Mary Nimmo Moran exhibits five etchings. (*Art Journal* 7 [Mar.], 96)

6 April. Sale of collection of Mr. David Jones, at Leavitt's galleries. Moran's *Castellated Colorado* sells to Mr. Lanthier for $500.00. (*Art Journal* 7 [May], 160)

22 April. *NY Post* quotes *London Spectator*'s review of SPE exhibition: "If the truth must be told, the majority of the British work is inferior both in method and imagination [to that of the Continental and American artists]. The London *Academy* says: 'It would take more space than is available here to distinguish as they deserve the works of Henry Farrer, Robert Swain Gifford, Thomas and Mary Moran, and F. S. Church.'"

23 April–21 May. At Boston Art Club Moran exhibits watercolors *Misty Morning, Neshaminy Creek, Pa.*; *Sunset, a Feudal Stronghold*; and *Near the Grand Cañon of the Colorado, N. Arizona* (nos. 123, 250, 262). (Chadbourne, Gabosh, and Vogel 1991, 277)

28 April. *Newark Daily Advertiser*: "Thomas Moran, the artist, who has been a resident of this city for the past twelve years, is about to remove to apartments in the Wyoming Flat [NY]."

7 May. Thomas and Mary Nimmo Moran invited to become Fellows of the SPE and to exhibit at Hanover Gallery, London. James D. Smillie later writes, "I sent 104 Etching pps by 15 American Etchers—12 of whom were afterwards elected 'Original Fellows'—Mrs. Moran sent six etching pps to that exhibit. She was the only woman elected, among the total 65 original fellows of all nationalities." Unidentified newspaper clipping attached to Smillie's letter: "The British Society of Painter-Etchers has invited Messrs. Henry Farrer, A. F. Bellows, F. S. Church, Thomas Moran, Mary Nimmo Moran, R. Swain Gifford, J. M. Falconer and James D. Smillie, who were among the prominent American contributors to the first annual exhibition of the Society, to become Fellows. This is properly regarded as a very just compliment to the artists named, all of whom are regarded at home as possessing a high order of talent as etchers." (Printed invitations, GA; Smillie to Moran, 19 Mar. 1895, with clipping, EHL)

7 May. *The Critic*, 126: "The etchings of Mr. and Mrs. Thomas Moran have been highly spoken of by the London art critics. Mrs. Moran, whose work some of them took to be that of a man, was especially complimented."

10 May. *NY Post*: "The catalogue of the recent exhibition of the London 'Society of Painter Etchers' mentions four hundred and ninety two examples. The New York names are Bellows, F. S. Church, Colman, Falconer, Henry Farrer, Swain Gifford, Thomas Moran, Mary Nimmo Moran, Sartain, and J. D. Smillie."

12 May. Moran is elected an Associate (ANA) of NAD at its annual meeting. (*American Art Review* 2, no. 1 [June], 89; *NY Post*, 13 May; printed notification, GA)

13 May. Moran elected to the executive committee of the NYEC at its annual meeting. Peter Moran elected a nonresident member. (*American Art Review* 2, no. 1 [June], 89)

24 May. From New York studio Moran writes artist-friend William H. Holmes: "I would very much like to do the work you speak of. For the best engraving, they would cost about one hundred & fifty dollars each. Add from $35.00 to $40.00 to that for drawing will make them cost 185.00 to 190.00 each. The number to be done might modify this price but not to any great extent. In my opinion it is always better to have a small number of good engravings than a large number of poor ones." Holmes accompanied Clarence Dutton's expedition to Grand Canyon in

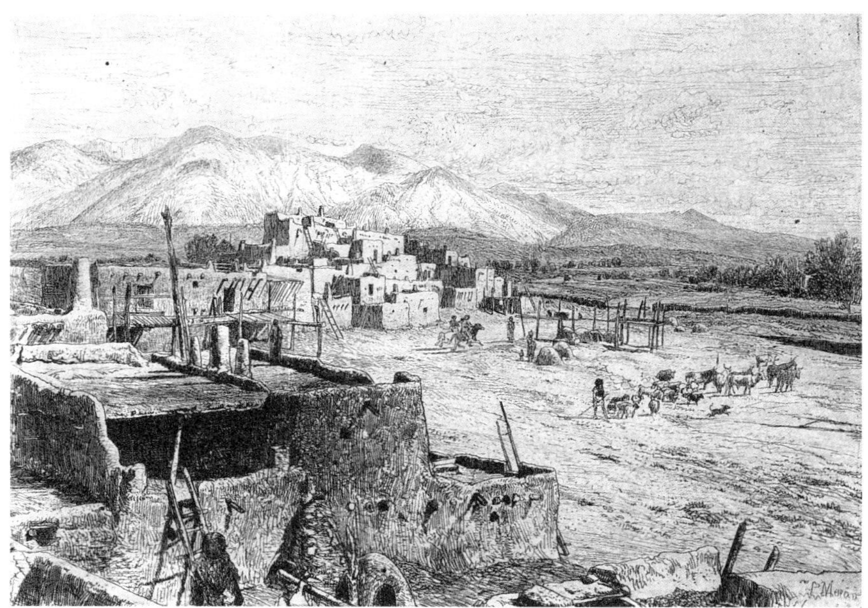

Peter Moran, *Pueblo of Taos, North*, 1881, etching, courtesy National Museum of American History, Smithsonian Institution, Graphic Arts Collection.

1880. He and Moran both produced illustrations for Dutton's *Tertiary History of the Grand Cañon District*, published 1882. Moran's illustration *The Transept* was based on a sketch by Holmes. (Fryxell, UW; Morand 1996, 96 n 62)

6 June. *Newark Daily Advertiser*: "Mr. and Mrs. Thos. Moran are comfortably situated in the new home in New York city, and are as industrious as ever, working steadily with a true love for their chosen profession; they are making many friends with their social, pleasant manners and agreeable entertaining."

Late June. Moran visits Niagara Falls to fulfill commission from engraving firm Schell and Hogan for 12 views for *Picturesque Canada*; provides 9 before end of the year. (Pringle 1989, 12 – 21; Morand 1996, 56; GA small notebook 1877/1882, 43)

Late June. Moran sketches *Under the American Fall from Goat Island*, inscribed June (Gilcrease).

29, 30 June. Sketches and dates *Rapids below Lower Suspension Bridge, Niagara Falls*, and *Niagara River from Brock Monument* (Gilcrease).

30 June. *The Independent* [NY]: "There are seven Morans in the last Academy Catalogue, and all of them artists of considerable note, some of them famous the world over.... Thomas Moran (Booth's Building) began his art life as a wood engraver—a good beginning for a man whose genius insures him immunity from the usual formal precision of that craft.... The grander aspects of Nature—towering rocks, primeval forests, mountain passes abounding in somber shadows, glowing skies, and sun-saturated seas of mist—all these things are so well done by Mr. Moran that he may be reckoned with the half dozen really successful painters of American scenery. He is less sensational than Bierstadt, less sentimental than Church, though he is far surpassed by the latter artist in the reproduction of delicate and subtle atmospheric gradations of color. One sees Turner's influence in his work continually; not an unpleasant influence when kept subordinate to the artist's strong personality and to a faithful regard for local facts of color and of atmospheric quality."

July. *Art Journal*, 221 – 224, commenting on American pictures at Metropolitan Museum: "'After a Thaw at Cummunipaw' [*sic*] is the best canvas that Mr. Thomas Moran has ever painted, to our mind. It is fairly 'ringing' with brilliant humidity, and its picturesqueness has the agreeably solid basis of actual truth which one misses in his Turneresque landscapes and in his bitumenized wood interiors. In other words, it is clever as all Mr. Moran's work is, but frank and real at the same time; whereas an obvious sophistication is sometimes characteristic of his more popular successes."

Art Journal also notes that "Thomas and Peter Moran will spend the summer in New Mexico, Arizona and the Yellowstone" and that London's SPE has elected Thomas and Mary Nimmo Moran as Fellows.

It further announces: "Thomas Moran has finished a large etching of his 'Conway Castle,' by Turner, but it will not be published until the fall.... The edition will be limited to 300.... The original picture, with proofs of the etching, have been taken to England by Mr. R.E. Moore of the American Art Gallery, for exhibition." Moran records: "Sold ½ interest in Turner plate to Moore for 500.00." (GA small notebook 1877/1882).

July. S.R. Koehler in *American Art Review*, 104, reports that since an earlier notice Moran has made a number of plates, including *The Rainbow*; *Montauk Ponds*; *Bridgehampton Road*; *Southerly Wind*; *Morning*; *Sassafras Grove*; *Three-Mile Harbor*; *Sounding Sea*; *Sand Dunes, Long Island Coast*; *In Northern Arizona*; *Tower Falls, Yellowstone Park*; and *Cedars on Sand Hills*: "Many of these plates were etched on Long Island, directly from nature, and the feeling of nature has been most admirably preserved in them.... It may unhesitatingly be affirmed that among these twelve plates is to be found some of the freshest and healthiest work yet done by an American etcher, and it is pleasant to know that, on the strength of their testimony to his abilities, Mr. Moran has been elected a fellow of the Society of Painter-Etchers lately organized in England."

7 July. Moran to S.R. Koehler: "Mrs. Moran has lately made a pretty large plate of 'The Cliff Dwellers of New York,' shanties on the rocks in our street which were removed a few days after she had finished her etching. As you say, it is a good field, and would have an historic value in time to come. The plate she has made is rather too large for the *Review* but if after you see it, you would like to have the plate, it can be cut down to a usable size without detriment to the etching. In a day or two I will send you the proof. I go to the Yellowstone." (EHL)

21 July. *Boston Transcript*: "Mr. Koehler has also a brief account [in *American Art Review*] of a new series of etchings by Thomas Moran, with an example of this later work, entitled 'Morning.'"

Late July. Moran travels with J.G. Pangborn, engraver John Karst, and a railroad official through Maryland, Virginia, West Virginia, and Pennsylvania to fulfill commission from railroad for illustrations for *Picturesque B. & O.: Historical and Descriptive*, to be written by Pangborn and published in 1882. Publication gives detailed account of trip. (GA small notebook 1877/1882, 26; Morand 1996, 56 – 58)

30 July. Moran sketches and dates *Potomac at Catoctin Mountain, Bald Eagle Island* (Gilcrease).

August. *Art Journal*, 256: "The Buffalo Academy of Fine Arts has purchased for $1,000 Thomas Moran's large and important painting, 'Bringing Home the Cattle—Coast of Florida.' The rejection of this picture at the exhibition of 1879 by the Society of American Artists, led to Mr. Moran's resignation from that body."

8, 9 August. Moran sketches and dates *Rawley* and *Idiotic Leap, Rawley* (Gilcrease).

13 August. *Boston Transcript*: "A few of the pictures in hand for the Charitable Mechanic Association's art gallery are as follows: Thomas Moran, 'A Moquis Town in Arizona' ($350) [cat. no. 143]."

22 August. *Boston Transcript* previews September periodicals: "A third article of note in [*Scribner's*] is John Muir's 'The Coniferous Forests of the Sierra Nevada,' illustrated by Vanderhoof, George Inness, Jr., and Thomas Moran."

Late August. Moran and John Karst go to Denver and join photographer W. H. Jackson, Ernest Ingersoll of Harper's, and Mrs. Ingersoll for trip following narrow-gauge rail lines through Colorado and New Mexico. Moran makes sketches for illustrations for Ingersoll's *Crest of the Continent* (1885) for the Denver & Rio Grande R. R., which provides private train and gives Jackson flat car to use as a photographer's platform. Moran designates drawings for illustrations for Harper's *Garden of the Gods*; Ojo Caliente for D & RG. Ingersoll's book gives detailed account of trip. (Morand 1996, 58–63, 206–210; Newhall and Edkins 1974, 145; GA small notebook 1877/1882)

September. *Art Journal*, 286: "The ninth Black and White exhibition at the Dudley Gallery in London, contains the following contributions from American artists. In wood engravings … 'The Bathers' after Thomas Moran."

4 September. *Denver Rocky Mt. News*: "Mr. Thomas Moran, the distinguished New York artist, is in [Leadville]. Mr. Moran's name has become almost a household word from his magnificent work in 'Scribner's Monthly,' and his well known view of the Mount of the Holy Cross. He will remain in the city for some days and spend his spare time sketching in the vicinity."

15, 16, 20 September. Moran sketches and dates *Upper Twin Lake, Wasatch Mountains*; then *Martha Lake*; then *Green River* and *Green River Buttes, Wyoming Territory* (Gilcrease; Stark Museum).

October. *Art Journal*, 319: "The great fair which is annually held in St. Louis constitutes one of the Art events of the season. … This year, as usual, the exhibition has been excellent. Among the New York artists represented were Thomas Moran." Moran records that he sent *Fort George Island, Florida* (sold from exh. for $400.00), and *Crossing the Stream*. (GA Partial Memorandum Concerning Pictures 1879–1882, 13)

October. Richard Watson Gilder becomes editor-in-chief of *Century Illustrated Monthly Magazine*; first issue is Nov. 1881. (Smith 1970, 24–25)

20 October. *The Independent* [NY]: "Thomas Moran has returned East from an extended tour in Colorado, Utah, and New Mexico."

November. *Art Journal*, 352: "At the recent Chicago-Interstate Industrial Exposition … 'The Cliffs of Green River,' Thos. Moran, [sold for] $1,000 … . The financial success of the smaller exhibition of the Milwaukee Industrial Exposition has also been very marked. Among the paintings sold were: 'Cloudy Day Near Waverly, N.Y.,' Thomas Moran, $250." Moran notes that he sent to Chicago, *Crab Pond East Hampton, L.I.*; *Three Mile Harbor*; and *Green River Cliffs* (sold to Mr. Clapp of Chicago); and sent to Milwaukee, *Near Waverly* (same as 1877 NAD cat. no. 253, sold for $250.00 from exhibition). (GA Partial Memorandum Concerning Pictures 1879–1882, 11–13; small notebook 1877/1882, 43)

December. *Art Journal*, 380: "The Christmas cards issued by Prang & Co. this season are of unusual interest through the impetus given by the prize competition of last spring. The reproduction of the prize cards meets every anticipation both in color and in the working out of the details. Among the new cards are … designs by … Thomas Moran."

3 December. *Newark Daily Advertiser* reviews paintings at Upper Library Hall: "The gallery as a whole is a very fair exhibit of modern art. It comprises one hundred and thirty-nine works by those whose names are familiar as household words with others we think entirely new to this city. Cropsey, Gifford … and Moran are as well known and appreciated here as they are elsewhere … . The finest of artists may be disappointing, however, and while we are in the vein of fault finding Thomas Moran may as well have a part of it." Reviewer judges *"Fiercely the red sun descending …"* a "failure."

9 December. *Boston Transcript*: "There is a thoroughly interesting collection of pictures by American artists at Messrs. Doll & Richards's just now … . Moran's sunset over the East Hampton sand wastes has much that is fine, the landscape being somewhat better than the sky."

• 1882 •

Moran moves residence to 166 W. 55th St., NY. (New York City Directory)

Moran becomes member of the Century Association. (*Century Association* 1947, 394)

Moran elected non-resident member of PSE. (Patterson 1994, 22)

Publication of J. G. Pangborn, *Picturesque B. & O.*

30 January–25 February. At NAD Moran exhibits with AWCS, *Noon—A Sketch in Cottonwood Cañon, Utah*; *Sketch from Nature—Little Cottonwood Cañon, Utah*; *Sketch from Nature—Green River, Utah* (cat. nos. 207, 329, 475); and with NYEC, *Montauk Point, L.I.*; *Old Church of San Juan, N. M.*; *Conway Castle, N. Wales (after J. M. W. Turner)* (cat. nos. 168–170), also serving on executive committee. Mary Nimmo Moran exhibits 11 works. (*NY Post*, 28 Jan. and 23 Feb.; *NYT*, 28 Jan.)

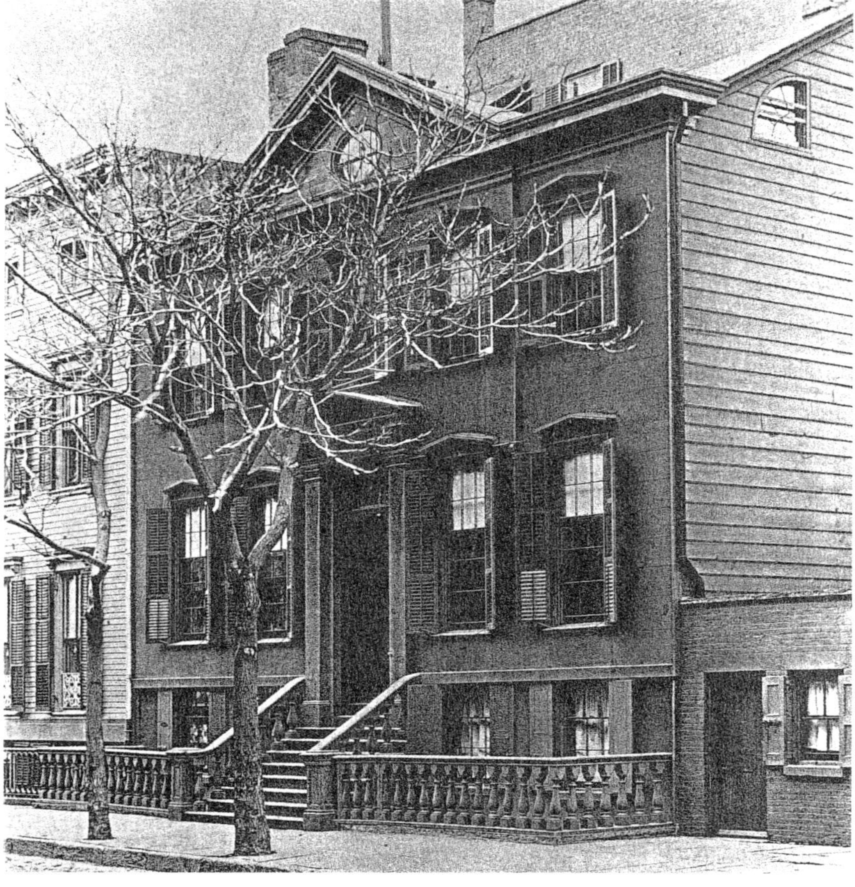

The Century Club, New York, 1882, published in *The Century, 1847–1946* (New York, 1947).

February. Samuel G.W. Benjamin in *Magazine of Art,* 89–93: "Never before has there been a nobler opportunity afforded the artist to aid in the growth of his native land, and to feel that, while ministering to his love of the sublime and the beautiful, he was at the same time a teacher and a co-worker with the pioneer, the man of science, and the soldier, who cleared, surveyed, and held this mighty continent, and brought it under the mild sway of civilisation.... as steamboats began to navigate the rivers, and railways covered the land with a network of steel, the landscape-painters kept pace with the march of improvement.... In considering the variety and excellence of Mr. Moran's attainments in art, it is impossible to assign him any other than very great ability. If he has not achieved the highest flights of art, he has yet exhibited extraordinary versatility in doing many things and doing them well, together with a very unusual exuberance of imagination. Furthermore, the public owe him a debt of gratitude for the enterprise and ability which have done so much to entertain and instruct."

February. *Art Journal* [NY], 63: "Thomas Moran has been invited to etch for 'The Portfolio.'"

12 February. Unidentified newspaper clipping: "In visiting Thomas Moran at his studio... one is surprised at the simple and unostentatious manner in which this great artist lives and works. Working in a room accessible to anyone... and surrounded by only such accessories as are required, Mr. Moran was found busily engaged on a large oil painting for the Royal British Academy. It was a scene in the green river country, and possesses many meritorious features, even in its sketched stage." (EHL scrapbook)

28 March–13 May. NAD annual exhibition. Moran exhibits *On the St. Johns River, Florida*; *Under the Trees*; *Pueblo of San Juan, N.M.*; *Three Mile Harbor, L.I.*; and *Outskirts of the Village—Twilight* (nos. 59, 250, 370, 555, 596). (*NY Post*, 4 Jan.; Naylor 1973, 654)

28 March. *Boston Transcript* reports that 46 works sold on opening day of the NAD exhibition, including Moran's *Under the Trees* for $150.

28 March. *Phila. Press* reviews NAD exhibition: "Mr. Thomas Moran appears by no means to so good advantage, his only important contribution being an extremely conventional and unsatisfactory landscape of largish size, but very limited interest."

April. *Art Journal*, 127, reports that Moran is on the board of control for AWCS.

April. *Harper's Monthly* publishes Ernest Ingersoll's "Silver San Juan" with illustrations by Moran.

18 April. *Boston Transcript*: "From New York:—Thomas Moran and Mary Nimmo Moran will sail for England, for a six-months' stay, in the first week of May. Mr. Moran, who sent to the Royal Academy ... his 'Cliffs of the Green River,' will take with him several paintings and studies."

22 April. *Bolton Journal* [England] publishes lengthy article on the Moran family. Mentions Moran's trip to England in 1862; exhibition of *Mountain of the Holy Cross* at the Royal Academy, London, and subsequent purchase by Englishman Dr. Bell; Yellowstone watercolor commission for Englishman William Blackmore; sale in England of the larger part of Prang's edition on Yellowstone Park. Second half of article features interview with Moran's mother, Mary Higson Moran, and biographies of Moran artists: "With such a distinguished roll of men and women possessed of genius of high order it will readily be believed that in America when the name Moran is found in a catalogue, the public expects a work of art." (Repr. *Bolton Evening News*, 24–25 Apr.)

12 May. Thomas and Mary Nimmo Moran and their children leave New York aboard steamer *Ethiopia* bound for Glasgow, Scotland. (*NY Post*, 13 May)

1 June. Moran sketches and dates *Strathaven Castle* and *Strathaven* in Scotland; undated sketches indicate he also visited Glencoe Pass and Fingal's Cave, Staffa (Gilcrease). Mary Nimmo Moran was born in Strathaven. (Morand 1996, 63–67)

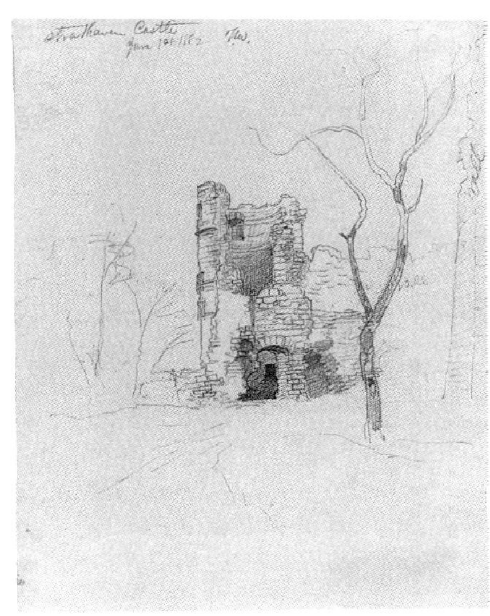

Thomas Moran, *Strathaven Castle,* 1882, graphite on paper, courtesy Gilcrease Museum, Tulsa, Oklahoma.

9 June. *Manchester Guardian* [England]: "There is at present on view at Mr. T. Bromley's Art Gallery... a collection of works which... will be interesting to Bolton people... [for] the talented artist who has produced them is a native of the town.... we have depicted in the works scenery of the Far West—of countries one often reads about, but which there is little chance of visiting by the vast majority of the people.... The artist is Mr. Thomas Moran, whose fame had reached Bolton some time ago.... In addition to the above there is a series of high class etchings by Mrs. Moran, and proof engravings by Mr. Moran of illustrations he had furnished in Scribner's, Harper's and other magazines. Mr. Moran likewise exhibits a work published in 1876, in which are 15 reproductions of water-colour drawings of scenery in the Yellowstone National Park... The collection will remain at Mr. Bromley's rooms during the whole of next week." In Bolton, the Morans stay with Tillotson family, owners of Tillotson's Newspapers, Ltd. (Fred L. Tillotson to Helen Comstock, editor of *Connoisseur Magazine,* 12 Jan. 1937, EHL)

June. *Bolton Evening News* publishes letter to the editor calling for a public honor for Moran. (EHL scrapbook)

June. *Bolton Evening News*: "Whether as a painter in oil or water colors, Mr. Moran will gain numerous admirers, his brilliant coloring in the former line of artistic work being as striking as the faithfulness and cleverness of the outlines of his less ambitious effects in water-color and in black and white sketches. His oil-paintings consist for the most part of representations of the wild force of Nature as displayed in the rugged scenery of the Far West; the spectator stands amazed before some of the artist's pictures, lost in admiring awe at the exhibition of the mighty agencies at work in the trackless West." (EHL)

3 July. *NY Herald* quotes *Bolton Journal*: "Bolton has many gifted sons of whom she may be justly proud, and among these must now be counted Mr. Thomas Moran. He has long been known to fame as an artist on the other side of the Atlantic, where his productions adorn the walls of Congress and are the joy of lovers of art; but until recently even his name was unknown in his native town. Mr. Moran, however, is just now paying a visit to Bolton, and a selection of his works will remain on exhibition for a few days at Mr. Bromley's art gallery. We venture to affirm that admirers of landscape and other art works of a high order will experience a pleasant surprise on viewing the productions of this truly great painter."

4 July. Sir Francis Seymour Haden of the SPE writes to invite Thomas and Mary Nimmo Moran to visit him at his home. (GA)

29 July. *The Critic*, 207: "Mr. Thomas Moran has given an exhibition of his oil- and water-color paintings at his native town, Bolton, England, and the local papers have praised them in the highest terms, commending also the paintings and etchings of his wife."

4 September. *NY Herald* quotes *Bolton Daily Chronicle*: "It will gratify our townspeople generally, and particularly those interested in art, to learn that upon a second visit to view the paintings and etchings executed by Mr. T. Moran, exhibited a short time ago at Mr. Bromley's Art Gallery... and now in London, Mr. John Ruskin, the great art critic, purchased two pictures and six etchings (including three by Mrs. Moran, who is the only lady member of the London Society of Painter-Etchers).... In addition to his purchases of paintings and etchings, Mr. Ruskin ordered a copy of Mr. Moran's work on the Yellowstone Park [Appendix 1]. Though he does not admire etching as a method of art expression, he was much pleased with the work in that line by both Mr. and Mrs. Moran, and thought that the latter had a 'grand style' for etching." Moran also recorded, "Small panel picture of Communipaw. Sold to John Ruskin in London 1882." (GA Old Book of Lists)

9 September. *The Critic*, 245: "Mr. Ruskin has just bought a number of the etchings and water colors of Mr. Thomas Moran, and some of the etchings of his wife. The veteran art-critic spent several afternoons in looking over Mr. Moran's portfolios, and expressed much surprise at the character of the country (mostly the Yellowstone) which they depict. He criticised the drawings with characteristic freedom and enthusiasm of utterance. Mr. Moran's power of painting rocks and drawing water was greater than that of any painter of whom he knew. An etching of an ocean-scene was pronounced 'the best thing ever done.' He termed Mrs. Moran's style of etching 'grand,' and ordered duplicates of the specimens he had bought."

10, 14–15 September. In North Wales, Moran sketches and dates two versions of *Conway* as well as a series dated 1882, including one inscribed, "Conway from across the River, near Turner's point of view"; then *Chwilog, Wales*; *Afon Wen, N. Wales*; *Criccieth Castle, Cardigan Bay, N. Wales*; *Harlech Castle and Snowden, N. Wales*; and *From Hotel Window, Harlech* (EHL; Gilcrease).

22 September. *Boston Transcript*: "Not many American artists have been more favorably received in England than Mr. Thomas Moran."

27 October. *NY Post*: "Thomas Moran has returned from Scotland with a portfolio full of sketches."

18 November. *The Critic*, 317: "One of the most picturesque and interesting plates in the series of American Etchings is Thomas Moran's view of 'Three Mile Harbor, Long Island,' which has just appeared.... Mr. Moran has brought home from his recent trip to Great Britain many studies of English, Welsh, and Scottish scenery, some of which he will utilize in future etchings."

2 December. Moran exhibits for the first time at Century Club, with *Pueblo of San Juan* and *Ringwood* (nos. 25, 30). (CA, AAA)

5–16 December. Fall BAA exhibition. Moran exhibits *Watering Place* and *Autumnal Woods* (nos. 89, 124). (Marlor 1970, 281, 393)

27 December–3 February 1883. Exhibition of PSE at PAFA. Thomas and Mary Nimmo Moran both exhibit. (Patterson 1994, 22–23)

27 December. John Ruskin writes Moran in New York: "I have your kind and interesting letter of the 11th with pamphlet on American art. Ward brought me yesterday the beautiful bridge by Mrs. Moran and your little landscape.—the Yellowstone Park—etc—will doubtless arrive later. I reply at once to send you Christmas greetings and hope you will not work as hard—or you will break down some day when you least expect it.—and I *do* wish with my whole heart you would give up—for a while all that flaring and glaring and splashing and rearing triumph—and *paint*, not etch—some quiet things like that little tree landscape absolutely from nature.... I hope you will come back to England to study [Turner's] work.... please do mind what I said, about a severer and simpler sincerity of study." (EHL)

• 1883 •

13 January. At Century Club Moran exhibits *Landscape* (no. 30). (CA, AAA)

20 January. *The Critic*, 24: "The Catalogue of the First Exhibition of the Philadelphia Society of Etchers is the most tasteful one we have ever seen. It contains etchings by F. S. Church, P. Moran, J. Simson, H. Farrar, S. J. Ferris, T. Moran, J. Pennell, and B. Uhle. There are 1070 etchings in the exhibition."

21 January. *NYT* quotes London *Academy* to say that Moran is "one of the most original and thoroughly national artists that America has produced, and his etchings are characterized no less by suggestiveness of light and space than by ready seizure of landscape character. That given in the thirteenth number of 'American Etchings' is quite representative and gives that interest to the meagre country at Three Mile Harbor, Long Island, which can only be seen by an artist and expressed by rare skill in selection of line."

29 January–25 February. At NAD Moran exhibits with AWCS, *Bridge of the Three Waters, Glencoe, Scotland*, and *Cliffs of Green River, Wyoming* (cat. nos. 275, 420); and with NYEC, *Harlech Castle, N. Wales*; *Pass of Glencoe*; *English River, Hampshire*; *Port Madoc, N. Wales*; *Strathaven Castle, Scotland* (cat. nos. 101–105), also serving on executive and hanging committees. Mary Nimmo Moran exhibits three works. (*Boston Transcript*, 27 Jan.; *NYT*, 24 Feb.)

Late January. Moran sails aboard White Star Line ship from New York to Mexico via Cuba, with Arthur G. Renshaw, British representative of the Mexican National Railroad, and mining engineer Mr. Hahn. (Envelope of fragmentary trip diary, GA; Morand 1996, 67–72)

29, 30 January. Moran sketches and dates *Double Headed Shot Keys*, *Elbow Key Light*, *Bahama Island Light*, and *Off the Bahamas*; then *Havana* (Gilcrease). (Christie's cat., 27 Sept. 1990; Sotheby's cat., 18 Dec. 1991)

February. M. G. van Rensselaer in *Century Magazine*, 494–495: "Mrs. Moran, is, as yet, the only woman who is a member of the New York Etching Club.... Her work...is, above all things, direct, emphatic, bold.... Mrs. Moran's immediate success with the needle was doubtless owing to the fact that she was her husband's pupil. Mr. Thomas Moran had etched for many years before the art became so popular as now, and has experimented in a score of ways, even with the little-practiced art of etching on glass. His plates are various in character, but to me his best results are those of delicacy and refinement and grace, rather than those of force. His seashore sketches are especially attractive. If there is a fault to be found with his work—which, by the way, has won him hearty praise from Mr. Ruskin, who is not a lover of the art in general—it will be that his compositions sometimes lack unity of conception and consequently of effect.... Mr. Thomas Moran's very large plate, after the Turner in his possession, is the most ambitious and also the most successful reproductive etching yet attempted in America."

3 February. Moran to Mary, from Vera Cruz: "[Havana] is I think the most picturesque place I ever saw. Everywhere it is a picture. The color is something indescribably beautiful. The people, the vehicles, churches, plazas, everything is pictorial.... I made some sketches from the vessel which are good. I would like to have made some sketches in the city but had no time.... We left Havana early in the evening [30 Jan.] and the effect of the setting sun on the towers and walls of the Moro Castle and the city was splendid.... Next day was spent in the open sea.... Plenty of flying fish and a fine sunset....

We arrived at Progresso in Yucatan [1 Feb.], a perfectly flat country.... left Progresso after sunset and today as I write

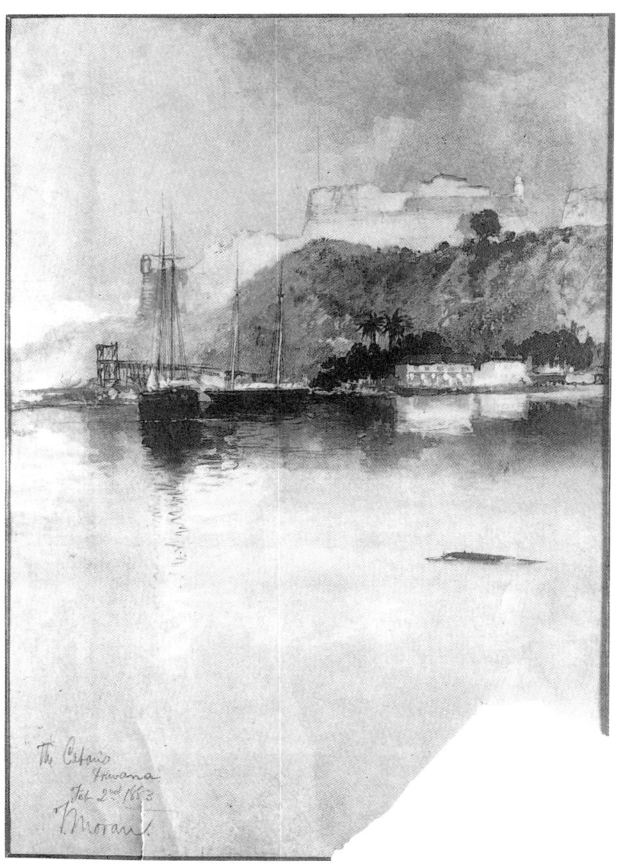

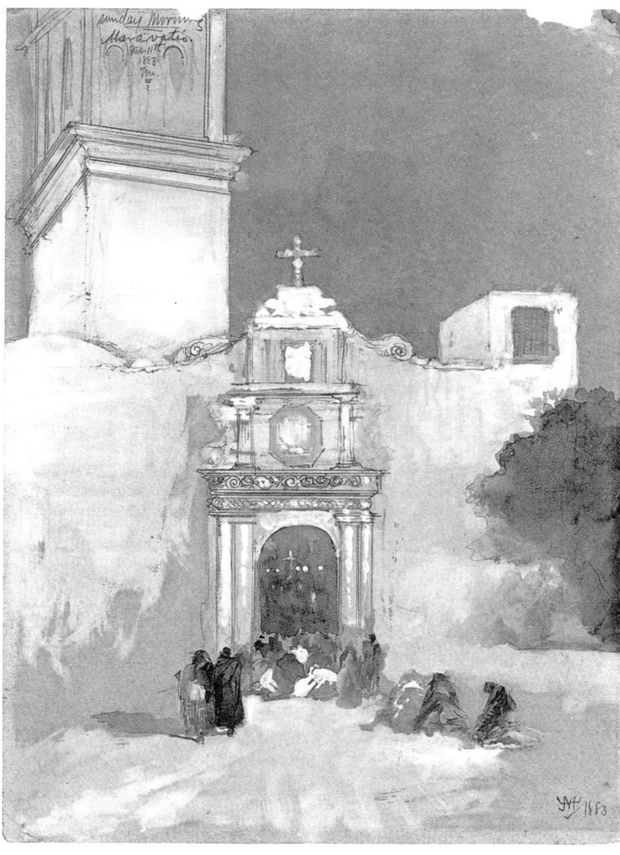

Thomas Moran, *The Cabaña, Havana,* 1883, watercolor and graphite on paper, courtesy East Hampton Library.

Thomas Moran, *Sunday Morning, Maravatio,* 1883, watercolor and graphite on paper, courtesy Gilcrease Museum, Tulsa, Oklahoma.

we are within 100 miles of Vera Cruz where we shall take the R.R. to Mexico City. The Captain says we shall be there very early in the morning. The Cap is a fine fellow with a taste for art ... [he] placed his cabin at my disposal and I have done all my sketching there. He is musical also ....

Here we are at Vera Cruz, another pictorial place like Venice. A quiet smooth sea reflecting the castle and buildings." (Bassford and Fryxell 1967, 61–62)

3–8 February. Moran sketches and dates *Vera Cruz*; then *San Juan d'Ulloa, Vera Cruz*; *Spanish Fort, Paso del Macho*; *On the Metlac River, Mexico*; *Cordova*; then two versions of *Orizaba*; then *Near Vera Cruz* and *Waterfall at Atoyac*; then two versions of *Mexico* and *Outskirts of Mexico City* (Gilcrease; EHL).

8 February. Moran to Mary, from Mexico City: "We had rooms in the Hotel Diligencia [Vera Cruz] overlooking the plaza and the cathedral with its variously colored tile roof and domes. The city with its numerous churches, from the ship looked much like Venice .... The Castle of San Juan and Ulloa is very pictorial and I made several sketches of both the castle and the city .... The country around Vera Cruz reminds me very much of Colorado and Idaho. From the ship on Saturday morning we had a glimpse of the great shining peak of Orizaba some 60 miles distant looming up high into the clouds and covered with snow. It is some 16000 feet high ....

We left Vera Cruz on Sunday morning ... for Orizaba. After leaving the Coast the tropical growth became very luxuriant and the dry sandy country soon gave way to a green and pleasant land, and as we rose toward the mountains the air became much cooler .... I succeeded in getting a couple of sketches before breakfast .... We left for Mexico [City] at 10:30, the R.R. going up a very steep grade through the mountains, but it was so cloudy and rainy that we could see but little of the country. Had it been clear, I think the scenery would have been very fine, as I think the great snow peak would have been in sight nearly all the way .... We reached Esperanza at two o'clock. This point is some 12000 feet above Vera Cruz and here we had a fine view of the snow-covered peak rising ... above us against an intensely blue sky. It was a grand sight. I made a sketch while the train was waiting, and I think I can do something with it when I get home. From this point the road begins to descend by a gradual slope toward the Valley of Mexico. Here we encountered the great dusty country of which I had heard so much, but it was not any worse than what I had often experienced in the west, and it is without the alkali .... [In Mexico City] we were met by some of [R.R. rep.] Mr. Renshaw's friends who took us in carriages to the Hotel San Carlos where rooms had been provided for us.

Next day I wandered about the town and found it very interesting and pictorial, and as it was a feast day everybody seemed to be out in the streets, bad smelling and dirty but just the thing for pictures.... In the evening the band played in the plaza opposite the great cathedral and maskers were plentiful. It was the Mardi-Gras in Mexico. Next day I and Mr. Hahn went to the imperial hill of Chapultepec the ancient residence of the Montezumas and Aztec kings, but I was disappointed as it was too cloudy to see the peaks of Popocatapetl and Istaccihuitl. The day was very hot and we came back tired out. In the afternoon I went into the outskirts of the city where the poor people live.... From the outskirts this morning I had a fine view of the two great mountains, snow covered and rising into the clear sky.... I have made some sketches about the city that I think I can make good use of, and Mexico has furnished me with lots of suggestions.... Today Renshaw told us... we had better start westward to Toluca and some other place with an unpronounceable name near the mines that Mr. Hahn is going to inspect.... I anxiously await a letter from you that I may hear how things are going with you and how mother is. I fear the worst for her and shall be glad if I hear that my fears are unfounded." (Bassford and Fryxell 1967, 63–67)

10 February. Moran's mother has died at age 75. (Interment records, Old Cathedral Cemetery, Phila.)

11 February. Moran to Mary, from Maravatio: "This place... is some 200 miles west of Mexico [City].... Yesterday I started out sketching but found the sun very hot, and after being out about 3 hours I returned to the Hotel, or rather stable, for it is little better than one, and in the afternoon worked up the sketches I had made.... The country here is very much like New Mexico and I feel a trifle disappointed with the scenery, which is rather barren than luxuriant. The towns however are always picturesque." (Bassford and Fryxell 1967, 69–71)

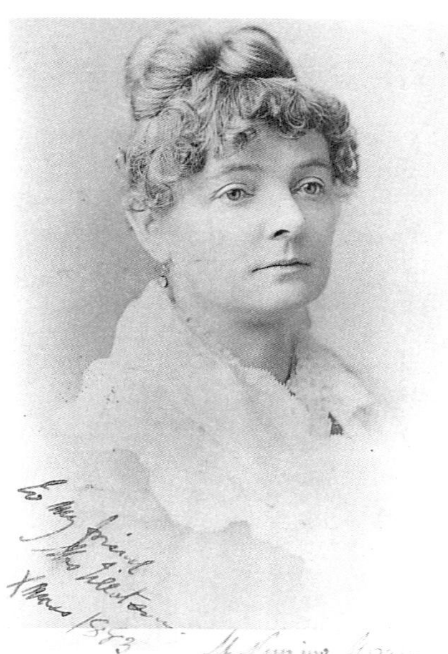

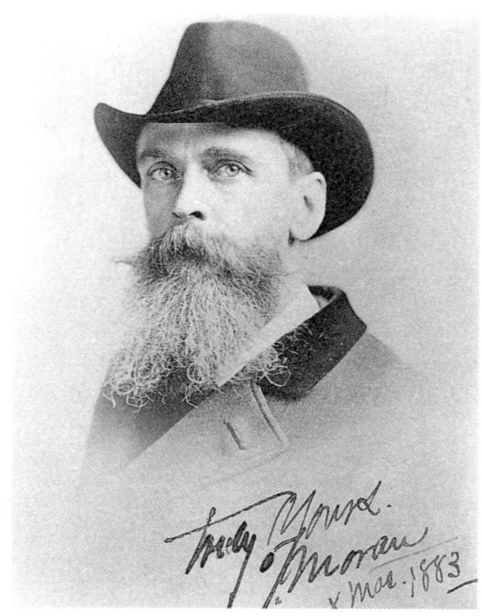

Mary Nimmo Moran and Thomas Moran in photographic portraits they sent with Christmas cards in 1883, courtesy Yellowstone National Park.

11–14 February. Moran sketches and dates *Sunday Morning, Maravatio*; *From Acambaro, West*; and *Payday, beyond Maravatio*; two sketches inscribed *Maravatio*; and *San José, beyond Maravatio*; and then *San José, Mexico* (Gilcrease; EHL).

17 February. Moran sketches and dates *Quirio, Mexico* (Gilcrease).

20 February. Moran to Mary, from Maravatio: "We left this place 4 or 5 days ago and went to Acambaro with a party of six. From there we went by Buck Board to Morelia 90 miles from this place. We stayed there one whole day and returned to Acambaro. Remained there over night and came here this morning on a special train. We are just about to start for Trojes mines where we shall remain a couple of days, return here, and then start northward for Monterey, and then home where Mr. Renshaw says we shall arrive about the 15th of March.... I have some good sketches." (Bassford and Fryxell 1967, 73)

25–27 February. Moran sketches and dates *From Hotel Window, Celaya*; *Calderon, Mexico*; then *Dolores, Hidalgo* (Gilcrease). Travels from San Miguel to Dolores via Sanctuario in the rain: "This morning we found it rainy & very cold & after the sample of the roads we had yesterday we decided to remain over until tomorrow as it would be almost impossible to make Jaral or San Francisco 50 to 60 miles without riding far into the night. Dolores is a poor & uninteresting town of about 8000 people. But the hotel kept by a Spaniard is one of the best we have stopped.... We obtained a change of mules as those we came with... were tired out." (Diary, GA)

28 February. Leaves Dolores for Chirimoya, passing through "the Gate or Gap of Chirimoya where the mountains are magnificent." Sketches and dates *On the Plateau above Dolores* and *Gate of Chirimolla* (Gilcrease). (Diary, GA)

1 March. Travels from Chirimoya to Jaral, "Queer town with conical granaries... [in] very fertile & large [valley] surrounded by fine Mts. & thickly wooded. Contains a large Laguna. The natives tell us it is 20 leagues from here to Potosi. Very cold & drizzly." Sketches and dates *Near San Francisco* and *Mountain Range on the West Side of San Louis Valley above San Francisco* (Cooper-Hewitt; Phillips Academy, Andover). (Diary, GA)

7–8, 11, 13 March. Sketches and dates *El Fraile near Catorce*; then *Yucca Grove beyond Cedral* and *Ojo de Agua, Saltillo*; then *Arroyo at Saltillo*; *Saltillo*; and *Santa Catarina near Monterrey*; then *Near Monterrey* (Gilcrease; EHL).

14–24 March. BAA exhibition. Moran exhibits watercolor *Cliffs of Green River, Wyoming* (no. 116) and four etchings. (Marlor 1970, 281, 393)

Mid-March. Returning from Mexico, Moran receives letter from Ruskin, dated 15 Feb.: "I had so much to say to you about your book [Appendix 1] that I could not say it when it came, and am still less able now. But it will be spoken of, I hope not in any way displeasing to you, at my first Oxford lectures in giving account of the new energies of modern art—and meantime, in justice to yourself, please.... Force yourself to show leaves and stones—and as God means us all to be shaded by, and to walk on—and be buried under.—till you see the daily beauty of these and make others see it." (EHL)

Spring. Moran rents Mulford House in East Hampton. (Wilkins 1966, 174)

2 April–12 May. NAD annual exhibition. Moran exhibits *On the Stour, Hampshire, England*; *Pass of Glencoe, Scotland*; and *Autumnal Woods* (nos. 165, 221, 388). Mary Nimmo Moran exhibits one work. (Naylor 1973, 654, 656)

7 April. At Century Club Moran exhibits *Cliffs of Green River, Wyoming Territory*, and *Pass of Glencoe—Scotland* (nos. 36, 37). (CA, AAA)

16 April. Moran sketches and dates a landscape he inscribes "After Claude" (Gilcrease).

5 May. At Century Club Moran exhibits *Maravatio, Mexico* (no. 1) and 12 watercolor studies of Mexico. (CA, AAA)

10 May. *The Independent* [NY] reviews NAD exhibition: "Thomas Moran, in his 'Pass of Glencoe,' has certainly gotten something of the grandeur of Nature on to his canvas. But the picture is rather sensational in its composition—would do for the background of a Highland battle in some stage drama of Scottish life."

19 May. *The Critic*, 236, mentions loan collection at Metropolitan Museum: "The skill displayed in Mr. Thomas Moran's big picture of Ponce de Leon in Florida will astonish many who saw it years ago, but who have seen nothing as good by Mr. Moran since then."

2 June. *Boston Transcript* quotes from *Pall Mall Gazette* [England]: "There is now on view in the drawing-room of the Egyptian Hall an interesting exhibition of American watercolor drawings and etchings, by a variety of painters, very few of whom have ever been heard of in England. The innumerable company of Morans, which is certainly the most artistic family since the days of the Van Huysums, sends specimens by five of its members...perhaps the most interesting and accomplished drawings in the gallery.... Mr. William Chase's 'Spaniard' is extremely clever, and so are many of Mr. Thomas Moran's etchings."

2 June. At Century Club Moran exhibits *Enquiring the Way* (no. 18). (CA, AAA)

July-August. On Long Island, Moran sketches and dates *Amagansett* and *Between Napeague Beach and Amagansett* (EHL; Gilcrease).

31 August. Sketches and dates *Gardiner Bay*; *Fresh Pond, Gardiner Bay*; and *Fresh Pond* (Gilcrease; EHL).

26, 27 September. Sketches and dates *East Hampton* and *At Foot of Fithian's Lot, East Hampton*; then another *East Hampton* (EHL).

10 October. Letter from American House, Denver, to Moran: "I have fulfilled my part of our compact of last spring...and am happy to inform you that you are a one third owner in the Thos Moran Lode. Which interest is valued at $2,500 today.... Location certificate filed 8:50 AM Sep 26th, 1883...All I ask of you is $154.75. That I was obliged to borrow in order to secure the claim we have.... It is far better than anything they are asking $50,000 for today in that section. I send by this mail the location certificate also a paper containing an opinion of a famous expert I have with me about four pounds of ore which you will see when I get to New York in about two weeks." (Letter and certificate, GA)

22 October. NAD autumn exhibition opens. Moran exhibits *Glory of Spring* and *Clouds and Sunlight, Long Island* (cat. nos. 127, 202), and serves on exhibition committee. (*NYT*, 20 Oct.)

15 November. Deed registered to Mary Nimmo Moran for about ⅔-acre property on Main St., East Hampton, from Edward and Phoebe Osborne, for $1,500. (Suffolk County records, Riverhead, NY, *Liber* 278, p. 36)

20 December. *Boston Transcript*: "In no work that we have seen has the present status of the art [of etching] in America been so well set forth as in the 'Twenty Original Etchings' just brought forth by Cassell & Co. of New York.... Thomas Moran [contributes] a Turneresque Mexican study."

Christmas. Thomas and Mary Moran send out Christmas cards with portrait photographs of themselves. (YNP)

28 December 1883–12 January 1884. Sale at American Art Galleries, Madison Square, NY, of American paintings owned by Thomas B. Clarke, to raise funds for figure study award at NAD annual exhibition. *Boston Transcript*, 1 Jan. 1884: "Thomas Moran has three delightful pictures—'Morning at Vera Cruz'—as full of rich color as a Venetian scene; 'Inquiring the Way,' suggestive of cool, shadowy paths in the mountains, and a study at Easthampton [cat. nos. 82–84]."

• 1884 •

Moran moves residence to 9 E. 17th St., NY. (Naylor 1973, 654)

Completes building of studio-cottage on Main St., East Hampton. (Whipple 1993, 21)

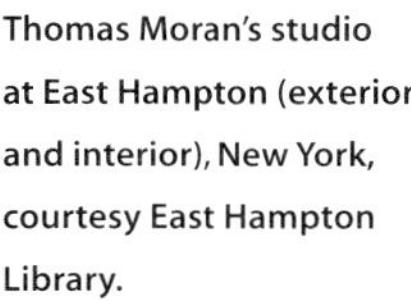

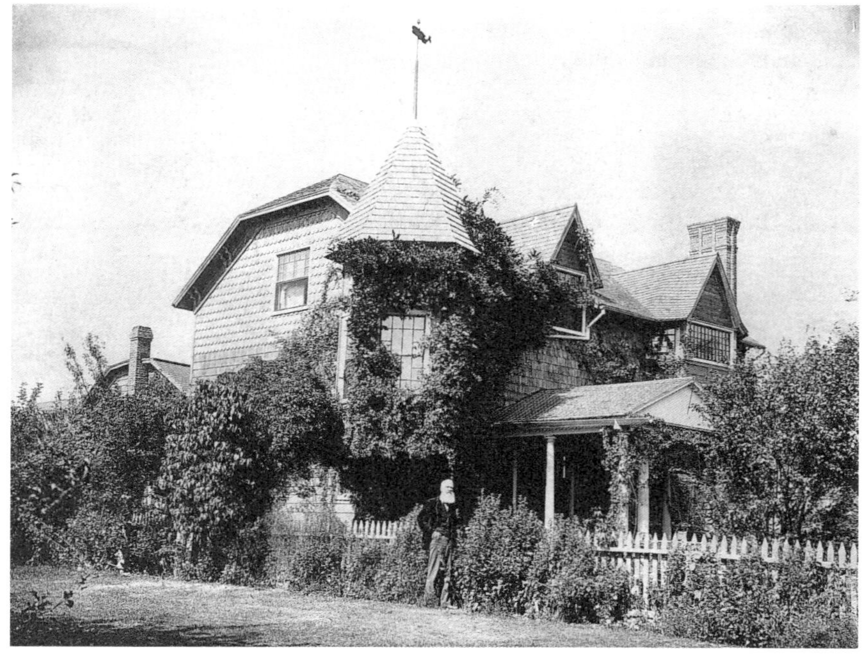

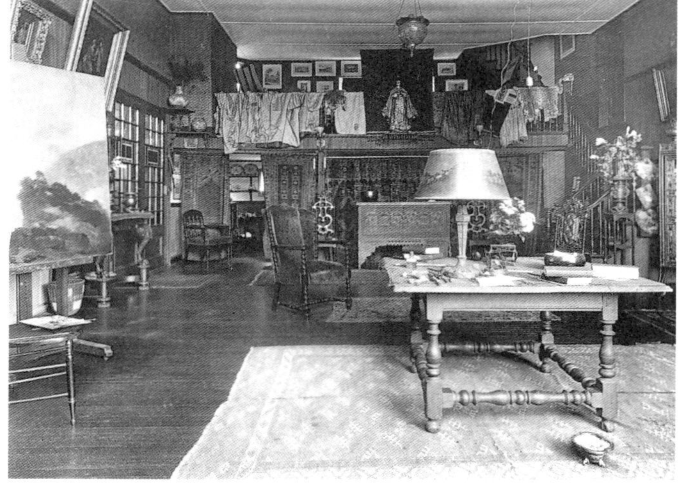

Thomas Moran's studio at East Hampton (exterior and interior), New York, courtesy East Hampton Library.

12, 26 January, 2 February. At Century Club Moran exhibits *Gathering Storm* (no. 7); 59 studies and sketches; then *Dream of the Orient* (no. 18). (CA, AAA)

4 February–1 March. At NAD Moran exhibits with AWCS, *City of Orisaba, Mexico*; *Maravatio, Mexico*; *Street in Maravatio, Mexico*; *Silver Mine of Trojes, Mexico*; *Castle of San Juan D'Ulloa, Harbor of Vera Cruz, Mexico*; *Tower of Cortes, Mexico*; *Off the Bahamas*; and *Havana, Cuba* (cat. nos. 188, 189, 194–199); and with NYEC, *Apple Orchard*; *Study of Buttonwoods*; *On the Shore of Gardiner's Bay, L.I.*; *Tower of Cortez* (nos. 136–138, and 139 from "Twenty Original Etchings by American Artists"), also serving on executive and hanging committees. Mary Nimmo Moran exhibits five works. (*Boston Transcript*, 14 Feb.)

1 March. At Century Club Moran exhibits *San Juan Abajo—Mexico* (no. 28). (CA, AAA)

5 April. *NY Herald* on varnishing day at NAD: "There is a large and strong study of waves at sunset, by Thomas Moran, and a large and well studied one of waves at midday, by Edward Moran."

5 April. *Boston Transcript* reports on varnishing day: "Thomas and Edward Moran occupy a good portion of the south wall with two large sea pieces, similar as to idea—the solitary grandeur of the ocean just after a storm—but very different in treatment. Of the two, the one by Thomas [*Norther in the Gulf of Mexico*] pleased me most, being deeper in tone, and having better perspective effects than the latter. The huge black, surging billows interpose their crests between the spectator and a thin stretch of golden sunlight on the horizon, giving a dash of welcome color to the scene. The spray in the distance is better managed than that in the foreground, which lacks lightness."

6 April. *NY Tribune* reports on sales at NAD exhibition: "There was the usual large attendance of 'Buyers' Day' at the Academy yesterday, and the sales opened in a not discouraging fashion. Among the pictures sold were…'A Gathering Storm, East Hampton,' Thomas Moran, $500."

7 April–17 May. NAD annual exhibition. Moran exhibits *Gathering Storm, East Hampton, L.I.*; *Norther in the Gulf of Mexico*; *Market Days in San Juan, Abajo, Mexico* (nos. 30, 241, 679), and serves on exhibition committee. (*NY Herald*, 4 Apr., 18 May; Naylor 1973, 654)

13 April. Morgan Molihenney reviews NAD exhibition for *NY Herald*: "Of the two elder brothers Moran, Thomas, in his large Turneresque view of 'A Norther in the Gulf of Mexico' shows more actual power as a painter than we have found in his work for some time, while Edward, though somewhat prosaic in his well drawn painting called 'The Sea,' shows a bright, attractive little work in the scene on 'Greenport Dock on Saturday Afternoon.'…Thomas Moran's principal landscape is 'A Gathering Storm—Easthampton, Long Island.' This is a thinly painted canvas, rich in color and dramatic in effect. It introduces the familiar windmill. He also shows a large and not particularly successful work picturing 'Market Day in San Juan Abajo, Mexico.'"

16 April. *NY Post* reviews NAD exhibition: "The veteran Moran allows his facility of treatment to carry him too far, and his 'Gathering Storm'…with a remarkable power over effect and large masses, has a glittering facility in rendering the detail and an exaggeration of the effective passages which suggest morbid feeling and a drift into the mechanical and formal…the tract that lies beyond wise and good conventionalization. Moran is a colorist in the proper sense of the term, and it is his own fault if he seems to some to be merely trying to catch the tricks of Turner."

27 April. *NY Tribune* announces recent election officers of NYEC: "Henry Farrer, president; J. C. Nicoll, secretary; F. S. Church, Thomas Moran and Frederic Dielman, members of the executive committee."

28 April. *NY Tribune* reviews NAD exhibition: "Now that our business men realize our nearness to Mexico we may expect some of our artists to follow in the footsteps of Messrs. Ferguson and Thomas Moran. The former sends a painting of the river and peak of Orizaba, the latter 'Market Days in San Juan.'... It is absurd that artists when they start on a search for subjects should overlook the riches within our own borders and so near as Mexico."

3 May. At Century Club Moran exhibits *Much-Resounding Sea* (no. 24). (CA, AAA)

4 May. *NY Herald*: "The names of C. F. Ulrich, F. D. Millet, C. Y. Turner, Arthur Quartley and Thomas Moran should certainly be found this year among those of the academicians elected." Moran is elected a full Academician (N.A.) and listed as such in the NAD autumn exh. cat. (p. 5). He presented *Three Mile Harbor* as diploma piece. (Clark 1954, 121)

8 May. *Boston Transcript*, 16 May: "A collection of etchings and engravings by ancient and modern masters formed the major part of the exhibition at the Union League Club, New York [8–10 May].... Among the ancient engravers and etchers represented were Rembrandt, Durer... among modern etchers, Haden, Whistler, Millet, Corot, Duveneck, Thomas Moran and Peter Moran."

17 May. *NY Post*: "We have received from Thomas Moran an etching after Turner, to which attaches an unusual interest, not only as etching of a sound and severe style, but on account of the quality of the picture, which we have seen and which leaves no doubt as to its originality, even if its pedigree were not unquestionable.... Mr. Moran in rendering it in white and black has not softened a defect or shirked a difficulty. Such as was the original he has given it with an exemplary fidelity and sympathy with the qualities of the picture. The etching is 16 x 21 inches, and is certainly one of the most important etchings yet done in this country, not only in size, but for its artistic excellence."

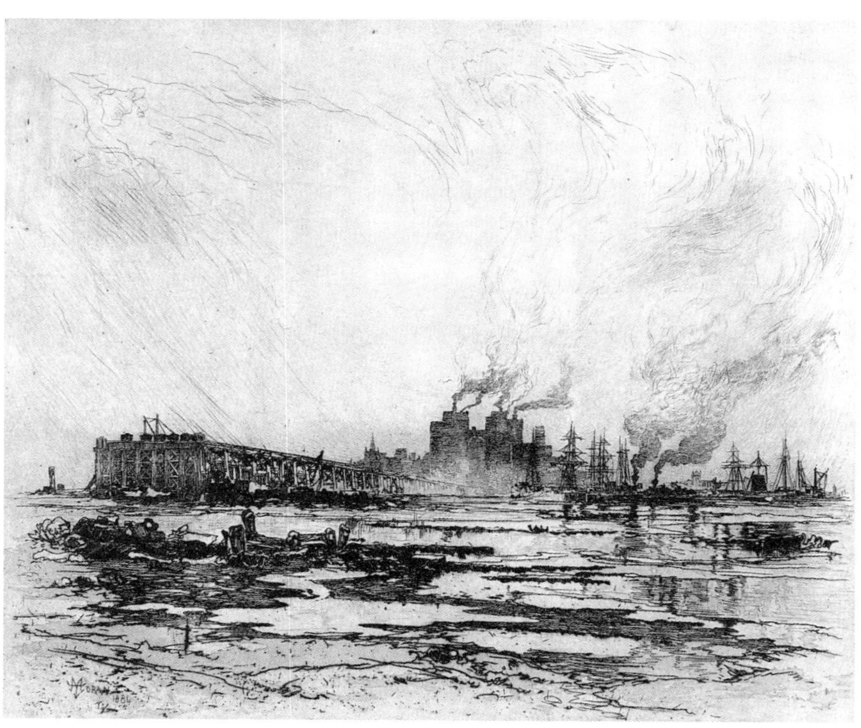

Thomas Moran, *Communipaw, N.J.*, 1884, etching, courtesy Gilcrease Museum, Tulsa, Oklahoma.

28 August, 18 September. *Boston Transcript*: "At the forthcoming exhibition of the Massachusetts Charitable Mechanic Association, opening Sept. 10, there will be an exceptionally interesting collection of the originals of Prang's publications—pictures by Thomas Moran, Murphy, Miss Bridges, F. S. Church, J. W. Champney, Jean Robie and others." Moran's original and lithographic work included in Prang display.

24 October. *Boston Transcript* comments on paintings at the Institute Fair: "Another remarkable canvas is Thomas Moran's 'Ponce de Leon in Florida,' in which wealth of foliate, luxuriant undergrowth and richness of coloring make up a most delightful whole and convey a vivid realization of the special beauty of the region."

10–28 November. NAD autumn exhibition. Moran exhibits *Sunrise—Harbor of Havana* (cat. no. 304). (*NY Tribune*, 25 May; *NYT*, 28 Nov.)

4 December. *Boston Transcript*: "There is now on public exhibition in New York a collection of designs for Christmas cards, entered in a limited competition established by Prang & Co. They were all ordered and paid for by the firm, and in addition compete for prizes of $1000, $500, $300 and $200. These prizes were awarded by the votes of about a hundred of the dealers in such cards. The first prize fell to Charles D. Weldon, the second to William H. Low, the third to Thomas Moran, and the fourth to Frederick Dielman. There are twenty-three designs in all by twenty-two well-known painters.... Mr. Moran [pictures] an angel trumpeting through a town at sunrise."

6 December. At Century Club Moran exhibits *Stormy Day at East Hampton* (no. 38). (CA, AAA)

12 December. *Boston Transcript* comments further about Prang prize designs: "Mr. Moran is represented by two views

of medieval cities, rich and glowing in color, one of them, while the other is dark and very blue, both being injured by somewhat theatrical perspective and angels poorly drawn."

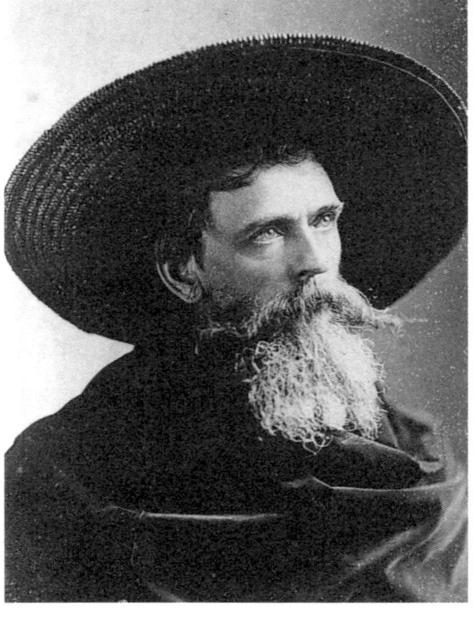

Thomas Moran, 1884, photograph by Napoleon Sarony, courtesy East Hampton Library.

Thomas Moran's daughter Mary with Edward Moran's son Percy in the East Hampton studio, courtesy East Hampton Library.

• 1885 •

10 January. At Century Club Moran exhibits *Fingal's Cave*; *Landscape*; and *Whirlpool Rapids—Niagara* (nos. 9, 11, 31). (CA, AAA)

24 January. *The Critic*, 43: "Opposite the New York home of Mr. Thomas Moran rise the high walls of Jefferson Market Police Court. From his doorstep, the other night, I saw the moon behind the clock-tower, the light and shadow making a most picturesque bit in the heart of this prosaic city. 'Why don't you put that scene into a picture?' I said to the artist. 'Because I have already done so,' he replied. 'I put an angel over the tower, and made a Christmas card of it, and it took the prize.' We both laughed involuntarily, for the combination of an angel and the Jefferson Market Police Court resulting in a Christmas card struck us both as very funny."

Flyer for "Prang's Christmas and New-Year Cards" says, "Season 1885–86. Third Prize Card.—By Thomas Moran. This design illustrates Christmas eve in a medieval city, over the cathedral spires of which hovers an angel, carrying a lighted torch against a dark blue night sky. The color effect is strong and eminently characteristic of Mr. Moran's genius." (NMAH archives, Norcross, box 42, folder 8)

2–28 February. At NAD Moran exhibits with AWCS, *Bridge in Lancashire, England*; *Hackensack Marshes*; *Gardiner's Bay, Long Island Sound*; *Showery Day, Long Island* (cat. nos. 299, 375, 423, 509); and with NYEC, *Communipaw* (cat. no. 160), also serving on executive and hanging committees. Mary Nimmo Moran exhibits five works. (*NYT*, 31 Jan., 15 Feb.)

7 February. At Century Club Moran exhibits *Return of the Life-Boat, East Hampton Beach* (no. 4). (CA, AAA)

15 February. *NYT* reviews NYEC exhibition: "Thomas, Peter, and Mrs. Nimmo Moran have works of more than common excellence, the first showing a view of Communipaw, in which the smoke from factory chimneys is felt delightfully."

19 February. *The Independent* [NY] reviews AWCS exhibition: "The Morans are out in full force.... There are four pictures by Thomas Moran, any one of which would be known for his work without the signature, which is equivalent to saying that they are excellent in motif and in technical qualities."

26 February. *The Independent* reviews NYEC exhibition: "The Morans are present in force, as usual."

7 March. *Boston Transcript*: "The Chautauqua Circle has just added a new and important branch.... This is an art 'circle,' to be called the Chautauqua Society of Fine Arts, in which it is proposed to give lessons in drawing and painting by correspondence.... Mr. Frank Fowler has been appointed director, and Messrs. R. Swain Gifford, Thomas Moran and Will H. Low will act as committee of award. The course of study will extend over two years, at the end of which time diplomas will be given and prizes awarded for the best work in the different classes."

23 March–4 April. BAA exhibition. Moran exhibits watercolors *Cliffs of the Upper Colorado*; *Gardiner's Bay, L.I.*; and *Near Beverly, N.J.* (nos. 61, 155, 266). (Marlor 1970, 281, 393)

4 April. At Century Club Moran exhibits *Lancashire Village* (no. 3). (CA, AAA)

6 April–16 May. NAD annual exhibition. Moran exhibits *Summer Afternoon*; *Abandoning Waterlogged Vessel, East Hampton, L.I.*; *Long Island Landscape*; *Fingal's Cave, Island of Staffa*; and *Morning at Vera Cruz, Mexico* (nos. 112, 271, 344, 479, 561). (Naylor 1973, 654)

11 April. *The Critic*, 174, reviews NAD exhibition: "Notable [is]...'Morning at Vera Cruz,' a marine full of light and blue by Thomas Moran."

18 April. *Boston Transcript* reports on exhibition and prizes at galleries of American Art Association, NY: "Mr. Thomas Moran shows a big canvas, 'The Pass of Glencoe,' with the mountains wrapped in clouds and mist."

17 May. *Brooklyn Eagle*: "Mr. Moran is about taking his summer quarters in Easthampton, L.I., which is becoming quite a resort for artists, and where he has built himself a cottage with a studio annex, or

studio with cottage annex, for the studio is 30 x 40 feet in dimension. He has of late given some attention to marine painting, aiming to produce pictures that indicate the force and vastness of the ocean."

October. *Century Magazine* publishes Lizzie Champney's "Summer Haunts of American Artists," with a photograph of the interior of Moran's studio in East Hampton: "Here, also, Mr. Thomas Moran has a house and studio, and his wife, Mrs. Nimmo Moran, has etched many of her vigorous plates."

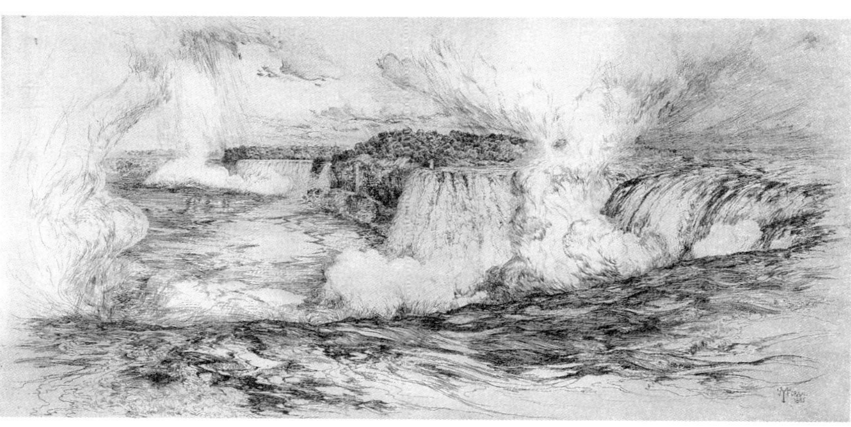

Thomas Moran, *Niagara, from the Canadian Side,* 1885, etching, courtesy Gilcrease Museum, Tulsa, Oklahoma.

12 October. Moran sketches and dates *Georgica,* and two drawings inscribed *Swamp, Georgica* (Gilcrease).

14 October. From East Hampton, Moran writes to art patron William T. Evans: "Would it be an inconvenience to you to let me have remainder due on 'The Dream of the Orient'? I would not ask it if it will put you to the least inconvenience & my only reason for doing so now is that the expense of my new studio has much exceeded my original calculations & has left me 'short' just now.... I have been hard at work this summer & have painted good things; especially a couple of subjects from Montauk point of boulders & wreckage under the cliffs." (Evans papers, AAA)

23 November. NAD autumn exhibition opens. Moran exhibits *Under the Trees, a Glimpse of Georgica Pond, L.I.*; *Misty Morning at Appoquogue, L.I.*; *Southerly Wind and a Cloudy Sky* (cat. nos. 199, 246, 505) and serves on Council. (*NYT*, 22 Nov.)

5 December. *The Critic*, 268: "'Etching' by S. R. Koehler (Cassell & Co.), is published at an opportune moment. It is at once a fairly complete work on etching, written from the standpoint of a contemporary amateur and student, and a handsome holiday art book.... Thirty full-page plates, by old and modern masters, are given. Those by the modern men have been selected with reference to their exemplification of some principle of technique as well as for representative artistic quality.... [Among] modern plates are ... 'Twilight in Arizona' by Thomas Moran, showing the quality of shadow and tone resulting from employment of the roulette ... and original etchings, in the characteristic manner of each artist, by ... Peter Moran ... and Mrs. Mary Nimmo Moran." (See also *Boston Transcript*, 19 Dec.)

10 December. *The Independent* [NY] reviews NAD autumn exhibition: "Thomas Moran's 'Southerly Wind and a Cloudy Sky' has much force, and recalls Diaz."

12 December. *Boston Transcript*: "As a companion in artistic beauty, though of a wholly different character, the same house [Estes & Lauriat] brings out a sumptuous volume entitled 'American Etchings,' consisting of a series of twenty choice etchings by Smillie, Moran, Parrish, Ferris, Garrett and others, printed in several styles." (See also *The Critic*, 19 Dec., 296)

18 December. *Boston Transcript* reports that at the American Art Association sale of the George Whitney collection (on exhibition at American Art Gallery, NY, 8–18 Dec.) Moran's *Autumn on the Wissahickon* sold for $255.

• 1886 •

Henry Teetor in *Magazine of Western History* (1889): "[*Mountain of the Holy Cross*] had a narrow escape from destruction in January 1886. A fire broke out at midnight which consumed Briarhurst and most of its contents. Dr. Bell was at the time in Boston. After rescuing the children, the first object Mrs. Bell sought to save was this picture. Its canvas measured seven feet and ten inches, by six feet, and the frame was too securely fastened against the wall to be moved. Mrs. Bell, with the aid of the butler, cut out the canvas and thus saved art an irreparable loss."

9 January. At Century Club Moran exhibits *Niagara* and *Coast Scene* (nos. 3, 4). (CA, AAA)

30 January–27 February. At NAD Moran exhibits with AWCS, *Mountain of the Holy Cross, Colorado*, and *Moonrise, Outskirts of the City of Celayo, Mexico* (cat. nos. 344, 707); and with NYEC, *Vera Cruz*; *Coming to the Anchor* (after Harry Chase); *On the Marne* (after Daubigny); *Twilight* (after N. V. Diaz) (cat. nos. 113–116), also serving on executive committee. Mary Nimmo Moran exhibits five works. (*NYT*, 30 Jan.)

6 February. At Century Club Moran exhibits *Rangeley Stream, Maine*; *Niagara Rapids*; and *Landscape* (nos. 39–41). (CA, AAA)

8 February. *NYT* reviews NYEC and AWCS exhibitions: "In many cases it is possible to examine the same artist as he works with watercolors and acid, noting which he excels in here, which there, and sometimes recalling his work in oils.... The difference is great between a large brilliantly wrought Turneresque 'Vera

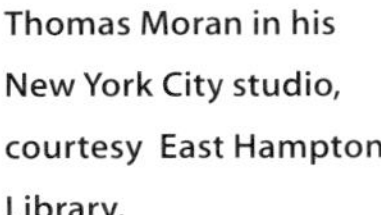

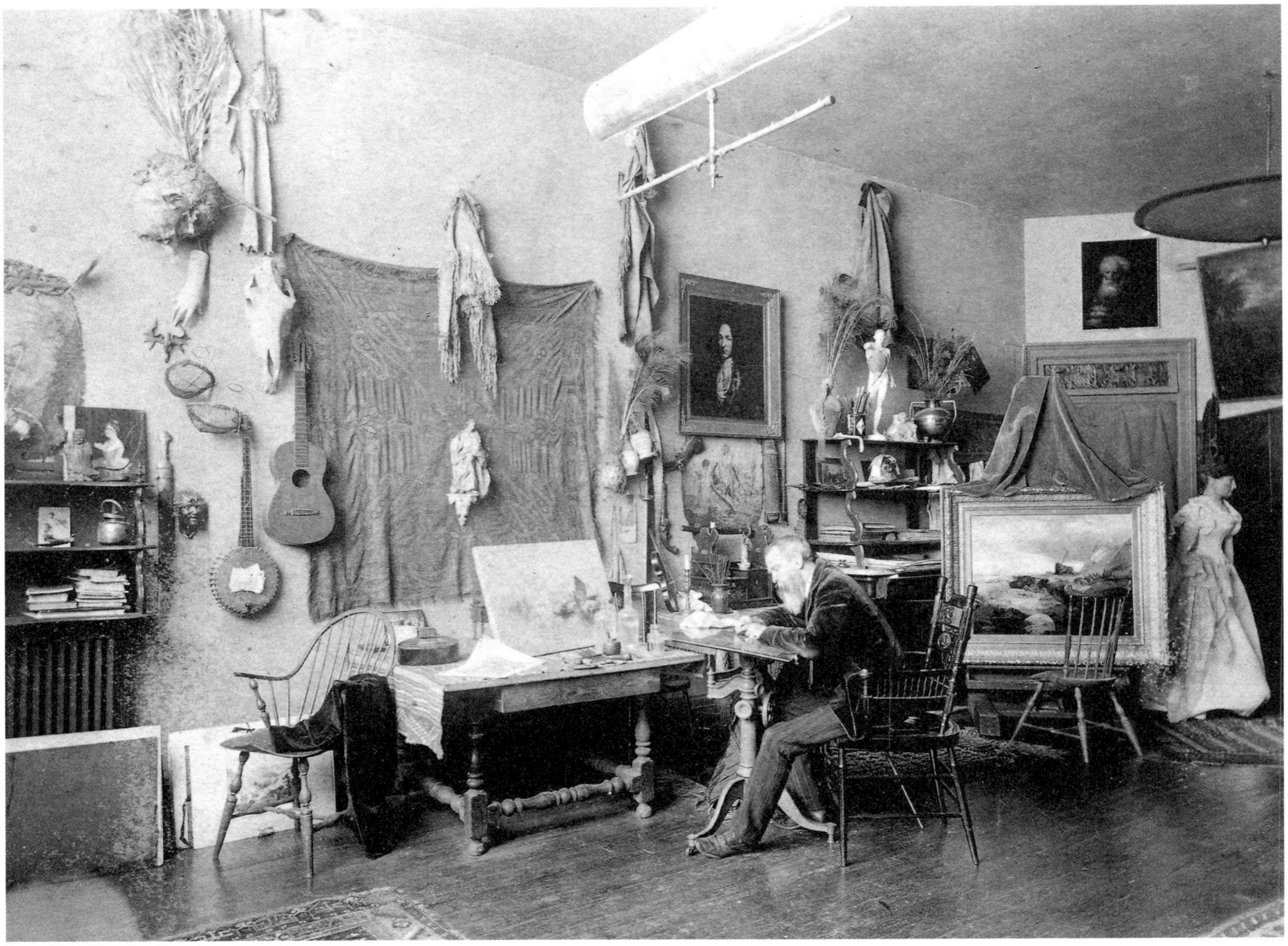

Thomas Moran in his New York City studio, courtesy East Hampton Library.

Cruz' by Thomas Moran, all [cirrus] cloud, sheeny water space, and knowing-looking sea craft, and the tragic effects produced by the heavy burin of Mr. Alexander Schilling.... 'Moonlight, Communipaw,' by J. C. Nicoll, recalls a very successful watercolor by Thomas Moran, being the same view from a slightly different point, and with more sentiment."

15 February. Moran to William MacLeod, curator of the Corcoran: "As you will see by the enclosed card and catalogue, I am about to have a sale of all my paintings, including the *Ponce de Leon in Florida,* which you will remember is a large size 6 x 9 feet and suited more to a public gallery than to an individual collection. I wrote to say that if the Trustees of the Gallery will forward a bid of $2000.00 to Ortgies & Co before the sale of the 24th of Feb, I would let it go to them if there were no higher bids. If you will place the matter before them in time for them to make a decision before the sale, I shall be much obliged to you." MacLeod responds 23 Feb.; Board meets 24 Feb., directing curator to inform Moran the sale date has passed. (Letter 3719, curator's journal, and letterpress volumes; all in director's records, Corcoran)

17–23 February. Moran exhibits 64 works at Ortgies & Co. Gallery preparatory to public auction. (Ortgies 1886)

18 February. *NY Herald* reviews Ortgies exhibition: "Mr. Moran is one of the most brilliant as well as technically one of the most dexterous of American painters. He draws and paints with a facility which sometimes verges on the fatal. His landscapes are often remarkable for truth of effect, and yet as often the artist is carried too far by his skill in picturesque rendition. Few if any landscape painters in the country could show such a wide range in subject and locality as are to be found in the collection of Mr. Moran.

Few painters can handle the grandiose in landscape with the sure, masterly hand that he possesses, and a few can paint the infinite depth and variety to be found in a clouded sky as he can. And yet there is often, with all this skill and power, a lack of sympathetic feeling and a coldness of *facture* to be found in Mr. Moran's work. It is nearly always picturesque, but rarely poetic. Of course, the influence of Turner is over it all, though the American painter has attained a strong individuality. Among the works in the present collection in which there is found the true poetic spirit are the robust and effective 'Lancashire Village

Twilight,' the brilliant, deep toned little view of 'A Moquis Town in Arizona, Evening,' and the superb and richly colored illustration of Browning's line, 'Childe Harold to the dark tower came.' These works, and especially the two latter, have fine qualities of color, and yet the painter cannot take high rank as a colorist. His coloring is often brilliant, but rarely beautiful....

The views of the Niagara Falls rapids and of the whirlpool ones show, like the Long Island shore scenes, remarkable *brio* and skill in the handling of turbulent water, in which the wet quality is, however, somewhat lacking. The various views of the striking scenery of Southern Utah and Colorado are highly picturesque. The 'Cañon of the Rio Virgin' is, however, also painty. The views of Vera Cruz and Havana are picturesque and Turneresque, and there are a couple of pleasing Corot-like effects called 'A Riverside Morning' and 'In the Meadows.' There are several Long Island landscapes and a large view of 'The Cliffs of Montauk.'

Among the watercolors will be found especially interesting the Mexican sketches. 'The Cabaña, Harbor of Havana,' and the earliest work shown, the very Turneresque 'Arundel Castle, Sussex, England.' There is a small oil by Mrs. Moran called 'The Newark Meadows.' There is a catalogue of the collection illustrated by light etchings, five by Mr. and three by Mrs. Moran."

18/23 February. Unidentified newspaper reviews Ortgies exhibition: "It has been said that 'Thomas Moran had he not studied Turner so deeply would be the foremost living American artist,' and the remark is often quoted. While it has much truth, its assertion is entirely too sweeping, for it infers a lack of originality which is by no means wanting in the artist's work. His pictures, while they give evidence in most instances of a perhaps unconscious striving after Turneresque effects, show deep appreciation of nature, charming atmospheric effects, are boldly handled and have for the most part delicious color schemes." (EHL scrapbook)

22 February. *NYT*: "An artist equally able as a painter in oils and water colors and as an etcher is about to sell 64 pieces from his studio, many of which have been exhibited, and none of which depart greatly from his usual grade of excellence. They range from a 5 x 8 sketch on the Potomac to the big 'Ponce de Leon in the Everglades of Florida,' and offer examples of work from Great Britain, such as 'Welsh Mountains Near Conway,' and 'Fingal's Cave, Staffa,' with its brilliant and spirited wave effects, to records of travel in the Yosemite and Mexico.... The way in which Mr. Thomas Moran can paint the life of the sea as shown in the wave near the sands is quite startling; it looks like an error to find him doing anything else when there are so few really great marine painters living."

24 February. Moran's collection auctioned by Thomas E. Kirby of American Art Association.

25 February. *NYT* reports on Ortgies sale: "Thomas E. Kirby sold at public auction last evening the pictures in oil and water colors of Thomas Moran.... The attendance was large and the bidding spirited. Sixty-one pictures were sold at a total of $10,321. The highest price obtained for a single picture was $2,000, for 'Ponce de Leon in Florida.' Following is a list of the paintings which brought $300 and upward: Cañon of the Rio Virgen, in Southern Utah $395; New York City from Communipaw 400; Havana (Cuba) Sunrise 315; The Rescuing Party 585; Rock Towers of the Colorado 560; A Stormy Sunset on the Upper Colorado 425; Blowing a Gale, Easthampton Beach 550; The Whirlpool Rapids, Niagara River 490; The Cliffs of Montauk 425."

27 February. *The Critic*, 108: "Thomas Moran's exhibition of his works at Ortgies gallery, which closed on Wednesday, served a good purpose in presenting to the New York public this painter's strong individuality in all its roundness. His is a many-sided talent, and while he is never negative, his degrees of positiveness are tolerably unequal as to force and artistic merit. In some of his Long Island subjects is visible that beauty of subdued color and gray tone which is distinctively modern."

6 March. At Century Club Moran exhibits *January Thaw at Communipaw*; *Wooded Landscape*; and *Sunset on a Rocky Coast*. (CA, AAA)

6 March. *EH Star* mentions Ortgies exhibition and sale, adding: "Mr. Thomas Moran, the celebrated painter, who has an extensive studio in this place, is going abroad."

3 April. At Century Club Moran exhibits *Communipaw*; *Gleaning from the Wreck*; and an untitled work (nos. 22–24). (CA, AAA)

14 April. Thomas Moran sets sail on the steamship *Fulda*, bound for Bremen, Germany, via Southampton, England. (Moran to S. R. Koehler, 13 Apr., EHL; *NYT*, 15 Apr.)

3 May. Moran writes Mary from the Grand Hotel, Venice: "Since my arrival [1 May] I have done nothing but wander about the streets & I have done no work as yet." During his stay in Venice, Moran sketches extensively. (Bassford and Fryxell 1967, 77; Morand 1996, 72–73)

6, 7 May. Moran sketches and dates *Venice* and *St. Michael's in Campo Santo* (Gilcrease).

August. Following return from Europe, Moran sketches *East Hampton Beach*, inscribed "Aug 1886" (Gilcrease).

15 December. *Boston Transcript* reviews new book *American Art*: "The New York house of Cassell & Co. bring out a magnificent volume illustrative of the work of American etchers and wood engravers. It contains twenty-five plates from paintings in public and private collections, printed on a large folio page of specially prepared paper, with text by S. R. Koehler.... the painters and etchers represented [include]... Thomas Moran."

• 1887 •

Thomas and Mary Nimmo Moran travel to Florida. (De Montaigu 1888/Fryxell 1958, 46–47; biographical notes by Ruth B. Moran, EHL; Morand 1996, 73)

15 January. *EH Star*: "At the monthly meeting of the Rembrandt Club of Brooklyn [5 Jan.], one of Mr. Moran's etchings was purchased.... some time ago the club decided to purchase an etching by some well known artist, buying the plate outright. A sufficient number of copies were to be struck to give one to each member and then the plate was to be broken up. Eleven etchings were submitted by different artists for the club competition.... About seventy-five of the one hundred members were present, and when the question was put to vote... [it] was unanimous in favor of Mr. Moran's plate. The price paid is $600.... A pleasant feature of the evening was the presence of Mr. Moran as a guest of the club. His picture is a landscape—a scene at Long Pond, Easthampton.... Mr. Moran has employed a free line in the execution of this plate, deepening the shadows in the foreground by a touch of mezzotint, and the clouds are drawn with a subtlety and force that suggest the glowing skies of Turner.

One of the other etchings submitted for the club's inspection was by Mrs. Moran, the artist's wife."

24 January. *Boston Transcript*: "The catalogue of the A.T. Stewart collection, soon to be shown in New York, preliminary to its sale, will contain etchings by R. Swain Gifford, W.M. Chase, Thomas Moran.... Besides the sixteen etchings there will be twenty to thirty process prints and eight or ten drawings by [Edward's sons] Leon and Percy Moran."

29 January. *The Critic*, 59: "The jury for selecting works in New York for the American Exhibition at London consists of Messrs. Bierstadt, J.Q. A. Ward, Thomas Moran, William M. Chase, Alden Weir and Frederick Dielman."

31 January–26 February. At NAD Moran exhibits with AWCS, *Giudecca, Venice*, and *Palace on the Grand Canal, Venice* (cat. nos. 208, 448); and with NYEC, *Morning on the Coast, East Hampton, L.I.*; *On the St. Johns River, Florida*; *Harbor of Vera Cruz, Mexico*; *Resounding Sea*; *Niagara Falls, from Canadian Side*; *Month of May* (after C.F. Daubigny) (cat. nos. 131–136), also serving on executive committee. Mary Nimmo Moran exhibits two works. (*The Critic*, 5 Feb., 69, which also notes that "Thomas Moran and M. Nimmo Moran have strong line-work in their various plates")

19 February. *The Critic*, 92: "The Rembrandt Club of Brooklyn recently offered a prize of $600 for the best original etching of an American subject. It was won by Thomas Moran, whose only serious rival in the competition was his wife. The judges were very evenly divided at first, but finally decided for the husband. What a happy frame of mind the man must be in who knows that if he doesn't win a $600 prize, his wife will! There is nothing like keeping the prizes in the family."

2 April. At Century Club Moran exhibits *Mountain of the Holy Cross*. (CA, AAA)

4 April–14 May. NAD annual exhibition. Moran exhibits *Church of Santa Maria della Salute, Venice*, and *Gate of Venice* (nos. 29, 213) and serves on hanging committee. (*The Critic*, 22 Jan., 47; Naylor 1973, 654)

21 April. Mrs. Schuyler van Rensselaer in *The Independent* [NY] reviews NAD exhibition: "Nor is there space left to say much of the landscapes.... Mr. Thomas Moran a view of Venice, quite in his old Turneresque manner."

7 May. At Century Club Moran exhibits two works titled *Venice* (nos. 1, 2). (CA, AAA)

9 May–31 October. American Exhibition in London. Moran exhibits *In the Yellowstone Park*; *Canon of the Colorado* (cat. nos. 1377, 1378); and six engravings. (*Times* [London], 9 May; exh. cat., 17–18, 29)

13 May. *Boston Transcript* reports election of officers of NAD at its annual meeting: "President, D. Huntington; vice-president, T.W. Wood; corresponding secretary, H.W. Robbins; treasurer, Alfred Jones; council—R. Swain Gifford, F.S. Church, J.G. Brown, F. Dielman, Thomas Moran, S.J. Guy."

4 June. *EH Star*: "Mr. Thomas Moran and family... arrived [31 May] and took possession of their cottage in this place."

14 July. *Daily News* [London] reviews American Exhibition in London: "Thomas Moran of New York, judging by his picture, 'In the Yellowstone Park... follows Turner, or more probably Pyne—but neither of these artists would be quite so brown in his foreground as this picture chances to be."

30 July, 13, 27 August. *EH Star* reports that Moran family participates in such social events in East Hampton as "Germans," "Assemblies," and "Concerts."

1 November. *Boston Transcript* announces special exhibitions of the work of American women etchers at MFA Boston and ULC [1 Nov.–31 Dec.; and 12–21 Apr. 1888]: "Easily first among the women etchers is Mrs. M. Nimmo Moran, pupil of her husband, Thomas Moran. Fifty-four of her plates are shown, constituting an exhibit of great variety and original force. In the movement of her skies Mrs. Moran occasionally reminds one of her husband's work, but with a difference. Her 'Haunted House' is a romantic and strongly colored plate, in a vein quite peculiar to herself."

21 November–17 December. NAD autumn exhibition. Moran exhibits *Morning in Venice* (cat. no. 109) and serves on Council and the selection committee. (*The Critic*, 26 Nov., 275)

3 December. *The Critic*, 287: "About 100 artists met at the Academy on Nov. 25th to arrange for sending a representative

collection of American pictures to the coming exhibition at Munich. The committee of arrangements consists of Eastman Johnson, Thomas Moran, Edward Gay and William M. Chase. The same artists will probably form part of the American Jury of Selection."

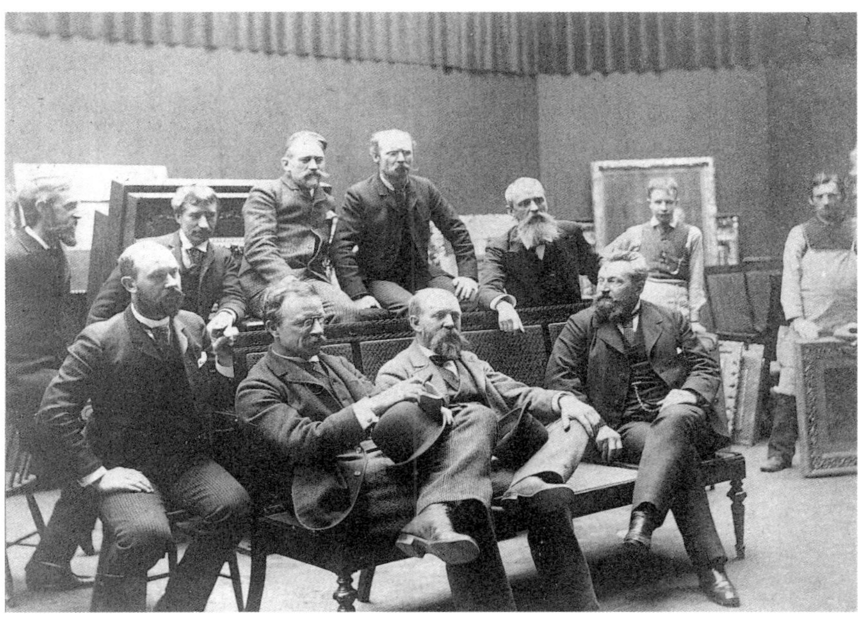

National Academy of Design jury of selection, Moran at right in second row, courtesy East Hampton Library.

22 December. F. V. Hayden dies in Philadelphia after a long illness. (*American Geologist* 1 [Feb. 1888], 110–113)

• 1888 •

Moran moves residence to 37 W. 22nd St., NY. (Naylor 1973, 654)

28 January. *NYT* previews the AWCS exhibition: "Full of good picture .... Thomas and Leon Moran ... and other steady contributors are represented as usual."

30 January–25 February. At NAD Moran exhibits with AWCS, *Santa Maria della Salute, Venice*; *On the Upper Colorado, Wyoming Territory*; and *Fondamenta Ca Dio, Venice* (cat. nos. 302, 308, 430); and with NYEC, *Venice* and *Dordrecht* (both after A. F. Bunner) (cat. nos. 131, 132), also serving on executive committee. Mary Nimmo Moran exhibits five works. (*The Critic*, 4 Feb., 58)

11 February. *EH Star* reviews AWCS exhibition: "Landscapes by Thomas Moran and Edward Moran are among the notable pictures."

31 March. *The Critic*, 158: "Last week's Loan Exhibition of etchings by the Young Men's Christian Association ... of Orange, East Orange, and South Orange [NJ] showed that valuable etchings abound in that neighborhood ....The Morans ... were present in force, with capital plates. ... An etching by T. Moran accompanied the special invitations to the exhibition."

2 April–12 May. NAD annual exhibition. Moran exhibits *Venice*; *Sand Dunes of Fort George Island, Florida*; and *Steam and Fog* (nos. 192, 329, 497). (*The Critic*, 31 Mar., 158; 12 May, 235; Naylor 1973, 654–655)

16 April. *Boston Transcript*: "At the sale of the Chapman collection ... in Chickering Hall, the bidding was rapid, and high prices were paid for some of the more notable pictures .... 'Near Westhampton,' Thomas Moran, $450."

28 April. *The Critic*, 210, reports election of officers of NAD at annual meeting: "Daniel Huntington was elected President, T. W. Wood, Vice-President, T. Addison Richards, Corresponding Secretary, and [Alfred] Jones, Treasurer .... The Hanging Committee consists of Charles H. Miller, F. D. Millet, Thomas Moran, J. Francis Murphy and J. C. Nicoll."

4 May. *Boston Transcript*: "The last of the important exhibitions ... for the season is that under the auspices of the American Art Association ... [which] consists solely of paintings and sculptures of American artists .... Thomas Moran has a conventionally brilliant Venetian scene."

5 May. *The Critic*, 223, reports sales of $17,000 at NAD: "Among recent sales are ... Thomas Moran's 'Venice' ($300)."

28 May–30 June. Annual exhibition of American oil paintings, AIC. Moran exhibits *Pass of Glencoe, Scotland*; *Morning, Fort George Island, Florida*; and *Misty Morning, Communipaw* (nos. 42, 49, 54). (Falk 1990a, 631)

9 June. *EH Star*: "Mr. Thomas Moran and family, are now occupying their cottage."

31 July. *Boston Transcript*: "The leading American etchers have formed a society [SAE], having for its objects: First, the elevation of the art of etching in this country; secondly, the limitation of editions, each publication by the members of the society being guaranteed by the stamp of the Society of American Etchers, in the same way as English prints are protected by the printsellers' stamp. The officers elected for the ensuing year are Thomas Moran, president, C. Y. Turner, secretary; and Frederick Dielman, treasurer." (Repr. *The Critic*, 11 Aug., 70)

3 September. Moran delivers etching plate for *Mountain of the Holy Cross* to printer J. D. Waring. On 29 Sept. he signs 30 proofs of the print for Waring and keeps 5 for himself as the first of 12 proofs he eventually reserves. On 1 Dec. he signs 20 more proofs for Waring. (GA account of etchings 1888–1895, 7)

4 September. Sketches and dates *Three Mile Harbor* (Gilcrease).

6 October. *The Critic*, 169: "Mr. Klackner has recently published several important new plates, among them being a large and effective etching, with considerable depth of color and good quality of tone, by Thomas Moran. It is called 'The Gate of Venice,' and is taken from a group of barges off the Riva dei Schiavoni, looking towards the Ducal Palace.... Thomas Moran's 'Mountain of the Holy Cross,' reproduced from his own large painting of that name, is the second plate issued by the Society of American Etchers, of which Mr. Moran is President."

19 November–16 December. NAD autumn exhibition. Moran exhibits *Ducal Palace, from the Giudecca, Venice*, and *Midsummer, Long Island* (cat. nos. 276, 361), and serves on selection and hanging committees. (*The Critic*, 29 Sept., 154)

19 November. *NYT* reviews NAD autumn exhibition: "From Thomas Moran comes an ideal presentment of a much-painted view in Venice."

19 November. First exhibition of SAE opens at Ortgies Gallery, NY. *The Critic*, 24 Nov., 261–262: "The present exhibition consists of fifteen plates, both original and reproductive.... Two brilliant original plates by C. A. Platt... and M. Nimmo Moran's 'St. Johns River, Florida,' are the most satisfactory plates in the exhibition.... Thomas Moran's 'Mountain of the Holy Cross,' is very elaborately treated and composed in the decorative way peculiar to this etcher. Simplification would add to its strength without injuring its effect."

Magazine also notes: "The Ohio Society of [NY] held an exhibition of pictures in connection with a ladies reception last Monday evening [19th]. Among the artists represented were Thomas Moran."

8 December. *The Critic*, 292: "At a social reunion at the Academy of Design, last week, Col. Rush C. Hawkins, the American Art Commissioner of the Paris Exposition next year, was the guest of the evening. The proposed display of American art at the exposition was discussed.... Thomas Moran [is on the jury].... Another jury will be chosen at Paris to cooperate with the New York jury, and special jurors will be appointed to represent other branches of art, such as architecture, engraving on metal, etc."

9 December. *NYT*: "The 400 or 500 pictures at the Academy of Design take their character as a collection from three groups—the marines, the French views and genre, and the Italian shores. With regard to the last named, Venice is, of course, the spot favored above all others. Besides the views of the Ducal Palace by Thomas Moran and Walter Palmer there is a bit from some quay of Venice by J. H. Twachtman."

• 1889 •

12 January, 2 February. At Century Club Moran exhibits *Venice* and *Wreck on Montauk*. (CA, AAA)

24 January–7 March. PAFA annual exhibition. Moran exhibits two etchings with SAE: *Mountain of the Holy Cross, Colorado*, and *Conway Castle, N. Wales* (after J. M. W. Turner). (Falk 1989, 342)

6 February–2 March. At NAD Moran exhibits with AWCS, *Entrance to the Grand Canal, Venice*; *Long Island Landscape*; and *Conway Castle, Wales* (cat. nos. 116, 232, 305); and with NYEC, *Mountain of the Holy Cross* (cat. no. 90), also serving on executive committee. (*The Critic*, 26 Jan., 46)

21 February. *Boston Transcript*: "The committee of artists selecting the [American] pictures to be included in the... coming international exhibition (... Moran [et al.]...) have accepted nearly 190 pictures out of a total offering of about three hundred. Most of the canvases are large, and, in the opinion of those in a position to know, the exhibits as a whole will be the most creditable to American art of any ever sent out of the country.... The American artists living in Europe have a jury of their own."

28 February. *Boston Transcript*: "Some of the American artists are not satisfied with the way in which they have been treated by the committee on American art at the Paris International Exposition.... Thomas Moran appears to be the spokesman for the malcontents. A list is given of the artists 'who will not be represented.' It includes the names of Bierstadt, De Haas, William Hart, the Morans, Homer, F. E. Church, Inness, La Farge, Lippincott, Shirlaw, Dielman, Millet, Warner and St. Gaudens. The list might be longer, and not prove anything to the prejudice of the committee. It is not to be expected that all, or even a majority, of the American artists will be presented at Paris. Many would abstain from exhibiting under any circumstances. It is to be expected naturally that those Americans who reside in France will be more interested than those who stay at home. Mr. Moran says he makes a distinction 'between American and Franco-American artists.' All very well; but what then? Shall we call him an Anglo-American because his pictures smack of Turner?"

3 March. *NYT*: "A very creditable showing of the etched work of Mr. and Mrs. Thomas Moran is in formation at Klackner's rooms. The high rank of Thomas Moran as an etcher is an old story, but the merits of Mrs. M. Nimmo Moran may not be so generally known. The walls are covered with the striking work of these two artists, among which the views by Mr. Moran in Wales, Venice, and the Yellowstone country are prominent, and those by Mrs. Moran from Long Island and Florida."

5 March. Exhibition of 129 etchings by Thomas and Mary Nimmo Moran opens at C. Klackner's, a commercial gallery in NY. (*NYT*, 3 Mar.; Trumbull 1889)

7 March. Exhibition of American art opens at new residence of Vice President Morton, 1500 Rhode Island Ave., Wash-

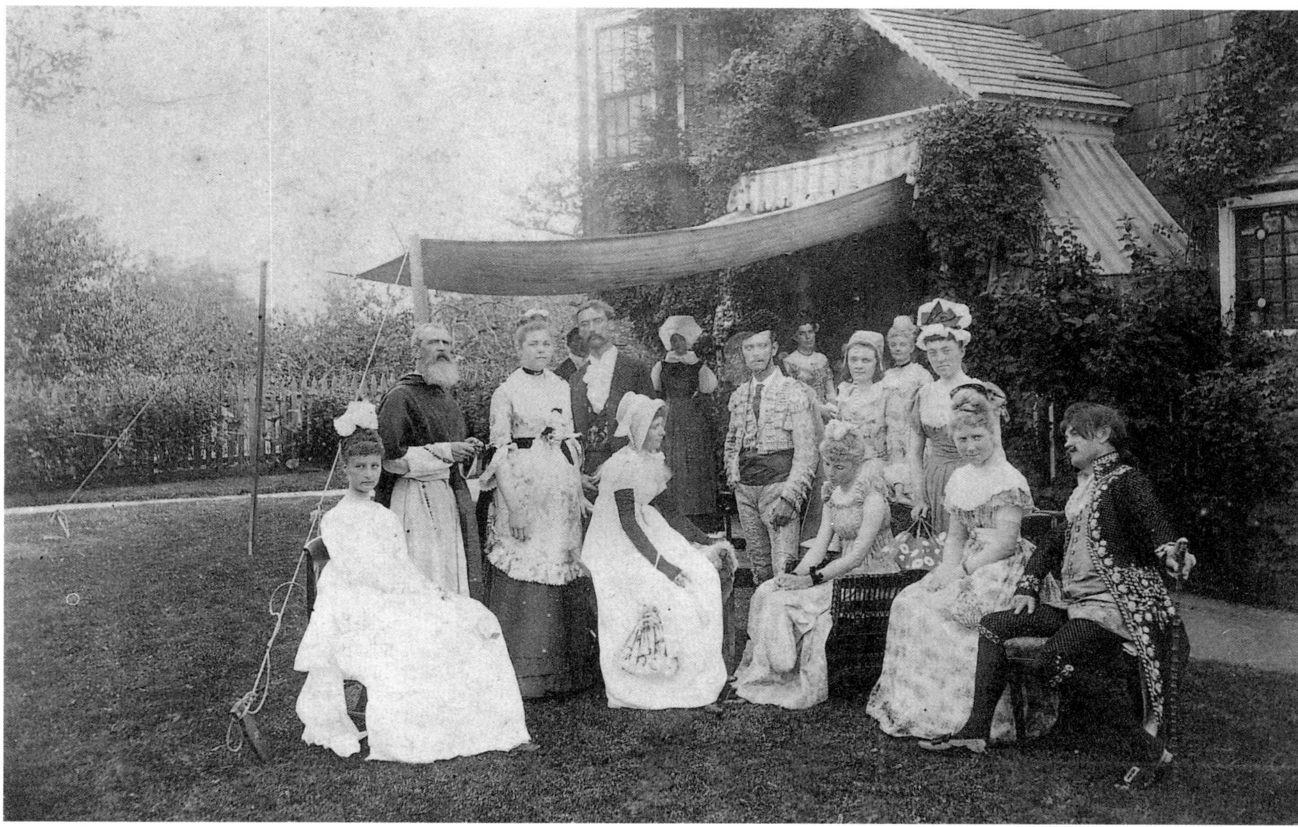

Fancy dress ball at Moran's East Hampton studio, August 1889, courtesy East Hampton Library.

ington, to benefit Garfield Memorial Hospital. Moran is among contributors. (*Evening Star* [DC], 2 and 7 Mar.; *The Critic*, 9 Mar., 122)

11 March. *NY Tribune* reviews Moran exhibition at Klackner's: "Both etchers have earned the esteem of the public.... Mr. Moran shows seventy-one etchings and Mrs. Moran fifty-eight.... [Mr. Moran's] command of technical resources has been frequently demonstrated... and the present collection illustrates fully the artist's range from pure line to mezzotint, and his facility in employing the diversified methods possible for the designer upon copper.... He is no narrow partisan of any special school or style. He has gone out among the Long Island sand dunes, selecting the characteristic phases of the scene before him and swiftly noting down the decisive lines, and again he has called to his aid roulette, scraper, all the aids within reach of the etcher and printer, and he has worked and reworked his plate to the last point of elaboration. The 'Gate of Venice,' etched after Mr. Moran's painting shown at the Academy in 1880 is exhibited as his most 'important' plate, and those who remember the strong serial chromatic effects of the original will agree that they have been very cleverly indicated in the reproduction.... All these large plates show a thorough acquaintance with the etcher's craft and remarkable energy and industry. Some of the smaller plates admit us to a closer intimacy with an artist whom we have learned to know as an etcher of vigor and spirit, sometimes lacking in tactful selection and in concentration, sometimes covering his plate with straggling or scratchy lines, which are devoid of truthful relations and apparently of genuine artistic purpose, but an etcher whose work is masculine, intelligent and versatile....

[Mrs. Moran's] rapid advance in self-confidence and certainty in execution may be traced in these plates, which present for the most part subjects selected at East-hampton.... [There are] plates characterized by reserve as well as by unusual vigor of line.... It may be possible to trace some resemblance between the linear work of these two etchers, but the merit of the results renders comparison futile."

16 March. *The Critic*, 135, reviews exhibition at Klackner's: "Though husband and wife, each, as is well-known to amateurs, sees and interprets nature in a different way. Mr. Moran likes complicated and difficult subjects, composes in the Turneresque manner, and is master of a technique equalled for range and subtlety by few living etchers. Mrs. Moran's work is bolder, broader, and more often displays sympathy with the ordinary aspects of nature."

1 April–11 May. NAD annual exhibition. Moran exhibits *Venice* and *A Pastoral* (nos. 183, 383). (Naylor 1973, 655)

May. Elizabeth Bisland in *Cosmopolitan*, 14, 18–19: "Thomas Moran, the etcher, and

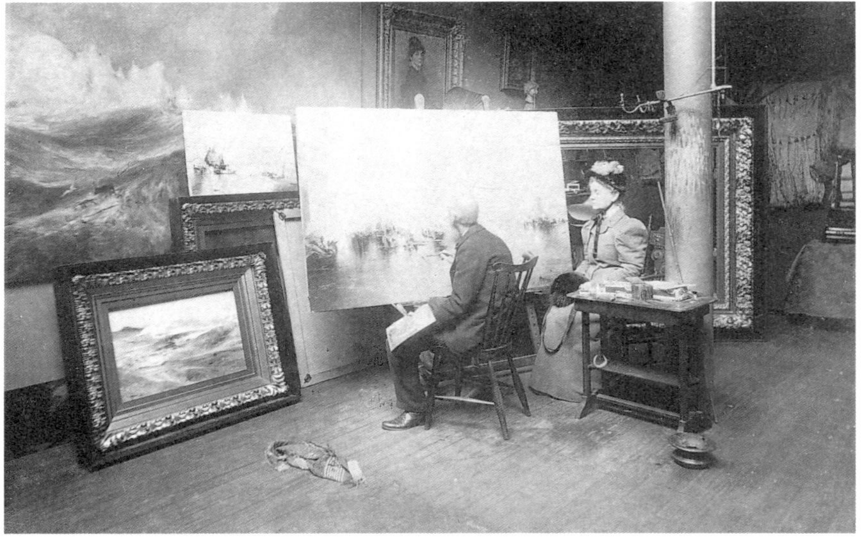

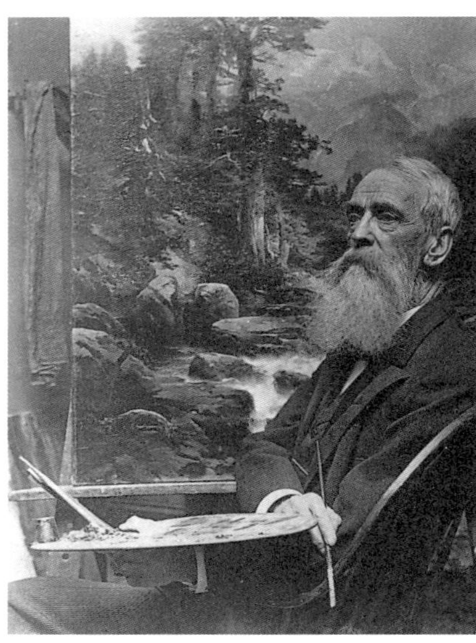

Thomas Moran in his New York studio, c. 1891, with his *Spectres from the North* identifiable on the wall, courtesy East Hampton Library. See also cat. 70.

Moran in his New York studio, c. 1897, with *Solitude* on his easel, courtesy East Hampton Library. See also cat. 84.

Mary Nimmo, his wife, work side by side down in their studio on Twenty-second Street. Big tables near the light, on which are laid the plates while the artists are at work, are an important feature of their furnishings; but there are easels, too, for before either of them was an etcher they were painters. There is not much attempt at decorative fittings here, the only adornments being Indian weapons, wampum belts, and other bits of savage finery, which were picked up by the artist when he was a member of a government surveying party and made the sketches for his great picture of 'The Mountain of the Holy Cross.'… Etching is comparatively a recent experiment with him; but how fully he was justified in abandoning in great part the brush for the needle is shown by the fact that among a number of plates in London Ruskin singled out one of Moran's as being the best that ever came from London, and one of the best that modern art had produced. Mrs. Moran is scarcely less famous in the use of the needle and acid than her husband, having, curiously enough, developed her artistic capacity through the influence of studio life."

30 May–30 June. Annual exhibition of oil paintings at AIC. Moran exhibits *Landscape* (no. 138, owned by James W. Ellworth). (Falk 1990a, 631)

19 August. Moran family gives "fancy dress party" called "Chalepa ta Kala" in East Hampton studio, with musicians and elaborate costumes. *EH Star*, 31 Aug., reports at length, concluding "Many of the costumes were photographed by Mr. Murray on the following afternoon."

18 November. Autumn exhibition opens at NAD. Moran exhibits *Venice* and *Sunset on Long Island* (cat. nos. 336, 393). (*The Critic*, 26 Oct., 204)

7 December. At Century Club Moran exhibits *Cloudy Day, Long Island*. (CA, AAA)

• 1890 •

11 January. At Century Club Moran exhibits *Gathering Storm*. (CA, AAA)

31 January. *Boston Transcript*: "James D. Gill's thirteenth yearly exhibition opens at Springfield today with one hundred and three pictures on the walls. Among the artists represented are Thomas Moran."

3 February–1 March. Annual AWCS exhibition at NAD. Moran exhibits *Bridge of Sighs, Venice*, and *Venice from the Giudecca* (cat. nos. 47, 617).

1 March. *The Critic*, 111: "Mr. Caroll Beckwith is President and Mr. Montague Marks Treasurer and Secretary of a new art organization, the American Society of Painters on Stone. The other members are Messrs.… Edward Moran, Thomas Moran.… The art of lithography will receive new life… from the organization of this society, which has no present intention of holding exhibitions, but will presumably publish works by its members."

7 April–16 May. NAD annual exhibition. Moran exhibits *Clouds and Sunshine*; *Bridge of Sighs, Venice*; *Autumn, Long Island*; and *Venice from the Public Gardens* (nos. 18, 172, 299, 411). (*The Critic*, 11 Jan., 23; *Boston Transcript*, 21 May; Naylor 1973, 655)

14 April. *NY Post* reviews NAD exhibition: "Thomas Moran still contributes stately, handsome, artificial landscapes."

28 April. On voyage to Antwerp from New York with his family, Moran sketches *Icebergs in the Middle Atlantic*; *Berg to the North of Us*; *Berg to the North after Passing*; *Icebergs*; *Tower of Spray*; and two drawings inscribed *Iceberg* (Gilcrease). (GA ledger, 3)

1, 9, 17–18, 20 May. Sketches and dates *At Sea*; then *St. Mark's Cathedral, Cologne*, and *Cologne*; then *Verona*; *Verona from the Bridge of St. Peter*; and *Castle of St. Peter and Bridge, Verona*; then *Venice*; then *San Giorgio Maggiore* and *Island from the Lido, Looking South* (Gilcrease; EHL).

22–23, 26, 29, 31 May. Sketches and dates *San Giorgio Maggiore from the Giudecca*; then *Burano from Murano* and two versions of *Murano*; then *Garibalde*; then *Burano* and *Canal Burano*; then *Picture of Sails from Chioggia*; *Venice from Malamocco*; and *Pellestrina* (Gilcrease; EHL).

19 July. *EH Star* reprints an article from *NY Herald*: "Among the many cottagers from New York already [in East Hampton] with their families are . . . the talented Moran family."

2 August. *EH Star*: "Thomas Moran, who owns a fine cottage on the main street, and is an all-the-year-round resident, has recently returned from a trip to London."

30 August. *EH Star* reports that Moran exhibited *Icebergs in Mid Ocean* [*Spectres from the North*] at Clinton Academy, East Hampton, on 29 Aug. Also quotes *NY Herald*: "The only busy class [in East Hampton] are the artists, who with palette and brush immortalize the surf and the woods. 'Tom' Moran spends his summers here in a weatherbeaten shingled house of a novel interior. The first floor is devoted to a studio, with an immense plate glass window looking out toward the north, and a winding stair leading to regions above. Great screens form partitions when necessary, and I hear that when meal time comes the table is set behind one of these."

6 September. *EH Star*: "Thomas Moran . . . while in Venice purchased the gondola and its outfit that belonged to the poet Browning. It was brought to this place by the steamer 'Shelter Island' [31 Aug.] . . . . Mr. Moran was in town overseeing its shipment, by teams to East Hampton, where he is to have it placed in Hook Pond."

18 October. *EH Star*: "We dropped into the studio of Thomas Moran, and were greatly surprised to learn that such a cosy and picturesque work-shop of art existed in our village. We found Mr. Moran working upon a Venetian painting which . . . showed several large palaces and public buildings well known to travelers in Venice, also the junction of several main canals, upon which floated numerous gondolas and together with the many figures represented, dressed in the striking costumes of the Venetians, makes a very lively scene in the heart of Venice. The artist informed us that the picture when finished would be topographically correct, even to the minutest details. Of course it is needless to say that such a picture from the brush of this artist is worth several hundred dollars. The artist kindly left his work and showed us around his interesting studio. First, a piece of etching work which he had under way, and described very minutely the process . . . . Mr. Moran has become quite expert in the art, and produces many handsome etchings. Mrs. Moran is considered one of the best etchers in this country. The artist then proceeded to show us his numerous curiosities, picked up during his travels . . . .

The studio was planned by the artist himself, and is of no particular style of architecture. The studio proper occupies the whole of the ground floor, and the ceiling is at least eighteen feet high. At one end of the room is a large plate glass window reaching from the floor nearly half way to the ceiling, and across the other end extends a gallery where are placed easy chairs and sofas, and a cabinet in which the artist keeps a large collection of pictures representing all branches of picture-making. From the corner of the gallery the door opens into an octagon-shaped room of glass in which one may keep warm by the sun's rays on a cold winter day. It is an interesting sight to sit in the gallery and look down into the studio ornamented with scores of pictures and endless bric-a-brac. Mr. Moran showed us a number of paintings he has under way, the prices of which will range from $200 to $1,000. Among the lot we noticed two or three East Hampton scenes."

1 November. *EH Star*: "Thomas Moran, the artist, has closed up his studio, and with his family, gone to New York where he has a winter studio between Fifth and Sixth avenues."

December. At ULC Moran exhibits *Bravo, Sunset*. (GA ledger)

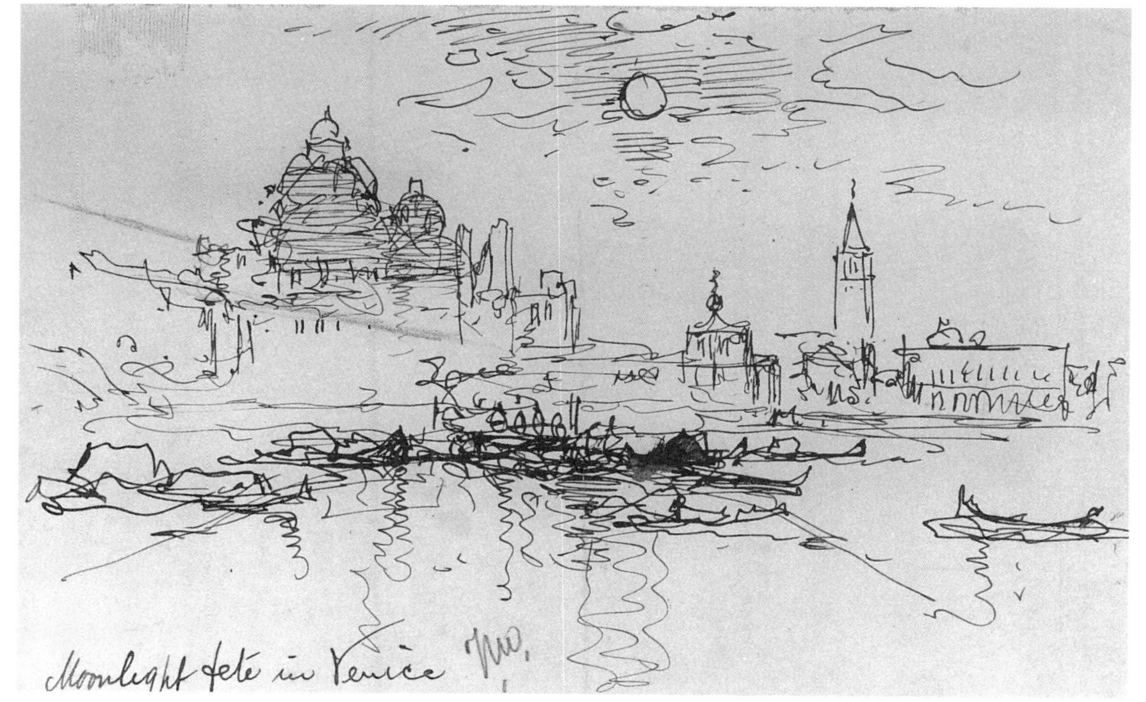

Thomas Moran, *Moonlight Fete in Venice*, graphite and pen and ink on paper, courtesy Gilcrease Museum, Tulsa, Oklahoma.

12 December. *NY Post* reviews ULC exhibition: "Modern painters, both American and foreign are by no means neglected.... American painters are represented by... Thomas Moran."

• 1891 •

10 January. At Century Club Moran exhibits *Spectres from the North* and *Venice*. (CA, AAA)

16–19 January. Exhibition of paintings by members at Salmagundi Club. *NYT*, 17 Jan.: "A place of honor is given to a large painting by Mr. Thomas Moran, 'Spectres from the North.'" *The Critic*, 23 Jan., 47: "About a hundred paintings... were exhibited at the new rooms of the Club.... Among the most interesting were... 'Specters from the North' (that is to say, icebergs) by T. Moran."

31 January. *NYT* previews of AWCS exhibition: "Mr. Thomas Moran's 'Old Tower of Torcello' is a Venetian view that does not lack style, but in 'Venice from San Giorgio' he lapses into mannerism."

1 February. *NYT* previews NYEC exhibition: "Thomas Moran contributes a brilliant and imposing landscape from Long Island."

2–28 February. At NAD Moran exhibits with AWCS, *Old Town of Torcello* and *Venice from San Giorgio* (cat. nos. 217, 638); and with NYEC, *Long Island Landscape* (cat. no. 92), also serving on executive committee.

7 February. *The Critic*, 71, calls the AWCS and NYEC exhibitions "unusually interesting" and praises Moran's *Long Island Landscape*, "with a marshy foreground and a row of fine old trees in the middle distance."

7 February. At Century Club Moran exhibits *Morning in Venice*; *Burano*; and *Cloudy Day*. (CA, AAA)

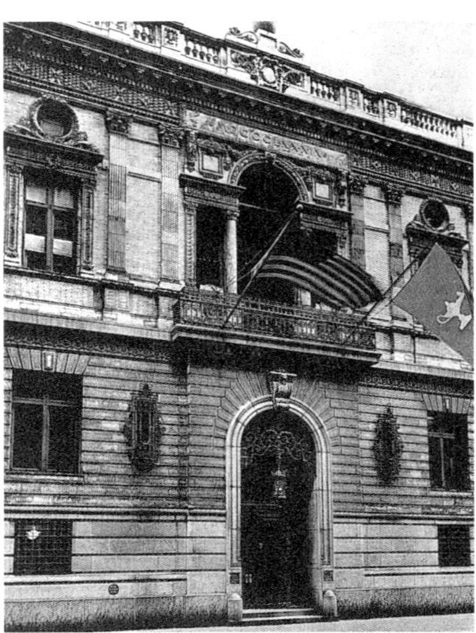

The Century Club, after 1891, published in *The Century, 1847–1946* (New York, 1947).

16 February. *NY Post*, reviewing shows at NAD, says Moran's watercolors were among "the principal things in the exhibition, and all extremely good."

21 March. Moran sketches and dates *Villa Alexandria*, in St. Augustine, FL, home of Mrs. Alexander Mitchell, a patron of Moran's since 1876 commission for Centennial Fair. Moran also painted *San Juan Abajo, Mexico*, for her in 1885, and *Venice from near the Public Gardens* (EHL). (GA ledger)

21 March. *The Critic*, 160, reports exhibition on 9–11 March of "about 150 works in black and white" by Salmagundi Club members, including Moran's india ink illustrations of Longfellow's *Hiawatha* among "the most notable exhibits."

The Critic also notes: "The New York Art Guild, which filed articles of incorporation at Albany on Tuesday, is designed to secure for its members guarantees of indemnity from damages at exhibitions where the works of its members are shown, or in transportation.... Any artist may join the Guild by paying the small initiation fee, and thus protect himself. Its affairs will be managed by seven trustees, those for the first year being Thomas Moran, John H. Dolph, Percival De Luce, J. H. Witt, Chester Loomis, Charles Y. Turner, and one other to be selected."

6 April–15 May. NAD annual exhibition. Moran exhibits *Spectres from the North*; *Morning—Venice*; and *Burano, Venice* (nos. 386, 449, 511). (*The Critic*, 17 Jan., 35; Naylor 1973, 655)

17 April. *NY Post*: "The Salmagundi Club opens with the usual festivities this evening another of its periodic exhibitions... confined to watercolors, with a few pastels.... [including] a 'Glimpse of Venice' by Thomas Moran."

29 May. *EH Star*: "Thomas Moran the artist, of New York, arrived at his studio cottage on Tuesday [26 May]."

August. Western Pennsylvania Exposition in Pittsburgh. Moran exhibits *Iceberg in Mid Atlantic: Spectres from the North* and *Reminiscence of Venice Sunrise*. (*NY Post*, 8 Aug.)

4 September. *EH Star* mentions entertainment for "the village improvement fund" that included "the Moran trio" and a violin obligato played by Thomas Moran.

11, 18 September. *EH Star* lists Moran as an incorporator and committee member on constitution and by-laws of the newly created, but not yet built, Maidstone Club in East Hampton. Moran chosen (12 Sept.) as one of nine directors of the club and elected vice president for one year.

2 October. *EH Star*: "The artists come year after year, producing beautiful pictures, many of which grace the exhibitions all over the country. Mr. Thos. Moran was the first to make his home here.... His work is so well known that comments on it are hardly necessary but one would like to see more of the local scenery from his hands; Mrs. Moran has given us more of it in her etchings, which prove what can be done with local bits. Their son Paul, who has lately been studying in Paris, is back again working with new ideas."

9 October. *EH Star*: "Thomas Moran is at work upon two paintings of East Hampton subjects, one being a picture of the surf and the other a scene at Town Pond."

15 October–28 November. Exhibition of the Thomas B. Clarke collection of American paintings at PAFA includes Moran's *At East Hampton, L.I.*, and *Vera Cruz* (cat. nos. 142, 143).

30 October. *EH Star*: "The only city people now remaining in town are Mr. Moran and family."

23 November–20 December. NAD autumn exhibition. Moran exhibits *Goose Pond, East Hampton*, and *Venice from the Lagoon, Fisherman's Wedding Party* (cat. nos. 341, 364).

3 December. *Boston Transcript* comments on December issue of *St. Nicholas* magazine: "The stupendous scenery of the Grand Canyon of the Colorado affords a most congenial theme for the pencil of Thomas Moran, who furnishes six grandiose drawings of it for the Christmas St. Nicholas. 'Within the Grand Canyon' (p. 125) is a thoroughly characteristic Moran, with a rocky world of castellated crags rising to dizzy heights on all sides, and the morning sun sending forth a flashing array of golden beams to light up the grim depths of the black chasm, after a most dramatic and time-honored fashion. The dark landscape on p. 129, 'Tree trunk petrified into an agate bridge,' is strongly effective."

10–11 December. Moran's *Old Tower of Torcello* included in exhibition and private sale to benefit Messiah Home for Children, held at Sherry's, NY. (*NY Post*, 1 Dec.)

• 1892 •

1–27 February. At NAD Moran exhibits with AWCS, *Morning in Chioggia*; *Pila in Saltillo, Mexico*; *Rock Tower of the Upper Colorado*; *San Juan, Mexico*; *Breezy Day*; *Outskirts of Venice*; *Grand Canal, Venice*; *Newtown Creek, L.I.*; *Communipaw*; and *Icebergs* (cat. nos. 43, 83, 93, 183, 190, 220, 280, 291, 298, 395). For NYEC serves on the executive committee but does not exhibit. (NYEC cat.)

5 February. *EH Star* quotes *The World*'s review of the AWCS exhibition: "Thomas Moran has ten of those vigorous, strongly colored compositions which so ably sustain from year to year his artistic reputation."

6 February. *NY Post* reports sales of $10,028 for 114 pictures at AWCS exhibition, including Moran's *Grand Canal* for $100.

13 February. *The Critic*, 106: "Of a large number of water-colors and some oil-paintings belonging to L. Prang & Co. of Boston, exhibited at the American Art Galleries, the water-colors are by far the best, and include some desirable examples of well-known artists. Among the most interesting may be mentioned Mr. Thomas Moran's views in the Yellowstone region."

16 February. *NY Post*: "It is obviously unfair to consider the Prang collection of pictures, on exhibition at the American Art Association Galleries, from a 'high art' point of view, for both collector and artist, recognizing the limitations of the art of reproduction, have plainly performed their work accordingly.... Not a few, however, afford genuine pleasure... Mr. Thos. Moran's 'Scenes in the Yellowstone' are quite equal to much he has since done."

27 February. *NY Post* announces latest sales at AWCS exhibition, including Moran *Icebergs* for $100 and *Breezy Day* for $175.

4 March. *EH Star* quotes *The Recorder*: "Given a subject which most accords with [Moran's] sentiment, his style of painting and his fondness for color, there is no native painter of our day who may hope to excel him in his chosen field."

21 March–17 April. Annual watercolor exhibition by American artists at AIC. Moran exhibits *Morning in Chioggia, Venice*; *Rock Tower of the Colorado*; and *San Juan, Mexico* (nos. 129–131). (Falk 1990a, 631)

4 April–14 May. NAD annual exhibition. Moran exhibits *Lotus Eaters*; *Clouds and Sunshine*; and *Ducal Palace and Prison—Venice* (nos. 6, 360, 420). (*NY Post*, 9 Jan.; Naylor 1973, 655)

29 April. *EH Star* mentions Moran's plans to return to the Rocky Mountains in the summer: "Mr. Moran went through the remoter parts of the West years before the rail-roads were carried through, and it was to his pictures of the wonderful peak and canon scenery that the public owed its first approximately correct knowledge of the region."

6 May. *EH Star*: "Mr. Thomas Moran and family arrived at the studio [2 May]... for the summer."

15 May. Thomas and Paul Moran leave East Hampton for the West. (*EH Star*, 20 May)

18 May. Moran to Mary, from Chicago. He and Paul arrived the night before and have made satisfactory arrangements with the Santa Fe Railroad: "They will have a special conveyance... for us to make the trip to the Cañon in one day." (Bassford and Fryxell 1967, 81, 83)

22 May. Moran to Mary, from Flagstaff, AZ: "We visited today the cliff dwellers house in a Cañon about 10 miles from here. The Cañon itself was not interesting and the buildings only curious because of their antiquity and the uncertainty of who built them.... We start tomorrow morning for the Grand Cañon with every comfort and convenience.... I think we shall be at the Cañon for a week." (Bassford and Fryxell 1967, 85)

25 May. Moran sketches and dates *Opposite Hance Camp* (Gilcrease). Writes to Mary from camp at the Grand Canyon: "Have just looked into the Cañon and am not yet sure whether this point is as good as the one I painted, but think it is. Today the party go on an expedition to find out the best points and then go to work. Our party consists of myself, Jackson, Paul, Mr. Higgins of [SFRR] Chicago, and Jackson's assistant [Sam Taylor]." (Bassford and Fryxell 1967, 87)

26 May. *Coconino Sun* [Flagstaff, AZ]: "The following visitors left for the Grand Canyon during the week: The ... party consisted of T. Moran, an eminent artist of New York, and his son, Paul N. Moran. These gentlemen will take a number of sketches of the Grand Canyon from which paintings will be made, and lithographs will be made from them for advertising purposes for the Santa Fe route.... The stage line is now a successful institution, and travel over it continues to increase each week."

27, 29, 31 May. Moran sketches and dates *Hance Canyon*; then *Grand Canyon of the Colorado*; *Looking North from Moran Point, Grand Canyon*; two versions of *Looking West from Moran Point*; and *Shadows, Grand Canyon*; then *Shiva Temple* (EHL; Gilcrease; JNEM).

1–4 June. Sketches and dates *San Francisco Mountains, from between Flagstaff and Cedar Ranch*; *The Needles*; *Rock Tower near Manuelito*; and *Laguna from East* (Gilcrease; Cooper-Hewitt; NMAA; EHL).

5 June. Moran to Mary, from Denver, describes trip to and descent into Grand Canyon: "The first descent of about 3000 feet is very steep, but we made it rapidly. The views on the way down are very magnificent. All our traps were on pack horses and how they could get down is remarkable as it was the most perpendicular trail I was ever on.... [three days later] started out with the pack animals and the big cameras for Bissel's point again where Jackson made negatives of the great sweep of the Cañon embracing a view of about 125 miles. His photographs will be nearly 7 feet long by 30 inches high. The following day we spent at various points along the Cañon edge and he made 100 negatives altogether.

On Monday...we had heavy rain..., and when it cleared we were treated to the most magnificent sight of all. Clouds and sunshine in the Cañon. He made many photos of it and will have some splendid effects. I have made some sketches that will serve my purposes well.

We left the Cañon on Tuesday...and reached Flagstaff Wednesday afternoon.... On the same afternoon Paul and Higgins left for home, and in the evening I and Jackson left for 'The Needles' on the lower Colorado in the Mohave Desert on the western edge of Arizona.... Jackson got his pictures of the bridge and we returned on another freight train to Needles early and loafed... until the East bound passenger train from San Francisco came along in the evening and took us eastward... and we arrived here in Denver on Saturday evening." (Bassford and Fryxell 1967, 89–93)

7 June. Moran's watercolor *Newtown Creek, L.I.*, contributed for sale at Ortgies to benefit the Grant Monument fund. (exh. cat., 13)

7 June. Moran to Mary, from Denver: "Yesterday morning I went down to Colorado Springs thinking to meet Dr. Bell but found that he had gone to New Mexico.... I saw his private sec'y, Lundstrom, and he showed me the picture of the H. Cross. It is in a terribly bad state. The whole of the lower end of the picture is rotted off from dampness and it is dreadfully discolored. It can however be put in good condition again. Stindolph can remove all the varnish and dirt and re-line it, and with some work... it will, I think, be as good as ever. Bell has leased a place at Maidstone in Kent, England, and is going to live there for some time to come and is going to take the picture there. His other two pictures, Venice and the Jersey City picture, look as fresh as the day he got them." (Bassford and Fryxell 1967, 95–96)

11 June. Moran to Mary: "Jackson has just heard from the Yellowstone people. They are ready to go whenever he is.... It is just a week since I arrived here [Denver] and it is getting very tiresome as well as expensive.... I have put in the time well however in working up sketches. Have worked up eight during the week. I have about 25 sketches altogether.

The best of them I shall send to Mr. White in Chicago until my return from Yellowstone as I do not want to risk their loss during the travelling there.

Jackson's negatives are turning out splendidly and they will furnish me materials for innumerable pictures.

Jackson and I are concocting a scheme for publication of six subjects of grand size of the Holy Cross, Yo Semite, Yellowstone, Shasta, and two others. He says they sell well." (Bassford and Fryxell 1967, 97)

12 June. Moran sketches and dates *Smelting Works at Denver* (Cleveland Museum).

14 June. Moran to Mary, about preparations for the Yellowstone trip: "We found that the party would consist of 8, Jackson and his assistant, myself, Mr. [Mead], Mr. Gilchrist, Mr. Williams of the Wyoming Commissioners [for the World's Fair], and a packer and cook. We have arranged to start on...June 21st.... It will take us some time to reach the park from Sheridan as our progress will be slow, it being a comparatively unknown region, and Jackson will make many photos on the way." (Bassford and Fryxell 1967, 99)

16 June. Moran to Mary: "I went to a little party at Jackson's and met a relative of F. D. Millet's.... I showed him the sketches I had painted and he was delighted with them. He is much interested in art and wanted me to meet a man named Hayden, one of Denver's rich men.... They are concocting a scheme for an Art Institute for Denver and want my advice about it.... Millet invited me to accompany himself and a few friends to a fishing lake." (Bassford and Fryxell 1967, 101)

18 June. Moran sketches *Wellington Lake near Denver* and *Nesmuth Fall, Wellington Lake* (Gilcrease; Cooper-Hewitt).

18 June. *Denver Rocky Mt. News*: "Thomas Moran, one of the greatest of American artists... is on his way to Yellowstone national park.... Mr. Moran stated that within the last month he has made a number of sketches of the Grand Canyon of the Colorado from which he will make selections for a painting to accompany the Yellowstone picture at the world's fair."

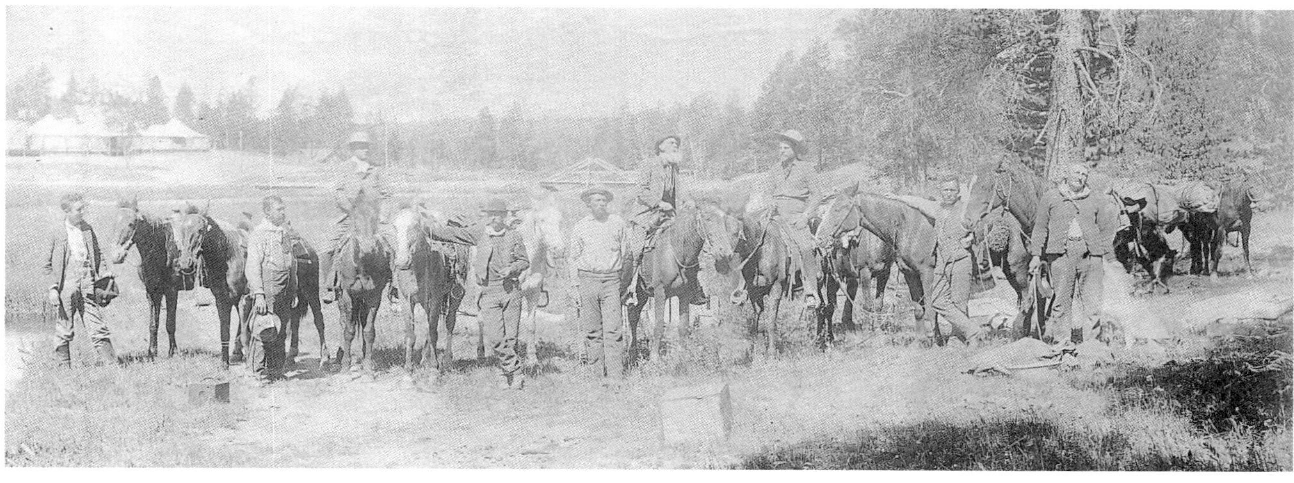

Group with which Moran traveled to Yellowstone in 1892 (Moran on horseback at center), photographed at Norris Basin by William Henry Jackson, courtesy East Hampton Library.

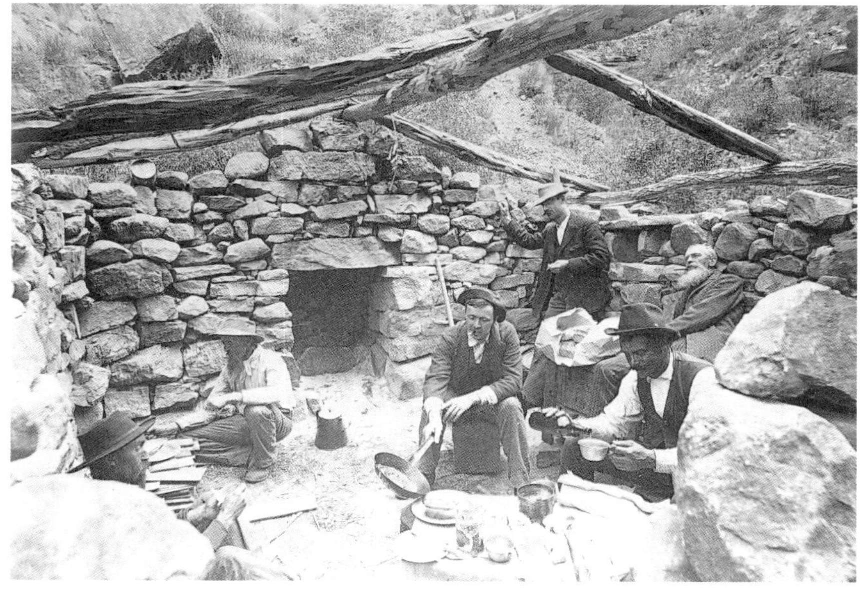

Interior of Hance's cabin, 1892 (Moran near wall at right), photograph by William Henry Jackson, courtesy East Hampton Library.

21 June. Moran to Mary,: "Last night I spent at the house of a Mr. Ward and he had 20 or 30 people to meet me there. I showed my sketches etc. I have been quite lionized in Denver the last few days, but I do not see any clear financial results from it. It may come later on." (Bassford and Fryxell 1967, 103)

22 June. Moran to Mary, from Aurora, NB: "Here we are in full swing for the Yellowstone. We left Denver last night at 8:30 and met the party from Wyoming." (Bassford and Fryxell 1967, 105)

23 June. Moran to Mary, from Newcastle, WY: "We left Aurora yesterday and arrived here this morning. About 200 miles farther on our way. We shall reach Moorcroft about noon, and from there we make a trip into the Black Hills to make some photos and shall not return to the R.R. until Monday next, and it will be the next Thursday before we reach Sheridan, the point where we take to the horses. From Gillette we take the stage for about 200 miles. All this makes a delay in time that I had not expected or calculated for." (Bassford and Fryxell 1967, 105)

24 June. Moran to Mary, from Gillette: "We arrived here yesterday afternoon and are just about to start for the 'Devil's Tower' some 70 miles away.... This place is a frontier R.R. town at the end of the line and the place is an awfully tough one." Party is overtaken by a violent hail storm and has to camp in the open. (Bassford and Fryxell 1967, 108; Moran 1894b, 452)

25 June. Group retraces route to Belle Fourche, stays at ranch of Burke and MacKenzie, finally reaching Devil's Tower the next day. (Moran 1894b, 454)

27 June. Moran to Mary, from Currycomb Ranch near Devil's Tower: "After an adventurous journey we have been to & photographed the 'Tower.'... We... return tomorrow to Gillette." (Bassford and Fryxell 1967, 109)

29 June. Moran to Mary, from Gillette: "We returned from our trip to the Devil's Tower last night & we had an unique experience during the trip. I commenced an account of it today with a view to a magazine article which I think would prove interesting." (Bassford and Fryxell 1967, 109)

1 July. Moran to Mary, from Sheridan: "We left Gillette yesterday and arrived here this morning after a tedious ride of 26 hours, going all night. This is a delightfully situated small town at the foot of the Big Horn range, a fine stream of water running right through the town." (Bassford and Fryxell 1967, 111)

3 July. Sketches and dates *Near Sheridan* and *Goose Creek, Sheridan* (NMAA).

5 July. Moran to Mary, from camp in Big Horn Mts.: "Jackson and a few of the others start today for Clouds Peak. I intended ... to go with them but backed out this morning as I was afraid the journey would be too dangerous and fatiguing.... Our camp is in a beautiful little valley on top of the mountains." (Bassford and Fryxell 1967, 113)

7 July. Moran sketches and dates *On the North Fork of Tongue River, Big Horn Mountains*; *Big Horn Mountains, Tongue River*; *Tongue River Cliffs*; and *On the Way from Tongue River* (Cooper-Hewitt; NMAA).

13 July. Moran to Mary, from camp on Stinking Water River: "We are progressing slowly toward the park but shall not reach it nearly so soon as I had expected. Jackson says we shall get to the Hot Springs on Gardiner's River on the 19th but I think it will be the 20th. This will leave me but a short time in the park, as my [railroad] passes only extend 3 days past the 1st of August." (Bassford and Fryxell 1967, 115)

13–16, 18–19 July. Moran sketches and dates *On Sunshine Fork of Clark's Fork*; *Heart Mountain, from Camp*; *South Fork of Clark's Fork, Sunshine River*; and *Yellowstone Range from Dead Indian Hill*; then *Peak on the Sunshine Fork*; *Mountain Top near Camp, Cooke City*; *On Soda Butte Creek*; and *Index*; then *Lower Falls of South Fork of Gardner River*; and two versions of *Sulphur Mountain* (NMAA; Cooper-Hewitt; JNEM).

20 July. Moran to Mary, from Yellowstone: "We have just arrived here after a most wearying journey.... We left Dayton on the 4th of July and have been in the saddle ever since. I have not yet gone up to look at the Springs, but from the Hotel it looks as if they had lost the color they had originally." (Bassford and Fryxell 1967, 117)

21, 23–24 July. Moran sketches and dates *Upper Basins* and *Dead Since First Visit in 1871*; then *Golden Gate Road*; *Golden Gate, Yellowstone Park*; and *Yellowstone Park, Golden Gate*; then *New Geyser, Norris*; *Norris Geyser Basin, Yellowstone Park*; *Hurricane Vent*; and two versions of *Norris* (Gilcrease; Cooper-Hewitt; NMAA).

26 July. Moran to Mary: "I have made [arrangements] with [F. Jay] Haynes [official Yellowstone photographer and owner of concessions in the park] to sell my Yellowstone pictures, which ... looks like a fine opening for me. We remained at the [Mammoth Hot] Springs two days. I stayed at the Hotel in preference to camp, as did Jackson and a couple of the others. We have all had enough of camp life. I made 4 or 5 color sketches of the Springs and I made a number of sketches that will work up well. After a day ... we left for the Grand Cañon where we stayed two days and made a great many photos. I saw so much to sketch that I have determined to return there myself after I have been to the Geyser Basins and the lake and spend a week at work there. It is as glorious in color as ever and I was completely carried away by its magnificence. I think I can paint a better picture of it than the old one after I have made my sketches.... At the Cañon we decided that we would not go further through the park.... So I and Jackson, Mead and Crosby have a Concord stage, four fine horses and a driver to go where and when we please. We left the Cañon this morning and following the road up the Yellowstone arrived at the lake this afternoon at 5 o'clock, and put up at the Hotel. The lake is fine but too large and the mountains too far off for good pictures. We stay here all day tomorrow to photograph and fish and the day after we go to the upper Geyser Basin.... I read a dispatch from Haynes asking the price of water colors and saying he had a customer. I told him they were the same price as oils, but nothing for less than $100.00.... I shall leave the party at the Lower Geyser Basin and return to the Cañon, do my work there and return home at once, via Northern Pacific.

I think I shall get home about the 8th of August. I am very well satisfied with the artistic side of the trip so far and I think the financial part will pan out all right when I get some work out. Altogether this trip will prove of great advantage to me I am sure.... I think I have opened the way to come out again whenever I want to without paying R.R. fares." (Bassford and Fryxell 1967, 119–122)

26, 28–29 July. Moran sketches and dates *West Wall of the Cañon*; then *Springs on the Border of Yellowstone Lake*; *Stevenson's Island, Yellowstone Lake*; and *From Old Faithful*; *Castle*; then three views of *Lower Geyser Basin*; *Lioness and Bear Cubs, Upper Geyser Basin*; *Fan Geyser*; and two views of *Excelsior Geyser* (Cooper-Hewitt; YNP; NMAA; Gilcrease).

29 July. Moran to Mary, from Lower Geyser Basin Hotel: "We left the upper Geyser Basin this morning and arrived here about noon today. The Great Blue Spring that I drew for Prang's work is about 10 times as large as when I saw it last and has become the greatest Geyser in the Basin.... each big spring seems finer and more beautiful than the last one." (Bassford and Fryxell 1967, 123)

30–31 July, 3–4 August. Moran sketches and dates *Beryl Spring*; then two views of *Moran Point, Yellowstone Canyon*; *Turreted Peaks in Yellowstone Canyon*; *Upper Fall*; and *Looking over the Lower Falls*; then *Cinnabar Mountain*; then *Yellowstone Badlands*; *Badlands of the Yellowstone*; *Yellowstone River near Rosebud*; *Badland near Boice*; and *Badlands of the Dakota* (NMAA; Cooper-Hewitt; Gilcrease).

19 August. *EH Star* reports opening of Maidstone Club on 13 August, its walls decorated with pictures loaned for the occasion, including several etchings by Mary Nimmo Moran.

August. Moran paints *Grand Canyon of the Colorado in Arizona*, giving copyright to Santa Fe Railroad "in consideration of paying expenses & transportation from N. York to the Canon & back of myself & Paul." (GA ledger)

October. Moran repairs *Mountain of the Holy Cross* in his studio for Dr. Bell of Colorado. (GA ledger)

8 October. *Boston Transcript* mentions Massachusetts Charitable Mechanic Association exhibition: "There is much to admire in Mr. Moran's picture of Venice, in the manner of Turner."

8 and 23 October. *NY Herald* reviews Columbian art exhibition at NAD (through 22 Oct.) that includes "Thomas Moran's fantastic and colorful *Dream of the Orient* (No. 114)... *The Mountain of the Holy Cross, Colorado* (No. 101, owned by Dr. Bell), and *A Northeast Gale at East Hampton* (No. 186)."

28 October. *EH Star*: "Mr. Paul Moran has returned to the city for the winter. Mr. and Mrs. Thomas Moran have been on a pleasure trip to Baltimore."

28 October. *EH Star*: "We dropped into Mr. Thomas Moran's studio on Thursday afternoon [27th] and found the artist at work upon the large painting of the Grand Canon of the Yellowstone. The picture is fourteen feet long and eight feet high, and to give a description of it in cold type is next to impossible. The banks of the canon are composed of ledges, peaks and bowlders [*sic*] of volcanic origin, presenting colors varying from a snowy white to a bright red, and representing curious growths of countless centuries. The coloring is grand, and it is upon such a subject that Mr. Moran finds himself right at home. He expects to have this picture together with more of his best works upon exhibition at the World's Fair."

4 November. *EH Star*: "Mr. Thomas Moran and family will leave town in a few days for their winter residence in New York."

21 November–17 December. NAD autumn exhibition. Moran exhibits *Napeague Beach, L.I.*, and *Moonrise—East Hampton Beach, L.I.* (cat. nos. 201, 366).

27 November. *Colorado Sun* quotes the prospectus of the Denver Art League: "The league... aspires, in the near future, to the establishment and maintenance of a permanent museum of art, which shall possess a suitable building and afford an opportunity for the collection and preservation and extension of the arts of design." In order to raise funds, the league will hold exhibitions, the next of which will be works by Moran, including about "250 oil paintings, water colors and engravings, among them a magnificent painting, 8 x 14, taken from a recent sketch in the Yellowstone country and intended for the World's fair. It will be here shown for the first time, with many other productions fresh from the easel of the same eminent artist."

28 November. *Denver Republican*: "To almost everyone who has traveled in the great West, and through the [railroad] car window or from the mountain trail, had the sublime panorama of its scenery unrolled before his eyes, the name of Thomas Moran, the artist, is familiar.

Perhaps no American artist is more widely known, for his work has not been confined to the galleries. Reproductions of many of his greatest works have enriched the monthly magazines, the guide books, folders and general literature of travel in the West.

That the largest collection of his works ever shown should be exhibited in Denver seems peculiarly fitting, as it was in Colorado that he found the material for some of his greatest work, and that the Denver Art league will give, not only its members but the general public, the opportunity of viewing so important a collection is promise that much good may be expected from that organization, if it receives a little of the encouragement it deserves."

1 December. *NY Herald*: "Thomas Moran, N.A., displayed yesterday at his studio his recently painted and huge painting of 'The Grand Canyon of the Yellowstone,' which he will exhibit first at Denver and then at the World's Fair. The... canvas is a forenoon effect, with spray rising from the falls, and is handled with great artistic skill and realism. Twenty years ago Mr. Moran exhibited a somewhat smaller picture of the same subject and from the same point of view, but with an afternoon effect. This is now in the Capitol at Washington."

3 December. *NY Post*: "Mr. and Mrs. Thomas Moran invited friends to their studio last Wednesday afternoon 'to a view of the Grand Canyon of the Yellowstone,' a large canvas even for Mr. Moran, giving a comprehensive view of that marvelous spot from an imaginary point of view."

Mid-December. Unidentified newspaper reports on Moran exhibition in Denver: "The hanging committee, consisting of Messrs. W. H. Jackson, S. Richards, Robert Long... hopes to be through with its work by Saturday." (EHL scrapbook)

18 December. *Denver Rocky Mt. News*: "Last evening at the Hayden & Dickinson building... a private full dress reception was given by the members of the Denver Art League, signalizing the opening of the display of the works of Thomas Moran. It was a very brilliant affair and largely attended.... The pictures were well hung in the spacious room allotted to them, affording ample distance for view....

The exhibition is well arranged for study, commencing in black and whites upon the first wall of the long side wall at the entrance, merging gradually into color works at the further end, until one arrives at the last compartment, where stands the colossal canvas 'Grand Canon of the Yellowstone.' The collection numbers over 260 pieces, a full list of which has been previously published."

Article goes on to mention etchings; wood engravings and photographic reproductions from original drawings, sketches, and paintings; preparatory sketches and lithographs; india ink drawings to illustrate *Hiawatha*; twelve color reproductions of the Yellowstone Park watercolors; and finally a series of watercolor paintings. It concludes: "There are few men in America who can show such a versatility of talent. This man has explored almost every material and method in his art, with an endless variety of subjects. Having visited different lands, always in search of the beautiful. While Mr. Moran has a poetic temperament and shows a poetic feeling all through his work, he is always faithful to nature in great things."

22, 25 December. *Denver Rocky Mt. News* publishes long admiring articles on Moran's etchings and other works in black and white.

• 1893 •

2 January. *Denver Rocky Mt. News*: "Thomas Moran, the artist, arrived in the city from New York yesterday and established himself for a week's vacation.... After six months of continuous work in the studio, Mr. Moran accepted the urgent invitation of Denver friends to visit the city while his paintings are on exhibition.... A reception will be tendered Mr. Moran at the rooms of the Art League....'I know of nothing new in art circles,' remarked the noted painter, in reply to an inquiry, 'except it be the apathy or antagonism American artists in relation to the art exhibit at the world's fair.'" Article discusses at length a controversy surrounding the jury's selection of paintings for the upcoming World's Fair, in which partiality for European works of art is alleged by American artists. "'If Americans had a fair chance for competition,' said Mr. Moran, 'I am satisfied the works of our own country would compare favorably with those of any country of the world.'... Moran's picture of the Yellowstone canon and the wonderful painting of the icebergs in the Atlantic, now on exhibition in this city, will be on exhibition at the world's fair. The 'Yellowstone Canon' Mr. Moran regards as the greatest work he has ever completed."

3, 8 January. Moran sketches and dates *Pike's Peak from the Bluffs East of Colorado Springs*; then two sketches inscribed *Lizard Head* (Gilcrease; Cooper-Hewitt). (Morand 1996, 79)

8 January. *Denver Rocky Mt. News* reports on Denver Art League's well-attended reception in honor of Moran. Also runs a letter to the editor: "As a governing member of the Denver Art League...I should like to know why the excellent collection of paintings of Thomas Moran is closed to the public on Sundays.... The Art league managers have done a good work in bringing this superb collection of pictures to this city and have spared neither time nor expense in doing so. Just why they should prevent a large number of citizens of Denver from seeing this collection by closing its doors upon the only day in the week when the breadwinners of Denver could make it possible to see the exhibition is most extraordinary and beyond comprehension.... This is the best exhibition ever made in Denver, and for study and instruction far and away better than most exhibitions which have ever come to the Western country, and its like may not come to us again soon."

Announcement in same issue of paper: "[The Moran] exhibition, which includes the well known pictures 'The Mount of the Holy Cross,' 'The Grand Canon of the Yellowstone' and 'Spectres from the North' together with 260 others, will be open on Sunday from 2 o'clock till 9. Admission 25 cents."

Extensive review of exhibition explores Moran's methods and styles; "astonishing" variety of subjects; use of blue or gray paper to affect images of sky and water, or warmer-toned paper for representations of sunlit scenes and arid landscapes. The review praises a "highly finished" Venetian picture as being "almost photographically true" yet admires "merest sketches" and "suggestive notes" as having "quite as much importance," continuing "Few artists would consent to make public their inside workings and methods of storing information for future work." With respect to Yellowstone watercolor sketches, whose unusual colors may "cause a majority of visitors who have never seen this region to doubt their fidelity to nature," the review defends Moran: "These subjects were never made with the intention of exhibiting them. They were made solely as his private truthful records of the scenes which he visited and as such were laid aside with numberless others for future reference at any time he might need them. It is not likely that he would have written in his own records things which were not true, or calculated to deceive only himself." In contrast to Europeans, the average American seems to deem it "his duty, first and last, to pick some flaw or fault instead of seeking for the beautiful. If he is fortunate enough to find anything which he does not understand he proceeds immediately in the broadest terms to 'roast the artist.'" This article calls on Colorado audiences to view Moran's watercolors in light of their experience of seeing the mountains, canyons, and related subjects "on a cold gloomy day" as well as "under the glow and glimmer of sunset [where] they become strange weird dreams of color, exceeding any and all resources of the artist's pallet."

15 January. *Denver Rocky Mt. News*: "The Moran exhibition, which was brought here under the auspices of the Denver Art league, will probably end at the close of the coming week unless the attendance should warrant the league in extending [it].... this exhibition is intended for the world's fair and must be delivered in Chicago within a prescribed time....

Mr. Moran was again in the city on Thursday [12 Jan.], after having made a student trip into the mountains with his old friend, Mr. William H. Jackson, in a special car provided by the president of the Rio Grande Southern road to select the most picturesque points en route, which will appear later in a special card of this company for circulation in Europe, setting forth the beauties of the natural scenery...to the intending visitors to the world's fair.

Attendance at the Moran exhibition has not been equal to expectations and the Art league managers are sadly disappointed. Having procured the choicest and latest of the famous artist's productions, the league certainly deserved more consideration from the public. Last week the average attendance was less than seventy-five daily, whereas the actual expenses can only be met by trebling that number. As this is the last week, it is hoped that the lovers of art will testify their appreciation by attending in large numbers."

21 January. *Denver Rocky Mt. News*: "A dispatch was received from the artist, Thomas Moran, last evening, granting to

the Denver Art league the privilege of continuing the exhibition another week. Messrs. Hayden, Dickinson and Feldhauser, the owners of the building at Sixteenth and California, promptly extended the use of the room for another week without charge. The collection is attracting general attention from art lovers, and it is expected that next week's attendance will be the largest of any week since the doors were thrown open."

22 January. *Denver Rocky Mt. News*: "Thomas Moran... exhibition will close on Monday, the 23d... when the 'Grand Canon of the Yellowstone,' 'The Spectres of the North' and 'The Lotus Eaters' will go to the world's fair at Chicago."

25 February. *Boston Transcript*: "New York Artists in a Ferment About the World's Fair Exhibit.... Here for the moment the dispute rests. The latest word of the indigenous, speaking through the mouth of Mr. Thomas Moran, declares that the exhibit from New York at the Fair 'will show American imitation of French art—that is all.'"

26 March. Moran writes Richard Watson Gilder regarding an article he is preparing for *Century Magazine*, saying he will get to it as soon as he can, but "I am worked night & day to fulfill work I have contracted to do by a certain time." (NYPL, mss)

27 March–13 May. NAD annual exhibition. Moran exhibits *Grand Canyon of the Yellowstone* and *Showery Day in Venice* (nos. 222, 324). (Naylor 1973, 655)

31 March. *EH Star*: "Thomas Moran will send his large picture of Yellowstone canon to the world's fair, after all."

Spring. Annual Exposition in St. Louis. Moran's *Vera Cruz* (cat. no. 174), lent by Thomas B. Clarke of New York.

April, May, June. Frances M. Benson in *Quarterly Illustrated*: "There are sixteen members of [the Moran family] who are marine, landscape, animal, portrait, and genre painters, etchers, and illustrators, and an even dozen of these are so near the head of their class that they are known as the 'Twelve Apostles.'... Thomas Moran is the landscape painter of the family, and he is the hardest-working one of the lot. Although not of robust build, his endurance is marvelous, and he may frequently be found in his studio from early morning until midnight. There is not a process of photography, lithographing, or etching, but he is familiar with it.... For his mastery of the processes, and his exact knowledge of cause and effect in nature, Thomas Moran has been dubbed the 'scientist-artist,' and his pictures of the Yellowstone are almost authoritative on rock formations and waterways... Thomas and Mary Nimmo are perhaps the most noted couple of the family.... In obedience to the parental wish, Paul went about the world searching for an education and a vocation, but finally returned with the conviction that he would rather be a poverty-stricken artist, if need be, than make money in any other profession, and now father and son are working side by side. Paul is essentially a painter of American subjects, believing there is ample opportunity for the native brush in the varying types of different sections.

What one has to consider in reviewing the achievements of this remarkable family of artists is not so much the vastness of its collective genius as the unceasing industry and enormous production of its individual members.... They are a rare company, are these Morans, and what they have done in the past, as well as what they are likely to do in time to come, will at least be individual, if not wholly remarkable. But what commendation could be greater?" (Benson 1893, 66–84)

1 May. World's Columbian Exposition opens in Chicago. Moran exhibits *Grand Canyon of the Yellowstone* and *Icebergs in Mid-Atlantic* [*Spectres from the North*] (World's Columbian Exposition rev. cat. nos. 1016, 1162). Mary Nimmo Moran exhibits 12 etchings and is awarded a medal and a diploma. Edward, Leon, and Peter and his wife Emily also exhibit.

5 May. *EH Star*: "Mrs. Thomas Moran arrived at the studio on Tuesday [2nd]."

1 June. Moran sketches and dates *Sand Hills back of East Hampton* (Gilcrease).

18 June. Moran to Gilder, following return from May trip to Baltimore, about article for *Century Magazine*: "I have now substantially finished it & will send it to you within three days at farthest." (NYPL, mss)

23 June. *EH Star* lists Moran among those now occupying their summer residences in East Hampton.

20 September. Moran sketches and dates *East Hampton* (Gilcrease).

4 December–18 January 1894. NAD autumn exhibition. Moran exhibits *Great Blue Spring, Yellowstone Park*; *Venice*; *Autumn, Long Island* (cat. nos. 110, 191, 262) and serves on the council, jury of selection, and committees on catalogue and decoration.

• 1894 •

January. *Century Magazine* publishes "Journey to the Devil's Tower in Wyoming (Artists' Adventures)," written and illustrated by Moran, an account of his trip to Yellowstone, the Tetons, and Big Horn Mts. with W. H. Jackson in 1892.

1 February. Gill exhibition opens in Springfield, MA. Moran exhibits *Bridge of Sighs*.

2 February. *Boston Transcript*: "The Gill exhibition... is the one art event of the year in that part of the State, and it has become an event of consequence to the artists who exhibit there, because of the impressive list of sales, which is duly published each winter at the close of the exhibition. The exhibition this winter contains, among other things, paintings by... Thomas Moran."

5 February–3 March. Annual AWCS exhibition at NAD. Moran exhibits *Cliffs of Green River, Wyoming*; *Effect of Mirage,*

Thomas Moran, 1897, courtesy East Hampton Library.

Bad Lands, Wyoming; *Mountain of the Holy Cross, Colorado*; *Santa Maria, Venice*; *Sunset, Long Island Sound*; *Tower Creek. Yellowstone Park*; and *Passage in Venice* (cat. nos. 61, 65–67, 165, 603, 605).

1 March. *The Collector*: "For upwards of twenty years a familiar visitor to the studios of New York artists has been Mr. James D. Gill... originally... a bookseller and stationer dealing incidentally in prints and other artistic objects.... But he was more than a mere tradesman. He had a natural love for pictures himself, and a good judgment of their merits.... He appreciated the fact that Springfield was a rich city in pretty much everything but the treasures of art, and the inspiration came upon him to supply the deficiency.... His catalogue enumerates one hundred and twenty-seven pictures, and these include examples of some of the best brushes in America. Such notable painters as... Thomas Moran... are worthily represented."

April. Moran gives *Passage Way in Venice* to Salmagundi Club. (GA ledger)

1 April–11 May. NAD annual exhibition. Moran exhibits *Golden Gate, Yellowstone Park*; *Sunrise after a Storm*; and *Morning in Venice* (nos. 169, 292, 350). (Naylor 1973, 655)

3 April–6 May. Annual watercolor exhibition by American artists at AIC. Moran exhibits *Tower Creek, Yellowstone Park* (no. 138). (Falk 1990a, 631)

7 April. *The Critic*, 244, reviews NAD exhibition: "Thomas Moran a 'Sunrise after a Storm,' in which [color] values are ignored... is beautifully composed."

27 April. *EH Star*: "Miss Ruth Moran arrived at her father's studio on Wednesday, and is preparing the house for occupancy by the rest of the family soon."

4 May. *EH Star*: "Thomas Moran, the famous painter, and family arrived in town for the summer on Monday [30 Apr.]."

25 May. *EH Star*: "The brothers Moran contributed greatly to the success of all the affairs at this place last year, and will of course, again."

8 June. *EH Star* lists Moran among cottage owners in residence.

10 December–5 January. NAD autumn exhibition. Moran exhibits *Sunrise in Mist—East Hampton*; *Venice*; and *Grand Canyon of the Yellowstone* (cat. nos. 122, 282, 287), and serves on council and committee on catalogue and decorations. Mary Nimmo Moran exhibits two works.

• 1895 •

4 February–2 March. Annual AWCS exhibition at NAD. Moran exhibits *Santa Maria della Salute, Venice*; *Old Tower of Torcello, Venice*; and *Icebergs in Mid-Atlantic* (cat. nos. 411, 454, 479).

29 March. *NY Post* previews NAD exhibition: "Upwards of 500 paintings have been hung with such judgment as the limited space and limited 'rights' of members permitted to the hanging committee, Messrs. Vinton, Low, and Inness.... places of honor are occupied by marines by William T. Richards and Thomas Moran."

1 April–11 May. NAD annual exhibition. Moran exhibits *Sunset over the Grand Canal, Venice*; *Gala Day in Venice*; and *Morning in Venice* (nos. 35, 283, 350). (*NY Post*, 29 Mar.; Naylor 1973, 655)

27 April. *NY Post*: "The exhibition of paintings now at the Lotos Club... [included] some marines by Edward and Thomas Moran [among] the list of better things.... the entire display is made by artist members of the club."

4 May. *NY Post* reports on at NAD, including Moran's *Sunset over the Grand Canal, Venice*, for $450.

17 May. *EH Star* announces Moran's election as a member of the Council at NAD and also a member of the jury of selections.

14 June. *EH Star* lists Moran among East Hampton summer residents who will occupy their own cottages during the season.

16 August. *EH Star*: "The most important social event among East Hampton's summer residents this season was the wedding, at St. Luke's chapel, on Thursday, Aug. 15, of Miss Mary Scott Moran, eldest daughter of Thomas Moran, N.A., the distinguished painter of landscapes, to Mr. Wirt DeVivier Tassin, of Washington, D.C."

1 November. *EH Star*: "Mr. Thomas Moran, the artist, left town with his family yesterday for New York."

11 November. E. S. Brooke writes to PAFA proposing to enter at the forthcoming Academy exhibition eight reproductions of pen drawings made by Moran to illustrate Lloyd Mifflin's poem "The Hills" and ten reproductions of wash drawings made by Moran to illustrate a volume of sonnets by Mifflin: "There will be 18 in the series.... these drawings will be found most attractive in the Black and White Department.... They will be exhibited, later, in New York." On 5 Dec. Brooks writes that Mifflin will send 18 drawings. (Letters, PAFA archives)

22 November. *EH Star*: "Mr. Thomas Moran, N.A., one of our summer residents, was recently elected president of the Salmagundi Club of New York. The club is composed of artists and literary men of the highest rank."

20 December. *EH Star*: "Among the notable pictures which have been exhibited in New York recently, previous to being seen at the Academy and other leading exhibitions of the year, are a group of characteristic canvasses by Thomas Moran. Several East Hampton landscapes, with their quiet pools, luxuriant foliage and distant windmills, form a pleasing contrast to the brilliantly colored scenes of Colorado canons and Venetians palaces. All of Moran's pictures are characterized by brilliant technical qualities

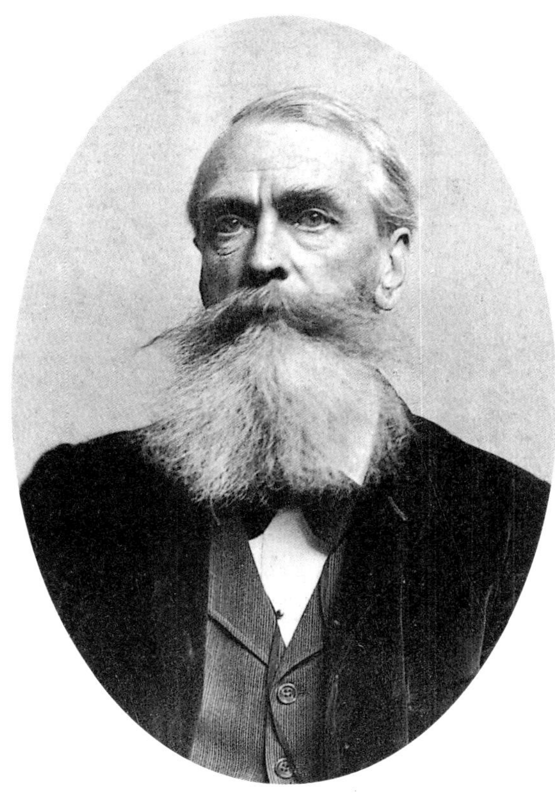

and a wealth of color which make them notable in any collection. Among the paintings exhibited by Mr. Moran were some Montauk pictures."

23 December – 11 January 1896. NAD autumn exhibition. Moran exhibits *June—East Hampton*; *Fort Pond Bay, Montauk*; *Three Tetons, Idaho* (cat. nos. 56, 148, 227), and serves on council, jury of selection, and committee on catalogue and decorations. Mary Nimmo Moran exhibits one work.

23 December – 22 February 1896. PAFA annual exhibition includes pen and ink drawings by Moran: *Autumn Strews Sod*; *Fields of Frozen Sleet*; *November: Dull and Sere*; *A Thousand Sheaves of Golden Grain*; *High upon Some Cloudy Crest*; *And Rest Them on My Paradise*; *Spring Comes Back in All Her Green*; and *Though in the Laurel Underbrush* (nos. 558 – 565)—illustrations for "The Hills" by Lloyd Mifflin. (Falk 1989, 342)

27 December. *EH Star* describes paintings in NAD autumn exhibition: "Three brilliant landscapes by Thomas Moran, one called 'June in East Hampton,' one a scene in the mountains of Idaho, and the other a view of Fort Pond bay, Montauk. The last named is a view over the waters of the harbor from the eastern side. The view is taken looking westward and shows the highlands of North Neck in the foreground with the bay and pond and the beach in the middle distance, with Hither woods and a glimpse of Gardiner's Island in the background."

• 1896 •

22 January. *NY Post* announces upcoming NAD exhibition, with Moran on the selection jury.

31 January. *NY Post* previews AWCS exhibition, with its "many ambitious works and examples of the pictures of leading watercolorists"; Moran's *Venice, from San Giorgio* (no. 140) is described as "bright with color."

3 – 29 February. Annual AWCS exhibition at NAD. Moran exhibits *Morning in Chioggia, Venice*; *Shrine of the Lagoon, Venice*; and *Venice from San Giorgio* (cat. nos. 10, 60, 140).

30 March – 16 May. NAD annual exhibition. Moran exhibits *Cliffs of Green River, Wyoming*; *Teton Range*; and *Venice from San Giorgio* (nos. 257, 311, 391). (*NY Post*, 22 Jan.; Naylor 1973, 655)

1 May. *EH Star*: "Thomas Moran arrived at his studio in this village yesterday."

29 June. Moran sketches and dates *Montauk* (Gilcrease).

23 August. *EH Star* writes that Moran hosted a reading by Richard Watson Gilder, editor of the *Century Magazine*, at his studio on 17 Mar., with about 80 people present.

2 October. *EH Star*: "Stepping into the picturesque studio of Mr. Thomas Moran on Wednesday morning, the Star reporter found Mr. Moran busy upon his pictures. Standing upon an easel was a handsome painting which Mr. Moran had finished the day before. The subject is from the story of the 'Arabian Nights.'... The rich coloring and delicate tones which one sees and the innumerable suggestions of things one doesn't see in the painting fascinate the beholder and make of it a picture which one could live with for all time.

Another beautiful painting was from the upper Colorado, Wyoming, and another, Lake Como, Northern Italy, was very pretty, giving one a clear conception of the rare beauty of those superb lakes of upper Italy.

A striking, and yet impressive picture among the group was a large painting from the biblical study of Rispah [*sic*], showing the bereaved woman watching over the dead bodies of her seven sons.

A painting of local interest was one of Montauk, taken from the northeast coast, between Shagwanac and the point. This is a very large painting, and like Montauk itself has a beauty about its coloring and composition that is all its own.

Mr. Moran says he has been hard at work all summer, and during the past five months spent in his East Hampton studio, has done the very best work of his life. And, indeed, from the standpoint of the lay spectator, it seemed to the reporter impossible that human hands could make more beautiful pictures."

16 October. *EH Star*: "Artist Thomas Moran and family left town yesterday."

23 November – 19 December. NAD autumn exhibition. Moran exhibits *City of Queen Marjaneh (from the "Arabian Nights")*; *Rizpah*; and *Fourth Voyage of Sinbad the Sailor (from the "Arabian Nights")* (cat. nos. 144, 150, 242).

24 November. *NY Post* reviews NAD autumn exhibition: "[There] is a landscape by Mr. Moran, called 'Rispah' [*sic*] (no. 150), that shows force and skill."

• 1897 •

14–16 January. At ULC of NY exhibition of paintings by American artists, Moran exhibits *Venice from the Giudecca* (cat. no. 23).

1–27 February. Annual AWCS exhibition at NAD. Moran exhibits *Outskirts of Venice*; *Low Tide, Venice*; *Venice from the Giudecca*; *Chioggia, Venice*; *Cliffs of the Upper Colorado, Wyoming*; *Roc's Egg (from the "Arabian Nights")*; *Sunset in Venice*; *Santa Maria della Salute*; and *Shrine in the Lagoon, Venice* (cat. nos. 58, 102, 126, 163, 168, 405, 419, 423, 427).

8 February. Moran one-man exhibition opens at C.W. Kraushaar Galleries, NY. Catalogue includes original verses by Edith M. Thomas.

13 February. *NY Post* reviews Moran exhibition at Kraushaar: "Twenty-five canvases . . . give a pretty fair impression of his abilities as a painter. In subject they range from Florida to Venice, and from Wyoming to Montauk Point. But it is impossible to mistake the familiar touch and scheme of color, be the pretext what it may."

Mid-February. *NY Sun* reviews Moran exhibition: "The pictures well exemplify Mr. Moran's characteristic methods, well-balanced composition, and effective contrasts of light and shade, in the Venetian scenes particularly, rich and varied color being the most striking elements. 'After Rain' . . . [is] one of the canvases in which a sober color scheme is well carried out in the gray and black of wind-driven clouds and the dull yellow of the seashore, while 'The Bride of the Adriatic' . . . is one of the most brilliant and unified . . . [and] 'Montauk' . . . is a large landscape showing a flat valley with a strongly handled sky." (Undated clipping, EHL scrapbook)

17 February. *NYT* reviews Moran exhibition: "A virile draftsman, a rich colorist, and a painter of unusual poetic thought and feeling, his work is known to all art lovers in America for its strength and individuality. He has been called 'an artist spoiled by too much study of Turner,' a criticism which has always seemed rather paradoxical, for it is difficult to conceive how the influence of the great English master could spoil any painter. If Thomas Moran sees Venice and even the majestic scenery of our far West as Turner might have seen them, the visions which he transcribes are none the less strong or entrancing on this account . . . . But there are in the present exhibition . . . other canvases which do not deserve the criticism above alluded to. 'Autumn on Long Island,' with its fine sweep of wind and sky, its clear atmosphere and rich deep color; 'Castle Lonely,' with its splendid flaming, sunset sky, and its strong poetic conception; 'Montauk,' with its superb distance and atmosphere, and 'June at Easthampton,' with its rich greens, are the work of an original, forceful painter."

20 February. *The Critic* reviews Moran exhibition: "The pictures . . . comprise a fair share of the artist's most interesting work. Four Venetian views are especially rich in color, high in key and satisfactory in composition . . . . The Yellowstone Valley and the colored cliffs of Arizona furnish subjects for several pictures, and, imaginatively treated, an impressive landscape setting for figures, such as that of Rizpah, and architectural fantasies from the 'Arabian Nights.' The artist is at his best when his imagination is moved, as in these cases, by something weird or wonderful in his subject; but even of such homely bits of nature as are to be found on Long Island he makes something out of the common."

13 March. *NY Post*: "A collection of modern paintings in oil and water color to be sold by order of Mr. Charles Knapp, executor, together with additions from two private galleries, is now on exhibition at the Fifth Avenue Galleries . . . . A landscape by George Inness . . . is one of the curiosities on display, and a 'Slave Hunt, Dismal Swamp,' by Thomas Moran, is not far behind it." (Executor's sale cat., 16 Mar.)

Spring. Annual Exposition in St. Louis. Moran exhibits *City of Queen Marjaneh (from the "Arabian Nights"* (cat. no. 349).

5 April–15 May. NAD annual exhibition. Moran exhibits *Sansovino in Venice—1540*; *Solitude*; and *Montauk* (nos. 121, 305, 402). Mary Nimmo Moran exhibits one work. (*NY Post*, 15 Jan.; Naylor 1973, 655)

25 October. Moran's early mentor John Sartain dies in Philadelphia at age 89. (*The Critic*, 30 Oct.)

30 October. Lucy Cleveland in *NY Post*: "Thomas Moran has . . . a studio where he is spreading the sun-mosaic from Fairyland with his brushes dipped in dreams . . . . You stand in delightful wonder at first as you look and catch the . . . butterfly's view of the room in which are gathered together in artistic confusion and charm relics from rambles . . . in every part of this variform world . . . Across that dark wood-carven gallery above are thrown the gorgeous vestments, now dulled, . . . of prelates of Brittany, ecclesiastical fragments from Hungary, fragrant moth-eaten robes from old Rome . . . . Suspended . . . swing bulbous bronze delights of mosque and seraglio lamps . . . deep-hued lustrous as the eyes of a Sultan's favorite, or the jeweled splendors of her little sandalled feet. Here are rugs from Persia and Afghanistan . . . here is an Egyptian rug with the coat of arms . . . of the Pharaoh—the winged disc of the sun . . . . There are on the easel four pictures from distinct Fairyland. No other of our artists is attempting these things. . . . Bluebeard's Castle . . . Sinbad the Sailor's Land . . . . These fairy pictures that open to you the lands of the ideal give one new courageous hope that the cult of realism is passing."

5 November. *EH Star*: "Thomas Moran, the artist, closed his studio here on Monday and with his family departed for the city."

12 November. *NY Post* previews NAD exhibition: "The adjoining east gallery is rendered attractive by such works as . . . Thomas Moran's 'A Feudal Tower.'"

15 November–18 December. NAD autumn exhibition. Moran exhibits *Feudal Tower*; *Santa Maria and the Ducal Palace, Venice*; and *Moonrise, Chioggia, Venice* (cat. nos. 171, 184, 264).

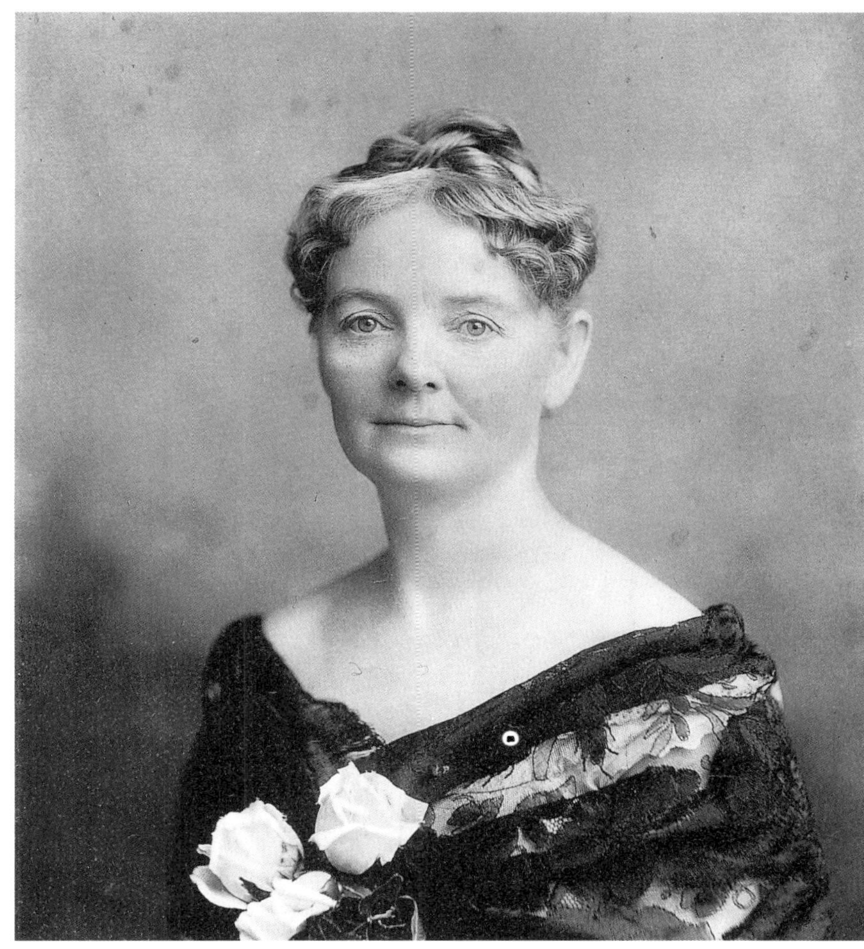

Mary Nimmo Moran, 1899, courtesy East Hampton Library.

• 1898 •

13–15 January. ULC of NY loan exhibition of paintings by American artists. Moran exhibits *Feudal Tower* (cat. no. 32).

21 January–26 February. Annual AWCS exhibition at NAD. Moran exhibits *In the Sierra Nevada*; *Yellowstone Range, National Park, Wyoming*; and *In the Big Horn Mountains* (cat. nos. 14, 68, 281).

28 March–14 May. NAD annual exhibition. Moran exhibits *Teton Range, Idaho*; *Story of the Third Sheik (from the "Arabian Nights")*; and *Sunset* (nos. 111, 177, 282). (Naylor 1973, 656)

3 June. *EH Star* lists Moran among cottage owners who will occupy their own residences during the summer.

19 August. *EH Star*: "Among the artists now in East Hampton are . . . Thomas Moran and Paul N. Moran."

5 August, 9 September. *EH Star* reports that troops have been removed from Santiago to Montauk because of yellow fever and that "some ladies of East Hampton have opened a small hospital for the care of sick soldiers from Montauk."

23 September. *EH Star* notes that Mary Nimmo Moran donated sheets and flannel bands to the Relief Corps Hospital in East Hampton.

7 October. *EH Star* notes that Mary Nimmo Moran and her daughter Ruth donate food "delicacies" once a week to the East Hampton Relief Corp.

28 October. *EH Star* lists Ruth Moran as a member of the Red Cross Society.

7 November–3 December. NAD autumn exhibition. Moran exhibits *"Childe Roland to the Dark Tower Came"*; *Dream of Venice*; and *Venice from the Lagoon* (cat. nos. 210, 222, 226).

15 November. *EH Star*, reviewing NAD exhibition, notes that Moran's *Long Island Landscape*, is included.

• 1899 •

13 February–11 March. Annual AWCS exhibition at NAD. Moran exhibits *Santa Maria and Ducal Palace, Venice*; *Chioggia, Venice*; and *Sunset, Venice* (cat. nos. 197, 299, 359).

24 February. *EH Star*: "At the great picture sale last week at Chickering Hall, New York, when Thomas B. Clarke's collection of American paintings [was] sold, many artists well known in East Hampton were represented. The sale was the largest of its kind ever held in this country, the prices paid during the four nights' auction being $234,495. In the list we noticed the following pictures which have a local interest: . . . Thomas Moran's 'Vera Cruz' was bought by C. M. Pratt for $725."

3 April–13 May. NAD annual exhibition. Moran exhibits *Stream in the Teton Range, Idaho*; *Venetian Fiesta*; and *Mountain of Lodestone (from the "Arabian Nights")* (nos. 159, 187, 195). (Naylor 1973, 656)

12 May. *EH Star*: "Thomas Moran, the landscape painter, and Mrs. Moran arrived at their studio yesterday."

14 May. For *NYT Magazine* Charles de Kay writes article about East Hampton that includes two pictures of Moran's studio: "The first artist to take root in East Hampton was Thomas Moran, whose pretty cottage studio looks from out its honeysuckle hedges across the old village pond, where the first settlers laid out their farms and established their graveyard. The painter of Venice, of Scottish moors and the Yellowstone found the even temperature and quiet landscapes of East Hampton just the kind he wanted, and his wife, Mrs. Nimmo Moran, has found in the surrounding fields, lakes, and beaches capital subjects for the art of which she has a mastery—the art of etching. With their son, who is also a painter, the Moran family forms a trio of artists that by this time has become one of the noteworthy points of the town." (Repr. *EH Star*, 19 May)

21 July. *EH Star* notes about the Village Fair: "Among other things of particular interest we noticed an etching, 'Meadow Grasses,' by M. Nimmo Moran, and another etching by Thomas Moran, entitled, 'A Road Near the Sea, East Hampton.'"

11 August. *EH Star* lists Moran among cottage owners in residence.

25 September. Mary Nimmo Moran dies from "enterocolitis" at age 57. She became ill caring for her daughter Ruth. (Death record, town clerk's office, East Hampton)

29 September. *EH Star*, In a memorial article: "East Hampton has sustained a sad and irreparable loss in the death of Mrs. Moran. Intimately associated with East Hampton scenes and East Hampton people for the past twenty years, in art, in society, and in her home life, Mrs. Moran has endeared herself to the hearts of all classes of our people.... She was...laid to rest in the South Burying-ground, opposite the old wind-mill that has so often been a feature in her paintings and etchings. She loved East Hampton and all that was associated with this village."

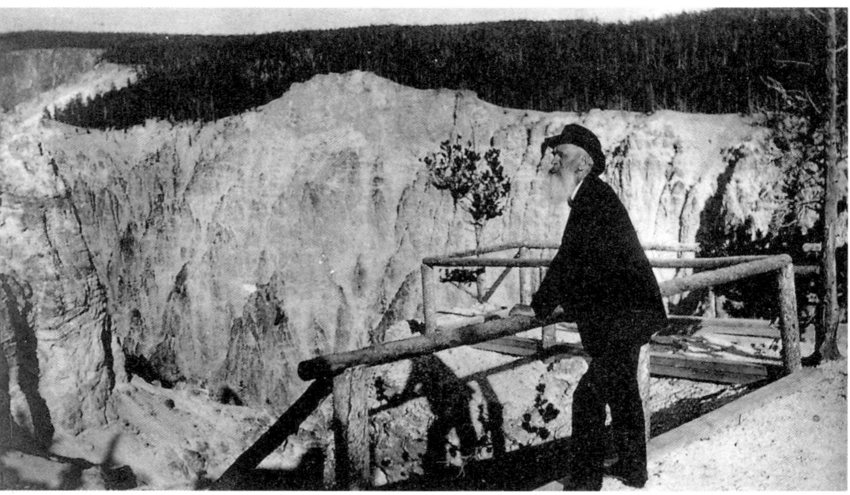

Thomas Moran in Yellowstone, 1900, courtesy East Hampton Library.

29 September. *EH Star*: "Miss Ruth Moran, daughter of Thomas Moran, who has been seriously ill for several weeks, is convalescing."

13 October. *EH Star*: "Thomas Moran will close his studio and return to the city on Monday next [16th]."

12 November. Moran moves to Mrs. Stimpson's Boarding House, 84 Irving Place, NY, making a dated inventory "of all the pictures and other material of value, in my studio, 37 West 22nd Street, at this date... and also the pictures that belong to me on loan at other places." (GA ledger)

22 December. *EH Star*: "The will of Mrs. Mary N. Moran, late of East Hampton, has been probated by Surrogate Petty. Mrs. Moran was the wife of Thomas Moran, the artist. The house and contents on Main street, East Hampton, are given to Ruth B. Moran, at whose death the property is to go to Mr. Moran, and if he is not living then to his heirs. All residue is given to husband, Thomas Moran. The will is dated March 20, 1898. The executors are Dr. Edward Osborne and Mrs. Phoebe H. Osborne, of East Hampton. The petition gives the personal estate at $1,500 and the real property is valued at $1,800."

• 1900 •

1–27 January. NAD annual exhibition. Moran exhibits *Teton Range, Idaho*; *Cliff Dwellers, Arizona*; and *Pearl of Venice* (nos. 66, 98, 115). (Naylor 1973, 656)

13 January. At Century Club Moran exhibits *Venice* and *Munroe's Cottage at East Hampton*. (CA, AAA)

1 February. Annual AWCS exhibition at NAD. Moran exhibits *Venice from San Giorgio*; *Cliffs of Green River, Wyoming*; and *Venice* (cat. nos. 14, 105, 161).

3 March, 7 April, 5 May, 3 June. At Century Club Moran exhibits *Long Island Landscape, Montauk* (watercolor), and *Rocky Mountain Stream*; then *Ulysses and the Sirens*; then *Venice*; *Fort Pond Bay, Montauk*; *Long Island Landscape*; *Mountain Stream, Idaho*; and *Rock Towers of the Rio Virgin, S. Utah*; then *Solitude*. (CA, AAA)

Summer. Thomas and Ruth Moran travel west, visiting Shoshone Falls on the Snake River, Blue Lakes in Idaho, and Yellowstone—Moran's last trip to the park. (*Salt Lake City Daily Tribune*, undated article in EHL scrapbook; Morand 1996, 81; Ruth Moran letter, 19 Feb. 1931, Fryxell, UW)

9 June. *Salt Lake City Daily Tribune* interviews Moran: "'You may quote me as saying anything complimentary about Utah

scenery.... It is unquestionably the greatest in the United States, and, in my estimation, Europe has no scenery that is really comparable with the American. Take the Swiss as an illustration of European scenery. It is what you might call very decent and well-behaved. Its lines are convincing and proper, as though built according to prearranged and well-proportioned design. It is rather on the order of grace and symmetry. You know from seeing one just what to expect in another, but the American—the Utah scenery, for instance—is ruggedly grand, inspiring, impressive. It is heaped up, massed up, and often in a profusion of irregularities, tempestuous combinations and stupendous effects that fairly daze the beholder, leaving him to wonder and admire by the hour.'...

On being asked as to his mode of traveling and working, the artist said he never carried an easel or any oil colors. These were left at home in the studio. All he was encumbered with was a good-sized portfolio for his paper and sketches, while for coloring he used water color. The rest of his equipment was the same as that of any other tourist on camping out. The artist said he had slept many a night in the open air without a tent, and had tramped many a hundred miles. But he could not do that now as much as formerly, as he was 63 years old. 'In working,' he said, 'I use my memory. This I have trained from youth up, so that while sketching and coloring, I impress indelibly upon my memory the features of the landscape and the combinations of coloring, so that when back in my studio the water color will recall vividly all the striking peculiarities of the scenes visited.'

The artist then remarked: 'While there are many American painters of American scenery, a majority of them secured their instruction in Europe and imbibed the spirit of the old masters. Now art is nature viewed through the temperament, and these foreign-instructed American artists show their foreign training in their American work. It is American scenery viewed through European spectacles, and as such it is not truly American. The way to present American themes on canvas, is to see them as they actually are, and not according to European models or standards. So I hold that American painters ought to get their fundamental instruction in this country, whose subjects they are to make their life study.'"

September. Richard Ladegast in *Truth Magazine*: "Essentially a colorist, a master of technique and form, Thomas Moran is beyond all else an 'individualist.' He has never been a mere copyist, even of Nature. All that he does is directed by an imagination so poetical, and yet so clear, and truthful, that his work is more akin to creation than reproduction."

October. Frederick W. Morton in *Brush and Pencil*: "It is not often that pioneers in a nascent art are privileged to share in its mature glory and take part in achievements that command the respect and elicit the admiration of critics and connoisseurs; but such is the unique distinction of Thomas Moran.... What is equally notable, Moran is to-day what he has been from the outset of his career—an American painter, with love for American subjects and pride in American work.... The reason of this—and the same dominant force is to be traced in all his subsequent work—is to be found in the character and temperament of the painter himself. His mental bent is poetic, and a rich, almost exotic, imagination is his chief characteristic."

3 November, 1 December. At Century Club Moran exhibits *Solitude*; then *Shoshone Falls of Snake River, Idaho*; *Yellowstone Cañon*; and *Passing Shower, Venice*. (CA, AAA)

• 1901 •

5 January–2 February. NAD annual exhibition. Moran exhibits *Yellowstone Cañon*; *Passing Shower, Venice*; and *Shoshone Falls of Snake River, Idaho* (nos. 4, 152, 208). (Falk 1990b, 367)

12 January. At Century Club Moran exhibits *In Arizona*; *East Hampton Meadows*; *Sunset, Wyoming*; and *Long Island Scene*. (CA, AAA)

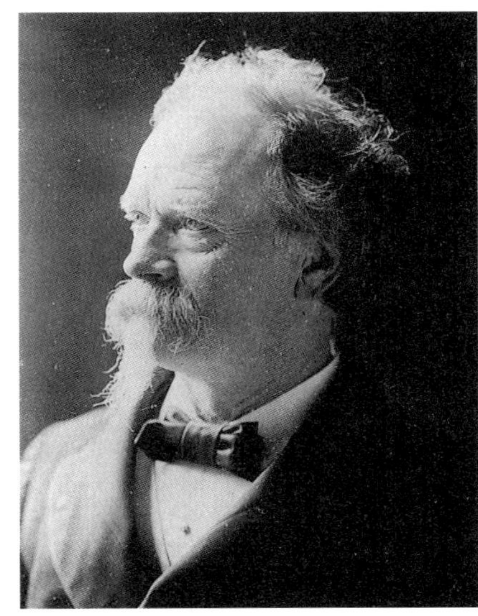

Edward Moran, photograph by Napoleon Sarony, New York, courtesy East Hampton Library.

19 January. Reviewing the NAD exhibition for *Harper's Weekly*, Charles Caffin singles out for praise Moran's *Shoshone Falls of Snake River*.

19 January. W. H. Jackson writes to Moran from Detroit about photograph of Shoshone Falls, discussing price and royalty arrangements for negatives and painting: "I have just been reading the... current number of *Harper's Weekly* of the opening of the exhibition, and from the fact that they start off with such an extended notice of your picture I judge that it is making a very decided impression.

There is one thing sure—and that is that such pictures as 'Shoshone Falls' will live many a long year after the eccentricities of the faddists have been lost sight of and forgotten." (EHL)

29 January. Moran to Mr. Nicholson at Santa Fe Railroad about an article requested: "I have decided that my literary capacity is 'Nil.' I tried it once before, & on rereading the article in the *Century Magazine* [T. Moran 1894] I felt ashamed of it, & have reresolved not to again take pen in hand for publication. I am of opinion that nothing finer or more descriptive of the Grand Canon can be written (for those who have not seen it), than the one done by our dear dead friend Higgins after the trip we made there together.

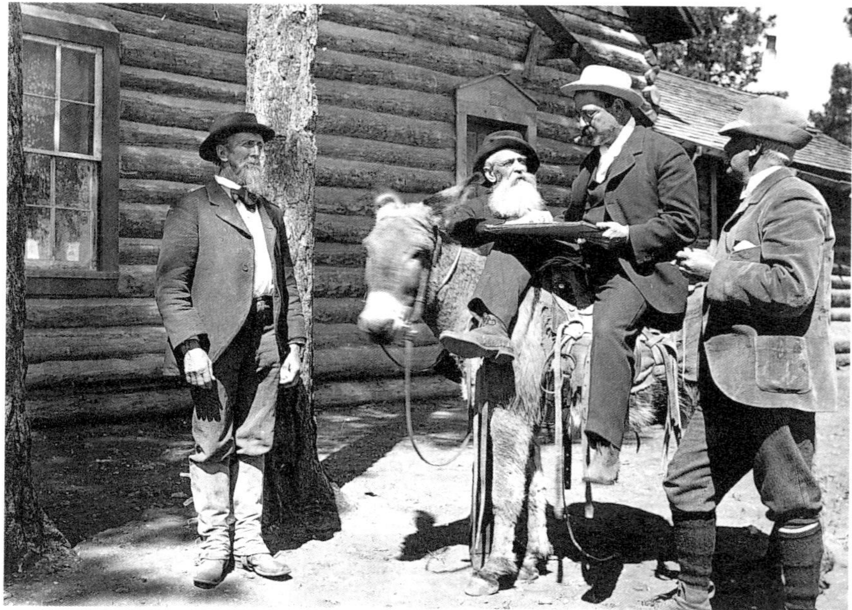

At Grand Canyon in 1901, John Hance, Thomas Moran, George Inness Jr., and George H. McCord (left to right), courtesy Museum of New Mexico.

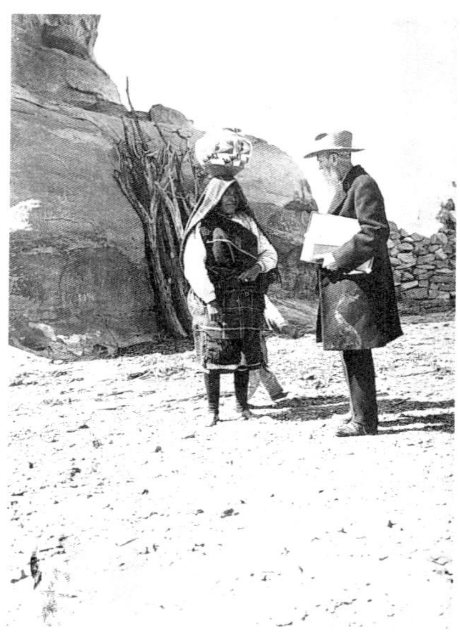

Moran at Acoma, New Mexico, 1901, courtesy East Hampton Library.

While I wish that I had literary capacity to give to others what I see in the Grand Canon I am convinced that I can only paint it, which I expect to continue to do until my hand ceases to work." (GA; yet see Moran 1903 and Moran 1906; see also Higgins 1897)

11 February–24 March. AWCS annual exhibition. Moran exhibits *Cliffs of Green River, Wyoming*; *Morning in Arizona*; *Walls of the Yellowstone Canyon*; *In Shoshone Village, Idaho*; and *Venice from the Lagoon*. (Wilson 1994, 4, 8)

2 March. At Century Club Moran exhibits *Ulysses and the Sirens*; and *Glen Eyrie, Garden of the Gods, Colorado*. (CA, AAA)

14 March. Moran copyrights *Shoshone Falls of Snake River, Idaho*. (LC doc. Class I. XXc. no. 542; EHL)

May. W. P. Lockington in *Brush and Pencil* reviews watercolor exhibition Philadelphia Art Club at which "sturdy Thomas Moran" exhibits *Morning in Arizona* and *Cliffs of Green River, Wyoming*.

May. Moran travels to Grand Canyon for Santa Fe Railroad with George Inness Jr., George H. McCord, Gustave H. Buek, their wives, and Ruth Moran. Trip organized by W. H. Simpson, assistant general passenger agent and head of advertising. Moran goes on to New Mexico and Colorado. (Simpson 1909, 23–25)

1 May–1 November. Pan American Exposition in Buffalo. Moran exhibits *Passing Shower, Venice*, and *Shoshone Falls of Snake River, Idaho*, which receives a silver medal. (Exh. cat., 90 and frontispiece; GA ledger)

4 May. At Century Club Moran exhibits *Yellowstone Cañon*; *Scene from Lalla Rookh*; and *Sunset in Arizona*. (CA, AAA)

24–25, 31 May. At Grand Canyon, Moran sketches and dates *From Rowe Point, Looking West*, and *From Havasupai Point, Looking East*; in New Mexico, sketches and dates *Sandstorm at Acoma* (JNEM; Cooper-Hewitt; Stark Museum).

2, 7 June. In Colorado, sketches and dates two drawings inscribed *Spanish Peaks, Colorado*; also *Pike's Peak and Cameron's Cove and Manitou Canyon*; and *Ruxton, Colorado at Manitou, from Cog Railroad* (Gilcrease; Cooper-Hewitt; Amon Carter).

9 June. Moran's older brother Edward dies in New York at age 71. (*NYT*, 10 June)

18 June. In New Mexico, Moran sketches and dates *Bit of Laguna* (Cooper-Hewitt).

July. Hugh Coleman in *Brush and Pencil*: "In the death of Edward Moran . . . America lost one of its ablest and most versatile artists. Coupled with his rare ability as a painter, he had an unusual aptitude for teaching his art, and, perhaps what is equally noteworthy, a genius for work. To him is due primarily the development of his brothers, Thomas and Peter, and also of the younger generation of Morans, Percy and Leon, all of whom have acquired enviable reputations . . . . In measure he lacked the ideality of his brother Thomas, and was not wooed as was the latter by the grander aspects of nature. His tastes were more pastoral, and his landscapes, therefore, were simpler and less pretentious than his brother's."

26 July. *EH Star*: "The largest and most attractive picture in the art gallery at the Pan-American is Thomas Moran's painting of the Shoshone Falls, Snake River, Idaho."

August. Moran sends *Grand Canyon of the Yellowstone* (1893) to Antlers Hotel, Colorado Springs, for display and sale, a practice he continues with other paintings. (GA ledger)

2 November. At Century Club Moran exhibits *In Arizona* and *Landscape in Summer*. (CA, AAA)

1 December–1 June 1902. Moran exhibits *Shoshone Falls* at exposition in Charleston (no. 244); Peter and Percy Moran also exhibit. (See *Fine Arts, South Carolina Inter-State and West India Exposition* cat.)

7 December. At Century Club Moran exhibits 16 works. (CA, AAA)

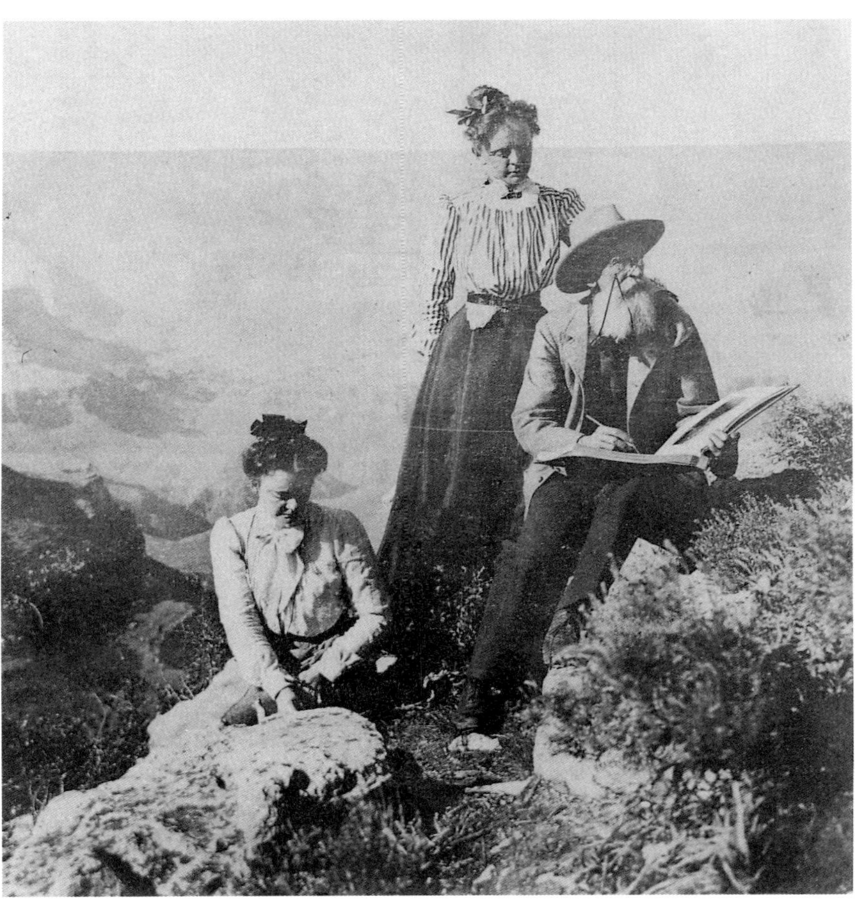

Thomas Moran sketching at Grand Canyon with daughters Ruth and Mary Moran Tassin, 1910, courtesy Museum of New Mexico.

• 1902 •

At American Art Society exhibition, Phila., Moran exhibits *Long Island Landscape* and *Sunset near La Rita* and is awarded a gold medal. (Ledger and certificate, GA)

3 January–1 February. NAD annual exhibition. Moran exhibits *Sunrise Venice*; *Windy Hilltop, Amagansett*; and *Morning in Arizona* (nos. 45, 78, 381). (Falk 1990b, 367)

6–7 February. Public auction of Edward Moran collection, 102 works, at Fifth Avenue Galleries, NY. (Collection cat.)

22 February. Moran's older brother John dies in New York at age 70. (Interment records, West Laurel Hill Cemetery, Phila.)

1 March. At Century Club Moran exhibits *At the Foot of Great Pond Montauk.* (CA, AAA)

21 April–4 May. Annual AWCS exhibition. Moran exhibits *Grand Canyon of the Yellowstone*; *Rock and Village of Acoma*; *Desert in Southern Utah*; *Venice*; *Rock Tower in the Grand Canyon of Arizona*; and *In a Side Canyon of the Colorado River.* (Wilson 1994, 11, 14)

3 May. At Century Club Moran exhibits *Edge of the Village, Long Island.* (CA, AAA)

20 May. George H. Yarnell, secretary of AFS of NY, to Moran: "In recognition of a kindly act on your part, by which several hundred dollars were paid into the Treasury of the Artists' Fund Society, and as an expression of their esteem and of their grateful feeling to you, the Board of Control . . . by a unanimous vote elected you an Honorary Member [13 May]. If accepted by you, they feel that they can in that way have you identified with a Society that will always feel glad to honor you in every way that lies in their power." (GA)

8 June. In New Mexico, Moran sketches and dates *Navajo Church near Wingate, N.M.* (EHL).

20 June. *EH Star* lists Moran among cottage owners who will be in residence in East Hampton this season.

1 November. At Century Club Moran exhibits *Bad Lands, Dakota*, and *Sunset, New Mexico.* (CA, AAA)

6 December. At Century Club Moran exhibits *Rock of Acoma, N.M.*; *Grand Cañon of Arizona*; and *Solitude.* (CA, AAA)

• 1903 •

In addition to Moran's residence in East Hampton, the artist is listed at Mrs. Stimpson's Boarding House, NY. (Falk 1990b, 367; GA ledger; *EH Star*, 19 June)

3–31 January. NAD annual exhibition. Moran exhibits *Forest Glade, East Hampton*; *Sunset near La Rita, New Mexico*; and *In the Land of the Dakotas* (nos. 112, 239, 306). (Falk 1990b, 367)

7 March. At Century Club Moran exhibits *Clouds and Sunshine.* (CA, AAA)

April. *Brush and Pencil* publishes "Knowledge a Prime Requisite for Art," written by Moran.

16, 28 April. In New Mexico, Moran sketches and dates *Albuquerque*; in

Mexico, sketches and dates *Cortés Palace* and *Ruins at Cuernavaca* (Gilcrease).

May. Sketches and dates *Cuernavaca, Bridge over the Baranca* (Gilcrease).

4 May. Moran in Mexico City. (Dated receipt from shop, "Antiquities Antiguedades," Mexico City, GA)

7 May. Sketches and dates *Huehuetoca, Mexico*, and *Lime Kilns at Tula* (EHL; Gilcrease).

June. *Brush and Pencil* publishes "Plea for a National Art Gallery," written by Moran.

19 June. *EH Star* lists Moran among cottage owners who will be in residence for the season.

7 August. Moran in East Hampton. (Dated inventory, GA ledger)

25 September. *EH Star*: "T. E. Babcock is building an addition to Thomas Moran's studio-cottage."

5 December. At Century Club Moran exhibits 11 works. (CA, AAA)

• 1904 •

2–30 January. NAD annual exhibition. Moran exhibits *Butterflies of Venice*; *Edge of the Grand Cañon, Arizona*; *Gossips at the Well, Mexico*; and *Cortes Palace at Cuernavaca, Mexico* (nos. 88, 179, 216, 269). (Falk 1990b, 367)

9 January, 5 March. At Century Club Moran exhibits *Valley of the Yuma* and 11 charcoal sketches; then *Woods in Autumn*; *Near Sag Harbor*; and *Venice*. (CA, AAA)

28 April–5 June. Annual watercolor exhibition by American artists at AIC. Moran exhibits *Desert in South Utah* (no. 241). (Falk 1990a, 631)

May–December. Universal Exposition in St. Louis commemorating Louisiana Purchase. Moran exhibits *Solitude* and *Cloud and Sunshine, Montauk, L. I.* (cat. nos. 534–535). (See also Holland art dept. cat.).

17, 27 May, 17 June. Sketches and dates *Grand Canyon*; then *Yosemite North and South Domes*; then another *Grand Canyon* (Gilcrease; Yosemite).

24 June. *EH Star* lists Moran among summer residents now occupying their cottages.

14 October. Charles de Kay, for *EH Star*: "No wonder the landscape and marine painters, Thomas Moran … and others, swear by East Hampton."

4 November. *EH Star*: "Thomas Moran closed his cottage here and returned to the city. Mr. Moran has been busily engaged in his studio here during the summer upon four of the grandest nature scenes to be found in America. They are the Yellowstone Park, the Yosemite Valley, the Grand Canon and the Petrified Forests of Arizona. The paintings will first go to the Century Club, after which they will be placed in some of the exhibitions."

3 December. At Century Club Moran exhibits *Grand Canyon of the Yellowstone*; *Grand Canyon of the Colorado*; *Domes of Yosemite*; and *Petrified Forest*. (CA, AAA)

10 December. In letter to the editor, *Art News*, marine painter Parker Newton comments on Comparative Art Exhibition: "An excellent opportunity … was lost sight of when the committee over-

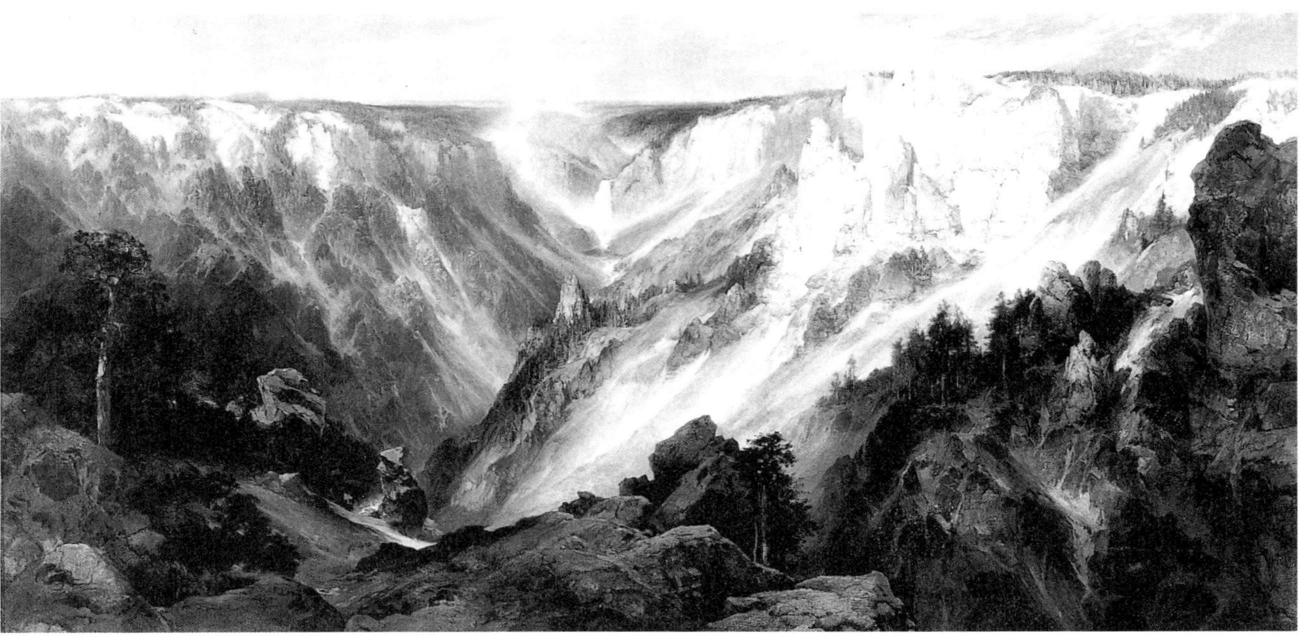

Thomas Moran, *Grand Canyon of the Yellowstone*, 1904, oil on canvas, courtesy Honolulu Academy of Arts, Gift of the Bank of Hawaii, 1970.

looked Thomas Moran in hanging Turner's 'Venice.' Moran painted the entrance to the Grand Canal from the same spot and it would not have been very difficult to have borrowed one of his pictures and placed it next to Turner's."

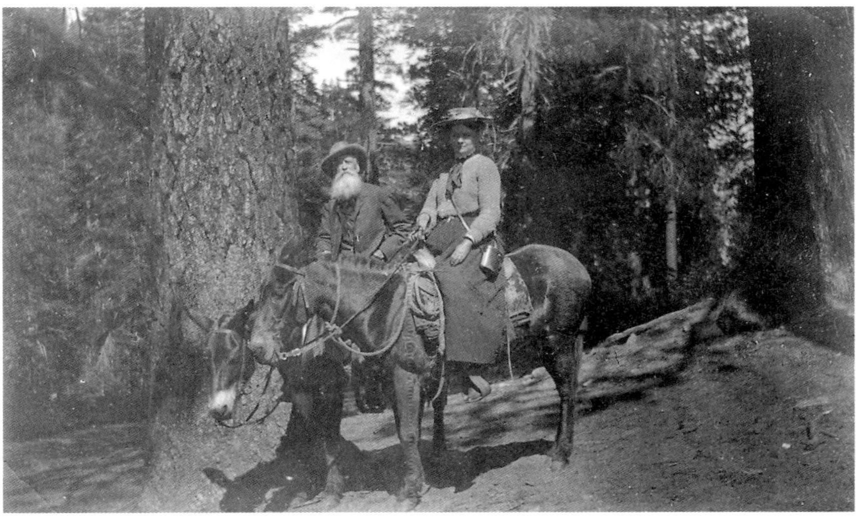

Thomas and Ruth Moran at Yosemite, 1904, courtesy East Hampton Library.

31 December–28 January 1905. NAD annual exhibition. Moran exhibits *Santa Maria and the Ducal Palace, Venice*; *Teoloyacan, Mexico*; and *Montauk Pond* (nos. 67, 128, 192). (Falk 1990b, 367)

• 1905 •

23 January–4 March. PAFA annual exhibition. Moran exhibits *Venice* (no. 101, owned by Edward Coates). (Falk 1989, 342)

14 January, 4 February. At Century Club Moran exhibits *Montauk*; *Autumn Woods*; and *Mount Moran*; then *Dark Tower*; *Indian Village*; and *Cloudy Day*. (CA, AAA)

12 March. Moran gives *Church of Teoloyucan* to poet Edith M. Thomas, who responds: "The scene is, for me, simple enchantment, like a mysterious revival of some romantic scene once known and long unvisited.... But... I am not quite unaware what a charming *reality* it is, in point of art,— in the breadth,—quietness—and richness of feeling, that pervades the whole canvas." (GA)

18 May. At Grand Canyon, Moran sketches and dates *Bright Angel [Trail]* (Gilcrease).

23 June. *EH Star*: "Thomas Moran, the noted landscape painter, and his family have arrived at his studio on Main Street."

25 July. Moran copyrights *Sunset at Amagansett, L.I.* (LC doc. class I. XXc. no. 15006, EHL)

28 July. *EH Star* lists Moran among owners occupying their cottages in East Hampton.

7 November. At Century Club Moran exhibits *At Close of Day* and *Yosemite Fall*. (CA, AAA)

23 December–20 January 1906. NAD annual exhibition. Moran exhibits *Sunset, East Hampton, L.I.*; *Entrance to Grand Canal, Venice*; and *Indian Pueblo of Laguna, New Mexico* (nos. 6, 104, 207). (Falk 1990b, 367)

29 December. Moran: "After this date all pictures will have a number in the order of their finish." He numbers eight paintings, then discontinues the practice. (GA ledger)

• 1906 •

5 January. Twelfth Night special exhibition at Century Club. Moran exhibits *Hitting the Pipe*. (CA, AAA)

25 January. Charles Cook to Moran, from Honolulu: "Am glad to report the safe arrival of the two pictures.... [they] have been hung in our Bank for the past three weeks and very much admired. I have hung the Venice picture in our Directors room.... at the Directors meeting of the Bank held yesterday, it was voted that the Bank of Hawaii purchase your 'Grand Canyon of the Yellowstone' for $1,500.00 and I herewith enclose... this amount. I forwarded... a notice from one of our papers regarding your pictures and also a report that you and your daughter would likely come to the islands in the summer.... I hope that you may find the Island scenery such that you may be tempted to represent some of it on canvas and I have no doubt but you will be able to sell several pictures." (EHL)

3 February, 7 April. At Century Club, Moran exhibits *Petrified Forest*; then *Childe Roland*; *Pueblo of Terra*; and *Mexican Well*. (CA, AAA)

12 May. Poet Lloyd Mifflin writes Moran, including a sonnet dedicated to the artist: "I find several blemishes in the Sonnet which I can correct, and I hope to improve it... and send you a better version... [in margin:]—I mean to publish it when I revise it—and why could not it be illustrated with one of your pictures?" (GA)

6 July. *EH Star* lists Moran among summer residents now occupying their cottages.

6, 8, 11, 12, 15 September. In Wales, Moran sketches and dates *Conway*; then two more versions of *Conway*; and *Queen's Tower, Conway Castle*; then *Conway from the Mountain* and *Gateway, Conway, North Wales*; then *Lighter at Conway*; then *Harlech* and *Dollwydellan Tower* (Gilcrease). (Morand 1996, 82–87)

22 December–19 January 1907. NAD winter exhibition. Moran exhibits *Desert, Southern Utah*, and *Mexican Well, Cuernavaca* (cat. nos. 19, 256).

• 1907 •

2 March. At Century Club Moran exhibits *Solitude*; *Mount Moran*; *Petrified Forest*; *Grand Canyon*; *Dark Tower*; and *Montauk*. (CA, AAA)

16 March–20 April. NAD annual exhibition. Moran exhibits *Morning, Venice*, and *Tower Creek, Yellowstone Park* (nos. 26, 356). (Falk 1990b, 367)

12, 21, 25 May. At Grand Canyon Moran sketches and dates *Clouds and Mist in the Canyon* and *Grand Canyon*; two drawings inscribed *Grand View*; then *Grand Canyon* (Gilcrease).

26 May. Paul Nimmo Moran, only son of Thomas and Mary Nimmo Moran, dies in Los Angeles at age 43. *NY Post*, 27 May: "Paul N. Moran, a painter... belonged to a remarkably gifted family.... He studied in Paris and was achieving a measure of success in this country when ill health obliged him to go West." (Also *NYT*, 27 May; Moran family monument, South End Cemetery, East Hampton)

21 June. *EH Star*: "Thomas Moran and family are now at their studio on Main Street."

7 December. At Century Club Moran exhibits *Mist in Grand Canyon*. (CA, AAA)

14 December–11 January 1908. NAD winter exhibition. Moran exhibits *Summer Shower, Venice*, and *Near Cuernavaca, Mexico* (nos. 51, 52). (Falk 1990b, 367)

• 1908 •

January. At Century Club. Moran exhibits *King Arthur's Castle*. (CA, AAA)

12 February. Lloyd Mifflin to Moran, thanking him for invitation to visit his New York studio: "How fortunate you are to be able to work and produce things which satisfy your sense of color & form and which delight so many people of cultivated tastes. It is a great blessing—this wonderful talent of yours. But you always treated it lightly yourself. And now men are painting literal views of ugly nature & calling it Art, and people are buying them, too. There seems to be no power of composition extant, and without it, what is painting but colored photography?" (EHL)

14 March–18 April. NAD annual exhibition. Moran exhibits *Harlech Castle, North Wales* (no. 35). (Falk 1990b, 367)

27 March–12 April. Newark Artists' Club exhibition. Moran exhibits *Petrified Forest*. (GA ledger)

1 May. *EH Star*: "Among the guests at the Osborne House the past week were... Thomas Moran, Miss Ruth Moran."

8 May. *EH Star*: "Thomas Moran, the well-known landscape painter and his daughter, Miss Ruth Moran, are spending a couple of months in Arizona. Mr. Moran has already painted many pictures depicting scenes in that region, which have become famous."

June. Moran sketches and dates *Hermit Chasm, Grand Canyon* (Gilcrease).

12 July. Sketches and dates *Rain in Canyon* and *Grand Canyon, Arizona* (Cooper-Hewitt). Charles Lummis in *Out West* recalls this visit: "Only a few weeks ago, after a gap of sixteen or seventeen years, I had the joy again of sitting there with 'Old Tom' Moran, who has come nearer to doing the Impossible than any other meddler with paints-and-canvas in the Southwest. No one knows better than he the hopelessness of painting God's masterpiece; but no one so well has made a transcript for our comprehension. He has just repainted his great picture of the Grand Canon; and I would like to see someone try to better it."

28 July. Sketches and dates *Street in Laguna, New Mexico* (Gilcrease).

7 August. *EH Star*: "Thomas Moran and his daughter, Miss Ruth Moran, who have been spending the past two months in Arizona, returned to East Hampton this week and are now at the Moran studio."

14 August. *EH Star* lists Moran among cottage owners settled in their summer homes in East Hampton.

28 November. *Brooklyn Times* publishes "Long Island Painter of World Wide Fame" on occasion of special recognition given Moran by the Huntington Culture Club. Artist is quoted: "I decided very early that I would be an American painter.... I like the comparatively flat land of eastern Long Island, such as I have near my studio at East Hampton... and then I like the rugged mountains of the Rockies.... Colorado and the Southwest in general is the field for me. I was the first painter except Bierstadt to work there.

The painter, of all men, must be a student of nature. He must be well informed upon all subjects. He must have knowledge before he begins to paint. He may get it in an educational institution, or he may have it in the form of intuition, but he must have it.... Science and art are vastly different. They have little in common, yet art must agree with science. Truth in all forms must agree."

5–13 December. At Century Club monthly exhibition, Moran shows *Petrified Forest*. (CA, AAA)

• 1909 •

8 January. *EH Star*, reporting on a meeting of the "Ramblers": "Thomas Moran, though mentioned as one of the Hudson River school, really belongs to a later period and has a wider knowledge of painting. Mr. Moran... kindly loaned one of his pictures to the society for this meeting. The picture was a drawing on canvas in charcoal and white of a scene in Mexico, and was a striking illustration of Mr. Moran's wonderful technical power in design, drawing and composition."

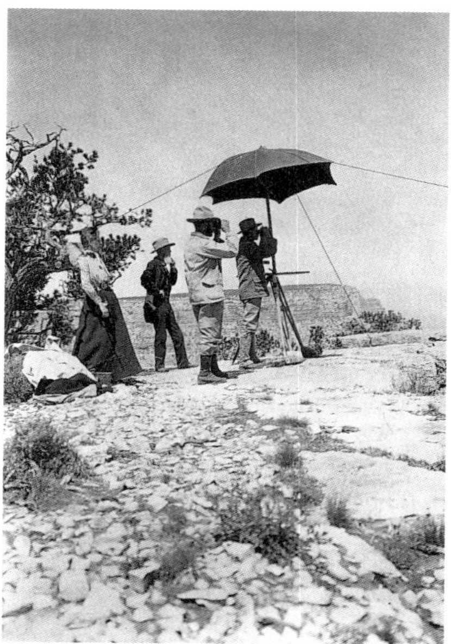

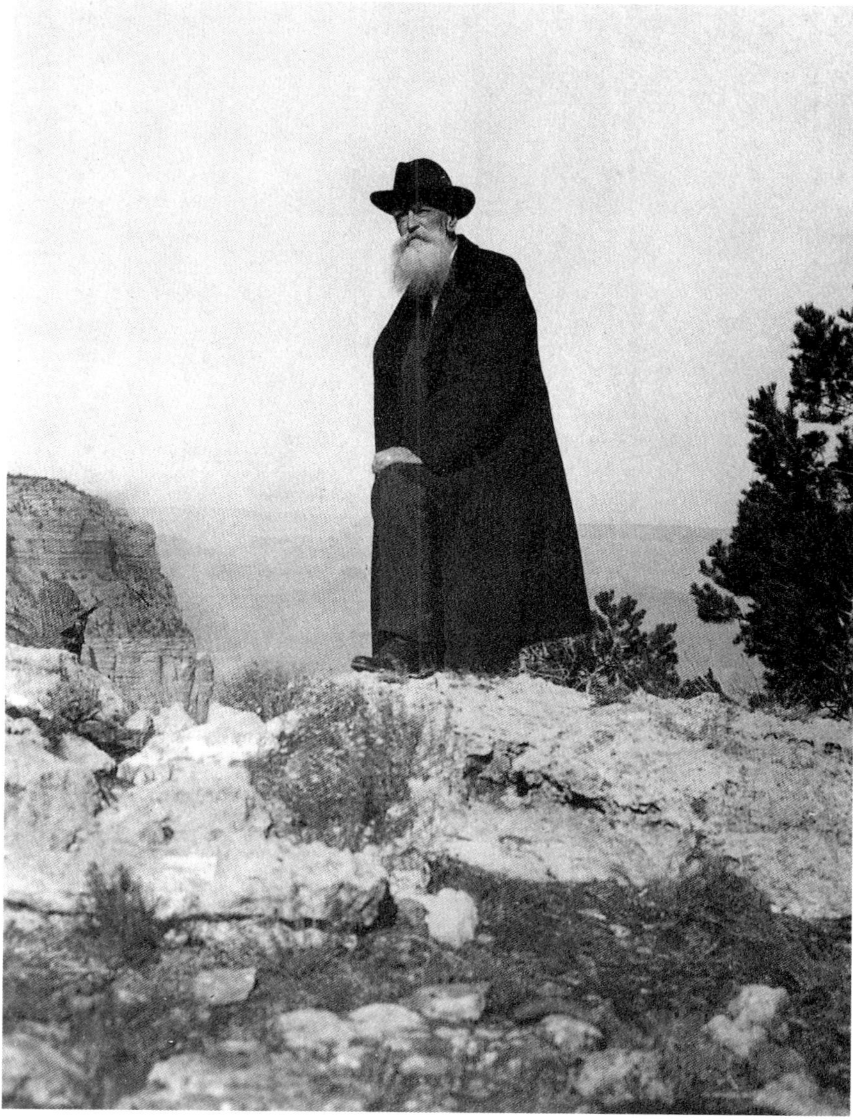

Thomas Moran and companions at the Grand Canyon, 1910, courtesy East Hampton Library.

Moran at the Grand Canyon, 1910, courtesy East Hampton Library.

4 February. Moran copyrights *Receding Wave.* (LC doc. class I. XXc. no. 28271, EHL)

6–12 February. At Century Club Moran exhibits *Icebergs.* (CA, AAA)

May. At Grand Canyon, Moran painted *Canons of the Colorado, Zoroaster.* (GA ledger)

2 July. *EH Star*: "Moran and family are now at their studio-cottage on Main Street."

14 September. From East Hampton, Moran to Gustave Buek (v.p., American Lithographic Company): "I had intended to call on you when you were down last week, but I got so busy on the pictures that I did not get around. Ruth tells me she saw you, & that your man wanted to know the price of the Turner. The price is $35000.00. The picture goes to Chicago on the 1st of October & will probably not come back to New York. There is to be an illustrated article on it in the October number of some Chicago magazine. As the picture is to go away so soon, I thought you might let the man who inquired about it know." (GA)

20 November. Lloyd Mifflin to Moran: "The Publishers will issue a small vol. of my Poems during Nov.—making my tenth vol.... and I have included in it a Sonnet on 'Thomas Moran, N.A.,' It is impossible to condense what I would like to say into the space of a sonnet, and it is necessary to give *discriminating* laudation, but I have refrained from saying what I would like to say, for if I should do so, it would recoil and do injury instead of good. I tried to have the poem published six months ago in a N.Y. paper, but I suppose they looked upon it as a 'puff' and declined to print it. So I reserved it for my Book." (GA)

4 December. At Century Club Moran exhibits *Woodland Pond.* (CA, AAA)

• 1910 •

8 January. At Century Club Moran exhibits *Yosemite Waterfall*; *Toltec Gorge, Colorado*; and *Tower Creek, Yellowstone Park.* (CA, AAA)

February. Lloyd Mifflin's tribute poem "Thomas Moran, N.A." is published in *Fine Arts Journal.*

5 February. At Century Club Moran exhibits *High Sierras, Nevada*, and *Petrified Forest.* (CA, AAA)

1 March. Moran notes: "Painted 20 pictures 1909–10 to date." (GA ledger)

25 March. *EH Star*: "Thomas Moran, the great painter, is occupying his cottage here during Easter week."

29 April. *EH Star*: "Thomas Moran and his daughter, Miss Ruth B. Moran, will sail from New York tomorrow for England."

Summer. Thomas and Ruth Moran travel in Britain along the southwest coast. Route follows the rail lines around the coast, between resort towns. (Morand 1996, 85–87)

25, 31 May. Moran sketches and dates *Bridge at Warwick*, then *Torquay* (Gilcrease).

1–3, 7, 9, 11–13 June. Sketches and dates two works inscribed *Anstey Cove*; then *Cockington Quarry* and *Cockington Lane*; then two works inscribed *Brixham*; then *Valley of Rock, Tintagel*; then *Tintagel*; then three versions of *Clovelly* (Gilcrease).

15, 17–19, 23 June. Sketches and dates *Ilfracombe*; then *Lynmouth Light Tower and Bay*; then *Castle, Valley of Rocks, Lynmouth*; then *Valley of Rocks, Lyn*; then *Lynmouth* (Gilcrease).

26 June, 13 July. Sketches and dates *Monnow Bridge, Monmouth*; then *Trossachs*; and *Near Silver Strand, Katrine, Scotland* (Gilcrease).

15 August. Thomas and Ruth Moran return to New York from Britain. Moran records: "Pictures painted since my return from England where we spent the summer of 1910. returned August 15 ... *Tantallon Castle, Scotland ... Cockington Lane, near Tourquay ... Trout Brook ... Wild Wales*." (GA ledger)

26 August. *EH Star*: "Thomas Moran and Miss Moran, who have been spending a portion of the summer in Europe, arrived in New York last week, and are now at their studio cottage in East Hampton, where they will remain until late fall."

13 September. Moran sends autobiographical sketch to Mr. Elliott Woods, Architect of the Capitol, at Woods' request. (Moran to Woods, 13 Sept., in A & R mss, Office of the Architect of the Capitol)

Fall. Thomas and Ruth Moran go to Grand Canyon with Gustave Buek, Mr. and Mrs. Elliot Daingerfield, Frederick Ballard Williams, Mr. and Mrs. DeWitt Parshall, Edward Potthast; Mr & Mrs. Charles Buek; Mr. and Mrs. Giles Whiting; Mr. and Mrs. W. H. Simpson (organizer of similar excursion in 1901); George Stevens (director of Toledo Museum), and wife Nina Spalding Stevens (biographer of Moran, who chronicles trip). Santa Fe Railroad provides private rail car for the journey and lodging at station hotels en route. (Stevens 1911, 107)

5 November. Grand Canyon party gathers in Chicago, beginning trip with dinner hosted by R. R. Ricketts at ULC. Group travels through Kansas City, La Junta, and Albuquerque by rail to Grand Canyon. At Grand Canyon, they stay at El Tovar Hotel, spending ten days seeing sights like Hopi Point, Pete Berry's Ranch, Grand View Point, and Bright Angel Trail. Artists work day and night, outdoors and in studio in El Tovar. (Stevens 1911, 107–113 and map)

12 November. "Artists' Souvenir Dinner" held at El Tovar. (Stevens 1911, illus. of souvenir menu)

• 1911 •

14 January, 4 February. At Century Club Moran exhibits *Grand Canyon, Arizona*; then *Twilight*. (CA, AAA)

1 April. At Century Club Moran exhibits *Roaring Forties*; *Hook Pond, East Hampton, L.I.*; and *A Bit of Acoma, New Mexico*. (CA, AAA)

21 April. *EH Star*: "Moran and his daughter, Miss Ruth Moran, sailed from New York for Antwerp on Saturday last, where they expect to remain until June 12."

12 June. Thomas and Ruth Moran return to New York on steamship *Minnetonka*. According to *NY World*: "Among the interesting passengers was Thomas Moran, the most famous of the old school of American artists whose work has been wholly landscape. His daughter, Ruth, accompanied him, having been his companion during the past four months on a tour of the European galleries .... The only living artist—he is now in his seventy-fifth year, strong and vigorous from a lifetime spent in the open—who has never painted anything but American mountain scenes, smiled at the suggestion that he may have made a study, and perhaps some sketches, of the Alps while in Switzerland. 'It has been my life-work' he said, 'to put on canvas only American natural life .... I want some typical winter scenes.'"

15 September. Fred Tillotson, proprietor of Bolton (England) newspapers, writes Moran, requesting photograph of him and details of his career for a future article. Clipping from *Bolton Journal and Guardian* with brief outline of Moran's career is enclosed, written on the occasion of a gift of a Moran painting to Bolton. Tillotson recalls Thomas and Mary Nimmo Moran's visit to Bolton in 1882 when he was a small boy, and sends regards from his mother, with whom the Morans had stayed. (GA)

10 November. *EH Star*: "Moran and his daughter, Miss Ruth Moran, left New York on Tuesday for the Grand Canyon, Arizona, where they will spend an indefinite time, Mr. Moran making sketches and studies of the wonderful works of nature to be found there."

26 November. Moran, Edward Potthast, Elliott Daingerfield, DeWitt Parshall, and Frederick Ballard Williams exhibit works from their trip to the Grand Canyon at Moulton and Ricketts' new gallery in New York. Gustav Kobbe in *NY Herald Sunday Magazine* reviews exhibition, which will travel to Buffalo, Toledo, St. Louis, and Chicago: "And a fine showing the results of this artists' painting expedition make—Mr. Moran's pictures, panoramic in scope, but softened by the draperies of mist that swathe the distant buttes and make them look like islands in a hanging sea."

December. Thomas and Ruth Moran stay at El Tovar and are joined by Mary Moran Tassin. Moran notes: "Dec 1911 ... spent the Winter 1912 at the Cañon." (GA ledger, 76)

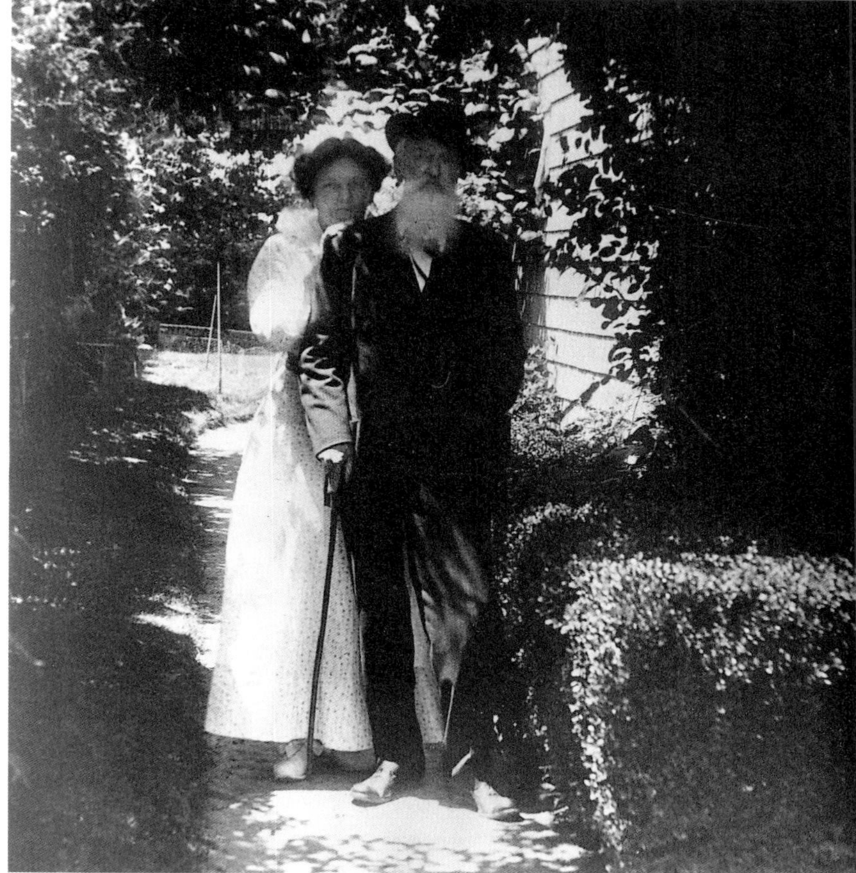

Ruth and Thomas Moran in Santa Barbara, California, courtesy East Hampton Library.

Christmas. Moran gives paintings as gifts to El Tovar employees: *Glimpse of Canyon, Pines*; *Canyon at Evening*; *Index Peak, Wyoming*. (GA ledger)

• 1912 •

16 February. Moran sketches and dates *Cyprus Point* [Monterey, CA] (Gilcrease).

26 April. *EH Star*: "Thomas Moran and his daughter Miss Ruth Moran, have returned from their trip to the Grand Canyon, and are now in New York.... The Morans will come to East Hampton early in the season."

4 May. At Century Club Moran exhibits *Point Lobos, California*. (CA, AAA)

8 November. *EH Star*: "Thomas Moran and his daughter, Miss Ruth Moran, closed their studio this week and returned to the city."

7 December. At Century Club Moran exhibits *Mexican Fiesta*. (CA, AAA)

Winter. Thomas and Ruth Moran at the Grand Canyon. (GA ledger, 77)

• 1913 •

10 January. *EH Star*: "Thomas Moran and his daughter, Miss Ruth Moran, are now at El Tovar, Grand Canyon, Arizona."

4 April. *EH Star*: "Thomas Moran and his daughter, Miss Ruth Moran, who have been spending the winter at Grand Canyon, Arizona, will arrive in New York this week, and will arrive at the Moran studio in East-Hampton early in the season."

25 April. *EH Star*: "Thomas Moran, Miss Ruth Moran, and [Mary Moran Tassin] are sailing on the steamer *Minnetonka* for England, to be gone until about July 1, when they will come to East Hampton for the remainder of the season."

4 July. *EH Star*: "Thomas Moran and daughter, Miss Ruth Moran, arrived in New York on Monday evening on the *Minnetonka*, after a two month rest in Europe."

11 July. *EH Star*: "Thomas Moran and Miss Ruth Moran arrived at their studio cottage here last week."

5 December. *EH Star*: "Thomas Moran and his daughter, Miss Ruth Moran, closed their cottage here this week and went to the city."

Winter. Thomas and Ruth Moran at Grand Canyon. (GA ledger, 78)

• 1914 •

Moran records that he is basing his prices on the size of the work: "20" x 30" $1,800; 25" x 30" $2,000; 30" x 40" $3,000; 22" x 42" $2,500." (GA ledger, 96)

6 March. Chicago art dealer Moulton and Ricketts goes into bankruptcy, owing Moran $9,400.00. (GA ledger, 82, and list of paintings 1899–1918, 59)

29 May. *EH Star*: "Thomas Moran, the world's greatest landscape painter, and his daughter, Miss Ruth Moran, have arrived at their cottage here after spending the winter at Grand Canyon, Arizona."

24 June. *Shoshone Falls* and *Spectres from the North* are released from Moulton and Ricketts bankruptcy and sent to storage in New York. (GA list of paintings 1899–1918, 60)

9 November. Peter Moran dies in Philadelphia at age 73. *Art News* (14 Nov.): "He was one of the best animal painters in the country and formed with his brothers Edward and Thomas..., a trio that did much to elevate the standard of American art as it was understood a few years ago." (See also *Phila. Evening Bulletin*, 10 Nov.; interment records, West Laurel Hill Cemetery)

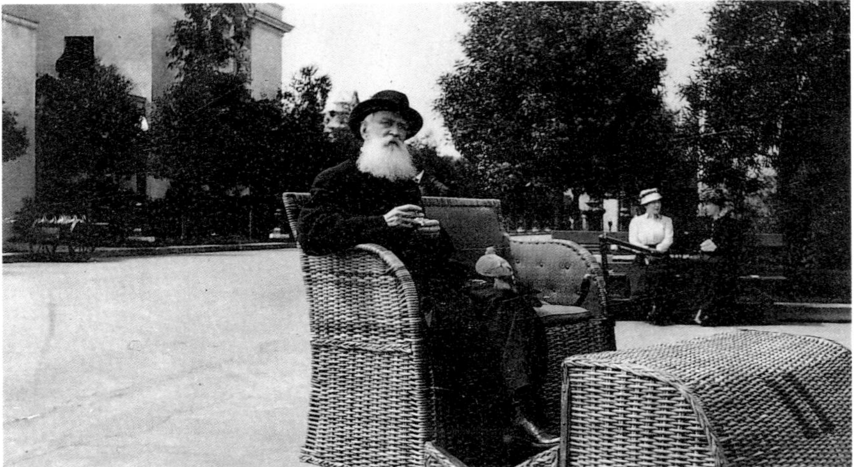

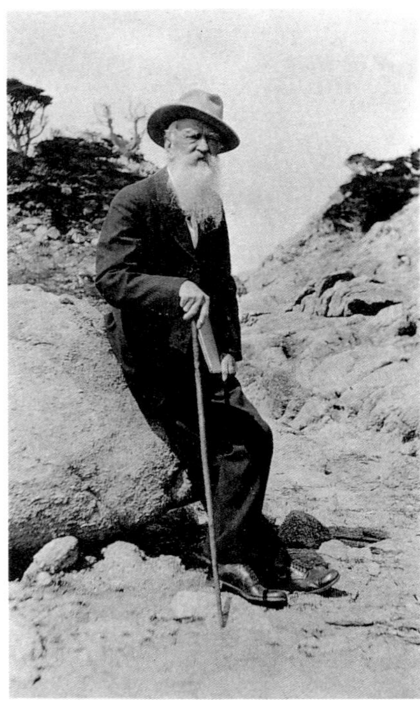

Thomas Moran at Panama-Pacific Exposition, San Francisco, 1915, courtesy East Hampton Library.

Moran at Point Lobos, California, 1919, courtesy East Hampton Library.

5 December. At Century Club Moran exhibits *Lair of the Mountain Lion*; *Zion Canyon, S. Utah*; *Point Lobos, California*; *Venice*; *Cypress Point, Monterey, California*; *Petrified Forest, Arizona*; *Mexican Fiesta*; *Green River Buttes, Wyoming*; *In Mid-Atlantic*; *North Perrin Cliffs, Devonshire*; *Index Peak, Wyoming*; *Ulysses and the Sirens*; and *Cliffs near Gallup, New Mexico.* (CA, AAA)

19 December–17 January 1915. NAD winter exhibition. Moran exhibits *Castle Rock, Green River, Wyoming* (cat. no. 117).

• 1915 •

20 February–4 December. Panama-Pacific International Exposition in San Francisco. Moran exhibits *Old Apple Orchard*; *Hook Pond, East Hampton*; *Breaking Wave*; *Light House*; *Solitude*; *California Forest* (cat. nos. 378, 388, 393, 395, 442, 2954); and seven prints.

8 April–8 May. Exhibition at Grolier Club (NY) of American book illustrations includes woodcuts by Moran for *St. Nicholas*, for Bryant and Gay's *Popular History of the United States*, and for Whittier's *Mabel Martin* as well as an engraver's proof and a "Vignette drawn ... on boxwood, ready for the Wood Engraver." (Anthony, Cole, and Kingsley 1916)

May. Moran at the Grand Canyon. (GA ledger, 85)

28 May. *EH Star*: "Thomas Moran, N.A., and his daughter, Miss Ruth Moran, have arrived at their cottage on Main Street."

24 June. Moran is notified he has been elected an honorary member of the Salmagundi Club. (Howard Giles to Moran, 24 June, GA)

25 August. Moran gives 1892 watercolor *In the Lava Beds* to Gustave Buek for his birthday, inscribed at lower left: "To G.H. Buek on his Birthday, Aug. 25th 1915 from T. Moran."

4 December. At Century Club Moran exhibits *Venice*; *Sunrise in Mid-Ocean*; and *Grand Canyon of Arizona.* (CA, AAA)

11–31 December. "Society of Men Who Paint the Far West" exhibition at Macbeth Gallery, NY. Moran's *Indian Peak, Wyoming*; *Mist in the Canyon*; and *Castle Rock, Green River, Wyoming* are included. *Art News* 14 (11 Dec.), 6: "The display is remarkable, aside from its pictorial interest, on account of the first public appearance of a new method of guaranteeing the authenticity of pictures by the thumb print, in the paint, of the artist. Thomas Moran, the originator of the scheme, has thus marked his three contributions, just over his signature.... So capable a painter is Mr. Moran, that it is no discredit to his co-exhibitors to say they, except perhaps in more modern, if not more skillful, ways of laying on paint, have gone little beyond him. And again he has poeticized, while they have in the main but realized.... The color of the locale is often so hot that in a few cases the landscapes seem to rise half-fused out of volcanic embers."

• 1916 •

Moran listed at 735 N. Los Robles Ave., Pasadena, as well as on Main St., East Hampton.

4 February. *Pasadena Star* reports on exhibition of Moran paintings to be held at Hotel Green, 15–29 Feb., while Moran winters in Pasadena: "Mr. Moran is a firm believer in the dictum of Ruskin that no picture can be successfully completed out of doors, but only in the studio, where there is opportunity for concentration and careful work.... 'Paint on a picture is not there to be seen,' declared Mr. Moran.... 'That is one fault I find with the modern departures.... The artist must know what to select and what to leave out, and paint his trees not leaf by leaf, nor yet with a splash

of green, but in such a way as the leaves appear to be there.... Modern art grew out of the ignorance of the beauty and laws of nature.'"

Moran exhibits *Santa Maria della Salute, Venice*; *Morning in a Storm, Mid-Atlantic*; *Cliffs of New Mexico, near Gallup*; *Grove of Sequoias, near Yosemite*; *Point Lobos, Monterey Coast*; *Mexican Fiesta, Cuernavaca*; *Castle Rock, Green River, Wy.*; *Buttes of Green River, Wy.*; *Landscape, East Hampton, L.I.*; *Blue Beard's Castle*; *Sinbad and His Companions*; and *Cypress Point, Monterey.* (Exh. list and invitation, GA)

11 March. *Pasadena Star* quotes Moran in an interview by Gussie Packard DuBois: "Nature always has something in reserve for the eye; so the best painting should have. The successful artist must know nature.... I have no patience with any of the modern fads in painting. Most of them have been deliberate frauds, attempts in the hands of unprincipled men to fool people who never think for themselves... The highest art lies in the concealment of art.... I don't care anything about paint; I want to see what [the artist] says with it." DuBois reports that Moran and his daughter will remain in Pasadena until late April, return to New York for a month, then go to their summer home.

2 June. *EH Star*: "Thomas Moran and daughter, Miss Ruth Moran will arrive today for the summer."

Winter. Moran writes William H. Holmes, curator for the National Museum, Washington: "I am sending to the Nat[ional] Parks Ex[hibit] two of my pictures that I consider the very best that I have ever painted. I hope you will like them & see that they are well displayed. I think the purpose of the exhibit is a fine idea and hope it will succeed.... It has been arranged that these two pictures are to be held over until May 1st. We are just on the eve of departure for the Arizona Canyon, from there we (I & my daughter Ruth) go to California until the latter part of April, then back to the Az. Canon for a time & then to New York." (Draft of letter, GA)

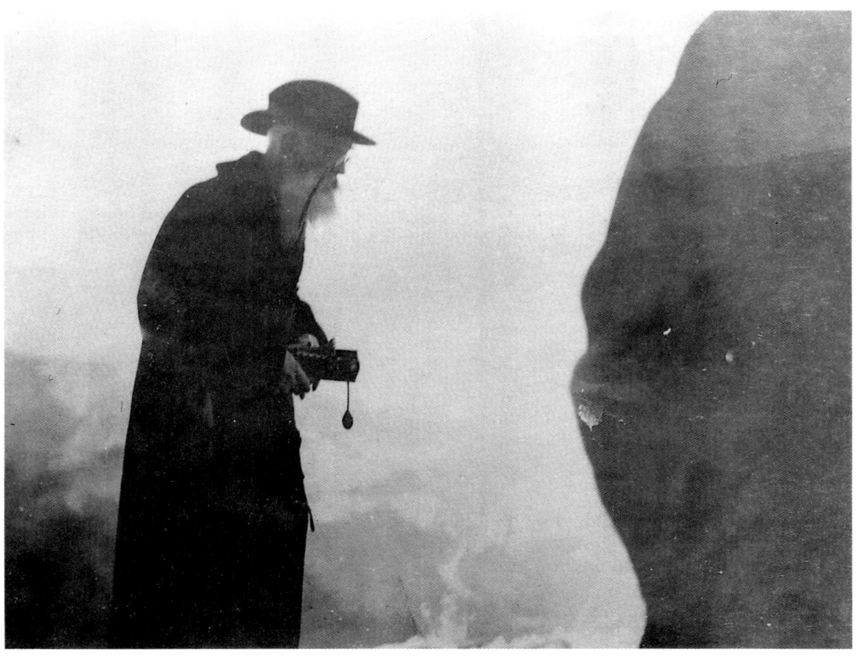

Thomas Moran with a camera, c.1920, courtesy East Hampton Library.

• 1917 •

2 January–9 March. National Parks Exhibition at National Museum, Washington, "designed to bring to the attention of Americans some of the marvelous natural attractions of their own country," includes four Moran works: *Grand Canyon of the Yellowstone* and *Rocky Mountain Solitude* lent by the artist; *Grand Canyon of Arizona on the Santa Fe* lent by Atchison, Topeka, and Santa Fe Railroad; and *In the Grand Canyon of the Colorado* lent by the National Museum. (Report, National Museum, 78–80, 126)

17 January. Holmes to Moran at El Tovar Hotel, Grand Canyon: "I must tell you that our National Parks Exhibit is a great success and that I have on the walls four of your works, namely: The great picture of the Grand Canyon which I regard as the greatest work in landscape that the world has produced; the 'Solitude' which is a beautiful work; a small painting of the Grand Canyon, and the side canyon which you presented to Major Powell—not a very large picture, but one of the best things you ever did.... and no end of other things which assist in telling the story of the Parks.

I do not get done admiring and praising your 'Grand Canyon of the Yellowstone,' which, choicely placed in our large room is lighted to the very best advantage, and I cannot but wish that it could stay there indefinitely. I have no idea whether the picture belongs to you, or to whom it belongs, but if it is not called for elsewhere, I trust that you will leave it with us as long as possible.

The exhibit has been, indeed, a great success. Thousands of people saw and admired it and it is to remain in place until after the 4th of March." (GA)

5 February. Holmes to Moran at the El Tovar Hotel, Grand Canyon, enclosing a copy of his remarks to the Parks Congress, reiterating the success of the National Parks exhibition, and asking for instructions regarding his works at the close of the show: "The light is perfect and your picture shows to enormous advantage. I wish that the fates might decide that it remain there for ever." (GA)

26 April. Meeting of the council of the Cooper-Hewitt Museum. Among the new acquisitions are "a series of sketches selected personally by the dean of Ameri-

can painters, Thomas Moran, from his own life work, intended to express it fully for the benefit of our students and such others as care to familiarize themselves with the methods of perhaps the only American painter eulogized by John Ruskin." Sketches are a gift from the artist. (Minutes, council of Cooper-Hewitt, GA)

22 and 29 June. *EH Star* reports that Thomas and Ruth Moran are in East Hampton for the summer.

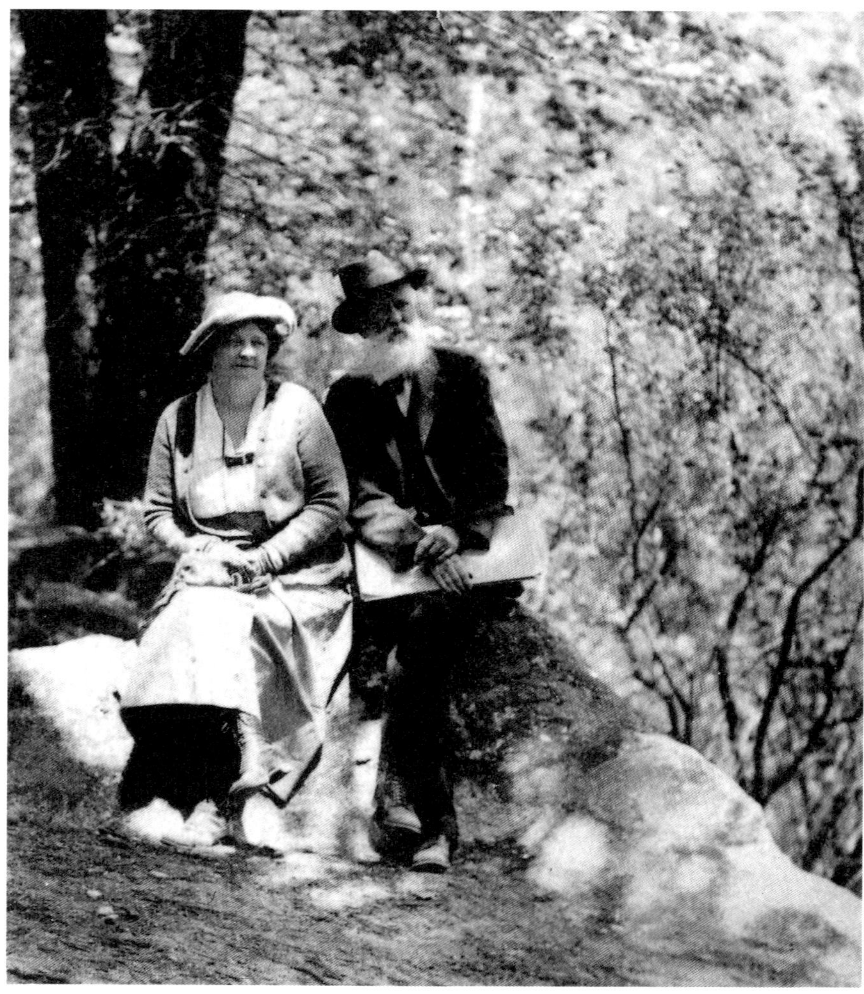

Ruth and Thomas Moran at Yosemite, 1922, courtesy East Hampton Library.

• 1918 •

Moran listed at La Morada Apts., 1821 Anacapa St., Santa Barbara, CA; as well as in East Hampton. (Santa Barbara City Directory; *EH Star*, 19 July)

• 1919 •

12 November. Holmes to Moran's daughter Mary Moran Tassin at "The Brackett," Santa Barbara, sending his regards to Moran: "I am greatly pleased to have your letter of November 5th and to know that your father is still in good shape and hard at work. . . . I consider him the greatest landscape painter that the world has ever known." (GA)

• 1920 •

Spring. Unidentified Santa Barbara newspaper: "The public library will have on exhibition during the next ten days a painting by Thomas Moran, an artist who has recently become a resident of Santa Barbara, after spending two winters as a visitor. The painting is of the Shoshone Falls, Snake River, Idaho, and is considered by connoisseurs one of the artist's most important canvases. It is one of three paintings that [he] has made of the most impressive landscapes of America: one of the Grand Canyon of Arizona, one of the Yellowstone Canyon and this of Shoshone Falls. The canvas is 6 by 12 feet, and was painted in 1900 immediately after the artist's visit to the west when the work was accomplished in one month. The picture has been exhibited in several large cities, and is now going to the Grand Canyon to take the place of a picture of the Canyon that was recently purchased by Mr. Lorimer, the editor of the Saturday Evening Post." (EHL scrapbook)

1 and 15 May. Thomas and Ruth Moran at Grand Canyon, where he sketches and dates two versions of *Desert View* (Gilcrease). (Morand 1996, 87–91)

9 July. *EH Star*: "Thomas Moran, the noted artist, and daughter Miss Ruth Moran, who have been spending the winter in Santa Barbara, Cal., have arrived at their studio on Main street."

October. Moran sends *Grand Canyon and Painted Desert* to Fred Harvey's gallery, El Tovar Hotel, Grand Canyon, to sell. (GA ledger)

17 December. *EH Star*: "Thomas Moran and his daughter, Miss Ruth Moran, are established in their winter home in the Mission City [Santa Barbara]."

• 1921 •

23 September. *EH Star*: "Thomas Moran and his daughter, Miss Ruth Moran, who have been at Santa Barbara, Cal., are at the Schuyler, New York City."

4 December. *Santa Barbara Morning Press*: "Thomas Moran, Santa Barbara's internationally famous artist, who left the city last September for a visit to New York City and his old home at East Hampton, Long Island, at which latter place he practiced his profession for many years, has returned to his home at 1821 Anacapa street, accom-

panied by his daughter, Miss Ruth Moran, his companion on all his travels.

Expressing his joy in his return, Mr. Moran exclaimed to the writer, with real enthusiasm: 'Santa Barbara is a beautiful place for an artist—or for anyone else! I am glad to note that there is afoot in this city a forward movement in art—and I must say, in simple candor, that I cannot see much progress in art in general in other parts, local or foreign. The salutary increase of interest in such matters in Santa Barbara I attribute principally to the beneficial influence of the new School of the Arts, one of the most commendable and admirable local enterprises of which I know.'...

A Venetian picture, now nearing its finish, is one of the few of Mr. Moran's recent works. It shows the entrance to the Grand Canal that would delight the artistic senses of the lover of the beauties of this ancient home of art—the abode of Titian, Paul Veronese and many others of the great painters of the world. The colors are brilliant and the painting shows the Doge's Palace, the Campanile and the Church of Salut, built as an offering to the saints in supplication for the banishment of a devastating plague." (EHL scrapbook)

• 1922 •

U. Seeley Jr. recounts a 1922 visit to Moran: "I have never enjoyed any meeting more. He is just as original and just as much of an individualist in his methods as he is in the great pictures he paints.

He was at work in his studio when Mrs. Seeley and I called there with one of his personal friends. The studio was large and almost square. Scattered about the room were little tabourets, on each of them an ash tray and a package of little cigars.

Mr. Moran was working on a picture. He had completed the general composition and was developing its completed glory. I was never told that when he was so engaged he would not stop to talk or eat. It was incredible that a man of 85 could put as much physical and mental energy into anything as he was giving to that labor of love.

He never took his eyes off the canvas. He would get far over to one side and then almost across the room, studying the painting closely. Then he would hurry across the studio with his brush poised, make one little stroke and back away, looking neither to right or left, studying again from some other angle. Again he would dash forward, make not more than one or two strokes—then back away.

It was fascinating. If his cigar went out or burned down, he dropped it into the nearest ash tray and without looking groped for a fresh smoke. He was a picture of intensity and energy. I never saw such concentration." (*Osborne Bulletin* 1924, 18–19)

10 March. *EH Star*: "Miss Ruth B. Moran and Thomas Moran, summer residents of this village, are among the recent arrivals at the Hotel Maryland, Pasadena."

Early Summer. Thomas and Ruth Moran visit Yosemite. (Draft of letter, Ruth Moran to Gustave Buek, 11 Mar., GA)

2 July. Charles Lummis visits Santa Barbara and photographs Moran at work in his studio. (Moneta 1985, 24)

7 October. From East Hampton, Ruth Moran to William H. Holmes of the National Museum: "Father and I are breaking up our old home and studio, before settling down in California." On behalf of her father, Ruth offers to send *Shoshone Falls, Idaho*, and *Spectres from the North* to Washington for exhibition. The offer is later accepted. (EHL; Smithsonian annual report, 54)

17 November–17 December. NAD winter exhibition. Moran exhibits *Venice* (cat. no. 201).

• 1923 •

24 February. Holmes to Ruth Moran in Santa Barbara, reporting that *Shoshone Falls, Idaho*, arrived at the National Museum on 20 Feb. and that when a frame has been made for *Spectres from the North*, both pictures will hang in the "hall devoted to Geology." (EHL)

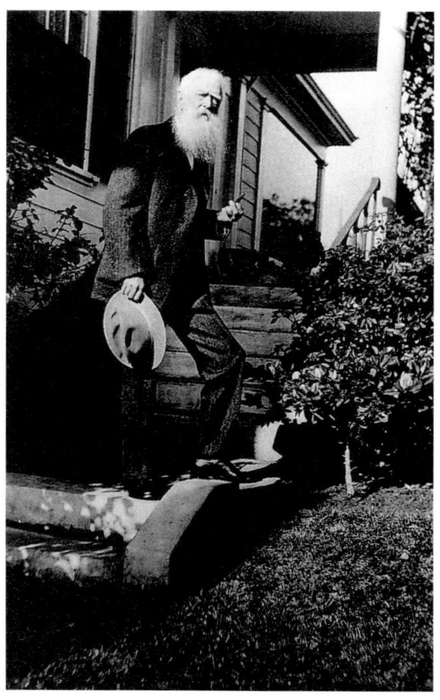

Thomas Moran in Santa Barbara, courtesy East Hampton Library.

29 March. Moran sketches and dates *Near Los Olivos* and two works inscribed *Near Los Olivos, California* (Gilcrease).

13 July. Holmes to Ruth Moran advising her that *Shoshone Falls, Idaho*, and *Spectres from the North* have been hung in the north lobby of the museum, "facing the entrance where everybody sees them," not in the geology division as previously stated. (EHL)

5 October. Describing Moran as the "grand old man of American art," *Kansas City Star* publishes extensive article, "Noted American Artist Still Sticks to His Easel at 86: Thomas Moran is confessedly America's greatest landscape painter, as he is also the painter of America's greatest landscapes.... his has ever been the perspective of a country upon which Nature has lavished colossal splendors.... he has evinced a combination of realism and idealism that sets his work superlatively apart from the many workers in the same field." Article is prompted by the exhibition of three Moran paintings at Findlay Gallery, Kansas City.

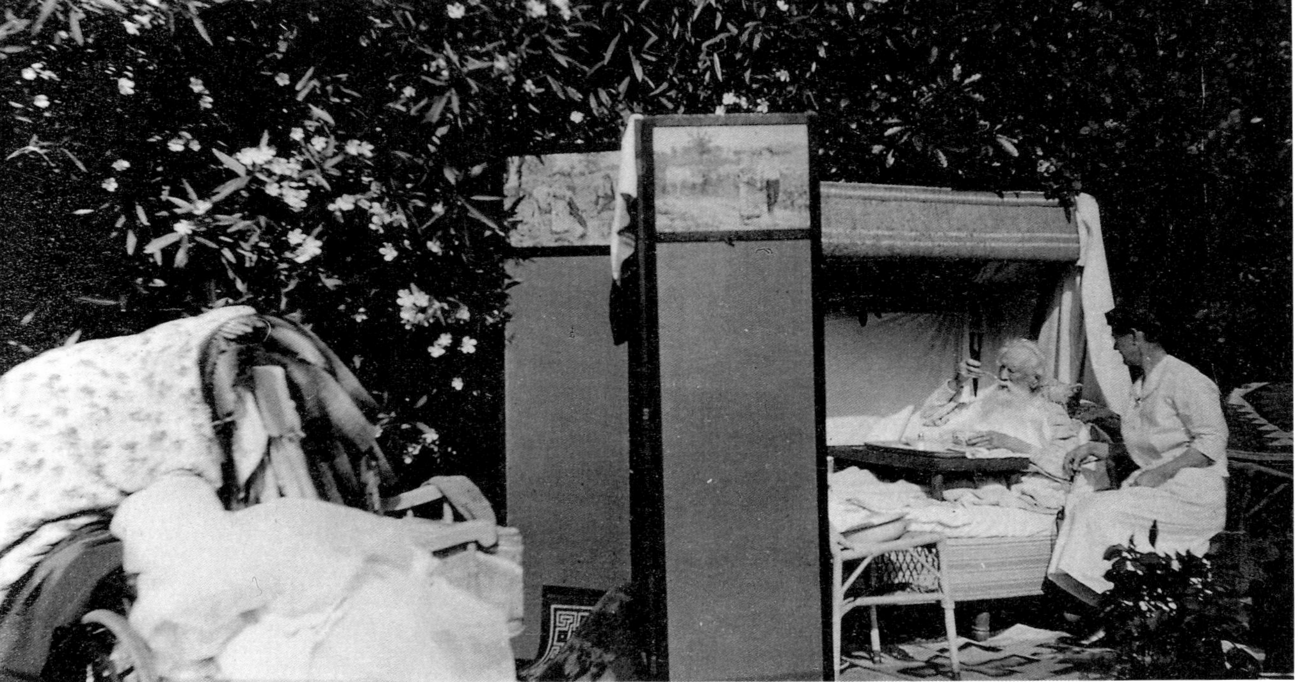

Moran's bed in his garden in Santa Barbara following earthquake in 1925, courtesy East Hampton Library.

• 1924 •

12 January. Article signed W. H. S., published in *Osborne Bulletin*, quotes Ruth Moran as saying, "father had recently felt the weight of the years and was painting very little."

15 March. Moran unanimously elected honorary member of Painters of the West. (Arthur M. Hazard [secretary] to Moran, 17 Mar., GA)

July. Ruth and Thomas Moran make brief visit to Grand Canyon. (Gillespie 1924, 366)

August. Harriet Sisson Gillespie in *International Studio*: "Despite the fact that Mr. Moran has spent the last eight years in California as a concession to the rigors of winter... he returns each autumn to spend a few months in his old haunts. Two spots on earth most completely satisfy Mr. Moran. One is the Grand Cañon, and the other is East Hampton, Long Island... He basks in the beauty of long-familiar scenes." (Repr. in part *Christian Science Monitor*, 14 Aug., and *Current Opinion* [Oct.], 447)

• 1925 •

10 February. *Spectres from the North* is shown at the National Museum along with sketches of icebergs made in 1890. (GA ledger)

16, 21 June. Laura Bride Powers in *Santa Barbara Morning Press*, reporting that Moran watercolors will be on view for two weeks at Santa Barbara Art Club, calls the works "lyric poems" and "records of fleeting moments of beauty" and singles out for praise *Smelting Works in Denver*. (Repr. *EH Star*, 3 July)

29 June. Earthquake in California. As a precautionary measure in the aftermath, Moran's bed is moved into the garden. (*LA Times*, 16 Aug.)

October. Davenport [IA] Municipal Art Gallery opens with exhibition of paintings presented to the museum by C. A. Ficke. *Welcoming the Return of the Boat* (cat. no. 188) by Moran is included.

17 October–15 November. Commemorative exhibition by members of NAD, 1825–1925, at Corcoran includes Moran's *Glory of the Canyon* (cat. no. 291). Travels to Grand Central Art Galleries (NY) 1 December–3 January 1926. (NAD, *Centennial Exhibition*, 14)

• 1926 •

25 August. Thomas Moran dies at his home in Santa Barbara. Ruth Moran telegraphs family friend Gustave Buek: "Father died peacefully this evening." (*Santa Barbara Morning Press*, 26 Aug.; *EH Star*, 27 Aug.)

27 August. *Santa Barbara Morning Press*: "Funeral services for Thomas Moran, N.A., dean of American artists and a leader of Santa Barbara's art colony... will be held in the Charles T. Holland chapel at 11 o'clock this morning, with Dr. Van Deering, acting rector of Trinity Episcopal church, officiating."

26 December. *NY American* reviews memorial exhibition at Milch Gallery (NY), noting that the 63 oil paintings and watercolors in the exhibition "present an amazing record of industry, imagination, exquisite color and superb painting in both mediums."

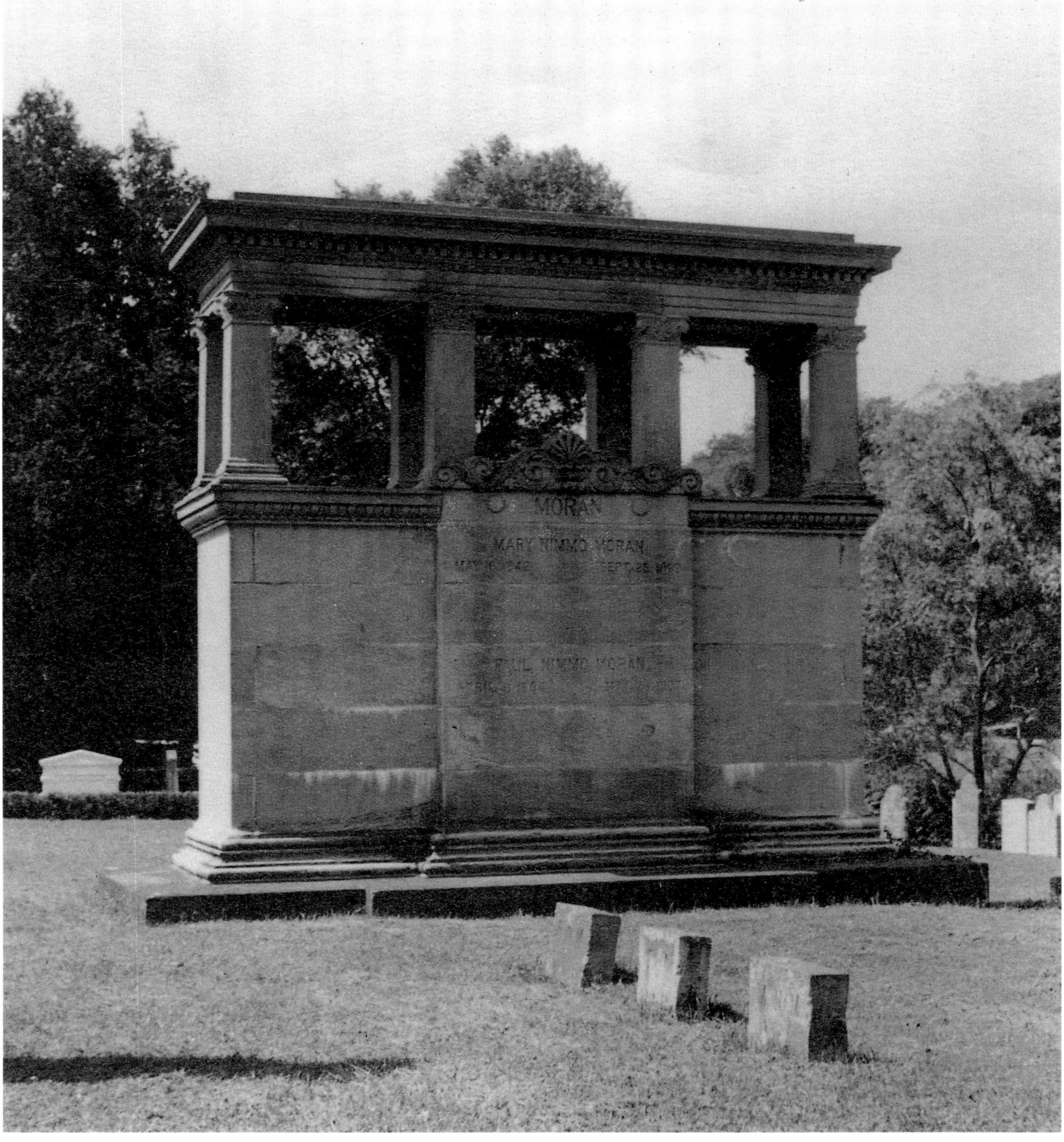

Moran family monument at South End Cemetery, East Hampton, New York.

Essays

Thomas Moran's involvement in printmaking opens a broad window onto American nineteenth-century print history. In one respect his graphic production was typical of many artists working from 1840 to 1890: his drawings and watercolors were reproduced as wood engravings or chromolithographs by professional printmakers. These images were then published in journals and in the popular literary press, or they were produced as larger pictures intended for framing. Until the 1890s, when the photographic halftone replaced the print as the principal means of visual reproduction, Moran enjoyed a continuous source of income from this form of employment.[1] The production of drawings and watercolors for reproductive illustration was not Moran's only connection with prints. Beginning about 1860 and continuing for thirty years—except for a hiatus from 1870 to 1878—Moran worked in lithography and etching. His lithographs represent one of the few instances in American printmaking before 1880 when an artist whose public recognition lay in painting worked directly and regularly in a print medium.[2] What Moran himself wrote about his etchings from the 1880s still holds true today: "His reputation as an etcher is of the first rank."[3]

Moran's first sustained foray into printmaking (1860–1869) was with lithography, although he initially experimented with *cliché-verre* and etching. His second concentrated effort (1878–1891) produced the etchings that have

BY THOMAS P. BRUHN

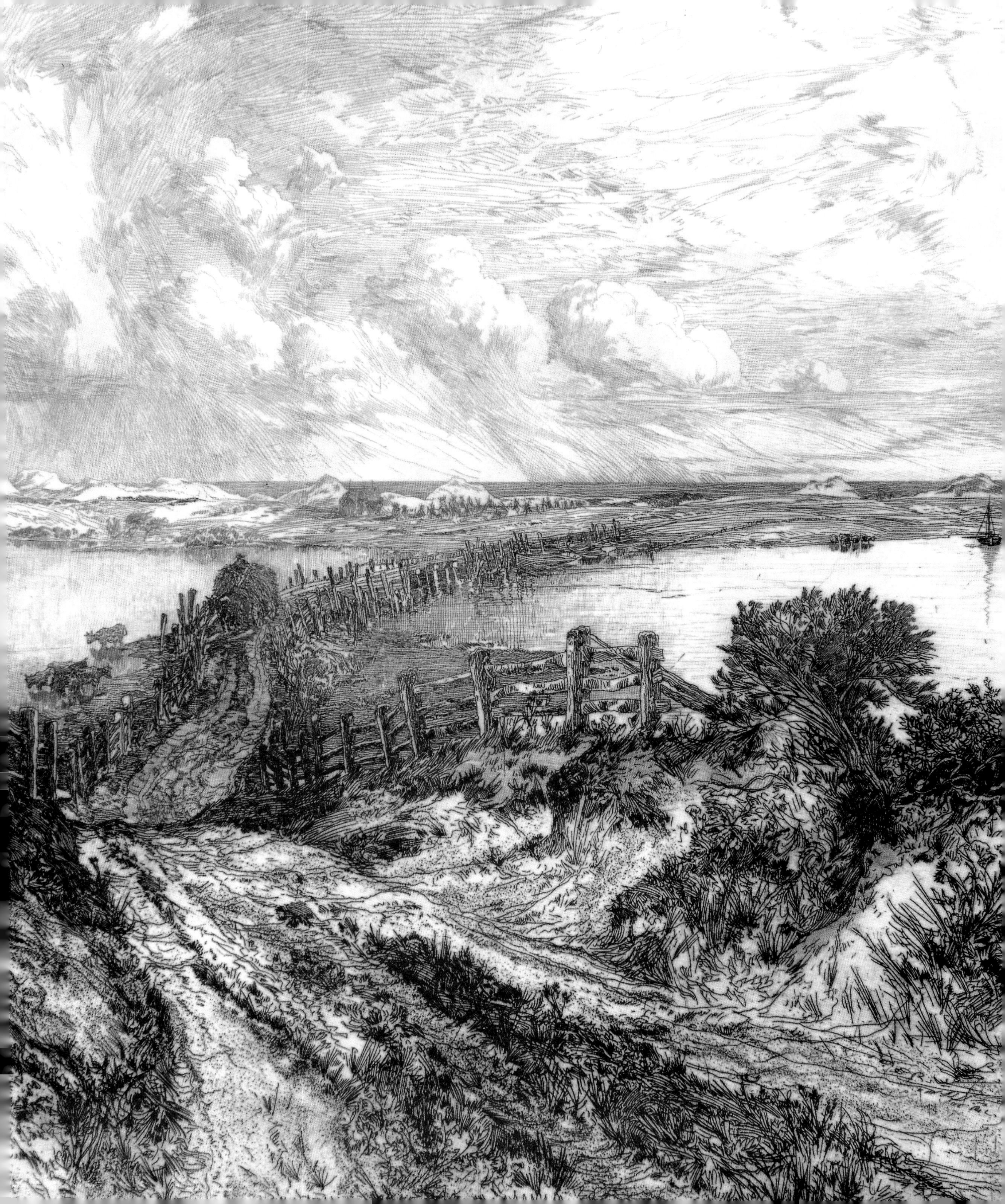

marked his most significant and best-known body of work as a printmaker. Indeed, Moran's prints span the two eras that define the mix of American printmaking in the nineteenth century. The lithographs from the 1860s lie within the period of the reproductive print, while the etchings of the 1880s appear at the beginning of the modern era of American printmaking, when prints were defined as a medium of artistic creativity.

1

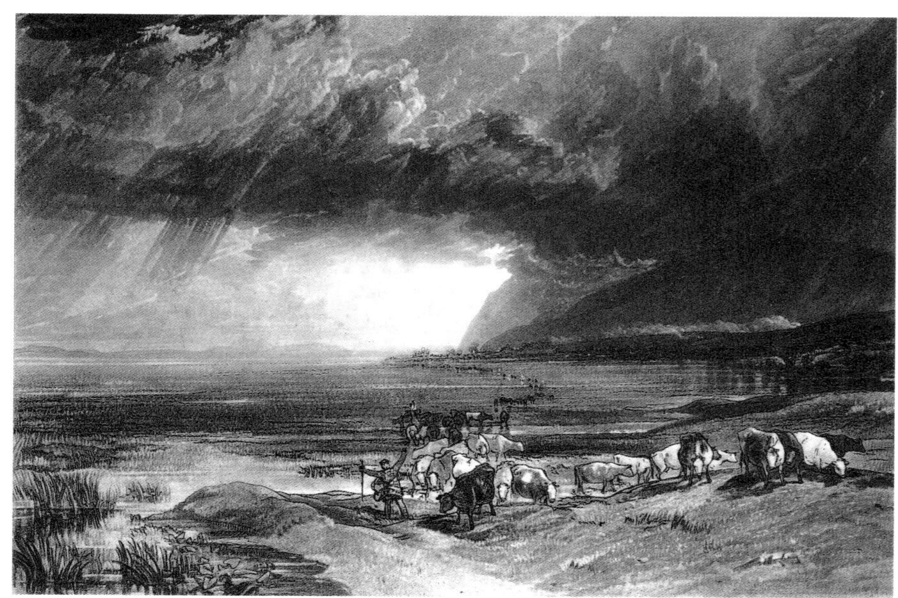

Preceding page: Detail of *Morning* (fig. 17)

1. J. M. W. Turner, *Solway Moss*, 1816, etching and mezzotint, courtesy National Gallery of Art, Washington.

Much of the value that we perceive in Moran's lithographs and etchings is determined by the very fact that Moran made them. In contrast, Moran's audience in the 1860s generally placed little significance on a print's execution except in a technical sense. Only in the 1880s did authorship of a print and the author's hand become an issue, although little distinction was perceived between prints an artist made that are unique to the medium and those based on the artist's work in another medium. Copies after another artist's work remained just that, but a reproductive etching by an artist of Moran's stature probably gained status from the presence of his name as etcher. In this shift lies perhaps the most important turning point in American print history: the realization by artists and public alike that the same values of artistic expression and creativity that give painting or sculpture its special significance are intrinsic to print media as well. Moran's printmaking is a reflection of the changes that the graphic arts underwent between the years of the Civil War and the 1893 World's Columbian Exposition, and his etchings and lithographs stand out as among the finest made in nineteenth-century America.[4]

Early Graphic Influences

In 1853, when Moran was sixteen, he entered into an apprenticeship at Scattergood and Telfer, wood engravers in Philadelphia. He was indifferent to the discipline necessary to become a practicing wood engraver, but he recalled that his apprenticeship "very directly led the way to an artistic career—drawing rather than engraving proved to be the outcome of this connection & after 3 years of this service Young Moran abruptly severed the connection and launched out on his own account as a water color painter."[5] His time spent in the firm—he left in 1857—proved important in two ways. First, the practical knowledge he gained of the medium's technical requirements and the linear qualities needed to draw for wood engraving likely contributed to his success as an illustrator in the 1870s. Second, during this period Moran first encountered the art and use of color of Joseph Mallord William Turner.[6]

Moran had become a proficient watercolorist while working for Scattergood and Telfer, and the charm and quality of his work enabled him to trade "his pictures to an old bookseller [C.J. Price & Co.], for 'The Rivers of France,' the 'Liber Studiorum,' and everything that contained the work of 'Turner.'"[7] Moran also obtained a volume of Richard Earlom's *Liber Veritatis, or a Collection of Prints after the Original Designs of Claude Le Lorrain. . . .*[8] Earlom reproduced in etching and mezzotint an album of drawings by Claude Lorrain, which the artist had sketched as a record of his paintings. Moran's initial interest in Claude is not surprising, given his Anglophile predisposition; a similar arcadian quality occasionally surfaces in his Pennsylvania lithographs of the 1860s and Long Island landscapes of the 1880s. But what the *Liber Veritatis* after Claude may have suggested to Moran was the possibility of creating a published compilation of an artist's work, a possibility that Turner's *Liber Studiorum* must have made explicit.

The *Liber Studiorum* represents Turner's efforts to bring his own artistic ideas and reputation before a larger public and to control the appearance of prints done after his own works.[9] Although Moran never spoke about the specific influence that Turner's prints—and the *Liber Studiorum* especially—may have had on his own printmaking, certain characteristics of Turner's *Liber* suggest qualities that Moran would exploit in his own work (fig. 1). Most apparent is the constant role light plays in Turner's prints. Moran could not help but respond to the way in which Turner evokes specific moods by the fall of light, by its density and directness, and by the interplay of clouds and light in the sky. What Moran could do in painting, he could equally well express in the media of prints. Parenthetically,

Moran was one of the only important etchers in the 1880s who used techniques such as the roulette and mezzotint rocker to lay down tonal passages in his etchings that compare to Turner's work.

A second possible association was what the *Liber Studiorum* might have meant to Moran by the middle 1860s. Throughout much of the decade Moran seems to have worked toward creating a publishable compilation of his own designs, which he variously referred to as "Studies for Pictures" and "Studies and Pictures." The drawings or lithographs of the landscape studies that would constitute these portfolios were often unique works, apparently drawn with this end in mind. Moran may have hoped that the publication of his drawings would enhance his still limited reputation and offer a compendium of landscapes that would have pedagogical value.

Despite Moran's interest in Turner, his two earliest etchings are copies after two English illustrators. On a print that copies a slight piece of landscape by Myles Birket Foster, Moran records in his own hand that this print was "My First plate, after Foster. 1856 about."[10] Although these works by Foster were etched plates, they have the style of wood engravings, with short, delicate strokes, a cleanly wiped plate, and shadowed areas created by an increased number of lines rather than more deeply etched ones. Moran's etching style is similarly cramped. Small, tight lines lend density to the landscape but provide no visual recession or structure to individual parts. The result is totally linear in execution and, like Birket Foster's designs, small in scale (3¼ x 3⅞ inches). Moran inscribed a second delicately executed landscape "No. 2. 2nd Experiment."[11] This one is clearly dated 1860 and thus was produced about the same time as his first lithograph in 1859 and his three *clichés-verre* in 1860. These protean efforts raise the question of where in Philadelphia and from whom young Moran learned to etch on copper, draw on stone, or scratch a photographic plate.

In his 1893 volume on the history of etching in America, Henry Russell Wray briefly describes the first lesson in etching that Moran and his friend and future brother-in-law Stephen Ferris received from the famous reproductive mezzotinter John Sartain. "As early as 1860, John Sartain, the veteran engraver, practically illustrated for Thomas Moran and Stephen J. Ferris, the process of etching....Before his enthusiastic audience of two, Mr. Sartain prepared a plate, made a drawing, and described the action of acids on different metals."[12]

As an artist, educator, and organizer of cultural events, Sartain stood out as a major figure in the Philadelphia print world. He excelled as a reproductive engraver of portraits, historical images, and sentimental genre subjects.[13] Technically he practiced the so-called mixed method, which combined mezzotint with etching, line engraving, and stipple or aquatint. The advantage of the mixed method was its greater facility in expeditiously producing sturdy printing plates. Young Moran probably had little interest in the historical set pieces or genre subjects that Sartain engraved, nor must he have cared much for the techniques of the metal engraver, which were more varied but as disciplined as those of the wood engraver. The immediacy and technical ease of etching may have momentarily intrigued him, but etching's role in the arts of this period was generally ancillary to that of engraving. Moran might well have turned away from etching because the medium showed little commercial possibility unless combined with engraving. He was nevertheless interested in printmaking, and if his two experiments with etching were unsatisfactory, he was willing to try others. Besides etching, he became involved with lithography and, most surprisingly, with *clichés-verre* prints in 1859 and 1860.

Clichés-verre are created through a chemically photographic technique that is mechanically similar to etching. One early writer on the artist exuberantly but mistakenly attributed the technique to Moran's invention, but *cliché-verre* in fact dates to the earliest years of photography.[14] Technically, *cliché-verre* mimics etching by

> the act of drawing through a prepared ground, generally printer's ink (dusted white for contrast) or fogged collodion. In *cliché-verre*, however, the ground rests on a transparent matrix surface [glass in the nineteenth century] rather than on metal corroded with acid. The drawing is most often done with an etching needle, quill pen, or other sharp instrument. Once drawn, the plate becomes a photographic negative and exposure to the sun, as printing agent, transfers the design to light-sensitive paper. Alternatively, the *cliché-verre* negative can be rendered as a monochrome painting, brushing emulsion in the form of oil paint onto the transparent matrix....By modifying the applied paint, thus altering the amount of light reaching the sensitized sheet, the artist can produce a complete range of tones.[15]

Cliché-verre lent itself to line drawing, and tonal gradations were difficult to achieve given this limitation. In spite of the autographic character of the medium, works tend to look more reproductive than freehand.

Two of Moran's *clichés-verre* from 1860 are of specific subjects, *The Flight into Egypt* and *The Haunted House* (fig. 2), while the third depicts a copse of trees and a swampy pond.[16] Both of the titled images were themes Moran had sketched or painted before—and would again—although one work did not strictly replicate another.[17] They are meticulously drawn, expressive pieces with diminutive figures enveloped in an exotic or eerie setting. The sky glows softly, and in some printings the moon has already risen. In turn, the landscape scene is reminiscent of Moran's two etchings in the contrast between lights and darks and in the handling of the sky and billowy clouds. Photographically, these *clichés-verre* are unusually sophisticated prints, and the subtle gradations of the sky make them quite unlike any ordinary *cliché-verre* of this period. In fact, some doubt has been expressed that they are *cliché-verre* at all but are instead "camera copies of Moran's work."[18] *The Haunted House*, however, has

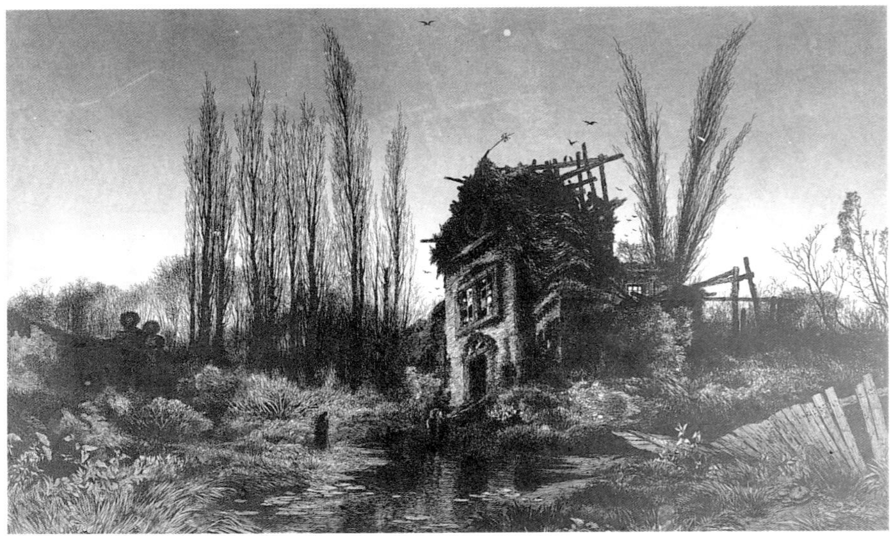

2

penciled on it "Etching through Collodian, on a glass plate. The Haunted House. T. Moran 1860," and *The Flight into Egypt* is inscribed in the image "The Flight into Egypt./Glass Etching. 1860."[19] This leaves little doubt that Moran personally drew them and that they are not photographic copies of his drawings.

If Moran did not learn *cliché-verre* on his own, his brother John most likely instructed him.[20] John first appears professionally as a photographer in 1859, and during the next decade he established himself in Philadelphia as the preeminent landscape and urban photographer. He worked closely with his younger brother Thomas during this period, and he was personally involved in the theoretical discussions surrounding photography as a fine art. John could have provided the technical knowledge necessary to make a *cliché-verre*, and his technical involvement offers a possible answer as to why these prints might reasonably be taken for photographic copies. Some examples of *The Haunted House* and *The Flight into Egypt* have a rising moon artfully placed in a delicately shaded sky. This suggests that variant printings were made from a tonal rather than a linear plate. Such was the case, according to a correspondent to the *Photographic News*, who saw at least one of Moran's *clichés-verre* in 1863. Although he probably confused John and Thomas, he was impressed by the quality of work. "Mr. Moran, of Philadelphia, has made some very fine moonlight pictures by double printing. He first prints the sky, making a full moon by laying a coin over the glass, and then prints from the negative. The effect of having a tree branch or chimney top appear against the moon is very fine. His photographic etching of 'The Haunted House' printed in this way, is exquisitely fine, and perhaps stands at the head of American Art Photography."[21] Moran was certainly curious about different print techniques. His brief forays into etching and *cliché-verre* suggest he may have sought a print medium that combined simplicity, ease, printability, and commercial acceptability, which neither of these did in 1860. But in lithography he found the medium that would occupy him for the next decade.

Lithography

Almost all of Moran's lithographs were meant to be black and white in an era when color played a dominant role in lithographic art. Chromolithography (color printing from lithographic stones) had been perfected by the 1850s, and artists such as Moran's contemporary Albert Bierstadt exploited its natural appeal as a mass-produced substitute for their paintings.[22] In a more popular vein Currier and Ives produced hand-colored lithographs that found great favor with the public. Black-and-white lithography, however, proved neither a high-end medium for the reproduction of works of art nor a commercially viable artistic medium. Lithography maintained too much of its own character to endear it to the general public and to compete with the textural capabilities and technical expertise of line engraving or the mixed style.

Moran probably learned lithography either in a lithographic shop or from one of his brothers—Edward or Peter—who were both practiced lithographers.[23] Thomas' training began about 1859, according to the inscription on the mount of his earliest dated lithograph, a small coastal scene.[24] The two known examples of this print bear pencil dates—in the image, on the sheet, or on the mount—of 1857, 1859, and 1860.[25]

The artist's lithographs fall into three groups that can be generally defined by subject and purpose. In the first group are the earliest works, which have the appearance of study pieces that were drawn in order to learn the lithographic technique through the example of others (fig. 3). Some seem to be variations on popular types, such as English coastal scenes, while others are direct copies, most notably after the work of Eugène Isabey (Sartain may have provided the prints from which Moran worked).[26]

2. Thomas Moran, *The Haunted House*, 1860, *cliché-verre*, courtesy Gilcrease Museum, Tulsa, Oklahoma.

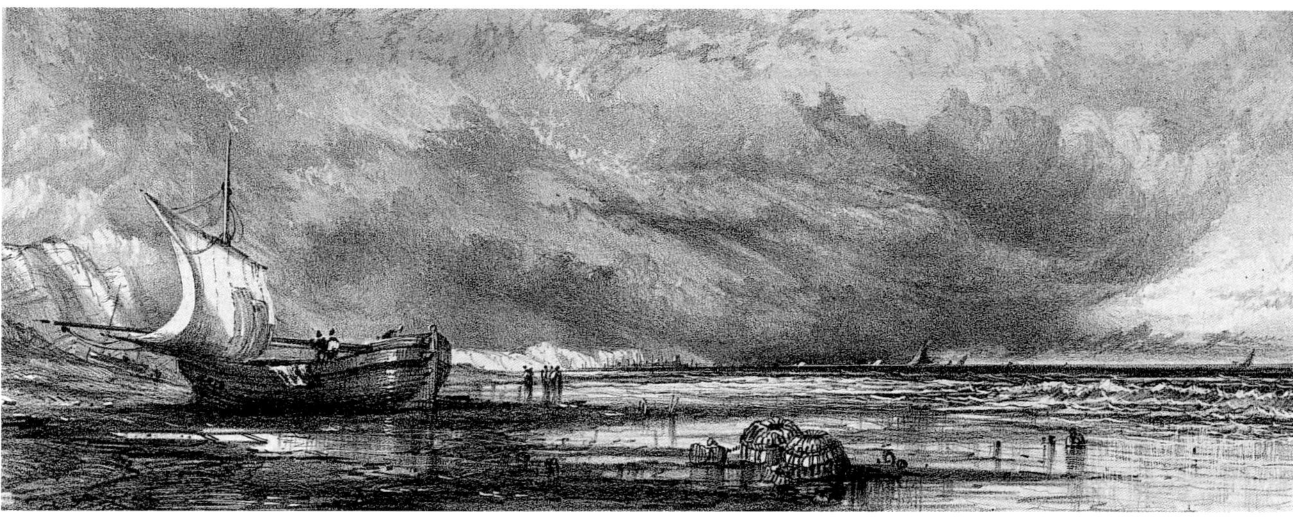

3. Thomas Moran, *Untitled (Seacoast—Low Tide)*, early 1860s, lithograph, courtesy New York Public Library; Astor, Lenox, and Tilden Foundations.

4. Thomas Moran, *Untitled (Six Fossilized Fish)*, 1863, lithograph, courtesy New York Public Library; Astor, Lenox, and Tilden Foundations.

Marine scenes are frequently encountered among the lithographs in this first group, and on the whole, the prints tend to be unsigned on the stone.

Purpose links the lithographs in the second group, which contains studies of fossil shells and fish (fig. 4) and sketches of fully detailed landscapes with railroads (fig. 7). None is dated in the stone, and the typical lithographed signature is a vertically conjoined "T" over an "M."[27] These lithographs were commissioned projects that represent early examples of the artist's illustrational skills.

The third group of lithographs postdates the trip to Europe taken by Thomas and his wife Mary from June 1866 to May 1867. These landscapes partially reflect the scenery he sketched in Italy and the Alps, and they share a common link to Moran's proposed portfolio of lithographs entitled "Studies and Pictures." Almost all are signed "T. Moran" on the stone, several have titles, and as a rule they are dated. These lithographs stand out as Moran's most mature work, and they show why, for an artist who thought in such coloristic terms, lithography proved a natural medium.

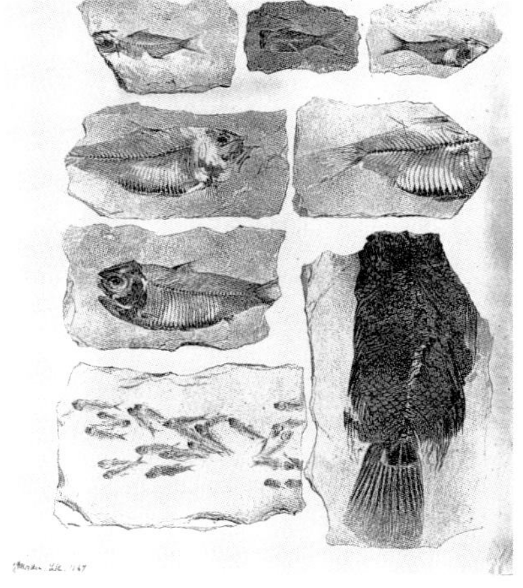

While the etchings and *clichés-verre* that Moran drew around 1859 and 1860 are all landscapes with small figures sometimes added, three of his earliest lithographs are seascapes, which suggest the influence in subject matter of his brother Edward as well as of Turner and English marine art in general.[28] Set on the English or Normandy coast, Moran's generic scenes depict a quiescent sea with fishing boats left stranded by the receding tide (see fig. 3). He emphasizes the sky with dense atmospheric clouds above a low horizon line and endows an otherwise ordinary setting with grandeur and sublimity by projecting the sky into a major role. While the earliest tidal scene is ill-drawn and poorly printed, one characteristic of Moran's lithographic style is already apparent: he draws tonally by emphasizing the broad edge of the crayon, not the tip. Moran then combines these heavy, broad strokes with a reductive approach to structural highlights and contours by scraping and scratching through the blacks. This technique permits him to conceive images that are both plausibly structured and subjectively defined by light and atmosphere. Although his early lithographs are still dominated by gray tones and his drawing is still tentative, he expresses a sensibility for the medium that differs from that shown by those few of his artist peers who attempted lithography.

One important influence on Moran was the energetic style and technique of Isabey, whose portfolio of lithographs, "Six Marines," was first published in 1833. From this set, which fully exploits the black and white potential of the medium, Moran chose *Retour de Port* (c. 1832) to copy almost line for line, retaining all the pictorial effects of the original (fig. 5).[29] He copied not just the roiling waters, cloudy sky, and thrashing boats but also Isabey's finesse at creating watery highlights and dense coloristic effects. In further emulation of Isabey, Moran's lithograph shows considerable scraping and some scratching to bring out highlights and to sculpt form. Moran felt strongly enough about the piece that on the margin of the only known impression he wrote, "Drawn on stone by TMoran after Isabey 1862."[30]

Three other subjects—a twilight landscape, cows by a stone bridge, and a study of a man and a wagon—belong to this same period.[31] Except for the twilight landscape, both of the other lithographs are probably copies. The source of the man and wagon is a small lithographic study by Paul Huet, whose handling of the crayon and the densely colored blacks must have attracted Moran. Of the remaining two lithographs, neither shows particularly strong drawing or compositional organization. The image of the cows by the crumpled stone bridge and rococoesque foliage seems unlike Moran, except when it is placed in the context of paintings such as *The Haunted House* (1858) and *Summer on the Susquehanna* (1860), in which organic forms become evanescent froth.

5

The other early work, with its indifferent technique and lack of defining edge, is either a scene of a rising or a setting sun. This lithograph easily would have been forgotten if not for its subsequent history. In 1880 Moran resurrected the composition and used it as the background for his etching *Twilight in Arizona.* The etching's limited printing in 1880 was succeeded by a widely circulated impression that had been liberally darkened to a mezzotint tone by heavy roulette work on the plate. This version, printed in 1885,[32] is the only etching known that is clearly based on an earlier lithograph.

Moran applied these lessons to the striking 1864 lithograph of tidal flats with fishermen and a boat (fig. 6).[33] Although drily and unevenly printed, the images created of sky, sand, and sea by Moran's handling of the crayon are strikingly redolent of Turner's mezzotinted effects. Moran drags the crayon across the stone in long curving or short twisted strokes to give the allusion of a sky of sunset reds and oranges. Fragments of white light are scraped out of the darker colors, and staccato strokes, almost like the teeth of a mezzotint rocker, delineate the foreground sand. Moran signed the stone "T. Moran 1864," suggesting his authorship of the image.[34]

How did Moran intend to use lithography? Two answers seem possible. By 1867 Moran clearly viewed lithography as another vehicle for expressing his artistic ideas and translating them into a multiple. In the early 1860s, however, he also saw the medium's practicality, and initially he may have undertaken it simply for its potential earning power. If Moran did make a living by producing lithographed illustrations, he never spoke of it. But just enough evidence exists to raise the possibility that unsigned, commissioned illustrational lithography by Moran might one day be found buried in mid-century reports or guides. In the 16 November 1869 issue of the *Philadelphia Evening Bulletin*, a correspondent wrote:

> Our Friendly readers will be interested in the large new lithograph of Swarthmore College, just drawn by Thomas Moran and printed by McGuigan. It is a spirited and handsome design. Mr. Moran does himself great credit whenever he lays his powerful hand to the lithographic crayon. His drawings for the guide-book now preparing by the West Chester Railroad Company (on which road, by the by, Swarthmore College is situated), are very brilliant and effective, and indicate in a curious degree the peculiar brushing and color of the artist's well-known oil-paintings.

An advertisement published the following day provides additional data, such as its price ($1.00) and its size (6 x 14 inches).[35] The brief notice offers considerable information: it confirms the existence of the Swarthmore lithograph; it identifies a set of small lithographs that were previously unidentified; it broadens our knowledge of Moran's activity as a quasi-commercial lithographer; and it underscores the relationship between Moran's paintings and lithographs.[36] Until this notice was found, Moran's only clearly commissioned lithographs were three sheets illustrating fossilized shells and fish (fig. 4), signed in pencil and variously dated to 1862, 1863, and 1867.[37] While the inscriptions might be later additions, the prints were intended "for scientific work" and are mentioned in lithograph inventories.[38] This is the type of straightforward visual illustration for which lithography was well suited. Yet even within the confines of this close replication of form, Moran's draftsmanship is firm.

Around 1869 Moran was offered a commission to sketch lithographic illustrations for the *Guidebook to the West Chester and Philadelphia Railroad* (fig. 7). This handbook, published in Philadelphia in 1869, offered a lengthy narrative description of the sights, towns, and manufactories that lay along the railroad's route. Typically, the railroads enlisted artists and writers

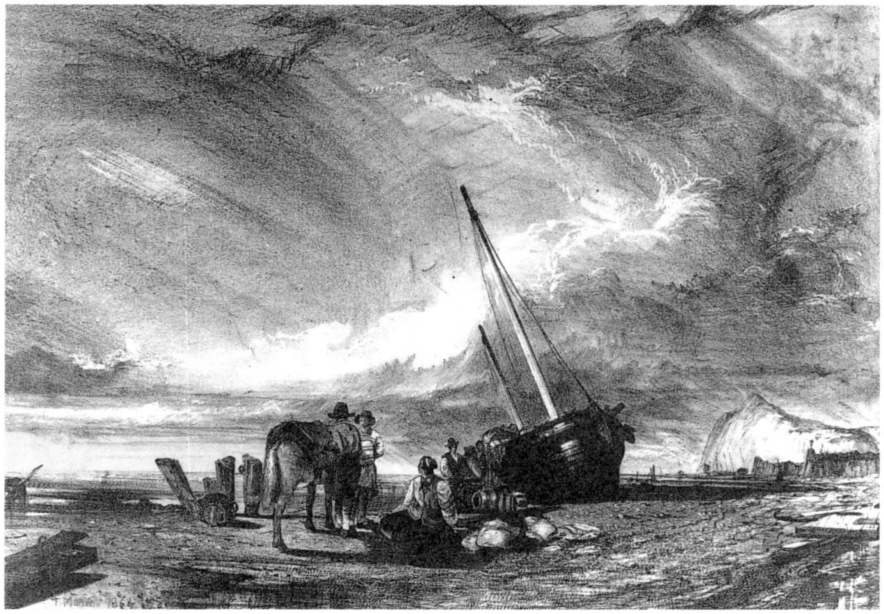

5. Thomas Moran after Eugène Isabey, *Return to Port*, 1862, lithograph, courtesy New York Public Library; Astor, Lenox, and Tilden Foundations.

6. Thomas Moran *Untitled (Beached Fishing Boats)*, 1864, lithograph, courtesy Cooper-Hewitt Museum of Design, Smithsonian Institution.

7. Thomas Moran, *Baltimore Junction*, 1869, lithograph, courtesy East Hampton Library.

to record their impressions of a particularly scenic route. The resulting guidebooks were then used as effective promotional tools. Moran had earlier done similar work for *Harper's Monthly*, when his sketches of views along the Susquehanna River appeared as woodcuts in June 1862. He had traveled on the Catawissa Railroad with his brother John, who photographed many of the same scenes that Thomas drew, and the two brothers may have again shared ideas.[39]

Eleven of the original fourteen lithographs were in Moran's collection after his death but were never included in any of his lifetime inventories.[40] As commercial work, they were probably proofs before the lettering was added. None is dated, but Moran did sign five of them with the early version of his monogram—the "T" over the "M" without serifs—that predates his first expedition to see the Yellowstone region in 1871. In addition to their uniform measurements (3¾ x 6 inches), these prints share a consistent range of middle tones, a straightforward drawing style, a preference for a broad view of the landscape, and a descriptive picture postcard-like image. Although tracks are prominent in several of the scenes, trains are seen in only two (including fig. 7).

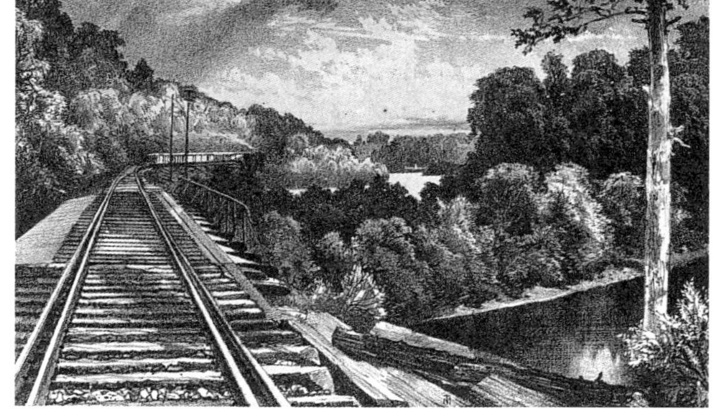

Two Portfolios

At some point in the early 1860s Moran decided to publish a portfolio, called "Studies for Pictures," of his own work in reproduction. In its earliest form it was to consist of photographs taken by John of large-scale landscape drawings by Thomas in charcoal and possibly lithography. By 1866, however, when Moran and Mary Nimmo visited England, France, and Italy, the idea was superseded. Referring to sketches from his travels in the Northeast, the Lake Superior region, and Europe, Moran intended to recreate scenes as a series of original lithographic drawings and publish them as "Studies and Pictures." Unfortunately, neither plan seems to have been realized. Yet the piecemeal results prove Moran was capable of some of the finest lithographic draftsmanship in nineteenth-century America.

The basis for the above works are the sketches Moran made both at home around Pennsylvania and on his several trips farther afield. His earliest distant excursion, to the south shore of Lake Superior and the scenically famous Pictured Rocks, took place over the summer of 1860. As he did on every trip, Moran sketched assiduously, paying special attention to the stratigraphy of the Michigan shoreline and the coloration of natural forms.[41] He traveled to England in 1862 and took an extended European journey with Mary between 1866 and 1867.[42] The myriad drawings he brought back formed the basis for subsequent paintings and lithographs well beyond the period in which he executed them.

While all of the lithographs for the portfolio "Studies and Pictures" were drawn from 1867 to 1869, its phantom predecessor "Studies for Pictures" should be briefly considered first. If Moran was overly presumptuous in thinking that a volume of his drawings reproduced photographically would find a market, he was at least correct in realizing that publishing photographic reproductions of artworks was a burgeoning industry. From the late 1850s to the middle 1860s, numerous volumes reproducing the art of contemporary artists, the old masters, and the collections of European galleries became available.[43] In an age before color photography, paintings were frequently reproduced first as a simplified line engraving or drawing and then photographed for reproduction, a process that clarified what otherwise might be tonal muddiness. Photography not only greatly simplified the process of reproduction but it also offered a record that could become the artist's perfect *Liber Studiorum*.

The earliest datable reference to the joint project of Thomas and John is a comment that appeared in the *Philadelphia Photographer* in 1866, written in regard to an earlier article on photography and the fine arts and how they do not have to be quarreling adversaries: "The Morans [Thomas and Edward] paint their gorgeous landscapes and draw their unsurpassed charcoal sketches, while another brother makes photographs of them, and saves the delay and expense attendant upon getting steel engravings made."[44] One example of this exists in a photograph by John of a landscape drawing by Thomas dated 1864. Judging from the photograph, this highly finished charcoal drawing appears to be worked in much the same way Moran worked the lithographic stone. It could easily be mistaken for a photograph of a lithograph.[45] In an ambiguous note, probably by Ruth Moran during one of her periodic inventories of her father's work, the writer states, "1862 & 64 was making charcoal drawings and lithographs—designs for pictures, & for a series—to be photographed by his brother John Moran."[46] The simplest interpretation is that the works were done in 1862 and 1864 and included studies for later pictures and "for a series—to be photographed by his brother John Moran." But if lithographs were also to be photographed for the series, would this have included Moran's 1864 beach scene of the English Channel (fig. 6)? While it might seem redundant to reproduce a lithograph, it was certainly not out of the question.

8

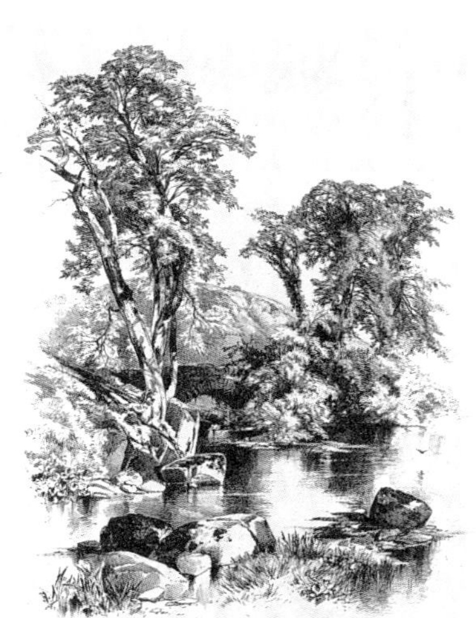

The final evidence that Moran planned a portfolio is found in his "Old Book of Lists, 1863–1909," which includes notations and diverse listings of works, such as:

Clearing. Charcoal. Canvas/size 30 x 45 in. Rubbed off to paint./ Made in Aug. 1864. Put in S. for Pic.

The Children of the Mountain/Charcoal on paper 52 x 62 inches Jan. 1865/pub. in Studies for Pictures.

Sentinels of the Coast/Charcoal on paper. Jan. 1865/Size 25 x 45. destroyed. Pub. in Studies for Pic.

A Canadian Waterfall. Charcoal/on Canvas. Made in May 1864/ Size 30 x 45 in. Rubbed off to paint on/published in my "Studies for Pictures."[47]

Twelve entries clearly state in one form or another that the cited work was published in "Studies for Pictures." Ten of the twelve drawings were charcoal on canvas or paper, and two are in "Vandyke Brown." The charcoal on canvas drawings were all subsequently rubbed off or "destroyed," and the canvases were painted over. The wording of the inventory suggests that these drawings no longer existed when inventoried. Perhaps Moran was working from existing photographs of the drawings taken by his brother John. With the exception of two titles listed under "Studies for Pictures"—*Solitude* and *The Wissahickon*—none of the titles in the inventory corresponds to any of the lithographs of 1867 to 1869, suggesting, in fact, that the drawings were not preparatory studies for the later lithographs.[48] Moreover, the constant reference to "Studies for Pictures" rather than "Studies and Pictures" is, as a title, closer to the function of the drawings, just as "Studies and Pictures" is to the later lithographs. Taken together, these points, but especially the remark about "designs for pictures, & for a series" being drawn in 1862 and 1864, suggest that a portfolio of works, possibly including lithographs, was under way before 1865. Prior to Thomas and Mary leaving for Europe, John was making photographs of these drawings in lieu of engravings. When they were gathered as a portfolio, they were possibly put on sale. Unfortunately, no set has yet been identified.

Following his and Mary's return from Europe in the spring of 1867, Moran's personal efforts in 1868 and 1869 centered on the production of a portfolio of lithographs entitled "Studies and Pictures." Seventeen lithographs still exist from this period and derive from the landscape drawings he had executed since 1860.[49] These late lithographs, with their interesting variations in design, exhibit the style and coherency of an artistically and technically mature artist. Moran alternates between a fully worked out image that is held within the limits of the picture frame and a vignetted image that "floats" on the surrounding white of the paper (fig. 8). The technique of isolating the scene in a field of white was common in illustration and approximates Moran's sketching method.

8. Thomas Moran, *Untitled (View of the Wissahickon with Stone Bridge)*, 1868/1869, lithograph, courtesy Library Company of Philadelphia.

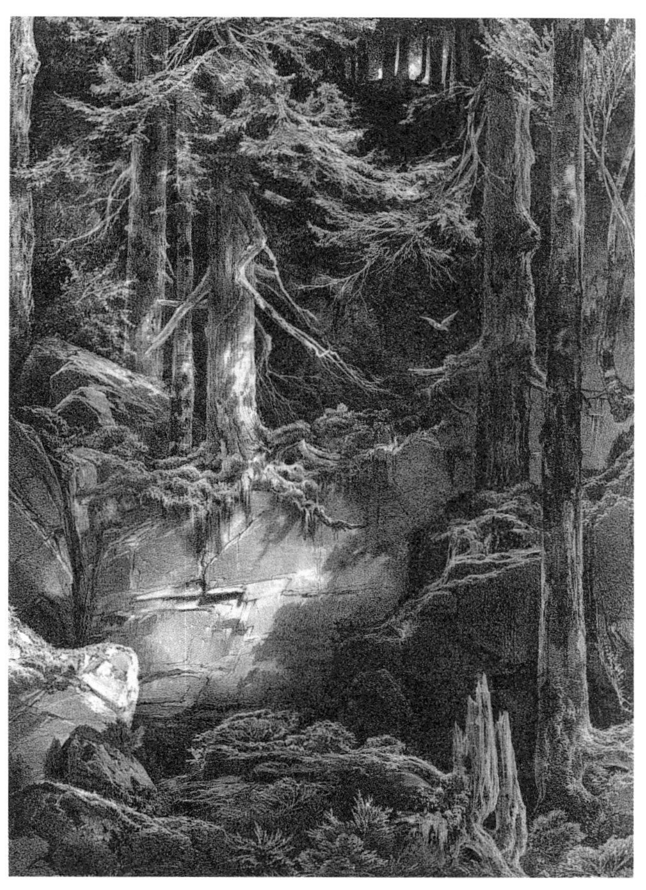

9. Thomas Moran, *In the Forest of the Wissahickon*, 1868, lithograph, courtesy Gilcrease Museum Tulsa, Oklahoma.

At whatever point the project ended, only three works had been chosen for inclusion: *In the Forest of the Wissahickon* (fig. 9), a claustrophobic, impenetrable woodland interior; *On the Susquehanna, Pa.*, a bucolic evocation of the American landscape; and *The Bay of Baiae* (fig. 10), which derives from his stay in Italy.[50] Typical of Moran's most evocative images, naturalistic details culled from the landscape and woods have been transformed to elicit a specific emotional response from the viewer. The rhythm of dark, light, dark, light in *Forest of the Wissahickon* selectively illuminates the solid rock ledge, dense trees, and decaying organic matter to produce a chilling but not wholly characteristic image. *On the Susquehanna* conjures an Edenic vision of the American landscape, with its lush, overarching tree, its placid, sun-dappled river, and its fishermen basking in the warmth of the summer sun. A similarly benign view of nature set in an exotic location is *The Bay of Baiae, Naples*. The barely discernible sun setting to the left casts shadows across the landscape. Like *On the Susquehanna*, a tree divides light from dark and becomes the perfect foil for visualizing the effects of light and shade. Technically, Moran now handles the lithographic crayon and scraper with absolute assurance.

How many lithographs would have been included in "Studies and Pictures" is unknown, since nothing indicates that it was ever completed and no published copy is known. More-

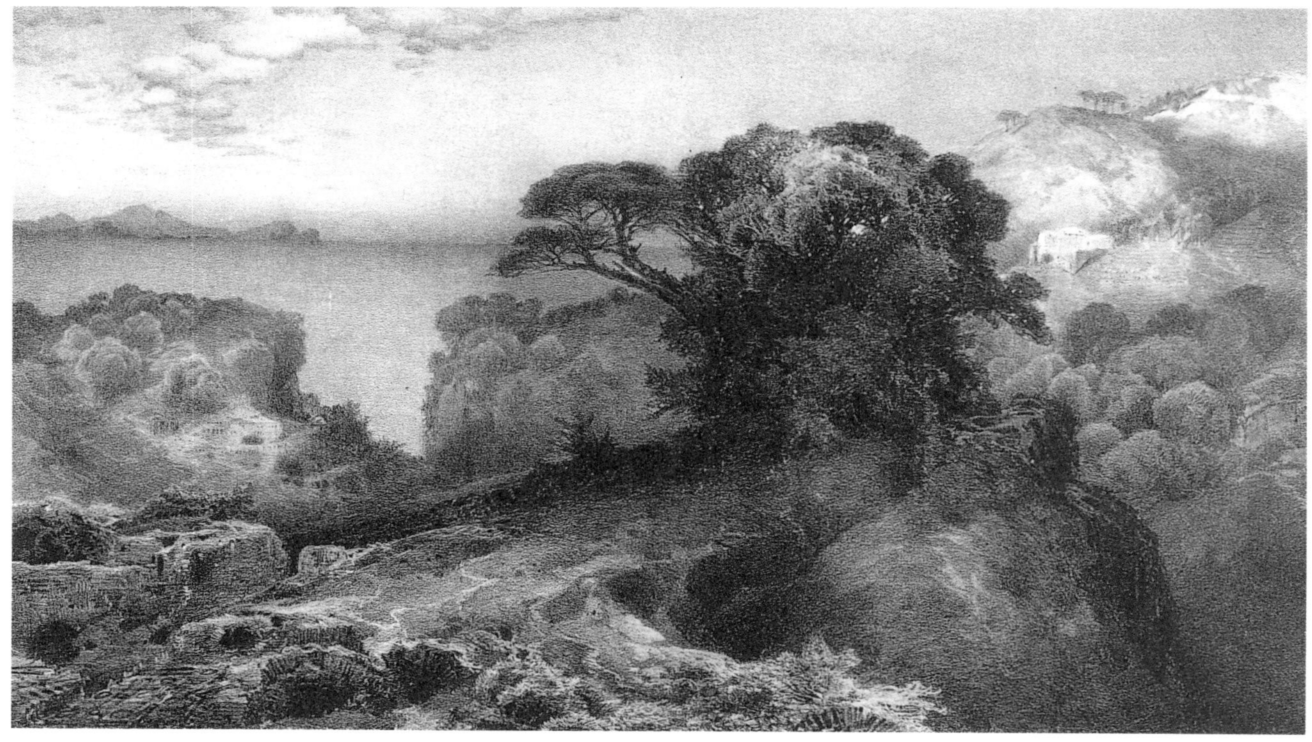

10. Thomas Moran, *Bay of Baiae*, 1869, lithograph, courtesy Gilcrease Museum, Tulsa, Oklahoma.

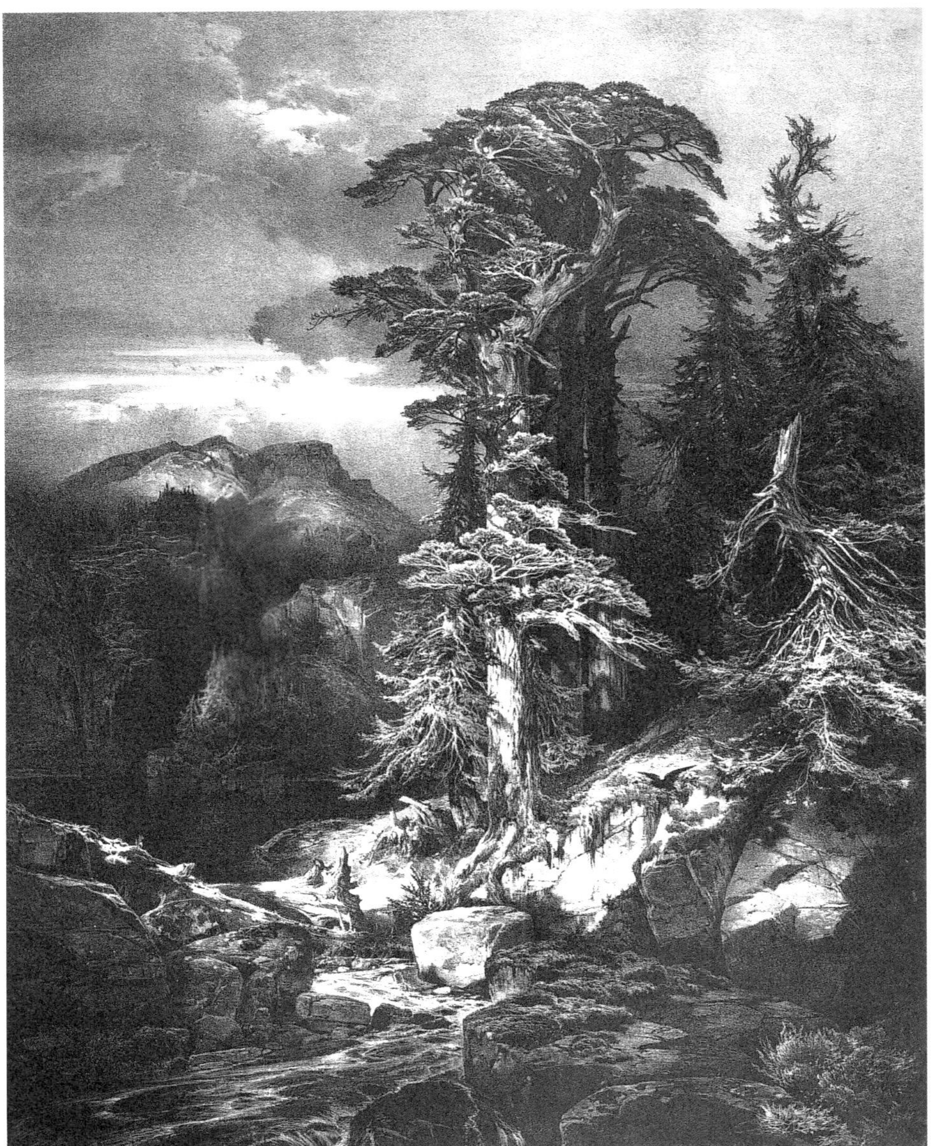

11. Thomas Moran, *Solitude*, 1869, lithograph, courtesy New York Public Library; Astor, Lenox, and Tilden Foundations.

12. Thomas Moran, *Desolation*, c. 1869, lithograph, courtesy Gilcrease Museum, Tulsa, Oklahoma.

over, with the exception of the lithographs for the West Chester and Philadelphia Railroad guidebook and one impression of *In the Forest of the Wissahickon*, every known impression of the lithographs is in a public institution, and the provenance is invariably the Moran family. Unlike his etchings, Moran's lithographs have rarely appeared in the marketplace.[51] The likelihood is remote that more than a dozen impressions of any image were ever made. Yet, they apparently were exhibited, perhaps individually, to the public at about the time they were made.[52]

Moran's two masterpieces in the lithographic medium are *Solitude* and *Desolation* (figs. 11, 12).[53] The monumental *Solitude* of 1869 measures 20⅝ x 16 inches, while its pair, the badly damaged, unique impression of *Desolation*, measures 21⅜ x 15⅝ inches. None of Moran's other lithographs exceeds 14 inches on a side. Including these disproportionately large images in the volume planned for "Studies and Pictures" would have required an elephant folio, and for reason of size alone they were probably never seriously considered. The genesis of both works lies at the beginning of the decade when Moran journeyed to the shores of Lake Superior to sketch the Pictured Rocks. There he found a grand, picturesque landscape more isolated by distance and geography than any he had yet encountered. This terrain mirrored Moran's own romantic inclinations about the soul of the landscape, and no more majestic image in print would come from his hand until he traveled farther west in 1871.

The artist identified the landscape with the human spirit and endowed it with qualities that cause the viewer to respond to its message. Through lighting and composition, a centrally dominant tree becomes the focal point for both images. In *Solitude* the tree, alive and growing, thrusts up into a heavenly light and stands in splendid isolation. The trees in *Desolation* are dead or rotted and overgrown, and the pond is stagnant. Birds hover over a clear running brook in *Solitude*, and a squirrel rests nearby. The only life in *Desolation* are birds high in the branches or overhead. In *Solitude* light and the breaking clouds in the distance play an important role in affirming life. In *Desolation* the sun is only faintly visible. Without light, there is no growth, no life. The power of these images lies in the intense and visceral way Moran depicts the immense sense of isolation and death in one and the uplifting feeling of quiet and self-containment in the other. Moran always tried to evoke a response from his viewer, and here the motivation is still genuine. Individually and in their pairing, the two works differ technically and histrionically from earlier prints and from American lithographs up to this time. On 15 January 1875 Moran wrote to L. Prang & Co., publishers of his chromolithographs, to inquire if they would be interested in printing an edition of *Solitude* and *Desolation*:

> The Stone of "Solitude" gave very good results on French india paper when it was printed from some 3 years ago; but may have deteriorated by want of care in the meanwhile. The other one "desolation" was never printed from save an experimental proof and I judge it might work up as good as it ever was. Both were somewhat spoiled in the original preparation of the stone by too much acid. I am desirous that you should try further and work them into the best possible condition and then send me proofs on French india paper (Buff Color) or if you have not got that, or cannot get it, on ordinary india paper. I should be sorry if the two drawings were now worthless through neglect.[54]

Nothing apparently came of the request, either from Prang's disinterest or the condition of the stones. If Moran had published "Studies and Pictures," and if *Desolation* and *Solitude* had been editioned, they would have been preeminent among nineteenth-century American lithographs conceived as original works of art.

Etching

In the 1870s Moran turned his energies to illustrations reproduced in woodcut and chromolithography. His drawings and paintings of the East and, more important, of the West clearly educated and influenced contemporary attitudes toward the American landscape, yet his black-and-white lithographs never achieved any great degree of circulation. A decade later he turned to etching and became one of the most successful printmakers of the 1880s. If Moran struggled against popular taste in pushing forward his lithography projects in the 1860s, his career as an etcher in the 1880s was fully caught up in the national enthusiasm for etching that swept "its way literally into the wilderness, and to the very extremities of the land."[55] In etching he found a print medium that not only bent to his needs as an artist but was also buoyed by a groundswell of popularity that lasted for ten years.

The new vision of etching that arose from 1878 to 1880 offered two basic tenets. One was the idea of the etched print as an original work of art and the creative product of the artist who etched the plate. The artist who copied his or her own work from another medium onto an etching plate was still considered to have created an original work, since the image copied and the etching made were both the product of a single individual. What made etching so accessible to the artist and capable of sustaining prolonged interest was the simplicity of drawing through an acid-resistant ground to the copper plate beneath.

12

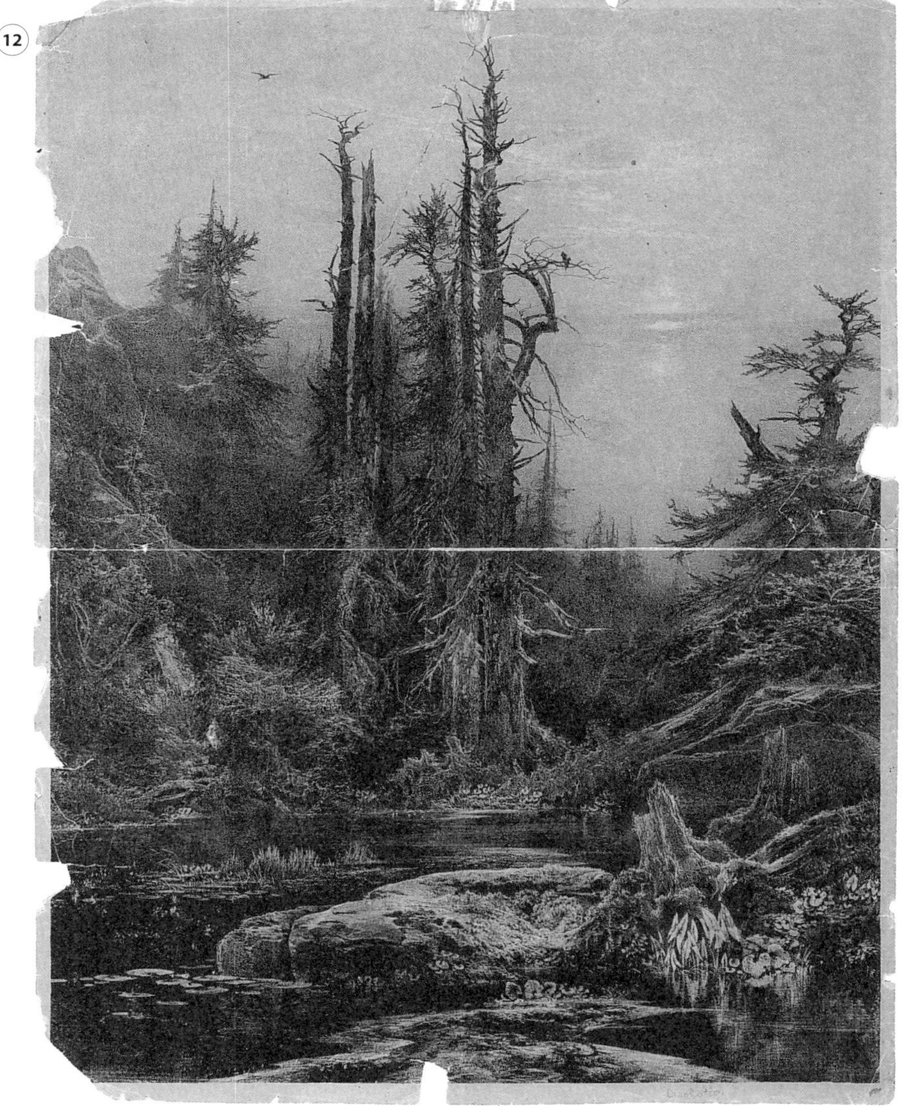

Biting the plate in acid and then proofing it required some technical knowledge, but compared to the complexities of lithographic printing or the time consumed in engraving a plate, etching was immediate and simple. To advocates of etching the technical characteristics that made it the preeminent artist's medium were the absolute freedom of stroke, where the point "plays upon the ground with even less friction than the pencil does on paper," and "a warmth of line and consequently a possibility of indicating color [that is] far beyond that obtainable in line engraving."[56] In its purest form, etching was an objective extension of the subjective act of creation, a medium directly expressive of the artist's spirit.

The second tenet proposed an imaginative use of the medium. Techniques that gave color, texture, and character to the plate were newly exploited. Retroussage, for example, was a manner of wiping the plate that left trails or films of ink outside the lines. When combined with a selective rather than wholly clean wiping of the plate, it could print tones that ranged from very rich to extremely subtle. Sandpaper pressed into the plate left pits that collected ink, and in a more controlled manner, the roulette wheel could add passages of darker tones.[57] The application of these techniques underscored the artistic and aesthetic choices that artists had to make when etching and printing a plate.

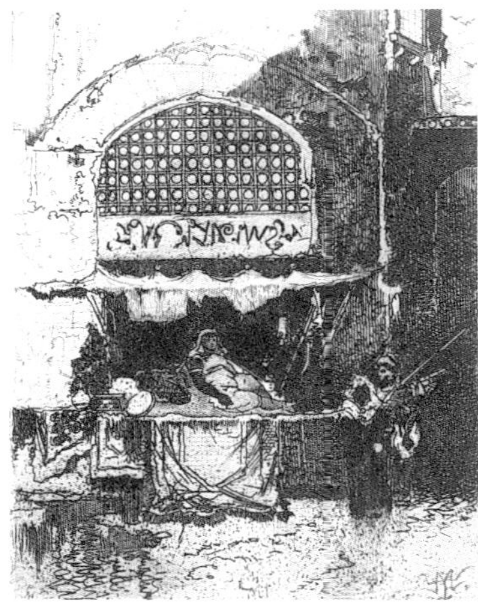

13

13. Thomas Moran, *A Bazaar*, 1869, etching and sandpaper ground, courtesy Gilcrease Museum, Tulsa, Oklahoma.

14. Thomas Moran, *Harlech Castle—Wales*, 1882, 2nd state, etching and roulette, courtesy Gilcrease Museum, Tulsa, Oklahoma.

15. Thomas Moran, *Harlech Castle—Wales*, 1888, 3rd state, etching and roulette, courtesy Gilcrease Museum, Tulsa, Oklahoma.

Already familiar with the technicalities of etching, Moran soon turned his attention to the medium and by the end of 1878 had drawn seven plates. Years later his daughter Ruth described the appearance in that year of a press in their home in Newark, New Jersey. "The old studio in Newark... had its floor strengthened and we got a press. Such excitement when the prints of the first plate were pulled—a small one called *A Bazaar*, characterized by vigorous, almost Rembrandtesque biting, with a curious effect added by means of sandpapering.... All of the plates were successes from the start" (fig. 13).[58]

Moran's earliest prints show a spirit of experimentation, but he quickly settled into a way of working that proved expressive for him. Etching in its simplest form was an exercise in drawing that created forms from lines. In *An Apple Orchard, East Hampton*,[59] Moran draws with clarity and uses a variety of lines to suggest the shape of organic forms, the dullness of wooden planks, and even the dryness of the earth. He did not usually build shadows by crosshatching, but instead he increased the number of lines or strengthened individual lines by biting deeper into the plate.[60] This method has a tendency to build areas of strong contrast, which can be very coloristic or almost seem splotchy at times. In *An Apple Orchard* Moran achieved an excellent visual balance of parts, with a sense of the organic texture of surfaces. Nuances of light were achieved by contrasting the lightly bitten background and more deeply bitten foreground and by the contrasting brilliance of the unbitten areas of the plate. This effect emerges even when a faint film of ink or plate tone is printed across the entire sheet.

Like Turner, Moran went beyond line to create atmospheric effects of shadowed light. *Bridge in the Pass of Glencoe* and *A Tower of Cortez—Mexico* (1883) contain broad areas of roulette work, which, when done with discretion, result in transparent darks that allow the viewer to see through them to the forms behind.[61] In both of these prints solid rocks and trees retain their identity despite being hidden in shadowed hollows or seen through dense foliage. Aquatint, sulphur tints, or selective wiping can achieve comparable results, but Moran seemed to prefer the absolute control he retained over the plate by leaving little to the vagaries of the printer. The more densely the roulette is rolled over the plate, the deeper become the shadows and the more atmospheric the blacks.

Moran's etching *Harlech Castle—Wales* (figs. 14, 15) clearly shows how the roulette could alter a print.[62] In its second state the peripheral parts of the composition were broadly sketched, with forms toward the center growing more solid. While a faint plate tone is evident, roulette work appears only across the center of the image, from the castle through the low trees to the small buildings on the right. Although the heavier shading visually draws the viewer to the center of the work, a sense of light pervades the scene. Yet the etched line from which the image is built remains undisguised in much of the print. When *Harlech Castle* was reissued in 1888, almost the entire plate had been reworked with the roulette to darken tints. To create highlights or patches of light, Moran burnished the plate smooth in selected parts, most obviously above the castle and partially across it. The desire must have been to heighten the romantic aura of the old castle, but the result is a visually heavy image dominated by atmospheric turbulence.

14

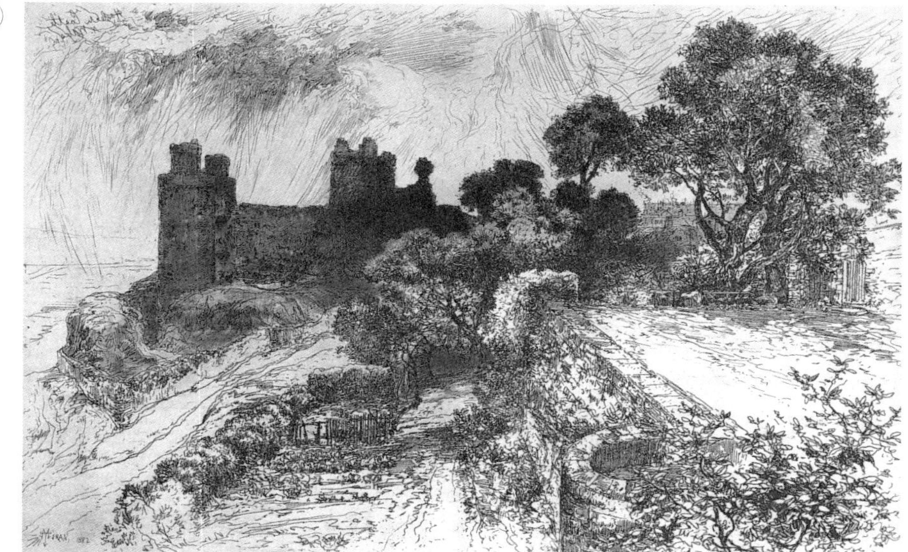

15

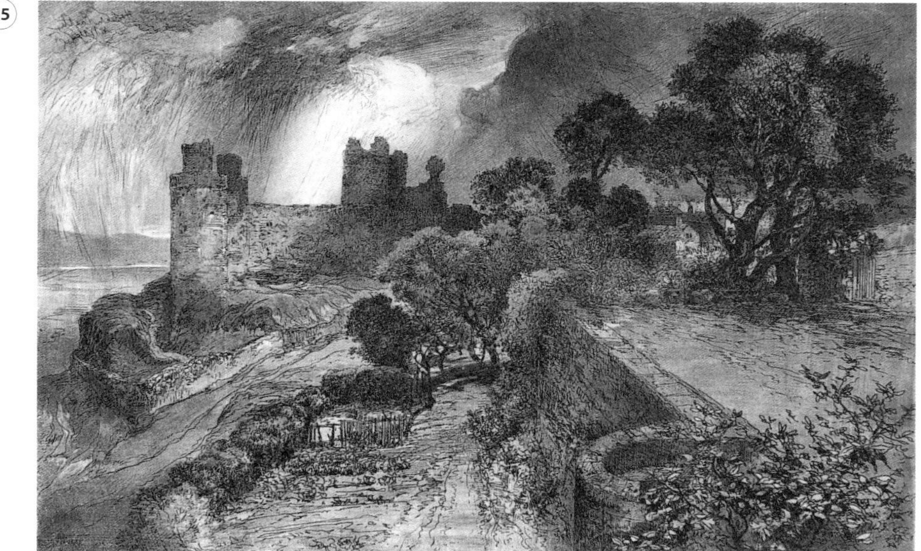

One motif Moran first explored in his lithographs and then expanded in his etchings was tumbling, cascading, breaking bodies of water. Rushing streams appear in the lithographs, and waterfalls and rolling waves became the subjects of several etchings. Summering in East Hampton, he painted, drew, and etched not only the habitable and benign landscape of the seaside but the ocean breaking on the seashore, a potent force of destruction that cast up debris and left ships floundering. The grandest and most elaborate of these studies is *The Much Resounding Sea* (fig. 16), published in 1886.[65] An earlier and more freely drawn etching without the shipwreck is *The Resounding Sea"* (fig. 2, p. 120), which the English critic John Ruskin thought "the finest piece of water drawing he had ever seen by any man."[66] The latter captures the froth of the waves, although they look somewhat like exotic lettuce, while the former establishes the weight and scale of the ocean's forces in one of Moran's most successful large-format etchings. Besides these two prints by Moran,[67] Christian Klackner published four by Winslow Homer: *The Life Line* (1884); *Eight Bells* (1887); *Perils of the Sea* (1888); and *Saved* (1889).[68] The most obvious difference between the two artists is the dominance of the ocean in Moran's prints and the dominance of the heroic figure in Homer's work. Moran was never happy drawing the figure, and his view of the natural world placed human presence secondary to nature.

Although the basis for Moran's national fame by the 1880s was his paintings of western and southwestern subjects, he etched relatively few plates with this theme. Of these, *A Pah-Ute Girl* and *The Empty Cradle* (both 1878) were done from photographs by John Hillers; and *Church of San Juan—New Mexico* (1881) was done after a photograph by William Henry Jackson.[69] *The Coyote—Arizona* (1880) is based on an untitled lithograph

Before they were reprinted in 1888, a number of Moran's prints were treated to this "improvement," the result of a growing taste for such enhancements. Four of the seven works reprinted—*Twilight* (1878); *Harlech Castle* (1882); *A Wreck—Montauk* (1886); and *Pass of Glencoe* (1886)—received extensive reworking with the roulette.[63] The decision to reprint a number of Thomas' prints was probably made for the exhibition of the Morans' collected etchings, which was organized by the New York dealer Christian Klackner in March 1889. An additional three images—*A Pah-Ute Girl* (1878); *The Lighthouse* (1879); and *Conway Castle* (1879)—were unchanged before they were reprinted or editioned for the first time in 1888.[64]

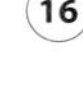

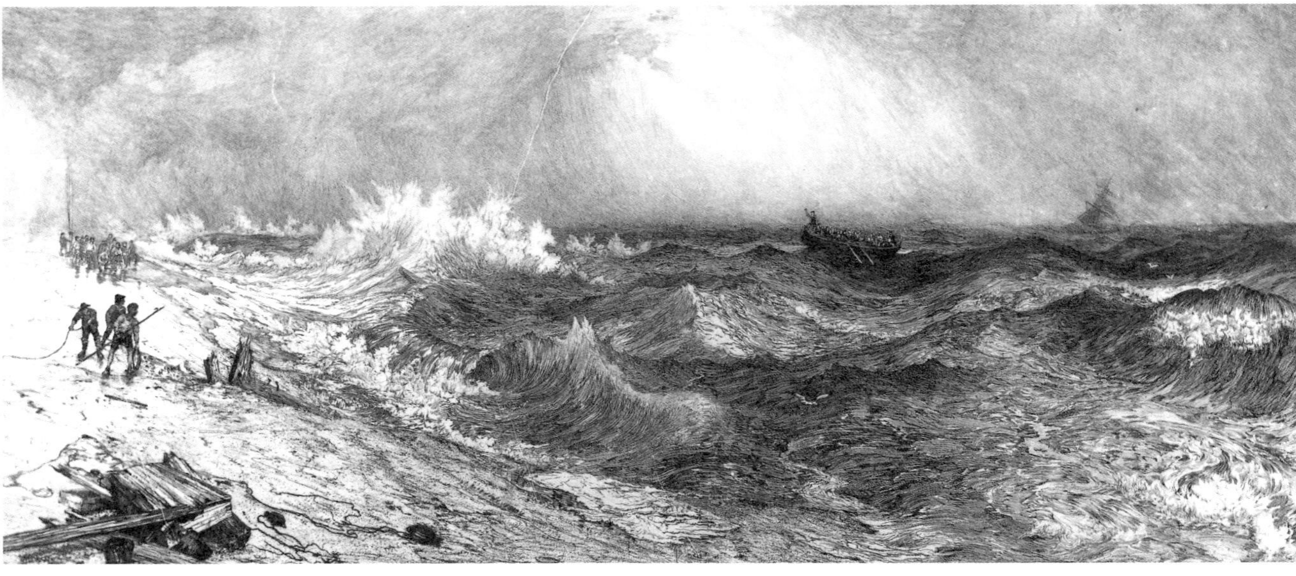

16. Thomas Moran, *The Much Resounding Sea,* 1886, etching, roulette, and sandpaper ground, courtesy Gilcrease Museum, Tulsa, Oklahoma. See also cat. 66.

17. Thomas Moran, *Morning*, 1886, etching, roulette, and sandpaper ground, courtesy Gilcrease Museum, Tulsa, Oklahoma.

18. Thomas Moran, *Conway Castle*, 1879, etching, roulette, and sandpaper ground, courtesy Gilcrease Museum, Tulsa, Oklahoma.

Moran did in the 1860s before he ever went west.[70] *Green River, Wyoming Territory* (1886), appeared in an auction catalogue of Moran's paintings that he and Mary illustrated; *The Harbor of Vera Cruz, Mexico* (1886), was commissioned by Christian Klackner; and *Mountain of the Holy Cross* was commissioned by the print publisher J. D. Waring.[71] *The Tower of Cortez—Mexico* (1883) and *The Castle of San Juan D'Ulloa, Vera Cruz, Mex.* (1884) appeared in portfolios of contemporary etchings. Only *The Head of the Yellowstone River* (1878, first exhibited in 1889) and the large and small versions of *Tower Falls —Yellowstone Park* (1880, after his watercolor) are relatively independent objects.[72]

Many of Moran's etchings were created for much the same purposes as these, and since Moran was clearly aware of the market value of his works, he would surely have made more western images if such etchings were marketable. Other than *Mountain of the Holy Cross*, the only printed western images that were truly successful among collectors were the Prang 1874 chromolithographs made after Moran's watercolors of Yellowstone (see Appendix 1). Quite possibly little market existed for black-and-white images of the distant western territories. Any reluctance on Moran's part to etch western scenes because of inherent limitations of scale, size, and line is out of keeping with his character.[73] Moran could conceive images of deep sublimity if he chose, and perhaps the singularly most convincing evocation of his vision is the 1886 etching *Morning* (fig. 17). It "shows a sunrise after a stormy night, the heavy cumulus clouds breaking away before the sun.... Long shafts of light are flung into vapory depths of sky, tinting the fragments of cloud that have broken from heavy masses rolling sullenly away to the left."[74]

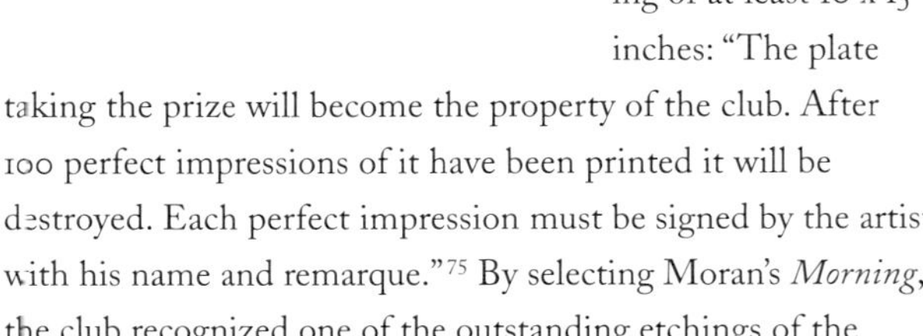

17

It had been announced in 1885 that the Rembrandt Club of Brooklyn was sponsoring a competition for an original etching of at least 10 x 15 inches: "The plate taking the prize will become the property of the club. After 100 perfect impressions of it have been printed it will be destroyed. Each perfect impression must be signed by the artist with his name and remarque."[75] By selecting Moran's *Morning*, the club recognized one of the outstanding etchings of the period.[76] Within the large image, Moran again evoked an animistic nature in which the vastness of the oceans, the flatness of the seashore, the struggle of natural forces, and the ragged flora of the foreground conjure intimations of the sublime over which man has no control. The medium never intrudes on the image; it does not attempt to be anything other than an etching. His style is fully mature, precise, and in balance with his aims, and the technical bravura of some later works plays no part.

The Rembrandt Club award was but one of several signs of Moran's importance to contemporary etching. Both he and Mary were invited in 1881 to join the newly founded Society of Painter-Etchers in London, and he was both a founding member of the New York Etching Club and a member of its executive board for much, if not all, of its existence.[77] Moran contributed to a number of notable publications as well. *Three-Mile Harbor* (1880) appeared in the *American Etchings* series published by the Art Interchange Publishing Company; and *Tower of Cortez—Mexico* was published in *Original Etchings by American Artists* (1883).[78] He traveled to Mexico in early 1883, and *Tower of Cortez* and *The Castle of San Juan D'Ulloa, Vera Cruz, Mex.* resulted from the large number of sketches and watercolors he made.[79] The latter was published in *Twenty Original American Etchings* (1885),[80] composed mostly of etchings by members of the New York Etching Club. Moran, a member of the publication's selection committee, seemed to have had a very good relationship with its editor, Sylvester Koehler, who promoted American

18

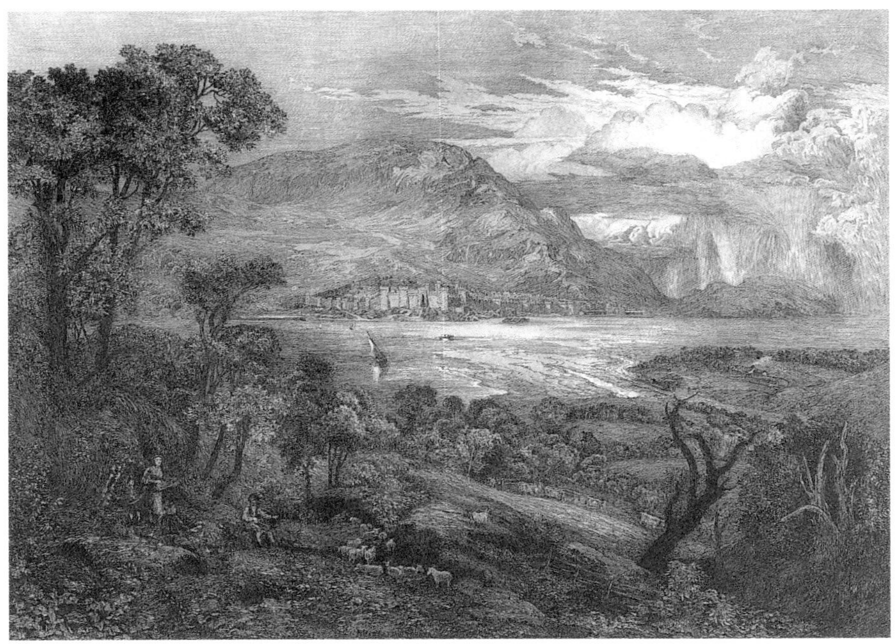

etching through the exhibitions he organized, the publications he edited, and his oversight of print collections in the Museum of Fine Arts, Boston, and the Smithsonian Institution.[81] Koehler wrote two brief notices about Moran's etchings in his *American Art Review* and mentioned the artist's paintings in his 1886 monograph *American Art.*[82] Koehler discussed *Morning on the St. Johns, Florida*, which Moran painted in 1881 and etched in 1886 to illustrate Koehler's volume.[83] By 1886 Moran was undertaking considerable etching after his own paintings and those by other artists. While those after his own watercolors or oils tend to be fine works in their own right—when he was etching and not just reproducing the image—the tastes of the late 1880s began to dictate different standards. Reproductive works dominated Moran's last years as a printmaker.

Conway Castle (fig. 18) was an important print for the artist because it reproduced the putative Turner oil painting that Moran had purchased in 1878. He worked on the reproductive etching over the next year, and judging from its size—almost 16 x 21 inches—he must have intended it to be a framing print. Despite the use of roulette work, especially in the foreground, this is a line etching. Although Moran avoids the freedom of drawing that his own etched compositions exhibit, his indifference in this work to a highly structured pattern of lines and to linear uniformity elicited praise from some critics.[84] Moran exhibited the print, but he must not have editioned it until Klackner "published" it in 1889.

By the late 1880s Moran was almost exclusively producing reproductive work, and *Conway Castle* was simply another in a growing number of such prints. Some large reproductions, after the works of American artists Henry Chase and Andrew F. Bunner, were meant for display on the wall. Smaller ones intended for collection catalogues reproduced works by Charles-François Daubigny and Narcisse-Virgile Diaz de la Peña.[85] Although these prints could reproduce the composition, tonalities, and "sentiment" of the original picture, they lack both Moran's style and that of the original artist. What Moran gave them was his name and the newfound cachet of etching.

While Moran's contemporaries felt that an etching after one's own design qualified as an original work, technically and stylistically no distinction can be found between Moran's "machines" after his own designs and those of another artist. The similarity is strikingly apparent when comparing Moran's copy after Andrew Bunner's *Venice* (1887) to his own *Gate of Venice* (1888) (figs. 19, 20).[86] Moran had visited Venice in early May 1886 and after his return painted the work on which the etching is based. According to Klackner, the etching "occupied the artist upwards of two years, and is by far the most important and completely artistic and elaborate plate that he has produced."[87] (This is hardly a surprising comment since Klackner published the etching and was profiting by its sale.) Klackner also published *Venice*, and both works in their comparably large size and their disciplined, meticulous etching have lost any sense of improvisation and individual style.

The attraction of reproductive work for Moran, as undoubtedly for other artists, was remuneration. The New York publisher J. D. Waring paid Moran $2,500 to etch a copy of *Mountain of the Holy Cross*. For this amount Waring received the plate and Moran signed impressions. By agreement Moran kept back twelve proofs for himself.[88] For the 1891 etched copy of his brother Edward's *White Squadron*, Moran received $2,000 from Radke, Lauckner and Co.[89] By the end of the 1890s, the glut of etchings, whether reproductive or original, had soured the market. Issues of fraud, unauthorized reproductions, and declining quality were sufficiently real to cause printmakers and dealers to become defensive and to seek reforms. Moran's interest was waning, and the large reproductive etchings he executed were symptomatic of his boredom. His last great etchings date to 1886, and the years from 1878 to 1886 were the most productive and inventive time for him and for his wife Mary.

Despite the loss of public interest in etching after 1890 and the appearance of a new generation of artists and printmakers with modernist ideas after 1900, Moran's career as a printmaker did not quite end in 1891. He never etched again, but a selection of his and Mary's etchings was reprinted in 1923. In a letter dated 21 February 1923, Ruth Moran wrote to Gustave H. Buek: "I have some beautiful prints of Fathers etchings (Mothers too) made while we were in New York by Peter Platt—and I am sending some soon to Milch—for sale, Fathers illness prevented them being all signed—now they are done—and I shall send a few of each to him."[90]

While these prints are marked in no special way, they do have two characteristics. One, they were apparently always printed with black ink, which is contrary to the warmer brownish blacks and even reddish browns in the 1880s but consistent with the 1920s. Two, they are printed on a soft, wove, slightly textured, faintly salmon-colored paper that has a slight deckle edge. This paper is unlike any used in the 1880s.[91] Impressions printed on this paper must have constituted much of what was left in the

19

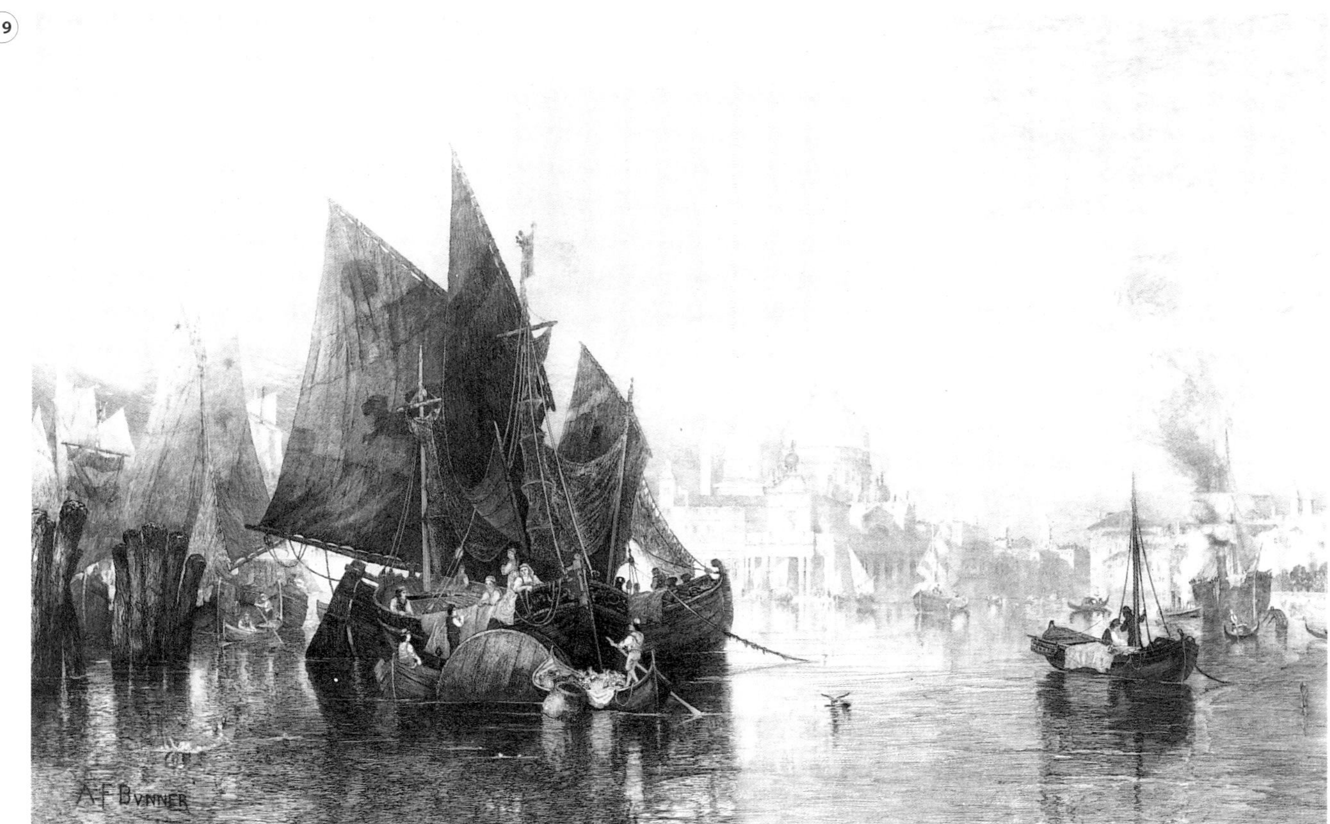

19. Thomas Moran after Andrew F. Bunner, *Venice*, 1887, etching and roulette, courtesy Gilcrease Museum, Tulsa, Oklahoma.

20. Thomas Moran, *The Gate of Venice*, 1888, etching and roulette, courtesy Gilcrease Museum, Tulsa, Oklahoma.

20

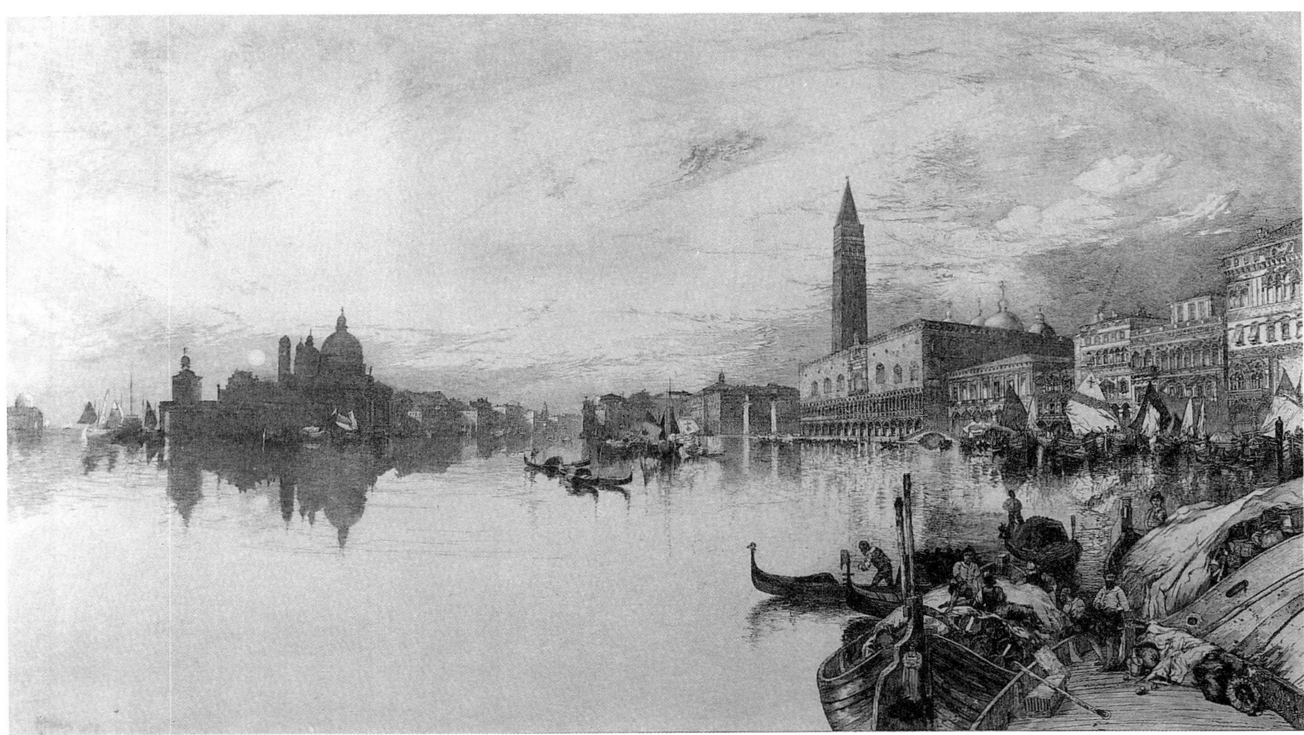

studio after Moran died. The quality of printing varies from impressions that look worn or lightly printed to others that are quite good. They mark, in any case, the end of Thomas Moran's career in the field of American printmaking.

Few artists in nineteenth-century America achieved as much as Thomas Moran did in the field of printmaking. While the discipline of wood or metal engraving ill suited his temperament and *cliché-verre* held little interest, etching and lithography exploited his strengths as a draftsman and colorist. Lithography offered Moran visually sophisticated results with little more technical knowledge needed than for sketching. Our loss was his inability to complete "Studies and Pictures" and the unfortunate paucity of existing impressions. Etching proved to Moran's liking as well, and the marketability of his work meant a substantial output. He became a leading figure in the decade of printmaking that witnessed a radical change in the attitude of artists, collectors, and the public toward the medium as a creative discipline. Moran's historical importance as a printmaker is marked by the stature his contemporaries accorded him, and his artistic importance by the beauty and creativity of the works that he etched and drew from 1860 to 1890. In his own words, he was a printmaker "of the first rank."

In 1878 a *Scribner's Monthly* article about tourism in Maine included the small wood engraving *Mt. Katahdin, a Famous Camping Ground* by Thomas Moran (fig. 1).[1] The modest image, one of several that accompanied the text and only one in a long series that Moran produced for the magazine over the course of many years, would be unremarkable if not for the self-conscious presentation of its subject and what that reveals about the artist and his commercial career.[2] The vignetted image of an interior corner focuses on a studio easel that supports a painted canvas. A painter's maulstick is propped against its side, and a palette and open paint box sit nearby, along with other canvases and a sketchbook. The canvas, a picture within a picture, is legibly signed "F.E. Church" in the lower right, and its mountain view replicates one of that artist's well-known compositions. Conspicuous in its tribute to the most famous American landscapist of the nineteenth century, the print is no less a meditation on the creative process, a contemplation of the relationship of nature to art, and an astute commentary on the role of reproductive imagery. As such it embodies a variety of concerns that preoccupied Thomas Moran throughout his long career.

By depicting a landscape within a studio and so prominently including the painter's tools, Moran emphasized the constructed nature both of Church's painted canvas and of the print that presumes to display it. Quite clearly

BY JONI L. KINSEY

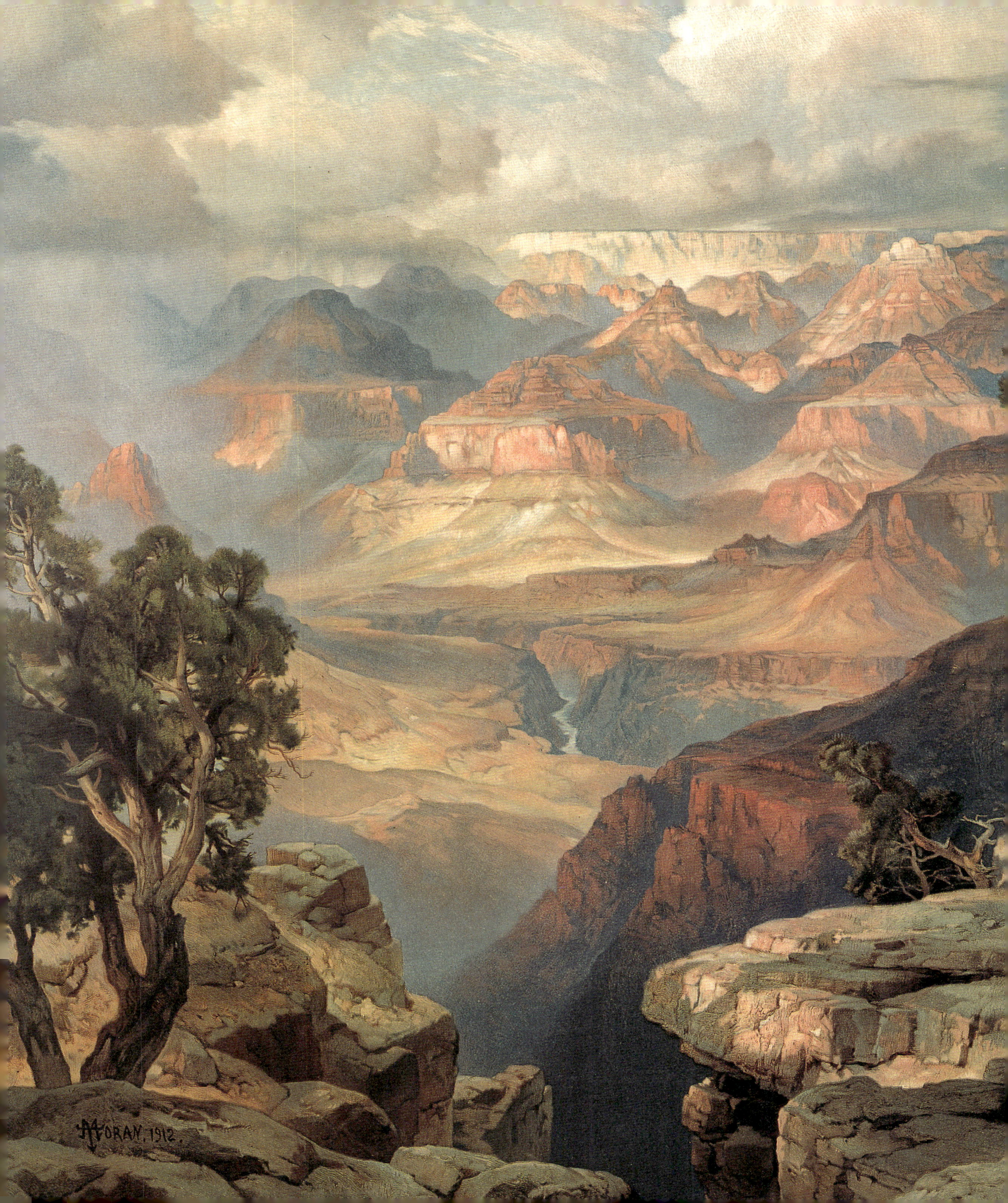
MORAN, 1912.

Preceding page: Color detail of *Grand Cañon from Hermit Rim* (fig. 17)

an artist has created this vision. The paradoxical caption, "Mt. Katahdin, a Famous Camping Ground, . . . Painted by Thomas Moran," and the additional signatures of both Moran and the engraver Frederick S. King, however, complicate the issue of authorship. The inclusion of the two extra signatures, for example, emphasizes the collaborative nature of the reproductive process and subverts the original artist's authority as primary intercessor between viewer and nature. These complications of course concern what Walter Benjamin so memorably defined as the "aura" of an original work of art and the problems that reproductions pose to it, but they also reflect Moran's understanding of the significance of different media in the late nineteenth century.[3] His illustration is in fact a sophisticated commentary on representation, reproduction, and land use.

Although the illustration is in one sense an homage to the "grand original" (Mount Katahdin itself) and a bow to Church's masterful rendition of it, Moran claimed it as an original composition by reinterpreting the subject and including his own monogram signature. Moreover, the work derives autonomy and cumulative power from its wide distribution through publication in *Scribner's* and by its subtle embodiment of attitudes toward American landscape. In *Mt. Katahdin* the subject is transformed from a sublime object of veneration to an enframed, consumable commodity. As he did in much of his art, Moran presents the land as *available*: for viewing, for contemplation, for tourism, or for purchase. The "Famous Camping Ground," as the article and picture imply, could be visited in Maine, hung on the wall in painted form, or held in the hand by magazine readers. In this way the illustration assumes a role different than a single, unique painting and makes land, art, and commerce available to a large audience. Recognizing this potential, Moran and his patrons used such published imagery to its full extent, especially in the decades after the Civil War when commercial publishing and land development reached unprecedented heights.

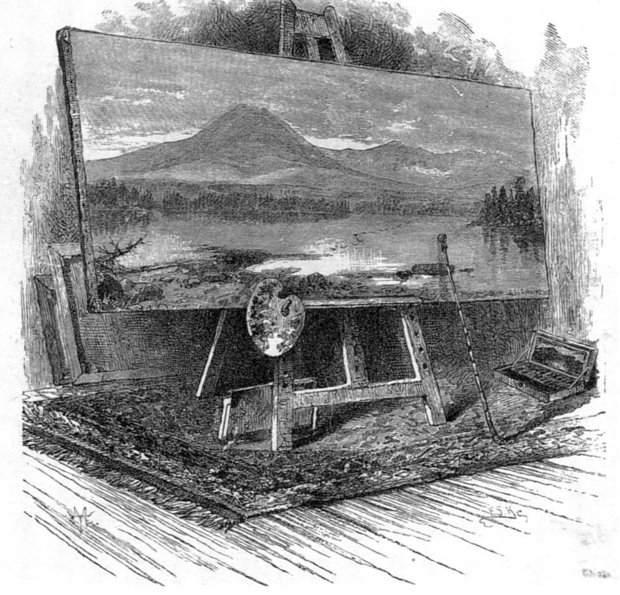

1. Thomas Moran, *Mt. Katahdin, a Famous Camping Ground,* wood engraving, published in *Scribner's Monthly* (May 1878), 33.

Availability: Problem or Achievement

At the same time Moran's commodification of landscape is a central issue in his commercial career, the very availability that it embodies in both subject and form impedes understanding of his achievements. His publishing activities helped make him professionally prominent, financially stable, and visually influential in shaping attitudes toward landscape after the Civil War, but they have also served to diminish his reputation in the twentieth century. Although his oeuvre is tightly integrated thematically, aesthetically, and circumstantially among various media, his published art, which too often has been displaced by his major paintings, has been relegated to a minor activity that is usually understood to have been driven by financial necessity. More than simply a shift in taste or aesthetic ideals, this perception can be attributed to efforts in the art world to devalue illustration as a fine art. While this has primarily been a twentieth-century phenomenon, its roots lay in the period during which Moran was most active and stem from many of the activities in which he was engaged. In its effect on attitudes toward his commercial art, this complex stratification of form and meaning is critical to understanding the significance of his work.

The artist himself did not argue that wood engravings or other published images were aesthetically equal to paintings, but neither did he dismiss them as mere reproductions or minor art. According to Moran, "Commercial work poses no threat to an artist. A good artist will express himself anyway."[4] For him such work was a vital part of his oeuvre, one that both benefited from and contributed to other aspects. For historians steeped in the aesthetic hierarchy that has elevated painting to the highest visual art, however, Moran's published work sacrificed its aura in its replication, diminished its prestige in its easy availability and prodigious quantity, and relinquished its soul in its service to commercial enterprise. For all these reasons and more, it is among the most intriguing aspects of his art.

Studying Moran's Commercial Oeuvre

Moran usually worked at painting and illustration simultaneously, creating oils and watercolors by day and drawing woodblocks at night when light was poor and color not a concern.[5] Subjects, motifs, and details recur in many images, both painted and printed, providing insights into the development of themes and into the artist's ideals and priorities. The correspondences between his paintings and commercial images are thus of primary importance for understanding his methods, aesthetic principles, and ultimate achievements as an artist.

Rarely focusing on other painters' work as he did in the *Mt. Katahdin* print, Moran more often created original designs for publication; and sometimes his paintings were inspired by his illustrations, inverting the expected process. The majority of his published imagery, estimated at over 2,000 images, was reproduced through wood engraving, the most common reproductive medium of his time, but he also created scenes that were replicated through steel engraving, lithography, chromolithography, and toward the end of his life, through photographically produced halftones and color letterpress.[6] His ability to complete so much work for publication was due to an indefatigable energy but also benefited from the assistance of his wife, Mary Nimmo Moran. Her involvement remains undetermined, since Moran never publicly acknowledged it, but a letter of 1873 indicates that it may have been substantial: "Work hard to improve your drawing, dear, as I shall have plenty of work for you this coming winter."[7] It was widely known by the 1880s that the couple shared an interest in printmaking, but beyond this provocative comment, little is known about Mary Nimmo's contributions to her husband's reputation as a major illustrator.

Studying Moran's reproductive work comprehensively is daunting, since he was so prolific and did not keep complete records of commercial assignments. Nineteenth-century publications did not always credit their illustrators, and articles that contain Moran's designs often include those of other artists as well. His monogram, which had the advantage of being legible in reverse in wood engraving, was not always included on the final carved blocks, and his prints sometimes lack signatures.[8] Yet although the subject matter in his images is often similar to that in works by other artists, his style is distinctive. The atmospheric subtlety and attention to chiaroscuro, texture, and detail that characterize his paintings are no less apparent in his graphic art and usually survived the wood engraving process.

Often confusing in Moran's published work are the frequent delays between original execution and publication. This, coupled with his tendency to repeat compositions and motifs in a number of versions and to date (sometimes erroneously) previously undated drawings in his later years, complicates attempts to determine correspondences among his sketches, paintings, and reproductive prints. An additional problem is the liberal sharing and outright pirating of illustrations by nineteenth-century publishers in the days before copyright enforcement.[9] This common activity resulted in identical or only slightly altered images appearing in very different publications, usually without notice or reimbursement to the artist. Signatures that appear in original versions were sometimes removed in secondary issues. In some instances these activities can be reconstructed, adding much to our understanding of the significance of illustrated material in the late nineteenth century and relationships among artists, publishers, government agencies, and railroads. Reproductions of Moran's work were most often acquired, however, through direct commissions by publishers, who, although interested in profit, sought to elevate public taste and to enhance the reputation of both the artist and their own publications through a judicious combination of text, illustrations, and high ideals. In so doing, they appealed to their readers' growing desire for visual imagery, provided an important venue for American artists' work, and allied themselves and their publications with the long-standing prestige of the fine arts.

Moran and the Rise of Publishing

Moran's commercial work is a virtual catalogue of the developments in reproductive technology during one of the industry's most formative periods, from 1850 to 1920. Not since the invention of moveable type had publishing experienced such change. New methods of making inexpensive paper, the refinement of wood engraving as a reproductive technique, the invention of steam-driven presses capable of exerting sufficient pressure to print engravings, and electroplating processes that transformed woodblocks into printable plates revolutionized the production of printed imagery.[10] Armed with the new technology, publishing houses and periodicals proliferated, prices for publications dropped, and more people than ever before gained access to published material in the United States.[11] A good deal of that material contained work by Thomas Moran.

Wood engraving, the medium of most of Moran's published work, was relatively new in commercial publishing in the nineteenth century, but it quickly became the medium of choice for printed illustrations. It differed from woodcut in that it used the end grain of boxwood rather than long-grain plank surface; and like other forms of intaglio, it printed from the incised lines rather than from the block's surface, allowing for much finer detail than the heavier woodcuts. It did have several disadvantages: it was limited to a single color, usually black, and was restricted to line, which ruled out true effects of continuous tone. Wood engraving also required craftspeople to engrave the blocks, resulting in translations that often caused artists great distress as they saw their drawings irrevocably altered. Moran was sensitive to this vulnerability and was appreciative when publishers, such as those at *The Aldine*, an art magazine that prided itself on its well-executed images, engraved his works well. He facilitated this as much as possible by working with publishers who employed the best engravers and by drawing directly on the blocks rather than submitting designs on paper that would have to be redrawn by others.[12] By working on the block, however, Moran sacrificed his original images, which were destroyed in the engraving process. This consequence prevents comparison of preparatory designs to their prints and accounts for the lack of drawings in Moran's oeuvre that correspond precisely to his published wood engravings.[13]

2

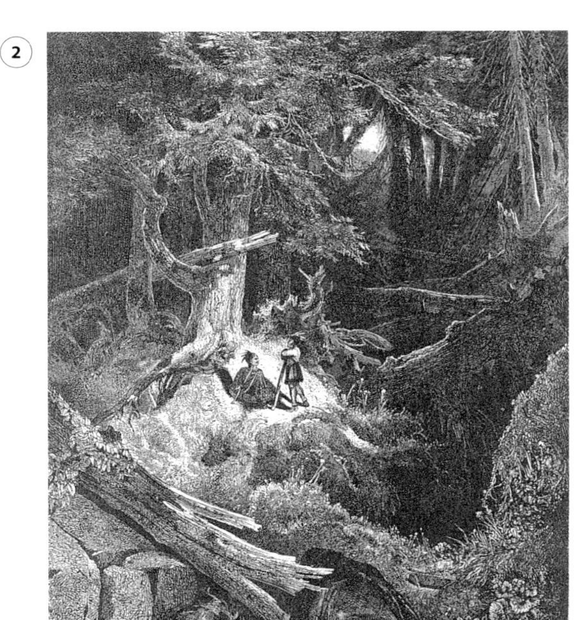

Moran was never explicit about the significance or potential meaning of his illustrative work. Other than brief mentions of profits or assignments and passing comments about being pleased or dissatisfied with the results, he rarely mentioned individual commissions and almost never reflected on his hopes for his commercial career as a whole. The fact that he did place his illustrative work almost exclusively with prominent publishers, however, suggests that through commercial work Moran hoped to contribute to illustration's position as a fine art and to enhance his own reputation as an artist.

Mass Production Versus Fine Art

Until photographically produced printing plates became the norm, which transferred pictorial replication into the realm of technology, the distinction between reproduction and creation, or illustrations and art, was slim. Wood engraving in the nineteenth century was recognized as a fine art form in the intaglio tradition, and it was not unusual to include wood engravings in exhibitions of more traditional media.[14] In 1875 the National Academy of Design exhibited three such prints by Moran within a larger display of paintings, and reviewers not only approved but also emphasized their appropriateness in such a context: "The mountain scenery of Utah, is represented with much force and grandeur in three large engravings on wood by Thomas Moran, that rank high as genuine works of art."[15] Late in life Moran also provided his biographer, Nina Spalding Stevens, with a series of prints and chromolithographs to be discussed with his paintings.[16] He considered this work part of his overall oeuvre and was never apologetic for its "lesser" status as art.

More problematic than arguments about art versus craft or commercialism that would later be employed to diminish the value of reproductions was the challenge to the art world posed by providing mass-produced visual imagery to an increasingly diverse public. The controversy concerned the role of art in society, the relative value of its different forms, and the impact of reproductive prints on America's cultural development.[17] Opinions were mixed: some regarded the growing plethora of visual media as a boon to the public's knowledge of art, while others saw it as the degradation of taste.[18] The latter perception became more dominant by the mid-twentieth century, but many critics during Moran's time considered reproductive imagery an important means of disseminating art and its ideals. In 1892, for example, William Coffin wrote, "More has been done through the medium of illustrated literature to make the masses of people realize that there is such a thing as art and that it is worth caring about."[19] Moran's illustrative career was thus grounded within a system that credited published art with elevating aesthetic values. Illustrations and reproductive images were to be encouraged for their contribution to a cultured society.

Literary Publications

Moran's first published illustrations seem to have been two small wood engravings in Nathaniel Parker Willis' *Sacred Poems* (1860).[20] The commission, which also included a view by Edward Moran, may have been recommended by James Hamilton, the Moran brothers' mentor, who was represented by four images. These unassuming vignettes are most notable for the author's prominence; Willis was one of the most popular writers and publishers of the time. His important early travel book, *American Scenery* (1838–1842), had been illustrated with 125 engraved views by William Henry Bartlett and set a standard for landscape promotion, making even Moran's modest contribution to the later publication rather prestigious.[21] It was an auspicious beginning to Moran's long career as a literary illustrator.

3

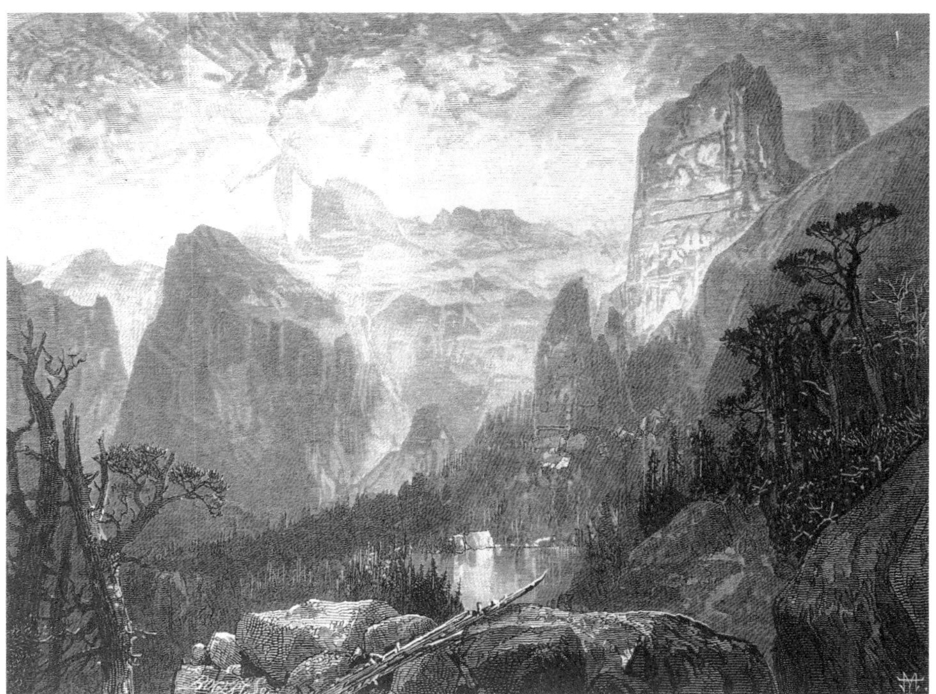

2. Thomas Moran, *Kwasind, the Strong Man,* wood engraving, published in *The Aldine* 5 (June 1872), cover.

3. Thomas Moran, *The Song of Hiawatha,* wood engraving, published in *The Poetical Works of Henry Wadsworth Longfellow* (Boston, 1882), 223.

Although Moran illustrated many different kinds of texts, one of his favorites was Longfellow's famous poem, *The Song of Hiawatha* (1855), which remained extremely popular throughout the nineteenth century. The artist produced several oils and a large number of wood engravings and wash drawings devoted to the theme and planned a special edition of steel engravings in the mid-1870s to capitalize on the commercial appeal of "America's first written epic."[22]

Moran's first wood engravings from *Hiawatha* were also his first for *The Aldine.* His *Kwasind, the Strong Man* (fig. 2), appeared on the June 1872 cover, followed the next year by two works in the article "The Pictured Rocks of Lake Superior."[23] The text in 1873 was devoted primarily to the area's geology, but the earlier publication not only recounted the tale of Kwasind and Longfellow's interest in the story but also offered intriguing commentary on contemporary interpretations of *Hiawatha.* Agreeing that the poem was very "American," the author noted that its appeal lay in the mythic heroism of Native Americans, a quality missing from their own time: "There is another side to America than that which its aborigines have turned to the gaze of the world. There is the early Puritan side, grim and stern as a battle-frieze on some old temple, alive with determined combatants; there is the Colonial and Revolutionary side, wherein pastoral and warlike scenes are strangely mingled; and there is the side of To-Day, bustling, money-making—unheroic."[24] The passage continued: "All these elements must be taken into consideration by the poet who shall aspire to write the one great American Poem." The same might be said, as Moran surely realized, of the one who aspires to create "great American art." Even his most idealized commercial works embodied *The Aldine*'s challenge: they aspired to a mythical heroism of a natural America but were firmly grounded within the "bustling, money-making [and] unheroic" context of his own era.

Moran's most ambitious use of the Hiawatha theme was his 1875 attempt to publish an illustrated edition of Longfellow's poem, with twenty-five large steel engravings of his drawings and his brother Peter as engraver.[25] Unlike other ventures in which he sold work or copyrights to publishers, this project was to be self-published and may have been meant to capitalize on nationalistic feelings as the centennial approached. The brothers enlisted a prestigious group of subscribers, including President Ulysses S. Grant, General William Tecumseh Sherman, the railroad magnate Collis P. Huntington, Mark Twain, and Longfellow himself. Unfortunately the project was never completed.[26] As early as May 1876 Moran reported without explanation, "Work on the etchings of Hiawatha has come to a stand still."[27] He exhibited several of the drawings at the Centennial Exposition that year but kept them, unpublished, for the rest of his life. He did contribute to a few Longfellow anthologies, including the lavishly illustrated, four-volume *Poetical Works of Henry Wadsworth Longfellow* (1879 and 1882; fig. 3), but his interest in the Hiawatha theme waned after 1876, perhaps because of the failure of the engraving project.

Despite its dissatisfying conclusion, the proposal's ambitiousness is undeniable, and although Moran never again attempted private publishing, he facilitated other special edition reproductions of his work throughout his life. His ability to enlist such significant support for the engraving project demonstrates the stature to which he had risen by the mid-1870s as well as the entrepreneurial spirit that sought a place for his art in the "money-making—unheroic" world.

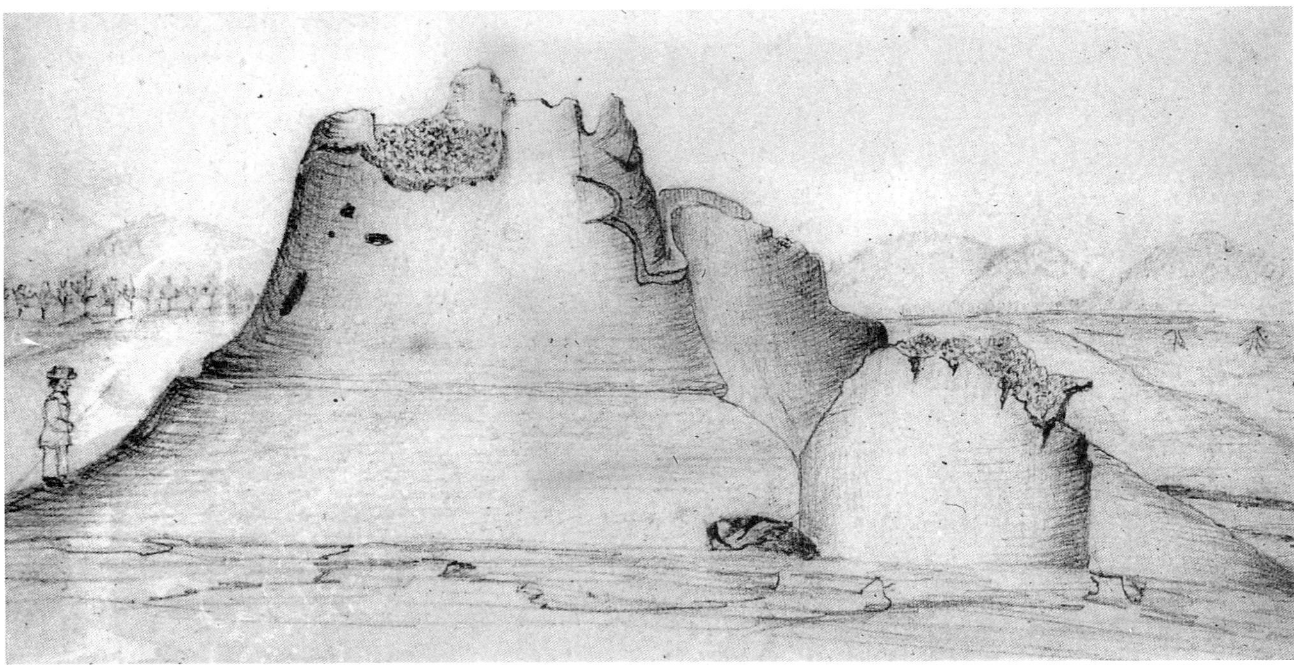

4. Walter Trumbull, *Castle Geyser Cone,* 1870, graphite on paper, courtesy Department of the Interior, Yellowstone National Park.

5. Thomas Moran after Walter Trumbull, *Castle Geyser Cone,* wood engraving, published in *Scribner's Monthly* 2 (May 1871), 125.

Scribner's Monthly

Although Moran aspired to illustrate literary epics, the impetus for his art usually came from magazines, book publishers, government surveys, and railroad publicity departments. In the decades after the Civil War—with an ever-expanding railway network, new sources of commercial enterprise, and a burgeoning reading public—each of these types of patrons sought the best means to promote American expansion and growth, and landscape art such as Moran's suited many of their needs. It suggested a progressive vision at the same time it underscored traditional aesthetic values, and when combined with text, it could accommodate a host of agendas, from the overtly commercial to the inspirational. While Moran constantly endeavored to monumentalize the prospect of the American land, he simultaneously worked in the service of industry, making such scenes available to an ever-wider public via his commercial imagery.

Of all Moran's patrons, *Scribner's Monthly* was the most faithful: he illustrated over one hundred articles for the magazine during its lifetime, 1870 to 1881, and he contributed images to many of the company's other publications, including books and magazines such as *St. Nicholas* for children and *Century Magazine*, which succeeded *Scribner's Monthly* in 1881.[28] *Scribner's Monthly* was conceived as a rival to *Harper's Monthly*, which had grown tremendously popular, largely because of its wood engraved illustrations, and *Scribner's* sought to supersede that position through its own essays, editorials, and stories, and its profusion of high-quality wood engravings.[29] Just as important, *Scribner's* took an activist position in promoting land for a variety of uses. It extolled the virtues of pleasure travel, applauded the achievements of industry, chronicled the progress of states and regions, and celebrated the government's role in making progress available to people. Although he always worked on commission rather than salary, Moran became the principal landscape illustrator for such stories precisely because his art visually underscored this agenda.

Moran's close relationship with *Scribner's* was due in part to his friendship with Richard Watson Gilder, the managing editor in charge of the art department, and Alexander Drake, the art editor. Gilder had been a childhood friend of Moran's in Bordentown, Pennsylvania, and all three men were neighbors, first in Philadelphia and then later in Newark and New York. Gilder became prominent in the literary world and was unfailing in his support for Moran. An erstwhile poet, Gilder and his wife, the artist Helena de Kay Gilder, surrounded themselves with leading writers and artists, including Moran, and they introduced him to many leading industrialists and potential patrons.[30]

Scribner's prided itself on its service to cultural advancement, and its defense of illustration and technological innovation reinforced that claim. Moran was equally committed to these issues, and his alliance with the magazine offered him many opportunities to contribute to the cause and to convey its merits to a growing audience.

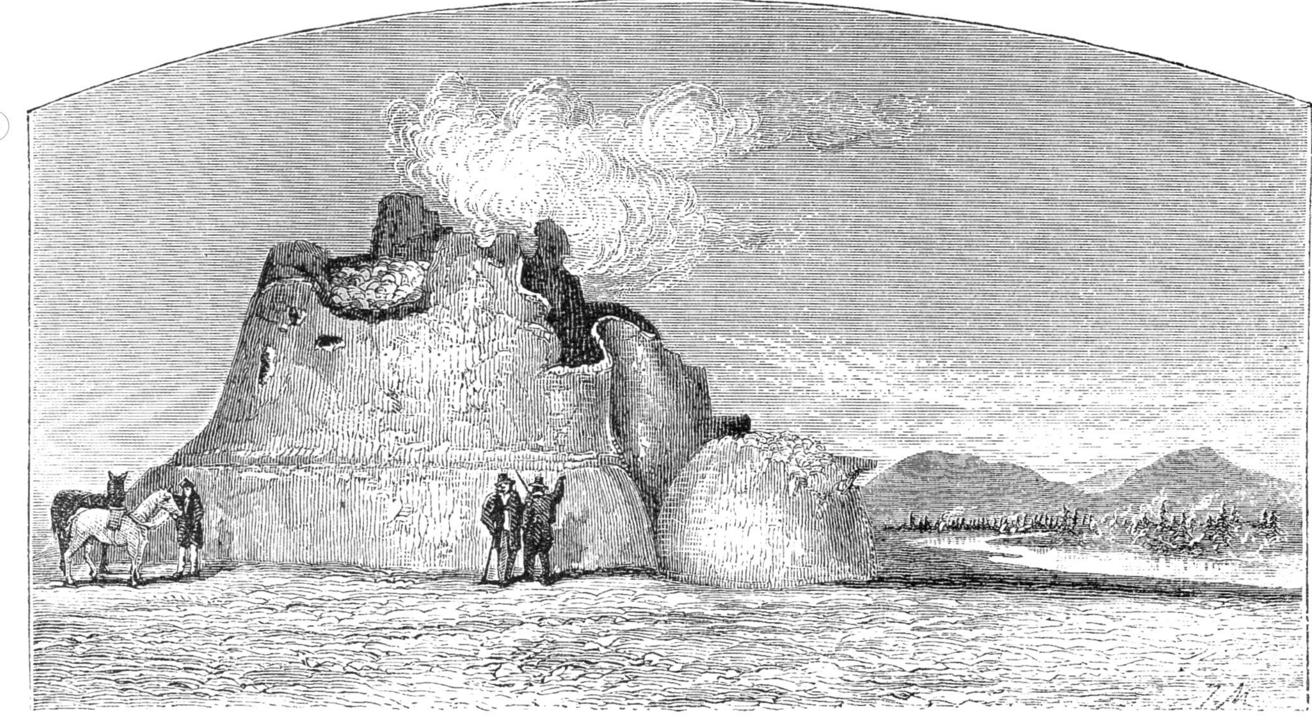

5

Popularizing Western Prospects

Moran's work appeared in *Scribner's* premiere issue in November 1870 and in five other articles during that journal's first year of publication. Almost immediately Gilder offered Moran a commission that ultimately changed the course of the artist's career—a story on the virtually undocumented region of Yellowstone. In this instance he was not asked to make original drawings but to rework the first sketches of the area that the Washburn-Doane expedition had just brought back. Those graphite views (fig. 4) had been produced by Walter Trumbull and Private Charles Moore, two amateur artists in the party. Although Moran had never seen the sights, he was able to enhance the scenes' appeal and approximate to a remarkable degree the appearance of the exotic formations (fig. 5).

Shortly before the illustrations appeared in the May and June issues of *Scribner's Monthly* in 1871, Moran was invited to join Ferdinand Hayden's Geographical and Geological Survey of the Territories.[31] The origin of the idea that Moran should go remains uncertain, but the 1870–1871 illustrative project and *Scribner's* close association with the Northern Pacific Railroad (NPRR) played a major role. Since the magazine was interested in obtaining images of the landscape, and the railroad was planning its line through the area, all involved recognized the value in having a noted artist bring back pictures of the mysterious region.[32]

To realize this visual product, *Scribner's* and the NPRR provided the means for Moran to travel with Hayden. Intriguingly, their assistance did not come in the form of an outright cash advance or even reimbursement of expenses. Instead, Moran left the painting *Children of the Mountain* (cat. 7) with *Scribner's* publisher Roswell Smith as collateral for $500, which he "did not redeem," and he received another $500 from Jay Cooke of the NPRR in return for a series of watercolors painted after the trip.[33] Moran said later it had not occurred to him that the magazine should have financed this trip, but although his way was often paid in future travels, he continued to make such arrangements from time to time.[34]

These negotiations reveal more about nineteenth-century business practice than either the lack of funding standards or mere penury on the part of publishing companies. By putting Moran in touch with railroad executives who could offer discount or free rail fare, and by smoothing his way into government surveys, the publishers were at once aligning themselves with the artists with whom they were working and with the leaders at the forefront of American expansionist enterprise in the hope of fostering good will. In working with the NPRR and with Hayden, the magazine agreed to promote the activities of both the survey and the railroad, and in turn it received primary reports that promised an edge in the competitive publishing world. The survey would receive favorable publicity that could lead to increased appropriations, and the railroad would benefit from free advertising, which would sell more bonds and eventually tickets. More generally, all of the parties were working together for what they perceived to be the common good of American progress. In their cooperative efforts they all focused on how Moran's art would advance their interests. He most certainly fulfilled their expectations.

A New Intensity

As if to confirm his more active involvement with the publishing industry, within months of his return from Yellowstone in the fall of 1871 Moran moved his family from Philadelphia to Newark to be closer to his publishing patrons.[35] He had been creating illustrations for over a decade, but it was at this time that the commercial part of his career developed most dramatically. Throughout the 1870s and 1880s his commissions, especially for wood engraving designs but increasingly for chromolithographs, grew substantially. His most important patron continued to be *Scribner's Monthly*, but he published as well with the rival *Harper's*, the fine art periodical *The Aldine*, and many others. All of these journals issued significant articles about Yellowstone and other regions, and they continued to support the artist for many years.

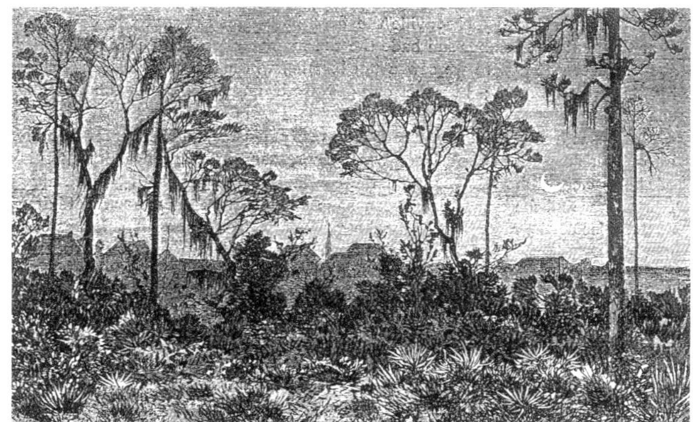

6

6. Thomas Moran, *Moonlight over Jacksonville, Florida,* wood engraving, published in Edward King's *The Great South* (1875), 377.

7. Thomas Moran, *Medmenham Abbey,* wood engraving, published in *Harper's Monthly* 62 (January 1881), 213.

Moran's work for *Scribner's Monthly* was exceptionally varied. Some of it focused on exotic sites that he would never encounter; other subjects were closer to home. Little correspondence is available to reveal how these commissions were arranged, but it is clear that Moran did not always create original compositions; prolific production required the expeditious use of sources. For Edward King's extensive series, "The Great South," for example, which ran in the magazine from 1873 to 1875 and was reprinted as a book in 1875, Moran made over fifty illustrations, working from the drawings of J. Wells Champney, the artist who had accompanied the author through the region.[36] The series, which was oriented toward southern conditions since the Civil War, was geographically and thematically comprehensive and included historical overviews and observations on race relations as well as commentary on notable sites and developments. Although not overly celebratory, it did consistently emphasize the region's promise for commercial reincorporation into the Union, among other issues of continuing interest to *Scribner's* readers.

Moran's images in the articles range from scenes in Indian Territory and San Antonio to industrial cityscapes, orange groves, and tropical swamps farther east (fig. 6). He often included small figures in the foregrounds as surrogates or metaphorical companions for his viewers and sometimes shaped his compositions into arched or circular vignettes to provide additional interest and three-dimensionality. Most often he presented elevated perspectives, a "magisterial gaze" or "prospect" that invited a sense of ownership and conveyed the idea of the availability and potential of the land.[37]

The Great South project resulted in a trip to Florida for an 1877 *Scribner's* article, "An Island of the Sea." The state's northern Atlantic coast near Jacksonville was being recognized as a tourist destination, and Moran was enlisted to visit Fort George Island at the mouth of the St. Johns River, just east of Jacksonville. The region was of special interest to northerners since it was accessible by water (rail service began in the early 1880s), and of course it boasted an exceptional climate that was touted for both its warmth and its curative properties. By the time Moran arrived in the mid-1870s, tourism was booming, with an estimated 50,000 visitors annually.[38] Moran's Florida work thus had much in common with his western activities, especially in its emphasis on tourism for pleasure, exotic scenery, health, and economic investment. Yet the Fort George Island vicinity, with its tropical vegetation and uniquely southern history, especially in regard to slavery, offered uncommon subject matter and posed special challenges that ultimately interested Moran less than those of other regions.

The sheer volume of Moran's work for Scribner and Company would require a lengthy study unto itself. In addition to the *Monthly*, he contributed to many of the company's books and to its children's publication *St. Nicholas*. When *Scribner's Monthly* became the *Century Magazine* in the 1880s, Moran was producing fewer illustrations in general, but he did provide some for that periodical as well. In November 1879, shortly before the magazine's title changed, the artist wrote in his ledger, "This is probably the last drawing I shall ever make for *Scribner's*."[39] Even though he did continue to work for the company in other ways, Moran recognized in this statement the significant role that

Scribner's Monthly had played in launching his career as an artist of national standing.

In summary, Moran provided illustrations to many general readership periodicals of the day. Most notable among these were *Scribner's Monthly*, *Harper's Monthly* (fig. 7), *The Aldine*, as well as a few images to *Harper's Weekly*.[40] All of these publications brought the American landscape to the public in important ways and contributed to Moran's growing reputation. They directed his printed art at a growing appreciation not only for the scenery of the United States but for art as well, and Moran's prolific work was an important means of satisfying those interests.

Railroad Guidebooks

Moran had a long history of working for railway companies, helping to promote them via illustrated travel articles. His first illustrations for *Harper's Monthly*, for example, complemented an 1862 article entitled "The Catawissa Railroad," based on drawings he made nearly a decade earlier during a family outing to Catawissa, Pennsylvania, on the Susquehanna River.[41] He later inscribed one view, *The Catawissa Valley*, as "one of my earliest drawings on wood," and it was published as *The Town of Catawissa* (fig. 8), complete with train tracks running through the scene.[42]

The earliest railroad publication to contain Moran's views, *Guidebook to the West Chester and Philadelphia Railroad*, appeared in 1869 and included fourteen lithographs advertising the scenery and amenities of a small trunk line into the Philadelphia suburbs (see fig. 7, p. 289). Some of the large number of guidebooks to which Moran later contributed also stand out. Several had their origins in 1881, an exceptionally busy summer for the artist. In July, having just returned from a sketching trip to Niagara Falls for *Picturesque Canada*, Moran joined writer Joseph Gladding Pangborn and engraver "Apple" Jack Karst on an extended tour along the Baltimore and Ohio Railroad. Pangborn, who had already published *The Rocky Mountain Tourist* (1877) with three of Moran's views, enlisted the artist as the sole illustrator in his more ambitious *Picturesque B. & O.: Historical and Descriptive* (1882), which eventually included sixty-eight of Moran's illustrations.[43]

7

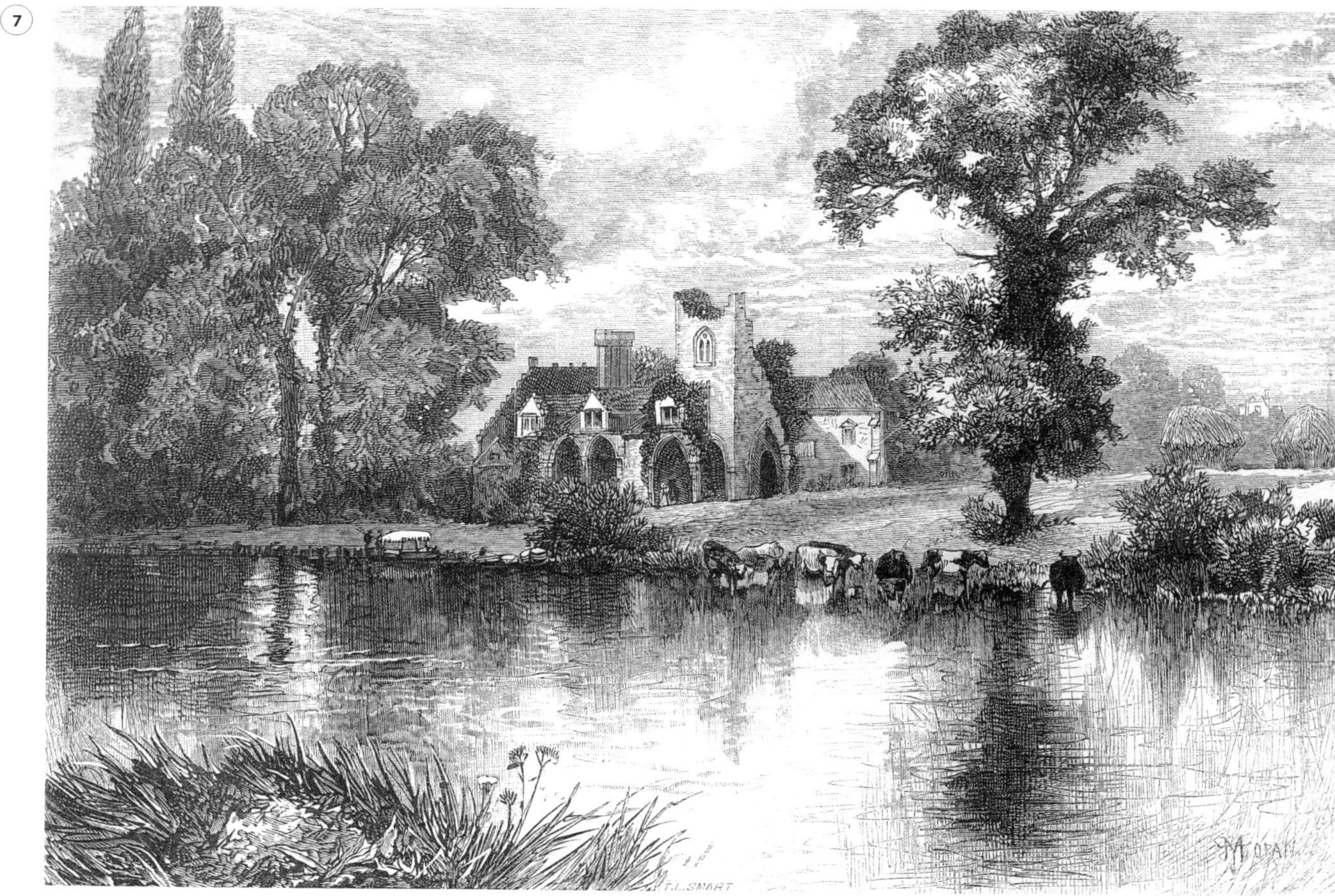

8. Thomas Moran, *The Town of Catawissa,* wood engraving, published in *Harper's Monthly* 25 (June 1862), 27.

9. *The Black Cañon,* c. 1881, photograph by William Henry Jackson, courtesy Colorado Historical Society.

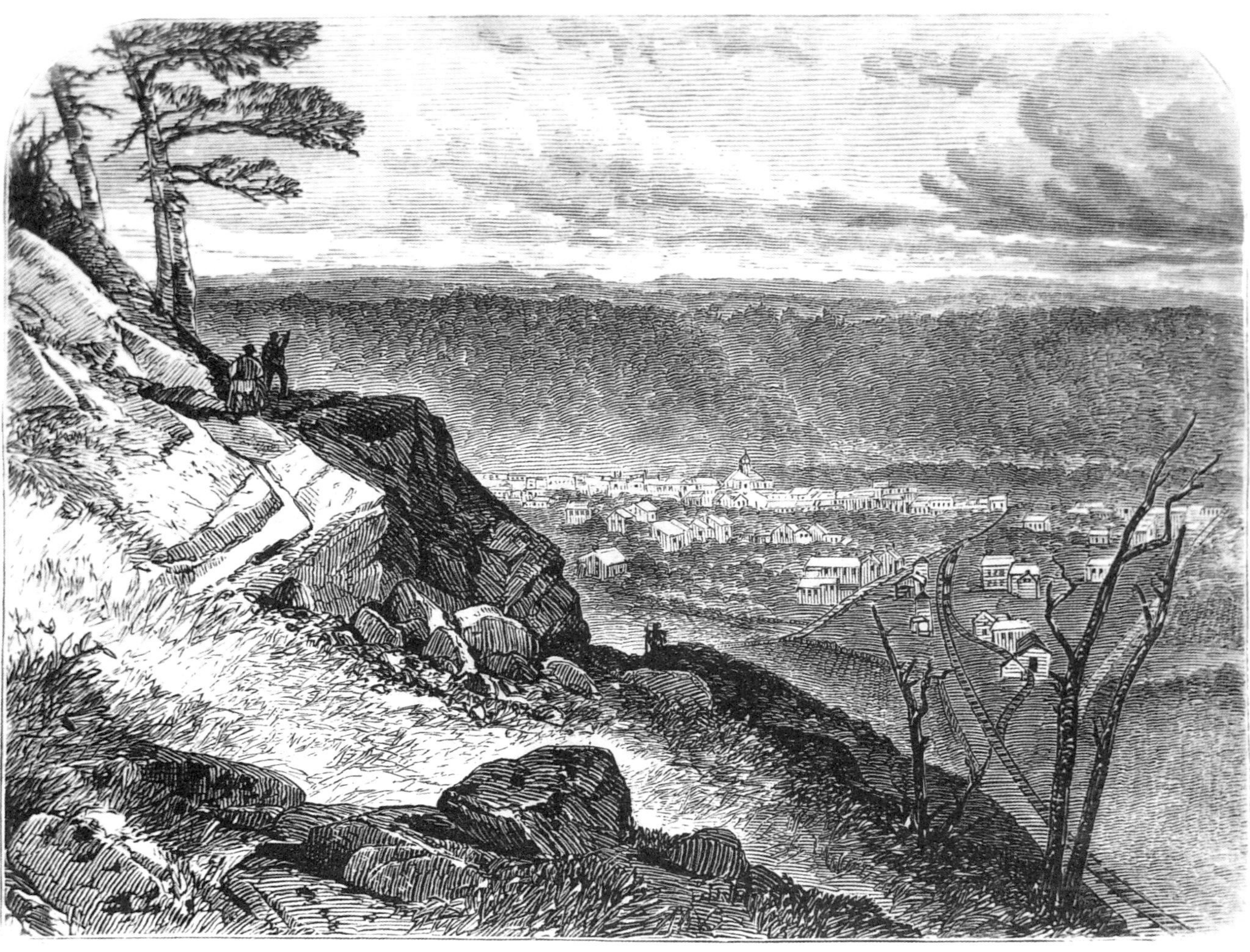

8

Pangborn's text is a much livelier narrative than most travel guides, even counting its lengthy attention to the history of the B. & O. Each member in the party, for example, acquired a nickname. Moran is referred to as "Yellowstone," and his contribution is noted more prominently than usual for such publications. The preface states, "The single fact that Thomas Moran furnished upwards of seventy entirely new drawings... would at once establish its surpassingly high character in the first artistic circles of the continent."[44] This was the greatest number of images he produced for any single publication.

In keeping with the book's visual emphasis, Pangborn constantly directed his reader to imagine the metaphorical trip in aesthetic terms. Ever mindful of presenting the railroad as a force for enlightenment in a growing country, Pangborn combined the visual, the industrial, and the natural as engagingly as possible. In similar fashion Moran drew several landscapes as he had done with *Mt. Katahdin* years before, depicting them as sketches or paintings propped on the floor, pinned to a wall, framed by curtains, or resting on an easel. The message is clear: the land is available, consumable, and transportable via the railroad. The combined efforts of Pangborn, Moran, and Karst made this project seem easy, fun, and creative.

Maintaining their breakneck pace in August that same summer, Karst and Moran headed to Denver to join photographer William H. Jackson and writer Ernest Ingersoll for a trip on the Denver and Rio Grande Railway. William Bell, vice-president of D & RG, had recently purchased Moran's painting *Mountain of the Holy Cross* (cat. 53), and he commissioned the men to help promote the new industrial and tourist lines that the company was building in the Rockies.[45] Moran and his companions were provided with a private train that had a special open car (fig. 9), and with such accommodations they created what would form the core of Colorado promotional material for many years to come.

A number of publications resulted from the 1881 excursion—several Ingersoll books, including *Crest of the Continent* (1885), an article in *Harper's Monthly* entitled "The Silver San Juan," an issue of the *Colorado Tourist*, and numerous guidebooks and literature—all containing Moran's illustrations. These wood engravings dominated the D & RG's public relations literature throughout the 1880s, especially the several editions of *Rhymes of the Rockies*, an illustrated book of poetry that linked Moran's views with literary musings on landscape.[46] Other railroads also used some of his D & RG illustrations, both with and without permission. The Chicago and Alton Railroad, for example, reprinted *Mountain of the Holy Cross* in several of its timetables in the 1880s and 1890s.

Moran worked for several other leading railroads. His 1879 trip through the Sierra Nevada with his brother Peter was at least partly funded by a commission from the Union Pacific, and as late as 1887 that line was republishing his illustrations in their guidebooks.[47] Throughout most of his long life Moran benefited from and in turn contributed to the vast changes in and perceptions about the transportation industry. His work provided ways of integrating those perceptions into a new vision of an industrial, incorporated America.

Guidebooks and Government Reports

Moran's work for government agencies, especially those "Great Surveys" headed by Ferdinand Hayden and John Wesley Powell, was intricately connected with his work for the publishing industry and the railroads. Both survey leaders recognized that well-illustrated reports and public attention from notable paintings resulted in increased government appropriations, and they consequently used Moran's art to the fullest. These men, in search of images for their official congressional reports, often worked closely with Moran's publishers rather than with the artist himself, and they provided illustrations to other publishers without notifying either the original owners or the artist. These interrelationships reveal the high level of interest in Moran's work and a passionate belief in its ability to convey a variety of ideas and ideals to a disparate audience.

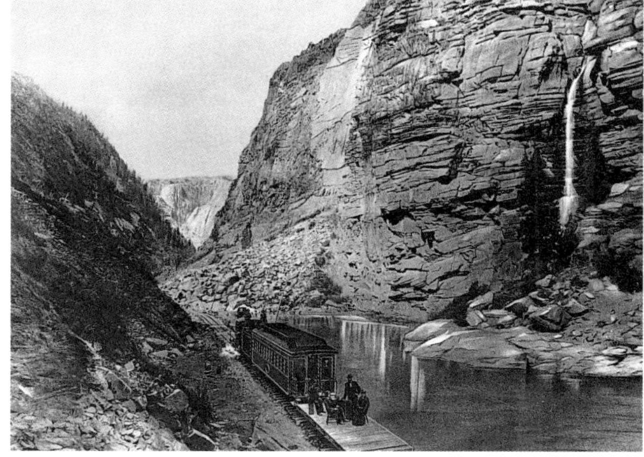

9

Although Hayden and Powell worked with many publishers, they relied heavily on *Scribner's Monthly* for Moran's illustrations and for an avenue to publicize their expeditions. Each wrote articles for the magazine and negotiated to use Moran's engravings in their own publications. These relationships began in early 1871, when *Scribner's* facilitated Moran's participation in Hayden's expedition. Shortly after his return, *Scribner's Monthly* commissioned Hayden to write a follow-up article to Langford's earlier introduction to the region.[48] Moran was already creating new illustrations, but a problem arose when Hayden assumed the magazine would allow him free reprinting rights in his federal report because he had accommodated the artist. In the end Hayden prevailed, but the approval came with a revealing admonition from editor Gilder.

> I enclose a check for $100 for your article....the publishers of the monthly really cannot afford to go to such large expense for original illustrations without getting back part of it from some quarter. Even Harper's, with its immense resources and circulation has largely depended upon reproductions. And it cheapens the illustrations to have them appear in reports, etc. We hardly ever allow the wood-cuts themselves to go out of our possession, even temporarily. The cuts accompanying your article cost about $500 and we thought that Uncle Sam would be rich enough to pay at least half [the] cost. But if it is a matter of your own purse, we will immediately pack up the blocks and send them to you that you may have electrotypes taken as you desire—*Providing* that you guarantee us against damage, and also against the use of the plates in any publications save your report....We will express the blocks to you to morrow. Now in this matter the publishers have acted promptly upon my suggestions and I look to you to stand by me my dear Dr.! If in the future we can get back some of this western money, legitimately, from the government, I hope you will help to that end—and that you will do all in your power to make the fourth of my articles, full, graphic, and *successful*![49]

Twelve of the sixty-four illustrations in Hayden's 1871 government report were thus provided free from *Scribner's*. Moran was not paid an additional fee, nor was he directly acknowledged in Hayden's text as their creator. Furthermore, Hayden did not comply with Gilder's request that the *Scribner's* wood engravings not be used elsewhere. He published his own book on the West in 1880 with ten of the illustrations and liberally provided them to guidebook writers in exchange for free publicity.[50] His unscrupulous sharing of electrotypes without credit or payment to the artist is ironic at best, since Hayden was sensitive to accounts of his discoveries that did not acknowledge him or his survey. He did contract Moran directly for some images, and he paid promptly for them, but his aggressive activities to secure their use demonstrates his own ambition and his recognition of the ability of Moran's imagery to convey his agenda.

John Wesley Powell, with whom Moran traveled to the Grand Canyon in 1873, also worked closely with Gilder, both in writing articles for *Scribner's Monthly* and in obtaining images for inclusion in his government report. Gilder, however, had learned a lesson with Hayden, and he drew up an official contract with Powell. In exchange for writing three articles for the magazine and a fee of $500 for the wood engravings, Powell assumed ownership of the electrotypes and their future use.[51]

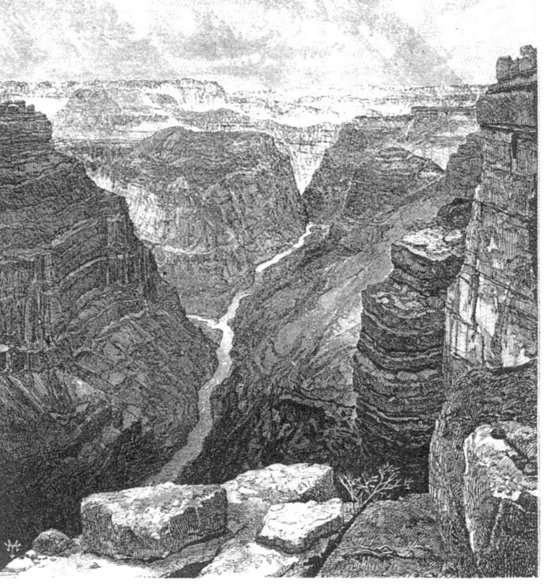

10

10. Thomas Moran, *Grand Cañon, at the Foot of To-Ró-Weap, Looking West,* wood engraving, published in *Scribner's Monthly* 9 (March 1875), 526.

11. Thomas Moran, *Springville Cañon,* wood engraving, published in *The Aldine* 7 (January 1874), 14.

The twenty-four illustrations Moran produced for Powell's three-part article, "The Cañons of the Colorado" (1875) number among the finest he created for *Scribner's*.[52] Although many of them were taken directly from Jack Hillers and E.O. Beaman's photographs from the Powell expedition, Moran redrew them in ways that accentuate his own style. The textural effects in *The Grand Cañon, at the Foot of To-Ró-Weap, Looking West* (fig. 10), for example, correspond closely to the painterly qualities in his color works. All the images ultimately reappeared in Powell's official report and later books.

Interested in promoting his own work, Powell generously shared the wood engravings. Henry T. Williams, for example, author and publisher of *The Pacific Tourist*, requested them, even though he worked directly with Moran for other illustrations.[53] Williams wrote to Powell in January 1876: "Mr. Thos. Moran is now engaged in making some drawings of Far Western Scenery for a new book which I am about to publish and I desire to include in it some mention of the Grand Cañon of the Colorado. I write to you at his suggestion to ask if you will sell me electrotypes of any of the illustrations which have appeared in Scribner's Mag [*sic*]—and at what prices—also if you can prepare for me an article description."[54]

Since Williams wrote three times with the same request for specific plates, it is uncertain whether Powell ever consented, but it is interesting that the request came at Moran's suggestion. The artist obviously considered illustrations for which he had been paid to be the property of their owners, and he did not expect to profit from their additional use. Much later, in the 1890s, some of these illustrations were reissued in several books, including Stanley Wood's *Over the Range to the Golden Gate* (rev. ed., 1895) and Charles Higgins' *The Grand Canyon* (1902). Obviously, the *Scribner's* wood engravings continued their usefulness long after the 1870s.

Through the alliance of government surveys, the popular press, and the railroads, Moran's images reached infinitely more viewers than they would have otherwise. Moreover, they contributed significantly to the understanding of the American continent in the late nineteenth century, to the development and industrialization of the American landscape, and to the establishment and popularity of the national parks. More than any original paintings could hope to affect, his published art helped establish the public's awareness of the natural wealth and potential of the United States as the country moved into its second century.

Art in *The Aldine*

In addition to the overtly commercial use of Moran's art to promote expansion and enterprise, his published work served more consciously aesthetic agendas. His wood engravings in *The Aldine*, for example, are among his most beautiful prints. The journal prided itself on quality illustrations, and Moran contributed more than thirty-nine images to its pages from 1872 to 1879.[55] He regarded them highly, as he remarked to Powell in 1873: "Will send you the January no. of the Aldine with the three of my Utah drawings which are the best pieces of engraving that have ever been made from my drawings.... Springville Cañon [fig. 11] is particularly fine."[56] The magazine employed the best engravers and often devoted entire pages to single images, making clear that it considered wood engravings an important art form.

Like most nineteenth-century periodicals, *The Aldine* went through a series of changes during its eleven years of production. As a "typographical art journal," its emphasis on illustrations was limited at the time of its founding in 1868. By the early 1870s, however, it focused more intently on art concerns, including landscape interpretation.[57] Moran's work is included in five of the nine volumes that the magazine produced.[58]

Even as *The Aldine* identified itself as an art journal, it was no less a lavish travel magazine, and Moran was one of its most important assets in this regard. Through his work it was able to join the fervent national enthusiasm for the West and for other established or potential tourist areas, such as Lake George (fig. 12); the Juniata, Vermont; and the Pictured Rocks at Lake Superior. The magazine featured his most dramatic compositions and combined them with text emphasizing their beauty and the sites' accessibility via rail, their climatic conditions and cultivation, and other issues of interest to tourists and investors.

11

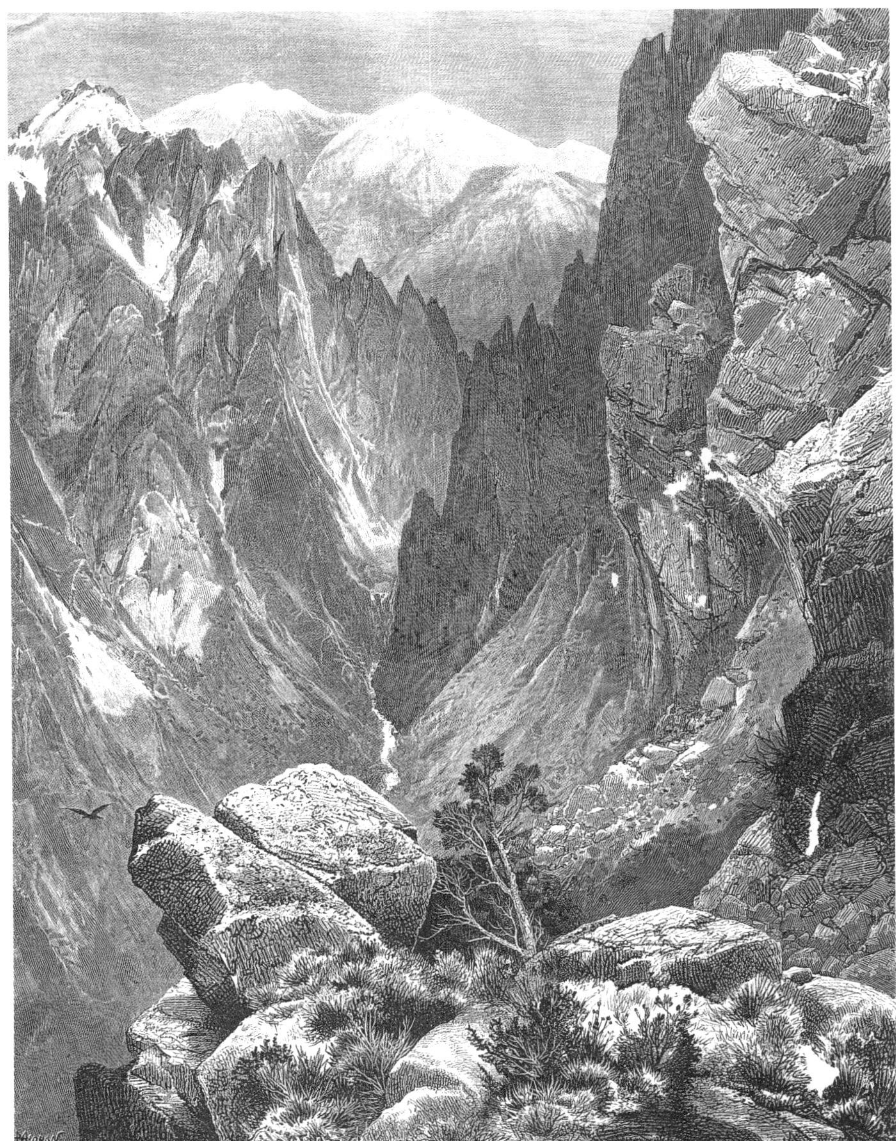

The Aldine was not usually overt in its industrial promotion, but it did consistently reiterate in both text and image that it was helping make American art and landscape available to its readers. Its article on Yellowstone, for instance, pointedly commends Moran's efforts to "open to us" that remarkable region: "The Yellowstone region evades description, and almost evades art. What art can do for it Mr. Thomas Moran has shown in his great picture painted for Congress, and in the illustrations which he has drawn for the present number of *The Aldine*. They open to us a world as wild as the one we see in dreams,—a strange and beautiful wonderland, and they are—but we will not bias the judgment of the reader with regard to them, he can see for himself what they are."[59]

The phrase "strange and beautiful wonderland" reveals that by 1873 this trope had become the conventional description of the new park. Moran's published and painted works accentuated the "wild" aspects of the West but had also been integral to transforming Yellowstone into a "wonderland." His art influenced attitudes toward American landscapes to the point that it offered entirely new discursive modes for a region.[60]

Special Commissions: The Illustrated Book

As all of Moran's publishers recognized, the most popular illustrated books in the nineteenth century in both the United States and England contained landscape views.[61] Armchair travel was a favorite pastime, and scenic images accompanied literary texts, poetry, history books, textbooks, and commemorative editions to appeal to this taste. Books had a special authority that influenced attitudes toward landscape in ways not possible with other publications, and Moran both benefited from and contributed to this development through a large number of commissions from book publishers.

Scribner and Company continued to be among his most important patrons in its book division, soliciting new work from him and reprinting images from its journal. New editions were certainly fiscally sensible in a competitive industry, but they also indicate the popularity and efficacy of the subject matter and, by extension, of Moran's images.[62] In addition to travel books, Scribner's also showcased his landscapes in history texts. One of the most important, and most influential in shaping American values, was the four-volume survey *The Popular History of the United States* (1876–1881), edited by the esteemed William Cullen

12

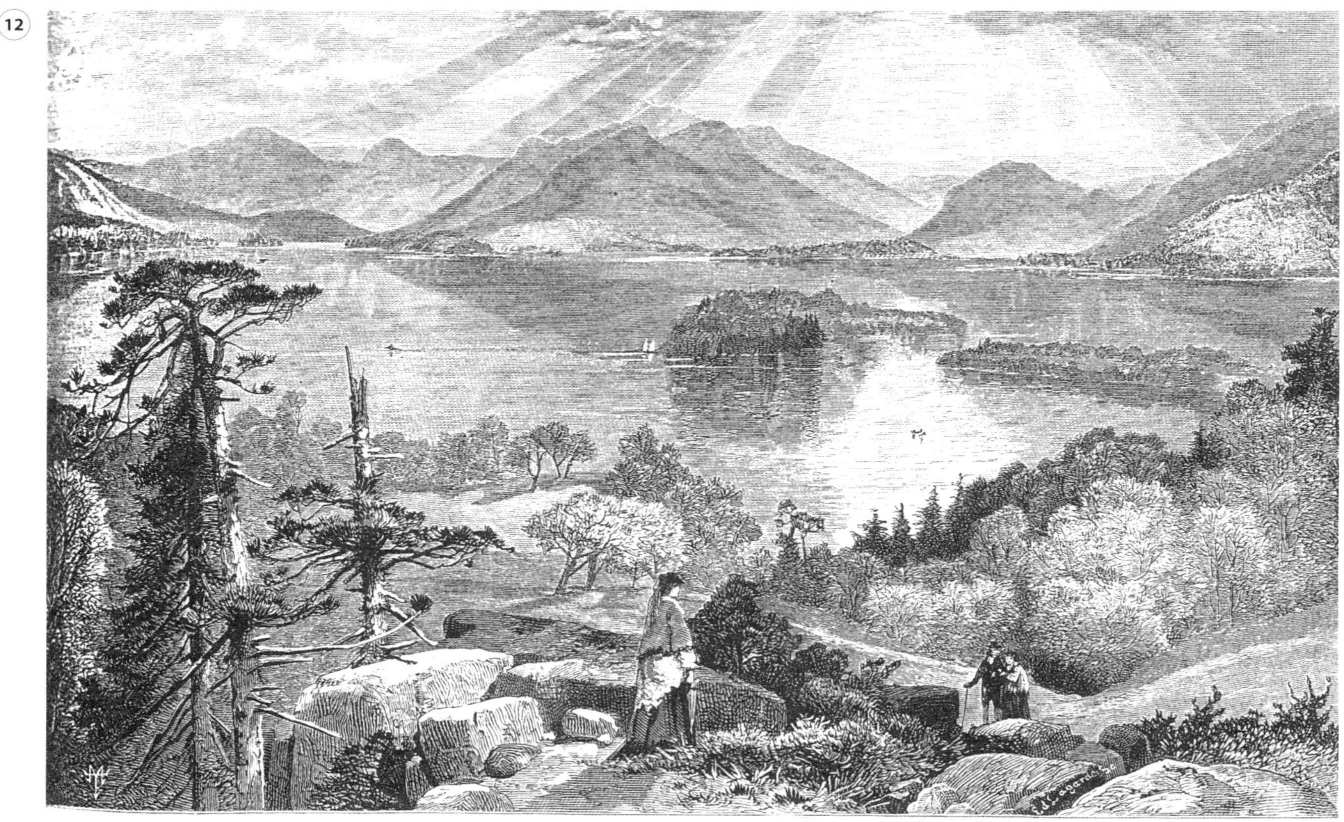

13

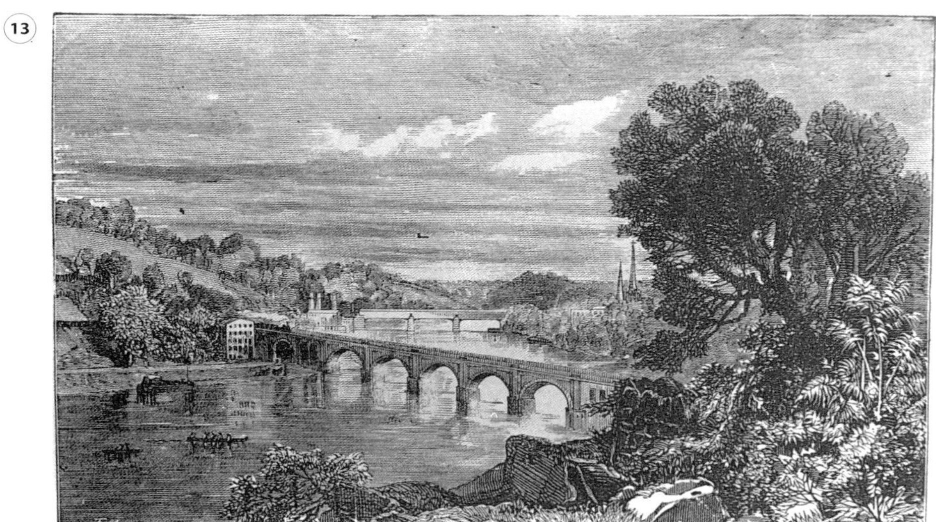

Bryant and Sydney Howard Gay. This centennial edition contained twenty-nine Moran illustrations that underscored the text's ideology of America's aesthetic and nationalistic qualities.[63] The artist also produced a large quantity of work for Ivison Blakeman and Company of New York, one of the largest textbook companies in the East.[64] The varied subject matter of these publications includes geography, oceanography, and elementary readers, but because they are little read today, such textbooks have been virtually forgotten and their impact discounted. At the time of their publication, however, they were an inestimable cultural force in helping young readers to construct their earliest understandings of landscape and its potential significance in their lives.

Tracing Moran's career through the many companies with which he worked is a lesson in the vagaries of the nineteenth-century publishing industry. At different times, for example, he worked for Hurd and Houghton; Houghton Osgood and Company; Houghton, Mifflin and Company; and Osgood and Company, all varying partnerships of several publishers. Of these, James Osgood and Company was among his most consistent patrons, and in 1875 it offered him yet another opportunity to work on Longfellow for its edition of *The Hanging of the Crane*.[65]

12. Thomas Moran, *Long Island, Lake George,* wood engraving, published in *The Aldine* 7 (April 1874), 75.

13. Thomas Moran, *View of the Schuylkill from Laurel Hill, Showing the Falls Bridge,* wood engraving, published in *The Illustrated History of the Centennial Exhibition* (Philadelphia, 1876).

14. Thomas Moran, *Upper Yellowstone Falls,* steel engraving, published in *Picturesque America,* 1874.

Moran also contributed to books written by friends. He illustrated poems by Lloyd Mifflin beginning in 1895. One of his last publications during his lifetime was for Henry Nehemiah Dodge's *Christus Victor: A Student's Reverie* (1926), a religious meditation that included nineteen of the artist's wash drawings reproduced through halftone. Included in this grouping were some of his old motifs, such as *Mountain of the Holy Cross* and the tree from *Solitude.*[66] It seems appropriate that in the year of Moran's death some of his favorite themes appeared via halftone, the new technique that had supplanted wood engraving.

Several deluxe books in which Moran published illustrations are especially notable. These luxuriously bound, embossed, and often gilded volumes were the forerunners of modern "coffee table" books and were frequently perused and prominently displayed in homes. As such, they carried a caché and legitimacy that reinforced the significance of their written and illustrative content. Within these expensive albums, wood engravings assumed added value as an art form. The constructions of landscape ideals in such books was a factor of both content and context.

Among the most interesting of these books are those published for the national centennial, such as James McCabe's *The Illustrated History of the Centennial Exhibition* (1876), one of the fair's official publications. Containing sixteen views by Moran, many of which had appeared earlier in *Scribner's Monthly*, along with countless other images by unnamed illustrators, this gilded tome of over 600 pages was meant to be both a guide and a souvenir of the exposition. Since the book also offered an exhaustive history of Philadelphia, Moran's work included typical views of the city. Among them was *View of the Schuylkill from Laurel Hill, Showing the Falls Bridge* (fig. 13), which focuses on the area's picturesque rivers as well as the newly constructed bridges that were such a point of pride.[67]

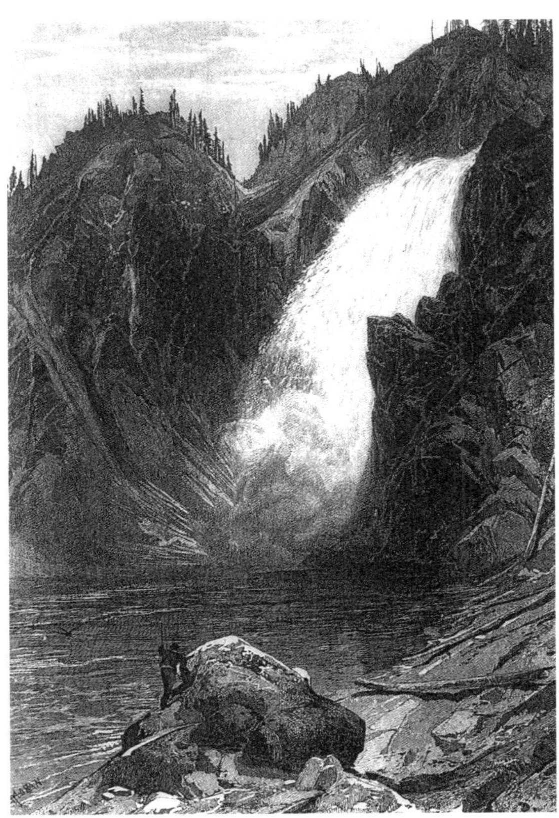

14

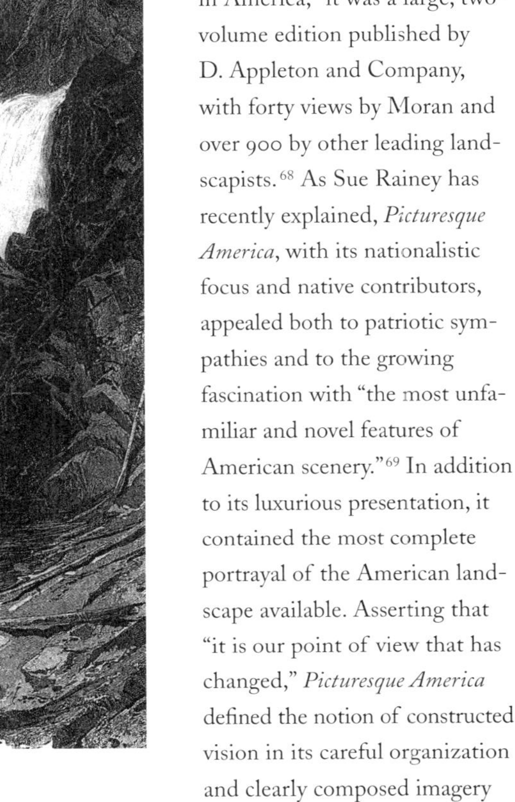

Picturesque America

Of all the deluxe books to which Moran contributed, *Picturesque America: Or the Land We Live In*, edited by William Cullen Bryant, was the most important both in form and influence. Called "the most magnificent illustrated work ever produced in America," it was a large, two-volume edition published by D. Appleton and Company, with forty views by Moran and over 900 by other leading landscapists.[68] As Sue Rainey has recently explained, *Picturesque America*, with its nationalistic focus and native contributors, appealed both to patriotic sympathies and to the growing fascination with "the most unfamiliar and novel features of American scenery."[69] In addition to its luxurious presentation, it contained the most complete portrayal of the American landscape available. Asserting that "it is our point of view that has changed," *Picturesque America* defined the notion of constructed vision in its careful organization and clearly composed imagery of the natural and industrial environment.[70] Enormously successful, it became a model for numerous imitators, most notably *Picturesque Canada* (1882), to which Moran also contributed, and it remains among the most beautiful publications of its kind from the nineteenth century.

Surprisingly perhaps, Moran was too busy to produce more than one steel engraving, *Upper Yellowstone Falls* (fig. 14), for the chapter on Yellowstone. He did, however, illustrate three other chapters: E. L. Burlingame's "The Plains and the Sierras," W. H. Rideing's "The Rocky Mountains," and J. E. Colburn's "The Cañons of the Colorado." As if to demonstrate the publication's importance to him, in 1872 Moran refused the "great inducements" that all four "Great Survey" leaders (Hayden, Clarence King, Powell, and Lieutenant George Wheeler) invited him to join their expeditions. Instead, he traveled via the Union and Central Pacific railroads to California to make images for Burlingame's chapter.[71]

Moran's views in the book focus on the exotic scenery of the West, glorifying its river valleys, unusual buttes, and close canyons, but they also emphasize the availability of such sites. Although the images are sometimes uninhabited, most often they contain a rider or two who serve as wandering surrogates for the reader. A few prints include trains, a reminder that civilization has indeed reached these wild places. The writer recommends: "It is worth the while to think, in this wonderful valley, of the engineering skill that was needed to carry the iron road through its depths....And, as if to mock it all Nature has tried her hand, too, at construction."[72] Nature and industry are thus conflated, both marvels of equal merit, both part of "Picturesque America."

Many of Moran's illustrations in the book are similar to his work in other media. Indeed, several have become his signature works. One of these, *Mountain of the Holy Cross* (fig. 15), in Rideing's chapter, both predates Moran's own trip to the mountain and anticipates his monumental oil of 1875. Basing his engraving on Jackson's photographs from 1873, he invented the lower portion of the composition, but even after he had visited the site in 1874 and realized that such a view did not exist, he retained the foreground in later versions. This striking example of Moran's reconstruction of nature was consistent with the popular promotion of landscape in general and with the Mountain of the Holy Cross in particular. Views of the actual cross were unavailable except at specific points well off the train routes, but this hardly prevented claims to the contrary from appearing in railroad publications.[73]

In April 1873 Moran wrote to Hayden that he "had finished up all the work" he was doing for *Picturesque America*.[74] Hayden had been involved with the project from the beginning, acquiring illustrations for his reports and sharing photographs.[75] Powell, in turn, had accommodated Colburn and Moran in 1873. Once again the government agents, publishers, and artists were working together to promote interest in the American landscape.[76] *Picturesque America* was among the most notable efforts, and its impact on shaping public perceptions of the landscape remains evident to this day.

One of the book's most immediate influences was *Picturesque Canada* (1881), which was directly modeled on its example.[77] Moran's commission to produce a series of views of Niagara, the most famous of Canadian /American attractions, for a Canadian publication indicates the esteem in which he was held in the 1880s.[78] In contrast to most earlier sketching trips, Moran took his entire family to the falls, and the experience resulted in at least seven major paintings. Some of these,

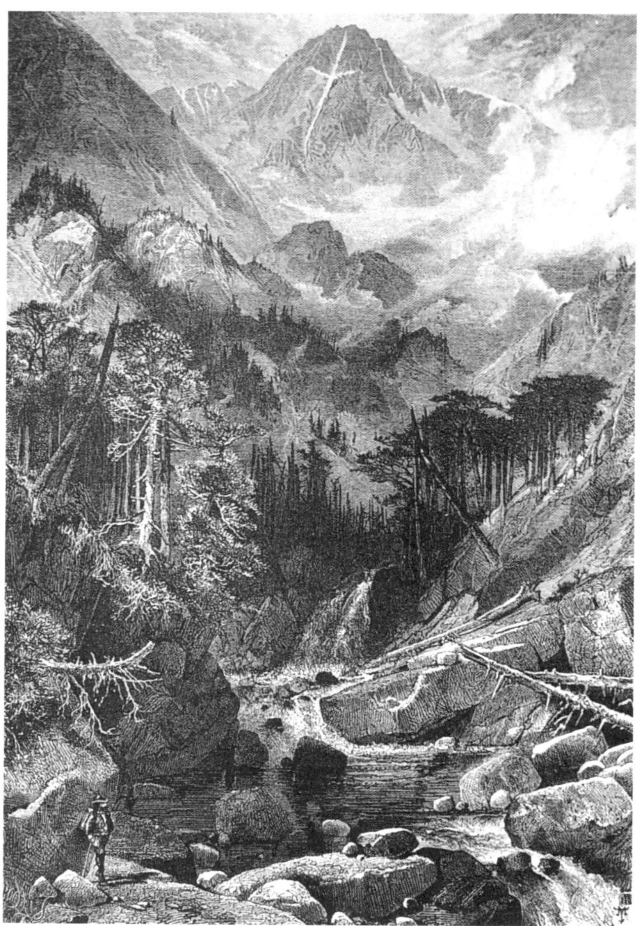

15. Thomas Moran, *Mountain of the Holy Cross,* wood engraving, published in *Picturesque America,* 1874. See also cat. 53.

16. Thomas Moran, *Rapids above Niagara,* wood engraving, published in *Picturesque Canada,* 1882.

such as *Rapids above Niagara* (cat. 68), correspond closely to the published wood engravings in *Picturesque Canada*, in this case an illustration with the same title (fig. 16). The position above the cataract in *The Rapids* and in the view entitled simply *Niagara* indicates Moran was recalling Frederic E. Church's famous 1857 painting, but in his focused attention on the foreground rocks and twisted tree, Moran was clearly formulating his own statement on one of the most frequently depicted scenes in the world. In the context of the Canadian publication Moran simultaneously claimed his own authority on the subject and acknowledged his artistic debt to his predecessors.

Through deluxe parlor books such as *Picturesque America* and *Picturesque Canada*, Moran influenced American thinking about landscape to an extent that is difficult to gauge. Today, the volumes' originality may be overshadowed by their similarity to countless modern coffee-table books, but this should impress more than demean. The early illustrated landscape books that packaged and glorified the natural world set a standard that endures into our own time.

The Prang Chromolithographs

Even considering the influence of *Picturesque America* and its emulators, the most extravagant reproductions of Moran's art were chromolithographs. The earliest may have been a special edition of two chromos issued by *The Aldine* in 1874.[79] As the advertisement that asserted their nationalistic significance indicates, one print depicts the White Mountains and the other the Green River.

> Premium for 1874. Every subscriber to *The Aldine* for the year 1874 will receive a pair of chromos. The original pictures were painted in oil for the publishers of TA [*The Aldine*] by Thomas Moran, whose great Colorado picture was purchased by Congress for $10,000. The subjects were chosen to represent "The East" and "The West." One is a view in the White Mountains, New Hampshire; the other gives the Cliffs of Green River, Wyoming Territory. The difference in the nature of the scenes themselves is a pleasing contrast, and affords a good display of the artist's scope and coloring. The chromos are each worked from thirty distinct plates, and are in size (12 x 16) and appearance exact facsimiles of the originals. The presentation of a worthy example of America's greatest landscape painter to the subscribers of TA was a bold but peculiarly happy idea, and its successful realization is attested by the following testimonial over the signature of Mr. Moran himself: "Newark N.J., September 20, 1873. Messrs. James Sutton & Co. Gentlemen: I am delighted with the proofs in color of your chromos. They are wonderfully successful representations by mechanical process of the original paintings. Very respectfully, Thos. Moran."
>
> These chromos are in every sense American. They are by an original American process, with material of American manufacture, from the designs of American scenery by an American painter, and presented to subscribers by the first successful American Art Journal. If no better because of all this they will certainly possess an interest no foreign production can inspire, and neither are they any the worse if by reason of peculiar facilities of production they cost the publishers only a trifle, *while equal in every respect to other chromos that are sold singly for double the subscription price of The Aldine*. Persons of taste will prize these pictures for themselves—not for the price they did or did not cost, and will appreciate the enterprise that renders their distribution possible.[80]

Clearly responding to the already vociferous debate over the merits of color reproductions, *The Aldine* asserted its aesthetic authority by quoting the artist himself and by reiterating the patriotic significance of the work. Also interesting is the reference to appreciating "the enterprise that renders their distribution possible." Only through the growth of many industries and inventions could every subscriber to a magazine receive free works of art, and the publishers of *The Aldine* were obviously proud of this effort to encourage art and culture.

16

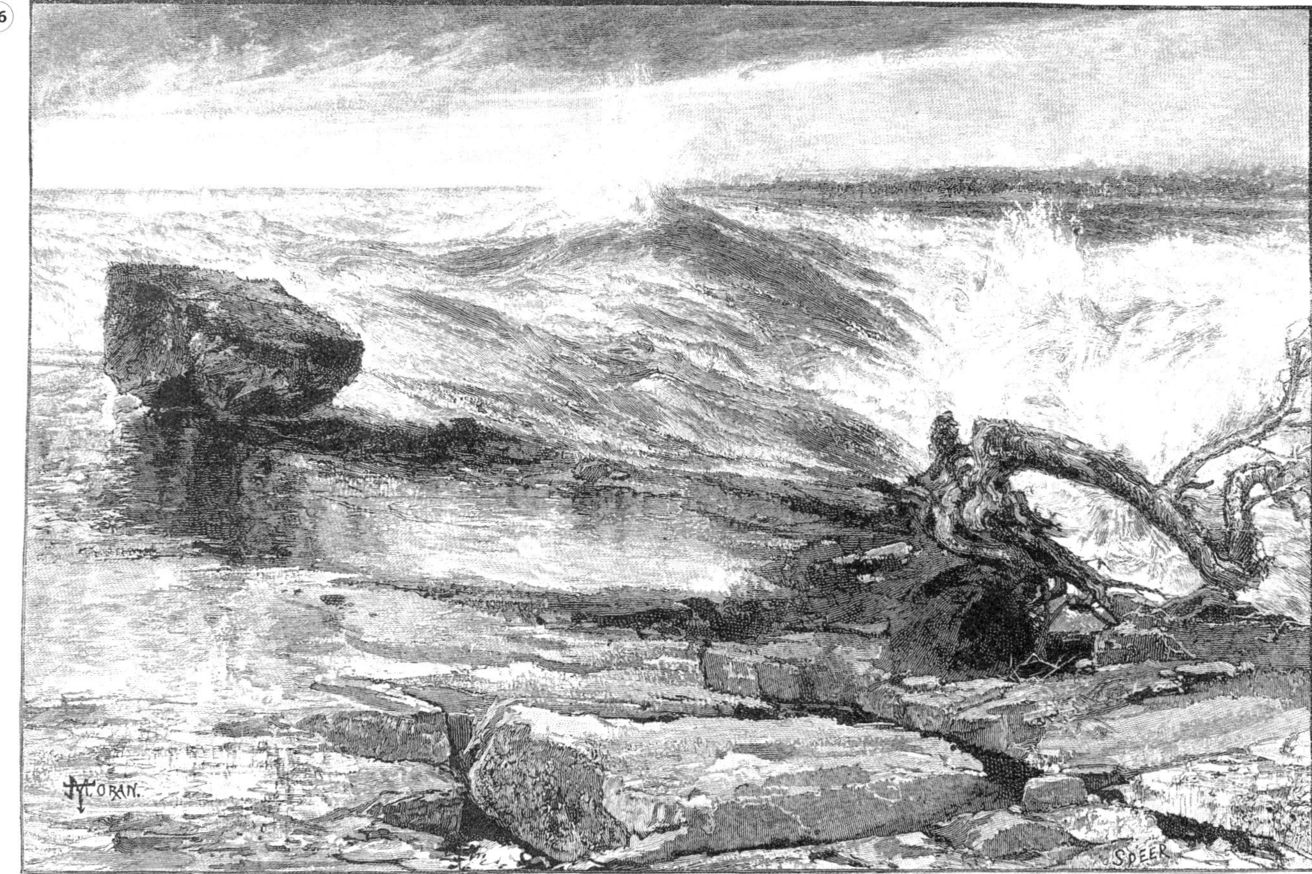

Several firms reproduced Moran's work chromolithographically, but none rivaled the quality of Louis Prang's 1876 edition of Moran's watercolors. Issued as a portfolio entitled *The Yellowstone National Park, and the Mountain Regions of Portions of Idaho, Nevada, Colorado, and Utah*, it contained some of the most beautiful chromos ever assembled and the most faithful reproductions of Moran's art. Rare today as complete sets, this publication is the most valuable of all of Moran's published work.[81]

The Yellowstone National Park featured fifteen chromolithographs from Moran's watercolors, which had been specially painted for the project (Appendix 1). Prang, who is renowned for the exceptional quality of his firm's chromolithographs, approached Moran about the project in 1873. The artist agreed, although he was initially wary.

> In reply I would intimate that my previous transaction with you in a similar business was anything but satisfactory to me, inasmuch as I made to your order three illustrations from the American poets for which you were to pay me $75.00. When I sent them to you, you returned them, merely saying that you had concluded that the publication of the work would prove too expensive. That, of course, was not my business and your declining to pay for the pictures you had ordered, was, to put it in the mildest form, taking a most unfair advantage of me.[82]

Moran continued, stating he would do the work but the order must be for at least eight watercolors, for which he would receive $100 each. He also specified his work schedule, payment plan, and the number of copies he desired. Within a few weeks, he wrote back to Prang with apologies, citing a misunderstanding with his brother Edward, who had apparently handled the earlier transaction. Moran expressed relief at being able to resolve the situation. "I have felt all along since that time I had been imposed upon. I now withdraw all that I said in my letter.... my brother Ed has the unfortunate faculty of muddling everything that he transacts for other people, and yours is not the only case where misunderstandings have arisen through very similar circumstances."[83] The artist subsequently finished three of the designs in 1874 and followed with a total of twenty-four, of which fifteen were published.[84] Many of the compositions were ones he had previously explored, and he maximized their potential by replicating them with only slight variations.

Although single prints from the group sold for as little as $1.50 each, the deluxe edition of *Yellowstone National Park* was limited to a thousand copies and sold for $60, a significant sum in the 1870s.[85] As one review described it:

> The book is not a book. It is a portfolio, each of those exquisite chromos being mounted upon pure white card board of imperial size. The chromos are 14 x 10 inches; the board is 23 x 18 inches, and the letter press, a gem of typography, is on card board of the same size and purity of color and texture. It is a genuine triumph of American graphic art, and some of the lake views almost ripple on the beach as we look at them. The coloring is perfect and the perspective admirably maintained. The two great pictures which adorn the Capitol at Washington are almost as beautiful, in this comparatively miniature form, as they are in the originals.[86]

Although E. L. Godkin had debunked "chromo-civilization" in *The Nation* in 1874, he published an admiring review of the Prang edition that only mildly damned it with faint praise. "It is especially to be commended.... the copying of such watercolors as these being one of the things that lithography is undeniably fitted to effect, and, indeed, its chief reason for existence."[87] An even more notable accolade came in 1882 when the preeminent aesthetician and English art critic John Ruskin bought a copy for the Sheffield Museum.[88]

Moran himself was extremely pleased with the Prang publication. He wrote to the publisher late in 1876: "It is in every respect a most sumptuous & magnificent work; if the faithfulness with which you have reproduced my water color drawings is beyond praise. It seems to me that Chromo-Lithography has, in your hands, attained perfection so skillfully have you reproduced every shade and tone of color in the originals. I naturally feel proud that a work so difficult and extensive should have been produced in America; & hope that your enterprise and skill will meet with the appreciation it deserves."[89]

Moran worked with Prang & Co. on other projects, but not on the scale of the 1876 publication. He produced at least two other works for chromo by the company: *On the Lookout: A Ute Camp, Utah*, and *Cliffs of the Upper Colorado River*. While creating the Yellowstone series, he also apparently asked Prang to print two of his early original lithographs, *Solitude* (1869) and *Desolation* (c. 1869).[90] And in the late 1870s, when Prang's attention turned to Christmas cards, Moran supplied a number of designs and won several prizes for them in the firm's annual competition.[91] The Christmas cards add an interesting dimension to an artist better known for landscapes and promotional material.

Prang's publication of Moran's work was unique in that it was an early effort to replicate the coloristic effects found in his paintings. It is equally interesting that the 1876 series was frequently mentioned in discussions of chromolithographs, but it was never criticized as an example of mass reproduction's detrimental effect on American taste. Other Prang chromos would be fuel for this debate, but Moran's prints, either by virtue of their patriotic significance or their technical excellence, seem to have transcended the fray. Had he done nothing else, Moran would be remembered for this series, which remains a landmark in publishing history.

Success and the Move away from Illustration

Throughout the 1870s Moran's commissions for illustrations grew steadily, and by 1878 he wrote, "During the past seven years I have made about 400 or 500 illustrations on wood, nearly all done at night."[92] In the opening years of the 1880s he exceeded even this remarkable output and earned a sizable income from his illustrative work.[93] After this hectic period, however, Moran produced fewer commercial illustrations. Increasingly he turned to original etching, and the steady sale of his paintings allowed him to reduce his attention to designs for wood engravings.

His account ledgers are instructive for determining the costs of publication and the financial significance of his commercial work. In 1873 Moran included prices of engraving in a letter to Hayden. "I find that first rate work costs about $60.00 for pictures ... 4 x 6 in." This was for the actual engraving of the blocks; the original designs usually brought less. By the end of the 1870s Moran was commanding between $10 and $100 per view, with an average being $35.[94] In 1880 alone he made $2,586 on commercial work and in 1881–1882 he earned nearly $7,000.[95]

Although estimates have varied as to the total number of Moran's illustrations, in 1882 Samuel Benjamin authoritatively stated: "He soon acquired repute as an illustrator of books and magazines. It was this which eventually let him to settle in New York; *Scribner's Monthly* gave him so many commissions that in order to be near the publisher he removed to that city. As proof of his readiness and popularity, it may be stated that during the last eight years, in addition to the large number of paintings and etchings he has produced, he has designed over 2,000 illustrations."[96] In just over twenty years Moran had compiled an impressive record of published work, but after 1882 he largely turned to other media. Later he would remark on this shift, saying in his third-person autobiography, "He has done much as an illustrator of books, magazines, etc., but has substantially abandoned that class of work and devotes himself entirely to painting."[97]

About the same time, printing technology moved toward photographic reproduction, and wood engravings were increasingly supplanted by halftone images. Instead of drawing directly on wood blocks that others carved, artists produced ink drawings that could be directly transferred to printing plates via the camera. This simpler process was much less expensive for publishers; in the early 1890s, for example, a halftone could be produced for less than $20, while a wood engraving cost at least $100.[98] Had Moran not chosen to move away from illustration, developments in technology would have made the decision for him.

Even as he turned to other activities, Moran considered commercial art an important part of his career. He included 160 examples of his published illustrations, prints, and reproductions among the 260 works in his 1892 retrospective exhibition at the Denver Art League. These were admired for their instructional potential.

> Of equal importance [to the oils] are fifty etchings and photogravures, all proofs, varied in method and treatment as well as subject. The list includes many wood engravings, lithographs and a large number of photographs from drawings and paintings. Of especial value to the student, as the reproduction of drawings in black and white is so important a factor in the art education of the country to-day, is a collection of drawings for illustration, which includes ten illustrations to "Hiawatha" in indian [*sic*] ink. The comprehensive exhibition closes with a list of water-color reproductions of Yellowstone park color drawings.[99]

Although one phase of his commercial career was thus closing, Moran's interest in reproductive art did not diminish. In the last decades of his life he turned his attention to the sale of paintings and their copyrights for publication.

"Posters" and Art Calendars

As advertising became more sophisticated, Moran's work was increasingly in demand for calendars, ink blotters, travel brochures, and other ephemera, and by the early 1890s his paintings were being reproduced on a large scale through chromolithography, letterpress, and eventually the new technique of offset lithography. These developments offered an entirely new way to promote his work, and Moran began selling copyrights of existing images rather than painting new designs for reproduction. Although mechanical processes distanced the final product from the original creation, photographically reproduced images printed via letterpress were touted by publishers as respectable substitutes for original works of art, and they were well received by average Americans. As a result, such ventures were important to Moran's commercial career, his reputation as an artist, and indeed the status of reproductions as art.[100]

In 1892 he returned to the Grand Canyon for the first time since his initial trip, with Powell in 1873.[101] As part of the three-month trip, he traveled for the Santa Fe Railway, which had extended its line nearly to the canyon, and he produced a major painting, *The Grand Canyon of the Colorado* (see fig. 6, p. 124), for the company in exchange for the trip.[102] The finished

17

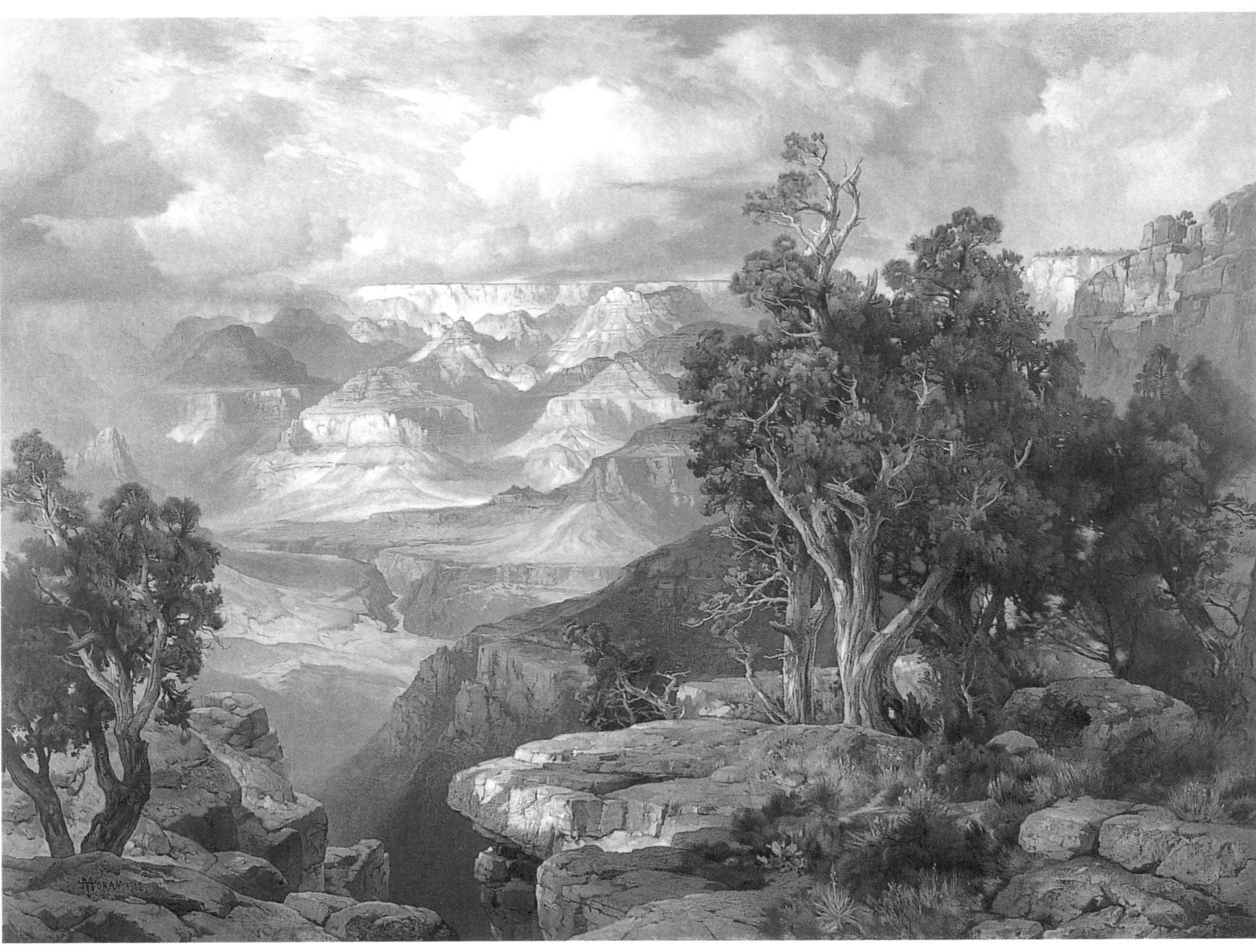

17. Thomas Moran, *Grand Cañon from Hermit Rim,* 1912, chromolithograph, courtesy Gilcrease Museum, Tulsa, Oklahoma.

18. Thomas Moran, *Toltec Gorge, Colorado,* published by Thomas Murphy Art Calendars, 1898. See also cat. 60.

oil hung for a number of years at the El Tovar Hotel at the Canyon, and chromolithographs of it became an important advertising tool in the early years of the Santa Fe Railway as the company established its identity as one of the most innovative patrons of art in the West.[103] Once the SFRR line actually reached the canyon in 1901, the railway began a program that enabled artists to visit the site in return for paintings that would adorn offices, hotel lobbies, and depots, and would appear in advertisements and calendars. To further encourage the visual promotion of this natural tourist attraction, "artists' excursions" were held in 1901 and again in 1910, and Moran participated in both.[104]

Recognized as an influential advocate for the area, Moran traveled via the SFRR to the Grand Canyon annually until about 1920 and was provided with lodging and a studio at the rimside El Tovar. He was consistently acknowledged in the company's tourist literature, and in 1912, twenty years after its first purchase of his art, the railroad bought another painting from which it printed 2,500 chromolithographs. This oil, *The Grand Canyon from Hermit Rim Road*, remains in the railroad's corporate collection, and the chromolithograph (fig. 17) has become a valuable collector's item.[105]

As chromolithographs were replaced by more efficient methods of reproduction, Moran enthusiastically sold copyrights of his work to emerging companies. This provided him the luxury of selling his work twice: each copyright brought an average of $500, and he could still sell the original oil painting.[106] He was obviously thinking of such benefits during his 1892 trip when he wrote to his wife, "Jackson and I are concocting a scheme for publication of six subjects of grand size of the Holy Cross, Yo Semite, Yellowstone, Shasta, and two others. He says they sell well right along and would be a steady source of income to me. He says he has paid Bell about a thousand already in royalty on the Holy Cross."[107] Although the details remain unclear, a later letter from Jackson written from the Detroit Publishing Company suggests that he arranged for the photography of Moran's work and acted as the broker to the publisher. The final outcome is uncertain, but correspondence as late as 1901 indicates it was an ongoing project.[108]

Similar to the reproductions Moran and Jackson planned were art calendars, a phenomenon in early twentieth-century printing and advertising. Moran's artworks were among the first to be reproduced and distributed in this way. Although many companies quickly replicated the idea, it was conceived in 1889 by Thomas D. Murphy and his friend and fellow newspaper editor Edmund B. Osborne in Red Oak, Iowa, as a way to supplement their newspaper business.[109] The calendars, adorned with a fine art reproduction and accompanied by advertising copy for local businesses, were given to clients as promotional gifts. To make his products distinctive, Murphy commissioned original art and purchased copyrights to paintings, and he quickly developed a unique industry that featured Moran's work prominently (fig. 18).[110]

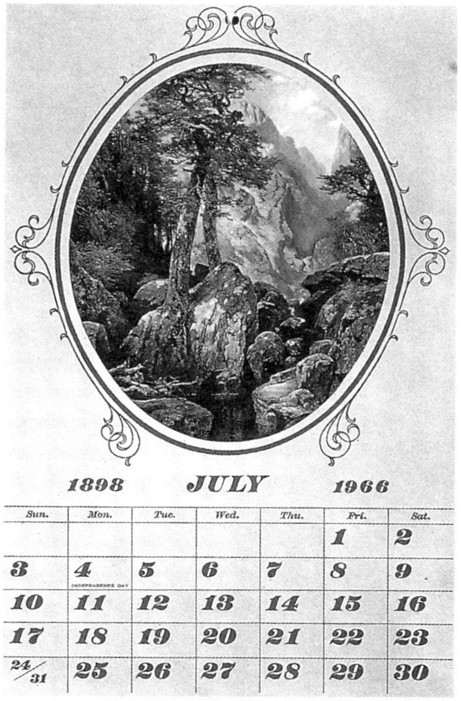

18

Murphy's calendars were produced to high specifications, and the company took great pride in its relationship with artists and its collection of original oils. Between 1910 and 1926 Moran sold the firm nearly sixty copyrights, and Murphy illustrated at least two of his own books with Moran's works.[111] He boasted in 1925 that "the pictures of [H.J.] Dobson and Moran are about the only ones that have not waned in popularity during the past fifteen years," and he took some pride in being a factor in that continuing popularity.[112]

In 1894–1895 Murphy's partner, Edmund Osborne, left Red Oak to establish his own art calendar company in Allwood, New Jersey. Osborne and Company also energetically promoted Moran's art, primarily through large-scale reproductions as well as calendars. In later years Murphy and Osborne rejoined forces to form the American Colortype Company, and it, along with Osborne and Company and JII/Sales Associates, heir to the Murphy Company, continued to publish Moran's work even after the artist's death.[113] In 1936 Osborne and Company produced a special anniversary calendar for the New York Emigrant Industrial Savings Bank, complete with a short biography of Moran and twelve reproductions of his paintings.[114] Moran's daughter Ruth wrote the company that "it would have pleased my father, Thomas Moran, to observe with what fidelity modern machinery and skill can now reproduce these miniature facsimiles of the artist's work. And it is also a pleasure to know that the public appreciates these reproductions."[115]

Too often overshadowed by his painting in art historical literature, commercial work was a primary means of economic support for Moran through most of his life. In the artist's own opinion and in that of many of his contemporaries, it comprised an important vehicle for his talent and vision. Commissions for illustrations provided him occasions for travel and artistic inspiration, and in many cases the resulting wood engravings formed the basis for more monumental work. Even after he left illustration, Moran continued to focus on reproducing his art through the most modern means available. His commercial art brought him into contact with some of the most influential individuals and corporations of his time, which in turn contributed to his success as a fine artist in the grand tradition.

The marginalization of Moran's career in reproduction is largely a product of twentieth-century attitudes toward aesthetic hierarchies and not something to which the artist himself ascribed. Indeed the period of his most prolific activity was precisely when illustration enjoyed acceptance as an art form. It should be remembered that Thomas Moran's commercial work, which extended over seven decades, profoundly influenced Americans' evolving conceptions of this country and its unique landscape. This aspect of his diverse career stands out as a major component of his development and his profound achievement as an American artist.

Appendices

The deluxe portfolio of chromolithographs of Thomas Moran's watercolors, *The Yellowstone Park, and the Mountain Regions of Portions of Idaho, Nevada, Colorado, and Utah,* published by Louis Prang of Boston in 1876, is a monument in the history of publishing. The fifteen prints of many of Moran's favorite western compositions are among the most faithful and beautiful reproductions of his art ever printed. The publication was composed of unbound folio plates, accompanied by a forty-eight-page text by Ferdinand V. Hayden, the leader of the United States Geological and Geographical survey that Moran accompanied in 1871, and packaged in an embossed case. The images reproduced here are from one of two sets in the collection of the Gilcrease Museum, Tulsa. Although single prints from the group sold for as little as $1.50 each, the deluxe edition was limited to one thousand copies and priced at $60, a significant sum in the 1870s.[1]

The appeal of the publication lay not only in the remarkable quality of the prints, achieved from some thirty lithographic stones for each image, but also, as Hayden pointed out in the introduction, in their color reproduction. "To a person who has not visited the Yellowstone and the territory adjacent to it," he wrote, "it is simply impossible to conceive of the character of the scenery, and even the most vivid description is utterly insufficient to give an accurate idea of it, unless accompanied by color illustrations." While Hayden's text is largely technical, explaining the geological origins of the various formations and the details of their location, he also includes a lengthy description of each site represented and emphasizes that the chromatic variety of the images was the key to their significance, especially in the decades before widespread color publishing. Moreover, his authority on the region testified to Moran's accuracy in conveying its appearance.

Prang's portfolio was heralded as one of the most spectacular publications of the age. Even *The Nation,* which had earlier criticized the modern era as a "chromo-civilization" and decried the cheapening effects of imitative reproductions, agreed that "the untraveled world is under vast obligation for these vivid reports of regions we shall not all live to see in any other form."[2] Virtually all the reviews acclaimed the work, calling it "beautiful," "exquisite," or a "sensation." *The Times* of London asserted that "no finer specimen of chromo-lithographic work had been produced anywhere."[3] But perhaps the most telling commentary was from the artist himself in a letter to the publisher, "It is in every respect a most sumptuous & magnificent work; & the faithfulness with which you have reproduced my water color drawings is beyond praise. It seems to me that Chromo-Lithography has, in your hands, attained perfection so skillfully have you reproduced every shade and tone of color in the originals. I naturally feel proud that a work so difficult & extensive should have been produced in America; & hope that your enterprise and skill will meet with the appreciation it deserves."[4]

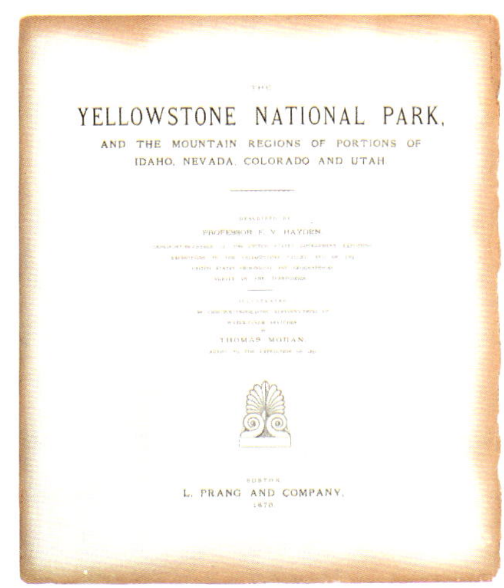

THE YELLOWSTONE NATIONAL PARK, AND THE MOUNTAIN REGIONS OF PORTIONS OF IDAHO, NEVADA, COLORADO, AND UTAH

Described by Professor F.V. Hayden, geologist-in-charge of the United States Government Exploring Expeditions to the Yellowstone Valley, and of the United States Geological and Geographical Survey of the Territories

Illustrated by chromolithographic reproductions of water-color sketches, by Thomas Moran, Artist to the Expedition of 1871

Boston. L. Prang and Company, 1876

Copyright, 1876
By L. Prang & Co.

Preface

The exquisite scenery of the Yellowstone National Park has become tolerably well known to the public by photographs, and by illustrations in magazines and books. But however accurate these illustrations may have been, they were all wanting in one particular, which no woodcut, engraving, or photograph can supply, and which, nevertheless, is of the greatest importance, especially in the case under consideration. All representations of landscape scenery must necessarily lose the greater part of their charm when deprived of color; but of any representation in black and white of the scenery of the Yellowstone it may truly be said that it is like Hamlet with the part of Hamlet omitted, for the wealth of color in which nature has clothed the mountains and the springs of that region constitutes one of the most wonderful elements of their beauty. To a person who has not visited the Yellowstone and the territory adjacent to it, it is simply impossible to conceive of the character of its scenery, and even the most vivid description is utterly insufficient to give an accurate idea of it, unless accompanied by colored illustrations. So strange, indeed, are the freaks of color which nature indulges in habitually in this wonderful country, that it will no doubt require strong faith on the part of the reader in the truthfulness of both artist and writer to enable him unhesitatingly to accept the statements made in the present volume by the pen as well as by the brush. For all the ordinary standards of landscape beauty fail in the presence of these marvels, which bear a closer resemblance to the fairy scenes sometimes represented on the stage than to the woods and hills which we are ordinarily accustomed to see.

Such being the case, it has long been my wish to have the most picturesque and interesting portions of the Yellowstone National Park illustrated in their natural colors, but the great expense to be incurred in such an enterprise deterred me from attempting it. I was therefore very agreeably surprised when I learned from the publishers of the present work that they had, of their own accord and at their own risk, determined to carry out a similar project, and I cheerfully assented to the request to take charge of the literary part of the work, more especially as I knew of my own personal knowledge that the sketches by Mr. Thomas Moran, who accompanied me on one of my expeditions, are not only of a high order of artistic merit, but that they can also be relied upon as exceedingly correct renderings of their subjects, interesting alike to the man of science, the lover of art, and the admirer of nature.

With the illustrations in this volume before the reader, I need hardly say that in the reproduction of Mr. Moran's water-colors Messrs. L. Prang & Co. have fully sustained the world-wide reputation to which they have attained by the conscientious and artistic practice of the difficult and beautiful process of chromo-lithography. It is a just subject for national pride to see a work of this character, which takes equal rank with anything of the kind ever undertaken in Europe, produced wholly on American soil. The public must now decide whether there is sufficient appreciation for work of so high a standard in the country, and whether the publishers were justified in incurring the very considerable out-lay involved in its production.

As to my own share in the work, it will be seen that I have confined myself to a short account of the discovery of the Yellowstone region, and of its natural features, together with a concise description of the illustrations. Those who desire to pursue the subject still further will find ample material in the reports published by me under the auspices of the United States Government. To these reports the series of views herewith submitted forms a most valuable and appropriate supplement.

F.V. Hayden. Office of the U.S. Geological and Geographical Survey of the Territories. Washington, D.C., August 1, 1876

Table of Contents

Introduction

Within the last two decades the remarkable scenery of the vast Rocky Mountain region has become more and more familiar to the travelling public at home and abroad. The completion of the railroad across the continent, connecting the Atlantic and the Pacific Oceans, has rendered accessible new worlds of grandeur and beauty. The far-famed Yosemite Valley, the snowy Sierras, the deep gorges of the Colorado of the West, the unrivalled views about the sources of the Yellowstone River, the great area of lofty mountain peaks in Central Colorado, — all these are unsurpassed, even by the world-renowned scenery of the

Alpine districts of Europe. Located in the northwestern corner of Wyoming Territory is a tract of country more remarkable for the wonderful phenomena of nature than any other region on the globe. It may very properly be called the "Northern Wonder Land," in contradistinction to a similar region in New Zealand, which is now known as the "Southern Wonder Land." It is a singular fact that this marvellous region has only been known to the world within a period of about six years. Vague rumors of burning plains, boiling springs, volcanoes ejecting water and mud, great lakes, and other wonders had indeed reached the civilized world from time to time; but as the most astounding stories of petrified forests, of animals turned to stone, and of streams flowing so rapidly that their waters became heated, were intermingled with these rumors, the latter were disregarded altogether and were looked upon as the wild vagaries of wandering mountaineers. Captains Lewis and Clarke, in their exploration of the head waters of the Missouri, in 1805, seem to have heard nothing of the marvels at the sources of the Madison and Yellowstone. They merely placed Yellowstone Lake on their map, as a large body of water, having in all probability derived their information from the Indians.

The first trustworthy accounts given of the region were the results of an expedition led by General Washburne, the Surveyor-General of Montana, and escorted by a small body of United States cavalry under Lieutenant G.C. Doane, in 1870. This expedition spent about a month in the interesting localities on the Yellowstone and Madison Rivers. Mr. N.P. Langford gave a popular account of it in two articles published in the second volume of "Scribner's Monthly"; while Lieutenant Doane submitted a report of the same expedition to the War Department, which report was published by the government (Executive Document No. 51, 41st Congress). In the summer of 1871 a small party under the command of Colonel J.W. Barlow, Chief Engineer of the Department of the Missouri, was sent to the Yellowstone by General Sheridan. On his return Colonel Barlow also prepared a brief report of his explorations.

The same season a large and thoroughly organized party, conducted by the writer, made a systematic survey of this region under the auspices of the Department of the Interior. Mr. Thomas Moran accompanied the expedition as artist, and it was at this time that he secured the studies from nature which he has so accurately and vividly embodied in the sketches reproduced by Messrs. L. Prang & Co. for this volume. The official report of this expedition, published after the return of the party, in the autumn of 1871, created so great an interest among the people, that in February, 1872, Congress was induced to pass an act withdrawing from settlement, occupancy, or sale, under the laws of the United States, an area about the sources of the Yellowstone River, consisting of 3,575 square miles, dedicating and setting it apart as a public park or pleasuring ground for the benefit and enjoyment of the people.

In the spring of 1872, a very liberal appropriation was made by Congress for a more detailed geological and geographical survey of the park and the adjacent territory. This appropriation permitted the writer to organize two well-equipped parties for the field work. The first party examined the Yellowstone River to its sources, made accurate charts of the Geyser Basins, and carefully investigated the previously unknown cañons of the Gallatin and Madison Rivers. The second party explored the remarkable basin of the Shoshone or Snake River, which latter has its source in the Yellowstone Park. Up to the time of these expeditions the great "divide," or water-shed, of the continent was probably the least known region in America, although it exceeds all other regions in geographical as well as geological interest. But by the scientific labors then performed our geographical knowledge of the territory under consideration has at last been placed upon a secure footing. The magnitude and the value of these labors will easily be understood, when it is considered that not less than forty small streams, which in their union form the upper portion of Snake River, were carefully surveyed; that new geyser basins were discovered, and that in the accurate and detailed reports subsequently published the wonders of the Yellowstone were for the first time authoritatively described.

As the wonderland of the National Park is attracting larger numbers of tourists from year to year, it will be of interest to learn something in regard to the routes by which it may be reached. A glance at the map will show that these routes are numerous, and it may confidently be asserted that at no distant period the Park will be as easily accessible as almost any other mountain region now visited by those who travel for pleasure.

The first route, which is the most practicable, the pleasantest, and the one in common use, is the following via Ogden: Ogden, Utah, is reached from the East by the Union Pacific Railroad and connecting lines, and from the West by the Central Pacific Railroad. From Ogden, take the Utah Northern Railroad to Franklin in Idaho Territory, whence there is a stage line to Virginia City and Bozeman, in Montana. The tourist has the choice of starting from either of these two places, at each of which a complete outfit of supplies, animals, and guides may be obtained. From Bozeman, the route is up the Yellowstone River and across to the Geyser Basins, and thence by the way of the Madison River to Virginia City. There is a wagon-road from Bozeman to the Mammoth Hot Springs, where there is said to be a hotel. From Virginia City there is the choice of two roads, one of which leads to the Madison and follows the trail up the river to the Geyser Basins. It will be best, however, to follow the wagon-road which is completed to the Upper Geyser Basin. This road leaves the southeastern limit of Virginia City, and strikes the Madison near Wigwam Creek, where it crosses the river, and follows it to a point just above the crossing of Lawrence Creek. Here it recrosses, and closely follows the river to Driftwood or Big Bend, three miles below the second cañon of the Madison. It then leaves the Madison Valley and crosses through Reynold's Pass to Henry's Lake, the head water of Henry's Fork of Snake River. From Sawtelle's Ranch, on Henry's Lake, the road follows the east shore of the lake for three miles in a southerly direction, when it turns to the northeast, and passes through Tyghee or Targee Pass, and down Beaver Dam Creek over the South Fork of the Madison, striking the mouth of the Fire Hole Cañon sixteen miles below the Lower Geyser Basin. It then follows the river closely, crossing twice before reaching the basin. From the basins, the route is either via Mud Volcanoes, Shoshone Lake, or Yellowstone Lake, to the Yellowstone and Bozeman.

A second route, and one which shortens the stage ride, will necessitate the purchase of an outfit at Salt Lake or Ogden. This outfit must be sent ahead to Market Lake in Snake River Valley, which point the traveller reaches by going by rail to Franklin, and thence by stage. This saves about 230 miles of staging. From Market Lake it is about 100 miles by a pack-train trail to Henry's Lake, from which point the Virginia City wagon-road is followed to the "Geyser Basins." Another route from Market Lake, which is long and somewhat out of the way, but more interesting, as it gives an opportunity to visit Mount Hayden, and passes some magnificent scenery, is to travel with a pack train up Pierre's River across Teton Pass, and up the main Snake River to Shoshone Lake, whence the other points of interest in the Park are readily reached. This is one of the routes followed by the Hayden Geological Survey in 1872.

A third route is by way of Camp Brown, a military post about 120 miles from Rawlins Springs Station, on the Union Pacific Railroad, with which it is connected by a stage-road. The trail from Camp Brown to Yellowstone Lake is said to be easy, and the distance only about 140 miles. It crosses the mountains at the head of the Upper Yellowstone River, which stream it follows to the lake. Captain Jones, in 1873, surveyed a route from Point of Rocks Station, on the Union Pacific Railroad, via Camp Brown, the Wind River Valley, and the head of Wind River, to the Yellowstone. He claims that it saves 482 miles in reaching Yellowstone Lake. The great drawback is that it is often unsafe on account of Indians, and very much obstructed by fallen timber.

As a fourth, the Missouri River may be mentioned. The river is navigable as far as Fort Benton until late in the summer, and thence 140 miles of staging will take the tourist to Helena, 118 miles from Bozeman. From Bismarck, the present terminus of the Northern Pacific Railroad, a trip of ten or fifteen days will bring the traveller to Fort Benton. It will be a tedious journey, however, over the "bad lands" of Dakota.

Another plan is to disembark at the mouth of the Mussel Shell River on the Missouri, and having ordered horses to be in readiness, to take the wagon trail to the Crow Indian Agency at the Big Bend of the Yellowstone. This would give 150 miles of land travel through a prairie country abounding in antelope and buffalo, and sometimes Indians.

The National Park may also be visited from the British Possessions, as well as by a road which follows the Hell Gate and Bitter Root Rivers from the west from Walla-Walla.

The following tables of distances are compiled principally from the reports of the United States Geological Survey:

Ogden, Utah, to Franklin, Idaho, by rail	80¼	miles.
Franklin to Virginia City, Montana (stage)	317	"
Virginia City to Bozeman (stage)	66	"
Franklin to Market Lake, Snake River Valley	152	"
Point of Rocks Station, Union Pacific Railroad, to Yellowstone Lake, by Captain Jones's route	289	"

BOZEMAN TO GEYSER BASINS, VIA YELLOWSTONE RIVER

Bozeman	0	miles.
Fort Ellis	3	"
Divide between Spring and Trail Creeks	16	"
Boteler's Ranch on Yellowstone River	39	"
Foot of Second Cañon of the Yellowstone	52	"
Devil's Slide at Cinnabar Mountain	60	"
Bridge near mouth of Gardiner's River	68	"
Cache Valley, the mouth of East Fork of Yellowstone	84	"
Crossing of Tower Creek	88	"
Divide on spur from Mount Washburn	94	"
Crossing of Cascade Creek	108	"
Mud Volcanoes	117	"
Yellowstone Lake at head of river	124	"
Head of Yellowstone River to Hot Springs on southwest arm of lake	15	"
Hot Springs to Upper Geyser Basin	15	"
Mud Volcanoes to Lower Geyser Basin	24	"
Bridge near mouth of Gardiner's River to Mammoth Hot Springs	4	"

MARKET LAKE TO YELLOWSTONE LAKE

Market Lake	0	miles.
Henry's Lake	100	"
Tyghee Pass	110	"
Gibbons' Fork	133	"
Lower Geyser Basin	140	"
Upper Geyser Basin	148	"
Divide	158	"
Shoshone Geyser Basin	162	"
Lewis Lake	172	"
Hot Springs, Yellowstone Lake	180	"

VIRGINIA CITY TO YELLOWSTONE LAKE VIA WAGON ROAD TO GEYSER BASINS

Virginia City	0	miles.
Madison River, half-mile from Wigwam Creek	14	"
Driftwood or Big Bend of Madison	42	"
Henry's Lake	60	"
Tyghee Pass	63	"
Gibbons' Fork	86	"
Lower Geyser Basin	93	"
Upper Geyser Basin	101	"
Yellowstone Lake	116	"

From a purely geographical point of view, the Yellowstone Park may be said to embrace some of the most remarkable and instructive features in North America. It forms the very apex, or "divide," of the continent. Within a radius of twenty-five miles may be found the sources of three of the largest rivers in America. The general elevation is from 7,000 to 8,000 feet above the sea, while the mountains, the eternal snows of which form the sources of the great rivers just mentioned, rise to a height of from 10,000 to 12,000 feet. Flowing northward are the numerous branches of the Missouri, Yellowstone, and Wind Rivers, all of which eventually unite in one great stream, the Missouri. To the south are the branches of Green River, which latter unites with the Colorado, and finally empties into the Gulf of California, while south and west flow the branches of Snake River, which, joining the Columbia, pour their vast volume of water into the Pacific.

The Yellowstone Lake, which is one of the most beautiful bodies of water on the continent, is always of a deep emerald-green color, and is set like a gem amid the surrounding volcanic mountain peaks. The view of it which is embraced in this volume is so true to nature that but few words of description are needed. On the south side of the lake, not more than half a mile distant from it, and not over three hundred feet above the level of its surface, is the divide between the drainage of the Atlantic and Pacific slopes. It would require but little labor to turn the waters of the lake into Snake River. Here is said to be located the supposed two-ocean stream, and it is indeed not improbable that on the summit of this low divide there is a small lake, the waters of which, at certain seasons of the year, flow in either direction.

From the summits of the snow-capped peaks surrounding the lake, which are seen in the sketch, the view is grand beyond description. From the top of Red Mountain, on the south side, the scope of vision embraces a circle having a radius of one hundred fifty miles, within which four hundred and seventy mountain peaks worthy of a name can be distinctly observed. The area swept by the eye from this point cannot be less than fifty thousand square miles, embracing large portions of Wyoming, Montana, Idaho, and Utah, and exhibiting every variety of the grandest and most beautiful scenery. Ten large lakes and several smaller ones are taken in by this view, and the entire Yellowstone Park is spread out under the eye. The purity of the atmosphere in these high latitudes is well known, so that these statements will not seem exaggerated. On the east side of the Yellowstone River, between the first and second cañons, we find one of the most symmetrical and remarkable ranges of mountains to be seen in the west. The Lower Yellowstone range Mr. Moran pronounced at once equal in beauty and artistic form to any that he had seen in Central Europe, and from it he obtained the sketch for one of the most beautiful and attractive illustrations in this volume. Sharp, jagged peaks and pyramidal masses stand out boldly against the sky, their snow-crowned heads glittering in the sunlight. The central portion of this range is composed of granite rocks, through the fissures of which the igneous matter has risen to the surface, covering the sides and summits, and giving to the entire mass a peculiarly sombre hue. At the west base of this range is one of the remarkable lake basins for which the West has now become famous. This basin has a length of thirty miles and an average width of about five miles. It is supposed that during the Pliocene period there was a series of these peculiar lake basins all along the upper portions of the great rivers of the West, in the sediments of which were entombed the remains of many extinct animals, such as the mastodon, elephant, rhinoceros, camel, horse, etc., which, thousands of years ago, roamed over this broad region unmolested by man. On either side of the river the view is grand and picturesque. Emigrant Peak, rising 10,629 feet above sea level and nearly 6,000 feet above the valley, stands at the head of the range, and from its melting snows are fed the numerous streams that water the hills and plains sloping to the river.

To the geologist the Yellowstone Park offers an endless field for observation and speculation. Even in comparatively modern geological times this entire area was the scene of the most wonderful volcanic activity, to a degree which has not been equalled in any other portion of our country. From innumerable craters or vast fissures in the earth's crust were ejected, in Pliocene or Post-Pliocene times, vast quantities of fragments of rocks, ashes, tuffs, etc., into the surrounding waters, where they were rearranged in horizontal beds from 3,000 to 5,000 feet in thickness. These beds of volcanic breccia or conglomerate must originally have covered an area about the sources of the Yellowstone and Missouri Rivers of from 8,000 to 10,000 square miles. It was from these beds that the strange, marvellous forms, which meet the eye at every point, have been carved out by the erosive action of water.

The Grand Cañon of the Yellowstone and the Towers of Tower Falls, which have furnished some of the most beautiful illustrations in the present collection, are types of this strange scenery. Immense gorges have been cut through the horizontal beds of breccia above referred to, with vertical walls 3,000 feet in height on either side. These walls are surmounted by a great variety of architectural forms, among which it does not require a vivid imagination to trace huge castles and fortress walls. The prevailing hue is a sombre black, although in many localities almost every shade of color is represented.

But perhaps the most prominent feature of the scenery of the Yellowstone National Park is its variety. The Yosemite Valley, the Shoshone Falls, and the great gorge of the Colorado have each some marked peculiarity which characterizes them as a whole. But here the traveller passes from one unique scene to another, and his vision never wearies and is never sated.

Among the natural phenomena of the Yellowstone National Park the thermal springs, which occur there in great numbers, have proved to be the leading objects of interest to scientific men, and in fact to all people of intelligence the world over. Almost all the known varieties of hot springs are found in the crevices of the rocks, which are the result of volcanic action. The geysers of Iceland are here surpassed in number as well as in magnitude; the wonderful Te Tarata Spring of New Zealand has its rival in the White Mountain Hot Springs; the mud springs and mud geysers of Java likewise have there representatives here; and sulphur and steam vents, such as occur in similar volcanic regions elsewhere, are distributed over a large portion of the Park. These hot springs, which are now slowly dying out, represent the last of a series of remarkable physical events. The evidence seems clear that, during the period of volcanic activity above alluded to, hot springs, and perhaps geysers, were very numerous over a large portion of the West. We find their remains or deposits everywhere in other States and Territories west of the Mississippi, and here and there a warm or hot spring is left as an indication of their former power.

A primary classification of the hot springs of the Park would divide them into two kinds with reference to their chemical constituents, namely, those in the deposits of which lime predominates, and those in which silica is most abundant. Of the first class the "Hot Springs of Gardiner's River," a view of which will be found among the illustrations, are a typical instance; while both the "Castle Geyser, Upper Geyser Basin," and the "Great Blue Spring," likewise depicted in this volume, are most beautiful examples of the second class. The nature of the deposits depends upon the character of the underlying rocks through which the heated waters reach the surface. Beneath the calcareous deposits of the Hot Springs of Gardiner's River there are from fifteen hundred to two thousand feet of limestone strata. The heated waters on their way upward dissolve the lime, and the latter reaches the surface in solution, and is left by evaporation in the beautiful and unique forms which so much excite the admiration of the observer. The silicious springs come to the surface through volcanic or other rocks in which silica is the preponderating constituent, and the silica is deposited about the orifice in the same way as the lime, but at a far less rapid rate. Here it is again the process of evaporation which forms the beautiful decorations about the springs.

It is, however, to the wonderful variety of exquisitely delicate colors, and the almost unnatural transparency of the waters, — characteristics which are common to both classes, — that these springs owe much of their attractiveness. The orifices through which the hot waters issue are beautifully enamelled with a porcelain-like lining, and around the edges a layer of sulphur is precipitated. Along the sides and bottoms of the numerous little channels of the streams that flow from these springs there is a striking display of the most vivid colors, consisting of various shades of red, from the fullest scarlet to a bright rose tint, and yellow, from deep bright sulphur through all conceivable shades to light cream-color. There are also various shades of green, arising from the peculiar vegetable forms with which many of the streams are filled, and which under the microscope prove to be diatoms. Great quantities of a fibrous, silky substance, which occur in the little streams that flow from the boiling springs, and vibrate with the slightest movement of the water, add still another element of beauty.

The remarkable transparency and deep, vivid blue of the waters, as shown in the illustrations of the "Great Blue Springs," and in the quiet, circular spring opposite the "Castle Geyser," are marvels in themselves, The sky, with the smallest cloud that flits across its face, is reflected in the clear depth of these waters; and the ultramarine colors displayed by them, more vivid even than the deep blue sea, are greatly heightened by the constant, gentle vibration. One can look down into the clear depth and see with perfect distinctness the minutest ornament on the sides of the basin.

These springs represent every stage of development, from the most active geysers of the first class to the entire extinction of all activity. In the Upper and Lower Geyser Basins of the Firehole River there are about fifty springs that might be regarded as geysers of the first class, throwing upward a column of water from a few feet to over a hundred feet in height. Then there is every grade downward to simple boiling or even quiet hot springs. All about are seen great numbers of dead springs which may once have been geysers of the first class. Among the hundreds of groups of springs that are distributed over the park the proofs of former intensity are everywhere to be found, showing that the springs still left are only remnants as compared with the number and power of those that must have existed at the cessation of the true volcanic forces. Next to the geysers are the mud volcanoes, mud springs, fumaroles, or salses, as they are usually termed. They also vary in grade from a simple bowl of turbid water to a vast crater of seething mud fifty to one hundred feet in diameter. Many of these mud springs are of great beauty, the silicious fire-clay presenting every shade of yellow and pink, from the mingling of sulphur and of ferric oxides, and a fineness of composition that would equal the purest meerschaum.

There are also deep, boiling caldrons from which are emitted clouds of sulphurous vapors and steam, that settle down upon the surrounding vegetation, incrusting it with a fine mud. Dr. Hochstetter, speaking of the same phenomena in the "Great Southern Wonderland" of New Zealand, describes them as follows:

> The entrance to the ravine is overgrown with a thicket and rather difficult of access; it also requires considerable caution, as suspicious places have to be passed where the visitor is in danger of being swallowed up in heated mud. Inside, the ravine has the appearance of a volcanic crater. The bare walls, utterly destitute of vegetation, are terribly fissured and torn, and odd-looking serratures, threatening every moment to break loose, loom up like dismal spectres from red, white, and blue fumarole-clay, evidently the last remains of decomposed rocks. The bottom of the ravine is of fine mud, scattered with blocks of silicious deposit, like cakes of floating ice after a thaw. Here, a big caldron of mud is simmering; there, lies a deep basin of boiling water; next to this is a terrible hole, emitting hissing jets of steam; and farther on are mud cones from two to five feet high vomiting hot mud from their craters with dull rumblings, and imitating on a small scale the play of large fire volcanoes. — Hochstetter's *New Zealand*, p. 414.

The probable origin of thermal springs is well known. The hot springs and geysers of Iceland have been studied with the greatest care by some of the ablest scientific men in Europe, as Bunsen, Bischoff, and Tyndall, and their conclusions have been accepted.

The same phenomena as those of Iceland are repeated in New Zealand and the Yellowstone National Park, only on a much more extensive scale. That all thermal springs are remnants of former volcanic action there can be no doubt. Geysers, or intermittent springs, may be regarded as volcanoes, except that the former throw out heated waters, while the latter eject melted materials, etc.

We may take it for granted that the hot springs derive their temperature from heated aqueous vapors rising from below; and the only question which remains to be settled regards the actual sources of these vapors. Shall we adopt the theory that the interior of our globe is in an incandescent state, and that the origin of the heat is deep-seated below the earth's crust, rising from the melted nucleus, or shall we look to a far more superficial force? In the first place, the water of the hot springs is derived from the surface. Passing down through fissures in the earth's crust it meets the heated vapors from below, and portions being expanded into steam a force is produced, the same as in a steam engine. If this force can rise freely in a continual column, a simple boiling spring is produced. If the channel or passage upward is complicated, we have the phenomena of the spouting spring. According to Bischoff, the intermittent springs are caused by the existence of caverns in which the heated vapors are retained by the pressure of the column of water from above. The violent escape of the vapor produces the thunder-like, subterranean sound, and the tremblings of the earth that precede the eruption. When so much vapor has escaped that the expansive force of that which remains has become less than the pressure of the confining column of water, tranquillity is restored, and this lasts until a quantity of vapor is again collected which is sufficient to produce a fresh eruption. The spouting of the spring is therefore repeated at intervals, depending on the capacity of the cavern, the height of the column of water, and the heat generated below.

The following extract from Dr. Von Hochstetter's description of the New Zealand hot springs is equally applicable to those of the Yellowstone Park, and explains the chemical as well as the thermodynamic forces which are in constant operation:

> Both kinds of springs owe their origin to the water permeating the surface and sinking through fissures into the bowels of the earth, where it becomes heated by the still existing volcanic fires. High-pressure steam is thus generated, which accompanied by volcanic gasses, such as muriatic acid, sulphurous acid, sulphuretted hydrogen, and carbonic acid, rises again toward the colder surface, and is there condensed into hot water. The overheated steam, however, and the gasses decompose the rock beneath, dissolve certain ingredients and deposit them on the surface. According to Bunsen's ingenious observations, a chronological succession takes place in the co-operation of the gasses. The sulphurous acid acts first. It must be generated there where rising sulphur vapor comes into contact with glowing masses of rock. Wherever vapors of sulphurous acid are constantly formed, there acid springs, or solfataras, arise. Incrustations of alum are very common in such places, arising

from the action of sulphuric acid on the alumina and alkali of the lavas; another product of the decomposition of the lavas is gypsum, or sulphate of lime, the residuum being a more or less ferruginous fumarole-clay, — the material of the mud pools. To the sulphurous acid succeeds sulphuretted hydrogen, produced by the action of steam upon sulphides, and by the mutual decomposition of the sulphuretted hydrogen and sulphurous acid sulphur is formed, which in all solfataras forms the characteristic precipitate, while the decomposition of silicious incrustations is either entirely wanting or quite inconsiderable, and a smell of sulphuretted hydrogen is but rarely noticed. These acid springs have no periodical outbursts of water.

In course of time, however, the source of sulphurous acid becomes exhausted, and sulphuretted hydrogen alone remains active. The acid reaction of the soil disappears, yielding to an alkaline reaction by the formation of sulphides. At the same time the action of the carbonic acid begins upon the rocks, and the alkaline bicarbonates thus produced dissolve the silica, which, on the evaporation of the water, deposits in the form of opal or quartz or silicious earth, and thus the shell of the springs is formed upon the structure of which the periodicity of the outbursts depends. Professor Bunsen, rejecting the antiquated theory of Makenzie based upon the existence of subterraneous chambers from which the water from time to time is pressed up through the vapors accumulating on its surface, according to the principle of the Heron fountain, has proved in the case of the Great Geyser that the periodical eruptions or explosions essentially depend upon the existence of a frame of silicious deposits with a deep, flue-shaped tube, and upon the sudden development of larger masses of steam from the overheated water in the lower portions of the tube. The deposition of silica in quantities sufficient for the formation of this spring apparatus in the course of years takes place only in the alkaline springs. Their water is either entirely neutral, or has a slightly alkaline reaction. Silica, chloride of sodium, carbonates, and sulphates are the chief ingredients dissolved in it. In the place of sulphurous acid the odor of sulphuretted hydrogen is sometimes observed in these springs.

The rocks from which the silicious hot springs of New Zealand derive their silica are rhyolites and rhyolithic tuffs, containing seventy and more per cent of silica; while we know that in Iceland palagonite and palagonitic tuffs, with fifty per cent of silica, are considered as the material acted upon and lixiviated by the hot water. By the gradual cooling of the volcanic rocks under the surface of the earth in the course of centuries the hot springs also will gradually disappear; for they too are but a transient phenomenon in the eternal change of everything created. — Hochstetter's *New Zealand*, English translation, p. 432.

The following statistics and chemical analyses have been derived from the reports of the survey of the Territories, and will prove of interest to the general reader:

HEIGHTS ATTAINED BY THE ERUPTIONS OF THE PRINCIPAL GEYSERS IN FIRE-HOLE BASINS, YELLOWSTONE NATIONAL PARK

Name of Geyser. Authority. Height in Feet.

Fountain in Lower Basin. Hayden, 1871. 30 to 60
Architectural in Lower Basin. Hayden, 1871. 60 to 80
Old Faithful, Upper Basin. Hayden, 1871. 100 to 150
Old Faithful, Upper Basin. Hayden, 1872. *132
Old Faithful, Upper Basin. Norton, 1872. 150
Old Faithful, Upper Basin. Comstock, 1873. 150
Old Faithful, Upper Basin. Dunraven, 1874. 100 to 150
Giantess, Upper Basin. Langford, 1870. 250
Giantess, Upper Basin. Hayden, 1872. *39
Giantess, Upper Basin. Norton, 1872. 100
Bee-Hive, Upper Basin. Langford, 1870. *219
Bee-Hive, Upper Basin. Hayden, 1872. 100 to 150
Bee-Hive, Upper Basin. Norton, 1872. 100
Castle, Upper Basin. Langford, 1870. 50
Castle, Upper Basin. Hayden, 1871. 10 to 15
Castle, Upper Basin. Hayden, 1872. *93
Castle, Upper Basin. Comstock, 1873. 30
Castle, Upper Basin. Dunraven, 1874. 250
Grand, Upper Basin. Hayden, 1871. 200
Grand, Upper Basin. Hayden, 1872. *173
Grand, Upper Basin. Comstock, 1873. 200
Turban, Upper Basin. Hayden, 1872. *25
Turban, Upper Basin. Comstock, 1873. 30
Giant, Upper Basin. Langford, 1870. 140
Grotto, Upper Basin. Langford, 1870. 60
Grotto, Upper Basin. Hayden, 1872. *41
Grotto, Upper Basin. Comstock, 1873. 25

* *Measured by triangulation; the others are estimated.*

ELEVATIONS IN THE YELLOWSTONE NATIONAL PARK

	Feet above Sea Level.
Mammoth White Mountain Hot Springs	6,278 to 7,035
Mud Volcanoes	7,756 to 7,800
Crater Hills Springs	7,828 to 7,979
Sulphur Springs on divide between Yellowstone and East Fork of Fire-Hole River	8,246
Lower Geyser Basin	7,250 to 7,350
Upper Geyser Basin	7,300 to 7,400
Third Geyser Basin	7,772
Shoshone Lake, Geyser Basin	7,900

LAKES

Yellowstone Lake	7,788
Shoshone Lake	7,870
Lewis Lake	7,750
Madison Lake	8,301
Henry's Lake	6,443

MOUNTAIN PEAKS

Mount Hayden	13,833
Mount Washburn	10,388
Mount Sheridan	10,343
Mount Blackmore	10,134
Mount Delano (Yellowstone Valley)	10,200
Mount Doane	10,118
Electric Peak	10,992
Emigrant Peak	10,629
Red Mountain, south of Yellowstone Lake	9,806
Lookout Hill, north of Shoshone Lake	8,257
Old Baldy, near Virginia City	9,711

PASSES AND DIVIDES

Teton Pass	8,464
Tyghee Pass	7,063
Reynold's Pass, Henry's Lake, north to Madison River	6,911
Divide, Yellowstone and Gallatin on road from Fort Ellis to Boteler's Ranch	5,721
Divide on Mount Washburn, where trail crosses	9,155
Divide between Yellowstone and Madison, on trail from Mud Volcanoes and Geyser Basins	8,164
Divide between Madison and Shoshone Lakes	8,717
Divide between Yellowstone and Lewis Lakes	8,024
Togwater Pass (Upper Yellowstone to Wind River)	9,621

ANALYSIS OF DEPOSIT FROM THE HOT SPRINGS OF GARDINER'S RIVER

Water and volatile matters	32.10	per cent
Lime	57.70	"
Silica	3.32	"
Ferric oxide	3.62	"
Alumina	3.31	"
Soda and magnesia traces	—	"
	100.05	"

ANALYSIS OF GEYERSITE FROM LOWER GEYSER BASIN

Water, etc.	9.00	per cent
Silica	88.60	"
Alumina and iron	1.60	"
Lime	0.95	"
Magnesia, soda, potash, and lithia traces	—	"
	100.15	"

ANALYSIS OF PINK MUD FROM MUD PUFFS IN LOWER GEYSER BASIN

Water	8.65	per cent
Silica	44.61	"
Alumina	45.09	"
Magnesia	2.66	"
Iron	1.86	"
Lime and soda traces	—	"
	102.87	"

ANALYSIS OF GEYERSITE FROM UPPER GEYSER BASIN

Water	13.42	per cent
Silica	79.56	"
Lime	1.54	"
Alumina	0.46	"
Magnesia	1.78	"
Iron, chlorine, and soda traces	—	"
	96.76	"

ANALYSIS OF GEYERSITE FROM SHOSHONE LAKE, GEYSER BASIN

Water	13.00	per cent
Silica	76.80	"
Alumina	9.46	"
Lime	1.80	"
Iron, magnesia, and soda traces	—	"
	101.06	"

As has been previously stated in this Introduction, during the session of 1871–72 a bill was introduced into both houses of Congress to set apart the area about the sources of the Yellowstone River, embracing these wonderful curiosities, as a Public Park for the benefit and instruction of the people. The bill was referred to the proper committee. At their request the writer prepared the following report, which explains the object of the bill, and on the strength of the information therein contained the bill became a law:

The Committee on the Public Lands, having had under consideration bill H.R. 764, would report as follows:

The bill now before Congress has for its object the withdrawal from settlement, occupancy, or sale, under the laws of the United States, a tract of land fifty-five by sixty-five miles about the sources of the Yellowstone and Missouri Rivers; and dedicates and sets it apart as a great national park or pleasure-ground for the benefit and enjoyment of the people. The entire area comprised within the limits of the reservation contemplated in this bill is not susceptible of cultivation with any degree of certainty, and the winters would be too severe for stock-raising. Whenever the altitude of the mountain districts exceeds 6,000 feet above tide water their settlement becomes problematical, unless there are valuable mines to attract people. The entire area within the limits of the proposed reservation is over 6,000 feet in altitude, and the Yellowstone Lake, which occupies an area 15 x 22 miles or 330 square miles, is 7,427 feet. The ranges of mountains that hem the valleys in on every side rise to the height of 10,000 and 12,000 feet, and are covered with snow all the year. These mountains are all of volcanic origin, and it is not probable that any mines or minerals of value will ever be found there. During the months of June, July, and August the climate is pure and most invigorating, with scarcely any rain or storms of any kind; but the thermometer frequently sinks as low as 26°. There is frost every month in the year. This whole region was in comparatively modern geological times the scene of the most wonderful volcanic activity of any portion of our country. The hot springs and the geysers represent the last stages — the vents or escape-pipes — of these remarkable volcanic manifestations of the internal forces. All these springs are adorned with decorations more beautiful than human art ever conceived, and which have required thousands of years for the cunning hand of nature to form. Persons are now waiting for the spring to open to enter in and take possession of these remarkable curiosities, to make merchandise of these beautiful specimens, to fence in these rare wonders so as to charge visitors a fee, as is now done at Niagara Falls, for the sight of that which ought to be as free as the air or water.

In a few years this region will be a place of resort for all classes of people from all portions of the world. The geysers of Iceland, which have been objects of interest for the scientific men and travellers of the entire world, sink into insignificance in comparison with the hot springs of the Yellowstone and Fire-Hole Basins. As a place of resort for invalids, it will not be excelled by any portion of the world. If this bill fails to become a law this session, the vandals who are now waiting to enter into this wonderland will, in a single season, despoil beyond recovery these remarkable curiosities which have required all the cunning skill of nature thousands of years to prepare.

We have already shown that no portion of this tract can ever be made available for agricultural or mining purposes. Even if the altitude and the climate would permit the country to be made available, not over fifty square miles of the entire area could ever be settled. The valleys are all narrow, hemmed in by high volcanic mountains like gigantic walls.

The withdrawal of this tract, therefore, from sale or settlement takes nothing from the value of the public domain, and is no pecuniary loss to the government, but will be regarded by the entire civilized world as a step of progress and an honor to Congress and the nation.

Department of the Interior, Washington, D.C., January 29, 1872

Sir: I have the honor to acknowledge the receipt of your communication of the 27th inst., relative to the bill now pending in the House of Representatives dedicating that tract of country known as the Yellowstone valley as a National Park.

I hand you herewith the report of Dr. F. V. Hayden, United States geologist, relative to said proposed reservation, and have only to add that I fully concur in his recommendations, and trust that the bill referred to may speedily become a law.

Very respectfully, your obedient servant,
C. Delano, Secretary

Hon. M. H. Dunnell, House of Representatives

The committee, therefore, recommend the passage of the bill without amendment.

The bill alluded to is as follows:

AN ACT TO SET APART A CERTAIN TRACT OF LAND LYING NEAR THE HEADWATERS OF THE YELLOWSTONE RIVER AS A PUBLIC PARK

Be it enacted by the Senate and House of Representatives of the United States of America in Congress assembled, That the tract of land in the Territories of Montana and Wyoming, lying near the headwaters of the Yellowstone River, and described as follows, to wit: commencing at the junction of Gardiner's River with the Yellowstone River and running east to the meridian passing ten miles to the eastward of the most eastern point of Yellowstone Lake; thence south along said meridian to the parallel of latitude passing ten miles south of the most southern point of Yellowstone Lake; thence west along said parallel to the meridian passing fifteen miles west of the most western point of Madison Lake; thence north along said meridian to the latitude of the junction of the Yellowstone and Gardiner's Rivers; thence east to the place of beginning, — is hereby reserved and withdrawn from settlement, occupancy, or sale under the laws of the United States, and dedicated and set apart as a Public Park or pleasuring-ground for the benefit and enjoyment of the people; and all persons who shall locate or settle upon or occupy the same, or any part thereof, except as hereinafter provided, shall be considered trespassers and removed therefrom.

SEC. 2. That said Public Park shall be under the exclusive control of the Secretary of the Interior, whose duty it shall be, as soon as practicable, to make and publish such rules and regulations as he may deem necessary or proper for the care and management of the same. Such regulations shall provide for the preservation, from injury or spoliation, of all timber, mineral deposits, natural curiosities, or wonders within said Park, and their retention in their natural condition. The Secretary may in his discretion grant leases for building purposes, for terms not exceeding ten years, of small parcels of ground, at such places in said Park as shall require the erection of buildings for the accommodation of visitors; all of the proceeds of said leases, and all other revenues that may be derived from any source connected with said Park, to be expended under his direction in the management of the same, and the construction of roads and bridle-paths therein. He shall provide against the wanton destruction of the fish and game found within said Park, and against their capture or destruction for the purpose of merchandise or profit. He shall also cause all persons trespassing upon the same after the passage of this act to be removed therefrom, and generally shall be authorized to take all such measures as shall be necessary or proper to fully carry out the objects and purposes of this act.

Approved March 1, 1872.

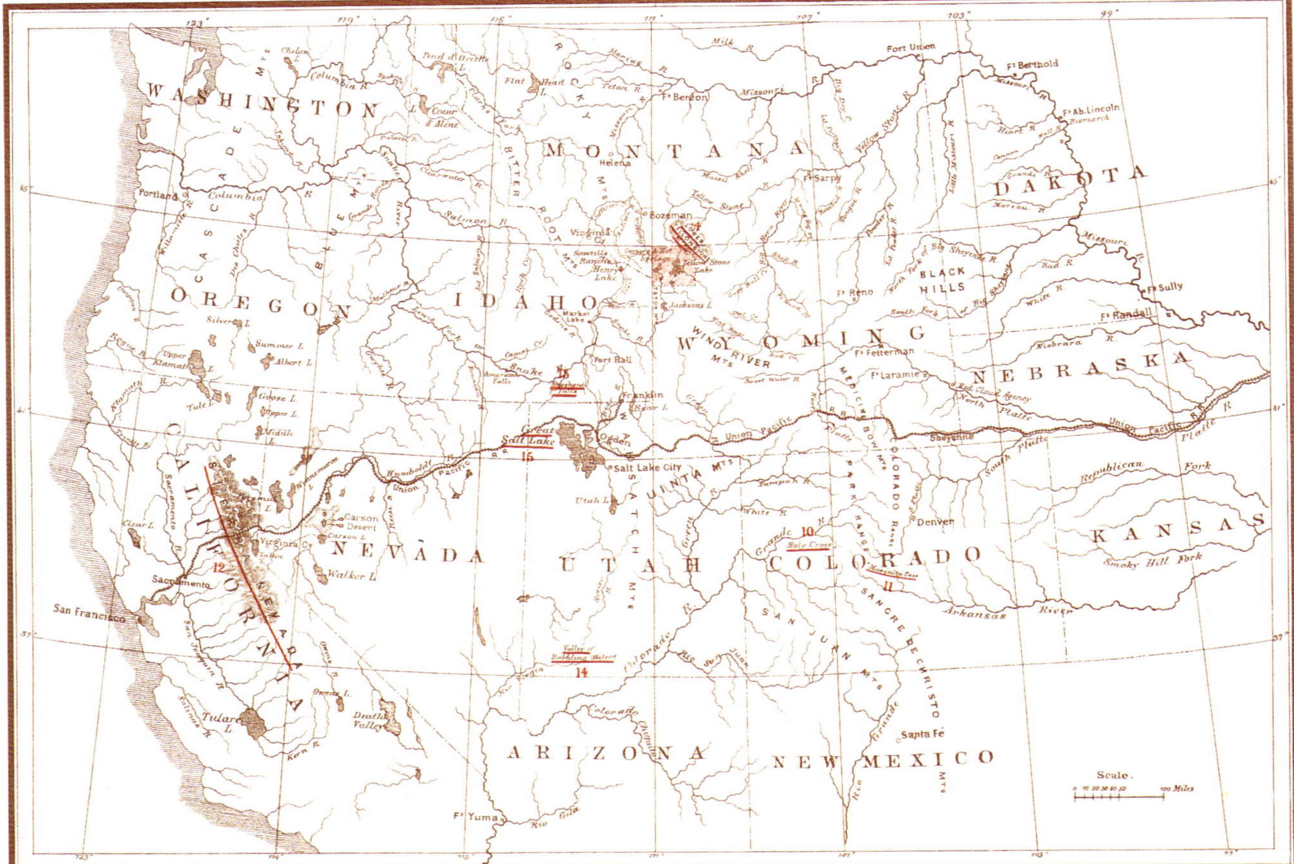

GENERAL MAP

showing the situation of the Yellowstone National Park and the location of views no. 4, 10, 11, 12, 13, 14, and 15.

The two maps which accompany this volume are designed to show the general geographical position of the regions described, the routes by which the Yellowstone National Park may be reached, and the location of the views sketched by Mr. Moran.

On the first map, which is the general map, and on which the National Park is indicated only on a small scale, the location of the following views will be found:

4. Lower Yellowstone Range
10. Mountain of the Holy Cross
11. The Mosquito Trail
12. The Sierra Nevada
13. Great Falls of Snake River (Shoshone Falls)
14. Valley of Babbling Waters
15. The Great Salt Lake of Utah

These seven views are all outside of the Park, although the point of view from which the Lower Yellowstone Range is taken is situated within the Park.

The second map, which is a detailed map of the Yellowstone National Park, shows the location of the remaining eight views, namely:

1. Hot Springs of Gardiner's River (White Mountain Hot Springs)
2. The Great Blue Spring of the Lower Geyser Basin
3. The Castle Geyser
5. Yellowstone Lake
6. Tower Falls and Sulphur Mountain
7. Head of Yellowstone River
8. The Grand Cañon of the Yellowstone
9. The Towers of Tower Falls

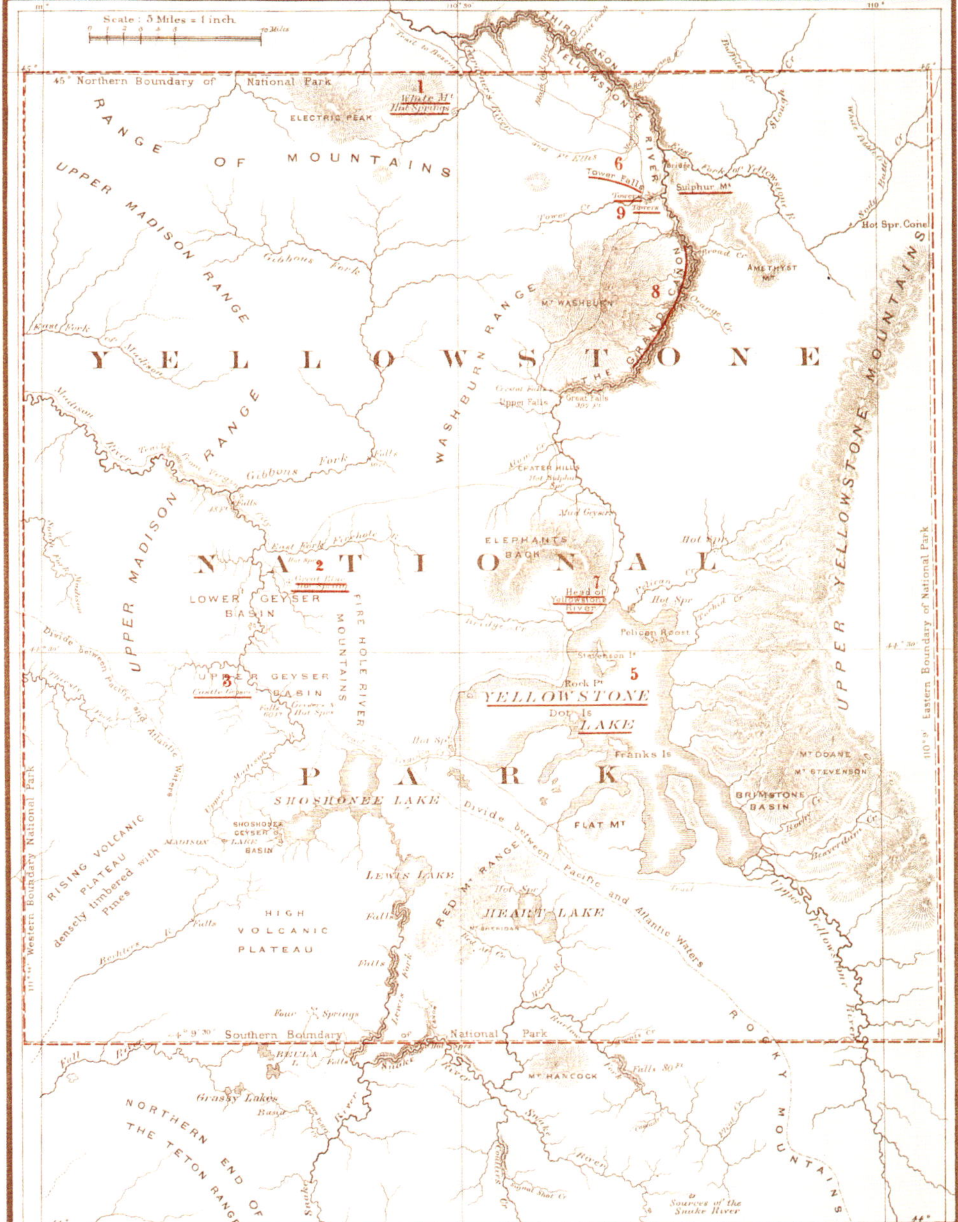

MAP OF THE YELLOWSTONE NATIONAL PARK

showing the location of views no. 1, 2, 3, 5, 6, 7, 8, and 9.

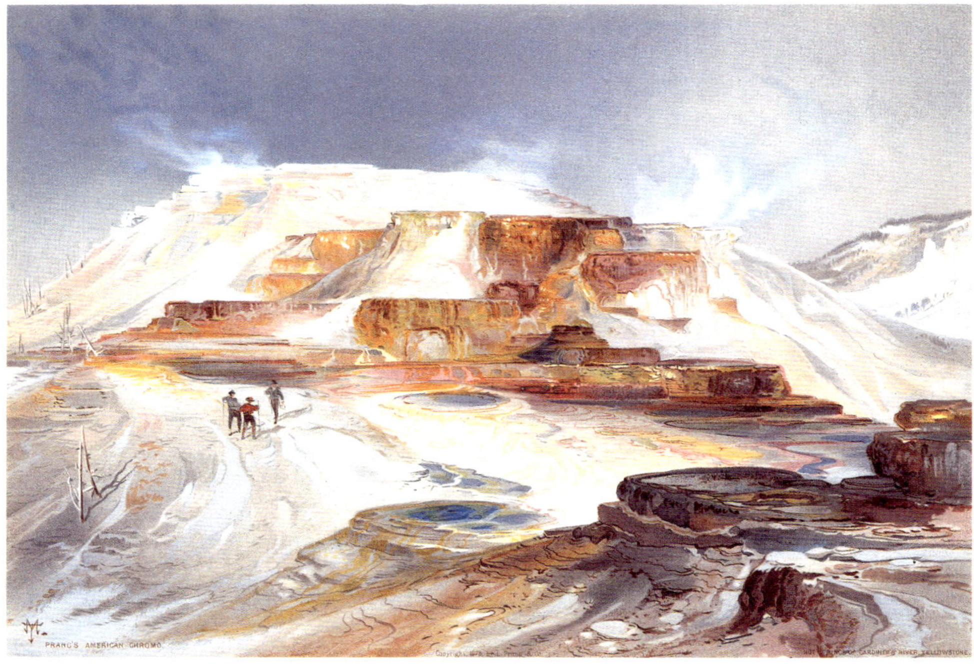

GARDINER'S RIVER HOT SPRINGS

The Mammoth Hot Springs are situated on the west side of Gardiner's River, a small tributary of the Yellowstone, joining it at the foot of the third Cañon in the northern part of the National Park.

In the springs and their beautiful variegated deposits we have one of the most remarkable displays of Nature's architectural work that can be found in the world. The famous "Te Tarata Spring" of New Zealand is its only rival.

The deposits cover a space of about two and a half square miles, extending from the river's edge to the head of a ravine one thousand feet above the level of the stream. The softness of the calcareous sediments renders them especially liable to the action of atmospheric agencies, and consequently we find a large proportion of the area covered with the ruins of former springs, which in many places are overgrown with pines, beneath which traces only are found of the beautifully sculptured basins that once were filled with emerald-tinted water. The weathering of these portions has given them a grayish color. The active springs are near the centre of the area, about halfway up the gorge. They represent but a portion of the activity that must once have had its seat here, and which is now gradually dying out. The springs are constantly changing their position. Where an active spring exists one season, the next we may find simply the ruins of its empty basin, while new springs will have burst through the crust, and the formation of new basins be progressing only to decay in their turn.

Ascending the hill from the river, we pass over a hard crust that gives forth a hollow sound under our feet. From beneath it streams of hot water pour into the river. Passing by several large pools of warm water in rusty-edged basins filled with bright green vegetation, we come suddenly in sight of the main mass of sediment in which the principal springs are found. It is two hundred feet high, and its snowy whiteness has suggested the name of "White Mountain Hot Springs." The general appearance is that of some huge cascade that has suddenly been arrested in its descent and frozen. Examining it more closely, we find that it is composed of a series of terraces rising one above the other like a series of steps, each containing semicircular basins resplendent with the most beautiful blue-tinted water. The basins are of all sizes and have exquisitely scalloped margins, their marble-like appearance contrasting beautifully with the turquoise-colored water. These pools have been called "Jupiter's Baths" and "Diana's Pools." They form elegant natural bathing-places, and one can choose a deep or shallow, large or small one, according to fancy. The water in the upper basins, near the principal springs, being warmest, as it descends, becomes cooled, so that it may be found of almost any desired temperature. As it pours from basin to basin, stalactites are formed, which ornament the bases of the pools. In some places they unite with stalagmites built up from below, thus forming columns. There are various other forms of ornamentation, some basins being beaded, while others have beautiful waved lines on their surfaces.

The presence of lime in the sediments has much to do with many of the peculiar forms that they assume. The color of the deposits is for the most part snowy white. On the lower terrace the basins are tinged with a delicate carmine.

In some of the groups of higher terraces the iron of the water has colored the edges of the pools most gorgeously, red predominating, mixed with creamy yellow, bright yellow of the sulphur, and greens where there is any vegetation. With the azure tints of the water itself, we have a scene surpassing all art.

The scenery in the vicinity of the springs is varied, and beautiful beyond description, especially at sunset, when the last rays of the sun throw a beautiful rosy light over the whole scene, intensifying the natural colors of the "Great White Springs."

The original sketch by Mr. Moran is true to nature; and the wonderful combinations and shades of coloring which form the most striking feature of many of the springs in the Park are shown with great perfection. The reproduction of the sketch by Messrs. L. Prang & Co. is in itself a marvel of accuracy and beauty.

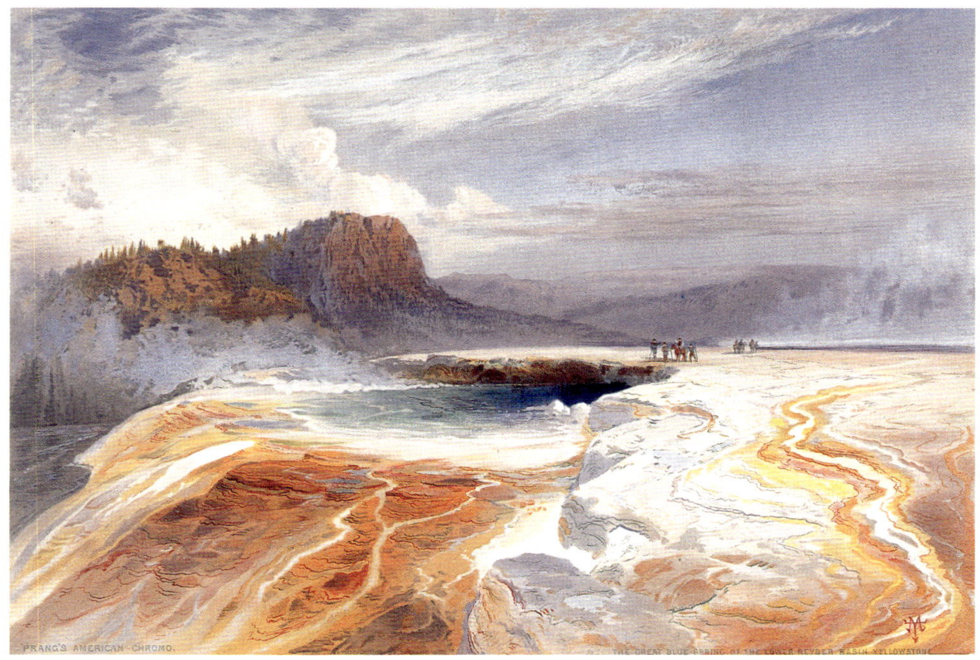

THE GREAT BLUE SPRING OF THE LOWER GEYSER BASIN

At the upper end of the Lower Geyser Basin is a group of springs that have been called the Half-way Springs, from the fact that they are about half-way between the centre of the lower basin and the lower limit of the upper basin. They are found on the left bank of the Fire Hole River, on the summit of a mound-like hill of silica, rising fifty feet above the level of the river. In this mound are several springs, among them the Great Blue Spring, one of the grandest hot springs ever seen by the human eye. It is near the margin of the river. Its edge is somewhat broken down on the river side, while the opposite edge is intact. At the latter place the lamination of the silicious deposit can readily be seen. The surface of this vast caldron, 250 feet in diameter, is intensely agitated, and steam is constantly rising, so that only when the passing breeze sweeps it aside can we gaze into the seething pit, where the water over the deepest part of the spring appears of the most intense blue color, fading toward the edge into a green. The overflow from the spring pours over the slope in small channels, or spreads over broad surfaces, where the evaporation of the water has deposited a crust of a marvellous combination of tints. The coloring is very vivid, and of many shades, from bright scarlet to delicate rose, mingled with bright and creamy yellows, and vivid green from the minute vegetation. Some of the channels are lined with a fine, delicate, yellow, silky vegetable growth, vibrating with every movement of the water. Back of the Blue Spring is another large pool 150 feet in diameter. It is almost impossible to give an idea either in words or picture of the exquisite beauty of the springs of which the Great Blue Spring is a type.

They are of all sizes, generally funnel-shaped, reaching unfathomable depths, and lined inside and out with delicate decorations. Looking into their depths we seem to see the interior of a fairy palace. The edge of the Spring is generally scalloped with exceeding regularity; while the sides, which sometimes slope inward gradually until lost to view in the depths, or again descend abruptly and perpendicularly, are corrugated and incrusted in the most varied manner. The tint of the clear water in these caverns is a beautiful blue or bluish green, to be compared only to the blue of a clear sky, and even then we must imagine the color intensified. It seems as though the cavity were lined with a portion of the heavens convoluted and rolled over the projecting ridges on the sides of the spring, each one of which throws back to us the sunlight resolved into its primary colors.

Around each spring extends a vast deposit of silicious sinter generally of a pure white color, except where the evaporation of the water has coated it, or where there is a low vegetable growth of a jelly-like substance of light red or green color, the surface of which yields beneath the foot like a cushion.

A similar substance is found lining springs when the temperature of the water is very low. When dry it resembles a brownish lichen. The temperature of most of the springs is at or near the boiling-point, and on a frosty morning the steam rises in dense clouds, and we might almost imagine ourselves in some great manufacturing village, the illusion being assisted by the noise of steam-jets and the throbbing of some of the large springs, or the falling of the water from the eruption of a geyser.

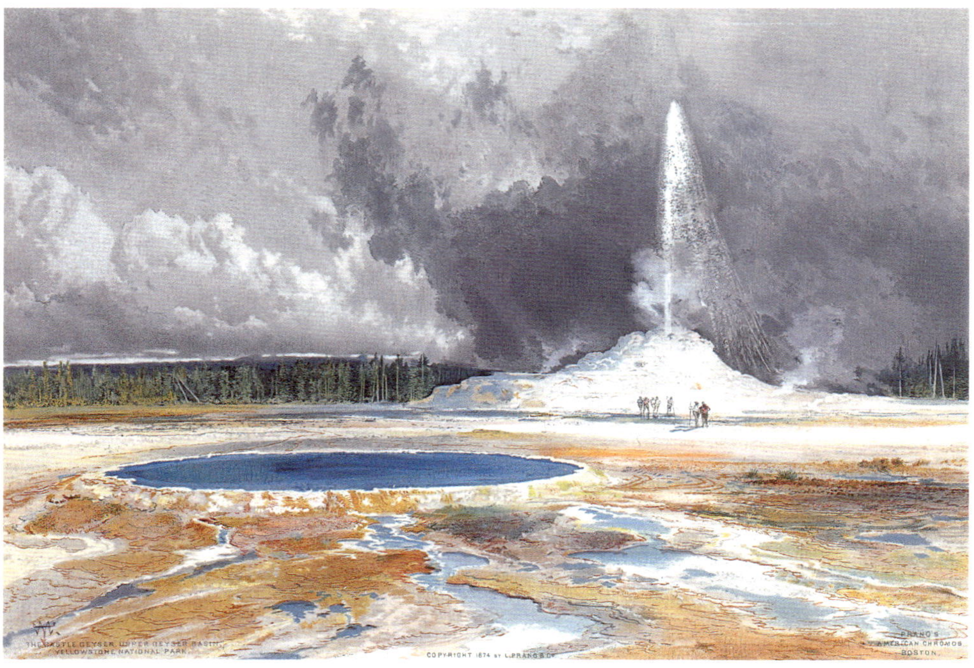

THE CASTLE GEYSER, UPPER GEYSER BASIN

A geyser is nothing more nor less than a column, or natural fountain of boiling water, projected at stated intervals from a tubular orifice in the ground. The word is Icelandic in origin, being derived from "geysa," meaning to rush out, to be impelled. It was formerly applied only to the great geyser of Iceland, but has become generic in its application.

Beside the geysers of the Fire Hole, or Upper Madison, those of Iceland sink into insignificance. The geysers of the Fire Hole are contained in two basins, — the lower basin and the upper basin, occupying altogether about seventy-five square miles. In this area are thousands of springs, mud-pools, and geysers, whose temperatures range from warm to the boiling-point. The water in the river itself, fed by these springs, is warmer than that of rivers ordinarily. Almost the entire area throughout the two basins is covered with a hard glaring-white siliceous sinter. The springs are of three classes: 1st. Those which are constantly agitated or boiling; 2d. Those which are only agitated at particular periods; and 3d. Those which are always tranquil. To the second class belong all the geysers in which the water is usually quiet until within a short time of the eruption, when it begins to bubble, and there is an escape of steam. The water rises gradually in the basin until it is suddenly projected into the air with great violence. Some of the geysers have built huge siliceous mounds or craters, from the summits of which the water is propelled in jets.

The lower geyser basin contains a larger number of springs than the upper basin, and the scene as we look out upon it on a cool frosty morning surpasses description. All about us rise columns of steam mingled with numerous fountain jets. The delicate wreaths of steam extend far up into the heavens. Interesting as is the lower basin, it must yield the palm to the upper for the magnitude of its geysers. Among the great geysers the "Castle," represented in the picture, plays an important part. It has a somewhat irregular crater in the centre of a gently sloping mound of sinter. From a platform three feet high, measuring 75 by 100 feet, its cone rises 11 feet. This cone is 120 feet in circumference at the base, and 20 feet in diameter at the top. The orifice of the tube is only three feet in diameter, and lined with large orange-colored globular masses. The eruption commences with a succession of jets of water and steam, which reach a height of two hundred feet. This continues about a quarter of an hour, and is succeeded by steam and spray escaping in pulsations, which soon change to a continuous volume of steam that entirely fills the orifice, being ejected with steady force and great noise. The noises are indescribable. It sounds as though the Castle had a thunder-storm in its interior, and to those noises of elemental war add the sounds of several steamboats letting off steam, and we can form some idea of the sounds heard during the eruption of the geyser. The entire eruption lasts about an hour and a half.

In front of the Castle is the beautiful blue spring, which has been given the fanciful name of "Circe's Boudoir." Words must fail to give an idea of the exquisite beauty of this spring. It is almost circular, measuring 19 by 21 feet. The edge is regularly scalloped. The basin is of marble-like appearance, and slopes to a funnel-shaped orifice, which is forty feet deep. The water in this basin is as clear as crystal, and of a beautiful blue tint, increasing in depth of color from the rim to the central orifice. The overflow from the spring in its meanderings spreads over a large surface, leaving brilliant streaks of color. On the side towards the river, shown in the foreground of the picture, it forms shallow pools, painting the white siliceous deposits with colors of the rainbow. Beds of rich creamy white, brilliant reds, and yellows are intermingled with patches of purple and delicate greens, surrounded with curious patterns of rich browns and grays. Where the water is warmest, the colors are most vivid. The form of the deposits and the blue color of the water add to the beauty of the picture.

This spring is not the only one of its kind. Scattered through the basins are numbers that will rival it in color and beauty of forms. They must be seen to be appreciated, for even the artist's pencil in this case falls short of nature.

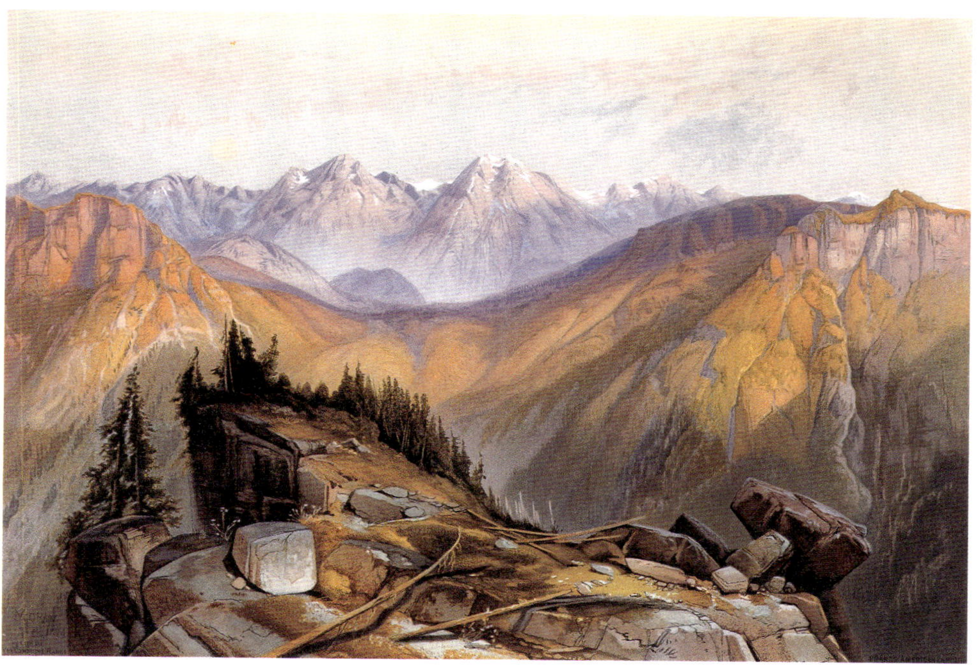

THE LOWER YELLOWSTONE RANGE

The Lower Yellowstone Range furnishes one of the most attractive views in that region of strange and beautiful scenery, the Northern Wonder-Land. This range of mountains is located on the east side of the Yellowstone River, just above the Lower Cañon, or Gate of the Mountains, and about thirty miles south-east of Fort Ellis, Montana Territory. Seen from the valley of the river, as in the sketch accompanying this description, it presents a series of cone-shaped peaks, resembling pyramids, and grouped alongside of each other in a row thirty or forty miles long. The sides of these peaks are almost vertical, and their summits are bald and covered with perpetual snow. Owing to this fact the whole chain was formerly called the "Snowy Mountains," a name frequently met with on old maps.

The Lower Yellowstone Range forms the great water-shed to the portions of the Yellowstone River immediately above and below the first cañon, and gives rise to some of the most important branches of that river. The latter, indeed, receives the waters from both of its declivities, a curious fact, which, as a reference to the map will show, is due to the position of the range within a bend of the Yellowstone. The deep gorges, which cut through the very core of the mountains, and form the wonderful gulches explored only by the hardy and daring miner, have been gashed out by the action of aqueous forces. One of these, named Emigrant Gulch, extends up into the mountain about eight miles. It is a deep, narrow gorge, with walls of green and dark brown quartzite and true gneiss, the peculiar hues of which are rendered still more sombre from their contact with volcanic rocks. At its bottom a fine stream of water flows swiftly over a rocky bed into the Yellowstone. It is estimated that $150,000 in gold dust was taken out of this gulch by miners in 1864. The western side of the range forms the eastern wall of one of the beautiful valleys of the Yellowstone, about thirty miles long, and with an average width of from three to five miles. This valley is really an ancient lake basin, one of the links in a chain of lakes which in past geological times extended from the sources of both the Missouri and Yellowstone Rivers far down into the plains. One of the highest cones of the whole range is Emigrant Peak, and from its summit there can be seen, as far as the field of vision extends, a vast mass of basaltic mountains rising to the height of from 10,000 to 11,000 feet.

The nucleus of the range is composed of granitic rocks, but the volcanic material has flowed up through the fissures, so that the sides and summits are covered with it. It is to these rocks that the mountains owe their varied and peculiar colors. As the rays of the setting sun rest upon them, they seem to possess an almost unnatural brilliancy from the blending of a great variety of hues. The color in Mr. Moran's painting is in no respect exaggerated, and in nature this beauty of color is still further enhanced by the remarkable delicacy of the innumerable shades which unite to form one glorious whole. The lower portions of the mountains are covered with a dense growth of pine, but the summits are bare of vegetation. Several members of the Geological Survey who have visited the far-famed mountains of Central Europe regard this range as in no way inferior in beauty to any in that country.

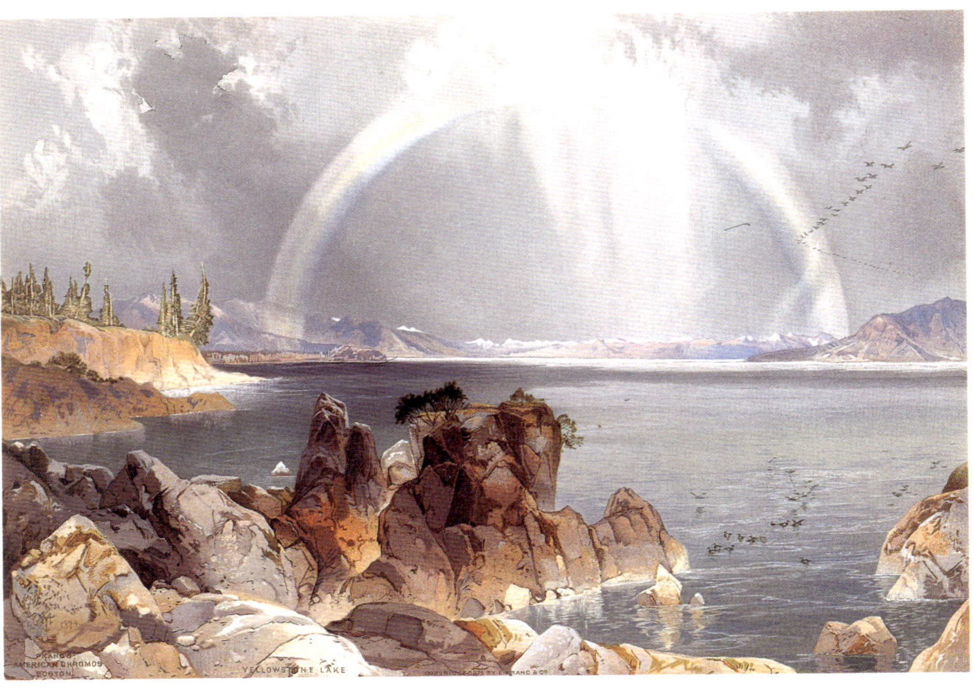

YELLOWSTONE LAKE

On the earliest maps of the West the Yellowstone River is represented as having its origin in a large lake called "Eustis Lake." On later maps it appears as "Sublette's Lake," and later still, the name "Yellowstone" is applied to it. It covers an area of about one hundred and twenty-five square miles, being about twenty miles long in its greatest length, and fifteen miles wide across the widest part. Its greatest depth is only three hundred feet. Its shape has been compared to that of an outspread hand, the main body of the lake representing the palm, while the four bays projecting southward represent the fingers, two of which are swollen and two dwarfed, and the southwestern bay represents a much-enlarged thumb.

The elevation of Yellowstone Lake is 7,788 feet. The only lakes of considerable size that have a greater elevation are the sacred lakes of Thibet, Lake "Nameho" of the Himalayas, and Lake "Titicaca" of Peru. The western side of Yellowstone Lake is densely wooded with tall pines, as also the southern shore, where there is a great deal of low land, which in the spring and summer is marshy. There are numerous small lakelets lying between Yellowstone Lake and the heads of Snake River.

To the south and west there are no high mountains; and ascending any one of the ridges in these directions we can see the streams rising at our feet flowing on either side with gentle descent, those on the one hand to join the Atlantic, and those on the other to mingle with the great Pacific.

The divides are so low that at one place is said to be a two-ocean stream that divides, one branch flowing to the Pacific side on the other towards the Atlantic.

The eastern side of the lake is well wooded, but more broken by beautiful grassy prairies, abounding with game, elk, deer, and grouse. On this side also there are some of the most beautiful shore-lines imaginable; some of the curves are as perfect as if drawn by hand. Mary's Bay, near Steamboat Point, on the northeast side, is one of the most perfect. Here also is Diamond Beach, so called from the crystals found in its sand mingled with particles of obsidian, or volcanic glass. The rocks about the lake are volcanic, trachytes predominating.

The country east of the lake rises very rapidly into a magnificent range of sharp volcanic peaks, about 10,000 feet above sea level, on whose slopes huge snow-banks rest until far into the summer, feeding numerous streams flowing into the lake. The principal peaks are Mounts Stevenson and Doane. The water of the lake is intensely cold at all times. It is filled with large salmon trout. If we visit the lake early in the morning, we find the surface perfectly placid, spreading out before us a quiet sheet of the most varied hues, from vivid green to delicate ultramarine. As the morning progresses, we notice a curious sound, a sort of whistle, which we find to be caused by gusts of wind in the air above our heads. Gradually the lower atmosphere is put in motion, and the tall pines sway back and forth in the western breeze, which grows stronger and stronger until the surface of the lake is broken into myriads of foam-capped waves that dash furiously on the shore, forming quite a heavy surf. This strong western wind is of almost daily occurrence.

There are three islands in the lake, "Stevenson's Island," "Frank's," and "Dot Island." They are probably elevated portions of the old lake bed, which have appeared as land by the gradual subsidence of the water of the lake, which once covered a much greater area than at present.

There are numerous hot springs, and the remains of many that are extinct, found on the shore of the lake. The most interesting are at Steamboat Point and on the south-western arm. At Steamboat Point there are several steam-vents from which the steam escapes in pulsations with a sound resembling that caused by the letting off of steam from some huge steamboat.

On the southwest arm of the lake are some unique springs whose conical silicious mounds rise above the surface of the water a short distance from the shore. The water in these springs is boiling hot, while that of the lake surrounding them is cold. Standing on one of these mounds the rod can be extended and trout caught, which, without being removed from the hook, may be cooked in the boiling spring. On the shore is a group of beautiful pink mud-springs near large pools of hot and warm water.

Brimstone Basin, on the east side of the lake, is an area of sulphur and alum deposits in which the springs have long been extinct.

From whatever point the lake is viewed, a scene of beauty will repay the observer. The student of science, the lover of nature, and the artist can all find something of interest on its shores.

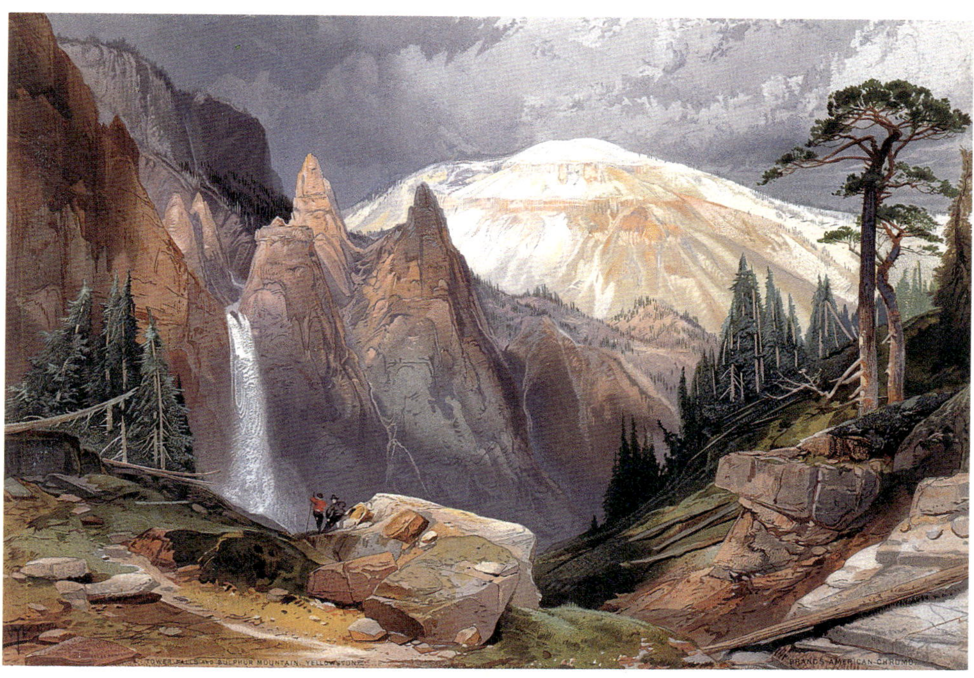

TOWER FALLS AND SULPHER MOUNTAIN

Tower Creek is a swift mountain torrent, rising near Mt. Washburn, in the divide between the Yellowstone, Gallatin, and Madison Rivers. For about ten miles it rushes madly along its course, the greater part of the distance through a cañon, the lower portion of which has been called "The Devil's Den." On either side of the creek are high tower-like masses, which stand there as if they kept guard over the stream. Passing between two of these rocky towers, after it has described a semicircular bend, the creek suddenly dashes over a ledge, which falls perpendicularly one hundred and fifty-six feet to a rounded basin, cut from the solid rock. Recovering from the shock, the stream hurries with frightful velocity in numerous rapids through a gloomy gorge, to join the Yellowstone a short distance beyond the fall. The upper course of the creek is obstructed by many bowlders, one of which at present stands at the extreme edge of the fall, waiting until the water shall have removed its foundation, when it will be precipitated to the bottom of the cañon, to join company with a similar mass, which once occupied a place on the brink, and is now continually bathed by the spray of the descending water.

Some of the lofty towers above referred to may be ascended by expert climbers. The view of the fall thus obtained is exceedingly grand, but the great height is calculated to cause dizziness in the head of even the boldest adventurer, as he gazes into the depths of the chasm far below.

A prominent object in the landscape is "Sulphur Mountain," on the opposite side of the Yellowstone. Two rows of basaltic columnar rocks, in a bluff wall that rises from 400 to 500 feet above the river, form a distinguishing feature of this mountain. The columns, which extend for two miles along the river and are plainly visible in the picture, are hexagonal in form, those in the upper line being from fifteen to twenty feet high, while those below reach thirty feet. Between the two rows there are strata of breccia and conglomerate, infiltrated with sulphur, from which latter the mountain has obtained its name. At the foot of the perpendicular wall the river is a perfect torrent of emerald-green water, capped with foam.

Tower Creek marks the lower end of the Grand Cañon of the Yellowstone, and the interest which it excites by reason of the grand scenery surrounding it is still further enhanced from the fact that there are several sulphur springs in its vicinity.

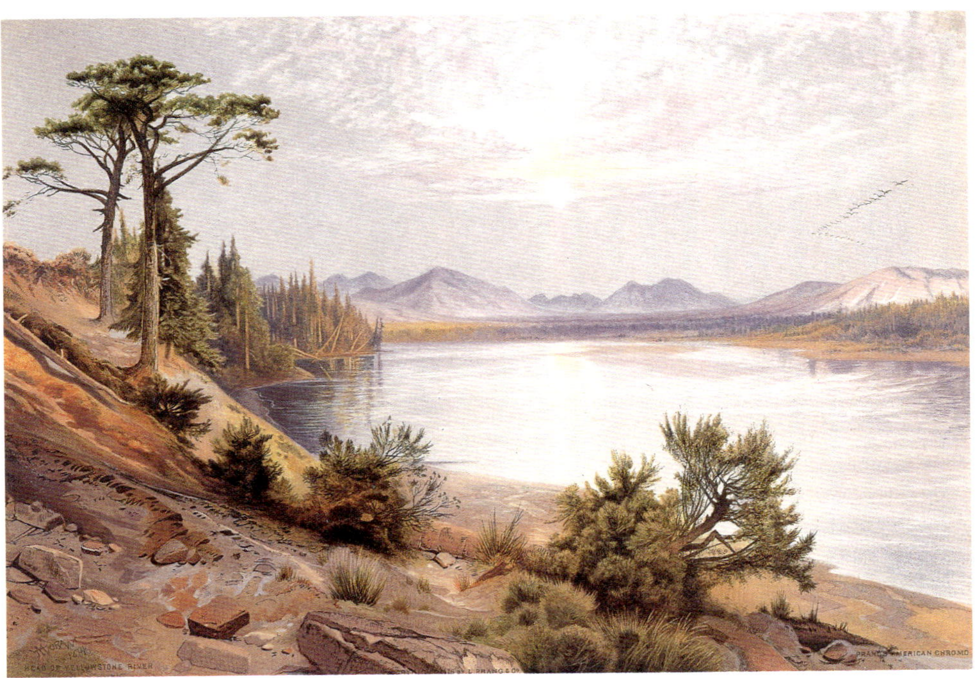

HEAD OF THE YELLOWSTONE RIVER

The Yellowstone River, or "Pierre Jaune" of the early French trappers, is one of the main branches of the Missouri, and from its source in Yellowstone Lake to its mouth at Fort Union, on the west line of Dakota, has a length of 1,300 miles, with a descent of nearly 6,000 feet. The river passes through a great variety of scenery, but at no point can it boast of more enchanting beauty than at its very head, near the magnificent lake of which it forms the outlet. Starting from the northwest extremity of the lake, it wanders in an aimless sort of a way to the northward, with sluggish current more like a lake than a great stream, its waters teeming with flocks of geese and ducks. Beautiful islands spot its broad surface, and beyond its pine-fringed shore the hazy outlines of distant mountains stand out boldly against the horizon. Along the shore there are numerous boiling mud and sulphur springs.

About ten miles below the head of the river the scene gradually changes, until finally the Yellowstone is converted into a rapid torrent, rushing along between rocky banks. Here and there huge rocks stand up in the middle of the rapids. The stream gains more and more in velocity as the slope of its bed increases, and soon it shoots over the Upper Fall, striking far out from the base of the cliff. At the foot of the fall it recovers itself, and, as if ashamed of its mad frolic, wanders quietly and demurely along for a quarter of a mile until it reaches the Lower Fall. At this point the water does not plunge or leap, it merely rolls over, forming a waterfall of the simplest kind, but nearly 400 feet in height. From the foot of the Lower Fall the stream pours tumultuously down a narrow chasm in a volcanic plateau, between cañon-walls 1,000 feet in height, and of colors of barbaric richness, yellows, reds, purples, and black. Through this chasm, which is known as the Grand Cañon, the river flows for thirty miles. At the mouth of Gardiner's River it again emerges into the light of day, and thence flows through a narrow valley, on either side of which rise snow-capped mountains. Down this valley, still flowing northward, the river holds its way. In two places the foothills of the mountains close in on the stream and grant it but a narrow passageway.

At the mouth of Shield's River the course of the Yellowstone sweeps around to the east, and but a short distance below this point it leaves the mountains to flow through broad and fertile bottoms, the home of the Crow Indians. It receives many large tributaries, among them the Big Horn, Clark's Fork, and Shield's River, and is navigable from its mouth to the intersection of the Big Horn.

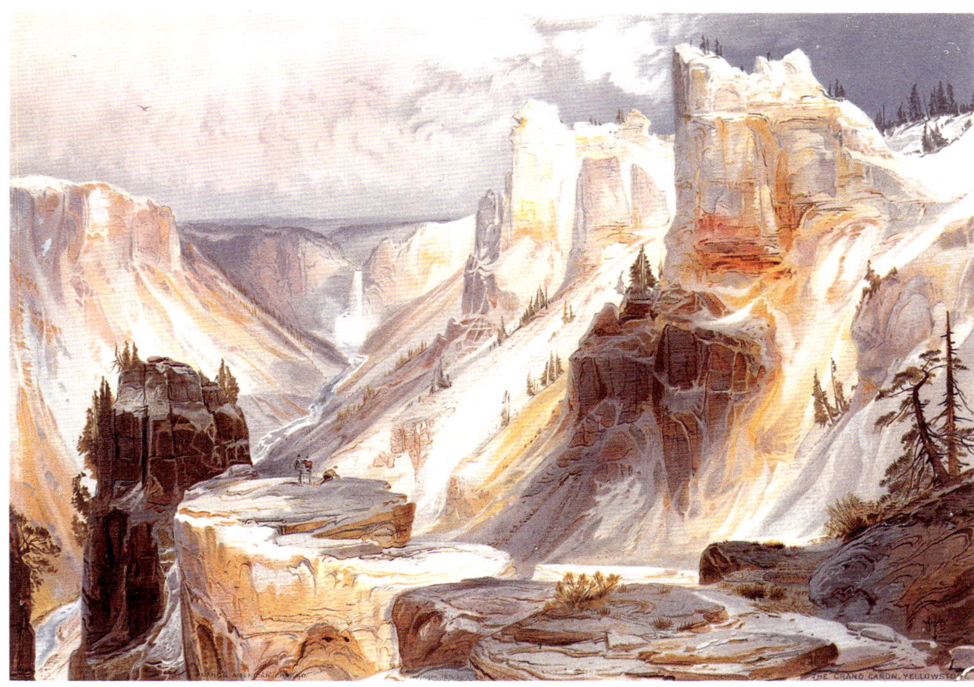

THE GRAND CAÑON OF THE YELLOWSTONE

One of the subjects of greatest interest in the Yellowstone National Park is the Grand Cañon, at the head of which is the Lower or Great Fall of the Yellowstone. It is one of the most remarkable cañons in the world, not only from its depth, but also from the brilliancy of its coloring. Even art must despair in attempting to reproduce the gorgeous tints displayed on its walls. The Yellowstone River on leaving the lake flows along peacefully between low banks over sandy reaches and pebbly bottoms, giving no indication of the turmoil into which it is to plunge but a short distance below. As it approaches the falls, the stream narrows and breaks into rapids. Having descended over the ledge forming the upper fall, 140 feet high, a farther run of a quarter of a mile brings it to the Lower or Great Fall situated at the upper limit of the Grand Cañon. Long before the Lower Fall is reached a deep roar like that of thunder gives warning of its presence. The river again suddenly narrows to a width of about 100 feet, and in one immense volume rushes over the precipice, falling nearly 400 feet. Let us approach the brink and look over. The cloud of spray obscures the view of the base of the fall. As we look into the abyss we realize the littleness of man when compared with the works of nature. Down goes the whirling mass, battling and writhing as the waters dash against the rocks with a noise like the discharge of artillery. Here and there a projecting rock is struck, and the water is resolved into myriads of drops. The bottom reached, the column breaks into a cloud of ascending spray, which, taken in connection with the varied tints of the cañon, produces a scene of unequalled magnificence.

The cañon extends from the falls to the mouth of Gardiner's River, a distance of about thirty miles. It is a gorge cut into volcanic rocks. No language can do justice to its wonderful grandeur and beauty. Standing at the edge of the fall we look into the chasm at the bottom of which the river appears like an attenuated thread of emerald green with silver edges. The walls, in many places vertical, slope to the water's edge, leaving no beach. In some places they are eroded into fantastic shapes, towers, spires, and Gothic columns; in others again they present fortress-like fronts, or long slides of brilliant-colored débris; while elsewhere they consist of massive rock, separated by jointage, resembling irregular masonry going to decay. Here and there a depression has been filled by sandstone, a remnant of the deposits left at the bottom of the lake, that once covered all this area. Stripes of bright red reach from the top to the bottom. The prevailing color is white, from the decomposing feldspar, streaked and splotched with red and yellow by deposits of iron and sulphur, while others of the rocks are black, relieved only by the green, where vegetation has gained a foothold. Here and there a pine sends it roots into the sloping débris, clutching the rocks as though its life were a continual struggle for existence.

An hour and a quarter of hard work will bring us to the bottom of the cañon. Now we see that the river is a succession of rapids, and its surface a mass of furiously agitated waves which dash madly against the rocky walls. The sense of danger which the place inspires is truly harrowing. The awful silence around us is broken only by the sounds of the waves. Looking up we see the pine-fringed margin of the walls, while farther down and yet far above our heads, some hawks disturbed by us in our descent float in the air in graceful circles. The rocks throw a dark gray shadow all about us. The sunlight does not reach us, but gilds the trees above us with its rays. The scene is fearfully grand and surpasses description.

The ascent of the cañon will take us over two hours, and we shall have to crawl on our hands and knees part of the way. We shall have to creep carefully around ledges, holding on with both hands and feet, knowing that a single misstep will precipitate us to the bottom, to become the prey of the angry waves.

The view of the cañon from the point selected for Mr. Moran's sketch, that is to say, some distance below the falls, is very fine, including the falls as the centre of the picture. The roar of the cataract is here partially suppressed by the distance. Far in the background we catch a shadowy glimpse of distant mountains, and beneath us in the foreground flows the river between the variegated walls of the gorge. The colors with which these walls are tinted — yellows, reds, browns, and whites, all intermingling and gradually passing into each other — show a greater variety of shade than ever adorned a work of human art.

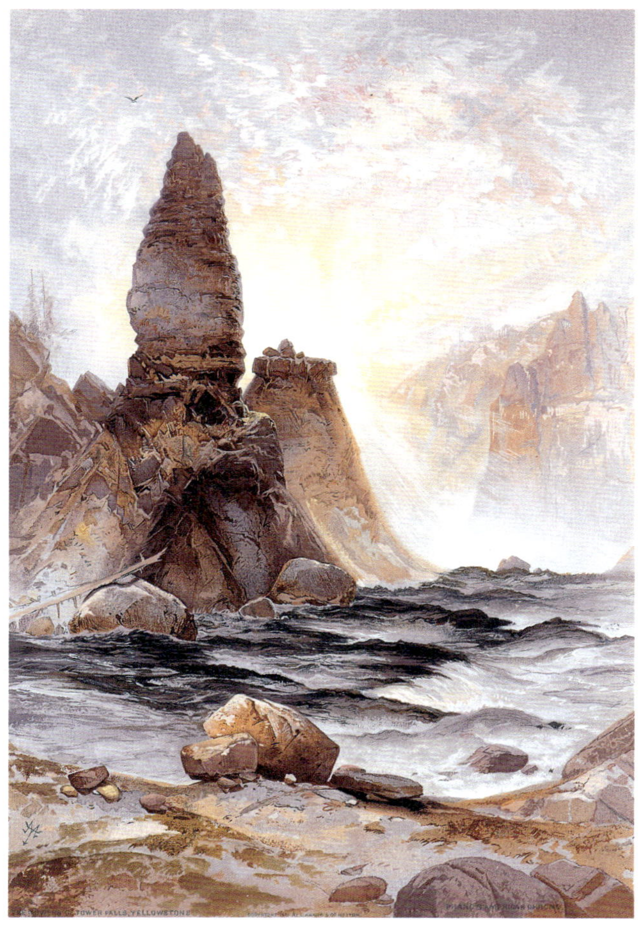

THE TOWERS OF TOWER FALLS

Tower Falls derives its name from the tower-like masses of breccia which form one of the most conspicuous features in the scenery surrounding the falls.

For countless ages the action of the water has been gnawing at the substance of the rocks, the remnants of which still stand on the banks of the creek. Some of these rocks are as slender as the minarets of a mosque, while others resemble rude towers, or Gothic spires. Two gigantic pillars stand at the edge of the fall, rising 100 feet above its angry waves. Many of the formations are so fantastic as to excite merriment. One mass has been named the Devil's Hoof, from a supposed resemblance to the proverbial hoof of his Satanic Majesty. The old mountaineers, who first travelled in the Yellowstone country, were particularly lavish in their use of the infernal vocabulary, and consequently we find many places bearing Satanic names, some of which, from their peculiar fitness, will never be superseded. Between the pillars which stand along the course of Tower Creek, the stream rushes madly along over huge bowlders that have fallen in the process of erosion. Many of these bowlders have already been carried over the fall, and others will doubtless share the same fate in the future. The scenery of rock, water, and forest in the neighborhood of the falls is strikingly picturesque. The view from the summit of one of the towers well repays the dangerous climb. The effect at sunrise is particularly striking. The gray dawn gradually gives place to a rosy light, and this again fades imperceptibly into the full yellow light of day which contrasts boldly with the dark colors of the pillars and the deep green of the rushing stream at their feet. This effect, which might have thrown into ecstasies the light-loving soul of a Turner, has been reproduced with consummate skill in Mr. Moran's brilliant sketch.

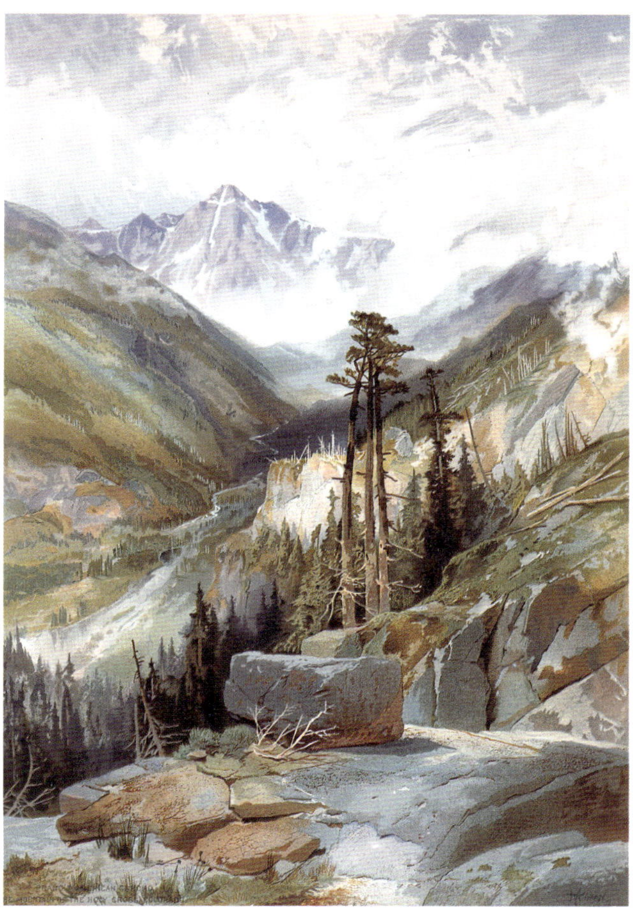

THE MOUNTAIN OF THE HOLY CROSS

The Mountain of the Holy Cross is in some respects the most remarkable peak on the American continent. Not, however, owing to its height of 14,176 feet above tide water, as there are from fifty to seventy-five peaks in Central Colorado which reach an elevation of over 14,000 feet; nor on account of the ruggedness and grandeur of its surroundings, for in this respect it is also equalled by many of its competitors. The distinguishing feature of the mountain, which may be seen by the naked eye as far away as the summit of Gray's Peak in the Colorado or Front Range, a distance of from 80 to 100 miles, is the cross on its south side. This cross, which forms one of the most attractive and most conspicuous landmarks in the West, is produced by snow lying in two intersecting seams of gneiss or granite. The face of the mountain, for about 3,000 feet in height, being nearly vertical, and so steep that no snow can lie on it, the cross remains visible throughout the whole year. The upright beam of the cross is about 1,500 feet in length, the snow in the crevice being from 50 to 100 feet deep. The length of the horizontal arm varies with the season, but averages about 700 feet in length. Under what circumstances, or at what time, the mountain received its exceedingly appropriate name is not now known. But it may be excusable to suppose that the words "Monte Santa Cruz" came almost spontaneously to the lips of some early, long-forgotten Catholic missionary, as, in his perilous wanderings, the uplifted symbol of his faith suddenly appeared before his wondering eyes.

From the summit of the Mountain of the Holy Cross the view in every direction is one of the grandest and most varied in the West, presenting whole groups of rugged peaks, which rise high above timber line and are covered here and there with masses of perpetual snow. Near the mountain crests repose beautiful green lakes, filled with ice-cold water from the melting snow, and forming the sources of the restless mountain streams which rush downward through the deep gorges. At the base of the Holy Cross there is a similar lake, and the stream issuing from it is seen to the left of the picture flowing down the valley in a series of falls and rapids so connected as to form a most picturesque cascade for several miles. This valley, which now forms the rocky bed of the torrent, was once the bed of an ancient glacier, and its bottom and sides, for a distance of 2,000 feet or more, are rounded and scarred by the action of ice. Looking down the valley from the summit of the mountain, the eye rests upon one of the most remarkable illustrations of what are called in Switzerland "Roches Moutonnes," or "sheep-backed rocks," so called because at a distance they look like a flock of enormous recumbent sheep. These rocks, which are scattered irregularly over the valley, vary in height from ten to fifty feet, and the inter stices between them are covered with fallen pines, sometimes forming a network several feet high.

It is impossible to approach on horseback within five miles of the base of the peak, and the reader may judge of the difficulties which were encountered by the members of the geological survey, if he will bear in mind that they had to travel over such a surface loaded down with instruments of all sorts. No other party has ever visited this spot before or since, and it is not probable that it will ever be accessible to the general public.

The Mountain of the Holy Cross is located at the north end of the great Sawatch or Sierra Madre Range, in latitude 39° 28' 4" and longitude 106° 28' 37", about 80 miles west of Denver, in the centre of the most rugged and mountainous region of Colorado. The Holy Cross group forms a portion of the water "divide" of the continent, the drainage of the eastern slope leading to the Atlantic, while that of the western leads to the Pacific Ocean.

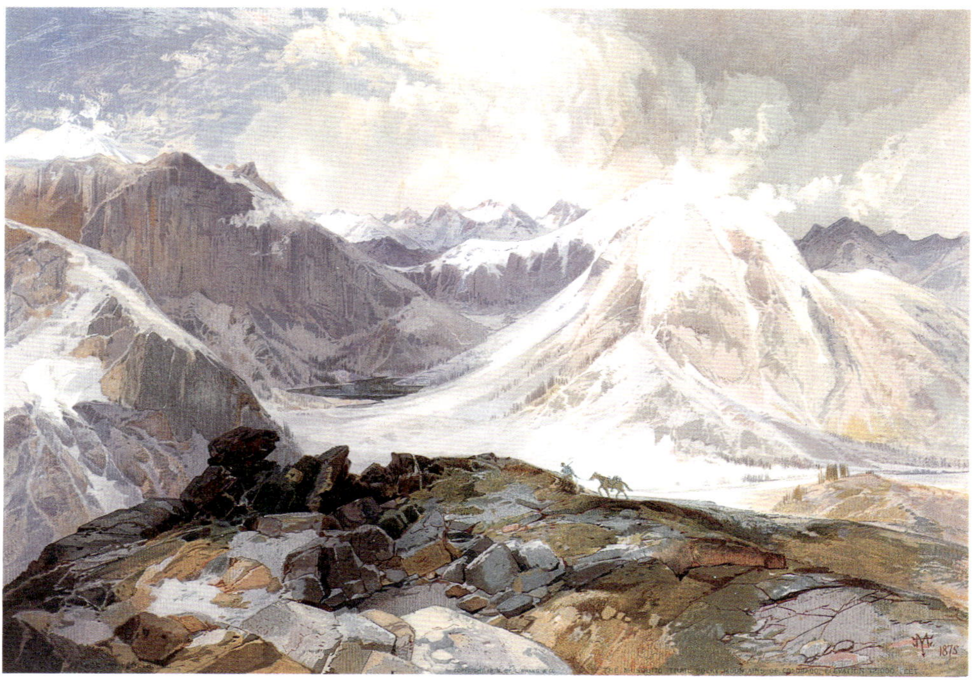

THE MOSQUITO TRAIL, ROCKY MOUNTAINS OF COLORADO

The view here given represents a portion of the great Park Range, which forms the west wall of the South Park. It is located in the vicinity of some of the rich gold and silver mines of Colorado, and the road to which it owes its name is in reality nothing but a miner's trail leading across the range from one mining gulch to another. The rocks are what are usually termed metamorphic, or primary, quartzitic, feldspathic, with a small addition of mica. They are everywhere traversed by veins of silver, while the loose superficial deposits on the sides of the mountains and in the gorges are filled with fine particles of yellow gold. The general level of the district is 10,000 feet above tide water; but the trails which lead over the ridges and passes carry the traveller above timber line, or, in other words, above the height of 11,500 feet, and into the midst of patches of perpetual snow. Mr. Moran has chosen one of these elevated passes for his sketch.

The scenery in the vicinity of the Mosquito Trail is not unlike that of the Holy Cross group, for as far as the field of vision extends on either side the eye encounters a wilderness of sharp granite peaks. Forming a portion of the immediate group is Mount Lincoln, with an elevation of 14,297 feet,— the highest point in the Park Range. Of the three mountain ranges — the loftiest on the continent — which loom up one after the other, the Sawatch is the most prominent, and literally bristles with high peaks for a distance of 80 miles from north to south. Conspicuous among the peaks of this range, which forms the water divide of the West, are Mount Harvard, with a height of 14,384 feet; Yale, 14,151 feet; Princeton, 14,199, feet and many others varying from 12,000 to 14,000 feet. At the extreme north end of the range stands the wonderful Mountain of the Holy Cross, while to the far south the Uncompahgre Peak, one of the highest points in America, is relieved against the sky. About ten miles to the westward, nestled in the glacier-worn gorge of Lake Fork, are distinctly seen the beautiful Twin Lakes, which at some period in the future will become one of the most attractive watering-places in the West. Looking down likewise to the westward, we can also see the beautiful valley of the Upper Arkansas River. To the southeast and east of the South Park the scope of vision finally embraces Pike's Peak, Gray's and Torrey's Peak, and numbers of others rising to a height of from 13,000 to 14,000 feet.

From the summit of any of the peaks in the vicinity of the trail the view in all directions of the compass is grand beyond description. But with the grandeur of the scene there is associated a keen sense of dreariness, loneliness, and desolation.

Returning once more to the spot which formed our starting-point in the survey just completed, we may remark that it offers a good example of what are called cirques or amphitheatres. These latter always occur at the sources of the small mountain streams which rise on either side of a mountain crest. All these streams have their origin at the head of a gorge or gulch, in a small lake, or reservoir, as it were, which is produced by the accumulation of the waters from the melting mountain snow. Some of these lakes are partially frozen the year round, and their water is so icy cold that little or no animal life can exist in them.

The average elevation of Colorado, the highest of all the States and Territories in the Union, is 6,600 feet. It may truly be said that in variety, beauty, and grandeur its scenery is inexhaustible.

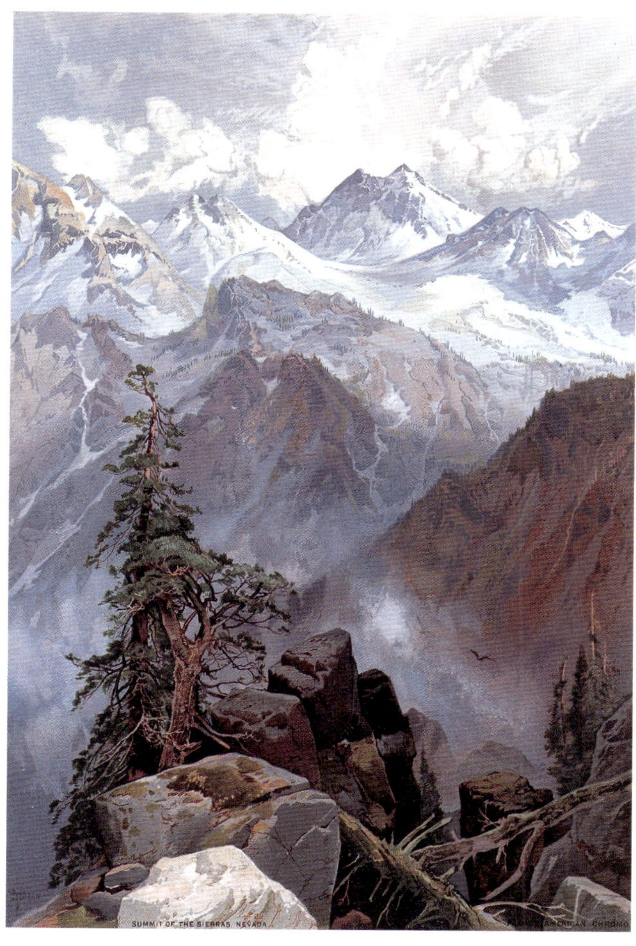

THE SUMMIT OF THE SIERRAS

The Sierra Nevada or "Snowy Range" of the Pacific Coast approaches more nearly the Alpine Mountains of Central Europe than any other range on the American continent. In extent or altitude, and in the abrupt ruggedness of its many lofty peaks, with their sides and summits covered by vast masses of snow and ice, it has no superior in any other part of the world.

The Sierra Nevada Range, of which the beautiful picture before us is a striking illustration, is situated on the border-line between California and Nevada, and extends from Tejou Pass to Mount Shasta, a distance of over 550 miles, its average breadth being about 80 miles. Its central mass or core is composed mostly of granite, flanked on both sides by metamorphic slates, capped with vast masses of basaltic and other kinds of lava, and heavy beds of ashes and breccia, witnesses of former subterranean volcanic forces which must have acted here on a tremendous scale, and of which at this time we are only reminded now and then by an earthquake shock. Among the peaks of this range is found the highest mountain in the United States, Mount Whitney, which rises to an elevation of 15,000 feet above the sea-level, while there are many others from 12,000 to 14,000 feet and upwards. In the same range also the Yosemite Valley is situated, — that unique and wonderful locality which has been set apart by legislative authority as a place of public resort and recreation for the people, unalienable for all time. The most striking difference between the Californian and Swiss Alpine scenery seems to consist principally in the much smaller quantity of snow in the Sierra as compared with equal elevations in Switzerland. The marks of old glaciers are very abundant, the polished surfaces, the extensive moraines or long trains of detritus, and the striae engraved on the walls of the cañons, testifying in most eloquent language to the icy covering which once clothed these mountains as it now clothes the Alps. The vast glacial masses still to be seen, although not true glaciers, likewise are silent witnesses of the past. The magnificent pine forests of the Sierras far surpass those of the Alps, and form one of the most attractive features of the scenery, even though they give a sombre tone to the landscape as seen from a distance in their dark shades of green.

The view before us is no doubt familiar to thousands who have crossed the Sierras on the Central Pacific Railroad. The clouds enveloping the snowy summits and the mists rising from the gorges can be seen at almost any season of the year. The beautiful green lakes, such as Donner Lake, Lake Tahoe, and hundreds of others of various sizes, attract the eye from every high point, as they lie nestled among the mountain peaks. These lakes are fed by the melting of the snows, and are usually the sources of the myriads of mountain streams which unite in the lowlands and form some of the large rivers of the Pacific Coast.

Up to the present day only a preliminary exploration has been made of the remarkable scenery of this region, although no portion of the globe is fraught with deeper interest to the mountaineer and lover of grand scenery than the Sierra Nevada of the Pacific Coast.

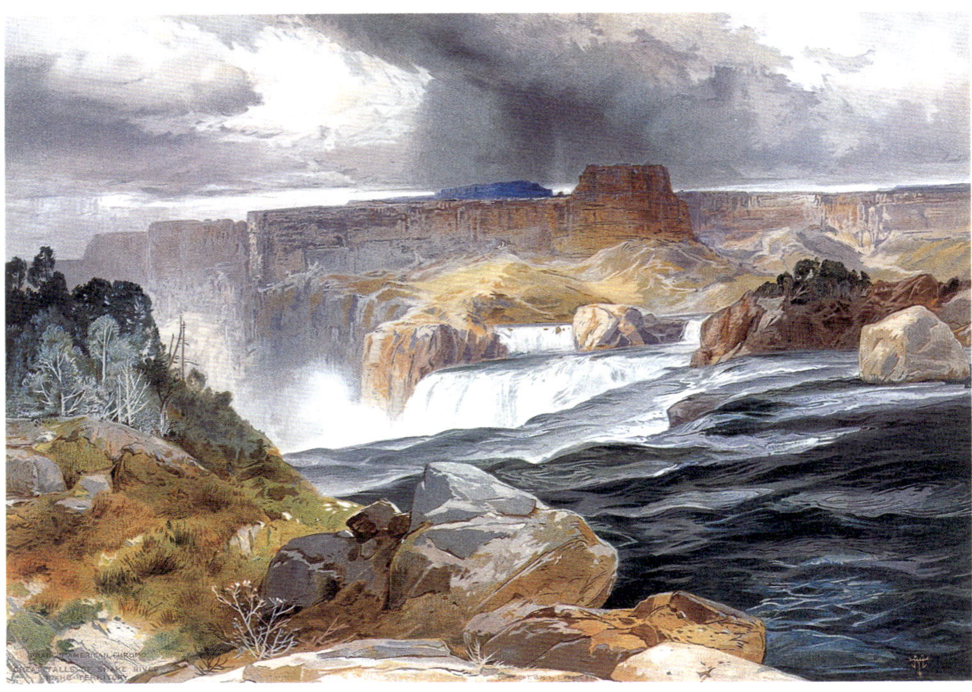

THE GREAT FALLS OF SNAKE RIVER, IDAHO TERRITORY

The following description is in part abridged from Mr. Clarence King's graphic account of a visit to the region of the Snake River in October, 1868.

The Snake River, or Shoshone, — the latter a far more appropriate Indian name, which ought in future to be used on all our maps, — forms the main branch of the great Columbia River, and rises in the southern portion of the Yellowstone National Park. Its course for the most part lies across a vast lava plain, into which it has cut deep cañons with almost vertical, black walls. An observer, standing upon the edge of the cañon-wall, at a point below the Falls, and somewhat lower down the river than the point from which Mr. Moran's sketch was taken, looks down into a broad, circular excavation, three quarters of a mile in diameter, and nearly seven hundred feet deep. The wall of the gorge opposite to him, plainly seen in the background of the picture, sinks, like the cliffs at his feet, in perpendicular bluffs nearly to the level of the river, while the broad excavation between the walls is covered by rough piles of black lava and rounded domes of trachyte rock. The whole aspect of the scene is strange and savage indeed, — a monotony of pale blue sky; olive and gray stretches of desert, extending afar off to the horizon, as level as the sea; a circling wall of jetty lava, the sharp edges of which are here and there battlemented in huge fortress-like masses; a smooth, broad river, the beryl-green waters of which, here and there reflecting the intense solemnity of the cliffs, flow quietly into the middle of the scene, there plunge into a labyrinth of rocks, tumble over a precipice two hundred feet high, and then, after having been broken up into a dazzling sheet of foam, move westward in a still, deep current, to disappear behind a black promontory, — such are the elements which in their combination leave upon the beholder an impression of weird and truly indescribable grandeur. In the early morning light, the shadows of the cliffs are cast over half the basin, defining themselves in sharp outline here and there on the river. Upon the foam of the cataract one point of the rock casts a cobalt-blue shadow. Where the river flows around the western promontory, it is wholly in shadow, and of a deep sea-green. A scanty growth of coniferous trees fringes the brink of the lower cliffs, overhanging the river. Dead barrenness is the whole sentiment of the scene. The mere suggestion of trees clinging here and there along the walls serves rather to heighten than to relieve the forbidding gloom of the place. Nor does the flashing whiteness, where the river tears itself among the rocky islands, or rolls in spray down the cliff, brighten the aspect; for in contrast with its brilliancy the rocks seem darker and more wild.

The descent of four hundred feet from the wall of the cañon to the level of the river above the falls has to be made by a narrow, winding path, among rough ledges of lava. The lower half of the cañon is excavated in a gray, porphyritic trachyte, and the ledge over which the Great Falls of Snake River are precipitated is composed of this material. Above the brink, the whole breadth of the river is broken up by a dozen small trachyte islands, which the water has carved into fantastic forms, now rounding some into low domes, then sharpening others into mere pillars, and wearing out deep caves elsewhere. At the very brink of the fall a few twisted evergreens cling with their roots to the rock, and lean over the abyss of foam, as if they were spell-bound by that same fatal fascination which is apt to take possession of men when standing above or by the side of masses of falling water.

In plan, the fall recurves up stream in a deep horseshoe, resembling the outline of Niagara. The total breadth is about seven hundred feet, and the greatest height attained at any one point is about one hundred and ninety. The whole mass of cataract is one ever-varying sheet of spray. Below the falls the river is very deep. The right bank sinks into the water in a clear, sharp precipice, but on the left side a narrow pebbly beach extends along the foot of the cliff. The trachytes are very curiously worn in vertical forms. Here and there an obelisk, either wholly or half detached from the cañon-wall, juts out like a buttress. Farther down, these projecting masses stand like a row of columns upon the left bank, while above them a solid capping of black lava reaches out to the edge, and overhangs the river in frowning precipices.

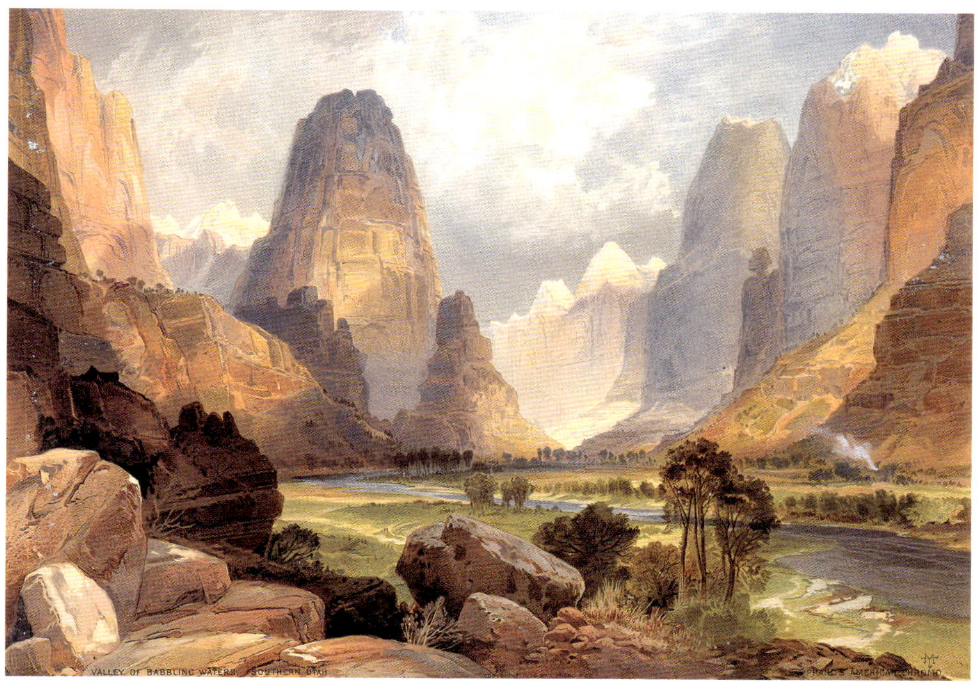

VALLEY OF THE BABBLING WATERS, SOUTHERN UTAH

The scenery of Southern Utah, along the Colorado River and its branches, is among the most remarkable and grand in this or any other country. The cañon of the Colorado, about two hundred miles in length, has been carved by running water out of the solid crust of the earth to a depth of from 2,000 to 5,000 feet. Innumerable side gorges open into the main gorge both to the right and to the left, and through them many extensive streams empty into the main river. One of these side gorges, which bears the poetical name of "The Valley of the Babbling Waters," is represented in the picture. It is traversed by a branch of the Rio Virgin (which flows into the Great Colorado of the West from the southeastern portion of Utah), and may be taken as a typical illustration of very much of the scenery of the Colorado River and its tributaries.

The character of this region is quite peculiar. The traveller, instead of ascending lofty mountain-peaks, with their summits far above timber-line, and clothed with perpetual snow, here descends into the interior of the earth, to the bottom of vast cañons, which are so deep that even the largest rivers rushing through them, when seen from the margin of the cliffs above, seem to be but threads. The cañons themselves present stupendous examples of the carving power of water, exercised during long periods of time, while the vast columns of rock, which stand like sentinels along the walls on either side, bear equal testimony to the efficiency of atmospheric agencies. The forms due to erosion, although presenting but little variety, occur here without number. The rocks are composed largely of sandstone, intermingled with some beds of limestone. The great variety of colors, such as different shades of red, green, yellow, etc., adds largely to the beauty of the scene, and intensifies the amazement of the beholder.

The whole of the region here described may be said to be almost inaccessible. In attempting to traverse it, one would be obliged to cross gorge after gorge, with nearly vertical walls, three thousand feet or more in depth. Hence this great country, above two hundred miles in length and one hundred and fifty miles in width, and rich in scenes as grand as the one before us, must ever be dedicated to nature, for it can never be inhabited by man. It is unique, grand, barren, and desolate.

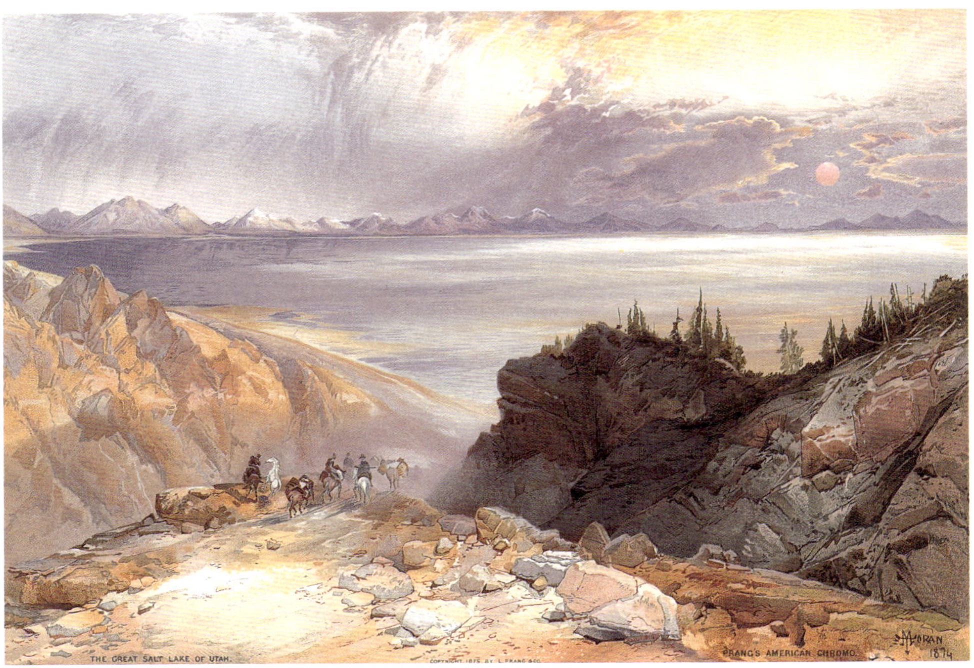

THE GREAT SALT LAKE OF UTAH

Our last illustration presents a view of the Great Salt Lake of Utah as it is seen in a westerly direction by an observer standing on the mountain-range which forms the eastern side of the lake basin. The view may be regarded as unique, for there is nothing, either in the western or in any other portion of the North American continent, that can compare with it. Its maximum of beauty is reached when the setting sun sends its slanting rays across the valley and the lake, and lends an air of enchantment to the entire region. The picturesque mountains which skirt the western horizon form a most befitting background for the magnificent scenery spread out at their feet.

Just underneath the mountains in the foreground is located Great Salt Lake City, in some respects the most beautiful city in the West. The cool mountain waters which flow continually along both sides of its streets serve to refresh animal as well as vegetable life, while the fruit and ornamental trees, which abound throughout the city, add greatly, not only to the beauty of the surroundings, but also to the comfort of the people.

The water of the lake, although it is as clear as crystal, is a very strong brine, the amount of salt held in solution being equal to about twenty per cent, which is a higher percentage than that of any other known body of salt water of so large a size. Until within a few years Salt Lake was supposed to be entirely destitute of animal life, like the Dead Sea. Thousands of waterfowl were, however, found to live around the islands on the lake; and as there must be something to attract these birds, it was inferred that after all there must be animated beings in the water. It has now been ascertained that the lake literally swarms with a small species of crustacean, capable of thriving in very strong brine.

Although such streams as the Jordan, Weber, and Bear Rivers, with numerous smaller streams, have for ages been pouring their vast volumes of water into this lake, it is nevertheless a well-known fact that it has no visible outlet. The question naturally arises as to what becomes of all the water thus gathered into one mass. The problem can only be solved by assuming that the water disappears by evaporation.

The great basin, at the bottom of which Salt Lake is situated, is enclosed by the Wahsatch Mountains on the east, the Sierra Nevada on the west, the crest or water-divide of the Columbia on the north, and that of the Colorado on the south. This vast area is supposed to have been occupied, long ages ago, by one grand inland sea of fresh water, which had an outlet into the basin of the Columbia River. At that time the summits of the smaller mountain-ranges projected above the surface of this sea in the shape of isolated islands. The water slowly passing away by evaporation, there were left those terraces which in their striking features reveal to us certain oscillations of level, and the various steps of progress toward the present order of things. The Salt Lake of our day is but a comparatively insignificant remnant of the ancient inland sea, its briny character being due to the concentration of the water in rocky basins without outlets.

The Wahsatch Mountains, which, as before stated, form the eastern wall of the basin, are gashed through with deep gorges almost to the level of the plains, and through these the traveller must pass as he approaches from the East. The Union Pacific Railroad, which opens into the great basin near Ogden, traverses a narrow channel cut through the range by the Weber River, and known by the name of the Devil's Gate.

In no portion of the inland West will the tourist so delight to linger, for the purpose of enjoying the novelty and beauty of the scene, as well as the exhilarating influences of the atmosphere, as in the valley of the Great Salt Lake.

Thomas Moran's "Opus List," from the collection of the Gilcrease Museum, is published here for the first time. As Moran himself wrote, "since Aug 1863 I have numbered every picture that I have painted, to which I attach any value." The artist's record includes forty-two of his most important early works, with their numbering ending in November 1868. Moran not only provided descriptions of the paintings on this list but often inscribed the opus numbers on his canvases near his signature.

The "Opus List" is significant for its wealth of original titles and for the telling glimpse it offers of Moran as a young artist whose comments reveal an evolving artistic direction. Although he had been painting and exhibiting for several years, this appears to be the first such record of his efforts.

Moran seems to have periodically taken stock of the contents of his studio and recorded sales in a timely fashion, yet entries in different colored inks indicate that he recorded additional information, such a changes in ownership of works, somewhat after the fact. In particularly busy times he may also have left gaps for which he reconstructed information at a later date (perhaps explaining works listed out of numerical sequence). The opus paintings share ledger pages with drawings and other works that Moran did not choose to number. He continued to use the ledger in which they are recorded sporadically until 1909 (titled "Old Book of Lists" on its cover, Gilcrease Archive 4026.4048).

4026.4048

Since Aug 1863 I have numbered every picture that I have painted, to which I attach any value.

No 1 The Wissahickon in Summer painted in July & August 1863 but never completed. Made an exchange with my brother Ned in which this unfinish picture was included. He finished it, sold it to Richardson the dealer, So among my numbered pictures, there is no No. 1. Got more knowledge of nature in painting this than any other study that I ever painted. It was all painted on the spot.

Size of the picture 29 in x 36 in. Upright

Four weeks labour upon it.

Since Aug 1863 I have numbered every picture that I have painted, to which I attach any value.

No. 1. *The Wissahickon in Summer*
Painted in July & August 1863 but never completed. Made an exchange with my brother Ned in which this unfinished picture was included. He finished it, sold it to Richardson the dealer. So among my numbered pictures, there is no No. 1
Got more knowledge of nature in painting this than any other study that I ever painted. It was all painted on the spot.
Size of the picture 29 in. x 36 in. Upright
Four weeks labour upon it.

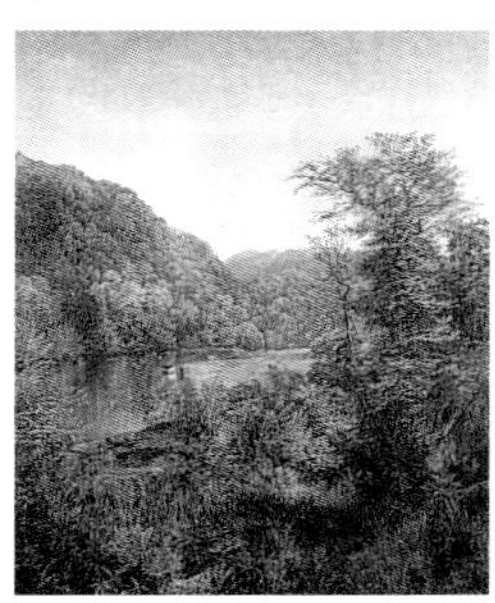

No. 2. *Autumn on the Wissahickon*
This picture was painted in October & November 1863. Incited by a most glorious Autumn. In finishing I decided that my forte lay in color & would prove my strongest point. More decided individuality than in anything previously painted but with less positive expression of sentiment than in many previous works.
Placed it in Earles for sale. Had offers of 150, 175, 225, & 250 dollars but determined not to sell for less than 300$ Hung five or six weeks. Then sold to A. Drexel the

Banker for	300.$
Deduct for frame	52.$
	248.$
Commission	24.$
Amt. Recd.	224.$

Size 29 x 36 inches

No. 3. *Okehampton Castle*
Painted in December 1863, in fulfillment of a commission from John Bohlen given previous to my going to England in 1862.
Amount — 50.$ Size 14 x 20 inches
Philadelphia [added in pencil]

No. 4. *A Canadian Waterfall, Sunset*
Painted in January 1864. Sold to J. S. Earle & Son for — 75$ Earl [*sic*] got $150.00
Size — 16 x 20 inches.

(No number) *Landscape, Scotland*
Free copy. Painted in Spring of 1864 for G. R. Orme. An old Commission.
60 x 40 inches price — 150.$

Ditto to Gabrylewitz

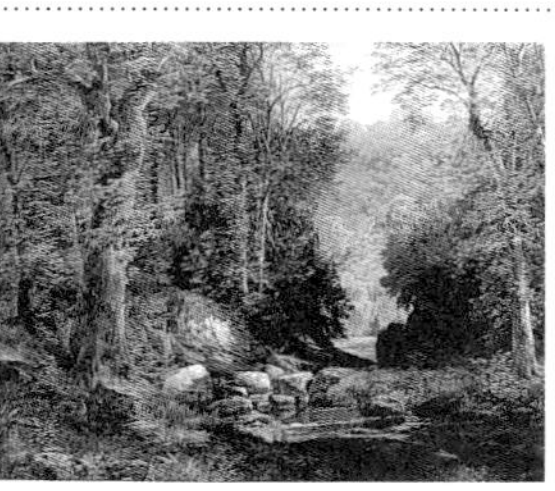

No. 5. *Creisham Glen, Wissahickon Autumn.* This was one of four Commissions from J. S. Earle & Son given on the strength of the popularity & sale of the *Wissahickon in Autumn* which was sold to Mr. Drexel. Received for it — 200$
Earle sold it to G. F. Tyler for — 350$
Painted in April 1864.
Size 29 x 36 — /Long/
My first creditable interior of a wood

No. 6. *A Reminiscence of the Passaic, Summer*
Size 20 x 30 inches.
Painted May 1864 for Horace B. Fry.
Broker. Price — 150$

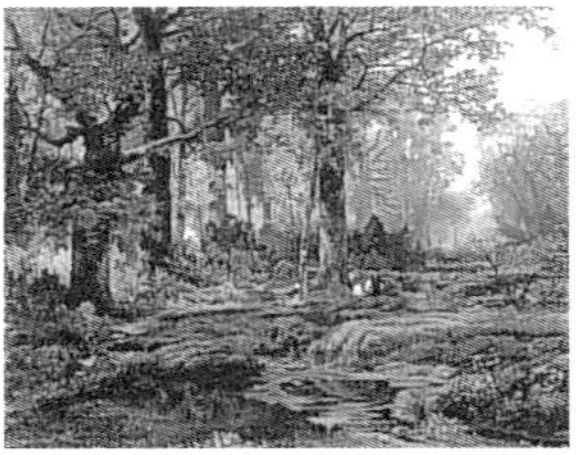

No. 7. *Nutting, Autumn*
Size 16 x 20 inches. Painted for & presented to the Sanitary fair in June 1864.
Brought at Sale — 75$

No. 8. *The Juniata, Evening*
Painted in September 1864 for G. F. Tyler — price — 200$ Size 20 x 30

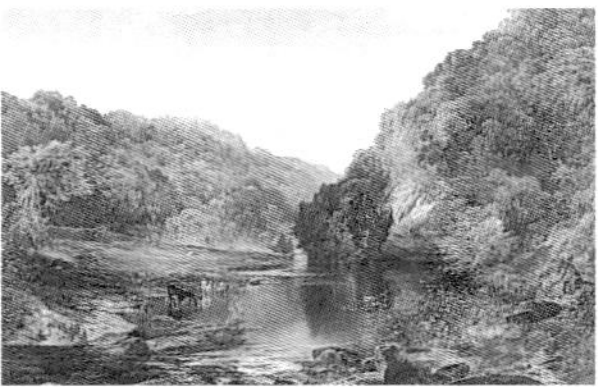

No. 9. *Autumn Afternoon, the Wissahickon*
Decidedly my best picture up to this time. Size 30 x 45 inches. Painted — November 1864. Earles Commission No. 2
Received for it — 300$ Earle sold it to Jas. S. Martin for 600$ Highest price yet obtained for any of my pictures. Cartoon in charcoal of this picture made June 1864.
Photographed & then destroyed

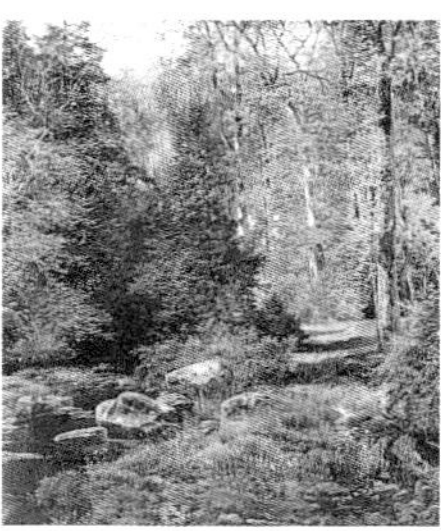

No. 10. *The Woods in Autumn*
A suggestion from Creisham Creek painted for & presented to the Artists Fund Society in November 1864. Sold at the sale to Geo Whitney for 180$.
Afterward received — 50$ for additional work upon it
Size of picture 20 x 24 inches

No. [crossed out]. *A Greenland Glacier*
From a sketch by Dr. Hayes. 8 x 12 inches
Given to A.F.S. Nov. 1864 Sold at
sale for — 7$ to Mr. Hurn

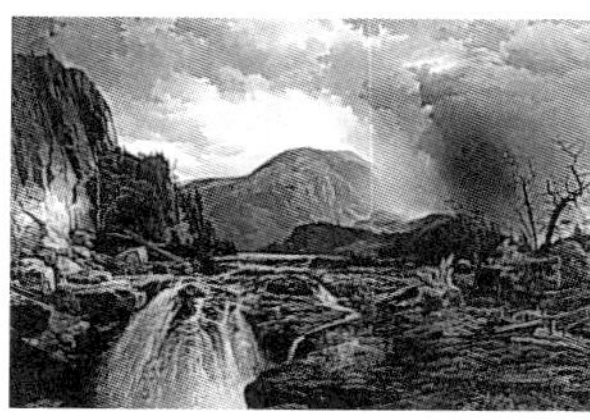

No. 11. *The Wilds of Lake Superior*
Earles Commission No. 3. painted in
December 1864 Size 30 x 45 inches
Received for it — 300$ Sold at Earles
sale in spring of 1865 to Leonard Grover
for — 610$

No. 12. *The Farewell of Summer*
Painted in February 1865 for Dr. J.M.
Sommerville. Motive from Geddes Run.
Bucks Co. Pa Size 30 x 45 in.
Price — 400$

No. 13. *The Conemaugh, Autumn*
Size 33 x 50 inches painted in March 1865
for C. Sharpless
price — 800$ Exhibited in the great Ex.
in Paris in 1867.

No. 14. *A Wood Scene, Autumn*
May 1865 for M.W. Baldwin
price — 150$ size 16 x 20

No. 15. *The Juniata, below Huntingdon*
Painted in June 1865 for J.V. Merrick
price — 1200$ size 36 x 58 inches

No. 16. *Clearing in the Mountains*
Size 30 x 45 inches. Painted for
the Annual Sale of the A.F. Society
in Nov 1865. Bought by C. McAllister
at sale for — 350$

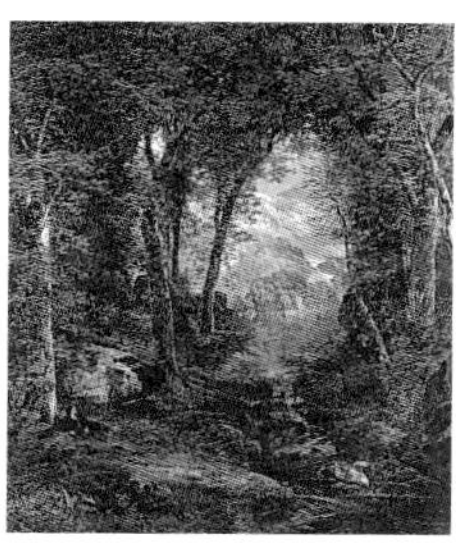

No. 17. *The Autumnal Woods*
Painted for M. Baird in September &
October 1865. from the Cartoon *Solitude*,
but very much altered, both in Arrangement & feeling. Size 34 x 40 inches.
price — 650$. A sketch to be thrown into
Bargain. Gave him the sketch in July 1868.

The Saco River. Painted for the
Benefit of Sanford Mason. Size 14 x 20
Nov 1865 Sold at the A.F.S.
Sale for — 45$ to Ashmead, Printer

Made 24 studies for the School of Design
for Women during 1865 & early part of
1866. price 350$

The Last Arrow
Charcoal on paper 23 x 34 inches
January 1866

No. 18. *Evening on the Juniata, Autumn*
Painted in January & May 1866
size 20 x 30 inches.
Commission from Joe Harrison.
price $300.00 poor picture

*A Landscape** in Charcoal. Paper
24 x 36 in. Jan 1866. used in S. for. pic.
*(under the trees)
(for Ashmead) (didn't paint it for
Ashmead)

Drawings in Charcoal etc.
A Canadian Waterfall. Charcoal on
canvas. Made in May 1864
size 30 x 45 in. Rubbed off to paint on
published in my "Studies for Pictures"

The Wissahickon. Charcoal on canvas. June
1864. 30 x 45 in. Rubbed off to paint on,
pub'd in S. for pic.

Solitude [crossed out]. Charcoal. Canvas.
Rubbed off to paint on. Same as
Farewell of Summer. 30 x 45 inches
June 1864. Pub in S. for pic.

The Shores of Lake Superior
Painted in Vandyke Brown June 1864
size 25 x 45. Pub in S. for pictures

Clearing. Charcoal. Canvas.
Size 30 x 45 in. Rubbed off to paint
Made in Aug 1864. Pub in S. for Pic

Valley of the Conemaugh
Charcoal on canvas. Made in
September 1864. size 60 x 40. Rubbed off
Pub. in Studies for Pictures

A White Frost
Drawn in Vandyke Brown Nov. 1864.
Size 30 x 45. Pub in S. for Pictures.

Sentinels of the Coast
Charcoal on paper. Jan 1865
size 25 x 45. destroyed
pub in Studies for Pic

The Children of the Mountain
Charcoal on paper 52 x 62 inches Jan 1865
pub in Studies for Pictures

Solitude. Charcoal on paper
25 x 30 inches. Upright. Made March 1865
Sold to H. Davids. Pub in S. for pictures

A Ravine. Charcoal on paper
25 x 30 in. March 1865. Gave it to Dr.
Rowe

The Juniata. Charcoal on canvas
38 x 56. Made in April 1865. Rubbed off
to paint over pub in Studies for Pics.

Morning. Charcoal on paper
20 x 30 in. Sepr. 1865

Evening. Charcoal on paper
20 x 30 inches Oct. 1865

No. 20. *A Morning in Autumn*
Painted in Paris (Paris) in October. 1866 for Henry B. Ashmead size of picture 30 x 45 inches Received for it $500 & an old picture in return that Ashmead paid $45 at the sale of the Artists F. Society in 1865

[added in black ink] Ashmead was dissatisfied with the picture & I painted No. 33 in exchange. Painted out the picture in June 1868 & turned it into a tropical picture. [added in purple ink] Dreamland

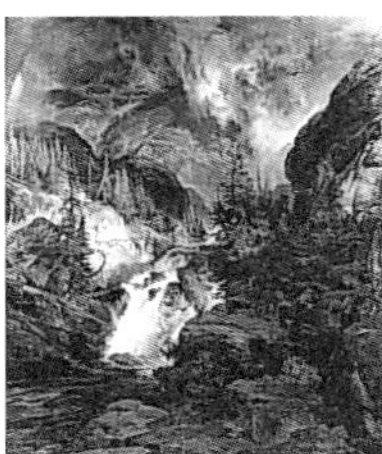

No. 21. *The Children of the Mountain, a Waterfall, Autumn*
Commenced the picture in the spring of 1866. Brought it with me to Paris & finished it in December of this year. Size of picture 52 x 62 inches Exhibited in the Universal Exposition of Paris 1867.

[added in black ink] Bought afterward by Roswell Smith of Scribners Magazine. that is I borrowed $500 from him with which to go on the Yellowstone expedition with Hayden & gave the picture as security & I did not redeem it. It is now 1909 in the possession of Geo Inness, Jr.

[added in pencil] since sold by Inness Jr.

The Track of the Storm
An allegory of the war for the republic. Charcoal drawing on paper Size 54 x 90 inches. February 1866. Pub in studies for pictures

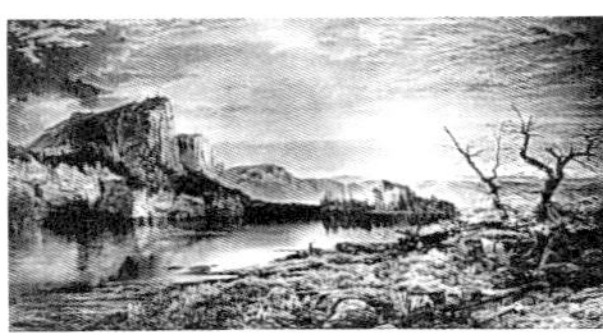

No. 19. *The Shores of Lake Superior*
Painted in May 1866 for Jas. S. Earle. Size 25 x 45 in. Old commission, price $300.00

A Subject from *Hiawatha*
Painted in black & white. 33 x 50 in. used in Studies for Pictures. [added in purple ink] Foolishly gave to A.W. Drake of Scribners in 1872 x 3.

(No numbers) *The Improvisatore & Evening in the Wilderness*
Painted & given to the A. F. Society sold at the Annual Sale in Jan 1867. painted in Paris Oct. 1866 *Improvisatore* to Dr. Holland 1871 for 100$ ["Dr. Holland" and "100" are in purple ink] *Wilderness* to [blank] [for 100]$

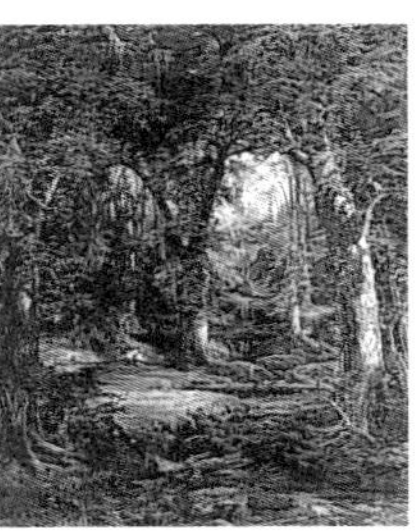

No. 22. *The Woods Were God's First Temples*
Commenced the picture in the Spring of 1866. Brought it with me to Paris & finished it in the spring of 1867. Size of the picture 52 x 62 inches Painted to the order of Dr. J.M. Sommerville for $1000

No. 24. *Rome, from the Campagna, Sunset*
Painted in June 1867 after return from Europe. Size 25 x 45. Shown at A.F.S. in Feb & March 1868. Sent to Chicago in April 1868. Returned in July 1868.

[added in purple ink] Afterwards sold to Gilbert for $75.00

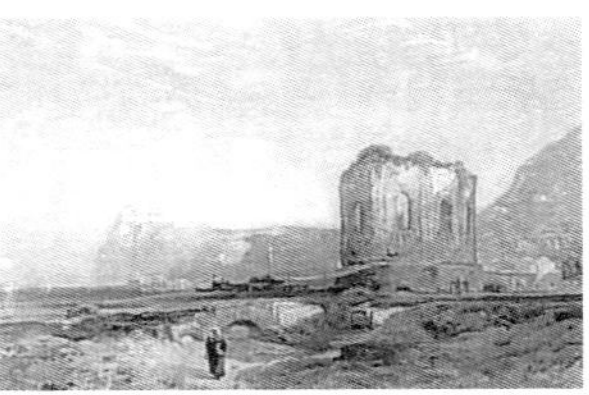

No. 23. *Temple of Venus & Castle of Baiae*
Size 20 x 30 in. Painted in July 1867 for J.S. Gilliams for Dentistry

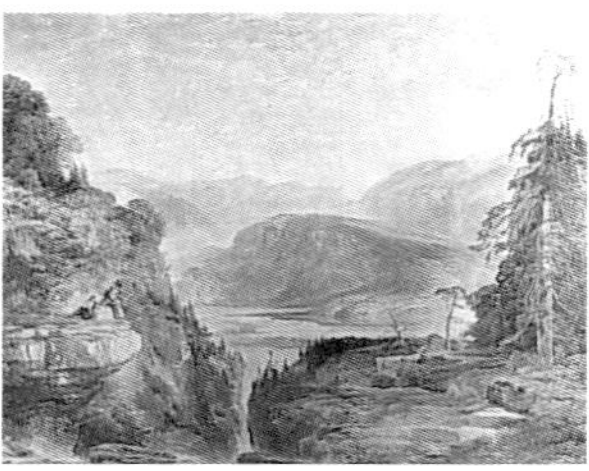

No. 25. *The Last Arrow*
Size 52 x 80 inches. Painted in June & July 1867. The figures were painted by Helmick. The male figure is a copy from Croome. The picture was commenced in Paris & nearly finished there *just like the drawing*, but was entirely remodeled & repainted on my return. 8 weeks in painting it.

[added in black ink] Exhibited at A. Fund S. in Feb & March 1868. Not sold. Previously offered 700 for it by W. F. Potts but declined. Sent to Chicago April 1868.

[added in sepia ink] Returned in July 1868. Sold in August 1868 to Mr. Baird for 700 dollars Baird afterwards paid 125 additional for the frame. Wretched price

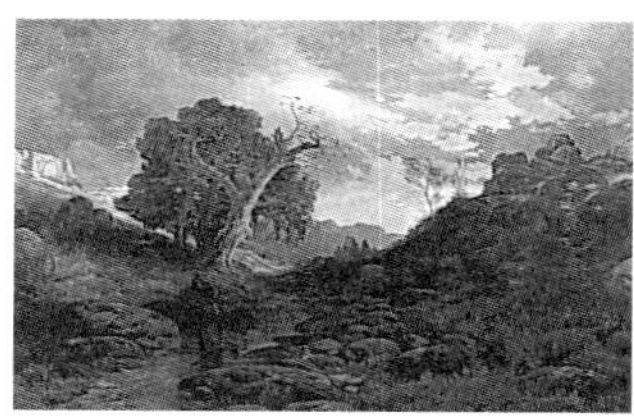

No. 26. *Evening after Rain, Fontainebleau*
Size 20 x 30 inches. Painted in September 1867. Sold to E. S. Handy for $80.00 in (December 1867)

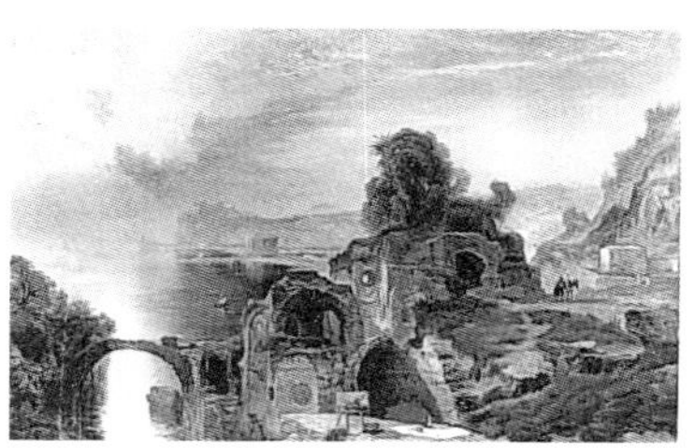

No. 28. *Bay of Baiae, Sunrise*
Painted in September 1867
Size 20 x 30 inches
Sold to E. S. Handy for $80.00 (Dec 1867)

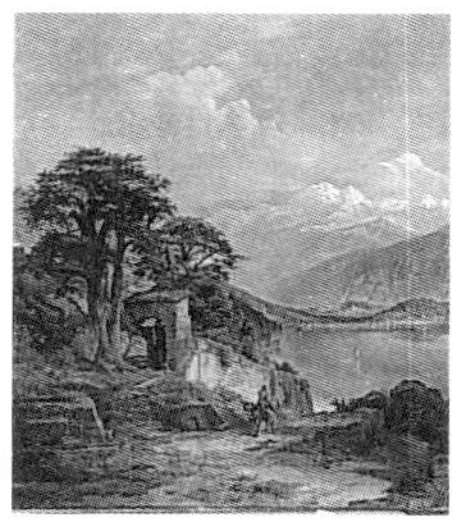

No. 27. *The Lake of Como*
Size 40 x 70 inches. Painted in August 1867. First picture sold after my return from Europe Sold to F. Gutekunst for $400 =

[added in sepia ink] Afterwards repainted many parts. G. dissatisfied with his purchase & traded it off to E. Moran.

[added in purple ink] Afterward E Moran cut the picture into two & repainted the two parts & sold them as mine at his sale in 1877

No. 29. *Pozzuoli & Bay of Baiae*
Size 25 x 45 inches
Painted in September 1867.

[added in purple ink] Sold to Mr. Gilbert for $75.00

No. 30. *The Forest of Fontainbleau*
Size 30 x 45 inches
Painted in October 1867 for annual contribution to the Artists Fund Society. Sold at the sale in December for $80.00 to W. F. Potts.

No. 31. [words crossed out] [added in black ink] *From the Quay at Naples*
Size 14 x 20 inches
Painted in October 1867. Contribution to fund for purchase of piano for A.F.S.

[added in black ink] to Josiah Brant for $25.00

No. 32. *Hiawatha*
Size 33. x 50 inches. Painted in Sepr. and October 1867. Sky & part of the coast repainted in March 1868. Exhibited at the Artists Fund Society in February & March 1868. Not sold. Sent to Chicago, April 1868

[added in sepia ink] Returned in July 1868. A picture that I esteem much but unsaleable in character

[added in purple ink] Afterward ruined it & is now in an unfinished state.

Charcoal Drawing
Moonlight with Owls & Ruined Castle
Size about 25.30. Sold it to C. F. Gristock for $20.00. Drawn in December 1867

Charcoal Drawing
A Hemlock Forest. Size about 25 x 30
Drawn in December 1867.

An Alpine Gorge
Drawn on canvas in pencil, Crayon. Lithographic crayon turpentine & black. Size 25 x 37 inches. January 1868.

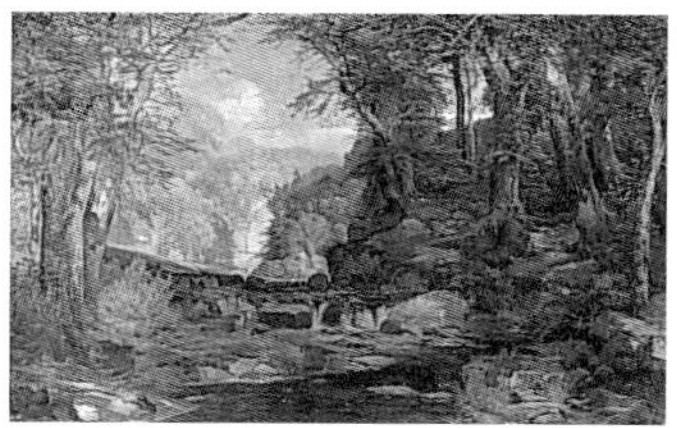

No. 33. *A Scene on the Tohickon Creek, Autumn.* Size 30 x 45 inches
Painted in Dec & Jan 1867-68 for H. B. Ashmead in place of the picture sent to him from Paris for which I received 500 dollars

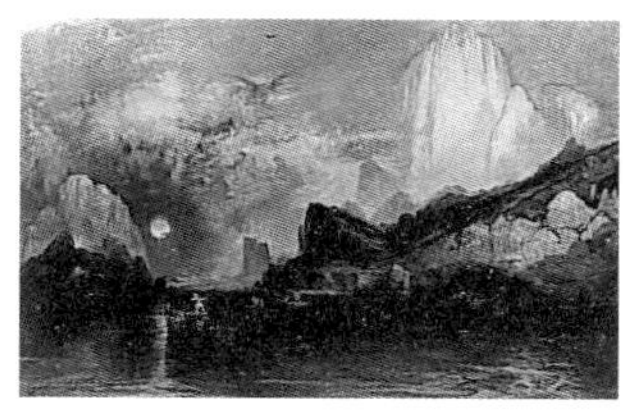

No. 34. *Hiawatha & the Serpents*
Copy from the larger picture size 20 x 30. Ordered by Dr. F. Lewis painted in March 1868. Received for it $150.00

No. 35. *The Remorse of Cain*
Size of the picture 52 x 62 inches painted in ten days in March 1868 Exhibited at the Spring Exhibition of the Artist's Fund Society same year.

[added in purple ink] On receiving it again in 1868 I think it is a beastly bad picture. I may yet repaint it.

No. 36. *The Sacrifice of Isaac*
First painted in June 1868 on canvas 30 x 36 long. Afterward cut it down to 25 x 30 which improved the picture much. Finished it in November 1868 Think it a good picture.

Sketch of same material with a monk reading. Given to Baird in July 1868 according to agreement size about 20 x 24.

No. 37. [drawing of a pot]
A Wood Scene, Autumn
Figures in boat & female figure in Foreground in red dress. Size 38 x 43 in. Painted to sell & in 8 days. All pictures with a pot at end of name, indicate pictures made to sell & not painted for love of subject. Painted in June 1868. Afterwards repainted it & consider it one of my good pictures.

Made 8 drawings in black & white for Bradley illustrating Dr. March's *Night Scenes in the Bible* for which received $115. Engraved by Saml [Samuel] Sartain. June 1868.

Painting in black & white
The Annunciation to the Shepherds
Size 20 x 30 in. June 1868. For Bradley Received for it $50. To be engraved 17 x 25 inches by S. Sartain.

Black & white. *Elijah Fed by Ravens*
20 x 30 For Artists Fund Society. Not used

November Morning. ditto ditto
Size about 16 x 22. Both in June 1868

10 sketches in sepia in life of Elijah

Elijah & the Widow of Zarephath. Sketch on panel about 20 x 24. May 1868

Small Autumn Wood Scene
May 1868. size 14 x 17. Painted for Gladwin of Worcester Mass. for $25

Creek Scene in Autumn.
Size 16 x 20 in summer 1868.
Marked with pot [crossed out]

painted out

No. 38. *Autumn on the Wissahickon*
Scene about ½ mile above the Red Bridge Size 25 x 30. Picture good. Painted in October 1868. Sold to F. Raig for $150 $50 in cash 100 in trade for clothing

No. 39. *Rome with St. Peters & the Castle of St. Angelo.*
Painted for Dr. Lewis in summer of 1868 Size 20 x 30 inches. A very good picture especially in tone. Received for it $200.00.

No. 40. *An Alpine Peak, Evening*
two large pine trees in foreground
Size 25 x 30 inches. Not yet finished Nov. 1st 1868. Never finished. 1870. Never will be 1874

Elaborate painting or drawing in Black & White made for Artists Fund Society in July 1868. Subject. *Lake Superior Morning* used in the A.F.S. Annual for 1868.

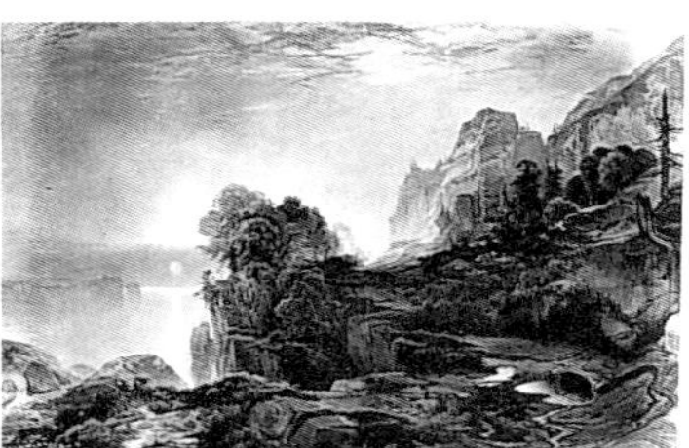

No. 41. *Lake Superior Morning*
Size about 22 x 34. Same as drawing in the A.F.S. Annual for 1868 with some alterations. Not yet finished Nov. 1st 1868 but in very promising condition.

No. 42. *A Waterfall.* Cliffs on right bank of river. Size about 13 x 18. Painted Nov 1868. Not of any account. [added in pencil] Gave it to Eakins Christmas 1868.

Sketch on panel about 16 x 24
July 1868. Subject. *Baths on the Coast near Naples.*

[added in purple ink] Afterward changed to *Elijah & the Woman of Zaripah* [*sic*]. Afterward to *Sunset on a Moquis Town.*

Sketch made from the end cut from *Sacrifice of Isaac.* Size 8 x 36 inches upright waterfall in the mountains gave to Howson

A river scene with dark thunder cloud coming up [illeg.] 20 x 30
very unpromising though generally liked by greenhorns. Uncertain at this time whether it is worth finishing

[added in black ink] never finished

Ceased numbering in 1868

ILLUSTRATIONS

Opening page: First page of the Opus List in Moran's ledger, Gilcrease Archive, Tulsa, Oklahoma.

No. 2. *Autumn on the Wissahickon*, 1863, oil on canvas, Drexel University, Philadelphia.

No. 5. *Creisham Glen, Wissahickon, Autumn*, 1864, oil on canvas, Hevrdejs Collection. See also cat. 4.

No. 7. *Nutting, Autumn*, 1864, oil on canvas, Collection of Conrad J. Kronholm Jr.

No. 9. *Autumn Afternoon, the Wissahickon* (now *Autumn on the Wissahickon*), 1864, oil on canvas, Terra Museum of American Art, Chicago, Daniel J. Terra Collection.

No. 10. *The Woods in Autumn* (now *Autumn Foliage*), 1864, Heckscher Museum, Huntington, New York, August Heckscher Collection.

No. 11. *The Wilds of Lake Superior*, 1864, oil on canvas, New Britain Museum of American Art, Charles F. Smith Fund. See also cat. 5.

No. 17. *The Autumnal Woods* (formerly titled *Under the Trees*), 1865, oil on canvas, Manoogian Collection. See also cat. 6.

No. 21. *The Children of the Mountain*, 1866, oil on canvas, The Anschutz Collection. See also cat. 7.

No. 19. *The Shores of Lake Superior*, 1866, present location unknown. Photograph by John Moran courtesy Gilcrease Museum, Tulsa, Oklahoma.

No. 22. *The Woods Were God's First Temples* (now *Woodland Temple*), 1867, oil on canvas, The Haggin Museum, Stockton, California.

No. 23. *Temple of Venus & Castle of Baiae*, 1867, oil on canvas, Private Collection. Photograph courtesy Sotheby's, New York.

No. 25. *The Last Arrow*, 1867, oil on canvas, The Berkshire Museum, Pittsfield, Massachusetts, Gift of Zenas Crane.

No. 26. *Evening after Rain, Fontainbleau* (also *The Evening Hunter*), 1867, oil on canvas, Private Collection. Photograph courtesy Gerald Peters Gallery, Santa Fe.

No. 27. *The Lake of Como* (now *Lake Como*), 1867, oil on canvas, The Metropolitan Museum of Art, New York, Bequest of Miss Emily Buch, 1963.

No. 28. *Bay of Baiae, Sunrise*, 1867, oil on canvas, courtesy Beacon Hill Fine Art, New York.

No. 33. *A Scene on the Tohickon Creek, Autumn*, 1867-1868, oil on canvas, The Minneapolis Institute of Arts, The Frances E. Andrews Wilderness Fund.

No. 34. *Hiawatha & the Serpents* (now *Hiawatha and the Great Serpent, the Kenabeek*), 1868, oil on canvas, The Baltimore Museum of Art, Friends of Art Fund.

No. 41. *Lake Superior Morning*, 1868, present location unknown (documented in charcoal drawing, also of unknown location). Photograph by John Moran courtesy Library Company of Philadelphia.

In the summer of 1873 Thomas Moran journeyed west to join John Wesley Powell on a trip to the Grand Canyon. Four years earlier Powell had captured the nation's attention when he led a small group of men in custom-crafted boats through the white water of the Colorado River. After listening to Powell describe the landscape through which the river had cut its path, Moran quickly perceived a subject equal in grandeur to that of Yellowstone. Already planning a pendant for his painting *Grand Canyon of the Yellowstone,* which Congress had purchased for the Capitol in 1872, Moran accepted Powell's invitation to join him the following summer. Accompanying the party was Justin E. Colburn, a newspaper correspondent, who, during the course of the journey, sent letters east for publication in the *New York Times.* Impatient with earlier promotional literature that painted the West as a lush garden, Colburn described it instead as a "rainless realm." Vivid, candid, and insightful, Colburn's letters offer a clear view of a forbidding landscape and a firsthand account of the often difficult journey he and Moran made with Powell to the Grand Canyon in 1873. Colburn's letters are published here as they appeared in the *New York Times* on 15 July, 7 August, and 4 September 1873.

On 13 August 1873, the day Colburn wrote his third letter, Thomas Moran wrote to his wife, Mary Nimmo Moran. Moran's letter, humorous and revealing, is also included here.

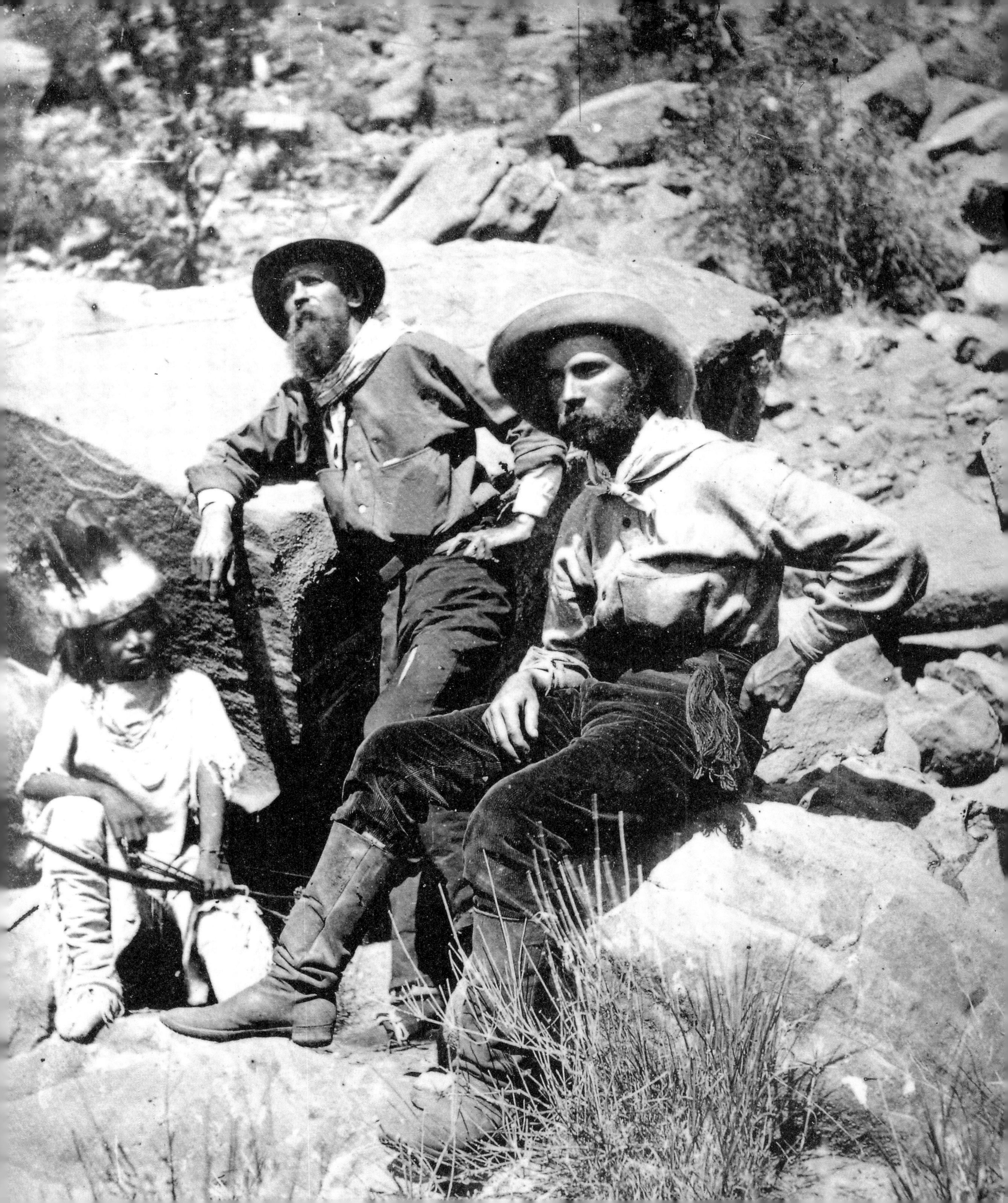

THE GREAT AMERICAN DESERT

FROM OMAHA TO SALT LAKE — A BARREN COUNTRY

From Our Own Correspondent
Salt Lake City, Tuesday, 8 July 1873

Preceding page: Thomas Moran (center) on the Powell expedition, 1873, with Indian boy and J. E. Colburn, photograph by John K. Hillers, courtesy East Hampton Library.

So many descriptions have been written of the route of the Union Pacific Railroad from Omaha to Ogden that any letter merely descriptive would be superfluous. Indeed I did not intend to write one word about it, and should not, except that I found my impressions and expectations, formed from reading, so at variance with the truth, and the facts so different from the notions that extensively prevail, that something new to many readers seems quite possible to be written.

There is but one express and mail train each day from Omaha west. That is due to leave at 11:30 a.m., but oftener does not start for one or two hours after that time, by reason of delay on some one of the roads from the East for whose Pacific trains the Union Pacific Railroad usually waits. The detention at Omaha is easily made up by the morning of the next day, and often much sooner; for there are but few trains to meet, and the time-table is very slow. There is, therefore, 150 to 175 miles of running by daylight after leaving Omaha, and during the entire afternoon the trains go directly toward the setting sun, over the fertile prairie, almost dead level, its vast expanse stretching out like the ocean — the horizon a straight, unbroken line, and in some of the varying atmospheric and sky effects hardly to be distinguished from the horizon at sea.

When one goes to sleep at night of the first day from Omaha, the last arable land on the whole journey has been seen. The supper-station, Grand Island, is on the verge of "The Great American Desert" of the maps of fifteen to twenty years ago. The train has entered the rainless realm, where drouth and aridity hold indisputable sway. This is the great fact, the fact gigantic in proportions when considered in its economical aspects and its importance to the American nation.

A correct impression of what one will see in a journey across the plains and of what one will realize who makes it for the first time, may be given in a few words. One leaves Omaha and the Missouri River, at noon. There is half a day of riding through a flat, fertile prairie, in which many thriving settlements have been planted. One retires to the berth of the sleeping car just as the furthest border of fertility has been reached. On looking out the next morning the train is moving up the valley of the North Platte, with the river to the south, a shallow, lazy, undetermined looking stream, listlessly moving back toward the Missouri, and low ranges of grassy hills, hardly high enough to be called hills, skirting a near horizon to the north. The vegetation is scant, and is, for the most part, a thin, short kind of grass that seems just ready to die. The country grows constantly more barren in appearance during the whole day, but maintains the same general characteristics. The Platte is left and the plains become slightly more rolling, narrowing the view and bringing the horizon nearer to the eye. The grades become heavier and the country more rolling after leaving Cheyenne, and during afternoon the highest point on the Pacific Roads, Sherman, is reached and passed, and one never would dream of being on the highest mountain range of North America, and really more than 8,000 feet above the sea, but for the information of the guide-books or the time-tables of the road. Before night the Laramie Plain, which is greener and more fertile looking than Platte Valley, but really worthless except for stock raising, is passed, and the train has entered a more desolate country than any yet seen. Nothing grows but sage brush, and even it looks disgusted with its habitation. It attains but a feeble, stunted growth. One has before this caught several glimpses of the snow-covered Rocky Mountain summits, many miles distant, and snow peaks are seen more or less frequently during the remainder of the journey.

The country is still but little broken. Perhaps rather rugged would convey an impression of the surface. The track winds among low earth hills, worn into curious forms by the action of wind and frost and sun on the peculiar soil of which they are composed. This ends the second day. There is another night, and in the morning the passenger looks out still on the sage-brush desert and curious low hills.

For a few miles near Green River station there is some interesting scenery, the hills becoming more prominent, and the forms more curious and beautiful. Church Buttes, so-called, give still new forms of the same general character and structure as those at Green River. But otherwise dull, monotonous barrenness continues till 2 o'clock in the afternoon, when, soon after leaving Wasatch, the train enters the beginning of Echo Canon, and the remainder of the trip to Ogden, about seventy miles, is made pleasant and exciting by striking, weird, and oft-times beautiful scenery. The road advertises that an observation car will be attached to the train while passing through this scenery. But it is not done, and has not been for some time, though still advertised.

Fortunately for myself and friends Superintendent Clark's car was attached to the train at Evanston, to be taken to Ogden, and by his kind permission we were afforded the best possible facilities for sight-seeing.

Most persons, I think, will be disappointed with the scenery of Echo Canon, though it is really grand and beautiful. Owing to some optical delusion, probably the clearness of the atmosphere, and the consequent distinctness with which details of form and color can be distinguished in the distance, as well as the homogeneous structure of the rock, precipices of a thousand feet do not impress one at first as very high; and it seemed to me that many a country highway of New England wound among higher hills and under loftier cliffs. This scenery, like Niagara, is disappointing at first, but it increases in magnitude rapidly after a little comparison and reflection. At first most persons will be likely to think the Cheat River scenery on the Baltimore & Ohio Road, or the scenery about and west of Kittaning Point on the Pennsylvania Central, grander and more interesting.

Many details of the trip — indeed, all the details — I have omitted, for they would prove tedious, as will the journey itself to nearly every traveler, and if introduced in a letter would but confuse the impression which ought to be conveyed. One keeping watch will find many things novel and entertaining by the way, as, for instance, the kinds and character of flowers, of which many varieties occur. A few antelopes and villages of prairie dogs satisfies all the curiosity about animal life. There are seen, also, a few birds, swallows being the most numerous.

But the one fact that impresses itself constantly, till it fixes an indelible impression, overlying all others made on the journey, is the utter desolation, the barrenness, the worthlessness of all the country passed through west of a point — say 150 miles from Omaha. Now and then one will see a stock ranch. This consists of a turf hut, a tent, or perhaps a small stockade, situated near the river or creek in some little valley that wears a brighter hue of green than the surrounding country. Around it a herder has gathered cattle, perhaps from twenty-five to fifty, and possibly sometimes 100. The stock appears to thrive; but how the man lives, or what he does with his stock when he has raised it, is a mystery into which I did not seek to pry. It was too profound. The Platte does not seem to irrigate even its own banks, for in the upper part of its course it is not marked by any line of increased growth of vegetation.

Viewed in the light of the facts, how absurd seems the contest about the Union Pacific land grant and the cry against giving away the agricultural lands west of the Mississippi to railroads; and how ridiculous the advertisement of the Road of "Twelve millions of choice farming, grazing and mineral lands" that "are being sold to settlers at prices varying from $2 to $10 per acre." The land of the Missouri River Valley is undoubtedly of very great value. It is choice farming land; though there are many obstacles to profitable culture. West of this there are absolutely no agricultural lands; and of all the lands owned by the Railroad, or to be owned by it when every obstacle to ownership is removed, except lands in the mountains which may prove to contain minerals, and lands east of Grand Island, not a thousand acres are worth more than a penny an acre. The Government, in reserving patents for half the lands located by the Company through Nebraska, retains all that is worth any thing that was ever granted to the Union Pacific, except the million acres for which patents have already issued.

I have spoken only of the country through which the railroad passes. Mentioning the impression the barrenness of the country made on my mind to a gentleman who has as great knowledge of the West as any man living, he made the astonishing general statement that excepting Oregon, which has a wet climate, not over two per cent of the whole country west of the 100th meridian could ever be made useful for agricultural purposes — not even when every river and brook and stream had been utilized to the utmost capacity for irrigation. In the whole Territory of Utah not an acre is productive without irrigation, and no further irrigation here can be undertaken without the outlay of great capital.

One other generalization will show how valueless for agricultural purposes this rainless country is. When, for purposes of irrigation, all the water west of the 100th meridian (a north and south line some 200 miles west of Omaha) has been spread upon the soil, all the agricultural product will not feed the mining population which may reasonably be expected to come hither.

The mineral wealth of the region, there is reason to believe, is greater than has ever been estimated or dreamed of. But the mines are in the mountains, and not on the plains, where the Union Pacific owns 12,000,000 acres of "choice" sage brush and alkali desert, excepting 2,000,000 acres of flat, fertile prairie in Nebraska.

The New York Times, 15 July 1873

THE LAND OF MORMON

THREE HUNDRED MILES THROUGH UTAH — SPANISH FORK CANON — MOUNT NEBO — OUT-DOOR BEDROOMS

From Our Special Correspondent
Toquerville, N. T., Wednesday, 23 July 1873

On the morning of July 10, your correspondent, in company with Major J. W. Powell and Mr. Thomas Moran, the artist, left the Utah Southern Railroad Depot, in Salt Lake City, for a visit to the Grand Cañon of the Colorado River. Twelve days of leisurely journeying brought Moran and myself to Toquerville, 300 miles on our way from Salt Lake, and still 100 miles, or more, from our destination. From Major Powell, who is charged with a special Government commission to the Indians of this Territory, we parted at Fillmore, 150 miles from Salt Lake, where he remained to meet and confer with Kanosh, one of the oldest and ablest of the Indian chiefs, who wishes his people to live like white men by cultivating the soil.

The Wasatch

At this Mormon village, where I am compelled to remain two days, I take the opportunity to jot down some notes about my trip of 300 miles through the land of the Mormons. The Southern Railroad, projected from Salt Lake to the southern limits of the Territory, does not advance very fast. It is now running to Lehi, a small village at the north end of Utah Lake, thirty miles from Salt Lake. The ride over this road is not without interest. South of Salt Lake is a chain of snowy peaks of the Wasatch range of mountains, rising abruptly from the level plain to a height of over 11,000 feet above the sea, or 6,500 feet above the valley. There are no more picturesque mountains in the world than this cluster, and the road runs toward its western angle, affording constantly changing views, and revealing new beauties in the landscape as the traveler approaches. The train passes over the "divide" between the Salt Lake and Utah Valleys, and down to Lehigh, on the margin of Utah Lake. This is a sheet of fresh water, very narrow, but about thirty miles long, and the valley which bears the same name is the most fertile in Utah.

A Western Valley

The term valley is one which needs a definition. In the Eastern mind it is associated with rich vegetation, a productive soil, and water, still or running, in low ground. But this notion must be reversed when one thinks of the valleys of these mountains. They are high — none lower than 4,000 feet above the sea, and some of them over 5,000, an elevation greater than the highest of the Green Mountain range. Instead of being well watered, some of them have scarcely a spring. Their only verdure is the gray, dwarfed sage-brush. They are barren deserts, utterly unfit for producing any useful plant without irrigation. Salt Lake Valley has the lake from which it is named, and the River Jordan. But not a drop of the water that flows into the valley from the surrounding mountains ever leaves it, except by evaporation. Part of the water of Utah Valley flows into Salt Lake, through the outlet of Utah Lake. But generally each valley drinks up all the water that flows into it, and, with the exception of a few small streams in the vicinity of the Colorado River, not a drop of water from this Territory reaches the ocean, or any stream emptying into it. If the reader can think of a tract of country, nearly circular, surrounded on all sides by mountains in an unbroken line, so that from the plain he can see no way out except by crossing mountains, and this plain parched and dried till no green thing is visible, nor a sign of water, with blasts of heated air scorching the face — if he can think of all these, accompanied by burning thirst, with no means of quenching it, he may realize the general character of the Utah valleys. Some are ten miles across, and others sixty or seventy miles. Taking a view of Salt Lake Valley, there are seen the lake and city, with patches reclaimed by irrigation, and covered with the most vivid green. Looking into Utah Valley several towns are to be seen, the furthest twenty-five miles distant. There is generally one town at least in each valley, but often so situated as not to be seen till quite near. Instead of being in the middle of the valley, it is at the edge, as near the sources of the creeks as good land can be found, for all the streams here are largest at the head, and decrease as they flow.

Open-Air Bedrooms

At Lehi we took stage for Spanish Fork, about twenty-five miles further, where we expected to remain overnight, and perhaps for a day or two, while Major Powell should see one or two bands of Ute Indians who are away from the Uintah Reservation. But upon arriving at Springville, five miles from Spanish Fork, occasion offered to collect the Indians there, and we stopped for the night. We slept between blankets, of which we had a plentiful supply, spread in the door-yard of Mr. Lyman Wood's house. This affords another point of departure in this discursive letter. No travelers, and few of the inhabitants of Utah, sleep indoors or in beds in Summer. So far as travel is concerned, there is little except of a local kind — that is to say, teamsters between the southern country and Salt Lake, or Mormons going up, Spring and Fall, to General Conference. These always carry a camping-mess and blankets, and stop wherever night overtakes them, cook their meals, and sleep by the wagons. The horses or mules, known here always by the general terms "animals" or "stock," are hobbled, and turned loose to graze, which, supplemented by a little wheat, barley, or oats, forms their subsistence on the road. For cooking purposes sage brush or cedar bushes, or anything that will burn, is gathered, and a very little serves the purpose. Miners and prospectors, going to and from the southern mining districts of Nevada, of which Pioche is the centre, travel in the stage which carries the mail. They sleep as much as they can in the coaches, and make a hundred miles a day. The dust follows the coach in dense clouds, so that the drivers cannot see their horses for several minutes at a time. The pleasures of that kind of travel for 500 miles without rest can be imagined. Any one who longs for it can be indulged in this Territory, and I can assure him he will find the fares enormously high, and the coaches generally miserably uncomfortable. He need make no provision for sleep. As for the dwellings, very rarely can more than one bed be found in a house, and, for that matter, oftener than otherwise there is no room for more. If a man has more wives than one he manages to provide a room and bed for each. The children, young and old, sleep out of doors in Summer. What they do in Winter is more than I can imagine. The "dwellers in Zion" do not seem to have even Ginx's knack for tucking away a round dozen of dirty babies. Sometimes there is a little bed in the yard near the door, or on the front porch, if there happen to be one. Sometimes it is an affair of dog-kennel architecture, placed near the wood-pile, or in some corner, into and out of which a big boy or a half-grown girl may crawl, sleeping like a spaniel. We have found our most luxurious couches under a hay-stack. But such good fortune has not fallen to us often. We go to bed early, sleep soundly, get up with the sun, and have no headaches from bad ventilation.

The Noble Red Man

To continue our journey. We stayed a night at Springville, so called from an immense spring, from which flows a large brook, supplying water to a village of a thousand inhabitants, in their houses, and enough to irrigate a large city lot for each. The next day Wanero, a Ute sub-chief, who was in Washington last Summer, came into town with a number of his band — a picturesque group — who were chiefly anxious to obtain tobacco and flour. They were peaceable and had been behaving themselves very well, begging a little but not stealing. Wanero has a herd of forty or fifty cattle in the mountains. His band seem willing to remain on the reservation if they are enabled to live there, but they could say little till they saw the head chief, who is himself on the reservation. Major Powell gave them a sack of flour for each of the three camps who had representatives present, with which they were mightily pleased. He learned that the most troublesome tribe in Utah, the one with which most difficulty was expected in negotiations, and called the Shi-vi-rets, had been broken up this season and scattered among other tribes. About twenty of their number had died suddenly of some disease which resembled cholera, and the Indians believed it was caused by some magical power of the whites exerted on them because they had not behaved themselves. The effect of the superstition has been excellent, and has reduced the difficulty of the Indian problem in Utah by one-half at least.

Spanish Fork Canon and Mount Nebo

The same day our party, with several citizens, went twelve miles up Spanish Fort cañon, and made a camp, where we remained two nights. The scenery is fine, and Moran made several sketches. Major Powell took advantage of the opportunity for geological research. The citizens attended to certain business of their own in regard to the cattle-herding in the cañon. When we returned to Springville we hired a span of mules, driver, and wagon, determined to avoid stage-riding as much as possible, and with this equipment we went to Fillmore, stopping to rest at night, and procuring our meals at the villages and ranches. There are seldom any hotels, but almost any family along the road will furnish such as they have of provisions at a very moderate price. Going to Fillmore from Salt Lake we passed through Utah, Juab, and Round Valleys. In Juab Valley, at Stewart's Ranch, we delayed a day to ascend Mount Nebo, the highest mountain of either Utah or Nevada. It is one of the Wasatch range, and 1,200 feet high. Starting from Stewart's about 4 o'clock in the afternoon, we drove to the base of the mountains, about five miles. Then, with our blankets and rations on our backs, we climbed till dark. We camped by a little spring, lighted a fire, and after a supper of coffee, bread, and chicken, roasted in the coals, we retired to our blankets. The night was cold, and we slept little. Early in the morning we renewed the ascent, and at 12:20 we stood upon the highest peak. Part of the ascent was difficult, and not without danger, perhaps, for often we had to go where a misstep might be instant death. We were repaid for our toil by a glorious mountain view, extending from the Rocky Mountain summits in Colorado, to the mountains of Nevada, and from Salt Lake on the north, almost to the Grand Cañon on the south. We descended with much greater ease and rapidity, reaching the base of the mountain before dark, and proceeded five miles on our way to Fillmore, stopping for the night at Willow Creek, or Mona. Many of the Mormon villages have in some manner come by two names. The second day after, we were in Fillmore early in the day. After a day's delay, having left Major Powell and Mr. Pilling, Moran and myself came here, 150 miles, in five days, on horseback most of the distance, in company with a team taking freight to Major Powell's party, who are now finishing up in the field the topographical work of the survey of the cañon country. We are already in sight of the wonderful cliffs and buttes of this wonderland, and have seen enough to know that a rich experience is before us in the weeks that we shall spend in it.

Mormon Propagandism

At this point I must close this letter. But first, a word about some excitement caused last year by a rumor in the East that the Mormons were preparing for a grand exodus from Utah. Nothing could be more absurd. The report was caused by the fact that a "mission" had been sent across the Colorado into Arizona. These "missions," as they are called, are simply colonies of settlement. The object of sending them into Arizona is to secure favorable locations for future growth. Except in a few small valleys in the east, all the settlements have been made in Utah that ever can be, and Mormon growth is near an end unless it expands beyond the boundaries of the Territory. The utmost possible increase within the Territory can hardly exceed the present number of inhabitants, making the limit of population that can be supported only about double what it is now. This statement will probably be a surprise to many readers, but I will make it plain in a future letter. It has great significance in relation to the solution of the Mormon problem. But it does not portend an exodus.

The New York Times, 7 August 1873

THE COLORADO CANON

A TRIP TO THE VERGE OF THE CHASM

MAJOR POWELL'S SECOND SURVEY — PECULIARITIES OF THE COUNTRY — WATER POCKETS IN THE ROCKS — LOOKING DOWN THE ABYSS — THE COLORADO AND NIAGARA

From Our Own Correspondent
Kanab, Utah Territory, Wednesday, 13 August 1873

From Toquerville, three weeks ago, I wrote a nasty sketch of my trip thither from Salt Lake, journeying toward the Grand Cañon of the Colorado. Since then, Mr. Moran, Mr. John K. Hillers, the photographer of the Powell Expedition, and myself, with a Mr. Adams, a resident of Kanab, for cook and "packer," and a Pi Ute Indian, whom we called "Jim," whose use was chiefly to consume rations and run for our "stock," consisting of mules and horses, have gone down to the brink of the vast chasm. The Grand Cañon is, perhaps, the least known, or, rather, known to fewer people than any of the great natural wonders of our country. Probably not more than a thousand or two of white men have ever beheld it in any portion of its length, while less than half a hundred have ever visited it at its two or three most interesting points. There is not a published map that gives its proper location in any considerable part of its course. Yet, generally unknown as it is, there is no unsettled portion of our country that has been so thoroughly explored, surveyed, and measured, and no similar extent of territory that has received so much and such careful and patient scientific investigation and study as the basin of the Grand Cañon. The results, both topographical and scientific, will be placed in the reach of all mankind within the next twelve months, by the publication of Major Powell's reports, or a portion of them, to the Smithsonian Institution. Furthermore, in the early part of the coming Winter, the Major will give to the public, through the regular channels of the trade, a work giving a popular account of his first trip through the cañon and subsequent explorations.

The Canon and Its Environs

Nature's work in this cañon country is on the most magnificent scale. The plains are wide, the mountains high, and the walls of perpendicular cliffs hemming it in unbroken, and for many miles altogether impassable. The gorges are deep, and the color intense. There is a prodigality of everything but water, and the vegetable and animal life which cannot subsist without it. The Grand Cañon, the central feature of the whole, is for 270 miles an impassable gorge, whose sides range from 1,000 feet to one mile and a quarter in perpendicular height, cut through the solid rock by the action of the wild, impetuous river that flows through it. Its general course is east and west; but it is exceedingly tortuous and irregular in its direction. Into it there break innumerable side cañons, whose united length is thousands of miles. Some of them run back into the country a hundred miles or more, and as they as well as the Grand Cañon are for the most part impassable, the edges of the Grand Cañon cannot be traversed without going around the side cañons also. It is practicable to reach the brink of the cañon by any ordinary effort only at a few points.

Major Powell's First Exploration

Lieut. Ives and party saw a portion of the canon in 1858, and he describes in his report some of its characteristic features. But he learned nothing of its extent, and added little to the knowledge that previously existed in regard to it. Few maps pretended to even hint at its course. Nothing of importance was ever made known in addition to what was conveyed by Ives' report till Major Powell, with a party of men in boats, passed through it from Green River Station, on the Union Pacific Railroad, to the running out of the canon in the North-western portion of Arizona. This was in the Summer of 1869. The whole length of the trip was 900 miles, and it was accomplished in three months and a day. Ten men in four boats started from Green River, and seven men and two boats came safely through. Two boats were destroyed. Three of the men, thinking there was certain death before them in the canon, chose a point where they attempted to climb out, hoping to find chances of life in a trip overland to some settlement. It was afterward ascertained that they were all murdered by the Indians when within two days' travel of the Mormon settlements. The seven who came through endured terrible sufferings and hardships, and nearly starved. Major Powell's papers, containing notes of the topography of the river, were partially lost, though, fortunately, the records for the part of the river below the mouth of the Kanab Canon were preserved. The brief accounts of this exploration that have been published will be remembered. There was no historian except the hero of the terrible voyage, who, instead of waiting to inform the world of his great achievement, turned his attention to repairing the loss of his papers. The Expedition had been undertaken at his own expense, mainly for the opportunity he believed it presented of geological study. He was not disappointed in his expectations, but a large portion of the material collected having been lost, another descent was necessary. The subject was brought before Congress, and $12,000 was first voted for the survey of the Colorado Canon, and subsequently $12,000 was added for the survey of Green River, as it was found to be only practicable to reach the head of the Grand Canon by descending the Green River in boats.

Preparations for the Second Survey

The Summer of 1870 was spent by Major Powell in a trip to the canon through Utah. He traveled among the frontiersmen, miners, and Indians and attempted to establish means of communication by trails leading down to the river. In this he was partly successful, and he made arrangements to have his supplies replenished when opposite the Uintah Indian Reservation, and again at the mouth of the Dirty Devil River, which points are both above the entrance to the Grand Canon proper.

Progress of the Survey

In the meantime, Prof. A. H. Thompson had been busy in Chicago making the necessary preparations for the second voyage, collecting information and material, and he has since had entire charge of the topographical labor, and has done the most of it himself. The experiences of the previous voyage were made use of in the preparations, and such precautions were taken that the survey on the river was continued during the Summer of 1871 and again during 1872, not without peril and accident, but still without loss of life. The Winters were spent in a careful survey of the country about the river by triangulation from base lines. So diligently and industriously has this branch of the work been pushed forward that from 58,000 to 60,000 square miles have been covered and very carefully mapped. Three very large and interesting fields, never before entered by white men, have been triangulated and mapped, and one of the three has never been penetrated by white men, except Prof. Thompson and Mr. Adams, who accompanied us to the brink of the canon. Meanwhile, Major Powell has devoted himself to a careful study of the geology of the region, and the result will be a most remarkable and valuable contribution to his department of scientific investigation. So quietly has all this labor gone forward that I fancy nine out of ten who read the accounts in the Winter of 1869 and '70 of the first voyage through the canon are wholly unaware of any further voyages and explorations having been made. Nearly all the material for the reports, both on physical geography and geology, has been collected, and the maps and reports will be presented to Congress early in the next session.

"Little Zion" Valley

Having written thus generally of the cañon and the exploration I turn back to give you an account of the trip we have just completed to the cañon at the foot of To-ro-weap Valley. After leaving Toquerville, Moran and myself, with a guide and a pack-horse, took an excursion of four days into and through the most interesting and beautiful region we had ever seen. It is called by the Mormons "Little Zion Valley"; but as this name has been only a short time applied, it is to be hoped some other, more consonant with the character of the place, may be adopted. If any name of religious origin is to be used, something suggestive of the idea generally entertained of the New Jerusalem should be taken. In beauty of forms, in color, in variety, in everything but size, the valley vastly excels the famous Yosemite. In a distance of a dozen miles are as many real domes, 3,000 feet and upward above the valley, dome-shaped from the very base, and most beautifully banded with lines of color. There are vast arches, cathedrals, columned temples, monuments and gates so perfect that the forms are recognizable without any aid from fancy. A river larger, and greatly excelling the Merced in beauty, flows through pleasant meadows and amid vast boulders, now forming emerald pools, and again breaking into cascades. At the foot of the valley, on the west, stands a mass of cliffs, 4,500 feet above the valley, called the Temple of the Virgin, which alone is worth the trip from Washington to Southern Utah. Having feasted our eyes with the endless beauties of this lovely valley we returned to Kanab, where we found Prof. Thompson and his working party encamped, and busy with their topographical labors.

A Trip to the Grand Canon

After some delay for preparation, we left for the Grand Cañon. Our "outfit" consisted, besides the animals we were to ride, of two pack-mules — one to carry Mr. Hillers' photographic apparatus, and the other our blankets and rations for ten days. Our rations were flour and "yeast-powder" for bread, "jerked" beef, bacon, coffee, tea, cheese, sugar, and dried peaches. A tin plate, knife, fork (not silver), and spoon for each person, was our table outfit, and a somewhat extravagant one it is generally considered by the men of the plains. We left here about noon of the 5th, and made our halt for the night at Pipe Spring, twenty miles distant. Kanab is in Utah, just north of the line. Pipe Spring is in Arizona, eleven miles south of the line. It is merely a large, fine spring, at the point of a high headland or butte, with a stone house, or rather two stone houses, connected with high stone walls, forming between them a kind of fortification. It was so built as a protection against Indians who, a few years ago, killed the keeper of the ranch. The spring is owned by the "Church," or "Brother Brigham." There is no other good water within twenty miles of it. Between Kanab and Pipe is a good wagon road. At Pipe we leave the road and strike directly across the desert, in a southwesterly direction, taking our course toward Mount Trumbull, which rises only fifteen miles from the foot of the To-ro-weap Valley. The second day we go from Pipe to the Wild Band Pocket, a round hole surrounded by low volcanic elevations, where the drainage from a shower that, with great good fortune for us, had fallen two days before, had settled in quantity to the amount of fifteen or twenty hogsheads. The pocket has a rock bottom, and water remains in it until carried away by evaporation. Wild horses, ranging over 500 to 1,000 square miles, sometimes come to the pocket for water. Hence its name. We chanced to see them grazing near a little bluff, five or six miles away. Wild Band is only sixteen miles from Pipe, and we reached it by mid-day. But we could go no further, for the nearest water in the direction of the cañon was twenty-five miles away, and it was not certain that it might not be dried up, or, as our Indian, Jim, expressed it in his language, "have died," in which case we should have to go seven or eight miles further, and out of our direct course, to find a spring. We therefore spent the rest of the day and the night at Wild Band.

"The Pigmies' Hole in the Rock"

The morning of the 7th we left camp, and proceeded to the next place where we hoped to find water, and were not disappointed. We continued direct toward Mount Trumbull from Wild Band, passing over a low bluff on which a few scraggy cedars grew through a sag, or bottom, up a sharp volcanic ridge, and around the base of an old volcano. Then a sharp turn to the south, and two miles brings us into the upper part of the To-ro-weap Valley. Then we turn toward the west, and the southern extremity of Mount Trumbull, near the base of which we find the "Unupits Pacavi" (pronounced oo-noo-pits pah-cah-vee). This is another "pocket" in a basin of volcanic rock. The Indian name signifies "the pigmies' hole in the rock." The Wild Band Pocket water was so muddy that one could not see the bottom in a teaspoonful of it. But it tasted sweet, except a little clayey. The water in the Unupits Pacavi was clearer, though discolored by organic matter. But it was thick with "wigglers" or mosquito larvae, and "tadpoles." It was also bitter, and left a prickling sensation in the throat. Men and animals drank from the same pool. We made coffee and tea from it, which I hope was not cruelty to animals, for a good many "wigglers" and "tadpoles" were unavoidably boiled to death. To our rations for dinner were added two rabbits, shot as we went along by a member of the party.

Poisonous Pocket Water

On the morning of the 8th we left the Unupits Pacavi, continuing down the To-ro-weap, and, after a fifteen miles' march, came to another water pocket in basaltic rock, a mile from the brink of the cañon. This water we thought good at first, but found it to leave the prickling sensation in the throat, mentioned above. We camped by it two days. The second day after dinner every member of the party was more or less ill, and one or two were taken with slight vomitings, which, however, soon passed away. We drank as little water as possible thereafter, and had little relish for food or drink again till we returned to Pipe.

On the Verge

As soon as we had eaten lunch, after our arrival at the last mentioned pocket, we proceeded to the brink of the cañon. Our view was obstructed by cliffs, or gulches, till we arrived almost at the very edge of the abyss, so that our first sight of it revealed it in all its mighty grandeur. We had looked across and seen the top of the wall on the opposite side. We had indeed seen as much as that when we were at Pipe — not the wall at To-ro-weap, but further up the cañon. But we had no view which gave us any idea of the vastness of the chasm. When we were 100 yards away, a sharp bend in the course of the stream appeared before us, and the gorge suddenly opened, almost as if the very crust of the earth had been instantly rent asunder. We stop and gaze in awe-stricken silence upon the wonderful spectacle. But still we do not yet comprehend, in the fullness of its power, the grand scene, nor have we all of it before our eyes. We go forward to the very edge, and creeping out on a projecting cliff, look directly down upon the river raging in its rocky bed, 3,000 feet beneath our standing-place. Although the river has a volume equal, at least, to the Ohio at Cincinnati, so distant is it that we see but a mere ribbon of sheen, like a little rivulet or creek. An object the size of a man by the water's edge, I am told, is invisible from our point, except as a speck before the eye, which cannot be distinguished as an object. Yet the water rushes along with such force that its motion can be seen, and what appear to be only ripples on its surface Mr. Hilliers, who came through the cañon in one of the boats, tells me are huge waves and swift rapids that hurry along with tremendous speed, and a deafening roar that is terrible to the navigator. This is easy to believe, for the roar of the dashing torrent bounds and echoes from wall to wall, reaching the point where we stand, intensifying the impression on the sense of sight. We seem to stand directly over the river, but when we come to consider and examine, we find we are at least 300 or 400 yards back from the water's edge. The opposite wall recedes in the same manner. The walls do not, however, recede by a regular angle, or inclination, but by a series of steep terraces, some very narrow and some quite wide. Between the terraces they shoot up perpendicularly hundreds of feet at a single leap. We judge the chasm to be 1,800 to 2,000 feet across at the top from where we stand, so it can be perceived that the angle of inclination from bottom to top is very slight. We spent the whole of the afternoon wandering about the verge of the cañon, selecting the most favorable points of view, receiving momentarily new revelations of magnitude, and new impressions of grandeur.

The Canon and Niagara

There is something in the character of the impression made upon the sense and feeling by the Grand Cañon peculiar to itself, and difficult of description. Perhaps comparison will reveal its real nature, though any close analysis of the emotion produced may not be attempted. At Niagara, the impression is one of tremendous power and activity. The beholder may stand at arm's length only from the mighty force he sees displayed, and all around him are the evidences of its recent energy. The wide, deep chasm below the Falls is not so deep but every movement of the whirling, seething waters is plain to see. It is not the effect of the force, but its activity, and the sense of its might, that produce the emotion of grandeur and sublimity. A mountain summit view is grand because of its vastness, and generally there is not impression like that made at Niagara, of force and power. At the Grand Cañon, the feeling of grandeur is not produced by power in activity, for the river is too far away, and forms too insignificant a part of the scene. Nor is it produced by the vastness of the chasm alone, for every one has seen other things giving a more distinct impression of great extent or size. I think the feeling is one of awe and wonder at the evidence of some mighty, inconceivable, unknown power, at some time terribly majestically, and mysteriously energetic, but now ceased. And yet the force that has wrought so wonderfully through periods unknown, unmeasured, and unmeasurable, is a river 3,000 feet below, so far away that one never thinks of it as an agency capable of such a work. Nor, indeed, without study and investigation and reflection can it be conceived that its ceaseless motion, through myriads of years, may have eroded and worn its rocky channel through plains and mountains, to such a depth that, in places, Mount Washington, plucked up by the roots, as Milton's contending legions plucked the heavenly hills, and thrown into the chasm, would not appear above the brink, nor form a dam for the rushing river.

The Upper Cliffs

I have mentioned only the lower and nearly perpendicular cleft of the rocky strata. The To-ro-weap has lead us down to its brink, and there rise all about us another series of terraces 1,800 or 2,000 feet high, which approach in places almost to the edge of the narrow chasm on which we stand, and in others recede a half mile or mile. This second series of terraces form a part of the cañon chasm, and it is only in places far distant from each other that the narrow plateau on which we stand can be gained. The upper cliffs are broken into beautiful shapes, extending out into splendid buttes and headlands, which are sometimes isolated, except at the bases, and stand as vast towers or castles beautifully painted and ornamented. The color of the walls below us is generally red, resembling in no slight degree the Seneca stone of Washington, of which the Smithsonian is constructed. The terraces above us are generally gray, marked in places by red and yellow. The effect at sunset on these cliffs, especially in the distance, as we see them looking up the cañon, is superb, and has a peculiar beauty.

The Return to Kanab

We spent two days at the foot of To-ro-weap, Hilliers and Moran made several photographs and sketches. We returned the way we came, but little fatigued from our trip, and well, owing to our good fortune in another series of showers which saved us from thirst and bad water. This good fortune will not always follow travelers to the To-ro-weap at this season of the year. Till the day before we started from Kanab there had been no rain-fall for many weeks, and a week earlier our excursion would have been attended, inevitably, with real suffering from bad water, or no water at all. We reached Kanab again on the evening of the 12th. Tomorrow, the 14th, we start with twelve days' rations for the Kai Bab Plateau, a still more wonderful and interesting portion of the cañon. This time we have the company of Major Powell and Mr. Pilling, and expect a trip of unusual interest and enjoyment.

The New York Times, 4 September 1873

LETTER FROM THOMAS MORAN TO MARY NIMMO MORAN

Kanab, 13 August 1873

My dear Wife,

The noon after my last letter was dated we left camp for the Grand Canon at the foot of To-Ro-Weap Valley. The first camp we made was at Pipe Springs 20 miles. The next day we reached what is called the Wild Band Pocket 20 miles. It is a gulch with a rock bottom that holds water after the rains and is frequented by a band of wild horses which we saw in the distance. All places that hold water after rain are called water pockets. The Wild Band Pocket is situated in as absolute a desert as I ever saw. The water was thick with a red mud, but was good, and when you want water you are not particular about the color of it. We shot some rabbits and had a game supper. The wolves were howling all round us but they did not come near. I ought to mention that we had an Indian guide named Jim, a Pi-Ute with whom we had a good deal of amusement. His business was to look after the horses of which we had seven with us. The next day we got into a volcanic country full of old craters and lava and reached the In-nu-pits peccavo, or *Witches pocket* in the lava rocks at the foot of Mt. Trumbull where we found a large pocket of clear water but of bad taste from decomposed vegetation. This day we travelled 35 miles. Luckily the weather was cool during the whole trip. From our camp at the pocket the wall of the Grand Canon was visible some 15 miles down the valley. The Indians are very superstitious and Jim did not much like our camping so near the pocket. During the night I was awakened by a wolf crunching the bones of a rabbit we had eaten. He was not more than 12 feet from where we were lying, and it being moonlight, I saw him clearly. Colburn had his gun in bed with him but when I rose up the animal took to his heels and disappeared. There must have been more than one in camp that night as Colburn's spur had disappeared having been carried off by a wolf for the leather on it. Indian Jim said that he had a bad dream, that an Indian shot him and he wanted to clear out very early. About noon we made another water pocket in the lava rocks about a mile from the Grand Chasm. The water was full of red mud again. After dinner (flour cake and bacon) we struck out for the Canon. On reaching the brink the whole gorge for miles lay beneath us and it was by far the most awfully grand and impressive scene that I have ever yet seen. We had reached the Canon on the second level or edge of the great gulf. Above and around us rose a wall of 2000 feet and below us a vast chasm 2500 feet in perpendicular depth and ½ a mile wide. At the bottom the river very muddy and seemingly only a hundred feet wide seemed slowly moving along but in reality is a rushing torrent filled with rapids. A suppressed sort of roar comes up constantly from the chasm but with that exception every thing impresses you with an awful stillness. The color of the Great Canon itself is red, a light Indian Red, and the material sandstone and red marble and is in terraces all the way down. All above the canon is variously colored sandstone mainly a light flesh or cream color and worn into very fine forms. I made an outline and did a little color work but had not time nor was it worth while to make a detailed study in color. We made several photos which will give me all the details I want if I conclude to paint the view. We stayed at the Canon all the next day. In the evening Jack Hillers the photographer was bringing a canteen of water from the pocket when a huge rattlesnake glided between his feet and he got a thorough scare. We searched for the snake with some burning sage brush and I killed it with a stone. It measured fully 3½ feet long. The stone mashed the rattles so we could not tell how many he had. On our trip to the Virgin River Jack had another narrow escape from a rattlesnake. He was talking to me and had both his elbows right over a rattler which Colburn shot. The Indian boy I told you had been bitten by one died after living nearly 3 days. We left the Canon pocket for camp at the In-nu-pits peccavo, and Indian Jim was very desirous that we should go somewhere else to camp as he said the little imps would hurt the horses as well as ourselves, but we told him the In-nu-pits were all dead long ago and we finally pacified him, though I don't think he slept much. Just after supper Colburn sitting by the fire found a large Tarantula beside him. He cleared out in a hurry and we killed him. This was the third Tarantula we killed. Between snakes and Tarantulas it made us feel a little uncomfortable at night down there, but we are very careful and there is but little danger of our getting bitten. The next day we cam back to the Wild Band pocket and it rained on us all afternoon and night. Yesterday we reached camp, having been away 8 days on the trip. When we got back we found Maj. Powell had arrived and he had all the Indians in camp and all the squaws making Indian toggery for him. He is going to get me an Indian suit made. This afternoon the Major and I are going up toward the Virgin River on a little trip to see some lakes in caverns about 7 miles from here and shall return this evening. Tomorrow morning a party of 8 including Colburn, myself, and Powell start for the Ki-bab plateau to see the Grand Canon at that point. It is 3500 feet deep at that point, and I am inclined to think it is a finer subject for a picture than the To-Ro-Weap view. This trip will take 8 days and I shall then be ready to come home. If I come down here again you must come too. You would just go wild over what there is to see here, and it is perfectly safe though a pretty hard trip to make. I have just received your letters, 4 in all, and the first I have gotten,.... I am so glad that everything is all right with you. I am sorry that Archie has to go to work in the way he has. The Major is waiting for me to go to the Lakes so I must close. I had a good many things to say but must cut short. This is perhaps the last letter I shall write from here as I expect to start for home on my return from the Ki-bab. Work hard to improve your drawing dear as I shall have plenty of work for you this coming winter. 70 drawings for Powell, 40 for Appleton, 4 for Aldine, 20 for Scribner's all from this region beside the water colors and oil pictures. Kisses and love to you all....

Your loving Hub, Tom

(Bassford and Fryxell 1967, 37–42)

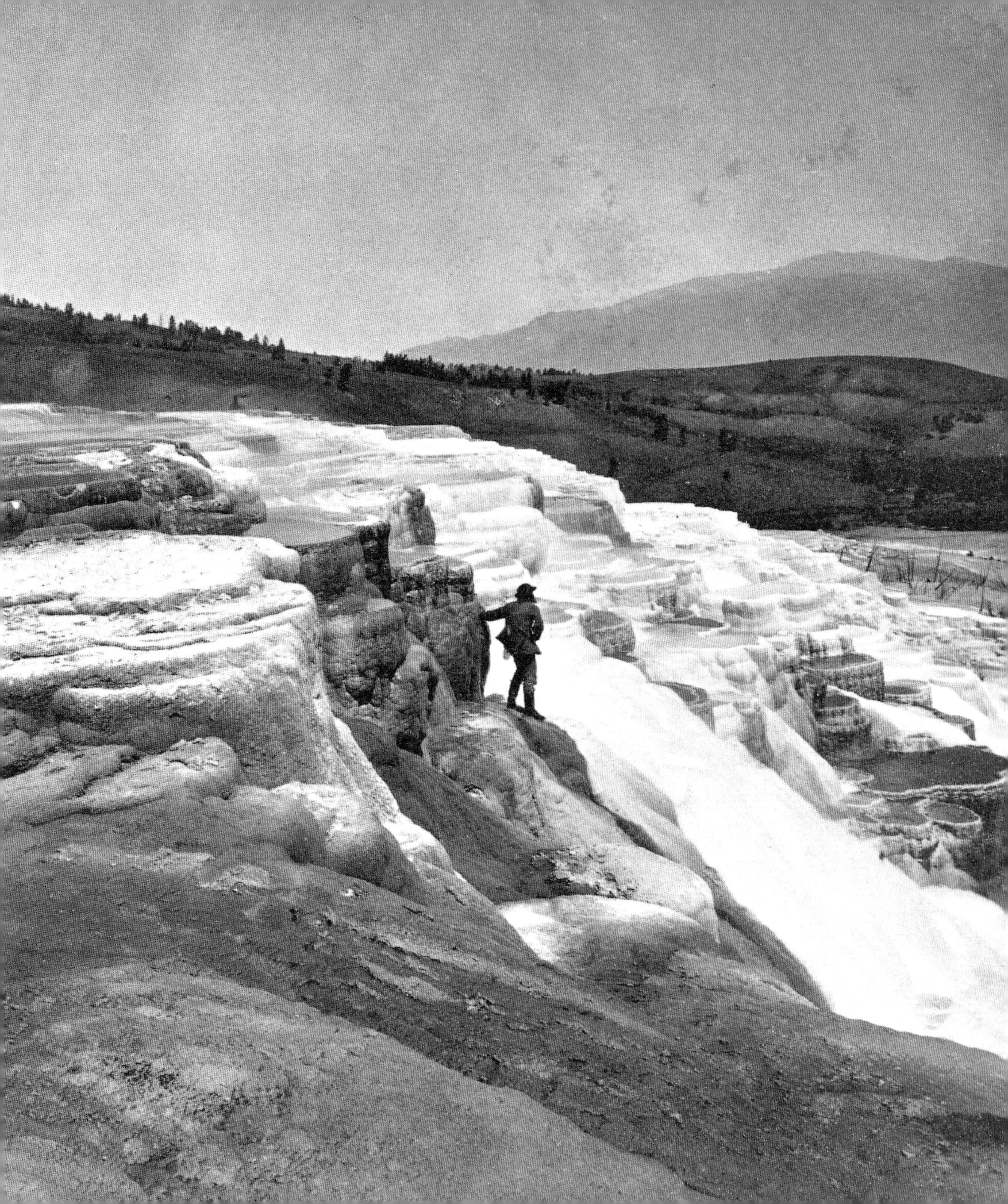

1837–1870: Emigrant Son

1. George Gordon, Lord Byron, "Frame Work Bill Speech," *Lord Byron: The Complete Miscellaneous Prose*, ed. Andrew Nicholson (Oxford, 1991), 22.
2. Engels 1993, 55.
3. Longworth 1987, 32.
4. Biographical notes by Ruth Moran, EHL.
5. Letter from Shaun Greenhalgh, 24 June 1987, quoting correspondence from Mary Higson Moran, Gilcrease research files.
6. *Bolton Journal*, 22 Apr. 1882, quoting Mary Higson Moran. Much of the information included in the article was published in the *Manchester Genealogist* 26 (Oct. 1990), 23–29.
7. Benson 1893, 70–71. E. Moran 1894, 52.
8. E. Moran 1894, 52.
9. Coleman 1901, 191.
10. According to some sources Thomas Moran became seriously ill and the apprenticeship was terminated for that reason. Other sources suggest that a disagreement over the sale by Scattergood and Telfer of drawings and watercolors by Moran precipitated the break. A biographical profile of Peter Moran published in *Art Journal* (May 1878), 135, reports that when Peter was sixteen he was apprenticed by his father "to learn the trade of lithographic printing in the establishment of Messrs. Herline & Hersel, of Philadelphia." After spending only a few "miserable" months with the firm, Peter "succeeded in picking a very serious quarrel with his employers, and in getting his indenture cancelled." His "matter-of-fact" relatives—most likely Thomas Moran Sr.—were described as displeased when Peter declared his wish to become an artist. His father had undoubtedly arranged for Thomas Moran's earlier apprenticeship as well. Peter's method of breaking his apprenticeship contract may reflect the example of Thomas.
11. E. Moran 1888, 101–103; 127–128.
12. John Sartain, "James Hamilton," *Sartain's Union Magazine of Literature and Art* 10 (Apr. 1852), 331.
13. Biographical notes by Ruth Moran, Mary Tassin Moran, and Thomas Moran, 1903, GA. In recalling books acquired in trade, Moran specifically noted Turner's *Rivers of France* and Cowper's "Task" and declared that he still (1903) owned a number of the books he had acquired in this manner. See also biographical notes regarding Thomas Moran, EHL.
14. As late as 1913 Moran's good friend, G.H. Buek wrote that Moran was "an indefatigable reader" with a "mind stored with the best that English literature has given to the world" (see Buek 1913, 30).
15. See Susan P. Casteras, "The 1857–1858 Exhibition of English Art in America and Critical Responses to Pre-Raphaelitism," in Ferber and Gerdts 1985, 109–133.
16. John Ruskin, *The Elements of Drawing; in Three Letters to Beginners*, (London, 1857), 132–148. Three copies by Moran after plates in Turner's *Liber* are at the Gilcrease Museum. Moran's copies are after pl. 13, *The Bridge in the Middle Distance*; pl. 23, *The Temple of Minerva Medica*; and pl. 41, *Procris and Cephalus*.
17. For a detailed discussion of "Studies for Pictures" see Thomas Bruhn's essay in this volume. The early technique Thomas and John Moran developed in preparing to publish "Studies for Pictures" may have had a lasting effect. In an interview in the *Kansas City Star*, 5 Oct. 1923, Thomas described his painting method to a reporter, who noted: "He first makes a close, careful drawing in charcoal on his canvas, photographs this drawing himself, then rubs out the charcoal sketch and begins to put on his colors, using the photograph merely to refresh his mind and referring to sketches made on the ground for his color and atmosphere."
18. Thomas Moran to Mary Nimmo, 9 Aug. 1860, in Bassford and Fryxell 1967, 23–24.
19. *The Complete Poetical Works of Longfellow*, (Boston, 1975), 113. See also Nickerson 1984, 49; and Carr 1986, 58–78.
20. See Foster and Whitney 1851.
21. Kinsey 1992, 24–25; Sweeney 1987, 34.
22. In 1873, thirteen years after his trip to Lake Superior, images based on his field studies appeared as illustrations for an article on the Pictured Rocks in *Aldine*. In 1876, at the Centennial Exposition in Philadelphia, Moran exhibited six drawings and a major painting (*"Fiercely the red sun descending,"* cat. 50) based on Longfellow's *Hiawatha*.
23. The International Exhibition in London opened 1 May 1862 and continued through 15 November. The number of American works of art exhibited was small, but John Sartain's engraving *Men of Progress—Inventors* was included. Several members of the Sartain family traveled to London during the exhibition period. The opportunity to see many works by European artists at the exhibition and visit with the Sartains may have contributed to Thomas and Edward's decision to go to England in 1862.
24. *The Golden Bough*, dated 1862, was offered at Sotheby's, New York, 10 Dec. 1970. The painting's present location is unknown.
25. E. Moran 1888, 101.
26. Benjamin 1879b, 42–43.
27. Paul Nimmo Moran was born 11 April 1864, Mary Scott Moran 16 June 1867, and Ruth Bedford Moran, 20 August 1870.
28. Benjamin 1880, 93, reviewing the 13th annual exhibition of the AWCS, described Moran's *Morning* as "an effective bit of work by an artist who, in the language of others, often gives us very clever thoughts of his own."
29. Tuckerman 1865.
30. Formerly titled *Under the Trees*. Moran's signature includes "Op 17," and Appendix 2 indicates that his original title for the picture was *The Autumnal Woods*.
31. As early as 1827/1828 Thomas Cole had included a similar reclining figure in the foreground of his painting *Autumn Landscape*. See Ellwood C. Parry III, *The Art of Thomas Cole: Ambition & Imagination* (Newark, DE, 1988).
32. Brown 1992, 84.
33. Brown 1992, 93.
34. *Phila. Evening Bulletin*, 26 Mar. 1868.
35. Throughout his life Moran cultivated the image of a poet-artist. Reviewers and critics often responded in kind. See an unidentified writer for the *Phila. Evening Bulletin* (13 Dec. 1867): "Avoiding the extreme of realism, and yet equally avoiding technical faults, Mr. Moran's works are poems as well as pictures. The romantic is a distinct but not obtrusive element in them and they create ever new impressions in the mind of the careful observer."
36. Morand 1986 credits Weitenkampf 1903.
37. Benjamin 1879b, 42.

1871–1880: Breakthrough

1. Moran to Richard Watson Gilder, Christmas 1872, NYPL Gilder papers.
2. Morand and Hirsch 1983.
3. Hayden undoubtedly read Langford's article about Yellowstone and perhaps heard Langford lecture on the subject in Washington, but as Kinsey 1992, 46, points out, Hayden's interest in Yellowstone had likely been roused several years earlier.
4. A.B. Nettleton to F.V. Hayden, 11 June 1871, Hayden IC, film 623, NA.
5. Nettleton to Hayden, 16 June 1871, Hayden IC, NA.
6. "Yellowstone Scientific Expedition," *Helena Herald* [MT], 11 July 1871.
7. YJ, 11 July 1871, YNP.
8. YJ, 7 Aug. 1871, YNP.
9. "Wonders of the Yellowstone Country," *Helena Herald*, 29 Aug. 1871.
10. Richard Watson Gilder grew up in Bordentown, NJ, not far from Philadelphia, and enlisted in the Philadelphia Artillery, a militia organization, in 1862. It is possible that Moran and Gilder knew one another in Philadelphia, although this has not been confirmed. In 1869 Gilder joined Robert Crane in founding the *Newark Morning Register*. To make ends meet, he took a second job as an editor for *Hours at Home*, a monthly publication of Charles Scribner and Company. He remained with the magazine until the debut of *Scribner's* in November 1870.
11. "A Picture Gallery of the Yellowstone," *Newark Daily Advertiser*, 6 Oct. 1871.
12. "Capitol and Departments," *National Republican* [DC], 20 Jan. 1872.
13. "Bills Reported," *National Republican* [DC], 24 Jan. 1872.
14. Hayden 1872a, 396. Yosemite had been set aside as a state park in June 1864. It became a national park in 1890.
15. Jackson 1936, 157.

16. Moran to Hayden, 11 Mar. 1872, Hayden IC, NA.
17. "New York," *Boston Advertiser*, 1 Apr. 1872.
18. Townley, Mar. 1872.
19. Moran to Hayden, 26 Apr. 1872, Hayden IC, NA.
20. Cook 1872a.
21. Cook 1872a.
22. Cook 1872a.
23. "Moran's 'Grand Canon of the Yellowstone,'" *Newark Daily Advertiser*, 29 Apr. 1872.
24. Moran to Mary Nimmo Moran, 18 and 21 May 1872, Fryxell, UW.
25. Moran to Mary Nimmo Moran, 22 May 1872, Fryxell, UW.
26. "Culture and Progress: Thomas Moran's 'Grand Canon of the Yellowstone,'" *Scribner's*, June 1872, 251–252.
27. Langford 1871, 118.
28. An undated list of books purchased by F. V. Hayden in a collection of letters to and from Hayden at the Western Reserve Historical Society includes books of poetry by Shelley and Coleridge and a copy of Byron's *Childe Harold*. I thank Mike Foster for his help with this reference.
29. Moran to Hayden, 28 June 1873, Hayden IC, NA.
30. Moran to Hayden, 20 May 1873, Hayden IC, NA.
31. Moran to Mary Nimmo Moran, 9 July 1873, in Bassford and Fryxell 1967, 29.
32. Bassford and Fryxell 1967, 41. In the same letter Moran encouraged Mary to "work hard" to improve her drawing as he "would have plenty of work" for her during the coming winter. What role Mary played in assisting Moran prepare images is not clear but such comments suggest that her contribution may have been more substantial than previously acknowledged. For an account of Moran's commissioned Grand Canyon work see Kinsey essay and last section of Bibliography.
33. Moran to Hayden, 25 Nov. 1873, Hayden IC, NA.
34. Moran to Hayden, 4 Dec. 1873, Hayden IC, NA.
35. Moran to Hayden, 29 Jan. 1874, Hayden IC, NA.
36. *Newark Daily Advertiser*, 1 May 1874.
37. The painting was shown privately on 11 May, then placed on public view at Goupil's, New York, the following day.
38. *Newark Daily Advertiser*, 13 May 1874.
39. *Appleton's*, 30 May 1874.
40. *Evening Star* [DC], 13 June 1874.
41. "The Pictures at the Capitol," *Evening Star* [DC], 14 July 1874.
42. "Culture and Progress: 'The Chasm of the Colorado,'" *Scribner's*, July 1874, 373.
43. Cook 1874, 375.
44. Cook 1874, 375.
45. Cook 1874, 376.
46. Copyright no. 3114E, 14 Mar. 1874, Copyright Office, Washington, DC. The photograph Moran submitted was most likely taken by William Henry Jackson.
47. Jackson 1940, 218, describes the journey to the Mountain of the Holy Cross in 1873; owing to the vagaries of the weather and the complexity of the photographic process at the time, Jackson was able to take only eight exposures.
48. Moran to Mary Nimmo Moran, 24 Aug. 1874, in Bassford and Fryxell 1967, 55.
49. "From the Mount of the Holy Cross," *Denver Rocky Mt. News*, 1 Sept. 1874.
50. "Moran's New Picture," *Newark Daily Advertiser*, 5 Apr. 1875.
51. "Mr. Moran's New Picture," *NYT*, 10 Apr. 1875.
52. *Aldine* (July 1875) published a review of *Mountain of the Holy Cross*, which also links Moran to Calame, "whose pupil Thomas Moran might have been." The Gilcrease collection includes three Calame prints once owned by Moran.
53. James Macleod to Moran, 14 June 1875, letterpress volumes, director's records, Corcoran.
54. "Art & Artists," *Boston Transcript*, 21 Dec. 1875.
55. For further details regarding Bierstadt's campaign to win the commission see Linda Ferber, "Albert Bierstadt: The History of a Reputation," in Anderson and Ferber 1990, 49–53.
56. "Art Notes," *Evening Star* [DC], 23 Feb. 1878.
57. "Art Notes," *Evening Star* [DC], 22 June 1878.

1881–1899: Home Fires and Distant Ports

1. "Art Matters," *Newark Daily Advertiser*, 6 June 1881.
2. Jackson 1940, 228–235.
3. Jackson 1940, 219–235; Jackson 1959, 257–334.
4. Ingersoll's article appeared in the *NY Tribune*, 3 Nov. 1874. Excerpts appear in Jackson 1940, 232–235.
5. Ingersoll 1885 included an account of the cliff dwelling trip and illustrations by Moran.
6. "Fine Arts," *NY Independent*, 20 Oct. 1881.
7. At the National Academy of Design annual exhibition in the spring of 1882 Moran exhibited *The Pueblo of San Juan, New Mexico*.
8. "Exhibition of Paintings in Bolton," *Manchester Guardian*, 9 June 1882.
9. "Art and Artists," *Boston Transcript*, 22 Sept. 1882.
10. "An American's Success in England," *NY Herald*, 4 Sept. 1882.
11. For possible reasons for the trip see Morand 1996, 67.
12. Thomas Moran to Mary Moran, in Bassford and Fryxell 1967, 62.
13. The *Catalogue of the Oils and Water Colors of Thomas Moran* issued for the sale at Ortgies Galleries, 24 Feb. 1886, lists sixty-four works. *NYT*, 25 Feb. 1886, reported that sixty-one pictures sold for a total of $10,321. The highest price paid for a single picture was $2,000 for *Ponce de Leon in Florida*.
14. "The Moran Exhibition," *NY Herald*, 18 Feb. 1886.
15. Moran left on the steamship *Fulda*, 14 Apr. 1886. *NYT*, 15 Apr. 1886; EHL.
16. Bassford and Fryxell 1967, 77.
17. Robert Browning, quoted in Julian Halsby, *Venice: The Artist's Vision* (London, 1990), 118. See also Bronson 1902, 145–171.
18. An excerpt from *Stones of Venice* appeared in *The Crayon* 1 (17 Jan. 1855), 42. Additional excerpts appeared in issues published on 4 July and 11 July 1855.
19. Turner altered Byron's lines, which read in the original: "I stood in Venice, on the Bridge of Sighs;/A palace and a prison on each hand" (*Childe Harold*, canto 4.1).
20. Henry James, "Venice," *Century Magazine* 25 (Nov. 1882), 3.
21. See both Lovell 1984 and Lovell 1989.
22. *EH Star*, 13 Sept. 1890. Moran's gondola is now in the collection of the Mariner's Museum, Newport News, VA.
23. Cleveland 1897.
24. "Artist Thomas Moran," *EH Star*, 4 Mar. 1892.
25. See Kinsey 1992, 132–133.
26. Bassford and Fryxell 1967, 91.
27. Bassford and Fryxell 1967, 89–93.
28. "A Mountain Painter," *Denver Rocky Mt. News*, 18 June 1892.
29. Bassford and Fryxell 1967, 119.
30. Bassford and Fryxell 1967, 123.
31. "Artist Thomas Moran," *EH Star*, 4 Mar. 1892.
32. "A Mountain Painter," *Denver Rocky Mt. News*, 18 June 1892.
33. Reports on the hospitals and community efforts to assist the soldiers appeared in the *EH Star*, 10 June, 29 July, 5 Aug., 26 Aug., 7 Oct., 28 Oct. 1898.
34. *Brooklyn Eagle* was quoted by the *EH Star*, 30 Sept. 1898.
35. A long article reporting Mary Moran's death was published in the *EH Star*, 29 Sept. 1899. The death record filed at the town clerk's office in East Hampton lists Mary Moran's cause of death as "enterocolitis."

1900–1926: "Old Guard"

1. "The Niagara of the West—The Great Shoshone Falls," *Phila. Evening Bulletin*, 17 July 1866.
2. Richardson 1867, 497; [Timothy O'Sullivan], "Photographs from the High Rockies," *Harper's Monthly* 39 (Sept. 1869), 475.
3. Clarence King, *Mountaineering in the Sierra Nevada* (Boston, 1872; repr. Lincoln, NE, 1970), 187–194.
4. Ruth Moran to Mr. [Horace] Albright, undated, EHL.
5. I thank Peter Boag for his assistance with references regarding early Idaho history, including Walgamott 1926.
6. Hults 1989, 89–102.
7. King 1872, 189–190.
8. "Great Irrigation Project," *Spokesman Review* [Spokane, WA], 18 Oct. 1900.
9. Caffin 1901, 74.
10. Caffin 1901.
11. *Shoshone Falls* remained unsold at the time of Moran's death. Ruth Moran was also unable to sell the picture. In 1948 the painting was acquired by Thomas Gilcrease.
12. Coleman 1901, 191.
13. *NY World*, 12 June 1911; typescript at EHL.
14. Ladegast 1900, 209.

15. Morton 1900, 1–16.
16. "Pictures in the Galleries," *NYT*, 17 Feb. 1897.

Printmaker "of the First Rank"

1. Rainey 1994 closely studies one of the major illustrated publications to which Moran contributed. See also Kinsey 1992.
2. For a general discussion of artists' prints in this country in the nineteenth century see Bruhn 1993, 5–23.
3. Morand and Hirsch 1983, 17.
4. Moran was not unique in creating prints both before and after the late 1870s. Other artists, such as Robert Swain Gifford, Henry Farrer, and Moran's brother Peter, were also painters, but none had the significance of Moran. Examples of their work and additional bibliographical information can be found in Bruhn 1993.
5. Quoted from Moran's autobiographical statement, written in the third person, GA; repr. in Morand and Hirsch 1983, 17.
6. For Moran's own words on Turner's color see Sheldon 1879, 123–124.
7. R. Moran 1926, 646.
8. On Earlom and the *Liber* see Lambert 1987, 102–103, 142–143; and Alexander and Godfrey 1980, 4.
9. The most recent publication to consider the *Liber Studiorum* in depth is Forrester 1996; for his prints in general see Lyles and Perkins 1989.
10. Klackner 1889, no. 1; Morand and Friese 1986, no. 1. The signatures and inscriptions found on Moran's etchings and lithographs, while generally in the artist's hand, may have been added by him at any time.
11. Klackner 1889, no. 2; Morand and Friese 1986, no. 2.
12. Wray 1893, 53–54. While the date Wray cited, 1860, contradicts the date Moran suggested for his first etching, 1856, no date seems absolutely certain for this work. The print went unmentioned in Koehler 1880. It first appears in Klackner 1889, 9. Klackner's text, however, gives the date as 1857. In lifetime inventories the print is also dated to 1858 and 1859.
13. On Sartain and reproductive printmaking see Philadelphia 1976, 369–371. See also Martinez 1983, 12 n 25; and Martinez 1987, 91–93, which lists several of Sartain's more important positions and accomplishments.
14. Benjamin 1882, 92. The most complete introduction to *cliché-verre* in English is Glassman and Symmes 1980, 29–44.
15. Glassman and Symmes 1980, 29.
16. Morand and Friese 1986, nos. 3–5. Besides the two prints of *Haunted House* at the Gilcrease, the NYPL (Stauffer Collection) has one copy.
17. Morand and Friese 1986, 59–60.
18. Glassman and Symmes 1980, 35 n 17.
19. Morand and Friese 1986, 59–60.
20. Two modern sources for John Moran's work, much of which is found in the LCP, are Reilly 1979; and Finkel 1980.
21. *Photographic News* (1863), 226. This clipping was found in the John Moran folder at the LCP. Nancy Friese suggests a similar method of printing in Morand and Friese 1986, 42.
22. Wright 1995, 267–294.
23. Until recently Edward Moran's only known lithograph was a reproduction dating to 1855 of Washington and his staff at Valley Forge by Veron Fletcher. Then Helena Wright, curator of graphic arts at the National Museum of American History, Smithsonian Institution, found a quarto-sized single sheet of six small landscape and seascape studies by Edward. The sheet is signed "Painted and drawn on stone by Edward Moran" and is in the John Sartain print collection at the Moore College of Art, Philadelphia.
24. Bruhn 1990, no. 1.
25. One is in the NYPL and one is in the EHL. By far the greatest number of lithographs are found in these two institutions, owing to the generosity of Moran's two daughters, Mary Tassin and Ruth. Moran was not overly scrupulous or interested in keeping records, and it is apparent that inventories of his prints, and even dates and signatures, were compiled or added sometimes much later in life.
26. Sartain's print collections are mentioned in Martinez 1987, 97, 100. In a letter to the author, Helena Wright raises the possibility that Sartain made his collection available to Moran.
27. The monogram generally associated with Moran is a vertically conjoined "M" over a "T" with serifs, but he did not use this version until after his 1871 trip to Yellowstone. Once Moran adopted the more elaborate monogram, he seems to have dropped the simpler "T" over "M"; see Wilkins 1966, 76.
28. Bruhn 1990, nos. 1 (EHL), 2, and 6 (both NYPL).
29. Hediard 1906, no. 8; Curtis 1939, no. 65.
30. Bruhn 1990, no. 6.
31. Bruhn 1990, nos. 3–5; Morand and Friese 1986, nos. 6, 7; Delteil 1911, no. 39. Huet's motif of the man and cart is one of six vignettes on the third sheet of four from his set Macédoine that was published in 1829.
32. Bruhn 1985, 36.
33. Bruhn 1990, no. 10.
34. The 1864 lithograph likely grew out of a compilation of coastal sketches he made in England in 1862. See sketches at the Gilcrease that include different elements of the lithograph. Morand 1996, nos. 52, 60, and 63.
35. Both notices were brought to my attention by Joni Kinsey.
36. The quotes confirm Wilkins 1966, 255: "At least one print issued by McGuigan, *A View of Swarthmore College*, was finished in color by hand."
37. Bruhn 1990, nos. 7, 8, 23. In a letter to the author, 3 August 1989, Professor Kennard B. Bork of Dennison University surmised, "The fishes are Actinopterygians ('ray-finned') of Cenozoic age (the last 65 million years). The 'school' bears a resemblance to Green River forms, but it is difficult to be overly definitive, given the lack of visible structure. The invertebrates... are a pectenoid (scallop), an oyster, and a turritellid snail. They are marine fossils and could be Cretaceous or Tertiary in age. Because of the abundance of similar forms, both in geographic and stratigraphic senses, it is difficult to know their specific origins. Also abundant are the potential books and professional articles which might have contained the lithographs." The letter is also quoted in Bruhn 1990, 19, with further remarks. These sheets, which were probably given to Moran, lack the text that would have accompanied the images, making it difficult to identify the subject and to track down their published source.
38. GA 4016.4022.2, AAA, reel 3275, frame 1070; reel 3272, frame 100.
39. Panzer 1990, 47–48. John had photographed the *West Town School* in 1864 (LCP, 8339.F.35/D162) and Thomas drew almost the same view in 1869 (Bruhn 1990, no. 19).
40. The lithographs with their correct titles are: *Glen Riddle*; *Baltimore Junction*; *Wallingford Bridge*; *Schuykill, from the "Woodlands"*; *Crozerville*; *Angora*; *Wilcox's Mills*; *West Town School*; *Ridley Creek from the Media Bridge*; *Market St. Hill, West Chester*; and *Osborn's Hill.* (Bruhn 1990, nos. 12–22). They are all in the EHL. The missing images are *Kellyville*; *Swarthmore College*; and *Residence of S.J. Sharpless, Street Road Station.*
41. Morand 1996, 14–16, and nos. 11–20.
42. Morand 1996, 29–34, and nos. 143–191.
43. Panzer 1995, 45–50.
44. *Philadelphia Photographer* 3, no. 28 (April 1866), 128.
45. The known examples are in the Gilcrease and the NYPL, whose copy is identified as a photograph of a Moran lithograph "in the style of Calame" (written on the mat).
46. GA 4027.3970.3; AAA, reel 3275, frame 260.
47. Moran papers, GA, AAA, reel 3275, frames 1249–1251.
48. The other works referred to in the Gilcrease inventory are by title: *The Track of the Storm: An Allegory of the War for the Republic* (1866); *Valley of Conemaugh* (1864); *White Frost* (1864); *Farewell of Summer* (1864); *Shores of Lake Superior* (1864); and *The Juniata* (1865). See AAA, reel 3275, frames 1235, 1249–1251.
49. Bruhn 1990, nos. 24–39 plus *View of the Wissahickon River with Stone Bridge* at the LCP, P.8065.3.
50. Bruhn 1990, nos. 27–29; Morand and Friese 1986, nos. 10–12.
51. An impression of *In the Forest of the Wissahickon* was sold by a dealer into a private collection a few years ago, and the LCP bought *The Wissahickon* (Bruhn 1990, no. 35) and *View of the Wissahickon with Stone Bridge* in 1973 from a dealer. See Finkel 1980, 46.

52. Cook 1872b: "Mr. Thomas Moran, an artist hitherto better known to the public interested in art by his lithographic drawings."
53. Bruhn 1990, nos. 30, 31; Morand and Friese 1986, nos. 13, 14.
54. I owe this quotation to Joni Kinsey, who found it among the Prang Papers, Hallmark Cards Collection, Kansas City, MO. The quotation clarifies the issue raised in Weitenkampf 1903, 544, which says the stone for *Solitude* "was broken by an unfortunate fall when but ten or twelve impressions had been taken." Weitenkampf was mistaken about the stone and must have meant *In the Forest of the Wissahickon*; see Bruhn 1990, 17, no. 27. A passage in *Art Amateur* 20, no. 2 (Jan. 1889), 30, which was brought to my attention by Helena Wright, states that the stones were "all destroyed by fire years ago in the big printing house in Philadelphia where they were stored." If this fire is dated to 1879, that would conveniently end the project.
55. NYEC 1882, 6.
56. Koehler 1880, 3–4.
57. For a discussion of some of these techniques and how they applied to Moran see Morand and Friese 1986, 43–48, and Bruhn 1985, 17 n 4.
58. Klackner 1889, no. 5, Morand and Friese 1986, no. 15. Ruth's characterization of *A Bazaar* is a quote from Koehler 1880, 151. For remarks on selected Moran etchings see Bruhn 1985, 27–52.
59. Klackner 1889, no. 36; Morand and Friese 1986, no. 45.
60. Obvious crosshatching, except in the sky, is the exception in his etchings, but it appears in prints such as *The Rainbow* (1880; Klackner 1889, no. 18; Morand and Friese 1986, no. 27).
61. Klackner 1889, nos. 29, 35; Morand and Friese 1986, nos. 39, 44. When *Bridge in the Pass of Glencoe* was reprinted in 1888, it probably received a slight amount of additional roulette work.
62. Klackner 1889, no. 33; Morand and Friese 1986, no. 42.
63. Klackner 1889, nos. 4, 34, 49, and 50; Morand and Friese 1986, nos. 42, 56, 57. Roulette work and mezzotinting are not the same, but both are used to create tonal passages. While the roulette wheel was used frequently in the 1880s, the results were often called mezzotinting. Mezzotinting uses a toothed "rocker" to lay down a dense ground of pits, which hold ink and print black unless burnished down. The greater the burnishing, the less ink is printed and the lighter the area. A roulette is a toothed wheel that adds pits to the plate as the wheel is rolled back and forth. Mezzotinting works from dark to light, and roulette from light to dark.
64. Klackner 1889, nos. 8, 13, 14; Morand and Friese 1986, nos. 17, 22, 23.
65. Klackner 1889, no. 45, Morand and Friese 1986, no. 53. On this work and the other etchings that are related see O'Brien and Mandel 1984, 38–39; and Bruhn 1985, 34, 36, 42, 44.
66. Klackner 1889, no. 21; Morand and Friese 1986, no. 29; Bruhn 1985, 34, 36. Quote from "An American's Success in England," *NY Herald*, 4 Sept. 1882.
67. Klackner also copyrighted a small-scale version of *The Much Resounding Sea* that is similar to its right two-thirds (Klackner 1889, unlisted; Morand and Friese 1986, no. 63). This plate illustrated first the Ortgies catalogue (Ortgies 1886, no. 19), and then the annual exhibition catalogue of the NYEC, 1887, no. 134.
68. Lloyd Goodrich, *The Graphic Art of Winslow Homer* (New York, 1968), nos. 91, 95, 98, 102.
69. Klackner 1889, nos. 8, 9, 28; Morand and Friese 1986, nos. 17, 18, 38.
70. Klackner 1889, no. 27a; Morand and Friese 1986, no. 36; Bruhn 1985, 36; Bruhn 1990, no. 3.
71. Klackner 1889, nos. 52, 53, 62; Morand and Friese 1986, nos. 59, 60; Ortgies 1886, pl. 9; and Bruhn 1985, 44–45.
72. Klackner 1889, no. 25, 26; Morand and Friese 1986, nos. 33, 34.
73. See Hults 1996, 34–36, for an intelligent argument based on the idea that Moran could not create in line "the operatic canvases of the American West, in which large size and scale, accurate color, geological and botanical detail and, above all, the sense of primeval wildness were important ingredients." Color limited Moran, but even Hults admits that Tower Falls achieves "with linear vigor the sublimity that might be diminished by the small, literally colorless format of the print."
74. Klackner 1889, no. 54, Morand and Friese 1986, no. 61; *EH Star*, 15 Jan. 1887.
75. *NYT*, 5 Dec. 1885, 2. Also quoted in Bruhn 1985, 45.
76. For an interesting discussion of this print and the role of the "sublime" in Moran's etchings see Linda Hults' essay in Morand and Friese 1986, 32–36.
77. Moran is listed on the board in all of the NYEC exhibition catalogues from 1882 to 1892.
78. Klackner 1889, no. 17; Morand and Friese 1986, no. 26; Bruhn 1985, 33–34. Little is known about the *American Etching* series other than it appeared in the early 1880s and its editor was Ernst Knaufft. *NYT*, 19 Nov. 1882, 6, criticizes plates by Moran, Stephen Parrish, Henry Hill, and Joseph Pennell, from which we can infer that Moran's print appeared in 1882: "Mr. Moran's *Three Mile Harbor, Long Island*, perhaps deserves the palm among the four; his hand is so sure, his touch so fine, his trees, outlines of beach and sand dunes, his rocks and small distant ships so clear and draughtsmanlike. There is more sentiment in Mr. Parrish's etching, but Mr. Moran's is full of the ease that belongs to a master." *Original Etchings*, edited by Sylvester Koehler and published by Cassell and Company, included the work of twenty major printmakers of the time; see Bruhn 1986, 18–19.
79. Klackner 1889, no. 41; Morand and Friese 1986, no. 49. Regarding the trip to Mexico and many of the resultant sketches see Morand 1996, 67–72.
80. Bruhn 1985, 20.
81. Ackley 1978, 143–150; Clark 1980b, 85–86.
82. Bruhn 1985, 22.
83. Klackner 1889, no. 56; Koehler 1886, pl. 11; Bruhn 1985, 47; O'Brien and Mandel 1984, 37–38.
84. Van Rensselaer 1883, 499.
85. The complete list is: J. Linnell (1883); H. Chase (1885); T. Rousseau (1886); C-F Daubigny (1886); C-F Daubigny (1886); J. F. Kensett (1886); A. F. Bunner (1887); A. F. Bunner (1887); G. Inness (1888); N-V Diaz (1888); J. F. Miller (1888); C. Wiggins (1888); C-F Daubigny (1888); H. Chase (1890); H. Chase (1890); and Edw. Moran (1891). See Klackner 1889, nos. 40, 43, 46–48, 55, 57, 58, 63–66, 70, and unlisted; Morand and Friese 1986, nos. 48, 51, 54, 55, 62, 64, 68–70, 73–75.
86. Klackner 1889, nos. 57, 61; Morand and Friese 1986, nos. 64, 67.
87. Klackner 1889, 15.
88. Klackner 1889, no. 62. "The prints from the/Mountain of the Holy Cross/in Account with J. D. Waring/price of plate $2500.00/ Delivered Sep. 3rd 1888." GA 4026.4024, 7; see AAA, reel 3275, frame 1140.
89. Klackner 1889, unlisted; Morand and Friese 1986, no. 75. GA 4026.4024, 47.
90. GA 3837.819.1; AAA, reel 3275, frame 641. Peter Platt was a copper plate printer who began working about 1878–1879 and continued into the 1930s. Schuyler Milch was a New York City dealer who carried Moran's works in the 1920s and to whom the etchings were sent. According to a list dated February 1924, Milch received twenty-five different prints and, with two exceptions, four of each. The list is in the EHL and includes: *Harlech Castle, N. Wales*; *January Thaw, Communipaw N.J.*; *Tower of Cortez*; *The Lane, E. H.*; *Tower Falls, Wyoming*; *Church of San Juan, N. Mex.*; *Light House*; *Port Madoc, N. Wales*; *3 Mile Harbor, L. I.* (small); *The Wreck* (small); *The Bridge*; *Sassifras Trees, L. I.* (small); *Sycamore Trees E. H.*; *Turkish Bazaar*; *Yellowstone River, Wyoming*; *Sand Dunes—E. H.*; *Montauk Point L.I.*; *Strathaven Castle Scotland*; *Pah Ute Girl*; *Fresh Pond L. I.*; *The Rainbow*; *An English River*; *The Wave*; *The Whirlpool Niagara*; and *The Empty-Cradle (Pah Ute Indian)*.
91. This paper is watermarked with a fleur-de-lis crowned escutcheon with a crown-like beehive within it. Above the design is the word "HANDMADE" and below is the word "SWEDEN." Most likely such paper was imported by the Japan Paper Company, New York, which began importing papers from Japan in 1901 and from Sweden at least by 1920. This was pointed out to me by Judy Walsh, paper conservator, NGA. For a discussion of papers used in the 1880s see Bruhn 1985, 10–11.

Moran and the Art of Publishing

I would like to express my appreciation for the assistance of many people. In addition to those acknowledged in my book of 1992, who contributed so much to my evolving understanding of Moran, I'd like to thank several individuals who offered their time and thoughts for this project. First of all, Nancy Anderson at the National Gallery of Art for her collegiality and able supervision of the project; her assistants Sally Mansfield and Sarah Kelly for their able assistance; and Merl M. Moore Jr. for his assiduous research. Many others have given willingly of their expertise, especially Anne Morand at the Gilcrease and Thomas Bruhn, University of Connecticut, but also Patricia Fuller of JII/Sales Associates, Red Oak, IA; Fran Krupka, National Park Service, Springfield, IL; Katherine Martinez, Karen McClendon, Red Oak Public Library; Bettie McKenzie, Red Oak Historical Society; Helen Murphy, Red Oak, Iowa; Janice Simon, University of Georgia; Roger Stein, University of Virginia; William Truettner, National Museum of American Art; and the Zamplin-Lampert Gallery, Santa Fe, NM. As always, scholarship is a collaborative effort and writing a solitary one. Many of the ideas herein are the gifts of others, but the mistakes are wholly mine.

1. Arbor Ilex, "Camps and Tramps about Ktaaden," *Scribner's Monthly* 16 (May 1878), 33–47.
2. Moran did similar illustrations, such as *Palisades of the Potomac*, which appeared in Pangborn 1882, 121.
3. Benjamin 1978.
4. *Pasadena Star*, 11 Mar. 1916, 6; cited in Wilkins 1966, 152.
5. Moran to Powell, 16 Dec. 1873, NA, RG 57, mfm. 156, roll 2, about his progress on illustrations from his experience with the explorer in Utah and the Grand Canyon the previous summer: "I'm awfully pleased with drawing on wood and have to work every night until one or two o'clock."
6. Benjamin 1882, 93.
7. Moran to Mary Nimmo Moran from Kanab, Utah, 13 Aug. 1873; quoted in Bassford and Fryxell 1967, 41–42.
8. Moran's first published use of the colophon seems to have been in Bromley 1872, 261–267.
9. Moran's friend and editor at *Scribner's Monthly*, Richard Watson Gilder, was among the most outspoken advocates for an international copyright law that would protect both writers and artists from unscrupulous copying of their work. This legislation was finally passed in 1891, and afterward Moran was quite active in copyrighting his paintings. See John 1981, 201–202; Gilder 1916, 191–204; Moran's ledgers at GA, esp. after 1900; and letters at EHL, 3–15, 3–16, 3–24.
10. For more on the development of printing techniques and the boom in publishing in the nineteenth century see Jussim 1983; and DeVinne 1880, 35.
11. It has been estimated that between 1865 and 1870 the number of American magazines grew at a rate of about a hundred per year. See Mott 1967, 5.
12. *Scribner's Monthly*, usually refused illustrations drawn on paper rather than woodblocks. See Linton 1880, 793.
13. Until the advent of photographic halftone printing, which preserved the original drawings, Moran only rarely provided images on paper for publication. His 1870 drawings for his first Yellowstone assignment for *Scribner's Monthly* was one such instance. These drawings are preserved in the Moran collection at Gilcrease.
14. Jussim 1983, 276–277, and passim. For more on this see Clapper 1995.
15. *Boston Transcript*, 9 Apr. 1875.
16. According to Stevens' lists in the Moran papers at Gilcrease these were *Polperro*, published by Gerlach & Barlow, 1907; *Green River Cliffs*, published by Frederickson, n.d.; and *Solitude*, published by Woodward & Tiernan, 1901.
17. For an extremely thoughtful essay on this issue and its importance to American intellectual history see "Iconography and Intellectual History: The Halftone Effect," in Harris 1990, 304–317.
18. Contemporary critics include Jarves 1871, 203, and Godkin 1874. For more see Marzio 1978, 76–102.
19. Coffin 1892, 108.
20. Willis 1860, 149, 167.
21. For more on the *American Scenery* commission see Myers 1987, 100–101. For Willis see Beers 1885 and Cortland P. Auser, *Nathaniel P. Willis* (New York, 1969).
22. *Chamber's Journal* (Jan. 1856), 7; cited in Nickerson 1984, 50.
23. *Aldine*, Jan. 1873, and frontispiece. *NY Post*, 13 May 1872, commented that "The 'Aldine' for June merits the warmest commendation for its varied excellence in typography, illustrations and literary contents. The full-page picture underneath the title, 'Kwasind, The Strong Man,' drawn by T. Moran, is a marvellous triumph in the representation of forest shade and dense foliage." *Harper's Monthly* also published an illustrated article on the Michigan region, but its images were not by Moran. See A. L. Rawson, "The Pictured Rocks of Lake Superior," *Harper's Monthly* 34 (May 1867), 681–697.
24. *Aldine* 1872. This view appears to have been based on the drawing *North Woods, Lake Superior, Michigan* (1860), reproduced in Bassford and Fryxell 1967, 22, but it is also quite similar to Moran's lithograph *In the Forest of the Wissahickon* (1868; Gilcrease), which is ostensibly a Pennsylvania woodland scene. Wilkins 1966, 55, states that *Kwasind, the Strong Man* was from Moran's Hiawatha series of steel engravings from 1875, but since it appeared in *Aldine* in 1872, this seems unlikely. Perhaps it was simply the other way around—the 1875 image was based on the earlier one.
25. Sixteen of the wash drawings were in progress the first year, and *Boston Transcript*, 1 Dec. 1875, looked forward to the publication: "Mr. Moran is a popular illustrator of books of travels and poems, some of the most sumptuous volumes ever published in this country having been enriched by the productions of his pencil.... Mr. Moran is at present engaged upon the most elaborate work which he has yet undertaken—a series of twenty-five illustrations of Longfellow's poem of 'Hiawatha' which his brother, Peter Moran a most skillful etcher, is reproducing on steel. These etchings will, we think furnish evidence of a versatility and originality of talent which entitles Mr. Moran to a foremost rank."
26. Wilkins 1966, 55.
27. Moran to Powell, 29 May 1876, NA, RG 57, mfm. 156, roll 4. The Hiawatha project was mentioned again in the *Boston Transcript*, 6 Dec. 1876, and also in *The Independent* [NY], 21 Dec. 1876, with the notice "Mr. Thomas Moran has nearly completed his series of illustrations in India ink of Longfellow's 'Hiawatha,' which are being etched by his brother Peter, who, by the way, was the only etcher awarded a medal at the Centennial." Moran reported in his ledgers, "In 1875 I commenced the series of illustrations to Hiawatha. Up to the present time I have finished about 16 out of an intended 25." GA Old Book of Lists, 4026.4048. For more on the project see Wilkins 1966, 55.
28. Wilkins 1966, 257, estimates that Moran produced more than 339 illustrations for *Scribner's Monthly*. See also Morand and Friese 1986, 240–243.
29. It was clear by 1853 that circulation rose when *Harper's* increased the number of illustrations in its monthly publication. See Levin 1980, 36.
30. For more on R. W. Gilder see Gilder 1916, Smith 1970, and John 1981.
31. Langford 1871. For more on the trip and Moran's various interactions with the survey, the publishers, and the railroads involved see Kinsey 1992, 45–92.
32. Nathaniel Langford to Jay Cooke from the Scribner's offices, 16 Mar. 1871, Cooke papers, Pennsylvania Historical Society. For more on this association and its agenda see Kinsey 1992, esp. 43–92.
33. GA ledger 21. Moran produced sixteen watercolors for Cooke, according to a letter he wrote Hayden, 24 Nov. 1872, NA, RG 57, mfm. 623, roll 2, frames 655–656.
34. Manuscript biography of Moran, probably by his daughter Ruth, Moran papers, AAA, NTM1, frame 190. Also see Moran to Hayden, 28 May 1873, NA, RG 57, mfm. 623, frames 370–371. In later years, especially with the Santa Fe, Moran traded paintings for rail fare.
35. Benjamin 1882, 90–91.
36. Wilkins 1966, 108; King 1875.
37. I would like to thank Roger Stein

for his prompting my thinking on this compositional effect. See also Rainey 1994, 34. For a discussion of "prospect" see Kinsey 1996, esp. 17–19. The term "magisterial gaze" is from Boime 1991.

38. Gannon 1996, 259. Promotion of the area began shortly after the Civil War, when Harriet Beecher Stowe settled there for her son's health. See Stowe 1873 and Lanier 1876.
39. GA ledger 1877–1882, 4026.4054, 27.
40. See last section of Bibliography.
41. H. D. Mears, "The Catawissa Railroad," *Harper's Monthly* 25 (June 1862), 20–28.
42. This view is similar to a photograph taken by Thomas' brother John, which was probably made at the same time as the drawing. *Town of Catawissa* is reproduced in Morand and Friese 1986, 172, no. 76, with the descriptive title *Village in the Valley* and dated 1853 by comparison to the East Hampton drawing.
43. For more see Danly and Marx 1988, 5–6.
44. Pangborn 1882. Moran was paid "about $1500.00" for his illustrations for the publication, according to his GA ledger, 4026–4054, 46.
45. For more on Bell and his company's development of eastern Colorado, especially regarding Colorado Springs and Manitou as a health resort and the use of Moran's images in D & RG publications, see Kinsey 1992, 153–173.
46. These small books are sometimes indexed in libraries, but more often they are found in vertical files of railroad and tourist ephemera, such as the Warshaw Collection of Business Americana at the National Museum of American History, Washington, DC; the Mercantile Library Collection in St. Louis; the Colorado Historical Society in Denver; and the California State Railroad Museum in Sacramento.
47. See Moran papers, GA 4026–4054, 26, 29, 33. Regarding the Sierra Nevada and Teton trip see Braff 1981, 10; Wilkins 1966, 123–130; and Fryxell 1932.
48. Hayden 1872a.
49. Gilder to Hayden, 24 Jan. 1872, NA, RG 57, mfm. 623, roll 2, frames 314–318.
50. Hayden 1880. Several of the views appeared in George Crofutt's *New Overland Tourist Guide* and other Crofutt publications in the 1870s and early 1880s. Crofutt to Hayden, 16 Feb. 1872, NA, RG 57, mfm. 623, roll 2, frame 373. For more on Crofutt and his publications see Fifer 1988. Correspondence with other guidebook writers indicates that Hayden was quite liberal in sharing the images. Harry J. Norton to Hayden, 6 Dec. 1872, NA, RG 47, mfm. 623, roll 2, frame 669.
51. The agreement is quoted in Kinsey 1992, 125–126.
52. Powell 1875b. The articles contain more than twenty-four illustrations, but the others apparently were engraved directly from Hiller's photographs.
53. Williams 1876. At this point in his career, Moran was generally paid an average of $35.00 per illustration. Moran papers, GA 6326.145, 41–44.
54. H. T. Williams to Powell, 20 Jan. 1876, NA, RG 57, mfm. 156, roll 4, frame 370.
55. There were twelve issues of *Aldine* per volume, but they do not indicate a monthly distribution. The journal was in press for eleven years, but only nine volumes were issued. By 1878 the magazine appeared bimonthly.
56. Moran to Powell, 16 Dec. 1873, NA, RG 57, mfm. 156, roll 2, referring to "Utah Scenery," *Aldine* 7 (Jan. 1874), 14–15.
57. I am especially grateful to Janice Simon at the University of Georgia for sharing her research on *Aldine*. See also Rainey 1994, 21.
58. Moran was obviously a valued contributor to *Aldine*. Early in 1872, for example, the publishers hosted a special celebration to mark its record circulation of 40,000 and the promotion of Richard Henry Stoddard to run the magazine. The event included luminaries such as Mark Twain, Bayard Taylor, and Thomas Moran. See *NY Mail*, 26 Feb. 1872.
59. "The Yellowstone Region," *Aldine* 6 (Apr. 1873), 73–75.
60. For more see Kinsey 1992, 82–83.
61. Hunnisett 1980, 135.
62. See Richardson 1874 and Brooks 1914, both of which reprint images from previous Scribner's publications.
63. Bryant 1876–1881. Moran contributed to history books by other publishers as well, such as Charles Coffin 1880, which contained two of his views.
64. The proper name of the firm was Ivison, Blakeman, Taylor & Co. See Madison 1966.
65. For more on Osgood and Company and its permutations see Weber 1959. The artist recorded in his account ledger for 1874 that Osgood paid him $62.50 for five illustrations for *Hanging of the Crane* in March and then $95.00 on 4 April for nine more. The last figure is crossed out and $102.50 is inserted, so it unclear how many Moran actually produced for the project and how much he was paid. Moran papers, GA 3626.145, 14.
66. Moran recorded in his ledger that he was paid $400 for the Dodge drawings from 1896 to 1899. GA 4026.4059, 106–107, 130–131.
67. The Schuylkill view, for example, had appeared previously in Crane 1871.
68. *Publishers' and Stationers' Weekly Trade Circular* (27 June 1872); cited in Rainey 1994, 77. Many of the chapters in *Picturesque America* first appeared in serial form in *Appleton's* and were revised for the final volumes.
69. The quote is from the original announcement for *Picturesque America*, which appeared in *Appleton's* (29 Oct. 1870); cited in Rainey 1994, 51.
70. Bryant 1874, 169.
71. Moran to Hayden, 24 Nov. 1872, NA, Rg 57, mfm. 623, roll 2, frames 655–656. Some of Moran's views in Burlingame's chapter were drawn from Jackson's photographs. For an itinerary of Moran's 1872 trip see Wilkins 1966, 74–76. While in California, Moran may have met John Muir, since one of his views of Half Dome in Yosemite was included in Muir's *Picturesque California*, but this could easily have been arranged in other ways.
72. Bryant 1874, 2:184. Wolfgang Schivelbusch, *The Railway Journey: The Industrialization of Time and Space in the 19th Century* (Berkeley, 1986).
73. See Kinsey 1992, 141–173.
74. Moran to Hayden, April 4, 1873, NA, RG 57, mfm. 623, roll 3, frame 263.
75. Hayden ended up paying $3,500 to reprint the illustrations in his 1874 *Eighth Annual Report* (not published until 1876).
76. Bunce to Hayden, 5 Nov. 1875, NA, RG 57, mfm. 623, roll 5, frame 1054. These negotiations were complex and drawn out over several years. For a thorough account see Rainey 1994, 159–175, and Kinsey 1992, 87–88, 130–132, 161–162.
77. The publication was originally offered in serial form beginning in 1882 in twenty-four parts, at $.60 each. Pringle 1989, 12, reports the commission was for fifteen illustrations, but Gilcrease records indicate Moran provided nine of the twelve before the end of the year and was paid about $50 each. See the small notebook with the list of paintings, GA 4026.4054, 43. See also Wilkins 1966, 145. Moran's commission did not come directly from the publishers but rather from Schell and Hogan, the engravers of the books.
78. Moran had already treated the theme in print. See Holley, "Niagara," *Scribner's Monthly* (Aug. 1876). The payment is recorded in Moran's account ledger for Apr. 1876, GA 3626.145, 45–46.
79. These may have been produced in collaboration with Louis Prang, with whom the magazine had worked since 1869. *Aldine* commissioned Prang to provide wood engravings of his company's "most celebrated pictures" for reproduction in the magazine. See "Increased Attractions," *Aldine Press* 2 (May 1869), 34; drawn to my attention by Janice Simon.
80. *NY Mail*, 3 Dec. 1873. *Aldine* also handled original art as an "art union." *Aldine Art Union Prospectus—1874–1875* (Nov. 1874) listed Moran's *Cliffs of the Green River* in a gold frame as the most expensive "Aldine Art Union Prize, Series A," at $500.
81. The most prominent and accessible collections of complete Prang portfolios include the Gilcrease (two sets from Moran's studio collection, one of which belonged to Hayden), the Buffalo Bill Historical Center in Cody, WY (one), and the Jefferson National Expansion Memorial in St. Louis (one). The edition was unbound, so the prints are easily scattered. Few sets exist intact.
82. Moran to Louis Prang, 22 Dec. 1873, Prang Papers, Hallmark Cards Collection, Kansas City, MO.
83. Moran to Prang, 8 Jan. 1874, Prang Papers, Hallmark Cards Collec-

tion, Kansas City. Edward Moran had produced at least one chromolithograph for Prang, *Launching the Lifeboat* (1869). *NY Post*, 22 Oct. 1869, 2:2–3. The Prang sale in Boston in 1899 also lists *Modesty*; *Girl with Roses*; *Rice of Plenty*; and *Winter Girl* by Edward's son Leon Moran as well as *Shepherdess*; *When the Wedding Gifts Arrive*; and *Going from the Church* by Edward's son Percy Moran. One previously unnoticed work Thomas produced for Prang, *Birth of Christ*, is included as well. *Christmas Designs* by all three artists are listed. Prang cat. 1899.

84. GA Old Book of Lists, 4026.4048.
85. *Illustrated Prang* 1889–1890, 19. National Museum of American History, graphic arts division, owns a copy of this publication.
86. *Newark Daily Advertiser*, 9 Mar. 1877.
87. "Fine Arts," *The Nation*, 15 Feb. 1877, 107.
88. GA Old Book of Lists, 4026–4048.
89. Moran to L. Prang & Co., Boston, 27 Dec. 1876. Copy of letter without source, NGA files.
90. These two works were reproduced in *Illustrated Prang* 1889–1890, 20. Mounted on boards measuring 9 x 14 inches and selling for $.75, these chromos were smaller and less expensive than the Yellowstone portfolio prints, which were 22 x 18 inches or 18 x 22 (mounted) and sold singly for $1.50.
91. In 1880 Moran was paid $100 each for two Christmas cards, one entitled *Christmas Wings*. *Boston Transcript*, 4 Dec. 1884.
92. EHL 1–14.
93. Small notebook with list of paintings and illustrations, 14 May 1877–Dec. 1882, GA 4026–4054, 45–48.
94. Moran to Hayden, 25 Nov. 1873, NA, RG 57, mfm. 623, roll 3, frames 597–598.
95. GA 4026.4054, 37–48.
96. Benjamin 1882, 90–91.
97. Moran's undated autobiography, GA 4026–3920.5.
98. Wagner 1995; Woodward 1974–1975.
99. "The Moran Pictures," *Denver Republican*, 28 Nov. 1892, EHL scrapbook, 56.
100. Moran worked with many publishing houses on these commissions, especially after the turn of the century, including Brown and Bigelow in St. Paul (for the Northern Pacific Railroad); Chicago Colortype Company; Knapp Company, New York; Charles Tabor and Company, New York; and Frederickson Company, Chicago. Others are listed in Moran's ledgers at GA.
101. Moran traveled that summer with his son Paul, William H. Jackson, Jackson's assistant Sam Taylor, and SFRR assistant general passenger agent Charles Higgins from Chicago.
102. Moran recorded that the copyright of the painting was provided "in consideration of paying expenses and transportation from N. York to the Canon & back of myself & Paul." GA 4026–4024, 67.
103. D'Emilio and Campbell 1991; and Weigle and Babcock 1996. The SFRR archives contain a sizable file on Moran's early relationship with the company. Unfortunately, they do not begin until 1904. See also Kinsey 1992, 132–137.
104. Simpson 1909, 23, 25. See also Stevens 1911; and Gustave Kobbe, "Artists Combine for Trip to Arizona," *NY Herald*, 26 Nov. 1911. The artists' works from the trip were exhibited together in 1911.
105. In 1996 the SFRR archives placed its remaining stock of these chromolithographs on sale through the Zaplin-Lampert Gallery in Santa Fe. An advertisement in the *American Art Review* (Aug. 1996) listed them for $4,800.
106. Moran's copyright sales are in GA ledger, 4016.4019. Some entries are listed twice in two different places and sometimes contain conflicting information.
107. Moran to Mary Nimmo Moran, 11 June 1892; quoted in Bassford and Fryxell 1967, 97.
108. Jackson to Moran, 19 Jan. 1901, from Detroit Publishing Company, Scenic and Art Publishers. EHL 3–131 and 3–132.
109. McKenzie 1994, 116; and May 1925, 38.
110. McKenzie 1994, 116–123; Murphy 1912; Murphy Press 1908; and May 1925, 36–42. The Thomas Murphy Art Calendar Company, although now absorbed by JII/Sales Associates, still conducts part of its work in the original plant, and it maintains a large collection of archival calendars and their original plates. These have all been photographed and slides are maintained by the Red Oak Public Library. I am grateful to Miss Helen Murphy and Pat Fuller, art director at JII/Sales, for their assistance with the Murphy company history and for providing a photograph of an 1898 calendar and permission to reproduce it as fig. 18 in my essay.
111. See the unpublished list of Moran images at Red Oak Historical Society, and Index 1991. The lists indicate that Percy Moran also sold many copyrights to the company.
112. May 1925, 40. See also "1919 Gift Calendars," *EH Star*, 3 Jan. 1919, 5:3; "Simmons Gives Calendars," *EH Star*, 10 Dec. 1920, 5:2; and "Present Calendars," *EH Star*, 9 Dec. 1921, 5:2. I would like to thank Merl M. Moore Jr. for his generosity in sharing these clippings with me.
113. McKenzie 1994, 116.
114. A copy of this may be found in the Artist Files, NYPL, M796D.
115. Letter to Osborne and Company, Allwood, NJ. Miscellaneous notes by Ruth R. Moran, Moran papers, AAA, frame 207.

Appendix 1: The Prang Commission

1. *Illustrated Catalogue of Fine Art Studies, Water Color Studies, Pictures, Etc. Published by L. Prang & Co.* (Boston, 1889–1890), 19. The National Museum of American History, division of graphic arts, owns a copy of this publication.
2. "Fine Arts," *The Nation* (15 Feb. 1877), 107. The reference to "chromo-civilization" is found in *The Nation* (24 Sept. 1874), 201–202.
3. *The Times* was quoted in *The Printing Times and Lithographer* (London), (15 Jan. 1878), 13; cited in Marzio 1979, 107.
4. Moran to L. Prang & Co., Boston, 27 Dec. 1876. Copy of letter without source, Moran archive, NGA.

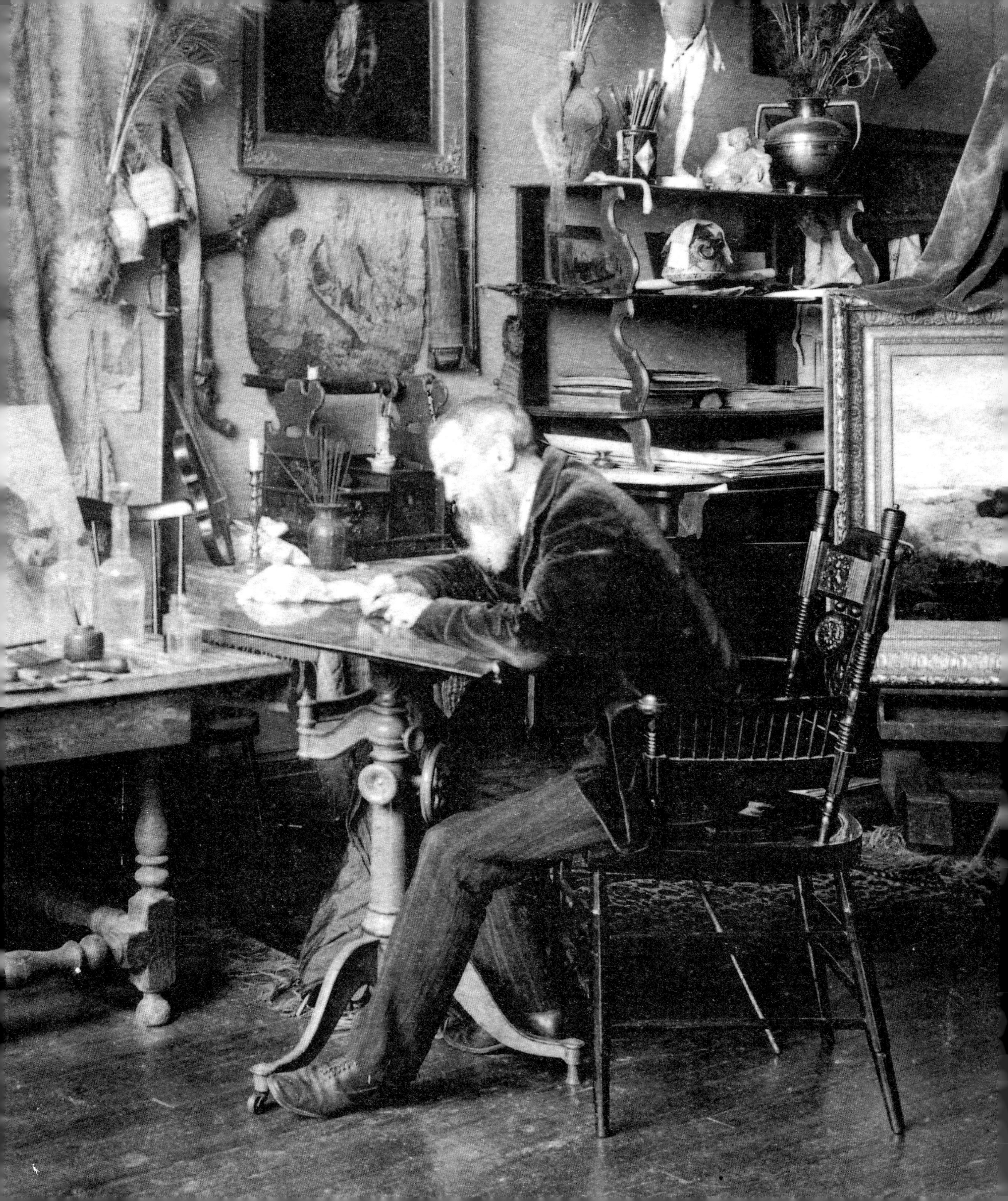

Bibliographic references are presented in two main sections. Critical references on the life and work of Thomas Moran are listed in chronological order, beginning in 1860 when reviewers first began to comment on his work, and continuing through 1996. By no means definitive, the list is offered as a starting point for those who wish to follow the rise of the artist's reputation and gauge the tenor of subsequent commentary in the order in which it appeared. The second part of the bibliography provides an alphabetical listing of additional general works consulted by the catalogue contributors.

A third reference section, compiled by Joni L. Kinsey, contains many publications to which Moran contributed illustrations (the number indicated in parentheses at the end of the entries). His images are not always identified by his signature, or the colophon he used after 1872, or in the accompanying texts. They are therefore sometimes difficult to attribute to his hand, and undoubtedly more will be discovered.

Archival Sources

American Heritage Center, University of Wyoming (Fritiof Fryxell papers)

Amon Carter Museum Archives, Fort Worth

Archives of American Art

Bolton Public Library, Archives and Local Studies Department, Bolton, England

Church of the Assumption, Blessed Virgin Mary, Philadelphia; records now held by St. John the Evangelist Church, Philadelphia

Cooper-Hewitt National Design Museum, Smithsonian Institution, New York

Corcoran Gallery and School of Art, Washington, DC

Frick Collection, New York

Grand Teton National Park, Wyoming

Hallmark Card Collection, Kansas City

Harvard University, Houghton Library, Cambridge

Jefferson National Expansion Memorial, St. Louis

Library Company of Philadelphia

Library of Congress, Washington, DC

Moran Archive, East Hampton Library

National Archives, Washington, DC

National Museum of American Art, Washington, DC

National Museum of American History, Washington, DC

New York Public Library (Gilder papers/Art Files)

New-York Historical Society

Old Cathedral Cemetery, Philadelphia

Pennsylvania Academy of Fine Arts, Philadelphia

Pennsylvania Historical Society (Jay Cooke papers)

Santa Fe Railroad Archive, Chicago

Gilcrease Archive, Tulsa

West Laurel Hill Cemetery, Philadelphia

Yellowstone National Park

Yosemite National Park

Chronological References

1860

21 April. "Fine Arts in Philadelphia." *Phila. Press.*

3 July. "Academy of Fine Arts." *Phila. Press.*

1862

June. "The Catawissa Railroad." *Harper's Monthly* 25:20–28.

3 June. "The Academy of the Fine Arts." *Phila. Evening Bulletin.*

13 November. "Landscape Art." *Boston Transcript.*

1864

30 April. "The Fine Arts." *Phila. Evening Bulletin.*

14 May. "Philadelphia Art Notes." *Round Table*, 344.

18 June. "Philadelphia Art Notes." *Round Table*, 10.

1865

7 April. "The Next Fine Arts Exhibition." *Phila. Press.*

25 April. "Fine Arts." *Phila. Press.*

29 April. "The Academy of Fine Arts." *Phila. N. American and Gazette.*

1 May. "Fine Arts." *Phila. Press.*

30 September. "Philadelphia Art Notes." *Round Table*, 60.

27 October. "The School of Design for Women." *Phila. Evening Bulletin.*

16 November. "What the Artists Are About." *Phila. Evening Bulletin.*

27 November. [Tuckerman, Henry T.]. "Art and Artists in Philadelphia." *NY Post.*

6 December. "What the Artists Are About." *Phila. Evening Bulletin.*

1866

6 March. "*Civil War.* The National Will out of Harmony with the Divine Will: Suggested by the Track of the Storm. *A Cartoon, by Thomas Moran.*" *Phila. Evening Bulletin.*

22 April. "Pennsylvania Academy of the Fine Arts." *Phila. Evening Bulletin.*

5 May. "Philadelphia Art Notes." *Round Table*, 279.

23 May. "Two Remarkable Pictures." *Boston Transcript.*

2 June. "Art and Artists." *Phila. Evening Bulletin.*

15 December. "The Artists' Fund Society." *Phila. Evening Bulletin.*

17 December. "The Artists' Fund Society." *Phila. Evening Bulletin.*

1867

Tuckerman, Henry T. *Book of the Artists.* [Reprinted New York, 1967].

23 February. "The Artists' Fund Exhibition." *Phila. Evening Bulletin.*

6 April. "American Contributors to the Paris Exposition." *Phila. Evening Bulletin.*

23 May. "The Annual Exhibition of the Pennsylvania Academy." *Phila. Evening Bulletin.*

13 December. "The Fine Arts." *Phila. Evening Bulletin.*

1868

14 February. "The Artists' Fund Exhibition." *Phila. Evening Bulletin.*

6 April. "Reception of the Artists' Fund." *Phila. Evening Bulletin.*

1869

26 April. "Academy of the Fine Arts." *Phila. N. American and Gazette.*

25 May. "Fine Arts." *Phila. Press.*

16 November. "View of Swarthmore College." *Phila. Evening Bulletin.*

1870

21 March. "Industrial Fine Arts for Women." *Phila. Evening Bulletin.*

15 April. "The Fine Arts." *Phila. Evening Bulletin.*

18 April. "Art Items." *Phila. Evening Bulletin.*

1871

11 July. "The Yellowstone Scientific Expedition." *Helena Herald* [MT].

29 August. "Wonders of the Yellowstone Country." *Helena Herald.*

16 September. "T. Moran." *NY Post.*

27 September. "T. Moran." *Boston Transcript.*

6 October. "A Picture Gallery of the Yellowstone." *Newark Daily Advertiser.*

1872

Bryant, William Cullen, ed. *Picturesque America*.... 2 vols. New York.

February. Hayden, F. V. "The Wonders of the West II. More about the Yellowstone." *Scribner's* 3:388–396. [Hayden 1872a; see General References for Hayden 1872b]

25 March. [Townley, D.O.C.]. "On the Easel." *NY Mail.*

1 April. "New York." *Boston Advertiser.*

18 April. "Art Gossip." *NY Mail.*

29 April. "Moran's 'Grand Cañon of the Yellowstone.'" *Newark Daily Advertiser.*

1 May. [Townley, D.O.C.]. "The Grand Canyon of the Yellowstone." *NY Mail.*

2 May. [Townley, D.O.C.]. "Thos. Moran's Picture." *NY Mail.*

4 May. [Cook, Clarence]. "Mr. Thomas Moran's 'Great Cañon of the Yellowstone.'" *NY Tribune* [Cook 1872a; see next page for Cook 1872b]

"A Newark Artist's Grand Masterpiece." *Newark Daily Advertiser.*

5 May. "Mr. Thomas Moran's Picture." *NYT.*

8 May. "A New Painting." *NY Post.*

9 May. "The Yellowstone." *National Republican* [DC].

13 May. "Literary." *NY Post.*

15 May. [Townley, D.O.C.]. "Art Notes." *NY Mail.*

20 May. "Moran's Painting of the Yellowstone Canyon." *San Francisco Evening Bulletin.*

25 May. "A Beautiful Painting." *Boston Transcript.*

30 May. "Moran's Painting of the Yellowstone Canyon." *Helena Herald.*

June. "Culture and Progress: Thomas Moran's 'Grand Canon of the Yellowstone.'" *Scribner's* 4:251–252.

[Gilder, Richard Watson.] "The Old Cabinet." *Scribner's* 4:242.

"The Noble Savage." *Aldine* 5:110.

1 June. "Art." *Appleton's* 7:612.

3 June. "Mr. Thomas Moran's Painting." *National Republican* [DC].

9 June. Nealy, Mary E. "Art at the Capitol." *Sunday Morning Chronicle* [DC].

10 June. *The Statutes at Large and Proclamations of the United States of America* [Mar. 1871 to Mar. 1873], 17:347, 362.

12 June. "Mr. Moran's Picture." *Newark Daily Advertiser*.

17 June. "The Canyon of the Yellowstone." *Boston Transcript*.

20 June. [Townley, D.O.C.]. *NY Mail*.

22 June. "The Fine Arts." *Boston Transcript*.

29 June. "Art Items." *San Francisco Daily Evening Bulletin*.

12 July. "Home Artists at the Great Show." *Newark Daily Advertiser*.

25 July. "The Grand Cañon of the Yellowstone." *NY Post*.

28 July. "Fine Arts." *NYT*.

August. [Cook, Clarence]. "Art." *Atlantic Monthly* 30:246–247. [Cook 1872b]

2 August. "The Goupil Gallery." *NY Post*.

3 August. "The Exposition of Newark Industries." *Newark Daily Advertiser*.

9 August. "Personal." *NY Post*.

14 August. "Local Matters." *Newark Daily Advertiser*.

23 August. "Local Matters." *Newark Daily Advertiser*.

5 September. "Fine Arts: The Yellowstone Landscape at Washington." *The Nation* 15:157–158.

Winter. Blackmore, William. *Catalogue of Water-Colour Drawings of the Yellowstone Region, Great National Park of the United States, Painted by Mr. T. Moran, for William Blackmore, and List of Photographs by Mr. W. H. Jackson*. N.p.

1873

January. "Culture and Progress: Thomas Moran's Water-Color Drawings." *Scribner's* 5:394.

"The Pictured Rocks of Lake Superior." *Aldine* 6:14.

"Songs of Nature." *Scribner's* 5:399.

21 January. "Personal." *Newark Daily Advertiser*.

February. "Art at the Capitol." *Scribner's* 5:493–500.

16 February. "The Water-Color Collection." *NYT*.

18 February. "Fine Arts." *NY Mail*.

25 February. "Water-Color Pictures." *Boston Transcript*.

15 March. "Art Notes." *Evening Star* [DC].

19 March. "The Aldine." *NY Post*.

April. "The Yellowstone Region." *Aldine* 6:74–75.

14 May. "Mr. T. Moran's Sketches." *NYT*.

June. Langford, N. P. "The Ascent of Mount Hayden." *Scribner's* 6:129–157.

15 July. Colburn, J. E. "The Great American Desert." *NYT*.

7 August. Colburn, J. E. "The Land of Mormon." *NYT*.

"Washington News and Gossip." *Evening Star* [DC].

4 September. Colburn, J. E. "The Colorado Cañon." *NYT*.

1874

January. "Utah Scenery." *Aldine* 7:14–15.

1 May. "The Chasm of the Colorado." *Newark Daily Advertiser*.

5 May. "Mr. Moran's Picture." *Newark Daily Advertiser*.

12 May. "Moran's Picture." *Newark Daily Advertiser*.

"Moran's 'Chasm of the Colorado.'" *NY Post*.

"Mr. Thomas Moran's 'Chasm of the Colorado.'" *NY Tribune*.

"The Chasm of the Colorado." *NYT*.

13 May. "A New York Criticism on Moran's Latest Picture." *Newark Daily Advertiser*.

18 May. "Fine Arts." *NYT*.

25 May. "Letters to the Editor." *NYT*.

30 May. "Art." *Appleton's* 11:700.

8 June. "Washington News and Gossip." *Evening Star* [DC].

13 June. "Local Art Notes." *Evening Star* [DC].

July. "Culture and Progress: 'The Chasm of the Colorado.'" *Scribner's* 8:373–374.

14 July. "The Pictures at the Capitol." *Evening Star* [DC].

September. [Cook, Clarence]. "Art." *Atlantic Monthly* 34:375–377.

"A Storm in Utah." *Aldine* 7:175.

1 September. "From the Mount of the Holy Cross." *Denver Rocky Mt. News*.

3 September. "Art Matters." *Denver Rocky Mt. News*.

18 November. "Art Notes." *NY Post*.

1875

The American Cyclopaedia: A Popular Dictionary of General Knowledge, s.v. "Moran, Thomas." Ed. George Ripley and Charles A. Dana. New York.

5 April. "Moran's New Picture." *Newark Daily Advertiser*.

10 April. "Mr. Moran's New Picture." *NYT*.

14 April. "Moran's 'Mountain of the Holy Cross.'" *NY Post*.

15 April. "Fine Arts." *The Independent* [NY].

17 April. "The Exhibition at the Academy of Design." *NYT*.

24 April. "The Academy Exhibition." *NY Post*.

"The Arts." *Appleton's* 13:535.

1 May. "The Arts." *Appleton's* 13:568.

22 May. "Thomas Moran's 'Mountain of the Holy Cross' at Schaus's Gallery." *NY Tribune*.

June. "Culture and Progress: Moran's 'Mountain of the Holy Cross.'" *Scribner's* 10:252–253.

12 June. "Sale of Paintings." *NY Post*.

July. James, Henry. "On Some Pictures Lately Exhibited." *Galaxy* 20:89–97.

"Moran's 'Mountain of the Holy Cross.'" *Aldine* 7:379–380.

19 October. "Art Notes." *Newark Daily Advertiser*.

25 October. "Mountain of the Holy Cross." *Boston Transcript*.

9 November. "Moran's Mountain of the Holy Cross." *Boston Transcript*.

10 November. "Art Matters in Newark." *Newark Daily Advertiser*.

14 November. "Art Notes." *Boston Evening Gazette*.

16 November. "Art and Artists." *Boston Transcript*.

1 December. "Thomas Moran." *Boston Transcript*.

7 December. "Art and Artists." *Boston Transcript*.

21 December. "Art and Artists." *Boston Transcript*.

1876

Hayden, Ferdinand V. *The Yellowstone National Park and Mountain Regions of Portions of Idaho, Nevada, Colorado and Utah*. Boston.

January. "Glories of Southern Utah." *Aldine* 8:34–35.

18 February. "Mountain of the Holy Cross." *St. Louis Republican*.

March. "Water-Color in New York." *Aldine* 8:91–92.

4 April. U.S. Congress. House of Representatives Debate on Loan of Thomas Moran's Paintings. 44th Cong., 1st sess. *Congressional Record* 4:2185.

5 April. "Moran's Pictures." *Newark Daily Advertiser*.

June. "Idaho Scenery." *Aldine* 8:195–196.

16 August. "Newark Art Items." *Newark Daily Advertiser*.

28 September. "Local Matters." *Newark Daily Advertiser*.

6 December. "Art and Artists." *Boston Transcript*.

11 December. "American Artist's Loan Exhibition." *Newark Daily Advertiser*.

12 December. "Local Matters." *Newark Daily Advertiser*.

28 December. "The Loan Exhibition." *Newark Daily Advertiser*.

1877

15 February. "Fine Arts." *The Nation* 24:107.

March. Review of Hayden 1876, *American Journal of Science and Arts* 13:229–230.

9 March. "A Splendid Work of Art." *Newark Daily Advertiser.*

20 March. "Art and Artists." *Boston Transcript.*

10 April. "The National Academy of Design." *Newark Daily Advertiser.*

17 April. "The National Academy of Design. *Newark Daily Advertiser.*

28 April. "The National Academy of Design: Some Landscapes in the Fifty-second Annual Exhibition." *NY Post.*

18 May. "Art and Artists." *Boston Transcript.*

6 December. "Exhibition at Library Hall." *Newark Daily Advertiser.*

27 December. "Art and Artists." *Boston Transcript.*

1878

13 March. "American Art." *Phila. Evening Telegraph.*

10 April. "The Academy Exhibition." *NYT.*

18 April. "American Art." *Newark Daily Advertiser.*

20 April. "Art Notes." *Evening Star* [DC].

27 April. "Art Notes." *Evening Star* [DC].

29 April. *NY Herald.*

22 June. "Art Notes." *Evening Star* [DC].

July. "Notes." *Art Journal* [NY] 4:223.

9 December. "A Turner Picture in Newark." *Newark Daily Advertiser.*

10 December. "Art and Artists." *Boston Transcript.*

1879

Benjamin, Samuel G.W. *Our American Artists.* Boston. [Benjamin 1879a; see General References for Benjamin 1879b]

Sheldon, George W. *American Painters.* London and New York.

February. [Sheldon, George W.]. "American Painters—Thomas Moran and Joseph Rusling Meeker." *Art Journal* [NY] 5:41–43.

"Notes." *Art Journal* [NY] 5:64.

March. "Thomas Moran." *Aldine* 9:265.

8 March. "Artistic Indignation." *Newark Daily Advertiser.*

14 March. "Art at the Union League Club." *NY Post.*

28 March. "Fifty-fourth Annual Exhibition of the Academy of Design." *NY Herald.*

2 April. "The Art Students' League." *NY Post.*

7 April. "Artists and Their Works." *NYT.*

May. "The Academy Exhibition." *Art Journal* [NY] 5:159.

8 May. "The Academy Exhibition—The Landscapes." *The Independent* [NY].

12 May. "Mr. Moran's Picture." *Newark Daily Advertiser.*

20 May. "Art and Artists." *Boston Transcript.*

20 May. "Pennsylvania Academy of Fine Arts." *Newark Daily Advertiser.*

June. Strahan, Edward [Earl Shinn]. "The National Academy of Design." *Art Amateur,* 4–5.

1880

Benjamin, Samuel G.W. *Art in America.* New York.

3 January. "Pictures at Library Hall." *Newark Daily Advertiser.*

February. Koehler, S. R. "Thomas Moran." *American Art Review* 1:151.

3 February. "American Water Color Society." *Newark Daily Advertiser.*

19 February. "Fine Arts." *NY Post.*

28 February. "The Painters in Water Colors." *NY Post.*

March. Benjamin, Samuel G.W. "American Water-Colour Society." *Art Journal* [NY] 6:91–93.

22 September. "Lovers of the Beautiful." *Denver Rocky Mt. News.*

26 October. "Art Matters in Newark." *Newark Daily Advertiser.*

22 December. "Art Matters." *Newark Daily Advertiser.*

1881

22 January. *Newark Daily Advertiser.*

February. "Exhibition of the American Water Color Society." *Art Amateur,* 49.

28 April. "Local News Briefs." *Newark Daily Advertiser.*

May. "Picture Sales of the Month." *Art Journal* [NY] 7:160.

7 May. "Art Notes." *The Critic,* 126.

10 May. "Fine Arts." *NY Post.*

13 May. "Fine Arts." *NY Post.*

6 June. "Art Matters." *Newark Daily Advertiser.*

30 June. "Fine Arts." *The Independent* [NY].

July. Koehler, S. R. "New Etchings by Thomas Moran." *American Art Review* 2:104.

July. "Art Notes." *Art Journal* [NY] 7:221–224.

August. "Minor Notes." *Art Journal* [NY] 7:256.

13 August. "Charitable Mechanic Association's Art Gallery." *Boston Transcript.*

September. "Exhibitions Present and Prospective." *Art Journal* 7: 286–287.

4 September. "Leadville." *Denver Rocky Mt. News.*

October. "St. Louis." *Art Journal* [NY] 7:319.

20 October. "Fine Arts." *The Independent* [NY].

November. "Chicago." *Art Journal* [NY] 7:352.

3 December. "The Paintings at Library Hall." *Newark Daily Advertiser.*

9 December. "The Fine Arts." *Boston Transcript.*

1882

Dutton, Clarence E. *Tertiary History of the Grand Canyon District.* Washington, DC.

February. Benjamin, Samuel G.W. "A Pioneer of the Palette: Thomas Moran." *Magazine of Art* 5:89–93.

28 March. "Art at the Metropolis." *Phila. Press.*

"Art and Artists." *Boston Transcript.*

18 April. "Art and Artists." *Boston Transcript.*

22 April. "Bolton Artists in the New World: The Moran Family—Interesting Personal Reminiscences." *Bolton Journal* [England]. [Reprinted in *Bolton Evening News,* 24, 25 April.]

9 June. "Exhibition of Paintings in Bolton." *Manchester Guardian* [England].

3 July. "Thomas Moran's Exhibition in His Native Town." *NY Herald.*

29 July. "Art Notes." *The Critic,* 207.

4 September. "An American's Success in England." *NY Herald.*

9 September. "Art Notes." *The Critic,* 245.

22 September. "Art and Artists." *Boston Transcript.*

18 November. "Art Notes." *The Critic,* 317.

1883

20 January. "Art Notes." *The Critic,* 24.

February. Van Rensselaer, Maria G. "American Etchers." *Century Magazine* 25:483–499. [Reprinted New York, 1886.]

10 May. "Fine Arts." *The Independent* [NY].

19 May. "The Fine Arts." *The Critic,* 236.

2 June. "Art and Artists." *Boston Transcript.*

16 June. "Art Notes." *The Critic,* 288.

1884

5 April. "National Academy Exhibition." *Boston Transcript.*

6 April. "The Week in Art Circles." *NY Tribune.*

13 April. "Notes About Artistic Subjects in the New World and the Old." *NY Herald.*

16 April. "National Academy of Design." *NY Post.*

27 April. "Art News and Comments." *NY Tribune.*

28 April. "The Academy Exhibition." *NY Tribune.*

4 May. "Fine Arts." *NY Herald.*

16 May. "Art and Artists." *Boston Transcript.*

17 May. "An Etching of Thomas Moran." *NY Post.*

28 August. "Art and Artists." *Boston Transcript.*

18 September. "The Lithographic Exhibit at the Mechanics Fair." *Boston Transcript.*

24 October. "Art Notes." *Boston Transcript.*

4 December. "Art and Artists." *Boston Transcript.*

12 December. "The Prang Prize Designs." *Boston Transcript.*

1885

Koehler, S. R. *Etching: An Outline of Its Technical Processes and Its History....* New York.

Koehler, S. R. et al. *American Etchings.* Boston.

24 January. *The Critic,* 43.

15 February. "The Water Colors and Etchings." *NYT.*

19 February. "Fine Arts." *The Independent* [NY].

7 March. "Art and Artists." *Boston Transcript.*

18 April. "Paintings by Americans." *Boston Transcript.*

17 May. "Gallery and Studio." *Brooklyn Daily Eagle.*

October. Champney, Lizzie W. "The Summer Haunts of American Artists." *Century Magazine* 30:845–860.

5 December. "Holiday Publications." *The Critic,* 268.

10 December. "Fine Arts." *The Independent* [NY].

12 December. "Art in Books." *Boston Transcript.*

18 December. "Art and Artists." *Boston Transcript.*

19 December. "New Books." *Boston Transcript.*

1886

Koehler, S. R. *American Art.* Boston.

8 February. "Etchers and Water Painters." *NYT.*

18 February. "The Moran Exhibition." *NY Herald.*

22 February. "Pictures by Thomas Moran, N.A." *NYT.*

24 February. "Art and Artists." *Boston Transcript.*

Ortgies Galleries. *Catalogue of the Oils and Water Colors of Thomas Moran, N.A.* New York.

25 February. "Sale of the Moran Paintings." *NYT.*

27 February. "Art Notes." *The Critic,* 108.

6 March. *EH Star.*

15 December. "American Art." *Boston Transcript.*

1887

15 January. "Another East Hampton Picture." *EH Star.*

29 January. "The Fine Arts." *The Critic,* 59.

19 February. "The Lounger." *The Critic,* 92.

13 May. "Art and Artists." *Boston Transcript.*

14 July. "Art at the American Exhibition." *Daily News* [London].

1888

Appletons' Cyclopaedia of American Biography, s.v. "Moran, Thomas." Ed. James Grant Wilson and John Fiske. New York.

31 March. "The Fine Arts." *The Critic,* 158.

16 April. "Art and Artists." *Boston Transcript.*

28 April. "Art Notes." *The Critic,* 210.

4 May. "American Paintings." *Boston Transcript.*

5 May. "The Fine Arts." *The Critic,* 223.

11 August. "The Fine Arts." *The Critic,* 70.

6 October. "The Fine Arts." *The Critic,* 169.

19 November. "The Autumn Academy." *NYT.*

24 November. "The Society of American Etchers." *The Critic,* 261.

"Art Notes." *The Critic,* 262.

8 December. "The Fine Arts." *The Critic,* 292.

9 December. "Some Academy Pictures." *NYT.*

1889

Clement, Clara Erskine, and Laurence Hutton. *Artists of the Nineteenth Century and Their Works,* s.v. "Moran, Thomas." Boston and New York.

21 February. "Art and Artists." *Boston Transcript.*

28 February. "Art Notes." *Boston Transcript.*

March. Trumble, Alfred. *A Catalogue of the Complete Etched Works of Thomas Moran, N.A., and M. Nimmo Moran, S.P.E.* New York.

3 March. "Etchings, Drawings, Pastels." *NYT.*

11 March. "Two American Etchers: The Work of Mr. and Mrs. Moran." *NY Tribune.*

16 March. *EH Star.*

"Etchings at Klackner's." *The Critic,* 135.

May. Bisland, Elizabeth. "The Studios of New York." *The Cosmopolitan* 7:2–22.

18 August. "Thomas Moran's Interview with 'Papa' Corot in Paris." *Brooklyn Daily Eagle.*

31 August. "Chalepa ta Kala." *EH Star.*

November. Teetor, Henry Dudley. "The Mountain of the Holy Cross." *Magazine of Western History* 11:4–8.

1890

31 January. "Art and Artists." *Boston Transcript.*

1 March. "Art Notes." *The Critic,* 111.

2 August. "Artists at East Hampton." *EH Star.*

30 August. "Summer in East Hampton" and "Notes." *EH Star.*

6 September. *EH Star.*

13 September. *EH Star.*

18 October. "An Hour in a Studio." *EH Star.*

12 December. "The December Exhibition at the Union League Club." *NY Post.*

1891

17 January. "The Salmagundi Exhibition." *NYT.*

23 January. "Art Notes." *The Critic,* 47.

23 January. *EH Star.*

31 January. "The Water Colors." *NYT.*

1 February. "New York Etching Club." *NYT.*

7 February. "The Fine Arts." *The Critic,* 76.

21 March. "The Fine Arts." *The Critic,* 160.

17 April. "The Salmagundi Club." *NY Post.*

8 August. "Art News Notes." *NY Post.*

4 September. *EH Star.*

2 October. "Artists of East Hampton." *EH Star.*

9 October. "They Could Not Make a Landing." *EH Star.*

1 December. "Exhibition and Sale of Paintings." *NY Post.*

3 December. "The Fine Arts." *Boston Transcript.*

1892

13 February. "Art Notes." *The Critic,* 106.

16 February. "Art Notes." *NY Post.*

27 February. "Art News." *NY Post.*

4 March. "Artist Thomas Moran." *EH Star.*

29 April. "Village and Town News." *EH Star.*

26 May. "Visitors to the Grand Canyon." *Flagstaff Coconino Sun* [AZ].

18 June. "A Mountain Painter." *Denver Rocky Mt. News.*

8 October. "The Fine Arts." *Boston Transcript.*

"The Columbian Art Display." *NY Herald.*

28 October. *EH Star.*

27 November. "Art Culture in Denver." *Colorado Sun.*

28 November. "The Moran Pictures." *Denver Republican.*

December. *Catalogue of Pictures of Thomas Moran, N.A., Exhibited under the Auspices of the Denver Art League.* Denver.

1 December. "His New Yellowstone Picture." *NY Herald.*

18 December. "Art Notes." *Denver Rocky Mt. News.*

22 December. "In Black and White." *Denver Rocky Mt. News.*

25 December. "Art Notes." *Denver Rocky Mt. News.*

1893

2 January. "Artist Moran Talks." *Denver Rocky Mt. News.*

8 January. "Art Notes" and "Reception at the Art League." *Denver Rocky Mt. News.*

15 January. "Denver Art League." *Denver Rocky Mt. News.*

21 January. "The Moran Collection." *Denver Rocky Mt. News.*

22 January. "Thomas Moran Exhibition." *Denver Rocky Mt. News.*

25 February. "The Artists and the Fair." *Boston Transcript.*

31 March. *EH Star.*

April. Benson, Frances M. "The Moran Family." *The Quarterly Illustrator* 1:66–84.

1894

January. Moran, Thomas. "A Journey to the Devil's Tower in Wyoming." *Century Magazine* 47:450–455.

2 February. "The Fine Arts." *Boston Transcript.*

7 April. "The Fine Arts." *The Critic*, 244.

1895

4 May. "Art News." *NY Post.*

17 May. *EH Star.*

16 August. "Married at St. Luke's. Tassin-Moran." *EH Star.*

22 November. *EH Star.*

1896

Benson, Frances M. "The Moran Family." In *Essays on American Art and Artists.* New York.

22 January. "Academy of Design Exhibition." *NY Post.*

2 October. "A Busy Artist." *EH Star.*

1897

8 February. Kraushaar, C. W. *Catalogue of Pictures by Thomas Moran, N.A., with Original Verses by Edith M. Thomas.* New York.

13 February. "Art News." *NY Post.*

17 February. "Pictures in the Galleries." *NYT.*

20 February. "Pictures by Mr. Moran." *The Critic*, 132.

13 March. "Pictures at Auction." *NY Post.*

30 October. Cleveland, Lucy. "In Thomas Moran's Studio." *NY Post.*

1899

14 May. De Kay, Charles. "A Happy Hunting Ground for Artists." *NYT Illustrated Magazine*: 8–9.

29 September. "Mrs. Thomas Moran." *EH Star.*

1900

Beck, Carol H., ed. *Catalogue of the W. P. Wilstach Collection.* Philadelphia.

9 June. "Thos. Moran on Utah Scenery." *Salt Lake City Daily Tribune.*

September. Ladegast, Richard. "Thomas Moran, N.A." *Truth* 19:209–212.

October. Morton, Frederick W. "Thomas Moran, Painter-Etcher." *Brush and Pencil* 7:1–16.

1901

19 January. Caffin, Charles H. "The Seventy-sixth Annual Exhibition of the National Academy of Design." *Harper's Weekly* 45:74.

May. Lockington, W. P. "Philadelphia Water-Color Exhibition." *Brush and Pencil* 8:65–72.

26 July. *EH Star.*

1903

April. Moran, Thomas. "Knowledge a Prime Requisite in Art." *Brush and Pencil* 12:14–16.

June. Moran, Thomas. "Plea for a National Art Gallery." *Brush and Pencil* 12:172–175.

1904

Official Catalogue of Exhibitors, Universal Exposition, St. Louis. St. Louis.

4 November. "Village and Town Notes." *EH Star.*

10 December. Newton, Parker. "Apropos of the Comparative Art Exhibition...to the Editor." *Art News* 3:54.

1905

Hosking, Arthur Nicholas, ed. *The Artist's Year Book*, 135–136. Chicago.

Isham, Samuel. *The History of American Painting.* New York.

1906

Moran, Thomas. "American Art and American Scenery." In *The Grand Canyon of Arizona*, 85–87. [Chicago]. [Reprinted SFRR 1909.]

1908

June and September. Lummis, Charles F. "The Artist's Paradise." *Out West* 28:437–451; and 29:173–191, 240–257.

28 November. "Long Island Painter of World Wide Fame." *Brooklyn Times.*

1909

January. Buckley, Edmund. "Thomas Moran a Splendid Example of American Achievement in Art." *Fine Arts Journal* 20:9–17.

Simpson, William H. "Thomas Moran: The Man." *Fine Arts Journal* 20:18–25.

8 January. "Rambler's Meeting." *EH Star.*

1910

February. Mifflin, Lloyd. "Thomas Moran, N.A." *Fine Arts Journal* 22: n.p.

Pattison, William. "Thomas Moran, N.A." *Fine Arts Journal* 22:91–92.

November. Stevens, Nina Spalding. *A Little Journey from New York to the Grand Canyon by Five Artists and Their Friends.* Privately printed.

1911

February. Stevens, Nina Spalding. "A Pilgrimage to the Artist's Paradise." *Fine Arts Journal* 25:105–113.

12 June. *NY World.*

26 November. Kobbe, Gustav. "Artists Combine for Trip to Arizona." *NY Herald Magazine*, 11.

1912

Murphy, Thomas Dowler. *Three Wonderlands of the American West.* Boston.

1913

January. Buek, Gustave H. "Thomas Moran." *American Magazine* 75:30–32.

1915

Offical Catalogue of the Department of Fine Arts, Panama-Pacific International Exposition, San Francisco.... San Francisco.

11 December. "Thumb Prints of the West." *Art News* 14:6.

1916

4 February. "Great Painter Finds Pasadena Ideal Environment for His Work." *Pasadena Star.*

11 March. DuBois, Gussie Packard. "Thomas Moran Knows Nature and Paints It." *Pasadena Star.*

1923

5 October. "Noted American Artist Still Sticks to His Easel at 86." *Kansas City Star.*

1924

12 January. W.H.S., "Thomas Moran on His 87th Birthday...." *The Osborne Bulletin*, 18–19.

4 April. "Gives Picture to School." *EH Star.*

August. Buek, Gustave H. "Thomas Moran, N.A.: The Grand Old Man of American Art." *Mentor*, 30–37.

Moran, Ruth B. "Thomas Moran: An Impression." *Mentor*, 38–52.

Gillespie, Harriet Sisson. "Thomas Moran, Dean of American Painters." *International Studio* 79:361–366. [Reprinted in *Christian Science Monitor*, 14 August, and *Current Opinion* 77 (October), 447.]

1925

Murphy, Thomas Dowler. *Seven Wonderlands of the American West*. Boston.

16 June. Powers, Laura Bride. "Early Art of Thomas Moran Shown in Art Club Exhibit." *Santa Barbara Morning Press*. [Reprinted in *EH Star*, 3 July.]

21 June. Powers, Laura Bride. "Art in Santa Barbara." *Santa Barbara Morning Press*. [Reprinted in *EH Star*, 3 July.]

1926

Fielding, Mantle. *Dictionary of American Painters, Sculptors, and Engravers*. s.v. "Moran, Thomas." Philadelphia.

22 January. "Winter and Summer Resorts." *EH Star*.

26 August. "Thomas Moran Famous Artist Dies in Home." *Santa Barbara Morning Press*.

27 August. "Capitol Has Great Paintings by Moran, Who Died Yesterday." *Evening Star* [DC].

"Thomas Moran, Artist, Dies at Santa Barbara." *NY Tribune*.

"Thomas Moran Died Wednesday." *EH Star*.

"Thomas Moran Dies; Painter of Rockies." *NYT*.

"Thomas Moran Funeral Today." *Santa Barbara Morning Press*.

28 August. "Rites Held for Thomas Moran." *Santa Barbara Morning Press*.

1 September. Gilder, J. B. "A Painter of the Far West." Letter to the Editor. *NYT*.

6 September. "Tribute to Moran." *LA Times*.

9 September. Vinton, Stallo. "An Artist's Mountain." Letter to the Editor. *NYT*.

17 September. "Thomas Moran: 'An Appreciation.'" *EH Star*.

18 September. "Obituary: Thomas Moran." *Art News* 24:6.

19 September. "American Etching Indebted to Moran." *NYT Magazine*, 14–15.

27 September. Biltmore Salon. *Memorial Exhibition: Thomas Moran, N.A., 1837–1926*. Los Angeles.

November. Butler, Howard Russell. "Thomas Moran, N.A.: An Appreciation." *Magazine of Art* 17:559–560.

December. Moran, Ruth. "The Real Life of Thomas Moran: As Known to His Daughter." *Magazine of Art* 17:645–646.

18 December. Watson, Forbes. "Art Notes." *NY World*.

19 December. *NY American*.

"Random Impressions in Current Exhibitions." *NY Tribune*.

20 December. *Christian Science Monitor*.

Milch Galleries. *Memorial Exhibition: Water Color Sketches by Thomas Moran, N.A.* New York.

26 December. "Thomas Moran Art in Milch Galleries an Amazing Record." *NY American*.

"Thomas Moran Memorial." *Brooklyn Eagle*.

28 December. "Pupil Recalls Thomas Moran." *NY Sun*.

1927

Mather, Frank Jewett, Charles Rufus Morey, and William James Henderson. *The American Spirit in Art*. New Haven.

Reports, Constitution, By-Laws, and List of Members of the Century Association for the Year 1927. New York.

U.S. Senate. *Art and Artists of the Capitol of the United States of America*. 69th Cong., 1st sess. S. doc. 95.

January. Biltmore Salon. *Water Colors by Thomas Moran, N.A., 1837–1926*. Los Angeles.

1 January. Walker, Caroline. "Genius of Dead Artists in L.A. Exhibit." *LA Herald*.

2 January. Mather, Stephen Tyng. "The Work of Thomas Moran." *NYT*.

4 January. "Geo. D. Pratt Buys Moran's Sketches." *NY World*.

9 January. Eddy, Frederick W. "Thomas Moran's Color Notes Helped to Make Yellowstone a National Park." *NY World*.

Parker, Robert Allerton. "The Water-Colors of Thomas Moran." *International Studio* 86:65–72.

27 March. "Showing at Biltmore." *LA Times*.

22 April. "Exhibit to Open Sunday Incites Interest in Art." *Peoria Star*.

June. Clark, Eliot. "Studies by American Masters at Cooper Union." *Art in America* 15:180–188.

5 June. *LA Times*.

October. Holmes, William Henry. "First Ascent of the Mountain of the Holy Cross." *Ohio Archaeological and Historical Quarterly* 36:517–527.

4 November. Anderson Galleries. *American Water Colors: The Collection Formed by the Late G. H. Buek, Easthampton, L.I.* New York.

5 November. "Water Colors Bring $12,460." *NY Tribune*.

1928

29 June. "Coming Exhibit Moran Paintings." *EH Star*.

July. "Exhibitions." *International Studio* 90:78.

1 July. Cary, Elisabeth Luther. "Summer Art Exhibitions Current Here and Now." *NYT*.

18 July. Clinton Academy. *Memorial Exhibition: Paintings and Etchings by Thomas Moran, N.A.,* East Hampton.

20 July. "Moran Memorial Exhibition at Clinton Academy." *EH Star*.

20 July. De Kay, Charles. "Moran the Pathbreaker." Letter to the Editor. *EH Star*.

August. "Finding Moran." *Art Digest* 2:6.

3 August. "Thomas Moran Memorial Exhibition Closes Sunday." *EH Star*.

September. "Mr. Pratt Presents Moran's Masterpiece to the National Gallery." *Art Digest* 2:1.

11 September. "Famous Moran Given to National Gallery." *Chicago Evening Post*.

15 September. "Pratt Gives Moran to National Gallery." *Art News* 26:14.

1929

Gabriel, Ralph Henry. *The Lure of the Frontier: A Story of Race Conflict*. New Haven.

1931

Artists' Fund Society of the City of New York, Triennial Report, 1929–1931. New York.

Neuhaus, Eugene. *The History and Ideals of American Art*. Palo Alto, CA.

19 August. Jewell, Edward Alden. "East Hampton's Gala Day." *NYT*.

20 August. "Guild Hall Opens at East Hampton." *NYT*.

6 December. Rainey, Ada. "Artists Nature's Press Agents." *Washington Post*.

1932

Fryxell, Fritiof. "Thomas Moran's Journey to the Tetons in 1879." *Augustana Historical Society Publications* 2:37–46. [Reprinted in *Annals of Wyoming* 15 (January 1943), 71–84.]

National Cyclopedia of American Biography, s.v. "Moran, Thomas." New York.

March. Cary, Elisabeth Luther. "The Morning of American Etching." *Parnassus* 4:5–7.

17 June. "Salute to Bolton Adventurers. Family which Found Fame in America." *Bolton Evening News* [England].

1934

Dictionary of American Biography, s.v. "Moran, Thomas." Entry by William Howe Downes. Ed. Dumas Malone. New York.

U.S. Department of the Interior. *Grand Teton National Park, Wyoming*. Washington, DC.

January. Fryxell, Fritiof. "The Mount of the Holy Cross." *Trail and Timberline*, no. 138, pp. 3–9, 14.

June. Fryxell, Fritiof. "Thomas Moran: An Appreciation." *Sierra Club Bulletin* 19:56–57.

21 October. Sheets, Nan. "Many Paintings by Thomas Moran Found in Oklahoma." *Oklahoma City Daily Oklahoman*.

1935

Cahill, Holger, and Alfred H. Barr. *Art in America: A Complete Survey.* New York.

29 May. California Pacific International Exposition, Palace of Fine Arts. *Illustrated Catalogue: Official Art Exhibition....* San Diego.

September. Fryxell, Fritiof. "Thomas Moran's Journey to the Mount of the Holy Cross in 1874." *Trail and Timberline*, no. 203, pp. 103–105.

October. "Art at the San Diego Exposition." *Magazine of Art* 28:591–596.

30 December. "Famous Boltonians." *Bolton Evening News* [England].

1936

Taylor, Rose. "Thomas Moran." *Yosemite Indians and Other Sketches*, 89–92. San Francisco.

4 January. "Coming Auctions." *Art News* 34:16.

11 January. "Art Is Sold for $39,000." *NYT.*

August. Fryxell, Fritiof. "The Thomas Moran Art Collection of the National Parks." *Yosemite Nature Notes* 15:57–60.

Moran, Ruth B. "Thomas Moran: An Impression." *Yosemite Nature Notes* 15:62–64.

15 August. "*Exhibit*: Moran Pictures Draw Crowds to Government Gallery." *News-Week*, 21.

December. Jackson, W. H. "Famous American Mountain Paintings, I: With Moran in the Yellowstone." *Appalachia* 21:149–158.

1937

January. Comstock, Helen. "In Recognition of Thomas Moran." *Connoisseur* 99:38–39.

7 January. "Memorial Exhibitions to Observe Centenary of Thomas Moran, Artist." *EH Star.*

"Moran Library Exhibit." *EH Star.*

9 January. "The Father of the National Parks: Thomas 'Yellowstone' Moran." *LA Saturday Night*, 5.

12 January. Newhouse Galleries Inc. *A Loan Exhibition of Paintings by Thomas Moran N.A. to Commemorate the Centenary of His Birth.* New York.

15 January. "Thomas Moran: He Sold a Nation's Wonders to Its People." *Art Digest* 11:10.

16 January. Jewell, Edward Alden. "Art Shows Honor Moran Centennial." *NYT.*

Vaughan, Malcolm. "Moran Centennial Leads Art Shows Opened this Week." *NY American.*

17 January. "About Well-Known Folk in Books, Art, Politics: National Gallery of Art Celebrates Centenary of Thomas Moran." *Evening Star* [DC].

"Thomas Moran." *NY Tribune.*

"Thomas Moran." *NYT.*

18 January. "Exhibition Marks Moran Centenary." *NY Sun.*

"Yellowstone Man." *Time* 29:46.

23 January. "The 'American Scene,' as Presented by Moran." *Evening Star* [DC].

"Moran and the Changing Western Landscape." *Art News* 35:20.

30 January. "Moran Memorial Devoted to His Prints." *NY Sun.*

"The Romantic Past of American Painting." *Art News* 35:15–16.

February. "A Thomas Moran Centenary." *Bulletin of the New York Public Library* 41:127–128.

Breuning, Margaret. "Thomas Moran." *Magazine of Art* 30:115.

1 February. "Moran in Washington." *Art Digest* 11:17.

7 February. Grafly, Dorothy. "Thomas Moran: Father of Our National Parks." *Philadelphia Record.*

"Exhibition at the New York Public Library." *NYT.*

March. Lane, James W. "Notes for New York." *Apollo* 25:157–158.

"Painter of the Western Scene." *Antiques* 31:136.

14 March. Cortissoz, Royal. "Moran: A Pioneer in Our Landscape Art." *NY Tribune.*

May. "Thomas Moran, N.A.: Centenary Exhibition." *LA Art Bulletin* 3: n.p.

4 May. Los Angeles Art Association. *Thomas Moran, N.A., Centenary Exhibition.* Los Angeles.

8 May. Kurtzworth, Harry Muir. "Art Leads to Parks." *LA Saturday Night*, 2.

29 May. "Art throughout America: Los Angeles: Moran Centenary." *Art News* 35:18.

2 July. Faulkner Memorial Art Gallery, Free Public Library. *Loan Exhibition Paintings and Etchings by Thomas Moran, N.A., 1837–1926.* Santa Barbara.

18 July. Paulding, Litti. "Moran Centennial Show Brings Honor to City." *Santa Barbara News-Press.*

1938

8 March. Springfield Museum of Fine Arts. *A Century of American Landscape Painting, 1800–1900.* Springfield, MA.

1939

June. Burroughs, Louise. "The Moses Tanenbaum Bequest." *Bulletin of the Metropolitan Museum of Art* 34:137–138.

15 December. "Where Is this Picture?" *Art Digest* 14:33.

1940

15 June. "New Exhibitions of the Week" and "Moran: An American in the British Tradition." *Art News* 38:12, 15.

15 November. "Public Picks Moran." *Art Digest* 15:17.

1941

"Arte Grafico del Hemisferio Occidental." *La Torre de Cortez, Mejico*, 73.

April. Draper, Benjamin Poff. "Thomas Moran: Painter, Adventurer, and Pioneer." *Art in America* 29:82–87.

1942

15–31 January. Lane, James W. "The Heritage of the National Academy." *Art News* 40:13–16.

June. Jackson, W. Turrentine. "Governmental Exploration of the Upper Yellowstone, 1871." *Pacific Historical Review* 11:187–199.

1943

Soby, James Thrall, and Dorothy C. Miller. *Romantic Painting in America.* New York.

1944

July. Godfrey, Elizabeth H. "Thumbnail Sketches of Yosemite Artists: Thomas Moran." *Yosemite Nature Notes* 23:64–68.

1 September. "New Britain Enriches Its Collections." *Art Digest* 18:6.

1 December. Breuning, Margaret. "From Our Artistic Background." *Art Digest* 19:11.

1945

Marshall, James. *Santa Fe: The Railroad that Built an Empire.* New York.

March. Sweet, Frederick A. "Painters of the Hudson River School." *Antiques* 47:158–161.

1–14 March. "Romantic Flow of the Hudson." *Art News* 44:11–12, 32.

17 April. Sweet, Frederick A. *The Hudson River School and the Early American Landscape Tradition.* New York.

1948

Born, Wolfgang. *American Landscape Painting: An Interpretation.* New Haven.

November. Evans, Raymond. "The McGuffey Readers." *Magazine of Art* 41:274–275.

1949

Larkin, Oliver W. *Art and Life in America.* New York.

1950

Barker, Virgil. *American Painting: History and Interpretation.* New York.

Huth, Hans. "The American and Nature." *Journal of the Warburg and Courtauld Institutes* 13:101–149.

March. U.S. Senate. *Transfer of Capitol Paintings to Interior Department.* 81st Cong., 2d sess., no. 1525.

June. U.S. House. *Transfer of Capitol Paintings to the Department of the Interior.* 81st Cong., 2d sess., no. 2427.

July. *U.S. Statutes at Large* 64: 321.

1951

11 February. "Moran Paintings in Tulsa Exhibit." *Tulsa Daily World.*

1952

McCracken, Harold. *Portrait of the Old West.* New York.

1953

12 December. Knox, Sanka. "Indian Gives Up Vast Art Collection in Deal to Clear $2,250,000.00 Debts." *NYT.*

18 December. "Christmas Collector's Item." *NY World Telegram and Sun.*

1954

Rathbone, Perry T., ed. *Westward the Way.* St. Louis.

Stegner, Wallace E. *Beyond the Hundredth Meridian.* Boston.

1955

Wilson, James Benjamin. "The Significance of Thomas Moran as an American Landscape Painter." Ph.D. diss., Ohio State University.

1956

Richardson, Edgar P. *Painting in America: The Story of 450 Years.* New York.

1957

The NY Historical Society's Dictionary of Artists in America, 1564–1860. s.v. "Moran, Thomas." Ed. George C. Groce and David H. Wallace. New Haven.

Huth, Hans. *Nature and the American: Three Centuries of Changing Attitudes.* Lincoln, NE.

1958

Fryxell, Fritiof. *Thomas Moran: Explorer in Search of Beauty.* East Hampton.

Hamilton, Sinclair. *Early American Book Illustrators and Wood Engravers 1670–1870.* Princeton. [Supplement published 1968.]

1960

8 October. *Famous Families in American Art.* Dallas.

1962

Flexner, James Thomas. *That Wilder Image: The Painting of America's Native School from Thomas Cole to Winslow Homer.* Boston.

Museum of Fine Arts. *M & M Karolik Collection of American Water Colors & Drawings, 1800–1875.* Boston.

October. Flexner, James Thomas. "The Rocky Mountain School of American Painting." *Antiques* 82:403–405.

1963

Sachs, Samuel. "Thomas Moran: Drawings and Watercolors." M.A. thesis, New York University, 1963.

Wilkins, Thurman. "Moran." *American Scene* 5:22–37, 57–59.

17 April. Gerdts, William H. *Thomas Moran, 1837–1926.* Riverside, CA.

May. Davidson, Ruth. "Special Events: Moran in California." *Antiques* 83:578, 580.

1964

Gerdts, William H. *Painting and Sculpture in New Jersey.* New Jersey Historical Series 21:157–161.

February. Gerdts, William H. "The Painting of Thomas Moran: Sources and Style." *Antiques* 85:202–205.

1965

Ewers, John C. *Artists of the Old West.* Garden City, NY.

5 June. Heckscher Museum. *The Moran Family.* Huntington, NY.

1966

Green, Samuel M. *American Art: A Historical Survey.* New York.

Wilkins, Thurman. *Thomas Moran: Artist of the Mountains.* Norman, OK.

15 May. "Moran House Made Landmark." *NYT.*

1967

Bassford, Amy O., and Fritiof M. Fryxell. *Home-Thoughts, from Afar: Letters of Thomas Moran to Mary Nimmo Moran.* East Hampton.

Lindquist-Cock, Elizabeth. "The Influence of Photography on American Landscape Painting, 1839–1880." Ph.D. diss., New York University.

May. Gerdts, William H. "Americans in Faraway Places in the Roderic H. D. Henderson Collection." *Antiques* 91:647–649.

1968

Wilmerding, John. *A History of American Marine Painting.* Salem, MA, and Boston.

1970

6 February. Heckscher Museum. *Artists of Suffolk County Part I.* Huntington, NY.

1971

8 April. Knox, Sanka. "American Art Sale Sets Auction Mark in First of 2 Days." *NYT.*

1972

20 August. Canaday, John. "Geysers and Canyons and Other Wonders." *NYT.*

17 September. Thornton, Gene. "His Landscapes Have No Beer Cans." *NYT.*

1973

Keene, Marie. "Moran." *American Scene* 14:6–11.

1974

Novak, Barbara. "Thomas Moran and the Grand Canyon of the Yellowstone." *Honolulu Academy of Arts Journal* 1:30–35.

1 October. Washburn Gallery. *Drawings and Watercolors of the West: Thomas Moran, from the Collection of the Cooper-Hewitt Museum of Design.* New York.

5 October. Kramer, Hilton. "Thomas Moran: Drawings and Watercolors of the West." *NYT.*

1975

Summer. "Moran, His Sketches: Blueprints for Masterpieces." *American Scene* 16:18–24.

1976

February. McClinton, Katharine Morrison. "L. Prang and Company Chromos." *Connoisseur* 191:97–105.

4 April. Fern, Thomas S. *The Drawings and Watercolors of Thomas Moran.* Notre Dame, IN.

9 May. Heckscher Museum. *Artists of Suffolk County Part X: Recorders of History.* Huntington, NY.

Summer. Fern, Thomas S. "The Drawings and Watercolors of Thomas Moran (1837–1926)." *Artists of the Rockies and the Golden West* 3:34–41.

June. "Paintings of the American West." *Kennedy Quarterly* 15:60–61.

Truettner, William H. "'Scenes of Majesty and Enduring Interest': Thomas Moran Goes West." *Art Bulletin* 58:241–259.

1977

Bartlett, Richard A. "From Imagination to Reality: Thomas Moran and the Yellowstone." *Prospects* 3:111–124.

1978

Patrick, Darryl. "The Iconographical Significance in Selected Western Subjects Painted by Thomas Moran." Ph.D. diss., North Texas State University.

May. Driscoll, John P. "Moran Watercolor Found in University Attic." *American Art Journal* 10:111–112.

July/August. Arkelian, Marjorie Dakin. "Artists in Yosemite." *American West* 15:34–47.

1979

January. Reilly, Bernard F., Jr. "The Early Work of John Moran, Landscape Photographer." *American Art Journal* 11:65–75.

March/April. Fisch, Mathias S. "Mount of the Holy Cross." *American West* 16:32–36, 57–58.

1980

Fahlman, Betsy. "Columbia Sublime: The Collaboration of Thomas Moran and Lloyd Mifflin." *Journal of the Lancaster County Historical Society* 84:167–178.

March/April. Clark, Carol. "'The Most Remarkable Scenery': Thomas Moran's Watercolors of the American West." *American West* 17:40–47. [Clark 1980a]

May. Duty, Michael. "Thomas Moran 1837–1926: 'The Most Remarkable Scenery.'" *Southwest Art* 9:128–131.

23 May. Clark, Carol. *Thomas Moran: Watercolors of the American West.* Austin, TX. [Clark 1980b]

December. Logue, John D. Review of Clark 1980b. *Southern Living* 15:98.

1981

Braff, Phyllis. *Thomas Moran: A Search for the Scenic*. East Hampton.

Clark, Carol. "Thomas Moran's Watercolors of the American West." Ph.D. diss., Case Western Reserve University.

January. Duty, Michael. "Thomas Moran's Watercolors of the American West." *Antiques* 99:212–215.

January/February. Ballinger, James K. "Visiting Artists Painted Arizona." *American West* 18:28–37.

1982

September/October. Schwarz, Ted. "The Santa Fe Railway and Early Southwest Artists." *American West* 19:32–41.

1983

Bienenstock, Jennifer A. Martin. "The Formation and Early Years of the Society of American Artists: 1877–1884." Ph.D. diss., City University of New York.

Lindstrom, Gaell. *Thomas Moran in Utah*. Logan, UT.

Morand, Anne, and Sarah Hirsch. *The Art of the Yellowstone, 1870–1872*. Tulsa.

Sparks, Esther. "Thomas Moran: Painter and Patriot." *Henry Ford Museum and Greenfield Village Herald* 12:60–65.

January. Broadd, Harry A. "The Art of Thomas Moran." *Gilcrease Magazine of American History and Art* 5:2–11.

King, Jeanne Snodgrass. "The Yellowstone: Thomas Moran's 1872 Watercolors." *Southwest Art* 12:106–113.

Morand, Anne. "Moran and the Yellowstone." *Gilcrease Magazine of American History and Art* 5:12–15.

Fall/Winter. Francis, Marilyn G. "Mary Nimmo Moran: Painter-Etcher." *Woman's Art Journal* 4:14–19.

1984

Leo, John Robert. "Landscape, Consumption, Redemption: Thomas Moran's 'Mountain of the Holy Cross' and the Signifying of Representation." *Substance* 13:47–70.

Lovell, Margaretta M. *Venice: The American View, 1860–1920*. San Francisco.

8 February. Risser, John. "Thomas Moran." *Susquehanna Magazine* 8:29–33.

Summer. Nickerson, Cynthia D. "Artistic Interpretations of Henry Wadsworth Longfellow's *The Song of Hiawatha*, 1855–1900." *American Art Journal* 16:49–77.

June/July. Tarshis, Jerome. "Painted on Water." *American Heritage* 35:36–47.

18 October. Ayres, Linda. *Thomas Moran's Watercolors of Yellowstone*. Washington, DC.

1985

Spassky, Natalie et al. *American Paintings in the Metropolitan Museum of Art*. 2:519–524. New York.

21 January. Bruhn, Thomas P. *American Etching: The 1880s*. Storrs, CT.

April. Lovell, Margaretta M. "American Artists in Venice, 1860–1920." *Antiques* 127:864–869.

May/June. Freeman, Judith. "Illuminating Yellowstone." *National Parks* 59:14–16.

26 October. Mottishaw, Barrie. "Explorers of the West." *Art Week* 16:5.

November. Brown, Hilton. "Unfamiliar Views and Distant Lands." *American Artist* 49:S30–S38, S53–S54.

1986

Morand, Anne, and Nancy Friese. *The Prints of Thomas Moran in the Thomas Gilcrease Institute of American History and Art, Tulsa, Oklahoma*. Tulsa.

22 February. Phoenix Art Museum. *Thomas Moran: Works from the Thomas Gilcrease Institute of American History and Art*. Phoenix.

6 March. Candlin, Enid Saunders. "The Home Forum: 'Art Is Not Nature.'" *Christian Science Monitor*.

July. McClinton, Katharine M. "Thomas Moran's Yellowstone Watercolours." *Apollo* 124:38–43.

Morand, Anne. "The Prints of Thomas Moran." *Gilcrease Magazine of American History and Art* 8:16–29.

October. Ewing, Norma. "The Metamorphic Drawings of Thomas Moran." *Southwest Art* 16:58–61.

1987

Ayres, Linda. *Yellowstone: The Poetry of Power, Works of Thomas Moran from the Gilcrease Museum*. Tulsa, 1987.

Manchester, Robert C. "Thomas Moran's Imaginative Ink-Blot Drawings." *Watercolor '87*, 52–57, 95, 97, 99.

January. May, Stephen. "River Frontiers in the Art of Bingham, Moran, and Russell." *Southwest Art* 16:71–77.

April-June. Oberlin College Library and Allen Memorial Art Museum. *Yellowstone National Park: The Oberlin Connection*. Oberlin.

1988

Arader, W. Graham. *Native Grace: Prints of the New World, 1590–1876*. Charlottesville, VA.

September. Collmer, Kathryn. "Museum Notebook: Moran's Yellowstone." *Southwest Art* 18:82.

1989

Kane, Arthur Conrad. "Thomas Moran: The Influence of His Art on Federal Legislation for the First United States National Park." M.A. thesis, California State University at Los Angeles.

Kinsey, Joni L. "Creating a Sense of Place: Thomas Moran and the Surveying of the American West." Ph.D. diss., Washington University.

February. Beesch, Ruth K., et al. *Florida Visionaries: 1870–1930*. Gainesville, FL.

February. Sweeney, J. Gray. "Carl S. Dentzel Collection." *Southwest Art* 18:34–38.

Spring. Pringle, Allan. "Thomas Moran: *Picturesque Canada* and the Quest for a Canadian National Landscape Theme." *Imprint* 14:12–21.

10 June. Guild Hall Museum and Florence Griswold Museum. *En Plein Air: The Art Colonies at East Hampton and Old Lyme, 1880–1930*. East Hampton, and Lyme, CT.

Summer/Autumn. Wagner, Virginia L. "Geological Time in Nineteenth-Century Landscape Paintings." *Winterthur Portfolio* 24:153–163.

Winter. Hults, Linda C. "Thomas Moran's *Shoshone Falls*: A Western Niagara." *Smithsonian Studies in American Art* 3:89–102.

1990

Spring. Bruhn, Thomas P. "Thomas Moran's Painter-Lithographs." *Imprint* 15:2–19.

Summer. Ogden, Kate Nearpass. "Sublime Vistas and Scenic Backdrops: Nineteenth-Century Painters and Photographers at Yosemite." *California History* 69:134–153, 223–224.

Kinsey, Joni L. "Sacred and Profane: Thomas Moran's *Mountain of the Holy Cross*." *Gateway Heritage* 11:4–23.

17 August. Morand, Anne, Joni L. Kinsey, and Mary Panzer. *Splendors of the West: Thomas Moran's Art of the Grand Canyon and Yellowstone. Paintings, Watercolors, Drawings, and Photographs from the Thomas Gilcrease Institute of American History and Art*. Birmingham, AL.

1991

Morand, Anne. "The Early Career of Thomas Moran, 1853–1870." M.A. thesis, Washington University.

Winter/Spring. Hults, Linda C. "Pilgrim's Progress in the West: Moran's *The Mountain of the Holy Cross*." *American Art* 5:69–85.

June. Rosenblum, Robert. "Art: Paintings of the American West." *Architectural Digest* 48:142–147.

October. May, Stephen. "The West as America." *Southwest Art* 21:100–109.

1992

Kinsey, Joni L. *Thomas Moran and the Surveying of the American West*. Washington, DC.

Ogden, Kate Nearpass. "Yosemite as Image and Symbol: Paintings and Photographs from 1855 to 1880." Ph.D. diss., Columbia University.

October. Mergen, B. Review of Kinsey 1992. *American Studies International* 30:85–87.

Fall. Morand, Anne. "Nocturnes: Paintings of Night." *Gilcrease Magazine of American History and Art* 14: 1–9.

1993

Fall. Nemerov, Alexander. Review of Kinsey 1992. *Gateway Heritage* 14:69–70.

Morand, Anne. "'Everywhere it is a picture': Moran in Mexico." *Gilcrease Journal* 1:46–57.

Rainey, Sue. "J. D. Woodward's Wood Engravings of Colorado and the Pacific Railways, 1876–1878." *Imprint* 18:2–12.

Winter. Hoss, Mary Louise. Review of Kinsey 1992. *Winterthur Portfolio* 28:293–296.

1994

Rainey, Sue. *Creating "Picturesque America": Monument to the Natural and Cultural Landscape*. Nashville and London.

February. Wilton, Andrew. Review of Kinsey 1992. *Burlington Magazine* 136:120–121.

July. Fernlund, K. J. Review of Kinsey 1992. *New Mexico Historical Review* 69:300–301.

Summer. Wilkins, Thurman. Review of Kinsey 1992. *Montana: The Magazine of Western History* 44:78, 80.

October. Schultz, W. J. Review of Kinsey 1992. *Journal of the West* 33:98.

1995

March. Landi, Ann. "National News: Washington, DC, the Vanishing 'Valley.'" *Art News* 95:36.

Spring. Reddick, S. Review of Kinsey 1992. *Oregon Historical Quarterly* 96:109–110.

1996

The Dictionary of Art, s.v. "Moran, Thomas." Entry by Carol Clark. New York.

Hults, Linda C. *The Print in the Western World: An Introductory History*. Madison, WI.

Morand, Anne. *Thomas Moran. The Field Sketches, 1856–1923*. Norman, OK.

Spring. Childs, Elizabeth C. "Time's Profile: John Wesley Powell, Art, and Geology at the Grand Canyon." *American Art* 10:7–35.

General References

Abbott, Austin. "The Eye and the Camera." *Harper's Monthly* 39 (Sept. 1869), 476–482.

Ackley, Clifford S. "Sylvester Rosa Koehler and the American Etching Revival." In *Art & Commerce: American Prints of the Nineteenth Century*, 143–150. Ed. Jonathan Fairbanks. Charlottesville, VA, 1978.

Adamson, Jeremy, et al. *Niagara: Two Centuries of Changing Attitudes, 1696–1901*. Washington, DC, 1985.

Alexander, David, and Richard T. Godfrey. *Painters and Engraving: The Reproductive Print from Hogarth to Wilkie*. New Haven, 1980.

American Artist 12 (June 1948), cover: "'Solitude': A Lithograph by Thomas Moran."

American Association for the Advancement of Science. *Centennial Program* [1848–1948]. Washington, 1948.

American Federation of Arts. *John Frederick Kensett*. Selected by John K. Howat. New Haven, 1968.

Amory, Dita, Marilyn Symmes, et al. *Nature Observed, Nature Interpreted*. New York, 1995.

Anderson, Nancy K., and Linda S. Ferber. *Albert Bierstadt: Art and Enterprise*. New York, 1990.

Anthony, A.V.S., Timothy Cole, and Elbridge Kingsley. *Wood Engraving: Three Essays with a List of American Books Illustrated with Woodcuts*. New York, 1916.

Appleton's 2 (26 Mar. 1870), 353–355: "Manifest Destiny."

Appleton's 7 (13 May 1871), 555–558: "Yosemite."

Art and Commerce: American Prints of the Nineteenth Century. Proceedings of a Conference, Museum of Fine Arts, Boston [May 1975]. Charlottesville, VA, 1978.

The Art Journal Illustrated Catalogue of the International Exhibition, 1862. New York, 1863.

Austin, George Lowell. "Something about Etching." *Art Journal* 2 (Apr. 1876), 124–126.

Avery, Kevin J. "*The Heart of the Andes* Exhibited: Frederic E. Church's Window on the Equatorial World." *American Art Journal* 18 (1986), 52–72.

Bachelder, John. *Bachelder's Illustrated Tourist's Guide of the United States: Popular Resorts and How to Reach Them*. New York, 1873.

Bailly-Herzberg, Janine. *L'Eau-forte de peintre au dix-neuvième siècle. La Société des aquafortistes 1862–1867*. 2 vols. Paris, 1972.

Baird, Joseph A., and Shirley Sargent. *Views of Yosemite: The Last Stance of the Romantic Landscape*. Fresno, 1982.

Baker, Paul R. *The Fortunate Pilgrims: Americans in Italy, 1800–1860*. Cambridge, MA, 1964.

Ballinger, James K., and Andrea D. Rubinstein. *Visitors to Arizona, 1846 to 1980*. Phoenix, 1980.

Bancroft, Hubert Howe. *The Book of the Fair: An Historical and Descriptive Presentation of the World's...Columbian Exposition at Chicago in 1893*. Vol. 3. Chicago and San Francisco, 1895.

Barrows, William. "The Railway System of the West." *Magazine of Western History* 4 (Aug. 1886), 413–431.

Bartlett, Richard A. "The Hayden Survey of Colorado." *Colorado Quarterly* 4 (Summer 1955), 73–88.

_____. "'Will Anyone Come Here for Pleasure?'" *American West* 6 (Sept. 1969), 10–16.

Baur, John E. "The Health Seeker in the Westward Movement, 1830–1900." *Mississippi Valley Historical Review* 46 (June 1959), 91–110.

Baur, John I.H. "American Luminism: A Neglected Aspect of the Realist Movement in Nineteenth-Century American Painting." *Perspectives USA* (Fall 1954), 90–98.

_____. "Early Studies in Light and Art by American Landscape Painters." *Bulletin of the Brooklyn Museum* 9 (Winter 1948), 1–9.

_____. "A Romantic Impressionist: James Hamilton." *Bulletin of the Brooklyn Museum* 12 (Spring 1951), 1–9.

Baxter, Jean Taylor. "Burdens and Rewards: Some Issues for American Artists, 1865–1876." Ph.D. diss., University of Maryland, College Park, 1988. Ann Arbor, 1988.

Becker, William B. "The American *cliché verre*." *History of Photography* 3 (Jan. 1979), 71–80.

Beers, Henry A. *Nathaniel Parker Willis*. Boston, 1885.

Benjamin, Samuel G.W. "Present Tendencies of American Art." *Harper's Monthly*. Mar. 1879. [Benjamin 1879b; see Chronological References for Benjamin 1879a]

Benjamin, Walter. *Illuminations*. Translated by Harry Zohn. New York, 1978.

Biographical Directory of the United States Congress 1774–1989. Washington, DC, 1989. [*Bio. Congress* 1989]

A Biographical Album of Prominent Pennsylvanians. 7 vols. Philadelphia, 1889.

Blake, William P., ed. *Reports of the United States Commissioners to the Paris Universal Exposition, 1867*. Washington, DC, 1870.

Bogart, Michele H. *Artists, Advertising, and the Borders of Art*. Chicago and London, 1995.

Boime, Albert. *The Magisterial Gaze: Manifest Destiny and American Landscape Painting, c. 1830–1865*. Washington, DC, 1991.

Borland, Hal. "A Camera Historian: William H. Jackson, Pioneer Photographer of the West...." *NYT Sunday Magazine*, 7 Apr. 1940, 4, 15.

Born, Wolfgang. "The Panoramic Landscape as an American Art Form." *Art in America* 36 (Jan. 1948), 3–10.

Bowles, Samuel. *Across the Continent: A Summer's Journey to the Rocky Mountains, the Mormons, and the Pacific States, with Speaker Colfax*. New York, 1865.

_____. *The Switzerland of America: A Summer Vacation in the Parks and Mountains of Colorado*. Springfield, MA, 1869.

Bradley, Frank H. "Explorations of 1872: U.S. Geological Survey of the Territories, under Dr. Hayden, Snake River Division." *American Journal of Science and Arts*, 3rd ser., no. 3 (Sept. 1873), 194–207.

Bradley, William A. "The Advantage of Wood Engraving." *Print Collector's Quarterly* 1 (1911), 382.

Brinton, Christian. *Impressions of the Art at the Panama-Pacific Exposition*. New York, 1916.

Bromley, Isaac. "The Wonders of the West, I: The Big Trees and the Yosemite." *Scribner's* 3 (Jan. 1872), 261–277.

Bronson, Katharine de Kay. "Browning in Venice: Being Recollections by the late Mrs. Katharine de Kay Bronson, with a Prefatory Note by Henry James." *Cornhill Magazine* 12 (Feb. 1902), 145–171.

Brooks, Van Wyck. *The Dream of Arcadia: American Writers and Artists in Italy, 1760-1915*. New York, 1958.

Brown, David Blayney. *Turner and Byron*. London, 1992.

Brown, Dee. *The Year of the Century: 1876*. New York, 1966.

Bruhn, Thomas P. *The American Print: Originality and Experimentation, 1790-1890*. Storrs, CT, 1993.

Burnham, Patricia M., and Lucretia H. Giese, eds. *Redefining American History Painting*. New York, 1995.

Burns, Sarah. *Inventing the Modern Artist: Art and Culture in Gilded Age America*. New Haven, 1996.

Butlin, Martin, and Joll, Evelyn. *The Paintings of J. M. W. Turner*. 2 vols. Rev. ed., New Haven and London, 1984.

Carr, Carolyn K., and George Gurney. *Revisiting the White City: American Art at the 1893 World's Fair*. Washington, DC, 1993.

Carr, Helen. "The Myth of Hiawatha." *Literature and History* 12 (Spring 1986), 58–78.

Catalogue of the American Exhibition of British Art: Oil Pictures and Water Colours. [New York], 1857.

Catalogue of the American Exhibition of British Art: Oil Pictures and Water Colours. [Philadelphia], 1858.

Catalogue of Louis Prang's Collection, Sold by Private Auction. Boston, 1899.

The Century, 1847-1946. New York, 1947.

Chadbourne, Janice H., Karl Gabosh, and Charles O. Vogel. *The Boston Art Club: Exhibition Record, 1873-1909*. Madison, CT, 1991.

Cikovsky, Nicolai, Jr. "Paintings of Florida in the Vickers Collection." *Antiques* (Nov. 1995), 694–703.

Cincinnati Industrial Exposition. *Report of the Board of Commissioners*. ... Cincinnati, 1873.

Clapper, Michael. "Art, Industry, and Education in Prang's Chromolithographic Company." *Proceedings of the American Antiquarians Society* 105 (1995), 145–161.

_____. "The Chromo and the Art Museum: Popular and Elite Art Institutions in Late Nineteenth-Century America." In *Domesticity and Modernism*. Ed. Christopher Reed. London, 1996.

Clark, Carol. "The Connoisseurship of Western American Drawings." *Drawing* 4 (Nov./Dec. 1982), 78–82.

Clark, Eliot. *History of the National Academy of Design, 1825-1953*. New York, 1954.

Clark, T. Edwards. "The Bottom of the Sea." *Scribner's* 1 (Nov. 1870), 18–35.

Cobb, Josephine. "The Washington Art Association: An Exhibition Record, 1856–1860." *Records of the Columbia Historical Society*, 122–190. Washington, DC, 1963–1965.

Coffin, William A. "American Illustration of Today." *Scribner's* 11 (Jan., Feb., Mar. 1892), 106–117, 197–205, 333–349.

Coleman, Hugh W. "Passing of a Famous Artist—Edward Moran." *Brush and Pencil* 8 (July 1901), 188–192.

Conklin, Enoch. *Conklin's Modern Nineveh and Babylon: Being a Description of the Ancient Pueblo People, and Their Dwellings....* N.p., 1883.

_____. *Picturesque Arizona*. New York, 1878.

Cook, Charles W. "The Valley of the Upper Yellowstone." *Western Monthly* 4 (July 1870), 60–67.

Cook, Clarence. [On the "Counterfeiting" of Art through Chromolithography]. *NY Tribune*, 20 Nov. 1866; 22 Oct. 1868.

Cope, E. D. "F. V. Hayden, M. D., L. L. D." *American Geologist* 1 (Feb. 1888), 110–113.

Cowdrey, Bartlett. *National Academy of Design Exhibition Record, 1826-1860*. 2 vols. New York, 1943.

Cozens, Alexander. *A New Method of Assisting the Invention in Drawing Original Compositions of Landscape*. London, [1784]. Reprinted as appendix in Oppé, Adolph P. *Alexander and John Robert Cozens*. Cambridge, MA, 1954.

Crane, Newton. "Fairmount Park." *Scribner's* 1 (Jan. 1871), 225–238.

Crofutt, George. *Crofutt's New Overland Tourist, and Pacific Coast Guide*. Omaha, 1883.

Crook, Sheila, Jean Joseph, and Eileen Voce. "Artisans to Artists." *Manchester Genealogist* 26 (Oct. 1990), 23–29.

Crosby Opera House Art Association, Its Plan and Objects: Descriptive Catalogue of Over Three Hundred Valuable Premiums!... N.p., [1867].

Cummings, Thomas S. *Historic Annals of the National Academy of Design, from 1825 to the Present Time*. Philadelphia, 1865.

Cunningham, Elizabeth. "Corporate Collections." *Artists of the Rockies and the Golden West* (Summer 1984), 118–125.

Curtis, Atherton. *Catalogue de l'oeuvre lithographie de Eugène Isabey*. Paris, 1939.

Curtis, John Trevor. *The Public Schools of Philadelphia*. Philadelphia, 1897.

Danly, Susan, Cheryl Leibold, et al. *Eakins and the Photograph: Works by Thomas Eakins and His Circle in the Collection of the Pennsylvania Academy of the Fine Arts*. Washington and London, 1994.

Danly, Susan, and Leo Marx, eds. *The Railroad in American Art: Representations of Technological Change*. Cambridge and London, 1988.

Darrah, William Culp. "Beaman, Fennemore, Hillers, Dellenbaugh, Johnson, and Hattan." *Utah Historical Quarterly* 16–17 (1948–1949), 491–503.

_____. "The Powell Colorado River Expedition of 1869." *Utah Historical Quarterly* 15 (1947), 9–18.

_____. *The World of Stereographs*. Gettysburg, 1977.

Delteil, Loys. "Paul Huet." *Le Peintre-graveur illustré*. Vol. 8. Paris, 1911.

D'Emilio, Sandra, and Suzan Campbell. *Visions and Visionaries: The Art of the Santa Fe Railway*. Salt Lake City, 1991.

De Montaigu, A. "A Pen Picture of Mrs. M. Nimmo Moran." *Art Stationer* 1 (July 1888), 4–6. Reprinted in Fryxell 1958, 41–48.

Detroit Institute of Arts and the Toledo Museum of Art. *Travelers in Arcadia: American Artists in Italy, 1830-1875*. Detroit and Toledo, 1951.

DeVinne, Theodore Low. "The Growth of Woodcut Printing." *Scribner's* 19 (Apr. 1880), 860–874; and 20 (May 1880), 34–45.

_____. *Printing in the Nineteenth Century*. New York, 1924.

Dickason, David Howard. *The Daring Young Men: The Story of the American Pre-Raphaelites*. Bloomington, IN, 1953.

Dodge, Julia E. "An Island of the Sea." *Scribner's* 14 (Sept. 1877), 652–661.

Driesbach, Janice Tolhurst, with William H. Gerdts. *Direct from Nature: The Oil Sketches of Thomas Hill.* Yosemite National Park, CA, 1997.

Dwyer, Britta C. "Nineteenth-Century Regional Women Artists: The Pittsburgh School of Design for Women, 1865–1904." Ph.D. diss., University of Pittsburgh, 1989. Ann Arbor, 1989.

Dyos, Harold J., and Michael Wolff, eds. *The Victorian City: Images and Realities.* Boston, 1973.

Dyson, Anthony. *Pictures to Print: The Nineteenth-Century Engraving Trade.* London, 1984.

Engels, Friedrich. *The Conditions of the Working Class in England.* Liepzig, 1845. Reprinted Oxford and New York, 1993.

Everett, Morris T. "The Etchings of Mrs. Mary Nimmo Moran." *Brush and Pencil* 8 (Apr. 1901), 7–16.

Everts, Truman C. "Thirty-Seven Days of Peril." *Scribner's* 3 (Nov. 1871), 1–17.

Exman, Eugene. *The House of Harper: One Hundred and Fifty Years of Publishing.* New York, 1967.

Fairbanks, Jonathan L. *Frontier America: The Far West.* Boston, 1975.

Fairman, Charles. *Art and Artists of the Capitol of the United States of America."* 69th Cong., 1st sess., Senate doc. 95. Washington, DC, 1927.

Falk, Peter Hastings, ed. *The Annual Exhibition Record of the Art Institute of Chicago, 1888-1950....* Madison, CT, 1990. [Falk 1990a]

_____. *The Annual Exhibition Record of the National Academy of Design, 1901-1950....* Madison, CT, 1990. [Falk 1990b]

_____. *The Annual Exhibition Record of the Pennsylvania Academy of the Fine Arts, 1876-1913.* Vol 2. Madison, CT, 1989.

Ferber, Linda S. "'My dear friend': A Letter from Thomas Eakins to William T. Richards." *Archives of American Art Journal* 34 (1994), 15–22.

_____. *William Trost Richards (1833-1905): American Landscape and Marine Painting.* New York, 1980.

_____, and William H. Gerdts. *The New Path: Ruskin and the American Pre-Raphaelites.* Brooklyn, 1985.

Fifer, J. Valerie. *American Progress: The Growth of Transport, Tourist, and Information Industries in the Nineteenth-Century West, Seen through the Life and Times of George A. Crofutt....* Chester, CT, 1988.

Fink, Lois Marie. *American Art at the Nineteenth-Century Paris Salons.* Washington, DC, and New York, 1990.

Finkel, Kenneth. *Nineteenth-Century Photography in Philadelphia.* New York, 1980.

_____. *Philadelphia ReVisions: The Print Department Collects.* Philadelphia, 1983.

_____. "Vintage Views of Historic Philadelphia: Antiquarian Photography, 1853–1870." *Nineteenth Century* 6 (Summer 1980), 52–56.

Flint, Janet. "The American Painter-Lithographer." *Art & Commerce: American Prints of the Nineteenth Century.* Ed. Jonathan Fairbanks. Charlottesville, VA, 1978.

Forrester, Gillian. *Turner's "Drawing Book": The "Liber Studiorum."* London, 1996.

Foster, John Wells, and Josiah Dwight Whitney. *Report of the Geology of Lake Superior Land District: Part II, The Iron Region.* Washington, DC, 1851. [32nd Cong., special sess., Mar. 1851, Senate exec. doc. 4]

Foster, Kathleen A. "Makers of the American Watercolor Movement: 1860–1890." Ph.D. diss., Yale University, 1982. Ann Arbor, 1982.

_____, and Cheryl Leibold. *Writing about Eakins: The Manuscripts in Charles Bregler's Thomas Eakins Collection.* Philadelphia, [1989].

Foster, Mike. *Strange Genius: The Life of Ferdinand Vandeveer Hayden.* Niwot, CO, 1994.

Fowler, Don D. *The Western Photographs of John K. Hillers: "Myself in the Water."* Washington, DC, 1989.

Francis, F. "The Yellowstone Geysers." *Nineteenth Century* 11 (Mar. 1882), 369–377.

Francis, Marilyn G. "Mary Nimmo Moran: Painter-Etcher." *Woman's Art Journal* 4 (Fall/Winter 1984), 14–19.

Friese, Nancy. *Prints of Nature: Poetic Etchings of Mary Nimmo Moran.* Tulsa, 1984.

_____. "Themes and Methods in the Etchings of Mary Nimmo Moran." *Gilcrease Magazine of American History and Art* 6 (Oct. 1984), 10–22.

Fryxell, Fritiof M. "Brilliant Western American Color Plate Book." *The Month at Goodspeed's* 27 (Jan.–Feb. 1956), 87–89.

_____. "Climbing the Cross of Snow." *Canadian Alpine Journal* 21 (1932), 28–32.

_____. "William H. Jackson, Photographer, Artist, Explorer." *American Annual of Photography* (1939).

Gannon, Michael, ed. *The New History of Florida.* Gainesville, FL, 1996.

Gardner, Albert Ten Eyck. "Scientific Sources of the Full-Length Landscape: 1850." *Bulletin of the Metropolitan Museum of Art* 4 (Oct. 1945), 59–65.

Gardner, James T. "Hayden and Gardner's Survey of the Territories, Under the Direction of the Department of the Interior." *American Journal of Science and Arts.* 3rd ser. (Oct. 1873), 297–300.

Great Central Fair. *Catalogue of Paintings, Drawings, Statuary....* Philadelphia, 1864.

Gerdts, William H. "The Influence of Ruskin and Pre-Raphaelitism on American Still-Life Painting." *American Art Journal* 1 (Fall 1969), 80–97.

_____. "Thomas Birch: America's First Marine Artist." *Antiques* 89 (Apr. 1966), 528–533.

[Gilder, Richard Watson]. "Culture and Progress: The Yellowstone National Park." *Scribner's* 4 (May 1872), 120–121.

Gilder, Rosamond, ed. *Letters of Richard Watson Gilder.* Boston and New York, 1916.

Glassman, Elizabeth, and Marilyn F. Symmes. *"Cliché-verre": Hand-Drawn, Light-Printed. A Survey of the Medium from 1839 to the Present.* Detroit, 1980.

Godfrey, Richard. *Printmaking in Britain: A General History from Its Beginnings to the Present Day.* Oxford, 1978.

[Godkin, E.L.]. "Chromo-civilization." *The Nation* (24 Sept. 1874), 201–202.

Goetzmann, William H. *Exploration and Empire: The Explorer and the Scientist in the Winning of the American West.* New York, 1986.

_____, and Goetzmann, William N. *The West of the Imagination.* New York, 1986.

The Golden Age of American Illustration, 1880-1914. Wilmington, 1972.

Goldman, Paul. *Victorian Illustrated Books, 1850-1870: The Heyday of Woodcut.* Boston, 1994.

Gonse, Louis. "Coup d'oeil à vol d'oiseau sur L'Exposition Universelle." *Gazette des Beaux Arts* 47, ser. 2 (1878), 481–492.

_____, ed. *Exposition Universelle de 1878, les beaux-arts et les arts decoratifs.* Paris, 1879.

Goodyear, Frank H., Jr. *Pennsylvania Academicians.* Philadelphia, 1973.

Gottfried, Herbert Wilson. "Spatiality and the Frontier: Spatial Themes in Western American Painting and Literature." Ph.D. diss., Ohio University, 1974. Ann Arbor, 1974.

Gries, John C. "Geological Exploration as Related to Railroad Development in Kansas and the Western United States." *Earth Sciences History* 3 (1984), 129–133.

Hallock, Charles. *Camp Life in Florida: A Handbook for Sportsmen and Settlers*. New York, 1876.

Hamerton, Philip Gilbert. *The Graphic Arts*. London, 1882.

Harper, J. Henry. *The House of Harper: A Century of Publishing in Franklin Square*. New York, 1912.

Harper's Monthly 56 (Apr. 1878), 764–765: "A New Departure in American Art."

Harper's Monthly 58 (Mar. 1879), 481–496: "Present Tendencies of American Art."

Harper's Monthly 60 (Apr. 1880), 447: "A Symposium of Wood-Engravers."

Harper's Weekly 16 (30 Mar. 1872), 243: "The Geysers of the Yellowstone."

Harper's Weekly 33 (18 May 1889), 403: "The Picture of Commerce."

Harris, Neil. *Cultural Excursions: Marketing Appetites and Cultural Tastes in Modern America*. Chicago, 1990.

Harrison, Eliza Cope, ed. *Voyages of the Packet Ship "Thomas P. Cope," 1839–1846*. South Bend, IN, 1978.

Hayden, Ferdinand V. *The Great West: Its Attractions and Resources*. Philadelphia, 1880.

_____. "The Hot Springs and Geysers of the Yellowstone and Firehole Rivers." *American Journal of Science and Arts*., 3rd ser., 3 (Feb. 1872), 105–115; (Mar. 1872), 161–176. [Hayden 1872b; see Chronological References for Hayden 1872a]

_____. *Sixth Annual Report of the U.S. Geological Survey, Embracing Portions of Montana, Idaho, Wyoming and Utah*.... Washington, DC, 1873.

Hayes, A. A. "Vacation Aspects of Colorado." *Harper's Monthly* 60 (Mar. 1880), 542–557.

Hédiard, Germain. *Eugène Isabey. Étude suivi de catalogue de son oeuvre*. Paris, 1906.

Hedges, James B. "Promotion of Immigration to the Pacific Northwest by the Railroads." *Mississippi Valley Historical Review* 15 (Sept. 1928), 183–203.

Higgins, Charles A. *Grand Cañon of the Colorado River, Arizona*. Chicago, 1897. Reprinted 1907.

Hitchcock, Ripley. *Etching in America*. New York, 1886.

Hoeber, Arthur. "A Century of American Book Illustration." *Bookman* 8 (1898–1899), 213–219; 316–324; 429–439; 540–548.

Holmes, William Henry. "Random Records of a Lifetime Devoted to Science and Art, 1846–1931." 21 vols. Mss, National Museum of American Art, [1931].

Honour, Hugh, and John Fleming. *The Venetian Hours of Henry James, Whistler, and Sargent*. Boston, 1991.

Hood, G., N. Rivard, and K. Pyne. "American Paintings Acquired during the Last Decade." *Bulletin of the Detroit Institute of Arts* 55 (1977), 69–108.

Horgan, Mary B. "Our Leading Illustrators." *The Independent* 59 (Dec. 1905), 1408.

Houfe, Simon. *The Dictionary of British Book Illustrators and Caricaturists: 1800–1914*. Woodbridge, Suffolk [England], 1978.

Howat, John K. "Uniqueness and Internationalism in American Landscape Painting." *Apollo* 111 (May 1980), 386–391.

Hudson, Frederic. *Journalism in the United States, 1690–1872*. New York, 1873.

Hudson River Museum. *The Book of Nature: American Painters and the Natural Sublime*. Yonkers, NY, 1983.

Hunnisett, Basil. *Steel-Engraved Book Illustration in England*. Boston, 1980.

Huntington, David Carew. *Art and the Excited Spirit: America in the Romantic Period*. Ann Arbor, MI, 1972.

_____. *The Landscapes of Frederic Edwin Church: Vision of an American Era*. New York, [1966].

_____. *The Quest for Unity: American Art between World's Fairs, 1876–1893*. Detroit, 1983.

Hussey, Christopher. *The Picturesque: Studies in a Point of View*. London, 1967.

Huxley, Aldous. "Unpainted Landscapes." *Encounter* 19 (Oct. 1962), 41–47.

Huyghe, René. "Delacroix and Baudelaire: A New Epoch in Art and Poetry." *Arts Yearbook* 2 (1958), 26–46.

Illustrated Catalogue of Fine Art Studies, Water Color Studies, Pictures, Etc. Published by L. Prang & Co. Boston, 1889–1890. [*Illustrated Prang*]

Index of Slides: The People's Art Calendars, 1889–1989. Red Oak, IA, 1991.

Ingersoll, Ernest. *The Crest of the Continent*. Chicago, 1885.

_____. *Knocking Round the Rockies*. New York, 1882. [Ingersoll 1882a]

_____. "Silver San Juan." *Harper's Monthly* 64 (Apr. 1882), 689–704. [Ingersoll 1882b]

Ingram, J. S. *The Centennial Exposition, Described and Illustrated*.... Philadelphia, 1876.

International Exhibition 1862: Official Catalogue, Fine Arts Department. London, 1862.

International Exhibition 1876: Official Catalogue, Part II. Art Gallery, Annexes, and Out-Door Works of Art. Philadelphia, 1876

International Review 1 (Jan. 1874), 1–16: "Our Late Panic."

International Studio 90 (July 1928), 78: "Exhibitions."

Ivins, William. *Prints and Visual Communication*. Cambridge, MA, 1953.

Jackson, William Henry. *The Diaries of William Henry Jackson, Frontier Photographer*. Ed. Ann W. Hafen and Leroy R. Hafen. Glendale, CA, 1959.

_____. "First Official Visit to the Cliff Dwellings." *Colorado Magazine* 1 (July 1924), 151–159.

_____. "Photographing the Colorado Rockies Fifty Years Ago." *Colorado Magazine* 3 (Mar. 1926), 11–22.

_____. *Pioneer Photographer: Rocky Mountain Adventures with a Camera*. Yonkers-on-Hudson, 1929.

_____. *Time Exposure: The Autobiography of William Henry Jackson*. 1940. Reprinted Albuquerque, 1986.

Jackson, W. Turrentine. "The Creation of Yellowstone National Park." *Mississippi Valley Historical Review* 29 (Sept. 1942), 187–206.

_____. "The Washburn-Doane Expedition into the Upper Yellowstone, 1870." *Pacific Historical Review* 10 (June 1941), 189–208.

Jacobowitz, Arlena. *James Hamilton, 1819–1878: American Marine Painter*. Brooklyn, 1966.

Jarves, James Jackson. *Art Thoughts*. New York, 1871.

Jenkins, Tom. "Summons to a Summit." *Westways* 75 (Aug. 1983), 40–42, 62.

John, Arthur. *The Best Years of the "Century": Richard Watson Gilder, "Scribner's Monthly," and the "Century Magazine," 1870–1909*. Urbana, IL, 1981.

Johnson, Barry C., ed. *"Ho, For the Great West!" and Other Original Papers to Mark the 25th Anniversary of the English Westerners' Society*. London, 1980.

Jussim, Estelle. *Visual Communication and the Graphic Arts: Photographic Technologies in the Nineteenth Century*. New York, 1983.

Kainen, Jacob. "Why Beewick Succeeded: A Note in the History of Wood Engraving." *Contributions from the Museum of History and Technology*. no. 218 (Washington, DC, 1959), 186–201.

Kellogg, Louise Phelps. "Wisconsin at the Centennial." *Wisconsin Magazine of History* 10 (Sept. 1926), 3–16.

Keppel, Frederick. *Catalogue of the Etched Work of Peter Moran*. New York, 1888.

Kinsey, Joni L. *Plain Pictures: Images of the American Prairie*. Washington, DC, 1996.

Klackner, C. *Proofs and Prints, Engravings and Etchings: How They Are Made... and How to Select Them.* New York, 1886.

Knoepflmacher, U.C., and G.B. Tennyson, eds. *Nature and the Victorian Imagination.* Berkeley, [1977].

Koehler, S.R. *American Art.* New York, 1886.

_____. "The Works of the American Etchers. XX—Mrs. M. Nimmo Moran." *American Art Review* 2 (1881), 153.

Kramer, Howard D. "The Scientist in the West, 1870–1880." *Pacific Historical Review* 12 (Sept. 1943), 239–251.

Laffan, W. Mackay. "The Tile Club at Work." *Scribner's* 17 (Jan. 1879), 401–410.

_____, and Edward Strahan [Earl Shinn]. "The Tile Club at Play." *Scribner's* 17 (Feb. 1879), 457–478.

Lambert, Susan. *The Image Multiplied: Five Centuries of Printed Reproductions of Paintings and Drawings.* New York, 1987.

Lane, Christopher W., and Donald H. Cresswell. *Prints of Philadelphia at the Philadelphia Print Shop, Featuring the Wohl Collection.* Philadelphia, 1990.

Langford, Nathaniel P. "The Wonders of the Yellowstone." *Scribner's* 2 (May and June 1871), 1–17; 113–128.

Lanier, Sidney. *Florida: Its Scenery, Climate, and History.* Philadelphia, 1876.

Lansdale, Maria Hornor. "Life-Work and Homes of Richard Watson Gilder." *The Century* (Mar. 1911), 716–733.

Larson, Judy L. *American Illustration, 1890–1925: Romance, Adventure & Suspense.* Calgary [Canada], 1986.

_____, with Cynthia Payne. *Graphic Arts & the South.* Fayetteville, AK, 1993.

Lears, T. J. Jackson. *No Place of Grace: Antimodernism and the Transformation of American Culture, 1880–1920.* Chicago, 1981.

Lee, Eric M. *Translations: Turner and Printmaking.* New Haven, 1993.

Leja, Michael. "The Illustrated Magazines and Print Connoisseurship in the Late 19th Century." *BlockPoints* (1993), 54–73.

Leslie, Frank. *Paris Universal Exposition, 1867: Reports of the United States Commissioners...on the Fine Arts.* Washington, DC, 1868.

Levin, Jo Ann Early. "The Golden Age of Illustration: Popular Art in American Magazines, 1850–1925." Ph.D. diss., University of Pennsylvania, 1980.

Levy, Florence N., ed. *American Art Annual.* New York, 1899.

Linton, William J. "The Engraver: His Function and Status." *Scribner's* 16 (June 1878), 237–242.

_____. *The History of Wood Engraving in America.* Boston, 1881.

_____. "Linton's Hints on Wood Engraving." *Scribner's* 19 (Apr. 1880), 793.

Longfellow, Henry Wadsworth. *The Song of Hiawatha.* Boston, 1856 [with extract (pp. 311–313) from Foster and Whitney 1851].

Longworth, James H. *The Cotton Mills of Bolton, 1780–1985: A Historical Directory.* Bolton, 1987.

Lovell, Margaretta M. *A Visitable Past: Views of Venice by American Artists, 1860–1915.* Chicago, 1989.

Lummis, Charles F. "Strange Corners of Our Country." *St. Nicholas* 19 (Dec. 1891), 122–129.

Lyles, Anne, and Diane Perkins. *Colour into Line: Turner and the Art of Engraving.* London, 1989.

Madison, Charles. *Book Publishing in America.* New York, 1966.

Manthorne, Katherine. "The Quest for a Tropical Paradise: Palm Trees as Fact and Symbol in Latin American Landscape Imagery, 1850–1875." *Art Journal* 44 (Winter 1984), 374–382.

_____. *Tropical Renaissance: North American Artists Exploring Latin America, 1839–1879.* Washington, DC, 1989.

Marlor, Clark S. *A History of the Brooklyn Art Association with an Index of Exhibitions.* New York, [1970].

Martinez, Katharine. "John Sartain (1808–1897): His Contribution to American Printmaking." *Imprint* 8 (Spring 1983), 1–12.

_____. "'Messengers of Love, Tokens of Friendship': Gift-Book Illustrations by John Sartain." In *The American Illustrated Book in the Nineteenth Century.* Ed. Gerald W. R. Ward. Winterthur, DE, 1987.

Marx, Leo. *The Machine in the Garden: Technology and the Pastoral Ideal in America.* New York, 1964.

_____. "The Railroad-in-the-Landscape: An Iconological Reading of a Theme in American Art" *Prospects* 10 (1985), 77–117.

Marzio, Peter C. *The Art Crusade: An Analysis of American Drawing Manuals, 1820–1860.* Washington, DC, 1976.

_____. *The Democratic Art: Pictures for a 19th-Century America.* Boston, 1979.

_____. "The Democratic Art of Chromolithography in America: An Overview." In *Art & Commerce: American Prints of the Nineteenth-Century*, Ed. Jonathan Fairbanks. Charlottesville, VA, 1978.

Mattes, Merrill J. "Behind the Legend of Colter's Hell: The Early Exploration of Yellowstone National Park." *Mississippi Valley Historical Review* 36 (Sept. 1949), 251–282.

May, Earl Chapin. "Murphy of Red Oak." *Everybody's Magazine* 52 (Oct. 1925), 36–42.

Mayor, A. Hyatt, and Mark Davis. *American Art at the Century.* New York, 1977.

McCabe, James D. *The Illustrated History of the Centennial Exhibition....* Philadelphia, 1876.

McClinton, Katherine Morrison. *The Chromolithography of Louis Prang.* New York, 1973.

McGreevy, Patrick V. *Imagining Niagara: The Meaning and Making of Niagara Falls.* Amherst, 1994.

McKenzie, Betty. "The People's Art: One Hundred Years of Calendar Art." *American Art Review* 6 (Feb./Mar. 1994), 116–123.

Miller, David C. *Dark Eden: the Swamp in Nineteenth-Century American Culture.* Cambridge and New York, 1989.

Miller, J. Hillis. *Illustration.* Cambridge, MA, 1992.

Miller, Lillian B. *Patrons and Patriotism: The Encouragement of the Fine Arts in the United States, 1790–1860.* Chicago, 1966.

_____, Walter T. K. Nugent, and H. Wayne Morgan. *Indiana Historical Society Lectures, 1972–1973: 1876 Centennial Year.* Indianapolis, 1973.

Mitnick, Barbara Jacobs. "Jean Leon Gerome Ferris: America'a Painter Historian." Ph.D. diss., Rutgers, The State University of New Jersey, 1983. Ann Arbor, 1983.

Modelski, Andrew M. *Railroad Maps of North America: The First Hundred Years.* Washington, DC, 1984.

Moneta, Daniela P. ed. *Chas. T. Lummis—The Centennial Exhibition Commemorating His Tramp across the Continent.* Los Angeles, 1985.

Montgomery, Walter, ed. *American Art and American Art Collections: Essays on Artistic Subjects by the Best Art Writers, Fully Illustrated with Etchings....* Boston, 1889.

Moran, Edward. "Marine Painting: ...Hints for Practical Study." *Art Amateur* 19 (Oct. and Nov. 1888), 101–103; 127–128.

_____. "Reminiscences of Mr. Edward Moran." *Art Amateur* 31 (July 1894), 52.

Moran, John. "The American Water-Color Society's Exhibition." *Art Journal* [NY] 4 (1878), 91–93.

_____. "Artist-Life in New York." *Art Journal* [NY] 6 (Feb. and Apr. 1880), 57–60; and 121–124.

_____. "New York Studios." *Art Journal* [NY] 6 (Jan. 1880), 1–4.

_____. "Reflections on Art." *Philadelphia Photographer* 12 (Oct. 1875), 294–295.

_____. "The Relation of Photography to the Fine Arts." *Philadelphia Photographer* 2 (Mar. 1865), 33–35.

_____. "Studio Life in New York." *Art Journal* [NY] 5 (Nov. and Dec. 1879), 343–345; and 353–355.

_____. "Thoughts on Art, Nature, and Photography." *Philadelphia Photographer* 12 (June 1875), 179–181.

Morgan, Lady. *The Life and Times of Salvator Rosa.* 2 vols. London, 1824.

Mott, Frank L. *A History of American Magazines, 1865–1885.* Cambridge, MA, 1967.

Moure, Nancy Dustin Wall. "Five Eastern Artists out West." *American Art Journal* 5 (Nov. 1973), 15–31.

Muir, John. "Feature of the Proposed Yosemite National Park." *Century Magazine* 11 (Sept. 1890), 656–667.

_____. *Picturesque California....* 2 vols. New York, 1888.

Mumford, Lewis. *The Brown Decades: A Study of the Arts in America, 1865–1895.* New York, [1931].

Murphy, Thomas Dowler. *The Art Calendar Industry: The Story of the Early Struggles of the Founders with a Short History of the Thos. D. Murphy Co.* Red Oak, IA, 1912.

Murphy Press. *Where Murphy Calendars Are Made: A Pictorial Study.* Red Oak, IA, 1908.

Museum of Fine Arts. *Exhibition of the Works of Women Etchers of America* [Nov-Dec. 1887]. Boston, 1887.

Museum of Fine Arts. *Nineteenth-Century American Landscape Painting: Selections from the Thyssen-Bornamisza Collection.* Houston, 1983.

Myers, Kenneth. *The Catskills: Painters, Writers, and Tourists in the Mountains, 1820–1895.* Yonkers, NY, 1987.

National Academy of Design Catalogue of the Sixth Winter Exhibition... of the American Society of Painters in Watercolors, and the English Collection of Watercolors and Sketches. N.p., 1873.

National Academy of Design. *Next to Nature: Landscape Paintings from the National Academy of Design.* New York, 1980.

National Gallery of Art. *Thomas Moran Memorial Exhibition.* Washington, DC, 1937.

Naylor, Maria. *The National Academy of Design Exhibition Record, 1861–1900.* 2 vols. New York, 1973.

Neuhaus, Eugene. *The Galleries of the Exposition: A Critical Review of the Paintings, Statuary, and the Graphic Arts in the Palace of Fine Arts at the Panama-Pacific International Exposition.* San Francisco, 1915.

New York Etching Club. *Catalogue of Etching Proofs.* New York, 1891, 1892.

New York World Telegram and Sun, 18 Dec. 1953: "Christmas Collector's Item."

Newark Industrial Exhibition. *Report and Catalogue of the First Exhibition of Newark Industries.* Newark, NJ, 1872.

Newhall, Beaumont. *The History of Photography: From 1839 to the Present Day.* New York, 1964; rev. ed. 1982.

_____, and Diana E. Edkins. *William H. Jackson.* Fort Worth, 1974.

Novak, Barbara. *Nature and Culture: American Landscape and Painting, 1825–1865.* New York, 1980. Rev. ed, 1995.

Nutty, Carolyn Sue Himelick. "Joseph Harrison, Jr. (1810–1874), Philadelphia Art Collector." Ph.D. diss., University of Delaware, 1993. Ann Arbor, 1993.

Oakland Museum. *Tropical Scenes by the 19th Century Painters of California.* Oakland, CA, 1971.

O'Brien, Maureen C., and Patricia C.F. Mandel. *The American Painter-Etcher Movement.* Southhampton, NY, 1984.

Oppé, Adolph P. *Alexander and John Robert Cozens.* Cambridge, MA, 1954.

_____. "Fresh Light on Alexander Cozens." *Print Collector's Quarterly* 8 (Apr. 1921), 61–90.

Pan American Exposition. *Official Handbook of Architecture and Sculpture and Art Catalogue....* Buffalo, NY, 1901.

Pangborn, J.G. *Picturesque B. & O.* Chicago, 1882.

_____. *The Rocky Mountain Tourist.* Topeka, KS, 1877.

Panzer, Mary. "Romantic Origins of American Realism: Photography, Arts, and Letters in Philadelphia, 1850–1875." Ph.D. diss., Boston University, 1990. Ann Arbor, 1995.

Parton, James. "Popularizing Art." *Atlantic Monthly* 23 (Mar. 1869), 348–357.

Patterson, William C. "The Philadelphia Society of Painter Etchers." *Imprint* 19 (Fall 1994), 17–29.

Pearson, Andrea G. "Frank Leslie's *Illustrated Newspaper* and *Harper's Weekly*: Innovation and Immitation in Nineteenth-Century American Pictorial Reporting." *Journal of Popular Culture* 23 (Spring 1990), 81–111.

Peet, Phyllis. *American Women of the Etching Revival.* Atlanta, 1988.

_____. "Emily Sartain: America's First Woman Mezzotint Engraver." *Imprint* 9 (Fall 1984), 19–26.

Pennell, Joseph. *The Adventures of an Illustrator.* Boston, 1925.

_____. *The Graphic Arts: Modern Men and Modern Methods.* Chicago, 1921.

_____. *Modern Illustration.* London and New York, 1895.

Peters, Harry T. *America on Stone: The Other Printmakers to the American People. A Chronicle of American Lithography....* [Garden City, NY], 1931.

Peters-Campbell, John R. "The Big Picture and the Epic American Landscape." Ph.D. diss., Cornell University, 1989.

Philadelphia Museum of Art. *Philadelphia: Three Centuries of American Art.* Philadelphia, 1976.

Philadelphia Photographer (Apr. 1872), 124–125: "Our Picture."

Philadelphia Sketch Club. *Catalogue of the First Annual Exhibition... Held at the Pennsylvania Academy of the Fine Arts.* Philadelphia, 1865.

Photographic News (8 May 1863), 226.

Pisano, Ronald G. *Long Island Landscape Painting.* 2 vols. Boston, 1985 and 1990.

Porte Crayon [Strother, David Hunter]. "Artist's Excursion Over the Baltimore and Ohio Rail Road." *Harper's Monthly* 14 (June 1859), 1–19.

Powell, John Wesley. "The Cañons of the Colorado." *Scribner's* 9 (Jan., Feb., Mar. 1875), 293–310, 394–409, 523–537. [Powell 1875a]

_____. *Explorations of the Colorado of the West and Its Tributaries.* Washington, DC, 1875. [Powell 1875b]

_____. "An Overland Trip to the Grand Cañon." *Scribner's* 10 (Oct. 1875), 659–678.

Prang, Louis. "Chromo-Lithography the Handmaiden of Painting." *NY Tribune*, 1 Dec. 1866.

Princeton University. *Early American Book Illustrators and Wood Engravers, 1670–1870.* Princeton, NJ, 1968.

Prown, Jules David, et al. *Discovered Lands, Invented Pasts: Transforming Visions of the American West.* New Haven and London, 1992.

Royal Academy. *The Exhibition of the Royal Academy of Arts. The One Hundred and Eleventh.* London, 1879.

Rambler [pseud.]. *Guide to Florida.* New York, 1875. Facsimile reprint edition with an introduction by Rembert W. Patrick, Gainesville, FL, 1964.

Rattray, Jeannette Edwards. *The Maidstone Club, 1891–1941.* East Hampton, 1941.

Raymond, R.W. "The Heart of the Continent: The Hot Springs and Geysers of the Yellow Stone Region." *Harper's Weekly* 17 (5 Apr. 1873), 272–273.

Report on the Progress and Condition of the United States National Museum for the Year Ending June 30, 1917. Washington, DC, 1918.

Richardson, Albert D. *Beyond the Mississippi: From the Great River to the Great Ocean. Life and Adventure on the Prairies, Mountains, and Pacific Coast.* Hartford, CT, 1867. Reprinted New York, 1968.

Richardson, Edgar P. *The World of the Romantic Artist; A Survey of American Culture from 1800 to 1875.* Detroit, 1944.

Richardson, James, ed. *Wonders of the Yellowstone.* New York, 1873.

Rindge, Debora Anne. "The Painted Desert: Images of the American West from the Geological and Geographical Surveys of the Western Territories, 1867–1879." Ph.D. diss., University of Maryland, 1993.

Ripley, George, and Charles A. Dana, eds. *The American Cyclopaedia: A Popular Dictionary of General Knowledge.* Vol. 11. New York, 1875.

Roberts, Edwards. *Shoshone and Other Western Wonders.* New York, 1888.

Rosenberger, Francis Coleman, ed. *Records of the Columbia Historical Society of Washington, D.C., the Fiftieth Volume.* Washington, DC, 1980.

Runte, Alfred. "The National Park Idea: Origins and Paradox of the American Experience." *Journal of Forest History* 21 (Apr. 1977), 64–75.

_____. "Pragmatic Alliance: Western Railroads and the National Parks." *National Parks & Conservation Magazine* 48 (Apr. 1974), 14–21.

Ruskin, John. *The Art Criticism of John Ruskin.* Ed. Robert L. Herbert. New York, 1964. Reprinted New York, 1987.

Rutledge, Anna Wells, ed. *Cumulative Record of Exhibition Catalogues: The Pennsylvania Academy of the Fine Arts, 1807–1870, The Society of Artists, 1800–1814, The Artist's Fund Society, 1835–1845.* Philadelphia, 1955. Rev. ed., Madison, CT, 1988.

Salon cat. *Explication des ouvrages de peinture, sculpture, architecture, gravure, et lithographie des artistes vivants, exposés au Palais des Champs-Elysees....* Paris, 1867.

Samson, John. "Photographs from the High Rockies." *Harper's Monthly* 39 (Sept. 1869), 465–475.

Sanders, Patricia B. *The Haggin Collection.* Stockton, CA, 1991.

Sandweiss, Martha A., ed. *Photography in Nineteenth-Century America.* New York, 1991.

[Sartain, Emily.] "Private Art-Collections of Philadelphia." *Lippincott's Magazine* 9 and 10 (Apr.–Dec. 1872), 437–446, 571–576, 702–709, 76–81, 221–230, 331–336, 454–458, 588–593, 705–710.

Sartain, John. *The Reminiscences of a Very Old Man.* New York, 1899.

_____, ed. *The American Gallery of Art.* Philadelphia, 1848.

Schantz, Michael W. *Peter Moran, 1841–1914.* Philadelphia, 1986.

Schneider, Rona. "The American Etching Revival: Its French Sources and Early Years." *American Art Journal* 14 (1982), 40–65.

_____. *American Painter Etchings, 1853–1908.* New York, 1989.

Schramm, Wilbur Lang. "Hiawatha and Its Predecessors." *Philological Quarterly* 11, no. 4 (Oct. 1932), 321–343.

Schweizer, Paul D. *Edward Moran (1829–1901), American Marine and Landscape Painter.* Wilmington, DE, 1979.

Scranton, Philip. *Proprietary Capitalism: The Textile Manufacture at Philadelphia, 1800–1885.* Cambridge, 1983.

Scribner's 18 (July 1879), 456: "Engraving on Wood."

Scribner's 21 (Apr. 1881), 941: "Wood-Engraving and the Scribner's Prize."

Sears, John F. *Sacred Places: American Tourist Attractions in the Nineteenth Century.* New York and Oxford, 1989.

Seckinger, Katharine Villard, ed. "The Great Railroad Celebration, 1883: A Narrative by Francis Jackson Garrison." *Montana* 33 (Summer 1983), 12–23.

Sellers, Coleman. "Foreign Correspondence." *British Journal of Photography* (15 Aug. and 2 Nov. 1863), 334, 435; (1 and 15 Jan. and 12 Aug. 1864), 18, 31, and 298.

[Sheldon, George W.]. "American Painters: Edward Moran." *Art Journal* [NY] 6 (Sept. 1880), 257–259.

Shikes, Robert H. "Colorado's First Physicians." *Colorado Heritage* 4 (1983), 18–24.

Simon, Janice. "'The Crayon,' 1855–1861: The Voice of Nature in Criticism, Poetry, and the Fine Arts." Ph.D. diss., University of Michigan, 1990. Ann Arbor, 1993.

Smalley, E.V. "The New North-West." *Century Magazine* 24 (Aug.–Oct. 1882), 504–512, 769–779, and 863–872; and 25 (Feb. 1883), 529–537.

Smith, Francis Hopkinson. *American Illustrators.* New York, 1892.

Smith, Henry Nash. "Clarence King, John Wesley Powell, and the Establishment of the United States Geological Survey." *Mississippi Valley Historical Review* 34 (June 1947), 37–58.

Smith, Herbert F. *Richard Watson Gilder.* New York, 1970.

Smith, R.A. *Philadelphia as It Is, in 1852.* Philadelphia, 1852.

Smithsonian Institution. *Annual Report of the Board of Regents.* Washington, DC, 1923.

Smithsonian Institution. National Collection of Fine Arts. *American Landscape: A Changing Frontier.* Washington, DC, 1966.

_____. *1876: American Art of the Centennial.* Washington, DC, 1976.

Stainton, Lindsay. *Turner's Venice.* London, 1985.

Staley, Allen, ed. *The Post-Pre-Raphaelite Print.* New York, 1995.

Statutes at Large and Proclamations of the United States [Mar. 1871 to Mar. 1873], 17:347, 362.

Statutes at Large of the United States [Dec. 1873 to Mar. 1875], vol. 18, part 3, pp. 204, 209.

Stebbins, Theodore E., Jr. *American Master Drawings and Watercolors.* New York, 1976.

Stegner, Wallace E. "Jack Sumner and John Wesley Powell." *Colorado Magazine* 26 (Jan. 1949), 61–69.

_____, and William H. Goetzmann. "'The Most Sublime of All Earthly Spectacles': The Grand Canyon, and Two of Its Most Eminent Biographers." *American West* 15 (May/June 1978), 17–29, 61–63.

Stein, Roger B. *John Ruskin and Aesthetic Thought in America, 1840–1900.* Cambridge, MA, 1967.

_____. *Susquehanna: Images of the Settled Landscape.* Binghamton, NY, 1981.

Stoddard, Richard Henry, ed. *A Century After: Picturesque Glimpses of Philadelphia and Pennsylvania....* Philadelphia, 1876.

Stowe, Harriet Beecher. *Dred: Tale of the Great Dismal Swamp.* Boston, 1856.

_____. *Palmetto-Leaves.* Boston, 1873.

Strahan, Edward [Earl Shinn]. *The Art Gallery of the Exhibition: A Selection from the Paintings and Sculpture.* Philadelphia, 1877.

_____. *The Masterpieces of the Centennial International Exhibition, 1876: Illustrated Catalogue.* Vol. 1. Philadelphia, 1875.

Strickler, Susan, ed. *American Traditions in Watercolor: The Worcester Art Museum Collection.* New York, 1987.

Stucker, Gilbert F. "Hayden in the Badlands." *American West* 4 (Feb. 1967), 40–45, 79–85.

Sutro, Theodore. *Thirteen Chapters of American History: Represented by the Edward Moran Series of Thirteen Historical Marine Paintings.* New York, 1905.

Sweeney, J. Gray. "The Artist-Explorers of the American West: 1860–1990." Ph.D. diss., Indiana University, 1975.

_____. *Artists of Michigan from the Nineteenth Century.* Muskegon, MI, 1987.

_____. *Great Lakes Marine Painting of the Nineteenth Century.* Muskegon, MI, 1983.

Szarkowski, John, ed. *The Photographer and the American Landscape.* New York, [1963]

Taft, Robert. *Artists and Illustrators of the Old West.* New York, 1953.

_____. *Photography and the American Scene; A Social History, 1839–1889.* New York, 1964.

Taylor, Colin. "'Ho, For the Great West!'...The West of William Blackmore." In Johnson 1980.

Tebbel, John William. *A History of Book Publishing in the United States.* Vol. 2, *The Expansion of an Industry 1865–1919.* New York, 1975.

Tobias, Michael. *A Vision of Nature: Traces of the Original World.* Kent, OH, 1995.

Toll, Roger W., ed. "The Hayden Survey in Colorado in 1873 and 1874: Letters from James T. Gardiner." *Colorado Magazine* 6 (July 1929), 146–166.

Trachtenberg, Alan. *The Incorporation of America.* New York, 1982.

Trask, John E.D., and J. Nilsen Laurvik, eds. *Catalogue De Luxe of the Department of Fine Arts Panama-Pacific International Exposition.* San Francisco, 1915.

Trenton, Patricia, and Peter H. Hassrick. *The Rocky Mountains: A Vision for Artists in the Nineteenth Century.* Norman, OK, 1983.

Troyen, Carol. "Innocents Abroad: American Painters at the 1867 Exposition Universelle, Paris." *American Art Journal* 16 (Fall 1984), 2–29.

Truettner, William H., and Robin Bolton-Smith. *National Parks and the American Landscape.* Washington, DC, 1972.

Tyler, Francine. *American Etchings of the Nineteenth Century.* New York, 1984.

_____. "The First American Painter-Etchers." *Print Review* 16 (1983), 34–47.

Union League Club. *Catalogue of the Work of the Women Etchers of America.* New York, 1888.

U.S. Christian Commission. *Catalogue of the Exhibition of a Private Collection of Works of Art... Held at the Academy of the Fine Arts, Philadelphia.* Philadelphia, 1864.

U.S. Congress. *Congressional Globe.* 42nd Cong., 2nd sess., 30 Jan. 1872, 697.

_____. *Congressional Globe.* 42nd Cong., 2nd sess., 27 Feb. 1872, 1228.

_____. *Congressional Globe.* 42nd Cong., 2nd sess., 5 Mar. 1872, 1416.

U.S. House. 43rd Cong., 1st sess., 1873–1874, H.R. 3600, 13–14.

Van Nostrand, Jeanne Skinner. *The First Hundred Years of Painting in California, 1775–1875.* San Francisco, 1980.

Verburg, JoAnn. "On the Re-photographing of the Mountain of the Holy Cross." *New Observations* (Sept.–Oct. 1995), 5–7.

Visitor's Guide to the Centennial Exhibition and Philadelphia. Philadelphia, 1875.

Voce, Eileen. "From Artisans to Artists." Pennsylvania Academy of Fine Arts Library, vertical files. Philadelphia, 1990.

Wagner, Ann Prentice. "The Graver, the Brush, and the Ruling Machine: The Training of Late Nineteenth-Century Wood Engravers." *Proceedings of the American Antiquarian Society* 105 (1995), 167–191.

Wainwright, Nicholas B. *Philadelphia in the Romantic Age of Lithography.* Philadelphia, 1958. Reprinted 1970.

Waldsmith, John S. *Stereo Views.* Radnor, PA, 1991.

Walgamott, Chas. S. *Reminiscences of Early Days: A Series of Historical Sketches and Happenings in the Early Days of Snake River Valley.* Twin Falls, ID, 1926.

Walker, Francis A., ed. *United States Centennial Commission, International Exhibition 1876: Reports and Awards....* Philadelphia, 1877.

Walker, J. B. "Great Railway Systems of the United States. Sixteen Hundred Miles of Mountain Railways." *Cosmopolitan* 19 (May 1895), 2–28.

Wallace, Marcia Briggs. "The 'Great Bear' and 'The Prince of the Evil Spirits': The American Response to J.M.W. Turner before the Advent of John Ruskin." Ph.D. diss., City University of New York, 1993. Ann Arbor, 1993.

Wallace, Richard W. *Salvator Rosa in America.* Wellesley, MA, 1979.

Walls, Nina de Angeli. "Art and Industry and Women's Education: Philadelphia School of Design for Women 1848–1932." Ph.D. diss., University of Delaware, 1995.

Walton, W. *The Chefs-d'oeuvres of the Exposition Universelle.* Vol. 3. Philadelphia, 1900.

Wasserman, Emily. "The Artist-Explorers." *Art in America* 60 (July–Aug. 1972), 48–57.

Watrous, James. *A Century of American Printmaking, 1880–1980.* Madison, WI, 1984.

World's Columbian Exposition. *Revised Catalogue Department of Fine Arts.* Chicago, 1893.

Weber, Carl J. *The Rise and Fall of James Ripley Osgood: A Biography.* Waterville, ME, 1959.

Weigle, Marta, and Barbara A. Babcock, eds. *The Great Southwest of the Fred Harvey Company and the Santa Fe Railway.* Phoenix, 1996.

Weinberg, Gail S. *Drawings of John Ruskin, 1819–1900.* Cambridge, MA, 1979.

Weitenkampf, Frank. *American Graphic Art.* New York, 1924.

_____. "Early American Landscape Prints." *Art Quarterly* 8 (Winter 1945), 40–67.

_____. "Painter-Lithography in the United States." *Scribner's* 33 (June 1903), 544.

West, Elliott. "Selling the Myth: Western Images in Advertising." *Montana: The Magazine of Western History* 46 (Summer 1996), 36–49.

Whipple, Enez. *Guild Hall of East Hampton.* New York, 1993.

White, Robert R. "An 1883 Etching of Santa Fe by Peter Moran." *Imprint* 20 (Spring 1995), 34–35.

_____. "The Southwestern Etchings of Peter Moran: A History and Catalogue." *Imprint* 19 (Spring 1994), 11–28.

Whiteman, Maxwell. *Paintings and Sculpture at the Union League of Philadelphia.* Philadelphia, 1978.

Whitney, J.D. "Geographical and Geological Surveys." *North American Review* 121 (July and Oct. 1875), 37–85, 270–313.

Whittlesey, Lee H. "Monarch of All These Mighty Wonders: Tourists and Yellowstone's Excelsior Geyser, 1881–1890." *Montana* (Spring 1990), 2–15.

_____. *Yellowstone Place Names.* Helena, MT, 1988.

_____, ed. "In Yellowstone Park, 1886–1889: George Tutherly's Reminiscences." *Montana* 33 (Winter 1983), 2–13.

Wilkins, Thurman. *Clarence King.* New York, 1958.

Wilson, Raymond L. *Index of American Watercolor Exhibitions 1900–1945.* Metuchen, NJ, 1994

Wilton, Andrew. *Painting and Poetry: Turner's "Verse Book" and His Work of 1804–1812.* London, 1990.

_____. *Turner and the Sublime.* London, 1980.

Winchester, Alice. "Maxim Karolik and His Collections." *Art in America* (Fall 1957), 34–41.

Wolfe, Gerard R. *The House of Appleton.* Metuchen, NJ, 1981.

Woodward, David. "The Decline of Wood-Engraving in Nineteenth-Century America." *Journal of the Printing Historical Society* 10 (1974–1975), 66–69.

Wray, Henry Russell. *A Review of Etching in the United States.* Philadelphia, 1893.

Wright, Helena E. *With Pen and Graver: Women Graphic Artists before 1900.* Washington, DC, 1995.

Yarnall, James L., and William H. Gerdts. *The National Museum of American Art's Index to American Exhibition Catalogues from the Beginning through the 1876 Centennial.* 6 vols. Boston, 1986.

Sources of Moran's Illustrations

BOOKS

Beadle, J. H. *The Undeveloped West, or Five Years in the Territories.* Philadelphia, 1873. (28)

Benjamin, Samuel G. W. *Art in America.* New York, 1880. (1)

Bowen, James A. *The Rand-McNally Grammar School Geography.* New York, 1897. (1)

Brewer, William H. *Warren's New Physical Geography.* Philadelphia, 1890. (6)

Brooks, Noah. *The Boy Emigrants.* New York, 1914. (3)

Bryant, William Cullen. *A Library of Poetry and Song.* New York, 1873 (3)

Bryant, William Cullen, ed. *Picturesque America. . . .* Vol. 2. New York, 1874. (40)

Bryant, William Cullen, and Sydney Howard Gay. *A Popular History of the United States. . . .* 4 vols. New York, 1876–1881. (29)

Catalogue of the A. T. Stewart Collection. New York, 1887. (1 etching)

Clemmer, Mary. *The Poetical Works of Alice and Phoebe Cary.* Cambridge, MA, 1876. (3)

Coffin, Charles Carleton. *Old Times in the Colonies.* New York, 1880. (2)

Cone, Mary. *Two Years in California.* Chicago, 1876. (1)

Conklin, Enoch. *Picturesque Arizona.* New York, 1878. (6)

Devens, R. M. *American Progress, or the Great Events of the Greatest Century.* Chicago, 1882. (17)

Dodge, Henry Nehemiah. "*Christus Victor*": *A Student's Reverie.* New York and London, 1926. (19 halftones)

Dutton, Clarence E. *Tertiary History of the Grand Canyon District.* Washington, DC, 1882.

The Eclectic Elementary Geography. New York, 1883. (5)

Fairmount Park Commissioners. *Annual Report.* Philadelphia, 1878. (4)

Fairmount Park Commissioners. *Third Annual Report. . . .* Philadelphia, 1871.

Fossett, Frank. *Colorado: A Tourist's Guide to the Rocky Mountains.* New York, 1879. (8)

French, Harry W. *Through Arctics and Tropics: Around the World by a New Path for a New Purpose.* Boston, 1892. (2)

Frye, Alex Everett. *Complete Geography.* Boston, 1895. (5)

Gill, William Fearing, ed. *Laurel Leaves: Original Poems, Stories and Essays by Henry W. Longfellow, John G. Whittier, and Others.* Boston, 1876. Reprinted Chicago, 1884. (1)

Grant, George Monro, ed. *Picturesque Canada. . . .* Vol. 1. Toronto, 1882. (13)

Guidebook to the West Chester and Philadelphia Railroad. Philadelphia, 1869. (14 lithographs)

Guyot, Arnold. *Physical Geography.* New York, 1873. (5)

Hall, Eugene J., *Lyrics of Homeland.* Chicago, 1881. (8)

Harper's School Geography. New York, 1894. (4)

Hayden, Ferdinand V. *Eighth Annual Report of the United States Geological and Geographical Survey of . . . Colorado and . . . Adjacent Territories . . .* [1874]. Washington, DC, 1876. (8)

_____. *The Great West: Its Attractions and Resources. . . .* Philadelphia and Bloomington, 1880. (10)

_____. *Preliminary Report of the United States Geological Survey of Montana and Portions of Adjacent Territories . . .* [1871]. Washington, DC, 1872.

_____. *Twelfth Annual Report of the United States Geological and Geographical Survey of . . . Wyoming and Idaho. . . .* [1878]. Washington, DC, 1883. (4 chromos)

_____. *The Yellowstone National Park, and the Mountain Regions of Portions of Idaho, Nevada, Colorado, and Utah.* Boston, 1876. (15 chromos)

Higgins, Charles A. *Grand Cañon of the Colorado River.* Chicago, 1892. (1)

_____. *Grand Cañon of the Colorado River, Arizona.* Chicago, 1897. (1)

Holland, Josiah Gilbert. *The Mistress of the Manse.* New York, 1877. (10)

Holmes, Oliver Wendell, et al. *Golden Songs of Great Poets.* New York, 1877. (11)

Houston, Edwin J. *The Elements of Physical Geography.* Philadelphia, 1891. (2)

Hows, John W. S. *Golden Leaves from the British and American Great Poets.* New York, 1865. (1)

Hunter, Thomas A. M. *Home Culture: A Self-Instructor and Aid to Social Hours at Home.* New York, 1884. (2)

The Imperial Galaxy of Poetry and Art. Philadelphia, 1890. (1)

Ingersoll, Ernest. *The Book of the Oceans.* New York, 1898. (6)

_____. *The Crest of the Continent.* Chicago, 1885. (16)

_____. *Knocking Round the Rockies.* New York, 1882. (5)

King, Edward. *The Great South: A Record of Journeys. . . .* Hartford, CT, 1875. (56)

Kirby, Thomas E., comp. *Catalogue of the Art Collection Formed by the Late Mrs. Mary J. Morgan.* New York, 1886. (2)

Linton, William J. *The History of Wood Engraving in America.* Boston, 1882. (2)

Longfellow, Henry Wadsworth. *Excelsior.* Boston, 1878. (3)

_____. *The Hanging of the Crane.* Boston, 1875. (5)

_____. *Longfellow Portfolio: Being a Selection of Seventy-five Artist-Proofs from the Original Wood-Cuts Illustrating a New Subscription Edition of Longfellow's Poetical Works.* Boston and New York, [1881]. (5)

_____. *The Poetical Works of Henry Wadsworth Longfellow.* 6 vols. Boston, 1879 (17); rev. ed., 1882, 2 vols. (10).

Lowell, James Russell. *The Poetical Works of James Russell Lowell.* Boston, 1880. (2)

Mabie, Hamilton W. *Footprints of Four Centuries: A Topical History of the United States.* Philadelphia, 1894. (5)

McCabe, James D. *The Illustrated History of the Centennial Exhibition....* Philadelphia, 1876. (16)

_____. *The Pictorial History of the World.* Philadelphia, 1884. (1)

_____. *A Tour around the World by General Grant.* Philadelphia, 1879. (1)

McGuffey's Second Eclectic Reader. Cinncinati and New York, 1879. (4)

March, Daniel. *Night Scenes in the Bible.* Philadelphia, 1868. (6)

Meredith, Owen. *Lucille.* Boston, 1894. (4)

Mifflin, Lloyd. *At the Gates of Song.* Boston, 1897. (12)

_____. *The Hills.* New York, 1895. (8)

_____. *The Slopes of Helicon and Other Poems.* Boston, 1898. (10)

Milburn, W.H. *The Royal Galaxy of Poetry and Art.* New York, 1886. (16)

Mitchell, S. Augustus. *Mitchell's New Primary Geography.* Philadelphia, 1885. (1)

Monteith, James. *Comprehensive Geography.* New York, 1882. (12)

_____. *Manual of Geography.* New York, 1868. (12)

Morton, Eliza. *Potter's New Elementary Geography—Teacher's Edition.* Philadelphia, 1888. (7)

Muir, John, ed. *Picturesque California.* ...2 vols. New York, 1888. (1, plus an etching by Mary Nimmo Moran after a painting by Thomas Moran)

Newton, Henry, and Walter Jenney. *Report on the Geology and Resources of the Black Hills of Dakota.* Washington, DC, 1880. (3)

Our Native Land. New York, 1882. (8)

Palmer, John W. *Songs of Nature.* New York, 1873. (3)

Pangborn, J.G. *Picturesque B. & O.: Historical and Descriptive.* Chicago, 1882. (68)

_____. *The Rocky Mountain Tourist.* Topeka, KS, 1877. (3)

The People's Illustrated & Descriptive Family Atlas of the World. Chicago, 1884. (8)

Pictorial Annual for 1885. San Francisco, 1884.

Platt, John James. *The Union of American Poetry and Art.* Cincinnati, 1880. (26)

A Portfolio of Proof Impressions Selected from "Scribner's Monthly" and "St. Nicholas." New York, [1879]. (4)

Powell, John Wesley. *Exploration of the Colorado River of the West and Its Tributaries....* Washington, DC, 1875. (22)

Rand, Edward A. *All Aboard for Sunrise Lands.* Boston, 1881. (13)

Redway, Jacques W., and Russel Hinman. *Natural Advanced Geography.* New York, 1898. (6)

Rhymes of the Rockies: What the Poets Have Found to Say of the Beautiful Scenery on the Denver & Rio Grande Railroad.... Chicago, 1887. Various editions.

Richardson, James, ed. *Wonders of the Yellowstone.* New York, 1874. (22)

Scudder, Horace. *A Short History of the United States.* New York, 1890. (2)

Sheldon, George W. *American Painters: With 104 Examples of Their Work Engraved on Wood.* London and New York, 1879. (2)

Sipes, William B. *The Pennsylvania Railroad: Its Origin, Construction, Conditions, and Connections....* Philadelphia, 1875. (12)

Smith, S. F. *America: Our National Hymn.* Boston, 1884. (3)

Steele, J.W. *Guide to the Pacific Coast: The Santa Fe Route.* Chicago, 1890. (11)

Strahan, Edward [Earl Shinn], ed. *A Century After: Picturesque Glimpses of Philadelphia and Pennsylvania....* Philadelphia, 1875. (8)

Sunshine at Home. Battle Creek, MI, 1883. (6)

Swinton, William. *Elementary Physical Geography.* New York, 1875. (4)

_____. *Grammar-School Geography: Physical, Political, and Commercial.* New York, 1880. (31)

Taylor, Bayard. *The National Ode.* Boston, 1877. (9)

Taylor, Benjamin F. *Dulce Domum: The Burden of the Song.* Chicago, 1883. (3)

_____. *Songs of Yesterday.* Chicago, 1875. (1)

Tenney, E.P. *Colorado: And Homes in the New West.* Boston, 1880. (8)

Tennyson, Alfred Lord. *The Poetic and Dramatic Worlds of Alfred Lord Tennyson: Household Edition.* Boston, 1899. (2)

Thayer, William H. *Marvels of the New West.* Norwich, CT, 1891. (7)

Union Pacific Sketchbook: A Brief Description of Prominent Places of Interest.... Omaha, 1887. (at least 2)

Valleys of the Great Salt Lake: Describing the Garden of Utah and the Two Great Cities of Salt Lake and Ogden. Chicago, 1890.

Von Steinwehr, A., and D.G. Brinton. *Primary Geography.* New York, 1870. (1)

Wheeler, A.C. *The Iron Trail.* New York, 1876. (3)

Whittier, John Greenleaf. *Mabel Martin: A Harvest Idyll.* Boston, 1876. (15)

Williams, David J. *American Illustrated.* Boston, 1883. (3)

Williams, Henry T. *The Pacific Tourist: Illustrated Trans-Continental Guide of Travel from the Atlantic to the Pacific Ocean.* New York, 1876. Various editions. (17)

Willis, Nathaniel Parker, et al. *Picturesque American Scenery.* Boston, 1885. (1)

_____. *Sacred Poems.* New York, 1860. (2)

Wood, Stanley. *Over the Range to the Golden Gate: A Complete Tourist's Guide to the Colorado, New Mexico, Utah, Nevada, California, Oregon, Puget Sound and the Great Northwest.* Rev. ed. Chicago, 1895.

Young, John Russell. *Around the World with General Grant.* New York, 1879. (9)

ARTICLES

listed chronologically within each periodical

Aldine

"Kwasind, the Strong Man." 5 (June 1872), cover.

"Pictured Rocks of Lake Superior." 6 (Jan. 1873), 14–15.

Untitled. 6 (Jan. 1873), inside back cover.

"The Yellowstone Region." 6 (Mar. 1873), 74–75.

"Utah Scenery." 7 (Jan. 1874), frontispiece, 14–15.

"Lake George." 7 (Apr. 1874), 73–75.

"Views in Vermont." 7 (June 1874), 114–116.

"A Storm in the Mountains." 7 (July 1874), inside front cover.

"A Storm in Utah." 7 (Sept. 1874), 175.

"The Scenery of Southern Utah." 7 (Apr. 1875), 306–307.

"Moran's 'Mountain of the Holy Cross.'" 7 (July 1875), 379–380.

"Glories of Southern Utah." 8 (Jan. 1876), 34–35.

"The Rock-Rover's Land." 8 (Feb. 1876), 62.

"A Foggy Morning in New York Bay." 8 (Mar. 1876), 83.

"Idaho Scenery." 8 (June 1876), 194–196.

"The Juniata." 8 (Aug. 1876), 264–266.

"River Scenery of Pennsylvania." 9 (1878), 156–161.

"The Watering Place." 9 (1879), 242.

"Thomas Moran." 9 (1879), 265.

Appleton's Journal of Literature, Science, and Art

"Scenes in the Yellowstone Valley." 7 (11 May 1872), 519–522.

"The Cañon of the Colorado and the Moquis Pueblos." 9 (18 and 25 Apr., 2, 9, 16, 23, and 30 May 1874), 481–484, 513–516, 545–548, 590–593, 623–626, 641–644, and 686–688.

The Art Journal [NY]

[Sheldon, George W.]. "American Painters: Thomas Moran and Joseph Rusling Meeker." 5 (Feb. 1879), 41–45. (I)

The Cosmopolitan

Cockerill, John A. "Brigham Young and Modern Utah." 19 (Sept. 1895), 501–512.

Harper's Monthly

Mears, H.D. "The Catawissa Railroad." 25 (June 1862), 20–28.

Cleveland, Henry W. "Alexander Hamilton Stephens." 52 (Feb. 1876), 389.

Mitchell, Marion. "In the Heart of the Hartz." 56 (Apr. 1878), 684–696.

Benjamin, Samuel G.W. "Along the South Shore." 56 (June 1878), 1–14.

_____. "Fifty Years of American Art." 59 (Oct. 1879), 673–688.

Whitman, James S. "Down the Thames in a Birch-Bark Canoe." 62 (Jan. 1881), 211–218.

Vane, Henry. "Adirondack Days." 63 (Oct. 1881), 678–686.

Bishop, W. H. "Commercial, Social and Political Mexico." 64 (Feb. 1882), 401–415.

Ingersoll, Ernest. "Silver San Juan." 64 (Apr. 1882), 689–704.

Wyckoff, William C. "Sunlight Mysteries." 67 (June 1883), 81–94.

Bianciardi, E.D.R. "Vallombrosa." 67 (Aug. 1883), 347–353.

Harper's Weekly

Raymond, R.W. "The Heart of the Continent: The Hot Springs and Geysers of the Yellow Stone Region." 17 (5 Apr. 1873), 272–273. (I)

"Fourteenth Exhibition of the American Society of Painters in Watercolors." 25 (5 Feb. 1881), 87–89. (I)

"The Grand Teton Range." 26 (9 Dec. 1882), 783–785. (I)

"The Yellowstone Park." 27 (25 Aug. 1883), 535, 537. (I)

The Illustrated London News

"Sketches in British Columbia." (5 Mar. 1887), 265. (I)

Scribner's Monthly

Clark, T. Edwards. "The Bottom of the Sea." 1 (Nov. 1870), 18–35.

Gladden, Washington. "The Hoosac Tunnel." 1 (Dec. 1870), 143–159.

Crane, Newton, "Fairmount Park." 1 (Jan. 1871), 225–238.

Riddle, M.F. "Strasburg After the Surrender." 1 (Jan. 1871), 311–319.

Wilkinson, W.C. "The Northern Lights." 1 (Jan. 1871), 310–311.

Bates, J.C. "Life in the Cannibal Islands." 1 (Mar. and Apr. 1871), 529–543, 577–596.

Langford, Nathaniel P. "The Wonders of the Yellowstone." 2 (May and June 1871), 1–17, 113–128.

Headley, J.T. "Philadelphia." 2 (July 1871), 225–240.

Burns, George W. "Pictures from Canada." 2 (Sept. 1871), 449–461.

Coan, T. M. "An Island on Fire." 2 (Oct. 1871), 561–573.

Austus-Johnson, J. "Cyprus—Afloat and Ashore." 3 (Dec. 1871), 177–186.

Bromley, Isaac H. "The Wonders of the West I: The Big Trees and the Yosemite." 3 (Jan. 1872), 261–277.

Hayden, Ferdinand V. "The Wonders of the West II: More about the Yellowstone." 3 (Feb. 1872), 388–396.

Seeley, R.H. "The Mormons and Their Religion." 3 (Febrary 1872), 396–408.

Taylor, Bayard. "The Heart of Arabia." 3 (Mar. 1872), 545–557.

Richardson, James. "Traveling by Telegraph: Northward to Niagara." 4 (May and June 1872), 1–23, 129–157.

Digby, H. S. "The City of Warwick." 4 (June 1872), 187–193.

Lossing, Benson J. "West Point." 4 (July 1872), 257–284.

Mallett, E.F., Jr. "Ascent of Gray's Peak." 4 (Sept. 1872), 576–581

Hotchkiss, Ted. "New Ways in the Old Dominion. The Chesapeake and Ohio Railroad." 5 (Dec. 1872), 137–160; (Jan. 1873), 273–293

Langford, Nathaniel P. "The Ascent of Mt. Hayden." 6 (June 1873), 129–157

King, Edward. "The Great South: The New Route to the Gold." 6 (July 1873), 257–288.

Magee, Thomas. "Mount Shasta." 6 (Aug. 1873), 441–444.

Avery, Benjamin P. "The Geysers of California." 6 (Oct. 1873), 641–651

Froude, James Anthony. "Annals of an English Abbey." 7 (Nov. 1873), 91–101.

King, Edward. "The Great South: Old and New Louisiana." 7 (Dec. 1873), 129–160;

_____. "The Great South: Glimpses of Texas I: A Visit to the San Antonio River." 7 (Jan. 1874), 203–230.

H.H. "The Singer's Hills." 7 (Jan. 1874), 257–259.

MacDonald, George. "The Haunted House." 7 (Jan. 1874), 302–330.

King, Edward. "The Great South: Among the Mountains of Western North Carolina." 7 (Mar. 1874), 513–544.

_____. "The Great South: A Ramble in Virginia, from Bristol to the Sea." 7 (Apr. 1874), 645–647.

_____. "Southern Mountain Rambles, in Tennessee, Georgia and South Carolina." 8 (May 1874), 5–33.

_____. "The Great South: The South Carolina Problem, the Epoch of Transition." 8 (June 1874), 129–160.

MacCalla, Clifford P. "Au Sable Chasm: The Gate of the Adirondacks." 8 (June 1874), 192–198.

King, Edward. "The Great South: Some Notes on Missouri, the Heart of the Republic." 8 (July 1874), 257–284.

_____. "The Great South: In the Cotton States." 8 (Aug. 1874), 385–412.

_____. "The Great South: Down the Mississippi—The Labor Question—Arkansas." 8 (Oct. 1874), 641–669.

_____. "The Great South: Pictures from Florida." 9 (Nov. 1874), 1–31.

Benjamin, Samuel G.W. "Rambles in Madeira." 9 (Dec. 1874), 211–217.

King, Edward. "The Great South: Notes on Kentucky and Tennessee." 9 (Jan. 1875), 129–157.

Powell, John Wesley. "The Cañons of the Colorado." 9 (Jan., Feb., and Mar. 1875), 293–310, 394–409, 523–537.

King, Edward. "The Liverpool of America." 9 (Apr. 1875), 681–695.

Waring, George E., Jr. "A Farmer's Vacation: I. Hollow-Land." 9 (Apr. 1875), 714–731.

_____. "A Farmer's Vacation: II. Droogmakerij." 10 (May 1875), 714–731.

_____. "A Farmer's Vacation: V. Old Jersey." 10 (Aug. 1875), 410–418.

Sheahan, J. W. "Chicago." 10 (Sept. 1875), 529–551.

Waring, George E., Jr. "A Farmer's Vacation: VI. Guernsey and Sark." 10 (Sept. 1875), 574–591.

Powell, John Wesley. "An Overland Trip to the Grand Cañon." 10 (Oct. 1875), 659–678.

_____. "The Ancient Province of Tusayan." 11 (Dec. 1875), 193–213.

Howell, Martin A., Jr. "Is There a Subterranean Outlet to the Upper Lake Region?" 11 (Apr. 1876), 784–789.

Wells, William. "Union College." 12 (June 1876), 229–241.

H.H. "Hide and Seek Town." 12 (Aug. 1876), 449–461.

Holley, George. "Niagara." 12 (Aug. 1876), 462–478.

Waring, George E., Jr. "The Bride of the Rhine II." 12 (Aug. 1876), 490–498.

Wheeler, A. C. "On the Iron Trail." 12 (Aug. 1876), 529–543.

Waring, George E., Jr. "The Bride of the Rhine III." 12 (Sept. 1876), 694–707.

_____. "The Bride of the Rhine IV." 12 (Oct. 1876), 749–761.

Wilkinson, A. G. "Notes on Salmon Fishing." 12 (Oct. 1876), 770–796.

Clark, Charles H. "The Charter Oak City." 13 (Nov. 1876), 1–22.

Mitchell, Donald G. "Lafayette College." 13 (Dec. 1876), 184–197.

Boyesen, Hjalmar Hjorth. "Norway and the Norsemen." 13 (Jan. 1877), 291–305.

McClellan George B. "A Winter on the Nile." 13 (Jan. 1877), 368–383; (Feb. 1877), 452–59.

Seymour, Edward. "Trout Fishing in the Rangeley Lakes." 13 (Feb. 1877), 433–451.

Hackleton, Mrs. M. W. "The Hills of Linganore." 13 (Apr. 1877), 746–747.

Pyle, Howard. "Chincoteague—The Island Ponies." 13 (Apr. 1877), 737–745.

Richardson, Leander P. "A Trip to the Black Hills." 13 (Apr. 1877), 748–756.

Rideing, William H. "Croton Water." 14 (June 1877), 161–175.

Thompson, Maurice. "Bow Shooting." 14 (July 1877), 271–287.

Montgomery, J. Eglinton. "A Railway in the Clouds." 14 (Aug. 1877), 449–464.

Dodge, Julia E. "An Island of the Sea." 14 (Sept. 1877), 652–661.

Stockton, Frank. "An Isle of June." 15 (Nov. 1877), 13–31.

Lanier, Sidney. "Under the Cedarcroft Chestnut." 15 (Jan. 1878), 3803–81.

Muir, John. "The Humming-Bird of the California Water-Falls." 15 (Feb. 1878), 545–554.

Westervelt, Ellsworth. "A Trip to Central America." 15 (Mar. 1878), 608–623.

Pyle, Howard. "Among the Thousand Islands." 15 (Apr. 1878), 823–842.

Wilcox, Julius. "How Lead-Pencils are Made." 15 (Apr. 1878), 801–810.

Ilex, Arbor. "Camps and Tramps About Ktaaden." 16 (May 1878), 33–47.

Morton, William J. "To South Africa for Diamonds." 16 (Aug. 1878), 551–563; (Sept. 1878), 662–675.

McClellan, George B. "The Engadine." 16 (Sept. 1878), 639–651.

Viele, Egbert L. "A Trip with Lincoln, Chase, and Stanton." 16 (Oct. 1878), 813–822.

Hardacre, Emma C. "The Cliff Dwellers." 17 (Dec. 1878), 266–276.

Ward, Charles C. "Caribou-Hunting." 17 (Dec. 1878), 234–247.

Muir, John. "The Mountain Lakes of California." 17 (Jan. 1879), 411–420.

_____. "The Passes of the Sierra." 17 (Mar. 1879), 644–652.

Bell, W. H. "The Stickeen River and Its Glaciers." 17 (Apr. 1879), 805–815.

Bishop, William H. "Over the Narrowest Gauge." 18 (Aug. 1879), 593–605.

Smith, Herbert H. "Rio de Janiero." 18 (Oct. 1879), 890–903.

Norris, Thadddeus. "The Michigan Grayling." 19 (Nov. 1879), 17–23.

Smith, Herbert H. "The Coffee Culture in Brazil." 19 (Dec. 1879), 225–238.

McClellan, George B. "From Palermo to Syracuse." 20 (July 1880), 400–406.

Endicott, Francis. "Striped Bass." 21 (Mar. 1881), 698–708.

Cumming, Constance F. Gordon. "The Greatest Active Volcano." 21 (Apr. 1881), 923–936.

Muir John. "Coniferous Forest of the Sierra Nevada I." 22 (Sept. 1881), 710–723.

St. Nicholas: An Illustrated Magazine for Young Folks. Ed. Mary Mapes Dodge. New York: Scribner & Co., and The Century Co.

Traverse, Major. "The Pony Express." 1 (Aug. 1874), 641–646. (1)

Rideing, William H. "Our Light-Houses and Light-Ships." 1 (Sept. 1874), 725–732 (1)

Brooks, Noah. "The Boy Emigrants." 3 (Nov. 1875), 3–9; (June 1876), 508–520; (Aug. 1876), 638–646. (3)

Taylor, Bayard. "The Story of Jon of Iceland." 3 (Mar. 1876), 305–310. (1)

Allison, Joy. "Pattikin's House." 4 (June 1877), 517–522. (1)

Untitled poem ["There's a Ship on the Sea"]. 4 (Oct. 1877), 773.

Rideing, William H. "Caught by the Snow." 4 (Oct. 1877), 792–795.

Coan, Sarah. "The Largest Volcano in the World." 5 (Nov. 1877), 13–15. (1)

Hodder, Edwin. "Drifted into Port." 5 (May 1878), 494–499. (1)

Alcott, Louisa M. "Under the Lilacs." 5 (Sept. 1878), 716–725. (1)

Drinkwater, Ella A. "The Dark Day." 6 (Nov. 1878), 26–27. (1)

Keiller, John. "Longitude One Hundred and Eighty." 7 (Mar. 1880), 366–368. (1)

Miller, Olive Thorne. "A Happy Thought for Street Children." 7 (Aug. 1880), 800–805. (4)

Marshall, James B. "The Swiss Glaciers." 8 (Nov. 1880), 14–17. (3)

H. H. "Christmas in the Pink Boarding House: The Story of Two Mining Camps." 11 (Jan. 1884), 187–200. (1)

Cavazza, E. "A Doll on Mount Etna." 16 (Oct. 1889), 894–900. (1).

Ford, M. Louise. "Fifteen Minutes with a Cyclone." 17 (Mar. 1890), 429. (1)

Spofford Harriet Prescott. "The Story of the Iceberg." 17 (Dec. 1889); 128–129. (1)

Lummis, Charles F. "Strange Corners of Our Country." 19 (Dec. 1891); 122–129. (6)

Hartt, Mrs. Charles F. "Volcanoes and Earthquakes." 19 (Oct. 1892), 883–893. (1 wood engraving and 7 wash drawings)

Gibson, Ewing. "The Earthquake at Charleston." 19 (Oct. 1892), 893–895. (1 wash drawing)

Harwood, W. S. "The Story of a Grain of Wheat." 20 (Oct. 1893), 883–891. (1 wash drawing)

Rollins, Alice. "Little Servants of the Sea." 20 (Apr. 1893), 444–449. (3 wash drawings)

Steele, John. "A Kansas Cyclone." 21 (Mar. 1894), 440–443. (4 wash drawings)

Lummis, Charles. "A Little Hero of Peru." 23 (Mar. 1896), 385–390. (1)

Smith, Herbert H. "What Lydia Saw." 23 (Mar. 1896), 404–410. (1)

Jenks, Tudor. "About Flying Machines." 23 (Apr. 1896), 443–454. (2 wash drawings)